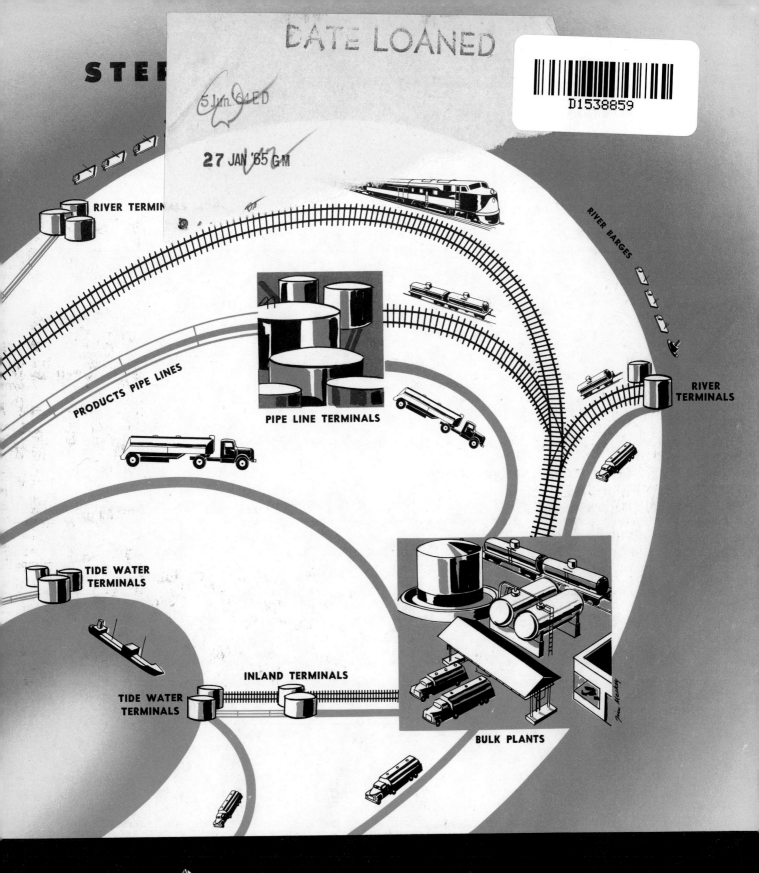

STE

RIVER TERMINALS

PRODUCTS PIPE LINES

PIPE LINE TERMINALS

RIVER BARGES

RIVER TERMINALS

TIDE WATER TERMINALS

INLAND TERMINALS

TIDE WATER TERMINALS

BULK PLANTS

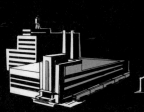     

FACTORIES   OFFICES   SERVICE STATIONS   HOMES   AIRPORTS   FARMS

The Growth of Integrated Oil Companies

ABSTRACT
THE GROWTH OF INTEGRATED OIL COMPANIES

This book is a study of the process of progressive adaptation which has resulted in the gradual emergence of large, integrated companies as the predominant form of business organization in the oil industry. The authors examine (1) the structure of the oil industry as it existed in 1950, (2) the technological, economic, and business circumstances which have encouraged vertical integration, (3) the differences and similarities in the structures of a selected group of oil companies and the nature of the managerial process by which the companies have continually adapted their structures to new conditions, and (4) the changes which have taken place in the participation of small business in the refining segment of the industry during the 30-year period 1920–1950 and the reasons why the changes have occurred.

The authors are two members of the Harvard Business School Faculty, John G. McLean and Robert Wm. Haigh. For the past seven years Professor McLean has been engaged in the development of a course of instruction which examines the organization of industries and the impact of changing technological and economic conditions upon management policies and programs. The plans for this research study were an outgrowth of methods of analysis being used in his teaching program.

PART ONE. THE STRUCTURE OF THE OIL INDUSTRY IN 1950

Part One of the book presents the results of a survey of the extent and nature of vertical integration in the oil industry in 1950. Statistical data were collected from 106 companies which represented 59.2% of the total number of operating refining companies in the industry and 94.7% of the refining capacity of the industry. From these data the authors establish *minimum* estimates of the amount of integration which actually existed in the industry in 1950. Among other things they report that:

(1) At least 48.6% of the total number of refining companies had some type of integrated structure. These companies as a group held 68.3% of the refining plants and accounted for 93.2% of the capacity of the industry.

(2) The share of the industry's facilities owned or leased by integrated companies was greatest in the middle of the oil process and declined toward both ends. The integrated companies held 93.2% of the refining capacity, 85.4% of the crude oil gathering lines, 82.1% of the crude oil trunk lines, and 92.2% of the products pipe lines. At the same time, however, the integrated companies held only 7.7% of the drilling rigs, 35.4% of the producing wells, and 51.6% of the service stations.

(3) Characteristically the integrated companies did not maintain an even balance among their activities in the different phases of the oil business. The typical producing-refining-wholesaling-retailing company (by far the most important type of integrated company) had crude production equal to 38.2% of its refinery runs, sold a volume equal to 63.8% of its refined products yield through its own terminals and bulk plants, and sold a volume equal to 26.7% of its gasoline and naphtha yield through service stations which it owned or leased.

(4) The large refining companies in 1950 were exclusively of the highly integrated type. All companies with capacities in excess of 50,000 barrels per day were engaged in producing, refining, wholesaling, retailing, and transportation activities, and there were not more than three companies with capacities in excess of 20,000 barrels per day which did not have some type of vertical integration. The small refining companies, on the other hand, had both integrated and nonintegrated structures.

PART TWO. THE EMERGENCE OF INTEGRATION IN THE OIL INDUSTRY

In Part Two the authors analyze the general environment in which the oil companies have operated and seek to isolate the circumstances that have brought the industry to the highly integrated state depicted in Part One. The authors present case histories of a number of large, integrated companies and examine in detail the points in their histories at which major integration steps were taken. From study of the management decisions made at these points and the circumstances which influenced the decisions, the authors evolve a general theory with regard to what has caused the gradual emergence of the large, integrated units.

The authors conclude that the large, integrated units have emerged because the economic climate in the oil industry has been generally favorable to the integration process for a long period of time. The favorable economic climate, in turn, they trace: (1) to certain general conditions which have been continually present in the industry, (2) to certain transitory conditions which have from time to time reinforced the general conditions, and (3) to a lack of serious obstacles to integration.

One of the most important of the general conditions was found in the behavior of the profit opportunities at the different levels of the industry. The authors present records of the gross margins available to producing, refining, wholesaling, and retailing companies over the 33-year period 1920–1952 and records of the profits earned by various types of integrated and nonintegrated companies.

These records reveal that the gross margins and profits in the different phases of the oil business have been continually changing and that the movements at one level have frequently differed in both timing and direction from the movements at another. By operating across two or more levels of the industry, oil companies have therefore been able to gain considerably in profit stability, to secure some protection from the short-term economic shocks developing from time to time in individual parts of the business, and thus to strengthen their opportunities for growth and survival.

A second series of general conditions favorable to integration was found in the economic characteristics of the physical facilities used in the oil process. The authors demonstrate that many of these facilities involve very large capital outlays, are highly specialized in terms of their economic utility, are extremely vulnerable to reductions in volume of throughput or output, and are heavily dependent for their competitive effectiveness upon supporting investments in other phases of the business. Investments in oil industry facilities have thus often been associated with a high degree of risk, and vertical integration has constituted one important means by which the risk might be reduced.

The authors find a third set of conditions favorable to the growth of integrated companies in the character of the managerial job involved in planning and conducting oil industry activities. The nature of the managerial job has been such that important benefits have been available to the companies that have been successful

in developing integrated structures together with sound techniques for administering their affairs on an integrated basis. Drawing upon actual case examples, the authors illustrate the way in which vertical integration may aid a company in planning capital investments and in handling the logistical problems involved in adjusting operating programs to changes in market conditions.

The authors demonstrate that these general conditions favorable to vertical integration have been reinforced by a continuing series of transitory conditions that have provided strong stimuli to the integration process during limited periods of time. Among other things, the transitory conditions have included the great crude oil discoveries of the late 1920's and early 1930's which for a time caused many crude oil producers to integrate forward into refining and marketing activities to secure an outlet for their products and the petroleum shortages following World War I and II which prompted many marketers and refiners to integrate backward to secure adequate sources of supply.

The presence of both general and transitory conditions favorable to vertical integration is not, in the judgment of the authors, fully sufficient to explain the strong receptivity of the oil industry to the integration process. In their research, they found certain other industries in which the business and economic reasons for vertical integration have been almost as persistent and powerful as in the oil industry but in which relatively little integration has ever taken place. Examination of some of these industries revealed that they have usually been characterized by major obstacles to vertical integration which have not been present in the oil industry. The authors conclude that the tendency toward vertical integration in the oil industry has been strong and enduring, not only because there have been important motivations for it, but likewise because there have been relatively few serious obstacles to it.

PART THREE. THE FORMATION AND ALTERATION OF INTEGRATION PATTERNS

In Part Three the authors analyze the integration programs of seven representative companies. Their purpose in this part of the research was to determine the differences and similarities in the structures and policies of the companies and to study the character of the managerial process by which the companies have adapted their structures to changing external conditions.

The companies selected for study were the Gulf Oil Corporation, The Texas Company, Sinclair Oil Corporation, The Ohio Oil Company, The Atlantic Refining Company, Standard Oil Company (Indiana), and Standard Oil Company (Ohio). These seven companies supplied the authors with a very large amount of statistical data which made it possible to define their structures in detail and to trace the changes made over a long period of time.

From their examination of the data, the authors conclude that the series of changes or steps by which the oil companies have continually shaped and reshaped their structures is closely akin to that which may be found at work throughout the entire world of living organisms. Living organisms are continually making a progressive adaptation to the physical environments in which they exist. As new conditions emerge, organisms which fail to make the necessary adaptations inevitably suffer a competitive disadvantage in nature's struggle for survival and, in some cases, gradually become extinct. So too it is, the authors conclude, in the economic world, and business corporations must continually alter their structures and seek new adaptations to the realities of their surroundings, if they are to remain strong and vigorous and able to withstand the relentless pressure of business competition.

More specific conclusions reached by the authors concerning the formation and alteration of integration patterns in the oil industry include the following:

(1) The forces and circumstances which influence the formation of integration patterns are multitudinous. Among other things they include: investment, cost, and profit considerations; competitive pressures; changes in economic, legal, and political conditions; managerial personalities; historical and accidental developments; changes in markets and products; and new technological discoveries.

(2) The formation and alteration of integration patterns is a continuing process; it has been going on throughout the industry's history and will probably continue for an indefinite period into the future. All the available evidence indicates that the oil companies have not been and are not moving toward any particular "integrated state" which once having achieved they will retain as a permanent form of organization. The structures of the seven

companies studied were found to be highly fluid in character and subject to continual rearrangement as the managements sought the optimum responses to new conditions.

(3) Management action with respect to the formation of integration patterns is taken in two closely related but very different ways: (a) through the development of management policies with regard to the balance a company should seek to maintain among its operations in different phases of the business, and (b) through the day-to-day executive decisions made on individual business problems involving integration arrangements. On the whole, it was found that the integration patterns of the companies studied were shaped more by the individual decisions made on the continuing series of day-to-day problems than they were by general management strategies.

(4) The formation of integration patterns in the oil industry has been characterized by a high degree of individualism. Just as any given physical environment fosters the growth and development of many different species of plant and animal life, so too has the oil industry fostered the growth and development of many different integrated structures. The records of the companies studied indicate conclusively that there have always been many different integration arrangements which would permit profitable operation and effective competition.

(5) The continual changes taking place in the structures of the integrated companies reflect the working of effective competition. The authors point out that if profits were easily won and competition generally soft in the oil industry, there would be no particular reason for a company to keep changing its structure. Changes in structure, the authors contend, are most likely to occur when and where the struggle for survival is most intense. The authors conclude that the degree of fluidity found in the integration patterns of the major oil companies is one excellent measure of the general intensity of competition in the industry.

PART FOUR. THE PARTICIPATION OF THE SMALL REFINER IN THE OIL INDUSTRY

In Part Four the authors examine the changes that have taken place in the activities of the small and substantially nonintegrated refiners as the integration process has gone forward in the industry and the reasons why the changes have occurred. This part of the research is based upon case histories of small refiners that have gone out of business in the past and of small refiners that are maintaining a profitable existence at the present time.

The authors find that over the past 30 years there has been a gradual contraction in the proportionate participation of the small refiners in the affairs of the oil industry. Among other things, they report that in the period 1920–1950 the proportionate share of the industry's refining capacity held by small firms declined from about 28% to 15% of the total. The authors further conclude that the decline has been an appropriate and natural part of the evolution of the industry and could have been avoided only by placing strong, artificial restraints on the economic, technological, and competitive forces at work in the industry.

The authors trace the evolution of refinery equipment in the period 1910–1950 and analyze carefully the effect which the size and type of equipment used by small refiners has had on their competitive position. They conclude that one of the most important things contributing to the decline in the position of the small firms has been the continued rapid advance in refinery technology which has made it necessary for the refiner to reinvest continually large sums in new plant facilities in order to maintain his operations on a competitive basis. The small refiners have often not had as ready access to large sums of new capital as have had the larger firms, and it is inevitable therefore that they should have suffered a loss in proportionate position.

The authors find that the development of the oil conservation laws was a second major circumstance which has contributed to the decline in the proportionate position of the small refiner. These laws tended to remove the large quantities of cheap crude oil which had from time to time in the past accompanied the discovery of new oil fields and which had often created a fertile field of opportunity for the small, oil field refiner. The authors' conclusions are based upon studies of the circumstances causing the entry and exit of small refiners in the East Texas field after 1930 and in the Illinois Basin fields after 1938.

A third circumstance which the authors find has contributed to the decline in the proportionate position of the small firm has been the general success which has attended vertical integration as a means of meeting the particular business and economic risks associated with oil industry operations. For a variety of reasons, the small firms have lagged behind the large firms in the use of integration arrangements, and it is understandable therefore that they should have suffered a gradual loss in position relative to the large firms that were ready and willing to undertake integration when and where it could be used to advantage.

Finally, the authors conclude that the decline in the proportionate position of the small refiners must be ascribed in large measure to the continuing pressure of competition. Had competition in the oil industry been generally weak and ineffective, the small refiners would have suffered no particular hardship from the technological and economic circumstances discussed above. Circumstances such as these, the authors point out, compel adjustments in industry and corporate structures only when the pressure of competition is strong.

Notwithstanding the decline which has taken place in the proportionate position of the small refiner, the authors find that the industry has been evolving in such a way that there are many profitable fields still open to small firms, *provided* that they select situations well suited to the financial and managerial resources at their command.

The authors present case histories which illustrate that the small refiners have been particularly successful when they have elected to operate in segments of the business which are of little interest to the large firms or in which the large firms are ill-equipped to compete. The authors find, for example, that small refiners have sometimes done extremely well by confining their operations to geographic areas which the large firms could not reach at low costs, by using special grades of crude oil which were not available in sufficient quantity to support a large operation, or by seeking markets which were too small or too specialized in their requirements for quality or service to interest large companies.

(Harvard Business School, Division of Research, Soldiers Field, Boston 63, Massachusetts. xxiv + 728 pages; 206 exhibits [maps, charts, diagrams, photographs, tables]; 23 appendix tables. $12.00. 1954)

THE GROWTH OF
INTEGRATED
OIL COMPANIES

John G. McLean
Professor of Business Administration

Robert Wm. Haigh
Assistant Professor of Business Administration

DIVISION OF RESEARCH
GRADUATE SCHOOL OF BUSINESS ADMINISTRATION
HARVARD UNIVERSITY
BOSTON
1954

HARVARD UNIVERSITY
GRADUATE SCHOOL OF BUSINESS ADMINISTRATION
GEORGE F. BAKER FOUNDATION

DONALD K. DAVID, *Dean*
BERTRAND FOX, *Director of Research*

Library of Congress Catalogue Card Number: 54–6417

Printed at
THE PLIMPTON PRESS
NORWOOD, MASSACHUSETTS

FOREWORD

In the research project on which this report is based, Professor McLean and Professor Haigh have concerned themselves with the processes by which the structure of the oil industry has been adapted to the changing conditions under which the concerns in this industry operate. The authors have sought to ascertain, company by company, what structural patterns now exist and how those patterns evolved. Since this industry has grown rapidly during the last forty years and since that growth has been achieved amidst rapidly and sometimes radically changing conditions, the industry seemed to afford a particularly fertile opportunity for such a study of structural adaptation.

In searching for a fruitful way of analyzing and interpreting their data, the researchers have developed a concept of industry structure and function which, it seems to me, will be useful, as circumstances permit, for making analogous analyses of various other industries. Sooner or later, every business concern faces adaptation to new conditions, and such studies as this are one means of learning more about the often misunderstood adaptation process.

This study was financed from the research funds of the School which include contributions from several companies in the oil industry. The project, however, was not proposed by anyone within the oil industry; it grew out of a method of analysis being developed by Professor McLean in his course of instruction at the Harvard Business School and was a completely independent undertaking of the Division of Research.

Melvin T. Copeland
Director of Research

Soldiers Field
Boston, Massachusetts
June 1953

NOTE TO THE READER

For the convenience of the hurried reader, we have placed at the end of each chapter a brief summary of the principal conclusions of that chapter. In addition, we have presented in Chapter Twenty-Four a general summary of the findings of the entire study.

PREFACE

In looking back over the course of this project, we find it difficult to acknowledge adequately our debt to the many organizations and people who aided us in our work. Rarely has one book owed so much to so many. In the following paragraphs we shall indicate some of the principal contributors to the study. We wish it clearly understood, however, that our selection of these few for special mention does not in any way imply a diminution of our gratitude to the numerous others who, for lack of space, shall have to go unmentioned.

First of all we wish to acknowledge the contribution which was made to the book by the many oil companies, large and small, whose activities and operations are discussed in the following pages. These companies welcomed us to their offices; their executives spent much time over a period of many months in discussions with us; and their staff departments devoted literally hundreds of man-hours to the task of compiling the statistical data and special records which we requested of them. Without the willing and extensive cooperation which the companies selected for study gave to us, the preparation of a book of this kind would have been impossible.

We were particularly impressed with the fact that while the oil companies willingly supplied us with facts and information, they at the same time respected our right to draw our own conclusions and make our own interpretations of the data. Once it was understood that our purpose was to make an impartial and objective analysis of industry experience, the oil companies joined wholeheartedly with us in the task. In our opinion, the increasing willingness of the oil companies to open their files and records to outside researchers and to make detailed facts about their operations available for publication represents a high order of business statesmanship.

Many individual executives in the oil companies reviewed various parts of the manuscript and were extremely helpful in checking the factual aspects of the study. We shall not attempt to mention all of these people by name, but our debt to them is great, and we herewith express our sincere appreciation to each and every one of them for the help which they gave to us.

Many statistical and historical data about the oil industry were secured through the cooperation of the American Petroleum Institute. The API was also very helpful to us in connection with the industry-wide survey of refining companies reported in Chapter Two. From the outset of our work, the officers and staff of the API were continually available to us for friendly counsel and advice and gave us many useful suggestions concerning sources of information.

For a period of about three years prior to the initiation of the study and during the time it was in process, one of the authors, John G. McLean, was retained as a consultant on management problems by one of the major oil companies. This consulting work, although it was in nowise connected with the research study, provided the author with a general background in oil industry economics which made it possible to conduct the research for the book more rapidly and efficiently than would otherwise have been possible.

Throughout the course of our work, we received much valuable assistance from several members of the Harvard Business School Faculty. Dr. Melvin T. Copeland, Director of the Division of Research until July 1, 1953, followed the project closely and gave us the benefit of his wise counsel and advice at all stages of the work. His long experience and breadth of vision were of invaluable assistance to us in defining the scope and objectives of the study and in determining the research methods to be employed. Dr. Copeland also read the entire manuscript and made many helpful suggestions which were incorporated in the final draft.

Grateful acknowledgment is also due Dr. Edmund P. Learned for his many contributions to our work. In the summer of 1950, Dr. Learned served as chairman of the group which developed the initial plans for this and a series of related research studies dealing with the place and function of big business in our industrial economy. Dr. Learned was subsequently called to Washington to serve for two years as special adviser to the Chief of Staff, United States Air

Forces. Despite the many heavy demands upon his time in Washington, he nevertheless maintained a close interest in our progress and reviewed the entire manuscript before publication. We valued our association with him not only because he gave us many excellent suggestions but also because he had the rare capacity to give us new inspiration and encouragement at the times when we needed them most.

Professors Richard S. Meriam and John Lintner were likewise of continuing assistance to us. Professor Meriam reviewed carefully the conclusions to each part of the study and gave us the benefit of the judgment derived from his many years of experience in analyzing oil industry problems. Professor Lintner gave us detailed comments and criticisms on each of the chapters, and we benefited greatly from his keen insight into the many economic aspects of the study. We should also like to acknowledge the help which Professor George S. Gibb gave to us in reviewing and criticising Chapter Two.

Very special recognition is due Miss Catherine C. Ellsworth who was associated with us as research assistant throughout the entire project. Miss Ellsworth conducted effectively many of the difficult jobs of library research, and her wide familiarity with the history of the oil industry and available reference materials proved of great assistance to us at many points. Her work in developing basic factual information for Chapters Three, Eight, Ten, Eighteen, and Twenty-One was particularly important. Miss Ellsworth also read the complete manuscript, and her careful comments and appraisals aided us greatly in preparing the final draft for publication.

The extensive statistical and computing work underlying Chapters Two, Five, and Six and many other parts of the book was done by the Bureau of Business Research at the Harvard Business School under the very able direction of Mrs. Rose W. Kneznek. Without the extremely effective support which Mrs. Kneznek and her associates in the Bureau gave to us, many important aspects of the study could not have been undertaken. We are also indebted to Mrs. Kneznek for much valuable advice on statistical procedures and methods.

The many graphs, charts, and maps in the book were prepared by Messrs. Robert W. Small, Joseph J. Lesko, George J. Feeney, and John Bailey. The excellent cooperation and helpful advice which these gentlemen gave to us made it possible to simplify the presentation of complicated data at many points in the book. Acknowledgment is also due Mr. Harold F. Craig and Mr. Albert Choules, Jr. for their help in preparing analyses of the earnings experience of different types of integrated companies and various other financial and statistical records.

Particular recognition is due Miss Carol Peterson who served as our secretary throughout the project, handled the manuscript through its several drafts, and participated in many ways in nearly all phases of the work. Her unfailing competence and willing spirit removed many obstacles from our path and speeded our progress at innumerable points.

We also wish to express sincere appreciation to Miss Ruth Norton who aided us in preparing the manuscript for publication, handled all the arrangements for the printing of the book, and helped us in many other ways. Special thanks are also due Mrs. William P. Gormbley, Jr., for her work in preparing the index.

Finally, we wish to make grateful acknowledgment of the help which was given to us by our wives, Patricia S. McLean and Jane S. Haigh. These ladies assisted in much of the statistical work, in the preparation of charts and tables, and in checking the various drafts of the manuscript. In addition, they patiently and willingly bore far more than their share of home and family responsibilities while our work was in process.

Although many people helped us in many ways, we wish to stress the fact that we undertook the study entirely on our own initiative. It was not suggested to or urged upon us by anyone within or without the oil industry. Moreover, we were at all times completely free to carry our research wherever we wished, to accept or reject the advice that was given to us, and to draw our own conclusions. It follows therefore that we and we alone must accept the responsibility for the final results.

JOHN G. MCLEAN
ROBERT WM. HAIGH

Soldiers Field
Boston, Massachusetts
January 1954

Table of Contents

PART THREE. THE FORMATION AND ALTERATION
OF INTEGRATION PATTERNS

PART FIVE. SUMMARY AND CONCLUSIONS

List of Exhibits

The Growth of Integrated Oil Companies

Introduction

THE PURPOSE of this study is to examine the processes which have led to the growth and development of integrated oil companies and which have brought the oil industry to its present, highly integrated state. Our interest in this matter was aroused by the divergencies in the patterns of corporate growth and development which may be found in different industries in the United States. In some industries, such as the oil and steel industries, large, vertically integrated units have gradually emerged as the predominant form of business organization. In other industries, such as the furniture and textile industries, large, vertically integrated units have been conspicuously lacking, and the majority of the business has tended to remain in the hands of organizations which are small in size and nonintegrated in structure.

These and other differences in general patterns of corporate growth and development have persisted among some of our industries for a hundred years or more, too long a period of time to be attributable merely to accident or solely to the personal desires and ambitions of the individuals who have been responsible for the management of the corporations. On the contrary, there is every reason to suppose that the divergencies have arisen from fundamental differences in the technological, economic, and business characteristics of the industries themselves.

In this book we shall present the results of our research on the oil industry as one "case example" of the processes by which business structures evolve and by which particular industries acquire their distinguishing characteristics. Our initial investigations indicated that it would be impossible in any short period of time to study all aspects of corporate growth and development in the oil industry, and we decided therefore to limit our research to the process of vertical integration and to the changes which have taken place in the participation of small firms at the refining level of the industry. In particular, we addressed our attention to three fundamental questions:

1. Why and how was it that over a long span of time the oil industry tended to develop large, vertically integrated units as the predominant way of doing business?

2. What differences and similarities exist in the structures of a selected group of oil companies and what is the nature of the process by which their structures have evolved?

3. What changes, if any, have taken place in the participation of small business in the refining segment of the industry and why have those changes occurred?

The need for better understanding of the processes of corporate growth and development is particularly great at the present time in view of the increasing tendency on the part of government agencies to regulate, or at least question, the structure of business units and the organization of industries. There has been a steadily growing controversy in legal, Congressional, academic, public, and business circles with regard to such things as the types of integration which corporations should be allowed to undertake and retain, the place and function of big and little business in our economy, and the relationships which should be maintained between large and small scale enterprises.

This controversy has focused attention on some profoundly disturbing and vastly complicated questions with regard to the behavior and values of large scale industrial enterprise. Among other things, questions have been raised concerning (a) the business efficiency of large scale enterprise, (b) the effect of large scale enterprise on the nature and intensity of competition, (c) the effect of large scale enterprise on the social values of our industrial economy, (d) the effect of big business on the opportunities for little business, and (e) the motives of those entrusted with the management of large, integrated corporations.

The appropriateness of the controversy which has centered on these and a host of related problems we do not wish to question. In our opinion, it is a healthy thing to subject the behavior and performance of the various parts of our economic system to continual challenge, examination, and review. Such processes play an important part in the development of the mores of our business and economic life. All too often, however, the process of probing and questioning and the controversy that has gone along with it have rested on inadequate facts and on inadequate understanding of the realities of the business situations involved. The arguments have thus frequently reached an impasse, a "Katy did, Katy didn't stage," with the protagonists on all sides lacking the basic information necessary to support their views. Professor M. A. Adelman draws to a close a recent study on "The Measurement of Industrial Concentration" with the comment, "The most obvious conclusion is also the most depressing one: how little we know of our industrial structure and its evolution." [1]

Our primary objective in this volume therefore will not be to argue whether vertical integration in the oil industry has been good or bad, nor shall we seek to pass a moral and economic judgment on the performance of the large, integrated companies. Our purpose will be to establish some of the underlying facts concerning vertical integration and with regard to how and why it occurred. Our effort will thus be to provide those who would attack or defend the social and economic consequences of vertical integration with a sounder basis for their argument than they have had heretofore; our own participation in the debate we will reserve (somewhat reluctantly) to later studies. The facts presented will to some extent, of course, speak for themselves, and we shall at certain points therefore draw such conclusions with regard to social and economic consequences as seem readily warranted by the particular set of facts at hand.

In short, our purpose in this study is to seek an answer to the question: Whence came the large, integrated oil companies and what caused them to grow in the particular way that they did? If we can gain an understanding of why and how the large, integrated oil companies have grown, we shall be in a far better position to evaluate their performance and to establish public policies concerning the kinds of structures which they should be allowed to develop and retain in the future.

[1] *The Review of Economics and Statistics,* Harvard University, Vol. XXXIII, No. 4, November 1951, p. 295.

PART ONE

The Structure of the Oil Industry in 1950

THE purpose of Part One of this study is to describe the structure of the oil industry as it existed in 1950 with particular reference to the nature and extent of vertical integration and the size of corporate units. It is important to realize that the data represent the industry as of but a single moment in the process of its evolution. As will be clearly demonstrated in later chapters, the structure of the oil industry and the structure of individual corporations in it are continually shifting and changing. The situation in earlier years was very different from that in 1950, and it is certain that tomorrow will witness rearrangements in the 1950 pattern. Part One of the study thus resembles a "still picture" of a scene full of action, a scene in which all the component parts are continually altering their characteristics and their relationships to each other.

The data presented in Part One are of two types. Chapter One consists of a qualitative examination of the different kinds of vertical integration that were present in the industry in 1950. Chapter Two presents a quantitative analysis of the extent of the various types of vertical integration at the successive levels of the industry.

The later sections of the study are devoted to the task of examining the nature and character of the evolutionary process by which the industry and certain corporations in it arrived at the positions depicted in Part One.

CHAPTER ONE

The Nature of Vertical Integration Processes and Arrangements

ONE of the questions most frequently asked of the authors in the course of the field research among oil companies was, "What do you mean by vertical integration?" This question was prompted by the fact that an almost infinite number of different kinds of integration processes are continually at work in the oil industry and have produced a multitude of different types of integrated companies. It is perhaps appropriate therefore that this study should begin with an attempt to describe and classify some of the more important integration processes and arrangements which we found to be prevalent in the industry.

The task of description and classification is complicated by the fact that there is no generally accepted terminology which can be applied to the problem. The literature on the subject of integration contains a number of useful definitions of kinds and types of integration,[1] but none of these definitions has as yet gained any widespread acceptance or usage in business practice. Moreover, the definitions have for the most part been couched in rather general terms and have not been sufficiently developed to cover the many variations in integration processes and arrangements which exist in the oil industry. In the discussion which follows, therefore, we will of necessity develop certain definitions and terminology of our own. No particular brief is held for the terms and categories which will be employed other than that we found them useful in classifying the particular kinds of integration present in the oil industry.

I. THE GENERAL TYPES OF INTEGRATION

The general term "integration," when used with respect to corporate growth and development, can perhaps best be defined as the process of extending the scope of the activities which are under the ownership, management, or control of a single company. In the oil industry, as in many other industries, it is useful to distinguish among three general types of integration: horizontal, vertical, and product integration.

Horizontal integration or combination is the process of extending a company's activities in fields in which it is already engaged. In the oil industry the actions of a refiner in building another refinery at a different location, of a jobber in building another bulk plant, of a service station operator in acquiring another service station, or of a pipe line company in constructing another pipe line may all be classified as horizontal integration. This type of integration is closely related to the simplest form of growth, expansion through an increase in sales volume. The term "horizontal integration" may, however, be used to distinguish that particular kind of growth and expansion which is brought about by the acquisition of additional facilities, separate and distinct from those already in operation. The reason for making such a distinction lies chiefly in the fact that the business considerations involved in the acquisition of a new facility are quite

---

[1] See the following: A. R. Burns, *The Decline of Competition* (New York, McGraw-Hill Book Company, 1936), p. 421; M. A. Adelman, "Integration and Antitrust Policy," *Harvard Law Review*, Vol. 63, November 1949, pp. 27–77; Temporary National Economic Committee, *Investigation of Concentration of Economic Power, Monograph 27, The Structure of Industry*, 76th Congress, 3rd Session (Washington, Government Printing Office, 1941), pp. 192–205; P. S. Florence, *The Logic of Industrial Organization* (London, Keegan Paul, Trench, Trubner and Co., Ltd., 1933), pp. 20–22; and Federal Trade Commission, *Report on the Merger Movement, A Summary Report* (Government Printing Office, 1948).

different from those involved in an expansion of the volume of business done through existing facilities.

Vertical integration, in its simplest form, is the process of increasing the number of distribution and processing steps in an industry's cycle of activities which are under the ownership, management, or control of a single company. The action of The Ohio Oil Company, an oil producer, in acquiring its Robinson refinery in 1924; the steps taken about 1942 by the Standard Oil Company (Ohio), a refiner and marketer, to engage in crude oil producing activities; and the building of the Keystone products pipe line in 1931 by The Atlantic Refining Company, a producer-refiner-marketer, constituted further vertical integration for the companies involved. Likewise the steps which many refiners have taken to own or operate terminals or bulk plants and which many jobbers have taken to acquire service station properties, fall in the vertical integration category. As will be noted later in this chapter, vertical integration may also take place when a company alters the depth, extent, or intensity of its integration arrangements.

Product integration, more commonly referred to as product diversification, is the process of increasing the scope of a company's activities by the manufacture or distribution of additional product lines. The steps which many oil companies have taken to engage in the distribution of tires, batteries, and accessories may be identified as product integration. Likewise the steps which a number of distributors of fuel oil have taken to sell fuel oil burners and to offer their customers burner maintenance service represent product diversification. An extreme case of product diversification may be found in the recent acquisition by the Allied Oil Company [2] of the distributorship for Snow Crop Frozen Foods in Cleveland, Ohio.

The boundary lines between these three general types of integration are by no means sharp and distinct. Although some integration moves can readily be classified as falling in one or another of the three categories, a great many such moves are likely to involve two or even three types of integration. For example, the acquisition of crude oil production by the Standard Oil Company (Ohio) beginning in 1942 was a clear case of vertical integration because it represented entrance into a new step in the oil process.[3] The effort initiated by the Sinclair Oil Corporation in 1949 to increase its crude production from about 36% to 50% of refinery runs, however, involved both horizontal and vertical integration; horizontal integration in the sense that it involved an expansion of the company's producing activities and vertical integration in the sense that it increased the crude oil supply the company had available for its refining operations. Similarly, the steps which many refiners have taken recently to enter the petrochemical business may be classified as product integration in the sense that they increase the range of products the refiners are manufacturing and selling and as vertical integration in the sense that they involve a further processing of intermediate products which might alternatively be sold to the chemical industry.

In some cases, horizontal, vertical, and product integration may all be involved in the same management action. An example may be found in the merger of the Standard Oil Company of New York and the Vacuum Oil Company in 1932. The Standard Oil Company of New York was active at all levels of the industry, and its product line included gasolines, kerosenes, fuel oils, automotive and industrial lubricants, and a wide range of miscellaneous products. The company and its subsidiaries had crude oil production equal to about 80%–90% of their refinery requirements in 1929 and owned or controlled over 9,000 retail outlets.

The Vacuum Oil Company was a specialist in the manufacture of high-grade automotive and industrial lubricants, and many of its industrial products were different from those manufactured by Socony. Such gasolines, kerosenes, and fuel oils as the Vacuum Oil Company produced were manufactured largely as by-products of the manufacture of lubricants, and the company in fact refined only about one-third of the gasoline and one-fourth of the kerosene which it marketed. The Vacuum Oil Company had a negligible amount of crude

---

[2] The Allied Oil Company was merged with the Ashland Oil & Refining Company in 1950.

[3] Before 1942 the company had had only a negligible amount of crude oil production.

oil production and owned or controlled only a relatively small number of retail outlets.[4]

The merger of the two companies thus represented horizontal integration at the refining level of the industry and to a minor extent at the producing and marketing levels. The merger also represented vertical integration in the supporting of Vacuum's refining activities with Socony's crude oil production and extensive system of retail outlets. Finally, the merger represented product integration in the joining of Vacuum's specialty lubricants, and particularly certain of its industrial products, with Socony's general line of petroleum products. A whole series of other types of integration, although of lesser significance, were also involved in the merger action.

Not only is there considerable interlocking among the three broad types of integration, but also within each type a vast range of different arrangements and gradations may be found. Since this study is concerned primarily with the process of vertical integration, the remainder of the chapter will be devoted to outlining some of the more important variations in the type and character of vertical integration processes and arrangements which we found in the oil industry.

II. THE TYPES OF VERTICAL INTEGRATION PROCESSES

We found that the various types of vertical integration which were continually taking place in the oil industry could be divided into three broad categories, which we shall designate as primary, secondary, and tertiary integration.

The term *primary integration* we shall use to designate the corporate growth which takes place when an oil company engages in the ownership, management, or control of another step in the sequence of activities directly involved in the processing and distribution of oil and its products. The meaning of primary integration may be clarified by reference to the end papers of this volume which show

in simplified form the more important steps which are commonly involved in bringing oil and its products from the well-head to the consumer. When a company engaged in any one of these steps, such as crude oil production, crude oil gathering, refining, barge transportation, bulk plant operation, truck transportation, or service station operation, undertakes the ownership, management, or control of another step in the process, the growth and expansion which results may be identified as primary integration. As will be noted later, the new step undertaken does not necessarily need to be that which immediately precedes or follows the one which the company is currently performing.

It is immediately apparent that primary integration can take on many different shades of meaning depending on how a "step" in the process is defined. Actually, the entire process of bringing oil and its products from well-head to consumers consists of an infinite series of small steps, performed one after another, and it is for all practical purposes impossible for a company to participate in the industry without performing more than one such step. In a modern refinery, for example, it would not be at all uncommon for even the simplest oil product to be carried through 10 to 20 distinct processing steps. Similarly, a firm engaged in barge transportation must at the very minimum participate in loading, transportation, and unloading activities.

It might thus be argued that all oil companies have engaged in at least some primary integration and that the differences among companies are simply matters of degree. For practical purposes, however, it seems desirable to define a "step" in the process as a group of activities which there is a reasonable business possibility of performing on an independent basis.[5] What constitutes a "reasonable business possibility" is, of course, a matter of business judgment. The jobber might argue that his ac-

---

[4] For a description of the business of the two companies, see Summary of the Evidence by Fred L. Williams, Master, in *United States* vs. *Standard Oil Company of New York and Vacuum Oil Company*, U. S. District Court, St. Louis, Missouri, September 4, 1930.

[5] Compare A. R. Burns, op. cit., p. 421. Burns treats this problem somewhat differently but arrives at substantially the same conclusion: "Almost every business unit brings under a single management a series of operations performed in sequence upon each unit of material. Where the series is short, or there are no points in the sequence at which the product is commonly thought of as salable, the series is not usually regarded as an example of vertical integration although logically it is such."

quisition and operation of truck transports do not really represent primary integration because there is no reasonable business possibility of performing the jobber activity without the operation of such equipment. Similarly, the refiner might contend that his acquisition of crude oil pipe lines does not properly represent primary integration on the grounds that the lines are an essential part of the refinery plant investment.

Moreover, it is clear that as the technological and managerial art of an industry advances, the number of activities at various points in the process which must be embraced under one management to provide a reasonable business opportunity will be continually expanding and contracting. Prior to 1930, for example, it was reasonably clear that the acquisition by a refiner of products transportation facilities would have represented primary integration. The recent extensive development of the products pipe line as a transportation device, however, alters the situation. It now is at least possible to argue that the products pipe line is merely an extension of the refinery plant facilities.[6]

Similarly, in the early days of the industry the crude oil distillation and cracking operations could easily be considered a single step in the process because cracking was accomplished by merely increasing the temperature and pressure in stills very much like those used for distillation purposes. At a later stage in the development of refining technology the two processes became separated and were for many years carried out in quite different units of equipment. There are, in fact, some refineries on the Gulf Coast today which operate only crude distillation equipment and sell their output as charging stock to companies with catalytic cracking equipment.[7] There is therefore a question whether the crude oil distillation and cracking operations should be treated as separate steps in the process or merely as elements in a broader "refining step." At the present time there is an increasing trend toward the use of combination distillation and cracking units, and the two processes may soon become, as they were at the

outset, so closely interrelated that there is no reasonable possibility of organizing a separate business activity around either step alone.[8]

It is thus evident that at any given stage in the industry's development there will always be boundary line cases where it is difficult to decide whether the term primary integration properly applies. The difficulties involved in classifying individual special cases do not, however, obscure what is meant by the *process* of primary integration, and it is with this process that our study is primarily concerned. Without attempting to be too precise about the matter therefore, we shall use the term primary integration with reference to what seem to be the generally recognized major steps in the process, such as crude oil production, crude oil transportation, refining, products transportation, terminal and/or bulk plant operation, and service station operation.

The term *secondary integration* we shall use to designate the corporate growth which takes place when an oil company engages in one of the peripheral activities which closely surround each of the main steps in the oil process.[9] The activities involved in secondary integration differ from those involved in primary integration in that they are not a direct part of the oil producing, refining, transportation, and marketing processes but are closely affiliated therewith and are supporting thereto. For example, in the oil producing end of the business there are a vast number of independent concerns available to handle such activities as well drilling, well cementing, well shooting, well acidifying, well logging, core analysis, well-tool manufacturing, tool sharpening, land surveying, lease brokering, seismic or geological work, and mud supply. The moves which oil producers from time to time make to engage in these activities on their own account represent secondary integration. The steps taken by a refiner to do his own laboratory test work or to undertake his own equipment and process design work rather than relying

---

6 See *Champlin Refining Company* vs. *United States et al.*, 329 U. S. 29 (1946).

7 See Chapter Twenty-Three.

8 It is recognized that the entire problem of vertical integration might be resolved and analyzed around the question of what groups of activities should be considered as a "step" in the process from a practical business standpoint. We pass this alternative in favor of the treatment which follows in the remainder of the study.

9 Compare P. S. Florence, op. cit., pp. 20–22. Florence defines this type of integration as "diagonal" integration.

upon outside concerns can also be identified as secondary integration. At the retail level, the action of the Standard Oil Company (New Jersey) in undertaking the manufacture of service station equipment through its subsidiary, the Gilbert and Barker Manufacturing Company, may likewise be placed in the secondary integration category.

The general relationship between primary and secondary integration is illustrated by the diagram in Exhibit I-1. A question at once arises as to what should be considered a peripheral activity and what should be considered an integral part of the major step in the oil producing process itself. No hard and fast line can be drawn, but for practical purposes peripheral activities may be defined as jobs associated with one of the main steps in the oil process which a company does not need to do itself but which it can, as a practical business alternative, get done by regularly established outside concerns. We have placed many of the oil finding activities in the peripheral category because an oil producer has as a very real alternative the possibility of buying proven reserves or producing properties and engaging in very few oil finding activities on his own account.[10]

As in the case of primary integration, it is clear that there will always be boundary line cases where it will be difficult to decide whether secondary integration is involved. Here again it is also clear that changes in the technological and managerial art may at one time require a different treatment of particular activities and types of management actions from that which was appropriate in an earlier period.

The term *tertiary integration* we shall use to cover the growth which takes place when an oil company engages in one of the more remote of the peripheral activities which surround each of the four or five main steps in the oil process. The distinction between secondary and tertiary integration is more a matter of degree than it is of kind. The activities involved in secondary integration may be differentiated from those involved in tertiary integration, however, on the grounds that the former are an integral part of the oil industry and would have little usefulness outside the oil industry whereas the activities involved in tertiary integration either are, or easily could be, supporting to other industries as well as the oil industry.

The acquisition of a shipyard for the construction of tankers by the Sun Oil Company in World War I, for example, may be classified as tertiary integration; the activity here involved was fully as much a part of the shipbuilding industry as it was of the oil industry. The steps which the Standard Oil Company (Indiana) at one time took to manufacture its own cans for packaging lube oils may be identified as tertiary integration because the activity might easily be considered a part of the can making industry. At the retail level of the industry, the steps which some companies have taken to construct and paint their own retail service stations or to lay their own station roadways may be placed in the category of tertiary integration because the activities involved are ones which the companies could, as many oil companies do, call upon well-established, outside industries to perform. Likewise, the steps which a number of oil companies have taken to maintain houses for employees in isolated areas are representative of tertiary integration.

There is, of course, no reason why the process of classification which has been followed up to this point need stop with tertiary integration. Actually, each of the major steps in the oil process may be envisaged as surrounded with an ever widening circle of supporting activities. The penetration of each successive layer of these activities might therefore be regarded as another stage in the integration process. For example, an oil producer might undertake to roll pipe for well casings, to make the steel for the pipes, to make the pig iron for the steel, to transport iron ore, to mine iron ore, to transport coal, to mine coal, to quarry limestone, and so on ad infinitum. The facilities which the Standard Oil group[11] once had for lithographing oil can labels and the timber tracts it once controlled as a source of shooks for wooden barrels might be classified

---

[10] It would have been equally appropriate to treat the cluster of activities involved in oil finding, as distinct from oil producing, as one of the main steps in the process.

[11] Reference here is to the group of companies that were at one time drawn together in the Standard Oil Trust. See Chapter Three, footnote 1.

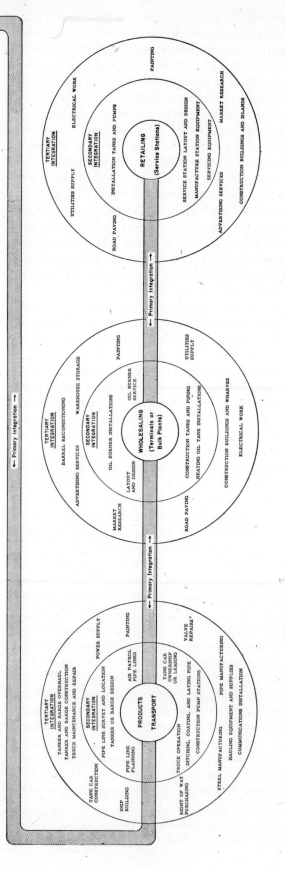

EXHIBIT I-1. RELATIONSHIP OF PRIMARY, SECONDARY, AND TERTIARY INTEGRATION

as lying in one of the remote, outer layers of integration possibilities.

While it is important to recognize the endless ramifications of the vertical integration process, no useful purpose would be served by attempting to set up categories for all possible cases. It seems reasonable therefore to classify as tertiary integration all vertical integration moves beyond those which are clearly in the primary or secondary categories.

Each of the various types of integration processes discussed above may be further classified as involving forward, backward, or "jump" integration. *Forward integration* carries a company closer to the consumer in the oil process. The acquisition of the Robinson refinery by The Ohio Oil Company, the construction of the Keystone products pipe line by The Atlantic Refining Company, and the fairly recent purchase of the Crown Oil Company, one of the largest distributors in Wyoming, by the Sinclair Oil Corporation may be classified as forward integration. Forward integration may also take place when a company engaged in one of the secondary activities undertakes one of the primary oil activities or when a company engaged in a tertiary activity undertakes either a secondary or a primary activity. For example, when the drilling firm of Helmerich and Payne formed the White Eagle Oil Company, a producing concern, in about 1921, the action represented forward integration.

Backward integration carries a company toward its raw materials and characteristically involves a "make or buy" decision. The recent acquisition of refining facilities by many of the farm cooperatives, The Atlantic Refining Company's construction of its two crude oil trunk lines in West Texas, and the acquisition of crude production by the Standard Oil Company (Ohio) may all be classified as backward integration moves. Similarly, all secondary and tertiary integration moves are backward in direction for a company engaged in the related primary step in the oil process. A move by a company engaged in one of the secondary activities to participate in a tertiary activity supporting thereto might also be classified as backward integration.

"*Jump*" integration takes place when a company undertakes some additional step in the oil process other than that which immediately precedes or follows the one it is already performing or when a company skips one of the intermediate steps in a series. Jump integration may, of course, be either forward or backward in direction. In some cases of jump integration the company making the move relies upon other concerns to handle the intervening steps; in other instances the intervening steps are entirely eliminated. Many small refiners, for example, have acquired an interest in producing properties or crude oil gathering lines without acquiring any interest in the common carrier trunk lines by which the oil is moved to their plants. Such moves may be classified as backward, jump integration with the intervening steps being left to other concerns. The recent moves which many refiners have made to by-pass bulk plants with direct, truck transport shipments to service stations, on the other hand, may be classified as forward, jump integration with the intervening step being completely skipped.

III. THE VARIATIONS IN INTEGRATION PATTERNS

The vertical integration processes outlined in the preceding paragraphs produce vertically integrated companies with a myriad of different structures or patterns. The patterns of individual oil companies are continually undergoing readjustments, and these readjustments are fully as important a part of the integration process as the original integration moves themselves. In general, we found that the integration patterns of the oil companies were subject to variations and readjustments with respect to *depth, extent,* and *intensity.* The meaning of the terms depth, extent, and intensity, and the options which management has with respect thereto will be discussed with reference to primary integration only, but it will be apparent that the same considerations apply to secondary and tertiary integration.

The term *depth of integration* we shall use with reference to the number of successive steps in the oil process which a company elects to cover. The Standard Oil Company (Ohio), for example, is engaged in crude oil production, crude oil transportation, refining activities, products transportation, the ownership and operation of terminals and bulk plants, and the ownership and operation of retail service stations. The Deep Rock Oil Company, on the other hand, is engaged in crude oil production, crude oil transportation, and refining activities, but the bulk of its output is turned over to independent distributors at the refinery gate. The difference between the integration arrangements of the two companies in this case may be classified as one of *depth of integration.*

The term *extent of integration* we shall use to designate the amount of a company's participation in successive steps in the oil process. For example, both the Standard Oil Company (Ohio) and The Atlantic Refining Company have engaged in primary integration with respect to crude oil producing activities. The former, however, produced in 1952 only about 29% of its own crude oil supplies while the latter produced about 58% of its refinery requirements. The difference between the two situations may be classified as a difference in *extent of integration.* A move by either company to increase its crude production to 75% of its refinery runs would represent an increase in extent of vertical integration but would at the same time involve further horizontal integration with respect to producing operations.

The term *intensity of integration* we shall use to designate differences in the strength of the integration bond between two successive steps in the oil process. The meaning of the term may be illustrated by listing in order of intensity some of the more common types of arrangements which we found existed between supplying companies (refiners or jobbers) and their retail outlets:

1. Supplier owns land and building and operates station
2. Supplier leases land, owns building, and operates station
3. Supplier leases land and building and operates station
4. Supplier owns land and building and rents to station operator
5. Supplier leases land, owns building, and rents to station operator
6. Supplier leases land and building and rents to station operator
7. Station operator owns or leases station, leases to supplier, and supplier rents back to station operator
8. Station operator owns or leases station from a third party; supplier owns and installs pumps
9. Station operator owns or leases station and all equipment; supplier sells to him for branded resale
10. Station operator owns or leases station and all equipment; supplier sells to him for unbranded resale

The list is by no means complete and could be extended almost indefinitely by taking into account variations in the time periods covered by the leases involved and variations in the conditions and terms of sale, particularly with respect to maximum and minimum quantities. Consideration might also be given to the extent of the formal and informal pressures which the supplying company may exert on the station operator to handle its products exclusively.[12] Finally, attention might be directed to the bonds established between supplying company and station operator by virtue of the merchandising, sales promotion, accounting, training, and managerial assistance which the former may extend to the latter and by virtue of the loans which the supplying company may advance to or notes which it may endorse for the station operator.

The list is, however, adequate to illustrate what is meant by intensity of integration. In case No. 1 the process of primary integration is complete and the intensity of integration at a maximum. In each of the subsequent cases the integration bond is gradually weakened until in case No. 9 it is of minor significance. There is, however, a very real difference between case No. 9 and case No. 10. If a station operator has built up over the years a good local business under the brand name of his supplying company, he will be less likely to shift his business to another supplier than might otherwise be the case.

The same general pattern of variations in intensity of integration was found at the wholesale level as at the retail level. In this case, however, the practice of consignment selling, which has been adopted by a number of oil companies, introduces a new variable to

[12] See *Standard Oil Company of California and Standard Stations, Inc.* vs. *United States,* 337 U. S. 293 (1949).

the problem. A refiner may own bulk plants and lease them to distributors for operation. If the refiner further arranges to ship products to the distributor on a consignment basis, he retains title to the properties through the wholesale level and puts himself in a position to establish the tank wagon selling prices for the products. The integration bond in such a case is clearly of a higher order of intensity than if the refiner makes an outright sale to the distributor.

At the refining level, the processing agreement provides a means of varying the intensity of integration arrangements. If a company engaged in marketing or producing activities enters into a processing agreement with a refining company, primary integration is accomplished but of a far lower order of intensity than if the company were to own or operate the refining facilities itself. The intensity of the integration bond involved in the processing agreement would, of course, vary depending on the time period covered and the character of the agreement with respect to the adjustments permissible in such things as quantities and processing fees.

The integration arrangements accomplished through the ownership of stock in affiliated companies permit a particularly wide range of variations in intensity. The Texas Company, for example, has a 30% stock interest in the Arabian American Oil Company and thereby gains access to a very important source of crude oil. The intensity of the integration bond in cases of this kind might be said to vary somewhat in proportion to the percentage of stock held in the affiliated company. Actually a sharp upward jump in intensity would take place when the 50% mark was crossed, and at all levels of ownership much would depend on how the residual shares were distributed and who held them.

A very complicated example of integration through affiliated companies which suggests the infinite gradations in intensity which are possible in such arrangements may be found in the relationships among the Skelly Oil Company, the Tide Water Associated Oil Company, the Pacific Western Oil Corporation, and their affiliates in December 1951. Paul Getty, individually or as a trustee, controlled about 84% of the stock in the Pacific Western

Oil Corporation which in turn held 11.59% of the stock in the Tide Water Associated Oil Company, 46.98% of the stock in the Mission Corporation, 67% of the stock in both the Pacific Western Oil Company, Ltd., and the Santa Fe Oil Company, Ltd., and 23.99% of the stock in the Mission Development Company.

The latter company held 38.57% of the stock in the Tide Water Associated Oil Company, and the Mission Corporation owned 59.37% of the stock in the Skelly Oil Company. The Skelly Oil Company owned 33% of the stock in both Pacific Western Oil Company, Ltd., and the Santa Fe Oil Company, Ltd., and the Skelly Oil Company and the Pacific Western Oil Corporation together had a 50% interest in a new Kuwait concession, the other 50% interest of which was held by the American Independent Oil Company which, in turn, was owned by a group of about seven other oil companies and two individuals.

Tide Water and Skelly were integrated companies operating in all phases of the oil business; the Pacific Western Oil Corporation, the Pacific Western Oil Company, Ltd., and the Santa Fe Oil Company, Ltd., were primarily producing companies; the Mission Corporation was a holding and producing company and the Mission Development Company was a holding company. In a case of this kind it is extremely difficult, and perhaps impossible, to form an opinion as to how much integration of what kind and of what degree of intensity is actually involved or could potentially be achieved.

The intensity of integration accomplished through the ownership of stock in affiliated companies does not rest upon the percentage of stock held alone, but is also much affected by the nature of the managerial and operating relationships among the companies involved. The Sinclair Oil Corporation, for example, has a 30.59% stock interest in the Richfield Oil Corporation. The latter corporation, however, operates almost entirely as an independent concern and the intensity of the integration link is thus much lower than would normally be suggested by a 30.59% stock equity. Similarly, the integration bond between the Standard Oil Company (New Jersey) and the Humble Oil and Refining Company is substantially weaker than might be inferred from the 72.41%

stock interest which the former has in the latter. The Ashland Oil & Refining Company, on the other hand, recently gained operating control for all practical purposes of the Southern Pipe Line Company by acquisition of about 40% of the stock in the firm.

Another type of integration arrangement which is subject to many gradations in intensity is that which is accomplished through common stock ownership by the owners of one company in other companies engaged in different operations in the oil industry. For example, the principal stockholders of small refining companies, either collectively or individually, frequently own stock in barge, pipe line, producing, or marketing companies. The intensity of the integration bond thus established varies in the first instance depending on the amount of stock which is held. Beyond that, however, it is entirely a matter of personal discretion with the individuals involved.

Many variations in the intensity of integration arrangements have also developed from the occasional usage of long-term contracts. When producing, refining, marketing, or transportation companies enter into long-term purchase, sale, or service contracts with each other they establish some measure of control over another step in the oil process. The intensity of the integration bond thus created varies according to the duration and terms of the contract. The very common practice of chartering tankers provides a good example of "contract integration."

In the light of the foregoing discussion of the integration processes and the many different integration arrangements which they have produced in the oil industry, it is possible to see the full ramifications of the problem of drawing a rigorous distinction between the so-called "integrated" and "nonintegrated" oil companies. Questions such as the following quickly arise: Should a company which performs only one of the major steps in the oil process but which has engaged heavily in secondary and tertiary integration be classed as an integrated company? How many steps in the oil process must a company cover and what must the extent of its participation at each step be before it can be classed as integrated? How intense must the integration

bond between two steps be before we can say that a company has become integrated?

As always in problems of this kind, the cases at the extreme ends of the scale are clear. The Standard Oil Company (New Jersey) with its 250-odd subsidiaries and affiliated companies engaged in extensive crude producing, transportation, refining, wholesaling, and retailing activities both in the United States and in a great many foreign countries is unquestionably an "integrated oil company." At the other end of the scale, the small refiner who buys all his crude oil and sells all his output in the cargo markets on an unbranded basis can be classified without hesitation as a "nonintegrated oil company." In between these two extremes there are any number of fine gradations, and an attempt to determine the exact spot where the nonintegrated companies leave off and the integrated begin is analogous to the task of trying to pick the precise point on the color spectrum where the color red ceases to be "red" and becomes yellow.

In the course of this study therefore we shall use the terms "integrated" and "nonintegrated" merely for the sake of convenience in differentiating companies lying well toward one end of the integration scale from those lying well toward the other end. In general, we shall not employ the term "integrated" unless a substantial amount of primary integration has taken place between at least two of the major steps in the process and unless the integration bond involves ownership, a leasehold, or active management.

IV. SUMMARY

1. In the oil industry, as in many other industries, it is useful to distinguish among three general types of integration: horizontal, vertical, and product integration. Horizontal integration or combination is the process of extending a company's activities in fields in which it is already engaged; vertical integration is the process of increasing the number of successive distribution and processing steps which are under the ownership, management, or control of a single company; and product integration or diversification is the process of increasing the scope of a company's activities by

the manufacture or distribution of additional product lines.

2. We found that there were at least three general types of vertical integration processes at work in the oil industry: primary, secondary, and tertiary. Primary integration takes place when a company engages in the ownership, management, or control of additional steps in the sequence of activities directly involved in the processing and distribution of oil and its products; secondary integration takes place when a company engages in one of the peripheral activities which closely surround each of the main steps in the oil process; and tertiary integration takes place when a company engages in one of the more remote of the peripheral activities related to each of the main steps in the process.

3. The vertical integration processes at work in the oil industry may further be classified as forward, backward, or jump integration. Forward integration carries a company into activities which are closer to the consumer in the oil processing and distribution cycle. Backward integration carries a company toward its raw materials and characteristically involves a "make or buy" decision. Jump integration occurs when a company undertakes some additional step in the oil process other than that which immediately precedes or follows the one it is already performing or when a company skips one of the intermediate steps in a series of three or more.

4. The various integration processes in the oil industry have been strongly at work for a long period of time and have produced a vast number of different types of integration arrangements. These arrangements or patterns are subject to variations in depth, extent, and intensity. Depth of integration has to do with the number of successive steps in the process which a company elects to cover, extent with the amount of its participation in each step, and intensity with the strength of the integration bond between the steps. The integration patterns of individual oil companies are continually undergoing readjustments which are fully as important a part of the integration process as are the original integration moves. themselves.

5. In view of the infinite number of variations which are possible in integration patterns, it is extremely difficult to draw a precise distinction between the so-called "integrated" and "nonintegrated" companies. In reality, the oil companies represent a continuum ranging from integrated to nonintegrated; and while the cases at one end of the scale can be easily distinguished from those at the other, it is almost impossible to pick the precise spot in the middle of the scale where the integrated companies leave off and the nonintegrated begin.

6. The difficulties involved in drawing rigorous distinctions among the many different species of integrated companies imply no ambiguity whatsoever with regard to the nature of the vertical integration processes, and it is with these processes that our study is primarily concerned. It is nearly always possible to classify individual business actions and to tell whether they represent a movement to the right or the left on the scale from integrated to nonintegrated.

CHAPTER TWO

The Extent of Vertical Integration in the Oil Industry in 1950

.ALTHOUGH it has long been recognized that the oil industry has been characterized by a high degree of vertical integration, relatively little systematic information has ever been collected with regard to the extent of the integration arrangements actually existing in the industry as of any particular date. As a result, misconceptions have frequently arisen with regard to such things as the prevalence of vertically integrated structures in the industry, the proportion of the industry's affairs which have been conducted by integrated companies as contrasted with nonintegrated concerns, and the extent to which vertical integration has been employed by small companies as contrasted with large ones.

The purpose of this chapter is to present such data as we were able to accumulate with regard to the vertical integration arrangements existing in the oil industry in 1950. The data pertain to four major topics: (a) the distribution of refining companies, refineries, and refining capacity by size and by type of integration; (b) the proportion of the industry's facilities held and operations conducted by various types of integrated companies; (c) selected operating ratios for various types and sizes of refining companies; and (d) the association of integration with large size at selected levels of the industry. It is our hope that these data may serve not only as a cross-section of the structure of the industry in 1950, but likewise as a bench mark against which future changes may be measured and evaluated.

NOTE: An advance release of the material in this chapter was contained in J. G. McLean and R. W. Haigh, *The Extent of Vertical Integration in the Oil Industry in 1950* (Boston, Harvard Business School, Division of Research, 1952). Extensive revisions and corrections were made in both the text and statistical tables for this publication.

I. NATURE OF THE DATA COLLECTED

As a means of collecting data on vertical integration arrangements in 1950, we found it necessary to make use of questionnaires to the oil companies. Careful study revealed that the statistical information regularly collected by the Bureau of the Census, other government agencies, and the various associations in the industry would not serve our purpose. The Census data, for example, are accumulated primarily by plant establishments rather than by companies, and although it is possible by means of special tabulations to convert the plant establishment figures to company figures, it is very difficult to determine the extent to which companies operating at one level of the industry are active at other levels of the industry. Similar limitations precluded the use of most of the other regularly reported data.

In view of the limitations on the time available for the study, it was impossible to direct a questionnaire to all levels of the industry. It was decided therefore to restrict the collection of data to companies engaged in refining operations. The refining companies represented the best segment of the industry from which to obtain data because their number was small and because the refining activity occupies a central position in the petroleum process. Moreover, it was known that a refining operation was included in nearly all the important types of integrated structures and that the accumulation of data on the activities of refining companies would thus make it possible to construct a fairly complete picture of the integration arrangements existing throughout the industry. It was recognized, however, that data from the refining companies would fail to provide information on all types of integration which did not involve a refining operation and particularly on integration across the wholesaling and retailing levels of the industry by companies engaged solely in marketing activities.[1]

The list of refining companies was compiled primarily from a survey of refineries and refining capacity prepared by the Petroleum Administration for Defense in cooperation with the Bureau of Mines as of January 1, 1951.[2] Individual refineries reported in the survey were grouped by companies, and to the resulting list of refining companies we added the names of a few more firms which we were able to locate in miscellaneous sources. The final mailing list included approximately 275 company names. A number of companies on the list replied to the questionnaire by indicating that they were not in operation during 1950 or that they had gone out of business as a result of liquidations or mergers sometime during 1950. The elimination of these firms from the original list, together with others representing refineries reported as shut down by the Bureau of Mines as of January 1, 1951,[3] established the fact that the number of refining companies in operation in the industry at the close of 1950 was not in excess of 179. Actually, the number of companies in operation was probably somewhat less than 179, because some of the companies which did not reply to our questionnaire were undoubtedly shut down, out of business, or a part of other companies by virtue of stockholding arrangements unknown to us.[4]

Proportion of the Industry Covered by the Survey:

From the 179 operating companies in the industry, we received usable data in response

to our questionnaire from 106. The 179 operating companies in the industry had 331 operating and shutdown refineries with a capacity of 6,943,853 barrels per day, whereas the 106 companies replying to the survey had 246 operating and shutdown refineries with a capacity of 6,576,809 barrels per day. Total industry refinery runs in the United States in 1950 were 2,094,867,000 barrels whereas the 106 survey companies reported domestic refinery runs of 2,038,537,000 barrels. The coverage of the industry by the survey may thus be summarized as follows:

	Percentage of Industry Total Covered by Survey
Number of Operating Refining Companies	59.2%
Number of Operating and Shutdown Refineries	74.3
Operating and Shutdown Refinery Capacity	94.7
Domestic Refinery Runs	97.3

More detailed information with regard to the coverage of the survey is shown in Exhibits II-1 and II-2. Exhibit II-1 shows the distribution of the operating *companies* in the industry and in the survey by their refining capacities and the total refining capacity of the companies in each size category. Exhibit II-2 shows the distribution of the operating and shutdown *refineries* in the industry and in the survey by size and the total capacity of the refineries in each size category. The data in the two exhibits differ because a company often fell in a size category different from its individual refineries. A company with four 2,000 barrels per day plants, for example, had its plants classified in the first size category in the refinery tabulations in Exhibit II-2 whereas the company itself fell in the second size category in the company tabulations in Exhibit II-1.

It is apparent from the data in the two exhibits that the survey covered *all* refining companies and refineries in the industry with capacities in excess of 40,000 barrels per day. Moreover, only five companies with capacities in excess of 15,000 barrels per day failed to respond to the survey. The coverage of companies and of company refining capacity[5] did

---

[1] A fairly large proportion of the wholesaling organizations in the industry own, lease, or operate service stations. Conversely, a number of firms operating one or more service stations also engage in some wholesaling activities. There are, however, a large number of service stations which are owned or leased by individuals active solely at the retailing level of the industry.

[2] Petroleum Administration for Defense, Supply and Transportation Division, *Transportation of Oil* (Washington, Government Printing Office, December 1951).

[3] U. S. Bureau of Mines, *Petroleum Refineries, Including Cracking Plants in the United States, January 1, 1951*, IC 7613, by J. G. Kirby (U. S. Department of the Interior, July 1951).

[4] The definition of "company" used for the purposes of the survey will be clarified by later discussion.

[5] Throughout the discussion "refining capacity" will mean the operating and shutdown capacity of *operating companies*, unless otherwise noted.

EXHIBIT II-1. DISTRIBUTION BY SIZE OF OPERATING REFINING COMPANIES IN INDUSTRY AND SURVEY:* DECEMBER 31, 1950

Company Refining Capacity (B/D)	Total Number of Refining Companies in the		Percentage of Companies Covered by Survey	Capacity of Companies in Each Group in ‡		Percentage of Capacity Covered by Survey
	Industry†	Survey		Industry†	Survey	
0– 5,000	96	40	41.7%	237,894	122,300	51.4%
5,001– 10,000	25	21	84.0	187,884	160,384	85.4
10,001– 15,000	14	6	42.8	171,200	76,000	44.4
15,001– 20,000	9	7	77.8	168,050	133,300	79.3
20,001– 25,000	3	3	100.0	66,000	66,000	100.0
25,001– 30,000	3	1	33.3	81,500	25,500	31.3
30,001– 35,000	2	2	100.0	63,500	63,500	100.0
35,001– 40,000	3	2	66.7	114,000	76,000	66.7
40,001– 45,000	3	3	100.0	132,500	132,500	100.0
45,001– 50,000	2	2	100.0	96,000	96,000	100.0
50,001– 60,000	..	..	....	....	....	....
60,001– 70,000	..	..	....	....	....	....
70,001– 80,000	..	..	....	....	....	....
80,001– 90,000	..	..	....	....	....	....
90,001–100,000	1	1	100.0	92,775	92,775	100.0
100,001–120,000	4	4	100.0	444,250	444,250	100.0
120,001–140,000	..	..	....	....	....	....
140,001–160,000	1	1	100.0	153,500	153,500	100.0
160,001–180,000	1	1	100.0	167,000	167,000	100.0
180,001–200,000	3	3	100.0	575,000	575,000	100.0
200,001–220,000	..	..	....	....	....	....
220,001–240,000	1	1	100.0	240,000	240,000	100.0
240,001–260,000	..	..	....	....	....	....
260,001–280,000	..	..	....	....	....	....
280,001–300,000	..	..	....	....	....	....
300,001–400,000	2	2	100.0	747,800	747,800	100.0
400,001 and over	6	6	100.0	3,205,000	3,205,000	100.0
Total	179	106	59.2%	6,943,853	6,576,809	94.7%

* Data tabulated for groups of less than four companies with permission of all companies in such groups.
† Excludes not more than 32 companies which were entirely inactive as of December 31, 1950.
‡ Includes operating and shutdown capacity of *operating companies.*

not drop below 31% of the industry total in any size category. The coverage of *refineries* was substantially better than the coverage of *companies* in the small-size categories because many of the small refineries were owned by large companies which responded to the survey. The coverage of refineries did not drop below 54% of the industry total or the coverage of plant capacity below 63% of the industry total in any size category.

Method of Consolidating Subsidiaries and Affiliates:

Each company was asked to report the drilling, producing, refining, transportation, and marketing facilities which it owned or leased as of December 31, 1950, and to report the extent of its operations at each level of the industry for the year 1950. The companies were asked to include in the data the facilities and operations of all subsidiary companies which they *normally consolidated* in the preparation of their annual reports.

We found that it was the practice of most of the oil companies to consolidate major subsidiaries in which they held important stock interests. For example, the Standard Oil Company (New Jersey) consolidated subsidiaries such as the Humble Oil and Refining Company, the Esso Standard Oil Company, and the Carter Oil Company; the Standard Oil Company (Indiana) consolidated subsidiaries such as the Utah Oil and Refining Company, the Pan-Am Southern Corporation, and the Pan American Petroleum and Transport Company (together with its subsidiaries, The American Oil Company and Lord Baltimore Filling Stations, Inc.); and the Socony-Vacuum Oil Company, Inc., consolidated subsidiaries such as the Gen-

EXHIBIT II-2. DISTRIBUTION BY SIZE OF REFINERIES OF OPERATING COMPANIES IN INDUSTRY AND SURVEY:* DECEMBER 31, 1950

Refinery Capacity (B/D)	Total Number of Refineries in the		Percentage of Refineries Covered by Survey	Capacity of Refineries in Each Group in		Percentage of Capacity Covered by Survey
	Industry†	Survey†		Industry†	Survey†	
0– 5,000	146	79	54.1%	384,019	244,425	63.6%
5,001– 10,000	65	56	86.1	492,084	428,584	87.1
10,001– 15,000	24	19	79.2	305,200	246,000	80.6
15,001– 20,000	15	13	86.7	273,650	236,900	86.6
20,001– 25,000	11	11	100.0	254,500	254,500	100.0
25,001– 30,000	11	10	90.9	313,400	283,400	90.4
30,001– 35,000	6	6	100.0	201,000	201,000	100.0
35,001– 40,000	7	6	85.7	272,700	234,700	86.1
40,001– 45,000	5	5	100.0	220,400	220,400	100.0
45,001– 50,000	4	4	100.0	192,600	192,600	100.0
50,001– 60,000	12	12	100.0	687,800	687,800	100.0
60,001– 70,000	1	1	100.0	69,000	69,000	100.0
70,001– 80,000	2	2	100.0	149,800	149,800	100.0
80,001– 90,000	4	4	100.0	355,000	355,000	100.0
90,001–100,000	1	1	100.0	100,000	100,000	100.0
100,001–120,000	4	4	100.0	453,000	453,000	100.0
120,001–140,000	5	5	100.0	652,700	652,700	100.0
140,001–160,000	2	2	100.0	300,000	300,000	100.0
160,001–180,000	1	1	100.0	165,000	165,000	100.0
180,001–200,000	2	2	100.0	382,000	382,000	100.0
200,001–220,000	..	..	....	....	....	....
220,001–240,000	1	1	100.0	230,000	230,000	100.0
240,001–260,000	2	2	100.0	490,000	490,000	100.0
260,001–280,000	..	..	....	....	....	....
280,001–300,000	..	..	....	....	....	....
300,001–400,000	..	..	....	....	....	....
400,001 and over	..	..	....	....	....	....
Total	331	246	74.3%	6,943,853	6,576,809	94.7%

* Data tabulated for groups of less than four companies with permission of all companies in such groups.
† Includes the shutdown refineries of operating companies; excludes 32 refineries which belonged to companies entirely inactive as of December 31, 1950.

eral Petroleum Corporation. The general effect of our procedure therefore was to show as one organization the facilities and operations of each parent company together with *all* the facilities and operations of its most important subsidiaries.

Each of the survey companies was also asked to list and report selected data for all *nonconsolidated* petroleum companies in which it held any stock interest and with which it had any significant operating relationship.[6] Wherever possible, we then added to each parent company's *refining* and *marketing* facilities a fractional part of the facilities and operations of all nonconsolidated companies in which it held a 50% or greater stock interest. The fractional part added was proportional to the company's

stockholding in the nonconsolidated affiliate.[7] The nonconsolidated companies in which a survey company held less than a 50% interest were treated as independent concerns wherever possible. For example, the Richfield Oil Corporation, in which the Sinclair Oil Corporation reported a 30.59% interest, was treated as an independent company and survey data were secured directly from it.

To each survey company's *pipe line* facili-

---

[6] The survey companies were not asked to report data for other companies in which they held very small amounts of stock for investment purposes only.

[7] The decision to handle *nonconsolidated* affiliates in this manner was an arbitrary one. A company may, of course, control the entire operations of an affiliate with anything over 50% of the stock. Moreover, under some circumstances a company may, for all practical purposes, gain managerial control of an affiliate with much less than 50% of the stock (see Chapter One). Actually, the matter was of no great significance, because the survey companies reported to us only 29 *nonconsolidated* affiliates which were engaged in refining or marketing and most of them were very small concerns. Of the 29 there were 16 in which the survey company held a 50% or greater interest.

ties and operations, we added a fractional part of the facilities and operations of all nonconsolidated pipe line companies in which it held any stock interest whatsoever. This procedure was followed because refining companies frequently accomplish integration into pipe line activities through joint ownership arrangements. We likewise added to each company's *producing wells* and *crude oil production* a fractional part, corresponding to its stock interest, of the wells and production of nonconsolidated producing companies in which it held any stock interest whatsoever. As in the case of the pipe lines, this procedure was followed because many refining companies gain control of significant quantities of crude oil, particularly in their foreign operations, through the ownership of less than 50% of a producing affiliate.

It was recognized, as pointed out in Chapter One, that many of the smaller refining companies accomplish vertical integration by virtue of the fact that the principal stockholders in the refining company are likewise stockholders of companies operating at other levels of the industry. The task of tracing these interlocking stockholdings would have required the accumulation of a great deal of data on the investment portfolios of individuals, obviously an impossible undertaking. We made no attempt therefore to reflect in our data vertical integration accomplished through the personal stockholding arrangements of the principal owners of refining companies.

Limitations of the Results:

In view of the manner in which the survey was conducted and tabulated, it is apparent that our data represent *minimum* figures. In other words, we know that there was *at least as much* vertical integration in the industry in 1950 as is reflected in the charts and tables presented in this chapter. There were clearly more vertical integration arrangements than our figures indicate for three principal reasons: (1) our survey covered only integrated structures which contained a refining operation; (2) 40.8% of the operating refining companies, principally very small concerns, representing 5.3% of the refining capacity and 2.7% of the refinery runs of the industry, did not reply to our survey; and (3) we were

not able to take account of integration accomplished through the stockholding arrangements of individuals. It should also be noted that our data reflect only those types of vertical integration involving ownership, lease, or operation of facilities and do not cover the integration arrangements of a lower order of intensity discussed in Chapter One.

We believe that the data returned to us by the survey companies was reasonably accurate and in accord with the records regularly compiled by the companies for managerial purposes, reports to stockholders, and reports to various government agencies. In some instances we were able to validate our returns against figures developed in other sources. The figures the survey companies reported for their refining capacity, for example, checked within 1% of the figures compiled by the Petroleum Administration for Defense and the Bureau of Mines for the same group of companies.[8]

It is extremely important to note, however, that technical problems of definition and various other difficulties made it impossible for the survey companies to give us precise figures on many points or for us to maintain strict comparability of data from one company to the next. There is, for example, considerable difference of opinion in the industry as to how bulk terminals, bulk plants, and service stations should be defined, and it is probable that some of the companies were not able to make their counts of such facilities conform precisely to the definitions we gave to them. There is also much difference of opinion as to how refining capacity should be rated and as to when a plant should be placed in the shutdown category. It is highly probable therefore that the reports of the individual companies on these matters were not all prepared on exactly the same basis. Moreover, as will be evident from later discussion, our estimates of the industry totals, against which we compared the data from the survey companies, were subject to an appreciable margin of error in several cases.

We should at this point therefore like to stress the fact that the figures we shall pre-

---

[8] Petroleum Administration for Defense, Supply and Transportation Division, *Transportation of Oil,* and U. S. Bureau of Mines, *Petroleum Refineries, Including Cracking Plants in the United States,* supra.

sent are *reasonable approximations;* we do not claim any very great degree of statistical precision for them. We are in this chapter attempting to paint a picture of the industry with a "broad brush," and we urge the reader to view the results of our survey with that understanding.

II. DISTRIBUTION OF REFINING COMPANIES, REFINERIES, AND REFINING CAPACITY BY SIZE AND TYPE OF INTEGRATION

The first significant approximations it was possible to make from the survey data had to do with the distribution of the refining companies, refineries, and refining capacity in the industry by size and type of integration. To make this analysis, the survey companies were divided into six major categories depending on the levels of the industry at which they were active, as follows: (1) producing-refining; (2) producing-refining-wholesaling; (3) producing-refining-wholesaling-retailing; (4) refining-wholesaling; (5) refining-wholesaling-retailing; and (6) refining alone. Each of these categories could have been split into four subgroups according to whether the companies were engaged in no transportation activities at all, crude oil transportation alone, products transportation alone, or both crude and products transportation. In the interests of simplicity, however, it was decided to use only the six main categories and to show the data on the crude and products transportation activities of the companies in each of the groups in later tables.

In all cases, a company was considered to be active at a level of the industry if it owned or leased facilities at that level. For example, a company was considered to be engaged in retailing if it owned or leased retail service stations, regardless of whether it operated the stations with company employees or under dealership arrangements.[9] Similarly a com-

pany was considered to be engaged in wholesaling if it owned or leased bulk plants or terminals.[10] We found one or two small companies which were engaged in refining and retailing but which by-passed the wholesaling operation entirely. To avoid setting up a separate category, these firms were arbitrarily classed as engaged in wholesaling on the grounds that the effect of their arrangements was to combine the wholesaling function with either the refining or the retailing activity.

Distribution of Companies by Size and Type of Integration:

The distribution of operating refining companies by size and type of integration is shown in Exhibit II-3. In 1950 at least 87 companies or 48.6% of the total in the industry had some type of vertically integrated structure. At least 19 companies or 10.6% of the total in the industry were nonintegrated refiners.[11] Information was not available from the survey with regard to the structures of 73 companies or 40.8% of the total in the industry. Since over three-quarters of these nonsurvey companies were small firms with capacities of less than 5,000 barrels per day, it is probable that a substantial number of them were in the nonintegrated category. If we assume that one-third of the nonsurvey companies were nonintegrated (about the same proportion as in the case of the survey companies in the corresponding size categories), the integrated refining companies in the industry would have outnumbered the nonintegrated by about three to one.

In terms of refining capacity, the integrated companies occupied a far more prominent position in the industry than did the nonintegrated companies, as may be seen from the distribution of the refining capacity of the

---

9 A company which has made the substantial capital investments or lease commitments necessary to acquire service station properties is in a very different competitive position in the market from one which has not. We therefore elected to treat companies owning or leasing service stations as having penetrated the retail level of the industry in an important way. It should be recognized, however, that companies leasing their stations to dealers did not actually participate in retail transactions. Moreover, it should

not be inferred that because the companies owned or leased service stations they controlled the retailing function or the dealers who operated the stations. See Chapter One, page 14, for a discussion of gradations in integration arrangements at the retail level of the industry.

10 An effort was made, however, to exclude bulk plants or terminals which were merely an adjunct to refinery operations.

11 For the purposes of the discussion in this chapter we shall use the term "nonintegrated refiner" to mean a company engaged in refining, but not in producing, wholesaling, or retailing. As noted above, such a company might or might not be engaged in transportation activities.

EXHIBIT II-3. DISTRIBUTION OF OPERATING REFINING COMPANIES BY SIZE AND TYPE:* DECEMBER 31, 1950

(Number of Companies in Parentheses)

Company Refining Capacity (B/D)	Total Industry	Total Survey	Refining Companies in Survey by Size and Type of Integration							Nonsurvey Refining Companies
			Producing and Refining	Producing, Refining, and Wholesaling	Producing, Refining, Wholesaling & Retailing	Refining and Wholesaling	Refining, Wholesaling & Retailing	Total Integrated Refining	Non-integrated Refining	
0– 5,000	100.0% (96)	41.7% (40)	7.3% (7)	1.0% (1)	12.5% (12)	3.1% (3)	6.3% (6)	30.2% (29)	11.5% (11)	58.3% (56)
5,001– 10,000	100.0 (25)	84.0 (21)	12.0 (3)	8.0 (2)	24.0 (6)	8.0 (2)	8.0 (2)	60.0 (15)	24.0 (6)	16.0 (4)
10,001– 15,000	100.0 (14)	42.8 (6)		7.1 (1)	28.6 (4)			35.7 (5)	7.1 (1)	57.2 (8)
15,001– 20,000	100.0 (9)	77.8 (7)		33.3 (3)	33.4 (3)			66.7 (6)	11.1 (1)	22.2 (2)
20,001– 25,000	100.0 (3)	100.0 (3)	33.3 (1)		66.7 (2)			100.0 (3)		
25,001– 30,000	100.0 (3)	33.3 (1)	33.3 (1)					33.3 (1)		66.7 (2)
30,001– 35,000	100.0 (2)	100.0 (2)			100.0 (2)			100.0 (2)		
35,001– 40,000	100.0 (3)	66.7 (2)			66.7 (2)			66.7 (2)		33.3 (1)
40,001– 45,000	100.0 (3)	100.0 (3)			100.0 (3)			100.0 (3)		
45,001– 50,000	100.0 (2)	100.0 (2)		50.0 (1)	50.0 (1)			100.0 (2)		
50,001– 60,000										
60,001– 70,000										
70,001– 80,000										
80,001– 90,000										
90,001–100,000	100.0 (1)	100.0 (1)			100.0 (1)			100.0 (1)		
100,001–120,000	100.0 (4)	100.0 (4)			100.0 (4)			100.0 (4)		
120,001–140,000										
140,001–160,000	100.0 (1)	100.0 (1)			100.0 (1)			100.0 (1)		
160,001–180,000	100.0 (1)	100.0 (1)			100.0 (1)			100.0 (1)		
180,001–200,000	100.0 (3)	100.0 (3)			100.0 (3)			100.0 (3)		
200,001–220,000										
220,001–240,000	100.0 (1)	100.0 (1)			100.0 (1)			100.0 (1)		
240,001–260,000										
260,001–280,000										
280,001–300,000										
300,001–400,000	100.0 (2)	100.0 (2)			100.0 (2)			100.0 (2)		
400,001 and over	100.0 (6)	100.0 (6)			100.0 (6)			100.0 (6)		
Total	100.0% (179)	59.2% (106)	6.7% (12)	4.5% (8)	30.1% (54)	2.8% (5)	4.5% (8)	48.6% (87)	10.6% (19)	40.8% (73)

* Data tabulated for groups of less than four companies with permission of all companies in such groups.

various groups of companies in Exhibit II-4. The 87 integrated refining companies had 93.2% of the refining capacity of the industry whereas the 19 nonintegrated companies reporting to the survey had only 1.5% of the total refining capacity. The remaining 5.3% of the capacity was held by the 73 small companies not reporting to the survey.

Among the integrated companies reporting to the survey, the firms which were active at all four major levels of the industry were by far the most important in terms of both numbers and refining capacity. Exhibits II-3 and II-4 indicate that at least 54 companies, representing 30.1% of the total number of companies in the industry and 89.1% of the refining capacity of the industry, fell in the producing-refining-wholesaling-retailing category. The integrated companies which were active at only two or three levels of the industry were relatively insignificant in terms of numbers and refining capacity.

The small refining companies in 1950 had a variety of integrated and nonintegrated structures, but the large companies were almost without exception highly integrated concerns. Exhibit II-3 reveals that there were not more than two companies in the industry with refining capacities in excess of 35,000 barrels per day which did not report activities at all four levels of the industry. One of these two companies was active at all levels except retailing, and the other did not reply to the survey. Conversely, it may be seen from Exhibit II-3 that the completely nonintegrated structures were found only among companies with refining capacities of 20,000 barrels per day or less. Moreover, even if the largest nonsurvey company is assumed to have been nonintegrated, the maximum size of the nonintegrated companies could have been only 40,000 barrels per day.

As noted earlier, we elected not to classify the refining companies in Exhibits II-3 and II-4 according to their ownership of various types of transportation facilities. It is important to note, however, that nearly all the integrated companies and a substantial number of the nonintegrated companies did own or lease pipe line facilities. Of the 87 integrated refining companies covered by the survey, 70 had one or more types of pipe line facilities;

68 had gathering lines, 41 had crude trunk lines, and 41 had products pipe lines. Of the 19 nonintegrated refining companies covered by the survey, 6 had one or more types of pipe line facilities; 4 had gathering lines, 2 had crude trunk lines, and 1 had products pipe lines. More detailed data on the transportation facilities and operations of the various types of companies are shown in Exhibits II-7 and II-8.

Distribution of Refineries by Size and Type of Integration:

In Exhibit II-5 the refineries in the industry have been classified by size and according to the type of company to which they belonged. The tabulation shows that in 1950 the integrated refining companies held at least 226 refineries or 68.3% of the total number in the industry. The nonintegrated refining companies held at least 20 refineries or 6.0% of the total in the industry. Information was not available with respect to 85 refineries, representing 25.7% of the total in the industry. If we assume that about 15% of these nonsurvey refineries might have belonged to nonintegrated companies (approximately the same proportion as in the case of the survey companies in the corresponding size categories), the integrated companies would have owned about nine times as many plants as the nonintegrated companies.

The integrated companies which participated in activities at all four of the major levels of the business held 178 refineries in 1950 or 53.8% of the total number in the industry. These plants included nearly all the large refineries. There were only three plants with capacities in excess of 20,000 barrels per day which were not reported as belonging to a producing-refining-wholesaling-retailing company. One of these plants belonged to a producing-refining-wholesaling company, and the other two belonged to nonsurvey companies. As a corollary, it may be noted that the plants of the nonintegrated companies and of companies active at only two or three levels of the industry were all relatively small in size and did not exceed 40,000 barrels per day capacity even if it is assumed that all the nonsurvey refineries belonged to such companies.

The distribution of the *capacity* of the re-

EXHIBIT II-4. DISTRIBUTION OF CAPACITY OF OPERATING REFINING COMPANIES BY SIZE AND TYPE OF COMPANY: *

DECEMBER 31, 1950

Company Refining Capacity (B/D)	Total Industry†	Total Survey†	Refining Capacity in Survey Classified by Size and Type of Company†							Nonsurvey Refining Companies
			Producing and Refining	Producing, Refining, and Wholesaling	Producing, Refining, Wholesaling & Retailing	Refining and Wholesaling	Refining, Wholesaling & Retailing	Total Integrated Refining	Non-integrated Refining	
0– 5,000	237,894	122,300	20,000	1,000	47,500	3,800	19,500	91,800	30,500	115,594
5,001– 10,000	187,884	160,384	25,000	15,834	45,600	16,000	15,000	117,434	42,950	27,500
10,001– 15,000	171,200	76,000	……	14,000	51,000	……	……	65,000	11,000	95,200
15,001– 20,000	168,050	133,300	……	58,300	55,000	……	……	113,300	20,000	34,750
20,001– 25,000	66,000	66,000	22,000	……	44,000	……	……	66,000	……	……
25,001– 30,000	81,500	25,500	25,500	……	……	……	……	25,500	……	56,000
30,001– 35,000	63,500	63,500	……	……	63,500	……	……	63,500	……	……
35,001– 40,000	114,000	76,000	……	……	76,000	……	……	76,000	……	38,000
40,001– 45,000	132,500	132,500	……	……	132,500	……	……	132,500	……	……
45,001– 50,000	96,000	96,000	……	50,000	46,000	……	……	96,000	……	……
50,001– 60,000	……	……	……	……	……	……	……	……	……	……
60,001– 70,000	……	……	……	……	……	……	……	……	……	……
70,001– 80,000	……	……	……	……	……	……	……	……	……	……
80,001– 90,000	……	……	……	……	……	……	……	……	……	……
90,001–100,000	92,775	92,775	……	……	92,775	……	……	92,775	……	……
100,001–120,000	444,250	444,250	……	……	444,250	……	……	444,250	……	……
120,001–140,000	……	……	……	……	……	……	……	……	……	……
140,001–160,000	153,500	153,500	……	……	153,500	……	……	153,500	……	……
160,001–180,000	167,000	167,000	……	……	167,000	……	……	167,000	……	……
180,001–200,000	575,000	575,000	……	……	575,000	……	……	575,000	……	……
200,001–220,000	……	……	……	……	……	……	……	……	……	……
220,001–240,000	240,000	240,000	……	……	240,000	……	……	240,000	……	……
240,001–260,000	……	……	……	……	……	……	……	……	……	……
260,001–280,000	……	……	……	……	……	……	……	……	……	……
280,001–300,000	……	……	……	……	……	……	……	……	……	……
300,001–400,000	747,800	747,800	……	……	747,800	……	……	747,800	……	……
400,001 and over	3,205,000	3,205,000	……	……	3,205,000	……	……	3,205,000	……	……
Total	6,943,853	6,576,809	92,500	139,134	6,186,425	19,800	34,500	6,472,359	104,450	367,044

* Data tabulated for groups of less than four companies with permission of all companies in such groups.

† Includes operating and shutdown capacity of operating companies.

EXHIBIT II-4 (CONTINUED)

(Percentages of Total Industry)

Refining Capacity in Survey Classified by Size and Type of Company †

Company Refining Capacity (B/D)	Total Industry †	Total Survey †	Producing and Refining	Producing, Refining, and Wholesaling	Producing, Refining, Wholesaling & Retailing	Refining and Wholesaling	Refining, Wholesaling & Retailing	Total Integrated Refining	Non-integrated Refining	Nonsurvey Refining Companies
0– 5,000	100.0%	51.4%	8.4%	0.4%	20.0%	1.6%	8.2%	38.6%	12.8%	48.6%
5,001– 10,000	100.0	85.4	13.3	8.4	24.3	8.5	8.0	62.5	22.9	14.6
10,001– 15,000	100.0	44.4		8.2	29.8			38.0	6.4	55.6
15,001– 20,000	100.0	79.3		34.7	32.7			67.4	11.9	20.7
20,001– 25,000	100.0	100.0	33.3		66.7			100.0		
25,001– 30,000	100.0	31.3	31.3					31.3		68.7
30,001– 35,000	100.0	100.0			100.0			100.0		
35,001– 40,000	100.0	66.7			66.7			66.7		33.3
40,001– 45,000	100.0	100.0			100.0			100.0		
45,001– 50,000	100.0	100.0		52.1	47.9			100.0		
50,001– 60,000										
60,001– 70,000										
70,001– 80,000										
80,001– 90,000	100.0	100.0			100.0			100.0		
90,001–100,000	100.0	100.0			100.0			100.0		
100,001–120,000										
120,001–140,000	100.0	100.0			100.0			100.0		
140,001–160,000	100.0	100.0			100.0			100.0		
160,001–180,000	100.0	100.0			100.0			100.0		
180,001–200,000	100.0	100.0			100.0			100.0		
200,001–220,000	100.0	100.0			100.0			100.0		
220,001–240,000										
240,001–260,000										
260,001–280,000										
280,001–300,000	100.0	100.0			100.0			100.0		
300,001–400,000	100.0	100.0			100.0			100.0		
400,001 and over	100.0	100.0			100.0			100.0		
Total	100.0%	94.7%	1.3%	2.0%	89.1%	0.3%	0.5%	93.2%	1.5%	5.3%

EXHIBIT II-5. DISTRIBUTION OF REFINERIES OF OPERATING COMPANIES BY SIZE AND TYPE OF COMPANY: *

DECEMBER 31, 1950

(Number of Refineries in Parentheses)

Refinery Capacity (B/D)	Total Industry†	Total Survey†	Refineries in Survey by Size and Type of Integration†							All Other Refineries in Industry
			Producing and Refining	Producing, Refining and Wholesaling	Producing, Refining, Wholesaling & Retailing	Refining and Wholesaling	Refining, Wholesaling & Retailing	Total Integrated Refining	Non-integrated Refining	
0- 5,000	100.0% (146)	54.1% (79)	8.9% (13)	3.4% (5)	24.7% (36)	3.4% (5)	5.5% (8)	45.9% (67)	8.2% (12)	45.9% (67)
5,001- 10,000	100.0 (65)	86.1 (56)	6.2 (4)	9.2 (6)	58.5 (38)	1.5 (1)	1.5 (1)	76.9 (50)	9.2 (6)	13.9 (9)
10,001- 15,000	100.0 (24)	79.2 (19)	4.2 (1)	4.2 (1)	66.6 (16)			75.0 (18)	4.2 (1)	20.8 (5)
15,001- 20,000	100.0 (15)	86.7 (13)	6.7 (1)	6.7 (1)	66.6 (10)			80.0 (12)	6.7 (1)	13.3 (2)
20,001- 25,000	100.0 (11)	100.0 (11)			100.0 (11)			100.0 (11)		
25,001- 30,000	100.0 (11)	90.9 (10)			90.9 (10)			90.9 (10)		9.1 (1)
30,001- 35,000	100.0 (6)	100.0 (6)			100.0 (6)			100.0 (6)		
35,001- 40,000	100.0 (7)	85.7 (6)		14.3 (1)	71.4 (5)			85.7 (6)		14.3 (1)
40,001- 45,000	100.0 (5)	100.0 (5)			100.0 (5)			100.0 (5)		
45,001- 50,000	100.0 (4)	100.0 (4)			100.0 (4)			100.0 (4)		
50,001- 60,000	100.0 (12)	100.0 (12)			100.0 (12)			100.0 (12)		
60,001- 70,000	100.0 (1)	100.0 (1)			100.0 (1)			100.0 (1)		
70,001- 80,000	100.0 (2)	100.0 (2)			100.0 (2)			100.0 (2)		
80,001- 90,000	100.0 (4)	100.0 (4)			100.0 (4)			100.0 (4)		
90,001-100,000	100.0 (1)	100.0 (1)			100.0 (1)			100.0 (1)		
100,001-120,000	100.0 (4)	100.0 (4)			100.0 (4)			100.0 (4)		
120,001-140,000	100.0 (5)	100.0 (5)			100.0 (5)			100.0 (5)		
140,001-160,000	100.0 (2)	100.0 (2)			100.0 (2)			100.0 (2)		
160,001-180,000	100.0 (1)	100.0 (1)			100.0 (1)			100.0 (1)		
180,001-200,000	100.0 (2)	100.0 (2)			100.0 (2)			100.0 (2)		
200,001-220,000										
220,001-240,000	100.0 (1)	100.0 (1)			100.0 (1)			100.0 (1)		
240,001-260,000	100.0 (2)	100.0 (2)			100.0 (2)			100.0 (2)		
260,001-280,000										
280,001-300,000										
300,001-400,000										
400,001 and over										
Total	100.0% (331)	74.3% (246)	5.8% (19)	4.2% (14)	53.8% (178)	1.8% (6)	2.7% (9)	68.3% (226)	6.0% (20)	25.7% (85)

* Data tabulated for groups of less than four companies with permission of all companies in such groups.

† Includes operating and shutdown refineries of operating companies.

fineries in the industry in 1950 by size of plant and type of company is shown in Exhibit II-6.

III. Participation of Integrated Companies in the Affairs of the Industry

The second major area in which it was possible to make approximations from the survey data concerned the proportion of the industry's facilities which were owned or leased by the various types of integrated companies at the close of 1950 and the proportion of the industry's operations which were conducted by the various types of integrated companies during the year 1950.[12] The information is tabulated in Exhibits II-7 and II-8 and represented graphically in Exhibit II-9.[13]

The first columns in Exhibits II-7 and II-8 show aggregate figures for the facilities or operations of the entire industry.[14] The succeeding columns then show the facilities or operations reported by the various groups of integrated companies covered in the survey. The figures in the last column in each table were obtained by deducting the facilities and operations of all survey companies from the total facilities and operations of the industry. The figures in the last column of each exhibit thus indicate the proportion of the industry's facilities or operations controlled by three kinds of companies: (1) refining companies, integrated or nonintegrated, which did not reply to the survey; (2) nonintegrated companies operating *solely* at the producing (including drilling), wholesaling, retailing, or transportation levels of the industry; and (3) companies engaged in both wholesaling and retailing. Any of the companies in the three groups might, of course, also have been engaged in transportation activities.

Since the nonsurvey refining companies represented only 5.3% of the refining capacity

and 2.7% of the refinery runs of the industry and since more than three-quarters of them were in the 0–5,000 barrels per day refining capacity range, their facilities and operations probably constituted only a very small proportion of the totals shown in the last column of the two tables, except in the case of refining facilities and operations. The figures in the last column of the two tables for producing, transportation, wholesaling, and retailing activities therefore reflect almost entirely the facilities and operations of the companies in groups (2) and (3) above.

Facilities Controlled by Integrated Companies:

Exhibit II-7 and Exhibit II-9 reveal that there were wide variations in the proportions of the industry's facilities owned or leased by integrated companies at the successive levels of the business. The control of facilities by integrated companies was of greatest significance in connection with refining and pipe line transportation equipment. As may be seen from the two exhibits, integrated companies at the close of 1950 controlled at least 68.3% of the industry's refineries, 93.2% of the crude charging capacity, and 93.8% of the cracked gasoline capacity. Integrated companies likewise controlled 85.4% of the industry's crude gathering lines, 82.1% of the crude trunk lines, and 92.2% of the products pipe lines. At the other end of the scale, however, the integrated companies controlled only 7.7% of the industry's drilling rigs and only 35.4% of the industry's producing oil wells. The control of facilities by integrated companies was also of moderate significance at the retail end of the process, amounting to ownership or lease of only 51.6% of the total service stations. The control of facilities by integrated companies was therefore heaviest in the middle of the oil process and declined toward both ends.

The data in Exhibits II-7 and II-9 also indicate that nearly all the facilities controlled by integrated companies were those held by companies engaged in operations at all four levels of the industry. The facilities owned or leased by all other types of integrated companies amounted to less than 6% of the industry totals, except in the case of number of refineries where their share of the industry total was 14.5%.

---

[12] In the case of tankers and tank cars our data cover only the facilities *owned* by the companies.

[13] In Exhibit II-9 the facilities and operations of the industry have been arranged somewhat in the order in which they occur in the oil process. Tankers were arbitrarily arrayed with the crude transportation facilities and tank cars with the products transportation facilities, although tankers and tank cars are used for hauling both crude oil and refined products.

[14] The methods used in establishing the industry totals are outlined in the Technical Note at the end of the chapter.

EXHIBIT II-6. DISTRIBUTION OF CAPACITY OF REFINERIES OF OPERATING COMPANIES BY SIZE OF PLANT AND TYPE OF COMPANY: * DECEMBER 31, 1950

Refinery Capacity (B/D)	Total Industry†	Total Survey†	Refinery Capacity in Survey Classified by Size of Plant and Type of Company†							All Other Refineries in Industry
			Producing and Refining	Producing, Refining, and Wholesaling	Producing, Refining, Wholesaling & Retailing	Refining and Wholesaling	Refining, Wholesaling & Retailing	Total Integrated Refining	Non-integrated Refining	
0– 5,000	384,019	244,425	32,500	17,800	124,325	9,800	26,500	210,925	33,500	139,594
5,001– 10,000	492,084	428,584	31,000	47,834	291,800	10,000	8,000	388,634	39,950	63,500
10,001– 15,000	305,200	246,000	11,000	13,500	210,500	....	....	235,000	11,000	59,200
15,001– 20,000	273,650	236,900	18,000	20,000	178,900	....	....	216,900	20,000	36,750
20,001– 25,000	254,500	254,500	....	....	254,500	....	....	254,500	....	....
25,001– 30,000	313,400	283,400	....	....	283,400	....	....	283,400	....	30,000
30,001– 35,000	201,000	201,000	....	....	201,000	....	....	201,000	....	....
35,001– 40,000	272,700	234,700	....	40,000	194,700	....	....	234,700	....	38,000
40,001– 45,000	220,400	220,400	....	....	220,400	....	....	220,400	....	....
45,001– 50,000	192,600	192,600	....	....	192,600	....	....	192,600	....	....
50,001– 60,000	687,800	687,800	....	....	687,800	....	....	687,800	....	....
60,001– 70,000	69,000	69,000	....	....	69,000	....	....	69,000	....	....
70,001– 80,000	149,800	149,800	....	....	149,800	....	....	149,800	....	....
80,001– 90,000	355,000	355,000	....	....	355,000	....	....	355,000	....	....
90,001–100,000	100,000	100,000	....	....	100,000	....	....	100,000	....	....
100,001–120,000	453,000	453,000	....	....	453,000	....	....	453,000	....	....
120,001–140,000	652,700	652,700	....	....	652,700	....	....	652,700	....	....
140,001–160,000	300,000	300,000	....	....	300,000	....	....	300,000	....	....
160,001–180,000	165,000	165,000	....	....	165,000	....	....	165,000	....	....
180,001–200,000	382,000	382,000	....	....	382,000	....	....	382,000	....	....
200,001–220,000	....	....	....	....	....	....	....	....	....	....
220,001–240,000	230,000	230,000	....	....	230,000	....	....	230,000	....	....
240,001–260,000	490,000	490,000	....	....	490,000	....	....	490,000	....	....
260,001–280,000	....	....	....	....	....	....	....	....	....	....
280,001–300,000	....	....	....	....	....	....	....	....	....	....
300,001–400,000	....	....	....	....	....	....	....	....	....	....
400,001 and over	....	....	....	....	....	....	....	....	....	....
Total	6,943,853	6,576,809	92,500	139,134	6,186,425	19,800	34,500	6,472,359	104,450	367,044

* Data tabulated for groups of less than four companies with permission of all companies in such groups.
† Includes operating and shutdown capacity of operating companies.

EXHIBIT II-6 (CONTINUED)

(Percentages of Total Industry)

Refinery Capacity (B/D)	Total Industry †	Total Survey †	Refining Capacity in Survey Classified by Size of Plant and Type of Company †							
			Producing and Refining	Producing, Refining, and Wholesaling	Producing, Refining, Wholesaling & Retailing	Refining and Wholesaling	Refining, Wholesaling & Retailing	Total Integrated Refining	Non-integrated Refining	All Other Refineries in Industry
0- 5,000	100.0%	63.6%	8.5%	4.6%	32.4%	2.5%	6.9%	54.9%	8.7%	36.4%
5,001- 10,000	100.0	87.1	6.3	9.7	59.3	2.1	1.6	79.0	8.1	12.9
10,001- 15,000	100.0	80.6	3.6	4.4	69.0	....	....	77.0	3.6	19.4
15,001- 20,000	100.0	86.6	6.6	7.3	65.4	....	....	79.3	7.3	13.4
20,001- 25,000	100.0	100.0	....	....	100.0	....	....	100.0	....	....
25,001- 30,000	100.0	90.4	....	....	90.4	....	....	90.4	....	9.6
30,001- 35,000	100.0	100.0	....	....	100.0	....	....	100.0	....	....
35,001- 40,000	100.0	86.1	....	14.7	71.4	....	....	86.1	....	13.9
40,001- 45,000	100.0	100.0	....	....	100.0	....	....	100.0	....	....
45,001- 50,000	100.0	100.0	....	....	100.0	....	....	100.0	....	....
50,001- 60,000	100.0	100.0	....	....	100.0	....	....	100.0	....	....
60,001- 70,000	100.0	100.0	....	....	100.0	....	....	100.0	....	....
70,001- 80,000	100.0	100.0	....	....	100.0	....	....	100.0	....	....
80,001- 90,000	100.0	100.0	....	....	100.0	....	....	100.0	....	....
90,001-100,000	100.0	100.0	....	....	100.0	....	....	100.0	....	....
100,001-120,000	100.0	100.0	....	....	100.0	....	....	100.0	....	....
120,001-140,000	100.0	100.0	....	....	100.0	....	....	100.0	....	....
140,001-160,000	100.0	100.0	....	....	100.0	....	....	100.0	....	....
160,001-180,000	100.0	100.0	....	....	100.0	....	....	100.0	....	....
180,001-200,000	100.0	100.0	....	....	100.0	....	....	100.0	....	....
200,001-220,000	....	....	....	....	....	....	....	....	....	....
220,001-240,000	100.0	100.0	....	....	100.0	....	....	100.0	....	....
240,001-260,000	100.0	100.0	....	....	100.0	....	....	100.0	....	....
260,001-280,000	....	....	....	....	....	....	....	....	....	....
280,001-300,000	....	....	....	....	....	....	....	....	....	....
300,001-400,000	....	....	....	....	....	....	....	....	....	....
400,001 and over	....	....	....	....	....	....	....	....	....	....
Total	100.0%	94.7%	1.3%	2.0%	89.1%	0.3%	0.5%	93.2%	1.5%	5.3%

EXHIBIT II-7. INDUSTRY FACILITIES OWNED OR LEASED BY VARIOUS TYPES OF COMPANIES: DECEMBER 31, 1950

Items	Total Industry	Facilities of Companies in Survey Classified by Type of Integration							All Other Companies in Industry
		Producing and Refining	Producing, Refining, and Wholesaling	Producing, Refining, Wholesaling & Retailing	Refining and Wholesaling	Refining, Wholesaling, & Retailing	Total Integrated Refining	Non-integrated Refining	
Number of Refining Companies	179	12	8	54	5	8	87	19	73
PRODUCING FACILITIES									
Number of Drilling Rigs	4,700 (a)	32	5	324	0	0	361	0	4,339
Rotary Rigs	3,300 (a)	22	4	281	0	0	307	0	2,993
Cable Rigs	1,400 (a)	10	1	43	0	0	54	0	1,346
Number of Producing Oil Wells	465,870 (b)	1,705	918	162,308	....	....	164,931	....	300,939
REFINING FACILITIES*									
Number of Refineries	331 (c)	19	14	178	6	9	226	20	85
Crude Oil Capacity (B/D)	6,943,853 (c)	92,500	139,134	6,186,425	19,800	34,500	6,472,359	104,450	367,044
Cracked Gasoline Capacity (B/D)	2,046,290 (c)	18,070	52,344	1,840,948	1,500	5,750	1,918,612	17,400	110,278
TRANSPORTATION FACILITIES									
Pipe Line Mileage									
Crude Oil Gathering	60,774 (d)	1,614	1,081	48,521	24	692	51,932	252	8,590
Crude Oil Trunk	72,436 (d)	317	287	58,529	232	105	59,470	9	12,957
Products Lines	24,192 (d)	53	268	21,975	0	14	22,310	1	1,881
Number of Tankers	432 (e)	0	0	207	0	0	207	0	225
Tanker DWT	6,801,500 (e)	0	0	3,138,267	0	0	3,138,267	0	3,663,233
Number of Tank Cars	111,451 (f)	140	107	19,408	0	116	19,771	0	91,680
MARKETING FACILITIES									
Number of Terminals and Bulk Plants	30,000 (g)	....	111	20,422	6	51	20,590	....	9,410
Number of Service Stations	188,000 (g)	....	....	96,619	....	371	96,990	....	91,010
Company Operated	....	....	....	3,037	....	23	3,060	....	....
Dealer Operated	....	....	....	93,582	....	348	93,930	....	....

* Includes operating and shutdown facilities of operating companies.

EXHIBIT II-7 (CONTINUED)

(Percentages of Industry Total)

Number of Refining Companies	100.0%	6.7%	4.5%	30.1%	2.8%	4.5%	48.6%	10.6%	40.8%
PRODUCING FACILITIES									
Number of Drilling Rigs	100.0	0.7	0.1	6.9	0.0	0.0	7.7	0.0	92.3
Rotary Rigs	100.0	0.7	0.1	8.5	0.0	0.0	9.3	0.0	90.7
Cable Rigs	100.0	0.7	0.1	3.1	0.0	0.0	3.9	0.0	96.1
Number of Producing Oil Wells	100.0	0.4	0.2	34.8	....	....	35.4	....	64.6
REFINING FACILITIES									
Number of Refineries	100.0	5.8	4.2	53.8	1.8	2.7	68.3	6.0	25.7
Crude Oil Capacity (B/D)	100.0	1.3	2.0	89.1	0.3	0.5	93.2	1.5	5.3
Cracked Gasoline Capacity (B/D)	100.0	0.9	2.5	90.0	0.1	0.3	93.8	0.8	5.4
TRANSPORTATION FACILITIES									
Pipe Line Mileage									
Crude Oil Gathering	100.0	2.6	1.8	79.8	0.1	1.1	85.4	0.4	14.2
Crude Oil Trunk	100.0	0.4	0.4	80.8	0.3	0.2	82.1	0.0	17.9
Products Lines	100.0	0.2	1.1	90.8	0.0	0.1	92.2	0.0	7.8
Number of Tankers	100.0	0.0	0.0	47.9	0.0	0.0	47.9	0.0	52.1
Tanker DWT	100.0	0.0	0.0	46.1	0.0	0.0	46.1	0.0	53.9
Number of Tank Cars	100.0	0.1	0.1	17.4	0.0	0.1	17.7	0.0	82.3
MARKETING FACILITIES									
Number of Terminals and Bulk Plants	100.0	....	0.4	68.0	0.0	0.2	68.6	....	31.4
Number of Service Stations	100.0	....	....	51.4	....	0.2	51.6	....	48.4

(a) *Oil and Gas Journal*, September 29, 1952, p. 166.

(b) American Petroleum Institute, *Statistical Bulletin*, Vol. XXXIII, No. 21, May 1, 1952. (Basic data drawn from *Oil and Gas Journal* and California office of A.P.I.)

(c) U.S. Bureau of Mines, *Petroleum Refineries, Including Cracking Plants, in the United States, January 1, 1951*, IC 7613, by J. G. Kirby (Government Printing Office), with minor adjustments made possible by survey information.

(d) U.S. Bureau of Mines, *Crude-Oil and Refined Products Pipe Line Mileage in the United States, January 1, 1950*, IC 7585, by A. T. Coumbe and I. F. Avery (Government Printing Office, October 1950); Interstate Commerce Commission, Bureau of Transport Economics and Statistics, *Selected Statistics of Oil Pipe Line Companies Reporting to the I.C.C. for the Year Ended December 31, 1950*, Statement No. 5152 (Washington, October 1951). See Technical Note at end of chapter for discussion of imputations.

(e) Petroleum Administration for Defense, Supply and Transportation Division, *Transportation of Oil*, December 1951 (Government Printing Office). Supplementary data secured through the courtesy of Mr. Benedict Saurino, Sun Oil Company. These sources also used for breakdowns by groups of companies. Survey data cover only tankers *owned* by oil companies.

(f) Interstate Commerce Commission, Bureau of Transport Economics and Statistics, *Selected Statistics from Annual Reports of Private Car Owners for Year Ended December 31, 1950*, Statement No. 529 (Washington, March 1952). This source also used for breakdown by groups of companies. Survey data cover only tank cars *owned* by oil companies.

(g) U.S. Census of Business, 1948, Volume IV, *Wholesale Trade — General Statistics; Commodity Line Sales Statistics, "Petroleum Bulk Stations,"* 14.07 and 14.47 (Government Printing Office, 1952). See Technical Note at end of chapter for adjustment of 1948 figures to 1950.

EXHIBIT II-8. INDUSTRY OPERATIONS CONDUCTED BY VARIOUS TYPES OF COMPANIES: 1950

Items	Total Industry	Operations of Companies in Survey Classified by Type of Integration							All Other Companies in Industry
		Producing and Refining	Producing, Refining, and Wholesaling	Producing, Refining, Wholesaling & Retailing	Refining and Wholesaling	Refining, Wholesaling & Retailing	Total Integrated Refining	Non-integrated Refining	
Number of Refining Companies	179	12	8	54	5	8	87	19	73
PRODUCING OPERATIONS									
Number of Wells Completed	43,287 (a)	220	148	10,975	....	....	11,343	....	31,944
Oil Wells	24,416 (a)	130	92	7,742	....	....	7,964	....	16,452
Gas Wells	2,837 (a)	25	6	741	....	....	772	....	2,065
Dry Holes	14,786 (a)	58	49	1,820	....	....	1,927	....	12,859
Service Wells	1,248 (a)	7	1	672	....	....	680	....	568
Net Crude Oil Production (1,000 barrels)	2,426,877	6,781	4,095	1,719,446	....	....	1,730,322	....	696,555
Domestic	1,726,877 (b)	6,725	4,095	1,022,386	....	....	1,033,206	....	693,671
Foreign	700,000 (c)	56	0	697,060	....	....	697,116	....	2,884
REFINING OPERATIONS (1,000 barrels)									
Domestic Refinery Runs	2,094,867 (b)	28,103	31,083	1,944,361	5,077	7,789	2,016,413	22,124	56,330
Yield of Refined Products	2,094,867 (b)	28,103	31,083	1,944,361	5,077	7,789	2,016,413	22,124	56,330
Gasolines and Naphthas	903,454 (b)	12,420	14,622	844,467	1,281	2,996	875,786	7,606	20,062
Kerosene and Distillates	517,424 (b)	7,439	9,090	474,037	1,130	1,538	493,234	5,043	19,147
Residual Fuel Oil	425,217 (b)	4,563	6,036	400,116	1,000	1,824	413,539	6,528	5,150
Other Products	256,132 (b)	3,537	428	212,785	1,414	1,119	219,283	2,151	34,698
TRANSPORTATION OPERATIONS (1,000 barrels)									
Crude Oil Runs from Wells	1,973,574 (d)	12,497	12,809	1,455,948	593	1,816	1,483,663	3,759	486,152
Crude Oil Delivered from Gathering and Trunk Lines	2,791,404 (d)	16,015	12,371	2,286,474	2,283	2,483	2,319,626	5,504	466,274
Products Delivered from Pipe Lines	576,978 (d)	906	4,631	524,391	0	596	530,524	0	46,454
Tank Car Miles (1,000)	1,864,681 (e)	3,436	3,360	325,214	0	1,808	333,818	0	1,530,863
MARKETING OPERATIONS (1,000 barrels)									
Terminal and Bulk Plant Sales*	1,661,000 (d)	....	15,003	1,000,257	600	4,216	1,020,076	....	641,275
Gasolines and Naphthas	1,150,000 (d)	....	9,083	702,124	339	2,860	714,406	....	435,437
Kerosene and Distillates	511,000 (d)	....	5,920	298,133	261	1,356	305,670	....	205,838
Service Station Sales of Gasoline†	480,000 (d)	....	....	277,656	....	1,025	278,681	....	201,735
Company Operated Stations	....	....	....	19,756	....	128	19,884	....	....
Dealer Operated Stations	....	....	....	257,900	....	897	258,797	....	....

EXHIBIT II-8 (CONTINUED)

(Percentages of Industry Total)

Number of Refining Companies	100.0%	6.7%	4.5%	30.1%	2.8%	4.5%	48.6%	10.6%	40.8%
PRODUCING OPERATIONS									
Number of Wells Completed	100.0	0.5	0.3	25.4	....	....	26.2	....	73.8
Oil Wells	100.0	0.5	0.4	31.7	....	....	32.6	....	67.4
Gas Wells	100.0	0.9	0.2	26.1	....	....	27.2	....	72.8
Dry Holes	100.0	0.4	0.3	12.3	....	....	13.0	....	87.0
Service Wells	100.0	0.6	0.1	53.8	....	....	54.5	....	45.5
Net Crude Oil Production	100.0	0.3	0.2	70.8	....	....	71.3	....	28.7
Domestic	100.0	0.4	0.2	59.2	....	....	59.8	....	40.2
Foreign	100.0	0.0	0.0	99.6	....	....	99.6	....	0.4
REFINING OPERATIONS									
Domestic Refinery Runs	100.0	1.3	1.5	92.8	0.2	0.4	96.2	1.1	2.7
Yield of Refined Products	100.0	1.3	1.5	92.8	0.2	0.4	96.2	1.1	2.7
Gasolines and Naphthas	100.0	1.4	1.6	93.5	0.1	0.3	96.9	0.9	2.2
Kerosene and Distillates	100.0	1.4	1.8	91.6	0.2	0.3	95.3	1.0	3.7
Residual Fuel Oil	100.0	1.1	1.4	94.1	0.3	0.4	97.3	1.5	1.2
Other Products	100.0	1.4	0.2	83.1	0.5	0.4	85.6	0.8	13.6
TRANSPORTATION OPERATIONS									
Crude Oil Runs from Wells	100.0	0.6	0.7	73.8	0.0	0.1	75.2	0.2	24.6
Crude Oil Delivered from Gathering and Trunk Lines	100.0	0.6	0.4	81.9	0.1	0.1	83.1	0.2	16.7
Products Delivered from Pipe Lines	100.0	0.1	0.8	90.9	0.0	0.1	91.9	0.0	8.1
Tank Car Miles	100.0	0.2	0.2	17.4	0.0	0.1	17.9	0.0	82.1
MARKETING OPERATIONS									
Terminal and Bulk Plant Sales*	100.0	....	0.9	60.2	0.0	0.3	61.4	....	38.6
Gasolines and Naphthas	100.0	....	0.8	61.0	0.0	0.3	62.1	....	37.9
Kerosene and Distillates	100.0	....	1.2	58.3	0.0	0.3	59.8	....	40.2
Service Station Sales of Gasoline†	100.0	....	....	57.8	....	0.2	58.0	....	42.0

(a) American Petroleum Institute, Statistical Bulletin, Vol. XXXII, No. 21, May 1, 1952. (Basic data drawn from Oil and Gas Journal and California Office of A.P.I.)

(b) U.S. Bureau of Mines, Mineral Industry Surveys, Annual Petroleum Statement No. P347, "Crude Petroleum and Petroleum Products, 1950 (Final Summary)" (Government Printing Office).

(c) Estimate of the Standard Oil Company (New Jersey), Coordination and Economics Department, modified on the basis of data secured directly from certain other companies. The figure represents the total crude oil produced in foreign countries by United States companies, including the share of such companies in the foreign production of foreign affiliates.

(d) See Technical Note at end of chapter.

(e) Interstate Commerce Commission, Bureau of Transport Economics and Statistics, Selected Statistics from Annual Reports of Private Car Owners for the Year Ended December 31, 1950, Statement No. 529 (Washington, March 1952). Survey data cover only tank cars owned by oil companies.

* Sales of light oil products only through terminals and bulk plants owned or leased by the companies in each group.

† Sales through stations owned or leased by the companies in each group.

EXHIBIT II-9. FACILITIES OWNED OR LEASED AND OPERATIONS CONDUCTED
BY VARIOUS TYPES OF COMPANIES: 1950

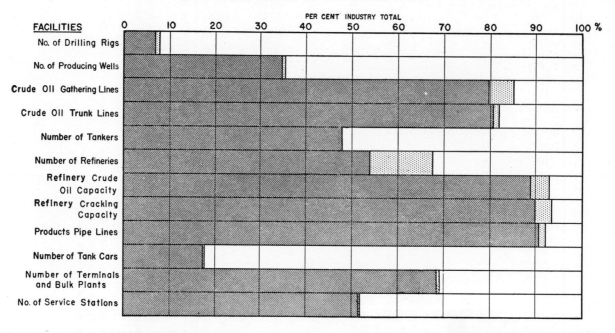

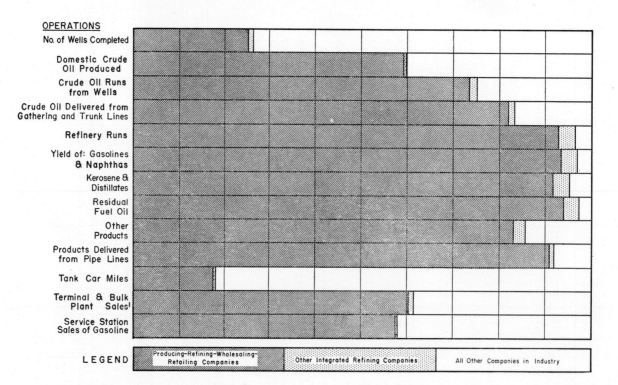

[1] Gasolines, naphthas, kerosene, and distillates

SOURCE: See Exhibit II-7 and II-8.

Operations Conducted by Integrated Companies:

Exhibits II-8 and II-9 show that there was also considerable variation in the proportions of the industry's operations conducted by integrated companies at the successive levels of the business. These variations were, however, less marked than in the case of facilities ownership. The control of operations by integrated companies was of greatest significance at the refining and pipe line transportation levels of the industry. In 1950 the integrated companies accounted for at least 96.2% of the industry's refinery runs, 75.2% of the crude oil runs from wells, 83.1% of the deliveries from crude oil gathering and trunk lines, and 91.9% of the deliveries from products pipe lines. The participation of the integrated companies in the activities of the industry dropped below 25% only in connection with the drilling of dry holes, where the integrated companies accounted for only 13.0% of the total for the industry.[15] As in the case of the facilities, the operations conducted by the integrated companies were particularly significant at the middle of the oil process and declined in relative importance toward both ends.

The producing-refining-wholesaling-retailing companies accounted for nearly all the operations conducted by the integrated companies. The operations conducted by all other types of integrated companies amounted to less than 4% of the total at all levels of the industry and to less than 2% at all levels except refining.

Comparison of Facilities and Operations of Integrated Companies:

The proportion of the industry's *operations* conducted by the producing-refining-wholesaling-retailing companies at most levels of the industry was substantially larger than the proportion of the industry's *facilities* owned or leased by such companies. To facilitate comparisons on this point, Exhibit II-10 was prepared. Similar charts were not developed for the other types of integrated companies because, as noted above, they constituted a relatively insignificant part of the total industry. Comparisons of facilities and operations for the other structures can, however, be made fairly easily from the data in Exhibits II-7 and II-8.

As may be seen from Exhibit II-10, although the producing-refining-wholesaling-retailing companies controlled only 6.9% of the total drilling rigs in the industry, they were responsible for the drilling of 25.4% of the total wells completed. This circumstance resulted from the general practice followed by the large, integrated companies of having the majority of their drilling work done by outside contractors (see Chapter Thirteen). It may further be observed that whereas the producing-refining-wholesaling-retailing companies drilled only 25.4% of the wells, they secured 31.7% of the oil producers and 26.1% of the gas producers. The higher ratio of producing wells secured by the integrated companies may reflect better geological work or a predisposition to concentrate drilling operations on the less hazardous projects.

There was a very wide discrepancy between the producing wells owned and crude oil produced by the producing-refining-wholesaling-retailing companies. Whereas the companies owned only 34.8% of the producing wells, they produced 59.2% of the domestic crude oil in 1950. These facts indicate that the average producing well of the heavily integrated company was far better than the average well of the companies with a lesser degree of integration or no integration at all. The situation may be explained largely by the fact that the producing-refining-wholesaling-retailing group embraced the majority of the large firms in the industry, and these companies have had a tendency to farm out their marginal drilling prospects to small, independent producers (see Chapter Thirteen) and likewise to turn over their very small producing wells to stripper-well operators.

The proportionate participation of the producing-refining-wholesaling-retailing companies in the refining activities of the industry was slightly greater than their proportionate control of refining facilities. Whereas the companies owned or leased 89.1% of the refining

---

[15] The integrated companies also accounted for only 17.9% of the tank car miles operated, but in this instance our figures represent only the cars owned by the integrated companies. Many additional cars were held under lease arrangements.

capacity, they accounted for 92.8% of the refinery runs, 93.5% of the production of gasolines and naphthas, 91.6% of the production of kerosene and distillates, 94.1% of the production of residual fuel oil, and 83.1% of the production of "other products." These facts indicate that the average refinery of the producing-refining-wholesaling-retailing companies ran at a slightly higher level of capacity than did the average refinery of other companies in the industry and secured an appreciably higher yield of gasolines, naphthas, and residual fuel oil and a significantly lower yield of "other products."

The higher than average operating level of the producing-refining-wholesaling-retailing companies may reflect a gain in stability of operations resulting from extensive vertical integration, as will be noted in the discussion on page 40, following. The higher than average yield of gasolines and naphthas reflects the fact that the plants of the producing-refining-wholesaling-retailing companies were somewhat better equipped with cracking facilities than were the average plants in the industry (see Exhibit II-7). The higher than average yield of residual which the producing-refining-wholesaling-retailing companies secured resulted from the fact that some of these companies had large refineries designed to run almost exclusively on very low gravity crude oils, particularly certain grades imported from Venezuela, which could only produce a high yield of residual. These very heavy grades of crude oil were customarily not handled in any very large volume by the small and substantially nonintegrated firms in the industry. The lower than average yield of "other products" obtained by the producing-refining-wholesaling-retailing companies reflects the presence in the industry of a number of small and substantially nonintegrated refiners specializing in asphalts and miscellaneous other products (see Chapter Twenty-Three).

Crude oil gathering was one of the few phases of the business in which the producing-refining-wholesaling-retailing companies appear to have controlled a larger share of the facilities (79.8%) than they did of the operations (73.8%). Our data, however, do not permit a precise comparison on this point because in a few cases we were unable to adjust the reports of the survey companies for the crude gathering activities of their affiliates. The producing-refining-wholesaling-retailing companies controlled very nearly the same proportion of the combined crude gathering and trunk line mileage (80.4%) as they did of crude oil deliveries from crude gathering and trunk lines (81.9%). In the case of products pipe lines, the producing-refining-wholesaling-retailing companies likewise controlled very close to the same proportion of the industry's facilities (90.8%) as they did of the industry's operations (90.9%). In addition, the producing-refining-wholesaling-retailing companies accounted for almost exactly the same proportion of the tank car mileage as they did of tank car ownership.

It appears from Exhibit II-10 that the producing-refining-wholesaling-retailing companies controlled a somewhat higher proportion of the industry's terminals and bulk plants (68.0%) than they did of the industry's wholesale marketing activities for light oil products (60.2%). The facts on this point are at variance with the general impressions we gathered in our field research; so far as we were able to determine, the terminals and bulk plants of the producing-refining-wholesaling-retailing companies normally did a larger volume of business than did the average terminal or bulk plant in the industry. We suspect that our comparison in Exhibit II-10 may be faulty because of certain approximations which it was necessary to make in developing the figures for the total terminals and bulk plants in the industry (see Technical Note at end of chapter). We have, however, no reason to doubt the absolute figures shown in the upper part of Exhibits II-7 and II-8 for the facilities and operations reported by each of the various groups of integrated companies.

The volume of gasoline sold through the service stations owned or leased by the producing-refining-wholesaling-retailing companies represented an appreciably higher proportion of the industry total (57.8%) than did the number of service stations owned or leased by such companies (51.4%). This fact corroborates the general belief in the industry that the average service station of the producing-refining-wholesaling-retailing company is larger than the average service station in the industry. It should be noted that 92.9% of the total volume sold through the service stations of the

Exhibit II-10. Comparison of Facilities and Operations of Producing-
Refining-Wholesaling-Retailing Companies: 1950

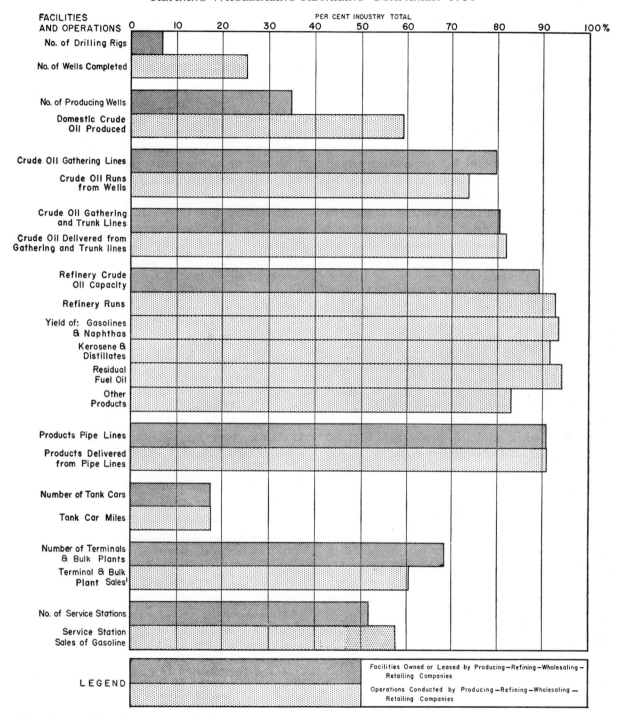

[1] Gasoline, naphthas, kerosene, and distillates

Source: See Exhibit II-7 and II-8.

producing-refining-wholesaling-retailing companies represented volume handled by independent dealers.

IV. SELECTED OPERATING RATIOS FOR VARIOUS TYPES AND SIZES OF REFINING COMPANIES

The data collected in the survey made it possible to develop a number of typical operating ratios for various types and sizes of refining companies. Exhibit II-11 shows selected operating ratios for the various groups of integrated refining companies and for the nonintegrated refining companies. Exhibit II-12 shows the same ratios for various sizes of refining companies. Among other things, the figures serve to reveal the balance which the various types and sizes of companies maintained among their activities at different levels of the industry. Throughout the two tables we have used interquartile averages (averages of the middle half of the companies) as measures of the *typical* experience of the companies comprising the various groups.

Operating Ratios for Various Types of Refining Companies:

The first group of figures in Exhibit II-11 reveals that the typical integrated refining company engaged in crude oil production in 1950 had net crude oil production equal to 32.7% of its refinery requirements. The typical integrated company, however, had its crude gathering lines connected to a far larger volume of crude production than it produced itself and had crude runs from wells equal to 64.5% of its refinery requirements. As will be noted in Chapter Fourteen, the extension of gathering lines to the wells of other producers constitutes a very effective alternative to the ownership of crude oil as a means of assuring a refinery of its supplies. Exhibit II-11 indicates that the companies which had low ratios of crude production to refinery runs had been extremely active in extending their gathering lines to the wells of other producers (see ratio of crude runs from wells to net crude oil production). Even some of the nonintegrated refiners, who had no production of their own, had gathering lines connected to producing wells. As a result, the positions of the various groups of refining companies with respect to crude runs from wells as

a percentage of refinery requirements were more uniform than with respect to crude production as a percentage of refinery requirements.

Exhibit II-11 reveals that the typical integrated refining company was able to maintain refinery runs equal to 81.6% of its operating and shutdown capacity whereas the typical nonintegrated company was able to maintain refinery runs equal to only 54.3% of its operating and shutdown capacity. Refining companies do not follow completely uniform practices with regard to the rating of refinery capacity, and it is therefore quite possible that the figures for the integrated and nonintegrated groups may not be strictly comparable and may in each case be subject to a certain margin of error.[16] After full allowance is made for possible discrepancies in methods of reporting, however, the data still permit the unquestionable conclusion that in the year 1950 the integrated refining companies maintained a substantially higher level of refinery runs as a percentage of their operating and shutdown capacity than did the nonintegrated companies.

Since the integrated companies were typically much larger than the nonintegrated companies (see Exhibit II-3), there was a possibility that the difference we observed in level of operations may have been a function of size rather than of integration. Examination of Exhibit II-12, however, revealed that although the larger refining companies typically had higher levels of refinery runs than did the smaller ones, the differences among companies of different sizes were significantly less than the differences between the companies in the integrated and nonintegrated groups shown in Exhibit II-11. Moreover, we found that the differences *between* successive size groups were characteristically less than the differences between the integrated and nonintegrated companies *within* each size group.[17]

---

[16] Our data did nevertheless check very closely with that regularly reported by the companies to the Bureau of Mines. See discussion on page 22.

[17] The companies in both the integrated and nonintegrated categories were classified by size. Median and arithmetic average operating ratios were then computed for each size group. The data revealed that in each size category the integrated companies had substantially higher (between 27% and 80%) median and average ratios of refinery runs to refinery capacity than did the nonintegrated companies. Among the integrated companies, there was a

Definitive conclusions cannot, of course, be drawn on the basis of the data for any single year. Our figures for the year 1950 do, however, bear some testimony to one of the major economic advantages often claimed for vertical integration; namely, greater stability of operations. The figures also reflect the presence among the nonintegrated companies of a certain number of "in-and-outer" refiners. These firms characteristically operate their plants when the refining margins are favorable and close them down when conditions are unfavorable (see Chapter Twenty-Three). As will be noted in Chapter Six, the refining margin contracted very sharply in the summer of 1949 and caused a number of small, nonintegrated firms to close their plants. The refining margin moved upward in the closing months of 1949 and throughout 1950, but some of the small, nonintegrated firms unquestionably remained closed down during the early months of 1950.

It is interesting to note that not only did the integrated companies maintain a higher level of operations than the nonintegrated, but that among the integrated companies the producing-refining-wholesaling-retailing companies secured a higher level of operations than did the companies with lesser depth of integration. In view of the high fixed costs associated with refining equipment, maintenance of a high level of operations is, of course, of critical importance to a company's profit position (see Chapters Eight and Twenty).

The integrated refining companies not only utilized a higher percentage of their operating and shutdown capacity than did the nonintegrated firms but also secured a substantially higher yield of gasolines and naphthas. Exhibit II-11 indicates that the typical integrated company converted 43.4% of its refinery runs to gasolines and naphthas whereas the typical nonintegrated company secured a gasoline and naphtha yield of only 27.0%. Again reference

to Exhibit II-12 reveals that the variations in the typical ratios among different sizes of refining companies were less than between the integrated and nonintegrated companies.[18] The data suggest that the integrated companies were better equipped with cracking facilities and probably concentrated more of their effort on the development of the gasoline markets than did the nonintegrated companies. As will be observed in Chapter Twenty-Three, many of the nonintegrated refiners have elected to concentrate on specialty products, other than gasoline, where the lack of well-recognized brand names is not a handicap to them.

The figures on terminal and bulk plant sales as a percentage of refinery yields in Exhibit II-11 provide an indication of the balance which the various groups of integrated companies maintained between their refining activities and their wholesale marketing operations.[19] The typical integrated refining company engaged in wholesale marketing activities in 1950 sold through its owned or leased terminals and bulk plants a volume of refined products equal to 66.8% of its refinery output, a volume of gasoline and naphthas equal to 81.8% of its refinery output, a volume of kerosene and distillates equal to 67.0% of its re-

---

slight increase in the median ratios for the companies in the larger size categories but no increase in the average ratios. Among the nonintegrated companies, both the median and average ratios for the 5,000–10,000 barrels per day group were appreciably higher than for the 0–5,000 barrels per day group. The differences *between* the two size groups were in each case, however, less than the differences between the integrated and nonintegrated companies *within* each size group. The fact that there were only two nonintegrated companies in the survey with capacities in excess of 10,000 barrels per day precluded further analysis.

[18] The validity of this observation was tested in the same manner as described in footnote 17 above. The companies in both the integrated and nonintegrated categories were classified by size. Median and arithmetic average gasoline and naphtha yields were then computed for each size group. In the 0–5,000 barrels per day group, the median and average yields for the integrated companies were approximately double what they were for the nonintegrated companies. In the 5,000–10,000 barrels per day group, the median and average yields were 30% to 40% higher for the integrated than for the nonintegrated companies. Among the integrated companies, the yield ratio for the 5,000–10,000 barrels per day companies was slightly higher than for the 0–5,000 barrels per day companies, but there was no significant increase in either the median or average yields for companies in the size categories above 10,000 barrels per day. Among the nonintegrated companies, the median and average yield ratios for the 5,000–10,000 barrels per day companies were substantially higher than for the 0–5,000 barrels per day companies. The differences *between* the two size groups, in this case, were only slightly less significant than were differences between the integrated and nonintegrated companies *within* each size group. The fact that there were only two nonintegrated companies in the survey with capacities in excess of 10,000 barrels per day precluded further analysis.

[19] As noted on page 23, for the purposes of this discussion we are treating the ownership or leasing of terminals and bulk plants as participation in the wholesaling field, regardless of the method by which the facilities were operated.

EXHIBIT II-11. SELECTED OPERATING FIGURES FOR VARIOUS TYPES OF REFINING COMPANIES: 1950

Interquartile Averages for Each Group

(Total Number of Reporting Companies in Parentheses)†

Items	Base	Companies in Survey by Type of Integration						
		Producing and Refining	Producing, Refining, and Wholesaling	Producing, Refining, Wholesaling, and Retailing	Refining and Wholesaling	Refining, Wholesaling, and Retailing	Total Integrated Refining	Non-integrated Refining
Net Crude Oil Production	% Refinery Runs	27.9% (12)	13.4% (8)	38.2% (54)	.....	.....	32.7% (74)	.....
Crude Oil Runs from Wells	% Refinery Runs	53.2 (11)	56.5 (7)	75.2 (49)	2.2% (5)	27.7% (7)	64.5 (79)	1.1% (17)
Crude Oil Runs from Wells	% Net Crude Oil Production	245.3 (11)	333.6 (7)	169.7 (49)	.....	.....	188.0 (67)	.....
Refinery Runs	% Refinery Capacity‡	79.0 (12)	68.3 (8)	85.4 (54)	75.1 (5)	62.7 (8)	81.6 (87)	54.3 (19)
Yield of Gasoline and Naphthas	% Refinery Runs	36.1 (12)	50.2 (8)	44.3 (53)	33.7 (5)	39.9 (8)	43.4 (86)	27.0 (19)
Terminal and Bulk Plant Sales§	% Yield of Refined Products		79.9 (8)	63.8 (45)	53.3 (5)	99.4 (6)	66.8 (64)	
Gasoline and Naphtha Sales	% Yield of Gasoline and Naphthas		68.2 (8)	83.2 (43)	54.0 (5)	131.7 (6)	81.8 (62)	
Kerosene and Distillate Sales	% Yield of Kerosene and Distillates		80.6 (8)	63.0 (43)	51.3 (5)	85.6 (6)	67.0 (62)	
Residual Fuel Oil Sales	% Yield of Residual Fuel Oil		81.6 (8)	30.9 (43)	87.2 (5)	72.2 (6)	44.4 (62)	
Service Station Sales of Gasoline‖	% Yield of Gasoline and Naphthas		.....	26.7 (47)	.....	35.2 (7)	27.4 (54)	
Sales through Company Operated Stations	% Yield of Gasoline and Naphthas		.....	1.5 (33)	.....	* (3)	1.5 (36)	
Sales through Dealer Operated Stations	% Yield of Gasoline and Naphthas		.....	26.1 (42)	.....	44.3 (4)	27.5 (46)	
Company Operated Bulk Plants	% Total Bulk Plants Owned or Leased	.....	* (2)	36.4 (49)	* (1)	62.9 (5)	43.9 (57)	.....
Company Operated Service Stations	% Total Service Stations Owned or Leased	.....	.....	1.6 (54)	.....	2.8 (7)	1.7 (61)	.....

* Insufficient data available to warrant computing averages.

† In the other exhibits dealing with aggregate amounts, some estimates were used to complete the data reported by certain companies. In this exhibit no estimated figures were used; thus each ratio reflects only the experience of those companies reporting the necessary data in comparable form. We have, however, included in each ratio all companies which might, in view of their classification by type of integration, have had the facility or operation in question; i.e., all companies engaged in retailing which reported the necessary comparable data were used in computing the ratio of company operated to total owned or leased service stations, even though some of them did not have company operated stations.

‡ Refinery Runs reflects operating and shutdown capacity of operating companies.

§ Includes all products sold through terminals or bulk plants owned or leased by companies in each group.

‖ Sales through stations owned or leased by companies in each group.

EXHIBIT II-12. SELECTED OPERATING FIGURES FOR VARIOUS SIZES OF REFINING COMPANIES: 1950

Interquartile Averages for Each Group

(Total Number of Reporting Companies in Parentheses)†

Items	Base	Refinery Capacity (B/D)					All Reporting Companies
		0–5,000	5,001–10,000	10,001–30,000	30,001–100,000	100,001 and Over	
Net Crude Oil Production	% Refinery Runs	26.0% (20)	23.5% (11)	21.2% (15)	59.8% (10)	50.0% (18)	32.7% (74)
Crude Oil Runs from Wells	% Refinery Runs	40.8 (35)	24.5 (18)	64.4 (17)	66.6 (9)	67.1 (17)	52.1 (96)
Crude Oil Runs from Wells	% Net Crude Oil Production	293.2 (18)	480.7 (8)	330.2 (15)	81.3 (9)	148.8 (17)	188.0 (67)
Refinery Runs	% Refinery Capacity‡	70.5 (40)	75.3 (21)	80.1 (17)	84.7 (10)	87.8 (18)	78.5 (106)
Yield of Gasoline and Naphthas	% Refinery Runs	32.2 (40)	39.7 (21)	47.3 (16)	47.7 (10)	44.2 (18)	41.4 (105)
Terminal and Bulk Station Sales§	% Yield of Refined Products	84.6 (18)	48.3 (10)	66.4 (10)	62.0 (9)	63.4 (17)	66.8 (64)
Gasoline and Naphtha Sales	% Yield of Gasoline and Naphthas	114.9 (17)	58.6 (10)	78.8 (10)	68.6 (9)	82.2 (16)	81.8 (62)
Kerosene and Distillate Sales	% Yield of Kerosene and Distillates	95.5 (17)	34.6 (10)	76.6 (10)	43.3 (9)	66.3 (16)	67.0 (62)
Residual Fuel Oil Sales	% Yield of Residual Fuel Oil	58.5 (17)	54.6 (10)	28.3 (10)	19.0 (9)	50.8 (16)	44.4 (62)
Service Station Sales of Gasoline‖ Sales through Company Operated Stations	% Yield of Gasoline and Naphthas	35.3 (15)	8.6 (8)	* (4)	15.2 (9)	33.0 (18)	27.4 (54)
Sales through Dealer Operated Stations	% Yield of Gasoline and Naphthas	5.7 (6)	0.4 (5)	* (3)	2.2 (6)	1.0 (16)	1.5 (36)
	% Yield of Gasoline and Naphthas	38.3 (13)	8.4 (6)	* (3)	20.8 (7)	29.7 (17)	27.5 (46)
Company Operated Bulk Plants	% Total Bulk Plants Owned or Leased	58.6 (17)	73.8 (7)	16.4 (8)	56.7 (7)	32.5 (18)	43.9 (57)
Company Operated Service Stations	% Total Service Stations Owned or Leased	3.9 (18)	6.1 (7)	0.2 (9)	5.6 (9)	1.0 (18)	1.7 (61)

* Insufficient data available to warrant computing averages.

† In the other exhibits dealing with aggregate amounts, some estimates were used to complete the data reported by certain companies. In this exhibit no estimated figures were used; thus each ratio reflects only the experience of those companies reporting the necessary data in comparable form. We have, however, included in each ratio all companies which might, in view of their classification by type of integration, have had the facility or operation in question; i.e., all companies engaged in retailing which reported the necessary comparable data were used in computing the ratio of company operated to total owned or leased service stations even though some of them did not have company operated stations.

‡ Includes operating and shutdown capacity of operating companies.

§ Includes all products sold through terminals or bulk plants owned or leased by companies in each group.

‖ Sales through stations owned or leased by companies in each group.

finery output, and a volume of residual fuel oil equal to 44.4% of its refinery output. In appraising these figures, it must be recognized that companies in any of the groups might have sold a portion of their own refinery output in the cargo markets and yet have purchased products from other refiners for resale through their own terminals and bulk plants. The data indicate that in 1950 the typical company in all groups had refining yields larger than its wholesale marketing operations, except the typical company in the refining-wholesaling-retailing group. The typical refining-wholesaling-retailing company apparently bought gasoline and naphthas equal to about 31.7% of its own refinery output for resale through its terminals and bulk plants.[20] It seems quite probable that several of the companies in the refining-wholesaling-retailing group may have been primarily marketing concerns which integrated backward into some refining activities to secure a portion of their refined products requirements.

The figures in Exhibit II-11 on service station sales of gasoline indicate the balance which the companies maintained between their refining activities and their retail marketing activities.[21] In 1950 the typical integrated refining company, among those that had owned or leased service stations, sold a volume of gasoline through such stations equal to 27.4% of its gasoline and naphtha yield. The typical company, among those that reported company operated stations, sold a volume of gasoline through such stations equal to 1.5% of its refinery output of gasoline and naphthas. The typical company, among those that reported dealer operated stations, sold a volume of gasoline through such stations equal to 27.5% of its refinery output of gasoline and naphthas. The latter two facts bear witness to the general withdrawal of integrated companies from the operation of their owned or leased stations, a development which will be discussed in Chapter Ten.

The last two ratios in Exhibit II-11 permit

a comparison of the extent to which the integrated refining companies used company employees to operate their bulk plants and service stations. In 1950 the typical company, among those that had owned or leased bulk plants, operated 43.9% of the plants with company employees whereas the typical company, among those that had owned or leased service stations, operated only 1.7% of the stations with company employees.

A general observation which may be made on the basis of the data in Exhibit II-11 is that in none of the groups did the typical company maintain an even balance among its activities in the various phases of the oil business. Moreover, in no case did the typical company in any group have activities in any other phase of the business exactly equal to its refining operations. The typical producing-refining-wholesaling-retailing company, for example, had crude production equal to 38.2% of its refinery runs, had crude runs from wells equal to 75.2% of its refinery runs, sold a volume equal to 63.8% of its refined products yield through its terminals and bulk plants, and sold a volume equal to 26.7% of its gasoline and naphtha yield through service stations which it owned or leased. The general topic of balance of operations in vertically integrated companies will be the subject of Part Three of this volume.

Operating Ratios for Various Sizes of Refining Companies:

Exhibit II-12 presents data on the same operating ratios as does Exhibit II-11, but whereas the analysis in Exhibit II-11 was for different *types* of refining companies, the analysis in Exhibit II-12 is for different *sizes* of refining companies. The data in Exhibit II-12 cover both integrated and nonintegrated refining companies, but the ratios were in each instance computed only for the companies in the size group which were engaged in the activity in question.

The first fact revealed by Exhibit II-12 is that the larger companies engaging in crude oil producing activities characteristically were able to supply a larger proportion of their refinery runs from their own production than were the smaller companies. The typical company with refining capacity in excess of 30,000 barrels per day had a ratio of crude oil production to re-

---

[20] The actual quantity purchased may have been more or less than 31.7% of the refinery yield, depending on the extent and direction of inventory changes.

[21] As noted on page 23, for the purposes of this discussion we are treating the ownership or leasing of service stations as participation in the retail field, regardless of the method by which the facilities were operated.

finery runs roughly twice that of the typical company with refining capacity of less than 30,000 barrels per day. It is important to note, however, that there were at least 20 companies in the industry in 1950 in the 0–5,000 barrels per day capacity range which were engaged in crude oil production and that the typical company in the group was able to supply 26.0% of its refinery requirements from its own production. Vertical integration between the producing and refining phases of the business was certainly by no means therefore confined exclusively to the large companies in the industry.

The typical companies in all size categories gathered a substantially larger quantity of crude oil than they produced. The small companies had particularly large crude gathering activities relative to their own crude oil producing operations, and our survey returns revealed that 10 companies in the 0–5,000 barrels per day capacity range and 3 companies in the 5,001–10,000 barrels per day range which had no crude production at all were engaged in crude gathering operations. It is very likely that a number of the small refining companies which were unable to finance crude producing programs, or only very small programs, undertook the construction of crude gathering lines as the next best means of assuring their crude oil supplies. As a general rule, the size groups which had low crude oil producing to crude oil refining ratios had relatively high ratios of runs from wells to crude oil produced. As a result, there was much more uniformity in the crude positions of the typical companies in the various size groups as measured by runs from wells than there was as measured by crude oil produced, except in the case of the 5,000–10,000 barrels per day group.

The large refining companies were typically able to maintain a higher level of operations at their refineries than were the smaller ones. As noted above, however, the percentage of operating and shutdown capacity utilized varied less among the various size groups than it did among the various integration groups analyzed in Exhibit II-11.[22] It would appear therefore that in the year 1950 vertical integration was a more significant determinant of a company's ability to maintain stable operations at the re-

fining level of the industry than was horizontal integration.

The companies with capacities in excess of 10,000 barrels per day typically secured higher gasoline and naphtha yields than did the companies with capacities of less than 10,000 barrels per day. Here again, however, the variations in gasoline yields among the various size groups were somewhat less than between the integrated and nonintegrated groups for which figures were presented in Exhibit II-11.[23] The data suggest therefore that it is primarily the *nonintegrated* refining companies and only secondarily the *small* refining companies which lack adequate cracking facilities and which tend to drift into the asphalt, fuel oil, and other specialty markets (see Chapter Twenty-Three).

The ratios dealing with extent of integration into marketing operations varied considerably from one size group to another. For many of these variations, we found no apparent explanation. It is difficult to understand, for example, why the ratio of residual fuel oil sales through company owned or leased terminals or bulk plants should have been so much higher for the very large and very small companies than for the companies of intermediate size. In our judgment the most significant general observation which may be drawn from the data is that the *extent* of integration by the very small refiners into marketing activities in 1950 was far greater than has generally been supposed. The typical company in the 0–5,000 barrels per day capacity range, for example, had appreciably larger terminal and bulk plant sales through its own facilities relative to refinery output than did the companies in any other size category. Moreover, the typical company in the 0–5,000 barrels per day capacity range sold a volume of gasoline through owned or leased service stations equal to 35.3% of its refinery output of gasolines and naphthas, whereas the comparable figure for the typical company in the over 100,-000 barrels per day range was only 33.0%. The figures in Exhibit II-12 demonstrate very clearly therefore that in 1950 vertical integration between refining and marketing activities was, like vertical integration between refining and producing, by no means confined solely to the large companies in the industry.

---

[22] See footnote 17.

[23] See footnote 18.

EXHIBIT II-13. FACILITIES AND OPERATIONS OF SUCCESSIVE GROUPS OF INTEGRATED REFINING COMPANIES: * 1950

Items	Number of Companies	Top Ten Companies	Top Twenty Companies	Top Thirty Companies	Top Forty Companies	Top Fifty Companies	Top Sixty Companies	Top Seventy Companies	Top Eighty Companies	All Integrated Companies in Survey
PLANT FACILITIES OWNED OR LEASED AS OF DECEMBER 31, 1950										
Number of Drilling Rigs	34									
Amounts		269	336	357	361					
Percentages of Industry Total		5.7%	7.1%	7.6%	7.7%					
Refinery Capacity as Per Cent of Industry Total†		54.9	64.6	71.5	71.7					
Number of Producing Oil Wells	74									
Amounts		102,278	146,198	160,098	163,250	164,354	164,790	164,924	164,931	
Percentages of Industry Total		22.0%	31.4%	34.4%	35.0%	35.3%	35.4%	35.4%	35.4%	
Refinery Capacity as Per Cent of Industry Total†		55.2	78.2	84.5	86.9	89.2	90.6	91.6	92.4	
Crude Oil Refinery Capacity	87									
Amounts (B/D in thousands)		4,393	5,675	6,041	6,227	6,328	6,391	6,436	6,463	6,472
Percentages of Industry Total		63.3%	81.7%	87.0%	89.7%	91.1%	92.0%	92.7%	93.1%	93.2%
Cracked Gasoline Capacity	69									
Amounts (B/D in thousands)		1,332	1,681	1,814	1,870	1,897	1,912	1,919		
Percentages of Industry Total		65.1%	82.2%	88.7%	91.4%	92.7%	93.5%	93.8%		
Refinery Capacity as Per Cent of Industry Total†		62.4	81.7	86.9	89.4	90.9	91.9	92.3		
Crude Oil Gathering Line Mileage	72									
Amounts		32,725	43,965	48,654	50,799	51,672	52,108	52,178	52,184	
Percentages of Industry Total		53.8%	72.3%	80.1%	83.6%	85.0%	85.7%	85.9%	85.8%	
Refinery Capacity as Per Cent of Industry Total†		50.6	75.4	83.6	86.5	88.1	89.5	90.2	90.9	
Crude Oil Trunk Line Mileage	43									
Amounts		49,366	57,982	59,256	59,471	59,479				
Percentages of Industry Total		68.2%	80.0%	81.8%	82.1%	82.1%				
Refinery Capacity as Per Cent of Industry Total†		55.7	79.2	83.9	85.5	85.7				
Products Pipe Line Mileage	42									
Amounts		16,448	21,454	22,261	22,309	22,311				
Percentages of Industry Total		68.0%	88.7%	92.0%	92.2%	92.2%				
Refinery Capacity as Per Cent of Industry Total†		53.7	75.3	81.6	85.7	85.8				
Number of Tankers‡	15									
Amounts		183	207							
Percentages of Industry Total		42.4%	47.9%							
Refinery Capacity as Per Cent of Industry Total†		51.8	60.0							
Number of Terminals and Bulk Plants	73									
Amounts		15,411	19,141	20,243	20,464	20,543	20,574	20,587	20,590	
Percentages of Industry Total		50.4%	63.8%	67.5%	68.2%	68.5%	68.6%	68.6%	68.6%	
Refinery Capacity as Per Cent of Industry Total†		61.7	74.3	84.0	85.8	87.8	90.0	90.8	91.1	
Number of Service Stations	62									
Amounts		75,799	92,490	95,896	96,679	96,936	96,988	96,990		
Percentages of Industry Total		40.3%	49.2%	51.0%	51.4%	51.6%	51.6%	51.6%		
Refinery Capacity as Per Cent of Industry Total†		62.8	81.6	84.4	86.2	87.5	88.8	89.6		

Exhibit II-13 (Continued)

OPERATIONS CONDUCTED DURING THE YEAR 1950

Item	No.									
Number of Wells Completed	66									
Amounts		6,880	9,521	10,623	11,021	11,253	11,332	11,343		
Percentages of Industry Total		15.9%	22.0%	24.5%	25.5%	26.0%	26.2%	26.2%		
Refinery Capacity as Per Cent of Industry Total †		59.0	76.3	84.9	87.0	89.6	91.4	92.0		
Number of Producing Oil Wells Completed	62									
Amounts		5,074	6,828	7,563	7,815	7,925	7,962	7,964		
Percentages of Industry Total		20.8%	28.0%	31.0%	32.0%	32.5%	32.6%	32.6%		
Refinery Capacity as Per Cent of Industry Total †		59.0	77.5	85.4	87.3	89.4	90.8	90.9		
Net Crude Oil Production — Domestic	74									
Amounts (bbls. in thousands)		708,324	965,446	1,013,887	1,025,530	1,030,267	1,032,386	1,033,166	1,033,206	
Percentages of Industry Total		41.0%	55.9%	58.7%	59.4%	59.7%	59.8%	59.8%	59.8%	
Refinery Capacity as Per Cent of Industry Total †		58.6	79.6	85.5	87.8	89.3	90.9	91.6	92.4	
Domestic Refinery Runs	87									
Amounts (bbls. in thousands)		1,382,941	1,786,415	1,893,102	1,948,343	1,977,570	1,994,878	2,007,836	2,014,646	2,016,413
Percentages of Industry Total		66.0%	85.3%	90.4%	93.0%	94.4%	95.2%	95.8%	96.2%	96.2%
Refinery Capacity as Per Cent of Industry Total †		63.3	81.6	86.6	89.5	91.1	92.0	92.7	93.1	93.2
Crude Oil Runs from Wells §	75									
Amounts (bbls. in thousands)		1,014,721	1,346,490	1,439,528	1,467,847	1,478,008	1,484,101	1,487,023	1,487,422	
Percentages of Industry Total		51.4%	68.2%	72.9%	74.4%	74.9%	75.2%	75.3%	75.4%	
Refinery Capacity as Per Cent of Industry Total †		61.8	80.7	85.4	86.9	87.9	89.3	90.2	90.4	
Crude Oil Delivered from Gathering and Trunk Lines §	67									
Amounts (bbls. in thousands)		1,670,993	2,184,834	2,277,034	2,304,684	2,317,975	2,324,003	2,325,130		
Percentages of Industry Total		59.9%	78.3%	81.6%	82.6%	83.0%	83.3%	83.3%		
Refinery Capacity as Per Cent of Industry Total †		56.7	75.4	79.5	81.4	82.4	83.2	84.1		
Refined Products Delivered from Pipe Lines §	34									
Amounts (bbls. in thousands)		398,451	515,099	529,529	530,524					
Percentages of Industry Total		69.1%	89.3%	91.8%	91.9%					
Refinery Capacity as Per Cent of Industry Total †		53.2	72.4	78.3	78.9					
Terminal and Bulk Plant Sales of Light Oil Products	73									
Amounts (bbls. in thousands)		731,810	926,789	985,113	1,005,813	1,014,762	1,018,713	1,019,982	1,020,076	
Percentages of Industry Total		44.1%	55.8%	59.3%	60.5%	61.1%	61.3%	61.4%	61.4%	
Refinery Capacity as Per Cent of Industry Total †		63.3	78.2	85.3	87.6	89.5	90.3	91.0	91.1	
Service Station Sales of Gasoline	62									
Amounts (bbls. in thousands)		211,476	268,167	275,395	277,623	278,402	278,677	278,681		
Percentages of Industry Total		44.1%	55.9%	57.4%	57.8%	58.0%	58.0%	58.0%		
Refinery Capacity as Per Cent of Industry Total †		62.2	80.8	84.2	86.5	87.4	88.9	89.6		

* Except in the case of transportation items, the data in this table pertain only to the facilities and operations of integrated refining companies, i.e., refining companies engaged in producing, wholesaling, or retailing activities. The data for crude gathering lines, crude trunk lines, products pipe lines, and tankers pertain to all refining companies which had such facilities.

† Figures are different for each item because the integrated refining companies ranked differently with respect to size on each item.

‡ Includes only tankers owned by survey companies; in all other cases data are for facilities owned or leased.

§ The figures for these items represent the absolute minimum amounts; for example, three companies with 721 miles of crude gathering lines did not report their crude runs from wells; three companies with 1,557 miles of crude trunk lines and two companies with 74 miles of crude gathering lines did not report the barrels of crude delivered from gathering and trunk lines; and eight companies with 829 miles of products pipe lines did not report the barrels of refined products delivered from pipe lines.

EXHIBIT II-14. FACILITIES AND OPERATIONS OF SUCCESSIVE GROUPS OF INTEGRATED
COMPANIES: 1950

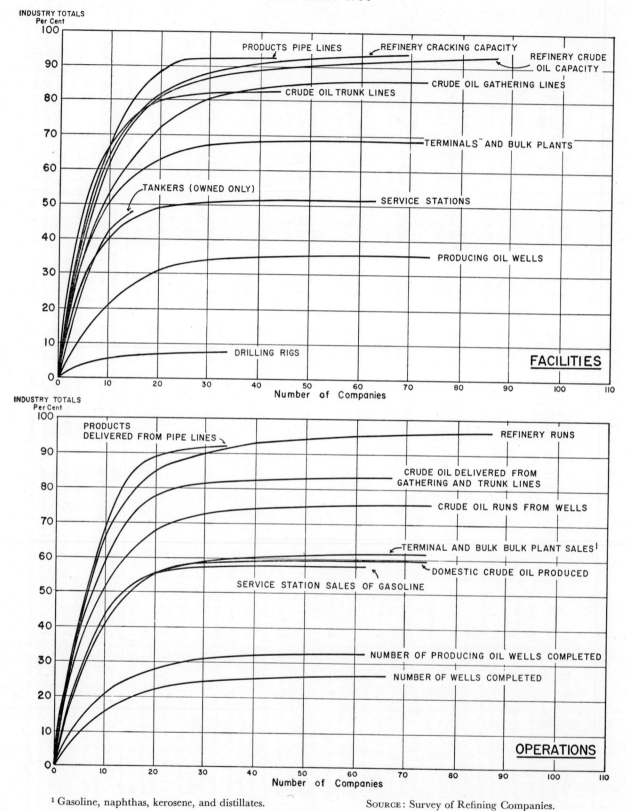

[1] Gasoline, naphthas, kerosene, and distillates.   SOURCE: Survey of Refining Companies.

V. Association of Vertical Integration with Large Size

As noted earlier in the chapter, the data in Exhibit II-3 demonstrate conclusively that in 1950 there was a very strong association between vertical integration and large size at the refining level of the industry. There were not more than three companies in 1950 with capacities in excess of 20,000 barrels per day which did not have some type of vertical integration, and there were no companies with capacities in excess of 50,000 barrels per day which were not engaged in producing, refining, wholesaling, retailing, and transportation operations. Whereas vertical integration sometimes was and sometimes was not associated with small scale refining, it was *always* a corollary of large scale refining.

As a means of examining the association between vertical integration and large size at certain other levels of the industry, the integrated refining companies owning or leasing facilities at a given level of the industry were arrayed by size with respect to their holdings of such facilities. The aggregate amount of the facilities owned by successive groups of 10 companies was then computed and expressed as a percentage of the industry total.[24] Likewise the refining capacity of each of these groups of 10 companies was expressed as a percentage of the industry total. The resulting figures, which are shown in Exhibit II-13, may be read in the following manner: the 10 refining companies with the largest number of drilling rigs owned 269 rigs or 5.7% of the industry total; these same companies owned or leased 54.9% of the refining capacity of the industry. It is important to note that the order of the refining companies with respect to one facility was not necessarily the same as with respect to other facilities. The data in the lower half of the table for operations conducted in 1950 were prepared in the same manner as the data for facilities owned or leased.

Exhibit II-14 contains a graphic representation of the data in Exhibit II-13. The plottings are, however, for successive groups of 4 integrated companies in order of size rather than

for 10; the data were not plotted for individual companies because of the necessity of avoiding disclosure of the operating ratios of individual concerns. In the upper chart in Exhibit II-14, the cumulative percentage of the industry's facilities owned or leased by successive groups of 4 companies is plotted against the cumulative number of companies. In the lower chart, the cumulative percentage of the industry's operations conducted by successive groups of 4 companies is plotted against the cumulative number of companies.

The data in Exhibits II-13 and II-14 indicate that there was a fairly strong association between vertical integration and large size at many levels of the industry in 1950. In other words, a relatively small number of integrated refining companies accounted for a substantial portion of the industry's facilities and operations in the refining as well as in other fields. The 10 largest integrated companies, for example, owned or leased more than 40% of the *facilities* at all levels studied other than at the drilling and producing levels. The 10 largest integrated companies, however, controlled only 5.7% of the industry's drilling rigs and only 22.0% of the industry's producing wells. Similarly, it may be noted that the 10 largest integrated companies conducted over 40% of the *operations* of the industry at all levels studied other than at the drilling level. The 10 largest integrated companies drilled only 15.9% of the total wells and 20.8% of the total oil producers. On the whole, the two exhibits provide considerable, but not necessarily conclusive, evidence that integrated refining companies were frequently among the largest participants at the various levels of the industry at which they were active except at the drilling level. At the drilling level there was no significant correlation, so far as can be determined from our data, between vertical integration and large size.

VI. Summary

1. The conclusions summarized in the following paragraphs are based on a survey which covered 106 operating refining companies or 59.2% of the total number in the industry. These 106 companies accounted for 74.3% of the operating and shutdown refineries, 94.7% of the operating and shutdown refin-

---

[24] No particular significance should be attached to our usage of the number 10; it was selected merely as a matter of statistical convenience in arranging the table.

ing capacity, and 97.3% of the domestic refinery runs. The data accumulated in the survey established the *minimum* amount of vertical integration which existed in the industry in 1950 because the survey covered only integrated structures which contained a refining segment, did not include a number of small refining companies representing 5.3% of the capacity of the industry, and did not take cognizance of integration accomplished through the personal stockholdings of individuals. Because of certain problems of definition and the difficulties involved in estimating industry totals, the figures should be regarded as an *approximation* of the structure of the oil industry as it existed in 1950.

2. At least 87 operating refining companies or 48.6% of the total number in the industry in 1950 had some type of integrated structure. These 87 companies held 226 operating and shutdown refineries or 68.3% of the total number in the industry and accounted for 93.2% of the refining capacity of the industry. At least 19 companies or 10.6% of the total number in the industry in 1950 were nonintegrated refiners. These 19 companies held 20 refineries or 6.0% of the total number in the industry and accounted for 1.5% of the total refining capacity of the industry. Rough approximations with regard to the structures of the 73 very small companies that did not reply to our survey suggest that the integrated companies in 1950 outnumbered the nonintegrated by about three to one and held about nine times as many refineries as did the nonintegrated.

3. There were wide variations in the proportion of the industry's facilities owned or leased by the integrated companies at the successive levels of the business. In general, the proportion was greatest in the middle of the oil process and declined toward both ends. The integrated companies held 93.2% of the crude charging capacity, 93.8% of the cracked gasoline capacity, 85.4% of the crude gathering lines, 82.1% of the crude trunk lines, and 92.2% of the products pipe lines. At the same time, however, the integrated companies held only 7.7% of the drill-

ing rigs, 35.4% of the producing wells, and 51.6% of the service stations.

4. There were likewise wide variations in the proportion of the industry's operations conducted by the integrated companies at the successive levels of the business. These variations were, however, less marked than in the case of facilities ownership. The integrated companies accounted for 96.2% of the refinery runs, 75.2% of the crude runs from wells, 83.1% of the deliveries from crude gathering and trunk lines, and 91.9% of the deliveries from products pipe lines. At the producing end of the business, the integrated companies accounted for only 26.2% of the total wells drilled and 32.6% of the oil wells completed as producers. At the retail level, the service stations owned or leased by integrated companies accounted for 58.0% of the total volume of gasoline sold through service stations (as defined by the Bureau of the Census).

5. By far the most important type of integrated company in 1950 was the producing-refining-wholesaling-retailing company. There were at least 54 such companies in 1950, representing 30.1% of the total number of companies in the industry. These companies held 178 refineries or 53.8% of the total and accounted for 89.1% of the refining capacity and 92.8% of the refinery runs of the industry. Moreover, all but a very small percentage of the facilities held and operations conducted by integrated companies at all other levels of the industry were those held and conducted by the producing-refining-wholesaling-retailing companies.

6. Characteristically the integrated companies did not maintain an even balance among their activities in the different phases of the oil business. The typical producing-refining-wholesaling-retailing company had crude production equal to 38.2% of its refinery runs, had crude runs from wells equal to 75.2% of its refinery runs, sold a volume equal to 63.8% of its refined products yield through its own terminals and bulk plants, and sold a volume equal to 26.7% of its gasoline and naphtha yield through service stations which it owned or leased.

7. The large refining companies in 1950 were exclusively of the highly integrated type. All companies with capacities in excess of 50,000 barrels per day were engaged in producing, refining, wholesaling, retailing, and transportation activities, and there were not more than 3 companies with capacities in excess of 20,000 barrels per day which did not have some type of vertical integration. The small refining companies, on the other hand, had both integrated and nonintegrated structures. There were at least 20 companies in the industry in 1950 in the 0–5,000 barrels per day capacity range which were engaged in crude production, and the typical company in the group produced 26.0% of its refining requirements. Moreover, the typical company engaged in marketing activities in the 0–5,000 barrels per day range had a greater extent of integration into wholesaling and retailing operations than did the typical company in the over 100,000 barrels per day capacity range.

8. The integrated refining companies in 1950 maintained a substantially higher level of refinery operations than did the nonintegrated companies, and the large refining companies maintained an appreciably higher level of operations than did the small companies. The differences in level of operations between the integrated and nonintegrated companies were significantly greater than the differences among companies in different size categories. It appears therefore that in the single year 1950 vertical integration contributed more to stability of refining operations than did large size.

9. There was a fairly strong association between vertical integration and large size at many levels of the industry in 1950. The 10 largest integrated companies,[25] for example, owned or leased more than 40% of the facilities at all levels studied other than drilling and producing, and conducted over 40% of the operations of the industry at all levels studied other than drilling.

TECHNICAL NOTE

As a preliminary step in the development of Exhibits II-7 and II-8, it was necessary to establish figures for the total facilities and operations of the industry in each major phase of the business in 1950. In a number of cases, the desired statistics were available from well-recognized industry or government sources. The sources for such figures have been indicated in footnotes to the tables and no further discussion of them is necessary. In other cases, however, it was necessary to employ various imputations or other special procedures to secure industry figures. The methods used in these instances will be outlined in the following paragraphs.

Pipe Line Facilities and Operations:

The Interstate Commerce Commission publishes annual figures covering the crude gathering, crude trunk, and products pipe line mileage of all companies which are required by law to file tariffs and other statistical data with the Commission.[26] These figures do not include the mileage of pipe lines which operate only in intrastate commerce and which are not required to report to the I.C.C. The Bureau of Mines, however, prepares at periodic intervals surveys of the pipe line mileage of the entire industry. One such report was made for the year 1949.[27] To obtain figures for the total industry crude gathering, crude trunk, and products pipe line mileage for the year 1950 therefore, we merely increased the I.C.C. figures for 1950 by the ratios between the Bureau of Mines and I.C.C. figures for 1949. The procedure assumed that the proportion of the total industry mileage represented by companies reporting to the I.C.C. was the same in 1950 as in 1949. The possible error arising from the assumption could not have been large, however, because (a) even in the case of products lines the I.C.C. figures

---

[25] Reference is here made to the 10 largest integrated companies at the level of the industry in question. As noted earlier, the array of companies by size at one level of the industry was not necessarily the same as at another. The number 10 is used for convenience in summarizing the data; we attach no particular significance to it.

[26] Interstate Commerce Commission, Bureau of Transport Economics and Statistics, *Selected Statistics of Oil Pipe Line Companies Reporting to the I.C.C. for the Year Ended Dec. 31, 1950,* Statement No. 5152 (Washington, October 1951).

[27] U. S. Bureau of Mines, *Crude-Oil and Refined Products Pipe Line Mileage in the United States, January 1, 1950,* IC 7585, by A. T. Coumbe and I. F. Avery (Government Printing Office, October 1950).

covered over 67% of the industry mileage, and
(b) the ratio of I.C.C. mileage to total mileage
does not vary greatly from one year to the next.

For the total volume of crude oil transported
by the industry's gathering lines, we used the
Bureau of Mines figure for total crude runs
from wells because it was known that all but
2% or 3% of the total moved from the wells by
pipe lines.[28] To obtain figures for the total
volume of crude oil delivered out of the industry's crude gathering and trunk lines and for
the total volume of refined products delivered
out of the industry's products pipe lines, the
following procedure was used: The total
volumes of crude oil and products delivered by
all companies reporting operations to the I.C.C.
were added to the volumes which companies
replying to our survey reported for their non-
I.C.C. lines. The total crude gathering and
trunk line *mileages* and products pipe line
mileages of the I.C.C. companies plus the non-
I.C.C. lines covered by the survey were then
compared with the figures for the total industry mileage.

The comparison revealed that the I.C.C.
lines plus the non-I.C.C. lines covered by the
survey represented 86.0% of the industry's
crude gathering and trunk line mileage and
93.8% of the industry's products pipe line
mileage. We therefore divided the total *deliveries* of the I.C.C. lines plus those of the non-
I.C.C. lines covered by the survey by 86.0% in
the case of crude oil and 93.8% in the case of
refined products to obtain our figures for the
crude oil and products volumes delivered out
of the entire industry's pipe line system. The
procedure assumes a direct relationship between pipe line mileage and volumes delivered, an assumption which is clearly open to
question. In view of the fact that the imputa-
tion was only necessary with respect to a very
small percentage of the industry's pipe line
facilities, however, the error in the final results
is probably of negligible significance.

Marketing Facilities and Operations:

There were no data available on the number of bulk terminals, bulk plants, and service
stations in the industry at the close of 1950 or
on the total volume of products sold through

such outlets during the year. We were forced
therefore to rely heavily upon the data developed by the Bureau of the Census in 1948 for
our estimates of industry totals for 1950.

Bulk Terminals and Bulk Plants: The Bureau of the Census reported the number of
bulk terminals and bulk plants in 1948 at 29,-
127. Of this total, 733 were bulk terminals and
28,394 were bulk plants.[29] We estimated that
there was probably a substantial increase in the
number of bulk terminals between 1948 and
1950 as a result of the general expansion in
the market for petroleum products and the extensive building of new products pipe lines.
We also estimated that many new bulk plants
were built between 1948 and 1950, but that
the increase in this case was partially offset by
the closing of a number of small bulk plants
which resulted from the advancement of the
bulk plant by-passing technique. On the
whole, therefore, we decided to take a figure
of 30,000 as a rough approximation of the total number of bulk terminals and bulk plants
in the industry at the close of 1950.

To obtain a figure for the total volume of
gasoline sold through bulk terminals and bulk
plants in 1950, we worked from the figure of
32,288,487,000 gallons reported by the Bureau
of the Census for bulk terminal and bulk
plant gasoline sales in 1948.[30] This figure was
first divided by 92.8%, the Bureau's estimate
of the proportion of the total bulk terminals
and bulk plants covered by its data. The resulting figure was then increased by the ratio
of domestic motor fuel demand in 1950 to domestic motor fuel demand in 1948 as reported

---

[28] American Petroleum Institute, *Petroleum Facts and
Figures,* Ninth Edition, 1950, pp. 271–272.

[29] U. S. Census of Business, 1948, Volume IV, *Wholesale
Trade—General Statistics; Commodity Line Sales Statistics,*
"Petroleum Bulk Stations," 14.07 and 14.47 (Government
Printing Office, 1952). The Bureau of the Census defined
bulk plants as establishments engaged primarily in the
storage and wholesale distribution of gasoline, oil, and
other petroleum products, usually from trucks, primarily to
retailers and other commercial users, and, in agricultural
areas, to farmers. Bulk terminals were defined as similar in
operation to bulk plants, but distinguished by the fact
that they had special equipment for the transfer of bulk
petroleum products from one type of transportation to another, were largely engaged in selling to bulk plants and
industrial accounts, and had larger operations than bulk
plants. We asked our survey companies to use the same
definitions in reporting their counts of facilities to us in
order that our data might be comparable with the Census
figures.

[30] Ibid.

by the Bureau of Mines.[31] A similar procedure was followed to develop a figure for the total volume of kerosene and distillates sold through bulk terminals and bulk plants in 1950.

Service Stations: The Bureau of the Census reported a total of 188,253 service stations in the industry in 1948.[32] The Bureau of the Census defined service stations as retail establishments primarily engaged in selling gasolines and lubricating oils, i.e., those deriving 50% or more of their total sales volume from gasolines and lubricating oils. This definition is a restrictive one because there are a very large number of outlets engaged in the distribution of gasoline which do not derive 50% or more of their sales volume from gasolines and lubricating oils.[33] Since we asked the survey companies to report their service stations to us in accordance with the Census definitions, however, it was appropriate for us to develop our estimate of the industry total in 1950 from the Census figures.

It was recognized that many new service stations were built in the two-year period 1948 to 1950. On the other hand, many old stations were eliminated as a consequence of the general movement in the industry over the past 10 years toward the development of a smaller number of larger size retail outlets. We concluded therefore that the 1948 Census figure was probably a reasonably satisfactory estimate for the number of retail outlets (as defined by the Census) in existence at the close of 1950 and used a round figure of 188,000 stations in our tabulations.

To develop an estimate of the total volume of gasoline sold through service stations in 1950, we began with the Census report of about $6,500,000,000 for the total dollar sales volume of the 188,253 service stations in operation in 1948.[34] In a merchandise line analysis covering 183,543 service stations, the Census found that the stations secured 70.3% of their dollar sales volume from gasoline.[35] We therefore took 70.3% of $6,500,000,000 to obtain a figure of $4,570,000,000 for the gasoline sales of the 188,253 service stations in 1950.

We next developed a weighted average of service station prices for regular grade gasoline, including tax,[36] as reported by The Texas Company in its survey of 50 cities.[37] As weighting factors we used the volume of gasoline consumed by passenger cars in the states in which the various cities were located.[38] The resulting figure of 25.9 cents per gallon, we divided into the total gasoline sales of $4,570,000,000 to obtain an estimate of 17,600,000,000 gallons for the total volume of gasoline sold by service stations in 1948. Finally, we increased the 17,-600,000,000 gallons by the ratio of passenger car consumption of gasoline in 1950 to passenger car consumption in 1948 to obtain our estimate of 20,100,000,000 gallons or 480,000,-000 barrels for the total volume of gasoline sold through service stations (as defined by the Census) in 1950.

---

[31] U. S. Bureau of Mines, *Mineral Industry Surveys,* Annual Petroleum Statement No. P347, "Crude Petroleum and Petroleum Products, 1950 (Final Summary)" and *Minerals Yearbook, 1949,* "Petroleum and Petroleum Products," by A. G. White, G. W. Cale, A. T. Coumbe, and A. L. Clapp (Government Printing Office, 1951), p. 866.

[32] U S. Census of Business, 1948, Volume IV, op. cit.

[33] Trade sources have sometimes placed the total number of outlets selling gasoline at retail at about 400,000.

[34] U. S. Census of Business, 1948, Volume IV, op. cit.

[35] U. S. Census of Business, 1948, Volume II, *Retail Trade—General Statistics, Part 2, and Merchandise Line Sales Statistics,* "Automotive Group, Gasoline Service Stations," 21.02 (Government Printing Office, 1952).

[36] We assumed that sales of premium gasoline would be approximately balanced by sales of gasoline below the prices reported for regular grade gasoline by The Texas Company.

[37] The Texas Company reported prices for at least one city in each state and the District of Columbia. In the one case where two cities were reported, we used a simple average of the two prices.

[38] American Petroleum Institute, *Petroleum Facts and Figures,* Tenth Edition, 1952, p. 5.

PART TWO

The Emergence of Integration in the Oil Industry

THE purpose of Part Two is to analyze the industrial environment in which the oil companies have operated in an effort to isolate the forces and circumstances which have led to the gradual emergence of large, integrated units as the predominant way of doing business in the oil industry. Part Two will thus constitute an examination of the processes by which the industry has acquired the characteristics described and measured in Part One.

The research method used in Part Two was to study in considerable detail a fairly large number of integration decisions and from those decisions to construct a picture of the forces and circumstances which have contributed to the integration process in various time periods. The examination of decisions was conducted primarily in, but by no means confined to, seven of the large, integrated oil companies. The group consisted of three independently organized firms, the Gulf Oil Corporation (1907), The Texas Company (1902), and the Sinclair Oil Corporation (1919), and four firms which were at one time components of the old Standard Oil Trust, The Ohio Oil Company (producing), The Atlantic Refining Company (refining), the Standard Oil Company (Indiana) (refining and marketing), and the Standard Oil Company (Ohio) (refining and marketing).[1] The latter four companies originally performed the functions indicated for the Standard Oil group, but each became an independent concern at the time of the dissolution decree in 1911. Each of the seven companies will be more fully introduced at the point where it is first taken up for discussion. In addition to the studies made in these large companies, integration decisions were likewise examined in about 30 of the small companies operating at the refining level of the industry in conjunction with the research done for Part Four of the book.

---

[1] The seven companies from time to time conducted certain of their operations through various wholly owned or partially owned subsidiaries, and in some cases the parent companies were reorganized under new names or reincorporated in different states. In the interests of simplicity we shall use the present names of the parent corporations, or simple contractions thereof, throughout the discussion in Part Two, unless there is some significant reason for distinguishing among the operations of a parent and its subsidiaries.

CHAPTER THREE

Integration in the Period Before 1911

THE year 1911 marked an extremely important turning point in the development of the oil industry. A relatively short span of time immediately before and after that date witnessed the emergence in the industry of an entirely new set of economic and competitive circumstances. For a period of fully 40 years prior to 1911 the entire activity of the industry was dominated by the Standard Oil group,[1] one of the greatest industrial combinations the United States has ever seen. In 1911 the group was broken up into 34 independent companies, out of which ultimately sprang a new and powerful group of competitors.

A second important development in the short period preceding and following 1911 was a fundamental change in the products and markets of the oil industry. In the period before 1911 the chief product of the industry was kerosene, of which roughly one-third to one-half and in some years over 60% was sold in foreign markets. In the period after 1911 the principal product was gasoline, a product for which the domestic market far surpassed the foreign in importance. In the first decade of the twentieth century there was also a very rapid development in the market for crude oil and residual oil as a fuel for industrial plants, marine engines, locomotives, and ships. A great increase likewise took place in the demand for a wide variety of other oil products. As state,

federal, and municipal agencies initiated road building programs, a market developed for road oil, asphalts, and macadam binders. At approximately the same time, the development and increased usage of motor cars, motorcycles, trucks, tractors, and all types of industrial machinery opened up a wide market for lubricants and industrial greases.

A third important development in the period immediately preceding 1911 was the increased acceptance accorded some new legal and public standards for the conduct of business affairs. These new standards had been in the process of evolution for some time and were gradually being formalized in business practices and in various statutes and court decisions, important among which were the Interstate Commerce Act of 1887, the Sherman Antitrust Act of 1890, the Elkins Act of 1903, and the Hepburn Act of 1906. Recognition and acceptance of the new standards were greatly stimulated by the trust-busting activities of Theodore Roosevelt's administration in the period 1901 to 1908. With the dissolution of the Standard Oil group in 1911 it became clear beyond all doubt that the public intended the oil companies, and business concerns generally, to conduct their competitive battles in the future with tactics very different from those employed in the past.

The oil industry was thus a very different world before 1911 from what it has been at any time since or probably ever will be again. We shall not therefore attempt to examine the period before 1911 in any great detail. We shall merely explore it sufficiently to find some of the roots of the integration process and to pick up the threads of the integration story.

The record of the oil industry reveals that in the years before 1911 vertical integration was very definitely a two-edged sword. To the Standard Oil group, vertical integration was

---

[1] In this chapter we shall use the term "Standard Oil group" to refer to the companies which became associated in an alliance shortly after the formation of the Standard Oil Company (Ohio) in 1870 and which were drawn together into the Standard Oil Trust in 1882. The Trust was dissolved ten years later in 1892, and the Standard Oil companies were held together for the next seven years by interlocking directorates and the close association of the principal stockholders in the companies. In 1899 the Standard Oil Company (New Jersey) was vested with the responsibility for holding the stocks and managing the affairs of the Standard Oil companies, an arrangement which was maintained until the organization was dissolved in 1911.

often used as a device to achieve, protect, and extend a virtual monopoly of the refining segment of the oil business. To the independent companies, on the other hand, vertical integration was often a means of escaping the dominance of the Standard Oil group, a means of challenging the industrial giant of the times. In Section I of this chapter we shall review briefly some of the major steps in the growth and development of the Standard Oil organization to indicate the part which vertical integration played in the strategy of Rockefeller and his associates. In Section II we shall then outline some of the early developments in the history of the Gulf Oil Corporation as an example of the integration movements among the independent firms.

I. Vertical Integration Moves of the Standard Oil Group [2]

The growth and development of the Standard Oil group was essentially a process of horizontal integration at the refining level which was later supported with various types and degrees of vertical integration. It would, of course, be impossible in this volume to trace all the many intricate moves involved in the evolution of the organization. We shall therefore merely select a few of the major steps to illustrate the way in which vertical integration was used by John D. Rockefeller and his associates to meet various problems which the Standard Oil interests encountered.

The Decision to Form a Combination of Refiners:

On January 10, 1870, the Standard Oil Company (Ohio) was organized with John D. Rockefeller as president to take over a refining business which had previously been conducted by Rockefeller and his associates under various partnership arrangements. The facilities of the new company consisted principally of two large refineries in Cleveland, the first of which was constructed at the time Rockefeller and

his associates entered the refining business in 1863 and the second of which was built in 1865. In the year following the formation of the new company, Rockefeller and his associates decided to attempt a combination of the refining interests in Cleveland. On the basis of the available facts and evidence, it appears that the motivations for this decision, apart from the desires which any group of able and aggressive businessmen might have had to expand their operations, lay chiefly in three primary circumstances: (1) the persistent instability of the petroleum industry, (2) the combinations which had already been formed by transportation agencies and the practices which existed with respect to shipping charges, and (3) the combinations which were from time to time being formed by producers, oil buyers, and the refiners in other areas.

Instability of the Petroleum Industry: In the twelve-year period from the discovery of the first commercial oil well in 1859 to 1871, chaotic conditions existed in all phases of the oil industry, and the prices of crude oil, the prices of refined products, and the refiner's margin were subject to violent fluctuations. The causes contributing to the instability of the industry were both external and internal in origin. The external causes included the Civil War boom and the sharp postwar depression which followed in 1866 and 1867; the crisis in the London money market in 1866 and the Austro-Prussian war, both of which were important to the petroleum industry because even in those days 20% to 50% of the American petroleum products were moving into foreign markets;[3] the American business depression of 1870; the $1.00 per barrel tax on crude oil passed by Congress in March 1865 and repealed in May 1866; and the fierce competitive struggles which were going on among the railroads.

The internal causes of disorder, which were of far greater significance than the external, stemmed in part from the nature of the crude oil discovery process, the spasmodic way in

2 For many of the facts in this section we have relied upon Allan Nevins, *John D. Rockefeller*, Vols. I and II (New York, Charles Scribner's Sons, 1940), and upon information and ideas given to us by Ralph W. and Muriel E. Hidy, who are currently writing a history of the Standard Oil Company (New Jersey), 1882–1911, under the auspices of the Business History Foundation, Inc.

3 U. S. Department of the Interior, Tenth Census of the United States, 1880, report on *Production, Technology, and Uses of Petroleum and Its Products* by S. F. Peckham, p. 278. In 1866 the quantity of petroleum products exported was 38.34% of production, and in 1867 the percentage exported amounted to 46.57%. See Table VII, p. 278.

which new crude supplies were brought forth, and the fact that new investments did not flow into the various branches of the new industry in a systematic manner. The discovery of the first commercial well in 1859 set off a great flurry of discovery activity, and soon vast quantities of oil were pouring forth from the wells. Much more oil was produced than could be accommodated by the existing storage, transportation, or refining facilities, and large quantities were run to waste on the ground or were dumped into the rivers. Production increased from 1,200 barrels per day in 1860 to over 5,000 barrels per day in 1861, and the price of crude oil at the wells dropped from about $10.00 per barrel in January 1861 to 10 cents per barrel at the close of the year [4] (see Exhibit III-1 for annual average prices).

The low price of crude oil and the demand for refined products stimulated a great influx of investment to the refining segment of the business, and a large number of small refineries were hastily constructed, often by individuals who lacked the financial resources and business ability to establish a sound enterprise. In 1864 a new oil boom was set in motion, partly as a result of the development of refining facilities, the enlargement of the market, and the sharp rise in the prices of all commodities, including crude oil and refined products. Several important new crude oil discoveries were made, and for a time both the producing and refining segments of the industry enjoyed a high rate of return. By the end of 1866, however, an excess supply of crude oil had been developed and far more refining capacity had been created than was necessary to meet the requirements of the market. The industry was thus doubly vulnerable to the postwar business depression which developed in 1866 and 1867.

During the postwar depression, the prices of crude oil and refined products moved drastically downward and the refiner's margin was reduced. Crude producers were reluctant to shut back their wells as the demand fell off for fear of losing their oil by drainage to adjacent wells, and some producers even attempted to increase their output as a means of offsetting the price drop. Eventually, however, many

producers were forced to abandon their wells, particularly those in the older fields where production was declining and costs were higher than in the new flush fields. The refiners attempted to operate their facilities as long as they could to secure any possible contribution to fixed costs, and severe price cutting developed in the refined products markets. Many of the smaller and less efficient refiners were forced into bankruptcy and numerous plants were soon standing idle.

EXHIBIT III-1. AVERAGE ANNUAL PRICE OF PENNSYLVANIA CRUDE OIL: 1860–1906 *

(Per Barrel of 42 Gallons)

Year	Price	Year	Price
1860	$9.59	1883	$1.00
1861	.49	1884	.84
1862	1.05	1885	.88
1863	3.15	1886	.71
1864	8.06	1887	.67
1865	6.59	1888	.88
1866	3.74	1889	.94
1867	2.41	1890	.87
1868	3.63	1891	.67
1869	5.64	1892	.56
1870	3.86	1893	.64
1871	4.34	1894	.84
1872	3.64	1895	1.36
1873	1.83	1896	1.18
1874	1.17	1897	.79
1875	1.35	1898	.91
1876	2.56	1899	1.29
1877	2.42	1900	1.35
1878	1.19	1901	1.21
1879	.86	1902	1.24
1880	.95	1903	1.59
1881	.86	1904	1.63
1882	.78	1905	1.39
		1906	1.60

* Based on reports of U. S. Geological Survey on Mineral Resources except 1906, for which year prices were computed from the quotations in the *Oil City Derrick*.

SOURCE: U. S. Bureau of Corporations, *Report of the Commission on the Petroleum Industry*, Part II, "Prices and Profits" (Washington, Government Printing Office, 1907), p. 84.

There was an upward movement in the prices of crude oil and refined products in 1869, and conditions in the industry improved somewhat. By 1870, however, excess production had again developed, a condition which was accentuated by the business depression which developed at that time. In addition, although some refineries had been eliminated, much spare capacity was still present in the industry. In 1870 and 1871 it was estimated that refining capacity was "already equal to three

---

[4] Paul H. Giddens, *Pennsylvania Petroleum 1750–1872* (Titusville, Pennsylvania, Pennsylvania Historical and Museum Commission, 1947), p. 223.

times the average [crude oil] production." [5] In 1870 therefore the industry again entered a period of severe price cutting and extreme competition which continued into the deep business depression of 1873.

A partial record of crude oil prices, kerosene prices, and the margin between the two prices for the period 1866–1873 is shown in Exhibit III-2. The reduction in the refiner's margin was, of course, less significant than the figures might at first seem to suggest because costs were being cut rapidly as volume increased and refining technology improved. The entire period was nonetheless characterized by continual uncertainty, violent fluctuations in prices and profits, wild speculation in crude oil and oil properties, and recurring intervals of ruinous competition. There is no question but what these chronic conditions of the industry had much influence on the decision which Rockefeller and his associates made late in 1871 to seek a combination of the refining interests in Cleveland.

Transportation Combinations and Rate-Making Practices: A second consideration which undoubtedly influenced Rockefeller's decision was the fact that some powerful combinations had already been formed in the transportation segment of the business. Crude oil trunk lines had not yet been developed, and the typical oil movement was by gathering line to a railroad shipping point and thence by tank car to refineries. The railroads were competing vigorously for oil traffic and found it expedient to own or control crude oil gathering lines as a means of gaining an assured business. It was therefore very natural for a close association of interests to form between the railroads and pipe lines. By 1871 four great systems of pipe lines and railroads—the Pennsylvania Transportation Company, the Empire Transportation Company, the Tidioute Pipe Line Company, and Vandergrift and Forman—had developed and completely dominated the transportation of crude oil. The first of these was associated with the Atlantic and Great Western Railroad (Erie system) and the second with the Pennsylvania Railroad. These systems, and particularly the railroad

---

[5] Nevins, op. cit., Vol. I, p. 308. The author quotes the Pittsburgh *Commercial*, January 1872.

EXHIBIT III-2. PRICES OF PENNSYLVANIA CRUDE AND ILLUMINATING OIL, WITH MARGIN BETWEEN THEM: 1866–1905 *

(In Cents per Gallon)

Year	Price of Pennsylvania Crude †	Price of Illuminating Oil ‡	Refiner's Margin
1866	6.33¢	30.08¢	23.75¢
1867	4.16	20.75	16.59
1868	6.13	21.16	15.03
1869	10.02	24.59	14.57
1870	8.08	22.96	14.88
1871	9.38	21.69	12.31
1872	7.92	20.97	13.05
1873	3.75	15.71	11.96
1874	2.63	11.65	9.02
1875	2.60	11.39	8.79
1876	5.51	17.22	11.71
1877	5.43	14.71	9.28
1878	2.78	10.75	7.97
1879	2.04	8.09	6.05
1880	2.24	9.15	6.91
1881	2.03	8.07	6.04
1882	1.87	7.42	5.55
1883	2.52	8.13	5.61
1884	2.00	8.29	6.29
1885	2.11	8.09	5.98
1886	1.70	7.11	5.41
1887	1.59	6.73	5.14
1888	2.07	7.49	5.42
1889	2.19	7.12	4.93
1890	2.06	7.31	5.25
1891	1.59	6.93	5.34
1892	1.32	6.07	4.75
1893	1.52	5.23	3.71
1894	1.99	5.19	3.20
1895	3.18	7.36	4.18
1896	2.84	6.97	4.13
1897	1.87	5.91	4.04
1898	2.16	6.32	4.16
1899	3.10	7.98	4.88
1900	3.22	8.46	5.24
1901	2.88	7.51	4.63
1902	2.95	7.38	4.43
1903	3.78	8.69	4.91
1904	3.87	8.30	4.43
1905	3.32	7.22	3.90

* Prices and margins 1866 to 1878, have been reduced to a gold basis for years when currency was not on a gold basis.

† The price of Pennsylvania crude oil for the years 1866 to 1899 are from U. S. Bureau of Corporations, *Report of the Commission on the Petroleum Industry*, Part I, "Position of the Standard Oil Company in the Petroleum Industry" (Washington, Government Printing Office, 1907), pp. 48–50. These figures do not coincide precisely with the per barrel figures shown in Exhibit III-1 because of minor differences in the data reported by the U. S. Geological Survey.

‡ New York export price for standard white kerosene in barrels.

SOURCE: U. S. Bureau of Corporations, op. cit., Part II, pp. 622–623.

portion thereof, did not offer producers and refiners a standardized service at a uniform price as the pipe lines and railroads are required to do today. The extreme competition among the railroads for traffic which began in the 1850's and reached strenuous proportions in the period following the Civil War resulted in the general practice of granting special rates and concessions to large shippers. The concessions took two general forms: rebates which were secret discounts granted at the time a shipment was made and drawbacks which were secret discounts granted at the end of the month on the basis of the volume shipped during the month. Large shippers were frequently able to demand and secure drawbacks not only on their own traffic but also on the volume moved by their competitors.

An oil refiner's transportation costs thus depended to a considerable extent on his ability to bargain with the railroads and pipe line companies. Transportation costs were then, as now, a critical factor in determining a refiner's competitive position, and the advantages to be gained from large size or a combination of refiners in one area were readily apparent. The Rockefeller interests began negotiating rebates with the railroads at least as early as 1867,[6] and much of their growth between 1867 and 1871 rested not only upon the fact that they conducted their refining business with efficiency and skill but also upon the fact that they constituted the largest refining concern in Cleveland and were thus able to negotiate more favorable rates than were their smaller competitors.

There was another aspect of the rate-making situation which suggested that advantages might be gained from a strong combination of refining interests. Throughout the 1860's and 1870's the three great trunk-line railroads [7] connecting the Atlantic coast and the Middle West engaged from time to time in vicious rate wars with each other. The maneuvers and adjustments involved in these rate wars sometimes placed the refiners in one region at such an extreme competitive disadvantage compared to those in other areas that they were threatened with complete extinction. Through

associations or combinations, it appeared that the refiners might marshal enough strength to bargain with the railroads and bring about a more stable rate situation.

Combinations of Producers, Oil Buyers, and Refiners in Other Areas: A third consideration which undoubtedly contributed to Rockefeller's decision to seek a combination of Cleveland refining interests was the fact that associations were from time to time already being formed by producers, oil buyers, and refiners in other cities. These associations threatened at any moment to become strong enough to place the Cleveland refiners at a severe competitive disadvantage. As early as 1866 the oil producers began to form groups to take action regarding the floods of crude oil which from time to time inundated the market and depressed prices. Moreover, speculation in crude oil was rampant, and many oil buying rings and combinations were formed to manipulate the price of crude oil by securing corners on the markets or by other means.[8] Early in 1871 one of these groups, working with the oil producers, was able to force so sharp an advance in the price of crude oil relative to refined products prices that many Pittsburgh and Cleveland refiners were forced to shut down their plants.[9]

The refiners as a group were somewhat slower to form associations than were the producers. One or two attempts had been made, however, to form alliances of refiners, and in 1871 it appeared that these efforts might be renewed with increased vigor in the near future. The abundant refining capacity in the industry had thrown the major refining centers of the country into intense competition with each other. The refiners in the Pennsylvania oil producing regions, Philadelphia, and New York, with their ally the Pennsylvania Railroad, were doing everything possible to take the oil business away from the refiners in Cleveland who were aided and abetted by the New York Central and Erie railroad systems. Meanwhile, the refiners in Pittsburgh, who were served by the Pennsylvania Railroad but at a disadvantage relative to the refiners in the

---

[6] Nevins, op. cit., Vol. I, pp. 255–256.

[7] The Pennsylvania, New York Central, and Erie railroads.

[8] Paul H. Giddens, *The Birth of the Oil Industry* (New York, The Macmillan Company, 1938), p. 184.

[9] Nevins, op. cit., Vol. I, p. 281.

oil producing regions and in Philadelphia, were attempting to work out favorable freight rates to the seaboard with the Baltimore and Ohio Railroad and the newly constructed Connellsville Railroad. On one occasion in 1869 while the Pennsylvania Railroad was engaged in a strenuous rate war with the New York Central and Erie railroads, the refiners in the Pennsylvania oil producing regions were able to form an alliance and negotiate a freight rate to the seaboard which gave them a distinct advantage over the Cleveland refiners. On the strength of this arrangement, it was "proclaimed in the public prints of Oil City, Titusville, and other places that Cleveland was to be wiped out as a refining center as with a sponge." [10]

In the light of the foregoing circumstances, it is not difficult to understand why Rockefeller and his associates came to the conclusion that a merger or combination was essential to the welfare of the Cleveland refining interests. A merger would first of all make it possible to eliminate some of the refining capacity and to exercise some control over prices. The smaller and less efficient refineries could be bought up and dismantled, and in times of depressed demand the production of the remaining refineries could be allocated and ruinous price competition thus avoided. A merger would likewise greatly increase the power of the Cleveland refiners in bargaining with the railroads over transportation rates and would put them in a position to battle any strong associations that might spring up among the producers or refiners in other cities.

In retrospect, it appears that a combination of the Cleveland refining interests offered many advantages from a business standpoint and that a failure to move in that direction might have represented a lack of business foresight and a failure to appreciate the character of the competitive and economic forces which were shaping up in the industry. It is not entirely clear at just what point Rockefeller conceived the larger scheme of merging nearly all the refining interests in the country. It was either in 1871 or very shortly thereafter. In

any case, the merger of the Cleveland refining interests was a necessary first step, and it was at this point that Rockefeller began his program of horizontal integration.

In the years that followed the Standard Oil group gradually proceeded with the acquisition of refineries in other refining centers. Many of the smaller and less efficient plants brought into the alliance were shut down and dismantled in accordance with the Rockefeller plan to reduce refining capacity. By the latter part of 1877 nearly all the refineries in the Pennsylvania oil producing regions had been purchased by the Standard Oil group. In 1878, after a successful battle with the Empire Transportation Company which will be discussed later, the Standard Oil group was able to take over several of the few remaining refineries in Pittsburgh and Buffalo. In the period 1878 to 1880 Rockefeller and his associates were able to draw into the Standard Oil group some large refiners in New York who had long held out against the combination. By the early 1880's the Standard Oil group was in control of perhaps 80%–90% of the refining capacity of the industry, and Rockefeller's objective of achieving a horizontal combination at the refining level had largely been realized.[11]

The methods used in drawing the independent firms into the organization have long been a subject of controversy. In retrospect, it appears that coercion, deception, rebates, drawbacks, and many other methods that would clearly be considered unethical by today's standards were sometimes used. Throughout the early years of its history, the Standard Oil group continued to press its case with the railroads and was able, largely because of the steadily increasing volume of its business, to negotiate some very favorable rates with the Atlantic and Great Western Railroad (Erie system) and the Lake Shore and Michigan

---

[10] Ibid., p. 294. Nevins quotes from General James H. Devereux, vice president of the Lake Shore Railroad in an affidavit, *Standard Oil Company* vs. *William C. Scofield and Others,* Court of Common Pleas, Cuyahoga County, Ohio.

[11] See Allan Nevins, *Study in Power* (New York, Charles Scribner's Sons, 1953), Vol. II, p. 7. Nevins reports the refinery capacity of the Standard Oil group in 1884 at 96,000 barrels per day or about 35,000,000 barrels per year. Accurate figures are not available on the total U. S. refining capacity in the early 1880's. Since total crude oil production in the period 1881–1884 did not exceed 31,000,000 barrels per year, however, the estimate of 80%–90% for the proportion of the refining capacity controlled by the Standard Oil group appears conservative, even if it is assumed that total U. S. refining capacity was substantially in excess of total U. S. producing capacity.

Southern Railroad (New York Central system). In later years these two railroads tended to form an alliance with the Standard Oil group against the Pennsylvania Railroad, the Empire Transportation Company, and the refining interests in the Pennsylvania oil fields. For the purposes of this study, it is important to observe that the quasi-vertical integration which resulted from the close association of the Standard Oil interests with the Erie and New York Central systems was certainly one important means of bringing pressure to bear on other refiners and of fostering the growth of the refining combination.

In appraising the record of the Standard Oil group, it must be remembered that the business methods it used did not differ greatly from those employed by its competitors. Moreover, much of the strength of the Standard Oil organization unquestionably lay in its highly efficient refining facilities and operating procedures. In addition, some of the refiners which found it expedient to sell out to the Standard Oil interests, particularly those in Pittsburgh, had long suffered from certain rate-making and other practices of the Pennsylvania Railroad, an organization which was certainly not under the Standard influence. Finally, it should be observed that the idea of a merger of refining companies appealed to many people in the period 1860–1881 as a means of bringing order out of chaos and as a means of placing the refiners in a position to bargain with the powerful groups that were from time to time being formed at other levels of the industry.

Integration Into Crude Oil Gathering and Trunk Lines:

In 1873 the Standard Oil group extended its activities to the ownership, operation, and control of crude oil gathering lines. This move appears to have been undertaken largely as a means of countering the growing strength of the Empire Transportation Company and its affiliate, the Pennsylvania Railroad, in the crude oil transportation field. The Empire Transportation Company owned the Mutual Pipe Line, one of the longest lines in the Pennsylvania oil regions, and in the summer of 1873 it acquired another important system, the Union Pipe Line. Moreover, the company was engaged in an aggressive program of extend-

ing its gathering lines to new fields as rapidly as they were opened up. The Standard Oil interests had suffered severely when the crude oil producers imposed an embargo in 1872 on shipments to refiners associated with the South Improvement Company, and Rockefeller and his associates clearly recognized how easily a strong combination in the crude oil transportation field could jeopardize their entire program with respect to refining operations.

For their part, the Empire Transportation Company and the Pennsylvania Railroad must have viewed with apprehension the growing strength of the Standard Oil alliance in the refining field, because it was apparent that the group could easily divert a large share of the oil business to its allies, the New York Central and Erie railroads, if it chose to do so. The Empire Transportation Company and the Pennsylvania Railroad probably pushed rapidly ahead therefore with the construction of their gathering lines as a means of protecting their oil traffic.

The Standard Oil group began the acquisition of pipe line properties in the latter part of 1873 and by 1877 had developed a system of pipe lines and storage facilities which was fully comparable with that of the Empire Transportation Company. Faced with the growing strength and power of the Standard Oil interests in both the refining and crude oil transportation fields, the Empire Transportation Company and the Pennsylvania Railroad entered into an agreement to establish an integrated operation of their own through the acquisition or construction of refining facilities at the eastern termini of lines controlled by the Pennsylvania Railroad.[12] The Empire Transportation Company acquired one refinery in New York and started construction of two new plants. Meanwhile it entered into alliances with the few remaining independent refiners in Pittsburgh, New York, and Buffalo and encouraged them to hold out against the Standard Oil group, thus blocking the efforts of the latter to form its national combination.

Rockefeller and his associates protested the entrance of the Empire-Pennsylvania group into the refining field and demanded that it withdraw. The demand was rejected and war-

---

[12] Nevins, *John D. Rockefeller,* Vol. I, p. 520.

fare promptly broke out between the two groups. The Standard Oil group immediately suspended all shipments over the Pennsylvania lines. The Standard Oil refineries in Pittsburgh were shut down until arrangements could be made for shipments eastward over the Baltimore and Ohio Railroad, prices were cut in all markets that the Pennsylvania Railroad served, and an aggressive effort was made to corner as much of the available supply of crude oil as was possible. The New York Central, Erie, and Baltimore and Ohio railroads cooperated with drastic rate reductions. The battle continued until the fall of 1877 when the Pennsylvania Railroad, weakened by the railroad strike of 1877 which was directed at it more than any other line, was forced to capitulate. The Empire Transportation Company was thereupon dissolved and its refineries, pipe lines, oil terminals, and barges sold to the Standard Oil group.

The Standard Oil interests thus came into control of nearly all the crude oil gathering lines in the country and were subsequently able to negotiate some very favorable freight rates with the railroads, including heavy drawbacks on shipments of their competitors. These moves made it very easy for the Standard Oil alliance to acquire some of the remaining independent firms in Pittsburgh and Buffalo. Vertical integration into crude oil gathering lines, which was undertaken as a means of protecting the horizontal combination of refining interests, thus became a means by which the horizontal combination was extended.

The Standard Oil group's first crude oil trunk lines were, like its first crude oil gathering lines, built to counter moves made by its competitors. In 1875 the Bradford field, the first really great producing area, came into production and in the subsequent years flooded the market with crude oil. The Standard Oil group made a tremendous effort to extend its crude oil pipe lines and storage facilities rapidly enough to handle the new supply, but by the early part of 1878 production had become so great that all existing facilities were jammed to capacity.[13] Crude oil and refined products prices were depressed (see Exhibit III-2), and

the Standard Oil group initiated the practice of taking only one-quarter of each man's oil for storage; the remainder was purchased at a discount for immediate shipment.

The producers, always suspicious of the Standard Oil interests and particularly so after the defeat of the Empire Transportation Company made Standard almost their sole outlet for crude oil, tended to blame their lot on the Standard Oil group and its associates, the railroads. The producers felt that Standard was taking undue advantage of the situation to depress the price of crude oil, was not building storage facilities or providing additional tank cars as fast as it should, and was engaging in various unfair practices with regard to the buying of oil. In the latter part of 1877, therefore, the producers held a general convention to discuss not only means of handling the overproduction of crude oil but likewise means of dealing with the Standard Oil interests.

The convention resulted in the formation of a producers' association which later came to be known as the Grand Council. This group was unable to develop any constructive measures for curtailing drilling or production, but it did initiate a number of legislative and court actions against the Standard Oil group. The producers also gave strong encouragement to the building of trunk pipe lines from the Bradford field by independent concerns, not only as a means of providing additional facilities for handling the oil but likewise as a means of gaining freedom from the Standard "monopoly." One of the projects sponsored by the producers resulted in the formation of the Tidewater Pipe Line Company which was successful in May 1879 in pumping oil from Coryville to Williamsport, Pennsylvania, a distance of about 108 miles, whence shipments could be made over the Philadelphia and Reading Railroad to New York harbor. The Philadelphia and Reading Railroad was outside the Standard influence and engaged in a battle with the Pennsylvania Railroad; it was so eager for oil traffic that it contributed about half of the capital required for the financing of the line. The new line represented a major technological advance in that oil was pumped a longer distance and at higher altitudes than ever before.

The successful completion of the Tidewa-

---

[13] Ida M. Tarbell, *The History of the Standard Oil Company* (New York, McClure, Phillips and Co., 1904), Vol. I, pp. 217–219.

ter line gave the independent refiners in New York a lower transportation cost than the Standard Oil plants could hope to achieve by rail, except when unusual concessions were obtained, and thus gave the independents great encouragement in their battle against the combination. Rockefeller and his associates immediately countered the new development: (a) by attempting to buy out the Tidewater interests, (b) by offering to contract for all the oil the Tidewater line could pump, (c) by acquiring a number of the remaining independent refineries in New York and Philadelphia in an effort to deprive the Tidewater line of its customers, and (d) by beginning construction of crude oil trunk lines of their own to New York, Cleveland, Philadelphia, and Buffalo. In addition, the United Pipe Line Company (controlled by the Standard Oil group) and the Pennsylvania, New York Central, and Erie railroads promptly initiated a vigorous rate war against the Tidewater pipe line and the Philadelphia and Reading Railroad.[14]

The battle between the Standard Oil interests and the Tidewater pipe line continued until 1883. By that time the Tidewater line had been weakened by financial difficulties, internal dissension among its stockholders, and the loss of independent refinery outlets in New York. The Standard Oil group had been able to complete the acquisition of the last of the major independent refining concerns in New York in 1880. It seems probable that the decision of the last of these refiners to sell out may have been influenced by the initiation of the Standard Oil trunk line to New York. The latter promised to give better service when completed than the Tidewater line because it permitted shipments over the entire distance by pipe line whereas the Tidewater shipments had to travel the last portion of the journey by rail.[15] An agreement was reached between

Tidewater and Standard in 1883 which provided that Tidewater would have 11.5% and Standard 88.5% of the traffic moving eastward from the Pennsylvania fields.[16] By 1885 the National Transit Company, which was organized in 1881 to consolidate the Standard Oil pipe line interests, was extending storage and pipe line facilities to almost every well as soon as it was drilled.

It would thus appear that the integration of the Standard Oil group into crude oil trunk lines was, as in the case of the crude oil gathering lines, a means of defending and extending the horizontal combination in the refining field. The building of the crude oil trunk lines might likewise be viewed as merely the substitution of one form of vertical integration for another in response to a new technological development. For all practical purposes, the Standard Oil group had already accomplished integration into crude oil transportation through its ownership of crude gathering lines and its close working relationships with the railroads. In building crude oil trunk lines the company merely replaced rail with pipe line transportation and at the same time increased the intensity of the integration bond by acquiring ownership of the facilities for its own account.

Integration into Marketing:

Before 1873 the Standard Oil group concentrated almost exclusively on the refining phase of the business and made no major effort to build a marketing organization of its own. Refined products were sold through the company's export agency to foreign marketers while in the United States the company sold to a variety of different types of marketing organizations, including commission merchants, sales agents, wholesalers, and jobbers. In the early years of the oil industry, the majority of the refiners preferred to concentrate on the job of manufacturing and to leave the marketing problems to others, a practice which cotton textile manufacturers have tended to follow almost to the present day. As a result, many different forms of petroleum marketing organizations quickly came into existence to handle the distribution job.

Beginning in 1873 the Standard Oil group

[14] Nevins, op. cit., Vol. I, pp. 579–589.

[15] The original contract between the builders of the Tidewater line and the Philadelphia and Reading Railroad provided that the former would forfeit $100,000 to the railroad if the line were built any closer to tidewater than Williamsport during the first eight years of operation. The line was extended to Bayonne, New Jersey, in 1888 whereas the Standard Oil line reached the seaboard in 1881. See in *Common Carrier Pipe Line Operations and Accounting,* edited by Paul J. Graber (Tulsa, Oklahoma, Ross-Martin Co., University of Tulsa, 1951) "Development of the Pipe Line Industry," by R. J. Andress, p. 4.

[16] Nevins, op. cit., Vol. I, p. 597.

acquired stock interests in a number of large, regional distributing companies, nearly all of which were later absorbed into the Standard organization. Some marketing properties also were acquired during the 1870's merely as a consequence of the fact that a few of the refineries purchased in the process of horizontal expansion also had marketing operations. By 1880 Rockefeller and his associates were fully embarked on the task of building a nation-wide marketing organization. Existing companies were bought in many cases, but for the most part the company expanded through the organization of new marketing companies and the extension of bulk plant facilities in areas where it was already represented.[17] The number of bulk plants which the Standard Oil interests had increased from 130 in 1882 to 313 in 1886 and to 3,573 in 1906.[18]

Once the Standard Oil group had decided to enter the marketing field, it did so with its characteristic aggressiveness and efficiency. Much has been written about the tactics and methods that were used by the Standard Oil marketing companies to gain entrance to new markets and to fight competition. From the mass of evidence that has been produced on the subject, it appears that at least the following generalizations are warranted: (1) The distribution system which the Standard Oil group built was extremely efficient from a competitive standpoint; the bulk plants were well-located, well-constructed, and well-kept, and the customer was offered the maximum in service and reliability of deliveries. (2) The marketing units of the organization were granted a good deal of autonomy in conducting their operations, and from time to time some of them, particularly the Waters-Pierce Oil Company, came under the management of people who employed unscrupulous methods in fighting competition. (3) The Standard Oil interests sought and gained rebates and drawbacks on shipments of refined products in much the same manner and for much the same reasons as they did on shipments of crude oil. (4) An extensive and detailed system was maintained for the purpose of collecting information about the activities of competitors, and Standard Oil employees sometimes went

to extreme lengths and used some very questionable methods to obtain the necessary data. (5) The Standard Oil marketing companies engaged in vigorous price wars to gain access to new markets and to drive out competitors, and in at least a few instances went so far as to supply groceries at discount prices to their dealers to aid them in competing with non-Standard dealers. (6) Considerable use was made of affiliated companies whose relationship to the Standard Oil group was carefully hidden as a means of securing the business of dealers who believed they were competing with the Standard Oil companies or as a means of entering markets with "fighting brands" which the company did not wish to have associated with the Standard name.

The decision of Rockefeller and his associates to enter the marketing field was apparently influenced by a number of different considerations, no one of which was of dominant importance. In the first place, the marketing field was probably considered a natural area of growth and expansion for the company and a source of additional profits. In addition, the marketing phase of the business, like the refining, was in a chaotic and disorderly state in the early years of the oil industry. During frequently recurring periods of large crude oil and refined products supplies, ruinous price cutting prevailed. Moreover, it was a common practice for unscrupulous jobbers to acquire low-quality or adulterated kerosene and sell it at prices which Standard found hard to meet, or indeed to sell it at low prices under the Standard brand names. It is therefore possible that Rockefeller may have felt that a strong combination of interests in the marketing field offered many of the same advantages that he believed existed for a combination in the refining field.

Rockefeller and his associates may likewise have believed that the exercise of considerable control over marketing activities was a necessary adjunct to the successful maintenance of the combination of refining interests. A number of the marketing organizations were at this time gaining considerable strength and power, and the Standard Oil interests may have feared the influence which they might some day come to exercise over refined product prices and thus over the margins on which the Standard Oil

---

[17] Nevins, op. cit., Vol. I, pp. 659–660.
[18] Ibid., pp. 657–661.

refineries operated. The growth of the refining business was, moreover, obviously limited to the growth in the use of refined products, and Rockefeller may have been dissatisfied with the attention which the jobbing companies were giving to the development of the market. The population of the country was moving westward, the railroads were rapidly extending transportation facilities to new territories, and the construction of a vast system of bulk plant facilities was clearly required to cultivate properly the potential market for kerosene and other petroleum products.

Finally, Rockefeller and his associates, who were always relentless in their pursuit of efficiency in business methods, may have felt that their entrance into the marketing field was necessary in order to extend the usage of the new bulk handling techniques that were becoming available and to get the marketing job done on an efficient basis. During the first few years of the oil industry's history, refined products were put up in barrels at the refineries and shipped by rail to jobbers who maintained warehouses and distributed to grocery stores and other dealers by horse and wagon. As soon as the tank car became available, refined products were shipped in bulk to local "barrelling and marketing" plants where they were put up in barrels, cans, and other containers for distribution to dealers and farm customers. These bulk plants, however, which called for storage tanks, a cooperage plant, and a barrel warehouse, were more expensive than the earlier warehouses, and the small jobbers may have been slow in constructing the new facilities.

The later adoption of the tank wagon to make deliveries to local retailers in populous areas, which likewise required additional investment, may also have proceeded more slowly than the Rockefeller interests thought desirable. The tank wagon not only lowered distribution costs by avoiding the packaging in barrels, but also relieved the customer of the inconvenience of handling the barrels. The tank wagon was drawn up to the customer's door and transfers were made to his storage tank usually by means of a five-gallon measuring can. In retrospect, it seems reasonably clear that the adoption of bulk handling techniques and of efficient methods in the marketing field was at least speeded by the entrance

of the Standard Oil group, with its great financial strength, into the field.

Integration into Crude Oil Production:

Rockefeller and his associates apparently intended originally to limit the activities of the Standard Oil group to the buying, transportation, and refining of crude oil and the marketing of refined products. Some miscellaneous purchases of producing properties were made in the 1870's and early 1880's, but before about 1886 the Standard Oil group made no sustained effort to develop crude oil production. In the period 1886 to 1890, however, the Standard Oil group initiated a program to acquire crude oil production of its own.

Lima-Indiana Oil Fields: The first step toward the development of crude oil production was taken in 1886 and 1887 when the Standard Oil interests made some purchases of oil lands in the newly discovered Lima-Indiana fields. This decision appears to have been made as a matter of long-run policy rather than of immediate necessity. In 1886 and the three-year period following, the oil producing regions were once again inundated with an oversupply of crude oil. Crude oil stocks rose to unprecedented levels and crude prices were severely depressed (see Exhibit III-1). In the early part of 1887 it was estimated that there were about 31,000,000 barrels of crude oil above ground [19] as contrasted with crude oil production for the year 1886 of only 28,000,000 barrels.[20] At the same time a flood of Russian crude oil was beginning to penetrate the European and Near Eastern markets. There was therefore no immediate prospect of a shortage of crude oil in either the domestic or world markets.

In addition, the new Lima crude oil was not particularly attractive as a source of supply for the Standard Oil refineries. The oil had a high sulphur content, and even the best refining techniques produced a kerosene with a slight odor which smoked and led to a rela-

[19] 50th U. S. Congress, 1st Session, 1887–1888, *House Reports, Vol. 9, Proceedings of the Committee on Manufactures in Relation to Trusts,* "The Standard Oil Trust," Testimony of David Kirk, April 7, 1888, p. 34.

[20] U. S. Bureau of Mines, *Mineral Resources of the U. S., 1911, Part II—Nonmetals* (Washington, Government Printing Office, 1912), pp. 339 and 340.

tively quick encrustation of the wicks. The processing cost was higher than for Pennsylvania crude oil, and the yield of kerosene and naphtha was about 57% whereas the yield of kerosene alone from Pennsylvania crude oil was 75%.

It would appear therefore that the decision to buy crude oil producing properties in the newly developing fields was made primarily as a means of securing a long-run source of supply for the Standard Oil refineries. Despite the current overproduction of Pennsylvania oil, no major new fields had been discovered for some time, and there was considerable geological opinion to the effect that the area had passed its peak and that the future would witness a slow but steady decline in production, an opinion which later proved to be correct. In view of their heavy investments in refining properties, Rockefeller and his associates must have felt keenly the need for assuring an ample, long-run supply of domestic crude oil. Moreover, as will be noted below, the Standard Oil interests were again at war with the producers in the Pennsylvania fields and the crude oil market was again in a chaotic condition. The Standard Oil executives may therefore have reached the conclusion at this time that the only long-run solution to their crude oil supply problem was to secure production of their own. Finally, it is highly probable that many of the Standard Oil executives may by this date have formed the opinion that good profits were available in the producing end of the business and that the Standard Oil group should seek to participate in them.

The Standard Oil group began purchasing in the Ohio fields in 1886, and in 1889 The Ohio Oil Company was acquired. This company had been organized in 1887 to consolidate the operations of a group of independent Ohio producers and to engage in the development of crude oil production in the Lima-Indiana fields on a large scale. The Buckeye Pipe Line Company was organized in 1886 to build crude gathering lines in the territory and to extend crude trunk lines to Chicago and to the western terminus of Standard's main pipe line system. A refinery was constructed at Lima, Ohio, and a short time later, in 1890, a much larger plant, the Whiting refinery, was built near Chicago. Both of these refineries

became the scene of extensive experimentation with refining techniques for handling the sulphurous Ohio crude oil. These experiments were successful in the commercial development of the Frasch process. By 1890 the Standard Oil interests were producing 56% of the crude oil from the Lima-Indiana fields and were hard pressed to provide adequate storage facilities for their own oil as well as that purchased from others.[21]

Pennsylvania Oil Fields: The second major step toward the development of crude oil production by the Standard Oil group was taken in the Pennsylvania fields. This step was taken shortly after the venture in Ohio producing under circumstances which also led to the organization of the Standard Oil group's first great competitor, the Pure Oil Company. As has already been noted, in 1886 and 1887 the oil regions were once again having trouble with an oversupply of crude oil, prices were depressed, and the situation appeared particularly gloomy in view of the new discoveries in Ohio and the movement of large quantities of Russian crude oil into the world markets.

The Pennsylvania producers recognized that much of their difficulty could be attributed to overproduction, but they nonetheless tended to blame part of their price difficulty on the Standard Oil interests whom they believed were using their pre-eminent position in the purchasing and transportation of crude oil to make capital out of the misfortunes of the producers. In the early part of 1887, therefore, the Producers' Protective Association was formed with two specific objectives: the first was to bring about a reduction of inventories and the second was to establish cooperative refining, transportation, and marketing facilities in order that the producers might dispose of their output independently and in competition with the Standard Oil group.

The Standard Oil interests cooperated in the first project, and over the next two years it proved fairly effective in reducing crude oil inventories to reasonable levels.[22] Vigorous

---

[21] U. S. Industrial Commission, *Preliminary Report on Trusts and Industrial Combinations* (Washington, Government Printing Office, 1900), Vol. I, p. 561.

[22] See 50th U. S. Congress, 1st Session, 1887–1888, *House Reports, Vol. 9,* op. cit., Testimony of James A. Goldsborough, April 7, 1888, p. 69, for memorandum of the agree-

work on the producers' second project was begun in 1888 and 1889. Plans were quickly developed for the construction of independent pipe lines, alliances with independent refineries, and selling crude oil and products to foreign distributors who owned tankers, storage, and marketing facilities. The venture was dealt a severe blow in 1890, however, when the Standard Oil group bought up four large producing companies which owned over 300,000 acres in Pennsylvania and West Virginia and which had an aggregate estimated production of 7,600 barrels daily.[23] By these purchases the Standard Oil group almost overnight became the largest single crude oil producer in the Pennsylvania region. Moreover, the owners of the four companies included several of the most prominent leaders of the independent movement.

The cooperative effort of the oil producers to create transportation, refining, and marketing facilities which would free them from the necessity of doing business with the Standard Oil group was renewed in 1891 at which time the Producers' Oil Company, Ltd., was formed. It was the intent of the producers not only to build their own transportation, refining, and marketing agencies, but also to unite in cutting off the crude oil supplies to the Standard Oil group. The new company built a few pipe lines in western Pennsylvania; constructed storage tanks; secured terminaling facilities at Bayonne, New Jersey; ordered fifty tank cars; and prepared to ship crude oil abroad.[24] The venture met with little success, however, because of a temporary decline in the foreign crude oil market, a lack of an adequate number of tank cars, and the fact that in 1888 the railroad rates on barrel shipments of crude oil were raised relative to the rates on tank car shipments by the Pennsylvania Railroad. The producers attributed the latter development to the Standard Oil interests and filed a vigorous protest with the Interstate Commerce Commission, but were unable to obtain relief.

In 1892 a new corporation, the Producers' and Refiners' Oil Company, Ltd., was formed

which represented a union of some 15 refineries and over 1,000 well owners.[25] The new firm built pipe line gathering systems in the oil fields and short trunk lines from the oil fields to the independent refineries at Oil City and Titusville. It was apparent, however, that the independent refineries in the oil regions would never be able to take but a small portion of the Pennsylvania output and that the producers could obtain no major success in competition with the Standard Oil interests until they had a pipe line to the eastern seaboard which would provide direct access to the foreign markets and the independent refining centers along the coast, particularly in New York.

In 1892 therefore the United States Pipe Line Company was organized with the support of the independent producers and refiners to build two trunk lines eastward, one for crude oil and one for refined products. Despite formidable opposition by the Standard Oil group and the Pennsylvania and Erie railroads which included court actions, the buying up of strips of land across the path of the pipe line, and attacks by armed gangs of men, the United States Pine Line successfully completed the two lines to Wilkes-Barre, Pennsylvania, in the summer of 1893 from whence shipments could be made by rail to New York harbor. The two lines were an unqualified success, and a short time later the company was able to extend them to within a few miles of New York and to arrange satisfactory rail rates for the remainder of the haul.

The three independent ventures (Producers' Oil Company, Ltd., Producers' and Refiners' Oil Company, Ltd., and the United States Pipe Line Company) suffered severely in the depression which began in the oil industry with declining crude and products prices in 1892, reached a peak in the general business panic in 1893, and continued on into 1894. Many producers and refiners during this period closed down their properties, sold out, or were forced into bankruptcy. The situation was particularly difficult for the refiners in 1893 because the crude oil price began to move upward while the refined products price continued to move downward (see Exhibit III-2), a phenomenon which was attributed to manip-

---

ment between the producers and the Standard Oil Company as of November 1, 1887.

[23] Nevins, op. cit., Vol. II, p. 308.

[24] Ibid., p. 310.

[25] Ibid., p. 311.

ulation by the Standard Oil interests. Moreover, the Standard Oil group during those years acquired substantial blocks of stock in all three of the new independent companies, often as a concomitant of its continued program of purchasing producing and refining properties, and in 1894 was almost successful in gaining control of the Producers' Oil Company, Ltd.[26]

To support the weaker independent units during the depression and to guard the independent movement against the inroads being made by the Standard Oil group's stock purchases, the leaders of the independent group organized the Pure Oil Company in 1895. Thirty independent refiners joined with the producing interests in this venture and agreed to contribute their plant facilities and tank cars in exchange for stock. In order to guard against the purchase of control by the Standard Oil interests, the plan of organization for the new company provided that half of the stock would be placed in the hands of five trustees who were bound by a trust bond to vote only for men and measures which would make the company forever independent.[27]

Fortunately, a great oil boom developed in 1895 from which the independent groups were able to gain considerable strength. In 1897 the capitalization of the Pure Oil Company was increased to $10,000,000 and to it was transferred control of the Producers' Oil Company, the Producers' and Refiners' Oil Company, and the United States Pipe Line Company. The Pure Oil Company subsequently developed rapidly and soon became a strong competitor of the Standard Oil group in both the domestic and foreign markets. By 1903 the company had 8,000 barrels per day of crude oil production, 14 refineries, 1,500 miles of crude oil pipe line, 400 miles of refined products lines, and owned one and chartered several tankers. In addition, it had developed marketing systems in England, Holland, and Germany and sold at both the wholesale and retail levels in the United States.

Most of the stockholders of the company, which numbered about 1,000, were producers.[28]

It is difficult to form a judgment as to the extent to which Rockefeller and his associates were motivated in their acquisitions of Pennsylvania crude oil production by a desire to block the growth of the independent organizations among the producers and refiners. In view of the Standard Oil group's earlier movement into crude oil production in Ohio, it would appear that a long-run policy decision to engage in the crude oil producing phase of the business was made several years before the big Pennsylvania acquisitions in 1890. The evidence clearly indicates, however, that the Standard Oil interests did everything in their power to block the growth of the Pure Oil Company and its predecessor organizations, and the furtherance of this effort undoubtedly became a very strong secondary reason why the Standard Oil group pushed the acquisition of Pennsylvania crude oil properties in 1890 and the years immediately following.

Position Attained by the Standard Oil Interests:

The acquisition of crude oil production completed the transformation of Rockefeller's original horizontal combination of refiners into a vertically integrated oil company, and thereafter the Standard Oil group followed an aggressive program of growth and expansion in all phases of the oil business. By 1907 the Standard Oil group owned or controlled a group of 67 subsidiary companies which included 9 refining companies, 5 lubricating oil and compounding companies, 3 producing companies, 12 pipe line companies, 1 tank car transportation company, 6 marketing companies, 16 natural gas companies, and 15 foreign companies. This listing relates only to the principal activities of the companies; a substantial number of them were integrated concerns operating at more than one level in the industry. As a group these companies gained a dominant position in the crude oil transportation, refining, and marketing phases of the business and an important position in crude oil production.

In 1898 the Standard Oil interests accounted

---

[26] U. S. Bureau of Corporations, *Report of the Commissioner of Corporations on the Petroleum Industry* (Washington, Government Printing Office, 1907), Part I, p. 11.

[27] Nevins, op. cit., Vol. II, p. 322. Nevins quotes from the prospectus of the new company.

[28] Ibid., p. 329.

for about 33.5% of the total crude oil production of the United States and produced sufficient oil to supply a large part of their refinery runs.[29] The position of the Standard Oil group in crude oil production declined thereafter, largely as a result of the dwindling output from the Appalachian and Lima-Indiana fields and the rapid development of the new fields in Kansas, Oklahoma, Texas, Illinois, and California. Whereas before 1900 the output of the Appalachian and Lima-Indiana fields accounted for about 95% of the United States total, by 1905 the output of the two fields amounted to less than 40% of the total.[30] At the time of the dissolution in 1911, the Standard Oil group controlled only about 14% of the total United States output. The Standard Oil interests produced a far higher percentage of the crude oil run to refineries, however, because much of the newly discovered oil in Texas and California was burned for fuel and not used for refining purposes.

Immediately before the dissolution in 1911, the crude oil pipe line system of the Standard Oil group included over 8,000 miles of trunk lines and 75,000 miles of gathering lines.[31] In 1904 the company collected 88.8% of the crude oil runs in the Appalachian fields and 96% of the crude oil runs in the Lima-Indiana fields.[32] In the Illinois and Mid-Continent fields the Standard Oil group also occupied a dominant position, although shortly after 1907 independent lines were built from the Mid-Continent fields to the Gulf Coast.

In 1904 there were about 100 refineries in the United States of which 18 were owned by the Standard Oil group and 5 by affiliated companies. Altogether the 23 plants accounted for 84.2% of the total crude oil consumed by refineries in the United States in 1904 and for 86.5% of the total illuminating oil output.[33]

The Standard Oil interests secured an even more important position in the marketing field than they did in refining activities. By 1904 the group had developed extensive marketing operations in almost every state in the Union. On the basis of replies to a questionnaire received from 5,397 dealers in 3,854 towns in 1904, the Bureau of Corporations estimated that 88.7% of the petroleum dealers were buying their supplies from the Standard Oil group and its jobbers or affiliates, 8.8% from independents, and 2.5% from unclassified concerns.[34] A total of 4,762 dealers or 88.2% of the total reported no purchases except from Standard Oil concerns.

II. THE FORMATION AND EARLY DEVELOPMENT OF THE GULF OIL CORPORATION [35]

While the Standard Oil group was carrying forward its program of horizontal and vertical integration, a number of independent petroleum companies were organized and likewise undertook either horizontal or vertical integration. Important among the independent concerns which were organized in the period prior to 1911 were the American Oilfields Company (California, 1910), the American Petroleum Company (California, 1908), the Associated Oil Company (California, 1901), the Gulf Oil Corporation (New Jersey, 1907), the Indian Refining Company (Maine, 1904), the National Refining Company (Ohio, 1906), the Pure Oil Company (New Jersey, 1895), The Texas Company (Texas, 1902), the Tide Water Oil Company (New Jersey, 1888), the Union Oil Company of California (California, 1890), and the United Petroleum Company (California, 1899).

---

[29] Since the Standard Oil group accounted for about 84.2% of the refinery runs in the United States in 1904 (see later paragraph), it would follow that the group probably had sufficient crude oil production in 1898 to supply somewhere in the neighborhood of 40% of its refinery runs. For crude oil production of Standard Oil group 1890–1898 see U. S. Industrial Commission, op. cit., p. 561.

[30] U. S. Bureau of Corporations, op. cit., Part I, p. 7.

[31] Moody's Manual of Railroads and Corporation Securities, 1912, p. 3603.

[32] U. S. Bureau of Corporations, op. cit., Part I, pp. 12–13. The figure for the Appalachian fields includes the runs of the affiliated Tidewater and Franklin lines and the figure for the Lima-Indiana field includes the runs of the Manhattan Oil Company which was under the control of the Standard Oil interests.

[33] Ibid., pp. 14–15 and 213.

[34] Ibid., pp. 17–18 and 295–297. In computing these percentages dealers buying from more than one source have been counted more than once, but the number of such dealers was small.

[35] The material in this section has been drawn largely from W. L. Mellon, Judge Mellon's Sons, privately printed 1948. Corroboration for many of the facts recorded by Mr. Mellon was found in other sources. We also drew at a few points upon Craig Thompson, Since Spindletop, 1952, a brief history of the Gulf Oil Corporation published by the company in commemoration of its fiftieth anniversary.

Mention has already been made of the circumstances which prompted the organization of the Pure Oil Company and its initial moves toward vertical integration. To illustrate further the character of and the motivations for the vertical integration moves made by some of the independent companies in the period before 1911, the following paragraphs will present a brief outline of the formation and early growth of the Gulf Oil Corporation.

Initial Mellon Operations in the Oil Industry:

The history of the Gulf Oil Corporation really began in April 1889 when Mr. William L. Mellon, excited by the discovery of the Legget gusher within a few miles of Pittsburgh, began acquiring oil-producing properties in the western part of Pennsylvania. Mr. Mellon at that time was 21 years of age and the capital for his operations was furnished by his two uncles, Mr. Andrew W. Mellon and Mr. Richard B. Mellon, who were managing the banking firm of T. Mellon and Sons which later became the Mellon National Bank.

Mr. W. L. Mellon's leasing and drilling operations were successful from the outset, and within a short time the Mellons had a number of producing wells. The initial crude oil production was sold almost exclusively to the Standard Oil group which maintained an extensive pipe line gathering system throughout the state of Pennsylvania. When a new producing field of any significance was discovered, the Standard Oil group usually extended its pipe lines to the wells and purchased the output from the well owners. A few other concerns were also engaged in the construction of pipe lines and the purchase of crude oil, but the Standard Oil group was by far the largest and the most important. As a practical matter, most crude oil producers had no real alternative other than to sell their output to the Standard Oil organization.

After he had been supplying oil to the Standard Oil group for about a year and a half, Mr. W. L. Mellon learned from a friend about an opportunity to sell crude oil to the French firm, Fenaille and Despeaux, which had one of the biggest refined oil businesses in France. This company had previously been one of the largest and best customers of Elkins and Widner, a firm of Philadelphia financiers which gathered oil in western Pennsylvania and shipped it in tank cars to its refinery and terminal in Philadelphia. Elkins and Widner was successful in developing vigorous competition for the Standard Oil group in the export market and was eventually bought out by Standard. In purchasing Elkins and Widner, however, the Standard Oil group did not acquire the goodwill of its customer, Fenaille and Despeaux. For one reason or another, the Frenchmen became dissatisfied with their arrangement with Standard, and Mr. W. L. Mellon was able to negotiate a contract to supply them with crude oil for a two-year period. Thereafter, instead of selling all their oil to the Standard Oil group, the Mellons shipped some of it in tank cars to New York where it was loaded on steamships owned by Fenaille and Despeaux.

Acquisition of the French account was the first step toward integration because it gave the Mellons marketing as well as producing activities; it also brought the Mellons for the first time into direct competition with the Standard Oil interests. The motivation for the move was clearly the desire of the Mellons to sell their output to someone other than the Standard Oil group and thus to escape dependence on a single large customer. Moreover, even at this early date Mr. W. L. Mellon was thinking in terms of developing a completely integrated oil company. On this point there is no doubt that his thinking was strongly influenced by that of his uncle, Mr. Andrew W. Mellon. In his autobiography, Mr. W. L. Mellon points out that his uncle frequently reminded him that the real way to make a business out of petroleum was to develop it from end to end; to get the raw material out of the ground, refine it, and distribute it.[36]

Mr. Andrew W. Mellon was a firm believer in integration as an efficient method of operation not only for the petroleum but for other businesses as well. For example, when the Aluminum Company of America, which was financed by Mellon funds, was in its formative years, Mr. Andrew W. Mellon was instrumental in urging a policy of complete integration. It was his firm conviction that only by having control of its own ore supplies, power, fabricating plants, and sales agencies could the firm

[36] W. L. Mellon, op. cit., p. 208.

bring about industrial acceptance of the new metal on the scale which was necessary for low-cost production.[37]

By 1891 the Mellons had developed sufficient crude oil production in Pennsylvania to justify construction of their own pipe line gathering system. Before undertaking construction of the pipe lines, however, Mr. W. L. Mellon decided that he should learn something about the refining process. Accordingly, he made arrangements to borrow a small refinery at Baden on the Ohio River which belonged to Mr. W. L. Dubbs.[38] Mr. Dubbs was having difficulty in maintaining profitable operations and was uncertain whether he wanted to sell the plant or to shut it down and resume operations later. He agreed to the loan as a means of keeping the plant in operating condition while he reached a decision.

Operation of the borrowed refinery soon led to the construction of the Mellons' first crude trunk line. At the outset, Mr. W. L. Mellon tried to bring the crude oil to the refinery by barge down the Ohio River from Coraopolis where he had producing properties. The barges leaked oil out and water in, and to end the difficulty a three-inch pipe line was laid from Coraopolis to the Dubbs plant. Additional pipe lines were then built from Coraopolis to producing fields in West Virginia and Pennsylvania where the Mellons had wells or where they could buy oil from others. Once the pipe line system was in operation, the Mellons found they had little difficulty in finding well owners who were willing to sell their output to them. The oil was pumped to Coraopolis and thence moved by tank car over the Pennsylvania Railroad to the East Coast for export trade. The business of producing, buying, and exporting crude oil grew rapidly throughout 1891, and by the end of the year the Mellons owned about 200 tank cars which were used to move the oil to the East.

The next major step toward integration was made in the summer of 1892 at which time the Pennsylvania Railroad raised shipping rates just enough to make the Mellons' export business profitless. The Mellons were therefore faced with the necessity of fulfilling all their existing foreign contracts at no profit or of building a pipe line to the East where a juncture could be made with another railroad. It is not unreasonable to suppose that the action of the Pennsylvania Railroad may have been influenced by the desires of its largest customer, the Standard Oil group, which was then finding the competition of the Mellons and other independent companies for the export market somewhat troublesome.

The Mellons decided to undertake the pipe line project and formed the Crescent Pipe Line Company. The original plan was to build the line from just outside Pittsburgh to Carlisle, Pennsylvania, where a juncture could be made with the Philadelphia and Reading Railroad which was then engaged in a competitive battle with the Pennsylvania Railroad. Mr. W. L. Mellon visited the president of the Philadelphia and Reading Railroad and was successful in negotiating a favorable shipping rate agreement. Shortly thereafter, however, the president was abruptly dismissed and the railroad served notice that it would not honor the contract. It thus became necessary to continue the pipe line to Marcus Hook, a distance of 271 miles from Pittsburgh.

The pipe line was not built without difficulty. Many crossings of the Pennsylvania Railroad were necessary, and nearly every crossing required a battle. The line would be laid in the daytime only to be torn up at night. The Mellons would then secure a court order to allow the work to proceed. Each time the line was torn up, a few of the Pennsylvania Railroad employees were arrested. The line was then relaid and there was no further difficulty at that particular point. The line was completed successfully in November 1892, and subsequently the Mellons were able to make shipments to the export trade from their terminal at Marcus Hook.

The final step in the integration of the initial venture of the Mellons in the oil business involved the acquisition of refinery capacity in the latter part of 1892 and early part of 1893. Construction of the pipe line had given the firm access to a great deal more crude oil than it had had before, and Mr. W. L. Mellon began to encounter some difficulty in finding customers. It soon became clear that many of the potential customers both at home and

---

[37] Ibid., p. 219.

[38] Later inventor of the important Dubbs cracking process.

abroad were not equipped, as was Fenaille and Despeaux, to do their own refining. Moreover, a demand was beginning to develop for a variety of different kinds of oil products in the various domestic and foreign markets. The Mellons concluded therefore that they would have to secure refining capacity as a means of finding an outlet for their crude oil and as a means of expanding their marketing operations.

As a first step, the Mellons purchased a half interest in the Bear Creek Refinery, a small independent plant located about 12 miles up the Allegheny River from Pittsburgh. This firm was owned by Mr. Benjamin B. Campbell who maintained an export clearing house for many of the little independent oil refiners in Pennsylvania. Acquisition of a half interest in the Bear Creek Refinery therefore gave the Mellons access to a substantial export business in refined products and solved to a considerable extent their problem of getting more customers for their constantly expanding volume of crude oil. Shortly after the Bear Creek acquisition the Mellon business expanded to the point where it justified the construction of a large refinery at Marcus Hook near the terminus of the Crescent pipe line. By the early part of 1893, therefore, the Mellons had in operation an integrated oil company engaged in producing, crude transportation, refining, and marketing activities. The total investment in these properties was in the neighborhood of two and a half million dollars.

On August 9, 1893, the Mellons entered into certain contracts which provided for the eventual transfer of the Crescent Pipe Line Company and five other petroleum companies which the Mellons owned to the Standard Oil interests. The willingness of the Mellons to sell their petroleum properties can be explained primarily by certain developments which were taking place in the crude oil producing field. It had been realized for some time that oil was no longer exclusively a Pennsylvania product. Oil had been discovered in Kansas, Ohio, West Virginia, California, and various other areas outside of Pennsylvania. It appeared that substantial deposits were available in Russia, and oil from that country was beginning to move into the European markets. These developments created consid-

erable apprehension throughout the oil industry that still further discoveries both at home and abroad might bring about a severe and prolonged depression in oil prices. The Pennsylvania producers had additional reason to be disturbed because the development of the Frasch process for refining high sulphur-content crude oil had brought Ohio oil into competition with Pennsylvania oil. Previously, the high sulphur-content Ohio oil had been almost worthless in the markets and had sold for as little as ten cents a barrel.

It therefore appeared to the Mellons that further participation in the oil industry would be likely to require nearly all the investment funds which they had at their disposal in order to keep pace with the expansion of producing operations into other areas and to survive a period of potential price depression. The Mellons had other business interests of considerable importance which required both their financial resources and their attention. As was noted earlier, the year 1893 was a time of severe depression both in the oil industry and in business generally. When the Standard Oil interests offered a price which afforded the Mellons a reasonable return on their investment, they were therefore willing to sell.

These initial experiences of the Mellons in the oil business have been recounted in some detail not only because they shed light on the forces and circumstances which led to the integration of oil companies in the days prior to the dissolution of the Standard Oil combination but also because there is no question but what these experiences did much to shape the policy of integration which Mr. W. L. Mellon later followed in the development of the Gulf Oil Corporation.

The J. M. Guffey Petroleum Company:

The Mellons re-entered the oil business through a series of financial developments which began in October 1900 when the Mellon National Bank made a loan of $300,000 to James M. Guffey and John H. Galey, one of the best-known and most successful oil prospecting partnerships of the time. Guffey and Galey had been approached by Mr. Anthony F. Lucas who wished them to join him in drilling a deep well on a hillock called "Round Top Mound" near Beaumont, Texas.

It had for some time been recognized that there might be oil in this area because gas had been found bubbling up through the water in some near-by springs. Two shallow wells had been drilled on the structure, one by Patillo Higgins and one by Higgins and Lucas in partnership. These wells were dry, but Lucas was convinced that oil could be found if a well were drilled to greater depths by means of one of the new rotary drills which were just then coming into use. The purpose of the $300,000 loan from the Mellons was to finance construction of the rotary rig. This rig was referred to by the natives of Beaumont as a "spindletop" and the field thus came to be known by that name.

The well, Lucas No. 1, blew in as one of the most fabulous gushers of all time from a depth of 1,020 feet on January 10, 1901. It is estimated that the well flowed at the rate of 40,000 barrels a day and produced over 400,000 barrels in the 10 days before it was capped. Lucas No. 2, which was drilled during the same month, likewise came in as a gusher, and within a short time Guffey, Galey, and Lucas had a vast quantity of crude oil stored in earthwork reservoirs in the vicinity of the wells.

At that time there were no significant refinery or pipe line facilities in Texas, and there were very few, if any, buyers for the crude oil where it stood. Guffey therefore found it immediately necessary to take the first step toward integration: the construction of 16 miles of 6-inch pipe line to Port Arthur from whence the oil could be moved by tank car or tanker to market areas.

During the early months of 1901, Guffey was successful in persuading Mr. Andrew W. Mellon to form a syndicate to take over the new producing properties in the Spindletop field and to organize the J. M. Guffey Petroleum Corporation. The members of the syndicate were all friends of the Mellon family and prominent men in Pittsburgh business affairs. The total amount subscribed was $1,500,000, and the new firm was capitalized at $15,000,000. The $1,500,000 went to Guffey to be used in payment for the properties which he owned jointly with Galey and Lucas. The properties turned over to the new firm consisted of one million acres of oil leases in Texas and Louisi-

ana, four producing wells in the Spindletop field, four wells being drilled, the pipe line from Spindletop to Port Arthur, one million barrels of storage tank capacity, 100 tank cars, about 375 acres of land in the vicinity of Port Arthur, and an assortment of contracts with railroads and the Port Arthur Dockage Company.

Almost as soon as the J. M. Guffey Petroleum Corporation was organized, Guffey found himself in need of additional funds to finance the construction of refining facilities, the purchase of tugs, barges, and tankers, and the building of a sales organization. In May 1901, 30,000 shares of treasury stock were therefore sold for a total return of about $2,000,000. These funds were used to begin work on a modern refinery and to purchase some tankers which could be used to haul crude oil from Texas to more heavily populated areas in the United States or abroad. Shortly thereafter, in November 1901, the Gulf Refining Company was organized with a capitalization of $750,000 to handle the refining and sale of the oil produced by the J. M. Guffey Petroleum Company. In terms of stock ownership and management the two firms were almost identical, and Guffey served as president of both companies.

The urgent need for refining and transportation facilities was a direct consequence of the large surplus of crude oil which was developed in Texas immediately after the Spindletop field was discovered. Extensive drilling operations were conducted not only on the Spindletop formation but throughout the Texas coastal plain. Within a few months the Sour Lake field, 24 miles west of Spindletop, and various others were brought into production. Aside from a few primitive stills which Guffey had established at Port Arthur, there were no real refineries in Texas, and the supply of crude oil was soon far in excess of that which could be moved to other markets with the available transportation facilities. In response to these conditions, the price of crude oil frequently dropped to 10 cents a barrel and in 1902 even went as low as 5 cents a barrel.

The need for the construction of satisfactory refining facilities was particularly acute because the Texas crude oil was totally unlike any oil which had previously been discovered. Whereas eastern crudes had a paraffin base and were light bodied and greenish in color, the new Texas crude oil had an asphalt base, was heavy in weight, black in color, and loaded with sulphur. Because of its characteristics, the Texas crude oil could not be refined by existing techniques to produce kerosene, then the most important oil product, which would burn without smoking. Likewise it was impossible with the existing technology to secure gasoline from the oil. The only important use which could be made of the crude oil was to burn it as a fuel in the boilers of industrial plants, locomotives, and steamships. Even in this market, however, the oil was not fully satisfactory because it had too high a sulphur content to meet the specifications of the British Navy, one of the most important customers. It appeared therefore that the J. M. Guffey Petroleum Company would be unable to expand its markets or to realize the potentialities of its producing fields until a solution to the refining problem was found.

The first refining facilities constructed at Port Arthur consisted of two small stills, one of 100 barrels capacity and the other of 375 barrels capacity. These proved inadequate in both capacity and the quality of product. As a next step, a petroleum chemist was brought in from Cleveland to superintend the construction of three "cheesebox" stills and five 1,000 barrel de-sulphurizing units to make the Texas crude oil acceptable to the British Navy. The new equipment solved the latter problem but still did not produce kerosene comparable in quality with that refined from Pennsylvania crude oil.

In the early part of 1902 it was decided to undertake construction of a large new refinery in an effort to solve the problem, and another specialist was brought in to superintend construction of Refinery No. 3, which consisted of 53 stills to make kerosene and 16 stills to produce asphalt. As soon as this decision was made, it was clear that the company would require additional financing, and the directors therefore authorized a bond issue of $5,000,000. A. W. and R. B. Mellon made a personal investment of $2,500,000 in these bonds, the Old Colony Trust Company of Boston subscribed $1,500,000, and the remainder of the bonds were held in the company treasury.

Two months later, in August 1902, the company was confronted by an even more critical problem than that presented by the refining situation because the Spindletop field abruptly stopped flowing. The two Mellon brothers, deeply concerned about the security of their own bonds and those held by the Old Colony Trust Company, which had been sold partially on their representations, immediately arranged for their nephew, Mr. W. L. Mellon, to go to Texas to investigate the situation. Mr. W. L. Mellon had previously made no personal investment in the J. M. Guffey Petroleum Company because he had little faith in Guffey, whom he regarded as more of a promoter than an oil man.

Mr. W. L. Mellon returned to Pittsburgh convinced that much more oil could still be produced from the Spindletop formation if the wells were put on pumps. He also reported that the refinery problem was as yet unsolved, that a sales organization was badly needed, and that an additional investment of $12,000,000 to $15,000,000 would be necessary to put the company on a sound operating basis. He also expressed the opinion that the bondholders would have little chance of salvaging their investment as long as the company remained under the Guffey management. It appeared that money had been spent lavishly, often for unnecessary things while necessities had been overlooked. Over one million acres of land had been leased but on a rather haphazard basis. As it actually developed, over 90% of the Spindletop production came from less than 100 acres. In this area, Guffey, who as driller of the discovery well should have been able to secure the entire field, had neglected to take up obviously important tracts adjacent to Lucas No. 1. Finally, the titles to the land in many cases were impaired, and subsequently involved the company in extensive lawsuits.

The Mellons were reluctant in 1902, when W. L. Mellon made his report, to become any more deeply involved in the oil business than they already were. Their first step therefore was to approach the Standard Oil group to see if it would be interested in taking over the company or in putting up the funds necessary for its further development. The Standard Oil management, however, refused to take any interest in the proposition. The Standard Oil subsidiary operating in the Southwest, the Waters-Pierce Oil Company, had been involved in continual litigation in Texas because of its unduly aggressive marketing tactics and certain of its pricing practices, and state authorities had sought to banish the company from the state.[39] In view of these experiences, the Standard Oil interests undoubtedly regarded the legal climate of the state of Texas as generally unfavorable to a further extension of the Standard activities. Moreover, the Standard Oil management was at this time having considerable difficulty in controlling the Waters-Pierce activities. Although a good majority of the stock was controlled by the Standard Oil interests, the terms of the stock acquisition had provided that management control should reside with Henry Clay Pierce, a very independent individual who fiercely resented any outside interference with his operations. Finally, the Standard Oil group was already embarked on the development of Mid-Continent crude oil which at the time appeared a great deal more attractive than did the Texas crude oil.

The refusal of the Standard Oil group to take any interest in the properties marked a turning point for the Mellons because from that time onward it was clear that they would have to make a major commitment of both funds and managerial effort to the oil business if their equity and that of the other bondholders, to whom they felt a real sense of obligation, in the J. M. Guffey Petroleum Company were to be preserved. The board of directors met and elected Mr. W. L. Mellon as vice president in charge of management, and he thereupon went to Texas to take over the active direction of the company's affairs.

Mr. W. L. Mellon brought to the job with him the conviction that complete integration was one of the broad objectives the company should seek in its long-run program of growth and development. In his own words,[40] he sized up the competitive situation in the industry as follows:

The Standard Oil Company at that time was the only oil company of major importance in existence, but it was not primarily a producing company. In fact, except in California, it had relatively little production of its own and had never made it a general policy to own or control production in a large way because it was practically the sole buyer of crude oil.[41]

Consequently, every wild-catter, every lease buyer, every owner of a producing well, was, in effect, a part of the Standard Oil Company's production department. Whatever price was posted by the Standard Oil Company at the well-head was the price the producer got for his crude. Standard made the price.

In saying this I do not mean to imply that the company took unfair advantage of the producers whose oil it bought. As a matter of fact, the producers who traded with the Standard Oil Company did very well, although some of them grumbled. Nevertheless, these producers were at the mercy of this company, which had a complete pipe line system. Normally, this was extended to any new field brought into production. Texas had been a significant exception. So it was to be expected that, as other fields were discovered and developed, Standard's pipe lines would be extended to these new fields.

This prospect did not leave much excuse for anybody to think he could operate an oil business on a big scale in competition with Standard if he tried to operate in the same way as Standard. I concluded that the way to compete was to develop an integrated business which would first of all produce oil. Production, I saw, *had* to be the foundation of such a business. That was clearly the only way for a company which proposed to operate without saying "by your leave" to anybody.

As Mr. Mellon had predicted, it was found that much additional production could be secured from the Spindletop field by the use of pumps,[42] and in the years 1903 and 1904 the new management made good progress toward putting the company's affairs in order. For the year 1904 the J. M. Guffey Petroleum Company was able to show a profit of $457,406 and

---

[39] See *Hathaway* vs. *State*, 1896 (36 SW 465); *Waters-Pierce Oil Company* vs. *State*, 1898 to 1900 (44 SW 936); and *State* vs. *Waters-Pierce Oil Company*, 1902 (67 SW 1057).

[40] W. L. Mellon, op. cit., pp. 272–273.

[41] It will be noted that W. L. Mellon's recollections on this point are somewhat at variance with the facts presented earlier in the chapter.

[42] At a later date large new reserves were found in the structure by deeper drilling.

the Gulf Refining Company a profit of $255,-598. By the middle of 1905 the company's crude oil production had risen to about 15,000 barrels per day. The value of the stock was, however, regarded as highly speculative. The volume of crude production still tended to run large relative to the market demand, prices were low, and profit margins small. Moreover, no satisfactory solution had yet been found to the problem of refining the crude into a good grade of kerosene.

Formation of the Gulf Oil Corporation:

The circumstances which brought about the formation of the Gulf Oil Corporation were likewise circumstances which called for further integration in the operations of the J. M. Guffey Petroleum Company and the Gulf Refining Company.

In an effort to solve the technological problems in processing Texas crude oil, one refinery unit after another was added to the facilities at Port Arthur until by the middle of 1906 capacity was about 12,000 barrels per day. To handle the transportation problem, the company had acquired three tankers and two barges of about 19,000 barrels capacity each and had three more tankers under construction with a capacity of 30,000 barrels each. Meanwhile, production in the Spindletop field as well as in many of the other new fields continued to decline at a rapid rate. In the summer of 1906 it appeared that the Spindletop field would soon be entirely exhausted. Moreover, experiments at the refinery were indicating that only certain types of the Texas crude oil could be processed satisfactorily into kerosene. It seemed apparent therefore that unless the company took prompt measures to secure an additional supply of crude oil, it would soon be hard pressed to keep its pipe lines, refinery, and tankers operating at capacity. Whereas the company had first been forced to build a refinery and transportation facilities to dispose of its large volume of crude oil output, it was now forced to search for new crude oil sources to keep these facilities adequately supplied.

It was at about this time that oil was discovered at the Glenn Pool [43] near Tulsa, Okla-

homa. This discovery had a profound effect upon the industry, because the oil was comparable in grade to the Pennsylvania crudes and yet it appeared that the reserves would be comparable in size to those which had been discovered in Texas. The new fields were 550 miles from Port Arthur, but the oil was nonetheless highly attractive to Mellon and his associates because it promised a solution not only to the supply problem but also to the extremely troublesome matter of securing a suitable grade of kerosene with which to meet competition in the market. Up to that time the products refined from Texas crude had been so poor that they sold for little more than did crude itself as fuel oil. The Oklahoma crude was also rich in its potential yield of gasoline, for which an important market was already beginning to develop. The situation was summarized in a letter to the stockholders in the fall of 1906 as follows:

The J. M. Guffey Petroleum Company was organized in May, 1901. At that time it got about 1,000,000 acres of oil land at Spindletop and issued $15,000,000 of capital stock. But it soon found that the Spindletop field was limited and that 90% of the entire production of the field comes from about 100 acres. Also the life of the field soon proved to be very short. In the five years since Spindletop came in, five new fields have been discovered. They are widely scattered—as much as 190 miles apart. All these fields, too, have had a short life. At present, the total oil production in Texas is about 30,000 barrels daily and of this only about 12,000 barrels are of a quality capable of refining. Also there are no pipe lines connecting these fields with the Port Arthur refinery. For nearly two years, no new fields have been found in Texas.

The capacity of the Gulf Refining Company, organized soon after the J. M. Guffey Petroleum Company, is 12,000 barrels daily. So if the company could get all the refinable crude produced in Texas, it would hardly be enough for the economic operation of the refinery. But it is able to get only about one-half of this daily production. So the present operation of the refinery depends for one-half of its output on the accumulated stocks of oil which at the present rate of depletion will be gone in nine months. Indian Territory [44]

---

[43] The discovery well at the Glenn Pool was drilled on November 22, 1905. It was drilled in such secrecy, however,

that its significance was not generally recognized until the early summer of 1906.

[44] Oklahoma was not yet a state and the region which it now occupies was Indian Territory.

oil is cheaper and better for refining than Texas oil. The oil is of 32 degrees gravity and better and is selling at 39 cents; while Texas oil averaging 22 degrees gravity is selling at 65 cents. So it is necessary for the company to enter the Indian Territory field if it aims to meet the competition of other companies.

It was apparent that at least $5,000,000 would be required for the acquisition of producing properties in the Tulsa territory and for the construction of a pipe line to Port Arthur. The Mellons were, however, unwilling to make an additional investment in the company unless a management reorganization could be effected. Mr. Guffey had remained as president of both the J. M. Guffey Petroleum Company and the Gulf Refining Company, but had never fully acquiesced in Mr. W. L. Mellon's assumption of authority as the managing head of the business. For some time it had been clear that a sound management organization could never be developed as long as Mr. Guffey remained as titular head of the two companies. Mr. Guffey, however, was not agreeable to any plan of reorganization which would result in any further curtailment of his authority. He held a large block of stock, and it was thus evident that the development of a new plan of corporate structure would require considerable time.

Nonetheless it was imperative that prompt action be taken if a share of the Oklahoma production was to be captured. The Standard Oil group, through its subsidiary the Prairie Oil and Gas Company, had already extended a pipe line to the field which carried the oil north to connect with Standard's main pipe line network. A few small refineries had also been constructed in the Tulsa area and were bidding for the crude oil output. While plans for the reorganization went forward therefore, two new companies were organized to begin work on the pipe line and to initiate an investigation of the Oklahoma producing fields with the thought that they could later be absorbed by the reorganized parent company.

The first of these, the Gulf Pipe Line Company of Texas, was organized with a capitalization of $3,500,000 to lay 413 miles of 8-inch pipe line from Tulsa to Sour Lake, Texas, where a connection could be made with the existing lines running to Port Arthur. Actual construction was begun on February 3, 1907. One crew worked southward from Tulsa, a second northward from Sour Lake, while two crews started in the middle and worked toward the ends. The pipe line was completed in August and represented the longest line yet laid in the United States by anyone other than the Standard Oil group.

The second new company, the Gypsy Oil Company, was formed for the purpose of acquiring producing properties in Oklahoma. Two important leases were secured; the Pittman lease at a price of $625,000 and the Berryhill lease at a price of $459,000. These properties subsequently proved to be two of the best leases in the area and by January 11, 1950 had produced a total of about 5,584,000 barrels of oil. The purchase of these leases was one of the few instances in the history of the company where it bought important properties already in production.[45] Throughout the first 25 or 30 years of the company's experience, it was a definite policy of the producing department to seek the discovery of new fields in preference to purchasing land in proven tracts.

Plans for the reorganization were completed in the early part of 1907, and on February 13 the Gulf Oil Corporation was formed as a New Jersey Corporation [46] with an authorized capitalization of $15,000,000 to acquire the stock of the J. M. Guffey Petroleum Company and the Gulf Refining Company. Most of the stockholders merely exchanged their shares in the old companies for shares in the new one. Mr. Guffey and a few others refused to participate in the reorganization, and their interest was purchased by the new concern. Cash amounting to $6,379,000 was paid into the Gulf Oil Corporation's treasury which provided funds to finance the operations initiated by the Gulf Pipe Line Company and the Gypsy Oil Company.

Mr. Andrew W. Mellon was elected president, Mr. W. L. Mellon, vice president, and Mr. R. B. Mellon, treasurer, of the new concern. Mr. W. L. Mellon became president in

---

[45] A second important occasion when the company departed from its usual practice was on June 28, 1922, when the Gypsy Oil Company purchased five tracts of Indian land in Oklahoma at an auction for $3,888,070.

[46] The company became a Pennsylvania corporation in 1922.

1909 and occupied that position until 1930. At that time he became chairman of the board of directors, a position which he occupied until 1948.

III. SUMMARY

1. In the period before 1911 there were two general movements toward vertical integration in the oil industry. The first was an integral part of the growth and development of the Standard Oil combination, and the second was a part of the growth and development of the independent firms which were stubbornly competing with the Standard Oil interests. The motivations for these two general movements were in some respects similar; in other respects, however, they were very different.

2. The Standard Oil group was originally a horizontal combination at the refining level of the oil business. John D. Rockefeller and his associates were prompted to form the organization largely as a means of dealing with certain fundamental competitive and economic forces which were at work in the industry. Horizontal integration was viewed by the Standard Oil interests as a means of correcting the persistent instability which characterized the early years of the industry's history and as a means of capitalizing on the prevailing business practices of the railroads with respect to rebates and drawbacks. An association of refining interests was also viewed as desirable to counter the combinations which were from time to time being formed by transportation agencies, crude oil producers, oil buyers, and competitive refiners in other areas.

3. Vertical integration of various types was frequently used by Rockefeller and his associates as a means of supporting and extending their horizontal combination of refining interests. Quasi-vertical integration achieved through close association with the railroads was used to force other refiners into the Standard Oil group. Crude oil gathering activities were undertaken in part to thwart the development of a strong combination in the transportation field by the Empire Transportation Company and the Pennsylvania Railroad which might have placed the Standard Oil refining interests in jeopardy. The Standard Oil group's first crude oil trunk lines were used to offset the Tidewater pipe line and the advantages which it gave to competing refiners in New York. Marketing activities were undertaken partially as a means of protecting and developing the market for the output of the Standard Oil refineries. And crude oil production was sought in part to assure a long-run supply for the Standard Oil refineries and to block the growth of a competitive combination of producing and refining interests.

4. Vertical integration was often used by the independent companies in the period before 1911 as a means of escaping the dominance of the Standard Oil group. The Pure Oil Company was born out of a cooperative effort by producers and refiners to form a vertical organization which would free them completely from the Standard Oil organization and all its agencies. In connection with their first crude oil producing business, the Mellons acquired foreign accounts and constructed pipe lines and refineries partially as a means of selling their output to someone other than the Standard Oil group. Moreover, the policy of vertical integration which the Gulf Oil Corporation adopted from its inception stemmed largely from W. L. Mellon's conviction that vertical integration provided the only means by which a company could compete successfully with the Standard Oil organization.

5. The experiences of both the Standard Oil group and the independent companies reveal that many of the motivations and business circumstances which later contributed much to the integration process throughout the industry were already at work in the period prior to 1911. The Gulf Oil Corporation built a crude oil pipe line and a refinery to provide an outlet for its newly discovered crude oil in the Spindletop field. Both the Standard Oil group and the Gulf Oil Corporation integrated backward to secure sources of crude oil for their refining facilities, the former as a matter of long-

run policy and the latter as a matter of immediate necessity to offset the decline in the output of the Spindletop field and to keep its Port Arthur refinery in operation.

The Standard Oil interests built their first crude oil trunk lines because a competitor had developed a lower cost method of transportation to the seaboard. The Standard Oil interests integrated forward into bulk plant operations partially as a means of assuring the standards of quality and service, provid-ing the capital, and carrying out the program of expansion necessary for the full development of the market. Finally, the convictions of A. W. and W. L. Mellon with regard to vertical integration and the strategies of John D. Rockefeller provide early illustrations of the manner in which the personal business philosophies of individuals have contributed to integration decisions. These and other factors which have played a part in the integration process will be more fully discussed in the following chapters.

CHAPTER FOUR

The Pressure of Crude Oil Before Prorationing

ONE of the most impelling forces underlying the integration process in the oil industry was the pressure of the enormous crude oil supplies which developed from time to time in the days before the prorationing laws were adopted. The character of the oil finding and producing process was such that the industry alternated between periods of great abundance and periods of severe shortage. In the periods of abundance, the oil producers frequently found themselves in possession of more crude oil than could be absorbed readily in the crude oil markets. Accordingly, they undertook the construction or acquisition of transportation, refining, and marketing facilities in an effort to secure and assure an outlet for their products. As will be noted in later chapters, the periods of scarcity, in their turn, contributed much to the backward integration moves of refiners and marketers.

Several early examples of forward integration taking place under the pressure of large crude oil supplies may be found in the experience of the Gulf Oil Corporation. As noted in the preceding chapter, the company built its first crude oil trunk line, began construction of its big refinery at Port Arthur, and acquired ocean-going tankers largely as a means of disposing of the vast crude oil output which flowed from the Spindletop field in 1902.[1] In 1911 the company was again faced with the problem of large crude oil supplies. Drilling operations in Oklahoma had been very successful, and some new discoveries had also been made in the central and northern part of Texas. Moreover, the important Caddo field in Louisiana, which was discovered in 1905, had proven very productive and was yielding in

1911 about two million barrels of crude oil per year. The management deemed it prudent therefore to divert some of the Oklahoma crude oil away from the Port Arthur refinery to another location. Accordingly, the company built a branch pipe line to Fort Worth, Texas, from its main crude oil trunk line, which extended from the Oklahoma fields to Port Arthur, and constructed at Fort Worth a 6,000 barrels per day refinery.

The pressure of large crude oil supplies as a stimulant to forward integration was particularly significant in the period from about 1920 to 1935. This interval was, moreover, one of the most active periods in the history of the industry with respect to integration moves of all types. The purpose of this chapter is to examine the circumstances which developed during the period and to indicate the manner in which they contributed to the integration process.

I. GEOLOGICAL, ECONOMIC, AND LEGAL CHARACTERISTICS OF CRUDE OIL PRODUCTION BEFORE PRORATIONING

The explanation of the large crude oil supplies which were generated at recurring intervals in the years prior to the adoption of the prorationing laws may be found in two primary circumstances, both of which stemmed from certain fundamental geological, economic, and legal characteristics of the oil finding and producing process.

In the first place, the oil finding process was, and still is, to a considerable extent a matter of chance. Wildcat drilling activity to some extent tends to increase and decrease in accordance with changes in crude oil demand and crude oil prices and there is some general correlation between the amount of such drill-

---

[1] Actually, this was the J. M. Guffey Petroleum Company, predecessor of the Gulf Oil Corporation (see Chapter Three).

ing activity and the volume of new crude oil reserves discovered each year. The major producing fields, however, have been very few in number, and their discovery has been largely a random occurrence. It has been estimated, for example, that only one well out of every 967 new-field (rank) wildcats in the years 1944–1946, inclusive, resulted in the discovery of a field with more than 50 million barrels of total ultimate recoverable reserves.[2] In the years 1945, 1948, and 1951 only 8 out of 1,233 new fields discovered had recoverable reserves in excess of 50 million barrels.[3] These occasional big fields, nevertheless, account for a very significant part of the total crude oil supply. From the beginning of the industry through 1951, 25 oil fields produced about 29% of the total United States crude oil output; in the year 1951, 24 fields accounted for about 22% of the total domestic production.[4] The random discovery of one of these big fields can therefore bring, and frequently has brought, large new crude oil supplies to the market at times when there is no particular need for them in terms of existing demand-supply relationships.

A second important reason for the periodic development of abundant crude oil supplies before the prorationing laws were adopted may be found in the fact that once a new field was discovered the leaseholders were under considerable economic and legal compulsion to produce their properties as rapidly as possible. Oil exists underground in reservoirs which frequently extend under the property of many different landowners. The oil has the capacity to migrate, and when a well is drilled into a reservoir the lowering of the subsurface pressure in the crude oil bearing formation causes oil from all parts of the reservoir to flow toward that well. The production of a well on one piece of property may therefore result in the subsurface drainage of oil from surrounding tracts of land.

The United States property laws with re-

spect to oil and gas reserves are based on the "rule of capture" and do not recognize the correlative rights of landowners in an underground reservoir.[5] In accordance with court interpretations of these laws, the driller of wells on a tract of land acquires title to all the oil and gas produced from his wells despite the fact that some of the oil and gas may be drained from under adjoining properties.

The discovery of a new field before the prorationing laws were adopted thus usually precipitated a wild scramble on the part of the lessees[6] to drill wells and produce them rapidly in order to capture the maximum possible share of the underground reservoir before it was drained by neighboring producers. If a lessee failed to drill and produce his oil promptly, he was not only exposed to loss of the oil but likewise to damage suits by his lessor for failure to protect the property adequately against drainage and to secure for the lessor the maximum possible amount of royalty oil. In some states under some conditions a landowner could even force cancellation of a lease if the lessee did not take adequate steps to capture a fair share of the oil pool.

The drilling and producing activity usually went ahead regardless of the price of the oil or the requirements of the market. Obviously it was to the advantage of a producer to sell his oil at any price in excess of his direct lifting costs rather than to lose it entirely. As long as one producer in a field continued his drilling and producing activities, there was thus unavoidable compulsion on all others to follow suit. Moreover, in conducting exploratory work and in drilling and equipping wells, a producer made heavy capital outlays which, once made, could not be withdrawn or directed to other purposes. Entirely apart from problems of drainage therefore, producers

[2] F. H. Lahee, "Exploratory Drilling in 1950," *Bulletin of The American Association of Petroleum Geologists*, Vol. 35, No. 6, June 1951, p. 1139.

[3] Ibid., "Exploratory Drilling in 1951," Vol. 36, No. 6, June 1952, p. 990.

[4] American Petroleum Institute, *Petroleum Facts and Figures*, Tenth Edition, 1952, pp. 94–97. (Original source of production by fields: *Oil and Gas Journal*.)

[5] The United States laws with respect to oil and gas property rights were developed from early decisions of the Pennsylvania courts which followed the English rule of percolating waters, established in *Acton* vs. *Blundell*, 12 M. & W. 324 (Ex. 1843). See Northcutt Ely, "The Conservation of Oil," *Harvard Law Review*, Vol. 51, No. 7, May 1938, p. 1218.

[6] Most oil lands are developed under lease arrangements. The lessor is usually paid an annual rental prior to the discovery of oil. Thereafter he is paid a fraction, usually one-eighth, of the oil produced as a royalty. The royalty oil is normally sold to the lessee at the well-head price at the time it is produced.

were usually willing to continue selling oil at very low margins over lifting costs to obtain some slight return on their investments.

The tendency of new discoveries to develop large supplies in the crude oil markets was accentuated by the fact that it was usually not feasible to shut down production temporarily in the older fields during the initial period of flush production in the new fields. The new wells often had far lower lifting costs than did the older ones and could operate profitably at much lower price levels. The owners of the older wells, however, were usually reluctant to shut in their production until prices returned to higher levels because of the possible loss from drainage by producers who elected to continue in operation. Moreover, it was frequently expensive and sometimes impossible to start up a well after it had been shut in for any very long period of time. The producers of older fields hence sometimes continued to operate even after prices had fallen below their direct lifting costs because it was cheaper to do so for a short period than to incur the costs and risks of shutting in production.

In view of the fortuitous character of the discovery process with respect to the major oil fields, the economic and legal compulsions to produce the fields at a maximum once they were discovered, and the difficulties involved in temporarily curtailing production in older fields, it was inescapable that the industry should from time to time accumulate huge crude oil supplies. As a corollary of the same circumstances, it was impossible for the industry to hold reserves underground for the purpose of providing a continuity of supply in the intervals between major discoveries. Inventories could be and were accumulated above ground, but the extent to which such inventories could be held was limited by the cost of storage facilities and the hazards of fire and explosion. Before the adoption of the prorationing laws, therefore, the industry alternated between periods of abundance and periods of scarcity and, as will be shown, both conditions contributed much to the development of integrated organizations within the industry.

It is important to note that the geological, economic, and legal aspects of the crude oil discovery and production discussed in the above paragraphs are quite different from those which are found in certain other mineral industries. It has been possible to locate the deposits of many minerals, such as coal, iron, and copper, with much more precision than it has the deposits of oil. Most of the major reserves of coal, iron, and copper in the United States were located many years ago, and new discoveries are not continually being made as in the case of oil. The development of coal, iron, and copper deposits, moreover, usually requires a period of several years, and the new supplies are not thrown abruptly into the markets in the short space of a few months as often happens in the case of oil. Finally, and most important, the owners of coal, iron, and copper deposits do not face problems of subsurface drainage and are free to store or produce their reserves as indicated by price levels and the requirements of the market.

II. THE BUILD-UP OF CRUDE OIL PRESSURE, 1920–1935

In the two- or three-year period immediately following the close of World War I, there was considerable anxiety about the adequacy of crude oil reserves in the United States. With the cessation of hostilities the automobile industry had resumed its growth, and the demand for gasoline was expanding very rapidly. An equally important expansion was likewise taking place in the demand for fuel oil. The United States Navy had abandoned the use of coal and was rapidly converting its ships to oil burners. Oil burners were also finding increased usage in the navies of foreign countries, in merchant marines, in industrial plants, and by railroads. Moreover, labor difficulties in the coal industries of the United States and several European countries suggested that the future might witness a continuing replacement of coal by oil for many purposes. The total United States demand for crude oil for consumption and export ran considerably above domestic production for several years after the war, and the deficiency was met only by large imports from the prolific Mexican fields. The Mexican supply, however, was associated with a number of uncertainties because of the hostile attitude of the

Mexican Government toward the development of the country's resources by foreign capital.

As a result of these conditions, there was considerable concern in industry and government circles that the United States might in the future encounter severe shortages with respect to its crude oil supplies. This concern, together with the rapidly expanding gasoline and fuel oil markets, the high and rising prices for crude oil, the general postwar inflation of the business economy, and the Internal Revenue Act of 1918 which allowed the use of "discovery value" in lieu of cost value [7] as a basis for depletion, stimulated a great deal of exploratory activity both in the United States and in foreign countries which resulted in the discovery and development of a number of important new oil fields.[8] The increased flow of crude oil from these new fields, together with the general business depression which began late in 1920 and deepened sharply in 1921, enabled domestic production plus imports from the Mexican fields to catch up with demand. During the first six months of 1920, demand ran ahead of supply, but the situation was reversed during the last six months of the year with the result that total stocks of crude oil and refined products were about 27,000,000 barrels higher at the close than at the beginning of the year.

The latter months of 1920 marked the beginning of a period of chronic oversupply in the petroleum industry which continued almost without interruption until about 1935. Total stocks of crude oil and refined products increased steadily throughout the period 1920 to 1929, inclusive, with the exception of the year 1926. In the period from 1930 to 1935, inclusive, the development of the prorationing laws brought about a reduction in total stocks in every year except 1933. In this period, however, the oversupply condition was manifested primarily in an underground reserve-producing potential rather than in above-ground stocks.

The record of industry conditions in the years 1920 to 1935 is clearly revealed in Exhibit IV-1 which shows the balance of supply and demand for crude oil and refined products in the United States. Total stocks are shown in the exhibit as of the close of each year in absolute amount and also in number of days' supply. Stocks began to move upward in the closing months of 1920. In March 1921 it was reported that the Mid-Continent Oil and Gas Association published rules designed to stop drilling in Oklahoma until demand returned to normal,[9] but stocks nonetheless continued to accumulate throughout the year. In 1922 the oversupply condition was further augmented by the flush output of newly developed fields in California, Arkansas, Texas, Oklahoma, and Louisiana. Of particular importance in 1922 was the development of the Long Beach field in California (3), which was discovered in 1921, and the Smackover field in Arkansas (8).[10] In the latter part of the year the output of the California fields became so great that crude oil and refined products began to move through the Panama Canal to Gulf and Atlantic Coast ports.

In 1923 the flow of imports from Mexico began to decline and dropped from a level of 126,195,000 barrels in 1922 to 3,404,000 barrels in 1935.[11] The reduction in Mexican imports, however, was more than offset by increased domestic production in the California, Arkansas, Texas, and Oklahoma fields. In 1923, for the first time in many years, total domestic production was in excess of the requirements for domestic consumption and exports. The movement of crude oil and refined products from California through the Panama Canal culminated in 1923 with a record shipment to eastern ports in the United

---

[7] Before 1918 oil companies had been allowed to take depletion on the basis of cost or valuation as of March 1, 1913, whichever was higher. The use of discovery value, which was permitted by the Internal Revenue Act of 1918, was superseded by the provisions for percentage depletion in the Internal Revenue Act of 1926.

[8] The most important new developments were in Mexico and California. The principal fields discovered in the United States in the period 1918 to 1920, together with the date found and rank in terms of over-all production as of 1951, were as follows: (Figures following the field indicate the year of discovery and rank in terms of over-all production as of 1951.) Santa Fe Springs, California, 1919 (6); Huntington Beach, California, 1920 (7); Burbank, Oklahoma, 1920 (22); Elk Hills, California, 1919 (32). See *Petroleum Facts and Figures*, Tenth Edition, pp. 96–97.

[9] Standard Statistics Co., Inc., New York, *Standard Daily Trade Service*, March 1, 1921, p. 6.

[10] Figures in parentheses indicate rank of field in terms of over-all production as of 1951. See *Petroleum Facts and Figures*, Tenth Edition, pp. 96–97.

[11] American Petroleum Institute, *Statistical Bulletin*, Vol. XXXII, No. 31, June 21, 1951.

EXHIBIT IV-1. UNITED STATES DEMAND, SUPPLY, STOCKS, AND PRICES FOR CRUDE OIL
AND REFINED PRODUCTS: 1918–1951

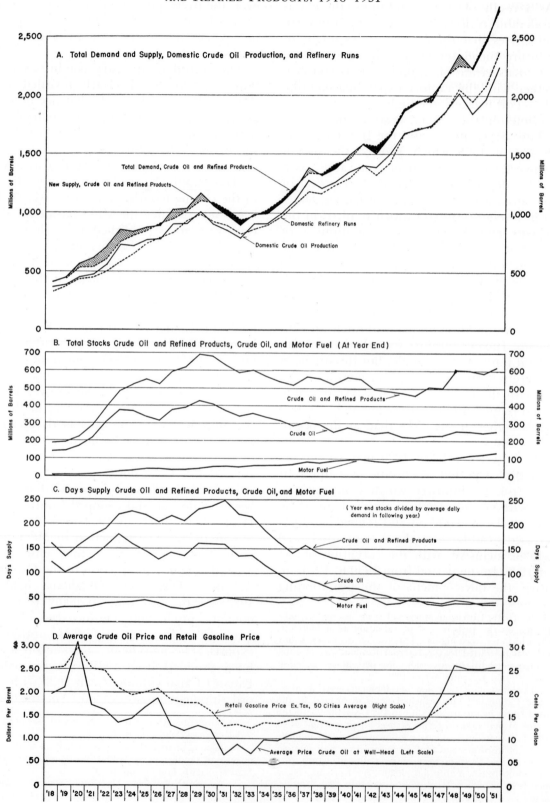

[1] Year-end stocks divided by average daily demand for following year.

SOURCES: American Petroleum Institute, *Statistical Bulletin*, Vol. XXXII, No. 31, June 21, 1951; Vol. XXXIII, No. 21, May 1, 1952; Vol. XXXIV, No. 19, April 16, 1953 (Demand, Supply, and Stock Figures); *Petroleum Facts and Figures*, Ninth Edition, 1950, and Tenth Edition, 1952 (Crude Oil Prices); The Texas Company (Gasoline Prices).

States of 52,350,000 barrels of crude oil and 3,369,000 barrels of refined products.[12]

Domestic production of crude oil declined in 1924 for the first time since 1906, largely as a result of a 13% drop in California production from the preceding year. There was also a slight further reduction in imports from Mexico, but domestic stocks of crude oil and refined products continued to increase. In 1925 there was a sharp drop in imports of crude oil from Mexico which was offset to some extent by imports from the Dutch West Indies, Venezuela, and Peru. Domestic production resumed its upward movement with the result that total stocks of crude oil and refined products were higher at the close of the year than at the beginning.

In 1926 there was an 8.5% increase in domestic consumption and exports which made it possible to absorb an increase in the supply of over 16,000,000 barrels and to bring about the only reduction in total stocks of crude oil and refined products which occurred in the period 1920 to 1929, inclusive. The year 1926, however, marked the beginning of a series of major discoveries which brought a tremendous flood of crude oil to the markets in the years that followed.[13] Important new fields discovered in 1926 included the Yates (13), Hendrick (25), McElroy (30), and Howard-Glasscock (49) fields in West Texas; the Seminole City (48) and Bowlegs (56) fields in Oklahoma; and the Seal Beach (62) field in California. In 1927 the Oklahoma production was further augmented by the discovery of the St. Louis (39) and Little River (64) fields. The year 1928 witnessed the discovery of the Oklahoma City (4) field in Oklahoma, the Kettleman North Dome (14) field in California, and the Eunice-Monument (26) and Hobbs (52) fields in New Mexico. The Van (23) field in East Texas was discovered in 1929, and the crude oil supply situation was brought to a climax in 1930 by the discovery of the main East Texas field, the greatest producer of all time. Another important discovery which followed in 1931 was that of the Conroe (17) field on the Texas Gulf Coast.

This series of discoveries crowded the development of 16 of the top 64 producing fields in over 90 years of oil industry history into the short space of six years, 1926–1931 inclusive. The crude oil supply in the United States was supplemented during the period by imports from Venezuela, Colombia, the Dutch West Indies, and Peru, which amounted to about 10% of the domestic crude oil output. As may be seen from Exhibit IV-1, total stocks of crude oil and refined products accumulated rapidly in 1927, 1928, and 1929. By 1930, however, the prorationing laws and other programs of curtailment, which were in the process of development by the various states, had become sufficiently effective to impose some restraint on domestic production. Total stocks thus declined in the three-year period 1930 to 1932, inclusive, despite the reduction in demand which accompanied the general business depression of that period. In 1933 crude oil production in the East Texas field got out of control, and there was an upward movement in domestic crude oil production and in stocks of crude oil and refined products. In 1934 and 1935, however, the prorationing procedures became well established in state and federal law, and the demand-supply situation in the petroleum industry assumed quite different characteristics from those it had had theretofore.

In view of the development of the prorationing laws, the mounting pressure of crude oil supplies after 1930 can best be seen by reference to the data in Exhibit IV-2 concerning crude oil reserves.[14] The general effect of the prorationing laws was to hold part of the crude oil supply underground. These underground stocks had a definite influence on the crude oil market because the prorationing laws were in a formative state and there was considerable doubt as to how effective they would actually be in controlling the crude oil production. Moreover, the existence of a large crude oil producing potential which could be brought to the market on short notice caused crude oil producers and refiners considerable anxiety

---

[12] U. S. Bureau of Mines, Bulletin 280, *Petroleum Refinery Statistics, 1916–1925*, by G. R. Hopkins, p. 8.

[13] *Petroleum Facts and Figures*, Tenth Edition, pp. 96–97.

[14] The data in this exhibit were made available to us through the courtesy of Mr. Earl S. Neal, general manager of the producing department of the Imperial Oil Company Limited and formerly of the Standard Oil Company (New Jersey).

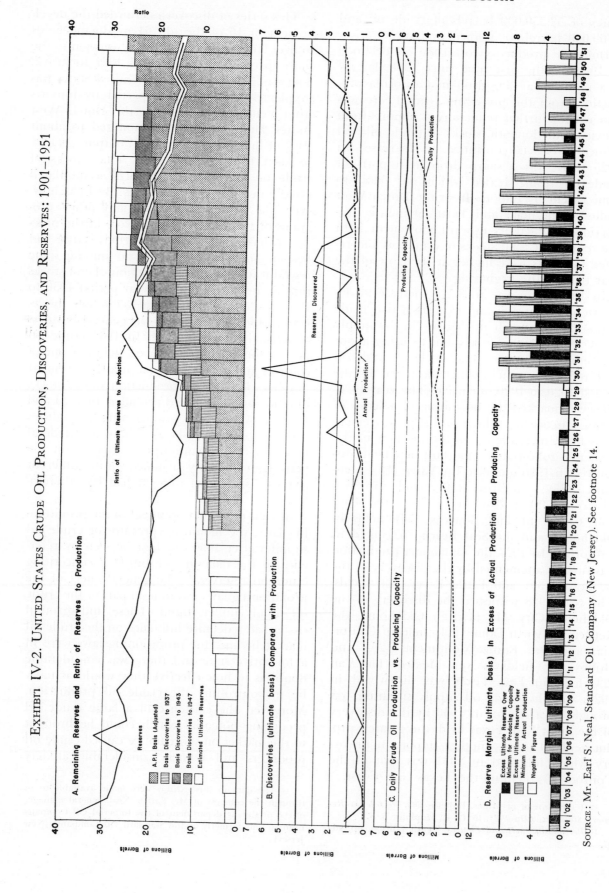

EXHIBIT IV-2. UNITED STATES CRUDE OIL PRODUCTION, DISCOVERIES, AND RESERVES: 1901–1951

SOURCE: Mr. Earl S. Neal, Standard Oil Company (New Jersey). See footnote 14.

about the security of their market outlets and contributed much to the development of forward integration programs.

Exhibit IV-2A shows the ultimate crude oil reserves in the ground at the end of each year over the period 1901 to 1951. Ordinarily it is not possible to estimate accurately the crude oil reserves in a field at the time of discovery because a good deal of further drilling is usually necessary before the limits of the pool can be determined. In the chart, therefore, the reserve figures for each year have been corrected to reflect later findings as to the actual size of the reservoirs uncovered by discoveries during that year. The chart shows the amount added to the discoveries of each year on the basis of knowledge available in 1937, 1943, and 1947 and an estimate of the ultimate reserves which subsequent development may show were associated with the discoveries.[15] Exhibit IV-2A also shows the ratio of ultimate reserves to production over the period 1901 to 1951.

Exhibit IV-2B presents a comparison of the crude oil discoveries in each year, in terms of estimated ultimate reserves, with crude oil production in the year. Exhibit IV-2C shows the relationship of actual daily crude oil production to the producing capacity of the industry in the period 1901–1951. Before the development of the prorationing laws it was assumed that crude oil production and producing capacity were synonymous.[16] To determine daily producing capacity for the period after the development of the prorationing laws, it was first assumed that the industry was producing at the maximum rate its reserves would sustain during the peak month of 1929. Production at this time was about 3,000,000 barrels per day and the ratio of reserves to production was at one of the lowest levels in the history of the industry (see Exhibit IV-2A). The producing capacity figures were then carried forward

from the 3,000,000 barrels per day base under the assumption that there was an annual decline in producing capacity each year equal to 10% of actual production in that year and that there was an annual increase equal to 34 barrels per day for each new producing well completed.[17]

Exhibit IV-2D contains an estimate of the extent to which the reserves in the ground at the end of each year were above or below the amount required to sustain the crude oil producing capacity of the industry. The producing capacity figures were determined in the manner outlined above. To obtain the reserves required to support producing capacity, the producing capacity figures for each year were multiplied by 13.5, the ratio of reserves to production during the peak month of 1929, since it was assumed that in the peak month of 1929 production was at the maximum rate the reserves would permit.

The data shown in Exhibit IV-2 reveal the magnitude of the reserves that were uncovered by the series of fortuitous discoveries in the period 1926 to 1931. During the early part of this period, demand was rising and there was a tendency, in the absence of any very effective prorationing laws, to produce the fields as rapidly as they could be developed. As a result, the ratio of reserves to production did not rise, although as noted earlier, above-ground stocks of crude oil and refined products accumulated rapidly. After 1930 a certain amount of the potential crude oil production was held underground. This situation resulted from the advent of the prorationing laws, the declining demand in the early years of the great business depression, and the fact that the production made possible by the discoveries of 1930 was so far in excess of market requirements. The extent to which reserve producing capacity hung over the market in the period 1930 to 1935 is suggested by the high ratio of reserves to production (Exhibit IV-2A), the estimated excess of producing capacity over crude production (Exhibit IV-2C), and the reserve mar-

---

[15] The reserves, A.P.I. basis, are the figures regularly reported by the A.P.I., with certain adjustments by Mr. Neal in the light of information available to the Standard Oil Company (New Jersey) from its own operations.

[16] There were nevertheless certain areas of the country where production was shut in before the development of the prorationing laws because of a lack of adequate transportation, refining, or marketing facilities. The crude oil production figures used in the chart were those assembled by the Bureau of Mines and do not reflect the "hot oil" produced in the early days of prorationing (see discussion in Chapter Twenty-One).

[17] The 10% and 34 barrels per day are estimates by Mr. Neal, based on the experience of the industry and the Standard Oil Company (New Jersey) over a long period of years. For 1950 and 1951 Mr. Neal substituted in his series the estimates of producing capacity prepared by the National Petroleum Council, Committee on Oil and Gas Availability.

gin in excess of that required to support producing capacity (Exhibit IV-2D).

The large crude oil supplies that tended to develop time and again throughout the period 1920 to 1935 were not due solely to the timing of crude oil discoveries and the compulsions to produce new fields at maximum capacity. A number of important changes were also taking place with respect to the demand for crude oil and its products. As noted earlier in the chapter, in the period immediately following World War I the rapid expansion of the automobile industry and the growth in the demand for fuel oil gave a great impetus to exploratory efforts. These efforts subsequently bore fruit in the discoveries which have been outlined above. Beginning about 1926, however, the rate of growth in the automobile industry began to slacken, as shown in Exhibit IV-3. The annual rate of increase in total motor vehicle registrations was appreciably less in the period 1926–1930 than it had been in earlier years, and during the business depression in 1931, 1932, and 1933 total motor vehicle registrations declined each year. These changes in motor vehicle registrations were partially offset by an increase in consumption of motor fuel per vehicle which resulted from the improvement of roads and more extensive traveling by car owners. As a result, there was no significant slackening of the growth in the demand for motor fuel until after 1929 (see Exhibit IV-3). In 1930 the percentage increase was much less than in earlier years, and for three successive years thereafter the total demand declined.

The effect of the changes in the demand for motor fuel on the demand for crude oil was accentuated by a number of improvements which were made in refining technology. Continuous thermal cracking processes were developed in about 1921, and throughout the next decade the refining segment of the industry was engaged in the installation of thermal cracking equipment. The new equipment made it possible to secure a higher yield of gasoline from crude oil and thus reduced the quantity of crude oil necessary to satisfy a given gasoline demand. Consequently, as shown in Exhibit IV-3, the rate of growth in the volume of crude oil required to satisfy the motor fuel demand began to slacken somewhat sooner and turned downward a year

earlier than did the demand for motor fuel itself.

The record of crude oil prices in the period 1920 to 1935 is indicated in Exhibit IV-1D. As might be anticipated from the foregoing discussion, the general movement of prices throughout the period was downward and particularly so in the years 1926 to 1933. There were, however, wide fluctuations in the crude prices from month to month and year to year. Many factors contributed to these fluctuations, but in general the prices tended to drop sharply as the flush production from newly discovered fields was thrown onto the market and to recover quickly as the large supplies were drained off. The bottom of the market was reached in 1933 when production in the East Texas field got temporarily out of control. The years 1934 and 1935 witnessed the beginning of the period of price stability which was brought into being by the development of the prorationing laws.

Exhibit IV-1D likewise contains a record of retail gasoline prices, ex. taxes, in the period 1920 to 1935. Gasoline prices moved downward throughout the period in much the same general manner as did crude oil prices. The timing of the short-term fluctuations in gasoline prices was, however, often quite different from the timing of the crude oil price fluctuations; a circumstance which, as will be noted in Chapter Five, contributed to occasional abrupt expansions and contractions in the refining and marketing margins. The downward movement in gasoline prices was chiefly a consequence of the general reduction in crude oil prices. In addition, however, the improvements in refining technology and the general intensification of competition in the refining and marketing phases of the business, which will be discussed later, contributed in some measure to the decline in gasoline prices.

It is important to note that the downward movement of crude oil and gasoline prices in the period 1920 to 1935 did little to alleviate the chronic condition of oversupply that tended to develop as a result of the disparity in the rate of growth of crude oil producing operations and the demand for gasoline and other refined products. The decline in crude oil prices did little to discourage drilling activities until after the discovery of the East

EXHIBIT IV-3. MOTOR VEHICLE REGISTRATIONS, DEMAND FOR MOTOR FUEL, AND
CRUDE OIL NECESSARY TO YIELD MOTOR FUEL REQUIREMENTS: 1918–1951

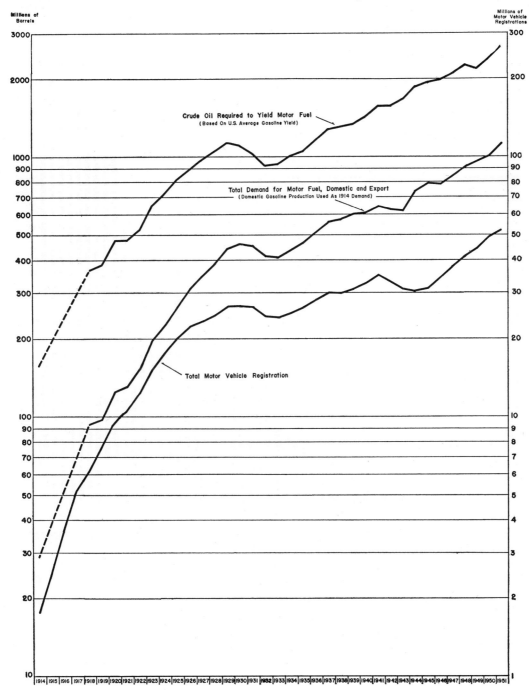

SOURCES: American Petroleum Institute, *Statistical Bulletin*, Vol. XXXII, No. 31, June 21, 1951; Vol. XXXIII, No. 21, May 1, 1952; Vol. XXXIV, No. 19, April 16, 1953 (Demand Figures); *Petroleum Facts and Figures*, Ninth Edition, 1950, and Tenth Edition, 1952 (Automobile Registrations and Gasoline Yield Ratios).

EXHIBIT IV-4. CRUDE OIL PRODUCTION BY STATES, 1900–1952

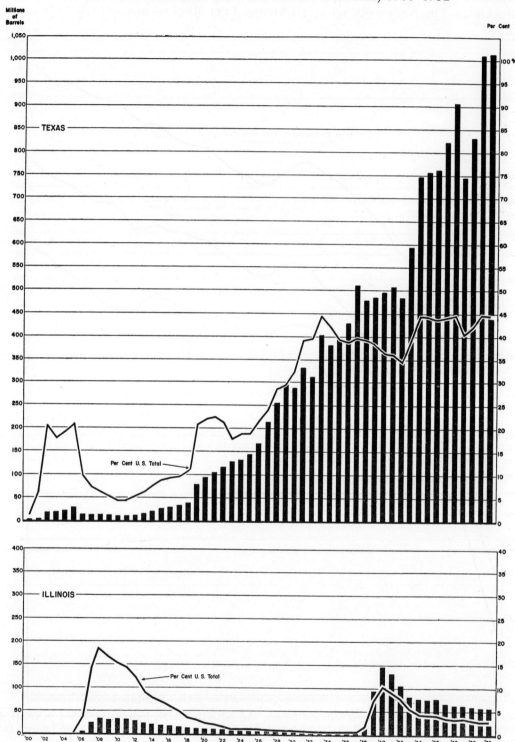

SOURCES: *World Oil*, February 15, 1952, for 1900–1951 data. Figures for 1952 from U.S. Bureau of Mines, *Mineral Industry Surveys*, "Crude Petroleum and Petroleum Products, 1952," Monthly Petroleum Statement No. 359.

EXHIBIT IV-4 (continued). CRUDE OIL PRODUCTION BY STATES, 1900–1952

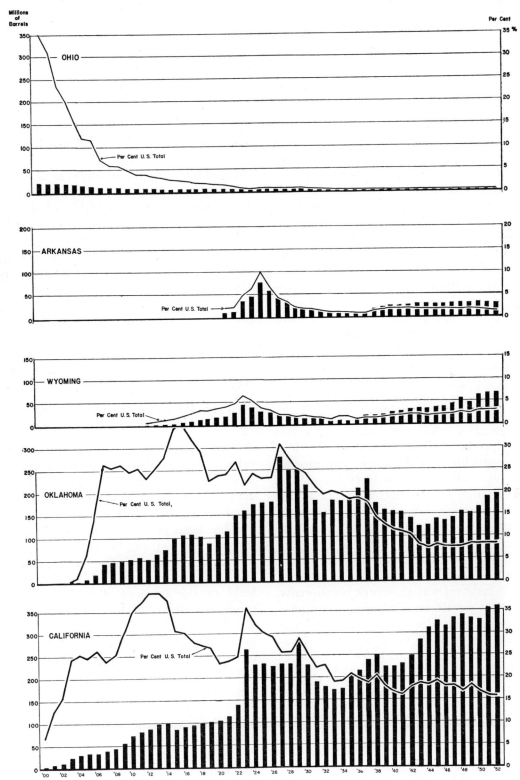

SOURCES: *World Oil*, February 15, 1952, for 1900–1951 data. Figures for 1952 from U.S. Bureau of Mines, *Mineral Industry Surveys*, "Crude Petroleum and Petroleum Products, 1952," Monthly Petroleum Statement No. 359.

Texas field in 1930 and the advent of the general business depression. Prior to that time the opportunities for gain from a single major discovery had such great speculative appeal that wildcat drilling tended to go ahead regardless of the state of the crude oil market; and development drilling, as pointed out earlier, was necessary to prevent loss of oil by drainage. At the same time, the decline in gasoline and refined products prices did not bring about any great expansion in the market. The total United States demand for gasoline, the most important refined product, is a derived demand and has generally been inelastic with respect to price changes, except perhaps over long periods of time.[18]

It should not be inferred from the above brief discussion of the crude oil supply situation in the United States in the period 1920 to 1935 that during these years all crude oil producers had excess crude oil on their hands or that all refiners had an easy time in locating sources of supply. For the country as a whole the period was generally one of chronic oversupply. Individual geographic areas, however, tended to alternate between periods of great abundance and periods of great scarcity depending on where the new discoveries were being made. Just as the new fields were developed and produced rapidly, so too were they exhausted quickly. The decline in one prolific field was often offset by a discovery somewhere else in the United States, but, as will be noted later, transportation costs place some very definite limits on the geographic areas from which a particular refinery can afford to draw its crude oil supplies. Crude oil in California, for example, is of little value to a refinery in Chicago. Crude oil was therefore occasionally in very short supply in particular geographic areas even though the total supply in the United States was ample to meet total require-

ments. Likewise the periods of abundance in particular areas were often far more acute than suggested by any of the data relating to the United States as a whole.

Some indication of the variations which occurred in the crude oil supply situation in particular areas as contrasted with that of the United States as a whole may be seen in Exhibit IV-4 which shows the production of some of the important producing states in barrels and as a percentage of the United States total for the period 1900 to 1952. It will be noted, for example, that the production of the state of Arkansas increased from 2.3% of the United States total in 1921 to 10.1% of the total in 1925 largely as a result of the development of the great Smackover field. Production declined in the state as the output of the field diminished and amounted to only 1.1% of the United States total in 1935. A more detailed discussion of the nature and significance of the fluctuations in crude oil supplies in particular fields and geographic regions will be presented in Chapter Twenty-One in connection with an analysis of the refining situation in the East Texas and Illinois fields.

III. FORWARD INTEGRATION TO FIND AN OUTLET FOR CRUDE OIL

The general condition of abundant crude oil supply which existed in the United States as a whole in the period 1920 to 1935 and the acute conditions of oversupply which developed from time to time in particular geographic areas provided a powerful stimulus to forward integration by crude oil producers. The series of new discoveries tended to generate intense competition at the producing level of the business. Established producers found themselves with more output than they could easily handle through their existing marketing arrangements. The new discoveries, moreover, gave birth to a number of new crude oil producing companies and made large producers out of ones which had previously been of minor size. Among the companies which secured the basis for their growth in the crude oil discoveries of the 1920's were the Phillips Petroleum Company, the Mid-Continent Petroleum Company, the Barnsdall Oil Company, the Lion Oil Company, the Skelly Oil Company, and the Champlin Oil Company.

---

[18] The demand for gasoline is heavily dependent upon the number of automobile registrations and the traveling habits of car owners, neither of which is much affected by short-run changes in the price of gasoline. As a result, the demand for gasoline usually does not increase significantly in response to price declines unless the declines are major in degree and persist over a long period of time. The total United States demand for gasoline is, of course, very different from the demand for the products of any single seller. Price reductions by one seller may enable him to take business away from others without bringing about any significant expansion in the total demand.

As was noted earlier in the chapter, the crude oil producers had little real alternative, prior to the development of the prorationing laws, other than to produce their oil as rapidly as it was discovered. It was readily apparent that in times of large supplies the producer who had assured access to refining, transportation, and marketing facilities was in a far better position to capture a share of the market than one who did not. Accordingly, many crude oil producers embarked on programs of forward integration as a means of disposing of their crude oil output.

The large crude oil supplies also tended to generate a good deal of new competition at the refining level of the industry and stimulated forward integration by refiners into marketing activities. As the new fields were discovered, refiners rushed into the areas and hastily constructed plants to take advantage of the low-cost crude oil in the periods of flush production (see Chapter Twenty-One). Once these plants were in operation, the owners were often confronted with the problem of disposing of their products in markets already overcrowded with supplies. As a means of securing a foothold in the market, the new refiners were frequently compelled to construct or acquire marketing facilities of their own.

Typical examples of the forward integration steps which were undertaken by producers, in whole or in part because of the pressure of crude oil supplies, in the period 1920 to 1935 may be found in the experiences of the Gulf Oil Corporation and The Ohio Oil Corporation outlined below. The forward integration of refiners into marketing in the period 1920 to 1935 will be discussed in Chapter Nine.

Gulf Oil Corporation:

The early history of the Gulf Oil Corporation was outlined in Chapter Three, and mention was made of the circumstances that led to the construction of the company's refinery at Fort Worth in the opening paragraphs of this chapter. For many years after construction of the Fort Worth refinery, the Gulf Oil Corporation accomplished expansion of its refining operations largely through successive enlargements of its main plant at Port Arthur. By 1925 the Port Arthur plant had become the largest refinery in the world. Marketing activities during this period were confined primarily to the southeastern section of the country and to the Atlantic Coast states. Products were shipped from Port Arthur by tanker to deep-water terminals all along the Gulf and Atlantic Coasts and were moved by barge to many inland destinations along the Mississippi and Ohio Rivers.

Throughout the period 1911 to 1923 the company's ratio of domestic crude production plus imports of its own foreign production to refinery runs gradually increased (see Chapter Twelve, Exhibit XII-10). Beginning in 1925 the company undertook a number of forward integration moves which were prompted to a considerable extent by the increasing supplies made available by successful exploratory and development work in Venezuela and the Mid-Continent area.

Bayonne and Philadelphia Refineries: In the period 1925 to 1927 the company built two new refineries, one at Bayonne, New Jersey, with a capacity of about 20,000 barrels per day, and a second at Philadelphia, Pennsylvania, with a capacity of about 40,000 barrels per day. These two plants, the combined cost of which was in excess of $20,000,000, were built primarily as a means of providing an outlet for the steadily increasing volume of production which the company was developing in Venezuela. The company had engaged in exploratory activities in Venezuela for a number of years in an effort to offset the decline in Mexican output and had secured its first production in 1925. By 1927 the company's production in Venezuela had jumped to 9,672,000 barrels for the year, and it appeared that an even greater rate of production could be expected in the future. The record of the company's foreign producing operations is shown in Exhibit IV-5.

The Gulf Oil Corporation had been shipping Mexican crude oil to its Port Arthur refinery and had been supplying the densely populated areas around Philadelphia and New York by shipments from Port Arthur to deep-water terminals at Philadelphia and Bayonne. Philadelphia and Bayonne, however, were nearly as close to Venezuela as was Port Arthur. As soon as it became apparent that Mexican crude oil would be largely replaced by

EXHIBIT IV-5. GULF OIL CORPORATION

Foreign Crude Oil Production: 1914–1952

(1,000 bbls.)

Year	Mexico	Total Venezuela	Kuwait (Gulf's Share)	Canada	Total Foreign	Venezuela Production Sold Under Long-Term Contract
1914	768	—	—	—	768	—
1915	871	—	—	—	871	—
1916	829	—	—	—	829	—
1917	1,199	—	—	—	1,199	—
1918	1,282	—	—	—	1,282	—
1919	4,281	—	—	—	4,281	—
1920	11,021	—	—	—	11,021	—
1921	17,201	—	—	—	17,201	—
1922	24,771	—	—	—	24,771	—
1923	7,192	—	—	—	7,192	—
1924	10,118	—	—	—	10,118	—
1925	5,406	1,181	—	—	6,587	—
1926	5,209	5,407	—	—	10,616	—
1927	2,848	9,672	—	—	12,520	—
1928	2,359	15,568	—	—	17,927	—
1929	2,186	26,000	—	—	28,186	—
1930	1,944	19,475	—	—	21,419	—
1931	1,890	15,044	—	—	16,934	—
1932	1,668	12,670	—	—	14,338	—
1933	2,062	11,214	—	—	13,276	—
1934	1,767	12,177	—	—	13,944	—
1935	1,594	14,298	—	—	15,892	—
1936	1,588	12,485	—	—	14,073	—
1937	1,563	18,621	—	—	20,184	—
1938	849	21,332	—	—	22,181	10,666
1939	361	22,123	—	—	22,484	11,062
1940	729	31,646	—	—	32,375	15,823
1941	286	38,694	—	—	38,980	19,347
1942	142	19,662	—	—	19,804	9,831
1943	115	17,341	—	—	17,456	8,670
1944	117	32,144	—	—	32,261	16,072
1945	225	43,709	—	—	43,934	21,794
1946	161	50,965	2,912	—	54,038	25,093
1947	182	54,954	7,600	—	62,736	26,605
1948	503	56,496	23,330	2	80,331	27,072
1949	267	51,924	48,035	210	100,436	24,207
1950	454	58,218	69,941	620	129,233	26,177
1951	99	70,405	106,281	1,499	178,284	32,209
1952	0	76,899	126,990	2,466	206,355	35,877

SOURCE: Gulf Oil Corporation.

Venezuelan, it was evident that it would be more economical to refine the oil at Bayonne and Philadelphia than to refine it at Port Arthur and ship products back to the Atlantic Coast.[19] Moreover, as will be noted below, the capacity of the Port Arthur refinery was al-

ready being strained by the steadily increasing volume of crude production available in Texas, Oklahoma, and Louisiana.

Expansion in North Central States: In the period 1928 to 1931, the Gulf Oil Corporation [20] undertook one of the most important expansion programs in its history. This program, which was accomplished through a care-

---

[19] In 1929 and 1930 the company's first thermal cracking unit was built at Philadelphia, together with a multisol unit for the manufacture of lubricating oils by the continuous solvent process at a cost of about $29,000,000. The Bayonne refinery was dismantled and moved to Staten Island, New York, in 1929 because of high tax rates at Bayonne.

[20] Actually the program was carried out through the Union Gulf Corporation, a subsidiary. The reasons for this arrangement will be discussed in Chapter Thirteen.

fully coordinated series of investments, involved the construction of a new pipe line from the Mid-Continent oil fields to Ohio, the building of new refining facilities at Toledo, Cincinnati, and Pittsburgh, and the acquisition of marketing outlets in Ohio, Michigan, Indiana, and Illinois.

These moves were initiated primarily because the Gulf Oil Corporation was developing more crude oil production in the Mid-Continent area than it could handle with its existing crude trunk line and refining facilities at Port Arthur and Fort Worth. As noted above, in the period preceding 1928 some very important new discoveries were made in Oklahoma and West Texas. Total production in Oklahoma jumped from 179,195,000 barrels in 1926 to 249,857,000 barrels in 1928, and the average value of crude oil at the well-head dropped from $2.31 to $1.39 per barrel; total production in the state of Texas increased from 166,916,000 barrels to 257,320,000 barrels and the average value of crude oil at the well-head fell from $1.85 to $0.92 per barrel.[21] The sharp increase which took place in the Gulf Oil Corporation's production in West Texas and Oklahoma in the period after 1926 is shown in Exhibit IV-6.

As a result of these and other discoveries, the Gulf Oil Corporation's domestic crude oil production increased by about 33% in the period 1926 to 1928 and by about 130% in the period 1920 to 1928 (see Exhibit IV-6). In the company's annual report for 1929, the management described the situation as follows:

The corporation has found itself in the position during the past two years of having a continually increasing oil production, even though it took every legal opportunity to curtail its production through cooperation in the conservation arrangements in the different districts. For this reason, it has been necessary to make important additions and improvements to plant and facilities as above shown. . . .

The Gulf Oil Corporation was also prompted to undertake the expansion program because of the growing importance of the market areas along the southern shores of the Great Lakes. In 1928 the four states of Ohio, Michigan, Indiana, and Illinois contained about one-sixth of the nation's population and were growing at a very rapid rate. The Gulf Oil Corporation had previously developed a very strong position in the South and East but had no good means of gaining access to the important North Central area. Moreover, it was apparent that some of the destinations which the company had been reaching by rail shipments from its tidewater and river terminals could be served far more economically from the new refineries.

The various steps in the expansion program were planned and executed on a coordinated basis. Construction of two new refineries having capacities of 12,000 and 8,000 barrels per day, respectively, was begun at Cincinnati and Pittsburgh. A third refinery at Toledo, Ohio, which was acquired with the properties of the Paragon Refining Company (see below), was modernized and expanded to a capacity of 12,000 barrels per day. Meanwhile, a crude pipe line was built from the company's existing line near Tulsa to the refinery location at Cincinnati. This line made connections at Lima, Ohio, with the Buckeye Pipe Line system, through which arrangements were made to ship oil to Pittsburgh and Toledo (see map, Chapter Twelve, Exhibit XII-3).

As a means of gaining access to the markets in the North Central states, the properties of the Paragon Refining Company were acquired. These properties included 344 bulk plants and service stations, various other marketing facilities in Ohio and Michigan, and an 8,000 barrels per day refinery at Toledo which also contained a complete lube oil and wax plant. The expenditure for the Paragon properties and various other marketing facilities in the North Central states was in excess of $22,000,000.

In the corporation's annual report for 1930, the management summarized the expansion program as follows:

The important development by the Union Gulf Corporation, consisting of a new pipe line system from the Mid-Continent field east into Ohio, connecting directly through its own line to the refinery at Cincinnati, and through a satisfactory operating agreement with the Buckeye Pipe Line Company to its refineries at Toledo and Pittsburgh, gives an increased outlet for the large pro-

---

21 H. J. Struth, Editor, *The Petroleum Data Book* (Dallas, The Petroleum Engineer Publishing Co., Second Edition, 1948), tables on pp. E-38, E-40, and E-77.

EXHIBIT IV-6. GULF OIL CORPORATION
Crude Oil Production by States: 1901–1952
(1,000 bbls.)

Year	West Texas	East Texas	New Mexico	Louisiana	Arkansas	Mississippi	Oklahoma	Kansas	Illinois	Indiana	Michigan	Kentucky	California	Total U.S.*
1901		1,204												1,204
1902		1,938												1,938
1903		2,158												2,158
1904		2,923												2,923
1905		3,361												3,361
1906		1,522		95										1,617
1907		1,581		102			1,662							3,345
1908		1,643		386			2,685							4,714
1909		1,345		765			4,535							6,645
1910	6	1,597		828			4,278							6,709
1911	34	1,614		1,989			4,048							7,685
1912	100	1,317		2,276			3,732							7,425
1913	483	972		3,192			4,385							9,032
1914	516	883		3,700			6,015							11,114
1915	355	920		4,734			6,205							12,215
1916	427	1,581		5,120			6,506	32						13,666
1917	530	4,954		3,980			4,333	2,538						16,335
1918	793	4,844		4,237			3,749	4,116				31		17,770
1919	4,279	4,060		3,768			3,733	634				128		16,602
1920	3,940	4,246		6,712			4,074	478				57		19,507
1921	3,362	5,562		4,321	563		3,449	426				57		17,740
1922	2,498	8,536		4,537	1,165		6,875	345				61		24,017
1923	2,249	10,098		3,903	3,203		12,923	372				59		32,807
1924	1,604	8,286		3,550	3,695		10,557	452				49		28,193
1925	2,146	9,290		3,263	7,264		8,769	530				40		31,302
1926	4,070	11,362		3,149	6,451		8,064	453				33		33,582
1927	10,548	8,516		3,486	4,882		14,381	407	3			29		42,252
1928	15,773	6,020		2,859	3,532		16,371	441	3			34	106	45,139
1929	17,668	8,117	1	2,564	2,600		16,454	2,353				58	244	50,059
1930	16,051	8,146	475	2,451	1,893		11,227	2,096				69	339	42,747
1931	10,716	12,884	828	2,398	1,346		7,890	1,551				53	328	37,995
1932	9,660	13,078	666	1,975	1,001		7,134	1,091				22	496	35,123
1933	8,694	16,000	831	2,169	930		6,714	1,539				26	591	37,494
1934	7,687	13,948	943	3,253	783		6,285	2,142				16	583	35,640
1935	7,745	14,003	1,411	3,496	737		6,595	2,379			23	11	982	37,382
1936	9,053	13,117	2,754	4,260	733		7,110	3,006			168	10	1,549	41,760
1937	10,362	13,673	4,778	3,961	718		7,494	3,721			48	10	1,552	46,317
1938	9,501	12,633	4,216	3,482	741		5,498	2,681	321		211	9	1,511	40,804
1939	10,762	13,063	3,985	3,786	666		4,517	2,484	272		495	9	1,196	41,235
1940	13,010	12,842	3,487	4,512	617		4,682	2,648	2,542	20	500	12	1,169	46,041
1941	13,286	12,545	3,546	5,486	607		4,340	3,122	2,089	73	942	12	1,148	47,196
1942	12,565	11,979	2,931	5,859	509		3,872	3,536	2,335	203	1,376	14	1,476	46,655
1943	14,887	16,165	3,416	6,496	420	1	3,694	3,726	2,244	159	1,654	874	1,907	55,643
1944	21,522	20,442	3,700	7,218	428	853	4,453	3,361	1,932	126	1,632	653	2,610	68,930
1945	23,008	20,426	3,558	7,960	420	2,482	5,271	3,303	1,977	133	1,732	576	3,168	74,014
1946	24,314	19,405	3,517	8,306	398	3,752	4,627	3,216	2,003	131	1,615	684	3,156	75,124
1947	24,783	19,817	3,783	9,328	367	5,893	4,978	3,303	1,680	102	1,145	534	3,170	78,883
1948	28,032	20,337	4,797	9,869	342	7,731	5,256	3,391	1,572	79	1,064	407	3,277	86,154
1949	22,708	16,307	5,158	9,846	337	4,008	4,445	2,761	1,429	84	1,139	322	3,317	71,861
1950	23,665	16,464	4,883	10,835	327	5,848	4,408	2,697	1,191	65	972	222	3,058	74,635
1951	28,432	19,115	4,868	12,431	310	6,641	5,085	2,749	1,168	69	787	198	3,237	85,094
1952	25,233	18,204	4,846	13,675	317	6,669	5,508	2,277	1,129	60	620	190	2,969	81,828

* In 1942, 1951, and 1952 the company had small amounts of production in certain other states which are not shown on the table.

SOURCE: Gulf Oil Corporation

duction of this corporation in the Mid-Continent fields, including Oklahoma, Kansas, New Mexico, Texas, Louisiana, and Arkansas, which will be more economically available to supply the present marketing facilities now served from the Atlantic Seaboard or the Gulf of Mexico, and to meet the expected growth and expansion of the business in the territory east of the Mississippi River, and the Great Lakes District. This construction of a new pipe line system and of refineries at Pittsburgh and Cincinnati was made necessary in order to effect substantial reduction in transportation costs, particularly in western Pennsylvania and along the Ohio and Mississippi Rivers as far south as Memphis, Tennessee, and to satisfactorily and economically meet competition.

Sweetwater Refinery: In 1929 the Gulf Oil Corporation built a 5,000 barrels per day refinery at Sweetwater, Texas. This move was unrelated to the expansion into the North Central states discussed above but was motivated in part by some of the same circumstances. The company's production from the newly discovered West Texas fields more than tripled in the period 1926 to 1928, and rose to a level of over 17,000,000 barrels in 1929 (see Exhibit IV-6). The company built the Sweetwater refinery largely as a means of providing an outlet for its crude oil supply in the West Texas area and also as a means of supplying its markets in western Texas at a lower freight cost than they could be supplied by shipments from Port Arthur or Fort Worth. At about the same time certain extensions were made in the West Texas pipe line system to permit the West Texas oil to move to the refineries at Sweetwater, Fort Worth, and Port Arthur and into lines connecting with the new pipe line extending to the North Central area.

In the light of the foregoing facts, it appears that the Gulf Oil Corporation's program of growth and development throughout the first 25 years of its history was much influenced by the need to provide physical facilities to handle the company's steadily increasing volume of crude oil production.

The Ohio Oil Company:

The experiences of The Ohio Oil Company provide a second example of forward integration moves which were influenced in part by a desire to find an outlet for crude oil. The

Ohio Oil Company was organized on August 1, 1887, by a group of 14 independent producers who were interested in cooperative action to impose some restraints on drilling and producing activities in the Lima-Indiana oil fields which had been discovered in 1885. Although the crude oil from the fields had a high sulphur content and posed difficult refining problems, it was being produced very rapidly. The tanks of the Buckeye Pipe Line Company, the principal crude oil gatherer in the field, had become filled to capacity, and the price of the oil had dropped to as low as $0.10 a barrel. The Ohio Oil Company bought a number of the producing properties in the area and tried to hold production at reasonable levels.

As was noted in Chapter Three, The Ohio Oil Company was purchased by the Standard Oil Trust in 1889 and thereafter became the principal producing agency of the Standard Oil organization in the Lima-Indiana region. Crude operations were expanded rapidly in the Lima-Indiana fields until about 1900, at which time output in the area began to decline. Total production in Ohio fell from 22,363,000 barrels in 1900 to 9,916,000 barrels in 1910.[22] The Indiana fields reached a peak production of 11,339,000 barrels in 1904; by 1910 production had slumped to 2,160,000 barrels.[23] To offset the dwindling production in the Lima-Indiana fields, The Ohio Oil Company entered the newly discovered Illinois fields in 1905 and soon became the largest producer in the state. In connection with the development of its Illinois properties, the company became engaged in the construction of crude gathering lines, trunk lines, and storage facilities and was soon purchasing practically all the oil produced in the state.

At the time of the dissolution decree in 1911, The Ohio Oil Company was the largest producer in the Illinois, Indiana, and Ohio oil fields and had extensive crude oil gathering and storage facilities in all three states. The terms of the dissolution decree limited the company's crude trunk line operations to a line extending from Wood River, Illinois, to the Ohio-Pennsylvania state line. In the years following 1911, the company confined its op-

---

[22] *Petroleum Facts and Figures,* Ninth Edition, pp. 145–148.

[23] Ibid.

erations to crude oil production, purchasing, and transportation. Production in the Illinois, Indiana, and Ohio fields declined so rapidly after 1912 that the company began to acquire oil leases in Wyoming and Montana and obtained its first Rocky Mountain crude production in 1914. In 1916 The Ohio Oil Company entered the Mid-Continent area as a producer through the purchase of the Mid-Kansas Oil and Gas Company. Operations were begun in Texas after the discovery of the Ranger field in 1918 and in Oklahoma and Louisiana in 1921.

Integration into Refining Operations: In 1924 The Ohio Oil Company integrated forward for the first time into refining operations. The step was taken through the purchase of a controlling interest in the business of one of the company's customers for crude oil, the Lincoln Oil and Refining Company, which had been operating a small plant of about 1,000 barrels per day capacity at Robinson, Illinois. The Lincoln Oil and Refining Company was in financial difficulties, and it appeared that it might soon be forced to shut down its plant.

The precise reasons why this initial venture into refining activities was undertaken by The Ohio Oil Company are not entirely clear. Some of the executives of the company recall that the move was undertaken primarily as a means of averting loss of an outlet for crude oil at a time when large stocks were accumulating; others recall that the decision was prompted largely by the attractiveness of the profit opportunities in the refining field. In retrospect and in the light of the circumstances prevailing at the time, it appears that the validity of both these reasons is open to question.

It is true, as noted earlier in the chapter, that there was an abundance of crude oil in the United States in the period 1921 to 1924. Stocks of crude oil and refined products accumulated throughout the period, and in 1923 domestic crude oil production exceeded domestic refinery runs plus exports for the first time in many years. There was at this time, nevertheless, considerable apprehension that the United States would soon run out of crude oil and become dependent upon foreign sources to meet the rapidly increasing domestic demand. Consequently, many producers

and purchasers of crude oil, including The Ohio Oil Company, were accumulating stocks with the hope that they might soon be able to realize large inventory gains as they had in the period of rising prices following World War I. It is thus quite possible that the management of The Ohio Oil Company may have had no great concern regarding the disposition of the company's crude oil output. Moreover, the company's total domestic crude oil production in 1924 was 12,678,789 barrels, whereas the Robinson refinery was capable of consuming only about 365,000 barrels per year. The one plant could not possibly therefore have been regarded as any major solution to a problem of disposing of surplus crude oil.

On the other hand, it seems doubtful that the attractiveness of the profit opportunity could have been a major factor in the decision. It is true that refining profits had been very attractive in the period 1918 to 1921. After the depression of 1921, however, the refining segment of the industry experienced declining margins and intense competition. In the period 1921 to 1924 refining capacity in the United States was approximately twice that needed to satisfy the domestic demand (see Chapter Eighteen, Exhibit XVIII-2). Moreover, the Robinson plant facilities were technologically obsolete and highly inefficient, and the Lincoln Oil and Refining Company was finding it very difficult to operate on a profitable basis.

Whatever the reasons for the original decision may have been, it seems quite clear that by the late 1920's the Robinson refinery had become important to The Ohio Oil Company as a means of disposing of its crude oil output in a market which was seriously oversupplied. The large crude oil supplies which were generated by the discoveries in Oklahoma and West Texas in 1926 have already been discussed. In 1926 The Ohio Oil Company purchased a half interest in a 10,000 acre block of land in Pecos County in West Texas from the Transcontinental Oil Company. A discovery well in about the center of the block uncovered the Yates field which by 1951 ranked 13th in terms of total crude oil production among the producing fields of the United States.[24]

----

[24] *Petroleum Facts and Figures,* Tenth Edition, pp. 96–97.

The initial flow from the discovery well was 3,000 barrels per day with a well depth of 1,032 feet. Three years later, the well was drilled to 1,150 feet and the capacity thereby increased to 72,000 barrels per day, based on a one-hour gage.

Largely as a result of the discovery of the Yates field, the production of The Ohio Oil Company increased from 11,238,087 barrels in 1926 to 20,917,513 in 1930.[25] These figures do not, however, fully reflect the company's crude oil situation because the operators of the Yates field very early initiated a voluntary program to regulate production as a means of avoiding waste and adjusting output to market demand. Their proposals for allocating production were submitted to and subsequently adopted by the Texas Railroad Commission in its first action with respect to the regulation of crude oil production.

Partially in recognition of the increasing supplies of crude oil in the United States after the discoveries of 1926, The Ohio Oil Company rebuilt the Robinson refinery in 1927 and enlarged it to a capacity of 5,000 barrels per day. Thereafter it became a well-established policy of the company to carry on a substantial refining operation as an adjunct to its producing operations. It is interesting to note that in the late 1920's and early 1930's The Ohio Oil Company accumulated about 30,-000,000 barrels of crude oil in storage, much of which it held until the early years of World War II. By this date the light ends had all escaped from the oil and it was sold as residual fuel. The company sold its crude oil tankage at this time and did not propose again to engage in the accumulation of large crude oil inventories for any reason, if it could possibly be avoided.

Integration into Marketing Operations: The Ohio Oil Company originally intended to market the output of the Robinson plant by selling at wholesale to other large oil companies. In view of the conditions of oversupply which developed in the late 1920's, however, it proved impossible to pursue such a program.

The company therefore found it necessary to integrate forward another step and engage in marketing activities. The program was begun by the purchase of the Show Me Distributing Company, the largest jobber customer of the Lincoln Oil and Refining Company. In the succeeding years the refinery output was sold in the states of Michigan, Ohio, Indiana, Illinois, and Kentucky under the trade name of "Linco." Marketing facilities were established in these areas through the purchase of the business of small jobbers and marketing companies and by the construction of the company's own bulk plants and service stations.

IV. DEVELOPMENT OF HARD COMPETITION IN THE MARKETING FIELD

The forward integration moves of producers and refiners under the pressure of large crude oil supplies in the period 1920 to 1935 eventually contributed, along with certain other circumstances, to some very hard competition in the wholesale and retail markets.

In the period from about 1914 to 1926 refining and marketing companies rushed into the construction of service stations as a means of serving the rapidly expanding market for automotive gasoline. As indicated in Exhibit IV-3, the demand for motor fuel increased between 1914 and 1926 from about 29 million barrels to 312 million barrels or more than 10 times.[26] The established oil companies did by no means, however, undertake to build all the marketing facilities required by the expansion of the demand for motor fuel, possibly because they lacked access to the necessary capital or because they elected not to make full use of their borrowing power. Instead they offered wide margins under the current retail prices to independent jobbers and dealers which served to attract much outside capital to the business.

By the middle 1920's when the growth in the demand for motor fuel began to slacken, the expansion of marketing facilities had been sufficient to provide reasonably adequate service to the market. The steadily mounting pressure of large crude oil supplies was at this

25 In 1930 The Ohio Oil Company also purchased the Transcontinental Oil Company and thereby acquired additional producing properties in the Yates field as well as in other areas.

26 The 1914 figure is U. S. gasoline production and the 1926 figure is total demand for motor fuel, domestic and export. See Exhibit IV-3 for sources.

time, however, placing the producing companies, and secondarily the refining companies, under great pressure to acquire marketing outlets as a means of disposing of their output.[27] The oil companies continued therefore to construct outlets of their own and to compete vigorously for the services of independent jobbers and dealers. Dealer margins continued to be attractive, and many indirect inducements were offered to the dealers in the form of special equipment, building repairs, and various other services. The gasoline output which refiners could not sell readily through their existing marketing arrangements was thrown onto the tank car market at low prices and thus provided an attractive business opportunity to the independent jobber. Both crude oil prices and tank car prices of refined products moved downward in the late 1920's somewhat in advance of the retail price of gasoline, and hence the marketing phase of the business was the last to feel the need for an abatement in the rate of expansion.

These three circumstances—the initial profit opportunities arising from the need to provide facilities to serve the growing automotive market, the drive to forward integration generated by the large supplies of crude oil, and the lag in the downward movement of retail prices with respect to tank car prices—combined to result in a great expansion of wholesale and retail market outlets. The expansion was, of course, facilitated by the fact that individual marketing properties required relatively small capital outlays and could be purchased fairly easily by small entrepreneurs. The great expansion of wholesale and retail outlets contributed to severe price competition and a narrowing of wholesale and retail gross margins in

[27] Beyond a certain point the further construction of marketing outlets did not contribute greatly to the solution of the industry-wide problem of handling the large supplies of crude oil. The acquisition of additional outlets by any one company did, however, help that company in disposing of its crude oil relative to other concerns.

1928 and 1929 (see Chapter Five, Exhibit V-2). By this time the expansion in market outlets had been so great that wholesalers and retailers suffered not only from a decline in gross margins but likewise from a decline in volume per outlet. In addition, by the late 1920's and early 1930's the crude oil producers had undertaken sufficient forward integration so that their distress with large crude oil supplies was transmitted fairly directly into tough competition in the retail and wholesale marketing fields.

The intense struggle for markets and market outlets which was generated in the late 1920's and early 1930's by the abundant supplies of crude oil, the forward integration moves of producers and refiners, and the great expansion of marketing facilities was manifested, in part, by some radical readjustments in the market positions of the leading marketers in the various states. The readjustment process was comprised of at least three distinct phases: (1) the large, well-established producing, refining, and marketing companies which found themselves with large supplies of crude oil on their hands, as did the Gulf Oil Corporation, frequently tended to branch out into new territories as a means of disposing of their output, (2) new producing companies or small producing companies which grew large with the discoveries of the middle 1920's integrated forward and pressed into any market they could reach, and (3) as new competition crowded into their home territories, the established marketers in the various states tended to expand into new areas as a means of recouping their losses.

In the period 1926 to 1935 the largest marketer in each of the 48 states and the District of Columbia suffered a loss in its *proportionate share* of the market in the state, as indicated in Exhibit IV-7. The largest marketer in each state in 1926 was, however, still the largest marketer in that state in 1935 except in the

SOURCES: The figures for 1926 are taken from the Federal Trade Commission, *Petroleum Industry, Prices, Profits, and Competition,* U.S. Senate Document No. 61, 70th Congress, 1st Session (Government Printing Office, 1928), p. 225, Table 68. The Federal Trade Commission secured statistics on the quantities of gasoline sold by each of 23 large companies in each state in 1926, but reported the data only on a combined basis for the marketing territories of the various Standard Oil Companies. As a result, the figures shown above are in error to whatever extent a company's share of the market in a particular state varied from the average share it held in the territory which embraced that state.

The figures for later years were taken from records prepared by various oil companies. The companies drew their data from reports on taxable gallonage of gasoline consumed in each state. In the few instances where tax records were not available, the data are estimates by the oil companies. The figures we secured from the various companies checked fairly closely against each other. In cases where there was a difference in the figures, we used the source that appeared to us to be the most reliable.

EXHIBIT IV-7. MARKET POSITIONS OF LARGEST MARKETERS IN INDIVIDUAL STATES FOR THE YEARS
1926, 1933, 1934, and 1935

Share of State Gasoline Market

State	Largest Marketer in 1926	1926	1933	1934	1935
Delaware	The Atlantic Refining Company	44.5%	18.4%	18.4%	18.0%
Pennsylvania	" " " "	44.5	22.9	22.0	21.7
Colorado	Continental Oil Company	47.2	18.1	18.5	18.4
Idaho	" " "	47.2	17.1	17.1	17.1
Montana	" " "	47.2	25.9	24.6	20.3
New Mexico	" " "	47.2	25.1	25.1	25.2
Utah	" " "	47.2	22.3	22.3	21.1
Wyoming	" " "	47.2	28.2	26.3	29.8
Connecticut	Socony-Vacuum Oil Company *	46.1	27.4	27.0	28.0
Maine	" " " "	46.1	29.8	30.9	27.8
Massachusetts	" " " "	46.1	27.0	27.5	27.5
New Hampshire	" " " "	46.1	30.8	30.2	29.3
Oklahoma	" " " "	18.1	5.8	6.0	6.4
Rhode Island	" " " "	46.1	20.4	19.1	19.2
Texas	" " " "	18.1	12.6	11.9	12.6
Vermont	" " " "	46.1	33.4	30.7	28.3
New York	" " " "	46.1	32.3	30.0	27.5
Arizona	Standard Oil Co. (California)	28.7	25.4	25.4	22.3
California	" " " "	28.7	21.0	21.0	19.5
Nevada	" " " "	28.7	30.7	30.7	24.8
Oregon	" " " "	28.7	25.5	25.5	24.6
Washington	" " " "	28.7	26.5	26.5	27.3
Illinois	Standard Oil Co. (Indiana)	35.5	23.4	25.3	21.7
Indiana	" " " "	35.5	24.6	23.5	23.6
Iowa	" " " "	35.5	23.0	20.2	21.1
Kansas	" " " "	35.5	13.4	15.1	12.7
Michigan	" " " "	35.5	20.0	18.9	20.5
Minnesota	" " " "	35.5	19.5	18.3	17.6
Missouri	" " " "	35.5	17.0	15.2	16.0
North Dakota	" " " "	35.5	30.0	30.0	29.2
South Dakota	" " " "	35.5	20.5	22.3	24.4
Wisconsin	" " " "	35.5	22.4	20.7	19.8
Alabama	Standard Oil Co. (Kentucky)	33.3	26.4	24.2	22.6
Florida	" " " "	33.3	24.1	24.3	23.3
Georgia	" " " "	33.3	21.8	21.3	20.6
Mississippi	" " " "	33.3	24.4	23.6	21.2
Kentucky	" " " "	33.3	30.5	29.7	29.13
Nebraska	Standard Oil Co. (Nebraska) †	23.6	11.6	13.4	10.9
Arkansas	Standard Oil Co. (New Jersey) ‡	35.5	18.3	20.7	22.1
Dist. of Col.	" " " "	43.2	29.6	34.7	29.7
Louisiana	" " " "	35.5	23.8	25.1	24.8
Maryland	" " " "	43.2	22.9	23.1	22.3
New Jersey	" " " "	43.2	27.1	27.4	28.0
North Carolina	" " " "	43.2	28.1	28.4	27.3
South Carolina	" " " "	43.2	31.6	31.6	31.6
Tennessee	" " " "	35.5	25.8	26.3	25.9
Virginia	" " " "	43.2	28.5	28.8	28.9
West Virginia	" " " "	43.2	37.4	35.1	34.0
Ohio	Standard Oil Company (Ohio)	37.6	25.6	24.0	23.0

* The Socony-Vacuum Oil Company was formed in 1932 by a merger of the Standard Oil Company of New York and the Vacuum Oil Company. The data for 1926 are for the Standard Oil Company of New York alone. The data for Oklahoma and Texas are for the Magnolia Petroleum Company, a wholly owned subsidiary.

† The Standard Oil Company (Nebraska) was affiliated with and supplied by the Standard Oil Company (Indiana). The latter did not acquire a controlling interest in the Standard Oil Company (Nebraska), however, until 1939.

‡ The data for Louisiana, Arkansas, and Tennessee are for the Standard Oil Company of Louisiana, a subsidiary of the Standard Oil Company (New Jersey). (For sources to Exhibit IV-7, see facing page.)

EXHIBIT IV-8. MARKET POSITIONS OF LEADING MARKETERS IN THE UNITED STATES: 1926–1935

Share of U.S. Gasoline Market

	1926	1933	1934	1935
Companies Listed in Exhibit IV-7				
Standard Oil Company (California)	3.4%	2.7%	2.8%	2.7%
Socony-Vacuum Oil Company *	9.6	9.3	8.8	8.7
Standard Oil Company (Indiana) †	10.6	8.7	8.7	8.5
The Atlantic Refining Company	4.2	2.7	2.6	2.5
Standard Oil Company (Ohio)	2.4	1.7	1.5	1.5
Standard Oil Company (New Jersey)	5.4	6.1	6.0	6.1
Standard Oil Company (Kentucky)	2.5	1.4	1.4	1.4
Continental Oil Company	1.4	1.8	2.0	1.8
Other Large Marketers				
The Texas Company	6.5	7.7	7.8	7.5
Sinclair Oil Corporation	7.8	6.0	6.0	6.0
Shell Oil Company	5.3	6.4	6.4	6.3
Sun Oil Company	(a)	3.2	3.2	3.2
Tide Water Associated Oil Company	3.3	3.5	3.3	3.3
Cities Service Company	(a)	2.5	2.5	2.5
Pure Oil Company	2.3	2.3	2.3	2.5
Phillips Petroleum Company	(a)	1.8	1.9	1.9
Union Oil Company	1.5	1.2	1.3	1.3
Skelly Oil Company	(a)	0.4	0.5	0.5
The Ohio Oil Company	(a)	0.6	0.6	0.6
Gulf Oil Corporation	7.0	5.8	5.8	5.3
All Other Companies	26.8	24.2	24.6	25.9

* See first footnote, Exhibit IV-7.

† Includes data for the operations of the Standard Oil Company (Nebraska). See footnote †, Exhibit IV-7.

(a) Share of market unknown. Included with "all other companies."

SOURCES: See sources to Exhibit IV-7, p. 102.

states of Oklahoma and Texas.[28] The largest marketers in each state were able to offset somewhat their losses in proportionate share of the market in their home states by expansion into new market areas, but all of them with the exception of the Standard Oil Company (New Jersey) and the Continental Oil Company had a smaller share of the total United States automotive gasoline market in 1935 than they did in 1926 (see Exhibit IV-8). It may also be observed from Exhibit IV-8 that certain large marketers which were *not the lead-*

[28] In Oklahoma the Standard Oil Company (New York) was replaced by the Continental Oil Company, and in Texas the Standard Oil Company (New York) was replaced by The Texas Company.

ing marketer in any state in 1926 made appreciable gains in their share of the total United States market between 1926 and 1935.

More detailed data on the readjustments in market positions which took place in the course of the competitive struggle for market outlets in the period 1926 to 1935 are shown in Exhibits IV-9 to IV-11 for the states of Ohio, Indiana, and Pennsylvania. These states were selected for illustration because the data shed light on the situations of the Standard Oil Company (Ohio), the Standard Oil Company (Indiana), and The Atlantic Refining Company which are to be discussed in later chapters. The charts clearly indicate the loss in *proportionate share of the market* experienced by the larger marketers in the three states and the crowding of new competition into the markets. Circumstances varied in other states, but for the most part the general course of developments was not very different from that shown for Ohio, Indiana, and Pennsylvania. No comparable readjustment in relative market positions took place in the 17 years after the great supplies of crude oil discovered in the period 1926 to 1935 were brought under control by the development of the prorationing laws. In the 17-year period 1935 to 1952 there was, of course, no major economic upheaval in the industry which had the same potential for disrupting market positions as did the crude oil discoveries of the period 1920 to 1935.

It should not be inferred that the readjustment in the market positions of the various companies indicated by the foregoing data was due solely to the competitive pressures generated in the wholesale and retail markets by large supplies of crude oil. The large marketing organizations were, at this time, finding other reasons for expanding their geographic areas of distribution. As a result of the improvement of roads and technological advances in automobile design, the public was beginning to travel greater distances, and some of the marketing organizations decided that they could strengthen their competitive positions by offering the customer service over a fairly wide geographic area. It was in the late 1920's, for example, that The Texas Company embarked on its program of developing nationwide distribution. Moreover, in the late 1920's and early 1930's there was a marked increase in the emphasis placed on brand names and advertising in the marketing of petroleum products, and some companies decided that their advertising programs could be developed more effectively and at a lower cost per unit of sale if their operations covered a fairly wide section of the country. After 1931 the products pipe line contributed to the general expansion of marketing territories because it gave companies access to markets from which they had previously been excluded by high transportation costs. Finally, a certain amount of geographic expansion undoubtedly took place merely because the companies sought the profit opportunities available in other areas.

V. DEFENSIVE RESPONSES OF ESTABLISHED COMPANIES

As new competition crowded forward into the wholesale and retail markets under the pressure of large crude oil supplies, the companies which had previously been well-established in the markets embarked on many different programs in an effort to protect their profit positions. As was noted above, one common response of the established companies to the inroads made on their markets was to expand into new geographic areas. In addition, some of the established companies intensified their programs of forward integration into wholesale and retail operations, undertook other backward and forward integration steps, revised their price policies, and increased their sales promotion efforts in many different ways.

In the face of the scramble for wholesale and retail outlets which developed in the late 1920's and early 1930's, companies that had been making considerable use of independent jobbers and retailers in their marketing programs found it necessary to take steps toward the acquisition or control of their outlets in order to prevent their capture by other concerns. An example may be found in the experience of The Atlantic Refining Company which was the leading marketer in the states of Pennsylvania and Delaware and which was also engaged in the expansion of its marketing operations into other Atlantic Coast states, primarily through the use of jobbers and distributors.

The Atlantic Refining Company did not have much crude oil production at this time and did not, therefore, have the problem of finding an outlet for its crude oil output. The company found it necessary, however, to acquire wholesale and retail outlets in order to protect its business from capture by companies which were under pressure to find an outlet for their crude oil. The company's situation is reflected in the following statement from its annual report for 1929:

While during the year, only about $1,000,000 was used for expanding your investments in several affiliated and nonaffiliated companies, nearly $19,000,000 was expended for physical properties of various kinds. Almost exactly one-half of this latter was used for the acquisition of marketing facilities in this country and abroad.

This concentration of expenditure points to the largest problem which confronted your management. The country-wide and world-wide excess production of crude oil and the products from the same which took place throughout the year, and which was a continuation of similar happenings during some prior years, has led all producers to seek market outlets for their goods. This search greatly disturbed previously existing individual relations between manufacturers, jobbers, and retail distributors, occasioned many changes in these connections and eventuated, to a large extent, in passing the full control of marketing outlets to the manufacturers through direct purchase or otherwise. In many instances, this, in turn, brought about the creation of new outlet facilities to replace connections that had been severed. *As a matter of protection, rather than of desire, your Company has been forced to participate in this general movement.*[29] Whenever possible it acquired previously existing distributor business, but, by force of circumstances was compelled to a large extent to undertake development and construction.

As the pressure of excess crude oil gradually intensified competition and narrowed profit margins at all levels of the industry, many of the oil companies embarked on backward and forward integration programs of many other types in an effort to reduce their operating costs. As will be noted in Chapter Eight, the Standard Oil Company (Ohio)'s program of integration into crude oil and products transportation activities was prompted, in part, by

[29] Italics added by authors.

EXHIBIT IV-9. PERCENTAGE OF THE GASOLINE MARKET

	1926	1927	1928	1929	1930	1931	1932	1933	1934	1935	1936
Gasoline Sales *(Millions of Gallons)*	663	752	830	910	927	983	857	838	955	1,015	1,134
Three Largest Marketers in 1926 (Percentage of Market)											
Standard Oil Company (Ohio)	37.6%		28.0%	23.9%	23.1%	28.6%	27.1%	26.7%	22.9%	22.5%	21.4%
Shell Oil Company	13.0		14.9	2.6	5.1	4.9	4.0	5.8	5.3	5.2	5.2
Sinclair Oil Corporation	7.7		8.5	4.9	5.2	5.2	4.5	4.5	4.2	4.6	4.6
Total	58.3		51.4	31.4	33.4	38.7	35.6	37.0	32.4	32.3	31.2
All Other Marketers (Percentage of Market)											
The Atlantic Refining Company	6.1		4.2								
Pure Oil Company	5.6			3.9	4.3	6.2	5.1	4.7	4.5	4.8	5.0
The Texas Company	1.0				1.1						
Ashland Oil and Refining Co.											
Cities Service Oil Co.			3.5	4.1	4.5	4.2	4.4	4.5	4.0	4.0	3.7
Farm Bureau Coop. Assn.											
Gulf Oil Corporation						4.2	5.3	5.6	5.6	5.3	5.7
National Refining Co.				1.3	1.6	1.8	2.1	2.2	2.2	2.2
The Ohio Oil Company							1.2	1.8	2.0	2.1	2.0
Rockwood Oil Terminals											
Canton Refining Co.											
American Oil Company											
Socony-Vacuum Oil Co.								1.4	1.3	3.0	2.7
Great Western Oil Co.						0.9			1.1	1.2	1.1
Texas Distributing Co.							0.9				
Sun Oil Company			4.4	3.0	4.5	4.2	4.3	6.0	7.4	7.4	7.1
Johnson Oil Ref. Co.			1.9								
Columbia Refining Co.				1.2	1.2	1.3	1.3	1.3	1.2	1.2	1.2
Caldwell and Taylor Corp.				1.4	1.5	1.8					
Solar Refining Company†			7.2								
Paragon Refining Company			6.9	3.3							
Refiners Oil Company‡			8.6	6.1	7.1						
Hickok Oil Corp.§			4.0	1.9	1.9	1.9	1.9	2.2	1.8	2.3	2.4
Indian Refining Company			2.7			1.1	2.3	2.7	2.8	2.7	2.7
Canfield Oil Company*			2.2	1.8	2.0	1.9	1.9	1.7	1.5	1.5	1.5
Boswell Oil Company			2.1	1.5							
Pocahontas Oil Company				1.3	1.5						
Miscellaneous Marketers	29.0		0.9	39.1	35.7	32.0	34.0	29.0	32.2	30.0	31.5
Total	41.7		48.6	68.6	66.6	61.3	64.4	63.0	67.6	67.7	68.8

* Included with Standard Oil Company (Ohio) beginning in 1950.

† Acquired by Standard Oil Company (Ohio) in 1931.

‡ Includes certain associated and affiliated companies. Merged with Standard Oil Company (Ohio) in 1931.

§ Owned by and included with the Pure Oil Company in 1952.

the company's urgent need to reduce its costs to the point where it could meet adequately the competitive situation in the state of Ohio. Similarly, The Atlantic Refining Company was motivated to undertake the construction of its first West Texas crude oil trunk line and its Keystone pipe line for refined products because of the difficulties it was having in the late 1920's and early 1930's in making a profit on its existing refining and marketing operations (see Chapter Seven).

The hard competition for markets and market outlets which developed in the late 1920's and early 1930's, also prompted the leading marketers in several states to make general revisions in their pricing practices. In the early 1920's a number of the large refining-marketing companies had based their price structures on their own refining and marketing costs, plus a liberal margin of profit, and had not been particularly aggressive in meeting the competition of newcomers into the market. The circumstances which developed in the late 1920's and early 1930's, however, convinced some of these companies that in the future they would have to follow the practice of

IN OHIO HELD BY PRINCIPAL MARKETERS: 1926–1952

1937	1938	1939	1940	1941	1942	1943	1944	1945	1946	1947	1948	1949	1950	1951	1952
1,234	1,216	1,302	1,398	1,548		1,333	1,105	1,216	1,569	1,708	1,869	1,976	2,152	2,269	2,350
21.0%	22.7%	24.9%	25.7%	26.5%		23.7%	23.8%	25.2%	28.8%	27.7%	28.8%	28.2%	28.6%	28.4%	30.4%
4.5	5.1	5.9	5.3	5.7		5.2	5.3	5.6	5.5	5.6	5.2	5.5	5.6	5.6	5.5
4.4	4.3	4.2	4.0	3.7		3.6	3.8	3.8	3.5	3.8	3.8	3.8	4.0	4.1	3.8
29.9	32.1	35.0	35.0	35.9		32.5	32.9	34.6	37.8	37.1	37.8	37.5	38.2	38.1	39.7
		1.3	1.2	1.0											0.2
6.5	4.7	5.3	4.8	4.6		4.8	4.4	4.9	4.2	4.0	3.8	3.7	3.7	3.8	4.0
						2.2	2.6	2.9	3.6	3.9	3.6	3.6	3.5	3.3	3.6
											1.2	1.3	1.4	1.6	2.1
3.4	2.6	1.6		1.3		2.4	2.5	2.5	2.1	2.2	2.2	2.2	2.1	2.2	2.2
1.3	1.4	1.3	1.3	1.1		1.8	1.9	1.8	1.8	1.8	1.7	1.8	1.7	1.7	1.7
8.3	9.1	7.1	8.4	9.7		6.4	6.7	6.7	7.2	7.0	6.9	6.8	6.9	7.2	7.4
2.1	2.0	2.6	2.4	2.3		2.6	1.3								
1.9	1.8	1.0				2.4	2.4	2.7	2.8	2.9	3.0	3.1	3.2	3.1	3.4
				1.0											0.1
		1.7	2.0												
									0.8	0.8		0.9	0.9	1.0	1.0
2.3	2.1	2.1	2.0	1.9		3.9	4.7	4.5	4.4	3.8	3.5	3.2	2.9	2.7	2.6
1.1	0.9							1.1							
7.1	6.9	7.0	8.2	7.8		5.5	5.0	5.7	7.3	8.4	8.7	8.7	8.5	8.9	8.9
2.1	2.0	2.3	2.5	2.6		2.9	2.9	2.6	2.3	2.3	1.9	2.0	1.8	1.8	
2.8	3.0	3.3	3.2	3.1											
1.1	1.1		1.1			1.5	1.4	1.2	1.1	1.1	1.1	0.9			
			1.7	1.8		1.5	1.5	1.3	1.2	1.0	0.9		0.9	0.9	0.9
30.1	30.3	28.4	26.2	25.9		29.6	29.8	27.5	23.4	23.7	23.7	24.3	24.3	23.7	22.2
70.1	67.9	65.0	65.0	64.1		67.5	67.1	65.4	62.2	62.9	62.2	62.5	61.8	61.9	60.3

Blank spaces indicate not in market or data not available.

SOURCES: 1926, see sources to Exhibit IV-7. 1928–1933, Ohio Petroleum Marketers Association, Inc. for records of individual companies; American Petroleum Institute, *Petroleum Facts and Figures*, Ninth Edition, 1950, pp. 388–392, for state motor fuel gallonage taxed. 1934–1952, all data from Standard Oil Company (Ohio).

meeting competitive market prices, regardless of their own costs of operation. The situation of the Standard Oil Company (Ohio) was summarized by the management in the company's annual report for 1928 as follows:

The over-production of oil and gasoline in recent years has resulted in an over-production of distribution facilities. As a class, the marketing companies operating their own refineries have tended to base their selling price of gasoline upon their own costs rather than upon the spot market for tank car gasoline. The past few years, therefore, have been characterized by rather wide margins between retail service station prices and the market tank car price of gasoline. Nowhere, perhaps, has this spread been so wide as in Ohio. The result of this wide margin has been the attraction into the distribution end of the business of many new people, and the over-development of distribution facilities. The gallonage of the industry per service station and per pump has steadily declined as a result of this over-expansion. Price cutting has been the method of most of the new-comers in the distribution end of the business. This price cutting not being met, the result has been an increasing proportion of the business to our competitors.

The situation outlined above has been more or

EXHIBIT IV-10. PERCENTAGE OF THE GASOLINE MARKET

	1926	1927	1928	1929	1930	1931	1932	1933	1934	1935	1936
Gasoline Sales †											
(*Millions of Gallons*)	242	289	285	411	429	451	418	407	439	472	526
Three Largest Marketers in 1926											
(*Percentage of Market*)											
Standard Oil Co. (Ind.)	35.5%							25.9%	25.1%	23.5%	23.1%
Sinclair Oil Corporation	10.8							5.5	5.6	6.0	6.0
Shell Oil Company	8.8							9.7	9.8	9.4	9.4
Total	55.1							41.1	40.5	38.9	38.5
All Other Marketers											
(*Percentage of Market*)											
The Texas Company	3.8							8.2	8.6	8.4	8.4
Pure Oil Company	3.4							1.7	2.1	2.0	2.2
Aetna Oil Service Co.										0.3	0.3
Cities Service Company	—							1.9	1.9	2.1	2.0
Continental Oil Co.	—							1.0	1.0	1.0	1.1
Deep Rock Oil Co.										0.2	0.3
Gulf Oil Corporation	—							3.7	4.2	3.9	4.0
Johnson Oil Ref. Co.										0.9	0.9
Mid-Continent Pet. Co.										3.0	3.0
The Ohio Oil Company	—							5.6	5.1	3.9	4.8
Phillips Petroleum Co.	—							3.2	3.4	3.7	3.7
Socony-Vacuum Oil Co.	—							2.1	2.6	2.8	2.9
Stoll Oil Ref. Co.										0.4	0.5
Sun Oil Company	—							—	—	—	—
National Ref. Co.										1.0	0.9
Barnsdall Oil Co.										0.1	0.2
Spur Distributing Co.										0.5	0.4
Miscellaneous Marketers	37.7							31.5	30.6	26.9	25.9
Total	44.9							58.9	59.5	61.1	61.5

† Motor-fuel gallonage taxed. See American Petroleum Institute, *Petroleum Facts and Figures*, Ninth Edition, 1950, pp. 388–392; Tenth Edition, 1952, p. 207. Figures for 1951 and 1952 supplied by A.P.I. (Compiled from records of Bureau of Public Roads.)

— Indicates were not in market so far as can be determined from available records.

less typical of the entire country, but from our observation the situation in Ohio has been much more acute than in most other parts of the country.

Last May, therefore, the new management was confronted with the problem of a vicious circle, to wit: a steadily declining gallonage and a resulting rise in cost per gallon. If our company continued to ask prices above the market fixed by our competitors, the gallonage would continue to decline and the costs would continue to rise. *The only solution appeared to be to meet the market,*[30] and reduce our costs by procuring a volume of sales sufficient to operate our equipment and organization at their maximum capacity. This appeared to be simply invoking one of the fundamental principles on which Standard Oil was founded, to-wit, a narrow margin of profit on a large volume of sales economically made.

The Standard Oil Company (Indiana) was likewise forced to abandon its policy of estab-

[30] Italics added by authors.

lishing base prices at its refineries and of attempting to secure those prices plus freight to all destinations. The Standard Oil Company (Indiana), however, made the adjustment somewhat tardily and did not begin to meet vigorously the competitive prices of the newcomers entering its markets from the Mid-Continent region until 1934 (see discussion in Chapter Seven).

Finally, the competitive conditions which developed under the pressure of large crude oil supplies led the established marketers to make many changes in their selling programs in an effort to protect their market positions. Increased attention was given to the use of advertising, the development of brand names, the upgrading of the quality of products, and the improvement of service station facilities and services. The intense competitive conditions of the time undoubtedly also contributed to the development of the practice of signing ex-

IN INDIANA HELD BY PRINCIPAL MARKETERS: 1926–1952

1937	1938	1939	1940	1941	1942	1943	1944	1945	1946	1947	1948	1949	1950	1951	1952
570	563	599	641	722	620	503	486	579	750	837	911	972	1,079	1,283	1,358
22.9%	24.0%	22.3%	21.5%	20.6%	22.3%	28.4%	23.4%	21.5%	21.7%	20.1%	19.5%	19.1%	18.6%	19.1%	18.5%
5.7	5.5	5.3	5.2	5.0	4.9	5.2	6.3	5.2	5.6	5.5	5.7	5.2	5.6	5.6	5.5
8.5	8.5	8.4	8.1	7.9	8.2	10.5	10.8	9.5	9.8	9.9	9.7	9.8	9.6	9.3	8.6
37.1	38.0	36.0	34.8	33.5	35.4	44.1	40.5	36.2	37.1	35.5	34.9	34.1	33.8	34.0	32.6
8.0	7.8	7.3	6.8	6.5	6.2	5.8	5.8	5.9	6.4	6.4	6.3	6.3	5.6	5.9	5.8
2.3	2.1	2.2	2.1	2.0	2.1	2.2	2.2	2.4	2.5	2.3	2.1	2.0	1.9	2.0	1.9
0.3	0.3	0.3	0.3	0.5	0.5	0.6	0.6	0.5	0.5	0.5	0.4	0.4	0.3	0.3	0.4
2.1	1.9	2.0	1.9	1.8	1.9	2.0	2.2	2.0	2.1	2.5	2.7	2.4	2.6	2.7	2.6
1.0	1.0	0.9	0.8	0.8	0.4	0.8	0.8	0.7	0.7	0.6	0.7	0.7	0.6	0.6	0.6
0.3	0.3	0.4	0.4	0.2	0.3	0.3	0.3	0.2	0.1	0.1	0.1	0.1	0.1	0.1	0.1
4.2	4.3	4.1	4.1	4.0	3.8	4.1	4.0	4.1	4.3	4.1	3.9	3.9	3.9	3.5	3.8
0.8	1.0	1.0	1.1	1.1	1.0	0.9	0.8	0.8	0.8	0.8	1.1	0.7	0.3	0.3	0.3
2.9	2.9	3.0	2.6	2.4	2.5	2.6	2.4	2.5	2.8	2.7	2.4	2.5	2.3	2.3	2.3
4.6	4.7	4.8	4.8	4.5	4.5	4.8	4.7	4.8	5.5	5.5	5.5	5.4	5.6	5.4	5.6
3.4	3.2	3.2	3.3	3.2	3.1	3.1	3.2	3.0	3.0	3.0	2.6	2.5	2.3	2.1	1.8
3.3	3.9	4.1	4.2	4.6	4.8	5.5	5.8	5.8	6.1	5.5	5.2	4.9	3.4	4.3	4.2
0.4	0.4	0.4	0.4	0.5	0.4	0.4	0.4	0.5	0.4	0.4	0.4	0.4	0.4	0.4	0.3
			0.1	0.1	0.1	0.1	0.1	0.3	0.3	1.0	1.0	0.9	0.9	1.0	1.4
0.8	0.7	0.8	0.8	0.6	0.7	0.8	0.1	—	—	—	—	*	*	0.1	*
0.2	0.2														
0.4	0.5	0.4	0.5	0.6	0.5	0.3	0.2	0.2	0.3	0.4	0.3	0.4	0.4	0.5	0.4
27.9	26.8	29.1	31.0	33.1	31.8	21.6	25.9	30.1	27.1	28.7	30.4	32.4	36.6	34.5	35.9
62.9	62.0	64.0	65.2	66.5	64.6	55.9	59.5	63.8	62.9	64.5	65.1	65.9	67.2	66.0	67.4

* Indicates were in market but share of market was negligible.
Blank space indicates information not available.

SOURCES: See sources to Exhibit IV-7, p. 102.

clusive contracts with dealers and distributors. In addition, the declining volume per station which resulted from the extensive building of marketing facilities prompted many marketing organizations to engage in the distribution of tires, batteries, and other automotive accessories as an aid in carrying the cost of their retail outlets.

VI. MODIFICATION OF THE PRESSURE OF CRUDE OIL BY THE PRORATIONING LAWS

The large crude oil supplies which developed in the late 1920's, together with the waste which accompanied wide-open production of flush fields, created a widespread interest among state, industry, and government agencies in measures for the regulation of crude oil production and eventually led to the enactment of the prorationing laws by the various producing states. These laws were developed only after several years of trial and error and much bitter controversy in the courts and throughout the industry. By 1935, however, most of the major oil producing states had developed some mechanism for controlling crude oil production.

The prorationing laws were developed and are administered by the states under various state laws covering the conservation of natural resources and under basic property laws assuring equality of opportunity to all landowners in an oil field. The Federal Government contributed to the state programs in four important respects. First, Congress approved in 1935 the Interstate Compact to Conserve Oil and Gas which gave the member states a means of taking cooperative action in the development of their conservation programs. The members of the Compact assume a moral, although not legal, obligation to enact and enforce laws to prevent physical waste, to cooper-

EXHIBIT IV-11. PERCENTAGE OF THE GASOLINE MARKET

	1926	1927	1928	1929	1930	1931	1932	1933	1934	1935	1936
Gasoline Sales †											
(Millions of Gallons)	588	692	733	1,048	929	1,082	1,010	1,025	1,114	1,171	1,277
Three Largest Marketers in 1926											
(Percentage of Market)											
The Atlantic Refining Co.	44.5%							22.9%	22.0%	21.7%	21.0%
Gulf Oil Corporation	20.8							9.5	9.5	8.9	9.0
Sinclair Oil Corporation	6.8							4.6	4.6	4.5	4.4
Total	72.1							37.0	36.1	35.1	34.4
All Other Marketers											
(Percentage of Market)											
The Texas Company	4.7							3.3	3.3	3.4	3.5
Tide Water Associated Oil Co.	4.3							2.5	2.5	2.5	2.5
Pure Oil Company	3.8							1.7	1.7	1.7	1.6
Standard Oil Co. (Calif.)	—							—	—	—	—
Cities Service Company	—							2.0	2.0	2.0	1.0
Standard Oil Co. (New Jersey)	—							9.4	9.4	10.0	11.4
Shell Oil Company	—							1.4	1.4	1.4	2.0
Socony-Vacuum Oil Co.	—							6.0	6.0	6.5	7.0
Standard Oil Co. (Ind.)	—							6.1	6.1	6.1	6.2
Standard Oil Co. (Ohio)	—							1.7	1.7	1.7	1.7
Sun Oil Company	—							10.9	10.9	10.7	9.6
Miscellaneous Marketers	15.1							18.0	18.9	18.9	19.1
Total	27.9							63.0	63.9	64.9	65.6

† Motor-fuel gallonage taxed. See American Petroleum Institute, *Petroleum Facts and Figures*, Ninth Edition, 1950, pp. 388–392; Tenth Edition, 1952, p. 207. Figures for 1951 and 1952 supplied by A.P.I. (Compiled from records of Bureau of Public Roads.)

— Indicates were not in market as far as can be determined from available records.

ate in carrying out the programs of the Interstate Oil Compact Commission, and to deny access to commerce of oil produced in violation of state statutes. The term "physical waste" is subject to many interpretations and is now sometimes taken to include the economic waste associated with production in excess of transportation, refining, and marketing facilities or in excess of market demand.[31]

The Federal Government made a second important contribution to the prorationing laws in 1935 by passage of the Connally Act. This act prohibits the transportation in interstate commerce of any oil produced in violation of a state's conservation laws and thus gave the states a powerful means of enforcing their conservation programs. The Federal Government has made a third contribution to the prorationing programs of the states through the action of the Bureau of Mines in publishing findings of fact with regard to demand-supply conditions in the industry which are useful to the states in setting their allowables. Finally, the Federal Government has contributed to the prorationing program through the enactment, beginning in 1932, of tariffs and various other measures to control the flow of foreign oil into the United States.

The programs of conservation and prorationing have developed along different lines in the various states and now involve a fairly complicated set of regulations covering the location, spacing, drilling, operation, and abandonment of wells and the maintenance of specified gas-oil and water-oil ratios. In general, however, the prorationing laws of most of the states which have such laws have two fundamental objectives: (1) the prevention of the waste of oil and gas resources, and (2) the protection of the correlative rights of property owners in underground reservoirs. To accomplish these ends, the prorationing programs of the major producing states have gradually come to embody three principal features as outlined in the following paragraphs.

[31] See American Bar Association, Section of Mineral Law, *Conservation of Oil and Gas, A Legal History, 1948*, edited by Blakely M. Murphy, Part III, pp. 572–573. The laws of some states, however, forbid the adjustment of production to market demand.

IN PENNSYLVANIA HELD BY PRINCIPAL MARKETERS: 1926–1952

1937	1938	1939	1940	1941	1942	1943	1944	1945	1946	1947	1948	1949	1950	1951	1952
1,410	1,397	1,476	1,575	1,694	1,371	1,046	1,109	1,246	1,653	1,801	1,961	2,052	2,210	2,359	2,467
19.8%	19.7%	20.5%	20.5%	20.5%	20.5%	20.0%	19.5%	20.0%	20.5%	21.3%	21.6%	22.5%	22.6%	22.5%	21.1%
9.1	8.9	9.5	9.5	9.5	10.0	10.0	10.0	9.5	9.0	9.4	9.2	10.2	10.4	10.0	9.7
4.3	4.7	4.5	4.5	4.8	4.5	5.8	6.8	7.3	7.5	6.7	7.0	7.3	7.9	7.4	7.0
33.2	33.3	34.5	34.5	34.8	35.0	35.8	36.3	36.8	37.0	37.4	37.8	40.0	40.9	39.9	37.8
3.6	3.7	4.3	4.5	4.5	5.1	5.1	5.0	5.1	5.5	6.3	6.1	6.5	6.8	6.8	6.5
2.3	2.3	2.5	2.3	2.5	2.5	2.7	2.7	2.8	2.7	2.3	2.1	2.3	2.3	2.3	2.4
1.9	1.6	0.7	0.5	0.7	0.5	0.2	0.5	0.8	1.0	0.5	0.5	0.5	—	—	—
—	—	—	—	—	—	—	—	—	—	—	0.0	0.3	2.5	0.7	2.3
1.6	1.2	1.5	1.8	2.3	2.0	2.3	2.2	2.2	2.5	2.3	2.6	3.1	3.3	3.4	3.2
12.5	12.7	14.0	14.4	15.3	14.6	14.7	14.8	14.9	14.8	15.1	15.1	15.4	15.3	16.1	16.2
2.0	1.6	1.6	1.0	0.5	0.2	0.1	0.2	0.2	0.2	0.2	0.2	0.1	0.1	*	0.1
6.7	6.9	7.0	7.3	7.0	7.2	7.0	7.5	7.5	7.7	7.7	7.5	7.4	7.1	7.0	6.9
6.1	6.2	6.6	6.6	6.7	7.0	7.0	6.7	6.7	7.0	6.9	6.7	6.7	6.0	5.9	5.4
1.7	1.6	1.5	1.2	1.2	1.2	1.2	1.3	1.2	1.3	1.2	1.2	0.5	—	—	—
9.8	9.6	9.7	9.8	9.9	9.5	9.3	9.8	9.2	9.0	9.5	9.8	10.2	10.4	10.9	11.5
18.6	19.3	16.1	16.1	14.6	15.2	14.6	13.0	12.6	11.3	10.6	10.4	7.0	7.3	7.0	7.7
66.8	66.7	65.5	65.5	65.2	65.0	64.2	63.7	63.2	63.0	62.6	62.2	60.0	59.1	60.1	62.2

* Indicates were in market but share of market was negligible.
Blank space indicates information not available.

SOURCE: See sources to Exhibit IV-7, p. 102.

First, and most important, the conservation laws of most of the states contain provisions of some type for preventing production in excess of a field's maximum efficient rate. Wide-open production under the rule of capture frequently left more oil in the ground than was recovered because the principal sources of reservoir energy, water and gas dissolved in the oil or associated with it, were dissipated irregularly or at uneconomic rates. In addition, more wells were frequently drilled into a pool than were necessary to produce the oil efficiently or than were desirable in terms of realizing the maximum ultimate recovery. Many of the provisions of the prorationing laws therefore have been designed to regulate the drilling and operation of wells in each pool in accordance with the reservoir characteristics in order that the natural gas-oil and water-oil pressures will not be wasted and the ultimate recovery thereby jeopardized.

A second important group of provisions in the prorationing laws are designed to allocate the production of a field fairly among the various property holders. Much trial and error have accompanied the development of the allocation formulas, and in many states the formulas still leave much to be desired. At the outset, production was frequently allocated among leaseholders on a flat per-well basis or on a per-well basis modified to take into account individual well characteristics such as bottom-hole pressures, gas-oil ratios, sand thicknesses, and production under open-flow conditions. Under these formulas, the production allowed from a particular lease could be raised by drilling more wells on the property. Lease operators therefore promptly began to drill many more wells than were necessary or desirable in order to capture as much of the oil in the reservoir as possible. The compulsion of the rule of capture which had previously applied to both the producing and drilling of wells was thus under the new prorationing laws merely transferred to and concentrated on the drilling of wells.

As the number of wells increased beyond that necessary to produce a field's allowable, further reductions in the per-well allotments became necessary. As a consequence, development costs per barrel of crude oil produced tended to rise, and in some fields the per-well allowable became so small that the well operator had no chance to recover his investment in a reasonable period of time. In recognition of these circumstances, most of the major producing states later adopted regulations controlling the spacing of wells and in a number of instances embodied acreage factors in their allocation formulas. Moreover, in recent years progress has been made in some of the states toward the operation of oil pools on a unitized basis. Under unit operation the property owners share in the total development cost and output of a field in accordance with a pre-arranged formula, and competitive drilling and producing in the field are thereby eliminated.

The third major feature of the prorationing laws has been the adjustment of production to market demand at times when production at maximum efficient rates would produce more oil than the market could readily absorb. This matter has been one of the most controversial aspects of the entire prorationing program and cannot be discussed here at any great length. Suffice it to say that those who favor the adjustment of production to market demand offer three general arguments in support of their position: [32] First, it is contended that the curtailment of production to market demand is necessary to protect the correlative rights of the leaseholders to the underground reservoirs. It is argued that in the absence of such restraints some producers of a pool would be able to sell their output while others could not and that the latter would thus suffer drainage of their properties. Second, it is contended that the adjustment of production to market demand is necessary as a conservation measure because the irregular withdrawals which would result from the fact that some producers could sell while others could not would interfere with the orderly development of a field and impair ultimate recovery. Finally, it is pointed out that a producer who cannot sell his oil in times of slack demand might store the oil

above ground, but that such a course of action would involve a large investment in tankage, hazards of fire and explosion, and waste because of the volatile character of the oil, and would be generally less desirable from an economic standpoint than storage of the oil underground.

In reply to these arguments, the opponents of prorationing to market demand point out that the amount of oil the market can absorb is a function of price and that if production were continued at the maximum efficient rates the price would fall in times of slack demand, the market would thereby be enlarged, and demand and supply would be brought into balance at a lower price level. The validity of this argument rests to a considerable extent on the assumption that the short-run demand for refined products is fairly elastic, a point which is certainly open to question, and on the amount of crude oil which happens to become available in a particular time period. At certain times in the history of the industry, the supplies of crude oil have unquestionably been so great that it would have been impossible to bring about a satisfactory adjustment of supply to demand through lower prices without serious disruption of the industry and the incurrence of economic waste in one form or another.

In 1952, 22 states were members of the Interstate Oil Compact Commission.[33] In addition, California had a conservation program which was carried out on a voluntary basis through the Conservation Committee of the California Oil Producer's Association. Wyoming, another important producing state, also had a conservation program, although it was not a member of the Interstate Oil Compact Commission and did not have comprehensive conservation laws.[34] The 22 members of the Commission, together with California and Wyoming, accounted for about 99.7% of the domestic crude oil production in 1952.

---

[32] See, for example, Hines H. Baker, *Achievements and Unsolved Problems in Oil and Gas Conservation*, a pamphlet embodying the substance of an address delivered before the Spring Meeting of the Southwestern District, American Petroleum Institute, Division of Production, at Galveston, Texas, March 10, 1949.

[33] Texas, Oklahoma, Louisiana, New Mexico, Kansas, Arkansas, Michigan, Florida, Alabama, Mississippi, Indiana, Tennessee, Illinois, Ohio, Colorado, Kentucky, Montana, New York, West Virginia, Pennsylvania, Arizona, and Georgia, the latter two being associate members.

[34] For a discussion of the prorationing laws of the individual states see American Bar Association, Section of Mineral Law, *Conservation of Oil and Gas, A Legal History, 1948*, edited by Blakely M. Murphy, Part II.

The 22 members of the Interstate Oil Compact Commission had a variety of different conservation programs. About 12 of the member states had comprehensive conservation laws and effective conservation programs.[35] These 12 states accounted for about 90.5% of the crude oil production in 1952. The remaining 10 members of the Interstate Oil Compact Commission had somewhat less effective conservation laws, or in some cases no laws at all. Two of these 10 states, Colorado and Montana, however, had been able to work out fairly satisfactory conservation procedures despite the absence of a fully adequate legal background for them.

At least six of the major producing states, and particularly the state of Texas, had prorationing programs which either explicitly in the state law or through administrative action provided for some adjustment of production allowables to market demand.[36] These six states accounted for about 72.6% of the total crude oil production in 1952. The laws of a few states, such as Mississippi, contained strong measures for the prevention of waste and the protection of the correlative rights of leaseholders but expressly forbid the adjustment of production to market demand.

The economic and legal implications of the conservation laws have for many years been a subject of great controversy in the oil industry. It is generally agreed, however, and there can be no question of the fact in the light of Exhibits IV-1 and IV-2, that the conservation laws provided for the more orderly development of oil fields and reduced the frequency and amplitude of crude oil price fluctuations.[37] To the extent that the conservation laws have

accomplished these ends, they have modified one of the major forces for forward integration from the producing level of the industry into refining and marketing operations. Since about 1935, the crude oil producer, notwithstanding special situations which have developed from time to time such as in the Illinois fields in 1938 and 1939, has had reasonable assurance that he could sell all the oil he was allowed to produce at the prevailing market prices on approximately equal terms with all other producers in the field, integrated or nonintegrated. The pressure of large crude oil supplies as a motivating force for forward integration has thus been of much less significance since 1935 than it was in earlier years.

It is important to note, however, that considerable forward integration is still undertaken today by crude oil producers as a means of disposing of their output. As will be noted in Chapter Seven, for example, crude oil producers have recently built crude oil pipe lines and other facilities in the Wyoming area as a means of providing a market outlet for their shut-in crude oil production. Similarly, producing interests have been planning the construction of refineries and pipe lines in Canada and in the Williston Basin of North Dakota as a means of providing an outlet for the newly discovered crude oil reserves in those two areas.

It is also important to note that while the prorationing laws have reduced the possibility of large crude oil supplies being thrown on the market and precipitating excessive competition for market outlets as frequently happened before 1935, the refiner still has a strong need for assured market outlets to protect his operations at times when the supply of refined products is running ahead of demand. As will be noted in Chapter Nine, the refining segment of the industry often tends to overproduce in times of slack demand because of the high fixed cost of refining equipment. The refiner therefore is still under considerable compulsion to integrate forward, although his need of assured outlets is not so great as it was before the development of the prorationing laws removed from the industry much of the hazard of the great crude oil supplies which characterized the period 1920–1935.

---

[35] Texas, Oklahoma, Louisiana, New Mexico, Kansas, Arkansas, Michigan, Florida, Alabama, Mississippi, Georgia, and Arizona.

[36] The other five states were Oklahoma, Louisiana, New Mexico, Kansas, and Arkansas. The adjustment of allowables to market demand in these states was, however, of far less importance than in the state of Texas.

[37] In times of slackening demand the supply of crude oil is often curtailed by state regulatory action before a decline in prices takes place. In many other petroleum markets a decline in prices is the means of bringing about a new adjustment of supply to a slackened demand. Crude oil producers may often suffer a loss in profits as a result of a loss in volume in times of slackened demand even though no reduction in crude oil prices takes place. See discussion in Chapter Five.

VII. SUMMARY

1. One of the most important circumstances contributing to the growth of vertical integration in the oil industry was the great crude oil supplies which were from time to time thrown onto the market in the period before the adoption of the conservation laws. The large supplies were occasioned by fortuitous oil discoveries and by legal and economic compulsions which prompted leaseholders to produce their properties as rapidly as possible once a new field was discovered.

2. The pressure of large crude oil supplies as a motivation for forward integration was particularly significant in the period extending from about 1920 to 1935. During these years a remarkable series of crude oil discoveries brought into being a far greater supply of crude oil than the market could readily absorb and generated much new competition at the producing level of the industry. As the large supplies of crude oil pressed forward into the market, companies operating at all levels of the industry were prompted to undertake forward integration programs as a means of gaining and securing their market outlets.

3. The large crude oil supplies and the forward integration moves of producing and refining companies, along with certain other factors, generated some extremely tough competition in the wholesale and retail markets. In the course of the intense struggle for markets and market outlets which developed in the period 1926 to 1935, all the leading marketers suffered a loss in their share of the market in their home states and nearly all of them a loss in their share of the total United States market.

4. As the established marketers sought to defend their positions against the onslaughts of new competition arising in their markets under the pressure of the large supplies of crude oil, they embarked on many new programs, some of which involved forward or backward integration. Forward integration into retailing operations was frequently undertaken to prevent the capture of market outlets by competitors and both backward and forward integration were undertaken in an effort to reduce costs of operation or to secure alternative sources of profits.

5. The development of the conservation laws in the period 1930 to 1935 reduced the likelihood that the discovery of new oil fields would generate crude oil supplies far in excess of market requirements and thus modified one of the important pressures for forward integration by crude oil producers. Forward integration is nevertheless still undertaken rather frequently by crude oil producers as a means of providing or improving the market outlets for their output.

CHAPTER FIVE

The Ebb and Flow of Profit Opportunities

ONE of the most important explanations for the development of all types of integrated structures in the oil industry in all time periods may be found in the contribution which vertical integration makes toward stabilizing a company's profit position. The gross margins and profits available at the different levels of the industry are continually shifting and changing, and the movements at one level frequently differ both time-wise and direction-wise from the movements at another. Gross margins and profits may thus be decreasing at one level while they are stable or increasing at other levels. By operating across two or more levels of the industry, a company may therefore gain considerable protection against wide fluctuations in its profit position. The president of one of the largest integrated companies summarized the situation as follows: "The chief explanation for the development of vertical integration in the oil industry may be found in the fact that vertical integration puts a company in a position to take advantage of the ebb and flow of profit opportunities at the different levels of the industry."

In gaining protection against wide fluctuations in its profit position, an integrated company not only avoids large, short-term losses but also foregoes the opportunity for large, short-term gains. As a result, the average profit opportunity available to the integrated company over the long run may not be much, if any, higher than that available to a nonintegrated company which is successful in weathering the economic storms which may arise from time to time in its particular phase of the business. There have always been small, nonintegrated operators in the oil industry who have frankly recognized that their profit experience was likely to be unstable but who have anticipated that their earnings in good times would be sufficient to tide them over the periods of adversity, provided that the earnings

were not withdrawn from the business for other use.

The stability of earnings which vertical integration often provides is nevertheless an extremely important asset to most companies under most types of circumstances. Of paramount significance is the fact that a company with stable earnings has a uniform flow of funds coming into the business which may be used for new capital investments. Stability of earnings likewise enhances the ability of a company to borrow or to float new stock issues when its capital needs exceed its own immediate resources. An integrated company drawing profits from several different levels of the industry can therefore often plan and carry out long-range programs of capital investments on a more orderly and efficient basis than can a nonintegrated company whose profits are continually fluctuating in accordance with economic changes at a single level of the industry. New plant facilities can be constructed at the times when business circumstances indicate that they should be constructed rather than only at the times when funds happen to be available for them.

Stability of earnings affords many other advantages. It permits a company to offer continuing employment to management and labor, to initiate and carry out long-range programs of research and development on an uninterrupted basis, and to give the stockholder a more uniform return on his investment. It likewise facilitates the development of pension plans and other employee benefits and contributes to stability in our national business expenditures for capital goods and in our national consumer purchasing power. For all these reasons, stability of earnings contributes much to the health and security of the individual firm and also to the health and security of our entire industrial economy.

The contribution of vertical integration toward the stabilization of company profits has not, however, often been recognized *explicitly* in integration decisions. We found, in fact, only a few cases where it could be said that a company made a particular integration decision primarily because its management believed that the move would *in general* help to stabilize the company's profit position. As will become clear from the discussion throughout this book, integration actions have usually been taken to solve the problems or capitalize on the opportunities of a particular situation. A marketer may, for example, find that he has difficulty in securing his supplies at reasonable prices in times of shortage and integrate backward into refining to solve his problem. Similarly, a refiner may see that crude oil producers are currently making good profits in a particular area, decide that "the grass is greener on the other side of the fence," and integrate into crude oil producing operations to secure the profit he thinks is available. Regardless, however, of the immediate reasons which may prompt vertical integration, once a company embarks on such a program it often gains in profit stability, secures some protection from the short-term economic shocks developing from time to time in individual phases of the business, and thus strengthens its opportunities for growth and survival.

The purpose of this chapter is to examine as closely as the available data will permit the effect which vertical integration has on the stability of a company's earnings. As our first approach to the problem, we shall examine: (a) the behavior of the gross margins at the producing, refining, wholesaling, and retailing levels of the industry, (b) the effect of various types of integration on the stability of *monthly* gross margins, and (c) the effect of various types of integration on the stability of *yearly* gross margins. From this examination of gross margins we shall draw certain *limited inferences* with regard to the effect of vertical integration on the stability of earnings. In the concluding section of the chapter, we shall then make a direct examination of the actual return on borrowed and invested capital earned by various groups of integrated and nonintegrated oil companies in the period 1920–1952. Our analysis of actual earnings was limited somewhat by the lack of published data on the operations of certain types of oil companies. The

analysis serves, however, to corroborate the inferences drawn from the examination of gross margins.

Throughout the discussion in this chapter we shall be concerned primarily with effects rather than causes. In Chapter Six, however, we shall direct attention to the underlying business and economic forces which bring about the dissimilarities in profit fluctuations at the different levels of the industry.

I. THE GROSS MARGINS AT THE DIFFERENT LEVELS OF THE INDUSTRY

The four gross margins which we examined are represented graphically in Exhibit V-1. The margins were not in all cases precisely the ones we would have liked to use, but we were necessarily limited in our selection by the availability of price records which could be projected backward to 1920 on a continuous basis. It will be noted, for example, that it was necessary to include refined products transportation activities with the wholesaling gross margin and crude oil transportation activities with the refining gross margin. However, since transportation costs change rather slowly, we do not believe that this arrangement impairs seriously the usefulness of the wholesaling and refining margins as general indicators of the short-term (i.e., monthly or yearly) fluctuations in the profit opportunities at the wholesaling and refining levels of the industry. As will be noted in later discussion, none of the gross margin series is particularly useful as an indicator of long-term trends in profit opportunities because, in the long term, changes in transportation and other costs of operation take place which may offset or accentuate the gross margin changes.

The record of the four gross margins in the Mid-Continent region for the period 1920–1952 is shown by months in Exhibit V-2. The Mid-Continent region was selected for analysis as a matter of convenience in compiling the statistical records; use of the Texas Gulf Coast or the Atlantic seaboard would, however, have been equally appropriate and would have yielded approximately the same general conclusions as we shall draw from our study of the Mid-Continent region. As will become clear in the following discussion, the gross margin series are in all cases designed to reflect the timing, direction, and amplitude of the fluctuations in

EXHIBIT V-1. PICTORIAL REPRESENTATION OF INDUSTRY GROSS MARGINS

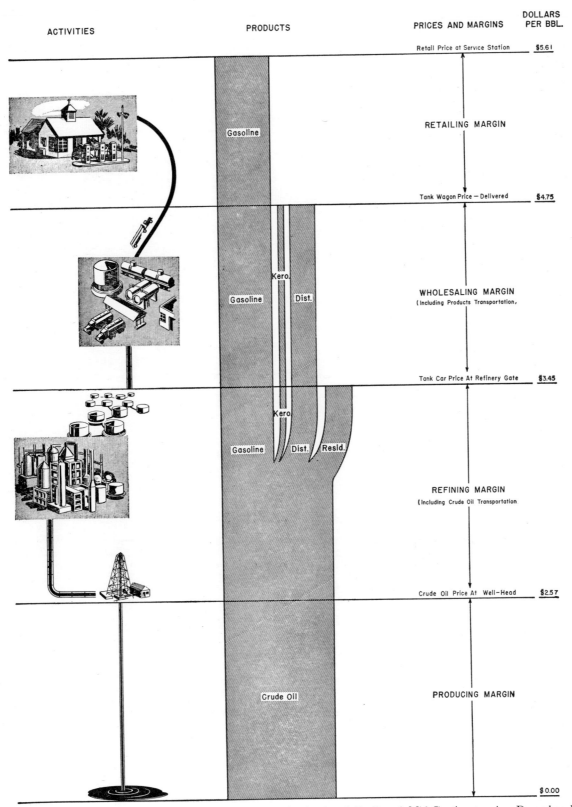

ACTIVITIES	PRODUCTS	PRICES AND MARGINS	DOLLARS PER BBL.
		Retail Price at Service Station	$5.61
	Gasoline	RETAILING MARGIN	
		Tank Wagon Price — Delivered	$4.75
	Gasoline Kero. Dist.	WHOLESALING MARGIN (Including Products Transportation)	
		Tank Car Price At Refinery Gate	$3.45
	Gasoline Kero. Dist. Resid.	REFINING MARGIN (Including Crude Oil Transportation)	
		Crude Oil Price At Well-Head	$2.57
	Crude Oil	PRODUCING MARGIN	
			$0.00

Note: Prices and margins are dollars per barrel of crude oil refined and distributed, Mid-Continent region, December, 1950.

EXHIBIT V-2. MONTHLY GROSS MARGINS AVAILABLE AT THE PRODUCING, REFINING, WHOLESALING, AND RETAILING LEVELS OF THE INDUSTRY

Mid-Continent Area: 1920–1952

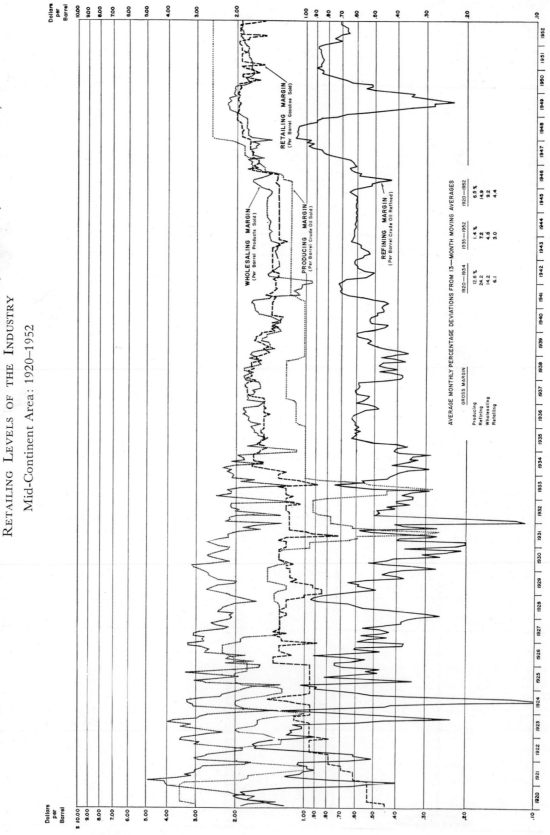

the unit gross margins available at the separate levels of the industry rather than to reflect the exact dollars and cents amount of the margin at each level. Had the latter purpose been our objective, many detailed refinements in the methods of computation would have been necessary, and the preparation of a comparable series for the entire period would have been virtually impossible.

Description of the Gross Margins:

For the purposes of the analysis, the producing level of the industry was defined as comprising the activities involved in finding oil, developing producing properties, and lifting oil to the well-head. To represent the producer's gross margin we used the average monthly price per barrel of 36° gravity Mid-Continent crude oil at the well-head. Since crude oil originates with the producer, he does not have a "gross margin" which is a difference between buying and selling prices as do firms at other levels of the industry. The crude oil price at the well-head, however, represents the amount per barrel which the producer has available to cover his finding, drilling, lifting, and other costs of operation and to provide his profit. The movements in crude oil prices may therefore be used as an indicator of the movements in profit opportunities at the producing level in the same sense that movements in gross margins may be used as indicators of the movements in profit opportunities at other levels of the industry.

The refining level of the industry was defined in the analysis as comprising the activities involved in getting oil from the well-head to the refinery, through the refining process, and into the tank car markets at the refinery gate (see Exhibit V-1). The refiner's gross margin was represented by the difference between the crude oil price and the tank car prices of the refined products secured from a barrel of crude oil. The yields of the different products were developed from the U. S. Bureau of Mines reports on the monthly output of refineries in the Mid-Continent area, which is comprised of Oklahoma, Kansas, Missouri, Arkansas, Inland Texas, and Inland Louisiana.[1] The percentage

yields of each product were multiplied by the Oklahoma tank car prices,[2] as reported in trade journals, to obtain the realization per barrel of crude oil run, and the crude oil price was then deducted from the latter figure to obtain the refiner's margin. The general method of computation is illustrated in Exhibit V-3 which shows the calculations for December 1950.

EXHIBIT V-3. CALCULATION OF REFINER'S GROSS MARGIN FOR DECEMBER 1950

Products	Monthly Yield, Total Barrels	Yield Per Barrel Run	Oklahoma Tank Car Price Per Barrel	Realization
Gasolines and Naphthas	11,842,000	.47	$4.36	$2.05
Kerosene	1,233,000	.05	3.80	.19
Distillate Fuel Oils and Gas Oil	5,782,000	.23	3.46	.79
Residual Fuel Oil and Still Gas	6,164,000	.24	1.71	.42
Loss in Refining	143,000	.01	—	—
	25,164,000	1.00		$3.45
Crude Oil Price Per Barrel				2.57
Refiner's Gross Margin Per Barrel Refined				$0.88

The prices used for gasoline were the monthly averages of the low quotations; the prices of all other products were the monthly averages of the high and the low quotations for the period 1920–1943 and the monthly averages of the low quotations for the period 1943–1952.[3] Because of the difficulties involved in segregating and pricing the various grades of gasoline, all the gasoline output was priced at

---

[1] For the years 1920–1930 the figures were computed from U. S. Bureau of Mines, *Petroleum Refining Statistics,* Bulletins Nos. 280, 289, 297, 339, and 367, by G. R. Hopkins. For the years 1931–1950 the figures were compiled by the American Petroleum Institute from U. S. Bureau of Mines data. For the years 1951 and 1952 the figures were computed from U. S. Bureau of Mines, *Mineral Industry Surveys,* "Crude Petroleum and Petroleum Products," Monthly Petroleum Statements Nos. 347 and 359, December 1951 and December 1952.

[2] The tank car price is an f.o.b. refinery price in tank car lots and thus represents the price at which a refiner might sell through brokers or to jobbers if he had no marketing facilities.

[3] For the years 1920–1938, inclusive, prices for the various products were taken from Sidney A. Swensrud, "The Relation Between Crude Oil and Product Prices," *Bulletin of the American Association of Petroleum Geologists,* Volume 23, No. 6, June 1939. For the years 1939–1950 a continuation of the price series used by Swensrud was furnished to us by the Standard Oil Company (Ohio). The company used the averages of the high and low quotations for products other than gasoline until prices were placed under wartime controls during 1943. After the price controls were removed, the averages of the low quotations were used. For the years 1951 and 1952 prices were taken from *Platt's Oil Price Handbooks.*

the price of the regular grade. The yield of lubricating oils and waxes was included and priced with the yield of distillate fuel oils and gas oil, and the yield of coke, asphalt, road oil, and other miscellaneous products was included and priced with the yield of residual fuel oil and still gas. Natural gasoline was excluded from the calculations (because of the difficulties in securing a realistic record of market prices) by omitting it from the input and by deducting the amount of it run to stills from the gasoline output. For these and other reasons which will be discussed later, the margin series does not represent the precise dollars and cents amount the Mid-Continent refiner may actually have received from his operations in any given month. The series is entirely adequate, however, to reflect the timing, direction, and amplitude of the fluctuations in the gross margin available to the Mid-Continent refiner.

The refiner's gross margin per barrel of crude oil refined represents the amount which the refiner had available to cover his inward transportation costs on crude oil, his overhead and operating expenses, and his profit. Since the Mid-Continent refiners are located fairly close to their sources of supply, the inward transportation was largely a gathering operation, and the cost thereof probably did not run much in excess of 10 cents to 20 cents per barrel. The refiner would have had no outward transportation charges to pay out of the calculated gross margin because the product prices used were all f.o.b. refinery quotations.

The wholesaling level of the industry was defined as comprising the activities involved in transporting refined products from the refinery to the bulk plant (or other distribution facility), in operating the bulk plant, and in delivering products to service stations or other customers (see Exhibit V-1). The wholesaler's gross margin was represented by the difference between the tank car and tank wagon prices for gasoline and kerosene in the period 1920–1942, inclusive, and by the difference between the tank car and tank wagon prices for gasoline, kerosene, and No. 2 fuel oil in the period 1943–1952.[4] In each case, it was assumed that the

products were handled in the same relative volumes as they were produced at the refining level of the industry, and the gross margin is thus a weighted average expressed in dollars per barrel of liquid products sold.[5] The tank car prices used in the calculations were identical to those employed in calculating the refiner's margin. The tank wagon price used for gasoline was an average of the dealer tank wagon prices, ex taxes, on the first of the month in Tulsa, Omaha, Des Moines, St. Louis, and Wichita as reported by The Texas Company. The tank wagon price used for kerosene was an average of the posted tank wagon prices, ex taxes, on the first of the month in the same five cities.[6] The tank wagon price used for No. 2 fuel oil in the period 1943–1952, inclusive, was the average of the prices, ex taxes, posted on the first of the month by the Standard Oil Company (Indiana) on its Stanolex furnace oil in Des Moines, St. Louis, and Wichita.

Tank wagon prices are, in general, the delivered prices at which wholesalers sell to service stations and various other customers.[7] The wholesaler's gross margin in Exhibit V-2 thus represents the amount per barrel the whole-

---

[4] Tank wagon prices on fuel oil were not available for earlier years. Moreover, fuel oil did not become a significant factor in bulk plant operations in the Mid-Continent area until at least the late 1930's.

[5] Whenever the wholesaling gross margin was used alone or in combination with the retailing gross margin in the analysis, it was expressed in dollars per barrel of liquid products sold. Whenever the wholesaling gross margin was used in combination with the refining gross margin or the producing-refining gross margin, it was expressed as dollars added per barrel of crude oil handled. See Exhibit V-1.

[6] The prices in Des Moines, St. Louis, and Wichita were those posted by the Standard Oil Company (Indiana) and were drawn from the records of that company. The prices for Tulsa and Omaha were drawn from Platt's Oil Price Handbooks.

[7] There are, of course, a variety of discounts occasionally used in some areas for different classes of trade. It should also be noted that in the period 1920–1935 it was a common practice for suppliers to grant discounts under the posted tank wagon prices for gasoline to their service station customers. For the period 1926–1935 The Texas Company has corrected its records (which are those used in our series) to reflect the actual prices at which tank wagon transactions were made. Between 1920 and 1926, however, the tank wagon prices in The Texas Company's records and in our series are probably somewhat higher than actual market prices. Moreover, as a result of the revision in the series beginning with the year 1926, the increase which appears in the retailing margin in Exhibit V-2 between 1920 and 1935 and the decrease which appears in the wholesaling margin between 1920 and 1935 are probably somewhat overstated. The overstatement is of no particular consequence because throughout the discussion we shall use the data to analyze the monthly and yearly fluctuations in gross margins rather than long-term trends in gross margins.

saler had available to transport products from the refinery to his terminal or bulk plant, to operate the terminal or bulk plant, to deliver products from the terminal or bulk plant to service stations and other customers, and to provide a profit. Here again, the series is not a completely accurate representation of the gross margin available at the wholesaling level of the industry because a wholesaler would normally handle other products, such as lubricating oils, tractor fuels, and sometimes tires, batteries, and accessories, which would increase and help to stabilize his gross margin situation. Gasoline, kerosene, and fuel oil are of sufficient importance, however, so that the fluctuations in the gross margin available on them are reasonably good indicators of the fluctuations in the gross margin on the entire wholesaling activity.

It is extremely important to note that the wholesaling gross margin as defined for the purposes of this analysis is not intended to represent the gross margin available to any particular kind of jobber or trade group. The wholesaling level of the industry contains many different kinds of firms which buy from their suppliers on a variety of different bases.[8] Some jobbers buy at a stated discount under delivered tank wagon prices, some buy at delivered tank car prices, and some have their choice of the two methods of purchase. Moreover, many jobbers have supply contracts which guarantee them a certain minimum gross margin. In addition, much gasoline and fuel oil is handled at the wholesale level on a consignment basis under which the operator of the bulk plant or terminal receives a commission of so much per gallon handled. The boundary line between refining and wholesaling activities is thus a rather fuzzy one with the wholesaling activity frequently being shared by refiner and wholesaler, and there are only a relatively small number of firms who buy exclusively in tank car lots at the refinery gate. The wholesaling gross margin shown in Exhibit V-2 should therefore be regarded as that available on the *entire wholesaling activity* or that which would be gained by a refiner if he sold his products in the tank wagon rather than the tank car markets. It should be related to the situations of particular kinds of jobbers or wholesalers only

if they happen to buy and sell on the same basis as that used in the preparation of the series.

The retailing level of the industry was defined as comprising the activities involved in the operation of service stations, and the retailing gross margin was represented by the difference between the average service station price, exclusive of state and federal taxes, of regular grade gasoline [9] and the delivered tank wagon prices in the five Mid-Continent cities noted above. The typical service station would, of course, sell other products, including premium gasoline, lubricating oils, tires, batteries, and accessories. The gross margin on regular grade gasoline does not, therefore, reflect the total margin available on the retailing operation. Moreover, the revenue from items other than regular grade gasoline would in all probability serve to offset to some degree the fluctuations in the gasoline gross margin. The regular grade gasoline is, however, by far the most important item handled at service stations and the gross margin available on it is a fair indicator of the timing and amplitude of the fluctuations in the gross margin available on the entire retailing activity.

Since all four of the gross margins charted in Exhibit V-2 were based upon published market prices, they may over- or understate the frequency and amplitude of the fluctuations which actually occurred at certain points in the industry's history. When demand and supply are reasonably well in balance, the published quotations are fair indicators of the prices at which most of the market transactions are made. When the markets are under the stress of either a shortage or a surplus, however, a great many transactions may be made at figures above or below the published quotations. During the winter of 1947–1948 when the Esso Standard Oil Company was attempting to "hold the line" on fuel oil prices,[10] for example, many marketers unquestionably sold above the Esso prices, which were those published in the trade journals for many locations. Similarly, in the period immediately after World War II, some refiners paid and some producers received premiums

---

[8] See Chapter Fifteen for a discussion of the arrangements used by several of the major oil companies.

[9] These prices were taken from The Texas Company's records of service station prices in the five Mid-Continent cities of Tulsa, Omaha, Des Moines, St. Louis, and Wichita on the first of the month.

[10] This situation is discussed in Chapter Six.

above the posted prices for crude oil at the well-head. For most of the industry in most time periods, however, we believe that the four series are reasonably good indicators of the gross margin movements in the four phases of the business as defined in Exhibit V-1.

Behavior of the Gross Margins:

The four gross margin series shown in Exhibit V-2 reflect in some degree almost every aspect of business and economic conditions in the oil industry throughout the 33-year period 1920–1952, and a complete discussion of the series would require treatment of many topics outside the scope of this study. In the following paragraphs we shall therefore merely direct attention to certain characteristic movements in the series which are particularly pertinent to our analysis of the effect of vertical integration on the stability of gross margins. To permit ready comparison of the relative magnitudes of the fluctuations in the four series, the margins have been plotted on a semi-logarithmic grid in Exhibit V-2. As a further means of comparing the relative stability of the series, we have tabulated in the lower right-hand corner of the chart the average monthly percentage deviations of each series from 13-month moving averages. The deviations are given for three different time periods: the period before the development of the prorationing laws (1920–1934), the period after the development of the prorationing laws (1935–1952), and the entire 33-year period, 1920–1952.

The most significant fact established by the records in Exhibit V-2 is that the dissimilarities in the monthly movements of the four gross margins were more pronounced than the similarities in the period 1920–1952. Rarely did the upward and downward movements and the periods of stability in all four series coincide with each other. There was a strong inverse correlation between the refining and wholesaling gross margins, and the movements in one series were very frequently offset by opposite movements in the other series. On at least 12 occasions in the 33-year period, steep declines in the refining margin occurred almost simultaneously with sharp increases in the wholesaling margin; on at least 9 occasions, steep rises in the refining margin coincided with declines in the wholesaling margin. In

only one or two instances did both series make major movements in the same direction at precisely the same time.

The monthly movements in the producing and refining gross margins had little correlation, direct or inverse, with each other. Before prorationing the refining margin frequently moved in the opposite direction to the price of crude oil. After prorationing the refining margin fluctuated both upward and downward in times of steady crude oil prices. The crude oil price made only three major upward movements in the period 1935–1952. On two of these occasions (1941 and 1946–1947), there was a corresponding upward movement in the refining margin; on the third occasion (1936–1937), the refining margin drifted downward as the crude oil price moved upward. There was only one downward movement in crude oil prices between 1935 and 1952 (in 1938), and it was accompanied by a temporary downward movement in the refining margin, followed shortly thereafter by an upward movement.

The monthly movements in the wholesaling gross margin in the period 1920–1952 had the relationship discussed above to the movements in the refining gross margin, but had no significant relationship to the movements in either the producing or retailing gross margins. The monthly movements in the retailing gross margin apparently had no clearly discernible relationship to the movements in any of the other gross margins in the period 1920–1952.

A second important fact established by the gross margin records in Exhibit V-2 is that there were marked differences in the monthly stability of the gross margins available at the four levels of the industry. The refining margin in particular was characterized by far greater monthly fluctuations both before and after prorationing than were the producing, wholesaling, and retailing gross margins. For the entire period 1920–1952, the monthly fluctuations in the refining gross margin were about 2.3 times as great as those in the producing margin, over 1.6 times as great as those in the wholesaling margin, and about 3.4 times as great as those in the retailing margin.[11] It is particularly sig-

---

[11] In the following discussion we shall use average monthly percentage deviations from 13-month moving averages as measures of the relative monthly fluctuations in the various series.

nificant that the refining gross margin was highly unstable both in times of general business prosperity and general business depression and both in times of fluctuating crude oil prices and relatively stable crude oil prices.

A third fact revealed by Exhibit V-2 is that the prorationing laws apparently had an important effect on the monthly stability of the gross margins available at all levels of the industry and particularly on the gross margin at the producing level. The monthly fluctuations in the producing gross margin were about nine times greater in the period before prorationing than they were in the period after prorationing. Similarly, the monthly fluctuations in the refining gross margin were more than three times greater before than after prorationing and the monthly fluctuations in the wholesaling and retailing gross margins were between two and three times greater in the period before than after prorationing.

All the gains in gross margin stability in the 18-year period 1935–1952 cannot, of course, be attributed to the adoption of the prorationing laws. A certain part of the gains unquestionably arose from the price controls which were in effect for a period of about three years during World War II. Moreover, there were significant differences in general business conditions in the periods before and after about 1934. The period 1920–1934 was marked by one of the greatest booms and greatest depressions our economy has ever experienced. The period 1935–1952, on the other hand, was characterized (with certain minor exceptions) by a steadily rising demand for most of the major petroleum products and by generally prosperous conditions in the petroleum industry. Notwithstanding these and other differences in general economic circumstances before and after 1934, the gross margin records in Exhibit V-2 still lend considerable support to the conclusion that the prorationing laws contributed significantly to gross margin stability at all levels of the industry.

II. Effect of Integration on the Monthly Stability of Gross Margins

In view of the dissimilarities which characterized the timing, direction, and amplitude of the monthly movements in the four gross margins in the period 1920–1952, it is apparent that a company could have increased significantly the monthly stability of the gross margin on which it operated by spanning two or more different levels of the industry. It is likewise evident from the behavior of the series that certain combinations of activities would have contributed more to stability of gross margins than others and that the contribution in each case would not necessarily have been the same in the periods before and after prorationing. In the following paragraphs we shall examine the effect of some of the more common vertical integration arrangements on the monthly stability of gross margins before prorationing, after prorationing, and in the 33-year period as a whole.

Forward Integration by a Producer:

The effect which forward integration by a crude oil producer would have had on the monthly stability of the gross margin received per barrel of crude oil handled is illustrated in Exhibit V-4. The bottom line on the chart is the crude oil price per barrel and thus represents the gross margin a firm would have received had it confined its operations exclusively to producing activities. The second line plots the sum of the crude oil price and the refiner's gross margin and thus indicates the total gross margin the firm would have realized had it integrated one step forward and carried all its oil through the refining operation. The third line represents the gross margin the firm would have received had it engaged in producing, refining, and wholesaling activities and sold all its gasoline and kerosene at tank wagon prices throughout the 33-year period, its distillates at tank car prices in the period 1920–1942 and at tank wagon prices in the period 1943–1952, and all other products at the refinery tank car prices.[12] The top line on the chart represents the gross margin the firm would have received had it engaged in the operation of service stations and sold all its gasoline output at the average service station prices, ex taxes, in the five Mid-Continent cities and all its other products on the same basis as in the previous case representing integration through the wholesaling level.

---

[12] The tank wagon and tank car prices were the same as those used in calculating the refining and wholesaling margins discussed above.

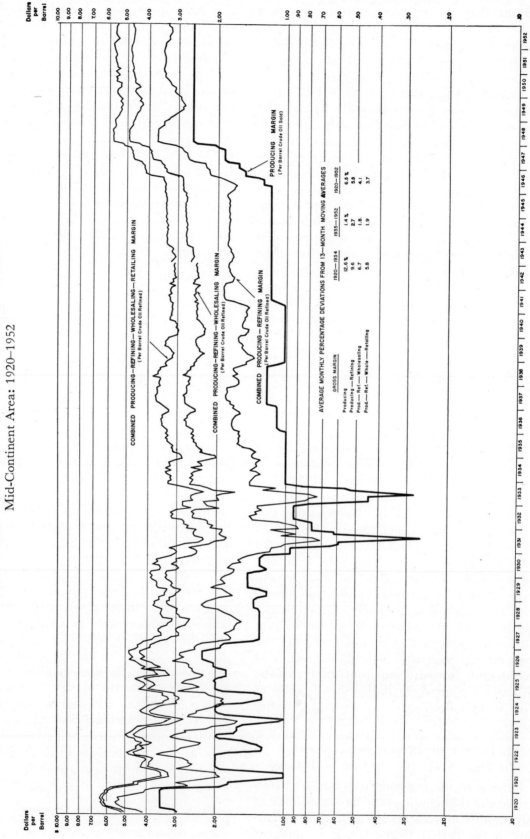

EXHIBIT V-4. EFFECT OF INTEGRATION ON MONTHLY STABILITY OF GROSS MARGINS:
FORWARD INTEGRATION BY A CRUDE OIL PRODUCER
Mid-Continent Area: 1920–1952

Examination of Exhibit V-4 indicates that before the development of the prorationing laws, a crude oil producer would have reduced the average monthly fluctuations in his gross margin from 12.6% to 9.6% through forward integration into refining activities and from 12.6% to 6.7% through forward integration into both refining and wholesaling activities. Further forward integration into retailing operations in gasoline, however, would have resulted in only a minor additional increase in monthly gross margin stability. After the development of the prorationing laws, a crude oil producer would have lost rather than gained in monthly gross margin stability by forward integration. By engaging in refining activities, he would have increased the average monthly fluctuations in his gross margin from 1.4% to 2.7%. By engaging in wholesaling or wholesaling and retailing operations in addition to refining activities, he would have increased the fluctuations in his margin from 1.4% to about 1.8%. For the entire span of 33 years, a crude oil producer would have gained slightly in average monthly margin stability with each successive forward integration step and from the combination of all four activities would have secured a gross margin of substantially greater monthly stability (average fluctuations of 3.7%) than that available on crude oil producing alone (average fluctuations of 6.5%).

Forward Integration by a Refiner Followed by Backward Integration:

The gains in monthly gross margin stability which a refiner would have secured by forward integration into marketing activities and then by backward integration into crude oil producing are illustrated in Exhibit V-5. The lower line on the chart is the gross margin per barrel available on refining operations alone. The second line shows the effect of forward integration by the refiner into wholesaling operations and the third line the effect of forward integration into both wholesaling and retailing operations. The gross margins for the combined refining-wholesaling and the combined refining-wholesaling-retailing operation have been developed in the same manner as discussed in connection with forward integration by a crude oil producer, only in this case the build-up starts from the refining margin rather than the

producing margin. The top line on the chart is the combined producing-refining-wholesaling-retailing margin and thus illustrates the additional stability in gross margin which a refiner would have gained by engaging in crude oil production after he had first integrated into wholesaling and retailing activities.

The first step of forward integration into wholesaling activities would have given the refiner a great gain in monthly gross margin stability as might be anticipated from the strong inverse correlation in the movements of the refining and wholesaling gross margins discussed above. The acquisition of wholesaling operations would have enabled the refiner to reduce the average monthly fluctuations in his gross margin from 24.2% to 7.4% before prorationing, from 7.2% to 3.0% after prorationing, and from 14.9% to 5.1% in the 33-year period as a whole. Further forward integration into retailing operations would have added slightly to the stability of the refiner's gross margin but not nearly so much as would have the first step forward into wholesaling operations.

Backward integration by a refiner into crude oil production, after he had first integrated into wholesaling and retailing operations, would have resulted in some further gains in monthly gross margin stability, particularly in the period after prorationing. In the 33-year period as a whole, the combination of all four activities would have yielded a gross margin with average monthly fluctuations of 3.7% as contrasted with average monthly fluctuations of 14.9% on the refining margin alone.

Backward Integration by a Refiner Followed by Forward Integration:

The gains in monthly gross margin stability which a refiner would have made had he first integrated backward into crude oil production and then forward into wholesaling and retailing activities are shown in Exhibit V-6. The series are similar to those in Exhibit V-5 but are arranged in a different order. The bottom line on the chart is again the gross margin per barrel available on refining operations alone, while the second line represents the gross margin available on a combined refining-producing operation. The third line represents the gross margin on a combination of refining-produc-

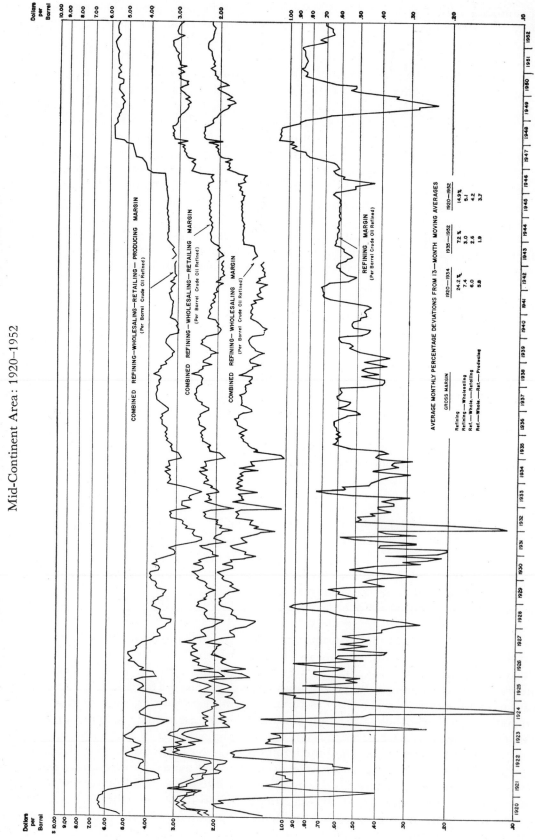

EXHIBIT V-5. EFFECT OF INTEGRATION ON MONTHLY STABILITY OF GROSS MARGINS: FORWARD INTEGRATION BY A REFINER FOLLOWED BY BACKWARD INTEGRATION

Mid-Continent Area: 1920–1952

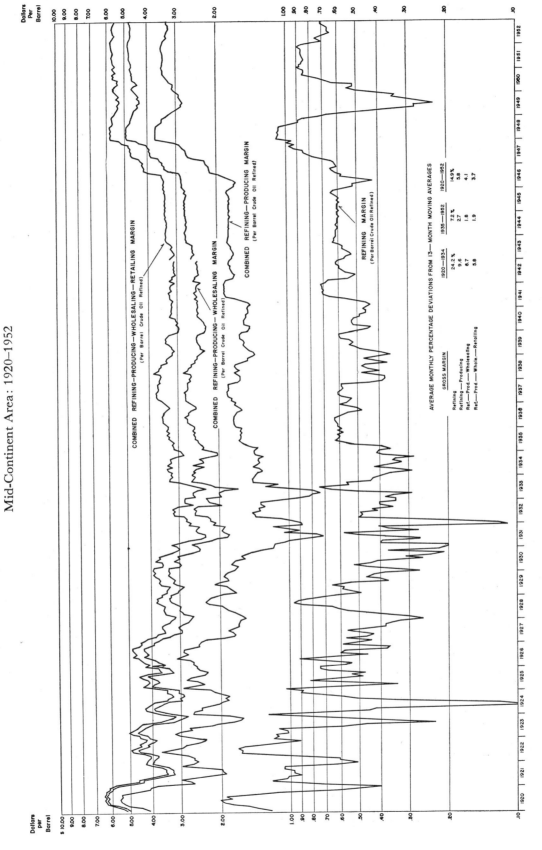

Exhibit V-6. Effect of Integration on Monthly Stability of Gross Margins: Backward Integration by a Refiner Followed by Forward Integration

Mid-Continent Area: 1920–1952

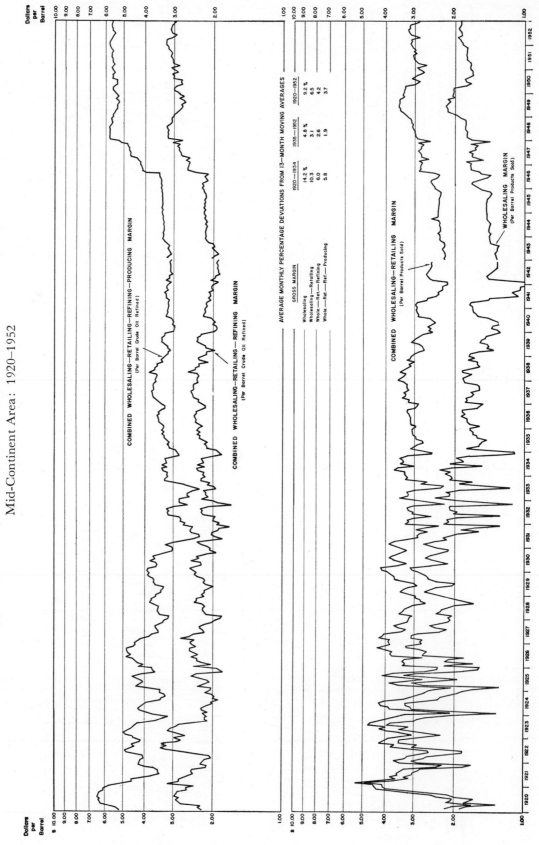

EXHIBIT V-7. EFFECT OF INTEGRATION ON MONTHLY STABILITY OF GROSS MARGINS:
FORWARD INTEGRATION BY A WHOLESALER FOLLOWED BY BACKWARD INTEGRATION
Mid-Continent Area: 1920–1952

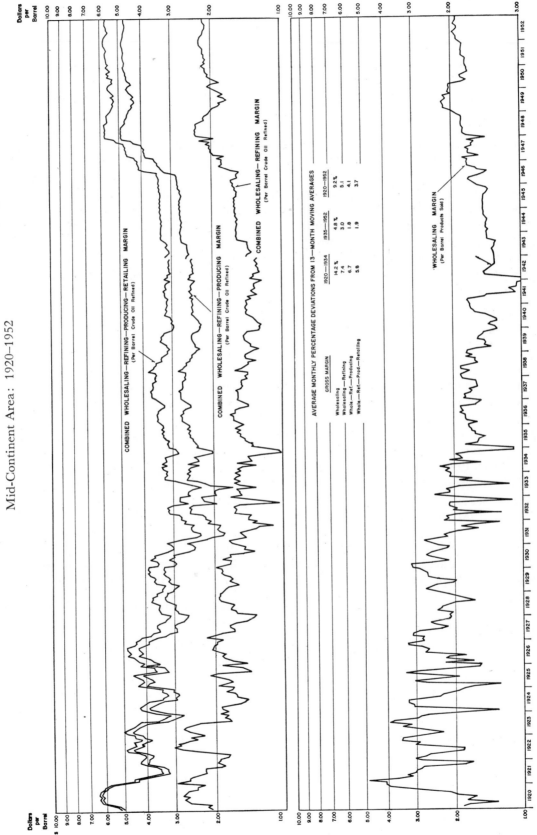

EXHIBIT V-8. EFFECT OF INTEGRATION ON MONTHLY STABILITY OF GROSS MARGINS: BACKWARD INTEGRATION BY A WHOLESALER FOLLOWED BY FORWARD INTEGRATION

Mid-Continent Area: 1920–1952

ing-wholesaling and the fourth line the gross margin on a combination of refining-producing-wholesaling-retailing.

Analysis of the chart reveals that backward integration into producing activities would have enabled a refiner to reduce the monthly fluctuations in his gross margin from 24.2% to 9.6% before prorationing, from 7.2% to 2.7% after prorationing, and from 14.9% to 5.8% in the entire period 1920–1952. The addition of wholesaling operations to the refining-producing activity would have provided a further increase in monthly gross margin stability, particularly in the period 1920–1934. The addition of retailing activities to the refining-producing-wholesaling combination would have added slightly to monthly stability in the periods 1920–1934 and 1920–1952, but not in the period 1935–1952.

Forward Integration by a Wholesaler Followed by Backward Integration:

The gains in monthly gross margin stability which a wholesaler would have secured had he integrated into retailing operations and then backward into refining and producing activities are represented in Exhibit V-7. The bottom line on the chart indicates the gross margin available on the wholesaling activity alone. The second line represents the gross margin on a combined wholesaling-retailing operation. In computing this margin, it was assumed that in the period 1920–1942, inclusive, the marketer bought gasoline and kerosene at tank car prices and resold the gasoline at retail service station prices and the kerosene at tank wagon prices. In the period 1943–1952, it was assumed that the marketer continued to handle gasoline and kerosene in the same manner and in addition bought fuel oil at tank car prices and resold it at tank wagon prices. The prices used were identical to those employed earlier in calculating the gross margins available at the separate levels of the industry. It has here again been assumed that the marketer handled the various products in the same ratio as yielded at the refinery level, and the gross margin is thus a weighted average expressed in dollars per barrel of liquid products sold.

The third line on the chart represents the gross margin on which a wholesaler would have operated if he had not only integrated

forward into retailing but also backward into refining. The line is the same as that shown in Exhibit V-5 to represent a combination of refining-wholesaling-retailing functions by a refiner. The fourth line is the same as in the other charts and indicates the gain in monthly gross margin stability a wholesaler would have secured by forward integration into retailing and backward integration into both refining and producing. As noted earlier, the wholesaling margin and the combined wholesaling-retailing margins are expressed in dollars *per barrel of liquid products sold* whereas the combined wholesaling-retailing-refining and the combined wholesaling-retailing-refining-producing margins are expressed in dollars per barrel of crude oil produced and refined (see footnote 5). The dollar amounts for the first two series cannot therefore be compared with those for the second two series.

The data in the chart reveal that a wholesaler would have reduced the monthly fluctuations in his gross margin substantially by forward integration into retailing in all three time periods. Each of the backward steps into refining and producing would have added still further to the wholesaler's monthly gross margin stability. The last step into crude oil production, however, would have yielded a gross margin only slightly more stable than that already available from the combined wholesaling-retailing-refining operation. The combination of all four activities would have reduced the monthly fluctuations in the wholesaler's gross margin from 14.2% to 5.8% before prorationing, from 4.8% to 1.9% after prorationing, and from 9.2% to 3.7% in the period 1920–1952.

Backward Integration by a Wholesaler Followed by Forward Integration:

The gains in monthly gross margin stability which a wholesaler would have secured by successive steps of backward integration into refining, backward integration into producing, and finally forward integration into retailing are illustrated in Exhibit V-8. The bottom line on the chart represents the gross margin on wholesaling operations alone. The second line is the combined wholesaling-refining margin and is identical to that shown in Exhibit V-5 for the combination of these two functions by a refiner. The third line is the combined whole-

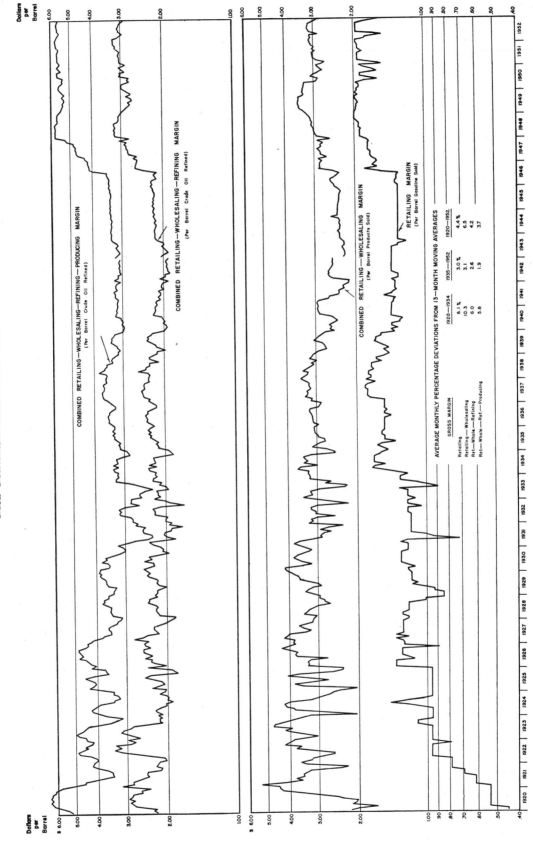

Exhibit V-9. Effect of Integration on Monthly Stability of Gross Margins: Backward Integration by a Retailer

Mid-Continent Area: 1920–1952

saling-refining-producing margin and is the same as that shown in Exhibit V-5 for the combination of the same three functions. The top line is identical to that in the preceding charts and represents the gain in monthly gross margin stability a wholesaler would have secured had he taken a final step of forward integration into retailing.

It is apparent that a wholesaler would have made a major gain in monthly gross margin stability by backward integration into refining just as would have a refiner by forward integration into wholesaling. Acquisition of refining activities would have enabled a wholesaler to reduce the monthly fluctuations in his gross margin from 14.2% to 7.4% before prorationing, from 4.8% to 3.0% after prorationing, and from 9.2% to 5.1% in the period 1920–1952. The second step of backward integration into producing would have added somewhat to monthly gross margin stability but not as much as the first step into refining. The addition of retailing activities to the combined wholesaling-refining-producing operation would have added slightly to monthly stability in the periods 1920–1935 and 1920–1952 but not in the period 1935–1952.

Backward Integration by a Retailer:

The effect which backward integration would have had on the monthly stability of the gross margin received by a retailing firm is shown in Exhibit V-9. The bottom line is the gross margin available on the retailing of gasoline alone. The second line represents the combined retailing-wholesaling margin and is the same as that shown in Exhibit V-7 for the combination of the same two functions. The top two lines are likewise identical to those shown in Exhibit V-7 for the combinations indicated.

The chart reveals that a retailer would have lost significantly in monthly gross margin stability by backward integration into wholesaling. Further backward integration into refining would have given the retailer approximately the same monthly gross margin stability as that which was available to him on retailing alone. A final step of backward integration into producing activities, however, would have yielded slightly greater monthly gross margin stability than that available on retailing operations. A combination of all four operations would have

enabled the retailer to reduce the monthly fluctuations in his gross margin from 6.1% to 5.8% before prorationing, from 3.0% to 1.9% after prorationing, and from 4.4% to 3.7% in the entire period 1920–1952.

In the light of the foregoing analysis, it appears that many of the important types of vertical integration constituted a means by which a company could have done a great deal in the period 1920–1952 toward increasing the monthly stability of the gross margin on which it operated. In fact, all vertical integration steps, backward or forward, by companies operating at any position in the industry would have added something to monthly gross margin stability except integration by a retailer into wholesaling, integration by a producer into refining in the period 1935–1952, and the addition of retailing to a producing-refining-wholesaling operation in the period 1935–1952. In general, it appears that the most significant gains in monthly gross margin stability would have been secured by arrangements involving: (a) forward integration by a refiner into wholesaling, (b) backward integration by a refiner into producing, (c) forward integration by a wholesaler into retailing, and (d) backward integration by a wholesaler into refining.

EXHIBIT V-10. RANKING OF GROSS MARGINS AND GROSS MARGIN COMBINATIONS IN ORDER OF MONTHLY STABILITY

Mid-Continent Area: 1920–1952

Order of Stability, 1920–1952	Average Deviations from 13-Month Moving Averages		
	1920–1934	1935–1952	1920–1952
1. Prod.-Ref.-Whole.-Retailing	5.8%	1.9%	3.7%
2. Prod.-Ref.-Wholesaling	6.7	1.8	4.1
3. Ref.-Whole.-Retailing	6.0	2.6	4.2
4. Retailing	6.1	3.0	4.4
5. Refining-Wholesaling	7.4	3.0	5.1
6. Producing-Refining	9.6	2.7	5.8
7. Producing	12.6	1.4	6.5
8. Wholesaling-Retailing	10.3	3.1	6.5
9. Wholesaling	14.2	4.8	9.2
10. Refining	24.2	7.2	14.9

The ranking of the various gross margins and margin combinations in order of average monthly stability is summarized in Exhibit V-10 for the periods 1920–1934, 1935–1952, and 1920–1952. In appraising the differences among the various situations, it is important to recognize that a very small difference in gross margin stability has the potential of occasioning a very large difference in net profit stability because an oil company ordinarily carries only a small fraction of its gross margin to net profits. If a company were, for example, carrying 20% of its gross margin to net profits, a 10% fluctuation in the gross margin would mean a 50% fluctuation in net profits in the absence of any changes in costs or other circumstances. By reducing the average monthly gross margin fluctuations from 10% to 5% in such a case, the company would reduce the average monthly fluctuations in its net profits from 50% to 25%. The small differences in average monthly gross margin stability which appear among some of the situations in Exhibit V-10 are therefore of greater significance than might at first glance appear to be the case.

III. Effect of Integration on Yearly Stability of Gross Margins

We anticipated that the effect of vertical integration on the *yearly* stability of gross margins might be somewhat different from the effect of integration on the *monthly* stability of gross margins. It was possible that a series which had wide fluctuations from month to month might be very stable on an annual basis. Conversely, it was possible (although not likely) that a series which was relatively stable on a monthly basis might have considerable fluctuation from one year to the next. We therefore examined the effect of integration on the yearly stability of gross margins in the same manner as we did the effect of integration on the monthly stability of gross margins. Our conclusion was that in the period 1920–1952 vertical integration had approximately the same general significance as a means of stabilizing yearly gross margins that it did as a means of stabilizing monthly gross margins, although the effect of particular combinations of activities on yearly stability was not always the same as on monthly stability.

The yearly gross margins available at the four levels of the industry are plotted in Exhibit V-11. The yearly figures were computed on the same general basis as were the monthly figures discussed above, and each yearly figure

represents a weighted average of the monthly figures for that year. In the case of the refining margin, for example, the monthly yields of individual products in barrels were multiplied by the monthly prices and the resulting monthly realizations were added together to secure a total realization figure for the entire year. From the total realization figure we deducted the total value of crude oil run to refineries during the year (calculated month by month) to obtain a net realization for the year. The net yearly realization was then divided by the number of barrels of crude oil run to refineries to obtain an average yearly gross margin per barrel.

The series have again been plotted on a semi-logarithmic grid to permit visual comparison of the relative magnitude of the fluctuations in one series with the magnitude of those in another. As a statistical measure of the relative stability of the series, we have tabulated in later charts the average percentage change of each series from year to year in the periods 1920–1934, 1935–1952, and 1920–1952. It will be noted that this measure of relative stability is different from the percentage deviations from 13-month moving averages used in connection with the monthly gross margins.

Inspection of Exhibit V-11 reveals that the behavior of the yearly gross margins at the separate levels of the industry in the period 1920–1935 was not greatly different from the behavior of the monthly gross margins. Each of the yearly gross margins was subject to continual fluctuations, and the timing, direction, and amplitude of the movements in one series were frequently different from the timing, direction, and amplitude of the movements in other series. There were substantial differences in the yearly stability of the four gross margins, and the refining gross margin was again by far the most unstable of the lot. The other three gross margins, however, ranked somewhat differently with respect to yearly stability than they did with respect to monthly stability. Finally, it may be observed that all of the yearly gross margins were substantially more stable in the period 1935–1952 than in the period 1920–1934, just as were the monthly gross margins.

We shall not undertake to discuss the effect of various types of integration moves on the yearly stability of gross margins in the same

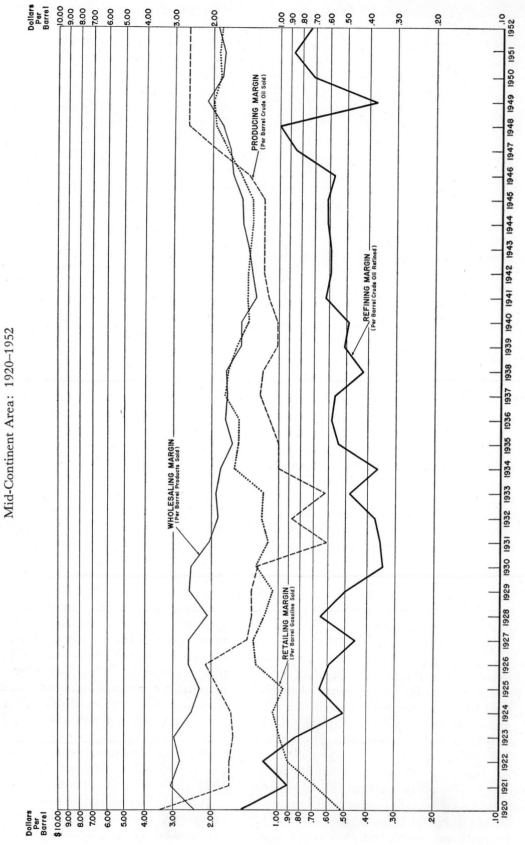

EXHIBIT V-11. YEARLY GROSS MARGINS AVAILABLE AT THE PRODUCING, REFINING, WHOLESALING, AND RETAILING LEVELS OF THE INDUSTRY

Mid-Continent Area: 1920–1952

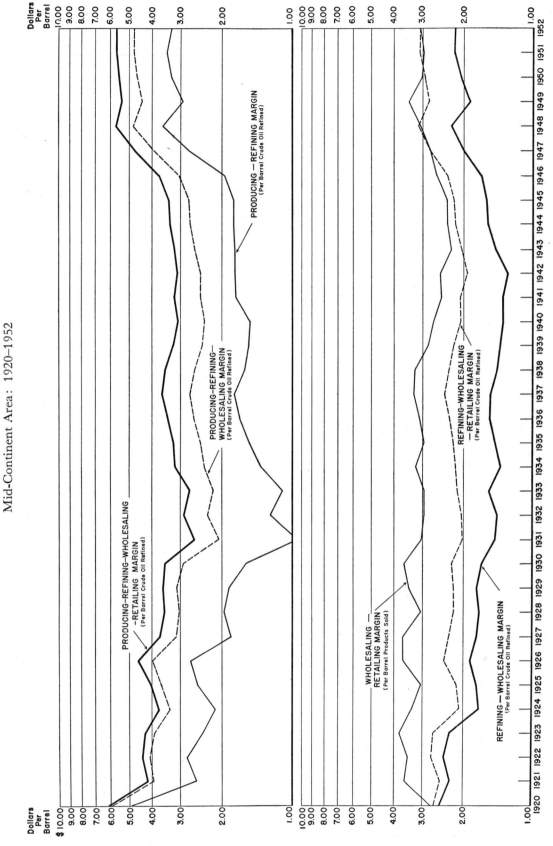

EXHIBIT V-12. EFFECT OF INTEGRATION ON THE YEARLY STABILITY OF GROSS MARGINS

Mid-Continent Area: 1920–1952

Exhibit V-13. Effect of Integration on Yearly Stability of Gross Margins

Average Percentage Changes in Gross Margins from Year to Year

	1920–1934	1935–1952	1920–1952
A. Forward Integration by a Producer			
Producing	23.2%	7.9%	14.5%
Producing-Refining	19.5	10.0	14.1
Producing-Refining-Wholesaling	11.8	6.8	9.0
Prod.-Ref.-Wholesaling-Retailing	11.4	6.3	8.5
B. Forward Integration by a Refiner Followed by Backward Integration			
Refining	25.3%	22.9%	24.0%
Refining-Wholesaling	7.5	6.9	7.2
Refining-Wholesaling-Retailing	6.3	5.9	6.1
Ref.-Whole.-Retailing-Producing	11.4	6.3	8.5
C. Backward Integration by a Refiner Followed by Forward Integration			
Refining	25.3%	22.9%	24.0%
Refining-Producing	19.5	10.0	14.1
Refining-Producing-Wholesaling	11.8	6.8	9.0
Ref.-Prod.-Whole.-Retailing	11.4	6.3	8.5
D. Forward Integration by a Wholesaler Followed by Backward Integration			
Wholesaling	11.1%	7.1%	8.8%
Wholesaling-Retailing	10.1	6.5	8.1
Wholesaling-Retailing-Refining	6.3	5.9	6.1
Whole.-Ret.-Refining-Producing	11.4	6.3	8.5
E. Backward Integration by a Wholesaler Followed by Forward Integration			
Wholesaling	11.1%	7.1%	8.8%
Wholesaling-Refining	7.5	6.9	7.2
Whole.-Refining-Producing	11.8	6.8	9.0
Whole.-Ref.-Prod.-Retailing	11.4	6.3	8.5
F. Backward Integration by a Retailer			
Retailing	15.3%	6.0%	10.0%
Retailing-Wholesaling	10.1	6.5	8.1
Retailing-Wholesaling-Refining	6.3	5.9	6.1
Ret.-Whole.-Ref.-Producing	11.4	6.3	8.5

Exhibit V-14. Ranking of Gross Margins and Gross Margin Combinations in Order of Yearly Stability

Mid-Continent Area: 1920–1952

Order of Stability, 1920–1952	Average Percentage Changes from Year to Year		
	1920–1934	1935–1952	1920–1952
1. Ref.-Whole.-Retailing	6.3%	5.9%	6.1%
2. Refining-Wholesaling	7.5	6.9	7.2
3. Wholesaling-Retailing	10.1	6.5	8.1
4. Prod.-Ref.-Whole.-Retailing	11.4	6.3	8.5
5. Wholesaling	11.1	7.1	8.8
6. Prod.-Ref.-Wholesaling	11.8	6.8	9.0
7. Retailing	15.3	6.0	10.0
8. Producing-Refining	19.5	10.0	14.1
9. Producing	23.2	7.9	14.5
10. Refining	25.3	22.9	24.0

detail as we did the effect on monthly stability of gross margins. The results of the full analysis of yearly stability are, however, shown in Exhibits V-12 to V-14, inclusive. Exhibit V-12 contains a yearly record of all the combinations of gross margins which were considered in the analysis of monthly stability. Exhibit V-13 shows the gains or losses in yearly gross margin stability (as measured by average percentage changes from year to year) which producers, refiners, wholesalers, or retailers would have realized through various successive integration steps in the periods 1920–1934, 1935–1952, and 1920–1952. Exhibit V-14 indicates the ranking of the individual gross margins and gross mar-

gin combinations in order of yearly stability for the three time periods.

Examination of Exhibits V-12 to V-14 reveals that many of the major types of vertical integration in the period 1920–1952 would have enabled a company to improve the yearly stability of its gross margin. All vertical integration steps backward or forward from any position would have contributed appreciably to yearly gross margin stability except the addition of producing operations to a refining-wholesaling or refining-wholesaling-retailing combination, the addition of refining to producing in the period 1935–1952, or the addition of wholesaling to retailing in the period 1935–1952. The most important gains in yearly gross margin stability would have resulted from: (a) forward integration by a refiner into wholesaling, (b) backward integration by a refiner into producing, and (c) forward integration by a producer-refiner into wholesaling. It is significant that these three types of integration were among the most common of those that took place in the industry in the period 1920–1952.

As was anticipated, the vertical integration arrangements that would have been effective in improving yearly stability of gross margins sometimes were and sometimes were not the same as those that would have been effective in improving monthly stability of gross margins. For example, forward integration by a refiner into wholesaling and backward integration by a refiner into producing would have had dramatic effects on both monthly and yearly stability. Forward and backward integration by a wholesaler would, however, have had much less effect on yearly stability than on monthly stability because the wholesaling margin itself ranked substantially higher in yearly stability than it did in monthly stability. It may also be observed that whereas a combination of all four activities would have yielded the greatest monthly stability in the period 1920–1952, the greatest yearly stability would have resulted from a combination of refining-wholesaling-retailing activities. Various other differences in the effect of particular integration arrangements on yearly and monthly gross margin stability may be ascertained by inspection of Exhibits V-2 to V-14. On the whole, the data support the general conclusion that most, although not all, of the important types of vertical integration in the period 1920–1952 provided a means whereby a company could have improved either or both its monthly and yearly gross margin stability.

IV. EFFECT OF INTEGRATION ON THE STABILITY AND AVERAGE LEVEL OF NET PROFITS

The findings outlined in the preceding pages concerning the effect of vertical integration on the monthly and yearly stability of gross margins are important because they contain an inference with regard to the effect of vertical integration on the stability of net profits. The inference is, however, only a limited one because a company's net profits are dependent not only upon the unit gross margin it secures but also upon its operating costs and the volume of business it handles.

Changes in operating costs may produce changes in net profits at times when gross margins are constant. Similarly, changes in operating costs may serve to accentuate or offset the effect of a particular gross margin change on net profits. Since changes in operating costs usually take place rather slowly, it seems probable that there is a fairly close correlation (in the absence of volume changes) between monthly and yearly fluctuations in gross margins and monthly and yearly fluctuations in net profits. Over longer periods of time, however, there is no question that changes in operating costs may greatly impair the usefulness of the unit gross margin series as indicators of what is happening

to profit opportunities. The downward trend in the wholesaling gross margin in the period 1930–1941, for example, was to a considerable extent offset by lower costs of transportation arising from the development of the products pipe lines and the use of truck transports to replace rail shipments for short hauls. Similarly, the downward trend in the refining gross margin during the 1920's was partially offset by the commercial development of the pipe still and the cost savings which it permitted (see Chapter Nineteen). In more recent years, the rise in the producing gross margin between 1946 and 1952 was sharply offset by increased finding and drilling costs. It appears therefore that while the gross margin series may be useful as indicators of monthly and yearly changes in net profits, they are of no particular significance as indicators of trends in profit opportunities.

Changes in the volume of products sold by a company may likewise produce changes in net profits while unit gross margins are constant or serve to accentuate or offset the effect of gross margin changes on net profits. The upward movement in retailing gross margins in the period 1920–1937, for example, did not result in a corresponding improvement in the net profits of many companies because during this period there was a great expansion of service station facilities which reduced sales volume per outlet to a greater extent than it was possible to reduce operating costs per outlet (see Chapter Six). It may also be observed that the stability of gross margins per barrel at the producing level of the industry after the advent of the prorationing laws was not fully reflected in a similar stability in net profits because the stability in crude oil prices was achieved, in part, through the curtailment of production in times of slackening demand and in times of rising supply. Since changes in volume may occur over either short or long periods of time, it is likely that they detract more from the usefulness of the gross margin series as indicators of monthly and yearly fluctuations in net profits than do the changes in costs of operation discussed above.

A third reason why care must be taken in drawing inferences with respect to the behavior of net profits from the behavior of gross margins lies in the fact that the effect of a given gross margin fluctuation on net profits varies depending on the percentage of the gross margin which is being carried to net profits at the time the fluctuation occurs. For example, a 5% variation in gross margins would have a corresponding effect on profits at each level of the industry, assuming operating costs and volumes remained constant, only if the proportion of gross profit carried to net profit was the same at each level of the industry. If at the time of the fluctuation, for example, the wholesaling level was carrying 5% of its gross margin to net profits and the refining level was carrying 10% of its gross margin to net profits, the 5% fluctuation in gross margins would produce a 100% change in net profits at the wholesaling level and only a 50% change in net profits at the refining level.

In view of the foregoing and various other limitations on the inferences which can be drawn from the analysis of gross margins with regard to the effect of integration on the stability of net profits, we undertook a direct examination of the per cent return on borrowed and invested capital actually earned by 98 different oil companies in the period 1920–1952. Because of limitations on the availability of published data, it was not possible to set up groups of companies corresponding to all the various integrated and nonintegrated situations discussed in the preceding pages. We were, however, able to find considerable evidence in the net profit records to corroborate in a general way the clear implication of the gross margin records to the effect that many types of integration arrangements in the period 1920–1952 would have enabled a company to improve the stability of its earnings experience.

The Net Profit Records:

The selection of companies for inclusion in the net profit study was determined largely by the availability of published financial and operating data. The core of the group was comprised of the 30 companies which have been analyzed since 1934 by Joseph E. Pogue and Frederick G. Coqueron of The Chase National Bank of New York in their annual study, "Financial Analysis of 30 Oil Companies." Selected financial and operating data on the individual companies included in this study were made available to us through the courtesy of The Chase National Bank and Frederick G. Co-

queron. Other companies for which published records were available were added to the group of 30 studied by Pogue and Coqueron, and the analysis of each company was then extended over as long a period of time as our data would permit.[13]

In the case of the 30 companies included in The Chase National Bank study, we accepted the figures compiled by Pogue and Coqueron for the per cent return earned by the individual companies on borrowed and invested capital. In Pogue and Coqueron's analysis, borrowed and invested capital was considered to include capital stock, surplus, long-term debt, and the equity of minority stockholders in consolidated subsidiaries. The net income figure used in the analysis was after taxes and all charges, except interest on long-term debt and earnings applicable to minority interests. In extending Pogue and Coqueron's figures back to earlier years and in computing figures for the companies we added to the group of 30, we followed the same general procedure as that used by Pogue and Coqueron. No attempt was made to adjust the figures of individual companies for changes in methods of handling intangible development costs and various other revisions in accounting practices which may have affected the comparability of earnings from one year to the next. Moreover, many arbitrary decisions were necessary with regard to the handling of special reserves and unusual charges against income and the determination of what constituted long-term debt. On the whole, however, we believe that the financial figures are sufficiently accurate to warrant the limited, general conclusions which we shall draw from them.

After the return on investment figures were prepared, the companies were divided into groups in each year according to depth and extent of integration. The six groups used in the analysis were as follows: (1) producing companies, (2) marketing companies, (3) refining-marketing companies (defined as companies producing less than 10% of their crude oil requirements), (4) producing-refining-marketing companies which produced 10% to 50% of their crude oil requirements, (5) producing-refining-marketing companies which produced

---

[13] For financial and operating data on a large number of companies in years prior to 1934, we are indebted to Mr. E. T. Knight of The Atlantic Refining Company.

50% to 100% of their crude oil requirements, and (6) producing-refining-marketing companies which produced 100% to 500% of their crude oil requirements.[14] Transportation activities were not considered in making the classification, but many of the companies in all groups, and particularly those in groups 4 to 6, were engaged in one or more kinds of transportation functions.[15]

Lack of information with regard to the activities of the companies made it impossible to establish separate groups of wholesaling and retailing companies, and as a result the "marketing" group includes all companies not engaged in producing or refining. We were able to secure data for only a small number of marketing companies, and these firms were in nearly all cases large organizations with extensive marketing facilities. Characteristically, they bought their products in the tank car markets and resold under well-established brand names of their own. Their operations were therefore quite different from those of the typical small jobber or commission distributor in the industry.

Lack of information with regard to specific activities of the companies also made it necessary to treat all companies engaged in refining as likewise engaged in "marketing." We believe, however, that most of the companies engaged in refining (groups 3 to 6 above) had substantially larger refining than wholesaling activities and substantially larger wholesaling than retailing activities. Moreover, the participation of these companies in the retailing field was usually confined primarily to the ownership or leasing of service stations, particularly after the middle 1930's. In only a few cases did these companies participate extensively in the operation of service stations.[16]

Companies were shifted from one grouping to another whenever changes in their depth and extent of integration took place. The use of an identical sample in each group throughout the 33-year period was found to be both impractical and undesirable because the majority of the companies made one or more changes in their integration arrangements sometime between 1920 and 1952. A company was not changed from one grouping to another, however, if the shift in its integration pattern was only of a minor or transitory nature. For example, if a company consistently produced from 50% to 100% of its crude oil requirements, but dropped slightly below the 50% level for one or two years, it was included in the 50% to 100% group throughout the entire time period. Companies were dropped out of the series at points where no data on their operations were available or at points where mergers, reorganizations, or other basic changes made their operations no longer representative of the groups under study. In order to minimize the effect of changes in the composition of the groups on the final results, a company usually was not included in any series unless its operations and the data available were such that it could remain in the group for a consecutive period of at least two or three years.

The number of companies included in the series ranged from 9 to 32 for the producing group, from 4 to 6 for the marketing group, and from 4 to 14 for all other groups. On the basis of the data contained in Chapter Two and such information as we were able to collect about each of the companies, we believe that our producing group accounted for a fairly large share of the volume of the nonintegrated producers in the industry but only a small share of the number of such producers. Our marketing group clearly represented only a very small portion of the nonintegrated segment of the industry in terms of both volume and numbers. The other four groups, however, probably represented in most of the years a substantial share of their corresponding industry segments in terms of both volume and numbers.

The profit records for each of the six groups of companies are shown graphically in Exhibits V-15 and V-16 and are tabulated in the Appendix, Table 1. The figures plotted in Exhibits V-15 and V-16 are unweighted, arithmetic aver-

---

[14] Crude oil producing ratios were based on net domestic production and crude runs to domestic refineries. Companies were dropped out of the series for years in which their foreign crude oil production was more than 20% of their domestic production *and also* more than 10% of their domestic refinery runs. This procedure was followed because the risks a company encounters and the profits it may earn are quite different in foreign than in domestic production.

[15] Further classification within each of the six groups by type of transportation functions would have greatly enlarged the number of categories and would have made it difficult to secure a reasonable sample in each category.

[16] See Chapters Two and Twelve for data on characteristic integration patterns in the oil industry.

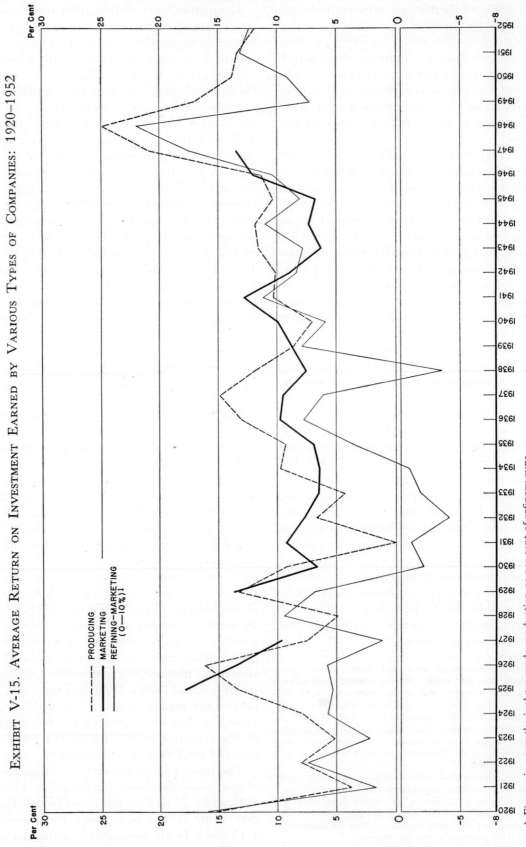

EXHIBIT V-15. AVERAGE RETURN ON INVESTMENT EARNED BY VARIOUS TYPES OF COMPANIES: 1920–1952

PRODUCING
MARKETING
REFINING–MARKETING
(0—10%)[1]

[1] Figures in parenthesis show crude production as per cent of refinery runs.

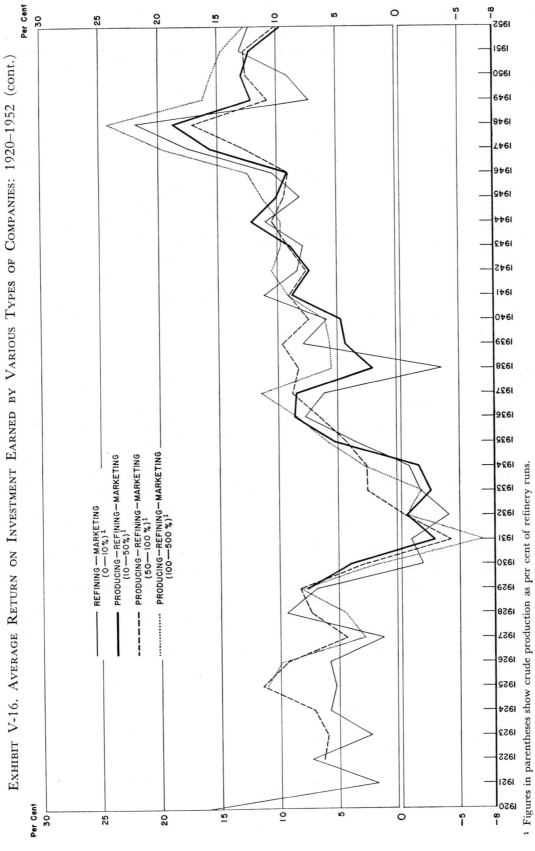

Exhibit V-16. Average Return on Investment Earned by Various Types of Companies: 1920–1952 (cont.)

REFINING—MARKETING
(0—10%)[1]

PRODUCING—REFINING—MARKETING
(10—50%)[1]

PRODUCING—REFINING—MARKETING
(50—100%)[1]

PRODUCING—REFINING—MARKETING
(100—500%)[1]

[1] Figures in parentheses show crude production as per cent of refinery runs.

ages of the per cent return earned on borrowed and invested capital by the companies in each group in each year. As may be seen from the Appendix, Table 1, the results would have been substantially the same had medians or interquartile averages been used. The rankings of the six groups of companies in order of net profit stability in the periods 1920–1934, 1935–1952, and 1920–1952, as measured by median percentage changes from year to year,[17] are shown in Exhibit V-17.

EXHIBIT V-17. RANKING OF VARIOUS TYPES OF COMPANIES IN ORDER OF STABILITY OF AVERAGE RETURN ON INVESTMENT: 1920–1952

Order of Stability, 1920–1952	Median Percentage Changes from Year to Year		
	1920–1934	1935–1952	1920–1952
1. Marketing	24.5%	16.4%	18.6%
2. Prod.-Ref.-Marketing (50%–100%) *	35.9	20.0	20.0
3. Producing	62.0	16.4	30.8
4. Prod.-Ref.-Marketing (100%–500%) *	72.8	15.0	33.4
5. Prod.-Ref.-Marketing (10%–50%) *	76.8	21.2	35.9
6. Refining-Marketing (0–10%) *	89.1	26.3	55.3

* Figures in parentheses show crude oil production as a percentage of refinery runs.

Effect of Integration on Stability of Net Profits:

There are many limitations on the inferences which may be drawn from the data in Exhibits V-15 to V-17 with regard to the effect of various types of integration on the stability of a company's net profits. The net profits of a company reflect many factors in addition to extent and type of integration, such as the calibre of management, the geographic location of plants and other facilities, the size of operations, the availability of financial resources for growth and expansion, and sometimes merely good luck in the discovery of major oil fields. The effect of

these and other factors on the data tends to be minimized as the number of companies included in each group increases. Lack of published data, however, made it impossible for us to build up as large or as well-balanced a sample in all groups as we would have liked. The conclusions drawn from Exhibits V-15 to V-17 must therefore be tempered with the realization that the series are in some cases based on relatively small samples and may reflect not only differences in integration patterns but likewise differences in the other characteristics of the particular companies that happened to be included in each group in each year.[18]

It is also extremely important to note that the series in Exhibits V-15 to V-17 do not by any means reflect the average or typical experience of all companies operating in any given category; on the contrary, the data reflect primarily the experience of the *large and successful* companies in each group. This situation results from the fact that many of the small and unsuccessful companies were closely held and data on their operations were not recorded in published sources. If a small producing company, for example, began operations sometime during the 1920's and was a few years later forced into bankruptcy, financial data on its operations would probably not be available at this date and its experience would not be reflected in the series. The data in Exhibits V-15 to V-17 thus undoubtedly overstate to some degree the typical earnings experience of the companies operating in each category, and the overstatement is not uniform to the extent that the mortality factor and the presence of small, closely held companies among some groups may have been higher than among others.

Finally, it should be recognized that the groupings of companies which it was necessary to use in the profit analysis obscures the effect of certain important steps in the integration

---

[17] Median rather than average percentage changes were used as measures of stability because in some years the profits of some groups declined to very close to zero, and the percentage change to a higher figure in the following year was sometimes so great as to impair the usefulness of average figures as measures of the typical experience of the groups in the time periods under study. (In the case of the yearly gross margin series discussed earlier, the use of either median or average percentage changes as measures of stability would have made no substantial difference in the general results.)

[18] It is particularly likely that the differences among the groups may have been influenced by differences in the relative size of companies included in each group. We would have liked to have prepared series for two or more different size categories in each group and to have compared the differences among size categories within a group with the differences among the over-all figures for each group. We were precluded from such an analysis by the small size of most of the groups which was partially a result of a lack of published data and partially a result of the fact that the total number of companies in the industry in some of the groups was extremely small.

process. For example, it is impossible to tell to what extent the profit performance of the "marketing group" reflects wholesaling operations, retailing operations, or a combination of wholesaling and retailing operations. Since all three types of operations were represented in the activities of the companies, however, the average figures for the group are probably fairly representative of the profits obtainable on a combined wholesaling-retailing operation. It is also impossible to tell to what extent the profit performance of the four groups of companies with refining-marketing operations reflect integration by the companies into wholesaling or retailing activities. As noted above, however, we believe that most of the companies in these four groups had substantially more refining than wholesaling and substantially more wholesaling than retailing. The record of the refining-marketing group (producing less than 10% of its crude oil requirements), in particular, we believe may be taken as representative primarily of profit conditions at the refining level of the industry, and we shall interpret it as such in the discussion which follows.

Notwithstanding the above and various other statistical and accounting limitations of the data presented in Exhibits V-15 to V-17, the profit records provide certain presumptive evidence to corroborate the inferences which may be drawn from the gross margin records concerning the effect of integration on the stability of a company's net profits. In our opinion, the data in Exhibits V-15 to V-17 permit the following general observations:

First, it appears from Exhibit V-15 that net profits at the producing, refining, and marketing levels of the oil industry were subject to continual fluctuations in the period 1920–1952 in much the same manner as were the gross margins, although the fluctuations in net profits did not always coincide precisely with the fluctuations in the corresponding gross margins. It likewise appears that the fluctuations in net profits at one level frequently differed in timing, direction, and amplitude from the fluctuations at other levels. Apparently therefore the behavior of net profits at the different levels of the industry was such that vertical integration *could easily have had* somewhat the same significance as a means of stabilizing a company's net profits that it did as a means of stabilizing

gross margins. In making this interpretation of the records in Exhibit V-15, we are assuming, as noted above, that the record of the refining-marketing group was representative primarily of profit conditions at the refining level of the industry.

A second observation which may be made from Exhibit V-15 is that net profits were generally more stable at the marketing level of the industry in the 33-year period 1920–1952 than they were at the producing or refining levels. (We are again taking the record of the refining-marketing companies as representative of the refining level for the reasons noted above.) The behavior of net profits in this instance is in full accord with the behavior of the gross margins at the separate levels of the industry. It will be recalled from Exhibit V-14, that the wholesaling, the retailing, and the combined wholesaling-retailing gross margins all had substantially greater yearly stability than did either the producing or refining gross margins. It is important to note, however, that the stability in the net profit record of the marketing companies may be partially a result of the composition of our sample. As noted earlier, lack of published records on the earnings of marketing companies made it necessary to use a very small group, and the companies in it were unquestionably among the largest and most successful firms in the industry.[19] Moreover, certain of them were fortunate in having close associations of long standing with their suppliers and thus secured in slight measure some of the advantages of backward integration into refining.

A third observation which is permitted by the data in Exhibit V-15 is that the refining-marketing companies had a less stable earnings record in the period 1920–1952 than did either the producing or marketing companies. Once again the net profit experience is in full accord with that suggested by the gross margin records when it is recognized that our refining-marketing companies probably had the major part of their operations in the refining field. As noted in earlier discussion, the refining gross margin was characterized by substantially greater fluctuations in the period 1920–1952 than were the

---

[19] It is particularly important to recognize that the results for the marketing group do not necessarily represent the activities of the typical small jobber or commission distributor in the industry.

gross margins on any other single activity or any combination of activities. It is particularly significant to observe that the sharp declines in net profits which the refining-marketing companies experienced in 1930–1934, 1938, 1940, and 1949 coincided closely with contractions in the refining gross margin (compare Exhibits V-11 and V-15).

A fourth observation permitted by the net profit records is that all six groups of companies gained in net profit stability after 1934 (see particularly Exhibit V-17). The profit records therefore bear out the conclusion which might have been inferred from the marked gain in gross margin stability which took place after 1934. As pointed out in earlier discussion, the improvement in stability after 1934 probably arose primarily from the adoption of the conservation laws and secondarily from certain fundamental differences in the general business and economic conditions characterizing the periods before and after 1934. It is important to note, however, that the net profits of crude oil producing companies after prorationing were distinctly less stable than the producing gross margin, a circumstance which resulted in part from the curtailment of allowables in times of falling demand. It will be noted, for example, that the net profits of the producing group dropped sharply in 1949, a year when crude oil production was cut back by state authorities. It should also be observed that the net profits of producing companies were not significantly more stable after prorationing than were the net profits of marketing companies and certain other groups.

The fifth and most important observation permitted by the net profit records is that the refining-marketing companies could have improved the stability of their net profit positions by backward integration into crude oil producing activities in the period 1920–1952. As may be seen from Exhibits V-16 and V-17, the refining-marketing companies (defined as those producing less than 10% of their crude oil requirements) had a substantially less stable earnings record than did the producing-refining-marketing companies which produced 10% to 50% of their crude oil requirements. Similarly, the companies producing 10% to 50% of their crude oil requirements had a slightly less stable earnings record than did the companies producing 50% to 100% of their crude oil requirements. The value which crude oil production would have had in offsetting the declines in profits which the refining-marketing companies suffered in 1938 and 1949 is particularly dramatic (see Exhibit V-16). It appears, however, that the expansion of crude oil producing activities beyond 100% of refinery requirements would not have added to net profit stability because the companies producing 100% to 500% of their requirements had a somewhat less stable earnings experience than did those producing 50% to 100% of their requirements.

The effect of backward integration into crude oil production on net profit stability discussed in the above paragraph seems at first glance to be at variance with the effect of a similar move on the stability of yearly gross margins, because as shown in Exhibit V-13 the addition of crude oil producing to a refining-wholesaling-retailing combination would have reduced rather than increased yearly gross margin stability. Here again, however, it must be remembered that our combined refining-wholesale-retailing gross margin represents that which a company would have secured by complete integration into the activities in question. Most of the companies covered in the profit study, on the other hand, probably had only partial integration into wholesaling and a very small extent of integration into retailing.[20] As a result, Exhibits V-16 and V-17 more nearly reflect the gains in net profit stability a refiner would have made by backward integration into crude oil production than they do the gains a refiner-wholesaler-retailer would have made by such a step. Viewed in this light, it is evident that the net profit records in Exhibits V-16 and V-17 reveal precisely the results which were implied by the corresponding gross margin records (i.e., Exhibit V-13 shows a major gain in yearly gross margin stability resulting from the addition of crude producing to refining operations).

In the light of the above observations, it appears that there was a general correlation in the period 1920–1952 between the movements in gross margins and the movements in net profits available from the various industry activities and combinations of activities. We may therefore infer that vertical integration would have made somewhat the same contributions to sta-

---

[20] See Chapters Two and Twelve.

bility of net profits as to stability of gross margins. Moreover, such evidence as was available concerning the actual earnings experience of various groups of integrated and nonintegrated companies lends support to the general conclusion that certain types of vertical integration provided a means by which a company could have improved the stability of its earnings record.

Effect of Integration on Average Level of Net Profits:

The net profit records do not permit definitive conclusions with regard to the effect of vertical integration on the *average level* of an oil company's net profits, because it was not possible to establish separate groups for completely nonintegrated refiners, wholesalers, or retailers. The net profit data do, however, make it possible to compare the records of producing companies, marketing companies, and producing-refining-marketing companies. The records also provide some indication of the effect which the addition of successively larger amounts of crude oil production might have had on the profit experience of a producing-refining-marketing company. For convenience in making these comparisons, the average net profits of each of the six groups of companies used in the profit analysis have been charted in Exhibit V-18 for the periods 1920–1934, 1935–1952, and 1920–1952.[21]

From inspection of Exhibit V-18 it is evident that the producing companies fared somewhat better in the periods 1920–1934, 1935–1952, and 1920–1952 than did any of the other groups covered in our study, except marketing companies in the period 1920–1934. It appears therefore that forward integration would not have enabled a producer to improve the average level of his profits. As will be noted in Chapter Six, the risks connected with exploration and producing activities are significantly greater than in other phases of the business, and there is probably a wider range between the earnings experience of successful and unsuccessful companies in the producing busi-

---

[21] The figures plotted in Exhibit V-18 are unweighted arithmetic averages. As may be seen from the Appendix, Table 1, substantially the same conclusions as those we shall draw in the following paragraphs would have been reached from an analysis of medians or interquartile averages.

ness than in other oil industry activities. Since our profit figures represent primarily the experience of the more successful companies in each group, it might be anticipated that the producing group would show a higher average return than the other groups. Our data should not be interpreted, however, as providing any clear indication that the average level of profits for all companies, *successful and unsuccessful,* in the producing field was generally higher than for companies in other phases of the oil business.

It is also evident from Exhibit V-18 that the marketing companies fared somewhat better than did any of the integrated groups in the period 1920–1934 and the period 1920–1952 as a whole. In the period 1935–1952 the integrated groups producing 50%–100% and 100%–500% of their crude oil requirements secured a slightly higher average return than did the marketing companies. On the whole therefore it appears that a marketing company would not have improved the average level of its profits by backward integration, except by making a very heavy commitment in crude oil producing activities and then only in the period 1935–1952.

As noted earlier, the comparatively favorable profit experience of the marketing companies can be partially explained by the fact that our group was comprised of a small number of the larger and more successful marketing firms in the industry. The comparatively favorable record of the marketing group also results in part from the fact that the marketing companies did not experience a major decline in earnings during the business depression of the early 1930's to the same extent as did nearly all other groups (see Exhibit V-16).

The refining-marketing companies (representing primarily the experience of the refining branch of the industry) had a lower average return on investment in the periods 1920–1934, 1935–1952, and 1920–1952 than did the producing companies or the marketing companies. In the period 1920–1934 the average earnings of the refining-marketing group were higher than the average earnings of the integrated companies producing 10%–50% and 100%–500% of their crude oil requirements but somewhat lower than the average earnings

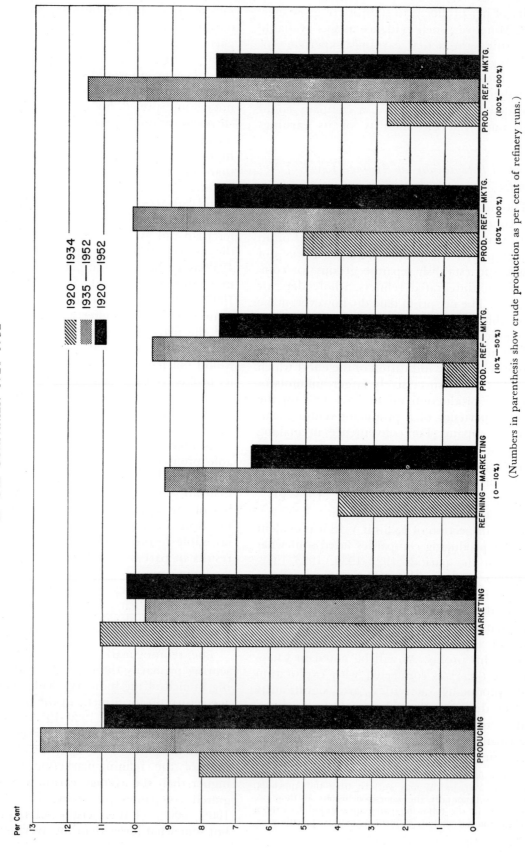

Exhibit V-18. Comparison of Average Level of Return on Investment Earned by Various Types of Oil Companies: 1920–1952

(Numbers in parenthesis show crude production as per cent of refinery runs.)

of the integrated companies producing 50%–100% of their crude oil requirements. In the period 1920–1934 therefore we find no significant evidence that backward integration into crude oil production would have improved the average earnings experience of a refining-marketing company.

In the period 1935–1952 and the period 1920–1952 as a whole, on the other hand, it appears that backward integration into crude oil production would have enabled a refining-marketing company to have improved its average return on borrowed and invested capital. In the period 1935–1952 the integrated companies show a clear increase in average earnings experience with increases in extent of integration into crude oil production. Moreover, in the period 1920–1952 as a whole the integrated companies producing 10%–50% of their crude oil requirements had appreciably higher earnings than did the refining-marketing companies. The integrated companies producing 50%–100% and 100%–500% of their crude oil requirements, however, had almost exactly the same average earnings experience in the period 1920–1952 as a whole as did the companies producing 10%–50% of their crude oil requirements.

We conclude therefore that our data provide no significant evidence that vertical integration would have increased the *average level* of a company's earnings, except possibly in the case of backward integration by a refiner into crude oil producing activities in the period 1935–1952. It should again be observed that our data did not permit an exhaustive study of the effect of integration on the average level of net profits because of the limited size of our samples and the fact that it was possible to develop records for only six different groups of integrated and nonintegrated companies. Had it been possible to study the earnings of completely nonintegrated refiners, wholesalers, or retailers, it might have been found that such groups had substantially higher or substantially lower average earnings than the six groups which we examined.

V. SUMMARY

1. The gross margins available at the producing, refining, wholesaling, and retailing levels of the industry were subject to continual fluctuations in the period 1920–1952, and the fluctuations at one level frequently differed in timing, direction, and amplitude from the fluctuations at other levels. There were marked differences in the relative stability of the four gross margins, and the fluctuations in the refining margin were characteristically more violent than at any other level of the industry. The gross margins at all levels were significantly more stable in the period 1935–1952 than in the period 1920–1934, primarily because of the development of the prorationing laws in the middle 1930's and secondarily because of fundamental differences in the economic and business conditions characterizing the periods 1920–1934 and 1935–1952.

2. In view of the differences in the timing, direction, and amplitude of the gross margin movements at the separate levels of the industry in the period 1920–1952, vertical integration constituted a means by which a company could have done a great deal toward stabilizing the gross margin on which it operated. With two or three exceptions, all of the major integration steps a company might have taken from any position would have contributed something to gross margin stability. The greatest gains in *monthly* gross margin stability would have arisen from integration by a refiner into producing or wholesaling and from integration by a wholesaler into refining or retailing. The greatest gains in *yearly* gross margin stability would have arisen from integration by a refiner into producing or wholesaling and from integration by a producer-refiner into wholesaling. These types of integration are among the more common of those that took place in the industry in the period 1920–1952.

3. The behavior of the gross margins available from individual activities and combinations of activities is important because it contains an inference that: (a) the profit opportunities at the different levels of the industry were continually shifting and changing in the period 1920–1952, (b) the movements at one level frequently differed in timing, direction, and amplitude from the move-

ments at other levels, and (c) vertical integration provided an important means by which a company could stabilize the net return earned on its borrowed and invested capital. These three inferences were corroborated in several respects by an examination of the earnings experience of 98 different oil companies with different types of integration in the period 1920–1952.

4. Although the analysis of monthly gross margins, yearly gross margins, and net return earned on borrowed and invested capital provided considerable evidence that many of the important types of vertical integration in the period 1920–1952 would have

resulted in an increase in *stability* of net profits, none of our data provided any significant evidence that vertical integration would have resulted in an increase in the *average level* of net profits, except possibly in the case of backward integration by a refining-marketing company into crude oil production in the period 1935–1952. We do not, however, consider our findings with regard to the effect of integration on the average level of net profits as exhaustive or definitive because of limitations in the size of our samples and the number of different types of integrated and nonintegrated companies it was possible for us to study.

CHAPTER SIX

The Causes of the Variations in Profit
Opportunities

THE preceding chapter revealed that vertical integration has often constituted an important means by which an oil company could increase the stability of its gross margins and annual net profits. Attention was also directed to the fact that vertical integration has had the potential for stabilizing a company's earnings experience because the profit opportunities at the separate levels of the industry have been continually shifting and changing and because the movements at one level have frequently differed in timing, direction, and amplitude from the movements at other levels. In this chapter our purpose will be to examine some of the causes of the variations in profit movements at the separate levels of the business and to appraise the significance and probable duration of the causes in the economic life of the oil industry.

In general, it may be said that the variations in profit movements arise from the resolution of the whole complex of business and economic circumstances which are relevant to the oil industry and to the separate activities of which it is comprised. A complete analysis of these circumstances would require a detailed review of almost every phase of oil industry life and of general business conditions throughout the period 1920–1952 and obviously cannot be undertaken in this volume. We shall therefore confine our discussion to a brief survey of some of the more important of the general causes of the dissimilarities in profit movements at the different levels of the industry and to a detailed analysis of one specific example, the sharp contraction in profit opportunities at the refining level of the industry which occurred in 1949. In a concluding section of the chapter we shall also comment briefly on the allegation that integrated companies "subsidize losses at one level of the industry out of profits made at another" because much of the substance of the chapter will be pertinent to the controversy which has arisen on this particular matter.

I. THE GENERAL CAUSES OF THE PROFIT VARIATIONS

The profit opportunities at each level of the oil industry are determined by the interplay of a particular set of business and economic forces. The forces at work at one level of the industry at any given time, however, are not necessarily similar in either degree or kind to those at work at other levels. As a result, it is entirely appropriate, and indeed inevitable, that the fluctuations in profits at the separate levels of the business should be characterized by differences in timing, direction, and amplitude. Among the more important of the economic circumstances from which the dissimilarities in profit movements arise are: (a) variations in the capital inputs to the different levels of the industry relative to requirements, (b) dissimilarities in price movements in the various petroleum markets, (c) differences among the various phases of the business with respect to such things as the mix of products handled, responsiveness to changes in external conditions, and the risk attached to capital investments.

Variations in Capital Inputs:

One of the most important factors determining the profit opportunities at a given level of the industry is the availability of capital facilities to perform the functions and services of that segment of the industry relative to the demand therefor. Funds for the construction of new facilities, however, rarely flow into any industry, or segment of an industry, smoothly and uniformly in accordance with the need for them. Characteristically, the capital input to a particular industrial activity sometimes runs ahead and sometimes lags behind the immediate requirements of the situation. As a result, the profit opportunities available from the activity are subject to continual fluctuations. Conversely, it may be said that the fluctuations in profit opportunities are the means by which new capital is attracted to a particular activity when the funds are needed and the means by which the input of capital is retarded when the funds can be put to better use elsewhere in the economy.

Consider, for example, the sequence of events which often follows a rapid rise in the demand for a particular industry service or product. The rise in demand often creates a shortage of facilities and results in wide profit margins which, in turn, attract new capital to the business. The influx of new capital very frequently, however, continues past the point justified by the enlarged requirements of the market for many reasons. Business firms may overestimate the extent and duration of the demand increase; buyers in shopping around for supplies in times of shortage may create the illusion that a greater shortage exists than is actually the case; several different firms may undertake expansion programs, each in the hope of capturing what is essentially the same piece of new business; and construction programs may be started which have to be carried to completion even though later developments may reveal that their conception was overly optimistic. Moreover, when a firm embarks on a major expansion of physical facilities, it is often a matter of sound business economics to provide not only for the immediate growth in demand but likewise for anticipated future growth, perhaps five to ten years in advance. If several firms undertake such programs, it is inevitable that the new capital facilities provided will be at least temporarily in excess of the needs of the situation.

The surplus of capital investment which is often generated in the manner outlined above by a rise in demand ultimately produces intensive competition and low profit margins. The low profit margins characteristically continue until some of the excess capital is squeezed out of the industry or until a further rise in demand either brings the situation into balance or starts the cycle all over again. In the latter case, however, business investors may be a little slow, because of the period of low profits which the industry has just experienced, to make major new commitments until the demand for them is clearly evident. As a result, the new cycle may start with capital input lagging behind the needs of the situation.

For the foregoing and various other reasons, the capital inputs to particular segments of an industry rarely maintain a precise adjustment to demand, but, on the contrary, tend to oscillate through periods of shortage and surplus. In the oil industry the capital inputs to the producing, refining, wholesaling, and retailing phases of the business have been subject to many such oscillations, and the timing, direction, and amplitude of the oscillations have not always been precisely the same in all phases of the business. As a result, there have frequently been dissimilarities in the profit movements at the different levels of the industry. A brief review of developments in the retailing, refining, and producing phases of the business during and subsequent to the initial period of rapid growth in the automotive gasoline market will serve to illustrate the point.

The developments in the retailing phase of the business which took place in response to the rapid increase in automobile registrations and the rise in the demand for motor fuel in the period 1914 to 1926 were mentioned in Chapter Four. The service station was found to be an effective means of serving the new automotive market, and nearly all companies engaged in marketing operations rushed into the construction of stations. In the middle 1920's the growth in the automotive gasoline market began to slacken, but new investment continued to surge into the retailing business because the steadily mounting pressure of large crude oil supplies was placing all companies under great compulsion (a) to construct or acquire retail outlets as a means of holding their markets, or (b) to offer wide margins to independent jobbers or dealers for marketing services.

The continued investment in retail outlets eventually led to tough competition in the retail field, a sharp decline in gallonage per outlet, and a reduction in the net profit which could be earned on investments in service sta-

EXHIBIT VI-1. THE ATLANTIC REFINING COMPANY

Experience of Company Operated Service Stations: 1925–1934

Year	Number of Stations	Total Cost of Stations ($1,000)	Total Gasoline Sold, Gallons (000)	Operating Costs Less Depreciation ($1,000)	Gallons Sold per Station (000)	Station Cost per Gallon	Operating Costs per Gallon
1925	173	$ 8,736	52,130	$2,364	302	16.7¢	4.47¢
1926	191	9,217	57,929	2,684	302	15.9	4.57
1927	210	9,512	59,798	2,791	284	15.9	4.60
1928	225	9,732	60,761	2,992	268	16.1	4.85
1929	303	10,739	61,987	3,495	205	17.3	5.55
1930	453	14,816	70,516	4,947	156	20.9	6.88
1931	550	18,024	82,007	5,365	149	22.0	6.40
1932	586	18,992	74,907	4,638	128	25.3	6.07
1933	603	18,689	72,385	4,593	120	25.8	6.17
1934	607	19,047	71,346	5,160	118	26.6	7.04

SOURCE: The Atlantic Refining Company.

tion properties. As the volume per outlet dropped, marketing expenses per gallon sold increased because a fairly large share of the expenses involved in the operation of a service station are of a fixed character and cannot be adjusted downward in proportion to volume changes. Moreover, as the oil companies struggled to maintain their volume in the face of severe competition, advertising, sales promotion, and various other marketing expenses tended to increase. The experience of The Atlantic Refining Company with its company operated service stations, which is shown in Exhibit VI-1, is typical of that of many oil companies in the late 1920's and early 1930's. In a study made in 1935, The Atlantic Refining Company estimated that its net profits on service station operations *before* depreciation and interest charges, expressed as a percentage of the undepreciated plant cost, declined as follows in the period 1921–1934: [1]

	Return on Investment
Prior to 1921 (rough approx.)	60.0%
1921	41.4
1924	27.1
1928	18.8
1930	7.5
1932	4.0
1934	2.1

The refining level of the industry, like the retailing level, experienced a great influx of capital in response to the initial rapid growth in the market for automotive gasoline, and here again the industry soon found itself with more capacity than was required by the immediate

situation.[2] The circumstances at the refining level, however, were somewhat different from those at the retailing level. As pointed out in Chapter Four, there was considerable anxiety in the period following World War I that the United States might not have sufficient supplies of crude oil to meet the growing demand for automotive gasoline. Moreover, the market for gasoline was growing much more rapidly than were the markets for other refined products. As a result, much attention was directed to the technological problem of increasing the yield of gasoline from crude oil. These efforts bore fruit in the commercial development of continuous thermal cracking processes which gained widespread acceptance in the industry during the middle 1920's and made possible an important increase in gasoline yields (see Chapter Nineteen).

As the more progressive refiners installed the new thermal cracking facilities, they automatically increased the gasoline producing capacity of their plants. At the same time, however, the refiners which did not choose or were not able to make the necessary investments in the new facilities continued to operate their old plants as long as they could without incurring an out-of-pocket loss. While the industry was in the process of making the transition in plant facilities required by the advance in refining techniques, there was therefore a mixture of

---

[1] Records of The Atlantic Refining Company

[2] Refinery runs did not average above 80% of refinery capacity in any year from 1920 to 1940; in about one-third of the years, refinery runs ranged from about 60% to 70% of capacity and in the remaining years from 70% to 80% of capacity (see Chapter Eighteen, Exhibit XVIII-2).

old and new equipment in existence which in total had somewhat more gasoline producing capacity than was required by the immediate market situation, particularly in the late 1920's when the growth in the gasoline demand began to slacken and in the depression of the early 1930's when the gasoline demand turned downward (see Chapter Four, Exhibit IV-3). The spare refining capacity together with the changes in demand resulted in a downward movement in refining profits which then served for a time to retard the input of new capital to refining activities.

The response of the crude oil producing level of the industry to the rise in the demand for automotive gasoline and to the threatened shortage of crude oil after World War I has been discussed in considerable detail in Chapter Four. At this point it need merely be noted that the measure of the large crude oil producing capacity which developed in response to the influx of new capital to the producing field was determined largely by the fortuitous circumstance of a series of major crude oil discoveries. It should also be noted that the impact of the large crude oil producing capacity on prices and profits was later cushioned to some extent by the development of the prorationing laws. In the refining and marketing fields, however, various attempts, voluntary and legal, to mitigate the economic effects of large capacity relative to demand proved largely unsuccessful.

From the foregoing discussion it is apparent that the rapid growth in the market for automotive gasoline precipitated inputs of investment capital to the retailing, refining, and producing phases of the business which were not at all times precisely in adjustment with immediate needs in the three phases of the business. The specific factors contributing to the lack of adjustment were, however, somewhat different in each of the three cases. As a result, the timing and significance of the lags and leads in capital inputs varied among the three levels of the industry and produced corresponding variations in the behavior of profit opportunities.

There are many considerations, in addition to those illustrated above, which contribute to lags and leads in capital inputs to the different levels of the industry and to the disparities in the timing and severity of the lags and leads in

one phase of the business as contrasted with another. One important consideration, for example, is the time lag between the initiation of new capital investments and the completion of projects. It is usually several months, or even years, after a change in market requirements has been recognized before new facilities can be brought into existence. During the period while new facilities are being built there is an inevitable temporary lag in the adjustment of capital facilities to industry requirements. Moreover, the time lag between the initiation and completion of projects varies among the different levels of the industry. In the marketing field, new facilities can often be constructed in a few months. In the case of pipe lines or refineries, two or three years may be required to complete a major project, while in the producing field, five to seven years may elapse before new expenditures are fully manifested in new producing capacity. Therefore, even though all levels of the industry are affected equally by and respond simultaneously to a given change in industry requirements, there will almost inevitably be differences in the speed with which capital facilities are adjusted to the new market conditions.

Dissimilarities in Price Movements:

A second important cause of the dissimilarities in profit fluctuations in the different phases of the oil business, and particularly the monthly fluctuations, may be found in the fact that prices at the successive levels of the industry do not move in complete harmony with one another. Exhibit VI-2 contains a record for the Mid-Continent area of the price of 36° gravity crude oil and of the tank car, tank wagon, and service station prices of gasoline. The crude oil price is plotted to reflect actual dates of change. The tank car price for gasoline is the monthly average of the lows of the published quotations for the Oklahoma, Group 3 market. The tank wagon and service station prices for gasoline are the average of the posted prices, ex taxes, on the first of the month in Tulsa, St. Louis, Wichita, Omaha, and Des Moines as reported by The Texas Company These prices are the same ones as those used in the computation of the gross margins available at the separate levels of the industry in Chapter Five. The series have been plotted on a semi-logarithmic

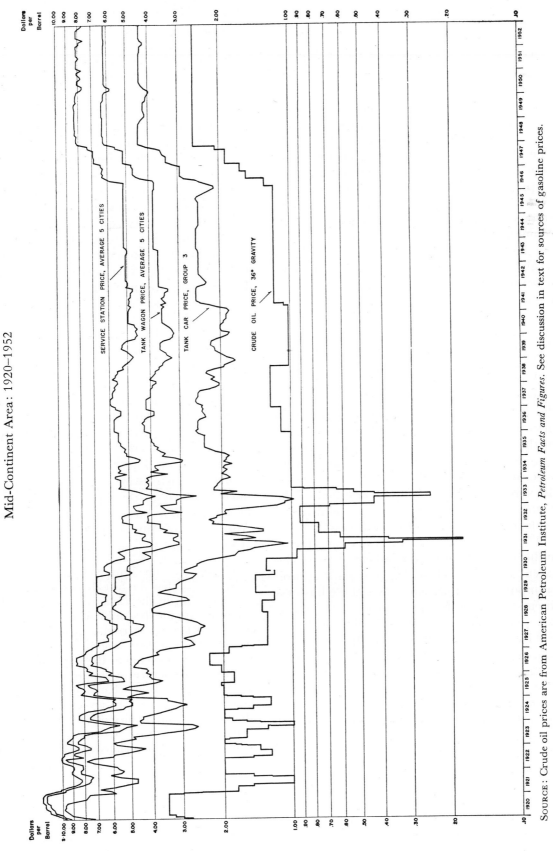

EXHIBIT VI-2. CRUDE OIL PRICE AND TANK CAR, TANK WAGON, AND SERVICE STATION
PRICES OF REGULAR GRADE GASOLINE
Mid-Continent Area: 1920–1952

SOURCE: Crude oil prices are from American Petroleum Institute, *Petroleum Facts and Figures*. See discussion in text for sources of gasoline prices.

grid to permit ready comparison of the relative magnitude of the fluctuations at one level versus another.

An examination of Exhibit VI-2 immediately reveals that the broad movements in the price series are of the same general pattern. This circumstance results from the fact that the segments of the industry involved in the production and refining of crude oil and the distribution of gasoline are subject, in general, to the same basic set of demand-supply conditions. It is apparent from the data in Exhibit VI-2, however, that marked dissimilarities in the short-run movements of the four price series are very common. Upward or downward movements at one level may take place while prices at other levels remain constant. Moreover, in times when prices generally are moving to either higher or lower levels, the timing of the adjustments made in each of the four prices may vary greatly. The tank car price of gasoline, for example, almost always moves both upward and downward in advance of the tank wagon and retail prices of gasoline and frequently moves upward and downward in advance of the crude oil price. These dissimilarities in price movements are reflected in fluctuations in the gross margins available at the separate levels of the industry and, in the absence of offsetting changes in the cost of operations or the volume handled, produce variations in the return which may be earned on capital invested in the different phases of the business.

The dissimilarities in the price movements at the separate levels of the industry are to some extent a corollary of the lags and leads in capital inputs to the different phases of the business discussed above. The price movements are, in fact, one of the important means by which lags and leads in capital investment adjustments are translated into fluctuations in profit opportunities. The variations in the movement of the four prices, and particularly the short-run variations, however, reflect many things other than lags and leads in capital inputs, as will be noted in the following paragraphs.

Differences in the Sensitivity of the Various Petroleum Prices to Market Conditions: One important reason why the prices at the various levels of the industry do not move in complete sympathy with one another may be found in the fact that the four prices differ in their sensitivity to changes in market conditions. It will be noted, for example, that the refined product prices have been far more sensitive than has the crude oil price. This circumstance results from a number of causes. Of primary importance is the fact that the operation of the prorationing laws automatically injects an element of stability into crude oil prices which is not present at the other levels of the industry. The prorationing laws in several of the important oil producing states operate in such a manner that changes in the demand-supply relationship for crude oil are often quickly compensated by legally imposed adjustments in the supply which, in effect, anticipate and preclude price changes. At the other levels of the industry, however, readjustments in demand-supply relationships are usually prompted by and brought about through the mechanism of price changes.

Crude oil prices also tend to be less sensitive than product prices because the character of the trading in the crude oil market is inherently different from that in the refined product markets. As indicated in Exhibit VI-2, the crude oil price showed a somewhat greater stability than the refined product prices even in the years prior to the development of the prorationing laws. The differences in the fundamental characteristics of the crude oil and refined products markets were well summarized by Sidney A. Swensrud in a speech before the Association of American Petroleum Geologists at Oklahoma City, March 23, 1939:

The reason refined product prices are more sensitive is doubtless the fact that trading is continually going on in these markets and price changes occur in minute fractions of a cent per gallon. Many sellers meet or contact many buyers almost continually, and there is no physical obstacle, such as a pipe line, to stand in the way of a buyer shifting from one source of supply to another or to hinder a seller from changing customers so far as wholesale transactions are concerned. Contrast this with the mechanics of the crude oil market where, under ordinary circumstances, buyers and sellers are closely associated together by pipe line connections. (Where this is not the case, as in a flush pool where oil is being shipped in tank cars, trucks, et cetera, crude oil prices frequently fluctuate widely during short periods.) These close physical connections between crude producer and purchaser make for delays in price changes because, in a competitive industry, price changes ordinarily come about through a buyer shifting or threatening to shift from one seller to another or vice-versa. In the case of crude oil producers and purchasers bound together by pipe line connections, however, there is difficulty and inconvenience in producers shifting to new purchasers or purchasers shifting to new sources of supply. In other words, there is the element of inertia. Furthermore so far as crude price *declines* are concerned, there is the fact that the initiative ordinarily comes from the purchasers in that they usually post their purchase price. For the buyer to cut the crude price is, therefore, to take upon himself considerable ill-will, however justified his action might be from the standpoint of supply and demand. This is in sharp contrast to the impersonal nature of the similar transactions in connection with commodities such as wheat or cotton, where there is no close physical or personal relation between the ultimate buyer and the producer.

These aspects of the crude oil price market explain, we believe, why it is a rather sluggish market in responding to changes in the supply-demand situation which have already been reflected in the prices of refined products. . . .[3]

Another reason for the stability of crude oil prices relative to refined product prices arises from the fact that there are very few individuals or companies anywhere in the oil industry who are interested in seeing crude oil prices move downward in times of declining product prices. The data in Chapter Two indicate that about 60% of the crude oil in the United States is produced by companies engaged in both refining and producing activities and that the remaining 40% is produced chiefly by companies engaged in producing operations alone. Since the refiners not engaged in producing activities consume less than 5% of the crude oil supply, it follows that such refiners can at the most buy only about one-eighth of the oil produced by nonintegrated producers and that the remaining seven-eighths must be purchased by the producing and refining companies.

In other words, approximately seven-eighths of the crude oil sold by independent producers is bought by companies which also have crude oil production of their own. In times of de-

clining product prices, such companies are naturally slow to bargain for lower crude oil prices because reductions in crude oil prices tend to prejudice the value of their own long-term investments in producing properties. Moreover, a reduction in crude oil prices brings about a reduction in the amount of the depletion allowance for tax purposes which a company may secure on a given volume of crude oil production. From an immediate operating cost standpoint alone, any company producing more than about 80% of its own crude oil requirements gains more from resisting a crude oil price decrease and thus maintaining the depletion allowance on the oil it produces than it would through bargaining for a price decrease and thus reducing the cost of that portion of its crude oil supply which it buys. As a result of these circumstances, the crude oil market may not develop pressures for a downward movement in prices as quickly as do some of the refined products markets.

The above paragraphs cover only a few of the many factors which influence the movement and behavior of crude oil prices. The points cited, however, constitute some of the more important reasons why crude oil prices are somewhat less sensitive to changing demand-supply conditions than are refined product prices. In a similar manner, the differences in the relative sensitivity of the tank car, tank wagon, and service station prices may to a considerable extent be explained by fundamental differences in the character of the markets involved.

Differences in Demand-Supply Conditions at the Separate Levels of the Industry: The dissimilarities in price movements at the different levels of the industry may be attributed in considerable measure to the fact that demand-supply conditions in the separate phases of the business are frequently quite different. It is true, as noted above, that the industry as a whole is, in general, responsive to essentially the same underlying demand-supply factors. In any short period of time, however, it is quite possible for stocks at one level of the industry to work into different positions than stocks at other levels. The refining branch of the industry, for example, may increase its refinery runs and fuel oil yields in order to build up fuel

[3] Sidney A. Swensrud, "The Relation Between Crude Oil and Product Prices," *Bulletin of the American Association of Petroleum Geologists,* Vol. 23, No. 6, June 1949, p. 773.

oil stocks for the winter season. In so doing, the refiners may draw crude oil stocks to low levels and permit gasoline inventories to decline to slightly lower positions than would normally be the case. If the winter subsequently proves unusually warm, a condition of oversupply may develop in the fuel oil markets whereas both the crude oil and gasoline markets may be in no distress, or certainly in no comparable degree of distress. It is entirely possible, therefore, that short-run price movements may be occurring in one market as demand-supply conditions there work out a new adjustment while prices in other markets remain constant or move in the opposite direction.

The Timing of Management Actions on Price Changes: Dissimilarities of short duration in the price movements at the separate levels of the industry sometimes arise from the timing of price changes by the price leaders in the various petroleum markets. Characteristically, there is a continual interaction in the petroleum markets among the price actions of companies of all types and sizes. A small marketer cannot hope to secure business at prices much above those charged by the large firms in the market, and the large firms cannot long maintain their volume in the face of persistent and deep price cutting by smaller competitors. A small company may choose to build its volume on a price basis and sell consistently below the prices charged by the large marketers, but such a firm ordinarily tends to use the prices of the large marketers as a target and to keep its prices as close to them as is consistent with its volume objectives. All marketers are therefore continually influenced in their price actions by the price decisions of their competitors, both large and small.[4]

In nearly all of the refined product markets, there are nevertheless usually one or more marketers, the so-called price leaders, who individually have a sufficient share of the business so that their decisions on price changes have a greater influence on the market than do the decisions of other firms. The decisions which these price leaders make from time to time with respect to price changes reflect their best judgment of the short- and long-term demand-supply situation, competitive conditions, the state of the economy, political sentiment, and all other factors they deem pertinent to the situation. The price leader in a particular market, however, cannot always make his price changes on precisely the day, week, or month that conditions indicate they can or should be made. On the contrary, the price leader may interpret demand-supply conditions incorrectly and may as a result make his changes early or late with respect to the new conditions developing in the market or may make changes which are larger or smaller than they should be. If the error made by the price leader is large, he is usually not followed by other marketers, and his action is of little significance. If, on the other hand, his error is small, he may be followed by many other marketers and thus lead the market to a new price level somewhat sooner or later than might otherwise have been the case.

The errors which individual price leaders may make in the timing of their price decisions cannot, of course, impinge uniformly on all products in all markets at all times. A company initiating a particular price change may be of importance in one product market but of little significance in another. Moreover, many companies which occupy positions of leadership in the refined products markets have little or no ability to influence the timing of price adjustments in the crude oil markets. As a result, dissimilarities in the price movements at the different levels of the industry inevitably occur. These dissimilarities are nearly always of short duration because the prices in all markets must sooner or later adjust to the level dictated by economic and competitive conditions. For short periods of time and on certain special occasions, however, the dissimilarities arising from lags or leads in the timing of price actions by large marketers may be of some significance.

A classic example of the way in which tardy managerial action by a price leader may contribute to dissimilarities in price movements at the different levels of the industry may be found in the experience of the Standard Oil Company (Indiana). In the years prior to 1933 the company continued to establish selling prices which were the sum of its own refinery

---

[4] For a thorough analysis of the mechanics of price making in the gasoline market, see Edmund P. Learned, "Pricing of Gasoline: A Case Study," *Harvard Business Review*, Vol. XXVI, No. 6, November 1948, pp. 723–766.

base prices plus freight to destination long after the discovery of the big Oklahoma fields and the development of new refining centers in the Mid-Continent area had indicated the desirability of basing product prices on the Mid-Continent market plus rail freight to destination. In 1933 the company began to base its selling prices on the Mid-Continent market and again clung to this practice long after the development of new methods of transportation and new refining centers in Michigan and Illinois had indicated that new pricing procedures were necessary to meet the competition of the local refiners and of the Mid-Continent refiners reaching the market by product pipe lines or other improved methods of transportation.[5] In both cases, the company suffered severe losses in volume to new competitors who crowded into the market under the price umbrella which it maintained, and eventually the management was forced to meet the price levels established by market conditions. The resistance the company offered to price reductions in both periods, however, unquestionably had some influence on the timing of the movements of the various refined product prices with respect to each other and with respect to crude oil prices.

A more recent example of the influence of managerial action by a price leader on the timing of short-run price movements in the various petroleum markets may be found in the experience of the Esso Standard Oil Company in 1947 and 1948 with its now famous "hold-the-line" price policy.[6] A severe shortage of crude oil and petroleum products developed in 1947 and 1948 largely because the industry as a whole underestimated the increases in demand which developed in the postwar period. In the winter of 1947–1948 the shortage of fuel oil proved particularly acute not only because of the very rapid growth which was taking place in the use of fuel oil for home heating purposes but also because weather conditions were unusually severe. As early as the summer of 1947 it was clear that strong inflationary forces were at work with respect to petroleum prices in

general and fuel oil prices in particular. The managements of Esso Standard and of the parent Standard Oil Company (New Jersey) were at this time of the opinion that the shortage of petroleum products was not due to a lack of crude oil in the ground but rather to a shortage of steel and other facilities necessary to produce, transport, and refine the oil and that price increases would not, therefore, be effective in bringing forth new supplies. The two managements were also of the opinion that the demand for petroleum products was inelastic in the short run and that price increases would not curtail the demand in any substantial degree. Finally, the Jersey management was sensitive to the strong public sentiment against price increases which existed in 1947 and recognized that price advances coupled with shortages of product and high profits might make the company very vulnerable to charges of profiteering.[7]

On July 24, 1947, therefore, Esso Standard announced its policy of "holding-the-line" on crude oil prices and on product prices at all levels with a statement which read, in part, as follows:

The present demand for oil products is higher than ever before in history. The ability of the industry to meet this unprecedented demand is strained, not by the lack of crude oil in the ground, but by limitations of transportation and other facilities occurring largely as a result of the war.

Most oil companies are having difficulty in meeting the full demands of their customers for products. Such a situation usually results in an increase in product prices which brings out added supplies and tends to balance supply and demand. A number of price increases have secretly taken place. It is our opinion, however, that under present conditions where a shortage of fabricated steel and other materials limits the industry's ability to produce, transport, and refine more crude oil, further price increases will not be effective in increasing the overall supply of petroleum products. We feel such price increases would only be inflationary and should be resisted.

Esso Standard believes so strongly that further increases in the price of crude oil or products under present conditions are not in the best interests of either the oil industry or the public that it is following a general policy of not increasing prices

---

[5] See discussion in Chapter Seven.

[6] For a detailed treatment of this situation, see Harry L. Hansen and Powell Niland, "Esso Standard: A Case Study in Pricing," *Harvard Business Review*, Vol. XXX, No. 3, May-June 1952, pp. 114–132.

[7] Ibid., p. 116.

unless such increases will tend to maintain or bring out additional supplies.[8]

Esso Standard marketed in 18 states along the Atlantic and Gulf Coasts and had traditionally been regarded as the market leader in New Jersey and most of the southern states in which it sold. The impact of the company's hold-the-line policy on price movements at the various levels of the industry was fairly complex, and space does not permit us to treat the matter in detail or to pass judgment on either the business wisdom or the social and economic implications of the action. In general, however, it can be said that the Esso policy with respect to refined product prices was followed by many, but by no means all, of the marketers in the territory in which it operated. The company was able to exercise a much lesser degree of influence on crude oil prices, and in order to maintain its crude oil buying connections [9] was forced to follow fairly quickly the upward movement initiated by the Phillips Petroleum Company in Oklahoma, Kansas, and Texas on October 15, 1947, and by the Sun Oil Company on November 28. In response to the advance in crude oil prices, Esso Standard raised its distillate prices 0.8 cents per gallon on October 30, and finally on December 22, after price increases had been made by several other large marketers, the company announced a general increase for all of its major refined products.

There is no question, however, that the hold-the-line decision of the Jersey and Esso managements tended to modify and retard the short-run movements in both crude oil and refined product prices. For our purposes, it is particularly important to note that the influence of the company on prices was significantly stronger in the refined product markets than it was in the crude oil markets and that the adoption of the hold-the-line policy inevitably, therefore, contributed to temporary dissimilarities in the movements of crude oil and refined product prices. The Jersey and Esso actions had no significant influence on the Gulf Coast cargo prices for refined products which rose

rather quickly as the shortages increased throughout the winter. As a result, wholesalers buying in the Gulf Coast for resale in the Esso territory along the Atlantic Coast protested that they were caught in a "price squeeze."

It should not be inferred from any of the foregoing discussion that the price leaders in any petroleum market have the power to set market prices. No managerial action with respect to prices which is contrary to competitive and economic conditions in the markets can stand for long or be of any lasting significance. It will be noted, for example, that in both of the cases cited above the leading marketer was soon forced to respond to the pressure of competitive conditions and to adjust his price policies accordingly. The intent of the above discussion therefore is merely to establish the fact that the managerial decisions of leading marketers sometimes have a bearing on the *timing* of price adjustments and the amplitude of short-run price fluctuations. It follows that these decisions may, for brief periods of time, contribute to dissimilarities in price movements at the different levels of the industry or may at times, on the other hand, keep those dissimilarities from being as great as might otherwise be the case under the pressure of other forces which contribute to them.

Other Factors Contributing to Dissimilarities in Profit Movements:

In addition to the variations in capital inputs and dissimilarities in price movements discussed in the preceding pages, there are many other factors which cause profit opportunities to fluctuate somewhat differently at the separate levels of the industry. Certain of these factors will be mentioned briefly in the paragraphs which follow:

To some extent, the dissimilarities in profit movements are simply a result of differences in the mix of products handled at the successive levels of the industry. The crude oil producer is, in general, subject to the entire range of demand-supply factors effecting all petroleum products.[10] The refiner is likewise subject to the full range of demand-supply considerations,

---

[8] See G. Ross McKee, Jr., "Jersey's Hold-Line Policy Draws Praise and Censure," *National Petroleum News*, July 30, 1947, pp. 9–10.

[9] The company was at this time purchasing approximately 50% of the crude oil supply for its domestic refineries.

[10] The producer of one grade of crude oil may, however, be exposed to a somewhat different set of demand-supply factors than is the producer of a significantly different grade of crude oil.

except to the extent that he may lack equipment for producing certain products, such as asphalts or lubricating oils, and may thus have his activities limited to certain phases of the business. The wholesaler, however, does not normally handle residual fuel oil and certain other important products which are usually sold by refiners directly to customers. Similarly, the retail level of the industry does not normally handle a number of products, such as heating oils, which are sold by wholesalers.

It is readily apparent, therefore, that a change in the demand-supply conditions with respect to any one of the petroleum products may have different implications with respect to profit opportunities at each of the levels of the industry. An oversupply of or drop in the demand for residual fuel oil, for example, might temporarily depress refining and producing profits without necessarily affecting wholesaling and retailing profits at all or in comparable degree. Similarly, the development of an oversupply of gasoline might lead to price cutting in the tank car, tank wagon, and retail markets but effect profits at the refining, wholesaling, and retailing levels differently depending on the extent of the price distress in each market and the relative significance of gasoline in the total profit position of each of the three phases of the business.

As a consequence of the differences in the mix of products handled at the separate levels of the industry, changes in general economic conditions may have a different bearing on the profit opportunities at one level than they do at another. During World War II, for example, there was a great increase in the demand by the armed services for many petroleum products. The armed services, however, did most of their buying in the cargo markets, and as a result the demand increase had a very different bearing on the activities of producers and refiners than it did on the activities of wholesalers and retailers. Similarly, the rationing of consumer purchases of gasoline during World War II tended to curtail the volume of business handled at the wholesaling and retailing levels of the industry but was of little significance to the producing and refining levels because their output was diverted to war uses. It will be noted from Chapter Five, Exhibit V-15, that the average net return earned by marketing companies declined during the period 1941–1944 whereas the net return earned by producing companies had a clear upward trend. Refining-marketing companies experienced a decline in net earnings during the war years, but in lesser degree than did the marketing companies.

Another factor which contributes to differences in the level and movement of profit opportunities in the separate phases of the oil business may be found in the differences in the risks which are associated with capital investments at each level of the industry. In any field of business endeavor, the return earned on invested capital tends to reflect the hazards to which the invested capital is exposed. Preferred stocks, for example, usually offer a lower rate of return than do common stocks because the preferred stockholder usually has a prior claim on both the assets and earnings of a company and thus has a lesser degree of risk associated with his investment than does the common stockholder. The factors which influence the flow of funds into the different fields of business activity are many and complex, but in general it can be said that higher rates of return are one of the oldest, the most universal, and the most important means by which capital funds are attracted to the more hazardous business ventures.

In the oil industry, the risk factors associated with operations at the different levels of the industry at any given time are usually quite different, and it should be anticipated therefore that the rates of return earned by *successful companies* in the different phases of the business should be different.[11] An investment in an exploratory well in the Gulf of Mexico, for example, may cost two or three million dollars and have only one chance in ten of yielding anything other than an empty hole covered by twenty feet of seawater. Such a project is obviously far more hazardous than an investment in a metropolitan service station where 30%

---

[11] Over very long perods of time, the composite returns earned on invested capital by all companies, successful and unsuccessful, in each segment of the industry may tend to draw together, because the high rates of return earned by successful companies in the more hazardous phases of the business may to some extent be counterbalanced by the losses incurred by the unsuccessful companies (see Chapter Five for discussion of earnings experience of different types of companies in the period 1920–1952).

to 40% of the total outlay may be for the purchase of land, which tends to have a fairly stable market value. Similarly, the typical refinery investment usually has far less risk associated with it than do many producing investments. In pressing their case for capital funds against the claims of producing departments, refinery executives sometimes take the stand that: "You producing fellows may show high anticipated rates of return on your projects, but you also drill plenty of dry holes; for our part, we never build a dry refinery."

Not only are the risk factors associated with investments at the separate levels of the industry different, but in addition, each set of factors may change independently of the others with the passage of time. The development of better techniques for estimating reservoir reserves and the adoption of the prorationing laws, for example, reduced the risks connected with investments in crude oil pipe lines without altering in any significant way the risks involved in the construction of service stations. Similarly, at some future time scientific progress may reduce the hazards accompanying the expenditure of funds for exploratory drilling without altering risks in other phases of the business. It may also be observed that progress in refinery technology does not always move ahead uniformly but tends to advance in fits and starts. In times of rapid technological change, the hazards of obsolescence in connection with refinery investments may increase although no corresponding changes may be occurring in the risks involved in other phases of oil industry operations.

As long as the risks associated with each phase of the oil business are different in degree and kind and are subject to change independently of each other, it is inescapable that the profit opportunities available at the separate levels of the industry should be different and change independently of each other.

Among the many other factors which may from time to time contribute to dissimilarities in profit fluctuations at the different levels of the industry are such things as: regulations with respect to taxes and particularly the provisions for the expensing of intangible drilling and development costs and the deductions for depletion on producing operations; government policies with respect to tariffs and imports; state

policies with respect to conservation and proration; economic developments in the coal and other competing industries; and new technological developments in the automotive industry.

In the light of the foregoing discussion, we believe that at least three general observations may be made concerning the general causes of the dissimilarities in profit fluctuations in the different phases of the oil business. *First,* it appears that many of the underlying forces which contribute to the variations in profit opportunities are an inherent part of oil industry life and that continual shifts and changes in the profits which can be earned at each level of the industry must be expected if oil companies are to be allowed any reasonable degree of freedom in deciding when and where to spend their capital funds, if new firms are to be allowed to enter and leave the business as they choose, and if business managers are to be allowed to exercise their own best judgment in adjusting their selling prices to meet competitive conditions. *Second,* it appears that it would be extremely difficult to eliminate the dissimilarities in profit movements even if it were desirable to do so (which we definitely do not believe to be the case). It is difficult to envisage any action by individual oil companies, by the oil industry, or the federal government which could regulate or contravene the many economic pressures influencing profits at the different levels of the industry in such a manner as to insure that profit opportunities at each level would move in unison with those at other levels. *Third,* it appears that the forces underlying the shifts and changes in profit opportunities are of such a character that there is little the individual firm can do to gain protection from them except through vertical integration or diversification into some other field of activity.

II. A SPECIFIC EXAMPLE, THE REFINER'S SQUEEZE IN 1949

The foregoing discussion has touched on some of the general business and economic circumstances which contribute to dissimilarities in profit movements in the different phases of the oil business. As a means of providing a specific illustration of some of these circumstances, attention is directed in the following paragraphs to the severe contraction in profit opportunities in the refining field which occurred in 1949. The data relate primarily to the Mid-Continent era, but somewhat similar contractions also took place at this time in the refiner's gross margin in other sections of the country.

As may be seen from Chapter Five, Exhibit V-2, the refiner's gross margin in the Mid-Continent area dropped from $1.09 per barrel in June 1948 to 23 cents per barrel in July 1949. During this period there was no significant change in refinery operating costs, and the volume of refinery throughput declined slightly. As a result, the contraction in the gross margin was reflected fairly directly in a severe decline in the net return on investment which could be earned at the refining level of the industry. Some indication of the contraction in the net profit opportunity at the refining level of the industry may be secured from Chapter Five, Exhibit V-15, which reveals that the return on investment earned by refining-marketing companies dropped from about 21.9% in 1948 to 7.3% in 1949 and rose again to 9.1% in 1950.[12] The contraction in profit opportunities for a completely nonintegrated refiner was probably greater than for refining-marketing companies because the former companies did not have the benefit of marketing profits to tide them over the period of adversity in the refining field.

It is important to note that the 1949 contraction in the gross margins and net profits at the refining level of the industry was not accompanied by comparable contractions in gross margins and net profits at other levels of the industry. Only a slight downward movement occurred in the wholesaling and retailing gross margins, and it may be inferred that the net profits earned by marketing companies probably remained more stable than did the net profits earned by refining-marketing companies.[13] Crude oil prices remained fairly stable throughout 1949, but a contraction did occur in the net profits earned by producers as a result of a reduction in the volume of crude oil produced.[13] The reduction in the net profits of producers was less severe, however, than

---

12 As pointed out in Chapter Five, we believe that most of the companies in our refining-marketing group had substantially larger refining than marketing activities.

13 See Chapter Five, Exhibits V-2 and V-15. Our marketing group was too small in the years 1948–1952 to permit computation of average profit figures.

EXHIBIT VI-3. COMPOSITION OF THE REFINER'S GROSS MARGIN, MID-CONTINENT AREA

	Yield	Price per Bbl.	Realization	Per Cent of Total Realization
June 1948				
Gasoline	.450	$4.41	$1.98	54.1%
Kerosene	.055	3.99	.22	6.0
Distillates	.187	3.78	.71	19.4
Residual Fuel Oil	.298	2.50	.75	20.5
Loss in Refining	.010	—	—	—
	1.000		$3.66	100.0%
Crude Oil Price per Barrel			2.57	
Refiner's Gross Margin per Barrel			$1.09	
July 1949				
Gasoline	.486	$4.20	$2.04	72.8%
Kerosene	.048	3.29	.16	5.7
Distillates	.168	2.52	.43	15.4
Residual Fuel Oil	.284	.60	.17	6.1
Loss in Refining	.014	—	—	
	1.000		$2.80	100.0%
Crude Oil Price per Barrel			2.57	
Refiner's Gross Margin per Barrel			$0.23	

NOTE: See Chapter Five for method of computation and grouping of products. The gross margin represents the difference between product realizations in the tank car markets and the posted price of crude oil at the well-head; it thus includes crude oil transportation costs.

was the reduction in the net profits of refiners. It is therefore apparent that the movements in refining gross margins and net profits in 1949 were dissimilar to the movements in gross margins and net profits at other levels of the industry.

Analysis of the Margin Contraction:

Analysis of the composition of the refiner's gross margin in June 1948 and July 1949 reveals that the contraction in the margin occured primarily because there was a sharp decline in the realization secured by the refiner on distillates and residual fuel oil which was not accompanied by a compensating reduction in crude oil prices. These facts are clearly established by the calculations of the refiner's gross margin in June 1948 and July 1949 shown in Exhibit VI-3. Since the crude oil price was the same in both months, the contraction of 86 cents per barrel in the gross margin may be attributed entirely to a loss in realization on refined products sold. The responsibility for the loss in realization may further be assigned to individual products as follows:

ANALYSIS OF LOSS IN PRODUCTS REALIZATION

(Per Barrel of Crude Oil Refined)

Products Realization, June 1948:	$3.66	
Products Realization, July 1949:	2.80	
Net Loss in Realization	.86	
Gain in Realization on Gasoline	.06	
Gross Loss in Realization	.92	100.0%
Loss in Realization on Kerosene	.06	6.5
Loss in Realization on Distillates	.28	30.4
Loss in Realization on Residual Fuel Oil	.58	63.1

It is therefore evident that almost two-thirds of the gross loss in realization arose from a decline in realization on residual fuel oil and that almost one-third of the gross loss arose from a decline in realizations on distillates. Less than 7% of the gross loss in realization was attributable to kerosene, and we shall not therefore consider it further in the discussion. In the case of both residual fuel oil and distillates the loss in realization resulted from a decline in the yield secured from a barrel of crude oil and a decline in the market price. From the margin calculations in Exhibit VI-3, it may be seen that in both cases the declines in prices were of far greater significance than the declines in yields.

The gross loss in realization of 92 cents per barrel refined was offset by a 6 cent gain in realization on the gasoline secured from a barrel of crude oil. This gain was the net result of a significant increase in the gasoline yield and a minor decline in the gasoline price. A record of refined product prices in the Mid-Continent area for the period 1946–1950 is shown in Exhibit VI-4. The exhibit also contains a record of product prices in the Gulf Coast cargo and New York Harbor markets which indicate that the Mid-Continent situation was not an isolated one.

On the basis of the above data, it is apparent that an explanation of the contraction of the refiner's gross margin in 1949 requires consideration of two basic questions: (1) what caused the decline in the prices for distillates and residual fuel oil, and (2) why was there no compensating downward movement in the price of crude oil?

The Decline in Distillate and Residual Fuel Oil Prices:

The decline in distillate and residual fuel oil prices was the product of a multiplicity of circumstances. In retrospect, however, it appears that the sequence of events was essentially as follows:

A tremendous increase in the demand for petroleum products developed immediately after World War II. The increase was far greater than that generally anticipated by the oil companies in planning their expansion programs, and even had it been fully foreseen it would have been difficult to have made adequate provision for it. As a result, the period from about 1945 to the fall of 1948 was a time of petroleum shortages, during which the oil companies made strenuous efforts to expand their producing, refining, marketing, and transportation facilities fast enough to meet the rapidly growing requirements of the market. As noted earlier in the chapter, the shortages were particularly great with respect to heating oils during the unusually cold winter of 1947–1948. During this period, heating oils were under allocation in many sections of the country; new customers were turned away; there was much public criticism of the oil companies for their failure to provide adequately for the consumer demand; the executives of many oil companies were called to testify before Congressional Committees; and there was considerable agitation for a government-financed synthetic fuels program.

The entire experience of the industry in the winter of 1947–1948 was a painful one from many standpoints, and the executives of the oil companies were generally anxious to avoid a repetition of it in the winter of 1948–1949. In the summer and early fall of 1948, therefore, the industry took steps to build ample stocks, particularly of distillates, in anticipation of the coming winter season. The accumulation of distillate heating oil stocks appeared particularly prudent in view of the fact that the installation of domestic oil burners was continuing at a high rate and the average number in use was steadily increasing, as indicated by the figures in Exhibit VI-5. At the same time, however, no major effort was made by the industry as a whole to develop new markets for distillate fuel oils or to secure new customers, because it was believed that new customers would merely add to a company's distress if shortages developed in the winter of 1948–1949 that were in any way comparable with those in the win-

Exhibit VI-4. Prices of Gasoline, Kerosene, No. 2 Fuel Oil,
and Residual Fuel Oil

Oklahoma, Gulf Coast, and New York Harbor: 1946–1950

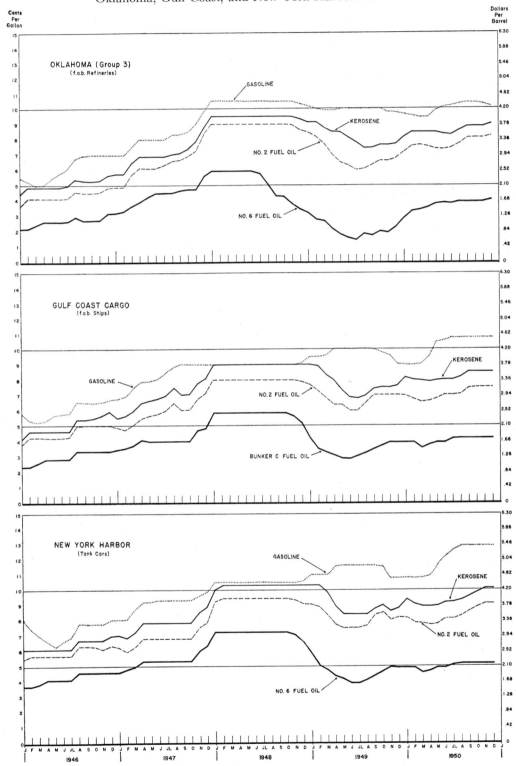

Note: All prices are monthly averages of low quotations.

Source: *Platt's Oil Price Handbooks.*

EXHIBIT VI-5. DOMESTIC OIL BURNERS AND RESIDUAL FUEL OIL BURNERS IN USE IN THE UNITED STATES: 1946–1950

Year	Total Installations	Net Installations*	In Use Dec. 31	Average No. in Use	Per Cent Increase Over Previous Year
Domestic Oil Burners in Use †					
1946	492,593	303,989	2,821,044	2,669,050	—
1947	888,083	829,470	3,650,514	3,235,779	21.2%
1948	455,245	325,259	3,975,773	3,813,144	17.8
1949	614,712	514,762	4,490,535	4,233,154	11.0
1950	846,815	681,599	5,172,134	4,831,335	14.1
Residual Fuel Oil Burners in Use ‡					
1946	15,200	13,700	142,300	135,450	—
1947	18,300	16,500	158,800	150,550	11.1%
1948	10,700	9,150	167,950	163,375	8.5
1949	9,500	7,800	175,750	171,850	5.2
1950	13,000	11,400	187,150	181,450	5.6

* Total installations minus withdrawals.

† Figures are for pump operated burners only.

‡ Figures are for space heaters only.

SOURCE: Standard Oil Company (New Jersey), Coordination and Economics Department.

ter of 1947–1948. The upward movements in distillate stocks which occurred in the latter part of 1948 in Districts 1, 2, and 3 and in the United States as a whole are clearly indicated in Exhibit VI-6. Data are shown for Districts 1, 2, and 3 only, because these are the areas which had the most direct bearing on market conditions in the Mid-Continent region.[14]

Residual fuel oil stocks likewise began to move upward in Districts 1, 2, and 3 and in the United States as a whole in the latter part of 1948 as may be seen from Exhibit VI-7. The situation in this case was somewhat different from that in the case of distillates because the demand for residual fuel oil had already turned downward in 1948 and there were not the same reasons to expect an increase in demand in the winter of 1948–1949 as there were in the case of distillates. The accumulation of residual fuel oil stocks was therefore to a considerable extent simply a result of the efforts to build distillate stocks and to continue the production of other products because a certain amount of residual

was inevitably obtained in refining operations.[15] In addition, there was some reason to believe that the demand for residual fuel oil might be at least fairly strong in the winter of 1948–1949 as a result of unsettled labor conditions in the coal industry and as a result of the continuing new installations of residual fuel oil burners. Data with regard to residual fuel oil burners installed and in use in the United States are shown in Exhibit VI-5.

In the light of the foregoing considerations, it is not hard to understand why the industry generally should have moved into the winter of 1948–1949 with ample stocks of distillates and residual fuel oil. The market demand during the winter of 1948–1949, however, did not develop as was generally anticipated, as may be seen from Exhibit VI-8. In the case of distillates, the strong upward trend in demand which had persisted since the close of World War II was sharply curtailed. The total demand for distillates in 1949 was 3.3% less than in 1948, despite a substantial increase in Diesel fuel sales to railroads. In the case of residual fuel oil, the demand in 1949 was 0.9% less than in 1948.

The tendency of the industry to develop strong stock positions in anticipation of the 1948–1949 winter coupled with the decline in demand for both distillates and residual fuel oil quickly produced excessive stocks of the two products, as may be seen from Exhibits VI-6 and VI-7. An abnormal accumulation of stocks of both products took place in Districts 1, 2, and 3 and in the United States as a whole. Of particular importance were the burdensome stocks of residual fuel oil in Districts 2 and 3. As the stocks of distillates and residual fuel oil continued to accumulate, refiners eventually approached the limits of their available storage capacity and price cutting was inevitable. The price declines began in the latter part of 1948 and continued until the stock situation was corrected in the summer of 1949.

The decline in the demand for distillates and residual fuel oil was the product of a number of circumstances. Of primary importance, particularly in the case of distillates, was the fact that the winter of 1948–1949 was substantially warmer than the winter of 1947–1948 (see Ex-

---

[14] District 1 includes the New England states, Atlantic Coast states, and West Virginia; District 2 includes the North Central states, Great Lakes states, Kentucky, Tennessee, Missouri, Oklahoma, and Kansas; District 3 includes New Mexico, Texas, Arkansas, Louisiana, Mississippi, and Alabama; District 4 includes Utah, Colorado, Idaho, Wyoming, and Montana; District 5 includes California, Oregon, Washington, Nevada, and Arizona.

[15] As will be noted later, both distillate and residual stocks were accumulated in part as a result of the continued demand for and production of gasoline.

EXHIBIT VI-6. DEMAND, SUPPLY, AND STOCKS OF DISTILLATES: 1946–1950

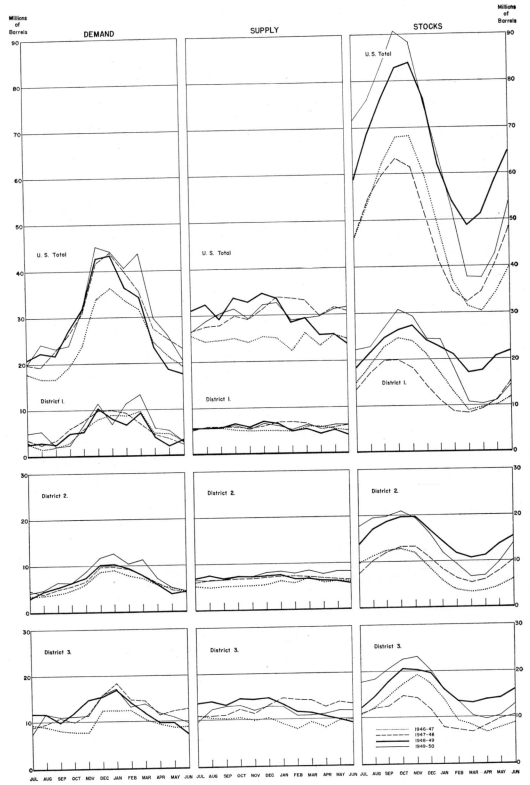

SOURCE: Standard Oil Company (New Jersey), Coordination and Economics Department (compiled from U.S. Bureau of Mines data)

EXHIBIT VI-7. DEMAND, SUPPLY, AND STOCKS OF RESIDUAL FUEL OIL: 1946–1950

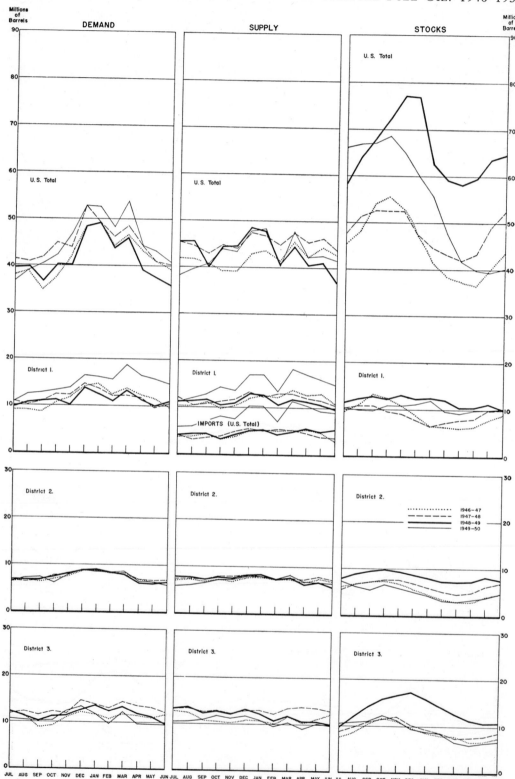

SOURCE: Standard Oil Company (New Jersey), Coordination and Economics Department (compiled from U.S. Bureau of Mines data).

EXHIBIT VI-8. DISTILLATE, RESIDUAL FUEL OIL, AND GASOLINE DEMAND BY USES
IN THE UNITED STATES: 1946–1950

Distillate Demand (1,000 Bbls.)

	Railroads	Vessel Bunkers	Gas and Electric Power Plants	Smelters, Mines, and Mfg. Plants	Heating Oil	No. 1 Fuel Oil Sold as Range Oil	Oil Company Use	All Other Uses	Total	Per Cent Change over Previous Year
1946	17,570	12,064	10,581	21,317	139,637	8,459	1,890	31,376	242,894	
1947	23,619	14,475	14,216	24,489	178,359	11,632	2,191	29,292	298,273	+22.8%
1948	31,006	14,511	14,856	29,932	200,024	13,534	3,625	33,088	340,576	+14.2
1949	38,604	13,121	12,550	26,424	190,387	12,279	4,151	31,762	329,278	−3.3
1950	48,703	12,872	13,207	37,121	220,947	14,793	5,692	41,550	394,885	+19.9

Residual Fuel Oil Demand (1,000 Bbls.)

	Railroads	Vessel Bunkers	Gas and Electric Power Plants	Smelters, Mines, and Mfg. Plants	Heating Oil	Oil Company Use	All Other Uses	Total	Per Cent Change over Previous Year
1946	100,305	88,185	50,921	99,011	49,734	58,054	33,819	480,029	
1947	97,500	101,900	60,964	115,108	56,402	62,649	23,987	518,510	+8.0%
1948	89,588	95,763	56,812	117,780	58,639	56,637	25,386	500,543	−3.5
1949	63,467	89,362	80,092	122,633	60,414	51,667	28,386	496,021	−0.9
1950	60,878	92,947	93,062	148,111	72,716	53,263	32,816	553,793	+11.6

Gasoline Demand (1,000 Bbls.)

	Passenger Cars	Trucks	Busses	Off Highway Agriculture	All Other Uses	Total Motor Gasoline	Per Cent Change Previous Year	Aviation	Total Demand	Per Cent Change over Previous Year
1946	441,455	162,937	18,900	55,300	43,920	722,512		12,905	735,417	+8.1%
1947	475,948	174,400	18,700	56,000	43,360	773,408	+7.0%	21,607	795,015	+9.6
1948	509,000	195,300	17,700	65,400	47,150	834,550	+7.9	36,720	871,270	+4.9
1949	540,500	203,000	16,300	74,200	45,721	879,721	+5.4	33,992	913,713	+4.9
1950	590,800	218,500	16,100	79,700	49,673	954,773	+8.5	39,517	994,290	+8.8

SOURCE: Standard Oil Company (New Jersey), Coordination and Economics Department.

hibit VI-9) and likewise substantially warmer than normal. In District 1 there were 4,711 degree days as contrasted with a normal of 5,519; in District 2 there were 6,136 degree days as contrasted with a normal of 6,475; in District 3 there were 2,408 degree days as contrasted with a normal of 2,432; and in the United States as a whole weighted average degree days were 4,992 as contrasted with a normal of 5,530.[16] The warm weather reduced the demand for all types of distillate fuel oils for heating purposes, as may be seen from Exhibit VI-8. The warm weather also had a further impact on stock positions and price movements because as soon as it became evident that the winter would be warmer than usual and that excess stocks were accumulating, there was a virtual buyers' strike

in the heating fuel markets as buyers withheld their purchases in the hope of a general crude oil price reduction and a still further drop in refined product prices.

A second important reason for the failure of the demand for both distillates and residual fuel oil to materialize as anticipated in the winter of 1948–1949 was the low rate of industrial activity. The Federal Reserve Board Index registered a decline of about 8% in 1949 as contrasted with 1948. The decline in industrial activity, in turn, occasioned a reduction of about 5.6% in total energy consumption (including coal, oil, natural gas, and water power).[17] The majority of the reduction in energy consumption was absorbed by the coal industry, which at that time was suffering from an adverse labor situation. The decline in

[16] Standard Oil Company (New Jersey), Coordination and Economic Department. Figures are weighted by burners in use.

[17] Standard Oil Company (New Jersey), Coordination and Economics Department.

EXHIBIT VI-9. DEGREE DAYS: 1946–1950

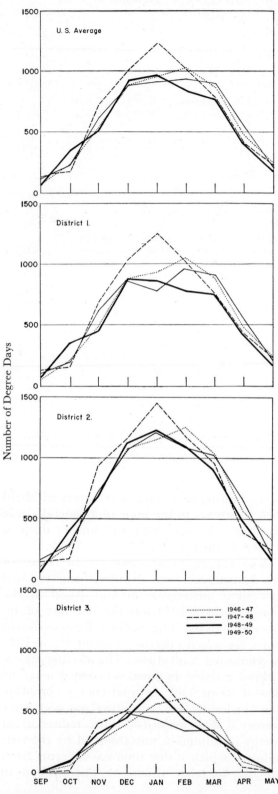

SOURCE: Standard Oil Company (New Jersey), Coordination and Economics Department.

energy consumption did, however, preclude the growth in petroleum consumption which might otherwise have taken place.

A third important development in 1949 was the increased use of Diesel locomotive equipment by the railroads. The conversion of locomotives to Diesel fuel brought about a reduction in the demand for residual fuel oil and, of course, some increase in the demand for Diesel fuels, which are a part of the distillate group of products. Since the volume of Diesel fuel required per railroad ton mile is far smaller than the volume of residual fuel oil required per ton mile, however, the decline in residual fuel oil utilization was far greater than the increase in Diesel fuel utilization. It will be noted from Exhibit VI-8 that residual fuel oil sales to railroads declined about 26,000,000 barrels in 1949 as contrasted with 1948, whereas distillate sales to railroads (reflecting primarily increased consumption of Diesel fuels) increased only about 7,600,000 barrels.[18] The decline in the demand for residual fuel oil by railroads was crucial to the Mid-Continent refiners because the railroads had previously constituted one of their most important markets for residual fuel oil. Eventually, as the situation worsened, the Mid-Continent refiners were forced to reduce their residual fuel oil prices to the point where the oil could be moved by tank car to the Gulf Coast and sold in competition with the residual fuel oil output of the Gulf Coast refiners as vessel bunkers and for various other purposes.

A fourth important cause of the lack of growth in the distillate and residual fuel oil demand in 1949 and of the price adjustments which took place beginning in the latter part of 1948 was the disparity which developed between the prices of the two groups of products and the price of an equivalent quantity of coal. The relationship between anthracite coal prices and No. 2 fuel oil prices and between bituminous coal prices and No. 6 fuel oil prices in New York City is shown in Exhibit VI-10. The disparities between the petroleum and coal prices arose because of the extensive installation of oil burners in the period immediately after World War II and the shortages of fuel oil in

[18] Diesel fuel sales to railroads increased by about 7,477,000 barrels; sales of other distillates to railroads increased about 121,000 barrels.

EXHIBIT VI-10. COMPARISON OF COAL PRICES WITH NO. 2
AND NO. 6 FUEL OIL PRICES: 1935–1951

Price of #2 Fuel
Versus Cost of Equivalent * Anthracite Stove Coal
New York City, Retail

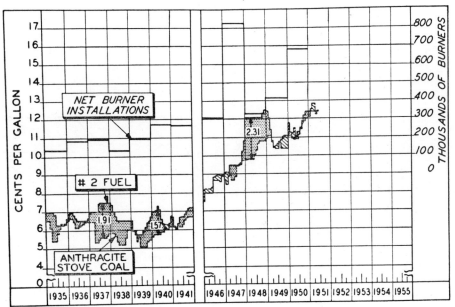

* B. T. U. Equivalent: .005453 Tons Stove Coal = One Gallon #2 Fuel

Price of #6 Fuel
Versus Cost of Equivalent * Bituminous Coal
F. O. B. New York City

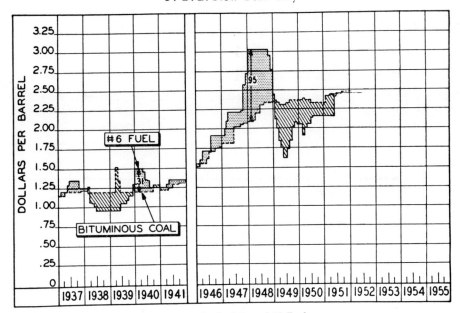

* B. T. U. Equivalent: .2400 Short Tons Bituminous Coal = 1 Barrel #6 Fuel

SOURCE: Standard Oil Company (New Jersey), Coordination and Economics Department.

EXHIBIT VI-11. DEMAND, SUPPLY, AND STOCKS OF GASOLINE: 1946–1950

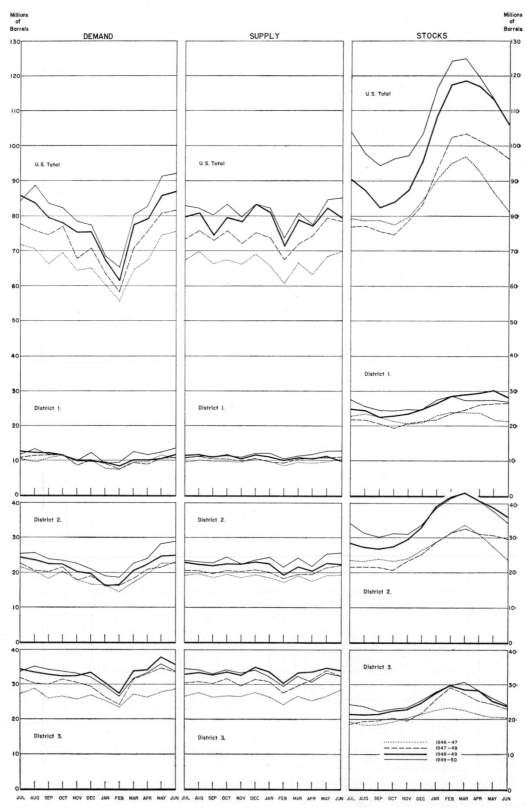

SOURCE: Standard Oil Company (New Jersey), Coordination and Economics Department (compiled from U.S. Bureau of Mines data).

the winter of 1947–1948. The disparities in the latter part of 1948 were clearly greater than warranted by the convenience of oil as contrasted with coal, and it was therefore inevitable that a price break should occur as soon as ample supplies became available.

Throughout the period from the middle of 1948 to the middle of 1949, the accumulation of distillate and residual fuel oil stocks was, in part, a consequence of the fact that the demand for gasoline continued to increase and the price of gasoline remained fairly stable (see Exhibits VI-4, VI-8, and VI-11). To meet the demand for gasoline, refiners tended to maintain their refinery runs (see Exhibit VI-12) and thereby inevitably generated a certain amount of distillates and residual fuel oil. Every possible effort was, of course, made to maximize gasoline and minimize distillate and residual fuel oil yields as soon as the character of the 1948–1949 winter demand had clarified (see Exhibit VI-13). As will be noted in Chapter Twenty, however, refiners without catalytic cracking facilities were not in a position to reduce their combined yields of distillates and residual fuel oil much below 50% of refinery runs. Many such refiners elected to continue in operation and to secure the realization on gasoline rather than to close down their plants and thereby contributed to the distress of the entire industry with excessive distillate and residual fuel oil stocks. Eventually some reduction in the industry's refinery runs did occur, but not until the accumulation of distillate and residual fuel oil stocks was far advanced. As may be seen from Exhibit VI-12, the reduction in refinery runs began in District 1 in about November 1948 but did not take place in Districts 2 and 3 in any significant degree until the spring of 1949.

The demand-supply situation in the winter of 1948–1949 might be analyzed in much greater detail.[19] The facts mentioned above,

19 Considerable attention was at the time directed to imports of residual fuel oil as a possible cause of the supply situation. As may be seen from Exhibit VI-7, imports of residual were about the same in the latter part of 1948 when domestic stocks of residual were accumulating as they were in the corresponding months of the two preceding years. Moreover, the total amount of residual imports was less in 1948 than in 1947. It is therefore unlikely that imports could have been an important cause of the excessive residual stocks. Imports of residual increased significantly in the spring and summer of 1949, but by that time the peak period of distress with residual stocks had already

(continued on page 173)

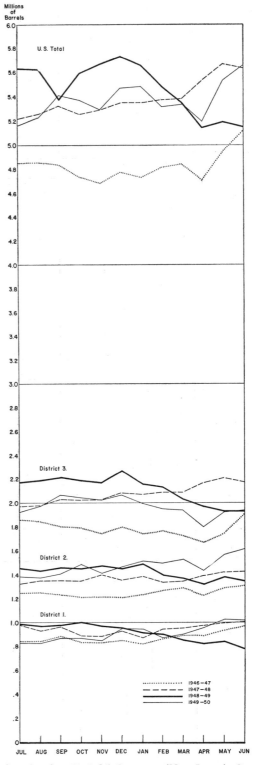

EXHIBIT VI-12. DOMESTIC REFINERY RUNS: 1946–1950

(Barrels per Day)

SOURCE: Standard Oil Company (New Jersey), Coordination and Economics Department (compiled from U.S. Bureau of Mines data).

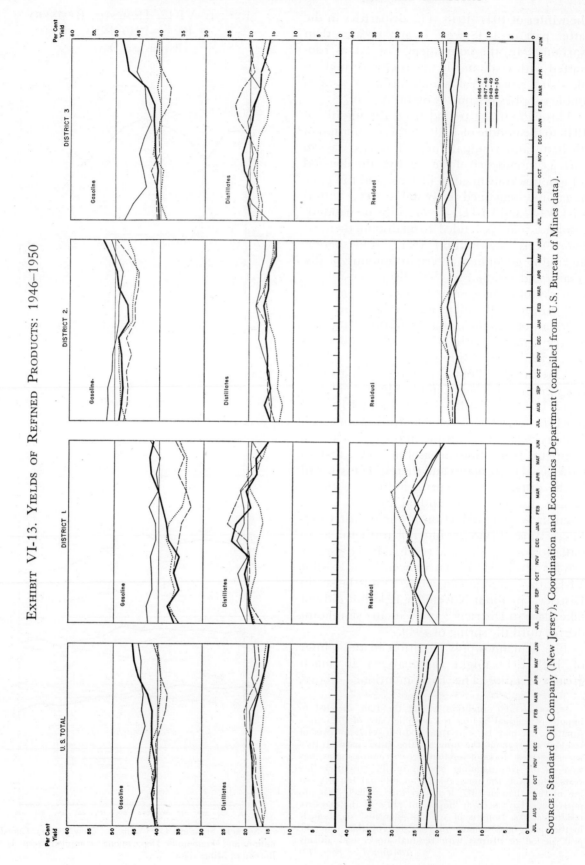

EXHIBIT VI-13. YIELDS OF REFINED PRODUCTS: 1946–1950

SOURCE: Standard Oil Company (New Jersey), Coordination and Economics Department (compiled from U.S. Bureau of Mines data).

however, were the main causes of the excessive stocks of distillates and residual fuel oils, and these stocks, in turn, were certainly sufficient to precipitate the price declines in the two groups of products and the resultant loss in the refiner's realization.

The Stability of Crude Oil Prices:

It was noted earlier in the discussion that the contraction in the refiner's margin in 1949 was a consequence not only of the loss in realizations on distillates and residual fuel oil but likewise of the fact that no compensating downward adjustment of any significance occurred in the price of crude oil (see Exhibit VI-2). Excessive stocks of crude oil tended to accumulate in the area east of California in much the same manner as in the case of distillates and residual fuel oil (see Exhibit VI-14). The failure of the crude oil price to move downward under the pressure of these stocks may be traced to at least three important circumstances:

In the first place, the various state production authorities, particularly the Texas Railroad Commission, took action to reduce allowable crude oil production as soon as it became apparent that large stocks were accumulating. The first reductions in allowables were made by the Texas Railroad Commission in January 1949, and similar action was taken by the authorities in other states shortly thereafter. Total domestic crude oil production in 1949 was about 1,842 million barrels or about 8.8% less than the 2,020 million barrels produced in 1948.[20] To a considerable extent, therefore, the adjustment of crude oil supplies to the market demand situation which developed in 1949 was accomplished through the action of the prorationing authorities rather than through the mechanism of price adjustments. As noted earlier, although the crude oil producing level of the industry did not experience a major decline in prices in 1949, it did experience a reduction in net profits as a result of the decline in total allowable production. It is im-

portant to note that the existence of the prorationing laws had a significant psychological effect on the market entirely apart from any formal action that was taken by the state prorationing authorities. On the basis of past experience, the entire industry was reasonably assured that state prorationing action would be initiated before any really serious distress with crude oil stocks developed, and as a result there was not the same incentive for price cuts as there was in the case of the refined products.

A second important reason why crude oil prices did not decline in 1949 was because there was an increase of 4.9% in the demand for gasoline (see Exhibit VI-8), which normally accounts for about 40%–45% of the yield from crude oil. Largely as a result of the increase in demand for gasoline, the total demand for crude oil and refined products in 1949 decreased by only 0.5% as contrasted with 1948.[21] Consequently, the pressure for a downward adjustment in crude oil prices was somewhat less than in the case of distillates and residual fuel oil which suffered a decrease in demand of 3.3% and 0.9%, respectively, as contrasted with 1948. Moreover, as may be seen from Exhibit VI-11, excessively large stocks did not accumulate in the case of gasoline as they did in the case of distillates and residual fuel oil.

A third reason why crude oil prices did not move downward in 1949 may be found in the fact noted earlier that crude oil prices are generally less sensitive to new developments in market conditions than are refined product prices. There is no question that pressure was developing for a reduction in crude oil prices throughout the early part of 1949. As early as December 1948 the price of Pennsylvania grade crude oil was reduced from $5.00 to $4.50 a barrel, and in January 1949 a further reduction was made to $4.00 a barrel. Early in July 1949 the Pure Oil Company reduced prices on Michigan crudes an average of 11 cents a barrel to "reflect changes in the relative values of crude produced in the various fields." At about the same time, the Three Rivers Refining Company reduced purchase prices for low gravity crude oil in a South Texas field by about 61 cents per barrel by declining to pay gathering and transportation costs, a form of price reduction which was employed by several

been passed. Residual imports as a percentage of the total United States supply of residual amounted to 10.3% in 1947, 9.8% in 1948, and 14.9% in 1949. (See U. S. Tariff Commission, *Hearing Memorandum for Standard Oil Company (New Jersey), Esso Standard Oil Company, and Creole Petroleum Corporation*, October 2, 1951.)

[20] American Petroleum Institute, *Statistical Bulletin*, Vol. XXXIV, No. 19, April 16, 1953.

[21] Ibid.

Exhibit VI-14. Demand, Supply, and Stocks of Crude Oil: 1946–1950

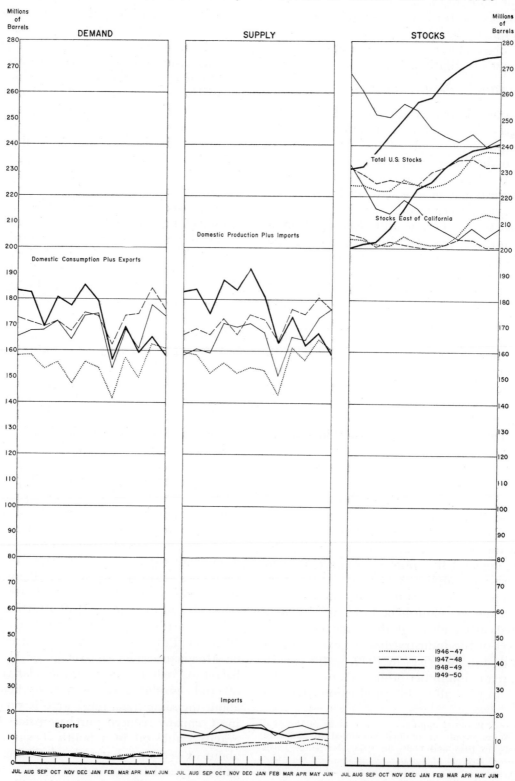

Source: American Petroleum Institute, *Statistical Bulletin*, Vol. XXIX, No. 34; Vol. XXXI, No. 30; and Vol. XXXII, No. 31.

companies in the first half of 1949. A few days later, the Humble Oil and Refining Company announced a reduction of ten cents a barrel in the price it would pay for low cold test crude oils in the Texas Gulf Coast and for low gravity Mirando grade crude oils. The Humble action was promptly followed with similar cuts by the Magnolia Oil Company, The Texas Company, the Gulf Oil Corporation, the Stanolind Oil and Gas Company, the Sun Oil Company, and the Sinclair Oil Corporation. Meanwhile, the Arkansas Fuel Oil Company reduced the price it would pay for oil purchased in the Urania, Tullos, and Georgetown, Louisiana, fields by ten cents per barrel. It seems likely, therefore, that if the depressed demand for distillates and residual fuel oil had persisted much beyond the summer of 1949, a reduction in crude oil prices would certainly have occurred.

In the light of the facts reviewed above, it seems reasonable to conclude that the contraction in the refiner's margin in 1949 was the result of an interplay of climatic and economic circumstances which an individual company could have done little to forestall. It is particularly important to note that the entire situation was precipitated in major degree by the building of ample stocks in anticipation of the winter demand for heating fuels, a course of action which would have been of great benefit to the public and likewise to the oil companies if the winter had turned out cold rather than warm. Finally, it may be observed that the situation was one in which an integrated oil company engaged in producing, refining, and marketing operations could not help but fare better than a nonintegrated company engaged in refining operations alone.

III. THE QUESTION OF SUBSIDIZING LOSSES

It is somewhat ironical that the stabilization of gross margins and net profits, one of the most important economic advantages resulting from vertical integration, should be one of the principal grounds upon which vertical integration has been attacked. For at least a quarter of a century, the opponents of vertical integration have been insisting that the vertically integrated companies "use profits made at one level of the industry to subsidize losses incurred at another." Precisely what is meant by the "subsidiz-

ing of losses" or why it should be considered an unfair or illegal competitive practice, if indeed it occurs, has rarely been explained. In general, however, the opponents of vertical integration have usually advanced either or both of two principal contentions: (a) that the integrated companies have gotten themselves into positions where they can and frequently do offset the losses incurred on one activity with profits made from another, and (b) that since the integrated companies are not completely dependent upon any single phase of the business, they sometimes inadvertently or deliberately precipitate a profit contraction at one or more levels of the industry while sustaining themselves on activities at other levels. In the following paragraphs, we shall seek to point out the relevance of the research data in Chapter Five and the preceding pages of this chapter to these two matters.

The first contention that the integrated companies can offset losses on one activity with profits drawn from another was well-summarized in a recent report to the Federal Trade Commission by its staff:

Moreover, the independents are at the mercy of a price squeeze, which may be effective at each stage of the integrated process of oil production, refining, and distribution, though not simultaneously. Independent operators of oil wells may be squeezed if the price of crude oil falls below their cost of production, a loss which the major oil companies can well incur if the prices of refined products do not fall in a corresponding manner. Independent refineries may be squeezed if the spread between the price of crude oil and the prices of refined products falls below the cost of refining, a loss which the major oil companies can again stand if the prices of refined products are high enough to cover the combined cost of producing, transporting, and refining oil, plus a reasonable profit. Independent distributors may be squeezed if the spread between the prices of refined products at the refinery and the prices of these products at retail is less than the margin necessary to make distribution profitable, a loss which the major oil companies can afford if the retail prices of refined products are high enough to allow a profit on the complete operation of producing, transporting, refining, and distributing.[22]

22 Staff Report to the Federal Trade Commission for the Subcommittee on Monopoly of the Select Committee on Small Business of the United States Senate, *Monopolistic Practices and Small Business* (Washington, D. C., March 31,

In the light of the data in Chapter Five, it is apparent that these statements by the staff of the Federal Trade Commission provide a reasonably accurate description of the relative positions of integrated and nonintegrated oil companies. As long as shifts and changes are continually taking place in the profit opportunities at the different levels of the oil industry, there is no question that an integrated company may at any given time make more money from one phase of its business than it does from another. It is likewise inescapable that when one level of the industry passes into a period of unprofitability, such as the refining level did in 1949, an integrated company may take losses on that activity and yet be sustained by profits made on other activities. As noted in earlier discussions, one of the most important results of vertical integration is that it frees a company from complete dependence on a single level of the business and aids it in weathering the economic storms which develop from time to time at different points in the industry.

An oil company cannot be criticized, however, for exercising reasonable business prudence and undertaking vertical integration as a means of stabilizing its profit position and of minimizing the risks to which it would be exposed if it attempted to operate at a single level of the industry. In our judgment, therefore, the contention that the losses of vertically integrated companies on one activity are sometimes offset by profits from other activities should be freely granted. All the available evidence indicates that the probability of experiencing such offsets is indeed one of the important consequences of vertical integration and that the stability of earnings arising therefrom contributes to the health and security of both the individual firm and the entire industrial economy. Moreover, the mere act of engaging in two or more activities which have offsetting profit characteristics cannot, with any reason or justice, be categorized as an unfair or illegal competitive practice.

The second principal contention of the opponents of vertical integration to the effect that the integrated oil companies inadvertently or deliberately *precipitate* the profit contractions from time to time occurring at various levels of the industry is a far more important matter and likewise much more difficult to resolve. The character of the arguments advanced by the opponents of vertical integration is suggested by the following statements from a report made in January 1952 by a committee of the South Carolina Jobbers' Association and from comments made by an officer of the South Carolina Jobbers' Association before the Florida Petroleum Marketers' Association on March 16, 1952: [23]

Competition in the marketing end of the oil business by integrated oil companies is unfair to those engaged only in marketing. As the trend towards extension and absorption of marketing outlets continues, the monopolistic hold on the oil industry grows more complete.

The integrated oil companies are fortified by profits from production of crude oil, refining operations, and pipe line and tanker transportation. They thus can use profits from the more profitable branches of the industry to absorb losses in marketing.

*   *   *

With such legislative guarantees of profit to oil producers [reference is to depletion allowance, duties on imported crude oil, state oil proration laws, Connally Act, Interstate Oil Compact, and monthly Bureau of Mines forecasts] it is unfair competition to allow any portion thereof to be used to absorb losses in oil marketing—absorbed losses that are injuring every oil marketer and driving them out of business.

*   *   *

The jobber is limited in the industry in securing his profits from the marketing function alone, and it is discouraging when he sees profits from other industry operations used to take his rightful busi-

---

1952), p. 45. The views of the Federal Trade Commission concerning vertical integration have changed from time to time depending upon the composition of the Commission's membership. In citing the above staff report therefore, we mean to imply nothing concerning the past, present, or future policies of the Federal Trade Commission regarding vertical integration. We use the statement merely to illustrate one of the focal points in the controversy over the so-called subsidization of losses.

---

[23] The first three paragraphs are from the committee report as recorded in *Platt's Oilgram News Service,* January 25, 1952, "South Carolina Jobbers Push Case for Divorcement," p. 1. The last two paragraphs are from a speech by the secretary-treasurer of the South Carolina Jobbers' Association as reported in *National Petroleum News,* May 21, 1952, p. 55.

ness, and his life investment become depleted with insufficient profits.

Many jobbers who have seen this trend have turned to other allied lines, such as transportation, farm equipment, orange groves, cattle farms, etc. If a jobber should use the profits from such other businesses to subsidize his oil business, it would be just as unsound from the standpoint of the economy as a whole, as it would be for an integrated company to use the depletion allowances, and profits from other divisions for expanding its markets or supporting a price war.

The issue raised by statements of this kind is one which has rarely been recognized explicitly or faced squarely in the welter of legal, Congressional, academic, and industry controversy on the subject of integration. It can be stated very simply: Has vertical integration in the oil business been largely a *result* of the dissimilarities in profit movements in the different phases of the business or has it been largely a *cause* of those dissimilarities and thereby a means of working a hardship on the small, non-integrated firm?

A complete and final judgment on this question would require an exhaustive study of industry conditions and the management practices of a fairly large group of integrated companies over a long period of time. The data presented in Chapters Five and Six and elsewhere in this book, however, provide considerable evidence to indicate that the growth and development of integrated oil companies has been far more a result than a cause of the variations in profit movements at the different levels of the business. Moreover, it appears that such minor influences as the integrated companies have had on the profit movements have been inadvertent rather than deliberate, at least during the past 33 years.

On the basis of the discussion in the preceding pages of this chapter, it seems reasonably clear that nearly all of the underlying business and economic circumstances which contribute to the dissimilarities in profit movements at the different levels of the business are of such a character that they would be operative regardless of the prevailing patterns of business organization in the industry. Such things as the weather conditions which precipitated the refiner's squeeze in 1949, the tendency of capital investments to lag and lead the immediate requirements of an industry situation, the differences in the sensitivity of prices in the various petroleum markets to changing conditions, the differences in the mix of products handled at the different levels of the industry, and the differences in the risks attached to capital investments in the several phases of the business—these are all forces and circumstances which would unquestionably continue to be of significance whether integrated companies were present or not.

The presence of integrated companies in the industry may from time to time have had some slight influences on the timing, direction, and amplitude of profit movements in the various phases of the business, but the exact nature of these influences is somewhat obscure and difficult to evaluate. The growth and development of integrated companies unquestionably resulted in a reduction in the volume of products handled and altered the character of the transactions in the intermediate markets. As noted earlier in the chapter, the fact that most of the large buyers of crude oil are also engaged in producing operations of their own has probably contributed in a minor way to the relative stability of crude oil as contrasted with refined product prices. It also appears possible that the price policies of some of the so-called price leaders might at certain times have been somewhat different had their operations been confined solely to wholesale or retail marketing. The timing of price changes by any marketer can at the most, however, have only a minor and transitory influence on the price adjustments which take place in the petroleum markets under the pressure of changing economic and competitive conditions.

On balance, it is by no means clear whether the net effect of the presence of integrated companies has been to accentuate or dampen the fluctuations and dissimilarities in the profit movements in the different phases of the business. To the extent that an integrated company can secure some measure of profit stability, it can carry out its capital investment programs on a more orderly basis and may thereby aid in keeping the capital inputs to the different phases of the business in better adjustment with industry requirements than might otherwise be the case. Moreover, as will be illustrated in Chapter Eleven, integrated companies are often in a more favorable position to manage their inventory programs in accordance with shifts and changes in demand-supply conditions than are nonintegrated companies. In this connection, it is significant to note that the violent fluctuations in profit opportunities which have persistently characterized the cotton textile industry have long been attributed by many economists and industry leaders to a *lack of vertical integration* (see Chapter Twenty-Four).

The contention that the integrated oil companies have *deliberately* attempted to precipitate profit fluctuations at one or more levels of the industry to serve their own ends appears particularly implausible, because there is little, if anything, an integrated company could hope to gain by such a move. The integrated companies have capital investments at each of the several levels of the industry and are under strong compulsion to protect each of those investments and earn an adequate return thereon, just as are the nonintegrated firms which have an investment at only one level of the business.

The only possible reason an integrated company might deliberately adopt price policies which would result in losses or inadequate returns on one phase of its operations would be in an effort to drive out competitors with the hope that after they were gone the losses incurred in the process of driving them out could be more than recouped. Under the conditions existing in the industry during the period 1920–1952, however, it is hard to believe that any responsible management would have embarked on such a course of action because there have been too many large, integrated competitors in each of the markets.[24] In no one of the states in 1949, for example, did any single company have more than 36% of the total market, and in 45 of the states and the District of Columbia, there were at least five big integrated companies in business, each holding at least 3% of the

total state market.[25] In the face of such circumstances, it is doubtful that the practice of depressing prices or margins in the hope of driving out competition long enough to reap so-called monopoly profits could have been used often or with much success. As one oil company executive put it, such efforts are a little "like trying to sweep back the ocean to get a dry place to sit down."[26] As soon as margins and prices are restored to their normal levels, competition flows back in, particularly in the marketing field where relatively small investments are required for individual plant facilities, and the aggressor gains little for his pains.

In the light of the data which will be presented in later chapters, we find considerable evidence to discredit the oft-made contention that the integrated companies have *for some years* been deliberately losing money in the refining or marketing fields while sustaining themselves on profits from producing and transportation operations. As will be noted in Chapter Seven, since the late 1930's profits on pipe line transportation have been held to very moderate levels, first by competition and second by the acceptance of the pipe line consent decree in 1941. Of even greater significance is the fact that nearly all the 20 or 30 largest refining and marketing companies have had a smaller operation in producing than in refining and marketing (see Chapters Two and Twelve). In addition, as will be noted in Chapters Twelve and Thirteen, at least some of these companies have in recent years expanded their marketing more rapidly than their refining and their refining more rapidly than their producing. It is hard to believe that such companies would deliberately seek to curtail profits on the larger and more rapidly growing phases of their business.

The foregoing considerations strongly suggest that the growth and development of integrated oil companies has been prompted by factors of risk and instability which were inherent in the business, particularly at the refining level, and that whatever effect the integrated companies may subsequently have had

---

[24] Before 1911 the old Standard Oil Trust and its successor organizations may at times have depressed prices in one area while sustaining themselves on profits made in other areas in an effort to drive competition out of particular markets (see Chapter Three). The Standard Oil organization, however, occupied a far more powerful position in the industry before 1911 than any single company has at any time since. Since 1911 it is very doubtful that such practices could have met with any significant or lasting success.

[25] The exceptions were Kansas, Wisconsin, and South Dakota. In these states the fifth largest marketers held 2.95%, 2.83%, and 1.00% of the market, respectively. See Chapter Four, Exhibit IV-7, for method of accumulating market shares data.

[26] E. P. Learnard, op. cit., p. 731.

on the profit movements at the different levels of the industry was a distinctly secondary and minor development. In other words, vertical integration in the oil business has been significant primarily as a means of providing protection against adverse profit fluctuations rather than as a means of precipitating those fluctuations in an effort to gain an advantage over non-integrated concerns.

IV. SUMMARY

1. The underlying causes of the dissimilarities in timing, direction, and amplitude which have characterized profit movements at the different levels of the industry have included such things as: variations in the adjustment of capital inputs to industry requirements, dissimilarities in the price movements in the various petroleum markets, differences in the mix of products handled at the successive levels of the industry, and differences in the risks applicable to investments in the separate phases of the business. The dissimilarities in price movements, one of the most important causes of the variations in profit opportunities, have in turn been a product of such things as differences in the sensitivity of the crude oil and various refined product prices to market conditions, temporary differences in demand-supply conditions at the separate levels of the industry, and occasional lags and leads in the timing of price adjustments by large marketers.

2. The refiner's squeeze in 1949 provides an excellent example of the way in which a contraction of profit opportunities at one level of the industry may be brought about through the interplay of business and economic circumstances. In the summer and fall of 1948, oil companies built ample stocks of distillates and residual fuel oil to make sure that the industry and the public would not again experience the shortages suffered in the previous winter. The demand for distillates and residual fuel oil did not develop as strongly as anticipated because the winter weather was much warmer than usual, there was a decline in general business activity, substantial progress was made in the dieselization of railroad equipment, and a major

disparity developed between coal prices and distillate and residual fuel oil prices. Stocks of distillates and residual fuel oil therefore soon became burdensome and precipitated price declines which continued until the stock situation was corrected in the summer of 1949. The price of crude oil did not begin to weaken until near the end of the period of distress largely because of reductions in allowables by state authorities and because the demand for gasoline was increasing. The declining distillate and residual fuel oil prices coupled with steady crude oil prices resulted in a sharp contraction in profit opportunities at the refining level which was quite different from the profit movements occurring at other levels of the industry.

3. The forces and circumstances which contribute to the profit fluctuations and dissimilarities in profit movements at separate levels of the oil business are deep-rooted in the economics of the oil industry and should be accepted as a natural part of business life in the industry and as a corollary of our system of private enterprise and open competition. To remove the dissimilarities in profit movements would require extensive controls over prices in all the petroleum markets, the timing of capital expenditures by business organizations, the selection of projects for investments, and the business entries to and exits from the industry. Even with such controls (the imposition of which would be entirely contrary to the spirit and philosophy of our business system), it is doubtful that all the many forces influencing profits could be so regulated that profit opportunities at all levels could be compelled to move in unison with each other.

4. As long as the profit opportunities at the different levels of the industry are subject to shift and change, it is inevitable that an integrated company will at times make more money on one phase of its business than it does on another and may at times lose money in one area of operations while sustaining itself on profits made in other areas. It by no means follows, however, that the integrated companies have been a *cause* of the variations in profit fluctuations in the different phases of the business. Nearly all of

the important causes of the dissimilarities in profit movements would continue in effect whether the integrated companies were present or not. Such influences as the presence of integrated companies in the industry may have had on the profit movements have probably been of minor and transitory significance, may have served to dampen rather than accentuate the profit movements, and have clearly not been the result of deliberate intent by the integrated companies. We conclude therefore that vertical integration in the oil industry has been significant as a means of providing protection from profit fluctuations in the separate phases of the business and not as a means of precipitating those fluctuations and thereby gaining competitive advantages over nonintegrated firms.

CHAPTER SEVEN

Integration into Transportation Activities: Crude Oil Trunk and Products Pipe Lines

THERE is probably no single point in the oil process where the tendency toward vertical integration has been more pronounced than with respect to the ownership and operation of crude oil trunk and products pipe lines. From the very early days of the oil industry down to the present time the great majority of the pipe lines have been constructed and operated by oil companies or by their subsidiaries and affiliates. It is true that one of the first great crude oil gathering and trunk line systems was developed by the Empire Transportation Company, an affiliate of the Pennsylvania Railroad (see Chapter Three). Likewise the first products pipe line was completed in 1893 by the United States Pipe Line Company which was an independent concern, although closely allied with producing interests. The Empire Transportation Company, however, was soon defeated and absorbed by the Standard Oil group, and the United States Pipe Line Company soon joined forces with producing and refining groups in the formation of the Pure Oil Company. With very few exceptions, all the great crude oil trunk and products pipe line systems which were constructed thereafter were initiated by companies already engaged in either the producing or the refining business.

As of 1950 companies engaged in refining activities or some combination of refining, producing, and marketing activities owned about 86% of the crude oil gathering line mileage in the United States, 82% of the crude oil trunk line mileage, and 92% of the products pipe line mileage (see Chapter Two). The remaining 14% of the crude oil gathering line mileage, 18% of the crude oil trunk line mileage, and 8% of the products pipe line mileage were owned by independent pipe line companies, producing companies, marketing companies, or refining companies which did not report to our survey. A substantial portion of the crude oil gathering and crude oil trunk line mileage owned by these latter companies was accounted for by the Buckeye Pipe Line Company, the Eureka Pipe Line Company, and the South West Pennsylvania Pipe Lines, which as a group owned about 12% of the total United States crude oil gathering lines and about 6% of the total crude oil trunk lines.[1] It is important to note that none of these three companies was originally established as an independent concern; all were associated with the Standard Oil group and became independent as a consequence of the dissolution decree of 1911.

The purpose of this chapter is to explore some of the circumstances which led producing, refining, and marketing companies to undertake the construction of crude oil trunk and products pipe lines.[2] The initial section of the chapter will establish certain facts with regard to transportation costs and the economics of pipe line systems. A series of examples will then be presented of specific pipe line projects undertaken by various oil companies. The concluding section of the chapter

---

[1] Industry data developed as in Chapter Two. Figures for three companies drawn from Interstate Commerce Commission, Bureau of Transport Economics and Statistics, *Statistics of Oil Pipe Line Companies Reporting to the ICC for the Year ended December 31, 1950,* Statement No. 5152 (Government Printing Office, October 1951). The figures for the Eureka Pipe Line Company include data for the New York Transit Company and the Northern Pipe Line Company. In 1952 the properties of South West Pennsylvania Pipe Lines were sold to the National Transit Company, and South West Pennsylvania Pipe Lines initiated liquidation proceedings.

[2] The circumstances which prompted the building of crude oil gathering systems will be discussed in Chapter Fourteen.

EXHIBIT VII-1. TRANSPORTATION COSTS FOR TYPICAL PETROLEUM MOVEMENTS: JANUARY 1952

GASOLINE TO SCRANTON

	Per Gallon
Crude Oil to Philadelphia	
Gathering Charge	$.0012
Trunk Line West Texas to Harbor Island	.0048
Terminal Charge, Harbor Island	.0006
Tanker Harbor Island to Philadelphia	.0090
Total	.0156
Gasoline to Scranton Service Station	
Pipe Line to Kingston	.0034
Terminal Charge, Kingston	.0010
Truck to Scranton Service Station	.0094
Total Transportation Expense	.0250
Tank Wagon Price, Less Tax	.1430
Transportation Expense As Percentage Tank Wagon Price	17%

GASOLINE TO PITTSBURGH

	Per Gallon
Crude Oil to Philadelphia	
Gathering Charge	$.0012
Trunk Line West Texas to Harbor Island	.0048
Terminal Charge, Harbor Island	.0006
Tanker Harbor Island to Philadelphia	.0090
Total	.0156
Gasoline to Pittsburgh Service Station	
Pipe Line to Pittsburgh	.0007
Terminal Charge, Pittsburgh	.0010
Truck to Pittsburgh Service Station	.0027
Total	.0094
Total Transportation Expense	.0250
Tank Wagon Price, Less Tax	.1560
Transportation Expense As Percentage Tank Wagon Price	21%

GASOLINE TO ALTOONA

	Per Gallon
Crude Oil to Philadelphia	
Gathering Charge	$.0012
Trunk Line West Texas to Harbor Island	.0048
Terminal Charge, Harbor Island	.0006
Tanker Harbor Island to Philadelphia	.0090
Total	.0156
Gasoline to Altoona Service Station	
Pipe Line to Eldorado	.0041
Terminal Charge, Eldorado	.0011
Truck to Altoona Service Station	.0030
Total	.0068
Total Transportation Expense	.0238
Tank Wagon Price, Less Tax	.1560
Transportation Expense As Percentage Tank Wagon Price	15%

KEROSENE TO ELMIRA

	Per Gallon
Crude Oil to Philadelphia	
Tanker Venezuela to Philadelphia	$.0090
Kerosene to Elmira Home	
Pipe Line Philadelphia to Big Flats	.0045
Terminal Charge, Big Flats	.0008
Truck to Elmira Home	.0122
Total	.0175
Total Transportation Expense	.0265
Tank Wagon Price, Less Tax	.1480
Transportation Expense As Percentage Tank Wagon Price	18%

FUEL OIL TO ROCHESTER

	Per Gallon
Crude Oil to Philadelphia	
Tanker Venezuela to Philadelphia	$.0090
Fuel Oil to Rochester Home	
Pipe Line Philadelphia to Rochester	.0002
Terminal Charge, Rochester	.0021
Truck to Rochester Home	.0096
Total	.0119
Total Transportation Expense	.0209
Tank Wagon Price, Less Tax	.1340
Transportation Expense As Percentage Tank Wagon Price	20%

GASOLINE TO PHILADELPHIA

	Per Gallon
Crude Oil to Philadelphia	
Tanker Persian Gulf to Philadelphia	$.0402
Gasoline to Philadelphia Service Station	
Truck Philadelphia Refinery to Service Station	.0042
Total	.0444
Total Transportation Expense	.0444
Tank Wagon Price, Less Tax	.1340
Transportation Expense As Percentage Tank Wagon Price	33%

FUEL OIL TO BOSTON

	Per Gallon
Crude Oil to Atreco	
Gathering Charge	$.0012
Trunk Line East Texas to Atreco	.0024
Total	.0036
Fuel Oil to Boston Home	
Tanker Atreco to Revere	.0100
Terminal Charge, Revere	.0028
Truck to Boston Home	.0111
Total	.0239
Total Transportation Expense	.0275
Tank Wagon Price, Less Tax	.1250
Transportation Expense As Percentage Tank Wagon Price	22%

FUEL OIL TO SPRINGFIELD

	Per Gallon
Crude Oil to Atreco	
Gathering Charge	$.0012
Trunk Line East Texas to Atreco	.0024
Total	.0036
Fuel Oil to Springfield Home	
Tanker Atreco to New Haven	.0093
Terminal Charge, New Haven	.0009
Truck to Springfield	.0084
Bulk Plant Charge, Springfield	.0035
Truck to Springfield Home	.0111
Total	.0332
Total Transportation Expense	.0368
Tank Wagon Price, Less Tax	.1380
Transportation Expense As Percentage Tank Wagon Price	28%

GASOLINE TO BALTIMORE

	Per Gallon
Crude Oil to Atreco	
Gathering Charge	$.0012
Trunk Line East Texas to Atreco	.0024
Total	.0036
Gasoline to Baltimore Service Station	
Barge to Baltimore	.0008
Terminal Charge, Baltimore	.0020
Truck to Baltimore Service Station	.0034
Total	.0060
Total Transportation Expense	.0482
Tank Wagon Price, Less Tax	.1460
Transportation Expense As Percentage Tank Wagon Price	33%

GASOLINE TO DANVILLE

	Per Gallon
Crude Oil to Atreco	
Gathering Charge	$.0012
Trunk Line West Texas to Atreco	.0048
Total	.0060
Gasoline to Danville Service Station	
Pipe Line to Baton Rouge	.0030
Pipe Line to Greensboro	.0092
Terminal Charge, Greensboro	.0035
Truck to Danville	.0056
Bulk Plant Charge, Danville	.0030
Truck to Danville Service Station	.0046
Total	.0265
Total Transportation Expense	.0325
Tank Wagon Price, Less Tax	.1540
Transportation Expense As Percentage Tank Wagon Price	21%

Legend:
Crude Trunk Line
Products Pipe Line
Tanker Route
Barge Route
Truck Route

SOURCE: The Atlantic Refining Company.

will discuss some of the reasons why the investment capital for pipe lines was characteristically supplied by producing, refining, and marketing companies rather than by outside concerns.[3]

I. SOME FACTS ABOUT TRANSPORTATION COSTS AND THE ECONOMICS OF PIPE LINE SYSTEMS

The strength of the integration process with respect to crude oil trunk and products pipe lines is explainable largely by a few simple facts with regard to transportation costs in the oil industry and the nature of the investment opportunity which pipe lines provide. As a background for the discussion of specific projects which is to follow, we shall therefore review briefly certain fundamental matters with regard to the significance of transportation costs to oil companies, the economic and operating characteristics of pipe lines, the government and state regulations with respect to pipe lines, and the record of pipe line earnings.

Significance of Transportation Costs in the Oil Business:

In general, it can be said that transportation costs are an extremely important element in the final delivered cost of oil products to the consumer and are a key factor in determining the competitive position of all firms engaged in the producing, manufacturing, and distribution cycle. The ratio of transportation costs to total delivered costs varies widely from one situation to another. Some refineries have a crude oil supply in their backyards and a gasoline service station at their front gates; in such instances transportation costs are of negligible significance. In other cases, however, crude oil may start out in a distant foreign country, such as Venezuela or Kuwait, and eventually be delivered as a refined product to a customer's house in, say, Akron, Ohio. In such instances transportation costs are an extremely high proportion of total costs.

As a means of illustrating the significance of transportation costs in some typical oil movements, the map in Exhibit VII-1 was prepared. The map is based on the experience of The

Atlantic Refining Company and shows cumulative transportation and terminaling costs as a proportion of delivered tank wagon prices at several different destinations. It was assumed that the crude oil originated in West Texas, East Texas, Venezuela, or the Persian Gulf, and that refining took place at either Atreco, Texas, or Philadelphia, Pennsylvania. The pipe line transportation rates used in the examples represent published tariffs. The vessel transportation rates represent calculations made on a basis equivalent to U. S. Maritime Commission rates. The truck transportation rates represent either published tariffs or costs of The Atlantic Refining Company, depending upon whether public or private carriers were used for the specific movements.

In the particular series of examples shown in Exhibit VII-1, the transportation costs, including terminaling charges, ranged from 15% to 33% of the delivered tank wagon prices. Examination of pipe line tariffs, rail rates, and the operating experience of other companies revealed that the costs and movements here shown were fairly representative of the industry as a whole. It seems reasonable to conclude therefore that transportation costs in the oil industry frequently represent about 25% of the delivered tank wagon prices.

Cost of Pipe Line Transportation Versus Other Methods:

Crude oil trunk and products pipe lines, under the proper circumstances, can make very substantial cost savings over other forms of transportation. It is extremely difficult to make any generalized comparison of the cost of transportation by one method versus another because the relative costs vary widely depending on such things as the volume to be shipped, the length of haul, and the terrain to be traversed. In the case of very small quantities involving short hauls over precipitous mountain roads, truck transportation would obviously be far cheaper than pipe line or rail transportation. Conversely, the use of trucks for moving large quantities over long distances would be prohibitive from a cost standpoint. Cost comparisons among the different methods of transportation are thus of very little significance except with respect to specific situations.

As a means of illustrating the magnitude of

---

[3] The companies originating the projects, of course, sometimes borrowed part of the capital from other sources.

EXHIBIT VII-2. COMPARATIVE TRANSPORTATION COSTS FOR
SELECTED CRUDE OIL AND GASOLINE MOVEMENTS: 1952

	Principal Carrier		
	Pipe Line	Railroad	Tanker
CRUDE OIL			
Scurry County,[a] Texas, to Bayway, New Jersey			
Gathering charge[b]	$ .050	$ .055	$ .055
Pipe line tariff	.730	—	.200
Loading	—	.025	.025
Tanker rate[c]	—	—	.375
Rail rate[d]	—	2.750	—
Total per Barrel	.780	2.830	.655
Scurry County,[a] Texas, to Chicago, Illinois			
Gathering charge[b]	.050	.050	
Pipe line tariff (average four companies)	.375		
Loading	—	.025	
Rail rate[e]	—	1.327	
Total per Barrel	$.425	1.402	
Scurry County,[a] Texas, to Toledo, Ohio			
Gathering charge[b]	.050	.050	
Pipe line tariff (average two companies)	.508	—	
Loading	—	.025	
Rail rate[f]	—	2.255	
Total per Barrel	$.558	2.330	
Scurry County,[a] Texas, to Houston, Texas			
Gathering charge[b]	.055	.055	
Pipe line tariff	.200	—	
Loading	—	.025	
Rail rate	—	1.214	
Total per Barrel	.255	1.294	
GASOLINE			
Houston, Texas, to Lynchburg, Virginia			
Pipe line tariff, Houston to Baton Rouge	$ .120		
Pipe line evaporation charge ($\frac{1}{4}$ of 1%)	.025		
Pipe line tariff, Baton Rouge to Greensboro, N.C.	.390		
Pipe line evaporation charge ($\frac{1}{4}$ of 1%)	.013		
Terminaling at Greensboro, N.C.	.063		
Truck rate, Greensboro to Lynchburg	.506		
Total per Barrel	$1.117		
Rail rate, Houston to Lynchburg		$3.152	
Tank car rental charge		.029	
Total per Barrel		$3.181	
Tanker rate, Houston to Norfolk, Va. (U.S.M.C.)			$ .309
Tanker evaporation loss ($\frac{4}{10}$ of 1%)			.015
Terminaling at Norfolk			.063
Rail rate, Norfolk to Lynchburg			.634
Tank car rental charge			.029
Total per Barrel			$1.050
Houston, Texas, to Pittsburgh, Pennsylvania			
Pipe line, total costs per barrel[g]	.400		
Rail charges,[h] total costs per barrel		3.149	
Tanker rate,[i] Houston to Philadelphia (U.S.M.C.)			.339
Tanker evaporation loss ($\frac{3}{10}$ of 1%)[j]			.015
Terminaling at Philadelphia			.063
Pipe line tariff, Philadelphia to Pittsburgh			.220
Pipe line evaporation loss ($\frac{1}{2}$ of 1%)			.027
Total per Barrel			$ .664

[a] Colorado City.   [b] Rates vary because different companies post different charges.   [c] U.S.M.C. rate for 36° A.P.I. gravity. [d] Estimated for continuing movement; published rate $3.4230 per barrel   [e] Estimated for continuing movement; published rate $1.6548 per barrel.   [f] Estimated for continuing movement; published rate $2.6506 per barrel.   [g] Estimated; a line from Houston to Pittsburgh is not now in existence.   [h] Includes tank car rental charge of $.029 per barrel.   [i] Includes 3% federal transportation tax.   [j] Evaporation loss based on full motor fuel cargoes.

SOURCE: Estimates by Standard Oil Company (New Jersey).

EXHIBIT VII-3. TARIFF REQUIRED TO EARN 7% NET RETURN ON INVESTMENT
FOR PIPE LINES OF DIFFERENT SIZES: 1948

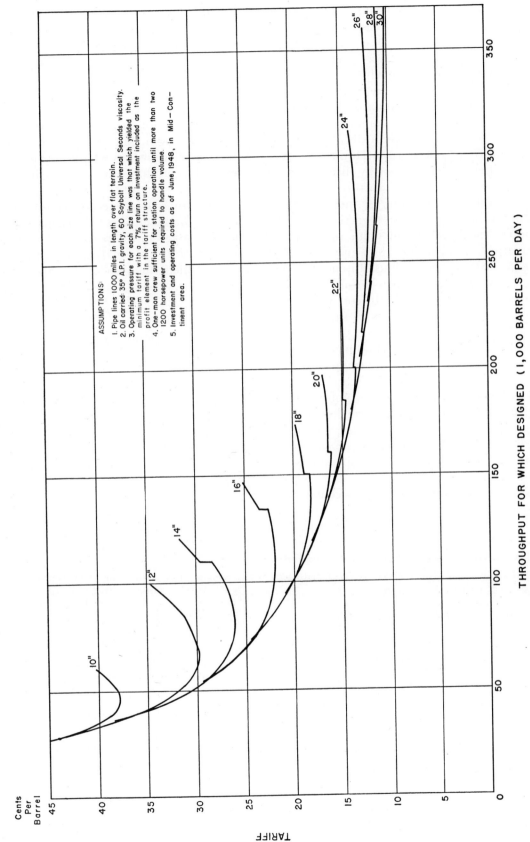

ASSUMPTIONS:

1. Pipe lines 1000 miles in length over flat terrain.
2. Oil carried: 35° A.P.I. gravity, 60 Saybolt Universal Seconds viscosity.
3. Operating pressure for each size line was that which yielded the minimum tariff with a 7% return on investment included as the profit element in the tariff structure.
4. One-man crew sufficient for station operation until more than two 1200 horsepower units required to handle volume.
5. Investment and operating costs as of June, 1948, in Mid-Continent area.

Cents Per Barrel

TARIFF

THROUGHPUT FOR WHICH DESIGNED (1,000 BARRELS PER DAY)

SOURCE: Standard Oil Company (New Jersey) and F. C. Whiteside, Continental Pipe Line Company.

the cost savings which can be made by crude oil trunk and products pipe lines, where the circumstances are such as to warrant the use of pipe lines, Exhibit VII-2 was prepared. The exhibit shows the cost of moving crude oil from Scurry County, Texas, to four different destinations by the various alternative methods of transportation that were commercially available in 1952. Similarly, the exhibit shows the cost of moving gasoline from Houston, Texas, to two different destinations by three different methods of transportation. In the examples, it was sometimes necessary to use more than one method of transportation to accomplish the complete movement from point of origin to destination. The exhibit therefore shows the *over-all cost* for the various shipments when pipe lines were used as the *principal carrier* as contrasted with the over-all cost when various other facilities were used as the principal carrier.

In these examples, the savings made possible by the use of pipe lines instead of rail transportation ranged from about $1.00 to $2.75 per barrel. In one case, however, a combined pipe line and tanker movement proved cheaper than did the pipe line movement alone, and in another case a combined tanker and rail movement was cheaper than the corresponding pipe line movement.

A series of examples could, of course, also be selected in which truck or rail transportation might show equal savings over pipe line transportation. The only conclusion that can be drawn with respect to pipe lines is that they permit great economies when the circumstances are such as to justify their use.

Economies from Large Diameter Pipe Lines:

Large diameter pipe lines achieve substantial cost savings over small diameter lines when a sufficient volume can be accumulated in one system to warrant their use. An indication of the significance of the cost savings made possible by the use of large diameter pipe lines may be obtained from Exhibit VII-3 which shows an illustrative example of the tariffs that would have to be charged to earn a return of 7% on the investment in pipe lines of different sizes, designed for different volumes of throughput. A 10-inch pipe line, for example, had its most favorable operating situation when

designed for a throughput of about 45,000 barrels per day and permitted, at this level, a tariff of approximately 37 cents per barrel. A 30-inch pipe line, on the other hand, when designed for 350,000 barrels per day of throughput, returned 7% on the investment with a tariff of slightly over 10 cents per barrel. The figures were for crude oil trunk lines 1,000 miles in length, but the general character of the cost relationships would not be greatly different for product lines or for lines of somewhat shorter length.[4]

Recognition of the economies made possible by large diameter lines led to a marked increase in their usage in the period 1941–1949 as may be seen from the analysis of crude oil trunk and products line mileage by pipe sizes shown in Exhibit VII-4.

EXHIBIT VII-4. CRUDE OIL TRUNK AND PRODUCTS PIPE LINES IN THE UNITED STATES: 1941 AND 1949

Size (Inside Diameter) *	Miles Crude Oil Trunk Lines		Miles Products Lines	
	1941	1949	1941	1949
Below 4-inch	1,050	1,233	162	391
4-inch	3,590	2,768	692	1,366
6-inch	12,570	12,254†	3,781	6,696
8-inch	29,380	27,780	4,230	9,979
10-inch	11,710	13,500	68	1,628
12-inch	6,710	9,027	68	817
Above 12-inch	170	4,811	—	4
Total U.S.	65,180	71,373	9,001	20,881

* Data for odd sizes are included in the next smaller size listed.

† Includes a small mileage of 5-inch pipe.

SOURCE: U.S. Bureau of Mines, *Crude-Oil and Refined Products Pipe-Line Mileage in the United States, January 1, 1950,* Information Circular 7585, by A. T. Coumbe and I. F. Avery, October 1950.

[4] The data for Exhibit VII-3 were based on design conditions and construction costs in the Mid-Continent area as of June 1948. The terrain traversed was assumed to be flat and the oil carried to be 35° API gravity and 60 SUS (Saybolt Universal Seconds) viscosity. Reasonable engineering practices were assumed with respect to pipe line materials and safety factors. The operating pressure used for each line size was that pressure which yielded the minimum tariff with a 7% return on the capital investment included as the profit element in the tariff structure. The operating pressure was then held constant and the station spacing altered to vary the throughput. It was assumed that a one-man crew was sufficient for station operations until more than two 1,200 horsepower units were required to handle the volume. Data courtesy Standard Oil Company (New Jersey) and F. C. Whiteside, Continental Pipe Line Company.

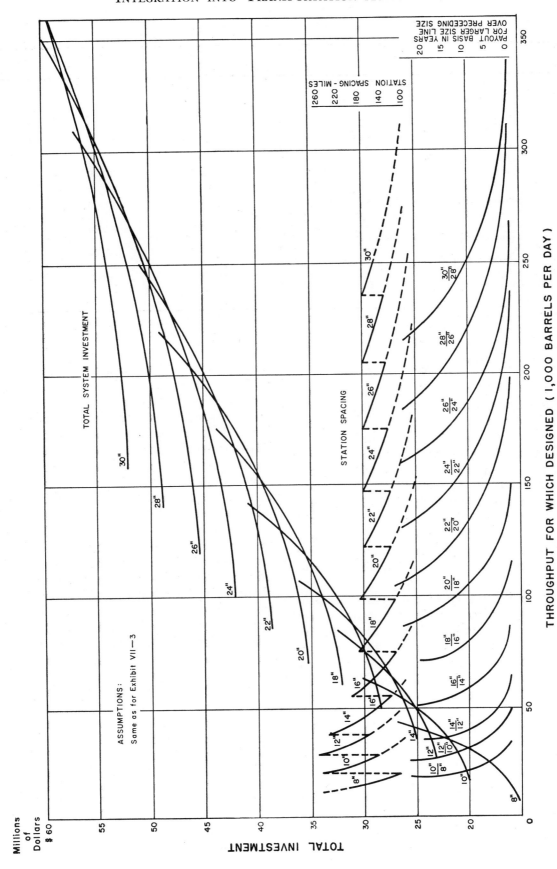

EXHIBIT VII-5. TOTAL SYSTEM INVESTMENT FOR PIPE LINES OF DIFFERENT SIZES: 1948

SOURCE: Standard Oil Company (New Jersey) and F. C. Whiteside, Continental Pipe Line Company.

EXHIBIT VII–6.   ESTIMATED COST OF RECENT PIPE LINE PROJECTS: 1952 *

	Length in Miles	Size	Capacity Barrels per Day	Estimated Cost
Crude Oil Trunk Lines				
Sinclair Pipe Line Co., Cushing, Okla., to Salisbury, Mo., and Chicago, Ill.	666	24, 22-inch	280,000	$51,943,000
Shell Pipe Line Corp., McCamey to Houston, Tex.†	463	24-inch	209,000	41,631,000
Platte Pipe Line Co., Wyoming to Wood River, Ill.	1,057	16, 20-inch	110,000	59,000,000
Pasotex Pipe Line Co., Wink to El Paso, Tex.	200	8-inch	11,500	3,283,000
Cities Service Pipe Line Co., Sour Lake, Tex., to Lake Charles, La.	64	18-inch	150,000	3,100,000
Products Pipe Lines				
Shell Oil Company, Wood River to Chicago, Ill.†	285	14-inch	85,000	10,588,000
Standard Oil Co. (Indiana), Sugar Creek, Mo., to Dubuque, Iowa†	316	12-inch	40,000	10,430,000
Pioneer Pipe Line Co., Sinclair, Wyo., to Salt Lake City, Utah	300	8-inch	12,000	7,840,000
Texas Pipe Line Co., Port Arthur, Tex., to Baton Rouge, La.†	198	16-inch	96,000	12,900,000
The Ohio Oil Company, East St. Louis, Ill., to Indianapolis, Ind.	255	8, 10-inch	14,000	2,893,000

* At the time these data were obtained, the lines were in various stages of planning or construction. The lines as finally completed sometimes had lengths, sizes, capacities, and costs different from those estimated in the early stages of the projects.

† *Platt's Oilgram News Service*, May 1, 1952, New York Edition, pp. 2–3.

Capital Costs of Pipe Lines:

Exhibit VII-5 reveals the high capital costs required for the construction of crude oil trunk lines. The curves show the total system investment required for 1,000-mile trunk lines of various capacities and various pipe sizes.[5] For example, an 8-inch line with a capacity of about 30,000 barrels per day would have cost in 1948 approximately $20,000,000; a 30-inch line capable of delivering 350,000 barrels per day would have cost about $58,000,000. The capital costs for products lines tend to run somewhat higher than for crude oil lines of similar diameter and capacity.

Further illustration of the large capital investments required for pipe line systems may be found in the estimated costs shown in Exhibit VII-6 for several recent pipe line construction projects. These costs cannot be compared directly with those shown in Exhibit VII-5 because of differences in conditions and because in some cases the companies building the lines listed in Exhibit VII-6 made partial use of existing facilities or of pipe taken up in other areas.

Importance of an Assured Throughput:

In view of the high capital costs required for the construction of pipe line systems and the fact that many of the operating expenses are relatively fixed irrespective of throughput, it is extremely important that a pipe line operate with a throughput very close to that for which it was designed. As may be seen from Exhibit VII-7, unit transportation costs tend to rise significantly if a line is operated above or below its designed rate. The curve shown in the exhibit was for a crude oil trunk line 1,000 miles in length, designed to operate with 12 pump stations at a capacity of 50,000 barrels per day.[6] With a throughput of 50,000 barrels, the transportation cost per thousand barrel miles was about 29 cents. For a throughput of about 33,000 barrels per day, however, the cost rose to approximately 36.4 cents per thousand barrel miles. For volumes below 33,000 barrels per day only 6 pump stations were required, and the unit operating costs at first declined as the volume dropped and then rose to about 40.9 cents per thousand barrel miles with a throughput of 25,000 barrels per day. Operation at a level in excess of 50,000 barrels per day required the installation of 12 additional pump stations (in this particular ex-

[5] The conditions on which the data are based are similar to those underlying Exhibit VII-3.

[6] The figures shown in Exhibit VII-7 should not be compared with the figures in Exhibit VII-5. Exhibit VII-7 shows the effect on unit costs of altering the volume of throughput in a line designed to operate at 50,000 barrels per day. Exhibit VII-5, on the other hand, shows the effect on unit tariffs of altering the volume at which a particular line was designed to operate.

EXHIBIT VII-7. EFFECT OF VARYING LEVELS OF THROUGHPUT ON OPERATING COSTS OF PIPE LINE DESIGNED TO CARRY 50,000 BARRELS PER DAY: 1952

(Exclusive of Income and Transportation Taxes)

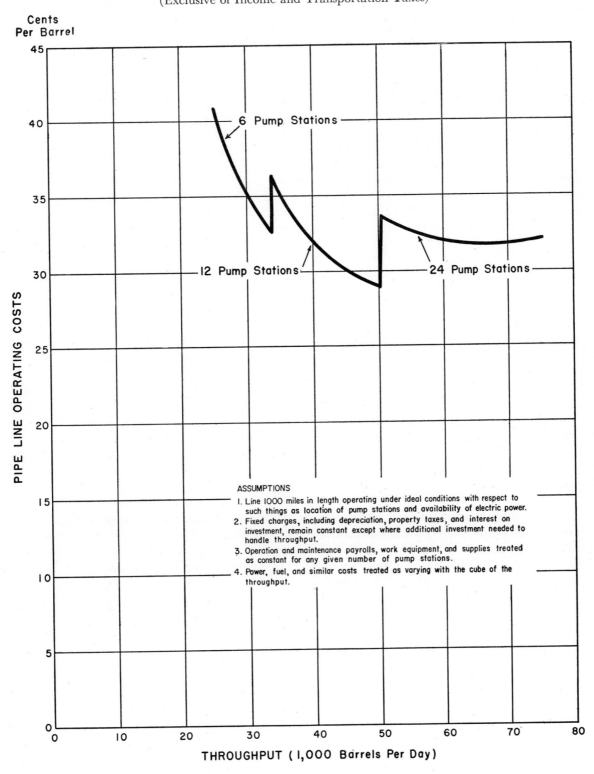

ASSUMPTIONS

1. Line 1000 miles in length operating under ideal conditions with respect to such things as location of pump stations and availability of electric power.
2. Fixed charges, including depreciation, property taxes, and interest on investment, remain constant except where additional investment needed to handle throughput.
3. Operation and maintenance payrolls, work equipment, and supplies treated as constant for any given number of pump stations.
4. Power, fuel, and similar costs treated as varying with the cube of the throughput.

SOURCE: T. R. Aude, Service Pipe Line Company.

ample) and resulted in costs ranging between 32 cents and 33.7 cents per thousand barrel miles, depending on the volume of throughput.

Further indication of the importance of predicting volume requirements accurately and of maintaining throughputs at designed levels may be found in Exhibits VII-3 and VII-5. The curves reveal that a pipe line of given diameter is competitive with the next larger or next smaller diameter line only over a very limited volume range. Consequently, if a line is constructed and subsequently required to operate at other than its designed rate, it may not be able to meet on a profitable basis the tariff schedules established by other lines of more appropriate size serving the same general area.

It is also important to note that the pipe line throughput ordinarily must be maintained over a fairly long period of years if the project is to be a financial success. As will be pointed out below, many of the pipe lines operate under the terms of the pipe line consent decree of 1941 which, in effect, requires them to set their tariffs at levels which will yield a return of only about 7% on the capital investment. Moreover, the Interstate Commerce Commission ordinarily requires the use of 30 to 40 year depreciation periods in the computation of earnings and pipe line valuations. The tariffs set by companies operating under the consent decree have an effect on rate structures established by all pipe line companies, and as a result the payout periods on many pipe line projects range from 15 to 25 years.

Specialized Character of Pipe Lines:

The ordinary pipe line is a highly specialized transportation facility. First, it is fixed with respect to its geographic location and cannot easily be moved from one area to another in accordance with shifts and changes in traffic patterns as may an oil tanker or a truck. Second, the pipe line is entirely dependent for its existence upon shipments of crude oil and refined products and cannot draw business from a variety of different fields as may a railroad. Third, the number of customers from which a pipe line must draw its main volume of business is usually very small. Refiners are the principal shippers over both crude oil and products pipe lines, and the number of plants which may be located in a single geographic area at the ter-

minus of a crude oil trunk line or the originating point of a products line usually ranges between one and five.

As a result of the specialized character of the pipe lines, there are a number of risks associated with their construction that are somewhat different from those associated with investments in other types of transportation facilities. When a crude oil pipe line system is built into a particular producing area, it becomes dependent upon the continued flow of oil from that area for its existence. If production in the field declines at an unexpectedly rapid rate, the pipe line may lose its traffic before its capital investment has been recovered. One such instance may be found in the experience of the Cumberland Pipe Line Company which at one time operated an extensive crude oil gathering system in the Kentucky oil fields. As a result of the decline in production in these fields, the company's revenues were greatly curtailed, and it was eventually forced to sell its properties at considerably less than their depreciated value.[7]

The sudden discovery of a major crude oil producing field at some other point may also drastically reduce the traffic of a pipe line. For example, when the new Illinois fields were developed in 1938, the refiners in the central states promptly shifted a large portion of their purchases from the Mid-Continent fields to Illinois, and the traffic of the crude oil pipe lines running north from Kansas and Oklahoma was correspondingly reduced. The Ajax Pipe Line, one of the largest trunk lines in the Mid-Continent area, lost about 67% of its traffic and about 77% of its operating revenues between 1938 and 1939.[8] Similarly, the development of a large volume of production in the Los Angeles Basin in 1923 temporarily resulted in the movement of substantial amounts of crude oil to Atlantic Coast refineries by tanker,

---

[7] 72d U. S. Congress, 2d Session, Committee on Interstate and Foreign Commerce, House Report No. 2192, *Report on Pipe Lines*, Part I, 1933, p. LXXIII. It is, of course, possible that the owners of this line received sufficient returns in earnings during the period of operation to recoup their capital outlay.

[8] Interstate Commerce Commission, Bureau of Transport Economics and Statistics, op. cit., Statements Nos. 3955 and 4044 for years ending December 31, 1938, and 1939. See also 76th U. S. Congress, Hearings Before the Temporary National Economic Committee, *Petroleum Transportation*, Testimony of Fayette B. Dow, October 4, 1939, pp. 43 and 59.

thereby reducing the volume handled by the pipe lines which had been moving crude oil eastward from the Mid-Continent fields. The traffic of the largest crude oil trunk line in the United States was abruptly cut in half by the Los Angeles development.[9]

A crude oil trunk line is furthermore always vulnerable to the possibility that one or more of its major customers may make other transportation arrangements. As was noted above, a pipe line has little opportunity to guard against this risk by increasing the number of customers it serves. A classic example of the loss of customers by a pipe line may be found in the experience of the Prairie companies [10] which originally constituted the crude oil purchasing and pipe line agencies of the Standard Oil group in the Mid-Continent area, but which operated independently after the dissolution decree in 1911. The Prairie companies encountered severe financial difficulties in the late 1920's and early 1930's and were eventually forced to sell out to the Sinclair Oil Corporation in 1932. There were many reasons for the failure of the Prairie companies but important among them was the fact that a number of their major customers in the Mid-Continent area in the late 1920's and early 1930's constructed crude oil pipe lines of their own.[11]

The Prairie companies were particularly hard hit in 1930 when one of their largest customers, the Standard Oil Company (Indiana), increased its ownership in the Sinclair Pipe Line Company from 50% to 100% and was thereafter able to handle most of its own crude

oil shipments. It is reported that the Indiana Company and the Standard Oil Company (New Jersey) attempted to secure rate reductions from The Prairie Pipe Line Company in 1929. The reduction was refused because the two companies would not make any commitments with regard to the volume they would transport through the lines. Subsequently, the Indiana Company increased its equity in the Sinclair Pipe Line and the Standard Oil Company (New Jersey) joined with the Standard Oil Company (Ohio) and the Pure Oil Company to build the Ajax Pipe Line. The Prairie Pipe Line Company lost approximately $13,500,000 in revenue from the Indiana Company alone between 1929 and 1931.[12]

The risks involved in the construction of products pipe lines are somewhat less than in the case of crude oil lines because there is usually a greater permanency in the flow of products from established refineries to market areas than there is in the flow of crude oil from producing fields to refineries. The products lines, like the crude oil trunk lines, however, are nearly always dependent for the major portion of their business on a very small group of shippers.

Government Regulations Covering Pipe Line Operations:

The Hepburn Act of 1906, which was later supported by the Supreme Court decision on The Pipe Line Cases [13] in 1914, established the status of the oil pipe line companies operating in interstate commerce as common carriers subject to regulation by the Interstate Commerce Commission. Among other things, the Interstate Commerce Commission requires the pipe line companies to file their rate schedules with the Commission, to maintain just and reasonable rates, and to establish rules and regulations covering minimum tenders and other shipping practices which will assure the availability of pipe line service to all shippers on a fair and equitable basis. Any interested party, or the Interstate Commerce Commission, may at any time challenge the rates and shipping practices of a pipe line company. Hearings are

[9] Joseph E. Pogue, *Economics of Pipe Line Transportation in the Petroleum Industry*, a pamphlet (New York, 1932), p. 19.

[10] The Prairie Oil and Gas Company was organized in 1900 as the Kansas Oil and Gas Company. The latter name was changed to The Prairie Oil and Gas Company in 1903. By 1915 the company had constructed and placed in operation approximately 5,523 miles of pipe line, originating at various points in the Mid-Continent fields and with principal terminals at Wood River, Illinois, and Griffith, Indiana. The Prairie Pipe Line Company was incorporated in Kansas in January 1915 to handle the transportation activities of The Prairie Oil and Gas Company; the entire capital stock of the pipe line company was distributed among the shareholders of The Prairie Oil and Gas Company. See 72d U. S. Congress, 2d Session, Committee on Interstate and Foreign Commerce, House Report 2192, *Report on Pipe Lines*, Part 2, 1933, pp. 132–133.

[11] Letter to the stockholders of The Prairie Oil and Gas Company and The Prairie Pipe Line Company from the Board of Directors, dated January 14, 1932.

[12] 72d U. S. Congress, 2d Session, Committee on Interstate and Foreign Commerce, House Report 2192, Part 2, pp. 146–149.

[13] 234 U. S. 548 (1914).

held on such complaints and remedial orders are entered by the Commission where required.

In 1940 the Department of Justice brought a suit against many of the pipe line companies charging that the dividends paid to shipper-owners constituted rebates and were thus in violation of the Elkins Act of 1903. The action was settled by the "pipe line consent decree" which was entered on December 23, 1941 [14] and which was signed by most of the major oil companies in the United States. The decree provides that a shipper-owner may not receive from a pipe line company more than its share of a 7% return on the Interstate Commerce Commission's valuation of the pipe line properties. Pipe line earnings in excess of 7% of the pipe line valuation are required to be held in special accounts in the pipe line companies and may be used for the extension of pipe line properties, but the value of the facilities so added may not be included in the valuation for dividend purposes.

The government regulations and legal decisions cited above have not been applied to products lines in quite the same manner as to crude oil lines, possibly because there were very few products lines in existence at the time of the decision on The Pipe Line Cases. The language of the Interstate Commerce Act is broad enough to cover products lines; and many products lines, such as the Great Lakes Pipe Line extending from northeastern Oklahoma to the North Central states, the Plantation Pipe Line running from Baton Rouge, Louisiana, to Greensboro, North Carolina, and the Keystone Pipe Line in Pennsylvania, have for years operated as common carriers under the jurisdiction of the Interstate Commerce Commission. Moreover, some of the products pipe lines belonging to companies that signed the pipe line consent decree have operated in accordance with the provisions of the decree. A number of products pipe lines, however, such as certain of those of the Standard Oil Company (Indiana) and that of the Champlin Refining Company running from its refinery at Enid, Oklahoma, to cities in Iowa and Nebraska, carry only the products of their owners and operate as private carriers. The ex-

act legal status of such lines has not yet been clarified by court decisions. In two decisions, one in 1946 [15] and one in 1950, the Supreme Court of the United States upheld the action of the Interstate Commerce Commission in requiring the Champlin Refining Company to furnish valuation information, file reports, and keep accounts in accordance with the provisions of the Interstate Commerce Act. The court did not, however, hold that the company was a common carrier or that it should be required to publish its tariffs.

Pipe lines that operate exclusively in intrastate commerce are, of course, not subject to the jurisdiction of the Interstate Commerce Commission. They must, however, comply with the regulations of the states in which they operate. About half the states have enacted some type of pipe line common carrier legislation. The regulations in a number of the states are patterned after the Interstate Commerce Act.

Pipe Line Earnings:

One general effect of the government regulations with respect to pipe line operations has been to bring about, in conjunction with other factors, a gradual reduction in pipe line earnings. Exhibit VII-8 indicates the return which pipe line companies reporting to the Interstate Commerce Commission earned on their borrowed and invested capital in the period 1923–1951. For the period 1923–1933, inclusive, the earnings figures represent the entire group of companies reporting to the ICC. In later years, the earnings figures represent a group of 19 or 20 companies for which corporate surplus figures were available in the ICC reports. Pipe lines which were operated as departments of an oil company were not, of course, able to report "corporate surplus" figures to the ICC.

The figures in Exhibit VII-8 are not strictly comparable from one year to the next because the Commission from time to time made changes in the methods permitted for the calculation of earnings. The data suffice, however, to give a reasonably clear picture of the decline in earnings which developed after about 1937. In the years before about 1937 the pipe line companies tended to establish tariffs which permitted fairly high rates of return on their capi-

---

[14] *U. S.* vs. *Atlantic Refining Company et al.,* Civil Action No. 14060, District Court of the District of Columbia (1941).

[15] *Champlin Refining Company* vs. *United States, et al.,* 329 U. S. 29 (1946).

EXHIBIT VII-8. TARIFFS, EXPENSES, AND EARNINGS OF PIPE LINE COMPANIES REPORTING TO THE INTERSTATE COMMERCE COMMISSION: 1923–1951

Year	Number of Carriers Reporting to ICC	Barrel Miles (Millions)			Trunk Line Revenue per Barrel Mile	Trunk Line Expenses per Barrel Mile	Borrowed and Invested Capital* ($1,000)	Pipe Line Operating Income* ($1,000)	Income as a Percentage of Borrowed and Invested Capital*
		Crude Oil	Refined Oil	Total					
1923	34						$574,944	$ 52,678	9.16%
1924	36						603,179	63,176	10.47
1925	35						448,158	70,966	15.84
1926	33						472,028	76,187	16.14
1927	32						537,774	92,719	17.24
1928	33						574,123	112,221	19.56
1929	37						613,907	135,421	22.06
1930	40						625,040	121,816	19.49
1931	49						644,680	116,767	18.11
1932	46						457,322	110,019	24.06
1933	48						452,210	107,811	23.84
1934	51						177,046	38,929	21.98
1935	53	213,798 †	17,196 ‡	230,994			169,957	33,171	19.51
1936	52	252,202 §	18,442	270,644			144,757	33,808	23.35
1937	58	280,670	22,347	303,016	$.632	$.238	176,267	44,096	25.02
1938	59	263,101	23,687	286,788	.674	.252	165,708	38,899	23.47
1939	63	265,181	24,430	389,610	.431	.184	165,157	32,798	19.85
1940	66	282,192	23,741	305,933	.583	.246	172,948	25,102	14.51
1941	71	324,037	26,749	350,785	.564	.234	158,764	26,664	16.79
1942	69	346,051	38,423	384,474	.498	.240	171,085	14,890	8.70
1943	74	393,030	60,896	453,926	.485	.251	177,503	19,329	10.89
1944	75	437,680	70,917	508,596	.487	.261	180,851	22,742	12.57
1945	74	429,943	65,360	495,303	.486	.303	201,133	18,993	9.44
1946	70	428,843	58,752	487,595	.468	.287	203,858	19,135	9.39
1947	71	465,504	71,555	537,059	.471	.304	214,425	17,711	8.26
1948	73	513,498	85,087	598,585	.491	.322	278,142	19,667	7.07
1949	73	497,179	92,563	589,741	.507	.323	355,104	22,347	6.29
1950	76	577,054	106,649	683,703	.518	.285	363,604	33,316	9.16
1951	76	694,723	122,188	816,911	.521	.274	398,913	31,318	7.85

* Borrowed and invested capital includes unmatured funded debt, capital stock, and corporate surplus. Pipe line operating income is after taxes but before interest and contingent charges and before income from outside investments. For the years 1923 to 1933 the entire group of companies reporting to the ICC was used. For the years 1934 to 1951 the data represent a group of companies for which corporate surplus figures were available in the ICC reports. The group included 19 companies in all years except 1934, 1935, 1937, 1938, 1939, 1948, and 1949, in which years it was comprised of 20 companies.

† Data not available for two companies.

‡ Data not available for five companies.

§ Data not available for one company.

SOURCE: Compiled from Interstate Commerce Commission, Bureau of Transport Economics and Statistics, *Statistics of Oil Pipe Line Companies Reporting to the ICC*, Annual Reports.

tal investments. In the early years of the industry's history the methods available for determining the extent of the crude oil reserves in newly discovered fields were even less precise than they are today. Moreover, the rule of capture tended to force wide-open production of the wells as a protection against drainage from adjoining properties, and many of the fields thus had very short lives. As a result, there was some reason for the pipe line companies to set their tariffs as high as they reasonably could in order to be sure of getting their investment back while the fields were still productive. Since the great majority of the producing fields in

the United States have turned out to have greater reserves than was anticipated at the time of the discovery, most of the pipe line companies were quite profitable.

The advent of the prorationing laws in the early 1930's led to a more orderly development of the producing fields, extended the life expectancy of the lines, and reduced some of the uncertainties connected with pipe line construction, thereby creating a situation favorable to the reduction of pipe line tariffs. Moreover, as a result of repeated complaints about pipe line earnings by refiners who did not have pipe lines of their own and who were forced to use the facilities of others, the Interstate Commerce Commission initiated a rate investigation in 1934, in the course of which it established a finding that earnings by a common carrier pipe line in excess of 8% on the valuation of its properties might be deemed excessive and subject to revision by commission order.

The downward movement of pipe line tariffs after 1937 was also occasioned to some extent by increasing competition among the pipe line carriers and between the carriers and other forms of transportation. During this period truck transportation became important as a method of hauling refined products and exerted a competitive pressure on pipe line tariffs so far as the shorter movements were concerned. Likewise barge and tanker transportation was developed in competition with the pipe lines for certain of the long-haul business. A further factor contributing to the downward movement of tariffs in the latter 1930's was the improvement of engineering practices with respect to pipe sizes, the spacing of stations, operating pressures, and other features of pipe line construction and operation. Finally, the pipe line consent decree in 1941 put a strong compulsion on the companies that were party to the agreement to set their tariffs so that the earnings of their lines would not exceed 7% on the ICC valuation of their properties. The mileage operated by the signers of the consent decree was sufficiently large so that their tariff schedules had an influence on pipe line rate structures throughout the country and thus affected the return on investment which might be earned by other pipe line companies.

In appraising the pipe line earnings records shown in Exhibit VII-8, it is important to recognize that a pipe line which is owned by integrated oil companies carries two types of traffic: shipments for the owners and shipments for outsiders. So far as the first type of business is concerned, the pipe line "profits" represent cost savings which the owners make in their own operations. Unfortunately the Interstate Commerce Commission does not require the pipe line companies to file records showing how much volume they carry for themselves as contrasted with outsiders. The findings of the Splawn Report,[16] the TNEC hearings, and our own investigations, however, all corroborate the fact that the majority of the volume carried by the pipe lines of integrated oil companies is for the account of the owners themselves. It appears therefore that the pipe line earnings reflect transportation savings which the owners make on their own business more than they do profits earned on transportation service provided to others.

It should also be recognized that the economic and operating value of a pipe line to the owners is frequently not fully reflected in the earnings of the pipe line company or in the dividends that may be paid to the owners. The owners may also make very important savings in their own transportation costs because the tariffs of the pipe line may be far lower than the costs associated with the next best method of transportation. In many cases the pipe line tariffs are set well below the costs of alternative carriers because of the various government regulations referred to above. Moreover, in some cases the applicable tax rates, the proportion of the stock a shipper-owner holds in a common carrier pipe line affiliate, and the percentage of the total volume the shipper-owner supplies to the line are such that a shipper-owner fares better by keeping the tariffs and earnings of the pipe line low in order to secure maximum freight savings on his own traffic than he does by raising the tariffs in order to increase the profits of the line on the traffic of outside shippers.

The bearing which the facts about transportation costs and the nature of pipe lines reviewed in the foregoing paragraphs have had on the tendency of producing, refining, or marketing companies to build their own crude oil trunk and products pipe lines will become clear as the discussion progresses.

II. CRUDE OIL TRUNK LINES AS A MEANS OF REDUCING TRANSPORTATION COSTS

The majority of the crude oil trunk lines we studied were built by refiners as a means of reducing their inward transportation costs on their own crude oil. The magnitude of the cost savings that may be achieved through the

---

[16] 72d U. S. Congress, 2d Session, Committee on Interstate and Foreign Commerce, House Report No. 2192, *Report on Pipe Lines*, Part I, 1933, p. LXIII. (This report was signed by Walter M. W. Splawn and is generally known as the "Splawn Report.")

construction of crude oil trunk lines when the circumstances are appropriate to their use have already been discussed. A typical example of backward integration by a refiner into the ownership and operation of crude oil trunk lines as a means of reducing transportation costs on inward movements of crude oil may be found in the experience of The Atlantic Refining Company in constructing its first crude oil trunk lines from the Gulf Coast to the East and West Texas fields in the period 1928 to 1931.

The Atlantic Refining Company was organized as an independent concern in 1870 but became a part of the Standard Oil group in 1874. At the time of the dissolution decree in 1911 when the company again became an independent firm, its principal properties consisted of three refineries located at Philadelphia, Pittsburgh, and Franklin, Pennsylvania. The dissolution action left Atlantic with no crude oil producing properties and no pipe lines or other transportation facilities. The company's marketing properties were limited to distributing stations in cities and large towns in Pennsylvania and Delaware. Over 60% of the output from the three refineries and 80% of the output of the Philadephia refinery had previously been sold in foreign markets under well-established brand names, which were assigned to Atlantic in the dissolution proceedings. The company did not, however, have a foreign sales organization because sale of the products had been accomplished through the Standard Oil organization.

In the period following 1911 Atlantic developed an extensive organization to handle direct sales to consumers and distributors in several foreign countries. In the United States the company integrated forward into both wholesale and retail marketing operations. In 1916 the company also initiated crude oil producing operations on a very limited scale and began the construction of a tanker fleet as a means of relieving the shortage of tankers in the coastwise service from the Gulf Coast to Philadelphia which developed as a result of wartime conditions. Throughout the period from 1911 to 1928, however, the company remained primarily a refining and marketing concern.

Before 1928 the company had no crude oil pipe lines of any significance and relied upon other concerns for overland transportation service. In the period 1928–1931 two major crude oil lines were constructed. The first was initiated in July 1928 immediately after the company secured its first important crude oil production in the Permian Basin in the West Texas and New Mexico fields. The line extended from Midland, a city in these fields, to Atreco on the Gulf Coast of Texas. It was 510 miles in length, cost approximately $7,500,000, and had a capacity of 48,000 barrels per day. The second line was built in 1931 shortly after the discovery of the great East Texas fields. It was 10 inches in diameter and extended from the East Texas fields to Atreco, a distance of 180 miles.

Examination of company records indicates that these two lines were built primarily because the company was experiencing difficulty in competing with refiners who had crude oil trunk lines of their own and were thus able to secure their crude oil at a lower transportation cost than could Atlantic. Atlantic was able to make use of the common carrier lines of other companies, but on shipments through these lines Atlantic made transportation savings only to the extent that the pipe line tariffs were below the rates charged by the railroads or other transportation agencies. The refiners who owned pipe lines, on the other hand, made similiar savings plus additional savings in cases where the pipe line tariffs were in excess of the amount necessary to cover pipe line operating costs and pay a reasonable return on the pipe line investment. The Atlantic management believed that the pipe line tariffs at this particular time were set so as to allow very liberal returns to the owners and that Atlantic was therefore under a severe handicap in competing with refiners who were in possession of them.

The Atlantic management observed that the company's profit showing relative to that of the other oil companies had declined steadily in the period following 1921. Whereas in the eight years before 1921 the company's rate of return on net worth was equal to or better than that of 34 other large oil companies, in the five years following 1922 its rate of return was equal to only 58% of that of the 34 other companies. In the period following 1922 the company's position in the industry also declined. Whereas

EXHIBIT VII-9. THE ATLANTIC REFINING COMPANY

Estimated Trend of Refinery Margins: 1923–1933

Col. (1) Value of products per barrel of crude oil run
Col. (2) Cost of raw materials per barrel of crude oil run
Col. (3) Gross margin per barrel of crude oil run
Col. (4) Total refinery expense per barrel of crude oil run

(Dollars per Barrel)

Year	United States			Oklahoma-Kansas Area			The Atlantic Refining Company			
	(1)	(2)	(3)	(1)	(2)	(3)	(1)	(2)	(3)	(4)
1923	$2.93	$1.72	$1.21	$2.86	$1.78	$1.08	$3.38	$2.51	$0.87	$0.76
1924	2.97	1.83	1.14	2.63	1.61	1.02	3.19	2.33	0.86	0.79
1925	2.99	2.10	0.89	3.14	2.05	1.09	3.61	2.66	0.95	0.76
1926	3.06	2.27	0.79	3.34	2.35	0.99	4.00	3.02	0.98	0.95
1927	2.38	1.68	0.70	2.27	1.46	0.81	3.20	2.36	0.84	0.80
1928	2.46	1.58	0.88	2.48	1.48	1.00	3.06	2.03	1.03	0.67
1929	2.38	1.70	0.68	2.37	1.48	0.89	3.01	2.13	0.88	0.64
1930	2.21	1.62	0.59	1.98	1.33	0.66	2.64	1.86	0.78	0.66
1931	1.54	1.06	0.48	1.31	0.71	0.60	1.81	1.23	0.58	0.55
1932	1.53	1.12	0.41	1.40	0.92	0.48	1.85	1.39	0.46	0.52
1933	1.47	0.97	0.50	1.17	0.71	0.46	1.68	1.14	0.54	0.48

SOURCE: Company memorandum of March 14, 1934.

in 1922 the company accounted for 4.1% of the industry refinery runs and 4.8% of the domestic gasoline sales, in 1928 it accounted for only 2.8% of the refinery runs and 3.3% of the domestic gasoline sales.[17]

The management believed that the decline in the company's profits relative to those of other oil companies and in its position in the industry was attributable in part to an industry-wide decline in the refiner's margin which Atlantic was unable to withstand as well as the companies that owned crude oil trunk lines. In reviewing in 1934 the pressures and circumstances that led to the decision to build the two crude oil trunk lines, the company prepared estimates of the trend of refining margins, as shown in Exhibit VII-9. The gross margin figures in the exhibit are the difference between posted prices in the field for crude oil and the selling prices for refined products at the refinery gate. They thus represent the amount which a refiner had available to cover his crude oil transportation costs and refinery operating expenses. The Atlantic management believed that the decline in the gross margin was occasioned by increased competition, by reductions in refinery operating expenses, and by the fact

[17] Company memorandum of March 14, 1934. See Chapter Twelve, Exhibit XII-2, for earnings record of Atlantic in the period 1912–1928.

that many refiners had reduced their crude oil transportation costs through the acquisition of crude oil trunk lines and tankers.

As another part of the general review made in 1934 of the circumstances leading to the construction of the two crude oil trunk lines, members of the Atlantic management staff prepared from reports of the Interstate Commerce Commission an analysis of the growth of pipe line systems of integrated oil companies in the area east of California (see Exhibit VII-10). The analysis suggested that during the middle 1920's the crude oil pipe line operations of integrated companies provided a very good return on investment and an important means of offsetting the reduction in refining margins shown in Exhibit VII-9.

Although the Atlantic executives did not have precisely the same data shown in Exhibits VII-9 and VII-10 before them in 1928 and 1931 at the time the decisions to build the two crude oil trunk lines were made, they were nevertheless keenly aware of the general facts presented in the two exhibits. From their awareness of these facts and related circumstances, the Atlantic executives concluded that the pipe line tariffs were being set at levels which were more than sufficient to pay the owners of the lines a fair return on their investments and to compensate them for the hazards involved in the

EXHIBIT VII-10. THE ATLANTIC REFINING COMPANY

Analysis of Growth of Pipe Line Systems of Integrated Oil Companies, East of California: 1919–1932

Year	Number Integrated Cos.	Number Controlled Lines	Miles Operated (Trunk & Gathering)	Pipe Line Investment ($1,000's)	Operating Income ($1,000's)	Net Income as % of Investment	Refinery Runs East of California (1,000 Bbls.)	Income per Barrel of Refinery Runs
1919	11	21	23,326	$187,306	$ 22,606	12.1%	288,587	7.8¢
1920	12	21	24,568	225,581	19,644	8.7	357,169	5.5
1921	13	22	25,063	236,208	5,611	2.4	357,613	1.6
1922	15	25	27,069	250,577	28,688	11.5	397,678	7.2
1923	14	24	33,739	294,365	34,659	11.8	431,032	8.0
1924	16	25	37,116	355,601	50,876	14.3	494,439	10.3
1925	16	25	39,100	375,384	55,256	14.7	555,823	10.0
1926	16	25	41,672	396,769	62,197	15.7	581,685	10.7
1927	15	24	44,009	460,174	74,872	16.2	619,743	12.1
1928	15	24	49,711	508,131	92,487	18.2	702,073	13.2
1929	16	28	52,949	582,724	113,662	19.5	744,598	15.2
1930	15	30	55,709	610,963	106,760	17.5	722,619	14.8
1931	15	35	59,222	649,038	112,390	17.3	721,600	15.5
1932	15	32	70,436	667,459	104,288	15.6	655,260	15.9

SOURCE: Company memorandum of March 14, 1934.

construction of the lines. To the Atlantic management it appeared that the refiners who owned such lines were obtaining: (a) cost savings on their own throughput which were not available to an outside company such as Atlantic, and (b) a very attractive secondary source of profits from the volume which they hauled for outside shippers.

The circumstances leading to the construction of Atlantic's first two crude oil trunk lines may thus be summarized in very simple terms: Atlantic was experiencing declining margins, declining profits relative to those of other oil companies, and a loss of its former position in the industry. The management diagnosed the difficulty as arising in large part from the fact that the company was, in effect, paying higher transportation costs on its crude oil than were its competitors who owned crude oil lines and decided the company should construct some pipe lines of its own as a means of correcting the situation.

In a semiannual report for the period ending June 30, 1931, the management announced construction of the second of the two crude oil trunk lines and of the Keystone products pipe line (discussed later in the chapter) with the following statement:

Your management can conceive no better way of attempting to meet the shrinkage in operating margins, as above discussed, than through efforts to reduce expenditures for crude materials and handling costs. . . . Again, because transportation charges on both crude oil and products decidedly affect operating margins, two new pipe line systems are under construction. One of these will be a 10-inch line, owned by Atlantic Pipe Line Company, extending over a distance of about 180 miles from the East Texas oil field to the already existing Atlantic Pipe Line deep water terminal at Atreco, near Port Arthur, Texas. Its purpose will be, of course, to transport oil produced and purchased by Atlantic Oil Producing Company and to serve other purchasers and shippers who may wish to use the facility under freight tariff regulations.

It should not be assumed that the decision to build the crude oil trunk lines was clear cut and easily made by the Atlantic executives. At that time, the company was headed by two very strong and able men of almost equal authority, Mr. J. W. Van Dyke, the chairman of the board of directors, and Mr. W. M. Irish, the president. Mr. Van Dyke and certain other executives were firmly convinced the lines were necessary if the company was to maintain its competitive position. Mr. Irish and another group of executives, however, felt that the hazards in the construction of the lines were greater than the possible gains and believed that the venture should be avoided. The construction was eventually undertaken while Mr. Irish was in Europe on a vacation.

III. Crude Oil Trunk Lines as a
Purchasing Agent for Crude Oil

From the very earliest days of the oil industry down to the present time, refining companies have integrated backward into the construction and operation of crude oil trunk lines as a means of gaining access to crude oil supplies that might not otherwise be available to them at a reasonable cost. The crude oil reserves in any oil field are subject to ultimate depletion. As the reserves in particular areas have played out, the refiners dependent upon them have time and again been forced to extend their crude oil lines to new producing fields as a means of remaining in existence and salvaging the value of their refinery investments.[18] A dramatic early example of a crude oil trunk line which was built by a refiner to secure new supplies of crude oil is the one which the Gulf Oil Corporation built to the newly discovered Oklahoma fields in 1907 after an abrupt decline had taken place in the Spindletop field from which the company had been drawing supplies for its big refinery at Port Arthur, Texas (see Chapter Three).

It may also be observed that the operations of the Standard Oil group in the period before 1911 were predicated to a considerable extent on the assumption that the construction of crude oil gathering systems and trunk lines constituted an adequate means of assuring the Standard Oil refineries of their crude oil supplies. The Standard Oil group, as was noted in Chapter Three, eventually became engaged in substantial producing activities, but never supplied much over about 40% of its refinery requirements from its own production. The Standard Oil group relied instead upon an aggressive policy of constructing crude oil lines to new fields as rapidly as they were discovered as a means of securing its requirements of crude oil.

A crude oil pipe line may serve not only as a means of gaining access to oil in a new producing area but likewise as a means of strengthening the buying position of a refiner relative to that of other buyers in the field. Producers,

like everyone else in the business world, want an assured market for their output, and tend to regard customers who have made a fixed investment and put their pipe lines on the ground as a more likely source of continuing business than those who have not. A refiner owning and operating a pipe line system is therefore, in times of short supply, often able to bargain more effectively and secure his well connections on more favorable terms than a refiner who does not have such facilities (see Chapter Fourteen).

A fairly recent example of the building of a pipe line to gain access to additional crude oil supplies and to improve a refiner's buying position may be found in the construction by The Atlantic Refining Company of its second major crude oil trunk line into the West Texas fields in 1948. This line cost about $8,000,000, was 10 inches in diameter and 417 miles in length, and terminated at Harbor Island on the Gulf Coast (see map, Chapter Twelve, Exhibit XII-7). It was selected as an example because the circumstances which prompted its construction are in such sharp contrast to those previously cited which prompted the construction of the company's first trunk line into the West Texas fields in 1928.

In 1947 and 1948 Atlantic was experiencing a sharply rising demand for its refined products and at the same time was encountering considerable difficulty in getting adequate supplies of crude oil for its refineries. The Harbor Island-West Texas line was built therefore as a "purchasing agent"; that is, as a means of strengthening the company's bargaining position as a buyer of crude oil in the West Texas market.

The need for additional pipe line capacity to carry the output of the West Texas fields began to assume significant proportions in 1947. At that time it developed that the production of and demand for West Texas crude oil was greater than the capacity of the existing pipe lines serving the field. As a result Atlantic and other oil companies began moving crude oil from the area by tank cars. In the company's annual report for 1947, the Atlantic management pointed out that the rail movement was an uneconomical one but that it was justified by the urgent need for crude oil.

In the early part of 1948 the Atlantic man-

---

[18] The impact of a decline in production in a producing area on the economic life of the refinery investment will be treated in Chapter Twenty-One in connection with a discussion of the East Texas and Illinois fields.

agement also became aware that the company would probably be facing a critical shortage of crude oil for its refineries in the near future. Analysis of the various alternative means of securing additional crude oil indicated that construction of the Harbor Island-West Texas line was probably the best solution to the problem. The facts of the situation, as summarized by the company's economics department, are reflected in the following excerpts from various company memoranda:

The Crude Oil Supply Situation: [19]

Our company faces a critical situation with respect to crude supplies in the very near future. We shall probably have to find new sources of supply for a minimum of 30,000 barrels a day just to maintain our present product sales volume. This is a large order, and it will require extraordinary effort and, possibly, extraordinary means to accomplish it. Since the first major loss of supply will hit us between May and July and the second at the end of the year, time is of the essence. We shall have to give priority to things which can provide us quick relief, even if it means deferring or slowing down other projects which are desirable but not immediately effective. Crude oil is our basic raw material. We must have it to stay in business.

The 30,000 barrels a day of new supply is indeed a bare minimum. By July 1 The Texas Company will be taking 9,000 barrels per day of Wasson production which we have run heretofore. At the end of the year Jersey will discontinue supplying us with 15,000 barrels per day of products from Aruba. We must also offset the natural decline in the producing capacity of our own wells and of others to which we have pipeline connections. This figure would probably amount to 5,000 to 6,000 barrels a day in a year's time, though it is not easily determinable without detailed analysis of field records. These three items account for the 30,000 barrels per day minimum. In addition, there is the risk of losing connections to premium-paying competitors, and as other companies bring into operation their expanded pipe line facilities out of West Texas, we may find it harder to buy crude in that area than we have in the past.

Venezuelan Crude Oil: In working out of the crude supply predicament we are in, it would be unwise to bank too heavily on the success of our Venezuelan program. This is not to say that that program should be cut back, as even moderate success in development drilling would make substantial amounts of oil available to us. The point is that we are in imminent need of real and tangible oil, while our Venezuelan results cannot at the present time be regarded as in the bag. Therefore, we should take steps which will assure us of our minimum requirements. Then, if our Venezuelan prospects materialize, we shall be able to go after new business.

Aside from our own production possibilities, it is somewhat uncertain whether additional amounts of Venezuelan oil would be available for sale to us over the near term. Although that country's rate of production will undoubtedly continue to increase, some of the major operators appear to have been pinched for supplies in a world-wide way and may require for their own refineries all the production increase they can get. Jersey Standard, the largest producer in Venezuela, is also the largest shipper of West Texas oil by tank car, and plans to import to the United States 15,000 barrels per day of Middle East crude over the next few months. Jersey was also hurt by the Tropical Oil Company strike in Colombia. All in all, the near term prospects for more oil from the Caribbean are cloudy.

Middle East Crude Oil: Oil can be purchased at the Persian Gulf for $1.75 a barrel, but we do not have boats of our own to move it. For what it is worth, the suggestion is advanced that our company operated tankers might be relieved for the Persian Gulf run by replacing them with barges in the Atlantic-Gulf-Caribbean run. War-surplus tugs are reported to be available, and new barges can be constructed quickly. Barge movements should be relatively safe during the better part of the year.

East Texas Crude Oil: If we cannot be certain of a Venezuelan supply of oil, and if we are unable to import Middle East oil, then we shall have to find means of filling our minimum requirements from domestic sources. Looking a year ahead, we cannot see any production increase for East Texas unless the Railroad Commission scraps the principles which have guided it in the past. The area consisting of the Louisiana and Texas Gulf Coast and South Texas will probably not gain a production increase of more than 200,000 barrels per day in the coming year, unless the regulatory commissions can be persuaded to revise upward the MER's [20] of the fields under their jurisdiction. We could not hope to buy more than a small fraction of this over-all increase since all East Coast and Gulf refiners will be competing for connections to the new wells.

---

[19] Company memorandum dated April 6, 1948. The memorandum was prepared by the company's economics department for consideration by the Atlantic management; it did not necessarily represent the conclusions of the Atlantic management.

[20] Maximum efficient rates of production.

West Texas Crude Oil: The most promising area for a near-term production increase is the Permian Basin of West Texas and New Mexico. Since our trunk pipe line from this area has been operating at or near capacity for some time, we have not been aggressive about running branch lines to the newly-developed fields. This is going to hurt us when the Wasson runs are lost, for we may have difficulty in replacing the loss with oil from other fields. The Mid-Continent refiners are bringing in increased pipe line capacity from West Texas this year and next. For this reason, the Permian Basin, which has been a region of chronic surplus producing capacity, may soon see the day when crude purchasers compete as sharply as they do elsewhere.

Whether or not there is going to be a scramble for West Texas oil, the fact remains that it is the best area in the country in which to try to pick up a new supply. On account of the past inadequacy of outlet, reserves have been drained at a slower rate than in other areas. Although the West Texas fields are now operating at their official MER's, it is probable that these MER's reflect past transportation shortages more than they do the principles of reservoir engineering, and if so, it ought to be easier to persuade the Railroad Commission to raise West Texas allowables than it would be for other areas. As a matter of fact, the Commission recently raised the allowables for Fullerton and Slaughter, materially but not spectacularly. It is possible that the transport bottleneck has acted to reduce the intensity of past development. Some operators may shortly see merit in closer well spacing in order to recover their oil more rapidly and to drill extra wells to tap reserves behind the pipe in multiple-pay fields.

Other companies looped their West Texas lines or built entirely new ones because they considered that area the best place to get the oil they needed. It is just as good a place for us. If we lay the pipe that will be delivered to us this fall, we shall not be too far behind the parade. With an aggressive campaign to push out feeder lines wherever oil can be obtained, it would not be long before our enlarged pipe line would be operating at a satisfactory rate.

* * *

In summary, the prospects for increased purchases of domestic crude do not appear very bright except in the Permian Basin area, and there only if we act aggressively to get new connections.

Premium Payments: Before passing from the subject of crude purchases, reference may be made to "premium payments." Even if we were willing to resort to this device, it is doubtful that we could acquire much additional supply without causing a round of general crude price increases. On the other hand we have suffered some losses of supply on account of premium prices offered by other crude purchasers. It is possible that government control of petroleum exports may curb or eliminate some of the buyers who paid premiums. Since the amount of oil sold for premiums appears to be a relatively small volume in comparison with the total supply, it may be that prospective production increases will shortly remove this thorn in our side.

Increasing Company Production: The most assured kind of new supply would be to increase our own production rate. There are three principal ways of doing this: get higher allowables for existing wells, drill new wells, and buy producing properties. If we have wells which we know can produce efficiently at rates higher than their allowables, we should spare no effort to get them increased. The Texas Commission, for one, has shown some receptiveness recently to the idea of larger allowables for fields that have adequate potentials. Where we have wells producing at rates lower than their official allowables, we should explore the possibilities of bringing them up. This might reduce their ultimate recovery to some extent, but if we lose many customers as a result of short supplies, we may not need the "ultimate" barrel. Our company's welfare demands emphasis on the "present" barrel whether or not it impairs the life-time financial record for a given lease.[21]

Our presently projected drilling program calls for many more new wells than we drilled last year. However, if we manage to drill as many as 100 full interest equivalent producers this year, the gross production rate would probably not exceed 15,000 barrels per day, which is half our minimum requirement. We appear to be reasonably well fixed for development drilling locations, though not as well as we should like to be. The pipe supply puts an unbeatable limitation on our drilling program. We probably cannot drill any more wells than we have presently budgeted for, since new orders for pipe will not be filled until some time next year.

Purchasing Producing Properties: We can increase our production rate by buying producing properties, but at current asking prices this is a very costly business. However, there are some possibilities for us in property transfers. The producing department has a number of assets that

---

[21] The management of The Atlantic Refining Company has definitely stated that it fully subscribes to the conservation policy of producing crude oil in accordance with the maximum efficient rate.

yield us income but furnish no oil for our refineries. Examples of such assets are our royalty interests and the Wasson leases where The Texas Company has a call on the oil. If such assets can be sold for anything like current prices, it would take the sting out of paying high prices for properties which would provide us with oil. The purchase of properties at current prices might well cause the producing department to show a poor profit and loss record in future years, but from the company's point of view we would not actually lose anything by trading, on even terms, an asset which did not supply us oil for one which did. The exigencies of our situation would justify trading on something less than even terms.

We know that asking prices for flush and semi-flush producing acreage are high in the Southwest, but we don't know much about the prices of properties operated by secondary recovery methods in the Pennsylvania Grade territory. It is just possible that such properties can be acquired on reasonable terms. We would not be able to run this crude in our own stills, but we might find some local refiner in the area who would run it for us and ship us the lubricating stock. This would ease our requirements for certain of the Southwestern crudes.

We hear of properties being offered for sale from time to time, but for several years the asking prices have been too high for us. However, they appear to be sold eventually to some buyer who will either take a chance or can work out a financing scheme which makes the deal attractive to him. Perhaps we could buy properties with only part of the purchase price being paid in cash and the rest of it to come out of the oil produced.

In cases where we are reluctant to buy a property we might be able to find an operator who would take it if we assist him to get a long-term insurance company loan so he could enjoy a reduced rate of interest, we to have a call on his oil in return for our assistance. Since the lenders do not make these loans without expert appraisal, we would not be likely to be required to make good on the loan. There are probably numerous variations to the financing method. They are worth looking into if they will get us new crude supplies with little or no immediate expenditure of cash.

Value of the Pipe Line as a Purchasing Agent: [22]

Opinion is nearly unanimous that the West Texas-New Mexico area is the most likely source of increasing domestic production of crude over the next five years. Ownership of a pipe line outlet from a producing region is second only to ownership of proven and developed acreage as a means of assuring a supply of crude. . . .

The following analysis shows that as long as the Midland-Atreco line had surplus capacity, we were able to increase the share of West Texas-New Mexico production received by our refineries; as soon as the line reached its capacity, our share of the production of this important region began an inexorable decline.

From 1935 to 1944 the mainline throughput of our West Texas line ranged from 6.74% to 8.56% of West Texas-New Mexico production, excluding the year 1942 when throughput was reduced because tankers could not sail. Since 1944, throughput as a proportion of West Texas-New Mexico production has steadily declined, reaching 5.13% in the first two months of 1948. The reason for the decline is clear: the pipe line reached substantially its capacity in 1944, but production continued to increase. Had materials to expand pipe line capacity been available in the 1944–47 period so that we could have maintained our 1935–44 average (ex. 1942) traffic of 7.65% of production, the West Texas line might well be moving currently 63,800 barrels per day instead of its present 42,750 (average for 1st two months of 1948). As appears in the supporting table,[23] when Atlantic West Texas Pipe Line had surplus capacity, the line moved two to three times as much oil for our company's account as we were able to produce by our own efforts, illustrating what an effective "purchasing agent" a pipe line can be. Even if under today's conditions of extremely tight crude supply no more of our own oil could be obtained in West Texas to fill an enlarged line than is currently the case, the hand of the crude purchasing and marketing division would certainly be strengthened by our ability to move oil for others, and the revenue of Atlantic Pipe Line Company would be increased.

Solely as an illustration of the fact that the potential volume indicated in the preceding paragraph is a commercial competitive opportunity and not a statistical abstraction, consider the history of the TXL pool which lies practically on Atlantic Pipe Line's right-of-way. The lease play on this pool occurred some years ago, around 1939

---

[22] Company memorandum dated April 9, 1948. The memorandum was prepared by the company's economics department for consideration by the Atlantic management; it did not necessarily represent the conclusions of the Atlantic management.

[23] The tables contained a record for the period 1931–1948 of: (a) total West Texas-New Mexico production, (b) Atlantic's West Texas-New Mexico production, (c) Atlantic's total pipe line throughput, (d) the pipe line throughput for others, (e) the estimated purchased oil in the throughput, and (f) the percentage of the total West Texas-New Mexico production which was available to Atlantic for movement through the pipe line.

and 1940, resulting in a complex arrangement of lease holdings with Shell, Phillips, Humble, our company, Amerada, Superior and Rowan Drilling Company among important holders. Several other interests were also represented. The discovery well was not drilled until 1945. By that time the Midland-Atreco line had reached capacity and our company was unable to establish a gathering system in a field lying right alongside the trunk line with a current production in excess of 64,000 barrels per day; our purchases: 15 barrels per day. If we had been able to establish a gathering system, we would have had at least a competitive opportunity to purchase additional oil.

* * *

From 1936 to 1939, when surplus pipe line capacity was available, our apparent share of "free oil" going through the West Texas Line rose steadily from 3.34% of West Texas-New Mexico production to 5.41%.[24] 1940 was an off-year and our apparent share dropped to 4.37%. But in 1941, still with surplus pipe line capacity available, our share of "free oil" increased to 4.79%. Conversely, our share of "free oil" has dropped from 2.77% to 2.70%, to 1.3% in November, 1947, according to [our] Dallas [office].

Assuming that with surplus pipe line capacity we could again command "free oil" to the extent of 4.16%, our 1936–41 average, our position by 1954 might appear as follows: [In the calculations which followed it was estimated (a) that total production in the West Texas-New Mexico area would increase from 848,000 barrels per day in February 1948 to 1,039,000 barrels per day in the fall of 1954, and (b) that with ample pipe line capacity available Atlantic would be able in the same period to increase its purchases of "free oil" from 11,070 barrels per day to 43,222 barrels per day.]

Estimated Production from and Pipe Line Capacity to West Texas Area: [25]

Our company's operation in [the West Texas] area has resulted in our acquisition of very complete information on both the territory and the details of individual properties. The expectation of the industry's geologists and engineering personnel is that production in that area will increase

materially; our own personnel foresee at least 189,000 barrels per day more oil coming out of West Texas-New Mexico in the fall of 1954 than is now being produced, and an increase of 288,000 barrels per day in MER, warranting still more pipe line facilities should demand for domestic production press upon MER. . . .

While present pipe line capacities out of the West Texas-New Mexico area adjusted for all known construction projects during the next six years, slightly exceed the predicted output of the area at the end of that period, after allowing for local consumption, the excess is so slight that even if our 10-inch line is built, the margin of reserve pipe line capacity is less than 8%, 82,000 barrels per day on a predicted production of 1,039,000 barrels per day. Such a narrow margin not only represents a slim margin of safety for the transportation system but also shows that there is room for our company to expand our line as an aggressive competitor. In addition, the predicted MER of the area, 1,156,000 barrels per day in 1954, exceeds the aggregate pipe line outlets from West Texas even after our line is built. The new line is therefore needed to service the area even if our company were not in such extreme need of additional oil.

Moreover, the crude producing department predicts that our company's controlled production in the area will approximate 52,000 barrels per day by 1954, a figure only slightly in excess of the capacity of our present line, but representing 60% operation of our West Texas Pipe Line System including the proposed addition. The original line did not reach this load factor until eleven years after its completion; and a 60% rate of usage permits profitable operation of a pipe line system both according to experience and in the opinion of pipe line personnel.

Long-Range Competitive Problems: [26]

[Another] important consideration which indicates the competitive necessity of materially increasing the capacity of the West Texas line, whether by looping or by building a second line, is this:

If we do not wish to be squeezed unmercifully between relative loss of domestic crude to inland refiners and a substantial inflow of foreign crude to coastal competitors, additional pipe line capacity in the best productive prospects in the United States, West Texas and New Mexico, is imperative.

---

[24] By "free oil" the writer of the memorandum means oil that could be purchased from other producers for Atlantic's own use.

[25] Company memorandum dated April 26, 1948. The memorandum was prepared by the company's economics department for consideration by the Atlantic management; it did not necessarily represent the conclusions of the Atlantic management.

---

[26] Company memorandum dated April 9, 1948. See footnote 25.

Consider the following data in support of this conclusion: Construction plans and commitments in the industry will increase West Texas pipe line outlets some 270,000 barrels per day, excluding our proposed line, by 1952. Virtually all of this construction is in the north and northeasterly direction. The five [27] major companies besides our selves who operate pipe lines from West Texas to the Gulf Coast are planning only minor additional changes in pipe line capacity leading to the Gulf Coast. But these five own important developed and producing acreages in the Middle East and Venezuela and are currently building here and abroad at least 23 super-tankers with a total loading capacity in excess of 5,000,000 barrels. We have no foreign producing acreage as far developed as have these five, nor are we either long on tankers, or building any. And even under the most favorable conditions a tanker at a loading dock is not the "purchasing agent" that is pipe line capacity in an expanding field.

In addition to all the above considerations, the company's decision to build the new line was also influenced by the fact that it already had on order a sufficient quantity of 10-inch pipe to complete the line, and delivery was scheduled to commence in the fall of the year. Pipe at that time was extremely scarce; the company was reluctant to release its order to competitors and had no other situation in which the pipe could be used to better advantage.

Some thought was given to the possibility of constructing the pipe line as a joint venture with some other oil company. This possibility was quickly discarded, however, on three grounds: first, the company did not need help in financing the project; second, the company estimated that it would soon have sufficient production of its own in the West Texas-New Mexico fields to guarantee at least about 60% of the throughput to both its old and new lines from the area; and third, it was believed that the most important function of the new line would be to serve as a "purchasing agent," and the company management saw no point in sharing this advantage with a competitor unless it was absolutely necessary to do so.

---

[27] Gulf Oil Corporation, Humble Oil and Refining Company, Magnolia Petroleum Company (Socony-Vacuum Oil Company, Inc.), Shell Oil Company, and The Texas Company.

IV. CRUDE OIL TRUNK LINES AS AN OUTLET FOR CRUDE OIL

Most of the crude oil trunk lines we studied were built by refiners in efforts to improve their crude oil supply situations in either or both of the respects outlined in the two preceding cases; that is, as a means of reducing inward transportation costs or as a means of gaining access to additional quantities of crude oil. We found, however, that crude oil trunk lines were also quite frequently built by crude oil producers as a means of providing an outlet for crude oil which might not otherwise have had a market.

The significance of forward integration by producers into crude oil trunk line activities has been somewhat obscured by the fact that many of the large producing companies have also been engaged in refining, and it has generally been assumed that the lines which they built were prompted by considerations associated with their refining operations. Moreover, the fact that a high percentage of the crude oil trunk lines has usually been owned by companies engaged in refining has also been taken as presumptive evidence that the building of the lines was prompted almost entirely by refining considerations. In 1950, for example, about 82% of the crude oil trunk lines were owned by companies engaged in refining and various other oil activities. Since most of the large refiners were also engaged in producing, however, it was equally true that almost 82% of the crude oil trunk lines in 1950 were owned by companies engaged in producing and various other oil activities.[28] In the case of crude oil trunk lines built or owned by companies engaged in both producing and refining operations, a scrutiny of the individual project is necessary before it can be determined whether the line was prompted by considerations associated with refining operations, producing

---

[28] See results of survey of refining companies reported in Chapter Two. Since some crude oil trunk lines were undoubtedly owned by companies engaged in crude oil producing alone, which were not covered by our survey, the percentage of the total crude oil trunk lines owned by companies engaged in producing alone or producing plus other activities was probably higher than the percentage owned by companies engaged in refining alone or refining plus other activities. Some of the companies classified as engaged in production, however, may have had only a small volume of production relative to their other activities.

operations, or both producing and refining operations.

We found several examples of crude oil trunk lines which were constructed by crude oil producers or by producing-refining companies primarily as a means of getting crude oil to markets. A very early example of the construction of a crude oil trunk line to provide an outlet for crude oil may be found in the Tidewater Pipe Line, the first important crude oil trunk line built in the United States. This line, which was constructed in 1879 and was 108 miles in length, extended eastward from the Pennsylvania oil fields, across the Allegheny Mountains, to Williamsport, Pennsylvania, from which point shipments were made over the Reading Railroad to the Atlantic seacoast. As was mentioned in Chapter Three, construction of the line was prompted largely by the need to provide an outlet for the production of the prolific Bradford field which was discovered in 1875. A second early example of a pipe line which was built to provide an outlet for crude oil was that which the Gulf Oil Corporation constructed from the Spindletop field to Port Arthur, Texas, in 1902 (see Chapter Three).

A present-day example of a pipe line built to provide an outlet for crude oil is the Platte Pipe Line which was completed in 1952. This line extended a distance of 1,057 miles from the producing fields of Wyoming to the important refining center at Wood River, Illinois. It was made up of a main trunk system of 16-inch and 20-inch diameter pipe with extended feeder lines consisting of approximately 182 miles of 8-inch, 12-inch, and 14-inch diameter pipe extending into the Big Horn and Wind River Basin areas of Wyoming. The pipe line was designed to carry about 110,000 barrels of crude oil per day and had an estimated cost of about $59,000,000. The project was initiated in 1950 by the Sinclair Oil Corporation (25%), the Continental Oil Company (20%), The Ohio Oil Company (25%), the Pure Oil Company (20%), and the British American Oil Company, Ltd. (15%).

The motives of the five companies in undertaking the project varied, depending upon their individual situations. All the companies were integrated concerns, engaged in producing, refining, transportation, and marketing operations. Only two of the companies, however,

Sinclair and the Pure Oil Company, were so situated that their participation in the project may have been motivated in any important degree by a desire to secure additional crude oil supplies for their refinery operations. Sinclair's crude oil production was at this time equal to only about 30% of its refinery requirements. The company had been very successful in its exploratory work in Wyoming, however, and about 21.5% of such crude oil production as it did have in 1950 was located in that state. The company was therefore anxious to move the Wyoming crude oil to its big refinery at Chicago, an arrangement that was possible because the new line crossed the company's main trunk line at a point near Carroltown, Missouri (see map, Chapter Twelve, Exhibit XII-5). Sinclair's acquisition of a refinery at Wood River, Illinois, in the summer of 1950, after the Platte project had been organized, made the new line appear even more attractive as a means of providing a source of supply for the company's refinery operations.

The Pure Oil Company was likewise short of crude oil production for its refinery operations; in 1950 its net crude oil production amounted to about 64% of its refinery runs. The company had five refineries, one of which was at Toledo, Ohio, and another of which was near Charleston, West Virginia. A common carrier pipe line which was not owned but was regularly used by the Pure Oil Company connected both of these plants with Wood River, Illinois. It is not unreasonable to suppose therefore that the Pure Oil Company's participation in the project was motivated at least in part by a desire to improve the crude oil supply situation of its refineries.

The situation of the other three partners in the project was quite different. The British American Oil Company's refineries were all located in Canada, and there was little possibility that the Platte Pipe Line would be of any material significance as a means of assuring their crude oil supply. The Ohio Oil Company had a large refinery at Robinson, Illinois, which could be reached from Wood River through the company's main crude oil trunk line system. The company's domestic crude oil production, however, normally was at least 200% to 400% of its refinery runs, and it certainly had no critical need of the Platte line to pro-

EXHIBIT VII-11. ESTIMATE OF ACTUAL AND POTENTIAL CRUDE OIL PRODUCTION IN ROCKY MOUNTAIN REGION AND OF CRUDE OIL AVAILABLE FOR PLATTE LINE: 1950

	Estimated Actual Production, Barrels per Day (1950)			Potential Production, Barrels per Day (1950)	Crude Available for Platte Line, Barrels per Day (1950)		
	Sweet	Sour	Total Sweet and Sour		Sweet	Sour	Total Sweet and Sour
Wyoming							
Big Horn Basin	2,927	76,088	79,015	95,163	750	36,347	37,097
Wind River Basin	1,919	17,105	19,024	27,455	285	10,902	11,187
Powder River Basin	42,930	45	42,975	42,042	17,600	140	17,740
Laramie Basin	2,725	1,420	4,145	4,518	2,700	1,691	4,391
Briger Basin	1,000	—	1,000	1,150	1,150	—	1,150
Great Divide Basin	1,222	16,186	17,408	15,908	10	9,555	9,565
Julesburg Basin	2,000	162	2,162	2,000	—	—	—
			165,729	188,236			81,130
Montana							
Sweet Grass Arch	8,500	6,515	15,015	15,200	—	—	—
Big Snowy	3,603	300	3,903	4,401	—	—	—
Big Horn Basin	762	350	1,112	1,006	300	300	600
Big Horn Uplift	—	—	—	50	—	—	—
Cedar Creek	—	—	—		—	—	—
			20,030	20,657			600
Colorado							
Unita Basin	10,975	55,141	66,116	71,366	485	7,500	7,985
North Park Basin	280	—	280	1,000	—	—	—
Julesburg Basin	330	—	330	—	—	—	—
			66,726	72,366			7,985
Utah							
——	—	3,500	3,500	5,500	—	—	—
Nebraska							
Gurley Area	850	—	850	850	850	—	850
Grand Total	80,023	176,812	256,835	287,609	24,130	66,435	90,565

SOURCE: The Ohio Oil Company.

vide for the requirements of the Robinson plant. The Continental Oil Company had eight refineries, but no one of them was so located that it could receive crude oil, economically, from the eastern terminus of the Platte line. Moreover, the Continental Oil Company's domestic crude oil production normally ran slightly in excess of its refinery requirements. Wood River was not only a very important refining center but also the juncture of several major crude oil pipe line systems, and it was clear that Wyoming crude oil available at Wood River would be extremely useful to the Continental Oil Company for trading purposes. Under the circumstances, however, it seems doubtful that the company was prompted to participate in the venture primarily as a means of securing crude oil for its refineries.

Whereas only two of the companies could have had any significant need for the Platte Pipe Line as a means of supplying crude oil to their refineries, all five of them had a very real need for the line as a means of providing an outlet for their rapidly mounting crude oil production in the Wyoming fields and in the adjacent fields in northern Colorado, which it was anticipated would be connected with the Platte line by means of a 70-mile, 12-inch line to be constructed by the British American Oil Company. The five companies had been very successful in their exploratory and development work in Wyoming and adjacent areas, and had reached a position where they were forced to produce their wells at less than the maximum efficient rate for lack of sufficient markets to absorb the output.

The current and estimated potential production in the fields which could be served by the new line and an estimate of the volume of crude oil which would be available immediately for shipment through the line is shown in Exhibit VII-11. The volume estimated

EXHIBIT VII-12. RATIO OF RESERVES TO PRODUCTION: COLORADO,
WYOMING, AND UNITED STATES TOTAL: 1937–1950

(1,000 barrels)

	United States Total			Wyoming			Colorado		
Year	Reserves*	Production	Ratio Reserves to Production	Reserves*	Production	Ratio Reserves to Production	Reserves*	Production	Ratio Reserves to Production
1937	15,507,268	1,279,160	12.1	265,922	19,166	13.9	19,125	1,605	11.9
1938	17,348,146	1,214,355	14.3	261,133	19,022	13.7	17,713	1,412	12.5
1939	18,483,012	1,264,962	14.6	305,616	21,454	14.2	20,162	1,404	14.4
1940	19,024,515	1,353,214	14.1	304,821	25,711	11.9	23,223	1,626	14.3
1941	19,589,296	1,402,228	14.0	304,053	29,878	10.2	23,443	2,150	10.9
1942	20,082,793	1,386,645	14.5	370,572	32,812	11.3	39,443	2,199	17.9
1943	20,064,152	1,505,613	13.3	499,394	34,253	14.6	45,111	2,320	19.4
1944	20,453,231	1,677,904	12.2	581,730	33,356	17.4	88,823	3,083	28.8
1945	20,826,813	1,713,655	12.2	599,881	36,219	16.6	259,830	5,036	51.6
1946	20,873,560	1,733,939	12.0	589,358	38,977	15.1	299,870	11,856	25.3
1947	21,487,685	1,856,987	11.6	679,311	44,772	15.2	381,882	15,702	24.3
1948	23,280,444	2,020,185	11.5	715,787	55,032	13.0	365,458	17,862	20.5
1949	24,649,489	1,841,940	13.4	691,602	47,890	14.4	344,812	23,587	14.6
1950	25,268,398	1,973,574	12.8	841,016	61,631	13.6	339,529	23,303	14.6

* Beginning with 1946 the figures are for crude oil only; prior to 1946 some condensate was included.
SOURCE: American Petroleum Institute, *Petroleum Facts and Figures*, Tenth Edition, 1952, and earlier editions.

as available for shipment was substantially greater than the amount of shut-in production because some of the current production was shipped out of the area at a high cost by tank car and some of it was refined in the area and the refined products moved to eastern markets on an uneconomical basis.

Not only did the companies operating in the Wyoming area have shut-in production; in addition, they were finding they could not proceed with their development drilling and exploratory work at the rate which was indicated by the proven and prospective reserves in the region. Some indication of the lag in developmental work in the area may be obtained from Exhibit VII-12 which shows the ratio of reserves to production in the states of Wyoming and Colorado as contrasted with the ratio for the entire United States. It will be noted that the ratio of reserves to production in both Wyoming and Colorado had for some time been above the national average. The figures for Colorado understate the case because the producing areas in the central and southern part of the state were served with pipe line connections; presumably the ratio of reserves to production in the northern fields which could be served by the new line was greater than for the state as a whole.

In 1951 the Petroleum Administration for

Defense estimated that the future availability of crude oil in Wyoming and Colorado would be as shown in the following figures, assuming that adequate pipe line outlets were provided to permit development of the reserves available in the two states. The anticipated increase in Wyoming production over actual production in 1950 is particularly striking.

ESTIMATED AVAILABILITY OF CRUDE OIL [29]

(1,000 barrels per year)

Year	Wyoming	Colorado
1950 (Actual production)	61,631	23,303
1951	75,920	28,288
1952	81,213	27,375
1953	87,235	26,463
1954	91,615	25,550
1955	94,900	25,185

At the time the Platte Pipe Line Company was formed, the only pipe line available for carrying crude oil out of the Wyoming area was that of the Service Pipe Line Company [30] which had a capacity of about 55,000 barrels per day (20,075,000 barrels per year) and

[29] Petroleum Administration for Defense, Supply and Transportation Division, *Transportation of Oil* (Government Printing Office, 1951), p. 71. Figures for 1950 actual production are from American Petroleum Institute, *Petroleum Facts and Figures*, Tenth Edition, 1952, p. 94.

[30] Subsidiary of the Standard Oil Company (Indiana).

which was already being fully utilized. The refining capacity in Wyoming was about 99,600 barrels per day (36,354,000 barrels per year),[31] and three of the participants in the Platte Pipe Line, Sinclair, Continental, and The Ohio Oil Company, had refineries in the state. The possibility of increasing local refining operations to take care of the producing potential of the state was, however, limited by the fact that the market for refined products in the surrounding region was small and already adequately supplied; much of the output of the Wyoming refineries was, in fact, already being moved far to the east into the North Central states in tank cars at very disadvantageous freight rates compared with those obtained by Mid-Continent refiners moving products north through the Great Lakes Pipe Line. One of the participants in the new line, The Ohio Oil Company, anticipated that as a result of the construction of the line it might even be able to shut down a small refinery at Lovell, Wyoming, which it had built in 1937 to absorb crude oil production in the area.

The construction of a products pipe line to permit the refineries in the state to serve a broader market was considered somewhat less desirable than the building of a crude oil trunk line because it would provide no solution to the problem of disposing of the residual fuel oil which would develop as a by-product of the refining operations and which was too viscous to move by pipe line. The industrial market in Wyoming was small, and the disposition of residual fuel oil had become increasingly difficult as the railroads converted their equipment to Diesel operation. As will be noted below, however, a products pipe line was later initiated as a partial solution to the Wyoming crude oil problem.

In the light of the foregoing facts, it seems reasonable to conclude that although the Platte line was initiated by integrated companies some of which were interested in securing Wyoming oil for their refining operations, the building of the line for the most part represented forward integration by producing interests as a means of finding an outlet for crude oil which would not otherwise have been able to reach a satisfactory market.

V. PRODUCTS PIPE LINES AS A MEANS OF REDUCING TRANSPORTATION COSTS

By far the most important motivation for the construction of the products pipe lines which we studied was simply the desire of the builder to reduce transportation costs on his own shipments. In all the cases examined, the lines were constructed by companies engaged in both refining and marketing operations, and it would be difficult to classify any of them as representing clear instances of forward integration by refiners or backward integration by marketers. For the most part, the companies involved had refineries at one point and marketing operations at another, and the pipe lines were built as a means of joining the two together. The decisions thus represented a mixture of both forward and backward integration. As may be seen from Chapter Two, Exhibit II-7, in 1950 about 92% of the products pipe lines were owned by companies engaged in both refining and marketing operations.

An early example of the construction of a products pipe line as a means of reducing transportation costs may be found in the Keystone Pipe Line system which was built by The Atlantic Refining Company beginning in 1931. Before 1931 Atlantic had no products pipe lines of any kind. At the time the Keystone system was planned, the company was operating a large refinery at Philadelphia and two small ones at Pittsburgh and Franklin, Pennsylvania. The company's marketing activities were concentrated primarily in Pennsylvania and Delaware, although some operations had been initiated in other Atlantic Coast states. Shipments from the refineries were made chiefly by tank cars to bulk plants from whence deliveries were made to service stations and other customers by tank truck.

The use of pipe lines as a means of transporting refined products did not become important in the United States until about 1930. In that year the Tuscarora Oil Company[32] reversed the crude oil pipe line which it had previously used to move crude oil from west to east across Pennsylvania, converted it to products operation, and began to pump gasoline from Bay-

---

[31] Petroleum Administration for Defense, *Transportation of Oil,* Exhibit 2, facing page 5.

[32] The Tuscarora Oil Company was owned by the Esso Standard Oil Company, a subsidiary of the Standard Oil Company (New Jersey).

way, New Jersey, to Midland, Pennsylvania, a distance of 370 miles. In the same year the Phillips Petroleum Company constructed a 735-mile line to pump gasoline from its refinery at Borger, in the Texas Panhandle, to Kansas City and St. Louis, and a group of Mid-Continent refiners began the construction of the 1,240-mile Great Lakes Pipe Line, extending northward from Oklahoma to the North Central states. In 1931 the Susquehanna Pipe Line Company, owned by the Sun Oil Company, completed construction of a products system with a branch extending westward from Marcus Hook across Pennsylvania to Akron and Cleveland and a branch extending northward to Syracuse, New York.

Two of the first major products pipe lines in the United States thus extended right through the heart of Atlantic's principal market territory. The company began construction of its Keystone system in 1931, and the chief motivation for the move was clearly the desire to reduce transportation costs on shipments out of the Philadelphia refinery and thus meet the competition of other companies being served by the two new systems. The first gasoline tariffs posted by the Tuscarora Oil Company were 25% to 60% below rail rates for equivalent distances, depending on the length of haul, and a few months after operations started the tariffs were cut 10% below the original levels.[33] Moreover, as was noted in the previous section, Atlantic was at this time under considerable pressure to make any savings in handling or other costs that it could as a means of offsetting the industry-wide decline in refining margins. On the basis of sales volumes for 1929 and 1930, it was estimated that the initial system would result in savings of about $1,040,000 per year.

Some indication of the transportation advantages offered by the line can be gained from the fact that in 1935 the rail rate from Philadelphia to Pittsburgh was 77 cents per barrel of gasoline whereas the first published pipe line tariff for the haul was 37 cents per barrel. Moreover, during the period 1935–1949, the rail rate from Philadelphia to Pittsburgh increased to $1.52 a barrel while the

pipe line tariff decreased to 22 cents a barrel.[34]

The initial Keystone system was confined to the eastern part of Pennsylvania, although it was anticipated from the outset that at a later date the lines would be extended to the western part of the state. The initial system proved so successful from a financial and operating standpoint that a program of expansion was undertaken in the period 1935–1937 which resulted in the extension of the lines west to Pittsburgh and north to the New York state line and in the formation of the Buffalo Pipe Line Corporation to construct a pipe line from that state line to Buffalo and Rochester in the western part of New York state (see map, Chapter Twelve, Exhibit XII-7).

The extension of the line into New York state involved somewhat different considerations from those related to other parts of the system. The original system and the extensions to Pittsburgh and the New York state line were built as a means of lowering the company's transportation costs to market areas in which it was already well established and as a means of enabling it to hold onto its existing business in the face of competition from other companies which were securing pipe line transportation to the territory. The extension into New York state, however, was built as a means of lowering the company's transportation costs to an area in which it had very limited distribution and was thus a means of permitting the company to develop a new market territory.

The management had decided that the company must expand its marketing activities into other states as a means of offsetting the encroachments of new competitors in Pennsylvania and had picked western New York state as a favorable territory because of its existing rate structures and competitive conditions. Moreover, it was believed that a pipe line terminal at Buffalo would be advantageous because it would permit the company occasionally to market bulk cargoes for shipment on the Great Lakes. The New York line also differed from other parts of the system in that it replaced a water movement over the New York State Barge Canal whereas other parts of the

---

[33] American Petroleum Institute, *Proceedings of 29th Annual Meeting*, Chicago, Illinois, November 7 to 10, 1949, Section V, Transportation. "History and Development of Products Pipe Lines," by John W. de Groot, p. 12.

[34] It is, of course, possible that the rail rates would have been entirely different if the gasoline traffic had not been diverted to pipe lines.

system for the most part replaced rail movements. The company had maintained a barge terminal at Rochester for a number of years which it supplied by barge shipments from its deep water marine terminal on the Hudson River at Rensselaer, New York, near Albany.

At the time the expansion of the initial system was undertaken, the company had such a limited volume of distribution in western New York state that it was estimated that the 75-mile extension to the New York state line would show a return on investment of only 7% *before* depreciation and taxes and that the extension to Buffalo and Rochester would show a return of only 4%. These estimates were based on Atlantic's existing volume of business; inclusion in the estimates of the volumes expected from other shippers raised the figure for the extension to the New York state line figure to 10% and the figure for the Buffalo and Rochester lines to 23%. It seems clear therefore that considerable risk was involved in the project and that it was undertaken largely on the anticipation that additional distribution could and would be developed in western New York state. It also seems evident that this particular line was certainly not built primarily in anticipation of profits to be made from the pipe line transportation business.

During the period 1935–1937 other shippers became interested in the Keystone and Buffalo lines. Terminals along various parts of the system were constructed by the Gulf Oil Corporation beginning in 1935, and by the Sun Oil Company beginning in 1937. These developments firmly established the Keystone and Buffalo systems as common carrier operations, and thereafter the lines carried products on a regular basis for other companies. In 1950 the system comprised 856 miles of pipe (including 12, 8, 6, and 4-inch lines) and 14 pumping stations. In addition, junctions with the Susquehanna Pipe Line made possible deliveries to 6 Atlantic terminals which had been built along that line.

The Keystone system at the outset pumped only White Flash gasoline and Atlantic Ethyl gasoline, but studies were soon initiated to determine the possibilities of moving kerosene and furnace oil through the same system. A model of the line between Philadelphia and Mechanicsburg was constructed from $\frac{1}{2}$-inch

pyrex glass tubing to permit measurement of the amounts of mixture which took place between adjacent products in the line. The experiment revealed that the interface portion, even after long travel through the line, was not a conglomerate mixture of the two products, but actually an orderly progression from one product to another. The studies also showed that the major part of the change from about 90% of one grade to 90% of the other grade took place very rapidly. The results of the tests were so favorable that in 1933, a little more than a year after the line went into operation, kerosene and furnace oil were pumped through the system for the first time. This development work resulted in the use of the Keystone and Buffalo pipe line systems for movement of the company's four major products some 13 years before competitive lines were generally used for products other than gasoline.

In 1949 comparative rail, truck, and pipe line transportation costs from Philadelphia to various points along the system in cents per gallon were as shown in the following table. The company estimated that for the year 1949 it would have paid about $5,000,000 more for transportation of products than the $1,800,000 it paid in pipe line tariffs had the pipe line not been available.

COMPARATIVE TRANSPORTATION COSTS FROM PHILADELPHIA TO POINTS ALONG KEYSTONE PIPE LINE: 1949 [35]

(Cents per Gallon)

Philadelphia to:	Rail	Truck	Pipe Line
Pittsburgh	3.399¢	3.94¢	.52¢
Williamsport	2.739	2.31	.29
Mechanicsburg	1.815	1.39	.19
Kingston	2.376	1.71	.29
Exton	1.287	.46	.12

While the Keystone and Buffalo systems were not built primarily as a means of earning a profit on the traffic of outside shippers, because of their common carrier status they ultimately did carry a substantial volume of such business and earned a good profit thereon. The initial investment in the Keystone line in 1931 amounted

[35] Records of The Atlantic Refining Company. Rail and truck costs include 3% transportation tax. Rail costs do not include car rentals; pipe line rates do not include the 1% or $\frac{1}{2}$% deductible allowance.

to $1,750,000 and the initial investment in the Buffalo system was $1,000,000. The Keystone Pipe Line Company subsequently borrowed $3,300,000 for construction purposes from The Atlantic Refining Company, and in 1949 this debt was still outstanding. In the period 1931–1949, however, the two products pipe line companies paid Atlantic $13,623,000 in dividends, and $3,769,000 was accumulated in frozen fund accounts as required under the consent decree. In addition to the dividends it received from the two products pipe line companies, Atlantic also made important direct savings on its own throughput as suggested by the above comparisons of pipe line tariffs with transportation costs by other carriers. Moreover, as of 1950 the two products pipe lines were valued by the Interstate Commerce Commission for rate-making purposes at about $10,000,000.

VI. PRODUCTS PIPE LINES AS PART OF A GENERAL COMPETITIVE STRATEGY

A number of the pipe lines we studied were built as part of a general program designed to strengthen the builder's competitive position in a particular market territory. An excellent example is provided by the products pipe line which the Standard Oil Company (Indiana) built from its big refinery at Whiting, near Chicago, to Indianapolis, Indiana, in 1941 (see map, Chapter Twelve, Exhibit XII-8). In the final analysis, the purpose of this line, like that of the products lines discussed in the preceding section, was to reduce transportation costs. The Indianapolis line warrants separate treatment, however, for two reasons. First, it illustrates the wide range of competitive pressures which may prompt the building of a products pipe line, and second, it illustrates the interrelationships which often exist between a pipe line project and a company's price policy, product policy, and many other aspects of its competitive program.

At the time of the dissolution decree in 1911 the operations of the Indiana Company were confined almost entirely to refining and marketing activities. The company had a 35,000 barrels per day plant at Whiting, which was reputed to be the second largest in the industry, a 20,000 barrels per day plant at Wood River,

Illinois, and a 15,000 barrels per day plant at Sugar Creek, Missouri. The company's marketing operations covered about ten midwestern and northwestern states. In these states the company was by far the largest marketer and undoubtedly held well over half and perhaps as much as 80% of the total market for light oil products.

In 1917 the company acquired its first crude oil producing properties, and by the later 1920's was fully embarked on a program of backward integration into crude oil production (see Chapter Eight). In 1921 the company became heavily engaged in crude oil transportation activities by acquiring a one-half interest in the Sinclair Pipe Line Company which at that time owned a pipe line extending from the oil fields of North Texas, Oklahoma, and Kansas through Missouri and Illinois to Chicago. In the following nine years a number of important additions were made to the pipe line system and in 1930 the Indiana Company acquired the remaining one-half interest in it.

By 1939 the Indiana Company and its subsidiaries had extended their marketing operations to 38 states and the District of Columbia and were operating 12 refineries with a total capacity of about 288,100 barrels per day. The parent company operated in Montana, Wyoming, Colorado, North and South Dakota, Kansas, Oklahoma, Missouri, Iowa, Minnesota, Wisconsin, Illinois, Indiana, and Michigan.[36] The Utah Oil Refining Company operated in Idaho and Utah; the Pan American Petroleum Corporation operated in Tennessee, Mississippi, Alabama, and Louisiana; and the American Oil Company operated in the Atlantic Coast and New England states, West Virginia, and Ohio. Product shipments from the company's refineries to its bulk plants and terminals were made almost entirely by rail, water, and truck. In 1939 the company had only one products pipe line, a 170-mile line which was built in 1939 from the refinery at Sugar Creek north to Council Bluffs. This line was extended in 1941 to Des Moines and Sioux Falls.

In the period 1934–1939, inclusive, the management of the Indiana Company observed that the company's market position was declin-

---

[36] The Standard Oil Company (Indiana) was also the principal supplier for the Standard Oil Company (Nebraska), a marketing concern which it acquired in 1939.

ing more rapidly in Illinois, Indiana, and Michigan than it was in other parts of the company's territory. The management therefore initiated a general study of competitive conditions in these three states.[37] Among other things, the study examined the company's price policies, the quality of its products relative to those of its competitors, the adequacy of its transportation arrangements, the calibre of its service station facilities and dealer personnel, inventory practices, and the circumstances underlying the loss and gain of dealer accounts. One outgrowth of the study was the decision to build the products pipe line from Whiting to Indianapolis. The management's analysis of the company's situation and the steps by which the decision to build the products pipe line was reached will be outlined in the following paragraphs:

Loss of Competitive Position in the Three Eastern States:

In the period following 1911 the Indiana Company, like most other oil companies, experienced an enormous expansion in its sales volume. At the same time, however, the company suffered a general long-run decline in the share of the market which it held in its original sales territory, a decline which was offset to some extent by expansion into new areas. In the six-year period 1934 to October 1939, inclusive, the parent company gained volume but lost relative market position throughout its territory. The decline in market position was particularly marked in the three eastern states of Illinois, Indiana, and Michigan. In these three states the company's share of the automobile gasoline market dropped from about 26% to 22% whereas in the seven western states of Iowa, Kansas, Minnesota, Missouri, North and South Dakota, and Wisconsin it dropped from about 20% to 18% (see Exhibit VII-13).[38]

As may be seen from Exhibit VII-14, the decline in market position in the three eastern states was not uniform nor was it necessarily continuous in any one state. In Illinois total consumption of automotive gasoline for the 12-month period ending November 1939, was about 31% above consumption in 1935 whereas the Indiana Company's sales over the same period increased only 12.5%. In Indiana total consumption increased 33% and the Indiana Company sales only 21%. In Michigan total consumption between 1935 and 1939 increased about 31% and the Indiana Company's sales only 17%. Analysis of individual areas in the three states revealed that the most disappointing sales trends relative to growth of the market were in the sales districts of Chicago, Indianapolis, and Grand Rapids.

Inadequacy of Price Policies:

Analysis of the situation in the three eastern states led the management of the Indiana Company to the conclusion that much of the loss in market position had resulted from the fact that the company's pricing practices were no longer adequate to meet the new competitive conditions which had been developing in the market for the past several years.

Direct Price Cuts by Competitors: Before 1934 the Indiana Company had established tank car prices at its refineries and added freight to these prices to arrive at delivered prices for various destinations throughout its territory. In general, the company attempted to maintain a normal price structure but frequently found it necessary to take losses in realization in low-price areas in order to meet competition. As was noted in Chapter Four, major crude oil discoveries in Oklahoma, Kansas, and East Texas in the middle 1920's and early 1930's brought a host of new competition to the Mid-Continent area. The output from newly established refineries soon began to move northward into the Indiana Company's territory, and the company suffered severe losses in its market position in the early 1930's.

In 1933 the company made a study of price-volume relationships in five cities in its territory for the period 1926 to June 1932 and found that its sales were influenced in major degree by the spread between its posted service station prices and the Group 3 tank car price.[39] When the spread was wide, competitors

---

[37] Source: Standard Oil Company (Indiana).

[38] The Rocky Mountain states were excluded from the comparison because they presented quite different competitive conditions than did other parts of the parent company's territory.

[39] The Mid-Continent area was known as Group 3 because a single freight classification covered movements from points of origin in that area.

EXHIBIT VII-13. STANDARD OIL COMPANY (INDIANA): TREND OF MARKET POSITION
IN THREE EASTERN AND SEVEN WESTERN STATES: 1934–1939

Indiana Company Sales as Percentage Total Consumption

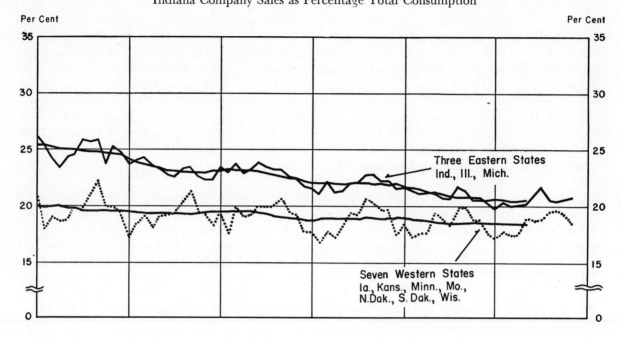

Comparative Rate of Decline of Indiana Company Market Position
in Three Eastern and Seven Western States (1934 = 100%)

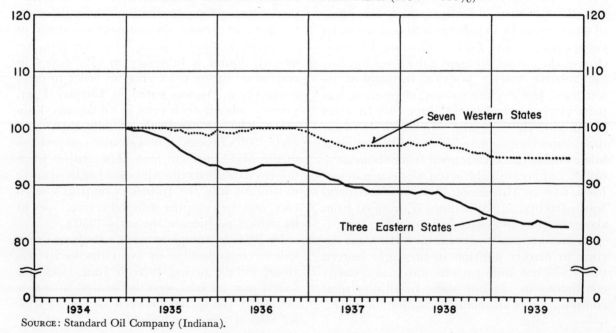

SOURCE: Standard Oil Company (Indiana).

EXHIBIT VII-14. STANDARD OIL
COMPANY (INDIANA)

Comparative Rate of Growth of Total Consumption
and Indiana Company Sales: 1936–1939
(1935 = 100%)

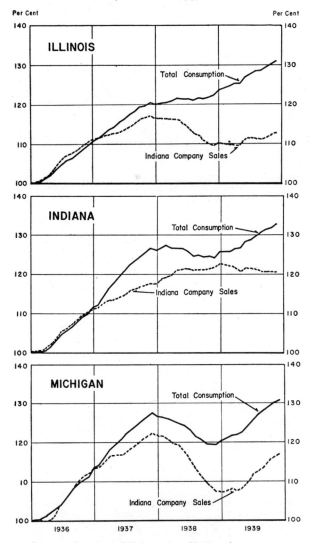

SOURCE: Standard Oil Company (Indiana).

of gasoline moving northward from the Group 3 area.

The "Group 3 plus" method of pricing adopted in 1934 was quite appropriate to conditions prevailing in the late 1920's and early 1930's because the trading area of the Group 3 refineries at this time was very wide and a large portion of the jobbers and other independent marketers in the Indiana Company's territory were receiving their supplies by rail shipments from the Mid-Continent area. The products pipe lines had just begun to come into usage with the construction of the Phillips Petroleum Company's line from the Texas Panhandle to St. Louis and of the Great Lakes Pipe Line from the Tulsa area to the North Central states. Moreover, crude oil production in Michigan and Illinois was very small and there was no significant independent refining center, such as later developed, in either state. As a result, delivered prices throughout the Indiana Company's territory tended to reflect Group 3 prices plus the rail cost of transportation to destination.

In the period 1931–1939 a number of important changes took place with respect to transportation facilities and refinery locations, the general effect of which was to make the Group 3 plus rail freight method of pricing completely obsolete. In the first place, this period witnessed the very rapid development of the products pipe line. With its new line the Phillips Petroleum Company was able to move gasoline from its refinery at Borger, Texas, to St. Louis, from which point gasoline could be moved northward along the Mississippi and Ohio Rivers by barge to many destinations in the Indiana Company's territory at very low transportation costs. The Great Lakes Pipe Line gave a number of Mid-Continent refiners lower laid down costs at many points in the North Central states than they had had before. In addition, new gasoline lines were built into St. Louis, Detroit, Effingham, Terre Haute, Indianapolis, and Muncie; the Illana pipe line was built from St. Louis to Chicago; and the Shell Oil Company converted a crude oil line across Illinois and Indiana to products operation (see Exhibit VII-15). The new products pipe lines were usually built large enough to provide for future growth in the market, and increased competitive activity, frequently including price

rushed in and took volume from the Indiana Company by selling at lower prices. In 1934 therefore the Indiana Company adopted the policy of setting its tank wagon gasoline prices on the basis of the going Group 3 price, plus rail freight from the Mid-Continent area to destination, plus a fixed differential of 3.5 cents per gallon. This policy was followed regardless of the refinery from which the gasoline was shipped and regardless of the Indiana Company's own cost of transportation. In effect, the prices were thus set to meet the competition

EXHIBIT VII-15. STANDARD OIL COMPANY (INDIANA)
Refineries, Pipe Lines, and Terminals Serving Three Eastern States: 1939

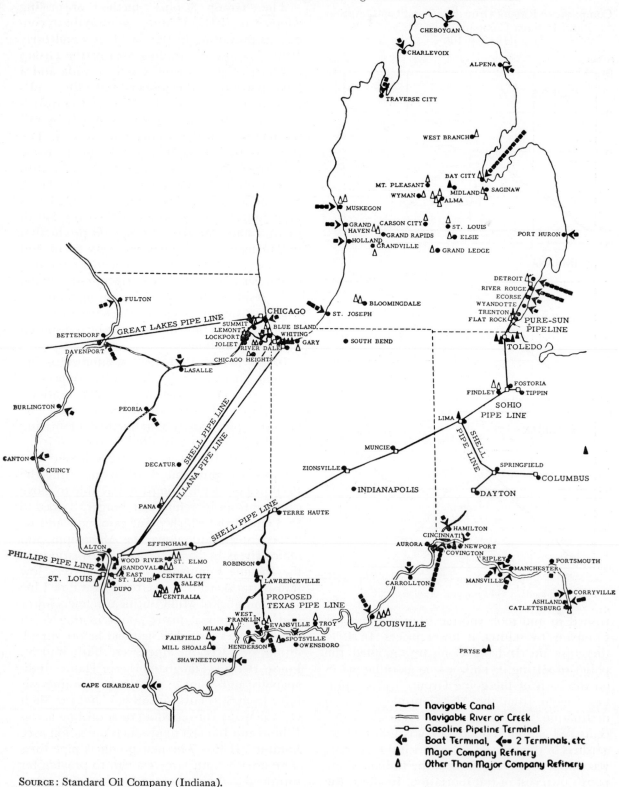

SOURCE: Standard Oil Company (Indiana).

cutting, usually followed their construction as the shipper-owners sought to gain as quickly as possible the economies incident to operation at full capacity.

The period 1931–1939 likewise witnessed a great expansion in the use of water and truck transportation which in many cases provided lower costs than did rail freight. Increased usage was made of barge movements on the Mississippi, Ohio, and Missouri Rivers and on the Illinois Waterways which were opened to commercial shipping in the middle 1930's. By 1939 there were about 70 terminals on the Mississippi River and about 90 terminals on the Ohio River (see Exhibit VII-15). Over the six-year period 1933–1939 the Indiana Company's records indicated that the volume of petroleum products moving on the Mississippi and tributary waters increased from about 12 to 54 million barrels per year. In addition, truck transportation for short hauls expanded rapidly during the 1930's with the development of hard-top roads and the improvement in trucking equipment.

Another extremely important development in the period 1931–1939 which contributed to the crumbling of the Group 3 plus rail freight price structure was the growth of independent refining centers in Michigan and Illinois following the discovery of new crude oil deposits in those states (see Exhibit VII-15). In Michigan, crude oil production jumped from 3,789,000 barrels in 1931 to 23,462,000 barrels in 1939 and the capacity of the independent refineries in the state increased from about 9,600 barrels per day to 61,000 barrels.[40] Total gasoline consumption in Michigan during this period increased only about 40%, and as a result the Group 3 plus price structure in Michigan and certain adjacent areas became completely untenable. In Illinois the growth in crude oil output was even more dramatic; production increased from 5,039,000 barrels in 1931 to 94,912,000 barrels in 1939. In October 1939 there were about 22 independent refineries

with a capacity of about 62,650 barrels per day in operation in Illinois and additional plants were under construction; in 1931 there were only about 3 independent refineries in the state with a capacity of approximately 9,500 barrels per day.[41] No similar growth in crude oil production or refinery capacity occurred in Indiana at this time, but the state was bordered on the north by the refineries in Chicago, central Michigan, and Toledo, and on the south by the Cincinnati, Louisville, and Evansville refineries. Moreover, the Ohio River brought much of the Indiana territory close to many refiners having access to the inland waterways, and the center of the state was crossed by the Shell pipe line running from Roxana to Toledo (see Exhibit VII-15).

As a result of the developments outlined above, very few of the marketers in Illinois, Michigan, and Indiana were bringing their supplies to the market in 1939 by tank car all the way from the Group 3 area; nearly all of them had secured in at least some degree the benefits of water or pipe line transportation or had gained access to products refined from local crude oil supplies. From the study it made in 1939, the management of the Indiana Company found that the company's competitors were making use of the economies they gained from lower transportation costs in one or another of three ways: (a) by lowering prices to tank car or tank wagon buyers, (b) by granting indirect price cuts in the form of various subsidies and allowances to dealers, and (c) by pouring capital into the market in the form of added distribution facilities.

The problem of direct price cuts became critical in Michigan sooner than it did in the other two states, and the company met the situation in December 9, 1936, by adopting a new normal price structure for its motor gasoline, kerosene, tractor fuel, furnace oil, and No. 1 fuel oil. Under the new policy a base price was established at River Rouge which was an arbitrary 1.9 cents (later 2.1 cents) per gallon above the Group 3 price; rail freight was then added to the River Rouge price to arrive at normal prices for various points in the state of Michigan. The new policy strengthened the company's competitive position in the

---

[40] The term "independent refineries" as used in this paragraph and in the following discussion will mean refineries not associated with the 20 or 30 largest oil companies. Data on number and capacity of independent refineries are from the Standard Oil Company (Indiana). Data on crude oil production and gasoline consumption by states are from American Petroleum Institute, *Petroleum Facts and Figures*, Ninth Edition, 1950, pp. 9 and 145.

[41] For a discussion of the growth of independent refineries in the Illinois fields, see Chapter Twenty-One.

River Rouge-Detroit area, but did little to help its situation in the central part of the state where it continued to lose volume to marketers supplied from local refineries.

The inability of the Indiana Company to hold to its normal price structure in Illinois and Indiana in the face of increasing competitive pressure in the period 1937–1939 is indicated by the following table which shows the difference between the company's actual average realization per gallon of gasoline sold in several of its sales districts and the average realization it would have secured had its normal price structure been maintained:

INDIANA COMPANY'S ESTIMATED LOSS OF REALIZATION FROM PRICE CUTS, ILLINOIS AND INDIANA

(Cents per gallon of gasoline)

Illinois Sales Districts	1937	1938	1939
Chicago	.06¢	.32¢	.45¢
Joliet	.01	.03	.08
Peoria	.06	.05	.16
Decatur	.06	.13	.38
Average	.05¢	.23¢	.35¢
Indiana Sales Districts			
South Bend	.03¢	.07¢	.18¢
Indianapolis	.04	.08	.16
Evansville *	.04	.16	.19
Average	.04¢	.09¢	.17¢

* District extends into Illinois.

Further evidence of the crumbling of the Group 3 price structure in the latter 1930's and of the difference between the prices the Indiana Company was attempting to charge and the prices its competitors would permit it to charge may be seen from Exhibits VII-16 and VII-17. Exhibit VII-16 shows the average realization secured by the Indiana Company in its various sales districts on all gasolines and naphthas sold through all channels less a weighted average freight cost to each district from the Group 3 area. The variations in the resulting net-back figures shown in the third column reflect differences among the various districts with respect to the volumes moving through different trade channels, differences in the ratio of products sold, and various other factors. Conditions in the districts were, however, sufficiently uniform so that the variations in the net-back figures may be taken as a partial

EXHIBIT VII-16. STANDARD OIL COMPANY (INDIANA)

Group 3 Net-Backs Based on Indiana Company Realizations: 1939

(Cents per gallon)

Sales Districts	Indiana Company Realizations, ex. Taxes, All Gasolines and Naphthas	Weighted Average Freight from Group 3	Net-Back at Group 3
Evansville	9.81¢	2.85¢	6.96¢
Indianapolis	10.26	3.22	7.04
South Bend	10.40	3.28	7.12
Detroit	7.86	4.22	3.64
Saginaw	9.47	4.42	5.05
Grand Rapids	9.50	4.03	5.47
Chicago	8.30	2.65	5.65
Joliet	9.82	2.71	7.11
Peoria	9.46	2.59	6.87
Decatur	9.12	2.52	6.11

SOURCE: Standard Oil Company (Indiana).

EXHIBIT VII-17. STANDARD OIL COMPANY (INDIANA)

Group 3 Net-Backs Based on Prices of Regular Gasoline of Cut-Price Distributors: 1939

(Cents per gallon)

Sales Districts	Realization, ex. Taxes, as Reported by Sales Fields	Weighted Average Freight from Group 3	Net-Back at Group 3
Evansville	10.83¢	2.85¢	7.98¢
Indianapolis	11.28	3.22	8.06
South Bend	11.23	3.28	7.95
Detroit	7.93	4.22	3.71
Saginaw	10.00	4.42	5.58
Grand Rapids	9.49	4.03	5.46
Chicago	9.84	2.65	7.19
Joliet	10.80	2.71	8.09
Peoria*			
Decatur	10.19	2.52	7.67

* Data not available.
SOURCE: Standard Oil Company (Indiana).

indication of the departure of market prices from the Group 3 basis.[42]

Exhibit VII-17 shows the posted retail prices of the so-called "cut-price marketers" in the various sales districts on regular grade gasolines netted back to the Group 3 area.[43] It is important to note that the price figures in Exhibit

[42] All other things being equal, maintenance of the Group 3 price structure would, of course, have resulted in uniform net-backs from all sales districts.
[43] Source: Standard Oil Company (Indiana).

EXHIBIT VII-18. STANDARD OIL COMPANY (INDIANA)

Comparison of Net Rent Costs Paid by the Indiana Company to
Dealers versus Those Paid by Competitors

Sales Districts	Indiana Company*		Competitors †	
	Annual Gallonage	Net Rent Cost Cents per Gallon	Annual Gallonage	Net Rent Cost Cents per Gallon
Evansville			499,296	.70¢
Indianapolis	392,722	.26¢	240,224	.79
South Bend	783,200	.38	376,745	.81
Detroit	611,500	.59	125,041	1.00
Saginaw	145,645	.50	69,731	.30
Grand Rapids	237,800	.48	241,785	.83
Chicago	1,264,347	.52	245,067	.60
Joliet	379,746	.34	367,843	.67
Peoria	39,700	.50	51,640	1.00
Decatur	334,100	.44	211,760	.85
Total	4,184,760	.46¢	2,429,132	.75¢

* Data covers only new accounts signed during the first 10 months of 1939 on which a net rent cost was incurred; new accounts on which the lease and sublease rentals equalized were not included.

† Data covers only the accounts lost by the Indiana Company to competitors in the period January 1, 1938, to October 31, 1939, on which competitors incurred net rent costs.

SOURCE: Standard Oil Company (Indiana).

VII-17 are posted consumer prices at service stations whereas the realization figures in Exhibit VII-16 reflect the Indiana Company's prices to all classes of trade. At this time the company sold very little gasoline through its own service stations to consumers; most of its sales were made at tank wagon prices to dealers. Exhibits VII-16 and VII-17 therefore are not comparable because Exhibit VII-17 includes the dealer margin as a part of the price which is not true of Exhibit VII-16. The variations in the net-back figures shown in Exhibit VII-17 were taken by the management as further corroboration of the fact that the Indiana Company's competitors were no longer pricing on the Group 3 basis.

As indicated by the above figures on loss in realization from price cuts, the Indiana Company departed from its normal price structure to meet the competition of other marketers when the management felt it necessary to do so. Ordinarily, however, the management did not take such steps until the company had suffered a significant loss in market position. Moreover, when the company cut its prices in a particular area, it could legally cut only to the competitive level because of the one-price laws in several of the states in which it operated. Under such circumstances, it was usually very difficult for the company to regain customers once they had been lost to other companies.

Indirect Price Cuts by Competitors: The management of the Indiana Company observed that the company was being undersold not only in terms of direct price cuts but likewise in terms of a variety of indirect price concessions that were offered to dealers. The indirect price concessions usually took one or another of three forms: (a) certain *special* types of resellers were placed on a distributor basis and, in effect, given the opportunity to buy at tank car prices, (b) stations were leased from dealers by supplying companies and then leased back to the dealers at lower rentals than those stipulated in the leases to the supplier, and (c) supplying companies installed special equipment, remodeled driveways, painted buildings, and made other improvements to dealer properties at no charge or at nominal costs.

In an effort to ascertain the extent to which it was being undersold in the matter of indirect concessions, the Indiana Company made a careful study of all the reseller accounts it lost in the period January 1, 1938, to October 31, 1939, and of all the privately owned stations which it leased and then subleased to dealers in the first 10 months of 1939. Exhibit VII-18 shows the estimates the company developed

EXHIBIT VII-19. STANDARD OIL COMPANY (INDIANA)

Comparison of Rent and Equipment Concessions Granted by the Indiana Company
to Dealers versus Those Granted by Competitors

| | Indiana Company* | | Competitors† | |
Sales Districts	Annual Gallonage	Net Rent and Equipment Cost Cents per Gallon	Annual Gallonage	Net Rent and Equipment Cost Cents per Gallon
Evansville	601,875	.14¢	849,026	.48¢
Indianapolis	2,555,133	.17	324,149	.63
South Bend	1,349,000	.32	865,687	.43
Detroit	2,203,039	.25	130,210	.98
Saginaw	644,595	.25	404,106	.18
Grand Rapids	1,057,650	.22	445,926	.54
Chicago	2,831,652	.35	311,426	.52
Joliet	1,013,750	.23	513,266	.53
Peoria	257,700	.22	257,438	.39
Decatur	1,221,950	.23	345,785	.59
Total	13,736,344	.25¢	4,447,019	.49¢

* Data covers new accounts signed during the first 10 months of 1939 on which rent and/or equipment concessions were granted.

† Data covers the accounts lost by the Indiana Company to competitors in the period July 4, 1938, to October 31, 1939, on which competitors granted rent and/or equipment concessions.

SOURCE: Standard Oil Company (Indiana).

from this study of the net rent costs (item (b) above) that it was incurring in contrast to those granted by competitors. Exhibit VII-19 shows the company's estimate of the total indirect concessions it had experienced to dealers in the form of net rent costs and equipment arrangements as contrasted with those given by competitors. As indicated by the two tables, the indirect concessions offered by competitors apeared to be approximately twice those being offered by the Indiana Company.

The management concluded that the only reason it was possible for competitors to take this position was that they had introduced some economy in reaching the particular market or that they were blind to their cost of doing business. The continued growth, expansion, and dividend records of some competitors did not indicate that the latter was the explanation. The margin over their costs was more likely to be wide enough to permit such practices on a sound competitive basis.[44]

Increase in Cut-Price Outlets: The management of the Indiana Company found further evidence of the inadequacy of the Group 3 plus rail freight price structure in the rapid increase in cut-price market outlets which occurred in the period 1936–1939. With the de-

[44] Source: Standard Oil Company (Indiana).

velopment of better transportation facilities and the new refining centers in Michigan and Illinois, the margins available under the price structure which the Indiana Company sought to maintain became very attractive and tended to draw new competition into the market. Company surveys indicated that in the period 1936–1939 the number of cut-price retail outlets increased by 98%, the number of bulk plants serving such outlets by 78%, and the volume of business done by cut-price marketers by 132%. The share of the gasoline market held by cut-price marketers in the period 1935–1939 was estimated as follows:

1935	8.8%
1936	9.7
1937	11.7
1938	13.1
1939	15.1

On the basis of the foregoing factors, the Indiana Company considered abandoning the Group 3 plus method of pricing and setting its prices in each market area on the basis of local competitive and economic conditions. New pricing procedures were established immediately in Michigan, and in 1941 the competitive situation in Indiana was recognized by a flat downward adjustment of $\frac{1}{2}$ cent per gallon in the prices computed from the Group 3 formula. The shortage of products which developed in the war and postwar period obviated the necessity of further adjustments in the company's normal price structure until 1949.

Competitive Quality of Gasolines:

The survey of competitive conditions in Michigan, Illinois, and Indiana revealed that a second major cause of the company's loss in market position in the latter 1930's was a narrowing of the quality differential between its gasolines and those offered by cut-price marketers. Company surveys indicated that whereas in 1935 only about 10% of the volume sold by cut-price marketers had an octane rating of over 70, in 1939 about 84% of the volume sold by such outlets had an octane rating of over 70. The improvement in the octane rating of the gasolines offered by cut-price marketers resulted largely from the liberalization of the Ethyl Gasoline Corporation's licensing agreements in 1939.[45] By the end of 1939 practically all of the cut-price marketers were offering either an ethylized premium or regular grade gasolines.

Field surveys indicated that most of the cut-price gasoline was being sold at a price differential of 2 to 3 cents per gallon below the price of the Indiana Company's regular grade, Red Crown gasoline. At this time, the company's Red Crown gasoline had an octane rating of about 74.5 to 75.5 and its premium gasoline a rating of about 78.

The management of the Indiana Company also observed that throughout the latter 1930's there was a growing recognition by the public of quality factors in gasoline and that some of the major companies were having outstanding success with the introduction and promotion of improved gasolines. The company records indicated, for example, that the Sun Oil

Company held about 18.2% of the gasoline market in Detroit in the 18-month period prior to the introduction of its new "Blue Sunoco," catalytic cracked gasoline. By the first week of December 1939, about 30 days after the gasoline was introduced, the company's share of the Detroit market had jumped to about 26.2%, according to the Indiana Company's figures. It was recognized that it would not be possible to judge the final effect of the introduction of the new gasoline until several months had elapsed, but the above figures were nevertheless regarded by the Indiana Company management as indicative of the increasing importance of quality as a selling feature.

In view of the increasing importance of competition in terms of product quality, the management of the Indiana Company decided that the company should seek to increase the octane rating of its regular grade gasoline as rapidly as possible as one means of correcting the downward trend in the company's market position in the three eastern states.

The Indianapolis Pipe Line:

The management of the Indiana Company recognized that while the proposed vigorous meeting of competitive prices in each local area and the proposed increase in the quality of regular grade gasoline might halt the company's loss of market position in the three eastern states, the company would in the long run be unable to operate profitably under these policies unless it was able to reach the markets at costs fully comparable with those of its competitors. The management therefore turned to an analysis of the company's transportation arrangements in the three eastern states. The decision to build the Indianapolis pipe line was one outgrowth of this analysis.

Exhibit VII-20 shows the supply point for each of the company's bulk plants in the three eastern states and the average transportation cost in cents per gallon incurred by each sales district for the movement of gasolines and naphthas, tractor fuel, and furnace oil from the supply points to the bulk plants. The data are based on volumes shipped during 1938 and rates in effect as of December 1, 1939. Total transportation costs by states, computed on the same basis, for the movement of naphthas, gasolines, tractor fuels, and furnace oil from

---

[45] In May 1939 the Federal Courts enjoined the Ethyl Gasoline Corporation's licensing agreements. The Ethyl Gasoline Corporation had previously entered into license agreements with approximately 123 refiners who together refined and sold about 88% of all the gasoline produced in the United States. The agreements with the refiners provided that they might sell lead-treated gasoline only to those jobbers which were licensed by the Ethyl Gasoline Corporation. The Courts held that the arrangement unreasonably restrained trade and violated the Sherman Anti-Trust Act. The Ethyl Gasoline Corporation was owned by the Standard Oil Company (New Jersey), the General Motors Corporation, and the E. I. du Pont de Nemours & Company.

EXHIBIT VII-20. STANDARD OIL COMPANY (INDIANA)

Normal Supply Points for Light Oil Products, Indiana, Michigan, and Illinois: 1939

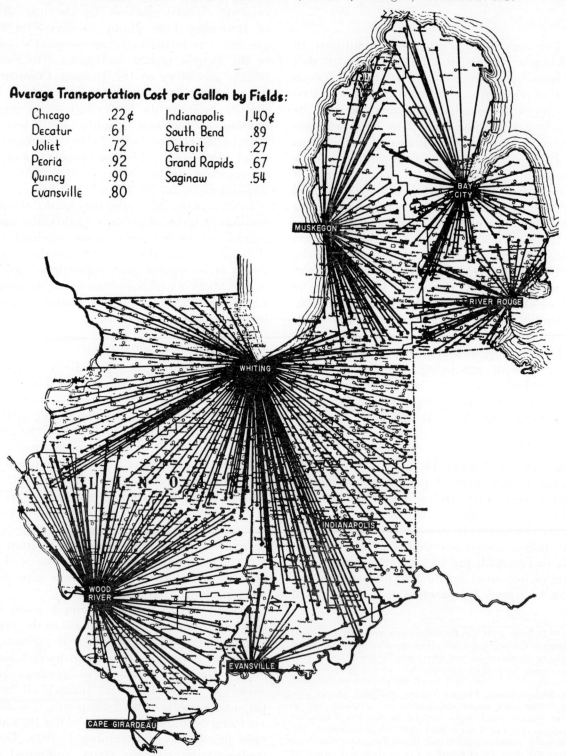

Average Transportation Cost per Gallon by Fields:

Chicago	.22¢	Indianapolis	1.40¢
Decatur	.61	South Bend	.89
Joliet	.72	Detroit	.27
Peoria	.92	Grand Rapids	.67
Quincy	.90	Saginaw	.54
Evansville	.80		

SOURCE: Standard Oil Company (Indiana).

supply points to bulk plants were found to be as follows:

INDIANA COMPANY'S TRANSPORTATION COSTS BY STATES, LIGHT OIL PRODUCTS: 1938

State	Thousand Gallons	Cost ($1,000)	Cost in Cents per Gallon
Illinois	303,048	$1,536	.51¢
Indiana	160,023	1,638	1.02
Michigan	214,598	946	.44
	677,669	$4,120	.61¢

Analysis of the data on transportation costs [46] revealed that the company was incurring particularly heavy transportation costs along a semicircular path running from Chicago, through South Bend and Fort Wayne, to Indianapolis. Moreover, it was found that the company's transportation costs in supplying the Indianapolis market were substantially higher than those estimated for many of its competitors, as indicated by the following figures:

COMPETITIVE DISADVANTAGE OF THE INDIANA COMPANY IN SHIPPING TO INDIANAPOLIS MARKET

Company	Method of Transport	Approximate Cost Cents per Gallon	Indiana Company Disability Cents per Gallon
Indiana Co.	Truck	1.31¢	—
Company A	Pipe Line & Truck	.45	.86¢
" B	" " " "	.45	.86
" C	" " " "	.45	.86
" D	Tank Car & Truck	.98	.33
" E	" " " "	.80	.51
" F	" " " "	.54	.77
" G	" " " "	.91	.40

The company found that of the reseller accounts lost by the Indianapolis sales district to competitors during 1939, 67.8% were lost to the three firms with the greatest transportation advantage over the Indiana Company. The company concluded as follows:

If we are to meet this competition in Indiana, our costs must be reduced to a comparable basis. Barge movement is impossible. Truck transportation has been extended to limits economically fea-

sible. If our transportation costs are to be reduced, it must be by pipe line movement.[47]

The transportation savings, before pipe line and terminal charges, which could be made by means of a pipe line from Whiting to South Bend, Fort Wayne, and Indianapolis were estimated as shown in the following table. Since the figures are before pipe line and terminal charges, they merely represent the advantage secured by supplying bulk plants in the area of the pipe line from the three proposed pipe line terminals by rail or truck as compared with the cost of serving them from their existing supply points.

ESTIMATED FREIGHT SAVINGS AVAILABLE BY SERVING BULK PLANTS FROM THREE PROPOSED TERMINALS

(1,000 gallons)

Terminal	Truck Shipments	
	Gallons	Saving
South Bend	22,741	$113,659
Fort Wayne	17,272	159,824
Indianapolis	64,239	623,575
Total	104,252	$897,058

	Rail Shipments	
	Gallons	Saving
South Bend	6,923	$ 24,273
Fort Wayne	6,757	53,546
Indianapolis	12,233	118,498
Total	25,913	$196,317

	Total Shipments	
	Gallons	Saving
South Bend	29,664	$ 137,932
Fort Wayne	24,029	213,370
Indianapolis	76,472	742,073
Total	130,165	$1,093,375

After an analysis had been made of the costs of constructing the pipe line and the terminals and of the operating expenses of the pipe line, it was decided to build a direct line only to Indianapolis. The line, which was 8 inches in diameter and about 150 miles in length, was laid in 1941.

Other Proposals for Strengthening the Company's Positions:

The survey in 1939 led to a number of other proposals for strengthening the company's competitive position in Illinois, Michigan, and Indiana. Among other things, the following were undertaken: (a) construction of an ad-

----

[46] The term "transportation costs" used hereafter in the discussion will refer to the cost of moving gasolines, naphthas, tractor fuel, and furnace oil from supply points to bulk plants, based on 1938 sales volumes and rates in effect as of December 1, 1939.

[47] Source: Standard Oil Company (Indiana).

ditional terminal on the Illinois Waterways, (b) construction of increased capacity for lake terminals at Muskegon, Bay City, and River Rouge as a means of reducing the company's transportation costs in serving the Michigan peninsula, (c) adoption of training programs and certain changes in rental policies in an effort to reduce dealer turnover, (d) modernization of some of the company's less attractive service stations, (e) increased promotional efforts on TBA items and the initiation of procedures to regulate TBA inventories in accordance with seasonal sales patterns, and (f) certain revisions in the commissions paid to the company's bulk station agents. In total, the survey resulted in 78 different recommendations, only two of which were concerned with the Indianapolis pipe line and terminal.

In summary therefore it appears that the Indiana Company's pipe line to Indianapolis was built in response to certain fundamental changes taking place in the economics of the petroleum industry in the Mid-Western section of the country which exposed the company to a new set of competitive pressures and made the reduction of transportation costs imperative. Moreover, it is evident that the pipe line was only one of a whole series of moves by which the company sought to hold its market position against the inroads being made by both new and established marketers.

VII. PRODUCTS PIPE LINES AS A MEANS OF MEETING SPECIAL REFINING AND MARKETING PROBLEMS

Although the great majority of the products pipe lines we studied were built simply to reduce transportation costs, we found a number of cases where products pipe lines were built to solve various problems a company was facing in its refining or marketing operations. Among other things, the lines were sometimes built to extend a refinery's market area, to provide a source of supply for a marketing operation, or to permit the closing down of an uneconomical refinery. These three cases might, of course, be classified as lines built to reduce transportation costs in the sense that they often made possible oil movements which would have been economically unfeasible by other transportation methods. There is, however,

considerable difference between the building of products pipe lines, such as those discussed above, to reduce costs on existing oil movements and the building of products pipe lines to permit new oil movements.

The Pioneer Pipe Line which was built in 1952 by Sinclair (35%) and the Continental Oil Company (65%) provides an interesting example of a pipe line which was built both to enlarge a refinery marketing area and to provide a source of supply for a marketing operation. The line was about 300 miles in length and extended from Sinclair, Wyoming, to Salt Lake City, Utah. It was 8 inches in diameter, had a capacity of 12,000 barrels per day, and involved a cost of about $8,000,000. To Sinclair the line represented a means of enlarging the marketing area of the company's refinery at Sinclair, Wyoming; to the Continental Oil Company it represented a means of supplying products to a large marketing operation in the Salt Lake area which had previously been served primarily through purchase arrangements. It might also be observed that in the case of both companies the line provided a supplemental means of providing an outlet for the surplus crude oil production in Wyoming which has already been discussed.

Sinclair had owned a small refinery at Sinclair, Wyoming, for a number of years. During World War II the capacity of the plant was enlarged from about 8,000 to 25,000 barrels per day capacity as a means of supplying high-octane gasoline to the armed forces. After the war the company found that the local market was insufficient to absorb the full output of the plant and that it could be run at capacity only if shipments were made far to the eastward. Such shipments involved high transportation costs and did not permit a reasonable profit in the face of competition from Mid-Continent refiners shipping to the North Central states via the Great Lakes Pipe Line.

In addition, there was at this time a general surplus of refining capacity in the Wyoming area, a situation caused by the fact that refiners in the Mid-Continent area had for some time been gradually encroaching on the Rocky Mountain market by extending their pipe lines to the North and West. In the future, it was anticipated that the market position of the Wyoming refineries would become increasingly difficult as a result of the building of refineries at the terminus of the Interprovincial Pipe Line near Superior, Wisconsin, to receive Canadian crude oil and as a result of the building of refineries near the newly discovered producing fields in the Williston Basin in North Dakota, such as that which had recently been announced by the Standard Oil Company (Indiana). It was believed that refineries at both of these locations would be able to ship their products westward for a considerable distance in competition with the Wyoming refineries.

To Sinclair the Pioneer Pipe Line thus represented a means of utilizing its excess capacity at the Sinclair refinery and a means of enlarging the plant's normal marketing area. The new line not only permitted access to the Salt Lake City market but also through a connection with the Salt Lake Pipe Line (Standard Oil Company of California) made possible shipments to the North and West through Idaho as far as Pasco, on the Columbia River in Washington. As evidence of the pressure of the general circumstances whch prompted Sinclair's interest in the Pioneer Pipe Line, it may be noted that the General Petroleum Corporation (Socony-Vacuum Oil Company), immediately after the Pioneer project was initiated, undertook construction of a 100-mile pipe line from Casper, Wyoming, to join with the Pioneer Line at Rawlins as a means of providing an outlet for its refinery at Casper, which was at that time operating at less than capacity.[48]

The interest of Continental Oil Company in the Pioneer venture was somewhat different from that of Sinclair. Continental Oil Company was originally the principal marketing agency of the Standard Oil group in the Rocky Mountain region in the 1880's. After the dissolution decree of 1911 the company secured products for its marketing operations in the Salt Lake area primarily through purchases from other companies. As a part of the Pioneer project, Continental arranged to give Sinclair crude oil near the origin of the Platte line for shipment to Wood River in exchange for Sinclair crude oil in the vicinity of the Sinclair refinery. It was further arranged that the latter oil would then be processed at

the Sinclair refinery for Continental and the products shipped through the Pioneer line to Salt Lake City. To Continental Oil Company the Pioneer line thus represented a means of replacing a long-standing products purchase arrangement with a source of supply which utilized, albeit somewhat indirectly, the company's crude oil producing potential in the Wyoming area.

We found a number of products pipe lines that were constructed as a means of replacing refineries which, as a result of changing conditions, could no longer be operated on a competitive basis. The extension of Atlantic's products pipe line system in the period 1935–1937 (discussed earlier in the chapter) was influenced in part, for example, by difficulties which the company was having in the operation of its Pittsburgh and Franklin refineries in western Pennsylvania. These two small refineries had been built before 1900 to operate on Pennsylvania crude oils. As the Pennsylvania production diminished, the company found it necessary to reach farther and farther into the Mid-Continent area to secure adequate crude oil supplies. For the movement of the oil it was necessary to pay either rail transport costs or the pipe line tariffs charged by other refiners who owned the crude oil lines. Moreover, the Pennsylvania crude oil made a very poor grade of gasoline and it was evident that both of the small refineries would sooner or later require extensive rebuilding and the installation of thermal cracking facilities to meet the octane requirements of the market.

Study of the problem indicated that it would be more economical to supply the markets served by the two refineries through the pipe line from the Philadelphia refinery than to make further capital commitments in them and attempt to secure a low-cost source of crude oil for them. The extension of the company's products pipe line system into western Pennsylvania was undertaken in part therefore to permit a closing down of the refineries at Pittsburgh and Franklin, which was done in 1936.

After World War II a number of companies found it desirable to extend their products lines as a means of serving certain parts of their market in lieu of installing the equipment necessary to produce high-octane gasolines in their

---

[48] George Webber, "Markets Shifting," *The Oil and Gas Journal*, April 28, 1952, p. 51.

smaller refineries. An example may be found in the experience of the Sinclair Oil Corporation. At the close of World War II, Sinclair had four small refineries in the Mid-Continent area with capacities as follows:

CAPACITY OF SINCLAIR REFINERIES IN MID-CONTINENT AREA: 1946

(Barrels per Day)

Refinery	Crude Capacity	Thermal Cracking Capacity
Kansas City, Kansas	12,000	7,000
Coffeyville, Kansas	11,000	7,000
Sand Springs, Oklahoma	7,200	3,000
Fort Worth, Texas	6,500	4,500

These refineries had for a number of years supplied the company's marketing operations in their immediate vicinities. Immediately after the close of the war there was a sharp upward movement in octane requirements, and it became apparent that the plants could no longer serve their markets on a competitive basis without extensive modernization and the installation of catalytic cracking equipment. At the same time, however, the plants were so small that the installation of catalytic cracking equipment of the size best suited for economical operations was not possible. The company decided therefore to convert the four refineries to products terminals and to supply their markets from its big refineries at Houston and Chicago by means of a products pipe line extending through the Mid-Continent region. Other reasons for the construction of this particular products pipe line will be discussed in Chapter Eleven.

VIII. CRUDE OIL TRUNK AND PRODUCTS PIPE LINES AS A SOURCE OF PROFITS

We found very few cases where it could be said that the building of either a crude oil trunk or products pipe line was motivated primarily by the desire to earn a profit on transportation service provided to other shippers. As was noted in the first section of the chapter, after 1934 the Interstate Commerce Commission tended to take the position that pipe line earnings in excess of 8% on the valuation of the properties might be deemed excessive. Moreover, after 1941 the signers of the consent decree were in a position where it was usually undesirable for them to generate earnings on

their pipe line operations much in excess of 7% of the pipe line valuations. Finally, in view of the high fixed costs associated with pipe line operations, a company was not ordinarily in a good position to build a pipe line unless it had producing, refining, or marketing operations of its own which enabled it to guarantee a sizable portion of the throughput to the line. As a result, the crude oil trunk and products pipe lines were usually built for one or another or some combination of the various reasons which have been illustrated in the cases cited above.

The builders of pipe lines frequently took in business from outside shippers as a matter of necessity under the common carrier regulations or because the incremental volume offered by the outside shippers could be handled on a profitable basis. In some cases the business of outside shippers permitted construction of a larger line than would otherwise have been possible, reduced the pipe line operating expenses per barrel, and provided the shippers with a source of additional revenue. In other words, the traffic of outside shippers was sometimes attractive as incremental business for lines which were being built for other reasons; rarely, however, were the profit opportunities associated with the outside business sufficient to be a *primary cause* for initiating a new line or for building a major extension to an existing line.

The operations of The Ohio Oil Company with respect to its pipe lines have been somewhat of an exception to the general rule, particularly in recent years. The Ohio Oil Company first became heavily engaged in pipe line activities in the period 1905–1907 while still a part of the Standard Oil group. After the dissolution decree in 1911 the company continued to own and operate its gathering systems and a trunk line extending from Wood River, Illinois, to the Pennsylvania border. In 1914, following the U. S. Supreme Court decision on The Pipe Line Cases holding the interstate lines to be common carriers, the Illinois Pipe Line Company was formed to take over the crude oil gathering and pipe line activities of The Ohio Oil Company, and the latter then temporarily withdrew from the pipe line business and concentrated on producing operations. In 1930, however, The Ohio Oil Company reacquired the common stock of the Illinois Pipe Line by issuing in exchange therefor $58,000,000 par value of preferred stock of its own.

In 1952 The Ohio Oil Company and its subsidiary, the Illinois Pipe Line Company of Texas, had in operation about 1,321 miles of gathering lines and 1,706 miles of trunk lines. The principal gathering systems were located in Texas, Indiana, Montana, Illinois, and Wyoming; the main trunk lines extended northeastward from Wood River across Illinois, Indiana, and Ohio to the Pennsylvania border (see map, Chapter Twelve, Exhibit XII-6). During the year 1952 the company transported about 163 million barrels of oil through its pipe line system.

The company's pipe lines were operated fully as much for their value as a transportation business as for their value as adjuncts to the company's producing and refining operations. The company's net crude oil production in 1952 was about 34 million barrels, and the consumption of its two refineries at Robinson, Illinois, and Lovell, Wyoming, was only about 14 million barrels. Had the company transported all its net crude oil production to market and had it supplied all its refinery requirements through its own pipe lines, it still would have had a substantial outside transportation business as indicated by the above figure of 163 million barrels of crude oil transported through the system. Actually, the company sold nearly all its crude oil production to other oil companies in the fields and used its pipe lines to handle its own products only in the case of intrastate shipments. Normally, shipments of the company's own oil for use at the Robinson refinery through the main trunk line system amounted to less than 10% of the volume handled by the line. For the most part, the main trunk line system operated as a common carrier and served a number of customers of long standing in the Mid-Continent area, such as the Pure Oil Company, the Sun Oil Company, the Ashland Oil & Refining Company, and the Midwest Petroleum Company.

At the time of the consent decree in 1941, the company was not carrying its own oil in interstate commerce; hence, it was not made a party to the complaint that led to the decree. Although the company was not subject to the 7% limitation in dividends, the earnings from the pipe line operations, according to company executives, did not usually run much above those of other pipe line carriers. The company was limited in the tariffs it could charge not only by the general review which the Interstate Commerce Commission exercised over pipe line rates, but likewise by the general level of tariffs established by competing carriers in the Mid-Continent areas, many of which were owned by companies subject to the consent decree.

The return which The Ohio Oil Company earned on its pipe line investments was, in the opinion of the management, substantially lower than that which the company earned on its investments in producing operations. The management believed, however, that the company should continue to own and operate pipe lines and to construct new ones when the circumstances warranted. The pipe line transportation business was regarded as a safe and secure source of reasonable profits which might be important in maintaining the company's earnings position should it encounter adversities in the somewhat more hazardous producing business in which the bulk of its activities were concentrated.

It should not be inferred from the above discussion that the company's only reason for integrating into the ownership of pipe lines was a desire to secure a transportation profit. As was noted earlier in the discussion of the Platte Pipe Line, the company sometimes engaged in pipe line projects as a means of providing outlets for its crude oil production despite the fact that it might sell its oil to other companies, as it planned to do in the case of the Platte line, prior to shipment through the line. Moreover, when the company built gathering lines to serve its own producing properties it quite naturally extended the lines to the near-by wells of other producers and thereby became engaged in transportation operations in excess of its own immediate needs. Likewise since the common carrier trunk lines are required to accept tenders from all customers on an equitable basis, it was inevitable that over the years the main line should become larger than any need the company might have for it in carrying oil to its principal refinery at Robinson, Illinois.

Before 1952, The Ohio Oil Company did not engage in the operation of any products pipe lines. In 1952, however, a products pipe line service was initiated between Wood River and Indianapolis. For many years The Ohio Oil Company had operated a crude oil trunk line between Wood River and Indianapolis as a part of its main trunk line system from Wood River to Lima, Ohio. As the demand increased, the company constructed additional lines parallel to the original line until in 1950 it had several small diameter pipes in the system. In 1950 the management decided to replace the multiple system of crude oil lines from Wood River to Lima, Ohio, with a single large diameter pipe. In connection with this decision, it was also decided to convert one of the old small diameter crude lines between Wood River and Indianapolis to products operation. The company had no intention of using the line for its own products and anticipated that it would serve entirely as a common carrier for other shippers.

IX. THE SOURCES OF INVESTMENT CAPITAL FOR PIPE LINES

As noted at the outset of this chapter, it is a matter of record that the great majority of the important pipe line projects in the United States were initiated by companies engaged in producing, refining, or marketing activities. In the light of the facts about transportation costs, pipe line operations, and the character of the circumstances giving rise to the need for pipe lines, it is not hard to understand why such should be the case.

As is illustrated by the projects discussed in this chapter, when a producer, refiner, or marketer needs a pipe line, he often needs it very badly. When the circumstances are appropriate to the use of a pipe line, very substantial cost savings may be secured over other forms of transporation. Transportation costs are an extremely important aspect of the competitive position of a refiner or marketer, and the lack of a pipe line may thus mean that he either suffers a competitive disability or foregoes a chance to gain a competitive advantage. Similarly, the lack of a pipe line may preclude a producer from developing his properties and recovering his capital outlays for exploration and development. Producers, refiners, and marketers are therefore frequently in positions where they cannot afford to wait for outside capital to discover and exploit the pipe line opportunity which may exist in a particular situation.

At the same time, moreover, pipe line investments have not been particularly attractive to firms not engaged in the industry. The ordinary pipe line usually requires a very large investment, it is highly specialized with respect to the markets and customers it can serve, and its profit position is extremely vulnerable to changes in the volume of throughput. To compensate him for the risks assumed in a pipe line project, the outside investor has only such profits as may be permitted to him by competition and by the government and state agencies which exercise jurisdiction over pipe line operations.

The integrated company, however, has these gains plus further savings on his own shipments to the extent that there is a difference between the pipe line tariffs and the rates charged by alternate carriers. Moreover, the integrated company may secure important corollary gains in other phases of its operations, as in the case of a producer who builds a pipe line to secure an outlet for shut-in crude oil production. Finally, the integrated company is often in a far better position to assure the future throughput to a line than is an outside investor, unless the latter enters into long-term contracts (which approach *de facto* integration) with the shippers he plans to serve. The integrated company thus usually has more to gain from a pipe line project than does an outside investor and can frequently undertake the projects with a good deal less risk. It is not surprising therefore that the capital for such ventures should, for the most part, have been drawn from the oil companies[49] rather than outside interests.

The relative attractiveness of pipe line investments to integrated companies and outside concerns which has just been discussed suggests one of the most important problems which would arise from legislation precluding the oil

---

[49] Reference here is to the companies that initiated the projects and *arranged* to supply the capital for pipe lines. In many cases, of course, the pipe line builders borrowed part of their funds from outside investors.

companies from pipe line construction. Such legislation would tend to freeze the competitive relationships among the oil companies in their present position. Companies now served by adequate pipe line connections would continue to be so served, but companies not so favored would be unable to build new lines to strengthen their competitive positions. Moreover, if one company happened to interest an outside concern in building a pipe line to serve its needs, it might immediately gain a significant advantage over its competitors which they would be powerless to offset through any investment action on their own initiative. Likewise a refiner who ran out of crude oil in the area of his existing pipe line connections or a producer who needed a pipe line to provide an outlet for his crude oil might go bankrupt while searching for outside capital to build the lines necessary to remedy their difficulties.

X. SUMMARY

1. The persistent tendency of producers, refiners, and marketers to engage in the construction of crude oil trunk and products pipe lines is explainable largely by a few simple facts with regard to transportation costs in the oil industry and the nature of the investment opportunity which pipe lines provide. Transportation costs are an extremely important element in the final delivered cost of oil products to consumers and are a key factor in determining the competitive position of all firms engaged in the producing, manufacturing, and distribution cycle. Under the proper circumstances, crude oil trunk and products pipe lines permit very substantial cost savings over other forms of transportation. As a result, when a producer, refiner, or marketer needs a pipe line, he often needs it very badly and cannot afford to wait for outside capital to discover and exploit the pipe line opportunity which may exist in a particular situation.

2. Pipe line investments have not been particularly attractive to firms not engaged in the oil industry for a number of reasons. A pipe line usually requires a very large capital outlay; it is highly specialized in terms of the products it may carry and the customers it may serve; and its cost characteristics are such that it must operate very close to the throughput for which it was designed to function efficiently. The risks associated with a pipe line investment therefore are different from those associated with many other transportation ventures and are generally large unless the builder is in a position to assure a substantial portion of the throughput to the line for a fairly long period of time. To compensate him for the risk assumed, an outside builder has only the profits arising from the difference between tariffs and operating costs which have in recent years run less than 10% of borrowed and invested capital for most lines. An integrated oil company, on the other hand, may gain further benefits from a pipe line through transportation cost savings on its own throughput and gains made elsewhere in its producing, refining, or marketing operations.

3. The majority of the crude oil trunk lines we studied were built by companies engaged in refining activities primarily as a means of: (a) reducing inward transportation costs on crude oil, or (b) gaining access to crude oil supplies that might not otherwise have been available. Crude trunk lines have also frequently been built by producing or producing and refining companies as a means of providing an outlet for crude oil which might not otherwise have had a market. The significance of the latter motivation for the construction of crude oil trunk lines has been somewhat obscured by the fact that most of the pipe line builders have been engaged in both producing and refining, and it has generally been assumed that they were prompted to build the lines by considerations associated with their refining interests alone.

4. The great majority of the products pipe lines we studied were built as a means of reducing transportation costs on the builders' own throughput. Some products pipe lines were also built to extend the marketing area of a refinery or group of refineries, to provide a source of supply for a marketing operation, to permit the closing down

of uneconomical refineries, or to solve other special refining and marketing problems. In many cases, the products pipe lines were built under a wide diversity of pressures and were an integral part of a general competitive strategy involving price policies, product policies, and many other aspects of a company's operating program.

5. We found very few cases where the building of either a crude oil trunk or products pipe line was motivated primarily by the desire to earn a profit on transportation service provided to other shippers. In recent years, and particularly since the advent of the pipe line consent decree, the opportunities for making profits on the handling of outside business have not been particularly attractive relative to the other profit opportunities which have been available to most of the oil companies. The great majority of the lines we studied were therefore conceived and initiated as a means of solving the builder's own transportation problems. The traffic of outside shippers however, has frequently been carried as a matter of necessity under the common carrier regulations or because it was attractive as incremental volume for lines which were being built for other reasons.

CHAPTER EIGHT

Backward Integration by Refiners into Producing Operations

THE DATA in Chapter Two reveal that there has been a very strong tendency for integration to take place between the producing and refining levels of the oil industry. In 1950 there were at least 74 companies engaged in both producing and refining operations.[1] These 74 companies represented 41.3% of the total operating companies in the refining industry and accounted for about 95.6% of the total domestic refinery runs and about 59.8% of the total domestic crude oil production. The typical company in the group of 74 was able to supply about 32.7% of its refinery requirements from its own net domestic production.[1] No accurate figures were available on the number of producing companies in the United States, but the number was probably in excess of 8,000 to 10,000. It is evident therefore that the 74 companies known to be engaged in both producing and refining constituted a much smaller percentage of the producing population than they did of the refining population and that there were far more nonintegrated producers than there were nonintegrated refiners.

The extensive integration existing between producing and refining interests in 1950 was the result of both forward integration by producers and backward integration by refiners. In Chapter Four some of the major circumstances which caused crude oil producers to integrate forward into refining operations were

discussed, and particular attention was directed to the acquisition of refineries by producers as a means of providing an outlet for their crude oil in times of large crude oil supplies. As was noted in Chapter Four, this particular motivation for forward integration appeared time and again throughout the history of the industry, but was considerably more important before the advent of the conservation laws than it was thereafter.

The purpose of this chapter is to examine some of the circumstances that led refining companies to integrate backward into crude oil production. The first part of the chapter will present some facts about refinery investments, refinery operations, and crude oil production which had a general bearing on the backward integration moves of refiners. Later sections of the chapter will then discuss in some detail the circumstances that prompted The Atlantic Refining Company, the Standard Oil Company (Ohio), and the Standard Oil Company (Indiana) to embark on their crude oil producing programs. Each of these three companies operated for a substantial period in its history without any appreciable crude oil production before arriving at its decision to integrate backward.

I. SOME FACTS ABOUT REFINING OPERATIONS AND CRUDE OIL PRODUCTION

In Chapter Seven attention was directed to the fact that the persistent tendency of producing, refining, and marketing companies to build their own pipe lines was explainable in large measure by certain fundamental facts about pipe line operations and the nature of the pipe line investment opportunity. So, too, we found

---

[1] See results of survey of refining companies in Chapter Two. The number of companies engaged in producing and refining was probably higher than 74, because certain of the companies not covered by our survey were probably engaged in both producing and refining. The nonsurvey companies amounted to 40.8% of the total refining companies and represented 5.3% of the total refining capacity of the industry. Most of the companies engaged in producing and refining were also engaged in marketing and transportation activities.

that there were certain economic facts about refining operations and the crude oil producing process which consistently played a part in the backward integration decisions of refiners. Included among them were the following:

Magnitude of the Refinery Investment:

The modern refinery, like the crude oil trunk and products pipe line, requires a very large capital investment. Refineries vary considerably in cost depending on their location, the type of crude oil on which they are designed to run, the range of products they are designed to produce, and the type of equipment installed. In 1950, however, the largest refineries in operation had capacities in excess of 250,000 barrels per day and represented investments (on the basis of 1950 costs) of over $100,000,-000. The average refinery in the industry in 1950 had a capacity of about 20,000 barrels per day and represented an investment of approximately $20,000,000.[2]

The concentration of such a large sum of money in a single plant facility compels the management of refining companies to take every possible precaution to insure the future economic life of the investment. As will be indicated below, one crucial precaution is that of assuring an adequate crude oil supply at reasonable prices.

Specialized Character of the Refinery Investment:

The refinery is likewise similar to the crude oil trunk and products pipe line in that it is a highly specialized piece of equipment. Although the modern plant can produce a vast range of specialized items in small quantities, a very large part of its output normally consists of three or four fairly standardized products, and the equipment cannot easily be converted to other purposes. In this respect a refinery differs, for example, from a general purpose machine tool plant which can be used with little difficulty to make many different products. The refinery is likewise a specialized investment in the sense that the geographic market areas it can serve are definitely limited by transportation costs. In certain other industries

the outward transportation costs are so low relative to the value of the product that the manufacturer can reach any market in the country on a competitive basis.

Finally, the refinery is specialized in the sense that it can draw its crude oil supplies only from near-by fields or from the particular geographic areas to which it has access by pipe line or other low-cost transportation methods. In certain other industries, such as the textile industry, where the inward freight cost is not quite such a high percentage of the delivered cost, a manufacturer can draw his raw materials by common carrier from almost any section of the country without being placed at any serious competitive disadvantage. As will be demonstrated in Chapter Twenty-One, the economic life of many refineries has been terminated by the drying up of crude oil supplies in the fields which were accessible to them.

The ordinary refinery can thus be used only for the processing of crude oil, drawn from a limited number of geographic areas, and only for the production of a few standardized products for a limited geographic market.

Importance of an Assured Throughput:

The refinery has a further point of similarity with the crude oil trunk and products pipe line in that its profit position is extremely vulnerable to a decline in the level of throughput. Operating practices vary considerably from company to company, but generally speaking a refinery cannot be run economically or maintain product standards at much less than 75% of the throughput for which it was designed. Moreover, as might be anticipated from the high capital cost of the plant, operating expenses per barrel processed tend to rise sharply with decreases in the volume of throughput and bring about a corresponding decline in unit profits. Exhibit VIII-1 illustrates the operating costs per barrel, including depreciation and overhead, for three different pieces of refinery equipment at different levels of throughput. Intermittent operation as an alternative to running at reduced levels of throughput is not attractive because the high capital investment results in high shutdown costs. The shutdown costs for the crude oil distillation unit shown in Exhibit VIII-1, for example, were es-

---

[2] The capital cost of refineries of different sizes will be discussed in greater detail in Chapter Twenty.

EXHIBIT VIII-1. EFFECT OF REDUCED THROUGHPUT ON OPERATING COSTS
OF SELECTED UNITS OF REFINING EQUIPMENT: 1951

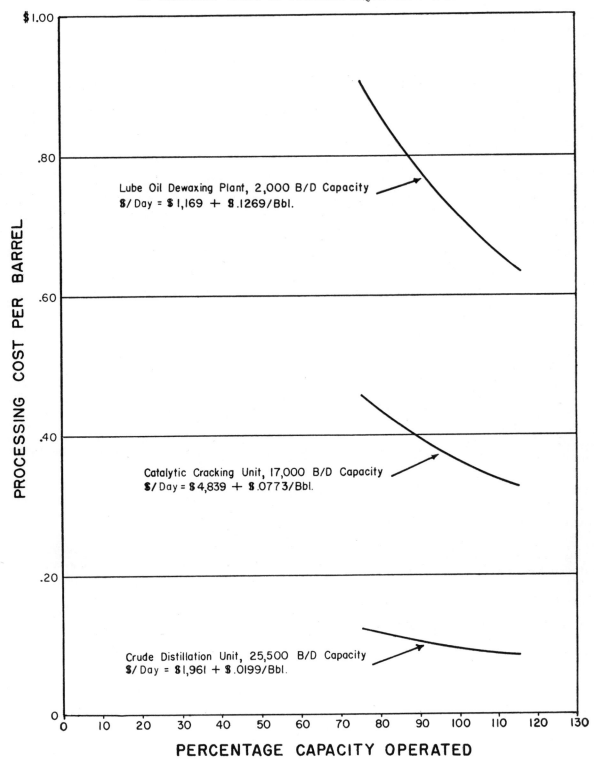

SOURCE: Gulf Oil Corporation.

timated at about 57% of the costs at full-capacity operation.[3]

The refinery is therefore extremely vulnerable to any curtailments in crude oil supply or other circumstances which require a reduction in the level of operations.

Importance of Crude Oil Costs to the Refiner:

The cost of crude oil constitutes a very high percentage of the value of the products sold by a refiner and is thus an extremely important factor in determining his competitive position. The Census of Manufactures reveals the following relationship between the cost of materials, fuel, electricity, and contract work and the value of products shipped in the petroleum refining industry: [4]

	(Millions of Dollars)			
	1939	1947	1949	1950
(a) Value of Products Shipped	$2,462	$6,624	$7,682	$9,410
(b) Cost of Materials, Fuel, Electricity, and Contract Work	1,934	5,129	6,471	7,926
Ratio (b) to (a)	78.6%	77.4%	84.2%	84.2%

The cost of crude oil made up by far the largest part of the cost of materials, fuel, electricity, and contract work. In 1939, the only year for which a breakdown of the figures was available, the cost of crude oil, plus a few minor supplies and containers, amounted to 96.3% of the total figure shown for materials, fuel, electricity, and contract work.[5] In contrast with the above figures, the ratio of the cost of materials, fuel, electricy, and contract work to the value of products shipped for all industries covered by the Census of Manufactures in 1939 was 56.6%.[6]

The importance of crude oil costs in the operating position of the refiner is further illustrated by Exhibit VIII-2 which shows an analysis of the service station price of gasoline in a fairly typical situation as of 1949. In this

---

[3] A more complete discussion of the behavior of refinery processing costs at reduced levels of throughput will be presented in Chapter Twenty.

[4] For 1939 and 1947 figures see U. S. Bureau of the Census, *Census of Manufactures, 1947*, Vol. II, p. 450. For 1949 and 1950 figures see U. S. Bureau of the Census, *Annual Survey of Manufactures: 1949 and 1950*, p. 44.

[5] U. S. Bureau of the Census, *Census of Manufactures, 1939*, Vol. I, p. 35.

[6] Ibid., p. 23.

EXHIBIT VIII–2. APPROXIMATE ANALYSIS OF COST ELEMENTS IN THE RETAIL PRICE OF GASOLINE DELIVERED TO NEWARK, NEW JERSEY: 1949

Cost Item		Cents per Gallon	Percentage of Total
Crude oil cost at well-head		7.2¢	28.4%
Gathering and pipe line transportation to Gulf Coast		0.6	2.3
Processing cost at large refinery on Gulf Coast		2.2	8.7
Cost to refiner, f.o.b. Gulf Coast		10.0	39.4
Profit to refiner		1.0	3.9
Refiner's selling price, Gulf Coast		11.0	43.3
Tanker transportation to East Coast terminal		1.0	3.9
Terminal charges		0.2	0.8
Barge transportation to bulk plant		0.1	0.4
Marketing costs:			
Bulk plant operations	0.2¢		
Tank truck delivery expense	0.4		
Advertising and administrative	0.4		
Accounting, sales, and other expenses	0.5	1.5	5.9
Delivered cost to marketer		13.8	54.3
Profit to marketer		0.8	3.2
Marketer's price to service station dealer		14.6	57.5
Dealer's margin to cover costs and profit		5.8	22.8
State and federal taxes		5.0	19.7
Retail price to service station customer		25.4¢	100.0%

SOURCE: Esso Standard Oil Company. See text for method of computation.

case, it was assumed that half of the crude oil required was purchased at the well-head in the East Texas fields and the remaining half at the well-head in the West Texas fields. It was further assumed that the oil was moved by pipe line to a refinery near Galveston, Texas. The gasoline manufactured from the oil was then moved by tanker to a deep water terminal in New York Harbor, by barge to a Newark bulk plant, and by tank truck to a Newark service station.

The cost of manufacturing the gasoline was developed under the assumption that the gasoline was produced by processing an incremental crude oil charge in an increment of new, complete refining capacity at an existing refinery while the volume of other products at the refinery was held constant, with the exception of residual fuel oil, coke, and gas. The cost at the well-head of the crude oil required to make the gasoline was determined by deducting from the delivered cost of the crude oil at the refinery the market value of the fuel oil, coke, and gas produced from it and the charges for gathering and pipe line transportation. The estimated manufacturing costs involved in processing the incremental crude oil run in the new plant facility, including all fixed charges and overhead, were allocated wholly against the gasoline. As may be seen from the exhibit, the delivered cost of crude oil at the refinery under these assumptions was 7.8 cents per gallon or about 71% of the refiner's gasoline selling price of 11.0 cents per gallon. The delivered cost of crude oil at the refinery was also 30.7% of the service station price of gasoline to the consumer.

The figures in Exhibit VIII-2 are estimates, and many questions might be raised about the methods of allocation which were used at various points in the calculations. The data suffice, however, to indicate the vulnerability of the refiner to any development in his crude oil supply situation which may put him at a crude oil price disadvantage relative to his competitors.

Characteristics of Crude Oil Production:

The above facts assume special significance when it is recognized that crude oil production in the United States has always been somewhat unpredictable. As was pointed out in Chapter Four, in the period prior to the development of the conservation laws the industry alternated between periods of surplus and periods of extreme shortage. The adoption of conservation procedures curtailed somewhat the periods of excessive production, but it did not remove the hazards which the refiner faced with respect to shortages. These shortages occur from time to time in the national supply and even more frequently in the local supply available in particular areas (see Chapter Four, Exhibits IV-1 and IV-4). As was noted earlier, a refiner often has only a limited number of producing fields from which he can draw his crude oil on an economical basis, and he may therefore experience crude oil supply problems even at times when the total United States supply is reasonably well in balance with demand.

In addition, since all crude oil fields are subject to ultimate depletion, every refiner must anticipate a long-run decline in the crude oil available in the fields from which he draws his supplies at any given time. The situation is thus entirely different from that in the case of an agricultural raw material, such as cotton, which may be in short supply from time to time but for which the ultimate supply is of a perennial nature. As the crude oil production in a particular area declines, as it ultimately must, the refiner can only anticipate increasing efforts by his competitors to secure for their own use such supplies as are available and increasing difficulties in purchasing his own needs in the market at a reasonable price.

Cost of Carrying Crude Oil Inventories:

It is important to note that a refiner can make only very limited use of crude oil inventories to guard against short-run shortages in supply. As was noted above, an average refinery has a capacity of about 20,000 barrels per day. A crude oil inventory equal to, say, six months' supply for such a refinery would amount to 3,600,000 barrels. With a delivered crude oil price of $2.65 per barrel this inventory would require a cash investment of $9,540,-000, to say nothing of the investment that would be required for storage facilities. At an interest rate of 6% the financial carrying charges on the inventory would amount to about $572,400 per annum or about 7.8 cents per barrel of crude oil run. The refiner's gross margin does not usually run much in excess of 60 to 80 cents per barrel (see Chapter Five, Exhibit V-2). A refiner who attempted to solve his crude oil supply problem through the carrying of any very large inventory would thus be at a distinct disadvantage relative to other refiners with more assured sources of supply.

In other industries where raw materials are not such a high proportion of the product value, it is often possible for a manufacturer to protect his raw materials position by carrying large inventories without incurring any substantial competitive disadvantage. Similarly, in industries where the raw materials consist of many different items, it is often relatively easy to carry inventories of the particular ones which are the most likely to present supply problems.

Instability of the Refining Margin:

Finally, it is important to note that the refining investment is made at a point in the industry where gross margins and profit opportunities have characteristically been extremely unstable. As was noted in Chapter Five, both the monthly and the yearly fluctuations in the refining gross margin in the period 1920–1952 were more violent than in the gross margins at any other level of the industry. The refining gross margin was characterized by a high degree of instability both before and after the adoption of the prorationing laws, in times of business prosperity and business depression, and in times of steady and fluctuating crude oil prices. It was likewise noted in Chapter Five that the net return on borrowed and invested capital earned by refining-marketing companies [7] was characteristically less stable than that earned by nonintegrated producers, nonintegrated marketers, and various types of integrated companies.

Throughout the period 1920–1952, backward integration into crude oil producing operations constituted one very important means by which a refiner could have improved the stability of the gross margin on which he operated. Backward integration into crude oil producing would have enabled a refiner to reduce the monthly fluctuations [8] in his gross margin from 24.2% to 9.6% before prorationing, from 7.2% to 2.7% after prorationing, and from 14.9% to 5.8% in the period 1920–1952 as a whole. Similarly, backward integration would have enabled a refiner to reduce the yearly fluctuations [9] in his gross margin from 25.3% to 19.5% before prorationing, from 22.9% to 10.0% after prorationing, and from 24.0% to 14.1% in the period 1920–1952 as a whole. It was also demonstrated in Chapter Five, Exhibits V-16 and V-17, that backward integration into crude oil producing in the period 1920–1952 would have served not only to have stabilized but likewise to have increased the net return on borrowed and invested capital earned by a refining-marketing company.

Taken in total, the points discussed above indicate that a refinery is an extremely expensive,

highly specialized piece of equipment which is very vulnerable to unfavorable developments, volume-wise or cost-wise, with respect to its crude oil supply. The nature of crude oil production is such that these developments can and frequently do occur, and the carrying of inventories to guard against them is feasible to only a limited extent. Finally, the refinery investment is made at a point in the industry where the gross margins and net profit opportunities are highly unstable, and the addition of crude oil production has constituted one effective means by which greater stability could be achieved. It is not surprising therefore that refiners should have taken steps toward the acquisition of crude oil reserves, entirely apart from the various other reasons for such moves which will become apparent in the discussion of the three cases which follow.

II. THE ATLANTIC REFINING COMPANY'S BACKWARD INTEGRATION INTO CRUDE OIL PRODUCTION

The Atlantic Refining Company was originally one of the principal refining subsidiaries of the Standard Oil combination. In the five-year period following the dissolution decree the company made no attempt to develop crude oil production of its own. Crude oil for the company's three refineries was secured by means of purchase contracts with independent producers or with integrated concerns having production in excess of their refinery requirements. Shipments to the Philadelphia refinery were made by tanker from Mexico and the Gulf Coast and by tank car from many points in Pennsylvania, West Virginia, Kentucky, Illinois, Kansas, and Oklahoma. Some use was also made of the National Transit Pipe Line which extended from Philadelphia to the fields in northwestern Pennsylvania. The company's Franklin refinery ran almost entirely on western Pennsylvania crude oil, and its Pittsburgh refinery drew supplies primarily from Pennsylvania, Ohio, and West Virginia.

The company began its search for crude oil in 1916. The subsequent growth of its producing operations may be divided into three distinct phases: the period 1916–1935, the period 1935–1941, and the period 1941–1952.

---

[7] The refining-marketing companies analyzed in Chapter Five produced less than 10% of their crude oil requirements and typically had larger refining than marketing operations. Their record therefore tends to reflect the situation of the substantially nonintegrated refiner.

[8] As measured by average monthly deviations from 13-month moving averages.

[9] As measured by average percentage changes from one year to the next.

Initial Producing Operations, 1916–1935:

Crude oil producing activities were begun in 1916 primarily as a means of guarding against the shortages which threatened to develop as a result of the wartime demand for petroleum products. In the period 1915–1918 domestic production in the United States was frequently less than domestic consumption plus exports. Atlantic, however, secured no commercial production until 1919 and did not produce more than a small percentage of its refinery runs until after the middle 1930's (see Chapter Twelve, Exhibit XII-14). The fact that the company did not develop its crude oil producing activities more rapidly during the period 1916–1935 may be attributed to two primary circumstances:

In the first place, throughout most of this period there was no urgent need for the company to have crude oil production of its own. The shortages of the war period were soon relieved by new discoveries, and the 15 years that followed were characterized by ample crude oil supplies in the domestic markets rather than by crude oil deficiencies. It is true that from time to time the company was hard pressed to find adequate supplies for its refineries and occasionally had to pay very high crude oil prices. In times of oversupply, on the other hand, the company was able to buy crude oil at distress prices and thus offset the losses incurred in times of shortage.

The company's position with respect to crude oil during the 1920's is reflected in the following excerpts from a letter to the stockholders dated May 9, 1927:

Existing demoralization in the industry results from an overproduction of crude oil, and crude oil has been made to suffer, in consequence, in the form of declining markets to a level certainly below the average cost of production. *As the producing of crude oil is one of the minor activities of your company, it will not suffer in this connection in the same proportion as probably will some others.*[10] Your company is, in fact, a buyer of crude for the conduct of its manufacturing to upwards of some 80% of its needs for such purposes. The effect, therefore, of the present depressed and demoralized crude oil market upon its manufacturing and product-marketing results will depend

principally upon two factors: one, the status of its crude oil purchase contracts; and the other, the secondary effect upon product prices.

Touching the first of these, it can be said that, with one very minor exception, all of our crude oil contracts move in price with the respective field markets and are as per the markets from day to day. We are not overbought, *and so are in a position to take advantage of any specially low priced crude, if and when any such comes to the market.*[11]

Further illustration of the way in which the company's crude oil buying position worked to its advantage in times of large crude oil supplies may be found in the situation which developed after the discovery of the East Texas field in 1930. In a semiannual report for the period ending June 30, 1931, the company explained the situation as follows:

In addition to the difficulties under which producers and marketers of commodities generally labored, because of the world-wide business depression, the petroleum industry in this country had to reckon with the rapid development of a new oil field (East Texas) of most extraordinary size and potentiality. Within a period of six months from the time of its discovery late last year this field was producing about 20% of the country's needs for crude oil, and this in the face of the fact that production from many other areas had been sharply curtailed for a long period of time by reason of lack of demand for their available production. The result was that the crude oil price structure, country wide, crashed under the pressure, bringing with it, to an even greater extent, a decline in all product prices.

The following brief statistical statement is fairly representative of the effect on marketing conditions generally, east of the Rocky Mountains: [The analysis which followed showed that during the first six months of 1931 the decline in gasoline prices, at service stations and for export, was substantially greater in cents per gallon than the decline in crude oil prices and that the decline in kerosene prices, to dealers and for export, was slightly less than the decline in crude oil prices.]

Operating under such conditions the company naturally experienced a sharp decrease in gross operating income as compared with other recent periods. *Fortunately such decrease was fully offset by reduced expenditures for crude materials and operating expenses.*[12] A somewhat itemized com-

---

[10] Italics added by authors.

[11] Italics added by authors.
[12] Italics added by authors.

parison for the first half of 1931 with the first half of 1930 is as follows:

(Figures in $1,000)

	1930	1931	Favorable or Unfavorable Difference
Gross Operating Income	$65,461	$50,966	$14,495*
Operating Charges			
Crude Materials	37,124	24,120	13,004
Operating Expenses	20,667	19,097	1,570
Insurance and Other Reserves	261	335	74*
Depreciation, Depletion, etc.	5,124	5,586	462*
Total Operating Charges	$63,176	$49,138	$14,038
Operating Margin	2,285	1,828	457*

* Unfavorable difference.

These figures are those of record for the respective periods and, as such, are without adjustments of any kind to compensate for differences in operating conditions such as the 4.4% increase in refinery operations during 1931, as referred to under "Volume of Business."

Throughout most of the period 1916–1927 the earnings of Atlantic were reasonably satisfactory (see Chapter Twelve, Exhibit XII-2), although as was pointed out in Chapter Seven, during the latter part of the period the management felt that the company was severely handicapped by its lack of crude oil pipe lines.

A second important reason why Atlantic did not develop a larger volume of crude oil production in the period 1916–1935 was the fact that the management of the company was not, at that time, particularly skilled in the producing phase of the business. Mr. J. W. Van Dyke, who became manager of the Philadelphia refinery in 1903 and president of the company in 1912, was an expert on refinery technology. Under his leadership, the management of the company tended to specialize in refining operations and made a number of important contributions to the advance of refining methods. When crude oil producing activities were initiated in 1916, Mr. Van Dyke elected to carry on the operations with the existing management team rather than with specialists hired from outside of the company. Moreover, the company undertook to find crude oil of its own rather than to purchase existing proven reserves.

As a result, such efforts as the company did make in the period 1916–1935 to develop crude

oil production were not particularly successful. In the first three years of operation the company drilled a number of wells, all of which were dry holes. It is reported that during this period the company tended to place too much emphasis on leasing acreage at a low cost rather than on leasing acreage that had good crude oil producing possibilities. Crude oil producing operations were conducted at a loss until about 1927 or 1928, despite the occasional assertions of the refining and marketing executives that their earnings were being dissipated in the producing effort.

Increased Emphasis on Crude Oil Production, 1935–1941:

In the middle 1930's the Atlantic management decided that the company's efforts to develop crude oil production should be substantially increased. This decision was reached primarily as a result of the adoption of the prorationing laws by the various producing states and of the management's interpretation of the effect which those laws would have on the price of crude oil and the profitability of the producing phase of the business.

It appeared to the Atlantic management that the prorationing laws would tend to modify the wide oscillations in crude oil prices which had developed in the past and to stabilize the prices at a level which, year in and year out, would probably permit a good return on producing operations. In the past the company had occasionally paid very high prices for crude oil in times of shortage and very low prices in times of surpluses. The losses taken in the former periods were about offset by the gains made in the latter periods. It now appeared that in the future the company would have very little opportunity to buy at distress prices, but would still be exposed to very high prices in times of shortage. The management interpreted the prorationing laws therefore as accentuating the need for a refiner to integrate backward and as reducing the need for a producer to integrate forward.

It also appeared to the Atlantic management that economic conditions in the refining and marketing phases of the business were such that these activities might not show good profits for some time to come. The management believed therefore that it would be desirable to develop crude oil production as an alternate source of profits, particularly in view of the fact that the prorationing laws seemed to be operating in such a way as to hold crude oil prices at artificially high levels. The thinking of at least some members of the management staff is reflected in the following excerpts from a company memorandum dated March 14, 1934: [13]

At this time our company's crude oil supply merits a larger share of our attention than at any time during the past twenty years. This statement will be amplified hereinafter. For the moment let this suffice: It is nearly inconceivable that refining and marketing expenses can be reduced sufficiently by improvements in efficiency to offset the premium now paid for crude oil under the cartel-made and governmentally supported crude oil price structure.[14]

In the last quarter of 1933 our refineries were charged for crude oil and total manufacturing costs about 14 cents per barrel more than they received for products from crude oil. In January, 1934, they were charged 8 cents per barrel more. The sales department did not recover the refineries' losses. Nor did the producing department's profits provide a sufficient subsidy to cover the deficits of the other named departments. With only short periods of respite, the margins made by crude and product prices have been insufficient to yield an average return on refining and marketing investments since July, 1929. Had it not been for crude pipe line profits, our published statements would have been unsatisfactory indeed.

Under proration and state action to uphold crude prices, the joint operating margin of our two largest divisions is likely to continue unsatisfactory. *A compensating source of profits must be found.*[15]

* * *

The new era, the era which began with proration, brought conditions which threaten our corporate security. In this respect the new era is like the era, 1922–30, which we may designate "the period of integration for crude oil transportation." For us the complications of the earlier period were created by governmentally approved, highly-profitable crude oil pipe line tariffs which we had to pay "out-of-pocket" to the great advantage of certain competitors. In the current era our chief obstacle takes the form of governmentally supported crude prices which we have to pay out-of-pocket regardless of the fact that we cannot recover their equivalent in product prices.

* * *

What we ought to get out of a study of the muddled crude situation are the answers to the series of questions above recited, the most practical of which is: Should we expand our investment for production?

The answer to this question might be yes or no, indifferently, if current conditions in the industry respecting the relation between crude and product prices were like those which existed *before proration,* and especially before 1921. *Certainly there would be no strong reason to engage in the hazardous business of production if crude oil could be bought as cheaply as it could be produced plus a nominal return on the production investment.*[16] But we are no longer assured of a relation between product prices and crude posted prices which provide a profitable margin for our refinery operations or indeed on our joint refinery-marketing investment.

The Atlantic Refining Company undertook its program of increasing crude oil production, despite the fact that the management fully realized that the effect of the proration laws might be to increase the financial investment necessary to develop a given crude oil output. The company's annual report for 1937 contains the following statement.

Although the company's crude oil is produced in those states where proration is the order of the day,—*a form of restraint which increases the financial difficulty of increasing crude production,*[16] —your company increased its daily average crude oil produced for 1937 over 1936 by more than 20%.

This statement is of some interest because, as will be noted in Chapter Thirteen, during this period one of the other companies we studied interpreted the prorationing laws and the increased investment for crude oil production which they seemed to entail as reasons for *reducing* its crude oil producing efforts, at least in areas where the new laws were operative.

Atlantic's crude oil producing program soon

---

[13] The memorandum was prepared by the company's economics department for consideration by the Atlantic management; it did not necessarily represent the conclusions of the Atlantic management.

[14] The writer undoubtedly refers to the period of the operation of the National Industrial Recovery Act.

[15] Italics added by authors.

[16] Italics added by authors.

created a need for additional capital, and in July 1938 the directors asked the stockholders to authorize an increase in the company's indebtedness by amounts not exceeding $50,000,-000 in the aggregate and an increase in the amount of common stock from 4,000,000 to 5,000,000 shares. A letter to the stockholders, dated July 9, 1938, states that the purpose of these arrangements was to put the company in a position: (a) to fund its bank loans and add to its working capital, (b) to achieve a closer balance of crude oil producing and marketing operations, and (c) to take advantage of any opportunity which might arise to purchase or develop additional crude oil production.

In addition to increasing the emphasis which it placed upon crude oil production, the company made certain other important changes in its crude oil operations during the 1930's. Whereas before the company had relied primarily upon its own efforts to find new crude oil producing reserves, in the period 1931–1938, it devoted a considerable proportion of its capital expenditures to the purchase of proven properties. In 1934, for example, about 80% of the new production secured during the year was obtained through the purchase of proven properties. During the early 1930's depressed crude oil prices and the adoption of the prorationing laws combined to create a situation in which many small crude oil producers were willing to sell their properties at fairly low prices. The small producers were in need of capital to continue their oil finding activities, and the general effect of the prorationing laws was to lengthen the payout period on their investments. In lieu of producing their properties slowly over a long period, many small producers chose to recover their capital by sale of their properties and thus to free their assets for reinvestment in further exploratory work or for other purposes.

The Atlantic Refining Company's decision to shift its emphasis from self-developed to purchased production undoubtedly helped to compensate for the management's lack of experience in oil prospecting and may have increased the effectiveness of the company's expenditures for crude oil production. An approximate breakdown of the company's crude oil production by method of development for the period 1930–1949 follows:

THE ATLANTIC REFINING COMPANY

Barrels per Day of Crude Oil Production[17]

Year	From Purchased Producing Properties[18]	From Company-Developed Properties[18]	Total
1930	2,000	7,000	9,056
1935	18,000	8,000	25,956
1940	18,600	18,300	36,875
1945	34,400	33,400	67,809
1949	22,200	42,000	64,210

A change was also made in the methods by which crude oil operations were managed after Mr. Robert H. Colley became president in 1937. Previously the producing department, which had its headquarters in Dallas, Texas, had been required to clear many of its more important actions through the company offices in Philadelphia. As a result, valuable leaseholds were sometimes lost to competitors while the Dallas office was waiting for administrative clearance to go ahead with the deals. After 1937 the department was given a great deal more freedom to take action on its own initiative.

Major Expansion of Crude Oil Production, 1941–1950:

The early years of World War II marked a third major shift in Atlantic's crude oil producing program. At this time the management decided to augment greatly the company's expenditures for crude oil producing properties (see Appendix, Table 20).

The decision rested primarily on two fundamental considerations. The first, and by far the most important, factor in the decision was the feeling of the management that the country was facing a long period of inflation and that a heavy investment in crude oil reserves would constitute a good hedge against rising costs and prices. Atlantic was at this time, like most other oil companies, enjoying good earnings and had substantial sums available for reinvestment in the business. The extent to which the funds could be used for the expansion of pipe line, refinery, and marketing operations was, however, limited by government controls on the use of materials. Moreover, the company was currently producing less than 40% of its crude oil requirements, and there was some question as to the wisdom of expanding other phases of

---

[17] Records of The Atlantic Refining Company.

[18] Figures are approximate and do not have the same accuracy as those in the total column.

the business without first securing additional crude oil producing reserves. From several standpoints therefore an increase in capital expenditures for crude oil production appeared attractive.

A second important consideration in Atlantic's decision to expand its crude oil producing operations was the fact that producing properties could at this particular time be purchased on favorable terms. As was noted earlier, during the period 1931–1938 Atlantic relied heavily upon the purchase of proven reserves as a means of expanding its crude oil production. In 1939 and 1940 the company found it difficult to make satisfactory purchase arrangements, but during the early war years the small producers were, as during the early 1930's, again confronted with conditions which favored sale of their properties.

Crude oil prices were frozen, which precluded any great advance in operating margins. At the same time, income tax rates were rising and appeared likely to remain at high levels for an indefinite period in the future.[19] A number of small producers, and particularly those in high income tax brackets, decided therefore that they could fare better by liquidating their holdings through sale arrangements subject to a capital gains tax of about 25% than they could by producing their properties under the prevailing high income tax rates. The producers who wished to continue in business reinvested the funds secured from the sale transactions in further oil finding efforts. The sale arrangements provided these individuals with a means of turning over their capital quickly and of translating much of their "income" from successful oil finding activities into capital gains subject to lower tax rates than would have applied if they had attempted to produce the properties themselves. As a result of these conditions, Atlantic was able to enter into a number of very satisfactory purchase arrangements in 1941, 1943, and 1944.

The Atlantic management was also probably influenced in its decision to expand crude oil production in 1941 by a desire to do everything possible to protect the company's refineries from a shortage of crude oil during the war period. At this time the shortage of steel pipe imposed some limitations on the extent to which the company could build new crude oil gathering lines as a means of augmenting its assured crude oil supply, and the controls on prices made it impossible to secure additional crude oil through overbidding competitors. The need to assure crude oil for the refineries was not a prime consideration in the problem, however, because throughout most of the war period the distribution of crude oil supplies was subject to government controls.

It is important to note that Atlantic's decision to increase its crude oil operations in the early war period was not influenced in any major way by the company's tax position. It is true that the company was subject to high income taxes and that a large share of any funds spent in finding and developing additional crude oil reserves on its own account could be used as tax offsets. The company's earning base for excess profits tax purposes, however, was so large that there was little danger that it would become subject to excess profits tax rates. As a consequence, tax considerations were far less important in the decision than might otherwise have been the case.

III. The Standard Oil Company (Ohio)'s Backward Integration into Crude Oil Production

The Standard Oil Company (Ohio) [20] was organized in 1870 by John D. Rockefeller and his associates as the first of the companies that later formed the Standard Oil alliance (see Chapter Three). At the time of the dissolution decree in 1911 Sohio became a small independent company engaged in refining and marketing within the state of Ohio. The company served a very high percentage of the Ohio market but had no crude oil production, crude oil purchasing organization, or pipe line transportation facilities of any kind.

For a number of years the company's refining facilities consisted of the two plants in Cleveland which were established as Rockefeller's first manufacturing activities. The com-

---

[19] The excess profits tax proved to be of particular significance to small producers who had recently made crude oil discoveries. Such firms often had both a low capital base and also a low earnings record; as a result their excess profits tax credits were often set at a low level relative to their current earning power.

[20] Hereafter sometimes referred to as "Sohio."

pany's marketing requirements were somewhat larger than its refinery output, and a substantial volume of products was therefore purchased from other refiners. In 1921, however, the company completed a new refinery at Toledo; in 1928 it purchased a refinery at Latonia, Kentucky; and in 1931 it acquired the Solar Refining Company, which had a refinery at Lima, Ohio. These moves served to bring the company's refining and marketing operations reasonably well into balance.

During the 1920's Sohio lost a large share of the Ohio market to new competitors that were crowding into the state under the pressure of the large crude oil supplies discussed in Chapter Four. By 1928 the company's competitive and economic position had become so precarious that a new management and an entirely new board of directors was placed in charge of the company's affairs. Many years later Mr. W. T. Holliday, who was selected as the new president in 1928, summarized the situation as follows:

We had lost most of our dealers. Half of our tank trucks were laid up. Many of our service stations were not selling enough gasoline to pay the rent or occupancy charge, or, in some cases, even the light bill. In other words, our unit costs were rising terrifically, but our selling prices were already too far above the market to be increased.[21]

In the years that followed, the new Sohio management revised the company's price policies to provide for the aggressive meeting of competition; previously the company had been attempting to set its selling prices on the basis of its own manufacturing and transportation costs without due regard for the pricing tactics of the newcomers entering the market. The new management also promptly took many steps to improve the efficiency of the company's marketing activities and products distribution arrangements (see Chapter Nine). In addition, the company gradually integrated backward during the 1930's into crude oil purchasing and transportation operations.

The company made no major effort to develop crude oil production of its own until about 1942. The decision to engage in crude oil production was prompted by certain general

problems which the company faced throughout the period 1928–1942 and which led it to take a number of steps in an effort to improve its crude oil supply situation. The timing of the move in 1942, however, was influenced to a considerable extent by tax considerations and other special circumstances which developed during the early years of World War II.

General Motivations for Integration into Crude Oil Production:

Throughout the period 1928–1942 Sohio was engaged in strenuous efforts to reduce the delivered cost of crude oil to its refineries. The management believed that the company's first and most pressing problem with respect to crude oil costs lay in the high charges the company was compelled to pay for purchasing, gathering, and pipe line transportation rather than in the prices it was charged for the oil at the well-head by the producers. Accordingly, most of the company's early integration efforts were directed toward the improvement of its crude oil purchasing and transportation arrangements. In addition, however, several members of the management group gradually developed the conviction that it would be highly desirable for the company to engage in crude oil production on its own account as soon as it accumulated sufficient financial strength and found a favorable opportunity to do so.

Protection Against Margin Squeezes: [22] In the first place, the management believed that the development of crude oil production would provide the company with some protection against the contractions which sometimes occurred in the gross margin on which it operated. Since the company purchased nearly all its crude oil at the well-head and sold a very high percentage of its gasoline through company operated service stations (see Chapter Twelve, Exhibit XII-25), it was interested

---

[21] *The Sohioan,* a company magazine, March 1950, pp. 2–3.

[22] In the following discussion, we shall endeavor to summarize the views of the Sohio management and the way in which the management's interpretation of economic conditions in the oil industry during the 1930's led to the decision to engage in crude oil production in 1942. Our own analysis and interpretation of the behavior of gross margins at the different levels of the oil industry are contained in Chapters Five and Six. It should be noted that conditions in the Mid-Continent region, which are reflected in the data and discussion in Chapters Five and Six, were occasionally somewhat different from those in the state of Ohio.

primarily in the spread between crude oil prices and retail gasoline prices, a spread which embraced a refining, wholesaling, and retailing margin.

Over a period of years the Sohio management observed that this margin sometimes contracted to the point where it was impossible for the company to operate at a satisfactory profit, regardless of the economies it was able to achieve in its manufacturing, distribution, and marketing arrangements. On some occasions the management had even found that refined products could be bought in the tank car markets at substantially lower prices than the company could manufacture them in its own refineries from purchased crude oil.

The Sohio management believed that the occasional margin contractions were to a considerable extent a natural and inevitable consequence of the fact that crude oil and refined products prices did not always move in precise harmony with each other. The company executives were of the opinion that crude oil and refined products prices responded to the same general set of demand and supply conditions but that crude oil prices were much less sensitive than the product prices and tended to lag behind the product prices in upward and downward adjustments. They further believed that the lag was greater on the downward movements than on the upward movements and that the company thus suffered more from the lags than it gained. The thinking of the Sohio management on these points is revealed in the following statements from the company's annual report for 1931:

The significance to your company of this lack of current synchronization between gasoline and crude oil prices is of course obvious in that during a period of generally declining prices it is obliged to sell gasoline at a market price which *anticipates* lower crude oil prices than have at that time become effective. . . . Of course in periods of rising prices, gasoline prices also tend to move upward first, but the crude oil price tends to follow upward changes in gasoline much more promptly than it follows downward changes.

. . . It is unfortunate that gasoline and crude oil prices do not move together more harmoniously, but it must be recognized that the tendency of gasoline price changes to take place first is for the most part a natural one due to the greater openness and more constant trading in the gasoline mar-

ket. Your company's gasoline prices, however, both wholesale and retail, must be based on the general gasoline price levels, regardless of the cost of crude oil, and it is intended here merely to point out the effect of these factors on your company's operating margins. They are factors which can greatly overshadow, in any particular year, all possible improvements in sales and economies in operation.[23]

The Sohio management also believed that the state prorationing laws were partially responsible for the contractions which sometimes took place in the refining-marketing margin during the 1930's. The Sohio executives believed that the prorationing laws *at this particular time* occasionally operated in such a way as to hold the price of crude oil above the level justified by current conditions in the refined products markets. Since Sohio had to purchase all its crude oil supplies, it suffered severely whenever crude oil prices failed to adjust promptly to a decline in refined products prices. Many of Sohio's competitors, on the other hand, had large crude oil producing operations of their own and were not particularly disturbed by the relationship between crude oil and refined products prices, provided that the over-all realization on refined products was sufficient to permit them a profit on the combined producing-refining-marketing operation.

The Sohio executives believed therefore that the adoption of the prorationing laws accentuated the difficulties arising from the company's lack of crude oil production and had the general effect of increasing the frequency of the occasions on which the company was at a disadvantage in meeting the competition of the producing-refining-marketing companies operating in the state of Ohio. The management reviewed the situation in the company's annual reports for 1932 and 1933 as follows:

Because of the strong economic forces tending toward lower oil prices in 1932, the proration machinery of the important oil states in that year, as never before, became dedicated to the ulterior purpose of price maintenance rather than of simply restricting production to marketing requirements or the avoidance of physical waste. The result was that during 1932 posted crude oil prices at practically all times of the year were kept at a level which made it impossible for the purchaser of crude oil at such posted prices to refine it and to

---

[23] *Annual Report for 1931*, p. 12.

secure a revenue from the finished products equal to the cost.[24]

*   *   *

The cause of this disparity between crude and refined product prices lies principally in the fact that the price of crude oil is to a large extent political, because the number of crude oil producers and royalty owners involved is very large, whereas the refineries which bear the brunt of the discrepancy are relatively few in number, especially after eliminating the refineries which are adjuncts of integrated companies operating on their own crude oil and who for that reason are not directly concerned with the posted price of crude oil as such. It was this political importance attaching to the crude oil price which was pointed out in last year's report as one of the difficulties. That difficulty still exists, and every observer of the industry knows that the present price of crude oil is not warranted on the basis of the value of its refined products. Yet most observers probably would agree that for the time being at least the entire program for the control of crude oil production depends in an important degree upon the maintenance of approximately the present crude oil price.[25]

It would appear therefore that Sohio suffered during the 1930's from somewhat the same circumstances that The Atlantic Refining Company anticipated might develop when it embarked on its first major crude oil producing effort shortly after the prorationing laws were adopted.

The Sohio management believed that the contractions in gross margins which the company experienced in the early 1930's were explainable not only by the circumstances discussed above, but also by the fact that the investment in marketing facilities in Ohio during the 1920's had exceeded the immediate requirements of the market. The management believed that marketing margins had increased during the 1920's as a means of inducing the necessary investment in marketing facilities and had then decreased in the early 1930's as a means of restricting further capital input. The management commented on the situation in 1931 as follows:

It is not intended to imply that all of the decline in the spread between the cost and the retail price of gasoline in 1931 is to be accounted for by

the failure of crude oil prices to decline in harmony with gasoline. It is believed that a substantial part of the shrinkage in this margin has been occasioned by developments in the marketing field alone, which are forcing upon the marketing branch of the industry a narrower spread between wholesale and retail prices. The oil industry through its competition for outlets has set up several times as many outlets as there is any reasonable or economic need for. These extra outlets, with consequent diminution of gallonage per outlet greatly increased the industry's cost per gallon of distribution, but it is useless to suppose that the retail prices necessary to yield a handsome return on such a gross overcapitalization can be secured. New types of marketers, usually not burdened by dealer margins, have entered the industry in recent years, and the cut prices at which they sell (with resulting large volume which reduces their unit cost of marketing) definitely limit the margins available to the marketing branch of the industry. It seems clear that the margin between the retail price and the wholesale tank car price of gasoline has narrowed permanently, and the only sound course is to get the cost of distribution into line with the margin.[26]

The Sohio management recognized that the producing phase of the business frequently had difficulties of its own during the 1930's, sometimes as a result of depressed prices and sometimes as a result of restrictions in the allowable production from wells under the state conservation laws. The management also recognized that Sohio occasionally profited from the fact that it was a buyer of crude oil, particularly during the early 1930's and during the development of the Illinois fields in 1938 and 1939 when distress sales of crude oil were not uncommon. On the whole, however, the Sohio management believed that the company would have had a somewhat more stable and perhaps higher earnings experience during the 1930's had it been engaged in crude oil production.

The interpretation of the Sohio management concerning the effect of backward integration on stability of earnings is corroborated in a general way by the data and discussion in Chapters Five and Six, although conditions in the Mid-Continent region were at times somewhat different from those in the state of Ohio. (In comparing the Sohio situation with the data in Chapters Five and Six, it is important to

24 *Annual Report for 1932*, p. 11.
25 *Annual Report for 1933*, p. 12.

26 *Annual Report for 1931*, p. 14.

note that Sohio did not have the full benefit of the stability of the refining-wholesaling-retailing margin which is revealed in Chapter Five because the company did not carry all its output through the wholesaling and retailing levels. The company sold some refined products in the tank car markets and approximately half of its gasoline in the tank wagon markets.)

An Attractive Source of Profits: A second general consideration which suggested to the Sohio management that it would be desirable for the company to integrate backward into crude oil production was the opportunity for profit which the producing business appeared to provide. The Sohio executives observed that the state conservation laws gradually corrected many of the chaotic and wasteful conditions which had frequently characterized the producing business in earlier years, reduced the violence of the fluctuations in crude oil prices, and generally enhanced the attractiveness of crude oil production from an investment standpoint. Toward the end of the 1930's it appeared to the Sohio management that crude oil producing had become a very profitable activity *for a successful concern* and perhaps the most profitable single phase of the oil business.

It appeared therefore that when Sohio was in a position to undertake a major expansion of its business, it might be desirable for the company to enter the crude oil producing field. The company's entire refining-marketing activities were directed primarily toward the intensive cultivation of the market within the state of Ohio. It was evident that the company might some day approach a saturation point with respect to the business it could secure in the state under one brand name and that further investments in refining and marketing opperations within the state might not yield so good a return as investments in crude oil production. At the same time a major marketing expansion outside the state of Ohio would have posed the difficult problem of developing consumer acceptance for a second brand name, because under the provisions of the dissolution decree of 1911 Sohio was not entitled to use the Standard Oil name in states where other Standard Oil companies were operating.[27] Con-

sequently, there was some reason to believe that it might be preferable for the company to continue its growth and development by engaging in crude oil production rather than by enlarging its refining and marketing operations.

Steps Taken as a Partial Solution to Crude Oil Supply Problems:

Although there was a growing sentiment among the Sohio executives that the company should engage in crude oil production, the company was not in a position to take such a step until sometime after 1940. As will be noted in later discussion, throughout the 1930's the management found it necessary to direct nearly all the company's efforts and financial resources to the task of improving the efficiency of refining, marketing, and transportation arrangements. Nevertheless, a number of steps were taken in the years before 1942 in an effort to improve the position of the company with respect to its crude oil supplies.

Long-Term Contract for Crude Oil: In 1930 Sohio joined with the Standard Oil Company (New Jersey) and the Pure Oil Company in the formation of the Ajax Pipe Line Company to build a crude oil trunk line extending from the Glenn Pool in Oklahoma to Wood River, Illinois. The arrangements for the organization and financing of the new company were somewhat complicated but, in general, provided that Sohio should have approximately a 22% interest in the project. Since there were common carrier pipe lines extending from Wood River to Ohio, the new Ajax line served to provide Sohio with a pipe line connection between its refineries and the Mid-Continent oil fields.

Under a related agreement Sohio entered into a contract to purchase 28,000 barrels of crude oil per day[28] from the Carter Oil Company (wholly owned subsidiary of the Jersey Company) for transmission through the Ajax Pipe Line. At this time 28,000 barrels per day represented about 100% of Sohio's refinery requirements. The original contract provided that Sohio would pay Carter the posted prices for crude oil in the field plus 10 cents per bar-

---

[27] The company had, however, begun to develop a jobber business in Ohio as well as in other states under the Fleet-Wing brand name (see Chapter Seventeen).

[28] The amount was revised to 31,000 barrels per day six months after the original agreement was signed.

rel for purchasing services and 20 cents per barrel for gathering services. The contract was negotiated for a five-year period but was extended in 1935 for an additional five-year period. The provisions of the original agreement were such that if Sohio had failed to renew the contract in 1935, it would have had to surrender its stock in the Ajax Corporation,[29] a holding company organized to hold the stock in the Ajax Pipe Line Company.

At the time the Ajax and Carter arrangements were made, the Sohio management believed that they would be of benefit to the company in that they would provide an opportunity for a material reduction in the delivered cost of crude oil and would assure the company of a large part of its crude oil requirements for a number of years into the future. The Sohio management soon concluded, however, that the charges the company was required to pay for crude oil purchasing, crude oil gathering, and the transmission of crude oil through the Ajax line were far higher than they should be, and the company struggled constantly throughout the early and middle 1930's to secure reductions in the rates.

As a part owner of the Ajax line, Sohio was in a position to receive dividends from the line as a partial offset to the tariffs it paid for pipe line transportation. Since the company provided about 45%–50% of the throughput for the line and had an equity of only about 22%, however, the company suffered far more from high tariffs than it could possibly recover through dividends from the pipe line company. The Sohio management's views of the Ajax and Carter arrangements are indicated by the following excerpts from a brief which Sohio prepared for presentation to the Standard Oil Company (New Jersey) in 1933.[30]

---

[29] In 1936 the Ajax Pipe Line Company and the Ajax Corporation were merged, and the name of the latter was changed to the Ajax Pipe Line Corporation. The Ajax Pipe Line Company was then dissolved and thereafter the pipe line business was conducted by the Ajax Pipe Line Corporation.

[30] It should be clearly understood that the Ajax and Carter contracts were extremely complicated and that we are not attempting to pass judgment on the equity of the arrangements. We are merely presenting the Sohio management's views of the situation as a means of illustrating some of the difficulties the company encountered in its efforts to work out satisfactory arrangements for its crude oil supplies during the 1930's.

In addition to the 20¢ gathering charge, this company pays 10¢ a barrel as a so-called marketing charge, sometimes referred to as commission or brokerage. When, as during the period from the war [World War I] up to 1926, crude was selling at an average price of almost $2.00 per barrel, such a marketing charge may have had some plausibility, but today, at the present price of crude, it represents approximately 23% of the value of the crude itself—a rather ridiculous amount or percentage for a brokerage fee to bear to the cost of the product, especially when the same company [Carter] receives a separate consideration for such transportation as it provides.

*   *   *

There apparently are plenty of producing companies which are glad of an opportunity to sell their oil and take their chances on a producing profit without attempting to collect any special charge for commission. We do not insist that the entire marketing commission should be eliminated in this case, inasmuch as we believe the Carter Oil Company purchases a substantial proportion of the crude furnished. We do believe, however, that it should be reduced to not over 1¢ or 2¢ a barrel. As in the case of the gathering charge, however, we should be glad to rest our case upon a fair consideration of the actual expenses incurred, plus a reasonable profit, as a means of arriving at a fair figure.

*   *   *

The profit for 1931 and 1932 of the Ajax Pipe Line Company, before Federal Income Tax, averaged over 22¢ a barrel—this profit arising solely from the excessive rates received as compared with the cost of operation, depreciation, and interest. If this company obtained the same share of this profit as it contributes thereto, there could be no objection to the high rates as such (except possibly that they tend increasingly to become the target of special tax levies and the like). The truth is, however, that this company contributes considerably more than twice as much of the profit revenue of Ajax as it can ever hope to obtain in return under the present schedule of common stock participation. Of the total crude run through the Ajax line in 1931, 49% was for the account of our company, and in 1932, 47.5%. We therefore contribute almost half of the total revenue and profits of Ajax. In return we have a chance of getting back only approximately 22% of the Ajax profits if our *contingent* participation in the common stock, of about that percentage, finally is made permanent. In other words, we are sharing with others money which does not represent cost of transportation or reasonable profit thereon.

EXHIBIT VIII-3. STANDARD OIL COMPANY (OHIO)

Delivered Cost of Mid-Continent Crude Oil at Toledo Refinery: 1932–1941

Dollars per Barrel

	12/16/32	1/20/33	5/8/33	6/19/33	7/6/33	8/25/33	8/28/33	9/6/33	9/8/33
Average Price at Well-Head	.69	.44	.25	.44	.54	.64	.64	.74	.89
Gathering Charge	.20	.20	.20	.20	.20	.20	.15	.15	.15
Purchasing Fee	.10	.10	.10	.10	—	—	.05	.05	.05
Pipe Line Tariff*	.595	.595	.595	.595	.595	.595	.595	.595	.595
Pipe Line Allowance	.01	.007	.005	.007	.007	.008	.008	.009	.011
Total	1.595	1.342	1.150	1.342	1.342	1.443	1.443	1.544	1.696

	9/29/33	7/20/34	1/9/36	1/28/37	10/13/38	10/15/38	4/1/41	5/21/41	7/30/41
Average Price at Well-Head	1.00	1.00	1.10	1.22	1.02	1.02	1.05	1.15	1.15
Gathering Charge	.15	.10	.10	.10	.10	.10	.10	.10	.10
Purchasing Fee	.05	.05	.05	.05	.05	.05	.05	.05	.01
Pipe Line Tariff*	.595	.5225	.5225	.5225	.5225	.40	.40	.40	.40
Pipe Line Allowance	.012	.0115	.0125	.0137	.0117	.012	.012	.013	.013
Total	1.807	1.6840	1.7850	1.9062	1.7042	1.582	1.612	1.713	1.673

* Includes tariff for Ajax Pipe Line and for other carriers involved in making the shipment. The Ajax tariff was usually about 50% of the total tariff.

SOURCE: Standard Oil Company (Ohio).

It is apparent, from the way in which the common stock participations in Ajax are arranged, that the two other principals in Ajax have an ulterior interest in the highest possible pipe line rates because they obtain a profit from such rates far in excess of the penalty they pay on the transportation of their own oil. Contrary, of course, our company has an interest in low rates, but such interest can hardly be said to be unjustified so long as the rate itself is not below the cost of transportation and does not therefore actually injure the other participants by forcing them to bear a part of the actual cost of transporting oil for our company. It can be seen, however, that it would take a reduction of about 22¢ a barrel in the present rates before this point would be reached.

*   *   *

Because of the payment by this company of total rates for gathering, commission, and main pipe line transportation of crude oil, which are inequitable and excessive to the extent of at least 37¢ a barrel, its cost of finished products delivered to the market is grossly out of line with the corresponding costs of its main competitors which, unlike our own, have been growing constantly less. We have reached the point where these disadvantages can no longer be offset or overcome by efficient and low cost marketing and economies in outbound transportation. We are faced, therefore, with the necessity of obtaining substantial reductions in the cost of getting to the point of sale the products which we can market effectively.[31]

[31] Standard Oil Company (Ohio), memorandum entitled *Arguments for Reduction in Pipe Line and Other Transportation Rates on Crude Oil*, April 20, 1933.

As may be seen from Exhibit VIII-3, Sohio was able to secure some reductions in the crude oil purchasing and gathering charges and in the pipe line tariffs in 1933 and 1934.[32] Further reductions in the pipe line tariffs were secured in 1938 after Sohio had appeared as a plaintiff in a hearing before the Interstate Commerce Commission.[33] Throughout the 1930's, however, the charges for purchasing, gathering, and pipe line transmission remained far higher than the Sohio management believed was warranted in view of competitive conditions and the services performed.

The terms of the Carter contract became particularly onerous when the prolific Illinois fields came into production in 1938 and 1939. These fields provided, temporarily at least, a low-cost source of supply close to the Sohio refineries, and it was apparent that the company could substantially reduce its crude oil costs by developing in Illinois a crude oil gathering and purchasing program of its own. Moreover, competitors quickly took advantage of the new sources of supply to undersell Sohio in the re-

[32] It should be noted that the pipe line tariff in this exhibit represents the cost for the entire haul from Oklahoma to Toledo and thus includes the Ajax as well as other pipe line tariffs.

[33] *Before the I.C.C., Docket No. 26,570, Brief for the Ajax Pipe Line Corporation, Oklahoma Pipe Line Company, Standard Oil Company of Louisiana, Transit and Storage Company, and Tuscarora Oil Company, Ltd.*, and *Reply of the Standard Oil Company (Ohio) and National Refining Company to Pipe Line Briefs of Exceptions*, July 2, 1936.

fined products markets. The situation became so difficult that Sohio was compelled to inform the Carter Oil Company that it could no longer comply with the provisions of the crude oil purchase contract. Fortunately, Carter did not seek the legal recourse available to it under the contract and permitted Sohio to withdraw from the arrangement.

In retrospect it appears therefore that Sohio's effort to assure its crude oil supplies by means of the long-term contract in 1930 eventually created more difficulties for the company than it solved.

Crude Oil Gathering System: In a second effort to strengthen its position with respect to crude oil supplies (and likewise as a means of escaping the high charges exacted for purchasing and gathering service by the Carter Oil Company), Sohio began in 1934 the development of an extensive crude oil gathering system of its own. As was noted in the discussion of Atlantic's second West Texas pipe line, small crude oil producers generally prefer to sell to a buyer who has made an investment in pipe lines and thus committed himself to a long-term purchasing program. Moreover, once a producer has had his tanks connected to a particular gathering system, he does not usually go to the trouble of changing to another buyer unless substantial price premiums or other strong inducements are offered. The development of crude oil gathering lines thus constituted a means by which Sohio could strengthen its position as a buyer of crude oil and gain considerable protection against the loss of supplies and the need to pay premiums in times of crude oil shortages.

The company began its crude oil gathering operations in 1934 with the purchase of a 60% interest in the Fordsville Pipe Line Company which had a small gathering system in Kentucky. In 1935 Sohio commenced the purchasing and gathering of crude oil in the new fields which were being developed in Michigan through the purchase of a 50% interest in the Simrall Corporation (later increased to 75%). In 1937 the Sohio Corporation, a wholly owned subsidiary, was organized to build an extensive crude oil gathering system and engage in direct purchasing activities in the new Illinois fields. By 1940 the Standard Oil Company (Ohio),

through its subsidiaries and affiliates, had become the largest purchaser and gatherer of crude oil in the Illinois, Indiana, and western Kentucky oil fields and one of the largest purchasers and gatherers in Michigan.

The growth of Sohio's crude oil gathering operations is clearly indicated in Exhibit VIII-4. Whereas in 1933 the company made 100% of its crude oil purchases from other gathering companies, in 1940 it made 100% of its purchases direct from producers. It may also be observed from Exhibit VIII-4 that, coincident with the development of its gathering operations, Sohio shifted the source of its crude oil purchases from the Mid-Continent oil fields to points much closer to its refineries. The average distance moved by the crude oil consumed in the company's refineries was reduced from 1,025 miles in 1935 to 465 miles in 1939, and significant savings were thereby made in the company's inward transportation costs.

While the crude oil gathering lines provided a very effective partial answer to Sohio's crude oil supply problem, they were by no means a complete solution to it. There were at least three distinct limitations on the extent to which reliance could be placed on the gathering lines as a device for protecting the company's raw material position. In the first place, Sohio was in a position to build gathering lines in only certain selected situations, such as the Illinois fields, where the crude oil production was developed by a large number of small producers who were anxious to sell to anyone who would make the necessary investment in the gathering lines or by large companies, such as the Amerada Petroleum Corporation, which characteristically sold their output to other concerns at the well-head. In areas such as West Texas, where much of the land was under lease to large integrated oil companies, there was little opportunity for Sohio to build gathering lines as a means of securing crude oil supplies. While the integrated companies might have been willing to have their oil collected by Sohio, they would certainly have reserved the right to use it for their own needs in times of shortage.

A second limitation on the use of crude oil gathering lines as a means of assuring a supply of crude oil arose from the fact that the crude oil reserves in the average producing field were

EXHIBIT VIII-4. STANDARD OIL COMPANY (OHIO)

Source of Crude Oil Purchases: 1929–1940

Percentage of Total

	1929	1930	1931	1932	1933	1934	1935	1936	1937	1938	1939	1940
Crude Oil Purchased from Other Gathering Companies												
Mid-Continent	92%	88%	89%	77%	89%	83%	78%	83%	61%	19%	4%	0
Michigan	5	3	6	7	4	11	8	0	8	2	0	0
Kentucky	0	0	0	7	3	4	0	0	0	0	0	0
Illinois	1	0	3	6	3	0	1	1	0	3	3	0
Ohio	2	2	2	3	1	1	1	1	1	0	0	0
Texas	0	7	0	0	0	0	0	0	0	0	0	0
Subtotal	100%	100%	100%	100%	100%	99%	88%	85%	70%	24%	7%	0
Crude Oil Gathered Direct from Producers												
Michigan	0	0	0	0	0	0	6%	7%	20%	35%	29%	7%
Kentucky	0	0	0	0	0	1%	6	8	7	8	5	4
Illinois	0	0	0	0	0	0	0	0	3	33	57	83
Ohio	0	0	0	0	0	0	0	0	0	0	1	2
Indiana	0	0	0	0	0	0	0	0	0	0	1	4
Subtotal	0	0	0	0	0	1%	12%	15%	30%	76%	93%	100%
GRAND TOTAL	100%	100%	100%	100%	100%	100%	100%	100%	100%	100%	100%	100%

SOURCE: Standard Oil Company (Ohio).

ordinarily subject to decline in a period of about 7 to 14 years. The building of a particular line therefore gave the company access to crude oil for only a limited period of time. Moreover, once the line was on the ground, the company became dependent on the producers in the area to carry on the development work necessary to maintain a satisfactory level of throughput.

A third limitation on the use of the crude oil gathering lines to assure crude oil supplies lay in the fact that most of the oil secured from the small producers was purchased, in accordance with the general industry practice, under arrangements which were subject to cancellation on a day-to-day basis. Consequently, although a crude oil producer might be slow to make a new crude oil gathering line connection, he was always free to do so on very short notice whenever the pressures on him became sufficiently great.

Crude Oil Purchasing Program: As a third means of strengthening and protecting its raw material position, Sohio gave a great deal of attention, along with the development of its crude oil gathering systems, to the task of establishing and maintaining favorable relationships with the many small producers which it

served. The company regarded the problem of crude oil supplier relationships as closely parallel to that of gasoline dealer relationships in the marketing field. The thinking of the executives on this matter is reflected in the following statements from a company memorandum dated November 11, 1939:

But let us look at the purchasing process itself in the fields. First, there is the job of lining up the "connection." Wooing a producer is just about the same as wooing a dealer, and I think most of our men in Simrall and Sohio would enter the typical producer against the typical dealer in any contest of temperamentality with great confidence. If one of the articles of faith of the average dealer is that he should get a lower cost price, then certainly it is one of the articles of faith of the average producer that he should get a higher price for his oil, to say nothing of larger runs and various other favors. We do not, however, say this in criticism of the average producer, who is simply a human being like most of us.

* * *

We have already mentioned the producer's problems, but studying, considering and dealing with customer complaints, and trying to keep him happy generally is a very large order. On occasions, it involves lending money to the producer whose development expenses may have outrun his cash balance, although he may have good equity.

On various occasions of this sort, we have loaned money, and tapping on wood, we are glad to say that we have not lost any of it yet.

Our sales officials are familiar with the problems involved in attempting to determine what gasoline prices to post. Here again we believe the men in our crude purchasing activities will refuse to yield to the sales department in the difficulties and problems involved in attempting to decide upon crude oil prices and price changes. Naturally, other things being equal, we are interested in buying at the lowest prices we can, but this must be tempered with the long-run question of retaining the good-will of the producer, and protecting his interest as well as our own.[34]

Sohio was among the first of the large oil companies to place major emphasis on the development of close ties with the small crude oil suppliers, and its efforts in this respect unquestionably stood the company in good stead in times of crude oil shortages.

Policy of Overbuying Crude Oil Requirements: As another means of making sure that it had access to adequate supplies of crude oil at satisfactory prices, Sohio developed the practice of purchasing quantities of crude oil somewhat in excess of its own immediate refinery requirements. The excess of crude oil purchased was regularly resold to others at prices which provided Sohio a small profit for handling. The policy of buying in excess of requirements helped the company to establish its position as a consistent and continuous buyer from many independent producers and also provided a small reserve supply to protect the company's refinery operations in times of shortage.

Limited Crude Oil Production: The final measure taken by the company as a partial solution to its crude oil supply problem in the period before 1942 was the development of a very small amount of crude oil production of its own. It is interesting to note that each of the initial steps involved a successively deeper penetration into the crude oil producing business. The first move was the purchase of 20,000 acres of oil and gas leases from the Kentucky Natural Gas Company in 1937. About 4,300 acres of this land were already proven and contained 218 producing wells which

were already connected to the Sohio gathering system. The second step, taken in 1938, involved the purchase of interests in some proven and semiproven leases in the Birk City field in Kentucky and the Freeman field in north central Michigan upon which the company did a good deal of its own development drilling. The third move, in 1939, involved the acquisition of a one-half interest in 60,000 acres in southwestern Michigan and smaller holdings in central Michigan, Illinois, and Indiana; upon this land the company planned to undertake exploratory drilling in the hope of finding oil. Notwithstanding these moves, however, the company's crude oil production never amounted to more than 2% of refinery requirements in any year before 1942.

Specific Motivations for Engaging in Crude Oil Production in 1942:

The Standard Oil Company (Ohio) might have continued to rely for some years upon the various partial solutions to its crude oil supply problem outlined above had it not been for certain special circumstances which developed in the early years of World War II. The possibility of engaging in crude oil production had been under discussion in the management group for a considerable period of time, and although some of the executives were thoroughly convinced that the move should be made, others were dubious about the wisdom of entering a new field so different from that in which the company had been engaged in the past.

By 1941 the company had got into a position where it could do a refining and marketing job in the state of Ohio on a highly competitive basis. It had developed low-cost transportation facilities for both its crude oil and refined products; its refineries were well located to serve the Ohio market and were fully comparable in equipment and efficiency with those of its competitors; its market outlets were among the best in the state; and its brand names were well accepted by Ohio consumers. Once the depression and the general contraction in refining and marketing margins in Ohio had been weathered, the company was able to earn reasonably good profits (see Chapter Twelve, Exhibit XII-2).

It was apparent that the development of

---

[34] Company memorandum, *The Supply and Transportation Department*, White Sulphur Springs Conference, November 4, 1939, pp. 31 and 32.

any substantial crude oil producing program would require the expenditure of very large sums of money and would provide the company with lower crude oil costs over the long run only if conducted very successfully. All the company's management skill and experience, however, were related almost exclusively to the transportation, refining, and marketing phases of the business. Moreover, there was a possibility that once the crude oil producing program was initiated, it might require so much management attention and such large capital investments that it might sap the company's strength in the refining-marketing field.

In spite of the general motivations for integration into crude oil production discussed above, there was therefore much to be said in favor of continuing to concentrate the company's efforts on the performance of a highly effective refining and marketing job in the limited geographic area of the state of Ohio. The decision to undertake the crude oil producing program was reached only after a fairly long period of careful deliberation within the management group. The specific circumstances which tipped the balance in favor of the decision were threefold:

Financial Position of Sohio: By 1942 the company had for the first time in 20 years got into a position when it was financially able to support a large-scale producing effort. In earlier years the company had faced such critical problems with respect to its refining and marketing operations that the management had deemed it prudent to concentrate the company's limited financial resources on the task of arresting and reversing the currently unfavorable trends in those phases of the business in preference to embarking on new programs. By 1942, however, the refining and marketing operations were in excellent shape, largely as a result of the development of adequate transportation facilities. Moreover, during the early months of the war the company's earnings were sufficient to make some excess funds available for investment purposes. In the company's annual report for 1944 the management commented as follows:

The outstanding development in your company in the last year or two has been the progress it has made in the production end of the business.

The company has for many years been conscious of the desirability of having substantial crude oil production of its own. With this in mind, it undertook a number of years ago to take some very minor steps in this direction.

The company could not of course have expected to solve the problem of procuring the large quantities of crude oil required for its refineries through the acquisition or development of its own production to any great extent at that time, and considering the fundamental importance of its refining and marketing position, it was felt more practicable first to attain as much independence as possible in the crude oil purchase and transportation ends of the business. For a number of years, therefore, the company concentrated its attention, so far as crude oil procurement was concerned, on these aspects of the problem rather than on production. *Relatively large capital expenditures for gathering, trunk pipe line and river transportation facilities were required, but nothing like the amounts that would have been needed to obtain any substantial quantity of crude oil production in relation to the company's refinery runs.*[35]

The gathering and transportation part of the solution was largely completed several years ago, and this fact, together with the increasing financial strength and profitable volume of operations of the company, enabled it to give real attention to the problem of crude oil production. . . .[36]

Availability of Crude Oil Producing Properties for Purchase: A second circumstance which contributed to the company's decision to integrate into crude oil production in 1942 was the fact, noted in the discussion of Atlantic's producing program, that there were during the early years of World War II a number of producing properties available for purchase. This circumstance was particularly important to Sohio because it provided a good means by which a company with limited experience in crude oil exploration activities could get into the crude oil producing business. In the period following 1942 the company acquired several crude oil producing concerns, including the Adams Oil and Gas Company (1943), The Margay Oil Corporation (1945), the Sharon Drilling Company (1946), the Aylward Production Company (1947), and the Felmont Corporation (1947).

---

[35] Italics added by authors.
[36] *Annual Report for 1944*, pp. 8–9.

Tax Position of Sohio: The most important reason why Sohio made the decision to begin crude oil producing operations at the particular time it did in 1942 may be found in the company's position with respect to the excess profits tax. Throughout the latter 1930's the company had made many improvements in its transportation facilities and had taken other steps to improve its operating position. By 1941 therefore its earnings potential was high relative to its earnings record in the years 1935–1939, the base period for excess profits tax purposes. In 1941 the company incurred an excess profits tax liability of $4,600,000,[37] and its total tax bill was $7,300,000, or about 54% of its net income before taxes. There was, moreover, every reason to suppose that the company would be exposed to taxes of comparable magnitude for the next several years.

The provisions of the Internal Revenue Act with respect to exploration and production activities, however, were such that a large share of the expenditures for the development of crude oil reserves and crude oil production could be charged off against current income for tax purposes. It was apparent therefore that the company could undertake a crude oil producing program and finance a large share of the necessary expenditures from sums which might otherwise be paid to the government in the form of taxes. In the company's annual report for 1942 the management commented as follows:

During 1942, your company considerably expanded its production activities. The generally accepted need of increased exploration activity to add to the industry's crude oil resources, together with the ability to charge off against current income unsuccessful exploration expenditures as well as the cost (other than equipping) of drilling productive wells, have made it seem desirable for the company to accelerate its activities in the field of production. These activities have taken the form of increased lease purchases and exploratory drilling not only in areas such as Michigan, Kentucky, and Illinois where most of the company's former production efforts were concentrated, but also in other areas, principally in Texas, Arkansas, and Louisiana.[38]

The relationship of tax considerations to the decision made by the Sohio management may be clarified by reference to Exhibit VIII-5. The table shows an approximate breakdown of the costs involved in finding and developing crude oil reserves and indicates how the costs would normally be separated between capitalized and expensed items for financial purposes and for tax purposes. Costs of this type cannot, of course, be determined with any very great degree of precision and vary considerably from company to company, from year to year, and from one geographic area to another. The figures shown, however, are sufficiently representative of general industry experience to be useful in illustrating the nature of the tax situation.[39]

The figures in the table include all costs except those involved in actually bringing the oil to the surface. They might thus be said to represent the cost of establishing a fully equipped "crude oil producing plant." As indicated by the table, approximately three-quarters of the costs may be charged off against current income in the year in which they are incurred. It is immediately apparent therefore that a company has much to gain from expanding its crude oil producing plant at times when it is subject to abnormally high tax rates, because in such periods a larger share of the expenditures for the plant may be drawn from sums that would otherwise be paid out in taxes than is normally the case. In effect, the mechanism of the tax laws provides for accelerated amortization on a one-year basis of about three-fourths of the cost of the crude oil producing plant.

In 1941 it appeared that Sohio would be facing an excess profits tax of about 90% on at least part of its income for the next several years.[40] The management decided therefore

---

[37] This amount was later much reduced through carry-back provisions on the amortization of refinery facilities and various other adjustments.

[38] *Annual Report for 1942*, p. 8.

[39] The analysis in Exhibit VIII-5 is based upon an estimated finding and development cost of $1.50 per barrel of proven reserves. Finding and development costs are usually estimated by the larger companies in the industry as falling somewhere between $0.80 and $1.50 per barrel of proven reserves.

[40] The Internal Revenue Act of 1941 provided for a normal tax of 24% and a surtax of 6% on the first $25,000 of taxable income; for taxable income in excess of $25,000 the surtax was 7%. The combined normal and surtax rate for a large corporation was thus very close to 31%. The excess profits tax was, however, deductible in determining the income tax base. The excess profits tax ranged from 35% on the first $20,000 of adjusted excess profits net income to

EXHIBIT VIII-5. COST OF FINDING AND DEVELOPING 10 MILLION BARRELS OF CRUDE
OIL RESERVES: 1952*

(Includes All Costs Prior to Actual Production)

Cost Item	Amount ($1,000)	Cost per Barrel	Percent-age of Total	Separation of Costs for Financial Purposes		Separation of Costs for Tax Purposes	
				Capitalized Items, % of Total	Expensed Items, % of Total	Capitalized Items, % of Total	Expensed Items, % of Total
Lands and Exploration	$ 3,700	$ .37	24.7%				
Geological, Geophysical, and Other Exploration	1,500	.15	10.0		10.0%	5.0% †	5.0%
Test Well Contributions	100	.01	0.7		0.7		0.7
Lease Rentals	700	.07	4.7		4.7		4.7
Overhead	1,400	.14	9.3		9.3		9.3
Leasehold Costs	1,400	.14	9.3				
Productive Properties	200	.02	1.3	1.3%		1.3	
Acquired and Surrendered	1,200	.12	8.0		8.0‡		8.0
Intangible Drilling Costs	7,100	.71	47.4				
Exploratory Wells: Dry Holes	1,700	.17	11.3		11.3		11.3
Productive	400	.04	2.7	2.7§			2.7
Development Wells: Dry Holes	800	.08	5.3		5.3		5.3
Productive	4,200	.42	28.1	28.1§			28.1
Lease and Field Equipment	2,600	.26	17.3	17.3		17.3	
Auxiliary Equipment	200	.02	1.3	1.3		1.3	
Total Expenditures	$15,000	$1.50	100.0%	50.7%	49.3%	24.9%	75.1%

* This table has been prepared to indicate the relative significance of various items of cost and the manner in which they are handled for financial and tax purposes. The figure of $1.50 per barrel for finding and development costs used in the analysis should not be taken as an industry average or as representative of the experience of any one company. Finding and development costs are very difficult to determine and are usually estimated as falling between about $0.80 and $1.50 per barrel of proven reserves.

† Assumes 50% of geological and geophysical expenses are capitalized for tax purposes.

‡ Leasehold costs are treated as a capital item at the time incurred but are expensed when surrendered.

§ A few companies expense these items for both financial and tax purposes.

SOURCE: Standard Oil Company (Ohio).

that the immediate future offered the company an opportunity to develop crude oil production at a far lower net cost after taxes than had been possible in prior years or might be possible in the years after the close of the war.

The foregoing discussion suggests that by properly regulating the flow of funds into crude oil exploration and producing activities, a company can modify the impact of an excess profits tax to a considerable degree. Some indication of the usefulness of a well-managed crude oil producing program as a buffer against an excess profits tax and of the

60% on excess profits net income in excess of $500,000. The excess profits tax credit was set at 95% of average earnings in the base period, 1936 to 1939, or at 8% of invested capital. A specific exemption of $5,000 was allowed in the computation of the excess profits tax net income. (See *National Tax Journal*, Vol. IV, No. 3, September 1951, pp. 241–250.)

peculiarly vulnerable tax position of Sohio in 1941 relative to that of the other major oil companies may be secured from Exhibit VIII-6. The table shows the normal and excess profits tax liabilities of 17 major oil companies in the year 1941 as a percentage of the net income they reported for financial purposes in their annual reports. The table also indicates each company's ratio of crude oil production to refinery runs. Three of the companies did not show excess profits taxes as a separate item, but if the normal taxes of these companies were about the same proportion of financial income as in the case of the other companies, their excess profits taxes could not have been very large.

It appears from the table that Sohio alone had a greater excess profits tax liability than at least 13 other major oil companies put to-

EXHIBIT VIII-6. COMPARISON OF PROFITS AND TAXES FOR 17 LARGE OIL COMPANIES; 1941

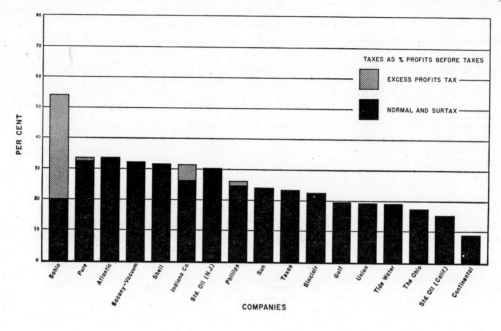

DATA FOR INDIVIDUAL COMPANIES: 1941

($ Figures in Millions)

		Federal Income Taxes			Taxes as % of Profits Before Taxes				Domestic Crude Oil Production As % of Domestic Refinery Runs
Company	Profits Before Taxes	Normal and Surtax	Excess Profits Tax	Total Taxes	Normal and Surtax	Excess Profits Tax	Total Taxes	Profits After Taxes	
Standard Oil Company (Ohio)	$ 13.5	$ 2.7	$4.6	$ 7.3	20.0%	34.0%	54.0%	$ 6.2	0.7%
Pure Oil Company	23.0	7.5	0.2	7.7	32.6	0.9	33.5	15.3	77.6
The Atlantic Refining Company	21.5	7.2	0	7.2	33.5	0	33.5	14.3	36.5
Socony-Vacuum Oil Company	63.6	20.5†	0	20.5†	32.2†	0	32.2†	43.1	43.2
Shell Union Oil Corporation	31.2	9.9	0	9.9	31.9	0	31.9	21.3	63.3‡
Standard Oil Company (Indiana)	70.8	18.5	3.9	22.4	26.2	5.4	31.6	48.4	35.6
Standard Oil Company (New Jersey)	201.2	60.6	*	60.6	30.2	*	30.2	140.6	48.8
Phillips Petroleum Company	23.5	5.8	0.3	6.1	24.7	1.3	26.0	17.4	109.2
Sun Oil Company	21.7	5.2	0	5.2	24.0	0	24.0	16.5	34.7
The Texas Company	67.9	15.8	*	15.8	23.3	*	23.3	51.9	64.0
Sinclair Oil Corporation	24.5	5.5	0	5.5	22.5	0	22.5	19.0	36.4
Gulf Oil Corporation	44.3	8.7	0	8.7	19.6	0	19.6	35.6	47.3
Union Oil Company	7.7	1.5	0	1.5	19.5	0	19.5	6.2	59.5
Tide Water Associated Oil Company	19.2	3.7	0	3.7	19.3	0	19.3	15.5	55.0
The Ohio Oil Company	13.1	2.3	0	2.3	17.5	0	17.5	10.8	378.4
Standard Oil Company (California)	39.0	6.0	*	6.0	15.4	*	15.4	33.0	63.4
Continental Oil Company	16.9	1.5	0	1.5	8.9	0	8.9	15.4	168.9
Average, 17 Oil Companies					23.6	2.5	26.1		
Average, Excluding Standard Oil Company (Ohio)					23.8	0.5	24.3		

⁰ Company annual report explicitly states " no excess profits taxes paid."

* Company annual report does not separate excess profits tax or indicate whether such taxes were paid in 1941, but reports one item for "income and excess profits taxes."

† Includes some small amount of state taxes.

‡ Ratio based on 1940 operations.

SOURCE: Annual reports of the oil companies. Adapted with modifications from an article by Paul Ryan, *World Petroleum*, November 1942.

gether. It is also clear that Sohio's normal tax bill was a substantially higher percentage of its net income than in the case of the other companies and particularly those companies with fairly large producing businesses relative to their refinery runs.

Whereas the combined normal and surtax rate for a large corporation in 1941 was very close to 31%, it may be observed from Exhibit VIII-6 that several companies with large producing businesses paid a tax bill of only about 15% to 25% of their financial income. This circumstance is explainable by the fact that a company engaged in crude oil production, if reasonably successful, usually has a very different and generally lower net income for tax purposes than it reports for financial purposes. Although accounting practices vary considerably from company to company, the difference between financial income and taxable income ordinarily arises from two principal causes, as outlined below.

In the first place, as indicated in Exhibit VIII-5, most companies capitalize their intangible development costs for financial purposes and expense them for tax purposes.[41] At times when a company is accelerating its exploration and development effort, its taxable income may therefore be substantially smaller than its financial income. Conversely, deceleration of the exploration and development effort has the effect of making the taxable income larger than the financial income.

A second reason for differences between financial and taxable income may be found in the fact that the financial income of most companies reflects primarily cost depletion whereas the taxable income reflects primarily percentage depletion. The tax law provides that a company may deplete the value of its leaseholds on a cost basis, or in lieu thereof may deduct $27\frac{1}{2}\%$ of the gross income from each property, provided that the amount so deducted does not exceed 50% of the net income from the property. In figuring the net income from a leasehold, however, all intangible development expenses incurred during the year must be charged against the gross receipts on oil produced from the property. In the first year or two of development, when the intangible costs are high, a lease often shows a loss and no percentage depletion may be taken. In such periods, depletion is taken on a cost basis for both financial and tax purposes. As soon as the lease produces sufficient income to permit a greater deduction by percentage depletion than by cost depletion, the percentage method is used for tax purposes and the cost method for financial purposes.

Percentage depletion on a producing leasehold usually far outstrips cost depletion because the income producing potential of the property is usually greater than was reflected in the leasehold cost which was incurred prior to the discovery of oil. As a general rule therefore the use of percentage depletion for tax purposes *in the case of a successful producing company* tends to state the taxable income at a substantially lower figure than the financial income.[42]

The extent to which the differences between taxable and financial income implied by the data in Exhibit VIII-6 were a product of the two considerations mentioned above or of other circumstances cannot be determined without a detailed examination of the records of each company. It is very clear, however, that

---

[41] If the intangible costs were capitalized as part of the leasehold investment for tax purposes, a company would forego the opportunity to write off such items whenever it claimed percentage depletion. This situation arises from the fact that percentage depletion is allowed in lieu of, rather than in addition to, cost depletion.

[42] A third general difference between the taxable and financial income of oil companies arose after 1950 from provisions in the tax law for the handling of geological and geophysical expenses. For financial purposes these costs are usually expensed as incurred. For tax purposes, however, the law now requires that a reasonable portion of the expenses must be capitalized as a part of the cost of the leases acquired or retained as a result of the survey work. In a typical exploratory program, the capitalized portion of the costs might amount to about 50% of the total. As a result, acceleration of the geological and geophysical work tends to reduce financial income relative to taxable income and deceleration of the work has the reverse effect.

The handling of geological and geophysical expense thus has an effect on the relationship of taxable to financial income opposite to that of the handling of intangible development costs discussed above. As indicated in Exhibit VIII-5, however, in an ordinary program geological and geophysical expenses are usually far smaller in amount than are intangible development expenses. Moreover, the effect of capitalizing geological and geophysical expenses is to some extent modified by the fact that the value of surrendered leaseholds, which are expense for both tax and financial purposes, always runs somewhat higher for tax than for financial purposes by virtue of whatever capitalized geological and geophysical costs may have been allocated to such leaseholds.

whatever steps the companies with producing activities took toward expansion of their exploratory and development work during the early years of the war certainly served to reduce their exposure to the excess profits tax. The Standard Oil Company (Ohio), on the other hand, was vulnerable to the prevailing high tax rates because it had no comparable opportunity to develop immediate tax credits through the expansion of its refining and marketing business, except to the limited extent of securing accelerated amortization on plant facilities.

Results of the Crude Oil Producing Program:

The operations of Sohio's crude oil producing department for the eight-year period 1942–1949 resulted in a net loss of $3.4 million so far as the financial records were concerned. At the end of the period the assets of the producing department had a net book value of $45.9 million as contrasted with a beginning value of $0.4 million. The net investment of the company in the program during the eight-year period was thus $48.9 million. At the close of the period the producing department estimated that it had 68.2 million barrels of developed reserves, 16.6 million barrels of proven, undeveloped reserves, and 25 million barrels of possible reserves. In one sense, the financial success of the program might be determined by measuring the market value of these reserves against the net investment of $48.9 million.

For tax purposes, however, the operations of the producing department over the eight-year period showed a loss of $38.6 million which was applied as a tax credit against the earnings generated by the company's refining and marketing operations. Because of the numerous adjustments which were made in the company tax status during the war years, it is almost impossible to determine what the company's tax rate would have been had the tax credits from producing operations not been available. Actually the company paid an effective tax rate of about 46% during the first four years of the eight-year period and a rate of about 38% during the remaining four years. If the tax credit generated in each of the years is valued at these conservative rates, the total tax saving to the company over the eight-year

period was $16.8 million.[43] It might thus be said that the actual out-of-pocket cost to the company of building the crude oil producing plant represented by the reserves on hand at the end of the period was not $48.9 million but $32.1 million. Moreover, to the extent that the tax credits were generated and applied in a period of abnormally high tax rates, the program was certainly less costly to the company than would have been the case in times of normal tax rates.

IV. THE STANDARD OIL COMPANY (INDIANA)'S BACKWARD INTEGRATION INTO CRUDE OIL PRODUCTION

For a number of years after the dissolution decree in 1911, the Standard Oil Company (Indiana) remained a refining and marketing company and made no significant attempt to acquire crude oil production. As noted in Chapter Seven, the company was at this time operating three principal refineries, a 35,000 barrels per day plant at Whiting, Indiana, a 20,000 barrels per day plant at Wood River, Illinois, and a 15,000 barrels per day plant at Sugar Creek, Missouri. All three of these plants were constructed while the Indiana Company was still affiliated with the Standard Oil combination. The Whiting plant was built in 1890 to handle the crude oil output of the newly discovered Lima-Indiana fields; the Sugar Creek refinery was constructed in 1904 to take advantage of the new discoveries of "sweet" crude oil near Neodesha, Kansas; and the Wood River refinery was built in 1908 to draw upon the crude oil reserves developed in southern Illinois in 1905. The company's fourth refinery was constructed at Casper, Wyoming, in 1914 as a result of the development of new crude oil production in the Rocky Mountain area.

To a certain extent therefore the Indiana Company solved its crude oil supply problems in the early years of its history by building its refineries near major new producing areas as they were developed, an expedient which was used time and again throughout the history of the industry by both large and small refiners as will be demonstrated in Chapter Twenty-One. Before 1911 the Indiana Com-

---

[43] It should be noted that the tax saving arose only because the company had profitable operations in other areas which were at this time subject to high tax rates.

pany was also, of course, assured of crude oil supplies by the crude oil producing, gathering, and transportation agencies of the Standard Oil group.

The crude oil for all the Indiana Company's refineries in the period 1911–1917 was obtained entirely through purchase arrangements. The company's principal supplier was the Prairie Oil and Gas Company which prior to the dissolution decree in 1911 had been the crude oil buying and transportation agency of the Standard Oil group in the Mid-Continent area. After the dissolution decree, the Prairie Oil and Gas Company continued for a number of years to supply the various members of the Standard Oil group in much the same manner as it had in the past.

The Indiana Company began its crude oil producing program in 1917 and thereafter gradually expanded its producing efforts until in 1952 it was supplying about 50% of its refinery runs from its own domestic output. For convenience in discussion, the development of the company's producing program will be divided into three time periods: (a) the period 1917–1921, a time of crude oil shortage in which the company acquired its first domestic producing properties; (b) the period 1921–1931, a time of ample crude oil supplies during which the company acquired both domestic and foreign producing properties; and (c) the period 1932–1952, which marked the company's disposal of its foreign properties and during which the company became firmly established as one of the major crude oil producers in the United States.

Development of Domestic Production, 1917–1921:

In March 1917 the stockholders of the Indiana Company voted to amend the company's charter in order that the company might engage in the production of crude oil and in the transportation of crude oil and refined products; [44] previously the company had been chartered to engage in refining and marketing activities alone. In August 1917 the Indiana Company started its acquisition of producing properties by purchasing some small properties from John A. Bell, Jr., which were located in Montgomery, Chautauqua, and Butler counties in

Kansas, at a reported price of $1,500,000.[45] In the following month Lauren J. Drake, a vice president of the Indiana Company, stated that the Bell acquisition was the forerunner of other purchases and that the company stood ready to increase its holdings of producing lands.[45]

The Bell acquisition and the subsequent efforts which the Indiana Company made to acquire crude oil production in the period 1917–1921 were apparently prompted by the immediate difficulties the company was encountering in obtaining adequate crude oil supplies for its refining operations. The entire period 1916–1921 was characterized by severe crude oil shortages in the United States which arose from two principal causes. In the first place, an enormous increase occurred in the demand for crude oil between 1916 and 1921 as a result of the rapid commercial development of the automobile and the corresponding growth in the domestic market for gasoline. A second major cause of the crude oil shortages was the great demand for oil products occasioned by World War I and particularly by the participation of the United States therein, beginning in 1917. The war drastically curtailed shipments of crude oil from the Middle East to France and England and also resulted in the destruction of certain European refineries. As a result, oil products were urgently needed not only to fuel the war machinery of the United States but likewise that of France and Great Britain. A particularly significant increase took place in the demand for fuel oil to supply merchant vessels and the British Navy and in the demand for gasoline to supply airplanes, tanks, motor trucks, and other mechanized military equipment.

One immediate manifestation of the crude oil shortages which began in 1916 was the formation of a large number of new producing companies. It was estimated that during 1916 about 210 new companies with a total capitalization of $419,000,000 were organized to engage in crude oil finding activities.[46] In the first six months of 1917, 260 new oil and gas companies were organized with a total capitalization of $355,000,000; 112 of these companies were organized in the months of May and

[44] *Moody's Manual*, 1918, p. 1544.

[45] Ibid.
[46] *National Petroleum News*, July 1917, p. 87.

June alone.[47] By August 1918 the shortage of crude oil at eastern refineries was so great that gasoline-less Sundays were inaugurated, and tankers were standing idle in seaports awaiting cargoes for overseas shipment. In October 1918 the United States Government, which had already assumed control of the oil industry, worked out plans for the allocation of crude oil to needy refineries. At the same time federal action was taken to prohibit the purchase of crude oil by refiners at premium prices, a step which was decried by many refiners on the grounds that it would make it impossible for them to obtain adequate crude oil supplies. The war ended early in November 1918, but the restrictions on premium prices were continued until December 18, 1918.

The crude oil shortages in the period 1916–1921 occasioned intense competition among refiners for available supplies, and the Indiana Company found it increasingly difficult to purchase the large quantities needed for its extensive refining operations. For a time in the early part of 1918 the company's Whiting refinery was receiving only 18,000 barrels of crude oil per day in contrast to its normal requirement of 55,000 barrels per day and it had 110 stills standing idle.[48] At the same time, however, the company's marketing operations continued to expand at an extremely rapid rate in response to the wartime increase in industrial activity and the increase in the domestic consumption of automotive gasoline. Since any expansion in refining operations was precluded both by the shortage of crude oil and by the difficulties involved in securing steel and other necessary materials, the Indiana Company was forced to meet a large share of the increase in demand from its customers through purchases from other refiners.

The Indiana Company purchased not only large volumes of gasoline and kerosene but likewise large volumes of distillate and residual fuel oil. The latter products were transported in tank cars to the Indiana Company's refineries where they were further processed in the company's Burton pressure stills, thus serving to augment the company's output of gasoline. The Burton pressure stills, which were developed by Dr. William M. Burton of the Indiana Company about 1911, represented one of the earliest commercially feasible thermal cracking processes. Most refiners in the period 1916–1921 had not yet installed thermal cracking equipment of any kind, and as a result the Indiana Company was often able to purchase distillate and residual fuel oil as charging stocks on very reasonable terms. In 1918 the Indiana Company's total purchases of crude oil, casinghead gasoline, distillate, and residual fuel oil in the Mid-Continent region were estimated at about $75,000,000.[49]

For a time, the Indiana Company made most of its refined product purchases through brokers. By 1919, however, the company's purchasing activities had become so extensive that the management decided to establish a buying office in Tulsa to deal directly with refiners. According to trade reports, the new buying office purchased some 3,000 tank cars of gasoline during November and December 1919 from independent refiners in Oklahoma. In January 1920 there were trade reports that the Indiana Company had contracted for the purchase of about 85,000,000 gallons of gasoline and 42,000,000 gallons of kerosene from the Cosden Refining Company in West Tulsa. In November 1920 there was a further report that the Indiana Company had renewed the Cosden contract for a period of one year for an amount of 200,000,000 gallons of gasoline and 50,000,000 gallons of kerosene.[50] Notwithstanding these extensive purchasing operations, there were a number of occasions during the period 1916–1920 when the Indiana Company's bulk plants were lacking refined products and the company's customers were forced to turn to other suppliers.

In the light of the foregoing circumstances, it is not difficult to understand why the Indiana Company began in 1917 to develop crude oil producing properties of its own. The next major step after the Bell acquisition in 1917 was the purchase of a 90% interest (later 100%) in the Dixie Oil Company, Inc., of Shreveport, Louisiana. The purchase was made in November 1919 at a price of approximately

---

[47] *National Petroleum News*, July 1917, p. 87.

[48] For data on this point we are indebted to Dr. Paul H. Giddens, president of Hamline University, who has been engaged in a historical study of the Standard Oil Company (Indiana).

[49] *National Petroleum News*, March 26, 1919, p. 32.

[50] *National Petroleum News*, November 17, 1920, p. 40.

$1,648,000.[51] The Dixie Oil Company, which had been organized in 1917, had producing properties in what was known as the "heavy" Caddo field of Louisiana. The company's crude oil production in 1917, however, was only about 1,500 barrels per day. As a subsidiary of the Indiana Company, the Dixie Oil Company subsequently acquired substantial prospective acreage and developed production in Louisiana, Arkansas, Kansas, Oklahoma, Texas, and Georgia.

The Indiana Company gained access to a very important source of crude oil in 1920 and 1921 by exchanging shares of its stock for 98% of the stock of the Midwest Refining Company. The Midwest Refining Company had been organized in 1914 pursuant to an agreement between the principal stockholders of the Midwest Oil Company and the Franco Petroleum Company. The latter two companies both had substantial producing interests in the Salt Creek field in Wyoming and operated small refineries at Casper, Wyoming, in competition with each other. The agreement under which the Midwest Refining Company was organized provided for the transfer of the refineries of the Midwest Oil Company and the Franco Petroleum Company to the Midwest Refining Company. At the same time the Midwest Refining Company was given a contract providing that it should have the right to purchase all the Salt Creek production of the Midwest Oil Company and the Franco Petroleum Company for a period of 20 years. Subsequently, the Midwest Refining Company became one of the most important refining and marketing companies in the Rocky Mountain area and eventually developed substantial crude oil production of its own.

The business association between the Indiana Company and the Midwest Refining Company began about 1914. At that time the latter was having difficulty in disposing of its distillate and residual fuel oil output because there was very little industrial activity in the Wyoming area. The Midwest executives learned of the Indiana Company's Burton cracking process

and negotiated an arrangement with the Indiana Company whereby the latter agreed to build Burton pressure stills in Wyoming to run on charging stocks supplied from the Midwest refineries, which were essentially skimming plants.[52] Pursuant to this arrangement, the Indiana Company built its Casper refinery in 1914 and its Greybull refinery in 1917. Both of these plants, which consisted almost entirely of Burton pressure stills, subsequently constituted a very important source of supply for the Indiana Company's marketing operations in the Rocky Mountain area.[53]

At the time of its acquisition by the Indiana Company in 1920 and 1921, the Midwest Refining Company was operating three refineries in Wyoming: a 60,000 barrels per day plant at Casper; a 15,000 barrels per day plant at Greybull, and a 5,000 barrels per day plant at Laramie. In addition, the company owned approximately 58% of the stock of the Utah Oil and Refining Company, which operated a 5,000 barrels per day plant at Salt Lake City, Utah; controlled through stock ownership the Merritt Oil Corporation, the Mid-Northern Oil Company, and the Western States Oil and Land Company; and held stock interests in various other oil concerns. The Merritt Oil Corporation was a producing concern which had about 6,620 acres of land under lease in the Big Muddy field near Casper and a crude oil output of about 3,000 barrels per day. The Mid-Northern Oil Company was the Montana operating subsidiary of the Midwest Refining Company and was active primarily as a crude oil producer in Montana. The Western States Oil and Land Company carried on exploratory and development work in Oklahoma and the Rocky Mountain area.

Acquisition of the Midwest interests gave the Indiana Company direct control of about 87% of the refining activities in the Wyoming area.[54] Of far greater importance, however, was the fact that with the acquisition the Indiana Company secured the Midwest purchase contracts with certain Salt Creek, Wyoming, oil

---

[51] U. S. Senate, 67th Congress, 2nd and 4th Sessions, *Report on High Cost of Gasoline and Other Petroleum Products*, Hearings Before a Subcommittee of the Committee on Manufactures, Pursuant to S. Res. 295, in two vols., Vol. I, pp. 762–771, "Standard of Indiana Co., R. W. S. Exhibit No. 2" (Government Printing Office, 1923).

[52] Dr. Paul H. Giddens. See footnote 48.

[53] Under a similar arrangement the Indiana Company also built Burton pressure stills at Florence, Colorado, to run on charging stocks furnished from the adjacent refinery of the United Oil Company, a subsidiary of the Continental Oil Company. See *Moody's Manual*, 1920, p. 2986.

[54] Dr. Paul H. Giddens. See footnote 48.

producers, which still had more than 10 years to run. These contracts, together with the production directly controlled by the Midwest Refining Company, gave the Indiana Company access to almost 65% of the Wyoming crude oil output.[55]

Another important step which the Indiana Company took in 1921 to strengthen its position with respect to crude oil supplies was the purchase of a one-half interest in the Sinclair Pipe Line Company (see Chapter Seven). At the same time, the Indiana Company joined with the Sinclair Oil Corporation in the formation of the Sinclair Crude Oil Purchasing Company to engage in the purchase, storage, and sale of crude oil. The Sinclair Pipe Line Company had crude oil trunk lines extending from the principal producing fields in Kansas, Oklahoma, and northern Texas to Chicago, and had been transporting crude oil as a common carrier to the Indiana Company's refineries at Whiting, Indiana, and Sugar Creek, Missouri. As noted in Chapter Seven, after 1921 the Sinclair Pipe Line Company extended its trunk lines and gathering systems throughout the Mid-Continent area and as far south as Houston, Texas. Meanwhile, the Sinclair Crude Oil Purchasing Company developed as one of the largest buyers of crude oil in the Mid-Continent area. Acquisition of a one-half interest in the two companies gave the Indiana Company a direct contact with crude oil producers and reduced its dependence upon the two Prairie companies as a source of supply.

It should not be inferred from the above discussion that the Indiana Company was in any particular financial distress as a result of its difficulties in securing adequate crude oil supplies in the period 1916–1921. The company may have lost business to competitors and may have been precluded from expanding its refining and marketing activities as rapidly as the company's executives would have liked, but for the most part the company continued to make substantial profits and to increase its size and financial strength. The company expanded its total assets from about $60,000,000 on December 31, 1915, to $305,700,000 on December 31, 1921.[56] The record of the com-

pany's net earnings in the period 1913–1921 is shown below:

STANDARD OIL COMPANY (INDIANA)

Net Earnings, Years Ended December 31[57]

1913	$14,687,696
1914	6,590,924
1915	15,898,376
1916	30,043,614
1917	43,808,930
1918	43,263,877
1919	34,604,416
1920	61,377,803
1921	23,288,348

Development of Foreign and Domestic Production, 1922–1931:

As was pointed out in Chapter Four, the period from the latter part of 1920 until about 1935 was, in general, a time of ample crude oil supplies in the United States. Throughout the 1920's, however, the Indiana Company continued its efforts to gain additional crude oil production both at home and abroad. In retrospect, it appears that whereas the company's entrance into the crude oil producing field in 1917 was prompted by the urgencies of its immediate crude oil supply problems, the continued emphasis which the company placed on crude oil production during the 1920's was largely a matter of long-run policy with respect to the company's general growth and development. It certainly seems unlikely that the Indiana Company could have had any serious difficulty in purchasing all the crude oil it needed in the 14-year period after about the middle of 1921.

It seems probable that sometime during the early 1920's the executives of the Indiana Company reached the conclusion that large crude oil producing operations would be necessary to support the continued growth and development of the company in the refining and marketing field. That the executives should have reached such a decision is not hard to understand in the light of all the difficulties the company had experienced in meeting the requirements of its marketing department in the period 1916–1921. Moreover, it will be recalled from the discussion in Chapter Four that in the early 1920's there was considerable opinion (despite the steadily mounting crude oil stocks) that the

[55] Dr. Paul H. Giddens. See footnote 48.
[56] Standard Oil Company (Indiana), Annual Reports for 1915 and 1921.
[57] *Moody's Manuals,* 1919, 1920, and 1925.

United States would soon be confronted with a serious, long-run shortage of crude oil and that the only solution to the situation lay in the development of foreign producing properties. The Indiana Company at this time had a very large refining and marketing investment in the North Central states, and the executives of the company probably regarded the development of adequate crude oil reserves as a necessary and prudent step to protect the company's existing commitments.

The Indiana Company's efforts to secure a large volume of crude oil production during the early 1920's must also be attributed in considerable measure to the personal ambitions and convictions of Colonel Robert W. Stewart, who at that time was chairman of the board of directors and chief executive officer of the company. Colonel Stewart had been elected chairman of the board in 1918, after 12 years of association with the company as attorney and general counsel, at the same time that Dr. William M. Burton was named president.

The available records indicate that Colonel Stewart was an imaginative, aggressive individual possessed with a driving ambition to build the Indiana Company into one of the most powerful oil companies in the world and to put it in a position where it could meet the Standard Oil Company (New Jersey) on equal terms in any market, at home or abroad.[58] Colonel Stewart was convinced that the Indiana Company's refining and marketing operations would always be vulnerable until the company secured a strong crude oil producing position. He was also among those who believed that the United States would soon have to turn to foreign sources for a large share of its crude oil supplies. Throughout his administration therefore Colonel Stewart relentlessly pursued the objective of developing a strong crude oil position for the Indiana Company.

Throughout the early 1920's there were various rumors that Colonel Stewart was negotiating a merger of the Indiana Company's refining and marketing properties with those of one or another of the large producing companies. In 1922 the Indiana Company unquestionably entered into negotiations with the Gulf Oil Corporation concerning a merger of the two concerns. The Gulf Oil Corporation at this time had a very strong crude oil position both in the United States and in certain Latin American countries (see Chapter Four) but had not yet developed a really large-scale domestic refining and marketing operation. Colonel Stewart later told a Senate Investigating Committee that he was particularly anxious to secure the Gulf properties because they fitted "end to end" with those of the Indiana Company. The negotiations were dropped, however, because the two parties were unable to come to an agreement over the terms of the merger.

In 1925 Colonel Stewart accomplished in large measure his ambition to make the Indiana Company a major crude oil producer through the acquisition of certain of E. L. Doheny interests in the Pan American Petroleum and Transport Company. The mechanism by which the acquisition was accomplished was somewhat complicated and need not be described in any great detail. Suffice it to say that as a result of the negotiations, the Indiana Company acquired control of the extensive producing properties held in Mexico by Pan American and its various subsidiary companies. The Pan American properties [59] included a large share of the production in the so-called "Golden Lane" along the Dos Bocas-Alamo fault. Some wells in this small area were reportedly capable of producing as much as 100,000 barrels per day unless their output was restricted. In 1925 the Mexican production of the Pan American company was about 50,000,-000 barrels per year. Other Pan American properties which were acquired by the Indiana Company in the transaction included a 105,000 barrels per day refinery at Tampico and two crude oil pipe line systems. Pan American also owned a fleet of tankers for moving Mexican crude oil to the United States and various foreign ports.

The Pan American properties in the United States which were acquired by the Indiana Company included a refinery at Destrehan, Louisiana, on the Mississippi River near New Orleans, and extensive marketing facilities

---

[58] Dr. Paul H. Giddens. See footnote 48.

[59] Actually, most of the Pan American properties in Mexico were held by a subsidiary, the Mexican Petroleum Company.

throughout the southeastern part of the country. Pan American was engaged primarily in the distribution of fuel oil but also had a fairly large number of gasoline outlets. Among other things, gasoline was barged up the Mississippi River from Destrehan to Memphis and then distributed to many inland points by tank car. Pan American also owned a 50% interest in the American Oil Company, a formerly independent marketing concern which had extensive distribution facilities in Baltimore and in other areas along the Atlantic seaboard.

An extremely important feature of the Pan American acquisition was that it gave the Indiana Company a 50% interest in the British Mexican Petroleum Company which, in turn, had bought into the Lago Petroleum Company. The latter had been formed in 1923 to purchase the Venezuelan concessions of the British Equatorial Oil Company. Among other things, these concessions included the petroleum rights to more than two million acres of land under the shallow waters of Lake Maracaibo, which later turned out to be one of the most important producing properties of South America. The British Mexican Petroleum Company was also one of the leading distributors of fuel oil in the world; it had marketing outlets throughout the United Kingdom and operated a fleet of tankers for making shipments to many foreign countries. The British Mexican Petroleum Company was under contract to purchase several million barrels of crude oil and gasoline a year from the Mexican Petroleum Company, the principal subsidiary of the Pan American Petroleum and Transport Company.

Acquisition of the Pan American properties placed "under the control of Colonel Stewart sufficient properties to give him the position of almost unequaled influence in the oil world that he [was] said to have desired since he became the executive head of the largest gasoline refining and marketing company in the world." [60] The Indiana Company was also placed in a position to enter the marketing field in foreign countries in competition with the Standard Oil Company (New Jersey) and other interests if it so desired. Of greatest im-

portance, however, was the fact that the acquisition of Pan American gave the Indiana Company the crude oil reserves necessary to support its refining and marketing operations. In 1925 the Indiana Company had a refinery capacity of about 160,000 barrels per day whereas the producing properties acquired from Pan American had a crude oil output of about 140,000 barrels per day.[61] After the acquisition Colonel Stewart expressed the opinion that the Indiana Company had solved its crude oil problems for a long time to come and could thereafter compete on equal terms with all comers.[61]

The six-year period following the Pan American acquisition marked somewhat of a lull in the development of the crude oil producing program of the Indiana Company. In March 1929 Colonel Stewart was not re-elected to his position as chairman of the board of directors and thereafter no longer held any official position with the Indiana Company. Mr. E. G. Seubert, who had been president of the company since 1927, when Dr. William M. Burton retired, was re-elected as president in 1929 and designated to act as chief executive officer of the company until such time as a new chairman might be elected.

The circumstances which culminated in Colonel Stewart's removal as head of the company have long been a matter of public record and need not be recounted in any great detail. According to one published source of information, the facts were essentially as follows: [62] Sometime between November 14 and 17, 1921, Colonel Stewart, Harry F. Sinclair (chairman of the board of the Sinclair Consolidated Oil Corporation), James E. O'Neil (president and a director of the Prairie Oil and Gas Company), and H. M. Blackmer (president and director of the Midwest Refining Company) arranged contracts for the purchase of 33,333,-333⅓ barrels of crude oil from the Humphreys Mexican Oil Company and the Humphreys Texas Company by the Continental Trading Company, Ltd., at a price of $1.50 per barrel. The Continental Trading Company

[60] Roger B. Stafford, "Indiana Standard Completes Deal for Mexican Petroleum Properties," National Petroleum News, April 1, 1925, p. 33.

[61] Dr. Paul H. Giddens. See footnote 48.

[62] See Colonel Stewart and the Standard Oil Company of Indiana, A Letter to the Stockholders of the Company from Winthrop W. Aldrich, dated February 8, 1929, published by Winthrop W. Aldrich, 15 Broad Street, New York.

was incorporated on November 17, 1921, and by contracts of the same date, it sold the 33,333,333⅓ barrels of oil to the Sinclair Crude Oil Purchasing Company and the Prairie Oil and Gas Company at a price of $1.75 per barrel.[63] The Sinclair Crude Oil Purchasing Company was at this time jointly owned by the Sinclair and Indiana companies and the latter also owned the Midwest Refining Company. The net effect of the transaction was to provide Stewart, Sinclair, O'Neil, and Blackmer with a profit of 25 cents per barrel for acting as intermediaries in the sale of oil to their own companies.[64]

On January 9, 1928, as an offshoot of investigations then being conducted of the leasing of Naval oil reserves [65] and particularly the Teapot Dome properties, the United States Senate passed Resolution No. 101 authorizing a specific investigation of the transactions of the Continental Trading Company. After giving testimony before the Senate Committee, Colonel Stewart was tried under indictments for contempt of the Senate and perjury. He was acquitted on both charges, but his conduct over the years 1921–1928 in connection with the Continental Trading Company, the incriminating nature of his testimony, and his attitude toward his own company, the public, and public authority resulted in his removal by the stockholders of the Indiana Company.

The administration of the Standard Oil Company (Indiana) by Mr. E. G. Seubert, after Colonel Stewart's removal was unquestionably more conservative than that of Colonel Stewart. Mr. Seubert had been associated with the Indiana Company for a great many years in accounting and financial capacities and had served as secretary and treasurer for eight years before his election as president in 1927. He did not have the ambitious expansionist tendencies of Colonel Stewart and was unques-tionably more interested in developing for the Indiana Company a sound, profitable position in the United States than in seeing the company become a major power in world oil markets. The transition from Stewart to Seubert therefore resulted in some modification of the Indiana Company's drive for crude oil during the late 1920's.

During the early years of the Seubert administration, however, three important steps were taken which served to strengthen the Indiana Company's position with respect to its crude oil supplies. The first step was taken about 1927 or 1928 when the company began in earnest to develop its own crude oil finding department under the leadership of Mr. A. W. Peake and Mr. F. O. Prior (president and executive vice president of the company in 1952).[66] Before that time the Indiana Company had acquired its crude oil production largely through purchases of proven properties rather than through exploratory work of its own.

A second important step was the acquisition, in 1930, by the Indiana Company of the remaining half interest in the Sinclair Crude Oil Purchasing Company and the Sinclair Pipe Line Company for a price of $72,500,000. This acquisition gave the Indiana Company complete control of one of the most important crude oil buying organizations of the time and of about 2,500 miles of crude oil gathering and about 4,400 miles of crude oil trunk lines which could be used to transport crude oil from the Mid-Continent and Texas fields to the company's refineries in Illinois, Indiana, and Missouri.

The third step, which was also taken in 1930, was the acquisition by stock exchange of the properties of the McMan Oil and Gas Company which was reported to have a potential production of 298,000 barrels per day from its holdings in the Mid-Continent fields and in the important Yates field in West Texas.[67] In January 1931 the Stanolind Oil and Gas Company was organized to take over and operate the Indiana Company's various producing properties, including the McMan Oil and Gas Company and the Dixie Oil Company.

[63] The contract was terminated on March 4, 1923, for a consideration of $400,000. Profits to the Continental Trading Company prior to that date had been $3,000,000. At the time of termination, over 24 million barrels remained to be delivered, and the contract thus had a potential value of about $6,000,000.

[64] Mr. H. S. Osler, a Canadian lawyer, received 2% of the profits for his services as president of the Continental Trading Company.

[65] Conducted by the Senate Public Lands Committee under Senate Resolution No. 282, April 29, 1922.

[66] Mr. Peake was elected president in January 1945 and Mr. Prior executive vice president in June 1951.

[67] Standard Oil Company (Indiana), Annual Report for the year 1930.

Withdrawal from Foreign Operations and Further Development of Domestic Production, 1931–1950:

Through a series of transactions carried out in the early part of 1932, the foreign properties of the Pan American Petroleum and Transport Company were sold to the Standard Oil Company (New Jersey). In return for its interest in the Pan American foreign properties, the Indiana Company received (payable over a four-year period) about $48,000,000 in cash and 1,778,973 shares of the Jersey Company's stock. The book value of the stock received as of December 31, 1931, was approximately $87,000,000.

As a result of the sale the Jersey Company acquired control of Pan American's subsidiary and affiliated companies operating outside the United States and of Pan American's fleet of tankers. The most important properties involved in the transfer consisted of 4.6 million acres of oil lands in Venezuela (principally the Lake Maracaibo properties) and Mexico, and of three foreign refineries with a combined operating capacity of about 140,000 barrels per day. The Pan American Petroleum and Transport Company, in which the Indiana Company at this time owned a 96% stock interest, retained its domestic properties which included oil and gas lands in Texas, Arkansas, and Louisiana; refineries at Destrehan, Louisiana, Baltimore, Maryland, and Savannah, Georgia; and storage, transportation, and marketing facilities in the southeastern states and along the Atlantic seaboard.

The decision of the Indiana Company to dispose of its foreign operations in 1932 was prompted to a considerable extent by the impending import tax on crude oil and refined products.[68] The Pan American crude oil and refined products had previously been used primarily to supply the Pan American refining and marketing operations in the southeastern area of the country. The Indiana Company executives feared that the import taxes would make it impossible to bring foreign oil and products into the United States for domestic refining and marketing on terms which would permit the Indiana Company to meet the competition of companies drawing their oil from domestic sources, particularly in view of the enormous supplies and low prices for crude oil then existing in the domestic market. If such proved to be the case, the Indiana Company would be faced with the task of developing new sources of supply for its domestic operations and of acquiring new outlets in foreign countries for the Pan American output. It appeared that the simultaneous undertaking of these two projects would pose insurmountable financial problems, and the sale to the Jersey Company was therefore adopted as a practical alternative solution. Mr. Seubert announced the sale in May 1932 as follows:

> Standard of Indiana has agreed to transfer its interest in the foreign property amounting to about 96% . . . The deal will materially improve the [Indiana] Company's position in relation to the world trade in oil. The foreign properties in which it has been interested have been dependent in large part upon outlets in the United States. If the threatened tariff on oil should be adopted, they would be obliged to seek additional outlets abroad in competition with established companies and at great cost. Standard of New Jersey, on the other hand, is in a position to provide foreign outlets by a mere adjustment in flow of business.
>
> By exchanging its interest in the Pan American foreign properties for an investment in the Jersey Company, Standard of Indiana will insure itself against loss through tariff developments and put itself in position to share not only in any benefits which the Jersey Company may gain from the transaction, but also in the earnings of that company's entire business, both foreign and domestic.[69]

It seems highly probable that the decision to make the sale also reflected the inherent conservatism of the Seubert administration as contrasted with the Stewart administration. If Colonel Stewart had remained as chief execu-

---

[68] Import duties on crude petroleum and major refined products became effective June 21, 1932. The import tax, which was authorized in the Revenue Act of 1932 and which was subject to various treaties, was imposed at varying rates on different products as follows: Crude petroleum, 0.5 cent per gallon; fuel oil, gas oil, and all liquid derivatives except gasoline and lubricating oils or other motor fuel, 0.5 cent per gallon; gasoline or other motor fuel, 2.5 cents per gallon; lubricating oil, 4 cents per gallon; paraffin and other petroleum wax products, 1 cent per pound. See National Industrial Conference Board, *The Petroleum Almanac* (The Conference Board, New York, 1946), p. 218.

[69] "Pan American Foreign Holdings Priced at $146,000,000," *National Petroleum News*, May 11, 1932, p. 23.

tive of the company, it seems likely that a wholly different policy might have been followed with respect to the development of foreign producing properties and that the Pan American sale might never have been negotiated.

Loss of Pan American's foreign production required the Indiana Company to enlarge its crude oil producing program greatly in the United States. Beginning in about 1932 the company initiated through its subsidiary, the Stanolind Oil and Gas Company, a very active program of exploration, wildcatting, and development and also made a number of purchases of proven properties. In the 21-year period 1932–1952, inclusive, the company's net domestic production increased from 10,676,000 barrels to 91,871,000 barrels per year, approximately a nine-fold increase.

In 1935, as one means of restoring the company's controlled crude oil supply, the Indiana Company purchased the properties of the Yount-Lee Oil Company for a price of approximately $42,000,000. The Yount-Lee properties included about 283,000 acres of oil lands and leases in Texas and Louisiana on which there were some 700 producing wells having an average daily allowable production under prorationing restrictions of about 20,000 barrels per day, an amount sufficient to increase the Indiana Company's production under prorationing by about 50%. The Yount-Lee properties also included certain pipe lines, deep water terminals on the Gulf Coast, and about 4,690,000 barrels of crude oil in storage.

Sometime during the early 1930's, perhaps at about the time of the Pan American sale, the Indiana Company executives gradually arrived at the conclusion that the company should seek as a long-run objective the development of domestic crude oil production equal to at least 50% of the company's refinery runs. Thereafter the company maintained a sustained effort to secure crude oil production, and in 1952 the executives still regarded a crude oil ratio of 50% or more of refinery runs as desirable and necessary to the company's operations. The company executives welcomed the adoption of the prorationing laws in the early 1930's, and, in general, the laws strengthened their conviction that the Indiana Company must seek a large crude oil supply of its own to support its refining and marketing operations. The results of the company's crude oil producing program in the period 1930–1952 are plotted in Chapter Twelve, Exhibit XII-15.

V. SUMMARY

1. Strong reasons for backward integration by refiners into crude oil producing activities may be found in certain economic facts with regard to refining operations, the crude oil producing process, and the nature of the investment opportunity at the refining level of the industry. A refinery is an extremely expensive, highly specialized piece of equipment which is very vulnerable to unfavorable developments, volume-wise or cost-wise, with respect to its crude oil supply. The nature of crude oil production is such that these developments can and frequently do occur, and the carrying of inventories to guard against them is feasible to only a very limited extent. The refinery investment is made at a point in the industry where the gross margins and profit opportunities are highly unstable, and the addition of crude oil production has constituted one effective means by which greater stability could be achieved. It is not surprising therefore that refiners should have taken steps toward the acquisition of crude oil reserves.

2. The experiences of the three companies discussed in this chapter illustrate the range of economic, business, and human considerations which have prompted backward integration moves by refiners in individual cases. The programs of all three companies, and particularly that of the Standard Oil Company (Indiana), were influenced by a general desire on the part of the company managements to protect refinery investments from shortages in crude oil supplies. In two of the companies, Sohio and Atlantic, the desire to gain protection from the violent fluctuations in the refining gross margin was an important consideration. The adoption of the prorationing laws had a bearing on the crude oil producing efforts of all three companies, and particularly on that of Atlantic, because the laws were interpreted as

increasing the exposure of a nonintegrated refiner to crude oil shortages and adverse margin fluctuations.

During the early years of World War II tax considerations had an influence on the programs of Sohio and Atlantic (and probably of the Indiana Company) in that the prevailing high income tax rates increased the availability of producing properties for purchase. In the case of Sohio, tax considerations assumed a further significance because of the vulnerability of the company's refining and marketing operations to the excess profits tax. The inflationary pressures which developed in the early years of World War II weighed heavily in Atlantic's decision to deepen its commitment in crude oil producing operations. Finally, the experiences of the Indiana Company in the middle 1920's illustrate the important influence which the personal philosophies and ambitions of individuals have sometimes had on backward integration programs of refiners.

3. The economic and business pressures for backward integration by refiners have been subject to continual changes and have not been constant in their intensity. In the period 1916–1921 a number of circumstances combined to create severe crude oil shortages, and at least two of the companies, Atlantic and the Indiana Company, suffered from a lack of assured supplies. The shortages were replaced by surpluses in the period 1921–1935, during which time the three companies appear to have suffered no major handicap from their lack of crude oil production. The Atlantic management even called attention in the latter 1920's to the benefits a company was able to secure from its buying position with respect to crude oil. The adoption of the prorationing laws once again altered the situation in that it reduced the refiner's opportunity to buy at distress prices but did not bring about a compensating reduction in his exposure to crude oil shortages. Another example of an important shift in the pressures for backward integration may be found in the inflationary and tax developments of World War II, as was illustrated in the experiences of Atlantic and Sohio.

4. The experiences of the three companies discussed in this chapter provide some preliminary evidence on a point which will be examined in detail in Part Three; namely, that the oil companies did not always react in the same way to the same circumstances and when they did make parallel moves it was not always for the same reason. Atlantic and the Indiana Company both started their crude oil producing programs in about 1916 or 1917 during a time of crude oil shortage for much the same reasons. During the period of surplus which followed in the 1920's, however, the Indiana Company drove ahead in a powerful effort to become one of the major crude oil producers in the world, while Atlantic conducted its crude producing program in a more or less desultory manner.

The adoption of the prorationing laws had about the same impact on both Atlantic and Sohio, and both companies interpreted the economic significance of the laws in somewhat the same manner. Atlantic, however, immediately embarked on a major crude oil producing program while Sohio, for some very good reasons, delayed its entrance into crude oil production for a period of about 10 years.

In the early years of World War II both Atlantic and Sohio saw a strong need for further integration into crude oil production and took steps accordingly, but for very different reasons. Atlantic was interested primarily in gaining some protection against long-run inflationary forces, and tax considerations played only a minor role in its decision in the sense that they increased the availability of purchase properties. In the case of Sohio, on the other hand, the excess profits tax was one of the most important factors determining the timing of the company's entrance into crude oil producing activities.

5. The backward integration programs of the three companies discussed in this chapter did not spring primarily from a desire to enter and develop a new business but rather from a desire to protect or enhance the profitability of the business in which the companies were already engaged. All three

companies were apparently content to concentrate their attention primarily on refining and marketing operations until they encountered difficulties in those fields. Backward integration into crude oil production was then undertaken as one means of solving their difficulties; the desire to engage in crude oil production as a source of profits in its own right was a secondary and in at least two cases, that of Atlantic and the Indiana Company, a much later consideration.

CHAPTER NINE

Integration Between Refining and Marketing Activities

ONE of the most important types of integration in the oil industry has been that which has taken place between the refining and marketing levels of the business. The data presented in Chapter Two reveal that in 1950 at least 75 of the 179 companies engaged in refining activities owned or leased wholesaling facilities, and at least 62 of these companies also owned or leased service stations.[1] All but 13 of the companies were likewise engaged in oil producing activities. The owned or leased facilities of the producing-refining-marketing and refining-marketing companies accounted for a minimum of 94.9% of the industry's refinery runs, 61.4% of the industry's light oil sales through bulk plants and terminals, and 58.0% of the industry's gasoline sales through service stations. The integrated companies typically distributed 66.8% of their refinery yields of all products through owned or leased bulk plants and 27.4% of their yields of gasoline and naphthas through owned or leased service stations.[2] Although the integrated refining companies accounted for about 42% of the total number of active refining companies in 1950, they represented only a very small fraction of the total number of business enterprises engaged in various types of wholesaling and retailing activities.

The development of integration between the refining and marketing levels of the industry has resulted primarily from forward integration by refiners and secondarily from backward integration by marketers. Certain of the general economic circumstances which contributed to both types of movements have already been suggested by the discussion in earlier chapters. In Chapter Five it was noted that the gross margin at the refining level of the industry was subject to violent fluctuations throughout the period 1920–1952 and that forward integration into wholesaling operations constituted a means by which the refiner could make very significant gains in both monthly and yearly gross margin stability. In the period 1920–1952 there was, in fact, no other single type of integration move which would have contributed more to gross margin stability than forward integration by a refiner into wholesaling. Additional gains in gross margin stability could also have been secured by a refiner through further forward integration into retailing activities. It seems reasonably clear therefore that one of the major circumstances encouraging forward integration by refiners was the important gain in gross margin and net profit stability which resulted from such moves.[3]

The data in Chapter Five also revealed that the wholesaling gross margin was subject to considerable fluctuation in the period 1920–1952 and that backward integration into refining constituted a means by which gains in monthly and yearly stability could have been secured. The wholesaling margin was not, however, subject to nearly so much yearly or monthly instability as the refining gross margin. It would appear therefore that the gain in gross margin and net profit stability obtained

---

[1] The number of refining companies that owned marketing facilities was probably greater than 75. The survey results in Chapter Two covered only 106 of approximately 179 refining companies active on December 31, 1950, and we had no way of knowing how many of the companies not responding to the survey owned or leased bulk plants or service stations. The respondents did, however, own 94.7% of the industry's refining capacity.

[2] Employees of the integrated companies typically operated 43.9% of the owned or leased bulk plants and 1.7% of the owned or leased service stations; the remaining bulk plants and service stations were operated by independent businessmen.

[3] See Chapter Five for a discussion of the relationships between gross margin and net profit stability.

by a wholesaler through backward integration into refining was probably a significant factor in encouraging such integration, but probably not so important as in the case of refiners integrating forward.

Another general circumstance contributing to the development of integration between the refining and marketing levels of the industry may be found in the characteristics of the refinery investment which were discussed in Chapter Eight. As was noted at that point, the modern refinery represents a very expensive and specialized piece of equipment which is extremely vulnerable cost-wise to any circumstance which causes refinery runs to be shut back below capacity. Attention has already been directed to the fact that investments in crude oil producing properties have sometimes been made by refiners to protect against the eventuality of supply shortages which would interfere with refinery operations. To maintain a high level of throughput at a refinery, the need for continuity of selling arrangements is no less important than the need for continuity of crude oil supplies. The substantial investment in specialized refinery equipment has therefore motivated refiners to invest in marketing properties for much the same reasons that it has prompted them to invest in producing properties.

In the following pages of the chapter we shall discuss and illustrate some of the other circumstances, in addition to those mentioned above, which have prompted forward integration by refiners and backward integration by marketers.

I. Forward Integration by Refiners into Marketing

Before 1911 there was not a great deal of integration between the refining and marketing levels of the industry. Although refiners sometimes maintained warehousing facilities, they owned very few retail outlets. Kerosene was then the principal petroleum product, and its market was of such a character that the building of retail stores solely or principally for the distribution of kerosene was not warranted. Distribution was accomplished primarily through multipurpose outlets such as livery stables and hardware, grocery, and general

stores which handled kerosene along with a wide range of other services or products. In addition, tank wagon deliveries of kerosene were sometimes made by oil companies directly to farmers, commercial accounts, and some household consumers.

After about 1911 a number of innovations and evolutionary circumstances prompted refiners to further greatly the extent of their integration into wholesaling activities and to enter the retailing business on a large scale. Among other things, forward integration took place to provide facilities and a high standard of service for the automotive market, to secure and hold market outlets during a period of heavy crude oil production, to capitalize on the economies of the products pipe line, and to reduce distribution costs through the by-passing of certain steps in the distribution process.

Integration to Provide Facilities and Service for the Automotive Market:

The very rapid development of the automotive market for gasoline created the need for a major expansion of the industry's wholesaling facilities and for the development of a type of retail outlet different from those which had formerly handled kerosene. The need which arose for a substantial enlargement in the number and capacity of marketing facilities is evident from the fact that the output of gasoline was almost 19 times as large in 1925 as it was in 1909.[4] The need which arose for a special type of retailing facility to fulfill the demands of the motoring public may also be inferred from the fact that the number of motor vehicle registrations in the United States increased as follows: [5]

Year	Number of Motor Vehicle Registrations
1900	8,000
1905	79,000
1910	458,000
1915	2,491,000
1920	9,239,000
1925	19,941,000

[4] Production figures obtained from The Conference Board, *The Petroleum Almanac* (New York, The Conference Board, 1946), p. 96. Original Source U. S. Bureau of Mines.

[5] *Collier's Encyclopedia*, "Automotive Industry" (New York, P. F. Collier & Son Corporation, 1950), Vol. 2, p. 567. Original data compiled by U. S. Public Roads Administration.

Refiners found it desirable to integrate into marketing operations to provide enough facilities to perform the enormous distribution job confronting the industry, to get the job done with acceptable standards of service to the public, and to take advantage of the lucrative profit opportunities afforded by marketing activities. The expansion of wholesaling facilities by refiners preceded somewhat their entry into retailing activities. Since a large number of jobbers did not enter the industry until after about 1925, it was incumbent upon refiners to build many new bulk plants for the intermediate storage of gasoline. The initial demand for new retailing facilities was, however, met largely by the same types of multipurpose outlets that had handled kerosene. In addition, a substantial volume of gasoline was sold through a new type of retail outlet, the automobile garage. The garage was established principally to repair motor vehicles and handled gasoline somewhat as a side-line item.

Although the number of multipurpose outlets handling gasoline, such as garages and general stores, was increased greatly after 1911, the standards of service provided for the public by these outlets were often very low. Motorists frequently experienced lengthy delays while store clerks attended to the sale of other products. Similarly, the garage operators usually regarded repair work as their primary business and viewed the sale of gasoline as somewhat of a nuisance. Moreover, the maintenance of unkempt facilities and the dilution of gasoline with kerosene were not at all uncommon occurrences. There was therefore the need for a new type of retail gasoline outlet which would offer an improved standard of service to motorists. The demand was met by the thousands of independent businessmen who erected service stations and by the refiners who integrated into retailing. Originally, the service stations had gasoline pumps at the curbside, but later "drive-in" stations were built, thereby avoiding a source of traffic congestion on narrow streets.

The experience of The Atlantic Refining Company provides an example of the motivations which refiners had to enter into retailing activities. In 1912 or 1913 a committee was formed to appraise the marketing program of The Atlantic Refining Company and to make appropriate recommendations with particular reference to the distribution of gasoline and motor oils. During the conduct of the study the committee toured Pennsylvania, visiting retail outlets and bulk plant establishments. One body of recommendations growing out of the study provided for certain improvements in Atlantic's existing mode of doing business, such as the installation and expansion of bulk plant facilities and the replacement of horse-drawn tank wagons with motor trucks. A second outgrowth of the study was the building and operation of service stations by The Atlantic Refining Company.

In retrospect it appears that the company built its first service stations primarily as a means of improving the standard of service at stations selling Atlantic products in the Pittsburgh area. The following excerpt from a company memorandum written in 1935 at the time a history of the domestic marketing operations was being prepared recaptures the findings of the committee with respect to the company's distribution through noncompany retailers.

In Allegheny County, particularly, it became very obvious that our distribution of gasoline to the public through dealers was a very uncertain and undesirable method of distribution. The majority of the dealers, most of whom were operating garages, were exceedingly poor credit risks. Their practices in this respect usually meant that when they became in debt beyond reasonable credit limits with one company, they turned to another, which resulted in a rather vicious circle as to supplying companies. In addition to their being poor credit risks, their standard of service to the public was comparatively poor. We had numerous complaints attributed to gasoline which, when traced down, were due to dirty storage tanks and to the blending of kerosene into gasoline.[6]

After reviewing the situation with dissatisfaction on several occasions, the Atlantic management decided to study at first hand the effectiveness of a service station owned and operated by the Pierce Oil Company in St. Louis. Apparently, the company operated service station of the Pierce Oil Company impressed the

---

[6] Company memorandum dated November 5, 1935. The term "dealers" is used in the memorandum to describe service station operators owning their own stations and buying products from The Atlantic Refining Company.

Atlantic management considerably. The management decided therefore that the company should construct its own service stations in Pittsburgh. The memorandum continues:

It became very obvious that as far as Pittsburgh and Allegheny County were concerned, that we should do something to raise the standard of service of gasoline to the buying public. . . . On Mr. Ablett's recommendation, we engaged the services of Mr. Kuntz, of Wilking & Company, Architects. He designed for us a white tile building with a green tile roof, with ample driveways around it and, as I recall it, about 10 or 12 points of service, with meter equipment.

The completion of this station and its opening represented the first company operated service station for The Atlantic Refining Company and, as far as I know, the first so-called modern company operated drive-in station in the eastern part of the United States. We acquired the land for this service station sometime during 1913 and the station was erected and in operation in 1915. [At completion, the service station represented a total investment of $52,000.] This station did a business averaging about 3,000 gallons a day and for a number of years did a business in excess of 1,000,000 gallons.

There is no doubt in my mind that the opening of this station, in over a relatively short period of time, did have the effect of substantially improving the service of gasoline to the public. Dealers were obliged to recognize the type of service that we were rendering on the Boulevard and, in order to compete and hold their business, did give much more attention to their service of gasoline to the public. The ultimate effect was that our relations with dealers improved very substantially. Instead of losing dealer business we actually, over a period of time, increased our dealer business.[7]

As a result of our experience with the station on Baum Boulevard, during the period of 1913 to 1917, we built several additional stations in Pittsburgh, including the station at the downtown entrance of Bigelow Boulevard, and East Liberty. These three stations, as I recall it, did a business of about 3,000,000 gallons a year. While the property for East Liberty was acquired in 1916, it did not get into actual operation until about 1919 (war period).[8]

The building of service stations by The Atlantic Refining Company in the Philadelphia area in 1916 and 1918 was motivated by the financial success enjoyed with the Pittsburgh stations and the desire to establish attractive stations selling under the Atlantic brand name in the Philadelphia area. In addition, commercial vehicles were coming into prominence in the larger cities, and while Atlantic solicited and contracted for commercial business with deliveries made by tank wagon, there was a growing need for a retail outlet to supply trucks. Since commercial buyers, such as department stores and express companies, did not ordinarily purchase from the company's retailers, Atlantic began to supply commercial accounts at its company owned and operated stations. Within a short period of time the sales made to commercial accounts at company stations comprised a substantial proportion of Atlantic's gasoline sales. Finally, the drive-in stations built by Atlantic became somewhat of a necessity in Philadelphia because the curb pumps in front of garages or accessory shops impeded the traffic flow. The company memorandum discusses the entrance into Philadelphia as follows:

Though we did not have the same reasons for building stations in Philadelphia that we did have in Pittsburgh, particularly as to our dealer distribution, our experience in Pittsburgh naturally led us to build stations in Philadelphia. Both these [Philadelphia] stations were built with the idea of offering very much improved service to the public. It had the result of creating a considerable amount of general goodwill with motorists and, incidentally, a very considerable amount of advertising value. Both of these stations were written up very considerably in magazines and in newspapers.

It became very obvious that the company owned and operated drive-in service station was to be an important factor in the gasoline business in the future. These service stations, at that time, became a marked convenience to passenger car owners and, particularly, to those that were storing cars in their own homes. It was a much needed service to the growing number of commercial accounts, many of which were operating an appreciable number of trucks, and with no opportunity for underground storage at their places of business.[9]

---

[7] There had originally been some apprehension that the operators of dealer stations selling Atlantic products might possibly raise objections to the building and operation of service stations by The Atlantic Refining Company and that these dealers might therefore choose to place their business with other suppliers. See also footnote 6.

[8] Company memorandum dated November 5, 1935.

[9] Ibid.

Subsequently, Atlantic built service stations in other areas of its marketing territory. Individual decisions were reached on the basis of the desirability of strengthening the company's position in individual marketing areas, the need for improved service, and the estimated profits that would be returned by the investment in new facilities.

Refiners continued to construct service stations until about 1926 as a means of servicing the rapidly expanding automotive market for gasoline. By about this time the number of service stations was reasonably adequate to provide satisfactory service to motorists, and thereafter the rate of growth in both the number of vehicles and motor fuel demand was not so appreciable as it had been in former years. Thousands of independent businessmen likewise built service stations from about 1914 to 1926 to satisfy the needs of the automotive market for gasoline. The retailing margin moved upward from about 1.7 cents in 1920 to 3.5 cents in 1926 which, together with the increases in gasoline demand, presented a profitable opportunity that attracted large investment funds into the retailing level of the industry.[10]

Integration to Secure and Hold Market Outlets:

From about 1920 through 1935 but particularly in the period 1926–1935 the forward movement by refiners into retailing activities was greatly accentuated by the desire to capture and hold a share of the market. As noted in Chapter Four, the intensive competition for retail outlets was generated principally by the large supplies of crude oil which came into being during the 1920's. The pressure of large crude oil supplies before the development of the prorationing laws caused aggressive marketing activity by two groups of companies. A group of new and expanding producing companies integrated forward into refining and then marketing activities as a means of disposing of their crude oil output. A second group of large, established companies moved into new marketing territories in order to utilize their additional crude oil producing potential and to offset the inroads made in their regular

marketing territories by the expansion of competitors. As noted in Chapter Four, the readjustments in the market also took place for a variety of other reasons, including the desire to operate refineries at high levels of throughput, to offer service to customers over wide geographic areas, to spread the cost of brand name programs over wider areas, and to take advantage of profit opportunities.

The struggle to secure and hold outlets was manifested in integration of two different types: the development of lease-and-license programs and an expansion in the number of company owned and operated service stations. The development of the lease-and-license programs, beginning in the early 1920's, provided a means by which a refiner could acquire and hold exclusive dealer outlets over time periods specified by contracts. The arrangements provided that a retailer would lease a previously unattached service station to an oil company in return for a rental fee. The owner would then operate the station under a license from the oil company, selling only that company's products. Stations acquired under the lease-and-license agreements represented integration of a lower order of intensity than the company owned and operated station because the dealer was under less restraints than the company employee and because the lease came up for renewal every several years whereas company owned facilities could be held indefinitely.

The competition among refiners for the more desirable retail accounts was very strong, and attractive inducements were offered to secure exclusive dealer patronage. It was not at all uncommon for refiners to offer retailers liberal rental terms for their stations, special price concessions on gasoline, and the free installation of gasoline pumps and storage tanks in return for a dealer contract. Moreover, refiners frequently agreed to paint service stations or pave driveways at little or no cost to retailers. As a result of the widening gross margins granted to retailers and the many indirect subsidies which were offered, a great many retailers became associated with supplying companies through lease-and-license agreements.

The competition among refiners for service station outlets forced the retailing margin, including subsidies, to such a high level that re-

---

[10] Retail margins determined from The Texas Company records of tank wagon and retail prices in 50 representative cities. See footnote 7, Chapter Five.

finers sometimes found that they could secure distribution for their products more economically by building their own stations than they could by soliciting either lease-and-license accounts or the business of contractor stations. The ownership and operation of service stations thus became a second important means by which refiners sought to secure and hold their retail outlets.

Refiners also built marketing facilities as a means of expanding their distribution in established marketing areas or as a means of gaining a foothold in entirely new territories. The competition for retailers was so keen that the more attractive, better managed stations soon became affiliated with one supplier or another under dealer arrangements. Therefore, the management of a refining company that was undertaking a program of expansion in an area was confronted with the alternatives of either accepting inferior outlets or of building stations of the caliber by which it wished to be represented to the trade. Many companies chose to build their own stations in order to acquire high volume stations and to protect their brand names.

Some of the former components of the Standard Oil group and other large companies were confronted with similar problems when they expanded beyond their traditional marketing territories around 1920 in an attempt to hold their market positions against the onslaught of new competitors. The experience of The Atlantic Refining Company, when it moved into direct distribution in New England after World War I, is illustrative of the problems encountered by companies in finding suitable outlets when they moved into new marketing territories. A memorandum reviewing the entrance into the New England region states:

In studying the channels of distribution which might be open to us, it became apparent that attempting distribution through the medium of dealers would be a very long drawn out operation, as practically all of the dealers were tied up in some form of contractual relationship with other major oil companies. The two channels of distribution that seemed to be open to us were, first, through the medium of our own company operated service stations to passenger cars and trucks and, second, to commercial business through the medium of tank wagon delivery.

[The company] started doing business at Providence, Worcester, Springfield, Hartford and New Haven, within a very short period of time in all places. In addition to the building of our storage facilities and warehouses, we had acquired properties for at least four or five service stations in all of these cities and, as previously stated, they were all put into service at all of these points within a relatively short period of time. Subsequently, we developed a dealer business at a great many points by making an investment of approximately $2,500 to $3,000 in the form of a small building with dispensing equipment in the driveway, having same operated by a dealer. With these three channels of distribution, namely, company operated service stations, tank wagon business with commercial accounts, and with dealers, it is my recollection that within the first year we acquired a volume of business of between 12,000,000 and 15,000,000 gallons of gasoline.

Our New England experience and the channels through which we established our distribution gave us a volume of business in a relatively short period of time that it would have taken many years to have acquired through dealers that were already being served by competitive companies.[11]

Subsequently, the company also moved into direct distribution in other parts of the East Coast. In some cases, integration was undertaken primarily to preserve the company's volume in the areas where jobber accounts were lost to other companies that were willing to offer better terms than the Atlantic management felt were justified. The experience of the company, as reflected in the company memorandum, is probably fairly representative of what was happening to other companies:

Our business in the South, and also in New York State, had previously been through the medium of jobbers. We lost a considerable amount of our jobber business due to major companies buying jobbers out at prices that we could not justify, or making contracts on wide differentials showing netbacks at our refinery points that seemed to be entirely unjustified. As a result of these losses of various jobbers, we were obliged to undertake marketing direct. It seemed necessary in the larger buying centers, both in the South and in New York State, and in order that we could evidence to the buying public that we were doing business, to build service stations.[11]

---

11 Company memorandum dated November 5, 1935.

Thus, the experience of The Atlantic Refining Company indicates that the building of service stations often proved to be the most expeditious way to break into a new market. The physical appearance of the stations and the standards of service offered gave the company prestige in a new area and made the acquisition of dealer accounts a much easier task. Beginning around 1930 most refining companies began to sublease their company owned or leased service stations to dealers for reasons which will be discussed in Chapter Ten.

Integration to Capitalize on the Products Pipe Line:

The development of the products pipe line precipitated a considerable amount of forward integration into marketing by refining companies. As demonstrated in Chapter Seven, the products pipe line is a very economical medium for transporting products in some circumstances. The pipe lines were built by refiners rather than marketers because the small marketer usually could not afford the very considerable capital investment needed to build a pipe line back to his source of supply. Moreover, the small marketer had no assurance that his source of supply would not shift at some future date, and he did not have a large enough volume to justify the building of a line. Since the pipe line investment opportunity was not particulary attractive to outside interests, it was incumbent upon refiners to build the lines if the potential savings in transportation costs were to be realized.

The building of products pipe lines prompted integration by refiners into both wholesaling and retailing activities. Integration into wholesaling activities was accomplished at the time a line was built, since it was necessary to erect new distributing facilities, pipe line terminals, in order that products might be drawn off the pipe line. Moreover, to the extent that pipe lines yielded the cost savings anticipated at the time of their construction, the owning companies were usually in a competitive position whereby they could increase their marketing efforts in the areas being served. The intensification of marketing efforts in areas served by pipe lines often involved the construction or acquisition of additional bulk plant and service station facilities.

The development of the Great Lakes Pipe Line System provides an excellent example of the impetus which a products pipe line sometimes gave for refining companies to expand their marketing facilities in a new area. In 1930 the Great Lakes Pipe Line Company, which was owned by a group of companies operating refineries in the Mid-Continent area, built a products pipe line extending from the heart of the Mid-Continent refining area into the North Central states. When the Great Lakes Pipe Line Company erected terminals along the route, the owning companies had, in effect, further integrated their refining operations into wholesaling. Moreover, the economical transportation provided by the pipe line and the availability of terminals put the pipe line builders in a position whereby they could very easily develop their bulk plant and service station facilities in the areas surrounding pipe line terminals.

The marketing expansion touched off by the Great Lakes Pipe Line system was not, however, limited to the companies owning the line. A group of small refiners in the Mid-Continent area seized upon the opportunity of using the newly provided common carrier facilities to enlarge the area of their marketing operations. Since the Great Lakes Pipe Line Company provided storage space at terminals for its shippers, it was unnecessary for companies using the line to build terminals of their own at the points they wished to draw products from the line. The small refiners frequently arranged with jobbers to receive shipments of their products at pipe line terminals. In addition, some small refiners built bulk plants in the territory served by the pipe line.

Integration to Lower Distribution Costs:

One of the most important integration movements by refiners into marketing immediately before and after World War II resulted from the pressure to lower distribution costs. In this period there was a growing tendency on the part of some companies to make deliveries of refined products by large truck transports directly from refineries or terminals to service stations and consumers. The traditional bulk plant activity was therefore by-passed. In moving products directly from primary sources of supply, such as refineries and terminals, to service stations and consumers without performing the usual wholesaling (bulk plant) function, the companies were engaged in "jump integration." [12]

The by-passing of bulk plants usually yielded two distinct types of savings in distribution costs. In the first place, the wholesaling costs of storage and transshipping at bulk plants were eliminated. Second, appreciable savings were generally made in the cost of moving refined products from storage points to service stations or consumers. Before by-passing, small delivery trucks were often used to transport products from bulk plants to outlets. When the by-passing of bulk plants was effected, products were moved from terminals or refineries to outlets by large, economical truck transports. Although both savings were significant, the savings in transportation costs were usually more important than the savings brought about in storage and handling costs.

The by-passing of bulk plants arose in response to the development of new facilities and expanding markets. A principal contributor to the by-passing technique was the network of products pipe line systems which sprang up throughout the country after 1930. As noted in Chapter Seven, the products pipe lines were built largely as a means of lowering the distribution costs involved in getting refined products from refineries to marketing areas. With the building of products pipe lines, refining companies frequently had both terminals and bulk plants in marketing areas where they had formerly owned only bulk plants. It was therefore possible to eliminate the bulk plants. In most cases, the per gallon costs of storage and transshipping at terminals were lower than those of the bulk plants they replaced because of the savings made possible through the handling of a large volume of products at a single installation. The development of barge and tanker transportation and the building of water terminals had much the same effect on the development of by-passing as did the building of pipe lines and pipe line terminals.

Two other developments which facilitated the extension of the by-passing method of distribution were the evolution of the tank truck and the improvements in road construction which made the use of heavier trucks feasible.

Subject to the loading and axle length limitations set forth in different state and city ordinances, the maximum capacity of tank trucks making direct deliveries increased in size from about 2,000 gallons in 1930 to about 8,000 gallons in 1952. The larger trucks could be operated at a much lower cost per gallon of refined products hauled than could smaller trucks.

The large volume service station with its large storage capacity was another innovation which was a prerequisite to the development of the by-passing technique. The continual growth in the demand for gasoline made it possible for many conventional service stations to install larger storage capacity and to sell much greater volumes than they had handled in former years. The large storage capacity enabled service stations to accept several thousand gallon "drops" from truck transports and meant that they could be serviced with fewer deliveries than would have been required with a lesser amount of storage capacity. The appearance of the multipump outlet and self-service stations in the postwar period also complemented the development of the by-passing technique. Although multipump and self-service stations were established primarily to reduce payroll costs rather than to permit direct deliveries, the fact that many of these stations attained high volumes and had large storage facilities permitted them to accept truck transport deliveries from terminals. The growth of commercial accounts for gasoline was still another factor which fostered the development of the by-passing method.

The practice of by-passing bulk plants originated before 1930, but it was after 1935 that the concept grew in importance. The Standard Oil Company of California, for example, applied the by-passing technique as early as 1929 when its small trucks were replaced with 2,000–2,550 gallon trucks for direct deliveries to service stations in the cities of Los Angeles, San Francisco, Oakland, and Seattle.[13] The numerous marketers that established large gallonage service stations at the points where railroads intersected well-traveled highways during the latter 1920's and 1930's also appreciated the by-passing principle and its potential advantages. These

---

[12] See Chapter One for a definition of jump integration.

[13] Frank Breese, "Direct Delivery Tank Trucks Become Bulk Plants on Wheels," *National Petroleum News*, Vol. 44, No. 18, April 30, 1952, p. 46.

"track-side" operators accepted bulk shipments of products which they sold on the same premises, thereby by-passing or at least consolidating the bulk plant activity.

The by-passing process has been employed more in some areas of the country and in some companies than in others. By-passing has, for example, reached an advanced state of development on the West Coast.[14] Some of the companies distributing in other areas that have made widespread use of by-passing are The Atlantic Refining Company, the Standard Oil Company (Ohio), and the Sun Oil Company. In the following paragraphs, we shall consider the effect of by-passing bulk plants on distribution costs, examine the process by which a decision to by-pass is reached, and discuss direct deliveries to large commercial accounts.

The Economies of By-Passing Bulk Plants: As a means of illustrating the economies made possible through the by-passing of bulk plants as well as other changes in distribution techniques, we shall present a record of the physical handling and transportation costs incurred by the Standard Oil Company (Ohio) to supply a typical dealer and a typical home heating oil consumer in five selected years from 1929 to 1950. The outlets selected as examples were located six miles west of Massillon, Ohio, and they were supplied from the company's Cleveland refinery throughout the entire time period.

The cost records together with an illustration of the different methods of distribution are shown in Exhibit IX-1 for the service station outlet and Exhibit IX-2 for the heating oil customer. The cost data included in the exhibits are in terms of original dollars and have not been adjusted in any way for subsequent price movements. The cost figures pertain only to these two typical outlets and they do not reflect average cost history of the Standard Oil Company (Ohio) either in the area or on a statewide basis. Although cost data were not available for 1952, a graphic representation of the methods of delivery in effect in 1952 was included in the exhibits to demonstrate the continuous progress in distribution techniques.

As shown in Exhibits IX-1 and IX-2, Sohio built a products pipe line from Cleveland to Canton in the period 1935–1940 and thereafter

14 Ibid.

the Massillon bulk plant was by-passed by direct deliveries from a terminal at Canton. In addition to showing the effects of by-passing in the period 1935–1940, however, the data in the exhibits reveal all the important changes in distribution operating equipment, modes, and techniques that affected the costs of supplying a typical dealer and a typical home heating oil account from 1929 to 1952. Thus, the changes effected in the period 1929–1935 show the developments in distribution techniques before the bulk plant was by-passed; the changes brought about after 1940 show the continual evolution of the by-passing method of distribution.

The first observation that may be made on the basis of the data revealed in Exhibits IX-1 and IX-2 is that the changes in distribution techniques in the period 1935–1940, which included the by-passing of the Massillon bulk plant, yielded a greater reduction in total transportation and handling costs than any of the changes in techniques effected in preceding or subsequent time periods. In the period 1935–1940 the total cost of moving gasoline from the Cleveland refinery to the service station near Massillon was reduced from 1.22 cents per gallon to 0.56 cent per gallon. The saving of 0.66 cent per gallon was approximately one-half of the entire saving in gasoline distribution costs effected in the entire period 1929–1950. In the period 1935–1940 the total delivery and handling costs for heating oil were reduced from 1.72 cents per gallon to 0.79 cent per gallon. The saving of 0.93 cent per gallon comprised 80% of the reduction in heating oil distribution costs realized in the entire period 1929–1950.

The data in the exhibits show very clearly the impetus given the by-passing method of distribution by the development of products pipe lines. Before the construction of the products pipe line (1935), the cost of truck transport movements of gasoline and heating oil from Cleveland to Massillon was 0.52 cent per gallon. The building of the products pipe line permitted Sohio to deliver gasoline and heating oil to a terminal at Canton for 0.07 cent per gallon in 1940. The products pipe line therefore permitted a saving of 0.45 cent per gallon on shipments to two cities which were approximately the same distance from Cleveland. Although the terminal costs at Canton amounted to 0.15 cent per gallon for gasoline and 0.18 cent per gallon for heating oil, it was possible to abandon the Massillon bulk plant and thereby eliminate its operating costs of 0.20 cent per gallon for both products.

In addition to the fact that all bulk plant costs were eliminated at the time by-passing was effected, Sohio realized another significant advantage through by-passing because the delivery costs to the service station and the heating oil account from the Canton terminal were far less than the delivery costs had been from the Massillon bulk plant. Despite the fact that the distance from Canton to the gasoline and heating oil outlets was approximately twice as great as the distance from Massillon to these outlets, the delivery costs for gasoline were reduced from 0.50 cent in 1935 to 0.34 cent in 1940 and the delivery costs for heating oil were reduced from 1.00 cent in 1935 to 0.54 cent in 1940. The savings on gasoline were made possible by the conversion from a small delivery truck operating out of Massillon to a truck transport operating out of Canton. In addition, the size of the individual delivery was increased from 750 gallons in 1935 to 1,500 gallons in 1940. The savings on heating oil delivery costs were brought about solely by an increase in the size of the truck utilized; there was no increase in the size of the individual home delivery.

The data in the exhibits also indicate the step-by-step reduction in distribution costs which a refiner-marketer may make over a period of years when the company is free to employ whatever types of integration arrangements are best suited to the needs of the situation. The replacement of railroad transportation from Cleveland to Massillon with truck transports in the period 1929–1935, for example, permitted a saving of 0.16 cent per gallon on gasoline and 0.22 cent per gallon on heating oil. The building of a products pipe line from Cleveland to Canton in the period 1935–1940 yielded an even more appreciable saving of 0.45 cent per gallon for both products in comparison with the trucking costs to Massillon. The employment of increasingly larger trucks for moving gasoline from storage points to the service station and the acceptance of larger deliveries at the service station permitted delivery costs from the storage points to the service station to be reduced 0.44 cent in the

period 1929–1950. The installation of larger storage capacity at the service station made it possible for the size of individual deliveries to be increased from 500 gallons in 1929 to 4,000 gallons in 1952. Progressively larger trucks were likewise used to deliver heating oil, and the delivery costs were reduced 0.61 cent in the period 1935–1950. The various changes made in distribution techniques were such that the total costs of handling and transporting both gasoline and heating oil were less in each successive year for which data were prepared.

The Decision to By-Pass: The experience of The Atlantic Refining Company serves to illustrate the types of facts upon which by-passing decisions are reached. The Atlantic Refining Company employed the by-passing technique extensively and was in 1952 distributing to its service stations largely from terminals. As a means of showing the types of economic considerations which led the company to use terminals rather than bulk plants as supply points for its service stations, we shall examine the factors which culminated in the by-passing of a bulk plant in Stroudsburg, Pennsylvania.

The Stroudsburg bulk plant was located approximately 50 miles northeast of Allentown, Pennsylvania, where the company owned and operated a pipe line terminal. The only product handled by the Stroudsburg bulk plant was gasoline. At the time the by-passing proposal was advanced, gasoline was being supplied to the bulk plant from the Allentown pipe line terminal by common carrier truck transports. The Atlantic Refining Company made deliveries to service stations in the Stroudsburg area from the bulk plant with two tank trucks of 1,000 gallon capacities. It was proposed that by-passing be effected by delivering gasoline in 4,500-gallon semitrailers directly from the Allentown terminal to the service stations in the Stroudsburg area. It was anticipated that, if the by-passing proposal was adopted, the Stroudsburg bulk station would no longer be used as a supply point for Atlantic's service stations. The bulk station would, however, remain open as a source of products supply for wholesale dealers in the vicinity.

The decision to by-pass the Stroudsburg bulk plant was reached largely on the basis of an estimate of the cost savings which might be

EXHIBIT IX-1. STANDARD OIL COMPANY (OHIO)

Illustrative Distribution Costs for Motor Gasoline: 1929–1952

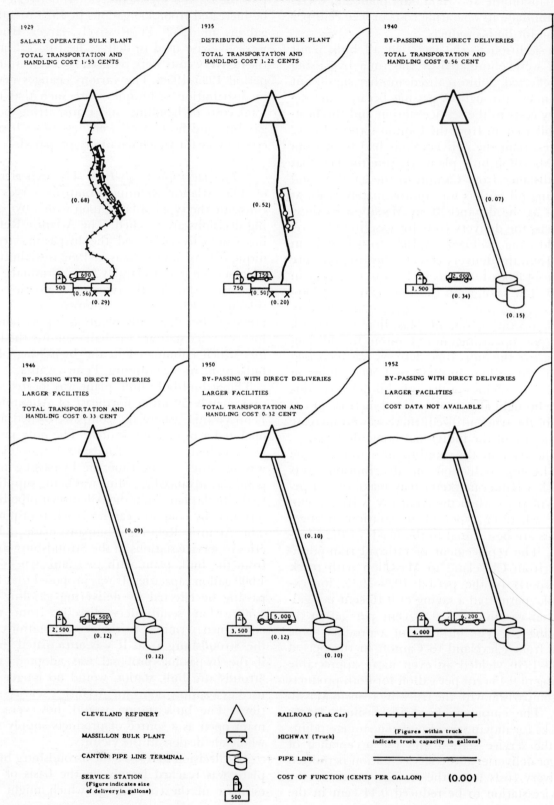

EXHIBIT IX-2. STANDARD OIL COMPANY (OHIO)

Illustrative Distribution Costs for Heating Oil: 1929–1952

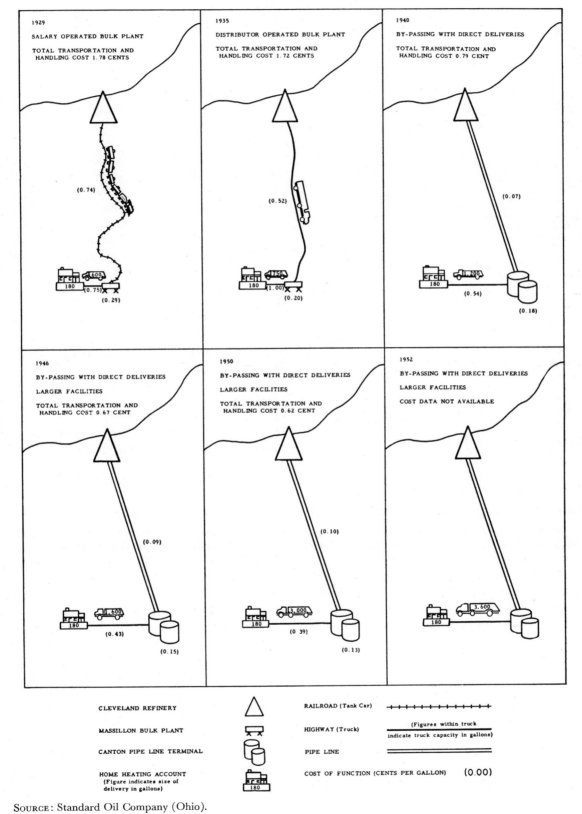

SOURCE: Standard Oil Company (Ohio).

made under the proposed method of operation. Exhibit IX-3 shows the cost figures upon which the by-passing decision was based. As the exhibit reveals, it was estimated that direct deliveries would result in a saving of $986 per month. On the basis of this estimate, the decision to by-pass was made and subsequent operations validated the accuracy of the estimate. It should be noted that the saving accrued almost entirely from the reduction of over-all delivery costs, a reduction made possible by the substitu-

EXHIBIT IX-3. THE ATLANTIC REFINING
COMPANY

Cost Savings Through By-Passing of Stroudsburg
Bulk Plant: 1951

Cost of Present Operation from Stroudsburg:		
Delivery by common carrier from Allentown to Stroudsburg		
150,550 gallons at 0.53 cent		$ 797.90
Stock loss (½ of 1%)		
752 gallons at 10 cents		75.00
Delivery cost from bulk plant		
Trucks: 2,702 miles/month at 10.10 cents/mile	$ 273.70	
Labor: 520 hours at $2.11/hour	1,097.30	1,371.00
Total Cost		$2,243.90
Cost of Proposed Operation from Allentown:		
Delivery cost from terminal		
Trucks: 4,800 miles*/month at 11.5 cents/mile		$ 518.00
Labor: 334 hours at $2.21/hour		740.00
Total Cost		$1,258.00
Monthly Saving Through By-Passing:		
($2,244 − $1,258)		$ 986.00

* 3,600 terminal miles and 1,200 route miles.
SOURCE: The Atlantic Refining Company.

tion of large for small delivery vehicles. Had the bulk plant been sold, additional savings would have resulted from the elimination of all costs associated with the plant.

One interesting aspect of the cost data is the saving gained in man-hours per month and consequently in labor costs despite the fact that the total miles traveled by Atlantic personnel were increased from 2,702 under the old system to 4,800 under the new plan. The labor saving came about largely through the greater flexibility which existed for utilizing each man's time effectively at the Allentown terminal. Three men working 10-hour shifts on staggered schedules were required at the Stroudsburg bulk plant. If one of the three men returned to the bulk plant several hours before the end of his shift, no effective use could be made of his

time. In other words, the number of men in Stroudsburg was out of balance; two men could not do the job, and full use could not be made of three men's time. Because of the many and varied assortment of jobs available in Allentown, however, a man could almost always be deployed from one job to another, thereby eliminating slack time.

Over a period of years The Atlantic Refining Company made hundreds of studies similar to the one which culminated in the by-passing of the Stroudsburg bulk plant. The end result of these analyses is apparent from the two maps of Pennsylvania shown in Exhibit IX-4. In 1930 the company was moving products, principally by rail, from three refineries in Pennsylvania to hundreds of bulk plants scattered throughout the state. In 1950 less than 50 Atlantic bulk plants remained in Pennsylvania. Replacing the earlier method of rail transportation was an elaborate products pipe line system. Product deliveries were made from pipe line terminals largely by truck transports to the remaining bulk plants or directly to service stations and consumers. The only Atlantic refinery remaining in Pennsylvania in 1950 was located in Philadelphia. The maps show very clearly how a company may gradually improve the efficiency of its entire distribution organization through hundreds of decisions with respect to bulk plants, terminals, pipe lines, and trucks.

By-Passing Bulk Plants with Sales to Commercial Accounts: In addition to the direct deliveries being made to many service station and household accounts, there was also a tendency in the period after World War II to by-pass the bulk station in making deliveries of gasoline to commercial accounts. Commercial accounts include certain large-volume consumers such as undertakers and bus, truck, and taxicab companies that maintain their own storage facilities. The commercial account often buys either under a yearly contract or in the open market, arranging for the delivery of several months' supply of gasoline at one time.

An important characteristic of the commercial business is the very heavy emphasis placed upon price. The commercial account is an avowed price shopper since his primary concern is to secure a low fuel cost per mile in the operation of his vehicles. Brand names and national advertising often mean very little to the commercial buyer. The customer buys on specifications and is interested only in the price he has to pay for a product of stipulated quality. The ordinary automobile operator is not much concerned about a fraction of a cent per mile in cost if he can be assured through branding or some other means that the product he purchases is at acceptable levels. A very small price differential is, however, extremely significant to the operator of a fleet of vehicles, and he is willing to go to great lengths to seek out an advantage.

Several factors have led to the institution of direct deliveries from refineries and terminals to commercial accounts. For one thing, the commercial market expanded greatly in recent years, and it now represents a far more important market segment than it formerly did. The trucking business grew rapidly during the war years to help relieve the load thrust upon overburdened transportation facilities. As this shift in the market went forward, some commercial accounts approached or even exceeded the size of individual bulk plant operations. In many cases, deliveries to bulk plants and then to commercial accounts involved unnecessary costs and the practice of by-passing bulk stations was therefore inevitable.

A great deal of controversy has arisen with regard to the propriety of refiners selling to commercial accounts at lower prices than they charge to their regular jobbers. To some extent the discounts to commercial accounts arise because the refiner frequently incurs lower costs in supplying commercial accounts than he does in supplying jobbers. The requirements of the commercial market are often quite different from those of the jobber market. Whereas the commercial buyer seeks only a low-cost product on which branding is of little significance, the jobber desires an array of services including a widely promoted product, credit cards, sales and technical advice, and point-of-sale advertising. Although the commercial account and the jobber may sometimes buy in approximately the same quantities, the costs to the refiner of serving the commercial account are often lower than those incurred to supply the jobber, and the commercial buyer feels he is entitled to a discount under the jobber price.

It is important to note that there are times when neither a jobber nor his supplier can secure or hold a commercial account unless the supplier quotes a price to a commercial account which is lower than his price to jobbers. In some areas, small refiners specialize in supplying commercial accounts on a price basis (see Chapter Twenty-Three). Since many small refiners sell on an unbranded basis and without the costs of advertising and sales promotion work, they are in a position to compete aggressively for commercial business. The decision which a supplier has to make often rests between losing a valuable commercial account to another refiner making direct deliveries or by-passing one of his jobbers with a competitive price and direct deliveries. For our purposes, the important thing to note is that the growth and evolution in the character of a market has been compelling jump integration. The commercial accounts have grown so markedly that a new type of supplier arrangement has been inevitable under the pressure of competition.

II. BACKWARD INTEGRATION BY MARKETERS INTO REFINING

Backward integration by marketers into refining has not contributed to the integrative bond between refining and marketing to the same extent as has the forward movement by refiners. The fact that a greater pressure for refining-marketing integration has come from refiners than from marketers may be attributed partially to the fact that refiners had more to gain from integration than did marketers. Attention has already been directed to the fact that nonintegrated refiners were subjected to greater profit instability than were wholesalers and retailers. Refiners were thus in a position to realize greater advantages in terms of profit stability through integration than were marketers. Moreover, refined products have more often tended to be in over- rather than undersupply. Refiners have therefore encountered somewhat greater difficulties in arranging to dispose of their products than marketers have encountered in seeking sources of supply.

The fact that backward integration has not been so prevalent as forward integration may also be explained partially by the fact that marketers had to overcome greater obstacles than refiners in order to build an integrated re-

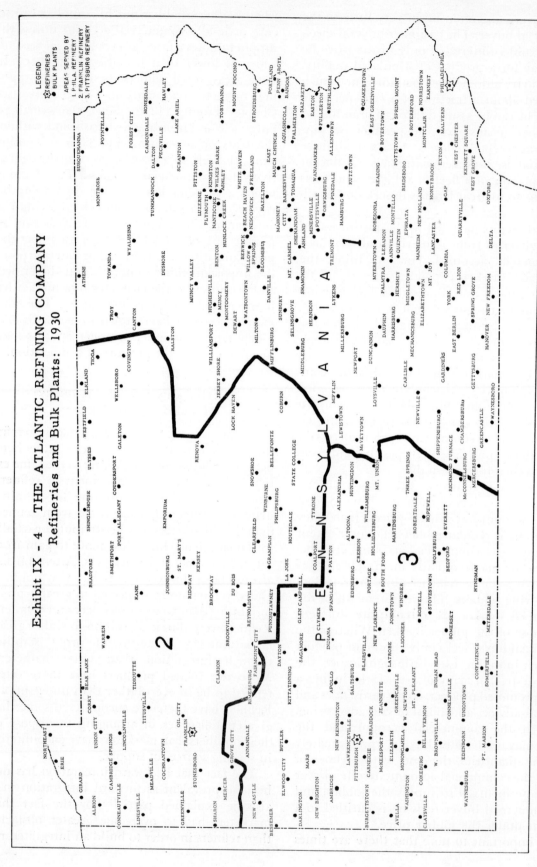

Exhibit IX - 4   THE ATLANTIC REFINING COMPANY
Refineries and Bulk Plants: 1930

SOURCE: The Atlantic Refining Company.

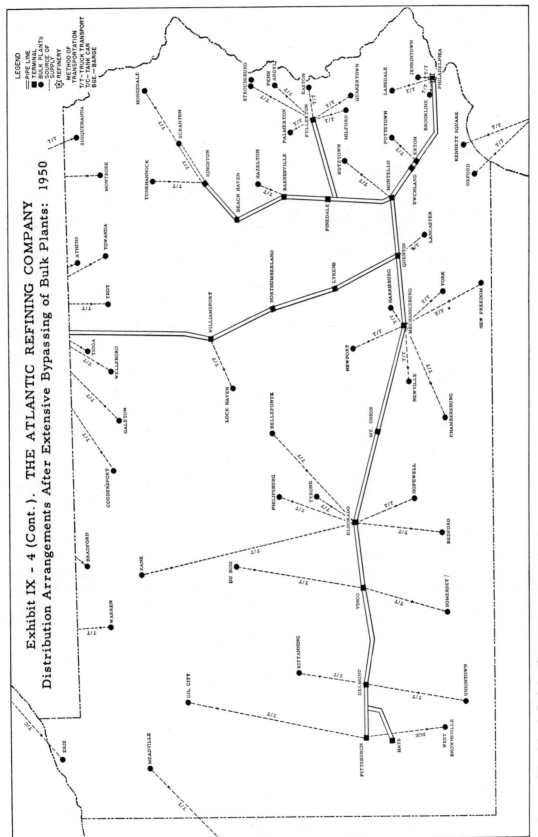

Exhibit IX - 4 (Cont.). THE ATLANTIC REFINING COMPANY
Distribution Arrangements After Extensive Bypassing of Bulk Plants: 1950

SOURCE: The Atlantic Refining Company.

fining-marketing structure. The acquisition of even a comparatively small refinery has entailed a very substantial financial outlay on the part of a marketer. A refiner could, however, purchase or construct bulk plants and service stations on a piecemeal basis and thereby spread his investment costs for marketing properties over a long period of time. It has also required a comparatively large marketing organization to provide an assured outlet for the products yielded by even a small refinery. A refiner could, however, absorb marketing outlets in gradual steps by directing additional increments of refinery output through any one newly acquired facility. Moreover, in the course of ordinary business operations a refiner was likely to gain a great deal of familiarity with the manner in which marketers operated their businesses, whereas a marketer had less opportunity to become familiar with the procurement and manufacturing problems of a refiner. From a management standpoint therefore, it was also a more difficult task for a marketer to integrate backward into refining than it was for a refiner to come the other way.

In the following paragraphs we shall discuss and illustrate some of the more important factors, other than those already considered, which led marketing companies to integrate into refining activities. These factors include the desire to assure supplies, to protect marketing investments, and to protect product quality.

Integration to Assure Supplies:

The quest for an assured source of supply has been one of the most important factors leading marketers to undertake refining activities. Access to refining facilities has given assurance to a marketing organization that it would not be caught short-handed when products were in short supply and that it would not need to enter the markets as a buyer when spot quantities were high in price. Backward integration into refining has, on the other hand, restricted the ability of marketing organizations to buy on the open market when prices were low. The effect of supply considerations on the integration decisions made by marketers has been clearly evident in the comparatively few periods over the past 30 years when refined products were in generally short supply on a national basis. For example, during World War

II and immediately thereafter many integration moves were made in response to an abnormally tight supply situation. As a means of illustrating the integration moves that took place during this period, we shall discuss: (a) the farm cooperatives which acquired refineries to protect their customers against shortages and to safeguard their petroleum marketing operations and (b) the Petroleum Heat and Power Company which integrated into refining to solve the problems in arranging for supplies which had beset its large and rapidly growing fuel oil marketing department.

Although both of these cases will illustrate integration decisions made during periods of short supply, it is important to recognize that certain marketers sometimes acquire refineries in order to gain an assured supply of refined products even during the periods when products are generally abundant throughout the country. Most of the period between the two World Wars was marked by a predisposition toward an oversupply rather than an undersupply of refined products. Refiners were hard pressed to find outlets and, as observed at an earlier point in the chapter, they pressed forward aggressively into the markets during most of these years. The forward movement by refiners placed an indirect pressure upon large marketers to reach back for refining facilities in order that they might be adequately hedged against a possible shift in the demand-supply situation in which refiners might supply their own outlets in preference to independent marketers.

Another reason why marketers sometimes seek refining facilities even when refined products are readily available on a national scale grows out of the very different demand-supply conditions which sometimes exist with respect to one or more refined products in certain geographic areas. A midwestern jobber is interested in the specific supply situation on the gasoline and heating oil economically available to his own territory. Recurring shortages or high prices for particular products in certain localized areas may therefore provide incentives for some marketers to secure refining facilities even though marketers in other sections of the country are encountering no difficulties in arranging for supplies at reasonable prices.

The Farm Cooperatives: The acquisition of refining facilities by farm cooperatives was a recent and significant development prompted largely by the desire of the distributing organizations to protect their customers in times of shortages.[15] Although farm cooperatives had long been engaged in the marketing of petroleum products, it was not until 1940 that two farm cooperatives constructed small refineries. The refining operations of farm cooperatives were performed by so-called "regionals."[16] In the nine years after 1940, 19 additional refineries were purchased by regionals, one of which was later resold. In 1950, 14 different regionals owned 20 plants with a total refining capacity of 106,900 barrels per day. There were throughout the United States 29 regionals supplying refined products to 2,110 local cooperatives which owned 2,565 bulk stations. The 14 regionals owning refineries conducted approximately 85% of the petroleum business held by all 29 regionals.[17]

The regionals integrated backward into refining in order to assure their customers of a continuing supply of products and to protect their own important petroleum marketing operations. Three-fourths of the refineries were acquired in just the two years of 1943 and 1948. In 1943 farm cooperatives found it exceedingly difficult to get sorely needed products. Refined products were in very short supply because of wartime restrictions and the very high domestic demand which existed. To alleviate the supply problem, five refineries were purchased by regionals in 1943.

In the period following World War II the demand for products rose very rapidly and cooperatives were once again confronted with shortages or, at best, the necessity of purchasing at premium prices. Under the particular set of economic conditions existing in 1948, regionals had the alternatives of: carrying on their petroleum marketing operations either on very low profit margins or unprofitably, substantially reducing or completely abandoning their marketing operations, or securing their own refining facilities as a solution to the conditions of short supply and high prices. Since the sale of petroleum products represented the greater part of the business of over half the regional cooperatives and was an important factor in others, any substantial cutback in petroleum marketing operations or unprofitable operations on this phase of their business were viewed with alarm. Consequently, cooperatives took positive steps to solve their short-term supply problem by acquiring refineries. The integration into refining represented a radical departure for the farmer cooperatives from a long-established way of conducting their petroleum operations.

It is interesting to note that 1948 ultimately proved to be a very inopportune time to enter the refining business. Toward the end of 1948 the supply situation was very suddenly overcorrected with respect to demand and the refinery prices of some products fell off sharply as indicated in Chapter Six. Only 6 plants out of the 20 owned by cooperatives managed to break even on refining operations in 1949, and each of the profitable plants was favored by either a freight rate differential or highly desirable outlets for fuel oil.[18] It is interesting to speculate whether this significant integration movement on the part of cooperatives would have proceeded with such rapidity if demand-supply conditions had changed just six months to a year earlier than they ultimately did. In any event, it is unquestionably true that the profit position of the farm cooperatives was enhanced in 1948 by the addition of refining facilities and that the refining operations were benefited in 1949 by the markets provided by the regional wholesaling organizations.

Petroleum Heat and Power Company: A second example of backward integration by a marketer during a period in which refined

---

15 The facts on farm cooperatives were drawn from J. Warren Mather *Petroleum Operations of Farmer Cooperatives,* Circular C-139, Farm Credit Administration, U. S. Department of Agriculture (Washington, Government Printing Office, May 1951).

16 Regionals are large buying organizations which make quantity purchases of supplies and equipment for local farm cooperative organizations. In general, bulk plant and service station operations are conducted by the local cooperatives and the regionals arrange for supplies. Most of the regionals serve a whole group of local cooperatives and are owned by the local cooperatives.

17 Most of the regionals acquiring refineries also secured crude oil production, pipe lines, and other transportation facilities. In 1950, 10 regionals were engaged in the production of crude oil, and their net crude oil production amounted to 16.3% of their refinery runs. Eight of the regionals operating refineries also owned pipe lines.

---

18 J. Warren Mather, op. cit.

products were in short supply is provided by the experience of the Petroleum Heat and Power Company. The company obtained an assured source of products supply as well as crude oil and natural gas production through a merger arranged with the Taylor Refining Company. The board of directors of the Petroleum Heat and Power Company voted to recommend the merger to stockholders on June 27, 1946, and the merger was consummated on June 23, 1947.

Prior to the merger the Petroleum Heat and Power Company was a substantial marketer of light and heavy fuel oils, a business originally established in 1903. The company did not engage in the marketing of gasoline. After World War II the company owned or leased large terminals along the East Coast from Boston to Washington as well as in Chicago. Light and heavy fuel oils were purchased either in local markets or on the Gulf Coast. Chartered tankers were used to transport products to eastern terminals from Gulf Coast locations. From terminals, distribution of fuel oils was made directly to household, commercial, and industrial consumers in a large fleet of company owned tank trucks. The company did not sell fuel oil for ship bunkering purposes. The company's wholesale and retail fuel oil marketing operations were well-balanced in the sense that all sales were made to ultimate consumers.

Petroleum Heat and Power also engaged in a complementary business activity, the manufacture and sale of fuel oil burners. In 1919 the company acquired the assets of Fess Rotary Oil Burners, Inc., and in 1929 the company merged with the American Nokol Corporation which also manufactured burners. In 1946 the company's plant located at Stamford, Connecticut, produced fuel oil burners for both residential and commercial installations. Oil burners were sold under the brand name Petro and distributed through the company's branch offices along the Eastern Seaboard and in the Middle West and through dealers and distributors in other areas throughout the United States. Over the years, however, sales of fuel oil contributed more substantially to the company's sales volume than did oil burner sales.

The actual and anticipated difficulties of arranging for a continuous supply of fuel oils in the period immediately following World War II were very important contributing factors in the company's decision to acquire refining facilities. In the years preceding World War II the company was supplied with fuel oils principally under long-term contracts arranged with the Taylor Refining Company. The contracts were however allowed to expire during the war period. At that time supplies of fuel oil were being allocated by the Petroleum Administration for War and a supply contract would have served no useful purpose. During the war years the company's sales of light fuel oil were greatly reduced due to rationing, and sales of heavy fuel oil were cut back as much as 64% by the conversion of industrial oil burning plants to the use of coal as a result of efforts to conserve petroleum products.

When the war ended the management was confronted with the unhappy task of supplying an unprecedented demand for fuel oils at a time when the company had not contracted with refiners for supplies. In the first postwar heating season, 1945–1946, much of the heavy fuel oil volume which had been lost by the company during the war years was regained and sales of light fuel oil exceeded figures for any preceding year in the company's history. Sales were expected to continue a sharp upward trend if adequate supplies of fuel oil could be obtained.

Petroleum Heat and Power was not in a position to arrange advantageous contracts with refiners because the company marketed only fuel oils rather than a more complete line of petroleum products. The volume of fuel oils sold by the company was sufficiently large so that the company might have contracted to buy the entire fuel oil output of a medium-size refiner. The management of Petroleum Heat and Power found that refiners were, however, often anxious to sell to very large accounts in package deals which included not only fuel oils but also gasoline in the contract terms. Since Petroleum Heat and Power had no marketing outlets for gasoline, the management was reluctant to enter into an arrangement whereby the company would market the entire output of a refiner, unless the refiner would agree to minimize the yield of gasoline. Refiners, on the other hand, were averse to any supply arrangement which would not permit them to maximize their gasoline yields when it would be profitable for them to do so. Because of its lack of facilities for handling the distribution of gasoline, therefore, Petroleum Heat and Power experienced greater difficulties in negotiating favorable supply contracts than might otherwise have been the case.

In 1946 when the board of directors decided to acquire the Taylor Refining Company through a stock exchange, Petroleum Heat and Power had no supply contracts for No. 1, No. 2, and No. 5 fuel oils and had little prospect of purchasing a volume of these products which would even approach its needs. The supply situation was particularly serious for the company because of the rapid sales expansion which had taken place in the two years preceding June 1946 and because of an anticipated sales increase of at least 30% in the forthcoming 1946–1947 heating season. In view of the existing shortage of fuel oils, the management did not want to assume the risks involved in buying spot cargoes. It was expected that price premiums would have to be paid for such spot cargoes as might be available. The management felt therefore that integration into refining was a necessity.

The decision to integrate into refining and, to a lesser extent, into crude oil and natural gas production was also strongly supported by the management's feeling that the producing and refining activities of the industry would offer greater profits than marketing operations over the long run. The fact that Coastal Refineries, a subsidiary of the Taylor Refining Company, held some potentially valuable oil and gas leases and reserves played an important part in making the merger particularly attractive to the management of the Petroleum Heat and Power Company.

The management was also anxious to integrate into refining and producing operations in order to secure a more stable gross margin position. On its fuel oil marketing business, Petroleum Heat and Power was dependent solely upon the margin available at the marketing level of the industry. At times in the company's history, this margin had narrowed to such an extent that profitable operations could not be maintained. The company had no opportunity to offset reduced marketing margins with an increased or stable margin at some other level of activity. It was believed that acquisition of the Taylor Refining Company would contribute to the firm's over-all profit stability by reducing the amplitude of its gross margin fluctuations.

The acquisition of the Taylor Refining Company gave Petroleum Heat and Power access to an assured supply of fuel oil and likewise provided an integrated company. On the effective date of the merger, June 23, 1947, the Taylor Refining Company owned a refinery at Corpus Christi, Texas, with a rated capacity of 28,000 barrels per day. Taylor also owned a small number of producing properties. Access to still more refining and producing facilities was gained through the controlling interest acquired in Coastal Refineries, Inc., a subsidiary of Taylor.[19] Coastal Refineries owned a 6,000 barrels per day refinery located at Port Isabel, Texas, and oil and gas producing properties in Texas. In the year ending June 30, 1947, gross crude oil production amounted to 2,838 barrels per day; net production amounted to 1,538 barrels per day.

The merger was effected through the exchange of 912,464 shares of Petroleum Heat and Power common stock for the entire capital stock of the Taylor Refining Company. Since Petroleum Heat and Power shares were selling for approximately $6 per share in the over-the-counter market, the purchase price was approximately $5,500,000. It is interesting to note that the stock received by the owners of the Taylor Refining Company represented a respectable return on the paid-in capitalization of approximately $100,000 existing at the time of Taylor's organization in 1930.

On May 27, 1952, the integration effects of the refining-marketing merger were nullified as Petroleum Heat and Power sold all its assets, except the stock and assets of the Taylor Refining Company, to the Pittston Company for $8,000,000 in cash. Thus, in the brief span of six years, Petroleum Heat and Power moved from a position in which it was a nonintegrated fuel oil marketer to a position in which it was a producer-refiner with no marketing facilities.

---

[19] At the time of the merger the Taylor Refining Company held a 75.53% stock interest in Coastal Refineries, Inc. During the period of the merger negotiations one year before, a 25% stock interest was owned.

The company had also become well established in the production of natural gas and had acquired 50% interest in a gas cycling plant. A discussion of the reasons for which the marketing properties were sold will be deferred to Chapter Ten.

Integration to Protect Marketing Investments:

Another general factor which prompted backward integration by marketers into refining was the desire to protect the very substantial investments which were sometimes accumulated in marketing businesses. As noted above, the individual investments made in marketing properties were not generally so large as those made in refineries or pipe lines. Over a period of time, however, some marketing companies made very heavy financial commitments in their operations by carrying out a program of individual investments. A marketer might, for example, expend large sums of money to cultivate a brand name, to acquire bulk plants and trucks, to build up a string of service stations, and to attract the patronage of independent distributors and retailers. When a marketer accumulated a substantial investment in his operation by virtue of such a program of investments, his desire to protect the investment with assured sources of supply was not unlike that of the refiner who sought to protect his manufacturing investment with investments at still other levels of the industry.

The larger marketers that made heavy financial commitments in their operations followed at least two general courses of action to obtain an uninterrupted supply of products. Some large marketing organizations worked out long-term supply contracts with refining companies. Others, such as the farm cooperatives and the Petroleum Heat and Power Company, employed backward integration as a means of protecting their marketing investments.

An excellent example of a situation in which the acquisition of a refinery was prompted by the desire to protect a marketing investment may be found in the experience of the Skelly Oil Company. In 1944 the Skelly Oil Company was a large, integrated concern whose operations were conducted principally in the Mid-Continent area. The company's sole refinery was situated at El Dorado, Kansas. Skelly had,

however, invested a considerable amount of money in the Rocky Mountain area to develop the company's brand name and to acquire marketing properties in the region.

Before 1944 the Skelly Oil Company serviced its Rocky Mountain marketing territory by tank car shipments from the company's refinery at El Dorado, Kansas. When the Interstate Commerce Commission approved a rate increase for the rail movement from El Dorado to the Rocky Mountain area, Skelly could not operate its marketing properties profitably on the basis of the higher delivered cost of products. In a very real sense therefore, the action of the Interstate Commerce Commission placed the Skelly Oil Company in a position whereby it was a nonintegrated marketer with respect to its Rocky Mountain territory. The company faced the alternatives of either withdrawing from the Rocky Mountain area or of finding a new supply of products that could be laid down in the area at a competitive cost.

The fact that Skelly was well entrenched from a marketing standpoint and had committed a considerable sum of money to its Rocky Mountain marketing operations caused the management to direct its attention toward finding a new source of products supply. In 1944 an opportunity was presented for Skelly to purchase the Perry Petroleum Company which owned a 1,000 barrels per day refinery in Denver, Colorado. The purchase of the Perry Petroleum Company was considered the best solution to the supply problem in the Rocky Mountain area and the refining company was therefore acquired.

Integration to Protect Product Quality:

Another general factor which motivated backward integration decisions by marketers, at least in so far as the *extent* of the integration is concerned, was the desire to secure the quality of products necessary for the development of an effective brand name program. Although we encountered no situation in which a nonintegrated marketer acquired a refinery specifically to improve the quality of his products, the maintenance of product quality has been an important factor leading refinery-marketing companies to bring their refining operations into balance with their expanding sales requirements.

The characteristics of motor fuels vary in terms of octane quality, vapor pressure, and the types and amounts of additives blended into gasoline, and the ingredients and characteristics are sometimes altered in accordance with a company's brand name promotional program. One company may stress "quick starting," another may feature "better mileage," another may emphasize "resistance to gum forming," and still another may stress "resistance to knocking in high compression engines."

Some companies reported that it would have been extremely difficult, if not impossible, to secure the differentiating characteristics in motor fuels upon which their brand name programs rested without direct control over manufacturing facilities. While outside suppliers could sometimes supply products of the desired specifications, it was difficult for any one supplying refinery to provide tailored products to several marketing companies. Products of basically high quality standards were, moreover, frequently in short supply, and a large marketing company could not easily secure all the premium products it needed without its own facilities. Finally, there was a feeling on the part of some sales executives that brand name programs in their companies could be endorsed more enthusiastically by sales people and the company's retail dealers if it were known that the products were manufactured in the companies own plants.

III. SUMMARY

1. The development of integration between the refining and marketing levels of the industry resulted primarily from forward integration by refiners and secondarily from backward integration by marketers. The predominance of forward integration may be explained partially by the fact that refiners had stronger business and economic reasons for seeking integration than marketers and partially by the fact that the obstacles to integration were less formidable for refiners than for marketers. Although both refiners and marketers were in a position to achieve very significant gains in profit stability through integration, refiners were in somewhat more need of the stability than were wholesalers or retailers. In general, the difficulties encountered by refiners in disposing of products were likewise more severe than those encountered by marketers in arranging for supplies. It was also easier for refiners to acquire marketing properties in a piecemeal fashion than it was for most marketers to finance the purchase of a refinery and to utilize its large manufacturing capacity.

2. Refiners made no major move to integrate forward into retailing activities until the automotive market for gasoline developed and created a need for new distribution facilities. After about 1911 refiners built drive-in service stations as a means of providing enough facilities to supply the rapidly expanding gasoline market, to provide higher standards of service to the public, and to take advantage of the strong profit potential offered by retailing activities.

3. From 1920 to about 1935 refiners undertook integration into retailing to secure and hold market outlets. The struggle for outlets resulted principally from the pressure of large crude oil supplies. Refiners developed the dealer lease-and-license program as one means of increasing the number of their assured outlets. Many new service stations were likewise built by refiners as a means of gaining a foothold in new territories where most of the reliable dealers were already dealing exclusively with some other supplier. In addition, refiners sometimes built service stations of their own as an alternative to the large financial inducements which it was necessary to offer in order to secure good dealers.

4. The building of products pipe lines by refining companies led directly to integration into wholesaling through the building of terminals at the delivery points along the line. The economical access gained to territories surrounding the lines also made it possible for refiners to expand other wholesaling and retailing facilities. Since refining companies were usually the only firms in a position to build products pipe lines, they had little alternative but to build the lines and the terminals if they wished to capitalize on a cost-saving innovation. Because of the common carrier status of most lines, how-

ever, the forward integration into marketing touched off by the products pipe line was not limited solely to the refiners building the pipe line systems.

5. An important factor prompting jump integration by refiners in the marketing field was the desire to reduce distribution costs. Marked economies have been made possible in some areas through the by-passing of bulk plants with direct deliveries from refineries or terminals to service stations, consumers, or commercial accounts. The by-passing technique developed under the pressure of competition as a means of realizing the cost savings made possible by innovations such as the products pipe line, better roads, bigger trucks, large volume service stations, and the growth of commercial accounts. The by-passing of bulk plants has been a step-by-step process justified in most situations by a comparative cost analysis of bulk plant operations versus those of direct distribution.

6. One of the most important reasons for backward integration by marketers into refining was the desire for an assured supply of products. The need for an assured supply was felt most strongly by large, rapidly growing marketing organizations and by companies that had made a heavy financial commitment in a marketing program. Marketers were most active in acquiring refining facilities during the comparatively few periods in which refined products were in short supply and spot quantities high-priced throughout the country. Even when supply and demand were fairly well in balance on a national scale, however, some marketers undertook integration to avert regional or particular products shortages or as a countermeasure to the forward integration movement by refiners.

7. The problem of maintaining the quality of products necessary for the development of a brand name program led many companies to keep their refinery output roughly in balance with their expanding sales requirements. Several companies featured distinctive characteristics of their motor fuels in their brand name programs. Since the product tailoring necessary to support the brand name programs was not easily accomplished through the use of outside suppliers, the companies expanded their own refining facilities.

CHAPTER TEN

Selected Examples of Disintegration

THE DEVELOPMENT of vertical integration in the oil industry has not been the result of a continuing, uninterrupted series of integration steps. The experience of the industry has been characterized by both integration and disintegration steps, and the industry has arrived at its present highly integrated state only because the integration moves have been somewhat more prevalent than the disintegration moves. The history of every company we studied revealed one or more situations in which the management had made deliberate decisions to *reduce* the depth, extent, or intensity of the company's integration arrangements for short or extended periods of time. We found some cases where companies had withdrawn completely or partially from producing, refining, transportation, or marketing activities and a fairly large number of cases where companies embarked on programs involving a weakening of the integrative ties among their operations at successive levels of the industry. In general, the experience of most of the companies was characterized by much trial and error with different types of integration arrangements.

As a means of illustrating the types of circumstances which sometimes cause the disbanding of integrative ties, we shall in this chapter discuss several examples of disintegration from marketing activities. Attention will first be directed to an industry-wide movement which brought about a general reduction in the intensity of integration between the refining and marketing levels of the industry: the leasing of company owned service stations to dealers during the 1930's. Attention will then be directed to individual company programs which led to the complete withdrawal from marketing activities: the decision of the Deep Rock Oil Corporation to sell its bulk plants and service stations in 1949, and the decision of the Petro-

leum Heat and Power Company to dispose of its fuel oil marketing properties in 1952. Examples of reductions in the extent of integration into particular marketing activities may be found in Chapters Fifteen and Sixteen. In addition, disintegration moves with respect to certain other industry activities will be discussed in other chapters of Part Three of the book.

I. THE IOWA PLAN

The withdrawal of most integrated oil companies from the direct salary operation of service stations was one of the most significant disintegration movements which has occurred in the history of the oil industry. Several integrated companies began to lease their company owned and operated service stations to private operators around 1930. In 1935 and the years immediately thereafter the program gained momentum and spread quickly throughout the industry. In many cases, service stations were leased to the persons who had formerly served as station managers. For purposes of discussion in this chapter, these new lessee operators will be referred to as dealers. The dealers purchased refined products from their suppliers and were responsible for the management of the stations as well as the selling prices at which the products were sold.

The process by which companies abandoned the direct salary operation of service stations is most widely known as the "Iowa Plan." The terminology was adopted in 1935 when practically every refining company and jobber selling in Iowa responded to a very severe chain store tax law by leasing out all of its company owned and operated stations in that state. In the strictest sense, the Iowa Plan of operation is one in which all a company's stations are leased, but the term is also applied to situations in which most stations are leased. The contracts originally drawn up in Iowa contained no provisions which would prevent dealers from switching from one supplier to another, whereas the modified Iowa Plans adopted in other states often required a lessee to handle the products of his supplier, although not necessarily on an exclusive basis.

The reasons which led the companies to lease their service stations to dealers are far more complex and diversified than the immediate response to the Iowa chain store tax might at first suggest. Many of the integrated companies, including the Mid-Continent Petroleum Corporation, the Sinclair Oil Corporation, The Texas Company, The Atlantic Refining Company, and the Standard Oil Company (Indiana) had experimented fairly extensively with lessee operations before the Iowa law was enacted. There is good reason to believe that the program would have proceeded, although perhaps more slowly than it ultimately did, even if chain store taxes had not been put into effect. In fact, the Iowa Plan of operation preceded the enactment of chain store taxation in many states, and it was adopted in other states where chain store taxes were never passed.

The Iowa Plan was adopted because many companies found that it was more profitable for them to lease their service stations to dealers than it was for them to operate the stations under the set of economic circumstances that developed in the late 1920's and 1930's. During this period company operated service stations suffered sharp losses in gallonage at a time when their operating costs were being forced to higher levels. With a combination of gallonage declines and higher costs, the company operation of service stations often yielded only very small profits or no profits at all. When the stations were leased to dealers, the supplying companies had two new sources of income which together frequently exceeded the retailing profits they had earned by operating the stations. In the first place, a rental income was secured from the dealers for the leased properties. Second, a gallonage increase was frequently obtained by the dealers which made it possible for the supplying companies to obtain higher profits on their refining and wholesaling functions. Moreover, since the total rentals paid by dealers increased with volume, in-

creased gallonage often meant higher rental fees for suppliers. In the following paragraphs we shall discuss (a) the reasons for the declining gallonage experience at company owned and operated stations, (b) the reasons for the rising costs at company operated stations, and (c) the results obtained under the Iowa Plan of operation.

The Declining Gallonage Experience of Company Owned and Operated Service Stations:

For reasons that have already been discussed in preceding chapters, the average gallonage sold by service stations began to decline markedly after about 1926.[1] The rate of growth in the automotive market for gasoline had begun to slacken but new investment funds continued to flow into the building of new service stations. Service stations had been built under the pressure of large crude oil supplies and because the spirited competition for retail outlets had forced unit gross margins to seemingly attractive levels. All types of retail stations, including company owned and operated service stations as well as contractor stations,[2] were adversely affected by the overexpansion in the number of outlets.

The company owned and operated service stations were, however, particularly hard hit by losses in gallonage because their selling prices were often not competitive with those of contractor stations or other marketers. Around 1929 or 1930 price competition was touched off by several new types of marketers. One such marketer was the trackside operator discussed in Chapter Nine. These firms were armed with both the wholesale and retail margins and frequently shaded one or two cents off going price levels to attract patronage. Trackside operators first appeared in rural areas (around 1925) and later spread to cities and towns. Cooperatives likewise began to develop positions of some importance in rural areas and a number of smaller marketing companies initiated price cutting at retail outlets. Contractor stations quickly met the challenge of the cut-price marketers by offering "under canopy" price dis-

---

[1] See Chapters Four, Six, and Nine.

[2] The term "contractor station" will be used in this chapter to describe an independently owned and operated station selling the brand-name products of a supplier under the terms of a supply arrangement worked out between the two parties (see Chapter Sixteen).

counts [3] to favored passenger car customers and to commercial buyers. As a result of the activities of avowed price cutters and the under canopy discounts offered by contractor stations, the company operated stations were no longer competitive and their volume of business declined sharply.

The pricing practices prevailing in the industry during the 1930's made it a very difficult task for the company owned and operated service stations to engage in price competition on an effective basis. Prior to the adoption of the Iowa Plan, retail prices were posted at company owned and operated stations. Contractor stations purchased gasoline at a stated discount off the retail prices posted at the stations of their suppliers and were, in effect, guaranteed a fixed margin in the amount of the discount. Many companies felt that the intense price competition which developed in the early 1930's, including under canopy price shading by contractor stations, was evidence that the contractor discounts could not be held at existing levels without a serious loss of gallonage by the company stations. Any one supplying company feared, however, that the announcement of a reduction in the amount of its discount to contractor stations might cause many of them to shift to other suppliers. Since contractor stations played an important role in distributing the gasoline of most companies, disastrous consequences could easily have followed the announcement of a cutback in the retail margin. One major oil company actually attempted to reduce the retail margin in Chicago but was forced to restore the cut as its contractor stations turned to jobbers as alternative sources of supply.

It should be noted that a general reduction in the prices posted at company stations would have aided company and contractor stations alike in combatting the inroads of cut-price marketers, but the contractor stations would still have enjoyed an advantage over company stations because they could have attracted business by giving away a portion of their "guaranteed margin." Many companies were therefore anxious to develop a distribution setup which would eliminate sales to contractor stations at a stated discount under the prices posted at their own company operated stations.

The complex administrative job of setting competitive prices at many different company operated stations and some uncertainties of a legal character were two other problems which made it difficult for company stations to meet the price cutting of contractor stations and other marketers. Companies found that it was not an easy task to set a comprehensive pricing policy under which their employees would be free to adjust prices to meet any type of situation, such as under canopy price cutting by contractor stations or open price cutting by only a few marketers in an area. Moreover, under the provisions of the Clayton Act and various state-wide one-price laws, it was possible that selling at a competitive price in one area of a state while a higher price was maintained in other areas might be considered as discriminatory pricing, thereby subjecting the company to possible court action. Companies were hesitant to suffer losses in realization throughout an entire state in order to meet the price competition in the most distressed areas of the state. Since companies were often reluctant to reduce any retail prices short of a compete collapse of the market, company stations in some cities and towns were placed at a severe handicap to other marketers.

The pressure for the Iowa Plan of operation found in the inadequacies of the pricing system was summarized by the Standard Oil Company (Indiana) in 1936 as follows:

Our company operated outlets are no longer competitive. Efforts to check declining sales have been unavailing under our present price and discount policies. . . . By placing our stations in the hands of independent dealers and by giving them the flexibility and private initiative of the independent operator, their sales trend should be reversed and our profits increased. [4]

One further circumstance bringing reduced gallonages to company owned and operated service stations was the loss of a large amount of commercial business in the 1930's. One provision of the Petroleum Code, instituted under the National Recovery Act, prohibited the granting of discounts below posted service station prices for any reason whatsoever. Pre-

---

[3] The terminology "under canopy" price discounts is used to describe a more or less secretive price concession which enabled a customer to purchase gasoline at a price lower than that posted on the pumps.

[4] Source: Standard Oil Company (Indiana).

viously, oil companies had sold large volumes of gasoline to commercial accounts from company operated service stations at discounts off posted retail prices. When the granting of discounts was banned, the large commercial accounts retaliated by installing storage facilities at their garages and accepting tank-wagon deliveries. The smaller commercial accounts that were unable to justify the building of storage facilities continued to purchase at company operated stations for awhile, but they were gradually lured away either by contractor stations offering under canopy price concessions in defiance of the code or by recognized price cutters. The experience of The Atlantic Refining Company, as related in a company report, is probably fairly representative of what was happening to company stations as a result of the abandonment of commercial discounts.

Under the terms of the Petroleum Code, we started the discontinuance of granting discounts at service stations, to commercial accounts. By this time we had developed a commercial business of 80 million gallons of gasoline a year, of which approximately 30 million gallons were through service stations and were sold at discounts ranging from 1 cent to $3\frac{1}{2}$ cents per gallon; the average discount for one year, the year 1930, was calculated to be 2.31 cents per gallon. Our commercial accounts under contract for the year 1935 show service station deliveries of less than half a million gallons for the year to this class of trade, all of which was at open market price. The studies of your Committee reveal that we would have had a lesser profit by $403,000 for the year 1930 in the Philadelphia and Eastern Pennsylvania Districts if we did not have the commercial gallonage at service stations, even though it was at a discount. Also, in these same districts, if we enjoyed the same relative volume of commercial business for the first 6 months of 1935, we would have had a greater profit by $170,000 or approximately $355,000 for the year.[5]

Rising Costs at Company Owned and Operated Stations:

Just at the time that retailers were under considerable pressure to reduce their costs as a means of maintaining profitable operations with lower volumes, the company owned and operated stations were confronted with several

new types of costs, such as chain store taxes and Social Security taxes, that other contractor stations and cut-price marketers were able to avoid. Self-employed retailers were, moreover, able to bring about a reduction in their labor costs by increasing the number of hours they worked per week for the same wages whereas the company operated stations were subjected to the overtime provisions of the wage and hour laws.

The enactment of chain store taxes in various states caused an important new cost to be incurred by company owned and operated stations. The Iowa tax made it virtually impossible for a company to operate a chain of stores on a profitable basis. Actually the statute levied two separate taxes against chain stores. One was a graduated store license tax based upon the number of stores in a chain, and the other was a tax on the gross receipts of chain stores. In both cases, the taxes were graduated sharply upward as the number of units or gross receipts increased. The maximum license tax per store amounted to $155 yearly for each store over fifty.[6] The graduated gross receipts tax ranged from $25 on gross receipts not in excess of $50,000 up to a maximum of $1,000 yearly for each additional $10,000 of gross receipts in excess of $9,000,000. On November 19, 1935, the Federal District Court invalidated the gross receipts tax provisions but upheld the per store tax. Later the United States Supreme Court affirmed the decree of the District Court and collection of the gross receipts tax was permanently enjoined.[7] The Iowa chain store tax law was apparently aimed originally at chain grocery and drug stores, but a small group of gasoline jobbers in Iowa was successful in its efforts to have the law apply to service stations as well.

The leading marketer in Iowa, the Indiana Company, responded immediately to the new tax law by leasing all its remaining company owned stations in the state prior to the effective date of the new statute. All the company's low-volume outlets had already been leased under

---

[5] Company memorandum dated June 1936.

[6] The yearly license taxes on the stores in a chain were as follows: second to tenth stores, $5 each; eleventh to twentieth stores, $15 each; twenty-first to thirtieth stores, $35 each; thirty-first to fortieth stores, $65 each; forty-first to fiftieth stores, $105 each; all over 50 stores, $155 each.

[7] *Valentine et al.* v. *Great Atlantic & Pacific Tea Co.*, 299 U. S. 32, 57 S. Ct., affirming *Great Atlantic & Pacific Tea Co.* v. *Valentine et al.*, 12 F. Supp. 760.

a program of selective leasing which had been in operation for approximately one year. Similarly, practically all other major oil companies marketing in Iowa adopted new marketing policies by leasing all company owned stations in the state. The enactment or threatened passage of chain store tax laws in other states caused the Iowa Plan of operation to spread very rapidly.

Wage and hour laws, the Social Security Act, and the growth of union activity were further factors which tended to make the company operation of service stations relatively more costly than that of an independent type of operation in many situations. A limitation on the number of hours which could be worked by company employees without the payment of a premium rate was of particular importance in placing company owned and operated service stations at a disadvantage relative to other independent retailers. Social Security legislation did not of itself impose a heavy enough burden to account for the shift to dealer operations, but the contribution by an employer amounting ultimately to about 6% of payroll charges was an added expense to the companies which other marketers did not share. The advent of service station unions was followed by strikes in some of the principal cities of the country. The wage increases granted in response to union demands placed the company operated stations at a cost disadvantage since the other marketers were self-employed and not usually interested in unionization.

Results Obtained Under the Iowa Plan:

The leasing of company owned and operated service stations to dealers proved to be a satisfactory solution to the problems which had placed many company outlets at a disadvantage to other retailers with respect to gallonage and costs. Under dealer operation the leased stations were able to compete on equal terms with other retailers and thereby increase their gallonages. They were also able to escape many of the burdensome cost factors that had impinged upon company owned and operated stations.

Certain changes in the pricing mechanism of the industry brought about by the Iowa Plan contributed very substantially to the improvements in gallonage shown by dealers under the new leasing arrangements. As noted above, company owned and operated stations were often at a price disadvantage in competing with contractor stations because contractor stations purchased gasoline at a discount under the prices posted at company stations and then undercut the company stations by offering under canopy price discounts off the posted retail prices. Under such circumstances, the operators of contractor stations had continually agitated for both higher retail prices and increased retailing margins on the basis that the increases would benefit both the contractor stations and company owned and operated stations. The experiences with cut-price marketers and under canopy price cutting, however, indicated that price or margin increases were not warranted. Under the Iowa Plan, supplying companies quoted tank wagon prices to both dealers and contractor stations and retail prices at all stations found their own levels according to local competitive situations. The newly leased stations had much to gain from the new pricing practices because their prices (when company operated) had often been out of line with the market.

The fact that dealers often showed greater personal initiative than company employees was a second factor contributing to the growth in gallonage at the newly leased stations. Under company operation the station employees were often paid a straight salary and there was not the same incentive to cultivate a continuing clientele as existed when the operators were independent businessmen.

Since dealers were self employed, they enjoyed a cost advantage in that they were not subject to the provisions of the chain store, Social Security, or wage and hour laws. They were, moreover, in a position to increase the length of their work week and to secure other economies by employing members of their families as attendants.

As an example of the results obtained under the Iowa Plan of operation, we shall draw upon the experience of the Indiana Company. The Indiana Company leased 907 of its low-volume accounts to dealers in 1934. In 1935 the company analyzed the policy of selective leasing of low-volume outlets. One finding of the analysis was that sales at leased stations increased 11.78% relative to the trend at company operated stations. There was no indication that the gain was a temporary spurt. Rather it appeared that the trend of sales had been reversed. Another finding of the analysis was that "operators of leased stations were more active in soliciting accounts and holding patronage on the basis of personal friendship than are the personnel of company operated stations." [8]

The Indiana Company had a second favorable experience with the leasing of stations in 1935 which, together with the results obtained at the low-volume stations leased in 1934, led the management to extend the Iowa Plan of operation throughout its marketing territory. Before July 1, 1935, all the Indiana Company's remaining stations in Iowa were leased to dealers in response to the state's chain store tax law. The conversion of stations to dealer operation benefited the Indiana Company as noted in the company's annual report for 1935 as follows:

The results have been rather surprising. While it has been impossible to maintain uniformity of free service, and there had probably been some decline in the employment provided in the stations, the company's sales have not suffered. On the contrary, the quantities of products distributed to the same stations have measurably increased.

On the basis of this experience, it has been decided to place the operation of company-owned stations as largely as possible in the hands of independent dealers . . . Large numbers of stations in other states have already been converted into such dealer outlets, and in the course of this conversion many former employees have become dealers in their own right, able to develop their own retail business as they see fit.

Subsequent to the development of the Iowa Plan in the 1930's, most companies found that independent dealers provided a more effective means for handling the retailing function than did company employees. Many companies, however, continued to operate a few service stations as a convenience in training their personnel or experimenting with new merchandising programs, and a few companies, such as the Standard Oil Company (Ohio), continued to rely upon company operated service stations to distribute an important part of their gasoline output (see Chapter Sixteen). Moreover, the companies adopting the Iowa Plan continued their participation in retailing activities through the

[8] Source: Standard Oil Company (Indiana).

construction of service stations and the continued ownership of service station properties.

II. EXAMPLES OF COMPLETE WITHDRAWALS FROM MARKETING

In this section we shall draw upon the experiences of the Deep Rock Oil Corporation and the Petroleum Heat and Power Company to illustrate the types of considerations upon which decisions to withdraw from marketing activities are based. The actions of these two companies portray a very different type of disintegration activity from that represented by the leasing of company owned and operated stations to dealers.

Both companies sold their marketing properties outright and thus ran the risk of losing completely their representation in a community should the new owners of their facilities have chosen to turn to other suppliers. In the case of the Iowa Plan, on the other hand, the oil companies retained their ownership and control of their marketing properties and merely placed them in the hands of independent businessmen for operation. Another distinction between the Iowa Plan and the Deep Rock and Petroleum Heat and Power situations may be found in the fact that after the sale of their marketing properties, the two companies sold refined products exclusively in the tank car markets whereas the concerns employing the Iowa Plan thereafter sold refined products in the tank car and tank wagon markets.

There are many shades and degrees of disintegration with respect to marketing activities between the type represented by the Deep Rock and Petroleum Heat and Power situations and the type represented by the conversion of service stations to dealer operation. Some companies have, for example, converted to branded jobber operations as a means of distributing in selected marketing territories and performing certain types of jobs. As a matter of policy most companies have for a long period of years been using several different types of wholesale and retail outlets (see Chapters Fifteen and Sixteen). The type of outlet and method of operation which companies employ in a given setting are continually being reappraised; at times the decision is made to strengthen the integrative tie while at other times the decision is made to decrease the strength of the integrative link.

Deep Rock Oil Corporation:

In 1948 the Deep Rock Oil Corporation was an integrated oil company of medium size. The operations of the company were conducted principally in the Mid-Continent area, and executive offices were maintained in Tulsa, Oklahoma. The company's crude oil exploration and producing activities were scattered over a wide area of the country, but most of the firm's crude oil production was obtained from Texas, Oklahoma, Kansas, and Arkansas. Net crude oil production in 1947 exceeded 7,500 barrels per day, which was more than 60% of the company's refinery runs of crude oil. The Deep Rock refinery at Cushing, Oklahoma, had a capacity of 12,500 barrels per day. The plant was inefficient in terms of operating costs and was not properly equipped to obtain the product yields and quality of products needed by the company.

Refined products were marketed in Oklahoma and ten states in the North Central section of the country. A large portion of the company's gasoline and heating oil was sold through 148 owned or leased bulk plants and 225 owned or leased service stations. Company employees operated 112 of the bulk plants and 43 service stations. Jobbers and nearly 400 contractor service stations were likewise employed in the company's distribution program. The company had no crude oil trunk lines but did maintain an extensive network of crude oil gathering lines in the territory surrounding its refinery. The company did not own any products pipe lines, but commencing in 1942 it made increasingly greater use of the common carrier facilities of the Great Lakes Pipe Line Company. On December 31, 1947, Deep Rock's assets exceeded $24,000,000 and the net profit for the year was nearly $2,600,000.

Beginning in 1948, shortly after Mr. W. D. Garbade became president of the company, several significant changes were made in Deep Rock's operating situation. Mr. Garbade and his staff took a six months' period to prepare a complete size-up of the company's position. As a result of the extensive appraisal of the company's operating situation, a new program

was initiated which involved three components: (1) the expansion of the company's crude oil finding and crude oil producing operations, (2) the enlargement and modernization of the Cushing refinery, and (3) the withdrawal from direct marketing through the company's own facilities. In the following discussion we shall concentrate on the marketing aspects of this program as well as those aspects of producing and refining activities which had a bearing on the marketing decision.

Deep Rock's sales of gasoline and heating oil were made in two different types of markets in 1948. The greater part of the sales volume was accounted for by sales to the farm trade. The farm business was scattered over a wide area and entailed many small deliveries from bulk plants to individual consumers. A certain number of small service stations were also maintained in farming areas. The company's second major market was in the metropolitan areas of Chicago, Milwaukee, Omaha, Grand Rapids, Minneapolis, and Des Moines where company owned bulk plants and service stations were maintained. In general there was a higher gasoline throughput at service stations and a stronger demand for home heating oil in the metropolitan areas than there was in the farm areas.

The first step taken in analyzing the marketing situation was to determine the territory in which Deep Rock could market competitively from a transportation cost standpoint. To determine the limits of this area, crude oil transportation costs were computed for all types of carriers from the major crude oil producing fields to each important refining center. From each refining center the cost of moving refined products to the county seats in many states was figured for all possible modes of transportation. The crude oil and products transportation costs were then added together in various combinations to ascertain the lowest possible total transportation cost incurred by any refiner in reaching each county seat in Deep Rock's potential marketing area. If Deep Rock's transportation costs to an area did not exceed the lowest estimated transportation cost of any competitor by more than one cent, it was decided that Deep Rock could market in the area competitively. Other factors weighed in evaluating potential marketing territories were the density and trend of population of specific areas. Furthermore, if a town was along a water route where refiners had historically "dumped products," it was considered a less desirable market than other towns which were not so located. As a result of the study, the company began in 1948 to withdraw from marketing activities in certain areas and to concentrate its operations in other locations where it could compete more effectively.

After the company's competitive area was defined in the manner outlined above, the question of company ownership of marketing facilities versus that of jobber operation was raised. The company's marketing facilities were in poor condition, and it was estimated that $3,000,000 to $4,000,000 would be required to put them in good shape. Thus, one primary consideration to be resolved was whether the marketing facilities warranted an expenditure of $3,000,000 to $4,000,000 or whether there were other aspects of the company's operation such as crude oil producing or refining activities where investment funds might be placed to better advantage.

A review of alternative outlets for investment funds led the management to the conclusion that producing operations should be expanded as rapidly as possible. The management felt that a small firm could compete very successfully with the large company in crude oil producing and crude oil finding activities. Moreover, it was the opinion of the management that Deep Rock could operate successfully as a nonintegrated producer if it was desirable or necessary to do so. One step taken in 1948 to improve the company's crude oil position was to purchase for approximately $8,500,000 a 79% common stock interest in the Sloan and Zook Company, a sizable crude oil producing firm. To finance this purchase, Deep Rock borrowed money from a syndicate of banks and an insurance company. Deep Rock also increased its holdings of developed and undeveloped acreage and stepped up its drilling program.

The company's crude oil producing operations were bolstered primarily for the profit opportunity presented by oil producing activities and not because the additional supplies were urgently needed for refinery operations. The company had net crude oil production equal to approximately 60% of its refinery runs and the company's gathering facilities gave it access to additional supplies of crude oil for refinery operations. The contemplated enlargement of the refinery discussed below may, however, have been partially responsible for the company's decision to expand its producing activities.

There was a critical need for a reinvestment of capital at the Cushing refinery if the company wished to remain in the manufacturing business on a competitive basis. The refinery was practically obsolete. The company was forced to purchase and use almost the maximum amount of tetraethyl lead permissible per gallon in order to obtain a regular grade gasoline of acceptable quality. A portion of the regular grade gasoline was traded to other refiners at a differential to obtain a premium grade gasoline for marketing purposes. Moreover, the company was confronted with a declining demand for residual fuel oil and the refinery was not properly equipped to curtail the output of this product. It was estimated that all necessary renovations including the installation of a fluid catalytic cracking unit and an enlargement of capacity would cost about $4,000,000.

The management doubted that the existing refinery could be sold for more than $2,500,000, whereas an incremental investment of $4,000,000 would provide a refinery with a replacement cost appraised by the management at $12,500,000. Moreover, the renovated refinery would have unit processing costs on a favorable scale with other refineries in the Mid-Continent area of the same general size. The management was also predisposed to continue refinery operations because the plant location was considered a good one. Cushing was a main trunk line terminal point at which several transcontinental lines intersected, and the management believed therefore that the company would always be in a good position to buy crude oil. The company could move products by truck competitively within a radius of 75 miles and access to the Great Lakes Pipe Line opened up a broad geographic market to the north for gasoline and heating oils.

Aside from crude oil producing operations, which the management had decided to expand as rapidly as funds would permit, the refinery seemed to be the next most profitable outlet for the limited capital resources which the company had at its disposal. As noted above, the amount of money needed to expand and modernize the refining facilities was approximately equal to that needed to renovate the marketing properties. It was estimated, however, that a $4,000,000 investment at the refinery would yield a return on the investment of 28% with a payback period of less than three years, whereas a $3,000,000 to $4,000,000 expenditure for marketing properties could be expected to yield only about a 7% to 8% return on the investment. The refinery modernization program was commenced in 1949 and completed in 1950. Refinery capacity was increased from 12,500 to 19,000 barrels per day.

Quite apart from the considerations of alternative uses of funds in different departments of the company, it was believed that jobber operations would, in the long run, prove more beneficial to Deep Rock than would the company retention of marketing facilities. It was expected that the wholesalers and retailers would be anxious to build up their businesses if they were given the full incentives of entrepreneurs. The management believed that the outright ownership of facilities would give marketers the greatest possible incentive for doing a good job. As a consequence of the incentive which their jobbers would have, it was expected that Deep Rock's sales volume and profits would likewise increase. In the short run, however, it was estimated that jobber operations would yield a lesser profit to the company than would continued company ownership of facilities. It was calculated that jobber operations would in the near future yield a rate of return on the value of the marketing properties approximately 2 percentage points less than that realized under the existing method of operation.

From a financial standpoint, the sale of the marketing properties was expected to be beneficial in two ways. Most important, the sale would obviate the necessity of spending $3,000,000 to $4,000,000 to modernize the facilities since this responsibility would be shifted to the new owners. Secondly, it was anticipated that the properties would be sold for $1,000,000, a sum which could then be diverted to other more profitable ends such as crude oil production. It should be noted, however, that the company did not have immediate access to this capital because Deep Rock was willing to, and ultimately did, grant mortgages covering the greater part of the sales price of the marketing properties.

One of the most important factors prompting the decision to withdraw completely from direct marketing activities was the strong feeling on the part of Mr. Garbade and other company officers that jobbers rather than large companies should own the marketing facilities of the industry. The officers felt that jobber distribution was a means by which independent businessmen could be given an opportunity to realize all the gains for which they personally were responsible. Mr. Garbade claimed that a place must be found for more entrepreneurs if the free enterprise system in America was to be preserved and expanded.

Deep Rock began to withdraw from direct marketing in 1949. At a conference held in June, jobber representatives and the Deep Rock management officials met together to discuss and work out details of the new distributor program. At this meeting, ideas for a new trademark design and a station color scheme were suggested. The first Deep Rock properties sold to jobbers were those in the rural areas. In the agricultural areas, particularly, the management felt that jobbers could do a more efficient marketing job than could the company. Subsequently, the remaining facilities in the cities of Omaha, Minneapolis, Chicago, Milwaukee, and Des Moines were likewise sold to jobbers.

The program was completed in 1951. In most cases the facilities were sold to the former operators such as commission agents or company employees. The buyers were required to have sufficient financial resources to meet their working capital requirements and to make a down payment on their properties. As noted above, Deep Rock granted mortgages to cover the remaining cost of the properties. In 1950 Deep Rock introduced a new distributor franchise agreement which was enthusiastically approved by jobbers throughout the industry. The agreement guaranteed all distributors a fixed margin and provided, initially, for a term contract between Deep Rock and its distributors to be followed by yearly contracts unless 90 days' notice of cancellation was given by either party.

The Deep Rock management was very well pleased with its rather distinctive marketing policy in which no company owned or leased bulk plants or service stations were maintained. Mr. Garbade emphasized that the management was convinced that the policy was "not only in the best interest of the economy but also good business for Deep Rock."

Petroleum Heat and Power Company:

A second situation in which an integrated company disposed of its marketing properties may be found in the experience of the Petroleum Heat and Power Company. As noted in Chapter Nine, Petroleum Heat and Power was a large fuel oil marketing organization which integrated backward into refining and producing operations in 1947 through the acquisition of the Taylor Refining Company and Coastal Refineries, Inc. The refineries were situated at Corpus Christi and Port Isabel, Texas, and the company's distillate and residual fuel oil marketing properties were located along the East Coast and in the Middle West. Deliveries of fuel oil were made by company trucks to household, industrial, and commercial customers from large terminals, and gasoline was sold in the Gulf Coast cargo market. The company also maintained a plant at Stamford, Connecticut, at which fuel oil burners were manufactured. In 1952 the nature of Petroleum Heat and Power's operations underwent a second sweeping change when the entire wholesale and retail fuel oil business as well as the burner manufacturing division were sold to the Pittston Company for $8,000,000. In the following paragraphs we shall consider the reasons which prompted the company to withdraw from the fuel oil marketing business.

When the two refineries were acquired in 1947, it was intended that maximum quantities of fuel oil should be produced to meet the requirements of the marketing division. The company maximized fuel oil production through the use of a straight distillation process; no thermal or catalytic cracking processes were employed. As a result, the company's yield of distillate and residual fuel oils was over 66% of refinery runs for the fiscal year ending June 30, 1948, as compared with a fig-

ure of approximately 50% for all refineries along the Texas Gulf Coast. The gasoline obtained from the distillation process was below domestic specifications for octane quality and was sold in the Gulf Coast spot cargo market for export to foreign markets. The fuel oils were transferred to the company's marketing division for sale.

Important among the factors leading to the sale of the fuel oil marketing properties were certain changes in refinery technology and marketing conditions which made it impossible for the company to maintain the balance of refining and marketing operations which it had employed in the past. In 1949 it became obvious that the refining division could not be operated profitably so long as it maximized fuel oil production and turned out a low quality gasoline. Only by maximizing fuel oil production, however, could the manufacturing division supply the fuel oil requirements of the marketing division. To protect the refining division under a new set of market conditions discussed below, it therefore became necessary to make certain changes in refinery equipment which deprived the marketing division of its source of assured supply.

Petroleum Heat and Power was unable to conduct its manufacturing operations on a profitable basis when the refining industry was confronted with a declining gross margin in 1949. As noted in Chapter Six, there was a particularly sharp decline in the refinery price of residual fuel oil and an appreciable decline in the refinery price of distillate fuel oils. Since Petroleum Heat and Power was maximizing the production of fuel oils, the company was considerably more vulnerable to the price declines than were other concerns that obtained higher yields of gasoline and other light products. In 1949 the company was also confronted with a declining demand for its exported gasoline. Since the gasoline did not meet domestic specifications for quality, it was very difficult to find a new market for the gasoline in the United States.

In view of the unprofitable refining operations caused by the declining prices of fuel oils and the lack of a market for the low quality gasoline output, the Corpus Christi plant was shut down on December 1, 1949, and operations at the Port Isabel plant were suspended early in January 1950. With large stocks of fuel oil readily available at low prices on the open market, it was at that time an easy matter for Petroleum Heat and Power to supply its marketing division by means of purchases. Fuel oils could in fact be secured at lower costs to the company by purchases in the open market than they could be obtained by manufacturing.

The management believed the character of future markets for refined products would be such that refining operations could seldom be carried on profitably if the company produced a low quality gasoline product and maximum quantities of fuel oil. It was apparent that it would be necessary to employ refinery equipment which would yield a high quality gasoline suitable for sale in the domestic markets and a product mix which would return higher refinery sales realizations than could be obtained from the products yielded by a simple distillation process. The management felt that the refineries could be operated profitably over the long run only by using cracking and reforming processes of both the thermal and catalytic types. Cracking processes would improve the quality of the gasoline product and give greater yields of the higher priced petroleum products such as gasoline, kerosene, and heating oils and reduce the output of the low realization residual fuel oils (see Chapters Nineteen and Twenty).

In view of the management's desire to put the manufacturing division on a firm competitive footing, a substantial modernization program was undertaken at the Corpus Christi and Port Isabel plants in the three-year period following the plant shutdowns. The refinery equipment at the Corpus Christi plant was first changed over from a simple distillation process to one in which distillation, thermal cracking, and reforming processes were utilized. These renovations were completed by February 1950, and refinery operations were then resumed with higher product quality and improved product yields. In the summer of 1950 the company took further steps to meet the domestic demand for a high octane gasoline by letting contracts for a thermofor catalytic cracking unit, a catalytic polymerization plant, and a gas concentration plant to be added to the Corpus Christi refinery. The new equipment was placed on stream during 1952. At the Port Isabel refinery, in which a one-half interest was sold in 1950 to Mayfair Minerals, Inc., a new 15,000 barrels per day crude distillation unit was completed and placed on stream on June 1, 1951. In 1952 a platforming unit was installed at the Port Isabel plant to upgrade the low octane gasoline then being yielded.

After the refineries had been put in shape to operate profitably, the refinery yields were out of balance with the requirements of the company's fuel oil marketing operations. The management anticipated that the gasoline yield would be about 50% of refinery runs, the output of No. 5 fuel oil completely eliminated, and the yield of No. 6 fuel oil negligible in amount with the new equipment operating economically. Although the company could have obtained very high yields of No. 5 and No. 6 fuel oil if it had desired to do so, increasing the relative output of these products would have jeopardized the chances of earning a favorable return on the investment in the new refinery equipment. Sales of residual fuel oils (No. 5 and No. 6 fuel oils), however, accounted for over two-thirds of the products volume of the marketing division. It was expected that the marketing division's requirements for only light fuel oil (No. 2 fuel oil) could be met by the refinery after the installation of the new processing facilities.

It was apparent therefore that if the company was to continue its marketing activities, it would once again be necessary for the company to buy large quantities of residual fuel oil from other refiners. The management was most reluctant to engage in a buying program because of the anticipated problems of arranging for adequate supplies. It will be recalled from Chapter Nine that the desire for assurance of supply was one of the primary reasons why the company had integrated backward into refining operations just five years before. The management considered the alternative of building up a wholesale and retail gasoline business along the East Coast to the point where the marketing requirements would be in balance with the new refinery yields. The possibility was rejected, however, because the management believed it did not have the funds necessary for such a program. The management decided therefore to withdraw from the marketing business and to concentrate upon producing and refining activities.

A second important factor resulting in the sale of the marketing properties was the management's belief that crude oil producing and refining operations would be likely to yield better returns on capital investments in the future than would marketing operations. It was believed therefore that such funds as were available for expansion should be diverted into the producing and refining divisions rather than into the marketing division. It was estimated that the sale of the marketing facilities would provide $8,000,000 which might be applied in furtherance of the company's producing and refining objectives.

The management also believed that the fuel oil burner manufacturing business would not return earnings commensurate with the investment required for this activity. The investment in the fuel oil burner business was very high because of the large inventories of spare parts which had to be carried. It was necessary for the company to do a high volume of business in order to make any money, and high volumes could not be attained consistently. Profits had been very erratic in the past. The management was therefore anxious to dispose of the burner activity along with the fuel oil marketing business.

The discovery of a vast gas reservoir in the McAllen field in Texas "tipped the scales" in favor of a future operation which would be based upon producing and refining operations rather than marketing activities. Petroleum Heat and Power and Mayfair Minerals, Inc., each owned an undivided half interest in the McAllen oil and gas field, and they had erected together a gas cycling plant in the field. The two companies signed a 20-year contract to supply natural gas from the field to the Trunkline Gas Supply Company. In 1951 Trunkline completed a gas line from northern Texas into Illinois, and Petroleum Heat and Power thus had prospects of a steady income from its gas operations for many years in the future.

In the light of the developments at the refineries, the firm's financial limitations, and the management's desire for the company to engage more heavily in producing activities, the stockholders of Petroleum Heat and Power voted on May 27, 1952, to sell all the assets of

the company, except the stock of the Tayor Refining Company, to the Pittston Company for a cash consideration of $8,000,000. The agreement provided for the sale of the marketing division with facilities along the East Coast and in Chicago and the fuel oil burner manufacturing business. The refinery at Corpus Christi, a one-half interest in the refinery at Port Isabel, and all the oil and gas properties of the company, including a one-half interest in the McAllen absorption and cycling plant, were the only properties not included in the transaction. Upon the consummation of the sale, Petroleum Heat and Power's activities were confined solely to its refining and producing operations in Texas.

Petroleum Heat and Power signed contracts to dispose of its refinery output after the sale of its marketing properties had been effected. The company contracted to sell its No. 2 fuel oil to the Metropolitan Petroleum Corporation, a subsidiary of the Pittston Company. Petroleum Heat and Power also arranged to sell its high quality gasoline output to a major company under a three-year contract. Thus, the company replaced ownership integration into marketing with contract integration. To assure an adequate supply of crude oil, a crude oil supply arrangement to supplement the company's own production was worked out with major companies.

III. SUMMARY

1. The oil industry did not arrive at its present highly integrated state by a series of integration steps alone, but rather by a combination of integration and disintegration steps. Although the integration moves were unquestionably more prevalent than the disintegration moves, deliberate decisions to reduce the depth, extent, and intensity of a company's integration arrangements were found in the history of every large company we studied. In general, the experience of most of the companies was characterized by much trial and error with different types of integration arrangements, and the processes of integration and disintegration were continually at work.

2. An important example of an industry-wide disintegration movement was the leasing of

company owned service stations to dealers during the 1930's. Company owned and operated service stations were leased to dealers because the stations were suffering serious losses in volume to other types of outlets and because the owners believed that the lease arrangements would permit a reduction in distribution costs. The company owned and operated stations were suffering losses in volume chiefly because their prices were not competitive with those of other marketers and because it was not easy to make quick adjustments in the prices at such stations to meet individual market situations. The factors tending to make the company operation of stations more expensive in many situations than a contractor or dealer type of operation were chain store taxes, wage and hour laws, the Social Security Act, the unionization of service station employees, and the difficulty of adjusting the working hours of salaried employees to the requirements of the service station business. The leasing of stations was greatly accelerated by the Iowa chain store law, and the movement thus came to be known as the Iowa Plan.

3. The experiences of the Deep Rock Oil Corporation and the Petroleum Heat and Power Company provide specific examples of the disintegration programs sometimes undertaken by individual concerns. Deep Rock sold all its bulk plants and service stations to jobbers because the management wished to expand the company's crude oil producing operations and modernize its re-

finery facilities and could not, at the same time, afford to make necessary improvements in the company's marketing properties. In addition, the Deep Rock management anticipated that the company's limited funds could be invested more profitably in producing and refining than in marketing activities, that jobbers might do a more effective selling job than company employees or commission agents, and that it would benefit the economy as a whole to increase the number of independent marketing enterprises.

Important among the factors prompting Petroleum Heat and Power to sell its marketing facilities were certain changes in refinery technology and marketing conditions which made it impossible for the company to maintain a satisfactory balance between its refining and marketing operations. The marketing properties handled distillate and residual fuel oils, but not gasoline. In order to secure profitable refining operations, it was considered necessary to install catalytic cracking facilities at the company's principal refinery to increase the yield of gasoline and to obtain a high quality product. The new refinery yields, however, deprived the company of a source of residual fuel oil for its marketing operations and the management was reluctant to operate without an assured supply. Moreover, the sale of the marketing properties provided funds which could be applied to producing, natural gas, and refining operation, activities which the management believed would prove more profitable in the future than would marketing.

CHAPTER ELEVEN

The Managerial and Operating Gains Realized from Vertical Integration

THE purpose of this chapter is to discuss the managerial and operating gains which some of the oil companies have been able to obtain from vertical integration. In the majority of the companies we studied, these gains were not recognized or developed in significant degree until long after a fairly advanced form of vertical integration had been achieved. The producing, refining, marketing, and pipe line departments usually operated on a fairly independent basis for a good many years after vertical integration had taken place. Each of the departments expanded as rapidly as it could, competed with the other departments for the capital funds available, and often made both its operating plans and commitments in plant facilities without much reference to the long-term planning of the other departments. In several of the large, integrated companies we studied, one or more of the executives made a statement to the effect that, "We have been an integrated company for a great many years, but it is only recently that we have begun to *manage* on an integrated basis."

It appears therefore that the managerial and operating gains permitted by vertical integration were rarely an important motivation for integration and were generally unanticipated at the time the moves were made. Ultimately, however, these gains may transcend in importance the specific forces and circumstances which have thus far prompted integration decisions. As noted in earlier chapters, integration decisions have usually been made under considerable competitive or economic pressure as a means of solving the problems which a company faced at a particular time. In later years changing circumstances frequently modified or completely nullified the original reasons for the decisions, and in some cases new pressures for

integration arose to replace the original ones. The specific, motivating forces for integration have thus been constantly shifting and changing in character and relative significance. The managerial and operating gains realized from vertical integration, on the other hand, have grown steadily in importance throughout the entire history of the industry, and there is considerable reason to believe that their full potentialities have by no means yet been realized.

Among the more important of the managerial and operating gains which some of the oil companies have come to realize from vertical integration, after having had some experience with it, have been (a) gains in the planning of capital investments, (b) gains in the planning of operations, and (c) gains arising from the enhancement of investment opportunities. In the following paragraphs we shall discuss and illustrate each of these three types of gains. A concluding section will then give brief consideration to various other managerial benefits which have often been associated with vertical integration.

I. GAINS IN THE PLANNING OF CAPITAL INVESTMENTS (SINCLAIR OIL CORPORATION)

The opportunity to plan capital investments in the different segments of the oil business on a coordinated basis is one of the most significant of the managerial benefits which oil companies have secured from vertical integration. Investments in oil wells, pipe lines, refineries, and marketing properties can have their maximum economic and business utility only if they are made at the right time and in the right places and only if the facilities have the proper capacities relative to each other. In an integrated company there is a managerial opportunity, albeit not always exercised, to see to it that the investments in the different segments of the business are properly correlated time-wise, place-wise, and size-wise with respect to each other and with respect to the requirements of the market. Frequently an integrated company can plan and make a whole series of investments in producing, transportation, refining, and marketing facilities as a single program. Moreover, since the management of each department usually has full access to the plans and programs of other departments, the chance of making unsound investment decisions is reduced.

The necessary correlation of investments in the different segments of the business may also, of course, be worked out among nonintegrated companies. The process of adjustment in this case, however, is far more likely to involve trial and error and to be accompanied by mistakes and attendant economic waste than it is in the case of integrated companies. Nonintegrated companies operating in different phases of the business cannot exchange information among themselves with respect to building programs, future plans, and future requirements as readily and as freely as may the department heads of an integrated company who meet each other day after day across the conference table and in the lunch room. In addition, a nonintegrated company is not often in a position to have firm commitments from all the many firms preceding and following it in the oil process with regard to the investments they will make in the future. The usefulness of a particular investment by a nonintegrated company may therefore sometimes be impaired by the failure of other companies to carry out their investment programs on schedule and to the extent originally anticipated.

If an integrated company were to construct a refinery in a new producing area, for example, it would probably at the same time initiate whatever other investments were necessary in crude oil gathering and trunk lines and in products transportation facilities to assure the plant a reasonable chance of operating successfully. If a nonintegrated company were to construct the same refinery, however, it would be dependent upon other concerns for the supporting investments, which might or might not be forthcoming in the immediate future. A classic, and perhaps apocryphal, example of an

error in an investment decision by a nonintegrated company may be found in the story of a refiner who hastily constructed a plant in Colorado on the strength of reports he had heard of extensive exploratory and drilling activity in one area of the state. The wells ultimately proved dry and the refinery, which was by that time fully completed, never ran a barrel of oil. An error of this kind in an integrated producing-refining organization would be possible but highly unlikely.

The gains which the integrated companies have frequently been able to make through the careful coordination of capital investment decisions are somewhat difficult to demonstrate in concrete terms. These gains usually become manifest only over a fairly long period of time and take the form of a generally improved utilization of capital funds and a general strengthening of a company's over-all competitive position. The situation may be likened to a chess game in which the white pieces are all under the control of a single person whereas the black pieces are moved by four or five different people, each of whom moves his particular pieces without too much reference to what his teammates are doing. In such a game the white player would usually win through the development of a superior over-all strategy and the better utilization of each individual piece under his command, but it would be difficult to explain precisely how he was able to gain his advantage over the black players. So too, many an integrated oil company develops a better over-all strategy in the use of capital funds than is usually possible in the case of nonintegrated companies, although the exact means by which the final result is accomplished may be difficult to demonstrate in detailed terms.

Some indication of the way in which producing, refining, marketing, and transportation investments may be related to one another in an integrated oil company may be gained from an examination of the program developed by the Sinclair Oil Corporation during and after World War II. In using the Sinclair Oil Corporation as an example, we do not mean to imply that all its decisions were sound ones, that it developed the best possible arrangement under the circumstances, or that the entire strategy of the various moves was fully conceived in advance of actual developments. We present the case merely as a good illustration of the way in which investments in one phase of an integrated company's business may be correlated, deliberately or fortuitously, with investments in other phases of the business.

Situation of the Sinclair Oil Corporation in 1941:

The Sinclair Oil Corporation [1] was organized in 1919 to consolidate the properties and operations of three other companies which as a group had extensive producing, refining, marketing, and transportation activities in the Mid-Continent area of the United States and limited operations in Mexico. Thereafter Sinclair grew and developed as an integrated concern active in all phases of the business.

In 1941 the company was operating three large refineries located at Marcus Hook, Chicago, and Houston and six small refineries located at Wellsville (New York), Sinclair (Wyoming), Kansas City (Kansas), Coffeyville (Kansas), Sand Springs (Oklahoma), and Fort Worth (Texas). These nine refineries had a combined crude oil charging capacity of about 200,000 barrels per day. The company's crude oil production amounted to about 27 million barrels a year, an amount sufficient to supply about 36% of its refinery requirements. The Sinclair crude oil pipe line system extended from Houston to Chicago (see map, Chapter Twelve, Exhibit XII-5) and was able to serve the four Mid-Continent, the Houston, and the Chicago refineries. The Corpus Christi, Sinclair, and Wellsville refineries were served by smaller crude oil pipe line systems in their immediate areas while the Marcus Hook re-

finery was supplied largely with crude oil from Texas and Mexico which was brought to Marcus Hook by tanker.

The company's marketing facilities in 1941 included 1,812 bulk plants and terminals, 20 company operated service stations, 9,626 dealer operated service stations, and 17,521 contractor service stations. These properties were spread throughout the 43 states east of the Rocky Mountains; the company was not represented in the 5 Pacific Coast states. For the movement of products from its refineries to bulk plants and terminals in the interior of the United States, the company relied heavily upon tank car shipments. The company had no investments of any significance in products pipe lines other than a 3% interest in the Great Lakes Pipe Line, and in 1940 only about 1.3% of its shipments from refineries moved via pipe lines which it owned or in which it had a stock interest. In many areas of the country, the company was unable to supply its market outlets on a competitive basis from its own refineries, and was therefore forced to enter into many exchange and product purchase arrangements.

By a series of well-coordinated moves with respect to its transportation, refining, marketing, and producing properties which were initiated during the latter part of World War II and carried to completion in the postwar period, the company was able to strengthen greatly its entire competitive position. The program may be divided into three major parts: (a) the construction of an extensive products pipe line system, (b) participation in the Platte and Pioneer pipe lines, and (c) the acquisition of a refinery at Wood River, Illinois. The strategy underlying this series of investments and the relationship of the investments to each other will be outlined in the paragraphs which follow. In reading these paragraphs, the reader will find it helpful to keep before him the map of Sinclair operations shown in Chapter Twelve, Exhibit XII-5, page 338.

Construction of the Products Pipe Line System:

The products pipe line system was begun in 1941 with the construction of a line from the Marcus Hook refinery to Steubenville, Ohio. This line, which had a branch to Baltimore,

---

[1] The company was organized as the Sinclair Consolidated Oil Corporation. Included in the consolidation were the Sinclair Oil and Refining Corporation and the Sinclair Gulf Corporation which had been formed in 1916 and 1917, respectively. The name of the company was changed to the Consolidated Oil Corporation on March 31, 1932, and to the Sinclair Oil Corporation on May 19, 1943. In 1952 the corporation operated almost entirely as a holding company and conducted its affairs through a number of subsidiaries, chief among which were the Sinclair Oil and Gas Company (producing and crude marketing), the Sinclair Pipe Line Company (transportation by pipe line), and the Sinclair Refining Company (refining, marketing, transportation by tank steamships, and petrochemical operations). In the interests of simplicity, the name "Sinclair" will be used throughout the discussion unless there is some need for designating the subsidiary connections.

Maryland, and Washington, D. C. was originally designed to transport products from Marcus Hook westward to market areas in central and western Pennsylvania. In order to obtain the critical materials required to complete the project under the provisions of Petroleum Administration for Defense directives, however, it proved necessary to construct a water terminal at Steubenville, Ohio, and to redesign the line so that it could pump from west to east. During the war period, these arrangements permitted products, moved from Gulf Coast refineries up the Mississippi and Ohio rivers by barge to Steubenville, to be pumped into the eastern markets. The line thus aided in relieving the shortages of petroleum products in the eastern markets which had developed because tanker movements from the Gulf Coast were interrupted by enemy submarine activity along the Atlantic and Gulf coasts. A large portion of the capacity of the line was reserved during the war for tenders of gasoline to the U. S. Navy.

In 1943 a second pipe line was constructed which extended from East Chicago, Indiana, to Toledo, Ohio. This line was constructed from reclaimed, secondhand pipe because wartime controls would not permit the use of new steel. The line made it possible to ship large quantities of products originating in the Chicago refining area to Toledo, from whence shipments could be made by lake tankers to many other points. As in the case of the Steubenville-Marcus Hook line, the East Chicago-Toledo line was useful in solving wartime distribution problems, and a large share of its capacity was reserved for U. S. Navy gasoline tenders.

It was apparent at the time of construction that both of the new lines would be of strategic importance to the company in its postwar operations. Crude oil normally moves to eastern markets from the Mid-Continent and Texas fields by two main paths: (a) north and east by pipe line, barge, and rail with refining taking place somewhere en route, or (b) south to the Gulf Coast, by tanker from there to the Atlantic Coast, and thence inland until products moving along the first path are met. In the case of the second movement, refining takes place at either Gulf Coast or Atlantic Coast plants.

The normal outlet for the East Chicago re-

finery was thus eastward to the heavy population centers along the southern shores of the Great Lakes. The East Chicago-Toledo line provided low-cost distribution to these markets. The Steubenville-Marcus Hook line, which it was anticipated would be reversed as soon as the war emergency was over, provided the Marcus Hook refinery with low-cost transportation to its normal markets inland and to the west. This refinery was essential to the company's operations because it was well located to receive crude oil from foreign sources, particularly from Venezuela where the company was developing substantial producing interests. Since the company had domestic crude oil production equal to only about 36% of its refinery requirements, it was important to have a large refinery in a position to make use of any future Venezuelan crude oil production. There was a definite limit on the extent to which products from Marcus Hook could be backhauled to Atlantic Coast points against competition from products moving directly to those places from Gulf Coast refineries, and hence access to inland markets was necessary to the refinery's operations.

At the close of the war the East Chicago-Toledo line was extended by the construction of branches from Toledo to Detroit and Columbus, and these two large industrial population centers were thus linked to the company's Chicago refinery. A line was next laid from Marion, Ohio (on the Toledo-Columbus line), to Clinton, Youngstown, and Steubenville, Ohio. This segment of the system was begun late in 1946 and completed about a year later. From Clinton, Ohio, a stub was then laid to Cleveland, Ohio. The completion of the line from Marion to Steubenville established a pipe line connection between Sinclair's two big refineries at East Chicago and Marcus Hook. Since products could be pumped through the system in either direction, the line made it possible to ship to the middle territory between the two refineries from either East Chicago or Marcus Hook in accordance with shifts in the economic boundary between the eastward and westward movements of oil and oil products discussed above.

The third segment of the pipe line system, extending northward from Corpus Christi to San Antonio and Austin, was constructed in

1947 to serve markets in southern Texas and to provide an outlet for the products of the Corpus Christi refinery. The Corpus Christi refinery was not particularly well situated with respect to the company's existing marketing facilities, and had it not been for the wartime demand for high-octane gasolines, the company would probably not have constructed a refinery of such size at the Corpus Christi location. In 1951, pending further development of the company's marketing program, a large share of the Corpus Christi output and of the deliveries from the Corpus Christi-San Antonio-Austin pipe line were used for exchange purposes.

Construction of the fourth major section of the Sinclair products pipe line system, a line running from Houston to East Chicago, resulted from certain considerations involving the four small refineries which the company had in operation at the close of the war in Kansas City and Coffeyville, Kansas; Sand Springs, Oklahoma; and Fort Worth, Texas. These four refineries had previously been used to supply the company's market outlets in the North Texas and Mid-Continent areas. At the close of the war it became apparent that the four refineries would all require extensive modernization in order to meet the demand for high-octane gasolines which developed in the postwar markets. The four refineries, however, had capacities ranging from about 6,500 to 12,000 barrels per day in 1946 and were thus too small to permit the installation of catalytic cracking equipment of an economical size. Moreover, analysis of the problem revealed that the products for the North Texas and Mid-Continent markets could be secured at a lower cost by producing them as incremental output from the big refineries at Houston and East Chicago and backhauling to Mid-Continent market locations via pipe line than by producing them in the four small refineries close to the market areas.

A new products pipe line was therefore constructed from Houston to Arlington, Texas, and stub lines were run from that point to Fort Worth and Dallas. The refinery at Fort Worth was then closed down and converted to a products terminal. The Houston line was extended northward into Oklahoma in 1948, and later in the same year the conversion of former crude oil lines made it possible to extend the system

to Kansas City and to convert the small refinery at that point to a products terminal. Former crude oil lines were used to continue the system to Griffiths, Indiana, where a junction could be made with an existing products pipe line running to East Chicago. Stub lines were then built from the main line to the Sand Springs and Coffeyville refineries which were retired and converted to products terminals.

The completed Houston-Chicago pipe line system not only provided a means by which the company could make shipments from its own refineries but likewise a basis for negotiating favorable product purchases and exchanges with other companies. Sinclair, for example, was subsequently able to make deliveries at terminals along its Houston-Chicago line to various Mid-Continent refiners in exchange for deliveries at terminals along the Great Lakes Pipe Line, which originated in Oklahoma and carried products to the North Central states (see map, Chapter Twelve, Exhibit XII-5).

Although the Houston-Chicago pipe line system represented a good solution to the problem of the four Mid-Continent refineries, it should not be inferred that it provided an ideal means of supplying refined products to the Mid-Continent area. The hauling of products from Houston north beyond the Texas border and the hauling of products from Chicago south beyond Fort Madison, Iowa, were not particularly economical arrangements. Moreover, the Houston-Chicago system was made up of small diameter pipe and involved higher costs per barrel mile than did the large diameter lines available to certain other companies. The Sinclair executives pointed out, however, that much of the system was built at a very low capital cost from old crude oil lines that were already in the ground. In addition, the cost of putting the old crude lines in service was deductible as a maintenance expense for tax purposes whereas it would have been necessary to have capitalized the cost of rebuilding the four refineries. On the whole, therefore, the Houston-Chicago pipe line represented a substantially better alternative than the modernization of one or more of the Mid-Continent plants.

In 1951 Sinclair was planning a further development of its products transportation arrangements which would give it access to the southeastern section of the United States. The company entered into an arrangement with the Gulf Oil Corporation and The Texas Company to build a large diameter products pipe line from Port Arthur to Baton Rouge where a connection could be made with the Plantation Pipe Line (see Chapter Twelve, Exhibit XII-5). The new line was to be owned 40% by Gulf, 40% by The Texas Company, and 20% by Sinclair. Sinclair planned to build its own line from its refinery at Houston to the beginning of the new line at Port Arthur. Concurrently with these arrangements, the company began the construction of eight terminals along the Plantation Pipe Line to serve as points of supply for marketing operations. Steps were also taken to gain access to the Southeastern Pipe Line, and Sinclair began the construction of eight terminals along that line. It was anticipated that in the future the company would pump products from its Houston refinery into the Plantation system and would ship products by tanker from Corpus Christi to Port St. Joe for movement through the Southeastern system.

The facts cited above were specific reasons for the construction of the individual segments of the pipe line system. Overriding all these reasons, however, were certain general considerations with regard to the company's competitive position in the postwar markets. At the close of the war the company was on balance a heavy purchaser of crude oil, and it competed in the final markets with more completely integrated companies which were, the Sinclair management believed, in a position to obtain their supplies of crude oil at a lower cost. It was therefore apparent that the company's only hope for competitive success lay in developing an extremely efficient refining and marketing operation. The company's refineries were reasonably well-located and well-equipped, but its marketing facilities were scattered throughout the 43 states east of the Rocky Mountains. Many of these locations were supplied at a high cost by rail shipments from the company's refineries or by purchase or exchange arrangements which lacked the stability necessary to permit further investments to modernize and improve the market outlets.

Study of the refining-marketing problem suggested that the most promising means of securing a low-cost operation was through the construction of the pipe line system. Refining costs normally ran in the neighborhood of 50 cents to 60 cents per barrel, and there was little opportunity for cost savings much greater than 5 cents to 10 cents per barrel no matter what improvements were made. Likewise marketing expenses normally were about 50 cents to 90 cents per barrel of products, and the most stringent economies seemed unlikely to produce savings much greater than 10 cents to 20 cents per barrel. The substitution of pipe line for rail transport, however, promised savings running as high as 50 cents or more per barrel, depending on the length of haul.

Construction of the pipe line system was thus undertaken as the means by which the company hoped to obtain a major competitive advantage in the immediate postwar period. Coincident with the construction of the new pipe lines, direct marketing operations were terminated in New Mexico, West Texas, Arkansas, Louisiana, Kentucky, and certain other areas which could not be reached by low-cost transportation. New marketing investments were concentrated in the vicinity of the refineries, in a path lying 60 to 70 miles to either side of the products pipe line, and in areas lying 60 to 70 miles inland from the company's Atlantic and Gulf Coast terminals. The pipe line system was therefore an integral part of a broad program designed to improve the overall efficiency of refining-marketing operations and involved a simultaneous consideration of refining, transportation, and marketing investments.

Participation in the Platte and Pioneer Pipe Lines:

Sinclair's decision to participate in the Platte and Pioneer lines resulted primarily from the necessity of providing an outlet for the company's crude oil reserves in Wyoming. The company had had extensive producing interests in Wyoming for many years, and during the 1940's the company's drilling operations in Wyoming were very successful. In 1950, 21.5% of the company's domestic crude oil production came from Wyoming, and some of its largest crude oil reserves were located in the state. During the war period a substantial portion of the available crude oil production was absorbed by the refinery at Sinclair, Wyoming, which was enlarged from 8,000 to 25,000 barrels per day capacity to meet the needs of the armed services for high-octane gasoline. This refinery, which Sinclair had acquired in 1932 as a part of the properties of The Prairie Oil and Gas Company and The Prairie Pipe Line Company, had previously been used primarily to serve a relatively small market in the adjacent Rocky Mountain states.

In the period following the close of the war it became apparent that the refinery could no longer be operated at the 25,000 barrels per day rate because the company's market in the area of the refinery was not large enough to absorb the output. The light oil products could be sold only by moving them eastward into Nebraska and North and South Dakota. In these markets the company was at a disadvantage because its transportation costs were higher than those of its competitors, and it had difficulty in realizing a satisfactory profit. An equally difficult problem was encountered in disposing of the residual fuel oil which was produced as a by-product of the refining operations. There was no major industrial market in Wyoming, and the only large buyers of residual fuel oil were the railroads. In selling to these buyers, Sinclair faced tough competition from other refiners in the area who were likewise anxious to find an outlet for their residual products. Moreover, the market was a declining one because the railroads were in the process of converting much of their equipment to Diesel operation.

As a consequence of these conditions, Sinclair found it necessary to cut back its refinery runs at the Sinclair refinery after the close of the war from 25,000 to 15,000 barrels per day. At the same time, however, the company's available crude oil production in Wyoming was steadily increasing, and it was apparent that the company would ultimately have an output substantially in excess of 25,000 barrels per day. In view of the fact that the company as a whole lacked sufficient crude oil to meet its refinery needs, the management considered it important to make effective use of such crude oil production as the company did have. The development of a new outlet for the crude oil was therefore clearly indicated.

The only crude oil pipe line out of the state of Wyoming was owned by the Standard Oil Company (Indiana).[2] This line was capable of carrying about 55,000 barrels per day and was being run at capacity. It was estimated that the shut-in crude oil production which Sinclair and other producing companies had in the state amounted to at least another 55,000 barrels per day. The management of the Standard Oil Company (Indiana), however, had shown no inclination to undertake an expansion of the pipe line facilities. Movement of the crude oil to the refining center at St. Louis by rail was not feasible because the cost per barrel would have been about $1.50 as contrasted with an estimated pipe line tariff of 40 cents per barrel. Sinclair therefore joined with the four other producing companies in the construction of the Platte Pipe Line, as outlined in Chapter Seven. Sinclair originally intended to move its crude oil to its main trunk line and thence into its refinery at East Chicago. As will be noted below, however, acquisition of the Wood River refinery provided a better alternative arrangement.

As a further means of providing an outlet for its Wyoming crude oil and also of utilizing the capacity of the Sinclair refinery, the company took two additional steps. First, it began an aggressive program for the expansion of its marketing operations in the Wyoming area which included, among other things, the construction of a number of new service stations and the purchase of the Crown Petroleum Company, one of the largest jobber organizations in the state. As a second step, the company joined with the Continental Oil Company in the formation of the Pioneer Pipe Line Company to build the products pipe line from Sinclair, Wyoming, to Salt Lake City, Utah, discussed in Chapter Seven. The new line connected with the Salt Lake Pipe Line,[3] which extended northward from Salt Lake City to a point on the Columbia River in Washington. As soon as plans for the Pioneer line were formulated, Sinclair began acquiring terminal, bulk plant, and service station sites in Utah and along the

---

[2] Before 1930 the line was owned jointly by Sinclair and the Indiana Company. In 1930 Sinclair sold its half interest to the Indiana Company (see Chapter Thirteen, page 389).

[3] Owned by the Standard Oil Company of California.

Salt Lake Pipe Line in order to provide market outlets for its share of the products moving through the line.

Acquisition of the Wood River Refinery:

In July 1950 Sinclair purchased a 30,000 barrels per day refinery located at Hartford, Illinois, about 15 miles north of St. Louis on the east bank of the Mississippi River. This refinery, which was owned by the Wood River Oil and Refining Company, had been built in 1940 and had been brought abreast of the latest developments in refinery processes in 1949 through the installation of new facilities, including a catalytic cracking unit. The refinery equipment was made of special corrosion-resisting alloys which enabled the plant to process a wide range of crude oils, including the high-sulphur content crude oils which were found in Wyoming. The equipment was sufficiently flexible to permit a high yield of high-octane gasoline and to provide a wide range of distillates, Diesel fuels, asphalts, road oils, and fuel oils. The properties of the Wood River Oil and Refining Company also included products terminals at Peru and Rockford, Illinois, and a short products pipe line connecting the two points. The company had intended to move products from the refinery to Peru by barge up the Illinois River and thence through the pipe line to Rockford. A right-of-way had been secured for a later extension of the pipe line to Madison, Wisconsin.

Sinclair purchased the Wood River refinery, the products pipe line, and the two terminals from the Wood River Oil and Refining Company for a price of approximately $15,500,000. Sinclair had little use for the pipe line in Illinois because it already had satisfactory means of reaching the markets which it served. The company did, however, want the Wood River refinery for two principal reasons: first, because it provided a natural home for the company's crude oil production in Wyoming, and second, because it provided a means of serving certain market outlets in the St. Louis area which the company was finding it difficult to supply on a competitive basis.

The problem of providing a market outlet for the company's increasing crude oil production in Wyoming has already been discussed. As noted above, it was originally intended to

take the Wyoming crude oil through the company's main trunk line to the East Chicago refinery. This arrangement would, however, have required considerable modification of the East Chicago equipment because the refinery had originally been built to handle Mid-Continent crude oils which did not have the high-sulphur content found in the Wyoming crude oils. The Wood River refinery was located close to the eastern terminus of the Platte line and was already fully equipped to handle the Wyoming oils.

Of even greater importance to Sinclair was the potential usefulness of the Wood River refinery in supplying certain marketing facilities which the company had in the St. Louis and Missouri areas. The company had had distribution in this region since its incorporation in 1919. Originally, products had been marketed primarily through an independent agency, the Puritan Oil Company. This company was acquired by Sinclair in the latter 1920's because the owners were anxious to sell and other oil companies were bidding for the properties. Additional marketing facilities were secured in Missouri, Arkansas, and Louisiana through the purchase of the Pierce Petroleum Company in 1930. For many years the company supplied its market outlets in the St. Louis region by shipments from its four small refineries in the Mid-Continent area. In the latter 1930's, however, the company began to feel considerable pressure from competitors who were reaching the markets at a lower cost, particularly from refineries located in St. Louis.

During the war the situation presented no problem because of the general shortage of petroleum products and the fact that the entire industry operated under government controls. Immediately after the close of the war, however, the company found that it could no longer ship products from its Mid-Continent refineries and still meet competitive prices in the St. Louis area. Accordingly, it began to supply the territory by means of various exchange agreements, particularly with the Standard Oil Company (Indiana). Sinclair gave products to the Indiana Company at the Sinclair refinery in Chicago and in return secured an equal volume from the Indiana Company's refinery at St. Louis. This arrangement was negotiated for short-term periods and was subject to frequent interruptions which required Sinclair to negotiate other exchanges or to purchase on the open market from suppliers such as the Wood River Oil and Refining Company. In one year, the company entered into as many as four different exchange agreements to supply products to the area.

The lack of an assured source of supply at St. Louis made it difficult for the company to compete effectively in the region and made the management reluctant to invest the funds necessary to modernize and improve the company's marketing outlets. The management was particularly reluctant to undertake construction of the expensive river terminals necessary to develop the markets at down-river locations, and it was chiefly for this reason that the decision was made to withdraw from direct marketing operations in Arkansas, Louisiana, and Kentucky. After the products pipe line from Houston to Chicago was in operation, it was decided to solve the St. Louis problem by converting one of the company's crude oil lines into the Wood River area into a products line and bringing it into a terminal in St. Louis. This move would have permitted shipments of products to the territory from Chicago or Houston and would have made it possible to develop the market in St. Louis. It would not, however, have been possible to reach the down-river locations in Arkansas and Louisiana at competitive costs.

Acquisition of the Wood River refinery provided a much better solution to the problem. From this refinery it was possible to supply the St. Louis market without backhauling from Chicago or Houston. Moreover, by converting one of the crude oil lines into Wood River into a products pipe line it became possible to ship products west from the refinery into Kansas and certain other Mid-Continent areas which the company had originally intended to supply by backhauling from Chicago or Houston on the main products pipe line. Finally, it appeared that the Wood River refinery would make it possible for the company to develop river marketing terminals along the Mississippi and Ohio rivers and thus re-enter the markets in Arkansas, Louisiana, and Kentucky, from which it had decided to withdraw as a part of the general marketing program discussed above.

Ultimately it was hoped that these marketing opportunities would permit enlargement of the refinery to a capacity of about 60,000 barrels per day. In the early part of 1952 the company began re-entrance into the Kentucky market with the purchase of the Stoll Oil Refining Company of Louisville, Kentucky. The Stoll properties included two river terminals, one at Louisville and one at West Point, Kentucky, each with more than 100,000 barrels of storage capacity; a 1,600 barrels per day lubricating oil and wax manufacturing plant at Louisville; a 2,000 barrels per day cracking plant at Louisville which had been idle for about two years; 50 bulk plants and 200 service stations in Indiana and Kentucky; and a number of barges, tank cars, and motor vehicles. The company planned to barge products from the Wood River refinery to Louisville and West Point.

The value of the Wood River refinery to Sinclair was further enhanced in 1951 by the decision of The Ohio Oil Company to build a products pipe line east from Wood River to Indianapolis. The misgivings of the Sinclair management with regard to the stability of the company's supply arrangements in St. Louis were proven justified in 1950 when the Standard Oil Company (Indiana) enlarged its own refinery at Whiting sufficiently to meet its requirements in the Chicago area.

The reasons why the owners of the Wood River Oil and Refining Company were willing to accept the offer of Sinclair for the refinery will be discussed in some detail in Chapter Twenty-Two. Suffice it at this point to say that the decision was prompted in large measure by problems which the owners were encountering in marketing the output of the refinery and in securing adequate supplies of crude oil. The solution to these problems appeared to require the expenditure of additional funds which the owners were unwilling or unable to advance and which they saw little chance of raising at a reasonable cost from outside sources.

For the purposes of this discussion, the most significant thing to be observed about the entire Wood River transaction is that a refinery which was of dubious future operating value to the Wood River Oil and Refining Company was of great future operating value to Sinclair because of its *relationship to other investments* which the company already had or was planning to make in producing, pipe line, and marketing facilities. In other words, the economic value of the refinery was greatly enhanced as soon as it became a part of an integrated program of investments in all phases of the petroleum business.

Position Achieved by the Sinclair Oil Corporation:

As a result of the program of refining, pipe line, and marketing investments outlined above, Sinclair arrived at a strategic position for the conduct of the refining and marketing phases of its business. In the first place, six of the company's seven refineries were extremely well-situated with respect to present and prospective supplies of crude oil. The Marcus Hook and, to a lesser extent, the Houston and Corpus Christi refineries were in a position to receive foreign crude oil if the balance of political and economic factors should dictate an increasing volume of imports in the future. The Houston, Corpus Christi, Wood River, and Chicago refineries were in a position to draw on the Texas and Mid-Continent oil fields; the Wood River, Sinclair, and Chicago refineries were able to tap the increasing volume of crude oil production in Wyoming; and the Chicago refinery was conceivably in a position to receive Canadian crude oil if such oil should move in large quantities into the Great Lakes area in the future. The Wellsville refinery was less well-situated with respect to crude oil supplies, but it was small in size and concentrated on the manufacture of special Pennsylvania lubricating oils. As a result, crude oil and inward freight costs were not so critical to its operations as in the case of the other refineries.

By virtue of its extensive products pipe line system, its refinery locations, and terminals along the Atlantic and Gulf coasts, Sinclair had access at reasonable transportation costs to nearly all the major markets in the eastern half of the United States. The main products pipe line which interconnected the four big refineries at Houston, Wood River, Chicago, and Marcus Hook was so arranged that products could be pumped in either direction. As a result the company had considerable flexibility in adjusting refinery runs and product movements in accordance with shifts in crude oil,

transportation, and refinery processing costs to arrive at the lowest possible delivered cost to various marketing points. The Corpus Christi refinery was in a position to move products inland by pipe line, by tanker to Atlantic and Gulf Coast terminals, or by tanker to Port St. Joe for movement through the Southeastern Pipe Line as market conditions required.

The Houston refinery could move products north via the Sinclair pipe line system, east via the Plantation Pipe Line, or by tanker to the tidewater terminals. The Wood River refinery was in a position to move products by barge along the Mississippi, Ohio, and Illinois rivers, by pipe line to the west as far as Kansas City where deliveries could be made to the Great Lakes Pipe Line, or to Indianapolis via The Ohio Oil Company's new products pipe line. The Marcus Hook refinery had the option of moving products inland through the main pipe line or to the tidewater terminals along the Atlantic Coast. The Chicago refinery could move products either east or west along the main trunk line or by barge to terminals on the Great Lakes. Each of these refineries thus had several alternatives with respect to the disposition of its output.

The Pioneer Pipe Line and the new marketing investments in Wyoming, Utah, and Idaho promised to provide a satisfactory outlet for the Sinclair, Wyoming refinery. Moreover, these investments together with the Platte Pipe Line provided a double-barreled outlet for the company's growing volume of crude oil production in Wyoming. The output of the seventh refinery, at Wellsville, New York, consisted chiefly of lubricating oils which presented no serious distribution problems. The small volume of light oils produced at Wellsville was sold in the immediate vicinity of the plant.

Through the careful correlation of producing, pipe line, refining, and marketing investments, Sinclair thus developed a very sound operating position in the six-year period after the close of World War II. As noted above, the company's arrangements were not ideal in all cases, but there were by 1951, nonetheless, few areas in the eastern half of the United States which the company was not prepared to reach on a competitive basis by direct shipments or by means of exchange arrangements. It is possible, but doubtful, that an equally effective arrangement of properties could have been secured in an equally short space of time by groups of nonintegrated companies working on an arms-length bargaining basis with each other.

II. GAINS IN THE PLANNING OF OPERATIONS (ESSO STANDARD OIL COMPANY)

A second area in which some of the vertically integrated oil companies have been able to make important managerial gains is in handling the logistical problems associated with the producing, refining, and distribution processes. The management of an integrated company is in a position to have an intimate knowledge of activities at all levels of the industry and can thus often do a more effective job of adjusting operating programs to shifts and changes in market demand than can the management of a nonintegrated company. An integrated company can likewise often plan its inventory positions on crude oil and the various categories of refined products with greater precision than can a nonintegrated company and can thus reduce somewhat the hazards of being caught short of supplies in times of rising demand or of being forced to liquidate excessive stocks at low prices in times of falling demand. It is therefore entirely possible that the presence of a large number of integrated companies in the industry may tend to protect the industry as a whole from some of the inventory maladjustments which have so long and so frequently distressed the cotton textile industry (see Chapter Twenty-Four).

The many contributions which vertical integration makes to the handling of logistical problems can be illustrated by considering the relative ability of integrated and nonintegrated companies to use inventory programs as a means of counterbalancing the seasonal fluctuations in the demand for petroleum products. The total demand for all refined products has a distinct seasonal peak in the winter months, as may be seen from Exhibit XI-1.[4] In addition, the demand for the two major refined products,

gasolines and distillates, have pronounced seasonal patterns which are approximately the converse of each other (see Chapter Six, Exhibits VI-6 and VI-11). As a result, if a company operated solely in accordance with market demands, it would be forced to make substantial changes in its refinery runs, refinery yields, and transportation activities from one season of the year to the next. Through the careful programming of inventories at refineries, market terminals, and bulk plants, a company can avoid to a considerable extent the necessity for making such changes and can thereby achieve significant savings in operating and investment costs.

In the following paragraphs we shall draw upon data developed by the Esso Standard Oil Company to illustrate the gains which may be made through the use of seasonal inventories to achieve more uniform refinery runs, refinery yields, and transportation requirements. A concluding section will then present the reasons why logistical gains of this type are generally more accessible to integrated than nonintegrated companies.

Use of Inventories to Secure Uniform Refinery Runs:

The accumulation of seasonal inventories permits a company to operate its refineries at close to capacity in the slack seasons of the year and thereby enables it to meet its annual marketing requirements with a smaller plant capacity than would otherwise be necessary. A company with adequate seasonal storage capacity might, for example, meet an average annual demand of 40,000 barrels per day with a refinery capacity of approximately that amount, whereas a company which was not able to accumulate seasonal stocks might be forced to operate at 35,000 barrels per day during the summer months and at 45,000 barrels per day during the winter months. In general, it may be said that every refinery has the alternative of meeting the seasonal peaks in the demand for petroleum products through the building of inventories or the maintenance of reserve refining capacity. Since storage tanks require a smaller capital investment than do the equivalent refining facilities, the maintenance of fairly uniform refinery runs through the accumulation of seasonal inventories permits some significant savings in capital costs.

---

[4] In earlier years, the seasonal pattern of the total demand was influenced more by gasoline than heating oils and had a seasonal peak in the summer rather than the winter. Increased winter driving and the development of the heating oil markets have recently shifted the seasonal peak to the winter months.

Exhibit XI-1. Production, Consumption, and Stocks of Crude Oil, Natural Gasoline, Benzol, and Refined Petroleum Products: 1946–1952

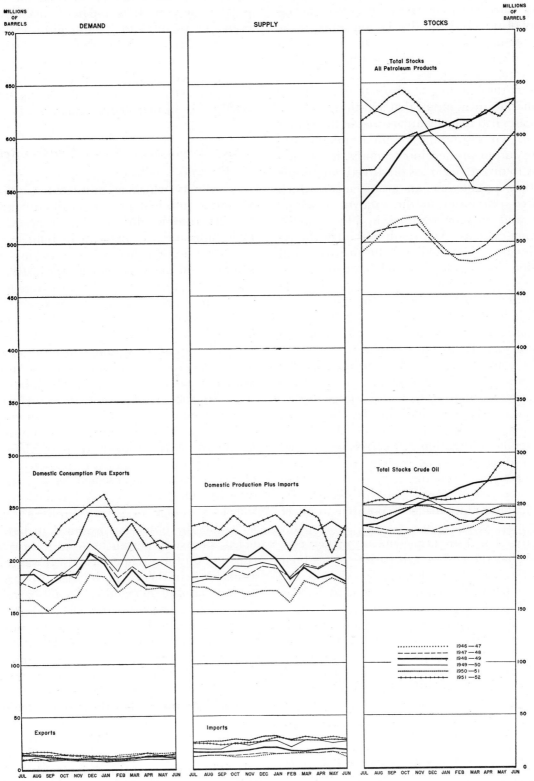

SOURCE: American Petroleum Institute, *Statistical Bulletin*, Vol. XXIX, No. 34; Vol. XXXI, No. 30; Vol. XXXII, No. 31; and Vol. XXXIV, No. 19.

In studies of its own operations, the Esso Standard Oil Company found that if adequate seasonal storage capacity was not available, refinery runs had to be reduced below the capacity of the crude oil distillation units in the summer months in order to keep the output of middle distillates within the limits of whatever storage tankage was available. The limitations on the building of distillate stocks in the summer, in turn, meant that additional middle distillates had to be manufactured in the winter season. To secure the required middle distillate output in the winter months, it was necessary to divert virgin gas oil directly to middle distillate production, an arrangement which reduced the input to the catalytic cracking units and thereby resulted in idle catalytic cracking capacity. As a result, although the refineries met their total middle distillate and gasoline requirements throughout the year, they did so by having: (a) some catalytic cracking capacity which operated in the summer and was idle in the winter, and (b) some crude oil distillation capacity which operated in the winter and was idle in the summer.

The construction of adequate capacity for the storage of middle distillates in the summer provided a means by which a large part of the idle refining capacity could be eliminated. The Esso management estimated that for a representative situation 220 barrels of seasonal storage capacity was equivalent to about one barrel per day of refining capacity, in the sense that the storage capacity avoided idle refining capacity and thus made it possible to meet given market requirements with smaller plant capacity. The Esso management further estimated that the cost of 220 barrels of seasonal storage capacity was about $350 whereas the cost of a barrel per day of refining capacity was about $1,400.[5]

The above figures do not take into account the additional investment in working capital required to enlarge the seasonal inventories of middle distillates. If a value of $3.50 per barrel is assigned to the middle distillates, however,

the average investment required for 220 barrels of products would be only $385. Moreover, the funds would be needed for only a part of the year. It is apparent therefore that even after taking into account additional working capital requirements, there would still be a substantial margin in favor of the inventory program over the maintenance of reserve refining capacity as a means of meeting the seasonal peaks in petroleum demand.

Use of Inventories to Secure Uniform Refinery Yields:

A refinery which accumulated seasonal inventories sufficient only to maintain uniform refinery runs would still find it necessary to make substantial changes in its refinery yields to meet the high demand for gasoline in the summer and the high demand for distillates in the winter, particularly if it had a large heating oil business. A refinery can, however, secure both uniform refinery runs and uniform refinery yields if it is in a position to accumulate the full amount of seasonal inventories necessary to do so. The maintenance of uniform refinery yields results in savings both in operating costs and in the capital investment necessary to handle a given volume of business.

To illustrate the value of using inventories to obtain more uniform refinery yields, the Esso Standard Oil Company prepared studies of two refineries of 100,000 barrels per day capacity. One refinery was assumed to have sufficient storage to permit uniform refinery runs and the other was assumed to have sufficient storage to permit both uniform refinery runs and uniform refinery yields. It was further assumed that the refineries had to meet an average gasoline demand of 42,000 barrels per day and an average distillate demand of 30,000 barrels per day, both subject to the seasonal variations characteristic of the Atlantic Coast markets. The manufacturing and inventory programs of the two refineries are summarized in Exhibit XI-2, page 316.

It will be noted that the refinery maintaining uniform refinery runs required a maximum gasoline inventory of 1,094,000 barrels and a maximum distillate inventory of 2,027,000 barrels. The refinery maintaining both uniform refinery runs and uniform refinery yields, how-

---

[5] Esso Standard Oil Company, *Tankage Requirements, Refineries, and Primary Terminals, 1951–1954,* a company memorandum prepared in 1951, p. 18. The figures developed in the original study were revised slightly in 1953 on the basis of discussions with the Esso management for use in this publication.

ever, required a maximum gasoline inventory of 1,275,000 barrels and a maximum distillate inventory of 2,522,000 barrels. The maintenance of uniform refinery yields thus required a total of 676,000 barrels more seasonal storage capacity than did the maintenance of uniform refinery runs (181,000 barrels more gasoline storage plus 495,000 barrels more distillate storage).

The Esso Standard Oil Company estimated that the refinery which maintained both uniform refinery runs and uniform refinery yields would be able to secure operating costs about one cent to two cents per barrel lower than the refinery which merely maintained uniform refinery runs. It was anticipated that the saving in operating costs would be the net result of three items as follows:

	Savings Cents per Barrel
1. Avoidance of need to crack cycle stock in summer months and to replace the cycle stock with virgin stock in winter months	1.1
2. Gain in flexibility to meet abnormal operating situations. Perhaps as much as:	1.0
3. Deduct additional tankage operating costs	(0.1)
Net savings in operating costs	1.0 to 2.0¢

The Esso management also estimated that the refinery maintaining only uniform refinery runs would require a larger investment in equipment than the refinery maintaining both uniform refinery runs and uniform refinery yields, chiefly because the refinery maintaining only uniform refinery runs would require additional catalytic cracking capacity to crack whatever cycle gas oil could not be placed in storage during the summer months. Comparative investment costs for the two situations were estimated as follows:

Investment	Refinery with Uniform Refinery Runs	Refinery with Both Uniform Refinery Runs and Yields
Refinery processing equipment	$ 97,000,000	$90,000,000
Seasonal tankage for gasoline and distillate	3,000,000	5,000,000
Total	$100,000,000	$95,000,000

Use of Inventories to Secure Uniform Transportation Requirements:

Seasonal inventories may be used to reduce the total investment required for transportation facilities in the same manner as in the case of refinery facilities. If a company can continue shipments from its refineries to terminals and bulk plants on a fairly uniform basis throughout the year, it can avoid developing a peak transportation requirement in the winter months. The Esso Standard Oil Company, which characteristically moved large volumes from the Gulf to the Atlantic Coast, for example, estimated that each 220 barrels of incremental storage capacity it established on the Atlantic Coast served to reduce tanker investments somewhere in the industry by about $900, on the basis of construction costs of 26,000 ton tanker ships in 1951.[6] The incremental seasonal storage capacity would also, of course, make possible a reduction in pipe lines and other crude oil transportation facilities.

As an alternative means of appraising the gains in transportation operations made possible by seasonal inventories, the Esso management compared the actual cost of its tanker charters for the movement of refined products from the Gulf to the Atlantic Coast in the 1950–1951 season with an estimate of what the costs would have been if sufficient storage had been available on the Atlantic Coast to permit uniform movements throughout the year. The data for the two situations are shown in Exhibit XI-3. The actual movement was accomplished with a total Atlantic Coast tankage of about 35,100,000 barrels; the potential even movement would have required an additional 8,500,000 barrels of tankage or an investment of about $14,200,000.

As may be seen from Exhibit XI-3, during the winter of 1950–1951, Esso moved about 152,100,000 barrels of products from the Gulf to New York by tankers which it had under time charters at an average cost of 36.6 cents per barrel. An additional 16,300,000 barrels of products were moved by tankers chartered as needed for individual voyages at an average cost of $1.008 per barrel. The Esso management estimated that if sufficient seasonal tank-

---

6 Ibid., p. 18.

EXHIBIT XI-2. MANUFACTURING AND INVENTORY PROGRAMS WITH UNIFORM REFINERY RUNS AND WITH BOTH UNIFORM REFINERY RUNS AND YIELDS

Programs for Distillate Demand

| Month | Middle Distillate Demand | | Refinery Runs | Refinery with Uniform Refinery Runs | | | Refinery with Both Uniform Refinery Runs and Yields | | |
	B/D	Bbls./Month	B/D	Distillate Production Per Cent Yield	Bbls./Month	Barrels in Storage 1st of Month	Distillate Production Per Cent Yield	Bbls./Month	Barrels in Storage 1st of Month
April	25,000	750,000	100,000	30.0%	900,000	500,000*	30.0%	900,000	600,000*
May	18,500	573,000	100,000	25.0	775,000	650,000	30.0	930,000	750,000
June	17,500	525,000	100,000	25.0	750,000	852,000	30.0	900,000	1,107,000
July	18,500	573,000	100,000	25.0	775,000	1,077,000	30.0	930,000	1,482,000
August	20,400	632,000	100,000	30.0	930,000	1,279,000	30.0	930,000	1,839,000
September	21,200	635,000	100,000	31.0	930,000	1,577,000	30.0	900,000	2,137,000
October	26,100	810,000	100,000	31.2	965,000	1,872,000	30.0	930,000	2,402,000
November	38,200	1,143,000	100,000	32.7	980,000	2,027,000†	30.0	900,000	2,522,000†
December	44,400	1,375,000	100,000	32.7	1,010,000	1,864,000	30.0	930,000	2,279,000
January	47,500	1,472,000	100,000	32.7	1,010,000	1,499,000	30.0	930,000	1,834,000
February	44,400	1,240,000	100,000	32.7	915,000	1,037,000	30.0	840,000	1,292,000
March	39,400	1,222,000	100,000	32.7	1,010,000	712,000	30.0	930,000	892,000
						500,000			600,000
Average	30,000			30.0			30.0		

Programs for Gasoline Demand

| Month | Gasoline Demand | | Refinery Runs | Refinery with Uniform Refinery Runs | | | Refinery with Both Uniform Refinery Runs and Yields | | |
	B/D	Bbls./Month	B/D	Gasoline Production Per Cent Yield	Bbls./Month	Barrels in Storage 1st of Month	Gasoline Production Per Cent Yield	Bbls./Month	Barrels in Storage 1st of Month
April	39,500	1,183,000	100,000	42.0%	1,260,000	876,000	42.0%	1,260,000	1,198,000
May	44,300	1,375,000	100,000	46.0	1,428,000	953,000	42.0	1,302,000	1,275,000†
June	44,000	1,320,000	100,000	46.0	1,380,000	1,006,000	42.0	1,260,000	1,202,000
July	45,200	1,400,000	100,000	46.0	1,428,000	1,006,000	42.0	1,302,000	1,142,000
August	45,600	1,413,000	100,000	42.0	1,302,000	1,094,000†	42.0	1,302,000	1,044,000
September	43,200	1,295,000	100,000	41.0	1,230,000	983,000	42.0	1,260,000	933,000
October	45,000	1,400,000	100,000	41.0	1,270,000	918,000	42.0	1,302,000	898,000
November	41,200	1,238,000	100,000	40.0	1,200,000	788,000	42.0	1,260,000	800,000*
December	38,400	1,190,000	100,000	40.0	1,240,000	750,000*	42.0	1,302,000	822,000
January	39,300	1,220,000	100,000	40.0	1,240,000	800,000	42.0	1,302,000	934,000
February	39,000	1,092,000	100,000	40.0	1,120,000	820,000	42.0	1,180,000	1,016,000
March	38,900	1,208,000	100,000	39.9	1,236,000	848,000	42.0	1,302,000	1,104,000
						876,000			1,198,000
Average	42,000			42.0			42.0		

* Minimum working tankage at end of seasonal demand period.
† Maximum tankage required to meet seasonal demand.

SOURCE: Esso Standard Oil Company. A study prepared for illustrative purposes in 1952.

age had been available, the company could have moved more of the 16,300,000 barrels handled with spot charter tankers earlier in the year when rates were lower and could thus have secured an average cost for the 16,300,000 barrels of 63.1 cents per barrel rather than $1.008 per barrel. The investment of $14,200,000 in seasonal tankage would therefore have enabled the company to reduce the total cost of the volume moved by spot charter tankers from $16,430,000 to $10,285,000, a saving of $6,145,000 for the one year, 1950–1951.

There was, moreover, a further possibility that the construction of sufficient seasonal tankage to permit uniform movements throughout the year would have justified expansion of the company's time chartered fleet to the point where all spot charters could have been eliminated. Such an arrangement would have made it possible to handle the entire 168,400,000 barrels at time charter rates and would have resulted in a total cost of $61,693,100 as contrasted with the total cost actually incurred in 1950–1951 of $72,099,000 for time and

Exhibit XI-3. Esso Standard Oil Company

Actual Tanker Costs Compared with Estimated
Costs for Uniform Movement: 1950–1951

(Volume in Millions of Barrels; Rates in Cents per
Barrel for 30°, Gulf to New York)

		Actual Loadings			
	Total Volume	Time Charter Volume	Rate	Spot Charter Volume	Rate
April 1950	11.6	12.7	31.8¢	(1.1)	23.8¢
May	11.9	13.0	31.4	(1.1)	24.1
June	12.2	12.5	30.9	(.3)	25.6
July	13.0	13.0	31.0	.0	27.5
August	13.7	13.0	31.3	.7	33.1
September	14.1	12.5	32.5	1.6	42.4
October	15.1	13.0	40.2	2.1	56.4
November	14.1	12.3	41.8	1.8	64.2
December	15.3	12.7	42.8	2.6	80.6
January 1951	15.7	12.7	42.0	3.0	102.6
February	15.2	11.7	41.0	3.5	116.6
March	16.5	13.0	42.9	3.5	112.4
Total	168.4	152.1		16.3	
Average Cost			36.6¢		100.8¢
Total Annual Cost		$55,669,000		$16,430,000	

		Estimated for Uniform Movement			
	Total Volume	Time Charter Volume	Rate	Spot Charter Volume	Rate
April 1950	14.0	12.7	31.8¢	1.3	23.8¢
May	14.0	13.0	31.4	1.0	24.1
June	14.1	12.5	30.9	1.6	25.6
July	14.0	13.0	31.0	1.0	27.5
August	14.0	13.0	31.3	1.0	33.1
September	14.1	12.5	32.5	1.6	42.4
October	14.0	13.0	40.2	1.0	56.4
November	14.0	12.3	41.8	1.7	64.2
December	14.1	12.7	42.8	1.4	80.6
January 1951	14.0	12.7	42.0	1.3	102.6
February	14.0	11.7	41.0	2.3	116.6
March	14.1	13.0	42.9	1.1	112.4
Total	168.4	152.1		16.3	
Average Cost			36.6¢		63.1¢
Total Annual Cost		$55,669,000		$10,285,000	

		Estimated for Uniform Movement with Enlarged Time Charter Fleet			
	Total Volume	Time Charter Volume	Rate	Spot Charter Volume	Rate
April 1950	14.0	14.0	31.8¢		
May	14.0	14.0	31.4		
June	14.1	14.1	30.9		
July	14.0	14.0	31.0		
August	14.0	14.0	31.3	None	
September	14.1	14.1	32.5		
October	14.0	14.0	40.2		
November	14.0	14.0	41.8		
December	14.1	14.1	42.8		
January 1951	14.0	14.0	42.0		
February	14.0	14.0	41.0		
March	14.1	14.1	42.9		
Total	168.4	168.4			
Average Cost			36.6¢		
Total Annual Cost		$61,693,100		None	

Source: Esso Standard Oil Company, *Tankage Requirements, Refineries, and Primary Terminals, 1951–1954*, a company memorandum prepared in 1951, page 19.

spot charter shipments ($55,669,000 plus $16,430,000). The saving resulting from the construction of seasonal tankage with the enlargement of the time charter fleet would therefore have been $10,405,900.

The provision for uniform shipments from the Gulf to the Atlantic Coast would have required some additional financial costs for the investment in inventories and some expenses for the operation of storage facilities, but even after liberal allowance for these items, it is apparent that the investment of $14,200,000 in the tankage necessary to permit the uniform movement would have yielded a very satisfactory return.

Accessibility of Gains in the Management of Inventories to Integrated and Nonintegrated Companies:

The gains arising from the use of inventories to offset the seasonal variations in the demand for petroleum products which have been discussed in the foregoing paragraphs are accessible in at least some degree to both integrated and nonintegrated companies. As a general rule, however, the gains arising from the effective management of inventories tend to be somewhat more accessible to integrated than nonintegrated concerns for at least three important reasons.

In the first place, an integrated company can embark on a program of building seasonal inventories with a good deal less risk than can a nonintegrated concern. The building of seasonal inventories necessarily requires certain estimates of future market demand, and the program can prove a success or failure depending on the accuracy of the estimates. Ordinarily a refiner who has integrated forward into wholesaling and retailing operations is in closer touch with the final markets and is in a far better position to develop accurate forecasts of the demand for his output than is a refiner who sells his products to jobbers or on an unbranded basis in the tank car markets. The nonintegrated refiner can, of course, draw upon his various customers for estimates of their stock positions and future needs, but the task of collecting accurate information quickly and systematically is more difficult than it is for an integrated company with extensive marketing operations of its own.

Moreover, even with the best of demand forecasts there is always the possibility that weather conditions or other unpredictable developments may result in market surpluses rather than shortages at the time anticipated for the liquidation of the inventories. In such circumstances, the integrated refiner has a well-established selling organization to aid him in working his way out of the problem. A nonintegrated refiner, on the other hand, can only sell his products for what they will bring in the tank car and cargo markets and may be forced to take far greater price reductions to move his stocks than the integrated concern.

It is also more difficult for a nonintegrated concern to carry out a program of building seasonal inventories on an orderly basis than it is for an integrated oil company. An integrated company controls market terminals and bulk plants and can proceed with the movement of stocks to these points without interruption, except when changes become necessary as a result of new market conditions. A nonintegrated refiner often finds, however, that his entire program is disrupted by efforts of his customers to anticipate changes in market prices. In times of slackening demand, cargo buyers and jobbers may retard their buying in the hope of obtaining lower prices; conversely, in times of rising demand they may accelerate their purchases abnormally in order to fill their tankage to capacity before a price increase takes place. As a result, a nonintegrated refiner may find his customers are refusing to buy at just the periods when he most urgently needs to make shipments to them and are buying heavily at times when he anticipated they would not. In other words, although the integrated and nonintegrated concerns face the same problems with respect to unforeseen changes in the demand by ultimate consumers, the impact of the changes on the noningrated refiner tends to be magnified by the buying activities of the wholesale and retail intermediaries which lie between him and the final consumer.

Finally, it is apparent that the gains arising from the use of inventories to obtain uniform transportation requirements are not available to nonintegrated concerns in the same degree as to integrated concerns. A nonintegrated refiner would ordinarily carry his seasonal stocks of refined products at his plant and would not have the opportunity to level out transportation requirements by building inventories at storage points throughout a market territory in the same manner as would an integrated concern. To the extent that the nonintegrated refiner sold on an f.o.b. plant basis, he would not be concerned with product movements, but the transportation costs incurred by his customers during the peak seasons of the year would to some extent be reflected in the prices he was able to secure at the refinery gate. Nonintegrated refining and marketing companies might, of course, work out arrangements with each other to handle product shipments in such a manner as to avoid peak loads on transportation facilities. As noted above, however, such arrangements are likely to be precluded by the efforts of the marketing organizations to anticipate price changes in their buying programs.

III. Gains from the Enhancement of Investment Opportunities (Gulf Oil Corporation)

A third means by which the integrated oil companies have been able to secure some important operating advantages has been through their ability to make certain types of investments which would appear unattractive to firms operating at only one level of the industry or to outside investors. By virtue of having activities in several different phases of the business, an integrated company is often able to reduce the risks incident to or increase the cost savings made possible by particular capital investment projects. By making a number of such investments over a long period of time, some of the integrated companies have been able to accomplish a gradual reduction in their over-all operating costs and to increase their competitive strength in the final markets relative to nonintegrated concerns. A company owning crude oil producing and refining or refining and marketing facilities, for example, can sometimes make pipe line investments which would be unattractive to other sources of capital. Nonintegrated firms, on the other hand, are dependent on other investors to supply the pipe line and other facilities which precede or follow them in the oil producing and distribution process. If these investments are not forthcoming, the nonintegrated firms inevitably operate

Exhibit XI-4. Southern Mississippi Oil Fields and Pipe Lines: 1951

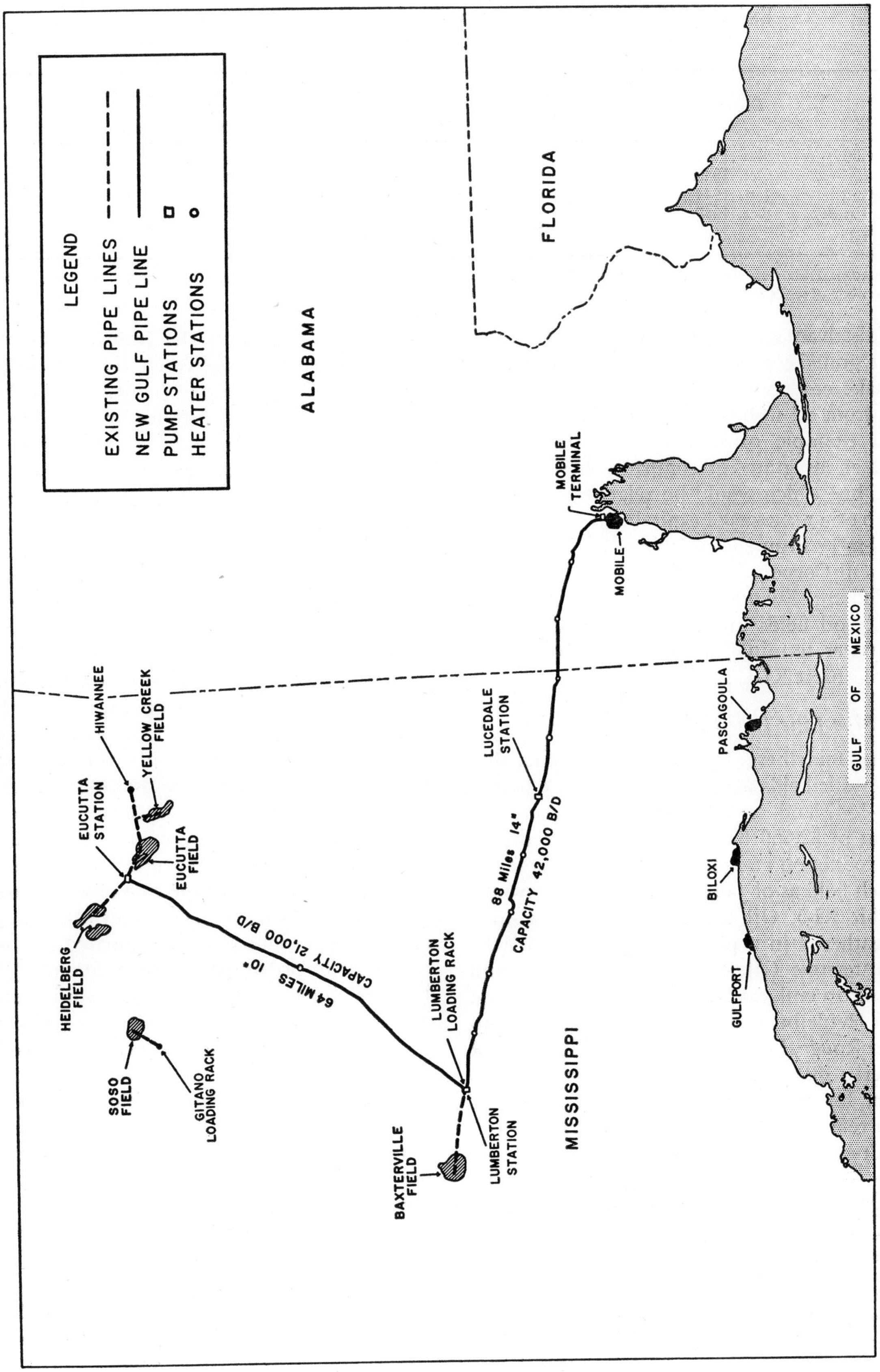

LEGEND

EXISTING PIPE LINES
NEW GULF PIPE LINE
PUMP STATIONS
HEATER STATIONS

FLORIDA

ALABAMA

MOBILE TERMINAL

MOBILE

HIWANNEE

YELLOW CREEK FIELD

EUCUTTA STATION

EUCUTTA FIELD

HEIDELBERG FIELD

LUCEDALE STATION

88 Miles 14"
CAPACITY 42,000 B/D

64 MILES 10"
CAPACITY 21,000 B/D

LUMBERTON LOADING RACK

SOSO FIELD

GITANO LOADING RACK

BAXTERVILLE FIELD

LUMBERTON STATION

MISSISSIPPI

PASCAGOULA

BILOXI

GULFPORT

GULF   OF   MEXICO

SOURCE: Gulf Oil Corporation.

EXHIBIT XI-5. PRODUCTION AND PROVEN REMAINING RESERVES IN
SELECTED MISSISSIPPI FIELDS: 1946–1950

Field	Discovery Date	Production of Oil and Gas Distillate (B/D)					Estimated Reserves (000's Bbls.)	Number of Wells
		1946	1947	1948	1949	1950		
Baxterville	Nov. 1944	3,489	13,606	20,708	6,485	13,558	73,866	160
Eucutta	Oct. 1943	6,550	6,878	7,306	5,267	5,460	22,992	123
Heidelberg	Jan. 1944	11,245	13,777	14,331	7,504	9,470	85,086	170
Yellow Creek	Dec. 1947	0	4	2,195	2,648	4,181	14,704	95
Total		21,284	34,265	44,540	21,904	32,669	196,648	548

SOURCES: Discovery dates and production figures from *Yearbooks of National Oil Scouts and Landmen's Association*. Reserves and number of wells from *Oil and Gas Journal*, January 25, 1951, page 258.

at a disadvantage in the final markets relative to integrated companies which are in a position to make cost-saving investments all along the road from oil well to service station.

An example of the types of investments which an integrated oil company can sometimes make but which would be relatively unattractive to other sources of capital may be found in a 155-mile steam heated pipe line which the Gulf Oil Corporation [7] built in 1951 from the Heidelberg, Eucutta, Yellow Creek, and Baxterville oil fields in southern Mississippi to a tide water terminal at Mobile, Alabama (see map, Exhibit XI-4).

The Pipe Line Investment Opportunity:

The Heidelberg, Eucutta, Yellow Creek, and Baxterville fields were discovered in the period 1943–1947 and in 1950 had a total crude oil output of 32,669 barrels per day. A record of the production and an estimate of the reserves in each field as of January 1, 1951, is shown in Exhibit XI-5. Oil from the Heidelberg field was gathered in a pipe line system owned by the Interstate Oil Pipe Line Company [8] and moved to a tank car loading rack at Heidelberg. From Heidelberg the oil was hauled by rail to Baton Rouge, Louisiana, for processing at local refineries or to Marrero (New Orleans), Louisiana, for transshipment by tankers to East Coast refineries. Oil from the Eucutta and Yellow Creek fields was gathered in a second pipe

line system owned by the Interstate Oil Pipe Line Company and delivered to a tank car loading rack at Hiwanee (see Exhibit XI-4). From Hiwanee the oil was customarily moved by rail to Mobile, Alabama, for transshipment by tanker to East Coast refineries. Oil from the Baxterville field was collected in a gathering system owned by Gulf and moved through a short pipe line to a tank car loading rack at Lumberton, Mississippi. From Lumberton the oil was usually moved by rail to Marrero for transshipment by tankers to East Coast refineries.

It was apparent that a crude oil trunk line which would extend from a point near the Heidelberg, Eucutta, and Yellow Creek fields to Lumberton and from Lumberton to a Gulf Coast port would permit substantial savings in transportation costs through the elimination of the expensive rail movements (see Exhibit XI-6). In its preliminary studies of the project, Gulf estimated that a pipe line of the required diameter could be built at a cost of about $7,000,000. The company also estimated that with tariffs set to provide a return of about 7% on the pipe line investment, the line would permit savings ranging from about 7 cents per barrel on oil movements from the Eucutta and Yellow Creek fields to about 20 cents per barrel on oil movements from the Baxterville field (see Exhibit XI-6). In view of the respective volumes moving from the fields, it thus appeared that the line would permit annual transportation savings of about $1,704,000.

Notwithstanding the apparent financial attractiveness of the project, no other oil company or outside investor had seen fit to provide the capital funds necessary for the line. Moreover, so far as the Gulf executives could deter-

---

[7] The Gulf Oil Corporation conducted certain of its domestic and foreign operations through various subsidiary companies. In the following discussion the name "Gulf" will be used to designate the operations of the corporation and its subsidiaries unless there is some need for designating specific subsidiary connections.

[8] Controlled by the Standard Oil Company (New Jersey).

Exhibit XI-6. Comparison of Rail and Pipe Line Tariffs for
Southern Mississippi Crude Oil: 1950 *

(Dollars per Barrel except as Noted)

| | | Producing Fields | |
	Heidelberg	Eucutta, Yellow Creek, and East Yellow Creek	Baxterville
Rail Destination	Baton Rouge, La.	Mobile, Ala.	Marrero, La.
Rail Tariffs			
Tank Car Loading	$.025	$.025	$.025
Freight and Switching †	.282	.186	.282
Terminaling into Tanker	.055	.087	.055
Total Cost by Rail, f.o.b. Tanker	.362	.298	.362
Pipe Line Tariff, f.o.b. Tanker at Mobile, Ala.	.225	.225	.165
Savings from Pipe Line vs. Rail Movement	.137	.073	.197
1950 Production (Barrels)	3,457,000	3,519,000	4,949,000
Potential Annual Savings ‡	$473,000	$257,000	$974,000
Potential Annual Savings: All Fields ‡			$1,704,000

* Figures assume pipe line allowance is equivalent to intransit and handling loss via rail movement.

† Rail rates are as of August 28, 1951.

‡ Based on 1950 production. Figures are a maximum because not all of the oil would move out by pipe line.

Source: Gulf Oil Corporation.

mine, there was little likelihood in 1951 that the line would be built by any other concern in the foreseeable future.

Unattractiveness of the Pipe Line to Other Investors:

The failure of other investors to undertake construction of the pipe line may be explained by a number of circumstances. In the first place, although the crude oil reserves in the four fields appeared ample to justify construction of the line (see Exhibit XI-5), it was known that the producing formations were of an unusual character and that the reserve estimates were open to a wider margin of error than was normally the case. There was therefore some possibility that the reserves might not last long enough to provide the pipe line builder with a good return on his investment. In addition, the performance of the wells had been somewhat unpredictable, and it was uncertain how long the wells would flow, how long they would pump, and what the future lifting costs might be. Thus, there was a slight chance that even though the reserves did prove adequate, high lifting costs in the future might make it uneconomical to move the crude oil to market.

Another consideration of importance was the fact that most of the crude oil in the four fields had a high sulphur content and a very low gravity (about 16°–26°). The oil from the Baxterville fields, in particular, was almost exclusively of about 16° gravity and almost tar-like in consistency. The output of the four fields was thus of marginal value in the crude oil markets. It was therefore evident that if crude oil surpluses should develop or if the volume of crude oil imports from Venezuela and other countries should be increased, the output of the southern Mississippi fields might be among the first to be taken off the market.

The low gravity and high viscosity of the oil presented another major problem in that heater stations would be necessary at intervals along the line to keep the oil sufficiently fluid to permit pumping. Heater stations had been used in other situations to move equally heavy crude oils, but never for the distances projected in the Mississippi pipe line. The Gulf engineers were confident the heating and pumping could be accomplished, but there was a real possibility that the costs of operation might prove far higher than anyone anticipated and make the entire project uneconomical.

A final circumstance which impaired the attractiveness of the project to outside investors was the manner in which the output of the four fields was divided among producing companies. As may be seen from Exhibit XI-7, about 50%

Exhibit XI-7. Crude Oil Production in Selected Mississippi Fields by
Lease Operators: 1950

(Barrels per Day)

Lease Operator	Baxterville	Eucutta	Heidelberg	Yellow Creek	Total
Large Integrated Companies					
Gulf (through Gulf Refining Company)	8,374	3,414	4,890	183	16,861
Humble Oil & Refining Co.	964	897		1,905	3,766
Sun Oil Company	1,373	300	599		2,272
Magnolia Petroleum Company		351	127	647	1,125
The Texas Company	649				649
Tide Water Associated Oil Co.	76	164	155	222	617
The Superior Oil Company	380				380
Skelly Oil Company			133		133
Sinclair Oil & Gas Co.			101		101
Lion Oil Company			82		82
Subtotal	11,816	5,126	6,087	2,957	25,986
Small Integrated Companies and Nonintegrated Producers					
Roeser & Pendleton, Inc.	853				853
Western Exploration Company		60		581	641
Jasper Oil Company			492		492
Midstates Oil Corporation			413		413
Texas Gulf Producing Co.			375		375
P. G. Lake, Inc.			308		308
Frank and George Frankel			272		272
Lyons and Prentiss		162	98		260
North Central Texas Oil Co.	258				258
S. C. Taylor	255				255
T. F. Hodge et al.			74	175	249
J. P. Evans	212				212
American Liberty Oil Co.			189		189
Fair & Billings		37	146		183
Southern Production Company	35		95	48	178
Texas Pacific Coal & Oil Co.				160	160
Graham & Lewis			157		157
C. L. Higgason			134		134
The Southland Company	116				116
Southern Oil Corporation		60	56		116
Lyle Cashion Company	6			104	110
Kingwood Oil Company			100		100
Walter E. Sistrunk				86	86
Claude B. Hamill			80		80
Hassle Hunt Trust			80		80
W. B. Johnson Drilling Co.			78		78
Southeastern Production Company			77		77
C. L. Morgan et al.			76		76
G. M. & O. Land Company				54	54
Ray Walker		48			48
R. W. Landrum			46		46
Owen & Bintliff			27		27
Grubb & Hawkins				17	17
Tacony Company				16	16
Deposit Guaranty Bank			15		15
Union Producing Company	8				8
W. C. Bedner			4		4
Subtotal	1,743	367	3,392	1,241	6,753
Grand Total	13,559	5,493	9,479	4,198	32,729

Source: Mississippi State Oil and Gas Board, *Petroleum Engineering Report on the Oil and Gas Reserves of Mississippi for Year Ending December 31, 1950.*

of the output of the fields was controlled by Gulf.[9] It was apparent therefore that the builder of the line would be heavily dependent for his throughput on a single large customer. Should Gulf elect to make other transportation arrangements or cease active development and producing efforts in the Mississippi fields, the economic value of the pipe line would be greatly reduced.

In view of the foregoing facts, the $7,000,000 pipe line investment had some significant business risks associated with it. At the same time, it appeared that the line would have to operate in interstate commerce [10] and that the tariffs would be subject to review by the Interstate Commerce Commission, which might or might not permit the builder to charge high enough rates to justify the hazards in the project. The attractiveness of the project was further qualified in the case of any oil company subject to the terms of the pipe line consent decree, which most of the larger producers in the fields were, because such a firm would have been forced to set its tariffs in the light of the 7% limitation on the payment of dividends to shipper-owners (see Chapter Seven).[11] These companies would therefore have been able to realize only a moderate return on the pipe line operation and would have been forced to give other shippers the benefit of approximately the full difference

between rail rates and pipe line tariffs (7% basis) shown in Exhibit XI-6. Since Gulf was by far the largest producer in the fields, the building of the line by another company subject to the consent decree would have provided Gulf with far greater financial benefits than the builder himself was able to secure, either from transportation on his own traffic or the provision of transportation service to other shippers.

Attractiveness of the Pipe Line Investment to Gulf:

Gulf was in a position to view the pipe line project in a somewhat different light from the other potential investors. In the first place, Gulf had enough present and prospective production of its own in the four fields to assure almost three-quarters of the throughput required for the line. Moreover, Gulf was in a position to exercise control over a large share of the future drilling and development work in the fields, and the decision to build the pipe line could, of course, carry with it a corollary decision to continue producing operations on an active basis. In making financial analyses of the project, for example, the Gulf engineers were able to plan on a 100% increase over 1950 production in the Gulf output from the Baxterville fields. Gulf was also one of the largest operators in Venezuela, and the Gulf management had both information and discretion regarding the extent to which Venezuelan crude oil might be brought into the United States in the future in competition with the Mississippi crude oil to supply the company's own refining operations.

Gulf's position also differed significantly from that of other possible investors in that the major part of the financial benefit it would derive from the line would come from transportation savings on its own throughput. These savings represented the difference between existing rail rates and the estimated pipe line operating costs, and the company was assured of them regardless of the level at which tariffs on the line might be set under applicable provisions of the pipe line consent decree or future rulings of the Interstate Commerce Commission. The Gulf management's payout calculations for the line are shown in Exhibit XI-8. The figures indicate that the company anticipated a saving of about $1,923,915 a year on its

---

[9] The exhibit indicates that the output from leases of which Gulf was the operating company was 16,861 barrels per day in 1950. Gulf's own net production in the four fields in 1950 was 14,191 barrels per day.

[10] The possibility of terminating the line within the State of Mississippi at the ports of Pascagoula, Biloxi, or Gulfport was carefully studied by the Gulf engineers. These ports were eliminated because the channels to them were not deep enough to accommodate T-2 tankers and larger vessels. There was a chance that the channels might be dredged to the required depth, but no assurance that the port authorities would maintain them at that depth in the future. The port of Marrero, Louisiana, located just north of New Orleans, was also considered as a possible terminus of the line but rejected because of the high costs of construction through swamplands along the route and because the direct route from Lumberton would have involved a crossing of Lake Pontchartrain. Such construction would have been undesirable under normal circumstances and was particularly so where it was necessary to heat the oil to reduce its viscosity for pumping through the line. The terminus at Mobile, Alabama, was thus selected as the best of several alternatives.

[11] A company can, of course, set its tariffs on any one line to produce earnings of more than 7% on the ICC valuation of the properties, if it so desires. The consent decree merely provides that from its pipe line operations *as a whole*, a company may not draw dividends in excess of 7% of the ICC valuation of the properties.

EXHIBIT XI-8. GULF OIL CORPORATION

Payout Calculations for Mississippi Pipe Line Constructed in 1951

Gulf Transportation Costs via Rail	Barrels Per Day*	Barrels Per Year	Cost Per Barrel	Cost Per Year
Heidelberg	3,700	1,350,500	$ .36176	$ 488,557
Eucutta				
Yellow Creek	3,600	1,314,000	.29810	391,703
East Yellow Creek				
Baxterville	17,800	6,497,000	.36176	2,350,355
Total	25,100	9,161,500	$ .35262	$3,230,615
Return from Pipe Line				
Gulf Transportation Costs via Rail Per Year				$3,230,615
Less: Pipe Line Operating Costs †			$941,300	
Depreciation @ 3½%			246,800	
Transportation Tax @ 4½%			109,600	
Total Pipe Line Expense				1,297,700
Gross Transportation Savings via Pipe Line				$1,923,915
Add: Tariff Revenue from Others (9,300 B/D @ $.225/bbl.)				763,763
Gross Transportation Savings and Tariff Revenue				$2,687,678
Less: Income Tax @ 54%				1,451,346
Net Return from Pipe Line				$1,236,332
Payout on Pipe Line				
Investment Cost				$7,052,000
Payout Funds				
Net Return				$1,236,000
Depreciation				247,000
Total				$1,483,000
Years to Payout				4.76

* Based on estimates of future production. It was anticipated that Gulf would increase substantially its production in the Baxterville field over the 1950 level.

† Costs include those incurred in transporting an estimated 9,300 barrels per day of Heidelberg, Eucutta, Yellow Creek, and East Yellow Creek crude oils for others.

SOURCE: Gulf Oil Corporation.

own transportation costs and a revenue from other shippers of only about $763,763 a year.

Other investors with little or no crude oil production of their own in the four fields were not in a position to make any significant cost savings on their own throughput and were dependent primarily on the difference between the pipe line operating costs and whatever tariffs they would be able to charge other shippers for the major part of the return they would earn from the line. As noted above, builders subject to the consent decree were subject to restraints (via limitations on dividends) in the tariffs they could charge and builders not subject to the consent decree were required to set tariffs that would meet with the approval of the Interstate Commerce Commission. A prospective pipe line builder could, of course, have secured somewhat the same situation as Gulf by buying large quantities of oil at the well-

head and conducting the transportation operation for his own account. Such a builder, however, would have always been exposed to possible loss of his traffic because the many small producers in the fields might transfer their business to new buyers coming into the area or cease active development work whenever they found more attractive opportunities for the use of their capital funds.

A final point on which the Gulf situation differed from that of other investors was that Gulf had a refinery at Staten Island, New York, which was in a good position to make use of the heavy Mississippi crude oil. As noted in Chapter Four, the Staten Island plant was originally built to run on heavy crude oil imported from the company's producing operations in Venezuela. In 1951, however, Gulf was selling most of its heavy crude oil in Venezuela and using its tankers to haul the more valuable, high gravity crude oils. The Staten Island refinery, which was little more than a skimming plant, could be used economically only for the production of a high yield of residual fuel oil from heavy crude oils, and there was some question as to whether it should be continued in operation as it was, closed down, or modernized. In 1951, however, the company was experiencing a strong demand for residual fuel oil in its marketing operations. Coincident with the decision to build the Mississippi pipe line therefore, it was decided to keep the Staten Island plant in operation and to charge to it the heavy crude oils from the Mississippi fields.

In the light of the above facts, it appears that the Mississippi pipe line presented a far more attractive investment opportunity to Gulf than it did to other investors by virtue of the relationship of the project to Gulf's operations in other phases of the oil business and particularly to its extensive producing activities in the southern Mississippi fields. Gulf was therefore able in this case to make an important cost-saving investment which might never have been made had all the various interests in the Mississippi fields been wholly nonintegrated concerns.

IV. Other Managerial and Operating Gains

There are many other managerial and operating gains which some of the oil companies have found to be associated with vertical integration. An integrated company may, for example, secure considerable benefit from the elimination of certain buying, selling, and promotional costs. When producing, transportation, refining, and marketing activities are owned and operated independently of each other, each unit must enter into buying negotiations with the units which precede it in the production and distribution process and into selling arrangements with the units which follow it. Every business unit in the line from oil field to filling station must thus incur the expense of maintaining its own buying and selling organizations. In a vertically integrated company, many of these expenses are eliminated because crude oil and its products are merely transferred from one department to another within the same company.

Extremely important managerial gains often arise in an integrated company simply from the free and easy exchange of information which integration makes possible among executives operating in several different phases of the business. Attention has already been directed to the manner in which the availability of information aids in the planning of capital investments and the handling of logistical problems in the distribution process. In addition, it may be observed that the making of good decisions on nearly all business matters depends in large measure upon having good information with regard to past, present, and future developments. In an integrated company, the constant interchange of formal and informal information among executives with regard to activities at all levels of the business provides an important means by which the general quality of a company's management decisions on many matters may be improved.

An integrated company is also in a position to do a more effective job in tailoring its products to meet the requirements of the market than is a nonintegrated concern. In recent years, a number of oil companies have adopted the practice of supplying different gasolines to different market areas in order to meet the requirements of local atmospheric and temperature conditions. The gasoline blends in a given market may, moreover, be altered as often as four times a year in accordance with changes in the seasons. In such cases it is usually easier for an integrated company to have the right quantities of the right blends available at the right times and in the right places than it would be for a nonintegrated marketer who is purchasing his requirements in the tank car markets.

A further illustration of the incidental benefits which some of the oil companies have derived from vertical integration may be found in the field of research. The handling of some types of research problems requires a knowledge of several different phases of the oil business. An integrated company can deal with such matters a little more easily than can a nonintegrated firm. In addition, there are certain types of basic and applied research which require continuing effort and financial support over a long period of years before any tangible results can be secured. Integrated companies are often in a better position to underwrite long-range research programs of this character than are nonintegrated concerns because of the increased stability of earnings which vertical integration often provides.

Many other managerial and operating gains which arise somewhat as by-products of the vertical integration process might be mentioned. Suffice it to say that the managerial opportunity for such gains is always present in an integrated company, and the nature and extent of the particular gains a company is able to realize rest largely on the skill of its management in administering the vertical form of organization.

V. SUMMARY

1. Some of the oil companies have been able to obtain important managerial and operating gains from vertical integration. These gains were usually not recognized or developed in significant degree until long after a fairly advanced form of vertical integration had been achieved, were generally not anticipated at the time the original integration steps were taken, and were certainly not a significant *cause* of vertical integration. The managerial and operating gains developed only after the companies had had considerable experience with vertical integration and had learned to *manage* on an integrated basis. To the extent that they have been realized, the managerial and operating gains from vertical integration have confirmed the oil companies in their original integration decisions and have come to be part of the reasons for integration.

2. One of the most significant managerial benefits which oil companies have secured from vertical integration has been the opportunity to plan capital investments in the different phases of the oil business on a coordinated basis. Investments in producing, transportation, refining, and marketing facilities can have their maximum economic and business utility only if they are properly correlated time-wise, place-wise, and size-wise with respect to one another. In an integrated company an entire series of capital investments can often be planned as a single program, and the chance of error in the making

of individual commitments can thereby be reduced. The gains realized from the improved planning of capital investments are difficult to demonstrate in concrete terms; they usually become manifest only over fairly long periods of time and take the form of a generally improved utilization of capital funds and a general strengthening of a company's over-all competitive position.

3. A second area in which some of the vertically integrated oil companies have been able to make many important managerial and operating gains is in handling the logistical problems associated with the production, refining, and distribution of crude oil and its products. An integrated company can, for example, often make more effective use of inventory programs to offset the seasonal fluctuations in the demand for petroleum products than can a nonintegrated company. By the strategic use of seasonal inventories to obtain more uniform refinery runs, refinery yields, and transportation requirements, an integrated company can often secure important savings in investment and operating costs. These gains are not equally accessible to nonintegrated companies because such companies incur more risks in the building of seasonal stocks, often have their inventory and refining programs interrupted by efforts of their customers to anticipate changes in market prices, and are not in an equally good position to level out transportation requirements by accumulating inventories at storage points throughout their market territories.

4. A third important managerial gain realized from vertical integration has been the enhancement of investment opportunities. Because it has activities in several different phases of the business, an integrated company can often increase the gains or reduce the risks associated with particular projects and can thus make certain types of investments which would appear unattractive to firms operating at only one level of the industry or to outside investors. By making a number of such investments over a long period of time, some of the integrated companies have been able to accomplish important reductions in their over-all operating costs.

Nonintegrated firms are dependent on other investors to supply the pipe line and other facilities which precede or follow them in the oil process. If these investments are not forthcoming, the nonintegrated firms inevitably have higher costs and operate at a disadvantage in the final markets relative to integrated companies which are in a position to make cost-saving investments all along the road from oil well to service station.

5. Many other opportunities for managerial and operating gains arise somewhat as by-products of the vertical integration process. Among them are the opportunities to eliminate intermediate buying, selling, and promotional costs; to improve management decisions through the exchange of business information; to do a more effective job in fitting product specifications to the requirements of the market; and to conduct more successful research and development programs. The extent to which these gains are realized depends on the skill of a company's management in administering the vertical form of organization.

6. The managerial and operating gains made possible by vertical integration may eventually transcend in importance the competitive and economic pressures which have thus far prompted integration decisions. These gains have grown steadily in significance, and there is considerable reason to believe that their full potentialities have not yet been realized. As the managements of integrated companies gradually increase their skill in administering the diverse activities under their control, the managerial and operating gains permitted by vertical integration may come to be an extremely important source of competitive and economic strength for the individual firm. To the extent that individual firms are able to make such gains from the judicious employment of vertical integration, the utilization of capital funds and the efficiency of operations throughout the industry may be improved. Ultimately therefore the managerial and operating gains made possible by vertical integration may prove to be an increasingly important reason for maintaining and developing vertical forms of organization.

PART THREE

The Formation and Alteration
of Integration Patterns

THE preceding chapters in Parts One and Two have dealt with the general economic forces and specific circumstances which have contributed to the gradual emergence of vertical integration as the predominant form of business organization in the oil industry. In Part Three of the book, we shall shift our attention from the industry as a whole to the integration programs of seven representative oil companies. Our purpose will be: (a) to examine the differences and similarities in the structures of the seven companies and in the policies the companies have been following with respect to vertical integration, and (b) to study the character of the managerial process by which the integration patterns of the companies have evolved.

The organization of Part Three will parallel that of Parts One and Two. It will be recalled that Part One established certain basic facts with regard to the structure of the oil industry as of 1950 and that the following chapters in Part Two then examined the process of evolution by which the industry arrived at the highly integrated state depicted in Part One. Similarly, we shall devote Chapter Twelve to the task of establishing some basic facts with regard to the integration patterns of the seven companies. The next four chapters will then discuss the differences and similarities in the patterns and the policies and objectives of the seven companies with respect to vertical integration. The concluding chapter in Part Three, Chapter Seventeen, will direct attention to the highly fluid character of integration patterns and to the kinds of influences which have continually brought about rearrangements in them.

CHAPTER TWELVE

Integration Patterns of Selected Oil Companies

A COMPANY's integration pattern may be defined as the whole matrix of arrangements the company has made with respect to vertical integration at all points in its operations. As was noted in Chapter One, integration patterns in the oil industry are subject to innumerable variations. First, a company has options with respect to *depth* of integration or the number of steps in the oil process which it elects to cover. Second, a company has options with respect to the *extent* of its participation in each step or the balance which it maintains among its operations at the successive levels of the industry. Third, a company has options with respect to *intensity* of integration or the strength of the bonds it establishes among its activities in the different phases of the business. All these options may be exercised not only with respect to each of the major steps in the oil process, but likewise with respect to the hundreds of peripheral activities which are associated with the major steps. The particular *combination* of these many options with respect to depth, extent, and intensity of integration which a company elects as of any particular time represents its integration pattern.

In this chapter it is our purpose to make a general examination of the integration patterns of seven major oil companies. The group of companies selected for study was comprised of three companies which were organized as independent concerns and of four companies which were important components of the Standard Oil group prior to the dissolution decree in 1911.[1] The three independently organized concerns were the Gulf Oil Corporation, The Texas Company, and the Sinclair Oil Corporation. The Gulf Oil Corporation and The Texas

Company, or rather their predecessor organizations, began operations in Texas in 1901 and 1902, respectively, as competitors of the Standard Oil group. These two companies were of particular interest to us because their operations covered a long span of the industry's history and because although they both were organized at about the same time and in about the same area as a result of the discovery of the Spindletop and adjacent oil fields, they subsequently developed their operations along quite different lines. The Sinclair Oil Corporation was added to the group as a third independently organized firm because it was incorporated at a much later date (1919) than the first two companies and because it had its origin in the Mid-Continent rather than the Texas oil fields.

The four former components of the Standard Oil group selected for study were The Ohio Oil Company, The Atlantic Refining Company, the Standard Oil Company (Indiana), and the Standard Oil Company (Ohio). As members of the Standard Oil group, these four companies concentrated on certain functions: The Ohio Oil Company was chiefly a producing organization; The Atlantic Refining Company was primarily a refining concern; the Standard Oil Company (Indiana) was both a refining and marketing company with somewhat larger refining than marketing operations; and the Standard Oil Company (Ohio) was both a refining and marketing concern with somewhat larger marketing than refining operations. At the time of the dissolution decree the four companies became independent, and each was faced with the task of developing the business connections necessary to sustain a separate existence. These four companies thus started from quite different positions with respect to vertical integration than did the first three companies in the group.

---

[1] Certain of the latter four companies were also organized as independent concerns but were absorbed by the Standard Oil group at an early stage in their development.

EXHIBIT XII-1. SELECTED FINANCIAL AND OPERATING DATA FOR THIRTY LARGE OIL COMPANIES: 1952

	Total Assets ($1,000)	Rank	Total Income ($1,000)	Rank	Net Income ($1,000)	Rank	Net Domestic Production* (1,000 Bbls.)	Rank	Foreign Production* (1,000 Bbls.)	Rank	Domestic Refinery Runs* (1,000 Bbls.)	Rank	Foreign Refinery Runs* (1,000 Bbls.)	Rank
Standard Oil Company (New Jersey)	$5,049,283	1	$4,156,977	1	$519,981	1	148,407	1	301,333	1	284,924	1	305,017	1
Socony-Vacuum Oil Company	2,011,337	2	1,626,518	2	171,092	4	80,028	7	17,958	3	185,702 #	2		
Standard Oil Company (Indiana)	1,983,756	3	1,616,895	3	119,981	6	89,737	5			185,326	3		
The Texas Company	1,786,081	4	1,587,148	4	181,242	2	110,505	2	11,346	4	172,900 ††	4	16,280	2
Gulf Oil Corporation	1,627,279	5	1,539,154	5	141,820	5	81,828	6	170,478	2	166,141	5	4,713	4
Standard Oil Company of California	1,407,198	6	1,087,116	7	174,030	3	94,641	4	7,683	5	147,468 ‡‡	6		
Cities Service Company	1,089,570	7	908,565	8	49,259	10	30,793 E	16	7	14	80,766 **	9	1,927	5
Sinclair Oil Corporation	1,035,308	8	873,107	9	86,475	8	40,230	10	3,680	6	132,281 **	8	6,706	3
Shell Oil Company	941,720	9	1,155,627	6	90,873	7	96,097	3	2	15	139,632	7		
Phillips Petroleum Company	922,936	10	723,092	10	75,284	9	45,286	8	2,738	8	79,881	10		
The Atlantic Refining Company	525,753	11	613,243	12	40,477	12	33,233	15	3,488	7	64,796	12		
Union Oil Company	440,227	12	288,344	17	27,580	17	33,553	14	115	13	52,155 ||	14		
Sun Oil Company	432,189	13	619,413	11	43,013	11	38,623	11	174	10	78,014	11		
Pure Oil Company	381,327	14	342,471	15	27,304	18	26,499	17			41,316 ‡	16		
Continental Oil Company	360,918	15	399,265	14	38,088	14	41,520	9			40,317 †	17		
Tide Water Associated Oil Company	341,550	16	431,573	13	31,117	15	34,986	12			54,947 †	13		
Standard Oil Company (Ohio)	295,872	17	304,497	16	17,697	20	11,766	21			43,361	15		
The Ohio Oil Company	284,118	18	225,694	18	39,354	13	33,723	13	135	11	13,774	21		
Skelly Oil Company	252,484	19	207,859	19	28,033	16	23,771	19			15,811	20		
Richfield Oil Company	239,487	20	181,800	20	25,625	19	21,161	20			38,383 ||	18		
Mid-Continent Petroleum Company	174,656	21	166,296	21	15,590	22	6,920	23			19,350 §	19		
Lion Oil Company	146,718	22	89,207	23	10,211	23	6,753	26			7,932	23		
Pacific Western Oil Company	128,286	23	18,768	28	8,890	25	3,429	29						
Amerada Petroleum Company	93,190	24	78,694	24	15,896	21	25,022	18	385	9				
Houston Oil Company	76,221	25	27,361	26	6,344	29	4,672	28						
Plymouth Oil Company	75,647	26	105,161	22	9,648	24	6,805	25			13,708	22		
Seaboard Oil Company	43,731	27	35,254	25	6,512	28	11,584	22	116	12				
Texas Pacific Coal and Oil Company	40,287	28	19,212	27	6,846	27	6,849	24						
Texas Gulf Producing Company	23,720	29	10,544	30	3,185	30	3,405	30						
Louisiana Land and Exploration Company	21,118	30	18,499	29	8,472	26	5,901	27						

Italics indicate companies selected for study.

E indicates estimate by Petroleum Department, Chase National Bank.

* Compilation only includes operations of companies and their *consolidated* subsidiaries. Note that the crude oil production figures shown in Exhibits XII-10 to XII-25 for certain of the companies sometimes include the company's net interest in the net production of affiliated, *but nonconsolidated,* companies.

† Includes crude oil processed by companies included in 30 oil company group.
‡ Includes crude oil processed by others not included in 30 oil company group.
§ Excludes 1,951 thousand barrels of natural gasoline and other products.
‖ Includes crude oil processed for others not included in 30 oil company group.
Includes 4,396 thousand barrels run for a company in California.

** Excludes crude oil processed for other companies included in 30 oil company group.
‡‡ Excludes crude oil processed by others.
†† Excludes 3,017 thousand barrels of purchased distillate.

SOURCE: Petroleum Department, Chase National Bank, except foreign production figure for Sinclair which was obtained directly from the company.

EXHIBIT XII-2. EARNINGS EXPERIENCE OF SEVEN OIL COMPANIES

Year	Net Income ($1,000)*							Percentage Return on Borrowed and Invested Capital**						
	Gulf Oil Corporation	The Texas Company	Sinclair Oil Corporation	The Ohio Oil Company	The Atlantic Refining Company	Standard Oil Co. (Indiana)	Standard Oil Co. (Ohio)	Gulf Oil Corporation	The Texas Company	Sinclair Oil Corporation	The Ohio Oil Company	The Atlantic Refining Company	Standard Oil Co. (Indiana)	Standard Oil Co. (Ohio)
1907	$ 1,809							8.5%						
1908	1,410							6.8						
1909	2,371							11.2						
1910	2,640							11.3						
1911	2,452							9.8						
1912	4,518				$7,298			16.2				31.5%		
1913	9,045				3,809			24.7				14.1		
1914	8,306				(991)			18.0				(3.8)		
1915	9,967				5,592			18.7				18.4		
1916	17,910				9,527			27.5				24.0		
1917	16,665				9,117			21.4				18.0		
1918	14,594				6,601			16.6				11.8		
1919	12,505		$11,880		8,832			10.6		5.5%		10.9		
1920	29,623		22,250		10,220			21.2		7.9		11.1		
1921	11,508		(1,253)		(2,994)			6.7		(.4)		(2.9)		
1922	24,277		10,325		8,050			12.4		3.3		7.5		
1923	17,357		2,146		1,610			8.3		.7		1.5		
1924	22,207		3,886		5,789			9.9		1.1		4.8		
1925	37,665		13,734		8,442			15.3		4.1		6.9		
1926	37,338	$36,464	25,370	$13,536	8,144			13.4	12.4%	7.4	13.3%	6.7		
1927	17,543	20,606	12,979	7,315	3,289			5.6	7.0	3.7	7.2	2.8		
1928	39,915	46,875	20,731	5,055	17,690			11.6	11.8	5.4	5.0	13.5		
1929	48,222	51,120	22,923	12,348	18,087		$4,276	12.6	9.0	6.1	11.6	12.5		11.4%
1930	16,008	21,658	18,145	10,630	3,433	$55,027	3,732	3.7	3.9	4.8	5.4	2.4	7.3%	8.7
1931	(16,578)§	(3,432)	(17,366)†	(21,489)§	1,280	21,202	2,400	(3.7)	(0.7)	(5.1)†	(12.4)§	.9	2.9	4.6
1932	8,952	4,458	5,260‡	7,243	4,689	19,560	(1,183)	2.1	0.9	1.5‡	4.2	3.3	2.9	(2.4)
1933	(5,243)	5,949	3,726	(122)	7,282	18,873	(808)	(1.3)	1.3	1.1	(.1)	5.0	2.9	(1.7)
1934	8,996	11,432	3,661	5,412	6,241	19,130	(1,905)	2.2	2.6	1.2	3.3	4.2	3.0	(4.3)
1935	14,985	22,554	13,719	5,488	4,707	30,796	2,695	3.7	5.2	4.5	4.2	3.2	4.7	5.8
1936	29,867	42,358	18,235	7,882	8,228	48,017	4,215	7.3	9.1	5.9	6.0	5.6	7.2	8.7
1937	34,771	58,801	22,761	11,862	10,256	57,703	3,557	8.1	10.9	7.2	9.0	6.7	8.4	7.0
1938	15,905	28,345	9,901	4,583	4,717	28,468	2,343	3.5	5.3	3.0	3.7	2.6	4.1	4.1
1939	17,675	39,154	10,228	1,492	5,835	35,853	5,888	3.9	6.6	3.1	1.7	3.2	5.2	9.6
1940	23,486	38,647	6,379	8,733	7,049	37,737	6,377	5.2	6.4	2.0	7.6	3.8	5.3	10.0
1941	34,602	56,718	19,119	10,800	15,167	50,820	6,490	7.5	9.1	5.7	9.2	7.6	6.9	9.1
1942	23,872	48,173	21,173	12,509	7,703	45,716	6,145	5.0	7.5	5.9	11.8	3.8	5.9	6.9
1943	30,437	51,657	26,542	14,147	11,644	52,363	5,559	6.2	7.4	7.1	13.4	5.3	6.5	6.0
1944	43,021	58,798	30,340	15,082	15,808	57,956	7,370	8.4	8.1	8.5	13.4	6.9	7.0	7.1
1945	46,122	55,983	18,335	13,950	2,630	52,605	4,298	8.5	7.6	4.5	11.7	1.1	6.1	3.9
1946	59,468	75,269	30,162	18,253	10,658	70,875	10,853	10.2	9.3	7.2	14.3	4.3	7.4	9.1
1947	98,274	110,624	51,652	29,161	16,849	100,912	16,944	14.3	11.1	10.3	20.6	6.0	8.9	11.4
1948	158,308	170,371	85,952	49,333	36,612	149,108	24,827	18.0	14.9	14.4	28.4	12.0	11.5	13.3
1949	105,994	137,653	58,641	33,659	28,319	113,405	17,264	10.4	11.1	9.3	17.5	8.6	8.1	8.9
1950	116,373	154,460	75,374	37,350	42,048	136,001	21,340	10.7	11.8	11.3	17.6	11.7	9.3	10.4
1951	145,111	184,307	87,982	41,682	46,031	160,834	24,309	12.6	13.2	11.5	17.8	11.7	10.3	10.4
1952	146,852	190,483	83,446‖	39,354	41,737	134,064	18,856	11.9	12.1	9.7‖	15.5	10.2	7.6	7.9

( ) Indicates loss.
* Net income after taxes plus interest charges and income applicable to minority interests. Note that figures are on a different basis than those shown in Exhibit XII-1.
** Borrowed and invested capital includes common stock, surplus, preferred stock, long-term debt, and equity of minority stockholders in consolidated subsidiaries.
† 13 months ended January 31, 1932. ‡ 11 months ended December 31, 1932.
§ Includes a charge against income in the amount of $16,306,503 for downward adjustment in property and inventory values.
‖ Does not include special gain of $9,630,351 on sales of Colorado Interstate Gas Company stock.

SOURCE: Company records.

In 1952 the seven companies ranked among the 21 largest oil companies in the industry. The relative positions of the companies with respect to various measures of size are shown in Exhibit XII-1, and the earnings record of each company is presented in Exhibit XII-2.

The seven companies from time to time conducted certain of their operations through various wholly owned or partially owned subsidiaries, and in some cases the parent companies were reorganized under new names or re-incorporated in different states. In the interests of simplicity, we shall use the present names of the parent corporations, or simple contractions thereof, throughout the discussion in this chapter and the following chapters in Part Three, unless there is some significant reason for distinguishing among the operations of a parent and its subsidiaries.

I. Statistical and Graphical Representation of Integration Patterns

A company's integration pattern involves a vast number of different kinds of relationships. Geographical considerations, physical volumes of products handled, number and capacity of producing, refining, transportation, and distribution facilities, and the business and contractual relationships of one unit in the structure to another are all a part of the picture. As a result, there is no single statistical or graphical device which may be used to portray a company's integration pattern. The representation of the pattern can be accomplished only through the use of several different kinds of statistical, graphical, and descriptive data.

In this chapter we shall present four types of data as a means of portraying and tracing the patterns of the seven companies which we studied: (a) a map showing the scope of each company's operations in 1952, (b) a record of the balance maintained among producing, refining, and marketing operations for as many years as available, (c) a record of the balance maintained among operations in all major phases of the business in 1935, 1940, 1946, and 1950, and (d) a record of capital expenditures by departments for as many years as data were

available. These data will suffice to give an overall view of the more important aspects of each company's integration pattern and of the manner in which the pattern has evolved. In later chapters we will introduce additional data on the activities and facilities of the seven companies as a means of scrutinizing more closely certain aspects of their integration arrangements.

In developing the data on integration patterns, we made every possible effort to secure comparable records from each of the seven companies. As might be expected, however, we found many differences in the kinds of statistical and accounting records which the companies kept with regard to their operations in various phases of the business. These differences stemmed from differences in operating situations and differences in managerial practices. In addition, the records of several of the companies were very sketchy, particularly with respect to operations in earlier years, and at a number of points it was necessary to make approximations and estimates. The data do not therefore permit rigorous cross-comparisons among companies at all points or rigorous comparisons of operations within a company from one year to the next. We are satisfied, however, that the data are entirely adequate to reveal in general terms the salient differences and similarities in the programs which the seven companies have been following with respect to vertical integration.

In the following paragraphs we shall present the facts about the integration patterns of each of the seven companies without analysis, discussion, or interpretation. With the facts before us, we shall then proceed in the latter half of the chapter to draw such conclusions as the combined experience of the seven companies seem to warrant.

Map of Operations in 1952:

As a means of defining the operations of the companies and of revealing certain geographical determinants of their integration programs, the series of maps shown in Exhibits XII-3 to XII-9 was prepared. For each company the maps show: (a) the proportion of the company's domestic crude oil production obtained from each state, (b) the location of the company's refineries and the crude oil distillation and cracking capacity of each, (c) the location of the major crude oil and products pipe lines owned, partly owned, and used by the company, (d) the location of major pipe lines and terminals, and (e) the geographic area in which the company marketed its products. In some cases, primary and secondary marketing territories have been shown as a means of differentiating between the areas in which a company had its own retail and wholesale outlets and the areas in which it was represented solely by jobbers. On the maps for The Texas Company and the Standard Oil Company (Indiana) we have also shown the location of individual bulk plants.

As will be indicated by later discussion, the location of a company's physical facilities and the area of the country in which it operates have a great deal to do with the character of its integration arrangements. A company with its refining capacity located along the Atlantic seaboard, for example, would obviously have a quite different situation with respect to backward integration into crude oil pipe lines from that of a company with its refining capacity located in the Mid-Continent region. A company with extensive marketing operations in sparsely settled farm areas might be expected to have different arrangements for wholesale and retail distribution from those of a company with marketing operations concentrated primarily in densely settled metropolitan areas. Similarly, a company with marketing operations spread over a broad geographic area would have a greater need to use purchase and exchange arrangements in securing its refined product requirements than would a company with its marketing operations concentrated in a small area close to its refineries.

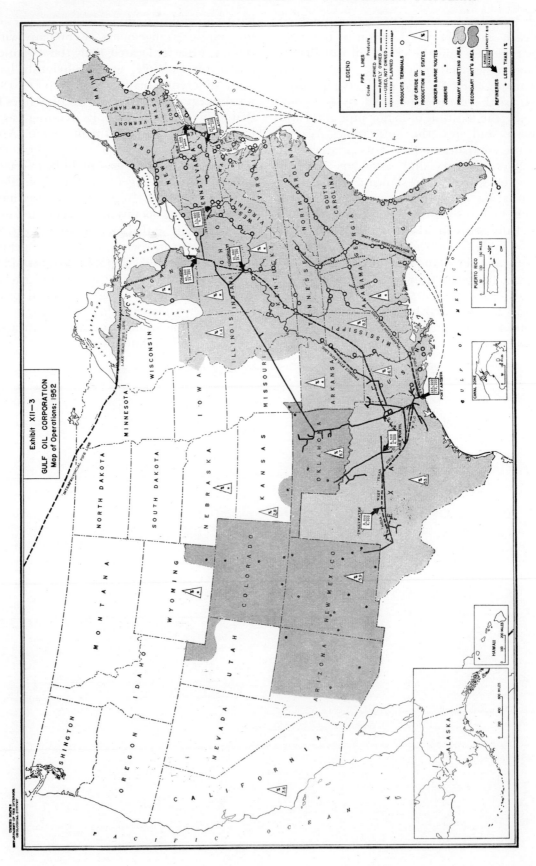

Exhibit XII—3

GULF OIL CORPORATION
Map of Operations: 1952

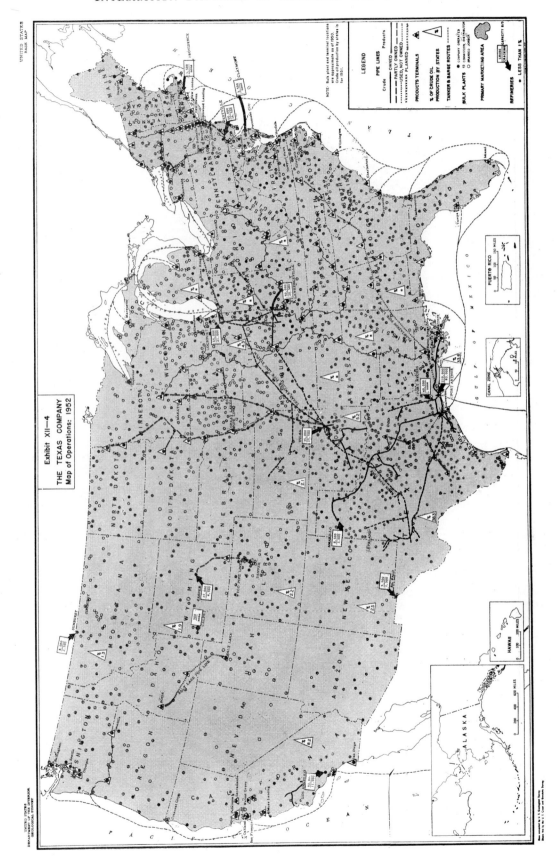

Exhibit XII—4

THE TEXAS COMPANY
Map of Operations: 1952

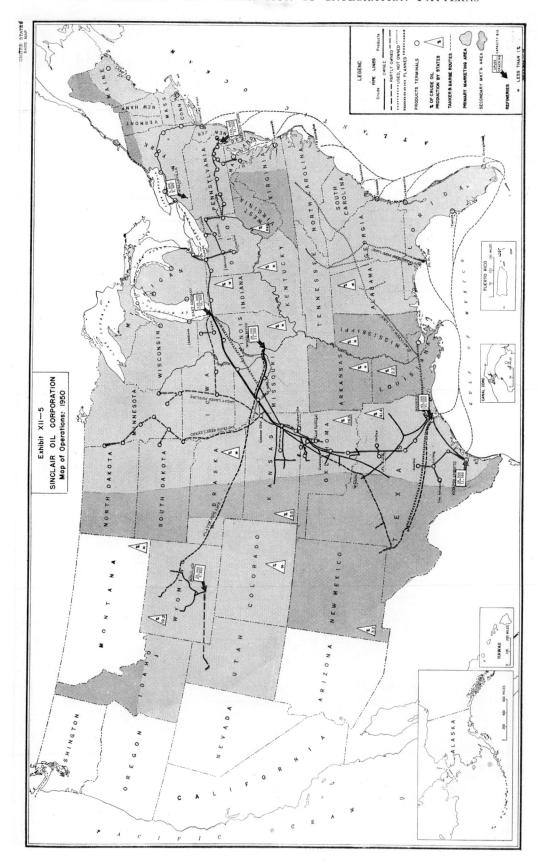

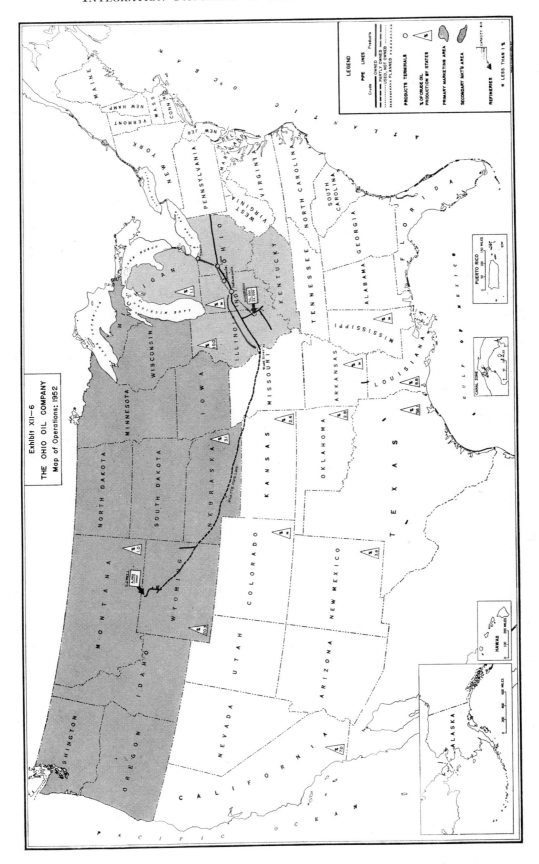

Exhibit XII—6
THE OHIO OIL COMPANY
Map of Operations: 1952

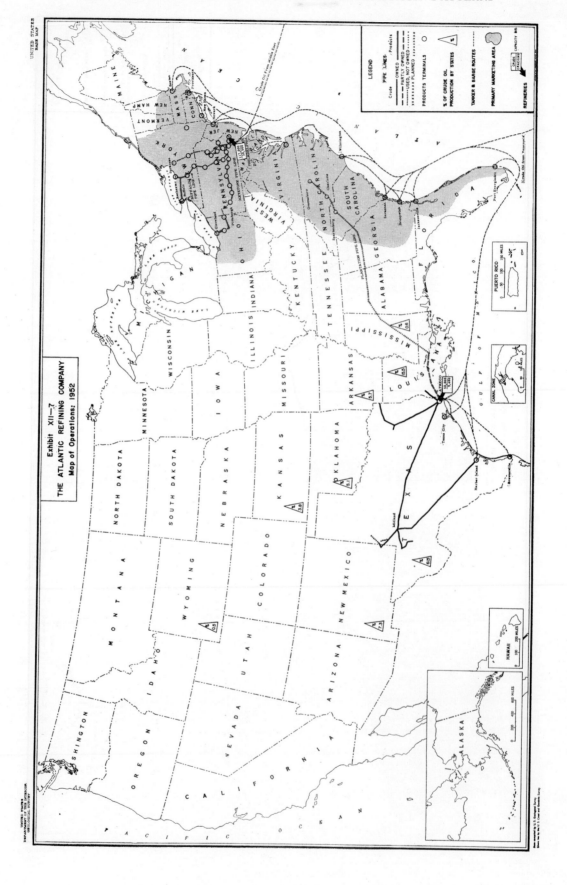

Exhibit XII–7
THE ATLANTIC REFINING COMPANY
Map of Operations: 1952

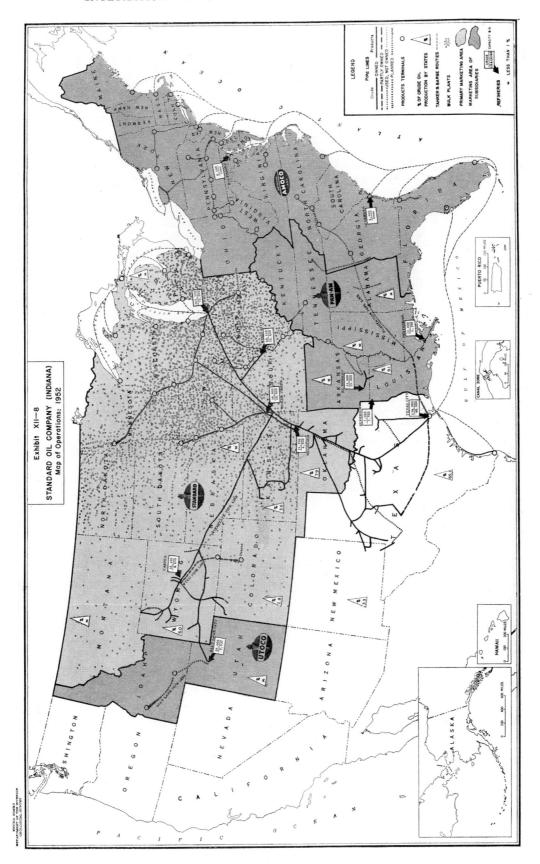

Exhibit XII—8
STANDARD OIL COMPANY (INDIANA)
Map of Operations: 1952

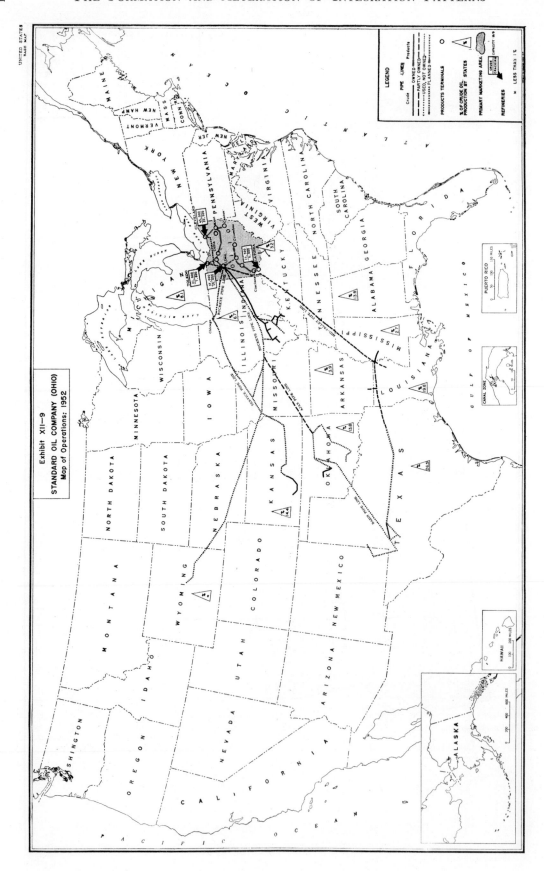

Exhibit XII—9

STANDARD OIL COMPANY (OHIO)
Map of Operations: 1952

Balance of Producing, Refining, and Marketing Operations:

As a second means of defining and tracing the integration patterns of the seven oil companies, we secured records of the balance which each company maintained among its producing, refining, and marketing operations for as many years as data were available. This three-way balance constitutes only a partial portrayal of a company's integration pattern, but it is extremely significant because it represents the extent of a company's participation in three of the most important phases of the business.

The data for the seven companies are shown graphically in Exhibits XII-10 to XII-16. The charts are designed primarily to reveal two relationships: (a) the proportion of a company's domestic refinery runs which were supplied from its own crude oil producing operations, and (b) the proportion of a company's total refined product sales which were supplied from its own refinery output. For these purposes, the supply of crude oil which a company had available for its domestic refineries was considered to consist of its net domestic production plus that portion of its foreign production which it brought into the United States. In many years, as indicated on the charts, some of the companies had additional foreign production which they sold abroad or ran to foreign refineries. Presumably this crude oil was not imported for cost, quality, political, or other considerations or because it was needed in foreign refining operations; it was not therefore considered as available for domestic refinery runs. In appraising the balance between crude oil supply in the United States and domestic refinery runs, it is important to note that the companies were at all times assured of a supply of royalty oil [2] to supplement their

own net domestic production, equal in amount to approximately one-eighth of their gross domestic production. Domestic crude oil production equal to about 87.5% of refinery runs would thus have been sufficient to assure the companies of a crude oil supply approximately equal to their refinery requirements.

The data in the exhibits for refined product sales include domestic sales plus shipments for export, except where otherwise noted. They thus represent total withdrawals from a company's domestic supply of refined products. To determine the proportion of the total sales volume which was supplied from a company's own refineries, the company's refined products purchases in each year were subtracted from its total refined product sales. In other words, we assumed that whatever portion of a company's marketing requirements was not met by product purchases must have been met by the output of its own refineries. We decided not to adjust the figures for increases and decreases in refined product inventories because in most cases such adjustments would have been of minor significance and would have added to the complexity of the analysis without improving appreciably the usefulness of the data. The figures for refined product sales supplied from a company's own refineries may therefore differ slightly in any one year from the figures developed in later charts for the yield of refined products from refining operations by the amount of whatever changes may have taken place in inventories during the year.

To facilitate comparisons among companies, the ratios for the proportion of refinery runs supplied from a company's own producing operations and the proportion of a company's total refined product sales supplied from its own refinery output have been consolidated in Exhibits XII-17 and XII-18. The data underlying all the charts on the producing, refining, and marketing operations of the seven companies have been reproduced in full in the Appendix, Tables 2–8.

---

[2] Leases on oil lands usually provide that the producing company will turn over to the lessor a certain amount of the oil, frequently one-eighth, as a royalty. As a practical matter, this royalty oil is usually retained by the lessee, and the lessor is paid in cash at the posted price in the field.

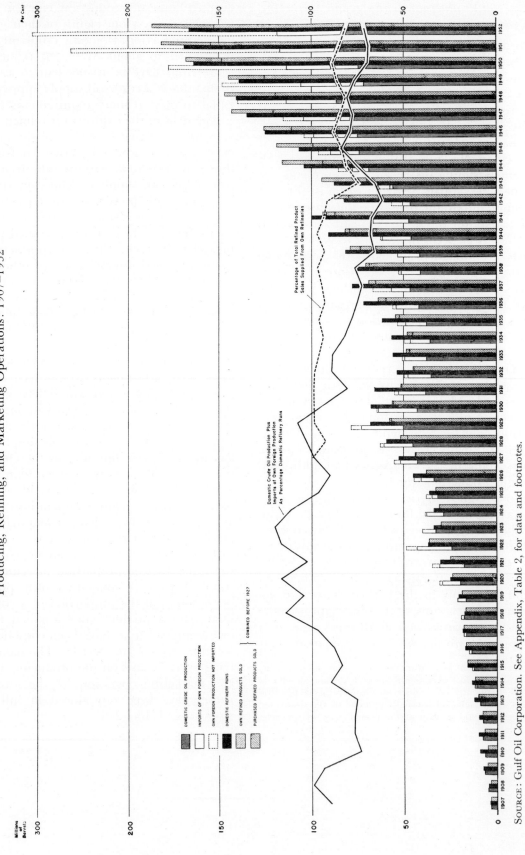

Exhibit XII-10. Gulf Oil Corporation
Producing, Refining, and Marketing Operations: 1907–1952

Source: Gulf Oil Corporation. See Appendix, Table 2, for data and footnotes.

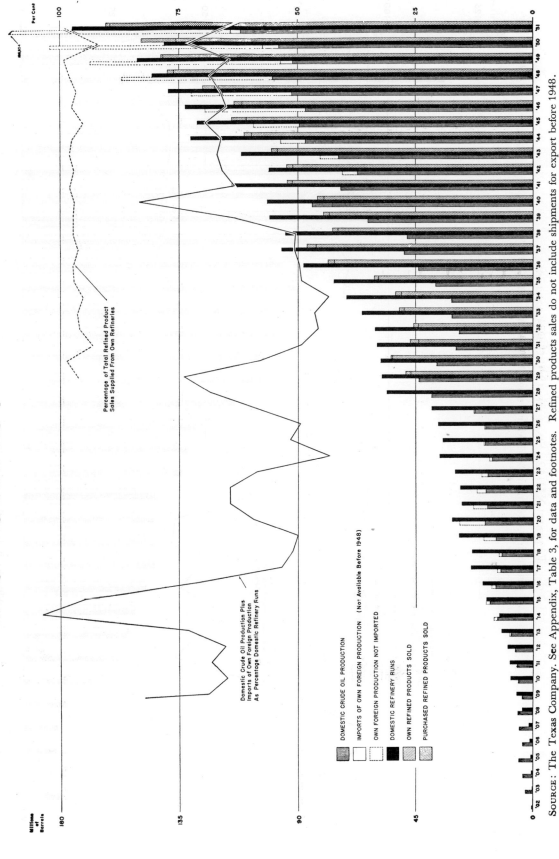

EXHIBIT XII-11. THE TEXAS COMPANY
Producing, Refining, and Marketing Operations: 1902–1951

Percentage of Total Refined Product
Sales Supplied From Own Refineries

Domestic Crude Oil Production Plus
Imports of Own Foreign Production
As Percentage Domestic Refinery Runs

DOMESTIC CRUDE OIL PRODUCTION

IMPORTS OF OWN FOREIGN PRODUCTION   (Not Available Before 1948)

OWN FOREIGN PRODUCTION NOT IMPORTED

DOMESTIC REFINERY RUNS

OWN REFINED PRODUCTS SOLD

PURCHASED REFINED PRODUCTS SOLD

SOURCE: The Texas Company. See Appendix, Table 3, for data and footnotes. Refined products sales do not include shipments for export before 1948.

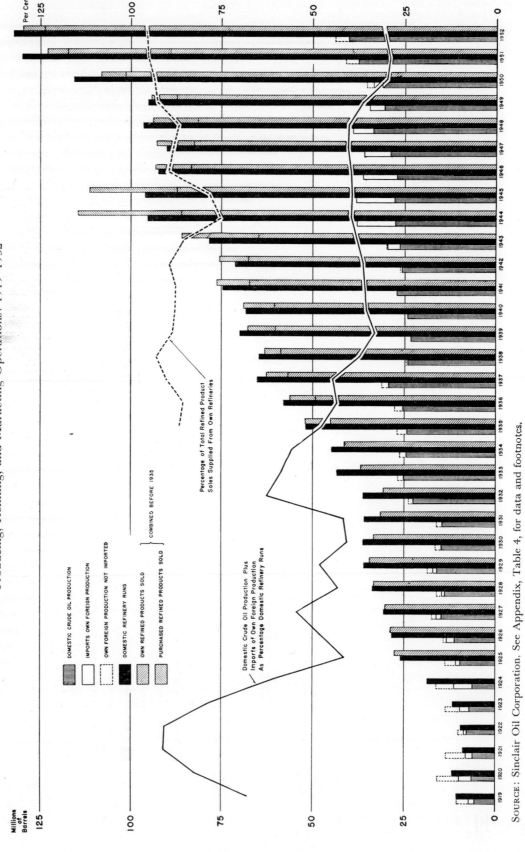

EXHIBIT XII-12. SINCLAIR OIL CORPORATION
Producing, Refining, and Marketing Operations: 1919–1952

SOURCE: Sinclair Oil Corporation. See Appendix, Table 4, for data and footnotes.

EXHIBIT XII-13. THE OHIO OIL COMPANY
Producing, Refining, and Marketing Operations: 1911–1952

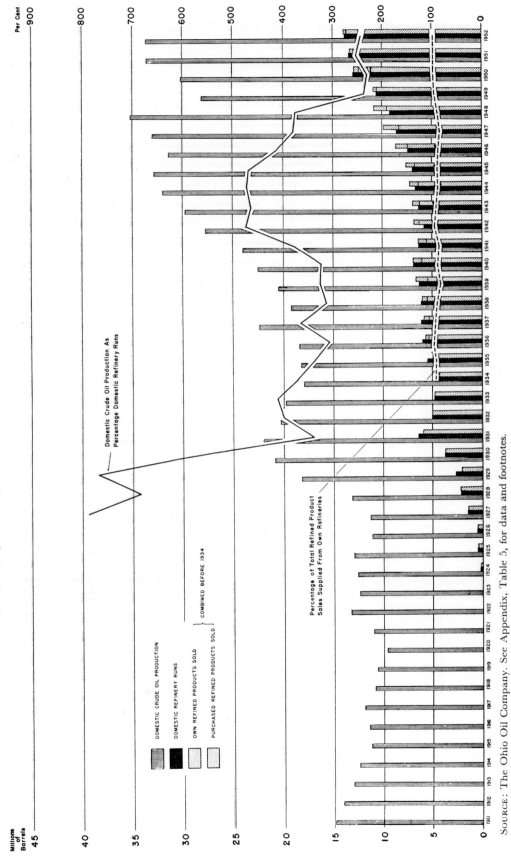

Millions
of
Barrels

Per Cent

Domestic Crude Oil Production As
Percentage Domestic Refinery Runs

COMBINED BEFORE 1934

Percentage of Total Refined Product
Sales Supplied From Own Refineries

DOMESTIC CRUDE OIL PRODUCTION

DOMESTIC REFINERY RUNS

OWN REFINED PRODUCTS SOLD

PURCHASED REFINED PRODUCTS SOLD

SOURCE: The Ohio Oil Company. See Appendix, Table 5, for data and footnotes.

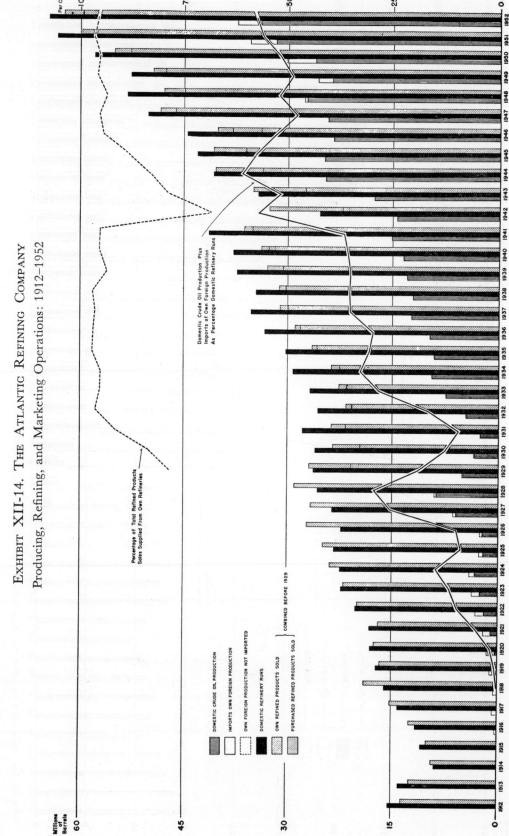

EXHIBIT XII-14. THE ATLANTIC REFINING COMPANY
Producing, Refining, and Marketing Operations: 1912–1952

SOURCE: The Atlantic Refining Company. See Appendix, Table 6, for data and footnotes.

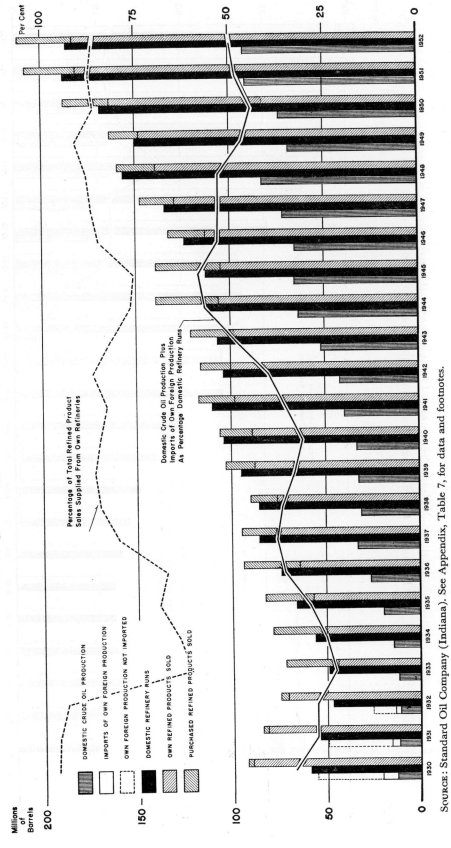

EXHIBIT XII-15. STANDARD OIL COMPANY (INDIANA)
Producing, Refining, and Marketing Operations: 1930–1952

Percentage of Total Refined Product
Sales Supplied From Own Refineries

Domestic Crude Oil Production Plus
Imports of Own Foreign Production
As Percentage Domestic Refinery Runs

DOMESTIC CRUDE OIL PRODUCTION
IMPORTS OF OWN FOREIGN PRODUCTION
OWN FOREIGN PRODUCTION NOT IMPORTED
DOMESTIC REFINERY RUNS
OWN REFINED PRODUCTS SOLD
PURCHASED REFINED PRODUCTS SOLD

SOURCE: Standard Oil Company (Indiana). See Appendix, Table 7, for data and footnotes.

EXHIBIT XII-16. STANDARD OIL COMPANY (OHIO)
Producing, Refining, and Marketing Operations: 1929–1952

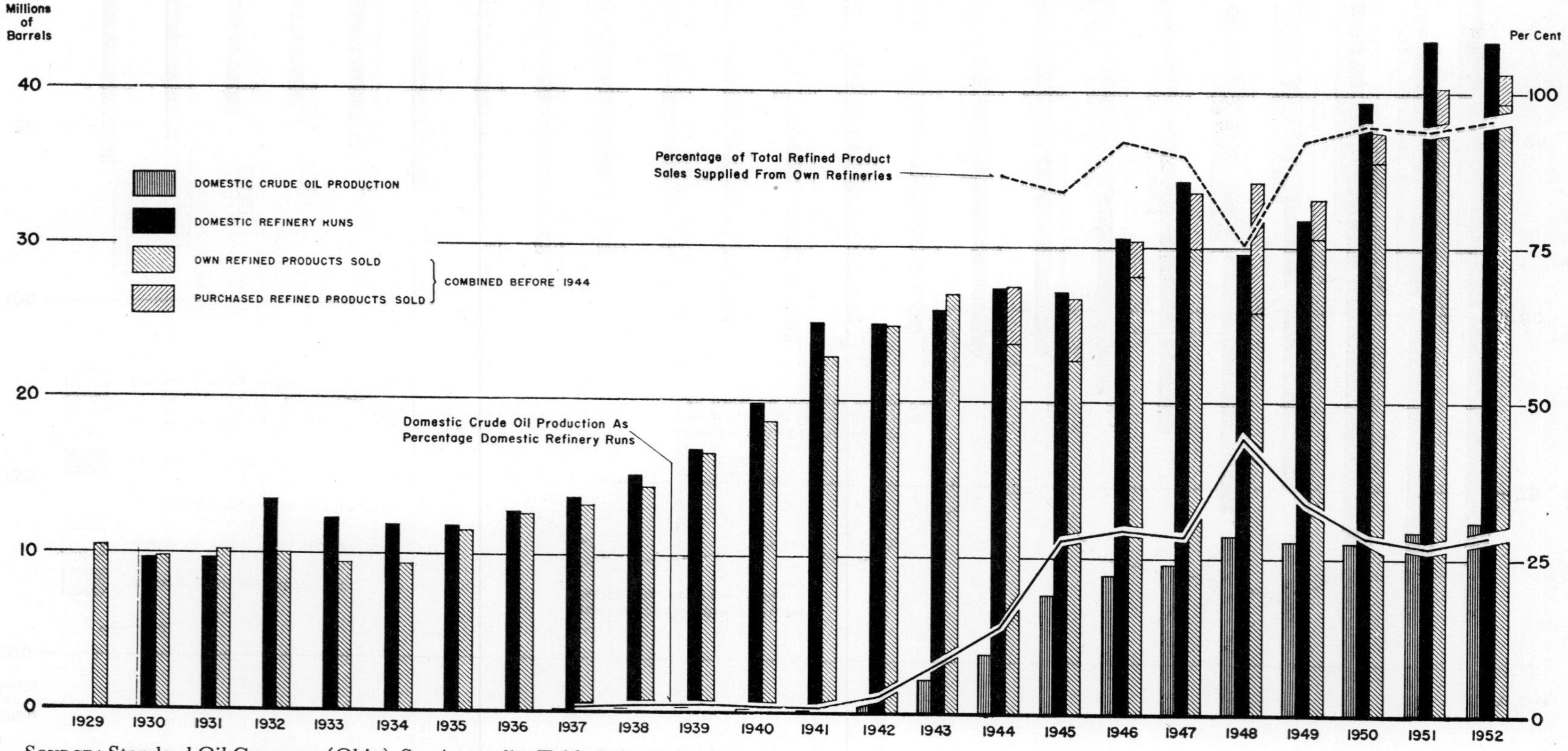

SOURCE: Standard Oil Company (Ohio). See Appendix, Table 8, for data and footnotes.

EXHIBIT XII-17. SIX OIL COMPANIES*

Ratio Crude Oil Supply in U. S. to Domestic Refinery Runs: 1910–1952

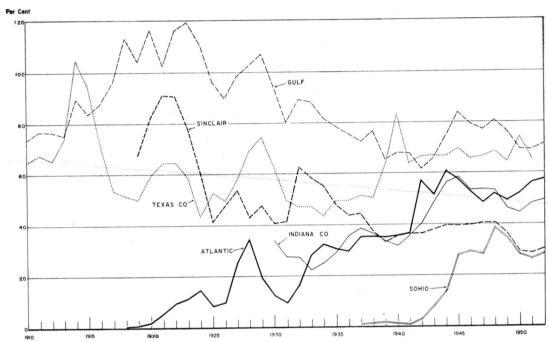

* The Ohio Oil Company was not included in this exhibit because its crude oil ratios ranged between 231.4% and 6000.9% in the period 1924–1952 and thus could not be plotted on the same scale with those of the other companies.

SOURCE: See Exhibits XII-10 to XII-16 and Appendix, Tables 2–8, for data and footnotes.

EXHIBIT XII-18. SEVEN OIL COMPANIES

Percentage of Product Sales Supplied from Own Refineries: 1927–1952

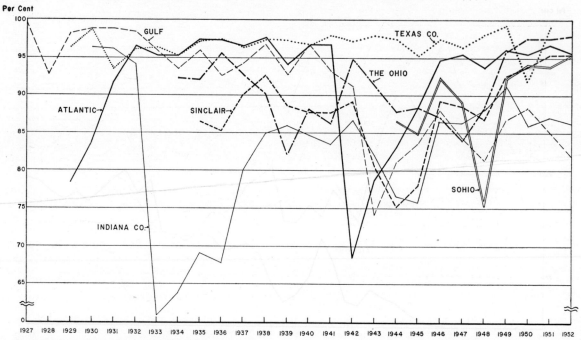

Note: Figures are somewhat overstated for The Texas Company before 1948 and for the Indiana Company before 1945. See Appendix, Tables 3 and 7, for explanation.

SOURCE: See Exhibits XII-10 to XII-16 and Appendix, Tables 2–8, for data and footnotes.

Balance of Operations in Selected Years:

As a third means of portraying and tracing the integration patterns of the seven oil companies, we secured fairly detailed data on the balance of their operations in all major phases of the business in the years 1935, 1940, 1946, and 1950. These data supplement the long-term records in Exhibits XII-10 to XII-18 in the sense that they provide more complete pictures of each company's integration pattern at selected points in its history. The year 1935 was chosen for the first reference point because it was the earliest year for which most of the companies were able to give us satisfactory records; the year 1940 was selected as a second reference point because it was the last year of normal operations before World War II; the year 1946 was used as a third reference point because it was the first year of normal operations after World War II; and 1950 was chosen as a terminal point because thereafter the activities of the companies were heavily influenced by the government controls and government buying associated with the Korean hostilities.

The data are presented in the form of bar charts in Exhibits XII-19 to XII-25. In general, the length of the various bars from left to right across the page represents the volume of business in barrels handled by a company at each major level of the industry. The grey segment of each bar indicates the volume handled through the company's own facilities, and the white segment, the volume for which the company was dependent upon outside organizations. The group of bars for any one year thus represents a "still picture" of a large sector of a company's integration pattern at that particular time.

The first bar on each of the charts represents a company's total supply of crude oil in the United States, and the subdivisions of the bar indicate the relative volumes obtained from domestic producing operations, imports from the company's foreign producing operations, and crude oil purchases. The purchases are a net figure representing the difference between gross purchases and gross sales of crude oil. Most of the companies engaged in extensive crude oil trading operations which involved the exchange of their own crude oil for other crude oil more advantageously located with respect to their refineries or of a grade and quality better suited to their manufacturing requirements. The exchanges were usually treated as purchase and sale transactions. The net purchase figure resulting from these activities thus represents the amount of crude oil the companies had to buy to supplement their own production.

The second bar on the charts represents a company's total receipts of either produced or purchased crude oil at its refineries, and the subdivisions of the bar indicate the relative volumes which moved via the company's own transportation facilities versus outside transportation facilities. In view of the fact that many of the important pipe lines in the United States are owned and used jointly by several different oil companies, any pipe line in which a company had a stock interest was classed as a company facility. Similarly, tankers under long-term charters were treated as company facilities. A precise classification of crude oil movements by type of carrier was, of course, impossible because in many instances the oil reached its destination via several different carriers. In general, however, an effort was made to classify the receipts at refineries according to the carrier by which the oil moved the longest distance.

The third bar on the charts represents domestic refinery runs, and the fourth bar represents a company's total new supply of refined products in the United States.[3] The subdivisions of the fourth bar indicate the proportions of the total supply which were obtained from the company's domestic refining operations, imports from its foreign refineries, and refined product purchases. The discrepancies between refinery runs and the yield of refined products represent, for the most part, losses in processing and fuel oil consumed for refinery heat. The discrepancies also reflect changes in the level of semifinished stocks, because some of the refinery runs may have terminated in such stocks and some of the refined products yield may have been produced from such stocks.

The fifth bar on the charts represents a company's total shipments of refined products from refineries. The subdivisions of the bar are similar to those used in the case of crude oil

---

[3] These figures differ from the refined products sales figures presented in Exhibits XII-10 to XII-18 by the amount of inventory changes during the year.

EXHIBIT XII-19. GULF OIL CORPORATION

Balance of Operations in Selected Years

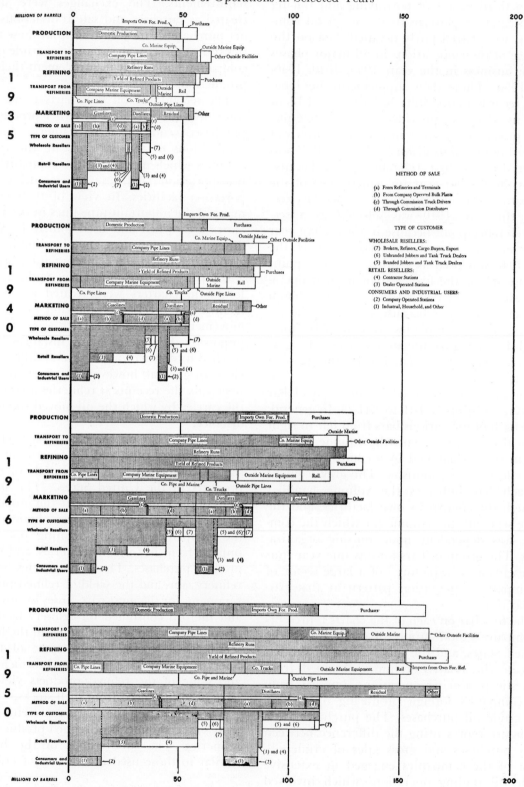

SOURCE: Gulf Oil Corporation. See Appendix, Table 9, for data and footnotes.

EXHIBIT XII-20. THE TEXAS COMPANY

Balance of Operations in Selected Years

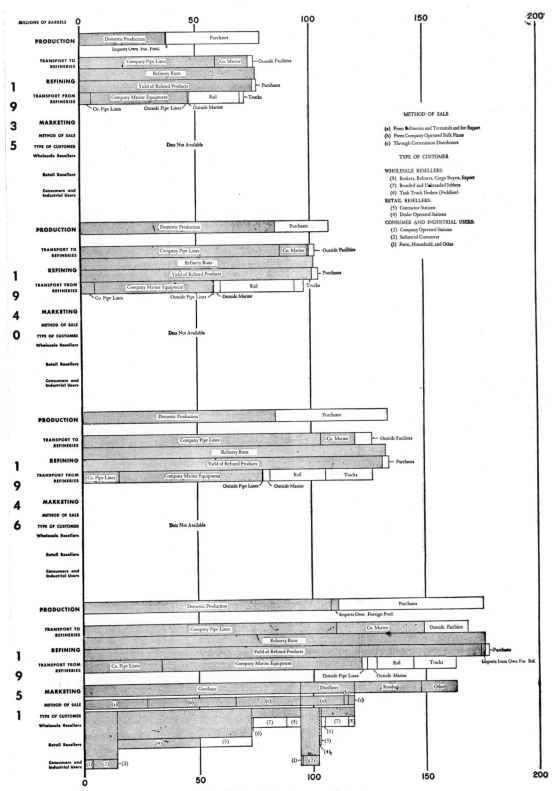

SOURCE: The Texas Company. See Appendix, Table 10, for data and footnotes.

EXHIBIT XII-21. SINCLAIR OIL CORPORATION

Balance of Operations in Selected Years

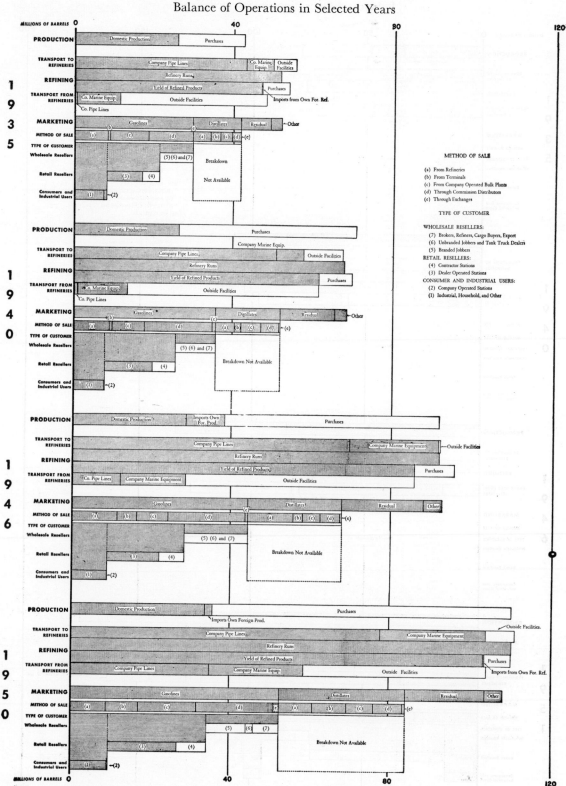

SOURCE: Sinclair Oil Corporation. See Appendix, Table 11, for data and footnotes.

EXHIBIT XII-22. THE OHIO OIL COMPANY
Balance of Operations in Selected Years

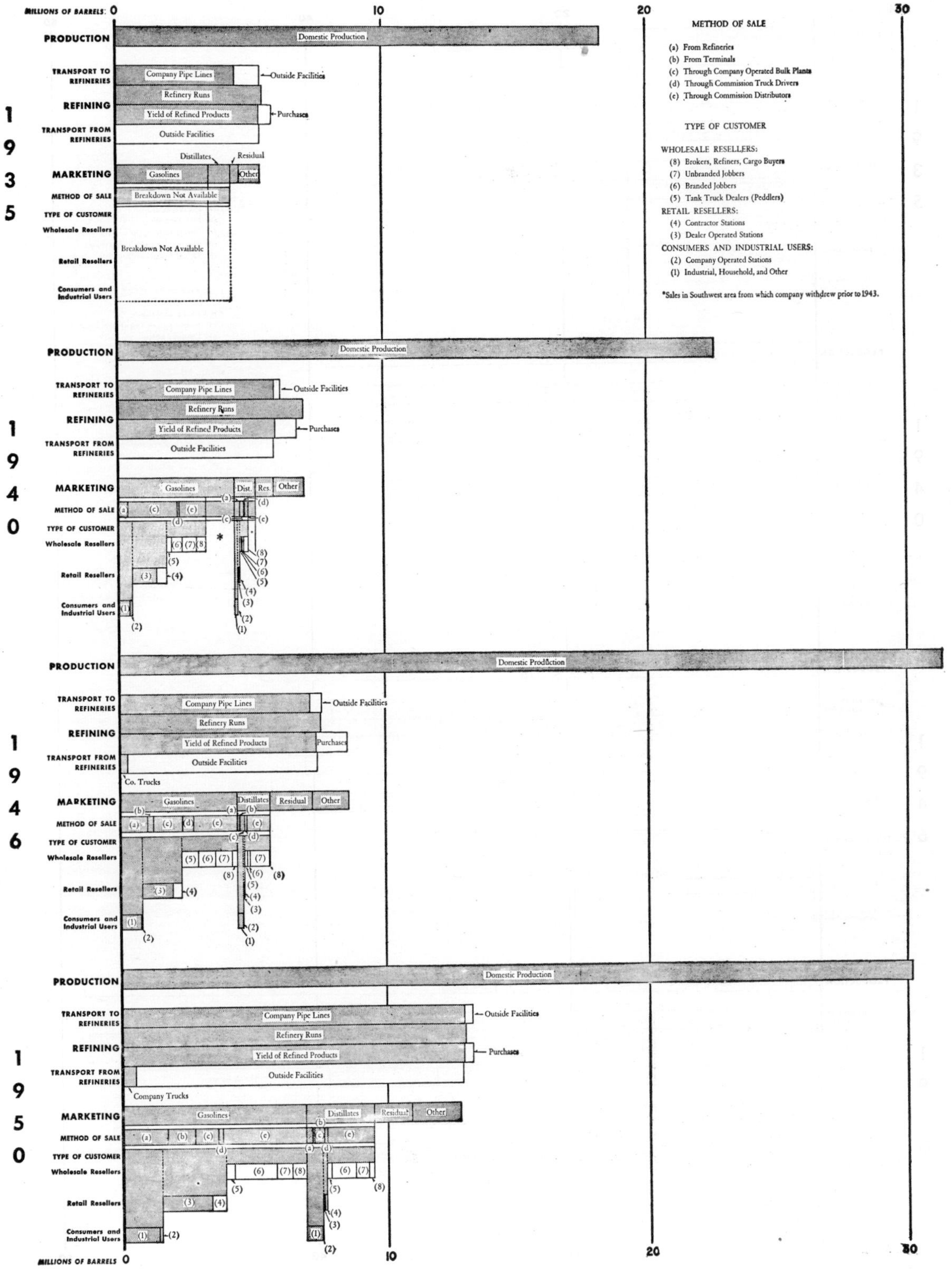

MILLIONS OF BARRELS: 0 — 10 — 20 — 30

1935

- PRODUCTION — Domestic Production
- TRANSPORT TO REFINERIES — Company Pipe Lines ← Outside Facilities
- REFINING — Refinery Runs; Yield of Refined Products ← Purchases
- TRANSPORT FROM REFINERIES — Outside Facilities
- MARKETING — Gasolines; Distillates; Residual; Other
- METHOD OF SALE — Breakdown Not Available
- TYPE OF CUSTOMER
  - Wholesale Resellers — Breakdown Not Available
  - Retail Resellers
  - Consumers and Industrial Users

METHOD OF SALE

(a) From Refineries
(b) From Terminals
(c) Through Company Operated Bulk Plants
(d) Through Commission Truck Drivers
(e) Through Commission Distributors

TYPE OF CUSTOMER

WHOLESALE RESELLERS:
(8) Brokers, Refiners, Cargo Buyers
(7) Unbranded Jobbers
(6) Branded Jobbers
(5) Tank Truck Dealers (Peddlers)
RETAIL RESELLERS:
(4) Contractor Stations
(3) Dealer Operated Stations
CONSUMERS AND INDUSTRIAL USERS:
(2) Company Operated Stations
(1) Industrial, Household, and Other

*Sales in Southwest area from which company withdrew prior to 1943.

1940

- PRODUCTION — Domestic Production
- TRANSPORT TO REFINERIES — Company Pipe Lines ← Outside Facilities
- REFINING — Refinery Runs; Yield of Refined Products ← Purchases
- TRANSPORT FROM REFINERIES — Outside Facilities
- MARKETING — Gasolines; Dist.; Res.; Other
- METHOD OF SALE — (a) (c) (e) (a) (c) (d) (c) (e)
- TYPE OF CUSTOMER
  - Wholesale Resellers — (6) (7) (8) (8) (7) (6) (5)
  - Retail Resellers — (3) (4) (4) (3)
  - Consumers and Industrial Users — (1) (2) (2) (1)

1946

- PRODUCTION — Domestic Production
- TRANSPORT TO REFINERIES — Company Pipe Lines ← Outside Facilities
- REFINING — Refinery Runs; Yield of Refined Products; Purchases
- TRANSPORT FROM REFINERIES — Outside Facilities
- Co. Trucks
- MARKETING — Gasolines; Distillates; Residual; Other
- METHOD OF SALE — (b) (a) (b) (a) (c) (d) (c) (e) (c) (d) (e)
- TYPE OF CUSTOMER
  - Wholesale Resellers — (5) (6) (7) (7) (8) (6) (8) (5)
  - Retail Resellers — (3) (4) (4) (3)
  - Consumers and Industrial Users — (1) (2) (2) (1)

1950

- PRODUCTION — Domestic Production
- TRANSPORT TO REFINERIES — Company Pipe Lines ← Outside Facilities
- REFINING — Refinery Runs; Yield of Refined Products ← Purchases
- TRANSPORT FROM REFINERIES — Outside Facilities
- Company Trucks
- MARKETING — Gasolines; Distillates; Residual; Other
- METHOD OF SALE — (a) (b) (c) (e) (b) (a) (d) (c) (e) (d)
- TYPE OF CUSTOMER
  - Wholesale Resellers — (6) (7) (8) (6) (7)
  - Retail Resellers — (5) (3) (4) (5) (8) (4) (3)
  - Consumers and Industrial Users — (1) (2) (1) (2)

MILLIONS OF BARRELS 0 — 10 — 20 — 30

SOURCE: The Ohio Oil Company. See Appendix, Table 12, for data and footnotes.

EXHIBIT XII-23. THE ATLANTIC REFINING COMPANY

Balance of Operations in Selected Years

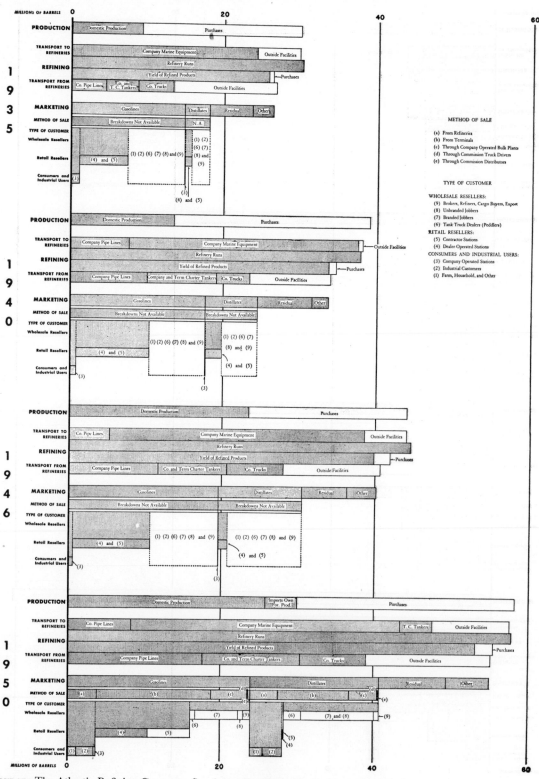

SOURCE: The Atlantic Refining Company. See Appendix, Table 13, for data and footnotes.

EXHIBIT XII-24. STANDARD OIL COMPANY (INDIANA)

Balance of Operations in Selected Years

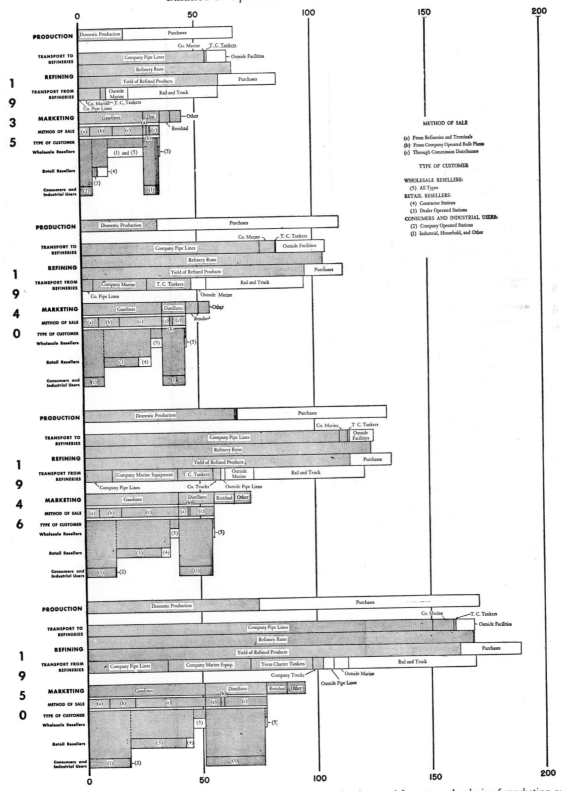

SOURCE: Standard Oil Company (Indiana). See Appendix, Table 14, for data and footnotes. Analysis of marketing operations is for parent company only.

EXHIBIT XII-25. STANDARD OIL COMPANY (OHIO)

Balance of Operations in Selected Years

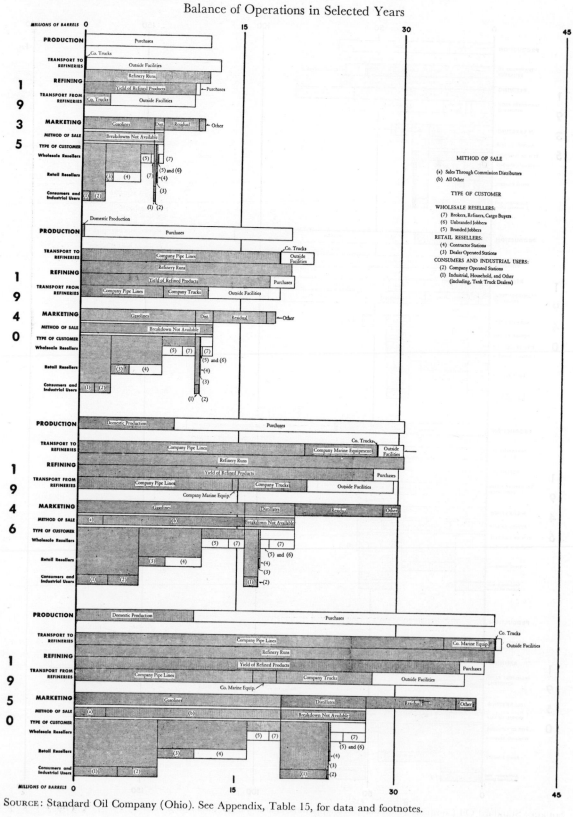

SOURCE: Standard Oil Company (Ohio). See Appendix, Table 15, for data and footnotes.

receipts at refineries and indicate the volume moving via company versus outside transportation facilities. Purchased refined products were included in the shipments only in cases where the purchases were taken into refinery inventories prior to resale. As a result, total shipments do not coincide precisely with refinery yields, refinery yields plus purchases, or refined product sales.

The sixth bar on the charts shows a company's refined product sales broken down into four major product groups. The remaining portions of the chart are then designed to reflect the depth, extent, and intensity of the company's forward integration into marketing activities for the distribution of gasolines and distillates (including kerosene). This part of the analysis was particularly difficult, not only because of the variety of channels and methods by which petroleum products are distributed, but likewise because the meaning of "vertical integration" varies considerably depending on the particular customer to whom the product is being sold. For example, if a company sells all its gasoline direct to industrial customers, it might be regarded as fully integrated into marketing operations despite the fact that it has no marketing facilities beyond the refinery gate. On the other hand, a company selling all its output direct from refineries to cargo buyers might be regarded as completely nonintegrated with respect to marketing activities. Similarly, a company may have no bulk plants but ship gasoline direct from its refineries to company operated service stations and thereby achieve a higher degree of vertical integration than one which has many bulk plants but which resells from them chiefly to dealer operated service stations. To gain an indication of the character of a company's integration into marketing activities, it was found necessary therefore to analyze its sales of individual products (a) by method of sale and (b) by type of customer.[4]

The seventh bar on the charts shows a company's sales of gasolines and distillates (including kerosene) broken down according to five methods of sale: direct from refineries, from

pipe line or marine terminals, from company operated bulk plants, through commission truck drivers, and through commission distributors.[5] In appraising the breakdown it is important to note that the figures have been compiled in terms of the *point at which the sale was made* rather than in terms of the physical volume *handled through* the various facilities. Much of the volume sold from all types of bulk plants would, of course, have first moved through a company's pipe line or marine terminals, and nearly all the volume sold by commission truck drivers would have first moved through company operated bulk plants.[6]

The analysis of methods of sale is significant primarily in the relationship revealed between the volume sold by company operated bulk plants and the commission truck drivers operating therefrom and the volume sold through commission distributors. Although the bulk plant facilities in both cases were usually owned or leased by the suppliers, the use of independent commission distributors to operate the plants clearly represents a lesser intensity of vertical integration than the use of company employees (see discussion in Chapter Fifteen). The relative volumes sold direct from company refineries or terminals have no particular significance except when considered in conjunction with the breakdown by type of customer as will be explained in Chapter Fifteen. As noted above, an increase in direct shipments from refineries or terminals could reflect either an increase or a decrease in depth of vertical integration.

The last portion of the exhibits breaks down the gasoline and distillate (including kerosene) sales according to the *level of the market* to which products were carried by the companies in their own operations. For this purpose the "wholesale level" was defined as consisting of cargo buyers, other refiners, export buyers, branded jobbers, unbranded jobbers, tank

---

[4] We would have liked a breakdown of sales by method of sale and by type of customer reached via each method, but such analysis was impossible in terms of the records which the companies had available, particularly for earlier years.

[5] Commission distributors and commission truck drivers will be discussed in Chapter Fifteen. In general, a commission distributor operates a bulk plant, usually leased from his supplier, receives products on a consignment basis, and is paid a commission of so much per gallon sold. A commission truck driver operates one or more trucks, hauls products from bulk plants or terminals to customers, and receives payments for his services on a commission basis.

[6] None of the companies had records of the volumes which their commission distributors, in their turn, sold through commission truck drivers.

truck dealers (peddlers),[7] and similar classes of trade.[8] Sales through brokers were also treated as "sales" at the wholesale level, because there was no way of classifying the customers reached in such transactions and because sales through brokers were much like wholesale sales in terms of the negotiations involved. The "retail level" of the market was defined as consisting of dealer operated stations and contractor stations. The distinction between the two types of stations lies chiefly in the fact that the former are owned or leased by the supplying company and subleased or rented to a dealer whereas the latter are owned by the station operator or leased by him from some third party.[9] The "consumer and industrial user level" was defined as consisting of all customers who bought for consumption rather than resale. For convenience in analysis, shipments to company operated service stations were simply treated as a "sale" to final consumers, although technically such shipments should have been shown in the breakdown by method of sale as a sale *through* company operated stations and in the breakdown by type of customer as a sale *to* the automotive market.

The breakdown of sales by type of customer may be read in three primary ways. In the first place, the relative volumes sold at the wholesale, retail, and consumer levels are a fairly direct measure of the depth and extent of a company's forward integration into marketing operations. Sales to final consumers represent greater depth of vertical integration than do sales to retail resellers, and sales to retail resellers, greater depth of vertical integration than do sales to wholesale resellers. In addition, differences in the intensity of integration are reflected by the relative volumes moving to different types of customers at each level of the market. Sales to branded jobbers, for example, represent a higher intensity of integration than

do sales through brokers, to other refiners, or to unbranded jobbers (see Chapter Fifteen).

Finally, the breakdown permits some general comparisons of the extent to which company versus various types of outside distribution facilities were used in the company's over-all marketing program. A fairly direct comparison, for example, may be drawn among sales through or to company operated, dealer operated, and contractor stations. Likewise a comparison may be drawn among: (a) sales by company operated bulk plants plus sales through commission truck drivers, (b) sales through commission distributors, and (c) sales to jobbers. In this instance, however, it must be remembered that some duplication of volumes is involved in the comparison because jobbers sometimes secured their supplies from company operated bulk plants or from commission distributors.

At no point in Exhibits XII-19 to XII-25 was any attempt made to take account of changes in inventory positions. The increases and decreases in inventories are therefore reflected in the discrepancies which appear on the charts among such things as: the new supply of crude oil in the United States and domestic refinery runs; crude oil receipts at refineries and domestic refinery runs; the yield of refined products plus purchases and refined product shipments from refineries;[10] and the yield of refined products plus purchases and total refined product sales.

In order to facilitate comparisons among the seven companies and to reveal the changes which individual companies made in their patterns from one period to the next, certain key ratios for each of the companies have been assembled in Exhibit XII-26. The underlying data for this exhibit as well as for Exhibits XII-19 to XII-25 are developed in Tables 9–15 of the Appendix. The footnotes to these tables indicate the various special groupings and arrangements of the data which were necessary to accommodate our analysis to the records of individual companies and should be carefully examined before detailed conclusions are drawn from Exhibits XII-19 to XII-26.

---

[7] Strictly speaking, tank truck dealers should probably have been classed as retail resellers, but it was necessary to treat them as wholesale resellers because several of the companies studied were unable to segregate sales to tank truck buyers from sales to jobbers.

[8] Whenever a company's records would permit, large quantity shipments to government agencies were treated as wholesale sales, but sales to local government agencies such as post offices and forestry offices were treated as sales to final consumers.

[9] The various types of retail accounts will be discussed in greater detail in Chapter Sixteen.

---

[10] As noted above, this discrepancy also reflects the fact that purchases were not included in the transportation figures unless they were received into refinery inventories before resale.

EXHIBIT XII-26. SELECTED OPERATING RATIOS: SEVEN OIL COMPANIES

		Gulf	Texas*	Sinclair	The Ohio	Atlantic	Indiana Co.	Sohio
CRUDE OIL OPERATIONS								
Net domestic production plus	1935	86.4%	48.0%	60.8%	432.8%	30.9%	28.7%	—
Imports own foreign production	1940	64.9	78.5	37.4	389.4	34.6	29.8	1.0%
As per cent total crude supply †	1946	77.2	63.0	41.7	380.8	53.4	50.4	29.4
	1950	70.2	63.2	32.5	260.2	51.7	43.6	28.1
Net purchases of crude oil	1935	13.6	52.0	39.2	(332.8)	69.1	71.3	100.0
As per cent total crude supply †	1940	35.1	21.5	62.6	(289.4)	65.4	70.2	99.0
	1946	22.8	37.0	58.3	(280.8)	46.6	49.6	70.6
	1950	29.8	36.8	67.5	(160.2)	48.3	56.4	71.9
CRUDE OIL TRANSPORTATION								
Crude oil receipts at refineries	1935	89.9	97.1	89.4	82.1	81.4	86.6	—
Via all company facilities	1940	86.3	97.4	85.8	95.9	98.4	79.8	85.8
As per cent total crude oil receipts	1946	87.6	94.4	99.3	93.6	87.3	91.6	92.2
	1950	82.2	88.3	93.7	97.8	82.5	95.3	98.6
Via company pipe lines	1935	74.6	78.0	77.0	82.1	—	85.2	—
	1940	75.7	84.9	75.6	95.9	20.0	72.9	85.5
	1946	75.1	82.9	75.5	93.6	12.2	87.9	70.2
	1950	61.4	65.6	70.0	97.8	14.4	88.9	86.2
Via company marine equipment‡	1935	15.3	19.1	12.4	—	81.4	1.4	—
	1940	10.6	12.5	10.2	—	78.4	7.0	0.3
	1946	12.5	11.5	23.8	—	75.1	3.7	22.0
	1950	20.8	22.7	23.7	—	68.1	6.4	12.4
Crude oil receipts at refineries	1935	10.1	2.9	10.6	17.9	18.6	13.4	100.0
Via outside carriers	1940	13.7	2.6	14.2	4.1	1.6	20.2	14.2
As per cent total crude oil receipts	1946	12.4	5.6	0.7	6.4	12.7	8.4	7.8
	1950	17.8	11.7	6.3	2.2	17.5	4.7	1.4
REFINING OPERATIONS								
Yield of refined products plus	1935	96.2	97.7	87.0	92.6	97.4	69.9	96.5
Imports from own foreign refineries	1940	96.9	97.4	88.0	87.7	97.0	85.7	88.6
As per cent total products supply	1946	88.6	97.9	89.6	86.7	94.9	86.0	92.2
	1950	88.7	99.0	93.9	97.6	95.6	86.8	94.2
Purchases of refined products	1935	3.8	2.3	13.0	7.4	2.6	30.1	3.5
As per cent total products supply	1940	3.1	2.6	12.0	12.3	3.0	14.3	11.4
	1946	11.4	2.1	10.4	13.3	5.1	14.0	7.8
	1950	11.3	1.0	6.1	2.4	4.4	13.2	5.8
PRODUCTS TRANSPORTATION								
Products shipments from refineries	1935	67.8	65.9	24.3	—	49.3	19.5	23.5
Via all company facilities	1940	66.6	59.8	22.2	—	69.0	49.2	64.0
As per cent total products shipments	1946	61.7	61.8	33.3	3.4	68.7	48.6	72.9
	1950	62.6	74.3	56.3	3.8	70.4	60.2	76.4
Via company pipe lines	1935	2.4	6.6	1.0	—	16.0	0.3	—
	1940	4.8	6.0	1.3	—	29.1	5.0	41.0
	1946	10.8	12.4	14.1	—	28.4	9.3	48.9
	1950	10.6	20.9	33.5	—	31.7	20.4	45.8
Via company marine and other equipment‡	1935	65.4	59.3	23.3	—	33.3	19.2	23.5
	1940	61.8	53.8	20.9	—	39.9	44.2	23.0
	1946	50.9	49.4	19.2	3.4	40.3	39.3	24.0
	1950	52.0	53.4	22.8	3.8	38.7	39.8	30.6
Products shipments from refineries	1935	32.2	34.1	75.7	100.0	50.7	80.5	76.5
Via all outside carriers	1940	33.4	40.2	77.8	100.0	31.0	50.8	36.0
As per cent total products shipments	1946	38.3	38.2	66.7	96.6	31.3	51.4	27.1
	1950	37.4	25.7	43.7	96.2	29.6	39.8	23.6

(For footnotes and source, see page 365)

EXHIBIT XII-26.   (CONTINUED) SELECTED OPERATING RATIOS: SEVEN OIL COMPANIES

		Gulf	Texas*	Sinclair	The Ohio	Atlantic	Indiana Co.	Sohio
GASOLINE MARKETING								
Methods of Sale:								
Sales from refineries and terminals	1935	15.7%	N.A.	30.3%	N.A.	N.A.	16.3%	N.A.
As per cent total gasoline sales §	1940	21.5	N.A.	29.5	9.3%	N.A.	19.8	N.A.
	1946	24.5	N.A.	37.9	26.9	N.A.	14.7	N.A.
	1950	19.7	28.8%	35.9	38.8	78.6%	17.6	N.A.
Sales from company operated bulk	1935	43.6	N.A.	32.6	N.A.	N.A.	35.5	N.A.
plants ‖	1940	37.6	N.A.	22.9	57.5	N.A.	26.3	N.A.
As per cent total gasoline sales	1946	37.6	N.A.	18.0	35.6	N.A.	23.5	N.A.
	1950	39.8	41.3	27.8	15.2	20.5	22.3	N.A.
Sales through commission distributors	1935	40.7	N.A.	37.1	N.A.	N.A.	48.2	N.A.
As per cent total gasoline sales	1940	40.9	N.A.	47.6	33.2	N.A.	53.9	N.A.
	1946	37.9	N.A.	44.1	37.5	N.A.	61.8	14.9%
	1950	40.5	29.9	36.3	46.0	0.9	60.1	14.8
Types of Customers:								
Sales to all wholesale resellers	1935	10.0	N.A.	28.9	N.A.	N.A.	N.A.	19.3
As per cent total gasoline sales	1940	16.2	N.A.	28.1	45.4	N.A.	14.7	29.4
	1946	23.1	N.A.	36.1	49.3	N.A.	10.0	25.6
	1950	16.9	22.7	34.1	44.5	33.6	9.9	16.2
To branded jobbers	1935	4.2	N.A.	N.A.	N.A.	N.A.	N.A.	14.3
	1940	7.5	N.A.	N.A.	13.0	N.A.	N.A.	18.0
	1946	5.4	N.A.	N.A.	15.6	N.A.	N.A.	16.0
	1950	8.6	N.A.	18.7	23.1	23.9	N.A.	10.6
To unbranded jobbers **	1935	1.5	N.A.	N.A.	N.A.	N.A.	N.A.	—
	1940	5.1	N.A.	N.A.	23.0	N.A.	N.A.	—
	1946	8.3	N.A.	N.A.	30.4	N.A.	N.A.	—
	1950	6.0	N.A.	2.7	13.6	5.6	N.A.	—
To or through brokers, refiners, and	1935	4.3	N.A.	N.A.	N.A.	N.A.	N.A.	5.0
other cargo buyers	1940	3.6	N.A.	N.A.	9.4	N.A.	N.A.	11.4
	1946	9.4	N.A.	N.A.	3.3	N.A.	N.A.	9.6
	1950	2.3	6.7	12.7	7.8	4.1	N.A.	5.6
Sales to all retail resellers	1935	64.4	N.A.	44.3	N.A.	N.A.	24.3	50.1
As per cent total gasoline sales	1940	62.9	N.A.	50.4	39.6	N.A.	59.4	44.3
	1946	56.4	N.A.	44.1	34.4	N.A.	57.9	37.7
	1950	62.1	62.2	47.8	35.5	51.8	55.2	43.5
To dealer operated stations	1935	N.A.	N.A.	29.8	N.A.	N.A.	7.2	11.1
	1940	26.5	N.A.	33.7	26.1	N.A.	44.0	15.8
	1946	25.0	N.A.	29.2	27.2	N.A.	48.2	15.7
	1950	25.3	38.4	33.1	27.8	28.5	48.8	17.6
To contractor stations	1935	N.A.	N.A.	14.5	N.A.	N.A.	17.1	39.0
	1940	36.4	N.A.	16.7	13.5	N.A.	15.4	28.5
	1946	31.4	N.A.	14.9	7.2	N.A.	9.7	22.0
	1950	36.7	23.8	14.7	7.7	23.3	6.4	25.9
Sales to all consumers and industrial	1935	25.6	N.A.	26.8	N.A.	N.A.	N.A.	30.6
users	1940	20.9	N.A.	21.5	15.0	N.A.	25.9	26.3
	1946	20.5	N.A.	19.8	16.3	N.A.	32.1	36.7
As per cent total gasoline sales	1950	21.1	15.1	18.1	20.0	14.6	34.9	40.3
Through company operated service	1935	8.0	N.A.	2.4	N.A.	N.A.	19.3	20.9
stations	1940	2.7	N.A.	0.1	2.6	N.A.	—	13.6
	1946	3.8	N.A.	—	0.8	N.A.	0.2	18.6
	1950	2.7	—	0.2	1.0	0.8	0.6	19.5
To industrial, household, farm, and	1935	42.2	N.A.	24.4	N.A.	N.A.	N.A.	9.7
other ††	1940	18.2	N.A.	21.4	12.4	N.A.	25.9	12.7
	1946	16.7	N.A.	19.8	15.5	N.A.	31.9	18.1
	1950	18.4	15.1	17.9	19.0	13.8	34.3	20.8

EXHIBIT XII-26. (CONTINUED) SELECTED OPERATING RATIOS: SEVEN OIL COMPANIES

		Gulf	Texas*	Sinclair	The Ohio	Atlantic	Indiana Co.	Sohio
DISTILLATE MARKETING								
Methods of Sale:								
Sales from refineries and terminals	1935	48.4%	N.A.	57.6%	N.A.	N.A.	19.8%	N.A.
As per cent total distillate sales §	1940	54.6	N.A.	42.3	43.6%	N.A.	32.1	N.A.
	1946	52.9	N.A.	59.6	7.4	N.A.	26.8	N.A.
	1950	50.4	79.6%	56.1	10.2	77.2%	25.6	N.A.
Sales from company operated bulk	1935	35.1	N.A.	25.8	N.A.	N.A.	18.7	N.A.
plants ‖	1940	27.0	N.A.	30.4	31.7	N.A.	12.2	N.A.
As per cent total distillate sales	1946	29.8	N.A.	18.9	21.9	N.A.	6.8	N.A.
	1950	35.4	8.0	21.3	17.5	22.4	6.0	N.A.
Sales through commission distributors	1935	16.5	N.A.	16.6	N.A.	N.A.	61.5	N.A.
As per cent total distillate sales	1940	18.4	N.A.	27.3	24.7	N.A.	55.7	N.A.
	1946	17.3	N.A.	21.5	70.7	N.A.	66.4	N.A.
	1950	14.2	12.4	22.6	72.3	0.4	68.4	N.A.
Types of Customers:	1935	46.7	N.A.	N.A.	N.A.	N.A.	2.9	63.9%
Sales to all wholesale resellers	1940	64.6	N.A.	N.A.	71.6	N.A.	4.7	66.5
As per cent total distillate sales	1946	60.3	N.A.	N.A.	78.6	N.A.	3.9	67.7
	1950	59.1	62.9	N.A.	69.4	74.6	3.8	40.3
To branded and unbranded jobbers **	1935	44.5	N.A.	N.A.	N.A.	N.A.	N.A.	5.2
	1940	62.8	N.A.	N.A.	28.0	N.A.	N.A.	7.7
	1946	47.5	N.A.	N.A.	76.8	N.A.	N.A.	17.1
	1950	54.2	49.1	N.A.	62.4	70.3	N.A.	15.1
To or through brokers, refiners, and	1935	2.2	N.A.	N.A.	N.A.	N.A.	N.A.	58.7
other cargo buyers	1940	1.8	N.A.	N.A.	43.6	N.A.	N.A.	58.8
	1946	12.8	N.A.	N.A.	1.8	N.A.	N.A.	50.6
	1950	4.9	13.8	N.A.	7.0	4.3	N.A.	25.2
Sales to all retail resellers	1935	10.9	N.A.	N.A.	N.A.	29.8	—	5.2
As per cent total distillate sales	1940	7.6	N.A.	N.A.	10.4	32.9	—	2.8
	1946	6.8	N.A.	N.A.	4.6	11.2	—	1.5
	1950	4.6	3.9	N.A.	3.9	0.6	—	1.6
Sales to all consumers and industrial	1935	42.4	N.A.	N.A.	N.A.	N.A.	97.1	30.9
users	1940	27.8	N.A.	N.A.	18.0	N.A.	95.3	30.7
As per cent total distillate sales ††	1946	32.9	N.A.	N.A.	16.8	N.A.	96.1	30.8
	1950	36.3	33.2	N.A.	26.7	24.8	96.2	58.1

— Indicates zero or negligible quantity.

* Data for the Texas Company are for the year 1951 in place of 1950.

† In the case of The Ohio Oil Company, the total crude supply figure was taken as the amount of crude oil the company had available for operations after deducting its net sales (total sales minus total purchases) from its net domestic production (see Appendix, Table 11).

‡ Term charter tankers included as company marine.

§ In case of Sinclair, includes exchange products sold through facilities of exchange partner.

‖ Includes sales through commission truck drivers operating from company bulk plants.

** Includes tank truck dealers in all cases except that of Sohio.

†† In case of Sohio, includes small volume sold to tank truck dealers.

SOURCE: Drawn from data for individual companies in Tables 9–15 of Appendix and subject to all footnotes appended thereto.

Capital Expenditures by Departments:

As a fourth means of examining the programs and policies of the seven companies with respect to vertical integration, we secured records of their capital expenditures in the major phases of the oil business for as many years as data were available. These data do not constitute direct measures of integration patterns in the same sense as do the maps and information on balance of operations presented in earlier parts of the chapter. The records of capital inputs, however, are useful as a device for tracing a company's integration efforts because it is through the allocation of funds to different phases of the business that a management controls the growth of a company and brings about changes in its integration pattern from one period of time to the next.

The full records of capital expenditures by departments for each company are contained in the Appendix, Tables 16–22. To facilitate comparisons among the companies, we have plotted in Exhibit XII-27 three-year moving averages of the proportions of each company's capital budget which were allocated to the producing, refining, marketing, and pipe line departments. The three-year moving averages have been used to reduce the influence of random fluctuations from year to year and to reveal more clearly the general trends in the capital spending of the companies.

In appraising the records in Exhibit XII-27, it is important to recognize that an oil company's relative capital inputs to the different phases of the business are normally subject to a good deal of irregularity and may reflect many things in addition to changes in integration policies. A company may, for example, make heavy expenditures in the refining department for two or three years merely to bring its equipment abreast of a new advance in refining technology. Similarly, a company may for one or two years make heavy expenditures in the producing department to develop a newly discovered oil field or heavy expenditures in the pipe line department to construct an addition to its pipe line system without any intention of changing the general balance among producing, refining, marketing, and transportation activities.

The changes in the proportions of a com-

pany's capital funds devoted to particular departments as shown in Exhibit XII-27 may or may not therefore, in any short period of time, reflect changes in management intent with respect to integration arrangements. At the same time, however, a company usually cannot accomplish a major change in its integration pattern without a major change in its capital spending program, and over long periods of time, the apportionment of capital funds to the different phases of the business has a very intimate relationship to the type of structure which a company develops.

II. GENERAL CONCLUSIONS ESTABLISHED BY THE EXPERIENCE OF THE SEVEN COMPANIES

The next four chapters of the book will be devoted to a detailed analysis of selected aspects of the data which have been presented in the preceding pages. At this point, however, we should like to view the entire collection of data in broad perspective and to establish four general conclusions with regard to the structures of the seven oil companies and the programs and policies they have been following with respect to vertical integration.

The Absence of Complete Integration:

It is readily apparent from Exhibits XII-10 to XII-26 that none of the seven oil companies was "fully integrated" at any time in the period covered by our data in the sense that it produced all its own crude oil, manufactured all its own refined products, owned and operated all its own transportation facilities, and carried all its output to customers exclusively through its own bulk plants and service stations. Either by necessity or intent, each of the seven companies was dependent in significant degree upon outside concerns at one point or another in its operations.

Consider, for example, the structure of the Gulf Oil Corporation in 1950 as shown in Exhibit XII-19. The company's domestic crude oil production plus imports of its own foreign production was sufficient to supply only 70% of its domestic refinery requirements, and the remaining 30% of the crude oil run to refineries had to be purchased from other concerns. The company's own pipe lines (including all those in which it had any stock interest) and marine facilities carried only 82% of the crude oil received at the Gulf refineries, and the remaining 18% was hauled by outside carriers. Similarly, of the total shipments from the company's refineries, only 63% moved via company owned facilities and 37% moved via outside pipe line, marine, and rail equipment. Of the total volume of refined products handled in the company's marketing operations, 89% was secured from Gulf refineries and the remaining 11% was purchased from other refiners.

The Gulf Oil Corporation was particularly dependent upon outside business units in its marketing operations. The company carried only 21% of its gasoline all the way to the final consumers; 62% of the gasoline was sold to service station operators and 17% was sold to independent jobbers and peddlers, to various other cargo buyers, or through brokers. Of the volume sold to service station operators, about 40% went to dealers who leased their stations from Gulf, but the remaining 60% went to station operators who had their own stations and were completely independent of the Gulf organization. The Gulf Oil Corporation likewise placed heavy reliance upon outside organizations for the distribution of its distillates (including kerosene). The company carried only 36% of its distillates all the way to final consumers; the remaining 64% of the volume was sold primarily to independent jobbers and peddlers, to various other cargo buyers, or through brokers.

Inspection of Exhibits XII-10 to XII-26 reveals that the Gulf situation in 1950 was, in general, characteristic of the experience of all the companies in the years covered by our data. During the 23-year period 1930–1952, for example, six of the seven companies were net buyers of crude oil in the United States and purchased amounts ranging from 6% to 100% of their refinery requirements. The seventh company was a net seller and was dependent upon outside buyers for the disposal of about 57% to 83% of its crude oil output. In the years 1935, 1940, 1946, and 1950, the seven companies all made considerable use of outside transportation facilities. Among the seven companies, crude oil receipts at refineries via outside carriers ranged from less than 1% to 100% of total receipts, and product shipments from refineries via outside carriers

ranged from 24% to 100% of total shipments. Likewise all seven companies made use of independent marketing organizations for the distribution of substantial portions of their refined product output. Among the seven companies in the years 1935, 1940, 1946, and 1950, sales of gasoline to unbranded jobbers ranged from zero to 30% of total gasoline sales; sales of gasoline to branded jobbers ranged from 4% to 24% of total gasoline sales; and sales of gasoline to contractor service stations ranged from 6% to 39% of total gasoline sales. In the case of distillates (including kerosene), sales to branded and unbranded jobbers ranged from about 5% to 77% of total sales.

It is evident therefore that the structures of the seven companies, in the years covered by our data, contained many interstices which provided an opportunity and a need for the companies to enter into purchase, sale, or exchange arrangements with nonintegrated companies or other integrated companies having a different balance of operations. The reasons why the interstices were maintained will be discussed in later chapters. At this point, it need merely be noted that in many cases the interstices reflected deliberate management decisions to confine a company's operations to certain fields in which it was well equipped to operate and to leave other functions which it was less well equipped to perform to outside concerns. We found no significant evidence that the interstices have been decreasing in size in recent years or that the programs of the seven companies are likely to result in an elimination of the interstices in the foreseeable future.

The Differences and Similarities in Integration Patterns:

In the years covered by our data, the integration patterns of the seven oil companies were characterized by both strong similarities and strong differences. As an example of the similarities, it may be noted that in 1950 the patterns of all seven companies were uniform with respect to depth of integration in the major phases of the business; that is, all the companies were engaged in crude oil production, crude oil transportation, refining, products transportation, wholesale marketing, retail marketing, and the sale of gasolines, kerosenes, and distillates to final consumers. It may also be observed

EXHIBIT XII-27. SEVEN OIL COMPANIES

Capital Expenditures by Departments: 1922–1952 (3-Year Moving Averages)

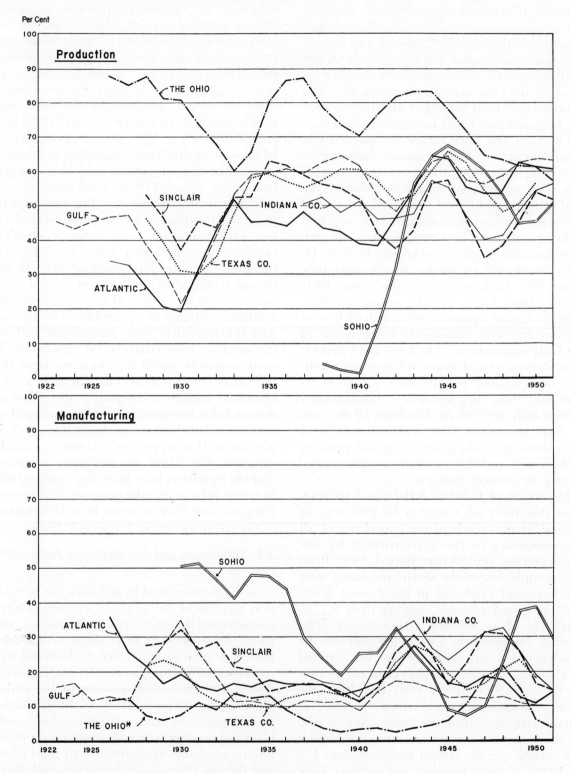

* Manufacturing and marketing figures are combined 1930–1932 and 1934–1937.

SOURCE: See Appendix, Tables 16–22, for data and footnotes.

EXHIBIT XII-27 (CONTINUED). SEVEN OIL COMPANIES

Capital Expenditures by Departments: 1922–1952 (3-Year Moving Averages)

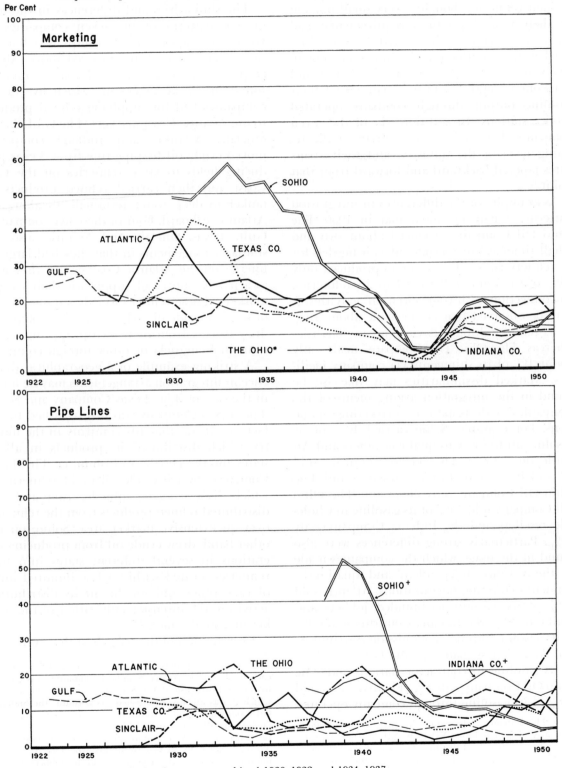

* Manufacturing and marketing figures are combined 1930–1932 and 1934–1937.
† Includes expenditures for all transportation facilities.
SOURCE: See Appendix, Tables 16–22, for data and footnotes.

that in 1950 all seven companies had their own transportation facilities for the movement of about 80% to 100% of their crude oil supplies to their refineries; bought a very small portion of their refined products requirements; had with one exception integrated forward into marketing activities for gasoline more extensively than for kerosenes and distillates; and with one exception sold less than 3% of their gasoline output through company operated service stations. In addition, six of the seven companies had their largest activity at the refining level of the industry, and their structures tapered backward and forward from that point.[11]

As examples of the differences in integration patterns, it may be noted that in 1950 The Ohio Oil Company produced about two and a half times as much crude oil as it needed for its refinery runs, whereas Sohio produced only 28% of the crude oil needed by its refineries. In connection with transportation activities, it may be observed that Sohio made about 76% of its refinery shipments via company facilities whereas The Ohio Oil Company made only about 4% of its shipments via company facilities. Marked dissimilarities may likewise be found in the integration arrangements of the companies with respect to marketing operations. For example, Sohio carried 40% of its gasoline all the way to final consumers and Atlantic only 15%; The Texas Company sold 62% of its gasoline to retail resellers and The Ohio Oil Company only 36%; and The Ohio Oil Company sold 45% of its gasoline to wholesale resellers and the Indiana Company only 10%. Particularly strong differences were also found in the usage which the companies made of the various independent and quasi-independent marketing organizations. Atlantic sold 24% of its gasoline to branded jobbers and Gulf only 9%; the Indiana Company sold 60% of its gasoline through commission distributors and Atlantic less than 1%; and Gulf sold 37% of its gasoline to contractor stations and The Ohio Oil Company only 8%. Finally, Sohio sold 20% of its gasoline through company operated

service stations whereas none of the other six companies sold more than 3% of its gasoline through such stations.

The similarities and differences in the integration patterns of the seven companies involved geographical relationships as well as the operating relationships discussed above. An example of a geographical similarity may be found in the arrangements which five of the companies had for supplying refined products to the Atlantic Coast markets. The Gulf, Texas, Sinclair, Atlantic, and Indiana companies moved crude oil by pipe line from Texas producing fields to large refineries on the Gulf Coast and then carried refined products by tanker to deep water terminals all along the Atlantic seaboard. Four of these five companies, Gulf, Texas, Sinclair, and Atlantic, also had similar arrangements in that they had large refineries on the Atlantic Coast which they used as a partial source of supply for their eastern markets. These refineries made substantial use of foreign crude oil, which the four companies drew in part from their own producing operations in Venezuela or other foreign countries.

A striking example of a geographical difference in integration arrangements may be found in the case of The Texas Company and Sohio. The Texas Company was distinguished by the fact that it was the only company in the industry which distributed its products in all 48 states and the District of Columbia. The Texas Company carried crude oil to 14 refineries at widely dispersed geographic locations and then distributed refined products from the refineries over an extensive market area. Sohio, on the other hand, drew crude oil from producing operations in several different states into four refineries located within a few hundred miles of each other and sought, in its distribution activities, the intensive cultivation of the market in a single state.[12]

Examination of the records of the seven com-

---

[11] This statement refers to the internal balance of operations as shown in Exhibits XII-19 to XII-25. Had the companies been assigned a full pro rata share of the volume of crude oil handled by all pipe lines in which they had stock interests, it is possible some of them might have had larger crude oil transportation than refining activities.

[12] Under the provisions of the dissolution decree in 1911, each of the newly created Standard companies was entitled to the exclusive use of the Standard name in the areas in which it was already established. As a result, the Standard Oil Company (Ohio) could not use the Standard name outside of Ohio, and some objection had even been raised to its use of the name "Sohio" outside the state boundaries. Through a wholly owned subsidiary, the Fleet-Wing Corporation, however, the company sold to jobbers in New York, Maryland, Pennsylvania, West Virginia, Michigan, and Indiana as well as in Ohio.

panies for earlier years reveals that the situation in 1950 was not at all unusual and that the integration patterns of the companies have always contained marked operating and geographical differences. Notwithstanding these differences, all the companies have made reasonably satisfactory returns on their investments (see Exhibit XII-2) and have steadily expanded their operations. It would appear therefore that there has been no single integration pattern which was necessary for successful operation in the oil industry at any given time. On the contrary, there have been many variations which have permitted successful and profitable operations.

The Fluidity of Integration Patterns:

One of the most important facts established by the data in the preceding pages is that the integration patterns of the seven companies have not been static but have been continually shifting and changing. Moreover, the shifts and changes have unquestionably involved both *increases* and *decreases* in the depth, extent, and intensity of the integration arrangements of the companies.

As examples of increases in the *depth* of integration, it may be noted that in the years covered by our data Atlantic, Sohio, and The Ohio Oil Company undertook the performance of new steps in the oil process. Atlantic and Sohio became engaged in crude oil producing operations and The Ohio Oil Company became engaged in refining and marketing activities. As examples of increases in the *extent* of integration, it may be observed that Sohio increased the proportion of crude oil shipped to refineries via company facilities from less than 1% to over 98% of the total; the Indiana Company tripled the proportion of its refinery shipments handled by is own products transportation facilities; and both Sohio and The Ohio Oil Company made significant increases in the proportions of their gasolines and distillates (including kerosene) carried to final consumers in their own operations. As examples of increases in the *intensity* of integration, it may be observed that The Ohio Oil Company, the Indiana Company, and Sohio made increases in the relative proportions of their gasoline sold at the retail level to dealer operated stations as contrasted with contractor stations.

The experience of the seven companies likewise provides ample evidence of decreases in the depth, extent, and intensity of integration. One important example of a decrease in *depth* may be found in the withdrawal of The Texas Company, The Ohio Oil Company, Sinclair, Atlantic, and the Indiana Company from the operation of service stations, beginning in the early 1930's. These companies reduced the proportion of their gasoline sold through company operated stations to 1% or less and thus virtually withdrew from the performance of one step in the distribution of gasoline to a major market. Significant examples of decreases in the *extent* of integration appear in the experiences of Gulf and The Texas Company. Both of these companies at one time in their histories produced well over 100% of their crude oil requirements, but subsequently their refining and marketing in the United States outgrew their domestic crude oil supply (including imports of their own foreign production). Similarly, Sinclair at one stage in its development produced three times as much (91%) of its crude oil requirements as it did in 1950 (29%). As an example of a decrease in *intensity* of integration, it may be noted that between 1935 and 1950, the Indiana Company reduced the proportion of its gasoline sold through company operated bulk plants from 36% to 22% of the total and at the same time increased the proportion of its gasoline sold through commission distributors from 48% to 60% of the total.

In the light of the above facts, it is readily apparent that the seven companies have not been engaged in a sustained drive toward further vertical integration in all phases of their operations. On the contrary, they have been continually adjusting their integration patterns and have been making changes which sometimes increased and sometimes decreased the depth, extent, and intensity of their integration arrangements.

The Timing and Direction of Integration Moves:

A fourth general conclusion established by the data in Exhibits XII-3 to XII-27 is that the changes which the seven companies have made in their integration patterns have sometimes been similar, but in other instances have been markedly different in either or both *direction* and *timing*. An example of a similar movement may be found in the development of company owned facilities for carrying crude oil to refineries, a step which all the companies took before 1940 in about the same degree. A second good example of a parallel movement was the general withdrawal from company operated service stations beginning in the early 1930's, although in this case Sohio followed a policy very different from that of the other six companies.

A striking example of a difference in the *direction* of integration movements occurred in the decade 1930–1940. During this period the ratio of crude oil production to refinery runs increased sharply in The Texas Company and The Atlantic Refining Company, decreased sharply in the Gulf Oil Corporation and the Sinclair Oil Corporation, and remained approximately constant in the Standard Oil Company (Indiana) and the Standard Oil Company (Ohio).

A clear difference in the *timing* of integration movements appears in the development of company owned facilities for the handling of products shipments from refineries. Gulf and The Texas Company had such facilities for handling a large portion of their output before 1935 and made no major changes after that date. During the period 1935–1950, however, the Indiana Company and Sohio tripled, Sinclair more than doubled, and Atlantic increased by 40% the proportion of refinery shipments handled through company facilities. The Ohio Oil Company throughout this period had only very limited company owned facilities for carrying its refinery output and did not attempt to increase the amount thereof.

Further evidence of similarities and differences in the timing and direction of integration moves may be found in the records of the capital spending programs of the seven companies shown in Exhibit XII-27. An example of a similarity appears in the gradual reduction which several of the companies made in the proportion of their capital funds devoted to marketing facilities in the period from about 1930 to the close of World War II.[13] As an ex-

---

[13] The records in Exhibit XII-27 are three-year moving averages and may therefore lag one or two years behind the dates on which changes in spending were actually initiated.

ample of a difference, it may be observed that during the early 1930's The Ohio Oil Company reduced its proportionate expenditures for production whereas several other companies increased the share of their funds devoted to producing activities. At this time, The Ohio Oil Company had ample crude oil production and was finding it desirable to expand its refining, marketing, and pipe line operations. Certain of the other companies, on the other hand, were finding it necessary to expand their expenditures for producing operations in order to offset the reductions in allowables which accompanied the development of the conservation laws in certain states.

In view of the foregoing and other differences in the direction and timing of integration moves which are readily apparent from Exhibits XII-3 to XII-27, it certainly cannot be said that the seven companies have been following uniform or parallel policies with respect to vertical integration.

III. THE INTERNAL VARIATIONS IN INTEGRATION PATTERNS

Our discussion thus far has been concerned with the integration patterns of each company as a whole. It should not be inferred, however, that these patterns were uniform throughout all sections of the country in which the companies operated. On the contrary, each company was found to be integrated quite differently in one or more areas from the way it was in others. The question of vertical integration cannot therefore be considered apart from the question of geographic location. Although highly unlikely, it is not inconceivable that the total operations of a company might show an even balance among producing, refining, and marketing operations, and yet the company might be conducting what for all practical purposes were three completely nonintegrated businesses; for example, a producing business in southern California, a refining business in Wyoming, and a marketing business in New York City.

The internal variations found in the integration patterns of the seven companies may be illustrated by the situation of the Sinclair Oil Corporation in 1950. In that year the company obtained about 30% of its over-all domestic refinery requirements from its own crude oil production and purchased the remaining 70%. For its Sinclair, Wyoming, refinery, however, the company had far more potential crude oil production than it could use. The company was charging about 15,000 barrels per day to the refinery whereas its actual crude oil production in Wyoming was about 20,000 barrels per day and its potential production was a much greater amount. In the area of the Sinclair, Wyoming, refinery therefore the company was in a selling rather than a buying position with respect to crude oil. At the other end of the scale, the company bought 100% of the crude oil supply for its refinery at Wellesville, New York, and thus conducted at this point a refining-marketing operation alone. The company also bought nearly all its crude oil for the Marcus Hook refinery. This plant was so situated that it could run more advantageously on crude oil from Venezuela and the Middle East than it could on crude oil hauled from the Gulf Coast. In 1950 the Sinclair Oil Corporation's Venezuelan production amounted to only about 9,700 barrels per day whereas the capacity of the Marcus Hook plant was about 90,000 barrels per day. The company therefore found it necessary to purchase the deficiency from other foreign producers.

A number of variations were also found to exist in the company's integration arrangements with respect to refined products supplies in different sections of the country. As indicated in Exhibit XII-21, the company as a whole bought about 6% of its total refined products requirements in 1950 from outside suppliers. In certain areas, however, such as that of the Sinclair, Wyoming, refinery, the company had the capacity to produce a substantially larger volume of refined products than it was in a position to market and bought no supplies whatsoever. Another type of internal variation was found to exist in the marketing arrangements which the company used in different sections of the country. In certain metropolitan areas the company marketed almost exclusively through its own bulk plants and service stations; in other areas it marketed almost entirely through branded jobbers; and at some points it sold entirely through unbranded jobbers.

Similar types of internal variations, as well as many different types, were found to exist in the integration patterns of all the companies studied. The explanation of these internal variations was found to lie in at least four general types of circumstances. In the first place, some of the internal variations were a matter of fortuitous circumstances with respect to such things as the location of crude oil discoveries. In the postwar period, for example, plentiful crude oil supplies happened to be developed in Wyoming, an area where the market for refined products was abnormally sparse. As a result, a number of companies, like Sinclair, were long on crude oil in Wyoming while they were short of supplies in other sections of the country. A second important cause of the internal variations was found to be management choice with regard to how a company conducted its business in different sections of the company. Each of the companies, for example, had certain geographical areas in which the management had elected to market through jobbers or commission distributors rather than the company's own bulk plants (see Chapter Fifteen).

The internal variations were also found in some cases to be temporary conditions which had developed in the normal course of a company's growth and expansion. Some companies, for example, had opened up marketing operations in new territories through the use of branded jobbers with the thought that they might later be replaced with company operations. Similarly, some companies were expanding their marketing operations in particular areas but were planning to purchase refined products until they had built up a sufficient volume to justify expansion of their own refining facilities. A fourth cause of at least temporary internal variations in integration patterns was unexpected shifts in market demand. Unusually severe winter weather conditions in a particular area sometimes forced a company to purchase fuel oils heavily in that territory whereas in other areas its own refinery output was ample to meet its market requirements.

The seven oil companies discussed in this chapter should in reality therefore be regarded as consisting of a conglomerate of many different types of integrated and nonintegrated activities which on the whole balanced out as shown in the various charts and tables. The internal variations are important because in the final analysis a company must meet prices and competition in each local market area. At the same time, however, the significance of the over-all patterns should not be discounted. Despite the many internal variations, the over-all patterns were usually found to represent the basis upon which the companies conducted the majority of their operations. Moreover, the mechanisms of crude oil trading and refined products exchanges are highly developed in the oil industry and provide a means by which geographical barriers may be overcome. The completion of the Platte Pipe Line, for example, put the Sinclair Oil Corporation in a position to trade its surplus Wyoming crude oil at the important Wood River refining center for crude oil to supply its Houston refinery. Similarly, although Sinclair could not easily move products from its own refineries into the Great Lakes Pipe Line for shipment to the North Central states, it could exchange products along its own pipe lines for deliveries by Mid-Continent refiners into the Great Lakes system.

IV. THE MANAGEMENT PROBLEM OF VERTICAL INTEGRATION

The data on integration patterns presented in this chapter shed much light on the character of the management problem involved in planning the growth and development of an integrated oil company. It is readily apparent from the experience of the seven companies that the problem is not simply a matter of deciding whether to build an "integrated oil company" or whether to engage in particular steps in the processing and distribution of oil and its products. On the contrary, the management problem of vertical integration is essentially one of resolving a vast matrix of individual integration problems with respect to particular phases of a company's business.

The management of an integrated oil company must, in the first place, exercise options with respect to depth, extent, and intensity of integration for the dozens of *different kinds of activities* in which the company is already engaged or might conceivably become engaged, such as well drilling, crude oil production, crude oil transportation, refining, products transportation, bulk plant operation, or service station operation. These decisions can rarely be made on a uniform basis for all sections of the country and appropriate modifications must therefore be made for the *different geographic areas* in which a company may operate. Moreover, the arrangements which are suitable for one product may not be satisfactory for another, and hence it may be necessary to plan specific integration programs for the *different products* which a company may have in its line. As may be seen from Exhibits XII-19 to XII-25, all the companies had somewhat different integration arrangements for the distribution of their gasolines from those they had for kerosenes and distillates.

A second general observation which may be made concerning the management problem of planning a company's integration program is that the problem goes far beyond the making of individual decisions with respect to depth, extent, and intensity of integration in particular cases. The effectiveness of vertical integration as a technique of organization and operation rests to a considerable extent on the interrelationships which are maintained among a company's activities in the several different phases of the oil business. The management of an integrated oil company cannot therefore treat integration problems as isolated cases, but must give continuing attention to the *combinations of options* which it elects with respect to vertical integration at various points in the company's field of activity.

Finally, it may be observed that the management problem of vertical integration never stays solved for any very long period of time. A company must continually *adjust its integration pattern* in response to changes in competitive and economic conditions, new technological developments, and many other things. The task of planning the growth and development of an integrated oil company thus involves the constant reappraisal of existing integration arrangements and the making of new decisions and new combinations of decisions with respect to depth, extent, and intensity of integration in all the many fields of endeavor in which a company may be engaged.

V. SUMMARY

1. An integration pattern may be defined as the whole matrix of arrangements a com-

pany has made with respect to depth, extent, and intensity of integration at all points in its operations. A company's integration pattern at any particular stage in its history is a manifestation of its management's policies with respect to vertical integration. Moreover, the changes which take place in the integration pattern from one year to the next provide concrete evidence concerning the direction in which a company is moving and the objectives its management is seeking with respect to vertical integration.

2. Examination of the integration patterns of seven major oil companies revealed that none of the companies was "fully integrated" at any time in the period covered by our data in the sense that it produced all its own crude oil, manufactured all its own refined products, owned and operated all its own transportation facilities, and carried all its output to customers exclusively through its own bulk plants and service stations. On the contrary, the structures of the companies contained many interstices where the companies were dependent in significant degree upon nonintegrated companies or other integrated companies. These interstices were often maintained as a matter of deliberate management policy, and we found no significant evidence that they were decreasing in size or were likely to be eliminated in the foreseeable future.

3. The integration patterns of the seven companies were characterized by both strong similarities and strong differences throughout the period covered by our data. Notwithstanding their many differences in integration patterns, all the companies have made reasonable profits and have steadily expanded their operations. It appears therefore that many variations in integration arrangements have been possible in the oil industry and that no single pattern has been necessary for successful operations at any given period in the industry's history.

4. The integration patterns of the seven companies have not been static but have been continually shifting and changing. The shifts and changes have unquestionably involved both *increases* and *decreases* in depth, extent, and intensity of integration arrangements. The record of these changes provides strong evidence that the seven companies have not been engaged in a sustained drive toward further vertical integration in all phases of their operations.

5. The changes which the seven companies have made in their integration patterns have sometimes been similar, but in other instances have been markedly different in either or both *direction* and *timing*. It certainly cannot be said therefore that the companies have been following uniform or parallel policies with respect to vertical integration.

6. The integration patterns of the seven companies have not been uniform in all sections of the country in which the companies have operated. On the contrary, each company was found to be integrated quite differently in one or more geographic areas from the way it was in others. A company's over-all integration pattern must therefore be considered as representing the net result of a conglomerate of many different types and degrees of integration in different geographic areas.

7. The management task of planning the growth and development of an integrated oil company requires resolution of the whole complex of individual integration problems with respect to depth, extent, and intensity of integration which a company may face in its various fields of operation. Integration decisions must be made for different kinds of activities, for different geographic areas, and for different products. These decisions must be considered not only as individual matters but likewise in relation to a company's integration pattern as a whole and must, moreover, be continually re-evaluated in the light of changing conditions in the oil industry.

CHAPTER THIRTEEN

Analysis of Integration Patterns: Crude Oil Producing Activities

THE PURPOSE of this chapter is to explore the programs and policies of the seven companies with respect to integration into crude oil producing operations. The discussion will be confined to three major topics: (a) the ratio of crude oil production to refinery runs, (b) the use of farm-outs and other producing deals in the exploratory program, and (c) the use of company versus contract rigs for drilling operations. We shall not attempt to discuss the policies of the seven companies with respect to the performance of the hundreds of secondary activities which are related to the producing job such as well logging, well cementing, well acidizing, well perforating, diamond coring, seismic work, core analysis, well workovers and repairs, and the supplying of mud for drilling operations. It is important to recognize, however, that a large company has the option of doing these jobs itself or of leaving them to outside concerns and that the arrangements which it makes with respect to such jobs form a part of its integration program.[1]

The discussion in the chapter will reveal some of the forces and circumstances which give form and shape to a company's integration pattern and which, from time to time, bring about fundamental changes in it. Full treatment of this matter, however, will be deferred until Chapter Seventeen.

I. THE RATIO OF CRUDE OIL PRODUCTION TO REFINERY RUNS

From the statistical data in the preceding chapter, it is apparent that the seven companies had arrived at quite different positions with respect to their ratios of crude oil production

---

[1] As noted in Chapter One, there are many independent companies in the industry which specialize in handling the secondary activities related to the producing job.

to refinery runs. It is also evident that the companies had from time to time throughout their histories made fundamental changes in their ratios. None of them, in fact, had anywhere near the same ratio in 1952 that it had in the early years of its history, and none of them maintained a constant ratio for any very long period of time. In the following paragraphs an analysis and comparison will be made of the timing, direction, and reasons for some of the changes made by the individual companies. Attention will then be directed to the present positions and objectives of the seven companies with respect to their ratios of crude oil production to refinery runs.

Throughout the discussion, the ratio of crude oil production to refinery runs will be understood to mean the ratio of a company's net domestic production plus imports of its own foreign production to its domestic refinery runs, in accordance with the statistical analyses developed in Chapter Twelve. In the interests of simplicity, we shall at times refer to this ratio as the "crude oil ratio."

Changes in Crude Oil Ratios Made by Individual Companies:

Chapter Eight discussed at some length the steps taken by The Atlantic Refining Company, the Standard Oil Company (Ohio), and the Standard Oil Company (Indiana) in the development of their crude oil producing programs, and Chapter Four discussed the circumstances that led The Ohio Oil Company into refining operations. These chapters contain sufficient information on the four companies to permit the comparison and contrast of policies which are to follow, and the discussion at this point will therefore be confined to the changes in crude oil ratios which were made by the Gulf

Oil Corporation, the Sinclair Oil Corporation, and The Texas Company.

Gulf Oil Corporation: The ratio of crude oil production to refinery runs which was maintained by Gulf throughout the period 1907 to 1952 is shown in Chapter Twelve, Exhibit XII-10. Although Gulf was formed as an integrated company and although it was Mr. W. L. Mellon's clear intent that it should develop along integrated lines, major emphasis was placed on producing operations during the first 23 years of the company's history. In his autobiography, Mr. Mellon makes the statement: "In all my thinking and the thinking of my associates, it was clearly understood that crude oil was what we were after." [2] As may be seen from Chapter Twelve, Exhibit XII-10, throughout much of the period from 1907 to 1929 the company's crude oil production was sufficient to cover the major part of its refinery requirements, and in many years the company was a net seller of crude oil.

After 1929 the company's crude oil ratio declined sharply, and the company was forced to begin buying crude oil to meet its domestic refinery requirements. The crude oil ratio continued to decline until 1942 at which time it reached a low point of 61.5%. After 1942 the ratio moved up sharply for a few years as the various producing states increased their allowables to obtain the output necessary for the war effort. In 1952, however, Gulf was still a net buyer of crude oil for about 30% of its domestic refinery requirements.

The shift in the balance of crude oil producing and refining operations which began about 1930 took place despite the best efforts of the management to prevent it and was the product of a number of circumstances. The first and perhaps most important circumstance was the adoption of the prorationing laws by the various producing states shortly after the discovery of the great East Texas field in 1930. The impact of the new laws on Gulf's crude oil producing position was particularly serious because the company had about 84% of its crude oil production in 1929 concentrated in Texas and Oklahoma,[3] the two states which were the first

to develop effective prorationing programs. As may be seen from Chapter Four, Exhibit IV-6, the company's domestic production dropped in the period 1929 to 1932 from about 50 to 35 million barrels per year, and most of the reduction took place in Texas and Oklahoma. Moreover, as noted in Chapter Four, the company undertook in 1928 a major expansion of its pipe line and refining facilities to take care of the increasing crude oil production it secured as one of the major participants in the development of the West Texas and Oklahoma fields in the period 1926 to 1928. The new pipe line, which extended from Tulsa to Cincinnati, and the new refineries at Toledo, Cincinnati, and Pittsburgh came into operation between 1929 and 1931, precisely the period in which the prorationing laws were developed.

A second important factor which contributed to the decline in the company's crude oil ratio after 1930 was the shortage of funds available for investment in producing properties. The cutbacks imposed by the prorationing laws could have been offset, at least in part, by the drilling of more wells and the development of new production or by purchasing producing properties from others. As noted in Chapter Eight, the middle 1930's was an excellent time to buy producing properties, and some of the large oil companies were quick to take advantage of the situation. Many small producing firms during this period were anxious to sell part or all of their holdings because the adoption of the prorationing laws automatically lengthened the pay-out period on producing wells and because they needed cash to carry their operations through the depression period.

The financial resources of the Gulf Oil Corporation, however, had been severely strained by the expansion of pipe line, refining, and marketing facilities initiated in 1928. To aid in financing the expansion program, the Union Gulf Corporation was formed in 1930; 45% of the capital stock in this firm was held by the Gulf Oil Corporation and the remainder by certain Gulf stockholders (principally the Mellon family). In the company's annual report for 1930, the Gulf management explained that:

This separate corporation was made necessary in order to issue $60,000,000 Collateral Trust Sinking Fund 5% Gold Bonds, due July 1, 1950, of the Union Gulf Corporation to provide funds for the

---

[2] W. L. Mellon, *Judge Mellon's Sons*, private printing, 1948, p. 278.

[3] See Chapter Four, Exhibit IV-6.

Exhibit XIII-1. Gulf Oil Corporation

Comparison of Refinery Capacities and Refinery Runs, Barrels per Day: 1923–1952

Year	Capacity	Refinery Runs	% Capacity Operated	Capacity	Refinery Runs	% Capacity Operated	Capacity	Refinery Runs	% Capacity Operated
	All Gulf Refineries			*Port Arthur Refinery*			*Fort Worth Refinery*		
1923	130,000	91,747	70.6%	125,000	87,380	69.9%	5,000	4,367	87.3%
1924	130,000	92,322	71.0	125,000	86,366	69.1	5,000	5,956	119.1
1925	130,000	98,987	76.1	125,000	93,733	75.0	5,000	5,254	105.1
1926	160,000	123,105	76.9	125,000	105,174	84.1	5,000	6,019	120.4
1927	190,000	143,982	75.8	125,000	113,106	90.5	5,000	5,953	119.1
1928	190,000	161,560	85.0	125,000	110,981	88.8	5,000	7,123	142.5
1929	206,000	186,249	90.4	125,000	118,155	94.5	6,000	6,074	101.2
1930	206,000	185,471	90.0	125,000	108,335	86.7	6,000	5,184	86.4
1931	236,000	179,770	76.2	125,000	100,220	80.2	6,000	5,151	85.9
1932	226,500	146,016	64.5	125,000	70,827	56.7	6,000	5,510	91.8
1933	190,000	152,642	80.3	100,000	73,666	73.7	6,000	4,992	83.2
1934	192,000	154,450	80.4	100,000	81,409	81.4	6,000	4,046	67.4
1935	192,000	169,075	88.1	100,000	87,615	87.6	6,000	3,565	59.4
1936	198,000	195,864	98.9	100,000	103,153	103.2	6,000	4,586	76.4
1937	214,000	213,410	99.7	110,000	116,039	105.5	6,000	5,303	88.4
1938	211,000	208,541	98.8	110,000	110,009	100.0	6,000	5,580	93.0
1939	226,000	223,549	98.9	125,000	127,271	101.8	6,000	5,793	96.6
1940	241,000	247,505	102.7	130,000	134,744	103.7	6,000	6,400	106.7
1941	277,000	273,104	98.6	148,000	144,513	97.6	7,200	6,739	93.6
1942	277,000	225,482	81.4	148,000	118,644	80.2	7,200	7,091	98.5
1943	299,300	240,514	80.4	153,600	131,526	85.6	7,200	7,518	104.4
1944	299,300	283,891	94.9	153,600	155,414	101.2	7,200	7,186	99.8
1945	312,600	292,096	93.4	163,000	155,326	95.3	7,200	7,336	101.9
1946	351,700	342,512	97.4	192,000	188,652	98.3	7,200	7,818	108.6
1947	363,900	369,582	101.6	198,000	203,173	102.6	7,800	7,923	101.6
1948	384,700	384,039	99.8	206,400	210,031	101.8	9,500	8,514	89.6
1949	428,700	380,241	88.7	230,000	205,872	89.5	9,500	7,816	82.3
1950	458,500	448,375	97.8	230,000	231,779	100.8	9,500	7,523	79.2
1951	473,500	463,259	97.8	245,000	245,440	100.2	9,500	7,448	78.4
1952	468,500	453,936	96.9	245,000	242,416	98.9	8,500	7,928	93.3

Year	Capacity	Refinery Runs	% Capacity Operated	Capacity	Refinery Runs	% Capacity Operated	Capacity	Refinery Runs	% Capacity Operated
	New York Refinery			*Philadelphia Refinery*			*Sweetwater Refinery*		
1923									
1924		Began Operations Feb. 1926							
1925					Began Operations Oct. 7, 1927				
1926	30,000	11,912	39.7%						
1927	30,000	21,491	71.6	30,000	3,432	11.4%		Began Operations Sept. 16, 1929	
1928	30,000	21,901	73.0	30,000	21,555	71.9			
1929	30,000	30,457	101.5	40,000	30,370	75.9	5,000	1,193	23.9%
1930	30,000	30,856	102.9	40,000	36,141	90.4	5,000	4,955	99.1
1931	30,000	22,328	74.4	40,000	29,288	73.2	5,000	4,816	96.3
1932	30,000	11,837	39.5	30,000	29,496	98.3	5,000	3,456	69.1
1933	15,000	13,155	87.7	30,000	30,349	101.2	5,000	3,807	76.1
1934	15,000	9,523	63.5	30,000	28,082	93.4	5,000	3,921	78.4
1935	15,000	9,749	65.0	30,000	30,663	102.2	5,000	3,996	79.9
1936	15,000	13,702	91.4	30,000	29,503	98.3	5,000	4,683	93.7
1937	14,000	9,791	69.9	33,000	31,858	96.5	5,000	5,620	112.4
1938	14,000	8,679	62.0	30,000	32,314	107.7	5,000	5,933	118.7
1939	13,000	8,783	67.6	30,000	35,151	117.2	6,000	6,038	100.6
1940	13,000	11,865	91.3	40,000	39,629	99.1	6,000	6,341	105.7
1941	13,000	12,190	93.8	50,000	50,388	100.8	6,400	6,387	99.8
1942	13,000	3,145	24.2	50,000	30,835	61.7	6,400	6,084	95.1
1943	13,000	1,158	8.9	58,000	34,431	59.4	7,300	7,416	101.6
1944	13,000			58,000	52,614	90.7	7,300	7,387	101.2
1945	13,000	7,310	56.2	58,000	53,953	93.0	7,300	8,280	113.4
1946	14,000	14,627	104.5	66,000	65,584	99.4	8,400	8,745	104.1
1947	16,000	17,845	111.5	68,000	71,145	104.6	10,000	9,028	90.3
1948	20,000	19,097	95.5	74,700	75,410	101.0	10,000	9,148	91.5
1949	20,000	13,569	67.9	76,700	83,560	108.9	10,000	9,301	93.0
1950	20,000	13,965	69.8	107,000	107,567	100.5	10,000	7,335	73.4
1951	20,000	12,978	64.9	107,000	106,136	99.2	8,000	7,328	91.6
1952	17,000	13,467	79.2	107,000	103,087	96.3	8,000	7,096	88.7

EXHIBIT XIII-1. (CONTINUED)

Year	Capacity	Refinery Runs	% Capacity Operated	Capacity	Refinery Runs	% Capacity Operated	Capacity	Refinery Runs	% Capacity Operated
		Pittsburgh Refinery			Toledo Refinery			Cincinnati Refinery	
1923									
1924									
1925									
1926									
1927									
1928									
1929		Began Operations Feb. 6, 1931			Began Operations April 4, 1931			Began Operations June 14, 1931	
1930									
1931	6,000	5,586	93.1%	12,000	7,662	63.9%	12,000	4,719	39.3%
1932	6,500	6,236	95.9	13,000	9,963	76.6	11,000	8,691	79.0
1933	8,000	6,700	83.8	13,000	10,137	78.0	13,000	9,836	75.7
1934	10,000	7,476	74.8	13,000	9,742	74.9	13,000	10,251	78.9
1935	10,000	8,733	87.3	13,000	12,537	96.4	13,000	12,217	94.0
1936	10,000	8,882	88.8	16,000	15,617	97.6	16,000	15,738	98.4
1937	10,000	9,830	98.3	18,000	17,503	97.2	18,000	17,466	97.0
1938	10,000	10,446	104.5	18,000	17,065	94.8	18,000	18,515	102.9
1939	10,000	10,594	105.9	18,000	10,315	57.3	18,000	19,604	108.9
1940	10,000	11,042	110.4	18,000	17,824	99.0	18,000	19,660	109.2
1941	11,800	11,633	98.6	19,700	19,845	100.7	20,900	21,409	102.4
1942	11,800	12,377	104.9	19,700	21,901	111.2	20,900	25,405	121.6
1943	12,400	12,089	97.5	21,200	20,249	95.5	26,600	26,127	98.2
1944	12,400	12,689	102.3	21,200	22,226	104.8	26,600	26,377	99.2
1945	14,500	14,207	98.0	23,000	20,770	90.3	26,600	24,914	93.7
1946	14,500	12,323	85.0	23,000	21,374	92.9	26,600	23,389	87.9
1947	14,500	14,180	97.8	23,000	22,001	95.7	26,600	24,287	91.3
1948	14,500	14,509	100.1	23,000	21,940	95.4	26,600	25,390	95.5
1949	14,500	12,928	89.2	40,000	22,977	57.4	28,000	24,218	86.5
1950	14,000	13,865	99.0	40,000	37,740	94.4	28,000	28,601	102.2
1951	14,000	13,677	97.7	40,000	39,313	98.3	30,000	30,939	103.1
1952	13,000	12,845	98.8	40,000	35,169	87.9	30,000	31,928	106.4

SOURCE: Gulf Oil Corporation.

acquisition of properties, improvements, extensions, and for other corporate purposes as stated above, without conflicting with the provisions of the Indentures of Trust executed in connection with the issue by the Gulf Oil Corporation of Pennsylvania of the 15-year 5% Debenture Gold Bonds due December 1, 1937 and the 20-year 5% Sinking Fund Debenture Gold Bonds due February 1, 1947. The Indentures securing these bond issues provide that as long as any of the bonds issued under these indentures are outstanding and unpaid, the quick assets of the corporation and its subsidiaries will, at all times, be equal to or in excess of the total liabilities of this corporation and its subsidiaries, including contingent liabilities and including the kinds issued under said Trust Indentures.

The Gulf Oil Corporation joined in the Union Gulf Oil Corporation's indenture of trust and agreed to maintain at all times collateral pledged with the trustee having a market value at least equal to 130% of the princi-

pal amount of bonds at any time outstanding. The collateral securities required for this purpose were leased by the company from certain of its stockholders, including the Mellons.

As a result of these arrangements, neither the Gulf Oil Corporation nor the Mellon family was in a position to make heavy commitments in the development or purchase of new producing properties in the period following 1930. As the general business depression deepened, the market value of the securities pledged with the trustee declined and required the continual pledging of more securities to comply with the terms of the trust indenture. Moreover, during the early years of the depression, Gulf incurred heavy financial losses from its operations which made inroads on the funds available for capital expenditures. As may be seen from Chapter Twelve, Exhibit XII-2, the company had a net loss before interest charges for the period 1931–1934, inclusive, of about $3,900,000. After interest charges the net loss for the period 1931–1934 was almost $30,000,000.

The lack of funds during the early 1930's to develop new crude oil production, and particularly to take advantage of the opportunity to buy proven properties at a low cost, was a matter of serious concern to the Gulf management and a source of keen regret for many years thereafter. The record of Gulf's capital expenditures by departments for the period 1910 to 1952 is shown in the Appendix, Table 16. The sharp decline in total expenditures and in expenditures for producing properties in the early 1930's is clearly evident.

For a short time after 1930, certain of the Gulf refineries were shut back as the company's crude oil production declined and were run at considerably less than capacity as may be seen from Exhibit XIII-1. This course of action was taken, in part, because certain of the executives of the company were strongly of the opinion that the profits in the petroleum business were primarily in crude oil production and that the company could make no money on the refining and marketing of purchased crude oil. A second reason for the reduction in refinery runs was the decline in gasoline consumption which accompanied the general business depression of the early 1930's and the fact that the company had not had a chance to develop adequately the markets for its newly acquired refineries in the North Central area. As may be seen from Chapter Twelve, Exhibit XII-10, the curtailment of refinery runs served to make the drop in the ratio of crude oil production to refinery runs much smaller than might otherwise have been the case.

After a great deal of discussion, the Gulf executives decided in July 1935 that the pipe lines and refineries should be run as close to capacity as the company's marketing operations would permit and that the company should enter the market as a buyer to obtain whatever crude oil it might need above its own production to meet the refinery requirements. The chief reason for the decision was that the pipe lines and refineries involved large capital investments and high fixed costs and the purchased crude oil could therefore be run at a relatively low incremental expense. In the following years, every possible effort was made to increase the company's marketing activities,

particularly in the North Central area, and to bring the pipe line and refinery facilities up to capacity operation. The development of the markets, the laying of crude oil gathering lines, and the establishment of crude oil buying connections required time, but nevertheless by about 1937 the company's pipe lines and refineries were brought close to capacity operations. The increase in refinery runs which took place after 1935, brought about a still further decline in the ratio of crude oil production to refinery runs, as shown in Chapter Twelve, Exhibit XII-10.

On December 15, 1937, Gulf's Venezuelan subsidiary, Mene Grande Oil Company, C.A. entered into a contract of purchase-sale of crude oil with International Petroleum Company Limited.[4] The Mene Grande Oil Company received $100,000,000, from International for a one-half interest in the physical plant and equipment of Mene Grande Oil Company as existing on December 15, 1937, and for one-half of all oil which might be produced from the concessions then held by Mene Grande or in which Mene Grande had an interest, International Petroleum also agreeing to pay one-half the cost of producing such oil. The purchaser also secured the right to obtain a one-half interest in all concessions subsequently acquired by Mene Grande upon payment of one-half the cost of acquisition. Twenty-five per cent of the $100,000,000 was payable upon execution of the contract, and the balance was payable over an 8-year period from December 15, 1937. After the negotiation of this contract, Gulf was financially able to take a stronger position with respect to the development of new producing properties both at home and abroad than it had been able to before.

In general, it might be said that before 1930 Gulf was primarily a producing company and made such investments in the refining, transportation, and marketing phases of the business as were necessary to dispose of its crude oil output. The years 1930–1935 were a time of transition. After 1935 the major departments were operated more or less independently of each other, and each was expected to develop profitable operations in its own right. The departments were headed by strong individuals,

---

[4] A Canadian corporation and a subsidiary of the Standard Oil Company (New Jersey).

and each strove to expand as rapidly as it could and competed with the other departments for the funds that were available for investment. The marketing operations were expanded as rapidly as competitive conditions permitted, the refining department expanded to keep pace with the marketing, and the producing department did the best it could to provide the raw materials required by the refining and marketing operations. It will be noted that this pattern of integration was more or less the reverse of that followed in the early years of the company's history when production was the keystone of the company's expansion, and refining and marketing operations were developed as a means of disposing of the crude oil.

Sinclair Oil Corporation: The Sinclair Oil Corporation, like the Gulf Oil Corporation, began its history with a very high ratio of crude oil production to refinery runs (see Chapter Twelve, Exhibit XII-12). In the period from 1922–1931, however, the company's crude oil production did not increase as rapidly as did its refinery operations. It is of particular interest to note that the company did not secure any large increase in production in the middle 1920's from the new discoveries in West Texas and Oklahoma. As a result, the company's crude oil ratio declined from 90.7% in 1922 to 41.4% in 1931. In 1932 a substantial increase in production was secured through the purchase of the Prairie Oil and Gas Company which brought Sinclair's crude oil ratio up to 62.5% and Sinclair's share of the United States output of crude oil up to about 2.9%. In the following seven years, the crude oil ratio was allowed to drop to 33.1% and the company's share of the domestic crude oil output to 1.8%. The crude oil ratio remained at the 35% to 40% level until 1949, at which time the company announced a major expansion program designed to bring crude oil production back up to at least 50% of refinery runs.

The steady decline in the crude oil ratio which took place after 1932 may be attributed almost entirely to the advent of the prorationing laws in the various producing states. As noted in Chapter Four, the prorationing laws functioned very imperfectly at the outset and did not contain adequate restraints on well-spacing or the number of wells drilled. It ap-

peared to the Sinclair management that the new laws were operating in such a way as to increase greatly the cost of finding and producing crude oil and the length of time necessary to recover investments in producing properties. The management's thinking on this point is reflected in the following excerpts from the corporation's annual reports:

Annual Report, 1934: The cost of oil production has been greatly increased by the administration of the proration laws. The allowable per well is so small that to obtain the quantity of oil needed the producer is required in some instances to pay a cost of developing and drilling greatly in excess of what was formerly necessary, creating a heavy burden on present day operations. Whether over a long period this increased investment will be retrieved in the form of greater recovery is problematical. We do know at this time that the investment necessary to secure current production and protect producing properties is far greater than ever before. From this situation there is no escape so long as existing laws, rules, and regulations are in force.

The East Texas field, for example, has been drilled to a density of one well to seven or eight acres, involving an expenditure estimated to be $100,000,000 more than the drilling cost actually necessary to recover the oil. The allowable production being on a per well basis, the property owner who does not have as many wells as the average for the field does not obtain his share of the total allowed to be taken out. In this way enormous waste of capital is forced upon the producer. "Dollar oil" did not cover the over-all cost of production under former conditions, and does not of course compensate the law-abiding producer for the increased cost imposed by the system of proration as now administered. The results of this system are now evident not only in respect to its cost, but also in the creation of imaginary potentials, arbitrary prices, evasions of law and "bootlegging," and in the establishment of political control of oil production by both federal and state agencies.

Annual Report, 1935: The Corporation participated in the drilling of 434 wells, of which 358 were wholly-owned. These, together with our interest in partnership wells, were equivalent to 382 wholly-owned wells. Under the restrictions of proration, the allowable from these wells was only 16,000 barrels per day, or an average of 42 barrels per well. The total crude production for the year was not materially greater than in 1934, viz.

26,000,000 barrels, an average of 71,000 net barrels per day.

The situation is not, of course, one peculiar to your Corporation. In the State of Oklahoma, for example, 1,321 oil wells were drilled by all companies in 1935, but the production of the State at the end of the year was approximately the same as it was at the beginning, mainly because the total allowable for the State was not materially changed; it was simply divided among a larger number of wells.

These figures as related to our own operations again illustrate the greatly increased capital outlay required to increase or even to maintain crude production because of the small amount of oil that may be taken from new wells. The only compensation is that greater available known reserves are created.

Annual Report, 1940: That your Company has been under the disadvantage of producing less oil than it consumes is due in part to its reluctance to make large capital investments for drilling in prorated areas where comparatively little oil could be obtained, and to the fact that the "payout" of the investment would be of long duration in restricted areas while other fields were unprorated. Production has been energetically sought and increased in areas not unreasonably restricted with the result that our average daily production in 1940 shows a substantial increase over 1939.

In the early 1930's great supplies of crude oil hung over the domestic market, the price of 36° gravity Mid-Continent crude oil dropped from a high of $1.45 per barrel in 1930 to 25 cents per barrel in 1933,[5] East Texas crude oil dropped to an all-time low of 10 cents per barrel in April 1933,[6] and it appeared that it would be possible to buy crude oil on favorable terms for an indefinite period into the future. In the face of these circumstances, the Sinclair management decided that the company would be better advised to buy crude oil, particularly in areas where the prorationing laws were operative, than to attempt to maintain its own production. Accordingly, in the following years Sinclair did little new drilling in the prorated areas other than that which was necessary to protect its properties from drainage by adjacent wells. The decline in the company's

expenditures for crude oil production may be seen from the Appendix, Table 18. Whereas in the period 1927–1930, inclusive, the company's average annual expenditures for crude oil production were about $14,400,000, in the period 1931–1939, inclusive, its average annual expenditures were only $11,300,000. The company went steadily ahead, however, with the expansion of its refining operations (see Chapter Twelve, Exhibit XII-12), and a decline in the ratio of crude oil production to refinery runs was an inevitable consequence.

The new production program which Sinclair announced in 1949 was designed to increase the company's crude oil production by at least 50,000 barrels per day and to bring the crude oil ratio up to a minimum of 50% of refinery runs. It was anticipated that it would require about five years and a total expenditure of about $100,000,000 to attain the desired increase in crude oil output. The decision to alter the company's crude oil ratio was the product of a number of circumstances. In the first place, by 1949 a number of changes had taken place in the crude oil producing phase of the business which made it a much more attractive field for investment, in the eyes of the Sinclair management, than it had appeared to be in the early 1930's. The mechanism of the prorationing had been greatly improved and many states had imposed restrictions on well-spacing; the demand for petroleum products had undergone an enormous expansion relative to the immediately available supply of crude oil in the United States; and the price of crude oil had tended to stabilize at levels which the Sinclair management believed would permit a satisfactory return over and above finding and producing costs.

Of even greater importance was the fact that the company had been experiencing considerable difficulty in securing adequate crude oil supplies in times of shortage, such as 1948. The company likewise had been experiencing difficulty in buying crude oil at prices which would enable it to meet competition in the final markets. The company had modernized its refineries, built its pipe line system, constructed new marketing facilities, and made every possible effort to improve the efficiency of its refining and marketing operations. It still found itself, however, unable to meet

---

[5] American Petroleum Institute, *Petroleum Facts and Figures*, Ninth Edition, 1950, p. 364–365.

[6] The average East Texas price for the year 1933 was $0.65 per barrel. See H. J. Struth, editor, *The Petroleum Data Book*, 1948, p. E-87.

severe price competition from companies with higher crude oil ratios at times when the margin between crude oil and refined product prices was depressed. On such occasions, the company sometimes found that its net-back at refineries, after deducting processing costs, was less than the price of purchased crude oil. The expansion of crude oil production was in one sense therefore undertaken as a last resort to place the company in a position to meet competition effectively at times when adverse fluctuations occurred in the gross margin available on refining and marketing operations alone.

A third consideration which influenced the Sinclair management in its decision to expand the company's crude oil production was the fact that the company's earnings appeared to be running somewhat lower than those of several other companies with higher crude oil ratios (see Chapter Twelve, Exhibit XII-2). The Sinclair management was also influenced in its decision by the fact that the economy as a whole appeared to be passing into a period of inflation. The management believed that at such a time the expenditure of funds for the discovery and development of underground oil reserves was a sound investment and a good hedge against depreciation in the value of the dollar. A fifth factor which contributed to the decision was the belief of the Sinclair management that corporate income taxes during the next few years were likely to be abnormally high and that in the near future the drilling and exploration work could therefore be carried on at a lower net cost to the corporation than at some later date. Finally, several of the executives who had been instrumental in urging the crude oil purchasing policy in the early 1930's, and particularly Mr. H. F. Sinclair, had by 1949 left the company or had ceased to be influential in the management of its affairs.

In the period 1949–1952 Sinclair increased its net domestic crude oil production by about 33%. The company's crude oil ratio, however, declined slightly because, in order to meet the requirements of its marketing program, the company expanded its refining operations somewhat more than it did its net domestic production. In addition, the company also reduced the imports of its own foreign production in the period 1949–1952 (see Chapter Twelve, Exhibit XII-12).

The Texas Company: The ratio of crude oil production to refinery runs went through the same general cycle in The Texas Company as in the Gulf Oil Corporation and the Sinclair Oil Corporation. The ratio was very high during the early years of the company's history, declined over a long period of time to a much lower level, and then increased substantially. The timing of and reasons for the changes, however, were quite different from those in the case of Gulf or Sinclair.

The Texas Company was organized on April 7, 1902, to take over the assets of the Texas Fuel Company which had been formed by Joseph S. Cullinan and some associates shortly after the discovery of the Spindletop field in Texas for the purpose of buying, transporting, and selling oil to northern refiners. During 1902 the new company completed a crude oil pipe line from the Spindletop field to Port Arthur, built extensive crude oil storage facilities, and began construction of a refinery at Port Arthur. The company also initiated crude oil producing operations through an affiliate, Producers Oil Company, which later became a subsidiary and which was absorbed by The Texas Company in 1917. The Producers Oil Company had extensive holdings in the prolific Sour Lake field, which was discovered in 1903 about 20 miles to the northwest of the Spindletop field, and likewise in the big Jennings field, which was discovered in Louisiana in 1904. By 1904 the net production of The Texas Company (including the Producers Oil Company) accounted for about 3.3% of the total United States crude oil output, and the company was one of the leading oil producers in the country.

In the following years, The Texas Company [7] participated in nearly all the important oil strikes in the Southwest. Like the Gulf Oil Corporation it participated in the development of the Glenn Pool in Oklahoma in 1905 and 1906 and constructed a crude oil pipe line from Oklahoma to connect with an existing line serving the company's refinery at Port Arthur. Meanwhile, the company pressed rapidly ahead with the development of transportation, refining, and marketing facilities. By 1905 it had acquired four tankers, by 1908 it had in opera-

---

[7] In the following discussion, it will be understood that reference to The Texas Company includes the Producers Oil Company.

tion a second refinery at West Dallas, Texas, and by 1910 it had 229 bulk plants distributed throughout the middle section of the United States and in certain eastern states. From the outset therefore The Texas Company was active in all phases of the oil business, and its initial experiences were closely parallel to those of the Gulf Oil Corporation.

During the first six or seven years of The Texas Company's history, crude oil producing activities were far larger than refining operations, and the company's profits were derived primarily from the sale of crude oil to northern refineries and for use as fuel to the Mississippi River sugar planters and the railroads. In the period 1902–1934, however, the company expanded its refining and marketing activities to a far greater extent than its crude oil producing operations. The company's crude oil ratio dropped below 100% in 1909 and followed a generally downward course until 1934, with the exception of three major occasions when temporary increases in the ratio took place as a result of special circumstances which will be discussed later. In 1934 the ratio was 43.7%, the lowest point it reached at any time in the company's history. After 1934 the ratio increased rapidly and by 1941 had reached a level of 64.0%. The ratio then remained fairly constant with the exception of the year 1950 when it increased to 74.0% as a result of a refinery strike which curtailed refinery runs. (See Chapter Twelve, Exhibit XII-11 for record of The Texas Company's producing, refining, and marketing operations.)

The reasons for the general decline in the company's crude oil ratio in the period 1902–1934 may be found in a number of circumstances. The first and one of the most important factors contributing to the decline was the rapid growth in the market for automotive gasoline which took place during the first quarter of the twentieth century. At the time The Texas Company began to develop its marketing activities, the Standard Oil group had a firm hold on the kerosene market in nearly all parts of the country (see Chapter Three). The Texas Company therefore elected almost from the outset to concentrate on the markets for automotive gasolines and lubricating oils. The company very quickly established distributing facilities over a wide area, developed an aggres-

sive marketing program under the "Texaco" brand name, and was one of the first to engage in an extensive advertising program.

The great expansion in the gasoline market, particularly from about 1910 to about 1926, brought about a correspondingly rapid growth in the marketing activities of The Texas Company. The rate of growth in the market was so rapid that the company found it difficult to expand its refining and producing operations fast enough to keep pace with it. By 1918 the company's gasoline sales were exceeding its refinery output, and throughout the period 1918–1924, inclusive, the company bought a substantial part of its gasoline supplies from other refiners. The Texas Company hastened to expand its refinery operations to meet its marketing requirements and as it did so its ratio of crude oil production to refinery runs declined. In a sense, The Texas Company's early commitment in widespread distribution facilities put the company in a position where it would have been very difficult for it to have avoided being pulled out of balance by the rapid expansion of the gasoline market.

A second important reason for the decline in The Texas Company's ratio of crude oil production to refinery runs in the period 1902–1934 may be found in the relative emphases which the executives of the company placed on the producing, refining, and marketing phases of the business. For many years before 1934 the executives tended to treat refining and marketing as the company's primary activities. Crude oil production was regarded largely as a means of obtaining a source of supply for the refineries rather than as a source of profits in itself. The executives were generally of the opinion that as long as the company had sufficient crude oil production to supply 50% or more of its needs it was in a sound position. It was also believed that the high prices which the company was sometimes forced to pay for crude oil in times of shortage could be offset by buying cheap oil in times of ample supply and storing it against future needs.

The tendency of The Texas Company's executives to give primary attention to refining and marketing operations is easily understandable in view of the urgent character of the refining and marketing problems which were associated with the early growth of the automotive gasoline market. The rapid expansion of the gasoline market created many pressing problems in the marketing field because of the need to create an entire new system of distribution facilities to serve the motoring public. At the same time, all refiners were placed under strong compulsion to obtain higher yields of gasoline from crude oil in order to provide the necessary gasoline supplies without excessive production of other petroleum products. Throughout the industry in the two decades after 1910 therefore, much attention was given to the development of continuous thermal cracking processes and to other means of increasing gasoline yields. This problem was a particularly pressing one for The Texas Company, because in the period from 1914 to 1922 the company lagged behind the rest of the industry in the gasoline yields it was able to

EXHIBIT XIII-2. THE TEXAS COMPANY

Yield of Gasoline from Crude Oil Compared with Industry Average: 1914–1926

Year	The Texas Company's Gasoline Yield	Industry Average Gasoline Yield
1914	16.9%	18.2%
1915	13.4	*
1916	16.1	*
1917	19.3	21.5
1918	20.0	25.3
1919	18.3	25.2
1920	21.0	26.1
1921	24.7	27.1
1922	26.5	28.8
1923	33.9	30.0
1924	40.0	31.2
1925	44.2	32.4
1926	44.6	34.9

* Data not available.

SOURCE: The Texas Company and *Petroleum Facts and Figures*, Ninth Edition, 1950.

obtain (see Exhibit XIII-2). Shortly after 1920, however, The Texas Company's Holmes-Manley continuous thermal cracking process proved highly successful in its first commercial installation at the company's Port Arthur refinery. The new process subsequently enabled the company to increase its gasoline yields substantially and served to strengthen the company's position in bargaining for patent rights with other concerns.[8]

---

[8] The Holmes-Manley process of The Texas Company, the tube-and-tank process of the Standard Oil Company (New Jersey), the Dubbs process controlled by the Universal

In 1926 Mr. R. C. Holmes was elected president of the company, and throughout the period of his administration, which continued until 1933, The Texas Company placed particular emphasis on the expansion and further improvement of its refining properties. For many years before 1926 Mr. Holmes had been head of the company's manufacturing department and together with Mr. Fred T. Manley had been instrumental in the development of the Holmes-Manley continuous thermal cracking process discussed above. Mr. Holmes recognized the importance of producing, transportation, and marketing activities but believed that the long-run success of the company rested largely on the efficiency of its refining operations.

During the Holmes administration it was clearly understood by the company executives that first attention was to be given to refining, and capital funds were more readily appropriated for manufacturing activities than for other phases of the business. The company's holdings of producing properties were not expanded so rapidly as some of the executives would have liked, and the resignation of board chairman Judge Amos L. Beaty in 1927 was due, in part, to his dissatisfaction with the company's producing efforts. During the period 1926–1933, on the other hand, the company almost doubled its refinery operations (see Chapter Twelve, Exhibit XII-11). In 1928 and 1929 the company purchased a new refinery at Amarillo, Texas; constructed new plants at Cody, Wyoming, and El Paso and San Antonio, Texas; and doubled the capacity of its refinery at Lockport, Illinois.

In the year 1928 The Texas Company also purchased from the Galena-Signal Oil Company a group of properties which included a 20,000 barrels per day refinery at Houston, cer-

Oil Products Company, and the Cross process controlled by the Gasoline Products Company were the four basic processes developed between about 1910 and 1925 to adapt the principles of the Burton pressure still, which was controlled by the Standard Oil Company (Indiana), to continuous operations. These four processes and the Burton process all became involved in extensive patent litigation which was not resolved until 1923 when a pooling agreement was negotiated between the Jersey Company, the Indiana Company, and The Texas Company. The agreement provided for a limited exchange of patents among the three parties and stipulated that each might go ahead with the development and licensing of its own processes without interference from the others.

tain terminals, bulk plants, and service stations, and the stock of four foreign marketing subsidiaries. In 1931 the Indian Refining Company was acquired. This concern had a 16,000 barrels per day refinery at Lawrenceville, Illinois, and marketing facilities in Illinois, Indiana, Ohio, Michigan, and Kentucky, areas in which the marketing program of The Texas Company was weak. It did not, however, have any significant producing properties. Another major acquisition in the period 1926–1933 was that of the California Petroleum Corporation. This company had extensive operations in all phases of the business, and, as will be noted below, its acquisition served to increase the crude oil ratio of The Texas Company.

A final circumstance which contributed to the general decline in The Texas Company's crude oil ratio before 1934 was a major reduction in the company's California production. In the period 1929–1933 the total output of the California fields declined from 292,534,000 barrels to 172,010,000 barrels, or approximately 41%. In the same period The Texas Company's production in California declined more than 12,000,000 barrels.

As noted above, there were three major occasions during the period 1902–1934 when the general downward movement in The Texas Company's crude oil ratio was interrupted for short periods of time. The first of these occasions was in 1914, at which time the company made an important discovery on the eastern flank of the Humble Salt Dome in Texas, developed substantial new production in the recently discovered Healdton and Cushing fields in Oklahoma, and acquired the Pasadena Oil Company which had producing facilities in Louisiana. The second occasion was in the period 1921–1923. In this instance, the crude oil ratio increased because of reductions in refinery runs which were made during the general business depression that began in 1921 and because of an increase in production in the West Columbia field in Texas.

The third major increase in the crude oil ratio occurred in 1928 when The Texas Company acquired the California Petroleum Corporation. Since the California Petroleum Corporation had crude oil production about equal to its refinery runs, the consolidation of its operations with those of The Texas Company resulted in a combined crude oil ratio which was substantially higher than The Texas Company had had before the acquisition. It appears that no one of the three occasions in the period 1902–1934, when a major increase occurred in The Texas Company's crude oil ratio, marked any change in the company's general policies with regard to the relative emphasis placed upon producing, refining, and marketing activities.

In 1933 President Holmes, after a bitter and prolonged controversy with the board of directors over certain matters of policy and administration, was replaced as president of the company by Mr. W. S. S. Rodgers.[9] Shortly thereafter The Texas Company, as a matter of long-run policy, increased significantly the emphasis which it placed upon producing operations and embarked on a general program designed to raise the company's crude oil ratio. The change in policy with respect to producing operations reflected a long-standing feeling on the part of some of the executives that the company's leaseholdings should be expanded more rapidly and a growing recognition among the executives that a large crude oil producing operation would be necessary to the company's operations in the future.

To implement the new policy with regard to producing operations, a number of important changes were made shortly after 1933 in the administration and conduct of the company's exploratory program. The producing department was given a greater degree of autonomy, a step which increased the speed and effectiveness of its land-leasing operations. In addition, the company's staff of geologists, geophysicists, petroleum engineers, and research scientists was substantially enlarged. The research group was subsequently very successful in developing improved geophysical equipment which made it possible for the company to select acreage for acquisition on a more scientific basis than had been the case theretofore.

The increased attention given to domestic producing operations after 1933 may be seen from Chapter Twelve, Exhibit XII-11, which shows the growth in the company's crude oil

---

[9] Mr. Holmes was elected chairman of the board of directors on April 25, 1933, at the same time that Mr. Rodgers was elected president of the company. On May 5, 1933, Mr. Holmes resigned as chairman of the board of directors.

production and from Exhibit XIII-3 which shows the increase in the number of seismic crews in operation, acreage acquisitions, and the company's share of the total United States production. The Texas Company's producing ef-

EXHIBIT XIII-3. THE TEXAS COMPANY

Seismic Crews in Operation, Acreage Acquisitions, and Share of U.S. Production: 1930-1950

Year	Seismic Crews *	Acreage Acquisitions	Net Crude Oil Production as Percentage of U.S. Production
1930			4.1%
1931	Not	Not	3.4
1932	Available	Available	3.6
1933	3	529,106	3.4
1934	5	1,157,490	3.4
1935	11	1,291,626	3.8
1936	14	3,016,826	4.0
1937	20	1,307,171	3.9
1938	15	482,707	4.0
1939	16	244,455	5.0
1940	13	896,704	6.3
1941	16	1,033,979	5.3
1942	18	1,214,479	4.8
1943	23	1,823,294	5.0
1944	27	4,362,985	5.2
1945	27	1,774,517	5.2
1946	22	1,165,652	5.0
1947	24	1,475,727	5.0
1948	33	1,801,826	4.9
1949	32	1,574,068	5.0
1950	32	2,008,532	4.9

* Company or contract crews in operation in the United States as of January 1.

SOURCE: The Texas Company.

forts were greatly benefited in 1939 by important new discoveries in the Illinois fields where the company had extensive leaseholdings. As a result of the rapid development of the Illinois fields, which were not controlled by conservation laws, The Texas Company's crude oil ratio rose to 83.3% in 1940. Production from the Illinois fields declined very rapidly, but from 1941 onward The Texas Company was able to maintain a crude oil ratio of about 60% to 70% of refinery runs.

Beginning in 1936 The Texas Company became heavily engaged in foreign producing operations.[10] The company had begun foreign

---

[10] The facts in the following four paragraphs have been drawn from United States District Court, Southern District of New York, Civil Action No. 86-27, *United States vs. Standard Oil Company (New Jersey), Socony-Vacuum Oil Company, Inc., Standard Oil Company of California, The Texas Company, Gulf Oil Corporation, Amended Answer of Defendant, The Texas Company*, dated September 21, 1953.

marketing operations in 1905 and in the succeeding 30 years established marketing organizations in South America, the Caribbean area, Western Europe, Africa, and the Far East. For many years substantially all the products sold abroad were refined in and shipped from the United States. As the foreign markets were developed, however, it gradually became clear that it would be much more economical for the company to supply them with products drawn from foreign refining and producing operations than with products shipped from the United States. The executives of The Texas Company also recognized that foreign crude oil might someday be highly desirable and perhaps necessary to support the company's refining and marketing operations in the United States in the event of a domestic crude oil shortage.

The Texas Company began its search for foreign crude oil in 1911 and 1912, but with the exception of certain properties which were developed in Mexico between 1918 and 1921 and later abandoned, the company was not successful before 1936 in finding any substantial quantities of crude oil in foreign countries. The company continued to be dependent upon domestic producing and refining operations to supply its foreign markets and experienced steadily increasing competitive pressure from other companies which had been able to develop producing and refining operations closer to the markets. By the 1930's it was clear that if The Texas Company wished to continue its foreign marketing operations it would have to find foreign crude oil or arrange to purchase refined products from its competitors.

In 1936 therefore The Texas Company took advantage of two major opportunities to secure foreign oil producing operations. As a first step, the company joined with the Socony-Vacuum Oil Company on a 50–50 basis in obtaining control of the Barco Concession in Colombia by acquiring the interest of the Gulf Oil Corporation in the South American Gulf Oil Company and the Colombian Petroleum Company. In the following 17 years The Texas Company and Socony-Vacuum invested and advanced a total of $60,000,000 in the project to build the pipe lines and carry on the other work necessary to the development of the concession.

The second major step taken by The Texas Company in 1936 was the acquisition of a one-half interest in certain crude oil concessions which the Standard Oil Company of California held or had the right to acquire on the Island of Bahrain (in the Persian Gulf), Saudi Arabia, Sumatra, Java, and Netherlands New Guinea. The Standard Oil Company of California had discovered oil in Bahrain, was building a small refinery on the island, and had hopes of finding oil on its other concessions. The company did not, however, have any marketing organization in the near-by countries. The Texas Company, on the other hand, had marketing organizations in near-by countries but no near-by sources of crude oil or refined products. The joining together of the interests of the two companies thus offered obvious advantages to both concerns and resulted in the formation of an integration organization for the production, refining, transportation, and marketing of petroleum and its products in the Eastern Hemisphere.[11]

Comparison of Policies With Respect to Changes in Crude Oil Ratios:

The experiences of Gulf, Sinclair, and The Texas Company together with those of the Indiana Company, Atlantic, Sohio, and The Ohio Oil Company, recounted in earlier chapters, reveal some of the differences and similarities in the direction, timing, and reasons for the changes which the companies made in their crude oil ratios. In some cases the companies moved in quite different directions at approximately the same time. In other cases they moved in the same direction at about the same time and under about the same circumstances but for very different reasons. In only a few cases could it be said that they did the same things at the same time for the same reasons.

---

[11] As a result of the arrangements initiated in 1936, The Texas Company and the Standard Oil Company of California became joint owners of the so-called Bahrain-Caltex group of companies operating in the Eastern Hemisphere. At the same time, The Texas Company acquired from the Standard Oil Company of California: (a) a 50% interest in the Arabian American Oil Company which owned the Saudi Arabian concession, (b) a 50% interest in N. V. Nederlandsche Pacific Petroleum Maatschappij which owned the concessions and rights in Sumatra and Java, and (c) a half interest in the Standard Oil Company of California's 20% interest in N. V. Nederlandsche Nieuw Guinee Petroleum Maatschappij which owned a concession in Netherlands New Guinea.

The decade from 1930 to 1940 provides a particularly good example of a situation in which several of the companies followed different courses of action with respect to their crude oil ratios, although in some cases the changes made were a matter of necessity rather than of choice. Gulf, Sinclair, and The Ohio Oil Company during this period experienced a significant decline in their crude oil ratios. The Atlantic Refining Company and The Texas Company, on the other hand, increased their crude oil ratios throughout most of the period. The Indiana Company was likewise aggressively seeking more crude oil production although no major changes occurred in its crude oil ratio. Sohio followed a third course of action during the 1930's and made no changes at all in its crude oil ratio, which at that time was approximately zero. Examination of the charts in Chapter Twelve reveals many other time periods in which the companies followed different courses of action with respect to their crude oil ratios.

The experiences of Gulf and Sinclair immediately after the adoption of the prorationing laws provide a good example of a situation in which two companies did the same thing at about the same time but for very different reasons. In both companies the crude oil ratio declined. In the case of Gulf, however, the decline was forced upon the company and was certainly not a matter of management choice. The management at this time was anxious to expand the company's crude oil producing operations and recognized that the mid-1930's provided an unusually favorable opportunity to do so. The management was unable to follow the course of action it would have liked because of the shortage of financial resources which resulted from the big expansion of refining and marketing properties undertaken in the late 1920's and the operating losses incurred during the early years of the depression. It may also be noted that Gulf made no further expansion of its refining facilities for eight or nine years after 1930 and even chose to run some of its plants at less than capacity for a time in preference to buying larger quantities of crude oil.

In the case of Sinclair, on the other hand, the decline in the crude oil ratio was a matter of deliberate management policy. The Sinclair management, or at least the controlling group therein, interpreted the development of the prorationing laws and the crude oil surpluses of the early 1930's as increasing the general desirability of buying as contrasted with producing crude oil for the company's refinery requirements. The analysis of the Sinclair management on this point differed from that of the managements of Atlantic and the Indiana Company. As noted in earlier discussion, the executives of the latter two companies interpreted the prorationing laws as accentuating the need for a refiner to have his own production, because they believed that the laws would eliminate the opportunity to buy crude oil at abnormally depressed prices but would still leave a refiner exposed to the necessity of paying high prices in times of shortage.

In contrasting the Gulf and Sinclair situations, it is particularly important to observe that the latter was not short of funds during the 1930's. In September 1930 the company sold its one-half interest in the Sinclair Crude Oil Purchasing Company and the Sinclair Pipe Line Company to the Standard Oil Company (Indiana), the owner of the other half interest, for the sum of $72,500,000. In January 1932 Sinclair then arranged to acquire the properties of The Prairie Oil and Gas Company and The Prairie Pipe Line Company and thus, for all practical purposes, replaced the properties sold to the Indiana Company. Since the sale to the Indiana Company was made for cash and the acquisition of the Prairie interests was accomplished by an exchange of common stock, the net effect of the two transactions was to increase greatly Sinclair's liquidity in a time of severe business depression. In December 1929 the company's ratio of current assets to current liabilities was about 3 to 1; immediately after the consolidation in 1932 it was slightly over 8 to 1.

Unlike Gulf therefore, Sinclair had the money during the middle 1930's to expand its crude oil producing operations if it had chosen to do so. As may be seen from Chapter Twelve, Exhibit XII-12, and the Appendix, Table 18, Sinclair used a substantial share of its capital funds during the 1930's to accomplish a steady expansion in its refining and marketing properties, whereas during the same period Gulf held its manufacturing facilities nearly constant.

Another interesting example of a situation in which two of the companies did about the same thing at about the same time, but for very different reasons, may be found in the experiences of Atlantic and Sohio during the early years of World War II. Both companies undertook a major expansion of crude oil producing operations beginning about 1942. As was noted in Chapter Eight, one of the most important among the many factors which influenced the executives of Sohio to undertake a crude oil producing program at this particular time was the large excess profits tax which the company had incurred in 1941 and which it appeared likely to incur throughout the war years. Atlantic, on the other hand, had a large earnings base for excess profits tax purposes, and the executives of the company were not influenced in their decision by tax considerations in any material way. On the contrary, the program was undertaken chiefly because the Atlantic executives believed that a heavy investment in crude oil production would provide a good hedge against inflation and because it appeared that there would be good opportunities to buy producing properties during the war years.

It is not difficult to understand why the experiences of the several companies reveal relatively few cases where two or more companies did the same thing at the same time for the same reasons with respect to their crude oil ratios. It is true that the companies operated in the same general environment and were subject to the influence of the same basic business and economic forces. The structures and situations of the individual companies were, however, quite different, as was illustrated in Chapter Twelve. At any given time therefore the economic forces at work in the industry might be expected to impinge on each of the companies in somewhat different ways. It might likewise be anticipated that the managements of the individual companies would make different interpretations of the shifts and changes taking place in the economic environment of the oil industry.

It is therefore not surprising that the differences in the timing, direction, and reasons for the changes the companies made in their crude oil ratios were somewhat more marked than the similarities. When the actions of the companies are viewed in long perspective, however, similarities can be found in the general efforts they made with respect to their crude oil ratios. Six of the seven companies, for example, at one time or another after 1930 made a strong effort to increase their crude oil ratios and were prompted to do so, at least in part, by somewhat the same general reasons, including the desire to assure continuity of supply to their refineries, the desire to guard against severe adverse fluctuations in the refining margin, and the desire to avoid paying high prices for crude oil in times of shortage. Moreover, as will be noted below, in 1952 six of the seven companies had somewhat the same general objectives with regard to the relationship between crude oil production and refinery runs.

Present Positions and Objectives:

We found that none of the seven companies had defined its objectives with regard to its crude oil ratio with any very great degree of precision. In the six companies which were net buyers of crude oil, most of the executives with whom we discussed the matter expressed the opinion that their companies might well produce a somewhat higher proportion of their crude oil requirements. Few, if any, of these executives had a specific figure in mind as to what the optimum ratio should be; their thinking was usually in terms of a range some 10 to 20 percentage points in width. There was general agreement, however, that it was important for a large refiner to produce at least about 50% of his crude oil requirements, that it was very desirable for him to produce as much as 75% or 80%, and that higher ratios were certainly welcome if they could be obtained at a reasonable cost.

The efforts which the six companies were making to enlarge their crude oil producing operations were dependent to a considerable extent on their existing ratios of crude oil production to refinery runs. In general, the companies producing less than about 50% of their crude oil requirements were making fairly strong efforts to produce a larger amount. The companies producing more than 50% of their crude oil requirements, on the other hand, were concerned primarily with seeing that their producing activities expanded rapidly enough to keep pace with the normal growth in their refining and marketing operations rather than

with altering the existing relationship between crude oil production and refinery runs.

All six companies which were net buyers of crude oil anticipated that their marketing activities would continue in the near future to expand at the rate of 3% to 5% per annum, in accordance with the normal growth of the industry, and that their refining operations would be kept roughly in balance with their marketing requirements (see Chapter Fourteen). The companies were all anxious to hold at least their existing share of the United States refining and marketing activities and were not disposed to improve their crude oil ratios by deliberately curtailing the growth of their marketing operations. Such a course of action would have posed at once the problem of initiating a program of "soft-selling" in the marketing organizations, a step which all the companies would have been very reluctant to take. All the companies, however, and particularly those with low crude oil ratios, were scrutinizing fairly carefully any proposals for expansion in refining and marketing activities which it appeared might result in a long-run reduction in their crude oil ratios.

Although the executives of the six companies were almost unanimous in the opinion that high crude oil ratios were generally desirable, they did not anticipate that their companies would ever be likely to close completely the gap between crude oil production and refinery runs and thus cease to be net buyers of crude oil in the United States. In most of the companies the bringing of crude oil production into balance with refinery runs would have required, in the opinion of the executives, capital expenditures far larger than the companies could have supported on their existing capitalizations or mergers with one or more large producing organizations.[12] It was also recognized that the prorationing laws operated in such a way as to keep the large refining companies in a net buying position. As noted in Chapter Two, the 30 largest integrated refining companies accounted in 1950 for about 87% of the refining capacity of the United States. As long as the nonintegrated producing companies are successful in finding more than about 13%

---

[12] In the case of one or two of the companies, the executives anticipated that mergers with large producing organizations might have been precluded by the antitrust laws.

of the domestic crude oil production plus imports, it is inescapable that the 30 large companies as a group should remain net buyers of crude oil because the prorationing laws operated in such a manner as to assure the nonintegrated producers of a market for their output on an equitable basis with the producing departments of the integrated companies.

In addition, the executives of several of the companies were of the opinion that their companies should continue to remain net buyers of crude oil in the United States because it was a healthy thing to have a strong group of nonintegrated producers in the industry, not only for political reasons but also because the oil-finding activities of the small, nonintegrated producers tended to supplement and complement those of the large, integrated firms in a variety of ways as will be noted in the following section of this chapter. Finally, it was believed by most of the executives in the companies that a refining company was in a fairly sound position with 75% to 80% of its crude oil supply secured and had no real need to produce 100%, particularly in view of the fact that it nearly always had access to royalty oil amounting to about $12\frac{1}{2}\%$ of its own gross production.[13]

The Ohio Oil Company occupied an entirely different position with respect to the relationship between crude oil production and refinery runs from that of the other six companies, and its policies and objectives with regard to the relationship were also quite different. As in the case of the other six companies, the executives of The Ohio Oil Company had no definite figure in mind as to the optimum crude oil ratio. Generally speaking, however, the executives believed that a ratio of 200% to 400% was entirely satisfactory and might well be continued into the future. The executives were of the opinion that the company's most profitable operations were in the producing field and that one of the company's strongest assets was the experience and ability of its management personnel in oil-finding activities. They believed that it was desirable, however, to have substantial refining and marketing operations to supplement the producing business because such activities were profitable in their own

right and provided a long-run hedge against the possibility, admittedly slight, that surpluses of crude oil might once again develop in the domestic markets as they had in the late 1920's and early 1930's.

In the future, it was anticipated that the company's investments in marketing properties would be sufficient to keep that phase of the business expanding at about the rate of growth for the industry generally and that refining operations would be kept approximately in balance with marketing requirements. The ratio maintained between crude oil production and refinery runs would then rest largely upon the success which attended the company's producing efforts. The executives anticipated that no deliberate effort would be made to alter the ratio unless in the course of the growth of the company it became substantially different than it currently was.

It is important to note that The Ohio Oil Company, the only one of the seven companies that was a net seller of crude oil, was not exclusively or primarily a source of supply for the six companies that were short of crude oil. Exhibit XIII-4 contains an analysis of The Ohio Oil Company's crude oil sales by size and type of customer for the years 1930, 1940, and 1950. It is apparent that after 1930 the company had far more little customers than big ones, that in the 20-year period 1930–1950 the number of its small customers increased more than the number of its large customers, and that the majority of its customers bought in fairly small lots.

Exhibit XIII-4 also reveals that the company made 23.4% of its gross crude oil sales in 1940 and 30.8% of its gross crude oil sales in 1950 to small concerns. These figures, however, greatly understate the significance of The Ohio Oil Company as a supplier of small concerns because a large share of the volume shown as sales to major companies merely represented crude oil trading arrangements which were handled as purchase and sales transactions. In other words, The Ohio Oil Company sold a much higher proportion of the net crude oil it had available, *after trading transactions,* to small concerns than is suggested by the analysis of gross crude oil sales shown in Exhibit XIII-4. It appears therefore that the close functional relationship which existed between

[13] See Chapter Twelve, footnote 2, for definition of royalty oil.

Exhibit XIII-4. The Ohio Oil Company

Analysis of Crude Oil Sales by Size and Type of Customer: 1930, 1940, and 1950

Quantity Purchased per Annum (1,000 bbls.)	Number of Customers by Size Groups					
	Major Companies *			Other Companies		
	1930	1940	1950	1930	1940	1950
0–99	12	9	7	30	45	62
100–499	6	9	8	5	9	11
500–999	2	1	4	2	4	4
1,000–1,999	1	5	3	2	1	2
2,000 and over	3	3	5	1	—	1
Total Customers	24	27	27	40	59	80

	Sales Volume by Type of Customer			
	1940		1950	
	Thousand Barrels	% Total	Thousand Barrels	% Total
Gross Sales Crude Oil	29,058	100.0%	42,203	100.0%
To Major Companies †	22,257	76.6	29,218	69.2
To Other Companies	6,801	23.4	12,985	30.8

* For the purposes of this analysis, major companies were defined as all companies included in the *Financial Analysis of 30 Oil Companies*, published annually by the Petroleum Department of The Chase National Bank of New York.

† Includes sales to subsidiaries of major companies. Many of these sales were crude oil trading arrangements which were handled as purchase and sale transactions.

Source: The Ohio Oil Company.

The Ohio Oil Company and other parts of the old Standard Oil group before 1911 probably became inconsequential sometime before 1930 and has not reappeared since that time.

II. The Use of Farm-Outs and Various Types of Cash Contributions in Exploratory Programs

We found that the exploratory programs of the seven oil companies embraced many different types of producing deals, such as farmouts, acreage contributions, dry-hole contributions, bottom-hole contributions, acreage purchase agreements, and joint interest wells. These arrangements, which were negotiated primarily but not exclusively with small, nonintegrated producers, are of interest for several reasons. In the first place, each such arrangement represents an integration decision in the sense that it marks a point where the companies decided to rely upon outside firms for a particular phase of their exploratory programs in lieu of assuming the risks and doing the jobs themselves. The arrangements are also of significance because they represent an important area of interdependence between the large and small companies in the oil industry, an area in which the two types of companies tend to complement and supplement each other in terms of the risks they assume and the functions they perform. Finally, the existence of these arrangements and the deliberate use of them by the seven large companies establishes and maintains a field of opportunity in the producing business for the small concern.

The Various Types of Producing Deals:

The seven companies employed a large number of different types of producing deals, many of which were subject to numerous variations and to use in combinations with other deals. In the following paragraphs we shall not attempt to cover all of the variations and combinations of the deals but merely to outline some of the more commonly used arrangements. For convenience in discussion, we shall treat the arrangements as deals between "large companies" and "small producers," for such is their usual pattern. It is very important to note, however, that the deals are sometimes made between two large companies, between two small producers, or in reverse fashion between a small company and a large one.

Farm-Outs: In the typical farm-out arrangement, a large company assigns to a small producer its lease on a particular piece of land, and the small producer in return agrees to drill a hole on the property. The types of land involved in farm-out transactions usually fall into three general categories: wildcat acreage, semiproved acreage, and proved acreage which is believed by the large company to be of marginal value. In the case of wildcat acreage, the large company usually (a) assigns a whole block of leases and reserves an overriding royalty on any oil and/or gas discovered, or (b) assigns portions of the land in a checkerboard pattern or an undivided interest in the land without reserving an overriding royalty. In the case of semiproved and proved acreage, the large company nearly always retains an overriding royalty interest in any production that may be developed. The amount of the overriding royalty retained by the large company varies depending on the chances of discovering oil on the property, the cost of drilling, and various other considerations, but it usually runs in the neighborhood of $\frac{1}{32}$ to $\frac{1}{8}$ of the net oil production after payment of the landowner's royalty. Ordinarily the small producer assumes the responsibility for making the lease payments to the landowner who originally granted the lease to the large company and for making the royalty payments to him if oil is discovered.

The company granting a farm-out is entitled to all well logs, cores, samples, and geological information that may be obtained during the drilling operation. The terms of the farm-out arrangement usually specify a limit of time during which a hole must be drilled by the small producer and often the depth of the hole or the geological horizon which must be reached. Moreover, the small producer becomes subject to whatever provisions with regard to the drilling of wells may have been included by the landowner in the original lease to the large company. The farm-out usually grants to the small producer all drilling rights on the property. In some cases, however, the large company grants only shallow drilling rights, down to say 5,000 feet, or in rare cases only deep drilling rights, from say 5,000 feet on down. The following are typical farm-out arrangements:

1. On March 28, 1951, a large company assigned two small operators several of its leases in a Texas area subject to their drilling an 8,500-foot test well on one of the leases assigned. The large company reserved an overriding royalty of $\frac{1}{16}$. The well was subsequently drilled to the required depth and abandoned as a dry hole.

2. On May 9, 1951, a large company assigned to a small operator checkerboard portions from a block of leases in a Texas area subject to his drilling a 6,300-foot test well on one of the leases assigned. No overriding royalty was retained by the large company on the portions of the leases covered in the farm-out. The well was drilled to the required depth and abandoned as a dry hole.

3. A large oil company, holding several thousand acres under lease in West Texas, farmed out 720 acres to a small operator subject to the requirement that he drill a 10,500-foot test well. The well was completed successfully and had an initial potential of about 500 barrels of oil per day. The small operator subsequently completed two additional wells on the property of approximately the same producing potential. Offsetting the original 720 acres, another farm-out deal was made whereby the small operator acquired a one-half interest in 640 acres subject to a 45-day drilling obligation. Two successful wells were completed on this tract. The underlying oil field had several million barrels of reserves, and the small operator was able as a result of his activities to secure an equity in about one million barrels of reserves.

Acreage Contributions: Acreage contributions are closely akin to farm-outs in that they involve the assignment of leases by a large company to a small producer. In this case, however, the small producer agrees to drill a well not on the property assigned by the large company but rather on a lease which he owns or controls in the same area. The small producer often contracts to sell the leases assigned to him by the large company to some third party, occasionally another large oil company. The acreage sales contract can then be used as a basis for borrowing money to finance the drilling operation. Acreage contributions are commonly employed in areas where there is a diversity of lease ownership and are sometimes combined with dry hole and bottom hole contributions. As in the case of farm-outs, the company making the contribution is entitled to the geological information obtained by the small producer when he drills his well.

Acreage contributions are so similar to farm-outs that they are commonly carried with farm-outs in the statistical records of the large oil companies.

Dry Hole Contributions: A dry hole contribution is a sum of money that a large company agrees to pay to a small producer if the latter drills a well to a specified depth at a specified location and the well turns out dry. Well logs, cores, samples, and all geological information obtained in the course of the drilling are made available to the contributing company. A small producer may, and frequently does, obtain dry hole contributions for a single well from several large companies holding property in the same area. Moreover, it is not uncommon for a small producer to obtain a farmout from one company and acreage or dry hole contributions from other companies. In rare cases, small producers have been known to drill nothing but dry holes during the year and yet to show profit on their operations because the dry hole and other contributions received were in excess of their drilling costs. Typical of the dry hole transactions are the following:

1. In October 1950 a large company agreed by letter to contribute $50,000 of dry hole money to a small operating company in support of the drilling of an 11,000-foot well in Louisiana. Oil was discovered at 9,800 feet, and the well tested 320 barrels per day on initial production. The small producer in this case did not receive the dry hole money but did, on the other hand, retain the full rights to the well, subject to whatever royalty stipulations may have been included in the lease of the property from the landowner.

2. In March 1951 a large company agreed by letter to contribute $5,000 of dry hole money to a small producing company in support of the drilling of a 7,400-foot well in Louisiana. The well was abandoned as a dry hole at 7,510 feet and the $5,000 of dry hole money was paid.

Bottom Hole Contributions: Bottom hole contributions are very similar to dry hole contributions except that in the case of the bottom hole contribution the money is payable when the drilling operation reaches a specified depth or geological horizon, regardless of whether the well is a dry hole or a producer. In some cases the bottom hole contribution is a final payment made when the bottom of the hole is reached; in other cases the contribution is repayable out of some fraction, usually $\frac{1}{8}$ or $\frac{1}{16}$, of the production from the well, if it turns out to be a producer. Bottom hole contributions are made far less frequently than dry hole contributions and are usually employed in cases where the contributing company has some unusual interest in seeing the well drilled. Typical cases of bottom hole contributions are the following:

1. A large company agreed by letter dated August 15, 1951, to contribute $4,000 bottom hole money to a small producer in support of the drilling of a 4,500-foot well in Texas; no provision for repayment of the contribution out of production was made. The well turned out to be a dry hole and the small producer received his $4,000. In a similar case, involving a $2,000 nonrepayable bottom hole commitment in Texas during 1950, the well resulted in a producer of gas and condensate. In this case likewise, final payment of the bottom hole money was made to the small producer since the deal did not involve any provision for repayment in the event that production was secured.

2. In March, 1951, a large company agreed to contribute $40,000 of bottom hole money to a small operator in support of the drilling of an 11,500-foot well in Louisiana. It was further agreed that the money would be repayable out of $\frac{1}{8}$ of production if oil was discovered. The well, however, was abandoned as a dry hole at the required depth and final payment of $40,000 was made to the small producer. In a similar case, involving a $50,000 repayable bottom hole commitment in Texas during 1951, the well resulted in a producer, and the large company was repaid out of $\frac{1}{4}$ of the production.

Acreage Purchase Agreements: Small producers quite often arrange to finance a test well wholly or partially through the sale of leases to large companies. In such cases, the small producer usually obtains control of a substantial body of leases in an area through direct purchases from the landowners and/or through acreage contribution letters from other lease owners in the area. He next approaches one or more large companies with his plan for drilling a test well and a map of his lease holdings. The large companies may then agree to purchase certain of the leases provided that the well is drilled as specified. The acreage involved in the purchase agreement is usually priced at several times its "untested" value, depending largely on the estimated cost of the proposed test well. Two examples of acreage purchase agreements are the following:

1. A large company made a deal in 1951 with a small operator who was planning to drill a 9,000-foot test well in a prospective area in East Texas. The large company agreed to pay for a spread of acreage an amount of money equal to approximately one-third the cost of the well provided that the well was drilled to the specified depth. The well was drilled and abandoned as a dry hole, and the sale of the leases to the large company was consummated.

2. A large company made a similar deal with a small producer in 1950 who was planning to drill a 3,500-foot test well in East Texas. In this case, the large company agreed to pay an amount equal to about two-thirds the cost of the test well for an undivided one-half interest in the small block of leases to be tested by the well, provided that the well was drilled to the required depth. Here again the well was drilled to the required depth and abandoned as a dry hole, and the leases covered by the deal were transferred to the large company.

Joint Interest Wells: A joint interest well is simply one in which two or more companies agree to share the cost of developing and operating the well and the production therefrom in some predetermined ratio. A joint working interest differs from a royalty interest in that the holder of a joint working interest usually, but not always, shares in the cost of developing and operating the property whereas the holder of a royalty interest usually receives a share of the production without bearing any of the costs of development or operation. Ordinarily, one of the companies involved in a joint interest arrangement is designated to act for the group as the operating company and to carry on the drilling and producing activities.

Joint interest wells arise in many types of situations. In the first place, the acreage in a particular territory may be split up among many different lessees, each of whom may hold, say, 10 or 20 acres. The conservation laws of the state may, however, provide for a minimum well spacing pattern of one well to 40 acres. Under such circumstances, joint interest arrangements are imperative as a means of conducting the exploratory and producing work. Joint interest wells may also arise when two or more companies decide to share the cost of acquiring leases as a means of spreading the expense and risk of an exploratory venture. Finally, joint interest wells may develop under some of the producing deals discussed above, if the large company elects to take a joint interest rather than a royalty interest for its participation in the project.

Combination Deals: As has already been suggested, the various producing deals discussed above are frequently used in combinations. An example of a combination deal, which was arranged in Wyoming in 1951, is shown in Exhibit XIII-5. The acreage was held by two large oil companies, both of which had "shot" the area and had about the same geophysical information. Both companies were interested in seeing a test well drilled, but neither wished to give the other the benefit of the geological information to be gained from the test well free of charge. The two companies had not been able to work out a mutually satisfactory joint arrangement, principally because Company B insisted on receiving a larger acreage contribution from Company A in return for its participation in the project than Company A was willing to give.

Company A therefore called in a small operator and agreed to give him one-half of its 10,880 acres plus $50,000 of dry hole money if he would drill a well to a depth of 10,000 feet at the location shown on the map in Exhibit XIII-5 to test the Dakota sandstone. The small operator accepted the proposition and then sold one-half of the acreage received from Company A to Company B for $150,000. The small operator thus secured a one-fourth interest in 10,880 acres plus $200,000 in return for drilling the required 10,000-foot well. It was estimated by the small operator that the cost of the well would be approximately $200,000.[14]

---

[14] The small operator was subsequently offered $250,000 for its one-fourth interest in the block by a third large company, an offer which it refused.

EXHIBIT XIII-5. EXAMPLE OF AN ACREAGE CONTRIBUTION, DRY HOLE
CONTRIBUTION, AND ACREAGE PURCHASE AGREEMENT

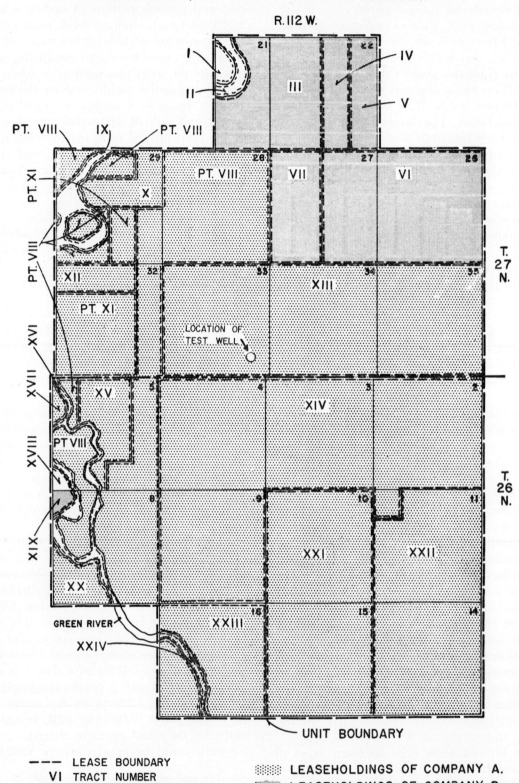

The deal thus involved an acreage contribution and a dry hole contribution on the part of Company A and acreage purchase agreement on the part of Company B.

Reasons for the Use of Producing Deals:

We found that producing deals, such as those described above, were used by the large companies as a regular and continuing part of their exploratory programs. The deals arose under a myriad of circumstances, but generally were employed either singly or in combinations for five general types of purposes, as described below.

Extending a Company's Exploratory Efforts:

One of the most important uses of the producing deals was to extend a company's exploratory efforts over a broader geographic area than it could possibly cover with its own resources. As a matter of general policy or occasional practice, a large company sometimes acquired extensive lease holdings in an area where little geological information was available and the cost of the leases was correspondingly low. The company then proceeded to evaluate the property by its own exploratory and drilling operations and by the judicious use of producing deals with smaller firms. Frequently in such situations, it was cheaper for the large company to determine the value of the properties quickly by means of extensive farm-outs and well contributions than it would have been to pay the lease rentals until such time as the large company was in a position and had the funds to do the work itself. Of primary importance, however, was the fact that the producing deals enabled the large company to handle far more acreage and to draw geological information from many more test wells than would have been possible with its own facilities and resources and thereby provided the means of locating oil reserves which might otherwise have been missed.

Meeting Drilling Needs and Obligations:

A second important use made of exploratory deals was to evaluate acreage which the large companies lacked funds to test at the time lease expiration dates or other considerations indicated that a test should be made. The typical oil and gas lease runs for a stated period of time, usually one to ten years, and the land-owner is ordinarily paid a cash bonus at the time the lease is negotiated plus an annual rental of a certain amount per acre. The leases frequently contain options with respect to renewals and may or may not contain stipulations with regard to wells to be drilled during the lease period. If production is secured on the property, the annual rentals cease, the landowner secures his royalty interest in the output of the well, and the lease is extended automatically for the life of the well.

Even the largest companies operated with an upper ceiling of some kind on the capital expenditures they could make in any given time period. As a result, the companies were continually finding that after they had allocated their capital budgets to their most attractive or urgent drilling prospects, they still had left certain properties which were approaching lease expiration dates and which they were reluctant to let go without testing. The large company might hold options to renew the lease, but developments since the original date of the contract might have increased the attractiveness of the property so that the landowner would be certain to demand much higher rentals for the renewal period. Under such circumstances, it was often greatly to the advantage of the large company to farm-out a piece of land to a small producer, subject to the stipulation that a well be drilled, or to make acreage, dry hole, bottom hole, or land purchase agreements as a means of getting a well drilled in the same general area before the lease expired. Farm-outs were also used in situations where a company had specific obligations to drill wells on a lease but had, at the moment, other more attractive uses for its own funds.

It is important to note that it was almost impossible, even with the best of planning, for a large producing company to avoid getting into situations where the drilling requirements arising out of its lease holdings sometimes exceeded the capital funds it had available in any one year. An active company usually held hundreds of leases each of which was negotiated on the best possible bases in the light of the information available at the time it was drawn. The relative desirability of various geographical areas, however, was continually changing on the basis of new discoveries and new geological information, and a company's plans with respect to where it could best do its drilling were, of necessity, subject to change on very short notice. A company was therefore sometimes forced to do a large amount of drilling by a sudden spurt of competitive activity in certain areas in which it had large holdings at just the time when it had important leases in other areas approaching their expiration dates.

Evaluating Acreage Which Was Highly Speculative: A third important use which the large companies made of the various producing deals was to evaluate acreage which was of a highly speculative character. A large company often held acreage which it believed had little prospect of producing oil or on which it had very little detailed geological information. The large company might wish to retain the leases, however, merely as a hedge against the possibility that oil might be discovered in the area. Occasionally a small producer would study one of these areas very intensively and on the basis of his information decide to hazard a test well. He might then approach the large company for a farm-out or some type of cash contribution to aid in financing the well. In such cases, the large company might enter into the deal as a means of getting the property tested at a relatively low cost.

The small producer in instances of this type usually performed one or another of several functions that the large company was not in a position or did not wish to perform. In some cases, the small producer undertook the well simply because he was willing to gamble on longer odds than was the large company. In other cases, by making a more detailed study of the particular sector than the large company could afford to make in view of the large territory over which it operated, the small producer might, in fact, reduce the risks on the well to a lower order than they appeared to be to the large company. Finally, by shopping around for various types of contributions among the major companies having an interest in the area, the small producer often served as the agent for spreading the risk on a hazardous venture and at the same time reduced his own commitment in the deal to the point where it was well warranted by the prospects of the site.

Evaluating Acreage Among Diversified Lease Holdings: A fourth use which the large companies made of the producing deals was to evaluate acreage in areas where the lease holdings were split up among several different companies, as in the example shown in Exhibit XIII-6. In such areas, the holdings of individual companies were sometimes so small that no one firm had much incentive to spend the money necessary to test the area by itself. Moreover, it was readily apparent that the driller of the first well would provide information of considerable value to all of the companies holding leases in the surrounding area, and it was to be expected that the interested parties should contribute to the cost of the project. The large companies in these situations sometimes contributed acreage or money to a small producer in order to get the test wells drilled and the land evaluated at a lower cost than if each did the drilling itself. The small producer, in effect, served as the intermediary to bring about the joint participation of several different companies in the well.

Drilling of Marginal Wells in Proven Areas: Producing deals were often negotiated as a means of getting wells drilled along the borders of producing properties where it was anticipated that the production obtained might scarcely be worth the cost of drilling and operating the wells. A typical situation is illustrated in Exhibit XIII-7. The large company leasing and developing the main tract of land might farm-out small leases along the edge of the property as a means of determining the boundaries of the producing formation and of securing a small share of whatever production might be developed. Similarly, it might contribute dry hole or bottom hole money to wells just beyond the property line in order to secure geological information with regard to the limits of the oil pool. Such contributions were sometimes accompanied by the stipulation that the large company have an option to purchase part or all of any production secured.

A large company also sometimes granted farm-outs along the borders of a producing property as a means of avoiding troublesome law suits by landowners. A large company might, for example, decide that lease "A" in Exhibit XIII-7 had some oil under it but not

EXHIBIT XIII-6. EXAMPLE OF DIVERSIFIED LEASE HOLDINGS
SUITABLE FOR A PRODUCING DEAL

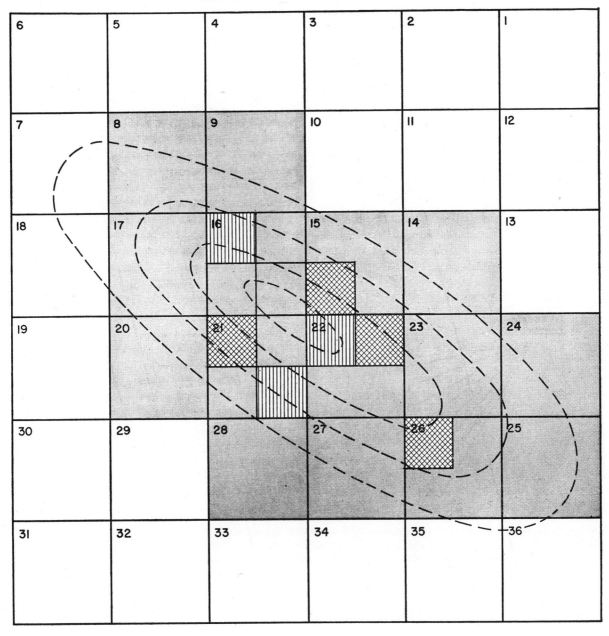

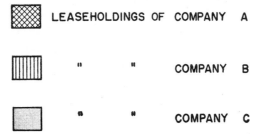

LEASEHOLDINGS OF COMPANY A

"   "   COMPANY B

"   "   COMPANY C

EXHIBIT XIII-7. EXAMPLE OF LAND SUITABLE FOR FARM-OUTS, DRY HOLE
CONTRIBUTIONS, AND BOTTOM HOLE CONTRIBUTIONS

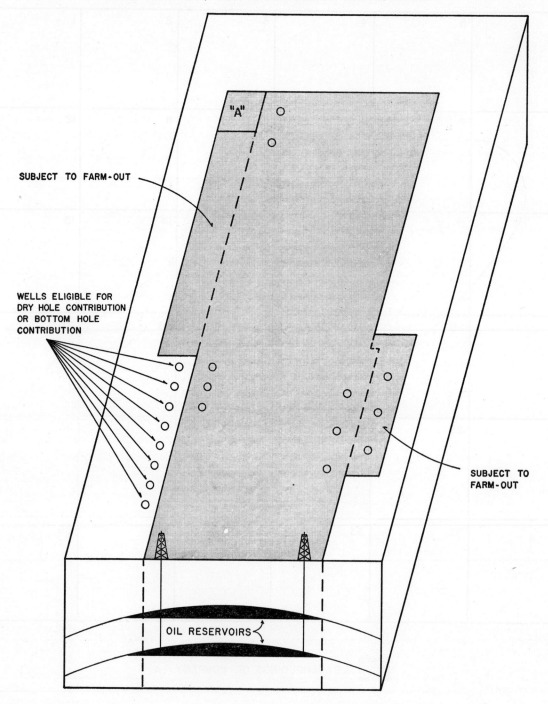

enough to justify the cost of a well. The owner of the land might, however, claim that oil was being drained from under his property by adjacent wells on the tract and that he was thereby being deprived of his rightful royalties. If the landowner were to take his case to court, he would stand a chance of forcing the large company either to drill an offset well on his property or to show good cause why such a well should not be drilled. To avoid the cost and trouble of the law suit and also the cost of the well, the large company might therefore farm-out the lease to a small producer, subject to the stipulation that a well be drilled.

The small producer sometimes took on these marginal drilling prospects in the hope of hitting permeable streaks or other irregular formations lying adjacent to the main pool but not revealed by the development drilling of the large company. Moreover, the small producers could sometimes afford to operate wells which would have been a losing proposition for the large companies because they had lower overhead and administrative costs than did the large companies. Finally, a well which promised such a low volume of production that it would hardly have been worth while to a large company was sometimes entirely satisfactory to a small producer who specialized in such operations and could give the well the individual attention that it required to maintain satisfactory operations.

Gaining Access to Specialized Geological Information: A final, but by no means the least important, reason why the large companies were interested in continually handling a fairly large volume of producing deals was to gain access to the geological ideas and information which the small producers might have. Oil finding is by no means an exact science, and successful exploratory work often depends to a considerable extent on the imagination and ingenuity of the prospector. The large number of small producers operating in the industry represents a vast pool of geological ideas, some of which are based upon very intimate studies of particular areas. By maintaining continuing contact with the small producers through the negotiation and arrangement of the producing deals, the exploratory department of a large company could often greatly increase the effec-

tiveness of its own geological work. There is an old saying in the industry that the large companies "know too much" to find oil; in other words, they have too much good scientific information why oil cannot be found in particular spots. The producing deals provide one means by which a large company could guard against "knowing too much."

In addition to the general reasons for the producing deals discussed above, there were a variety of miscellaneous cost, tax, and economic considerations which sometimes prompted the arrangements. For example, farm-outs were sometimes arranged simply because the recipient of the farm-out had a drilling rig in the vicinity and could thus afford to drill a well on a site which offered little prospect of yielding any very large volume of production. Producing deals were also sometimes arranged because the recipient was in a very high personal income tax bracket and thus in a position to risk his money on drilling prospects which were not attractive to the large companies.

Similarities and Differences in the Usage of Producing Deals:

We found it somewhat difficult to gather statistical information with regard to the number and type of producing deals employed by the seven large oil companies which we studied because the companies did not have detailed historical records of the arrangements readily available. Moreover, it proved impossible to secure comparable data in all cases because the companies kept their records of number of wells drilled on somewhat different bases.[15] The data which we were able to accumulate, however, are shown in Exhibits XIII-8 to XIII-12 and serve to establish some of the major points of similarity and difference among the

---

[15] Some of the companies kept records of "wells drilled as operator" while others kept records of "net interest wells drilled." Wells drilled as operator are all wells in which a company has a 100% interest plus all joint interest wells for which it has the responsibility for drilling operations. Net interest wells drilled are all wells in which a company has a 100% interest plus the company's net equity in all joint interest wells. Wells drilled as operator might be greater than, equal to, or less than net interest wells depending on a company's practices with regard to the operation of joint interest properties. Wells drilled as operator and net interest wells would be equal only when the proportion of a company's joint interest wells which it drilled as operator happened to be equal to its net equity in the joint interest wells.

EXHIBIT XIII-8. STANDARD OIL COMPANY (INDIANA)*

Selected Data on Producing Deals: 1942–1952

(Dollar figures in $1,000)

	1942	1943	1944	1945	1946	1947	1948	1949	1950	1951	1952
Capital expenditures for production ($1,000) †	$17,117	$47,202	$59,981	$51,420	$66,031	$85,313	$111,242	$64,231	$79,029	$119,345	$112,859
Net interest wells drilled ‡	255	242	324	341	440	762	842	479	725	829	701
Number of farm-outs	102	145	207	248	259	291	313	379	445	505	673
Dry hole contributions											
Number	34	84	122	124	112	142	131	88	144	217	258
Amount ($1,000)	$113	$362	$490	$649	$644	$1,094	$907	$737	$1,186	$1,982	$2,238
Bottom hole contributions											
Number	47	36	36	36	46	38	34	24	45	31	48
Amount ($1,000)	$433	$338	$305	$301	$663	$535	$558	$332	$655	$480	$934
Other arrangements											
Number	5	18	22	25	23	30	30	18	36	39	46
Amount ($1,000)	$29	$573	$724	$995	$1,160	$1,332	$2,903	$3,514	$2,473	$2,289	$3,569
Total dry hole, bottom hole, and other arrangements											
Number	86	138	180	185	181	210	195	130	225	287	352
Amount ($1,000)	$575	$1,273	$1,519	$1,945	$2,467	$2,961	$4,368	$4,583	$4,314	$4,751	$6,741
Number of farm-outs as percentage net interest wells drilled	40.0%	59.9%	63.9%	72.7%	58.9%	38.2%	37.2%	79.1%	61.4%	60.9%	96.0%
Number of dry hole, bottom hole, and other arrangements as percentage net interest wells drilled	33.7%	57.0%	55.6%	54.3%	41.1%	27.6%	23.2%	27.1%	31.0%	34.6%	50.2%
Total number of producing deals as percentage net interest wells drilled	73.7%	116.9%	119.5%	127.0%	100.0%	65.8%	60.4%	106.2%	92.4%	95.5%	146.2%
Amount of dry hole, bottom hole, and other contributions as percentage capital expenditures for production	3.4%	2.7%	2.5%	3.8%	3.7%	3.5%	3.9%	7.1%	5.5%	4.0%	6.0%

* Data cover Stanolind Oil and Gas Company, Pan-American Petroleum and Transport Company, and Pan-American Southern Corporation. Information for Utah Oil Refining Company not available.

† Domestic and foreign; includes dry holes costs. Foreign expenditures are not a large part of the total.

‡ Includes wells drilled by the Indiana Company alone plus company's net equity in joint interest wells.

SOURCE: Standard Oil Company (Indiana).

EXHIBIT XIII-9. THE TEXAS COMPANY*

Selected Data on Producing Deals: 1942–1951

(Dollar figures in $1,000)

	1942	1943	1944	1945	1946	1947	1948	1949	1950	1951
Capital expenditures for production ($1,000)†	$31,437	$47,916	$63,730	$55,651	$50,356	$81,437	$112,688	$92,020	$94,353	$130,980
Wells drilled as operator‡	644	677	1,114	707	454	709	857	813	974	1,108
Number of farm-outs	29	36	35	44	49	60	49	74	114	136
Dry hole contributions										
Number	10	30	52	40	32	56	88	97	136	194
Amount ($1,000)	$12	$81	$124	$128	$169	$258	$443	$648	$920	$1,249
Bottom hole contributions										
Number	1	1	4	0	2	0	2	1	9	15
Amount ($1,000)	$5	$1	$5	0	$11	0	$59	$4	$42	$70
Total dry and bottom hole contributions										
Number	11	31	56	40	34	56	90	98	145	209
Amount ($1,000)	$17	$82	$129	$128	$180	$258	$502	$652	$962	$1,319
Number of farm-outs as percentage wells drilled as operator	4.5%	5.3%	3.1%	6.2%	10.8%	8.5%	5.7%	9.1%	11.7%	12.3%
Number of dry and bottom hole contributions as percentage wells drilled as operator	1.7%	4.6%	5.0%	5.7%	7.5%	7.9%	10.5%	12.1%	14.9%	18.9%
Total number of farm-outs and dry and bottom hole contributions as percentage wells drilled as operator	6.2%	9.9%	8.1%	11.9%	18.3%	16.4%	16.2%	21.2%	26.6%	31.2%
Amount of dry and bottom hole contributions as percentage capital expenditures for production§	0.1%	0.2%	0.2%	0.2%	0.4%	0.3%	0.4%	0.7%	1.0%	1.0%

* Data not available on land purchase agreements and other arrangements.
† Foreign and domestic; includes intangible development costs.
‡ Includes wells drilled by The Texas Company alone plus all joint interest wells for which The Texas Company was the operator.
§ Understates significance of producing deals because capital expenditures figures include expenditures in foreign countries where opportunity for producing deals is not usually available.

SOURCE: The Texas Company.

EXHIBIT XIII-10. GULF OIL CORPORATION

Selected Data on Producing Deals: 1935–1952

(Dollar figures in $1,000)

	1935	1940	1946	1949	1950	1951	1952
Capital expenditures for production *	$26,116	$37,619	$60,637	$102,568	$90,465	$117,552	$139,680
Wells drilled as operator †	524	610	441	677	709	594	431
Number of farm-outs	36	64	61	116	165	155	139
Dry hole contributions							
Number	27	50	63	76	129	238	171
Amount ($1,000)	$99	$101	$315	$716	$870	$1,904	$1,647
Bottom hole contributions							
Number	56	38	21	22	20	14	7
Amount ($1,000)	$202	$174	$135	$452	$624	$235	$230
Bottom hole purchases							
Number					23	28	14
Amount ($1,000)					$415	$899	$400
Number of farm-outs as percentage wells drilled as operator	6.9%	10.5%	13.8%	17.1%	23.3%	26.1%	32.3%
Number of dry and bottom hole contributions and bottom hole purchases as percentage wells drilled as operator	15.8%	14.4%	19.0%	14.5%	24.3%	47.1%	44.5%
Total number of producing deals as percentage wells drilled as operator ‡	22.7%	24.9%	32.8%	31.6%	47.6%	73.2%	76.8%
Total amount of dry and bottom hole contributions and bottom hole purchases as percentage capital expenditures for production §	1.2%	0.7%	0.7%	1.1%	2.1%	2.6%	1.6%

Note: Blank spaces indicate data not available.
* Foreign and domestic; includes intangible development and dry hole costs.
† Includes wells drilled by Gulf alone plus all joint interest wells for which Gulf was the operating company.
‡ Does not include small number of bottom hole purchases in the years 1935–1949.
§ Does not include bottom hole purchases in the years 1935–1949. Understates significance of producing deals because capital expenditures figures include expenditures in foreign countries where opportunity for producing deals is not usually available.

SOURCE: Gulf Oil Corporation.

EXHIBIT XIII-11. THE OHIO OIL COMPANY, ATLANTIC, AND SINCLAIR

Selected Data on Producing Deals: 1935–1952

	1935	1940	1946	1947	1948	1949	1950	1951	1952
The Ohio Oil Company									
Capital expenditures for production ($1,000)*	$7,311	$6,871	$11,604	$18,169	$19,988	$20,260	$20,044	$23,196	$27,481
Wells drilled as operator**			109			181	213	326	269
Number of farm-outs			48			34	64	47	49
Number of dry hole and bottom hole contributions and other arrangements			79			48	73	92	76
Number of farm-outs as percentage wells drilled as operator			44.0%			18.8%	30.0%	14.4%	18.2%
Number of dry hole and bottom hole contributions and other arrangements as percentage wells drilled as operator			72.5%			26.5%	34.3%	28.2%	28.3%
Total number of producing deals as percentage wells drilled as operator			116.5%			45.3%	64.3%	42.6%	46.5%
The Atlantic Refining Company									
Capital expenditures for production ($1,000)*	$5,541	$6,794	$23,506	$19,841	$35,427	$30,478	$31,159	$44,680	$45,372
Net interest wells drilled†	206	169	96	89	204	192	273	270	225
Number of farm-outs	23	34	37			84			
Dry hole and other contributions									
Number			3	10	8	12	15	35	33
Amount ($1,000)			$96	$525	$359	$264	$368	$975	$957
Number of farm-outs as percentage net interest wells drilled	11.2%	20.1%	38.5%			43.7%			
Number of dry hole and other contributions as percentage net interest wells drilled			3.1%	11.2%	3.9%	6.3%	5.5%	13.0%	14.7%
Total number of producing deals as percentage net interest wells drilled			41.6%			50.0%			
Amount of dry hole and other contributions as percentage capital expenditures for production			0.4%	2.6%	1.0%	0.9%	1.2%	2.2%	2.1%
Sinclair Oil Corporation‡									
Capital expenditures for production ($1,000)*	$11,531	$15,399	$23,213	$28,238	$38,712	$36,322	$47,377	$75,624	$76,953
Wells drilled as operator**	465	309	216			303	433	759	716
Number of farm-outs	37	18	52			42	52	42	115
Dry hole contributions									
Number	54	43	75	122	130	99	110	223	251
Amount ($1,000)			$301	$488	$550	$578	$506	$1,422	$1,646
Number of bottom hole purchase agreements	13	35	42			28	3	4	2
Number of farm-outs as percentage wells drilled as operator	8.0%	5.8%	24.1%			13.9%	12.0%	5.5%	16.1%
Number of dry hole and bottom hole purchase agreements as percentage wells drilled as operator			54.2%			41.9%	26.1%	29.9%	35.3%
Total number of producing deals as percentage wells drilled as operator			78.3%			55.8%	38.1%	35.4%	51.4%
Amount of dry hole contributions as percentage capital expenditures for production§			1.3%	1.7%	1.4%	1.6%	1.1%	1.9%	2.1%

Note: Blank spaces indicate data not available.
* Domestic and foreign; includes dry hole costs. Foreign expenditures are not a large part of the total.
** Includes wells drilled by company alone plus all joint interest wells for which company was operator.
† Includes wells drilled by company alone plus company's net equity in joint interest wells.
‡ Company reports no bottom hole contributions
§ Data not available on dollar amount of bottom hole purchase agreements.
SOURCE: Company records.

EXHIBIT XIII-12. INDIANA COMPANY, SINCLAIR, AND GULF

Analysis of Producing Deals by Type of Partner: 1942–1952*

(Dollar figures in $1,000)

	Number or Amount ($1,000)											Percentage of Total										
	1942	1943	1944	1945	1946	1947	1948	1949	1950	1951	1952	1942	1943	1944	1945	1946	1947	1948	1949	1950	1951	1952
Standard Oil Company (Indiana)†																						
Number of farm-outs	102	145	207	248	259	291	313	379	445	505	673	100.0%	100.0%	100.0%	100.0%	100.0%	100.0%	100.0%	100.0%	100.0%	100.0%	100.0%
To major companies	4	14	37	32	31	24	39	30	38	37	40	3.9	9.7	17.9	12.9	12.0	8.2	12.5	7.9	8.5	7.3	5.9
To other companies	98	131	170	216	228	267	274	349	407	468	633	96.1	90.3	82.1	87.1	88.0	91.8	87.5	92.1	91.5	92.7	94.1
Number of dry hole contributions	34	84	122	124	112	142	131	88	144	217	258	100.0	100.0	100.0	100.0	100.0	100.0	100.0	100.0	100.0	100.0	100.0
To major companies	2	7	28	19	16	15	23	15	17	23	23	5.9	8.3	23.0	15.3	14.3	10.6	17.6	17.0	11.8	10.5	8.9
To other companies	32	77	94	105	96	127	108	73	127	194	235	94.1	91.7	77.0	84.7	85.7	89.4	82.4	83.0	88.2	89.5	91.1
Amount of dry hole contributions	$113	$362	$490	$649	$644	$1,094	$907	$737	$1,186	$1,982	$2,238	100.0	100.0	100.0	100.0	100.0	100.0	100.0	100.0	100.0	100.0	100.0
To major companies	12	95	149	170	170	173	235	173	156	399	176	10.6	26.2	30.4	26.2	26.4	15.8	25.9	23.5	13.1	20.1	7.8
To other companies	101	267	341	479	474	921	672	564	1,030	1,583	2,062	89.4	73.8	69.6	73.8	73.6	84.2	74.1	76.5	86.9	79.9	92.2
Number of bottom hole contributions	47	36	36	36	46	38	34	24	45	31	48	100.0	100.0	100.0	100.0	100.0	100.0	100.0	100.0	100.0	100.0	100.0
To major companies	0	0	2	0	2	1	1	1	0	0	0	0	0	5.6	0	4.3	2.6	2.9	4.2	0	0	0
To other companies	47	36	34	36	44	37	33	23	45	31	48	100.0	100.0	94.4	100.0	95.7	97.4	97.1	95.8	100.0	100.0	100.0
Amount of bottom hole contributions	$433	$338	$305	$301	$663	$535	$558	$332	$655	$480	$934	100.0	100.0	100.0	100.0	100.0	100.0	100.0	100.0	100.0	100.0	100.0
To major companies	0	0	40	0	14	18	48	4	0	0	0	0	0	13.1	0	2.1	3.4	8.6	1.2	0	0	0
To other companies	433	338	265	301	649	517	510	328	655	480	934	100.0	100.0	86.9	100.0	97.9	96.6	91.4	98.8	100.0	100.0	100.0
Number of other arrangements	5	18	22	25	23	30	30	18	36	39	46	100.0	100.0	100.0	100.0	100.0	100.0	100.0	100.0	100.0	100.0	100.0
With major companies	3	12	8	8	13	18	16	7	16	19	14	60.0	66.7	36.4	32.0	56.5	60.0	53.3	38.9	44.4	48.8	30.4
With other companies	2	6	14	17	10	12	14	11	20	20	32	40.0	33.3	63.6	68.0	43.5	40.0	46.7	61.1	55.6	51.2	69.6
Amount of other arrangements	$29	$573	$724	$995	$1,160	$1,332	$2,903	$3,514	$2,473	$2,289	$3,569	100.0	100.0	100.0	100.0	100.0	100.0	100.0	100.0	100.0	100.0	100.0
With major companies	15	347	245	318	631	1,066	1,369	1,312	1,689	1,102	1,077	51.7	60.6	33.8	32.0	54.4	80.0	47.2	37.3	68.3	48.1	30.2
With other companies	14	226	479	677	529	266	1,534	2,202	784	1,187	2,492	48.3	39.4	66.2	68.0	45.6	20.0	52.8	62.7	31.7	51.9	69.8
Sinclair Oil Corporation																						
Number of dry hole contributions					75	122	130	99	110	223	251					100.0	100.0	100.0	100.0	100.0	100.0	100.0
To major companies					12	21	23	14	14	23	29					16.0	17.2	17.7	14.1	12.7	10.3	11.6
To other companies					63	101	107	85	96	200	222					84.0	82.8	82.3	85.9	87.3	89.7	88.4
Amount of dry hole contributions					$301	$488	$550	$578	$506	$1,422	$1,646					100.0	100.0	100.0	100.0	100.0	100.0	100.0
To major companies					80	103	131	132	131	217	252					26.6	21.1	23.8	22.8	25.9	15.3	15.3
To other companies					221	385	419	446	375	1,205	1,394					73.4	78.9	76.2	77.2	74.1	84.7	84.7
Gulf Oil Corporation																						
Number of farm-outs									165	155	139									100.0	100.0	100.0
To major companies									10	14	13									6.1	9.0	9.4
To other companies									155	141	126									93.9	91.0	90.6
Number of joint interest wells					88			235	206	257	223					100.0			100.0	100.0	100.0	100.0
With major companies					43			100	89	119	117					48.9			42.6	43.2	46.3	52.5
With other companies					45			135	117	138	106					51.1			57.4	56.8	53.7	47.5
Number of dry hole contributions									129	238	171									100.0	100.0	100.0
To major companies									11	44	31									8.5	18.5	18.1
To other companies									118	194	140									91.5	81.5	81.9
Amount of dry hole contributions									$870	$1,904	$1,647									100.0	100.0	100.0
To major companies									134	566	332									15.4	29.7	20.2
To other companies									736	1,338	1,315									84.6	70.3	79.8
Number of bottom hole contributions										14	7										100.0	100.0
To major companies										1	1										7.1	14.3
To other companies										13	6										92.9	85.7
Amount of bottom hole contributions										$235	$230										100.0	100.0
To major companies										30	20										12.8	8.7
To other companies										205	210										87.2	91.3

Note: Blank spaces indicate data not available.

* For the purposes of this analysis, major companies were defined as all companies included in the *Financial Analysis of 30 Oil Companies*, published annually by the Petroleum Department of The Chase National Bank of New York.

† Data cover Stanolind Oil and Gas Company, Pan American Petroleum Transport Company, and Pan-American Southern Corporation. Information for Utah Oil Refining Company not available.

SOURCE: Company records.

programs of six of the companies. No data were available from the seventh company, the Standard Oil Company (Ohio).

The first point established by the records in Exhibits XIII-8 to XIII-12 is that the producing deals played a very important part in the programs of all six companies in the period for which data were available. The relative importance of the deals is difficult to measure on a statistical basis, but some idea as to their significance may be gained from comparisons of the number of such deals with the number of wells drilled by the companies in their own operations. In 1949, a year in which data were available from all six companies, for example, the total number of producing deals negotiated (exclusive of joint interest wells) ranged from 21.2% of wells drilled as operator in the case of The Texas Company to 106.2% of net interest wells drilled in the case of the Indiana Company.[16] These figures are minima because some of the companies did not have records of certain of their deals. The various producing deals were used more frequently in connection with exploratory wells than with development wells and were therefore of even greater relative significance in the exploratory drilling programs of the companies than is suggested by the above comparisons.

The relative importance of the producing deals may also be measured by comparing the cash value of the dry hole, bottom hole, and various other arrangements for each company with its total capital expenditures for production. The records in the exhibits indicate that the cash value of the deals ranged from less than 1% to 7.1% of the total capital expenditures of the companies for production in the years covered by our data. This comparison, however, understates the significance of the deals because the capital expenditure figures, and particularly those for Gulf and The Texas Company, included expenditures in foreign countries where opportunities to use produc-

ing deals would not normally be present. In addition, there was no way to express in dollar figures the value of the farm-outs which were used in the programs of all the companies. Finally, it must again be remembered that the deals represented a substantially higher proportion of expenditures for exploratory work than of total expenditures for production.

The second important fact established by the records in the exhibits is that the usage of producing deals by the six companies either increased or remained approximately the same in the period covered by our data. The records for The Texas Company and the Gulf Oil Corporation reveal a very clear upward trend in the number of producing deals and also in the number of producing deals as a percentage of wells drilled as operator. The records for the Indiana Company show a strong increase in the number of deals, but no particular trend in the number of deals as a percentage of net interest wells drilled. The records for the other three companies are fragmentary and contain mixed evidence, but taken as a whole permit the conclusion that producing deals probably maintained about the same relative significance in the programs of the companies in the period covered by our data.

A third point established by the records in the exhibits is that although the producing deals were important in the programs of all the companies, there were some wide variations among the companies with respect to their usage of the deals. The most striking difference appears in the relative usage of the deals by the Indiana Company and The Texas Company. In the period 1942–1952 the Indiana Company's farm-outs ranged between 37.2% and 96.0% of net interest wells drilled whereas in the period 1942–1951 The Texas Company's farm-outs ranged between 3.1% and 12.3% of wells drilled as operator. Similarly, the Indiana Company's dry hole and bottom hole contributions ranged between 19.6% and 49.6% of net interest wells drilled [17] in the period 1942–1952, whereas The Texas Company's dry hole and bottom hole contributions ranged between 1.7% and 18.9% of wells drilled as operator in the period 1942–1951.

---

[16] The ratios are not strictly comparable because The Texas Company figure is based on wells drilled as operator and the Indiana Company figure is based on net interest wells drilled (see footnote 15). Moreover, The Texas Company data did not include land purchase agreements and certain other arrangements which were included in the Indiana Company data. The two figures serve, however, to indicate the general importance of producing deals in the programs of the companies.

[17] These figures are not shown in Exhibit XIII-8 which contains the Indiana Company data but were derived therefrom.

As noted earlier, the data for the two companies are not strictly comparable because the Indiana Company records are based on net interest wells drilled and The Texas Company figures on wells drilled as operator. After making due allowance for the lack of comparability, however, the data still permit the unquestionable conclusion that the Indiana Company made far more usage of farm-outs and dry hole and bottom hole contributions in its exploratory work than did The Texas Company. A comparison of the total number of producing deals negotiated by the two companies was not possible because The Texas Company did not have a record of its land purchase agreements and miscellaneous arrangements.

Another point of difference in the programs of the six companies may be found in the relative usage made of the different types of deals. It may be noted, for example, that the Indiana Company consistently made far more use of farm-outs than it did of dry hole contributions. Sinclair, on the other hand, made far more use of dry hole contributions than it did of farm-outs. The Texas Company made slightly more use of farm-outs than dry hole contributions in the period 1942–1947, but in the period 1948–1952 reversed the relationship and made more use of dry hole contributions than farm-outs. The Gulf Oil Corporation likewise changed its relative usage of farm-outs and dry hole contributions in the years covered by our data. Gulf usually made more use of farm-outs in the years before 1951 and then reversed the relationship and made more use of dry hole contributions in 1951 and 1952.

We were able to secure an analysis of producing deals by type of partner for only three of the companies, the Indiana Company, Sinclair, and Gulf (see Exhibit XIII-12). The data indicate very clearly that the three companies negotiated the great majority of their producing deals with smaller concerns. In the period 1942–1952 the Indiana Company negotiated 82.1% to 96.1% of its farm-outs, 77.0% to 94.1% of its dry hole contributions, 94.4% to 100% of its bottom hole contributions, and 33.3% to 69.6% of its "other" arrangements with small producers. Sinclair's dry hole contributions to small firms ran between 82.3% and 89.7% of the total made by the company.

In the years for which data were available on Gulf's operations, the company negotiated over 90% of its farm-outs, over 80% of its dry hole, and over 85% of its bottom hole arrangements with small producers. Moreover, approximately half of the company's joint interests wells were ventures with small producers.

In the case of all three companies, the dry hole, bottom hole, and other cash contributions to major companies were usually proportionately larger than the number of deals arranged with such companies. In other words, the average dollar value of the deals arranged with major companies was greater than the average dollar value of the deals with small producers. This circumstance undoubtedly reflects the fact that the large companies were generally able to finance and were frequently engaged in more costly drilling propositions than were the small producers.

Although The Texas Company, The Ohio Company, and The Atlantic Refining Company were not able to furnish us with an analysis of their producing deals by type of partner, the executives of the companies stated that the great majority of their deals, exclusive of joint interest wells, were with small rather than large concerns. All the companies drilled joint interest wells with both large and small companies, and the number drilled with each group tended to vary depending upon the lease holdings in the areas in which the companies were operating.

There was no reason why the six companies could not have entered into farm-out, dry hole, bottom hole, and other arrangements with other major companies just as well as with small producers and, as indicated by Exhibit XIII-12, they occasionally did. As suggested by the discussion earlier in the chapter, however, the character of these deals is often such that they are uniquely suited to the operations of a small firm specializing in them. The small firm, for example, can often function very effectively as a "go-between" in arranging the participation of several large companies in a test well. The farm-out arrangement, in particular, is handled almost exclusively by small firms. The large companies have a high regard for each other's geological information and are much more inclined to grant farm-outs to small operators than they are to large competitors.

Moreover, it is somewhat less embarrassing for the management of a large company to have oil discovered on a farm-out to a small producer than it is to have oil discovered on a farm-out to a major competitor.

All the foregoing discussion has related to granting of farm-outs and cash contributions by the six companies to other firms and to the participation of the six companies as buyers in land purchase agreements and other arrangements. It should not be inferred, however, that the producing deals were exclusively unidirectional arrangements. Occasionally the six companies *received* farm-outs or cash contributions from both large and small companies and sometimes were on the selling rather than the buying side of land purchase agreements and other arrangements.

III. THE USE OF CONTRACT VERSUS COMPANY DRILLING RIGS

We found that the seven companies studied had a definite policy of using contract rather than company rigs for the great majority of their drilling operations. Some of the companies had never operated any appreciable number of company rigs; others had made considerable use of company rigs at one time or another in their histories but had greatly reduced the number thereof sometime prior to 1952. It appears therefore that the drilling of oil wells represents a point in the oil industry where the integration process has come to a halt or has gone forward and later been set in reverse and a phase of the oil business in which experience seems to have proven that the small, nonintegrated firm can operate more effectively than the large integrated one. As was noted in Chapter Two, at the close of 1950 only about 7.7% of the drilling rigs in the oil industry were owned by integrated refining companies.[18]

The records of the number of wells drilled by company as compared with contract rigs for six of the seven companies are shown in Exhibit XIII-13. In 1935 Gulf drilled 395 wells with company rigs and 129 with contract rigs;

in the following years, however, the company steadily decreased its use of company rigs until in 1952 it drilled only 33 wells with such rigs as contrasted with 398 wells drilled by contract rigs. Sinclair drilled 35 wells with company and 430 wells with contract rigs in 1935, but later completely abandoned the company rigs and drilled all its wells in 1940, 1946, and 1949–1952 with contract rigs. Atlantic apparently never used any company rigs or at least not after 1935. In the period 1938–1952 the Indiana Company decreased the number of its wells drilled by company rigs from 90 to 31 and increased the number of its wells drilled by contract rigs from 491 to 670. The Texas Company in the period 1942–1951 held the number of its wells drilled by company rigs fairly constant but almost doubled the number of its wells drilled by contract rigs.[19]

In the period 1949–1952 The Ohio Oil Company drilled more wells with company than it did with contract rigs. Ordinarily, however, it was the company's practice to drill the majority of its wells with contract rigs. The preponderance of wells drilled with company rigs in the years 1949–1952 resulted from the fact that the company happened to have a large number of very shallow wells to drill in the Toborg area in Texas and elected to do the job with company tools. In 1951 and 1952 the company also made extensive use of company rigs in the Julesburg Basin of Western Nebraska.

The executives of the six companies were almost unanimous in the reasons they gave for doing most of their drilling with contract rather than company rigs. The first and most important consideration mentioned was the problem of moving rigs. The drilling operations of the six companies extended over a wide geographic area, and the use of company rigs would have required the continual shifting of crews and equipment from one location to another. Such shifts involved high transportation costs and frequently created labor problems. Drilling contractors were able to keep both the moving costs and the labor problems to a minimum by having individual rigs do work for a number of companies in the same general area. Many of the drilling contractors,

---

[18] As indicated in Chapter Two, the 7.7% is a minimum because certain of the companies that did not reply to our survey may have been integrated refining companies owning drilling rigs.

[19] The data for the several companies are not strictly comparable because of the different bases upon which the records of wells were kept. See footnotes to Exhibit XIII-13.

EXHIBIT XIII-13. SIX OIL COMPANIES

Wells Drilled by Company and Contract Drilling Rigs: 1935–1952

Year	Gulf Oil Corporation* Company Rigs Rotary	Cable	Total	Contract Rigs Rotary	Cable	Total	Sinclair Oil Corporation* Company Rigs	Contract Rigs	The Atlantic Refining Company† Company Rigs	Contract Rigs	The Ohio Oil Company* Company Rigs‡	Contract Rigs	Standard Oil Company (Indiana)† Company Rigs	Contract Rigs	The Texas Company* Company Rigs	Contract Rigs
1935	286	109	395	108	21	129	35	430	0	206						
1936									0	190						
1937									0	329						
1938									0	225			90	491		
1939									0	108			105	448		
1940	143	98	241	349	20	369	0	309	0	169			68	363		
1941									0	155			60	458		
1942									0	80			33	222	130	514
1943									0	61			17	225	110	567
1944									0	115			20	304	133	981
1945									0	101			32	309	104	603
1946	24	37	61	352	28	380	0	216	0	96	28	81	32	408	106	348
1947									0	89			36	726	127	582
1948									0	204			32	810	128	729
1949	40	31	71	507	99	606	0	303	0	192	97	84	40	439	139	674
1950	44	25	69	567	73	640	0	433	0	273	132	81	40	685	143	831
1951	39	21	60	476	58	534	0	759	0	270	241	85	43	786	128	980
1952	16	17	33	382	16	398	0	716	0	225	179	90	31	670		

Note: Blank spaces indicate data not available.
* Includes wells drilled by company alone plus all joint interest wells for which company was the operator.
† Includes wells drilled by company alone plus company's net equity in joint interest wells.
‡ Large number of wells drilled by company rigs 1949–1952 reflects special situations in Toborg area in Texas and Julesburg Basin of western Nebraska.

SOURCE: Company records.

EXHIBIT XIII-14. HELMERICH AND PAYNE, INC.

Rig Moving Costs for a Typical Group of Wells: 1950

Well Name	Rig Number	Rig Move	Move Distance	Rig Days	Well Depth	Moving Cost	Total Drilling Cost	Moving Cost as Percentage Total Drilling Cost
McLaughlin #27	8	Oklahoma to Scurry County, Texas	350 Miles	35	6,820 ft.	$7,498	$ 37,785	18.8%
McLaughlin #40		Location Move to Scurry County		38	6,852	923	30,721	3.0
Strom #6		" " "		33	6,806	1,487	30,373	4.9
Onlenbusch #4		" " "		33	6,820	1,138	29,791	3.8
Onlenbusch #5		" " "		31	6,817	889	27,665	3.2
Onlenbusch #8		" " "		32	6,799	751	28,436	2.6
Strom #13		" " "		32	6,909	959	31,333	3.1
Strom #19		" " "		32	6,915	793	28,551	2.8
Strom #24		" " "		37	6,876	533	33,006	1.6
Gertie #4	24	" " "		36	6,760	1,284	31,763	4.0
Jack #6		" " "		34	6,775	1,490	29,531	5.1
McLaughlin #34		" " "		45	6,849	1,159	39,568	2.9
Jack #8		" " "		37	6,825	1,341	33,704	4.0
McLaughlin #47		" " "		90	6,863	3,342	73,662	4.5
McLaughlin #46		" " "		35	6,889	1,327	33,600	4.0
Strom #14		" " "		36	6,875	1,036	31,469	3.3
Strom #21		" " "		35	6,902	1,062	32,614	3.3
McLaughlin #28	26	Oklahoma to Scurry County, Texas	350 Miles	51	6,866	4,028	43,819	9.2
McLaughlin #41		Location Move to Scurry County		41	6,852	2,139	35,786	6.0
Strom #5		" " "		38	6,815	2,024	32,792	6.2
Holt A–1		Scurry County to Eaton County	120 Miles	34	5,195	3,538	28,104	12.6
Holt A–2		Location Move to Scurry County		35	5,197	1,232	25,628	4.8
Haines #3		Eaton County to Scurry County	120 Miles	47	6,841	3,817	39,845	9.6
McLaughlin #29	36	Kansas to Oklahoma to Texas, Scurry County	350 Miles	38	6,878	1,345	39,028	3.5
McLaughlin #42		Location Move to Scurry County		58	6,862	3,244	52,474	6.2
Holt #1		" " "		46	6,839	2,722	41,637	6.4
Holt #4		" " "		44	6,845	903	34,659	2.6
Stewart #3		" " "		35	6,887	1,727	34,502	5.0
Lemons #1		" " "		39	6,859	2,162	36,639	5.9
University "AH" #2	9	Upton County, Texas to Crane County, Texas	125 Miles	134	9,215	6,053	133,826	4.5
L. Hutto #1	25	Upton County to Howard County, Texas	125 Miles	126	9,347	6,607	125,300	5.3
University "BL" #1		Howard County to Reagan County, Texas	150 Miles	76	8,940	7,777	87,130	8.9
T. A. Loc. #1	32	Odessa Yard to Dawson County, Texas	90 Miles	77	10,005	7,472	115,764	6.5

SOURCE: Helmerich and Payne, Inc.

in fact, were local firms which confined their operations to a radius of a few hundred miles.

Moving costs were a very significant item in drilling operations. To transport a rig and supplies from one location to another often required more than 25 large transport trucks. The major items transported were drill pipe, sheds and warehouses, and the rig itself. The drill pipe was extremely heavy, and state highway regulations with regard to maximum axle loads sometimes made it impossible to move more than 20 or 30 pieces of pipe on one truck. In some states overload permits could be secured but the cost thereof frequently ran as high as $800 or $900 for a single moving job.

The moving costs incurred by one drilling contractor in connection with his drilling operations in the West Texas area for the year ending September 30, 1950, are shown in Exhibit XIII-14. As may be seen from the exhibit, short moves from one location to another in the same area frequently cost as much as $1,000 to $3,000 and amounted to from about 2% to 5% of the total well costs. Longer moves sometimes cost as much as $6,000 to $8,000 and in one case amounted to 18.8% of the total well cost.

A second reason which the executives of the companies gave for the use of contract drilling rigs was the frequent fluctuations which occurred in their drilling requirements. The amount of drilling a company found it necessary to do varied considerably from time to time depending on current discoveries and the company's situation with respect to lease expiration dates. The use of contract rigs made it easy for a company to expand and contract its drilling activities in accordance with its needs, whereas the use of company rigs presented the problem of carrying idle equipment and idle drilling crews through slack periods.

A third important reason for the use of contract rigs was the high cost and specialized nature of both rigs and equipment. The large producing companies operated over a wide area and encountered a variety of geological conditions. As a result, they required a variety of different kinds of drilling rigs, different sizes of drill pipe, and different types of tools and well equipment. The investment necessary to maintain an inventory with a full range of rigs, pipes, and equipment was large. Moreover, it was more difficult for a single company to keep costly, specialized rigs and tools busy on a full-time basis than it was for a drilling contractor who was in a position to secure work from a number of different producing firms.

The executives of the six companies also stated that the contract drilling firms were frequently able to operate at lower costs than could a large company. Some contract drillers secured lower costs because they used cheaper or less equipment, allowed smaller safety margins, spent less for maintenance, and had less expensive employee benefit plans than did the large companies. In addition, contract drillers were sometimes able to do a more effective job in supervising rig crews than could a large company. Drilling contracts were usually let on a fixed price per foot basis, and consequently the small contractors, and often their tool pushers, had a personal financial interest in the progress of each well. As a result, they sometimes spent 18 hours a day on the job and drove their crews harder than could the supervisors of a large oil company. The tool pushers of some drilling contractors even made it a practice to maintain their living quarters at the drilling sites. The cost of maintaining a rig on location usually amounted to $700 to $1,000 a day, and the speed of drilling operations was therefore of critical importance.

A final circumstance which contributed to the tendency of the large companies to use contract drilling rigs was the highly competitive situation which had existed for some years in the contract drilling industry. Drillers and tool pushers with a good reputation for rapid drilling could secure a $100,000 rig, satisfactory for shallow drilling, from mill supply houses on credit with a down payment of about $10,000 and go into business for themselves. As a result, a large number of one-rig firms had crowded into the industry. Many of these firms did not have an adequate understanding of overhead and depreciation costs and tended to set their bid prices solely on the basis of out-of-pocket costs for such things as labor, bits, supplies, and rig transportation. A 10,000-foot well requiring 50 to 60 days drilling time, for example, might involve a total cost of $12.00 per foot and a reasonable bid to cover total costs and profit might be $13.00 per foot. The out-of-pocket costs on such a project, however, might be only about $8.50 per foot, and a small firm hard pressed for cash might bid $11.00 per foot. Eventually, of course, such firms were forced out of business, but their rigs were then merely repossessed by the rig supply houses and resold to other newcomers. The constantly revolving population of small, marginal operators in the industry tended to keep bid prices low, and the large companies were thus generally assured of getting contract drilling work done on favorable terms.

Although it was their policy to use contract rigs for most of their drilling work, the large companies did follow the practice of using company rigs for certain special types of situations. Company rigs were used for drilling operations in foreign countries where contract crews were not readily available, for trying out experimental drilling equipment, and for drilling "tight holes," i.e., holes where the driller was anxious that no geological information should leak out before the well was completed. Company rigs were also frequently used for off-shore drilling or for drilling in areas where geological knowledge of the substructure was scanty and unexpected rock formations might be encountered. In such cases, the drilling contractors were of necessity forced to include high safety factors in their bid prices, and by using its own rigs a company could at least be assured of getting the jobs done at cost. The companies likewise occasionally used their own rigs where they had a large amount of drilling work to do in one spot and could keep one or more rigs busy for a fairly long period of time. As noted above, for example, The Ohio Oil Company used its own rigs to drill a large number of shallow wells in the Toborg area in Texas in the years 1949–1952. Finally, some of the companies made it a practice to keep one or two drilling rigs in operation simply as a means of maintaining a constant check on the bid prices of the drilling contractors.

IV. SUMMARY

1. At several points in their histories, the seven large companies which we studied made fundamental changes in their ratios of crude oil production to refinery runs. In some cases the companies did about the same thing at about the same time for about the same reasons. More frequently, however, they either moved in different directions at the same time or moved in the same direction but for very different reasons. The dissimilarities in the timing, direction, and reasons for the changes the companies made in their crude oil ratios reflected differences in operating situations, differences in management interpretations of economic developments in the oil industry, good fortune in the discovery of major oil fields, and many other things.

2. The six companies which were net buyers of crude oil in the United States were all interested in raising their ratios of crude oil production to refinery runs. The executives of these companies were generally in accord that it was important for a large refiner to produce at least about 50% of his crude oil requirements, very desirable for him to produce as much as 75% or 80%, and certainly to his advantage to produce larger amounts if he could do so at a reasonable cost. None of the companies anticipated, however, that it would be able in the foreseeable future to close the gap between its domestic production plus imports of its own foreign production and its domestic refinery runs. Each of the companies anticipated that its refining and marketing operations would continue to grow in pace with the industry, and none of them was sufficiently interested in altering its crude oil ratio to deliberately curtail the intensity of its competitive effort in the wholesale and retail markets.

3. The Ohio Oil Company's position and objectives with regard to its crude oil ratio were quite different from those of the other six companies. In 1952 the company had a crude oil ratio of 244.8%, and the executives anticipated that the ratio would remain somewhere between 200% and 400% for an indefinite period into the future. The executives anticipated that the company would spend enough on refining and marketing to expand those activities at the normal rate of growth for the industry and that the exact relationship maintained between crude oil production and refinery runs would then rest largely on the success of the company's oil finding efforts.

4. The seven companies made extensive use of various producing deals, including farmouts, acreage contributions, dry hole contributions, bottom hole contributions, and bottom hole purchase agreements as a regular part of their exploratory programs. The large companies used the deals to extend their exploratory efforts over a broader area than they could cover with their own resources, to meet drilling needs and obligations when they were short of capital funds, to evaluate acreage which was highly speculative, to evaluate acreage among diversified lease holdings, to get wells drilled on marginal properties, and to gain access to specialized geological information. While the general policies of the seven companies with respect to the producing deals were found to be basically the same, there were many differences among the companies with respect to the relative emphasis placed on the different types of deals and with respect to the relative significance of the deals in their over-all exploratory programs.

5. The large companies negotiated their producing deals primarily, but not exclusively, with small producers. The producing deals characteristically involved functions and risks which were uniquely suited to the

small operator and often represented activities which the large companies preferred not to handle because (a) they had other uses and needs for their funds, or (b) they had found from experience that the work could be accomplished most easily and effectively through the deals with small operators. The records and present policies of the seven companies suggest that the producing deals may constitute a continuing and perhaps increasing field of opportunity for small business.

6. It was the policy of the seven companies to drill the majority of their wells with contract rather than company rigs. Some of the companies had never operated any appreciable number of company rigs. Others had experimented with backward integration into drilling operations but had later decided to restrict the use of company rigs to very special situations. The executives of the seven companies reported that they could usually get much of their drilling work done more economically on a contract basis because of the cost of moving company rigs from one location to another, the fluctuating nature of their drilling requirements, and the variety of specialized equipment necessary to meet their needs. It was also recognized that drilling contractors could often operate with lower costs than large companies and that competitive conditions in the contract drilling business were such as to keep bid prices at very reasonable levels.

7. As in the case of the producing deals, the records and policies of the seven companies suggest that contract drilling may constitute a continuing and perhaps increasing field of opportunity for small business. Somewhat in contrast to the producing deals, however, it appears that the small business opportunity in the drilling field rests not on the performance of specialized functions or the assumption of specialized risks but rather on the fact that the independent drilling contractor is often in a position to meet the requirements of drilling situations and to do the drilling job more economically than can a large, integrated company.

CHAPTER FOURTEEN

Analysis of Integration Patterns: Transportation, Refining, and Marketing Activities

THE PURPOSE of this chapter is to continue the analysis of the integration patterns of the seven oil companies that was begun in Chapter Thirteen. The discussion will be confined to two topics: (a) the balance maintained between transportation and refining activities, and (b) the balance maintained between refining and marketing activities as revealed by the magnitude of a company's product purchases and product exchanges. As in Chapter Thirteen, the primary objective of the discussion will be to explore the differences and similarities in the integration arrangements of the seven companies, the reasons for the changes which the companies made from time to time in their structures, and the future intentions of the companies with respect to vertical integration.

I. TRANSPORTATION ACTIVITIES

We found that the seven oil companies were engaged in a large number of different kinds of transportation activities, including the gathering of crude oil by pipe line; the transportation of crude oil from the producing fields to refineries by pipe line, tanker, barge, and truck; the transportation of products from refineries to terminals and bulk plants by pipe line, tanker, barge, and truck; the transportation of products from terminals and bulk plants to service stations, farms, homes, and industrial plants by truck; and the ownership or leasing of tank cars for the movement of both crude oil and refined products. In addition to these activities, which were all directly connected with the movement of crude oil and refined products, the companies were also engaged in many secondary transportation activities, such as the operation of airplanes for the patrolling of pipe lines, the transportation of executive personnel, and the conduct of certain types of exploratory work; the operation of motor launches to carry crews to and from off-shore drilling platforms; and the operation of specialized trucks for the transportation of geophysical and seismic crews and equipment.

With respect to each of these activities the seven companies were continually making integration decisions; that is, decisions as to whether they would do the jobs themselves or rely upon outside concerns. It was, however, impossible for us to examine the practices and policies of the seven companies with respect to all these many and diverse activities, and of necessity therefore we limited our study to crude oil gathering, crude oil trunk line, and products pipe line operations.

Crude Oil Gathering Lines:

The seven oil companies were all heavily engaged in the ownership and operation of crude oil gathering lines. In general, we found that there were at least three reasons why the seven companies had found it desirable to integrate into crude oil gathering operations. In the first place, as noted in Chapter Seven, some of the companies began the construction and operation of gathering lines during the 1920's and 1930's as a means of reducing the high gathering charges which were sometimes exacted by outside carriers. The executives of the seven companies reported, however, that from about 1940 onward competitive conditions had kept gathering charges at a low level and that the profits their companies or other companies had been able to earn on the gathering function alone were of negligible significance. We were told therefore that as of 1952 few, if any, gathering systems were being built primarily as a source of profits or as a means of reducing the cost of the gathering service.

A second and far more important reason for the construction of gathering lines was to gain access to a supply of crude oil. As was noted in earlier chapters, crude oil producers are not unlike sellers of all products the world around; they want a continuing and assured outlet for their product and are inclined to place their confidence in the buyer who has made a financial commitment of his own in the producing area through the building of a pipe line gathering system. Moreover, once lines have been laid into a producer's well by a gathering company, the producer is not likely to transfer his business to some other buyer unless he is offered a considerable price differential or other considerations of importance. As a result, a company has a far stronger buying position and a far more assured source of supply if it builds crude oil gathering lines to the producer's wells than if it merely buys crude oil from other carriers in large quantities at pipe line terminals. The ownership of crude oil gathering lines has long been regarded therefore as the next best thing to the ownership of crude oil production as a means of assuring a source of supply for refinery operations. As was noted in Chapter Two, many small refiners who are not in a position to make the financial commitments necessary to engage in crude oil producing operations have attempted to assure their sources of supply through the construction of gathering lines.

A third general reason why the seven companies were interested in the construction of crude oil gathering lines was simply one of expediency; they frequently had found it necessary to build the lines as a means of getting their crude oil production to their own refineries or to crude oil trunk line terminals for sale to other concerns. As was noted above, crude oil gathering charges had been worked down to fairly low levels, and there was no particularly strong motivation for any company to build a gathering system simply for the purpose of earning a profit on the gathering function. Ordinarily, the question of who built the gathering systems in a producing field was determined largely by how the crude oil production was distributed. If a fairly large num-

ber of the producing leaseholds were in the hands of nonintegrated producers, almost any refiner anxious to gain crude oil might build a gathering system, regardless of whether he had much production of his own in the field. Under such circumstances, the refiner would be able to count on the output of the nonintegrated producers to provide the throughput necessary to pay out the investment in the line and would also regard the preferred position he gained as a buyer of their output as worth his trouble in building the line.

On the other hand, if the producing leaseholds were largely in the hands of producers who were also refiners, there was little likelihood that the gathering systems would be built by refiners not holding production in the field. Under such circumstances, the builder might arrange to buy the output of the refiner-producers in the field but he would also be fairly well assured that they would cease to sell to him, or sell only subject to trading arrangements, whenever crude oil was in tight supply and they needed the production of the field for their own refining operations. Moreover, the builder would always be exposed to the hazard that the refiner-producers would build their own gathering systems and leave him without a throughput for his line. Consequently, a refiner had little to gain and much to risk by building gathering systems in fields where the production was largely in the hands of the producing departments of other refiners. By default therefore the large producer-refiners in a field were sometimes in a position where they had little alternative other than to build their own gathering systems, even though they might have no urgent immediate need for the output of the field in their own refining operations.

The extent of each company's commitment in gathering activities is indicated by Exhibit XIV-1 which shows three relationships: (a) the ratio of domestic crude oil production plus imports of a company's own foreign production to domestic refinery runs,[1] (b) the ratio of domestic crude oil gathered plus imports of a company's own foreign production to domestic refinery runs, and (c) the ratio of domestic crude oil gathered to domestic crude oil production. Imports of a company's own for-

---

[1] As in Chapter Thirteen, this ratio will sometimes be referred to as the "crude oil ratio."

eign production were included in the first two ratios to make the data comparable with that used throughout Chapters Twelve and Thirteen. In all cases, however, the imports were very small relative to a company's producing or gathering activities, and we shall not therefore consider them further in the discussion.

The first fact which is apparent from the data in Exhibit XIV-1 is that the companies which were short of crude oil for their domestic refinery operations characteristically gathered a great deal more crude oil than they produced,[2] with the possible exception of The Texas Company for which very limited data were available. Gulf's ratio of crude oil gathered to domestic crude oil production ranged between 135.5% and 171.6% in the period 1939–1952; Sinclair's ratio ranged between 188.2% and 253.2% in the period 1935–1952; Atlantic's ratio ranged between 104.2% and 275.4% in the period 1935–1952; and the Indiana Company's ratio ranged between 130.6% and 338.2% in the period 1930–1952. Sohio had extensive gathering activities long before it had any significant amount of crude oil production and never had a ratio of crude oil gathered to crude oil produced of less than 243.8%.

A second fact apparent from Exhibit XIV-1 is that the six companies which were net buyers of crude oil in the United States maintained relatively high ratios of crude oil gathered plus imports[3] to domestic refinery runs. In other words, the companies guarded against interruptions in their crude oil supplies by building gathering lines and buying at the well-head a large part of their crude oil deficiencies, or in some cases substantially more than their deficiencies. At no time in the years covered by our data did Gulf, The Texas Company, Sinclair, or Sohio have ratios of crude oil gathered plus imports to domestic refinery runs of less than 60%, and characteristically the ratios were

much higher than 60%. The Indiana Company had a ratio of crude oil gathered plus imports to domestic refinery runs of 46.5% in 1939, but thereafter the ratio increased rapidly and did not fall below 86% at any time after 1942. Atlantic had somewhat lower ratios of crude oil gathered plus imports to domestic refinery runs than did the other companies, a circumstance which can probably be explained by the fact that the company had a relatively high proportion of its refinery capacity at Philadelphia and purchased a substantial part of its crude oil abroad. Crude oil purchased abroad would not normally be susceptible to purchase at the well-head.

A third fact evident from the data in Exhibit XIV-1 is that the companies with low crude oil producing ratios typically had higher ratios of crude oil gathered to crude oil produced than did the companies with high crude oil producing ratios. This circumstance follows somewhat as a corollary of the fact noted above that the companies which were net buyers of crude oil tended to buy a large part of their deficiencies, or sometimes more than their deficiencies, at the well-head as a means of assuring their sources of supply. Naturally therefore the companies with low crude oil producing ratios had higher ratios of crude oil gathered to crude oil produced than did the companies with high crude oil producing ratios.

It may be observed from Exhibit XIV-1, for example, that Sinclair, the Indiana Company, and Sohio, all companies with low crude oil ratios, had substantially higher ratios of crude oil gathered to crude oil produced as a general rule than did Gulf and The Texas Company, two concerns with fairly high crude oil ratios. Atlantic was somewhat of an exception to the general pattern; although the company had a low crude oil ratio, its ratio of crude oil gathered to crude oil produced was not much higher than that of Gulf or The Texas Company. The explanation probably lies in the fact noted above that Atlantic drew a large part of the crude oil for its largest refinery from foreign sources.

It may also be noted from Exhibit XIV-1 that The Ohio Oil Company usually had lower ratios of crude oil gathered to crude oil produced than did the other companies (with the possible exception of The Texas Company for

---

[2] It does not follow that the companies gathered all their *own* production. A company might, for example, gather crude oil equal to 120% of its production and yet have a large share of the output of its own wells gathered by other companies.

[3] In the following discussion it will be understood that "imports" mean imports of a company's own foreign production. In the interests of consistency, we shall refer to "crude oil gathered plus imports" in the case of all companies, although some of the companies had no imports of their own foreign production. See Appendix, Tables 2–8.

EXHIBIT XIV-1. SEVEN OIL COMPANIES

Relationship Among Crude Oil Produced, Crude Oil Gathered, and Domestic Refinery Runs: 1924–1952

Year	Gulf Oil Corporation			The Texas Company			Sinclair Oil Corporation			The Ohio Oil Company		
	Domestic Production Plus Imports* as % Domestic Refinery Runs	Crude Oil Gathered Plus Imports* as % Domestic Refinery Runs	Crude Oil Gathered as % Domestic Production	Domestic Production Plus Imports* as % Domestic Refinery Runs	Crude Oil Gathered Plus Imports* as % Domestic Refinery Runs	Crude Oil Gathered as % Domestic Production	Domestic Production Plus Imports* as % Domestic Refinery Runs	Crude Oil Gathered Plus Imports* as % Domestic Refinery Runs	Crude Oil Gathered as % Domestic Production	Domestic Production Plus Imports* as % Domestic Refinery Runs	Crude Oil Gathered Plus Imports* as % Domestic Refinery Runs	Crude Oil Gathered as % Domestic Production
1924	111.0%			43.9%			60.6%					134.0%
1925	96.1			52.9			41.4			6009.0%	8053.6%	135.3
1926	89.9			49.5			47.9			2994.9	4052.8	173.0
1927	98.5			58.1			53.8			2542.5	4398.0	182.0
1928	102.7			69.1			43.0			788.0	1434.2	186.6
1929	107.1			74.8			47.8			686.3	1280.3	176.5
1930	94.0			63.0			40.8			768.7	1356.4	144.7
1931	80.3			49.3			41.4			584.8	846.3	118.6
1932	89.2			47.0			62.5			339.2	402.5	129.8
1933	88.2			47.1			58.3			400.8	520.3	123.3
1934	81.9			43.7			55.2			411.4	507.2	124.1
1935	78.6			49.4			47.7	89.7%	188.2%	372.0	461.8	131.4
1936	75.6			49.7			43.9	91.9	209.4	336.4	442.0	122.4
1937	72.8			51.4			44.4	93.8	211.2	307.1	375.9	123.0
1938	76.7			50.8			37.3	78.7	210.8	365.5	449.6	131.2
1939	65.3	94.3%	157.4%	63.1			33.1	78.5	237.3	313.2	411.0	106.5
1940	68.0	96.5	156.1	83.3			35.4	80.1	226.0	326.2	347.3	97.8
1941	67.9	92.4	151.8	64.0			36.4	75.3	207.2	324.0	316.9	94.7
1942	61.5	100.7	169.2	66.4			36.6	79.7	217.7	378.4	358.2	90.1
1943	65.3	110.7	171.6	67.0			38.0	88.0	248.2	474.0	427.1	95.8
1944	74.8	118.9	166.5	66.7			39.8	83.8	253.2	465.1	445.6	94.5
1945	83.8	108.8	136.0	69.7			39.5	81.9	248.2	472.7	446.8	96.3
1946	79.2	106.3	145.1	65.7			39.7	80.6	240.8	468.8	451.6	106.9
1947	77.1	101.3	141.4	66.7			40.5	86.4	242.9	416.7	445.5	110.3
1948	80.6	104.4	138.8	68.5			40.4	97.0	233.8	381.3	420.8	115.0
1949	76.1	94.5	135.5	64.4			36.4	78.0	230.5	377.5	434.0	126.4
1950	69.3	91.1	147.6	74.0†	73.4%	114.8%	29.2	63.4	224.6	263.3	332.9	123.0
1951	69.2	99.5	160.2	65.2	79.7	108.2	28.9	60.7	210.0	231.4	284.7	131.6
1952	71.3	104.1	166.5		66.6	102.2	30.4	61.6	202.7	244.8	334.4	136.0

EXHIBIT XIV-1 (CONTINUED)

Year	The Atlantic Refining Company			Standard Oil Company (Indiana)			Standard Oil Company (Ohio)		
	Domestic Production Plus Imports* as % Domestic Refinery Runs	Crude Oil Gathered Plus Imports* as % Domestic Refinery Runs	Crude Oil Gathered as % Domestic Production	Domestic Production Plus Imports* as % Domestic Refinery Runs	Crude Oil Gathered Plus Imports* as % Domestic Refinery Runs	Crude Oil Gathered as % Domestic Production	Domestic Production Plus Imports* as % Domestic Refinery Runs	Crude Oil Gathered Plus Imports* as % Domestic Refinery Runs	Crude Oil Gathered as % Domestic Production
1924	14.6%								
1925	8.8								
1926	9.9								
1927	25.3								
1928	34.6								
1929	19.1								
1930	12.7			34.0%	80.6%	316.3%			
1931	9.4			27.7	73.8	313.0			
1932	16.8			27.5	72.5	299.7			
1933	28.2			22.5	76.2	338.2			
1934	32.6			25.1	56.2	224.2			
1935	30.6	82.8%	271.2%	29.2	56.4	192.9			
1936	29.6	81.5	275.4	35.8	63.6	177.8			
1937	35.2	90.5	257.3	38.6	62.3	161.5	0.8%		
1938	35.3	77.9	220.4	36.6	47.8	130.6	1.1		
1939	35.0	73.7	210.4	33.4	46.5	139.0	1.6		
1940	35.7	75.2	210.7	31.8	48.9	153.7	1.0		
1941	36.5	61.7	168.9	35.6	68.8	193.3	0.7		
1942	57.0	73.9	129.9	40.2	88.0	219.0	2.8	153.3%	5572.0%
1943	51.6	72.1	139.8	48.7	92.9	190.7	8.0	115.5	1445.7
1944	60.6	81.8	135.0	56.5	96.8	171.3	13.8	117.0	845.7
1945	57.5	73.7	128.2	58.4	86.3	147.9	27.9	144.4	518.2
1946	52.8	69.2	131.2	53.2	91.4	171.9	29.4	131.8	448.4
1947	48.3	60.7	125.5	53.6	97.6	182.0	28.3	111.6	394.8
1948	52.0	57.6	111.0	53.2	98.7	185.6	38.8†	121.9	314.4
1949	49.2	51.1	104.2	46.1	92.0	199.4	34.9	102.5	293.6
1950	52.0	55.4	107.7	44.4	90.3	203.6	28.1	78.2	278.2
1951	56.1	63.1	125.8	48.2	102.1	211.9	26.9	71.2	264.3
1952	57.5	66.6	127.5	49.6	110.7	223.2	28.6	69.8	243.8

Note: Blank spaces indicate data not available.

* Imports of company's own foreign production. In the interests of consistency, the same column headings were used for all companies, although some of the companies had no imports of their own foreign production. See Appendix, Tables 2–8.

† Operations influenced by a refinery strike.

SOURCE: Company records.

which only limited data were available). Moreover, The Ohio Oil Company was the only company ever to gather an amount of crude oil equal to less than 100% of its own production. The unique position of the company in these respects can be explained by the fact that it always had far more of its own crude oil production than it needed for its refinery requirements and, as a result, had no particular motivation to gather much beyond its own production plus whatever other production might be readily accessible to its lines. The question might be raised as to why The Ohio Oil Company did not leave the gathering function to the buyers of its oil. The answer appears to lie in the fact that The Ohio Oil Company was one of the few in the industry which had found it worth while to engage in crude oil gathering and trunk line operations solely for the profits to be made therefrom and had over the years built up a substantial business in the tranportation of crude oil for other concerns. The company's sales of crude oil, however, were always made at the wells and before the oil crossed interstate lines.

So far as we could determine, the seven companies made no major changes in their policies and practices with respect to crude oil gathering activities in the years covered by our data. In general, the six companies which were net buyers of crude oil in the United States sought to develop or maintain sufficient gathering lines so that their crude oil gathered (plus imports) would be a high proportion, or perhaps somewhat in excess, of their domestic refinery runs. In these companies therefore the ratio of crude oil gathered to crude oil produced usually tended to decline as a company increased its crude oil producing ratio (see particularly the records of Atlantic, the Indiana Company, and Sohio). The Ohio Oil Company apparently sought to maintain gathering operations about equal to or somewhat in excess of its own crude oil producing activities. As a result, its ratio of crude oil gathered to domestic refinery runs tended to decline as the company expanded its refining operations and reduced its crude oil producing ratio.

We found no indication that any of the seven companies contemplated changes in their general program of integration into crude oil gathering operations in the near future.

Crude Oil Trunk Lines:

We found that the practices and policies of the six large companies which were net buyers of crude oil in the United States were substantially the same with respect to the construction, ownership, and operation of crude oil trunk lines. In general the companies built crude oil trunk lines wherever and whenever they needed them in their operations. Ordinarily, the chief objective of a company in building a line was to get crude oil to its refineries at costs comparable with or, if possible, lower than those of its competitors, although as was noted in Chapter Seven, lines were occasionally built for other purposes. The question of whether to participate in a particular project was usually simply a matter of business economics; that is, a matter of deciding whether the cost savings and other benefits to be secured from the line were sufficient to justify the required capital investment. All six companies, however, unquestionably regarded the ownership and operation of crude oil trunk lines as subordinate and supporting to the other phases of their business. The chief value of the lines was regarded as lying in the transportation savings which they enabled a company to make on its own throughput. In no case did we find that one of the six companies had participated in a crude oil trunk line project in recent years simply for the profits to be earned by providing transportation service to outside shippers or that it had participated in a trunk line which it did not plan to use in one way or another in its own producing or refining operations.

With the exception of a few, short intrastate lines, the crude oil trunk lines of the six companies were operated as common carriers, subject to the regulations of the Interstate Commerce Commission and the various state authorities, and carried oil for outside shippers as well as for the owners. The six companies were all signers of the pipe line consent decree of 1941 and hence could not receive dividends from their pipe line subsidiaries in excess of their share of a 7% return on the ICC valuation of the pipe line properties.

We found that it was a very common practice for two or more companies to build crude oil trunk lines under joint ownership arrangements when they had need for transportation in the same general direction, because by so doing they could build larger lines and secure the operating economies resulting therefrom. We also found that a company sometimes acquired a stock interest in a line which other companies had already built or were planning to build regardless of whether the company in question participated in the project. We examined some of these cases rather carefully because off-hand it would appear that under such circumstances a company would be better advised to use the line as a common carrier and to avoid the commitment of its own capital funds in a project which at the best promised a return of only about 7%. The companies, however, gave several reasons why they sometimes secured a stock interest in a line that was important to their operations even though the building of the line was not contingent upon their participation in the ownership thereof.

The first reason was to gain participation in the management of the line, a voice in the allocation of capacity among shippers at times when the line was pressed to capacity, and the right to participate in decisions as to when, where, and under what circumstances the line might be enlarged in capacity or extended to new territories. A second reason was to gain a share in the terminal value of the properties. Even though dividends to shipper-owners were limited to 7%, the tariffs on the lines were usually set so that the lines could be maintained and the capital investment returned over a period of about 15 to 25 years. In some cases it was anticipated that the lines might have a fairly high investment value at the end of the depreciation period. Some of the companies took the position therefore that if they were to provide part of the throughput to the line and thus, in a sense, to guarantee its successful operation, they should also acquire stock in the line and gain a share in the residual value of the properties.

In addition, we found that although legally a company did not need to hold a stock interest in a pipe line to gain access thereto, as a practical matter the large oil companies usually did acquire stock interests in lines which they planned to use for any very large volume of shipments. In other words, the large companies did not often take advantage of the common carrier provisions of the law to force their way into lines owned by other companies. It was generally expected in the industry that if a company planned to use any very substantial part of the capacity of a line, it should bear a share of the capital investment in the line.

The crude oil trunk lines of the seven companies as of 1952 are shown on the maps in Chapter Twelve, Exhibits XII-3 to XII-9. The volumes of crude oil which the companies moved to their refineries through crude oil trunk lines in which they had a stock interest are indicated in Chapter Twelve, Exhibits XII-19 to XII-25 for the years 1935, 1940, 1946, and 1950, and summary figures for each company are shown in Chapter Twelve, Exhibit XII-26. As noted in Chapter Twelve, the oil movements were difficult to classify because sometimes a shipment traveled by several different carriers before it reached its destination. Wherever possible, however, the data in Chapter Twelve and the figures which will be used in the following discussion indicate the carrier by which the oil moved the longest distance.

In the years 1940, 1946, and 1950, all the companies which were net buyers of crude oil in the United States, except Atlantic, carried 60% or more of their crude oil to refineries through crude oil trunk lines in which they had at least a partial interest. Atlantic, however, carried only 12%–20% of its oil to refineries through crude oil trunk lines in which it had an interest. This circumstance may be explained largely by the fact that the company had the majority of its refinery capacity at Philadelphia, a point which it was practical to serve only by tanker shipments. As may be seen from Chapter Twelve, Exhibit XII-23, Atlantic's extensive tanker fleet was to a considerable extent the counterpart of crude oil trunk lines in other companies. Atlantic nevertheless did move about 40% of its crude oil for the Philadelphia refinery to the Gulf Coast for transfer to tankers through crude oil trunk lines in which it had a stock interest.

We found that various other differences that existed among the six companies which were net buyers of crude oil with respect to the proportion of crude oil moved to refineries via company owned pipe lines arose primarily from differences in the geographic location of refineries rather than from differences in the policies of the companies with respect to the ownership of crude oil trunk lines. It may be noted, for example, that Gulf and Sinclair, both of which had about 25% of their refinery capacity on the Atlantic seaboard, moved a smaller proportion of their crude oil supplies via company pipe lines than did Sohio which had all its capacity inland or the Indiana Company which had the great majority of its capacity inland or on the Gulf Coast. It is interesting to observe that Gulf and Sinclair, both of which had about the same proportion of their refinery capacity on the Atlantic Coast, had almost exactly the same proportion of their crude oil carried to refineries by company owned pipe lines in the years 1935, 1940, and 1946.

The data in Chapter Twelve, Exhibit XII-26, indicate that the six companies from time to time altered the proportions of their crude oil requirements which they carried to refineries via company owned pipe lines. These alterations usually reflected the construction or expansion of pipe line facilities. In some instances, however, the alterations merely reflected changes in operating situations. For example, if a company enlarged a refinery served primarily by tankers but left the capacity of its inland refineries unchanged, a reduction usually took place in the proportion of the company's crude oil requirements which moved to its refineries by company owned pipe lines.

Similarly, changes in the proportions of incoming crude oil carried to refineries via company owned lines were precipitated by such things as changes in the geographic location of a company's sources of crude oil and changes in the relative costs of different types of carriers. In 1940, for example, Sohio brought 85.5% of its crude oil to refineries via company owned lines. Between 1940 and 1946, however, the company found an opportunity to purchase a substantial volume of crude oil in the Tinsley fields in Mississippi from whence oil could be shipped very economically along the Mississippi River by barge to Latonia. In 1946 therefore the company brought 70.2% of its crude oil to refineries by company owned pipe lines and 21.8% by barge. Between 1946 and 1950 the company found that the use of a large diameter pipe line would permit substantial

economies over barge transportation, and as a result the company sold most of its barges and participated in the construction of the Mid-Valley trunk line (see map, Chapter Twelve, Exhibit XII-9). In 1950 the company carried 86.2% of its crude oil via company owned pipe lines and only 12.4% via barges.

The policies and position of The Ohio Oil Company with respect to the ownership and operation of crude oil trunk lines differed in several respects from those of the other six companies discussed above. In the first place, as noted in Chapter Seven, The Ohio Oil Company was not carrying any of its own crude oil in interstate commerce at the time of the pipe line consent decree in 1941, and suit was not brought against it by the Department of Justice under the Elkins Act, as it was against most of the shipper-owners in the country. The company has not subsequently shipped its own oil in interstate commerce. The Ohio Oil Company therefore operated under no restraints as to the dividends it could receive from pipe line operations, although like all other companies it was required to operate its interstate lines as common carriers and to file tariffs with the Interstate Commerce Commission.

The policies of The Ohio Oil Company with respect to the ownership and operation of crude oil trunk lines also differed from those of the other six companies in that the company executives did not regard pipe line operations merely as supporting activities for other phases of the company's business. In most instances, the company certainly could have disposed of its crude oil output without engaging in transportation activities, and only a small trunk line system would have been necessary to take care of the requirements of the Robinson and Lovell refineries. The extensive crude oil trunk line system, of which the company was sole or partial owner, thus reflected the tendency of the company executives to view pipe line operations as a source of profits in their own right and as a separate field of investment for the company's capital funds. It should not be inferred, however, that the company earned a significantly higher return on its pipe line investments than did the other oil companies. In certain cases the company filed joint tariffs with companies who were subject to restraints as to the amount of dividends they could receive, and in all cases the pipe line tariffs charged had to be reasonably in line with those of competitive carriers in order to obtain business.

We found no evidence that any of the seven large companies was contemplating major changes in its practices or policies with regard to the ownership and operation of crude oil trunk lines. There was, however, some evidence that the large companies were tending to build an increasing number of their trunk lines under joint ownership arrangements with other companies. The increase in joint ownership arrangements was prompted by several considerations. During the postwar period large diameter lines were developed very rapidly and were found to yield some very significant savings in operating costs over small diameter lines. The large diameter lines required such a large volume of throughput and such a large capital investment that a single company was not often in a position to build one by itself alone. Moreover, in view of the common carrier status of the crude oil trunk lines and the ICC regulations concerning tariffs and dividends to shipper-owners, there were not many situations in which a company could gain any significant advantage over its competitors through sole rather than joint ownership. Ordinarily therefore the companies were anxious to get the crude oil trunk lines built and to assure their positions in them with the minimum commitment of their own capital funds and were thus receptive to joint ownership arrangements.

Products Pipe Lines:

As in the case of crude oil trunk lines, it was the general policy of six of the companies (The Ohio Oil Company excepted) to build products pipe lines wherever they were necessary to meet competition or wherever it could be demonstrated that the cost savings derived therefrom would be sufficient to justify the capital costs. Ordinarily, the six companies regarded the cost savings made on their own throughput as the chief gains secured from the construction of the lines. We found no cases where the six companies were participating in the construction of products lines primarily in anticipation of earning a profit on transportation service provided to other shippers. Likewise we found no cases in which the companies were participating in the construction of lines they did not plan to use in their own operations. In general, the products pipe lines were regarded as supporting facilities for refining and marketing operations.

The Ohio Oil Company had policies somewhat different from those of the other companies. As noted in Chapter Seven, in 1952 the company converted an old crude oil trunk line running from Wood River, Illinois, to Indianapolis, Indiana, to operation as a products pipe line. It was anticipated that this line would carry only products for outside shippers and would be operated by The Ohio Oil Company solely for the profits to be earned on the transportation service. So far as the company's own transportation requirements for refined products were concerned, the same general policies were followed as in the case of crude oil. In other words, the company did not engage in the transportation of its own products in interstate commerce. The company, for example, constructed a products pipe line from its refinery at Robinson, Illinois, to Indianapolis but immediately upon completion of the line sold it to the Buckeye Pipe Line Company for operation.

In the years 1935, 1940, 1946, and 1950 we found that six of the companies (Atlantic excepted) were far more extensively integrated into pipe line transportation activities for the movement of crude oil into their refineries than they were for the movement of refined products out of their refineries. In 1950, for example, whereas the volume of crude oil moved into refineries via company pipe lines varied among the six companies from 61.4% to 97.8% of total crude oil receipts, the volume of products moved out via company pipe lines ranged from zero in the case of The Ohio Oil Company to 45.8% in the case of Sohio. The Atlantic Refining Company developed its products pipe lines somewhat earlier than did the other companies and in 1950 made 31.7% of its refinery shipments via company owned pipe lines. The company made a larger share of its products shipments from refineries via company pipe lines than it did of its crude oil shipments to refineries merely because of the fact noted above that the company's largest refinery at Philadelphia was in a position where it could receive crude oil more economically by tanker than by pipe line.

All the companies, with the exception of The Ohio Oil Company, showed a marked increase in the proportion of their refinery shipments made via company pipe lines in the period 1935 to 1950. The most dramatic increases occurred in the case of Sinclair and Sohio; the former increased its shipments via company pipe lines from 1.0% to 33.5% and the latter from zero to 45.8% of total refinery shipments. The increases can be easily understood when it is recalled that it was in the period from about 1930 to 1950 that the products pipe line gained widespread commercial acceptance in the United States. As long as the generally accepted method for the overland transportation of refined products was the railroad, a multipurpose carrier capable of serving many customers, the companies relied upon outside concerns for transportation service and did not attempt to integrate forward beyond the ownership and leasing of tank cars. When as a result of technological developments, the products pipe line, a unipurpose carrier capable of serving only a few shippers, became the preferred method of transportation for many situations, the oil companies found it both necessary and desirable to integrate more heavily into transportation activities (see Chapter Seven). Here, as at other points in the industry's history, integration took place as a means of securing the reductions in operating costs made possible by a new technological development.

There were many differences among the companies with respect to the extent to which they had established company owned products pipe lines to serve their refining and marketing operations. In 1950 Sohio made 45.8% of its refinery shipments via company owned pipe lines, Sinclair 33.5%, Atlantic 31.7%, The Texas Company 20.9%, the Indiana Company 20.4%, and Gulf 10.6%. These differences were explainable in the first instance by the fact that the products pipe line was a relatively new facility, and it was to be expected that the several companies should have made different degrees of progress with respect to its usage in their own operations. As in the case of the crude oil trunk lines, moreover, the differences were in many cases partially explainable by differences in the geographic situations of the

companies. Sohio, for example, had its marketing activities confined to a relatively small, inland area and was in a position where particularly good use could be made of products pipe lines as contrasted to other methods of transportation. Atlantic, Sinclair, and Gulf, on the other hand, had their refining and marketing operations so located that the preferred method of transportation for much of their volume was via tankers or barges. The Texas Company had its marketing operations distributed over such a wide area that there were not many places where it had enough volume concentrated in one spot to warrant the construction of pipe lines. The Indiana Company had much of its volume in the farm markets and likewise had only certain points at which it could make effective usage of products pipe lines.

As a general rule, we found that there were far more variations in the practices and policies of the companies with respect to the ownership and operation of products pipe lines than there were with respect to crude oil trunk lines. These variations arose in the first instance from the fact, noted in Chapter Seven, that the legal status of the products pipe lines had not been fully clarified and, as a result, the seven companies were not bound by a common set of rules and regulations as they were in the case of crude oil trunk lines. The terms of the Interstate Commerce Act were broad enough to cover products pipe lines and the courts had held that the lines must publish tariffs and keep accounts in accordance with the ICC regulations, but it had not been determined whether the lines which crossed state boundaries were required to serve outside shippers. As a result, the companies had elected in some cases to operate the pipe line facilities in which they had an interest as common carriers, while in other cases they had chosen to reserve their lines exclusively for their own use.

The Standard Oil Company (Indiana), for example, operated the major products pipe lines of the parent company exclusively as private carriers and did not handle any products for outside shippers.[4] Similarly, Sinclair did not ordinarily make shipments for other con-

[4] The subsidiaries of the Indiana Company, however, operated or participated in the operation of certain products pipe lines which were common carriers. In addition, the parent company had an interest in the Wyco Pipe Line which was a common carrier.

cerns in its products pipe line system. The products pipe lines which Sohio owned in partnership with other companies were likewise operated as private carriers. In this case, of course, the lines were confined to the state of Ohio, and there was no particular reason why they should have had a common carrier status so far as federal statutes were concerned.

In contrast to these three companies, Atlantic had always operated its Keystone and Buffalo pipe line systems as common carriers. Gulf had both common and private carrier pipe lines in its system; the company and its partners operated the Southeastern and Detroit Southern pipe lines as common carriers and the Project Five Pipe Line as a private carrier. The Texas Company likewise had both common and private carrier pipe lines. The products pipe lines which were given a common carrier status by the companies were operated on much the same basis as the common carrier crude oil lines, except that in the case of the products pipe lines the owners did not usually provide terminaling facilities for outside shippers,[5] a service which was required in the case of crude oil trunk lines.

Another point of difference found among the seven companies was with respect to the use of joint ownership arrangements. The economic arguments for joint ownership arrangements were somewhat the same in the case of products pipe lines as in the case of crude oil trunk lines. The possibility of operating the products pipe lines as private carriers and of drawing dividends from them free of the restraints of the pipe line consent decree, however, favored single ownership in certain cases. As of 1952 the Indiana Company, Sinclair, and Atlantic were the sole owners of their more important products pipe lines. Gulf, The Texas Company, and Sohio, on the other hand, owned the majority of their products pipe lines jointly with other concerns.

These differences in ownership arrangements, however, appeared to us to reflect largely matters of historical accident and expediency in individual cases rather than basic differences in policy among the companies. None of the companies had a firm policy of confining its operations to one type of owner-

ship arrangement or the other, and each company apparently decided the question of single versus joint ownership on the merits of the individual cases as they arose. In 1951, for example, the Indiana Company, which previously had usually not shared the ownership of its major products pipe lines, gave careful consideration to the use of a joint ownership arrangement for a new 243-mile line it was planning to build from its Whiting refinery to River Rouge, Michigan. In this case, the company eventually decided on single ownership largely for public policy reasons; that is, the company recognized that the line would give it low costs in reaching the Michigan peninsula and wished to avoid any possible accusation that it was joining with others to exert undue competitive pressure on the small refiners in Michigan. Moreover, the Indiana Company had a sufficient volume of throughput to permit the construction of a line on its own account.

We found every indication that six of the seven oil companies (The Ohio Oil Company excepted) were intending to press ahead with the construction of products pipe lines wherever the lines could be used effectively in their operations. Several of the companies were working very rapidly toward the elimination of rail shipments and toward a position in which their products shipments from refineries to market territories would move almost exclusively by pipe line, tanker, or barge. This objective was being achieved primarily through: (a) the extension of products pipe lines to new areas, and (b) the elimination of market territories which it was not feasible to reach via pipe line, tanker, or barge. Moreover, three of the companies, Sinclair, Sohio, and the Indiana Company, had either established, or expected to establish in the very near future, pipe line connections between several of their major refineries in order that they might be able to shift products from one refinery area to another in accordance with changes in economic conditions and market demand.

II. THE BALANCE OF REFINING AND MARKETING ACTIVITIES

In Chapter Thirteen attention was directed to the changes which from time to time oc-

5 The Great Lakes Pipe Line was an exception and did provide terminaling service to shippers.

curred in the balance the seven companies maintained between their crude oil producing and refining operations. In the following pages the discussion will be concerned with a similar problem, the practices and policies of the seven companies with respect to the balance maintained between refining and marketing activities.

The balance of a company's refining and marketing activities is difficult to define and likewise difficult to measure on a statistical basis. The relationship involves at least three considerations: (a) to what extent does the company purchase products to supplement its own refinery output, (b) to what extent does the company make use of outside wholesale and retail intermediaries in getting its refinery output into the hands of final consumers, and (c) to what extent does the company exchange [6] or purchase refined products as a means of getting supplies to marketing territories which it cannot reach on a competitive basis from its own refineries? The first two considerations have to do with balance in terms of relative volumes handled at the refining and marketing levels while the third consideration has to do with the geographical balance of operations.

From a strictly theoretical standpoint, it might be said that a company's refining and marketing operations are in perfect balance volume-wise when it purchases no refined products and when it makes all its sales directly through its own marketing facilities to final consumers. It might further be said that a company has a deficiency in refining capacity to the extent that it purchases refined products to supply its own outlets or that it has a deficiency in marketing facilities to the extent that it sells to outside wholesale or retail re-

sellers. In the case of a company which both purchases refined products and sells to outside wholesale and retail resellers, the degree of imbalance volume-wise might be expressed as the difference between the volume purchased and the volume sold to outside resellers. The volume of a company's product exchanges plus any purchases beyond those necessary to offset a refining deficiency might then be taken as a measure of the geographical imbalance of refining and marketing facilities. A company might, of course, have either a volume or a geographical imbalance or some combination of the two.

This general concept of refining-marketing balance is satisfactory for descriptive purposes, but it is almost impossible to develop a satisfactory statistical measure of it. The difficulty arises from the fact that there is no single volume figure which can be used to designate the extent of a company's reliance upon outside wholesale and retail resellers and which can be related to a company's refined products output.[7] A figure can be secured for the percentage of a company's refinery output sold to outside resellers, but the use of such a figure fails to distinguish between sales to outside resellers at the wholesale and at the retail levels and, in effect, treats on equal terms a company which sells 50% of its volume to wholesale resellers at the refinery gate and one which has extensive bulk plant facilities but nevertheless sells 50% of its volume to retail resellers. An adequate appraisal of the extent of a company's reliance upon outside marketing intermediaries really involves the full range of statistical measures which were used in Chapter Twelve in analyzing depth, extent, and intensity of integration into marketing operations.

We shall not attempt at this point therefore to analyze all aspects of the refining-marketing balance of the seven companies but shall limit the discussion to two important relationships: (a) the ratio of refined product purchases to total refined product sales, and (b) the ratio

---

[6] In an exchange arrangement a company trades products at one location in return for an equal volume of products at another location. The exchange may be made on equal terms or may involve the payment of a "place differential" of so much per gallon by one company to the other. The amount of the place differential is subject to bargaining and depends upon demand-supply conditions at the two locations, the relative transportation costs involved in getting products to the two points, and various other considerations. Exchanges usually involve identical products, but in some instances may involve products different in grade or kind. In the latter cases, appropriate differentials are paid by one company to the other to reflect the relative market value of the products involved in the trade.

[7] Working with dollar figures it would perhaps be possible to establish a relationship between the f.o.b. refinery realization value of a company's products and the actual realization value. Such a ratio would, however, reflect types of customers as well as the extent of a company's marketing facilities. Moreover, it would be difficult to decide what particular ratio constituted a "balanced" refining-marketing situation.

of refined product exchanges to total refined product sales. These two ratios reflect the first and third aspects of refining-marketing balance noted above; i.e., the extent to which a company purchases products to supplement its own refinery output and the extent to which it exchanges or purchases refined products as a means of getting supplies to marketing territories it cannot reach on a competitive basis from its own refineries. Consideration of the second aspect of refining-marketing balance, the extent to which a company makes use of outside wholesale and retail intermediaries as a means of getting its refinery output into the hands of final consumers, will be deferred to Chapters Fifteen and Sixteen and will be taken up as one phase of the general problem of integration into marketing activities.

It should be noted at the outset that since a company must ultimately sell in one way or another all the products it refines, purchases, or acquires by exchange, the ratios of purchases and exchanges to total refined product sales can never exceed 100%. The two ratios are measures of refining deficiencies and approach zero as a company's dependency on outside refiners decreases. As will become clear in the following discussion, the ratio of purchases to sales is a measure of both volume deficiencies and geographical imbalance whereas the ratio of exchanges to sales is largely a measure of geographical imbalance alone.

Ratio of Refined Product Purchases to Total Refined Product Sales:

We found that none of the seven companies was completely self-sufficient with respect to its supply of refined products for marketing operations. As may be seen from Exhibit XIV-2, each of the companies had for many years purchased some part of its requirements from other refiners. The largest volume of purchases relative to refined product sales in the years for which records were available was made by the Indiana Company in 1936, at which time the company's purchases amounted to 32.2% of its product sales.[8] The smallest volume of purchases rela-

---

[8] In the years 1935–1944 our figures understate the purchases of the Indiana Company because they include only the purchases of subsidiaries and not the purchases of the parent company. In the period 1945–1950 purchases by the parent company amounted to about 15% of total purchases.

tive to refined product sales was made by The Ohio Oil Company in 1952, at which time the company's purchases amounted to only 2.1% of its product sales. (The Texas Company had an even lower volume of purchases in some years, but the company's data cover purchases by the refining department only.)

Reasons for the Purchases: There were many different reasons why the seven companies found it both necessary and desirable to purchase a certain part of their refined product requirements from other refiners. In the first place, a need for refined product purchases arose from the fact that it was usually not possible for a company to expand its refining and marketing operations in precise step with each other. In the normal course of events, a company's marketing operations tended to expand by a series of relatively small annual increments. Refining operations, on the other hand, were usually expanded spasmodically in fairly large increments by periodic building or reconstruction projects. Because of the high costs involved in carrying idle refinery equipment, the companies sometimes elected to delay their refinery construction projects until their sales volume was somewhat in excess of their existing refinery output and the market for the new capacity thus well assured. Companies breaking into new market areas, for example, often found it desirable to purchase products and withhold any commitment in refining facilities until they were reasonably sure of gaining a foothold in the market. When the expansion of refining capacity was undertaken, however, it was often carried somewhat beyond immediate needs in order to provide for future marketing expansion. In the intervals of these cycles when refining capacity was less than marketing requirements, it was necessary for a company to secure part of its supplies from other concerns.

A second reason for occasional purchases of refined products was to take care of spot shortages. It was not always possible for a company to predict the demand for the various petroleum products with sufficient accuracy and to handle the logistics of the distribution function with sufficient precision so that it could maintain adequate supplies of each product at all times at all points throughout its entire mar-

EXHIBIT XIV-2. SEVEN OIL COMPANIES

Relationship Among Purchases, Exchanges, and Total Sales of Refined Products: 1935–1952*

Year	Gulf Oil Corporation — Purchases as % Total Sales	Gulf Oil Corporation — Exchanges as % Total Sales	Gulf Oil Corporation — Purchases + Exchanges as % Total Sales	The Texas Company — Purchases as % Total Sales†	The Texas Company — Exchanges as % Total Sales	The Texas Company — Purchases + Exchanges as % Total Sales†	Sinclair Oil Corporation — Purchases as % Total Sales‡	Sinclair Oil Corporation — Exchanges as % Total Sales	Sinclair Oil Corporation — Purchases + Exchanges as % Total Sales‡	The Ohio Oil Company — Purchases as % Total Sales	The Ohio Oil Company — Exchanges as % Total Sales	The Ohio Oil Company — Purchases + Exchanges as % Total Sales
1935	4.0%	5.9%	9.9%	2.9%	0.5%	3.4%	13.4%	6.9%	20.3%	8.0%		
1936	7.3			2.6	0.5	3.1	14.7	8.4	23.1	4.4		
1937	5.8			3.6	0.4	4.0	9.8	9.2	19.0	7.3		
1938	3.2			2.7	0.2	2.9	7.3	13.4	20.7	9.7		
1939	7.2			2.7	0.5	3.2	11.3	13.2	24.5	18.0		
1940	3.2	13.2	16.4	3.2	1.6	4.8	12.2	17.0	29.2	11.8		
1941	6.8	13.1	19.9	2.0	1.2	3.2	12.3	19.7	32.0	13.8		
1942	8.8	16.1	24.9	2.8	6.9	9.7	10.8	17.8	28.6	5.1		
1943	25.9			2.0	7.2	9.2	19.5	16.4	35.9	8.6		
1944	18.9			2.5	7.2	9.7	24.9	11.4	36.3	12.2		
1945	16.5			4.7	6.5	11.2	22.0	9.7	31.7	11.6	31.0%	42.6%
1946	12.0	15.4	27.4	2.5	4.0	6.5	10.7	10.8	21.5	13.0	27.5	40.5
1947	15.7	13.9	29.6	3.6	4.6	8.2	11.4	12.8	24.2	15.9	29.2	45.1
1948	18.7	18.3	37.0	1.9	3.2	5.1	13.2	11.8	25.0	11.7	31.4	43.1
1949	13.3	15.3	28.6	0.6	2.9	3.5	7.4	13.7	21.1	4.1	41.5	45.6
1950	11.5	14.5	26.0	8.1§	3.9	12.0	6.2	16.2	22.4	2.4	38.1	40.5
1951	15.0	17.2	32.2	1.0	3.9	4.9	4.6	3.3	7.9	2.4	34.7	37.1
1952	18.1	20.9	39.0				4.5	3.7	8.2	2.1	31.1	33.3

Year	The Atlantic Refining Company — Purchases as % Total Sales	The Atlantic Refining Company — Exchanges as % Total Sales	The Atlantic Refining Company — Purchases + Exchanges as % Total Sales	Standard Oil Company (Indiana) — Purchases as % Total Sales‖	Standard Oil Company (Indiana) — Exchanges as % Total Sales	Standard Oil Company (Indiana) — Purchases + Exchanges as % Total Sales‖	Standard Oil Company (Ohio) — Purchases as % Total Sales	Standard Oil Company (Ohio) — Exchanges as % Total Sales	Standard Oil Company (Ohio) — Purchases + Exchanges as % Total Sales
1935	2.6%			31.0%					
1936	2.7			32.2					
1937	3.5			20.0					
1938	2.4			15.1					
1939	6.0			13.9					
1940	3.1			15.2					
1941	3.2			16.4					
1942	31.6			13.2				8.1%	
1943	21.3			17.9	11.4%	29.3%		9.7	
1944	16.9			23.4	11.1	34.5	13.4%	10.5	23.9%
1945	11.7			24.2	8.1	32.3	15.1	9.9	25.0
1946	5.3	6.6%	11.9%	13.6	8.6	22.2	7.7	10.9	18.6
1947	4.4	7.9	12.3	13.6	9.5	23.1	10.8	8.8	19.6
1948	6.3	7.3	13.6	11.8	9.3	21.1	24.7§	14.4	39.1
1949	3.9	6.6	10.5	8.8	10.2	19.0	7.7	8.2	15.9
1950	4.4	6.5	10.9	14.0	8.1	22.1	5.9	5.5	11.4
1951	3.2	6.4	9.6	13.0			6.2	9.6	15.8
1952	4.3	10.7	15.0	13.8			4.5	7.0	11.5

Note: Blank spaces indicate data not available. Purchase data include products acquired under processing agreements except as noted in the case of Sinclair.

* Purchases of refined products 1942–1945 were in accord with government directives during the war.

† Includes purchases by refining department only. Data on other purchases not available but reported to be small part of total supply.

‡ Data do not include products acquired under processing agreements before 1950. Such acquisitions were less than 1% of refined product sales.

§ Operations influenced by a refinery strike.

‖ Data do not include purchases of parent company in years 1935–1944. In the period 1945–1950, purchases by parent company amounted to about 15% of total purchases.

SOURCE: Company records.

keting territory. When as a result of unexpected weather conditions, strikes, transportation tieups, or other factors, a shortage of products developed in a particular market, the companies sometimes found that they had no alternative other than to purchase their requirements or that it was more economical to make such purchases than to increase temporarily their own refinery outputs.

Some of the companies also made it a regular practice to purchase a small portion of their refined product requirements as a means of making sure that their own refineries always ran at capacity. The executives of these companies pointed out, for example, that the demand for domestic fuel oils was heavily dependent upon climatic conditions and could not be predicted in advance with any very high degree of accuracy. If therefore a company attempted to manufacture all its own fuel oil, it was required either to carry very large inventories or to make abrupt adjustments in its rate of refinery output. These difficulties could be avoided, however, if a company deliberately sold some 15% to 20% more fuel oil than it expected to manufacture. If the demand subsequently developed as anticipated, spot purchases could be made from independent refiners;[9] if it fell short of the estimates, the company was at least assured of operating its own refineries at capacity. The reasoning of the executives on this point was parallel to that which has often been advanced in favor of maintaining a larger marketing than manufacturing capacity in an integrated textile company.

A fourth reason for the refined product purchases was found in the fact that some of the companies deliberately planned product purchasing programs as a means of meeting the normal seasonal variations in the demand for fuel oil and gasoline. The Indiana Company, for example, sold its products at several points along the shores of the Great Lakes which it could not reach by barge or tanker shipments during the winter months when the lakes were frozen. To carry these terminals through the winter months without resorting to purchases, it would have been necessary for the company to build stocks of both gasoline and distillate during the summer and fall. The company executives recognized, however, that during the winter months other refiners usually pressed their crude oil runs to a maximum to meet the requirements of the domestic fuel oil market,[10] and, as a result, often had surplus gasoline to sell at favorable prices. The Indiana Company therefore confined its stock building program at the Great Lakes terminals primarily to distillates and planned to purchase a substantial share of the winter gasoline requirements for these terminals from other concerns.

We found a fifth reason for the refined product purchases in the fact that some of the companies used purchases to compensate for disparities between the ratio of products yielded from their normal refining operations and the ratio of products required in their marketing programs. As the companies pressed ahead with their marketing programs, it was not always possible to keep the sales volumes of the various products in the same general proportions as normal refinery yields. A company might, for example, as the result of an unusually successful advertising program, a particularly good piece of promotional work, or the activities of an outstanding salesman, develop a larger market for a particular product than it could readily supply without increasing its refinery runs and thereby producing an excess quantity of other products. Under such circumstances, the companies sometimes purchased part of their product requirements until the market for the other products could be expanded sufficiently to justify the higher level of refining activities. Similarly, the companies occasionally purchased products which their own refineries were not equipped to manufacture in order that they might offer a complete line of products to their customers.

A sixth purpose of product purchases in the case of some of the companies was to take ad-

[9] It had been the experience of some of the companies that spot purchases of this kind often had to be made at such high prices that the products could not be resold at a profit. These companies therefore reversed the practice outlined in the paragraph and made sure that they had ample manufacturing capacity and stocks to take care of their customers under extreme weather conditions. If it later developed that all the available products were not needed in the company's own marketing program, sales were then made in the cargo markets, often at low prices, to other concerns.

[10] The total demand for petroleum products in the Great Lakes area was also somewhat greater in the winter than in the summer.

vantage of favorable buying opportunities. As was noted in Chapter Five, the prices of the various refined products tend to fluctuate over a fairly wide range. Occasionally a company found that it could purchase certain products at lower prices than it could manufacture them in its own refineries. In such cases, a company might forego an increase in its own refinery runs or under exceptional circumstances might even reduce its own refinery runs in favor of purchasing in the cargo market.

The executives of some of the companies were also not unaware that if a large company maintained a buying position in the refined products markets, it could occasionally absorb the distressed cargoes which were from time to time thrown into the markets and thus aid in avoiding violent fluctuations in the prices of refined products in the territory in which it operated. It was not uncommon for refiners, and particularly the small ones, to maintain their refinery runs in the face of rising stocks and falling demand until they were in real distress from a marketing standpoint and forced to unload their supplies at any prices they could get. A large company could occasionally absorb these cargoes in its own operations and market them over a period of time in an orderly manner. If, however, these distress cargoes passed into the hands of cut-price jobbers, price wars were sometimes precipitated all along the line to the retail level.

A final reason for the product purchases was to obtain supplies for market territories which a company could not reach economically by shipments from its own refineries. As will be noted below, these situations were often handled by product exchanges. In cases where exchanges could not be arranged on a favorable basis, however, product purchases were used.

Practices of the Seven Companies With Respect to Product Purchases: For one or another of the above reasons, the seven companies were continually engaged in the purchasing of refined products from other refiners. Needless to say, the relative significance of the various reasons varied depending on the individual situations of the companies and upon the policies established by their executive personnel. Considerations such as purchasing to assure capacity refinery operations or purchasing to

round out a product line which were of significance in some companies were regarded as completely inconsequential in others. Moreover, the reasons why the individual companies purchased refined products varied from year to year depending upon current circumstances. Each company, however, had some reason or combination of reasons for purchasing a part of its marketing requirements.

The extent to which each of the companies engaged in product purchases is shown in Exhibit XIV-2. As might be anticipated in view of the kinds of reasons for which the purchases were made, the volume purchased by each company as a percentage of its total refined product sales tended to fluctuate considerably from one year to the next. During the war years, many special product purchase and sale arrangements were negotiated at the request of the government, and these years should therefore be disregarded in judging the typical experiences of the companies. Ignoring the war years, it appears that the purchases of the seven companies customarily fell somewhere between 2% and 20% of their refined products requirements.

In the period 1935–1941 the Indiana Company characteristically made more use of refined product purchases than did any of the other companies.[11] In the period 1946–1952, however, Gulf characteristically made the most use of purchases, although its usage was only slightly greater than that of the Indiana Company. For the period 1935–1952 as a whole (war years excepted), The Atlantic Refining Company made somewhat less use of product purchases than did the other companies. The low volume of purchases by Atlantic may be explained by the fact that the company's market territory was, for the most part, confined to areas which could be reached economically from the Atlantic refineries by water transport or by the extensive products pipe line system which the company had developed in Pennsylvania and New York (see map, Chapter Twelve, Exhibit XII-7).

The Texas Company also apparently made very little usage of product purchases in the years covered by our data, although in this case the record is not entirely clear because our

---

[11] No data were available for Sohio in the period 1935–1941. See footnote 8 concerning purchases of the Indiana Company in the period 1935–1944.

data cover only purchases by the company's refining department. The company executives reported, however, that other purchases were a small part of the company's total supply. The rather limited usage of product purchases by The Texas Company is of particular interest in view of the company's widespread market territory and the fact that it also made little use of product exchanges.

No particular trends were discernible in the purchasing activities of the companies, except in the case of Gulf and the Indiana Company. Gulf secured a substantially larger share of its products by means of purchase arrangements in the postwar than in the prewar period, whereas the Indiana Company purchased a substantially larger share of its requirements in the prewar than in the postwar period.[12] It may likewise be noted from Exhibit XIV-2 that both Sinclair and The Ohio Oil Company reduced their refined product purchases very sharply in the period 1949–1952. This reduction may probably be attributed to the fact that both companies initiated refinery expansion programs fairly early in the postwar period and brought new equipment into operation in about 1949. Moreover, Sinclair in 1948 and 1949 elected to withdraw from certain market territories far removed from its refineries and extended its products pipe lines to reach certain other areas which it had not previously been able to serve at economical transportation costs from its own plants.

An analysis of the purchasing programs of the companies by individual products is shown in Exhibit XIV-3. It is apparent from the data that some of the companies which had low ratios of total purchases to sales nevertheless purchased a fairly large part of their requirements of certain products. In 1952, for example, The Ohio Oil Company purchased 18.6% of its requirements of "other products" (chiefly lubricating oils), although its total purchases of all products amounted to only 2.1% of total sales. Similarly, Sohio purchased 14.7% of its requirements of residual in 1952, although its total purchases of all products amounted to only 4.5% of total sales.

Exhibit XIV-3 also reveals that there were wide differences among the seven companies

with respect to the proportions of their requirements of individual products which they secured by means of purchase arrangements. In 1952, for example, Gulf purchased 21.2% of its gasoline requirements whereas Sohio purchased only 1.2% of its gasoline requirements. Sohio, on the other hand, purchased 14.7% of its residual requirements whereas Gulf purchased only 10.2% of its residual requirements.

The analysis of purchasing programs is carried one step further in Exhibit XIV-4 which shows for selected years the proportion of each company's total volume of purchases which was accounted for by each of the major product groups. The data indicate that the composition of each company's total purchases often varied widely from one year to the next. For example, gasoline comprised 51.2% of Atlantic's total purchases in 1946 but only 11.4% in 1951; similarly, kerosene and distillates comprised only 7.2% of the company's purchases in 1951 but 57.7% in 1952. It may also be observed that Sohio's purchases of kerosenes and distillates were only 6.3% of total purchases in 1950 but were 21.3% of purchases in the following year and that Sinclair's purchases of gasoline amounted to only 9.5% of total purchases in 1951 as contrasted with 32.2% of total purchases in 1952. These irregularities and sudden changes in the composition of the total product purchases of the companies were, of course, wholly consistent with the character of the circumstances noted above under which product purchases were ordinarily made.

A further fact revealed by Exhibit XIV-4 is that there was often a great deal of difference in the relative significance of individual products in the purchasing programs of the companies. In the postwar period, for example, a far larger share of The Ohio Oil Company's purchases was made up of kerosene and distillates than was true in the case of the other companies for which data were available. On the other hand, residual apparently accounted for a larger share of the purchases of Sohio, Sinclair, Atlantic, and the Indiana Company in the postwar period than it did of the purchases of The Ohio Oil Company or Gulf. Differences of this kind in the composition of total product purchases might be anticipated in the light of the circumstances under which purchases were normally made.

[12] See footnote 8 concerning purchases of the Indiana Company in the period 1935–1944.

EXHIBIT XIV-3. SEVEN OIL COMPANIES

Analysis of Refined Product Purchases as Percentage of Product Sales: 1935–1952*

Year	Gulf Oil Corporation					The Texas Company†					The Ohio Oil Company					Sinclair Oil Corporation‡				
	All Products	Gasoline	Kerosene and Distillates	Residual	Other	All Products	Gasoline	Kerosene and Distillates	Residual	Other	All Products	Gasoline	Kerosene and Distillates	Residual	Other	All Products	Gasoline	Kerosene and Distillates	Residual	Other
1935	4.0%	5.9%	1.1%	2.4%	4.3%	2.9%					8.0%	16.8%	30.2%	Neg.	34.2%	13.4%	18.4%	8.4%	0.2%	16.6%
1936	7.3					2.6					4.4	6.7	1.6	0.4%	1.1	14.7				
1937	5.8					3.6					7.3	7.4	17.8	1.2	1.7	9.8				
1938	3.2					2.7					9.7	13.3	10.5	1.0	4.6	7.3				
1939	7.2					2.7					18.0	24.7	14.1	0.1	8.5	11.3				
1940	3.2	1.9	6.0	3.4	5.4	3.2					11.8	17.1	8.7	0.2	6.7	12.2	9.0	24.1	5.8	14.8
1941	6.8					2.0					13.8	20.7	9.6	0.6	10.4	12.3				
1942	8.8					2.8					5.1	7.2	5.7	0.6	12.3	10.8				
1943	25.9					2.0					8.6	15.0	3.0	1.1	32.2	19.5				
1944	18.9					2.5					12.2	21.4	6.9	1.8	15.3	24.9				
1945	16.5					4.7					11.6	19.9	8.2	1.1	15.2	22.0				
1946	12.0	15.5	14.9	5.6	5.1	2.5					13.0	22.6	7.5	Neg.	29.4	10.7	7.7	18.5	9.6	4.4
1947	15.7					3.6					15.9	24.1	17.2	0.1	54.0	11.4				
1948	18.7					1.9					11.7	16.5	17.7	0.5	13.5	13.2				
1949	13.3	16.9	10.2	11.2	5.6	0.6	0.5%	Neg.	1.7%	0.1%	4.1	2.4	13.2	0.8	14.9	7.4				
1950	11.5	9.9	12.4	13.5	8.4	8.1§					2.4	Neg.	10.0	0.9	16.8	6.2	1.5	7.5	16.9	6.8
1951	15.0	13.8	17.6	13.5	19.2		1.4	0.1	0.7		2.4	0.1	8.3	1.4	16.1	4.6	0.9	6.1	9.7	11.8
1952	18.1	21.2	20.1	10.2	18.6	1.0			0.7	1.1	2.1	0.4	6.5	0.7	18.6	4.5	3.1	3.0	9.4	10.3

Year	The Atlantic Refining Company					Standard Oil Company (Indiana)‖	Standard Oil Company (Ohio)				
	All Products	Gasoline	Kerosene and Distillates	Residual	Other	All Products	All Products	Gasoline	Kerosene and Distillates	Residual	Other
1935	2.6%					31.0%	3.3%	2.0%	2.1%	5.1%	8.8%
1936	2.7					32.2					
1937	3.5					20.0					
1938	2.4					15.1					
1939	6.0					13.9					
1940	3.1	1.1%	0.7%	7.0%	14.2%	15.2	12.4	14.6	9.7	9.1	9.8
1941	3.2					16.4					
1942	31.6					13.2					
1943	21.3					17.9	13.4				
1944	16.9					23.4	15.1				
1945	11.7					24.2					
1946	5.3	5.6	4.1	3.4	10.4	13.6	7.7	8.0	2.7	10.2	6.4
1947	4.4					13.6	10.8				
1948	6.3					11.8	24.7§				
1949	3.9	2.3	1.4	10.9	6.2	8.8	7.7				
1950	4.4	2.5	0.8	16.2	5.0	14.0	5.9	4.5	1.8	12.1	10.8
1951	3.2	0.9	0.7	13.0	4.4	13.0	6.2	3.2	6.3	13.7	5.9
1952	4.3	1.7	7.3	5.2	3.7	13.8	4.5	1.2	3.3	14.7	4.5

(Analysis by products not possible because data on purchases are for parent company and consolidated subsidiaries whereas data on sales of products are for parent company only. See Chapter Twelve.)

Note: Blank spaces indicate data not available. Data include products acquired under processing agreements except as noted in the case of Sinclair.

* Purchases of refined products 1942–1945 were in accord with government directives during the war.

† Includes purchases by refining department only. Data on other purchases not available but reported to be a small part of total supply.

‡ Data do not include products acquired under processing agreements before 1950. Such acquisitions were less than 1% of refined product sales.

§ Operations influenced by a refinery strike.

‖ Data do not include purchases of parent company in years 1935–1944. In period 1945–1950, purchases by parent company amounted to about 15% of total purchases.

Source: Company records.

EXHIBIT XIV-4. SEVEN OIL COMPANIES

Analysis of Refined Product Purchases by Type of Product as Percentage of Total Purchases: 1935–1952 *

Year	Gulf Oil Corporation				The Texas Company †				Sinclair Oil Corporation ‡				The Ohio Oil Company			
	Gasoline	Kerosene and Distillates	Residual	Other	Gasoline	Kerosene and Distillates	Residual	Other	Gasoline	Kerosene and Distillates	Residual	Other	Gasoline	Kerosene and Distillates	Residual	Other
1935	72.1%	4.6%	18.8%	4.5%	99.5%	Neg.	Neg.	0.5%	78.4%	14.5%	0.2%	6.9%	81.7%	15.0%	Neg.	3.3%
1936													92.8	4.3	1.9	1.0
1937													66.5	29.4	3.2	0.9
1938													84.4	11.4	2.5	1.7
1939													90.2	6.7	1.1	2.0
1940	29.0	31.5	31.7	7.8	35.5	0.2	63.9	0.4	38.4	47.2	9.2	5.2	89.6	8.3	0.4	1.7
1941	69.7	11.0	15.2	4.1									90.0	6.6	1.2	2.2
1942	51.3	15.7	29.3	3.7									72.6	17.3	3.4	6.7
1943	42.7	25.1	27.5	4.7									80.8	7.6	3.9	7.7
1944	46.4	17.6	30.4	5.6									82.0	10.3	5.0	2.7
1945	49.9	18.5	28.0	3.6	80.5	Neg.	17.6	1.9	34.3	44.1	19.7	1.9	81.6	12.6	3.0	2.8
1946	58.7	25.8	13.6	1.9									86.7	8.4	0.1	4.8
1947	45.5	26.1	27.2	1.2									76.2	17.6	0.1	6.1
1948	42.3	21.7	35.0	1.0	48.7	0.2	49.6	1.5					71.8	25.0	1.4	1.8
1949	57.3	17.4	23.8	1.5									31.6	58.4	5.2	4.8
1950	36.1	27.9	33.1	2.9	76.9	1.2	12.2	9.7	11.3	35.2	48.9	4.6	0.7	90.0	9.6	8.7
1951	38.6	33.2	23.1	5.1					9.5	38.7	42.1	9.7	1.4	77.9	13.1	7.6
1952	52.2	30.5	13.6	3.7					32.2	19.3	39.8	8.7	11.1	72.6	7.0	9.3

Year	The Atlantic Refining Company				Standard Oil Company (Indiana) §				Standard Oil Company (Ohio)			
	Gasoline	Kerosene and Distillates	Residual	Other	Gasoline	Kerosene and Distillates	Residual	Other	Gasoline	Kerosene and Distillates	Residual	Other
1935	18.3%	4.9%	47.7%	29.1%	38.2%	7.9%	47.6%	6.3%	34.4%	5.0%	44.5%	16.1%
1936												
1937												
1938												
1939												
1940									68.7	7.3	20.0	4.0
1941												
1942												
1943												
1944												
1945												
1946	51.2	20.9	9.4	18.5					54.2	5.5	35.9	4.4
1947												
1948												
1949	27.7	9.0	44.8	18.5	24.6	11.3	60.3	3.8	39.1	6.3	45.5	9.1
1950	24.7	5.6	58.4	11.3					26.9	21.3	46.4	5.4
1951	11.4	7.2	66.6	14.8								
1952	15.8	57.7	17.9	8.6					13.5	16.8	63.6	6.1

Note: Blank spaces indicate data not available. Data include products acquired under processing agreements except as noted in the case of Sinclair.

* Purchases of refined products 1942–1945 were in accord with government directives during the war.

† Includes purchases by refining department only. Data on other purchases not available but reported to be a small part of total supply.

‡ Data do not include products acquired under processing agreements before 1950. Such acquisitions were less than 1% of refined product sales.

§ Data do not include purchases of parent company in years 1935–1944. In the period 1945–1950, purchases by parent company amount to about 15% of total purchases.

SOURCE: Company records.

So far as we were able to determine, the differences in the records of the seven companies with respect to refined product purchases, such as those mentioned in the preceding paragraphs, were largely reflections of differences in their refining-marketing situations rather than reflections of differences in their fundamental policies with respect to the use of refined product purchases. To be sure, the executives of the several companies had different ideas as to when, where, and to what extent refined product purchases should be made, but these differences in thinking did not seem to be the prime causes of the differences in the purchasing records of the seven companies.

We found no indication that any of the seven companies expected to make any significant changes in the immediate future in its policies with respect to purchases of refined products. The executives of each of the companies indicated that their firms would probably continue to make refined product purchases for much the same reasons as in earlier years. It was anticipated that the amounts of the purchases would continue to vary from time to time in accordance with changes in operating situations.

Sources of Product Purchases: The executives of the seven companies indicated that the majority, or at least a large share, of their product purchases were normally made from small refiners. The Gulf Oil Corporation corroborated the point by providing us with the analysis of its refined product purchases shown in Exhibit XIV-5. This record shows the company's total purchases and purchases of each major product group divided into three categories: purchases under processing agreements, purchases from major companies,[13] and purchases from other companies.

Assuming that all the processing agreements were with major companies, which was not necessarily the case, it is evident from the data that in the years 1946 to 1951, inclusive, Gulf made about 63% to 83% of its total refined product purchases from small refining companies. There were, however, some significant variations with respect to the sources of the individual products. In 1951, for example, the

company made 64.9% of its purchases in the gasoline group and 69.0% of its purchases in the kerosene and distillate group from small refiners. In the same year, however, the company made only 47.8% of its residual purchases and only 0.4% of its purchases of lube oils and other products from small concerns. It may also be noted that whereas in the period 1946–1951 the proportion of the company's gasoline and kerosene and distillate purchases made from small firms remained approximately constant, the proportion of its residual and other product purchases made from small firms decreased very sharply.

The proportion of the company's total refined product purchases made from small refiners showed a slight decrease in the period 1946–1951. The executives of the company reported, however, that the decrease was largely the result of random circumstances and stated that the company would probably continue in the future to place the great majority of its over-all purchases of refined products with small concerns. The executives further stated that Gulf had a long-standing relationship with about three small refiners and made it a policy to patronize them regardless of the state of the market. During the period of oversupply and sharply reduced refining margins in 1949, for example, the company paid these three refiners a premium of about one cent a gallon above the market prices for certain of their products in order to assure them a reasonable operating margin.

Ratio of Product Exchanges to Total Refined Product Sales:

We found that all seven companies were engaged to some extent in refined product exchanges. The ratio of each company's exchanges to its refined product sales for selected years is shown in Exhibit XIV-2. For the years in which data were available, the exchanges ranged in the seven companies from a low of 0.2% of sales in the case of The Texas Company in 1938 to a high of 41.5% of sales in the case of The Ohio Oil Company in 1949.

Reasons for the Exchanges: The most important reason why the companies engaged in refined product exchanges was to supply market areas which they could not reach from their

---

[13] Defined for the purpose of this analysis as approximately the 20 or 30 largest refining companies.

EXHIBIT XIV-5. GULF OIL CORPORATION

Analysis of Refined Product Purchases by Source: 1946–1951

	1946	1947	1948	1949	1950	1951
All Products, % Purchased From:						
Processing Agreements	9.6%	5.0%	8.2%	9.6%	6.1%	15.4%
Major Companies*	18.0	15.4	9.3	27.3	25.0	25.6
Other Companies	72.4	79.6	82.5	63.1	68.9	59.0
Gasolines, % Purchased From:						
Processing Agreements	6.0	4.8	9.1	8.3	8.6	16.7
Major Companies*	16.9	14.3	7.5	16.0	11.5	18.4
Other Companies	77.1	80.9	83.4	75.7	79.9	64.9
Kerosene and Distillates, % Purchased From:						
Processing Agreements	9.3	5.5	12.2	14.8	6.4	18.3
Major Companies*	22.2	25.4	7.5	19.0	20.0	12.7
Other Companies	68.5	69.1	80.3	66.2	73.6	69.0
Residual, % Purchased From:						
Processing Agreements	27.0	5.0	4.8	9.3	3.7	12.4
Major Companies*	8.6	5.6	10.1	57.2	37.4	39.8
Other Companies	64.4	89.4	85.1	33.5	58.9	47.8
Other Products, % Purchased From:						
Processing Agreements	0	0	0	0	0	0
Major Companies*	62.3	59.2	97.0	81.4	99.6	99.6
Other Companies	37.7	40.8	3.0	18.6	0.4	0.4

* For the purposes of this analysis, "major companies" were defined as roughly the 20 or 30 largest refining companies.

SOURCE: Gulf Oil Corporation.

own refineries on an economical basis. The companies were continually developing such areas in their marketing territories as a result of changes in the various logistical factors upon which their refining-marketing operations were originally planned. The construction of a new products pipe line by competitors, for example, often placed a company in a position where it could no longer reach a part of its market on equal terms with other shippers. New crude oil discoveries and the development of new refining centers sometimes tended to exclude a company from a portion of its market. Likewise such things as changes in labor costs, the gradual depletion of near-by oil fields, or changes in tanker charter rates, rail charges, or pipe line tariffs often resulted in a contraction of the geographical area a company could serve from an existing refinery point. In addition, companies occasionally found it necessary to shut down one of their refineries and thus lost their sources of supply for particular markets. A number of situations of this type developed in the immediate postwar period as a result of the rapid increase in the octane ratings of gasoline. At this time some companies elected to close down certain of their plants because they were too small to permit the installation of catalytic cracking equipment, and as a result were left with market areas for which a new source of supply had to be arranged.

When, as a result of one or another of the above circumstances, it developed that a sector of a company's market could no longer be reached by direct shipments from its refineries, the company had only the alternatives of withdrawing from the area or seeking new supply arrangements. In some cases, the companies had such heavy investments in marketing facilities and brand name promotion that withdrawal from the area was out of the question. There were, of course, many steps a company could take as a means of improving its supply position and remaining in the market; new refineries could be built, old plants could be modernized or enlarged to reduce their operating costs and thus increase their shipping areas, and new pipe lines could be laid or access gained to the lines of other companies. Moves of this kind, however, frequently took time and in some cases were not feasible in terms of a company's existing financial situation. Exchange arrangements were therefore frequently used as temporary or fairly long-run solutions to the problem of supplying areas which a company could not reach from its own plants.

Product exchanges served a second general purpose in that they provided a convenient means by which two or more companies could share the economic advantages of well-located refineries, pipe lines, or terminals with each other on mutually advantageous bases. Two companies occasionally found, for example, that each was shipping products into an area where the other had a refinery and ample supplies available. In such cases, an exchange arrangement reduced or eliminated the transportation cost for both companies and enabled each to do the distribution job at a lower cost than would otherwise have been possible. Similarly, a company which did not ordinarily make its products pipe lines available to other shippers might nevertheless accept products from a shipper at one point along its pipe lines in exchange for deliveries at another point. The shipper thus, for all practical purposes, was provided with the advantages of the line and merely paid a differential on the exchange tantamount to a pipe line tariff. Sinclair, for example, accepted products from a number of large and small refiners at several points along its pipe line in the Mid-Continent area and returned the products to the shippers as exchanges at other points along the line further to the north.

Exchanges were also used as temporary expedients to handle a variety of situations in much the same manner as were product purchases: to take care of spot shortages in particular areas, to supply new markets in which a company was seeking to gain a foothold, and to compensate for disparities between a company's refinery yields and its marketing requirements. Exchanges of the latter type, of course, involved the trading of one kind of product for another.

It should not be inferred from the foregoing discussion that all exchanges originated as "force-plays"; that is, as defensive moves under competitive pressure or in response to a shift in the economic factors affecting a company's supply and distribution arrangements. Some exchanges were planned and executed solely as aggressive moves in an effort by companies to gain lower supply costs and better positions in the market than those of their competitors. A company which happened to have ample refining capacity at a point where supplies were temporarily short could, for example, often capitalize on the situation by a series of exchange arrangements and get products delivered to many other parts of its market territory on very favorable terms.

Practices of the Seven Companies With Respect to the Use of Exchanges: As may be seen from Exhibit XIV-2, there were some marked differences among the seven companies with respect to the extent to which product exchanges were used. In the years covered by our data, Atlantic and The Texas Company usually had ratios of exchanges to total sales of less than 8%; Sohio, the Indiana Company, Gulf, and Sinclair ratios somewhere between 8% and 20%; and The Ohio Oil Company ratios of about 28% to 42%. It may also be noted that all the companies made approximately the same proportionate use of exchanges and purchases except The Ohio Oil Company and the Indiana Company. The Ohio Oil Company used exchanges more heavily than purchases, whereas the Indiana Company customarily used purchases somewhat more heavily than exchanges.

As in the case of product purchases, these differences in practice with respect to exchanges were at least partially a reflection of differences in the refining-marketing situations of the companies. Sohio and Atlantic, for example, had relatively little need for exchanges because their major markets were limited to small geographic areas readily accessible to their refineries and because each had well-developed products pipe line systems. The Ohio Oil Company, on the other hand, as may be seen from the map in Chapter Twelve, Exhibit XII-6, marketed in several states along the northern border of the United States which were far removed from its refinery locations. The company's Robinson plant was, however, well situated to supply products to many other firms and thus placed the company in a strong position to negotiate exchange agreements. It is also possible that the large volume of exchanges used by The Ohio Oil Company stemmed, in part, from its policy of not owning pipe lines to carry its own products in interstate commerce.

To a far greater degree than was true in the case of product purchases, we found that the differences in the practices of the seven companies with respect to exchanges reflected fundamental differences in policies as well as special circumstances with respect to distribution situations. With but one or two exceptions, all the companies were actively seeking to work into positions where their exchanges would be at a minimum and nearly all their markets would be supplied by direct shipments from their own refineries. There were, however, marked differences among the seven companies in the vigor with which this general objective was pursued, and these differences in policy were manifested to a considerable degree in the differences in exchange ratios shown in Exhibit XIV-2.

There were a number of reasons why the companies had sought and were continuing to seek a reduction in the volume of their product exchanges. In the first place, the executives of several of the companies stated that their marketing organizations had a distinct dislike for exchanges. Salesmen reported that it was very difficult for them to convince customers that the products of their company were of superior quality when it was well known that the products were drawn from the tanks and sometimes delivered in the trucks of a competitor. Exchange agreements were likewise regarded by the executives of some of the companies as lacking sufficient permanency to warrant the extensive capital commitments in the transportation and marketing facilities necessary to develop a market area properly and effectively.

Another important objection to product exchanges lay in the fact that it was not easy for a company making extensive use of them to maintain a consistent program with respect to the specifications and quality of its products. The products of each refiner were usually at least a little bit different in octane ratings or other specifications from those of other refiners. As a result, a company which secured any very large volume of its supplies on exchanges often had to do a good deal of mixing and blending to maintain its product standards.

The executives of The Texas Company, for example, reported that they tried to avoid exchanges because of the difficulty under such arrangements of maintaining the quality specifications for their gasolines in different sections of the country at different times of the year in accordance with the requirements of the company's marketing program. The company sold two grades of gasoline in 48 states. The states were divided into 25 geographic areas, and the specifications of the two grades of gasoline were changed four times a year in each area. These changes were made because the optimum volatility of gasolines depended to a considerable extent on weather conditions. The dates on which the changes were made in each geographic territory varied somewhat, depending on the timing of the season changes. A quality program of this kind would, of course, have been somewhat difficult to maintain had any very large volume of purchases or exchanges been used since there was always a certain amount of variation in the octane ratings and other specifications of the products produced by different refiners.

The executives of the Sinclair Oil Corporation had experienced similar difficulties in getting fuel oil of satisfactory specifications on an exchange basis. The company had developed a "dual purpose" No. 2 fuel oil which served not only as a Diesel fuel for tractors, trucks, and busses but also as a fuel oil for domestic ranges and space heaters. Most other refiners did not make a comparable product, and hence it was difficult for Sinclair to enter into exchanges for its fuel oil requirements.

A final reason why some of the companies were interested in reducing the volume of their exchanges lay in the fact that there was a slight possibility that the arrangements might some day be subject to legal criticism on the grounds that they involved misrepresentation of products.

Sources of Products Acquired on Exchanges: Whereas the seven companies customarily entered into purchase arrangements with small refiners, they negotiated the great majority of their exchanges with other large concerns. This circumstance was simply a natural result of the fact that the small refiners were not often in a position to participate as partners in product exchanges. Ordinarily, the small refiners had only one plant and confined their marketing operations to a limited geographic area. Accordingly, they did not often have products at one point which they might wish to offer in trade for products at another point. Whenever it was mutually desirable to do so, however, the large companies entered into exchange arrangements with small firms just as readily as they did with other large companies.

III. Summary

1. The seven oil companies were heavily engaged in crude oil gathering activities, and characteristically gathered an amount of crude oil equal to between 100% and 300% of their own crude oil production. The gathering lines were not built primarily to earn a profit on the gathering function but rather to gain access to crude oil or as a matter of expediency in getting oil out of the fields. It was the general policy of the six companies which were net buyers of crude oil in the United States to develop or maintain sufficient gathering lines so that their crude oil gathered (plus imports of their own foreign production) would be a high proportion, or perhaps somewhat in excess, of their domestic refinery runs. It was the practice of The Ohio Oil Company, on the other hand, to gather an amount of crude oil about equal to or somewhat in excess of its domestic crude oil production. None of the companies was contemplating major changes in its crude oil gathering programs in the foreseeable future.

2. Six of the companies had by 1950 developed company owned pipe line facilities for the movement of between 61.4% and 97.8% of their crude oil requirements to their refineries. The seventh company, The Atlantic Refining Company, was so situated that a large part of its crude oil requirements could best be received by tanker. There were marked differences in the extent to which the various companies had established crude oil trunk line facilities, but these differences were occasioned more by differences in the geographic location of refineries than by differences in integration policies.

Six of the companies regarded crude oil trunk lines as supporting facilities for other phases of their businesses and rarely, if ever, built lines which they did not plan to use in their own operations or lines primarily for the purpose of earning a profit on transportation service provided to other shippers. The policies of The Ohio Oil Company differed from those of the other companies in that it did not carry its own oil in interstate commerce and in that it did build crude oil trunk lines for the purpose of earning a profit on transportation service provided to other shippers. We found no indication that any of the companies was contemplating changes in its policies with respect to crude oil trunk lines, although there was some evidence of a trend toward the increased usage of joint ownership arrangements.

3. The volume of refined products moved from refineries via company pipe lines by the seven companies ranged from zero in the case of The Ohio Oil Company to 45.8% of total shipments in the case of Sohio. As in the case of crude oil trunk lines, all the companies except The Ohio Oil Company regarded products pipe lines as supporting to other phases of their business and rarely built lines which they did not plan to use themselves or lines primarily for the purpose of earning a profit on service provided to other shippers. The Ohio Oil Company, on the other hand, established a products pipe line in 1952 for the specific purpose of providing transportation service to other shippers.

There were variations among the seven companies with respect to the extent to which they had developed products pipe lines, the use of joint ownership arrangements, and the carrying of products for other shippers. These differences were in part a consequence of the fact that products pipe lines were a fairly recent development and in part a consequence of historical accidents, matters of expediency in individual cases, and differences in the geographical location of refineries. We found every reason to believe that the companies would press ahead with the construction of additional products pipe lines and would handle an increasing volume of their refinery shipments through such facilities in the future.

4. With the exception of the war years, the seven companies customarily purchased 2% to 20% of their refined product requirements. Purchases were used to compensate for lags in refining versus marketing expansion, to handle spot shortages, to assure a company's own refineries of capacity operations, to meet seasonal variations in demand, to compensate for disparities between refinery yields and market requirements, to take advantage of favorable buying opportunities, to relieve the market of distress cargoes, and to supply market areas remote from refineries. There were wide variations in the purchasing programs of the seven companies and in the programs of each company from one year to the next. So far as we were able to determine, the differences among the seven companies arose more from differences in their refining-marketing situations than from fundamental differences in their policies with respect to the use of purchases. Each of the companies anticipated that it would continue its existing practices with respect to product purchases and that the amounts and items bought would vary from year to year depending upon current circumstances.

5. The executives of the seven companies reported that their product purchases were made largely from small firms, a fact which was fully corroborated by statistical data in the case of one company, the Gulf Oil Corporation. It would appear therefore that in continuing their existing practices with respect to product purchases, the seven large companies will maintain an important field of opportunity for the small refiner.

6. The seven companies all engaged to some extent in refined product exchanges. Exchanges were made to supply market areas a company could not reach from its own refineries; as a means of sharing the economic advantages of well-located refineries, pipe lines, or terminals on mutually advantageous bases; and for many other purposes. There were marked differences in the usage of exchanges by the seven companies; two companies characteristically obtained less than 8% of their products on exchanges whereas another company obtained about 28% to 42%.

The differences in the exchange practices of the seven companies were, in part, a reflection of differences in refining-marketing situations, but to a much greater degree than in the case of product purchases, they were also a matter of differences in company policies. Most of the companies had been seeking to reduce the volume of their exchanges, but some companies were pressing the matter far more vigorously than others. The desire to avoid exchanges arose from the fact that the exchanges hampered the activities of salesmen in stressing quality characteristics, made it difficult to maintain quality standards, lacked sufficient permanency to encourage commitments in marketing facilities, and exposed a company to some slight possibility of legal criticism.

CHAPTER FIFTEEN

Analysis of Integration Patterns: Wholesale Marketing Activities

THE PURPOSE of this chapter and the one which follows is to analyze and compare the integration patterns of the seven companies with respect to marketing activities. As was noted in Chapter Fourteen, this topic embraces and should be considered as one aspect of the problem of balance between refining and marketing operations, because as a company alters its forward integration into the marketing field, it automatically increases or decreases its dependency upon outside wholesale and retail intermediaries for the distribution of its refinery output and thereby alters the balance of its refining and marketing activities. As in the case of the two preceding chapters, the discussion will relate to the data presented in Chapter Twelve, and the primary purpose of the analysis will be to examine the present positions of the seven companies, the recent changes they have made in their structures, and their future intentions with respect to integration in the marketing field.

We found it far more difficult to draw comparisons among the integration patterns of the seven companies with respect to marketing activities than with respect to any other phase of their operations. There were possibilities for variations with respect to the *depth* of integration or the number of steps covered in the distribution process, the *extent* of integration or the amount of participation in each step, and the *intensity* of integration or the character of the bonds established with the various wholesale and retail intermediaries and with different types of customers (see Chapter One). We found no satisfactory means of reducing these several kinds of differences to a common denominator, and it was therefore necessary to make separate comparisons with respect to each point of difference.

A second problem of analysis arose from the fact that the differences in integration patterns in the marketing field did not, in general, run parallel to the policies and business decisions from which the differences arose. In other words, the differences in depth, extent, and intensity of integration among the seven companies sprang, not from policies and decisions made explicitly with respect thereto, but rather from policies and decisions with respect to the types of outlets to be used in particular market situations. A company might, for example, consider the use of a company operated bulk plant, a commission bulk plant, a branded jobber, or an unbranded jobber to serve a particular market territory and might have general policies with respect to the circumstances in which each type of outlet should be used. Decisions on such matters embraced decisions on the depth, extent, and intensity of integration, but the latter were usually secondary rather than prime focal points for executive thinking. We found therefore that the differences in structure among the seven companies could not be related directly to policies with respect thereto but could only be regarded as secondary reflections of policies and practices with respect to the selection of market outlets.

In view of the above considerations, we shall first compare the depth and extent of integration found among the seven companies as reflected in the volumes sold at the wholesale, retail, and consumer and industrial user levels of the market.[1] We shall then direct attention to the practices and policies of the companies with respect to the usage of different types of wholesale and retail outlets as the underlying

---

[1] See footnotes to Exhibit XV-1 for types of business embraced by each level of the market.

source of the differences in depth and extent of integration. The analysis with respect to wholesale outlets will be included in this chapter, and the analysis with respect to retail outlets will be presented in Chapter Sixteen. The discussion of practices and policies with respect to the usage of wholesale and retail outlets will also cover the question of intensity of integration because intensity is largely a matter of the types of outlets a company uses and the character of the relationships it establishes with them by contracts or other means.

I. COMPARISON OF DEPTH AND EXTENT OF FORWARD INTEGRATION INTO MARKETING ACTIVITIES

We found that the structures of the seven companies were uniform with respect to depth of integration into the marketing field; that is, all the companies sold to wholesale resellers, retail resellers, and consumers and industrial users.[2] Moreover, our statistical data revealed that the companies had been active at all three levels of the market for at least 15 years before 1950, and the executives of each company informed us that their company's practice of selling at the three levels of the market went back approximately to the beginning of its refinery operations. There were, on the other hand, many differences among the seven companies with respect to the extent of integration or the relative volumes of refinery output sold at each level of the market. There were likewise important differences among the companies with respect to the changes made in the extent of integration during the period 1935–1950, or during such parts of the period as were covered by the available data.

Gasoline Marketing Activities:

The proportions of each company's gasoline volume which were sold to wholesale resellers, retail resellers, and consumers and industrial users in the years 1935, 1940, 1946, and 1950 are shown in Exhibit XV-1. The data for this exhibit were drawn from the information on

balance of operations presented in Chapter Twelve, Exhibits XII-19 to XII-26, and in the Appendix, Tables 9–15. The figures are subject to all the notations in Chapter Twelve and in the footnotes to the tables in the Appendix with regard to the manner in which the data for each company were prepared or estimated.

The seven companies have been listed in Exhibit XV-1 in order of extent of forward integration in 1950. It is readily apparent that the Indiana Company and Sohio[3] had a substantially greater extent of forward integration into gasoline marketing activities in 1950 than did any other company. Both companies sold a higher proportion of their gasoline volume to consumers and industrial users and a smaller proportion to wholesale resellers than did the other companies. Sohio sold a larger volume to consumers and industrial users than did the Indiana Company, but it also sold a larger volume to wholesale resellers than did the Indiana Company. We have placed the Indiana Company ahead of Sohio in extent of integration because the relative difference between the two companies was greater at the wholesale level (where the Indiana Company showed the greater extent of integration) than it was at the consumer and industrial user level (where Sohio showed the greater extent of integration).

The Gulf Oil Corporation had a substantially lesser extent of forward integration than did Sohio because, although it sold about the same share of its volume to wholesale resellers, it sold only about half as much to consumers and industrial users as did Sohio. The Texas Company ranked below Gulf in degree of integration because it sold more to wholesale resellers and less to consumers and industrial users than did Gulf. Sinclair sold slightly more to consumers and industrial users than did The Texas Company but ranked below The Texas Company in extent of integration because it sold a much larger share to wholesale resellers than did The Texas Company. Atlantic sold about the same amount to wholesale resellers as did Sinclair, but ranked below Sinclair in extent of integration because it sold a smaller share to consumers and industrial users than did Sinclair. The Ohio Oil Company sold more

[2] For simplicity in discussion, we shall speak of sales "to" particular levels of the market. It will be understood that we mean sales "to" or "through" the particular outlets embraced by the level of the market under discussion, depending on the types of transactions involved. See discussion in Chapter Twelve and footnotes to Exhibit XV-1.

[3] See footnotes to Exhibit XV-1 regarding the arrangement of the Sohio data.

Exhibit XV-1. Seven Oil Companies

Proportions of Gasoline Volume Sold at Different Levels of the Market:
1935, 1940, 1946, and 1950

Companies (Listed in Order of Extent of Integration in 1950)		Proportions of Gasoline Volume Sold to or Through		
		Wholesale Resellers *	Retail Resellers †	Consumers and Industrial Users ‡
1. Indiana Company	1935	N.A.	24.3%	N.A.
	1940	14.7%	59.4	25.9%
	1946	10.0	57.9	32.1
	1950	9.9	55.2	34.9
2. Sohio	1935	19.3	50.1	30.6
	1940	29.4	44.3	26.3
	1946	25.6	37.7	36.7
	1950	16.2	43.5	40.3
3. Gulf	1935	10.0	64.4	25.6
	1940	16.2	62.9	20.9
	1946	23.1	56.4	20.5
	1950	16.9	62.1	21.1
4. The Texas Company§	1935	N.A.	N.A.	N.A.
	1940	N.A.	N.A.	N.A.
	1946	N.A.	N.A.	N.A.
	1951	22.7	62.2	15.1
5. Sinclair	1935	28.9	44.3	26.8
	1940	28.1	50.4	21.5
	1946	36.1	44.1	19.8
	1950	34.1	47.8	18.1
6. Atlantic	1935	N.A.	N.A.	N.A.
	1940	N.A.	N.A.	N.A.
	1946	N.A.	N.A.	N.A.
	1950	33.6	51.8	14.6
7. The Ohio Oil Company	1935	N.A.	N.A.	N.A.
	1940	45.4	39.6	15.0
	1946	49.3	34.4	16.3
	1950	44.5	35.5	20.0

* Includes sales through brokers and sales to cargo buyers, all types of jobbers, and tank truck dealers, except in the case of Sohio. In the Sohio data tank truck dealers were grouped with consumers and industrial users. Since the volume of gasoline sold by most companies to tank truck dealers was very small, we do not believe that the inclusion of such dealers in the consumer group in the case of Sohio distorts the comparisons by more than two or three percentage points.

† Includes sales to dealer operated service stations and contractor service stations.

‡ Includes sales through company operated service stations and sales to homes, farms, and various types of industrial and commercial accounts.

§ The Texas Company data are for 1951 rather than 1950.

Source: See Chapter Twelve, Exhibits XII-19 to XII-26, and Appendix, Tables 9–15.

to consumers and industrial users than did Atlantic, but was placed last in extent of integration because it sold much more to wholesale resellers than did Atlantic and because the differences were greater at the wholesale level (where Atlantic showed the greater extent of integration) than at the consumer and industrial user level (where The Ohio Oil Company showed the greater extent of integration).

It is important to note that the differences in extent of forward integration into gasoline marketing activities among the seven companies covered a very wide range. The Indiana Company sold about two-thirds as much of its volume at the wholesale level as did any other company and only about one-fourth as much as did The Ohio Oil Company. Sohio sold substantially more of its volume at the consumer and industrial user level than did any other company and about two and one-half times as much as did Atlantic. As will be noted in Chapter Sixteen, Sohio's unique position in the consumer and industrial user market was attributable almost entirely to the large share of its volume which it sold through company operated service stations. In other words, all the companies, with some exception in the case of Atlantic, sold about the same share of their volume to other than service station customers; that is, to industrial plants, farms, homes, commercial transport concerns, and city, state, and government agencies.[4]

The foregoing discussion has related to the differences among the companies at the wholesale and consumer and industrial user levels of the market as a matter of convenience in discussion. Since the remainder of each company's volume was sold at the retail level, the differences at the retail level were necessarily parallel to those at the wholesale and consumer and industrial user levels.

The data in Exhibit XV-1 reveal the changes which the companies made in their extent of forward integration into gasoline marketing activities in the period 1935–1950. These changes are important because, as will become clear later in the chapter, they reflect the net result of a vast range of executive decisions with regard to the usage of different types of wholesale and retail outlets and provide a general indication of whether the companies were accelerating or decelerating their forward integration programs. The figures in Exhibit XV-1 have some distinct limitations as a basis for analyzing trends because they fluctuate considerably and cover only four selected years in the 15-year period. They do, however, permit some unequivocal conclusions with regard to the relative positions of the companies at the beginning and end of the period.

The data indicate that (a) several of the companies altered their extent of integration into gasoline marketing activities appreciably between 1935 and 1950, and (b) that the alteration represented further integration in some cases and disintegration in others.

Two of the companies, Sinclair and Gulf, *decreased* their extent of integration. Sinclair

increased its sales to wholesale resellers from 28.9% to 34.1%, increased its sales to retail resellers from 44.3% to 47.8%, and reduced its sales to consumers and industrial users from 26.8% to 18.1%. Gulf increased its sales to wholesale resellers from 10.0% to 16.9%, decreased its sales to retail resellers from 64.4% to 62.1%, and decreased its sales to consumers and industrial users from 25.6% to 21.1%.

On the other hand, three of the companies, Sohio, The Ohio Oil Company, and the Indiana Company, *increased* their extent of integration. Sohio decreased its sales to wholesale resellers from 19.3% to 16.2%, decreased its sales to retail resellers from 50.1% to 43.5%, and increased its sales to consumers and industrial users from 30.6% to 40.3%. The Ohio Oil Company in the period 1940–1950 decreased its sales to wholesale resellers from 45.4% to 44.5%, decreased its sales to retail resellers from 39.6% to 35.5%, and increased its sales to consumers and industrial users from 15.0% to 20.0%. The Indiana Company in the period 1940–1950 decreased its sales to wholesale resellers from 14.7% to 9.9%, decreased its sales to retail resellers from 59.4% to 55.2%, and increased its sales to consumers and industrial users from 25.9% to 34.9%.

The data for Atlantic and The Texas Company are not sufficient to permit an analysis of net changes in position.

Kerosene and Distillate Marketing Activities:

The proportions of each company's kerosene and distillate volume which were sold to wholesale resellers, retail resellers, and consumers and industrial users are shown in Exhibit XV-2. The data have been drawn from the same sources, are subject to the same notations, and have been arranged in the same manner as the data for gasoline marketing activities in Exhibit XV-1.

Exhibit XV-2 reveals that the seven companies in 1950 had about the same relative rank with respect to extent of integration into kerosene and distillate marketing activities as they did with respect to extent of integration into gasoline marketing activities. As in the case of gasoline, the Indiana Company and Sohio had the greatest extent of integration. The position of the Indiana Company, however, was much further removed from that of

---

[4] As noted in Chapter Twelve, most of the companies treated sales to local government agencies, such as the post office and forestry service, as "consumer sales" and sales to the military services as "cargo sales."

EXHIBIT XV-2. SIX OIL COMPANIES*
Proportions of Kerosene and Distillate Sold at Different Levels of the Market:
1935, 1940, 1946, and 1950

Companies (Listed in Order of Extent of Integration in 1950)		Proportions of Kerosene and Distillate Volume Sold to or Through		
		Wholesale Resellers†	Retail Resellers‡	Consumers and Industrial Users§
1. Indiana Company	1935	2.9%	—	97.1%
	1940	4.7	—	95.3
	1946	3.9	—	96.1
	1950	3.8	—	96.2
2. Sohio	1935	63.9	5.2%	30.9
	1940	66.5	2.8	30.7
	1946	67.7	1.5	30.8
	1950	40.3	1.6	58.1
3. Gulf	1935	46.7	10.9	42.4
	1940	64.6	7.6	27.8
	1946	60.3	6.8	32.9
	1950	59.1	4.6	36.3
4. The Texas Company ‖	1935	N.A.	N.A.	N.A.
	1940	N.A.	N.A.	N.A.
	1946	N.A.	N.A.	N.A.
	1951	62.9	3.9	32.2
5. The Ohio Oil Company	1935	N.A.	N.A.	N.A.
	1940	71.6	10.4	18.0
	1946	78.6	4.6	16.8
	1950	69.4	3.9	26.7
6. Atlantic	1935	N.A.	29.8	N.A.
	1940	N.A.	32.9	N.A.
	1946	N.A.	11.2	N.A.
	1950	74.6	0.6	24.8

* No data were available on the activities of Sinclair in the kerosene and distillate markets.

† Includes sales through brokers and sales to cargo buyers, all types of jobbers, and tank truck dealers, except in the case of Sohio. In the Sohio data tank truck dealers were grouped with consumers and industrial users.

‡ Includes sales to dealer operated service stations and contractor service stations.

§ Includes sales through company operated service stations and sales to homes, farms, and various types of industrial and commercial accounts.

‖ The Texas Company data are for 1951 rather than 1950.

SOURCE: See Chapter Twelve, Exhibits XII–19 to XII–26, and Appendix, Tables 9–15.

Sohio and the other companies in the case of kerosene and distillate than it was in the case of gasoline.

It should be noted that the statistical data for Sohio had an important limitation in that tank truck dealers were grouped with consumers and industrial users whereas in the case of all other companies tank truck dealers were grouped with wholesale resellers. This limitation in the comparability of our data is more important here than it was in the case of gasoline, because although the seven companies sold very little of their gasoline to tank truck dealers, some of them sold as much as 10% to

15% of their kerosene and distillate volume to tank truck dealers. Nevertheless, even if Sohio had sold as much as 18% of its kerosene and distillate volume to tank truck dealers, which is quite unlikely, it would still have ranked second in extent of forward integration in 1950.

The positions which Atlantic and The Ohio Oil Company held with respect to extent of forward integration into gasoline marketing activities were reversed in the case of kerosene and distillate marketing activities. The Ohio Oil Company sold an appreciably smaller volume of kerosene and distillate to wholesale resellers and an appreciably larger volume to consumers and industrial users than did Atlantic. Both companies, however, had a substantially lesser extent of forward integration than did the other five companies.

The data in Exhibit XV-2 permit an analysis of changes in position for only four of the companies, Gulf, Sohio, The Ohio Oil Company, and the Indiana Company. The direction of the change made by each of these companies in extent of integration into kerosene and distillate marketing activities was usually the same as the direction of the change in the case of gasoline marketing activities. Gulf *decreased* its extent of integration just as it did in the case of gasoline. Sales to wholesale resellers increased from 46.7% to 59.1%, sales to retail resellers decreased from 10.9% to 4.6%, and sales to consumers and industrial users decreased from 42.4% to 36.3%.

Sohio and The Ohio Oil Company, on the other hand, *increased* their extent of integration. Sohio decreased its sales to wholesale resellers from 63.9% to 40.3%, decreased its sales to retail resellers from 5.2% to 1.6%, and increased its sales to final consumers from 30.9% to 58.1%.[5] The Ohio Oil Company decreased its sales to wholesale resellers from 71.6% to 69.4%, decreased its sales to wholesale resellers from 10.4% to 3.9%, and increased its sales to final consumers from 18.0% to 26.7%. The Indiana Company made no significant change in its position in the kerosene and distillate marketing field as far as may be determined from our data.

[5] It should again be noted that these comparisons are somewhat faulty because tank truck dealers were grouped with wholesale resellers in the case of Gulf, the Indiana Company, and The Ohio Oil Company and with final consumers in the case of Sohio. The tank truck dealers are usually very active in the home fuel oil market which expanded enormously in the period 1935–1950. Any increase in sales to this class of account would show up in the Gulf, the Indiana Company and The Ohio Oil Company figures as a decrease in degree of integration and in the Sohio figures as an increase in degree of integration. It is not likely, however, that the general direction of the changes indicated for each company would have been different had it been possible to handle tank truck dealers as retail resellers. In other words, the changes in sales to tank truck dealers probably accounted for only a part of Gulf's increase in sales to wholesale resellers and for only a part of Sohio's increase in sales to final consumers. In the case of The Ohio Oil Company, separate figures were available for sales to tank truck dealers, and it may be seen that the share of the company's volume sold to them was about the same in 1940 as in 1950 (see Appendix, Table 12).

Comparison of Exhibits XV-1 and XV-2 reveals that the integration patterns of the seven companies with respect to kerosene and distillate marketing activities were quite different from those with respect to gasoline marketing activities. The differences were not, however, quite so marked as would appear at first glance to be the case. In the kerosene and distillate markets, the counterparts of the retail resellers in the gasoline market were in reality the tank truck dealers. Unfortunately, it was not possible to show separate figures for tank truck dealers except in the case of The Texas Company, Atlantic, and The Ohio Oil Company, and in the interests of uniformity therefore tank truck dealers were grouped with wholesale resellers in all cases except that of Sohio where they were treated as noted above.

As may be inferred from the data for The Texas Company, The Ohio Oil Company, and Atlantic (see Appendix, Tables 10, 12, and 13), if it had been possible to treat these tank truck dealers as "retail resellers," the integration patterns of the seven companies with respect to gasoline and kerosene and distillate marketing activities would have shown a greater degree of similarity than is suggested by the present arrangement of the data. Nevertheless, the data unquestionably permit the conclusion that all the companies except the Indiana Company had a greater extent of forward integration into gasoline than into kerosene and distillate marketing activities. It should also be noted that all the companies for which data were available sold somewhat more kerosene and distillate directly to consumers and industrial users than they did gasoline.

As was suggested in earlier discussion, a company's position with respect to forward integration into gasoline and kerosene and distillate marketing activities is derived from the summation of the decisions the company makes with respect to the selection and usage of different types of wholesale and retail intermediaries for the distribution of its products. It follows that the future objectives of the companies with respect to extent of integration into marketing activities can best be expressed in terms of their objectives with respect to the usage of different types of outlets. We shall therefore defer discussion of objectives with respect to extent of integration until we have first considered practices, policies, and objectives with respect to the usage of different types of market outlets.

II. THE TYPES OF WHOLESALE OUTLETS

We found that there was considerable confusion in the industry with respect to the terminology applied to the various types of wholesale outlets. Practices varied widely from one geographical area of the country to another and likewise varied among different companies in the same geographical area. The terms "jobber" and "distributor" were particularly ambiguous and either term was often used to cover operations which were distinctly different in character. In the following paragraphs therefore we shall establish certain terminology and definitions of our own as a basis for the contrast and comparison of the policies of the seven companies which are to follow in later sections of the chapter.

We shall define "wholesale outlet" as an activity which involves the maintenance and operation of a bulk plant or terminal. This definition arbitrarily excludes from consideration the many different types of intermediaries, which we shall term tank truck dealers or peddlers, who customarily buy gasoline and/or kerosene and distillate "under the rack" at the bulk plants or terminals of their suppliers but who do not operate bulk plant or terminal facilities of their own. The tank truck dealers will be treated as retail resellers because their principal field of activity is in the home fuel oil market where they make their sales to final consumers rather than to retail resellers.[6] So far as gasoline is concerned, however, many of these buyers might have been treated equally well as a special layer of wholesale intermediaries operating between bulk plants and service stations.

In the interests of simplicity, we shall confine the discussion largely to bulk plants, although conceivably each type of outlet could exist for either bulk plants or terminals, because it is principally with respect to bulk

plants that the market outlet selection problem arises. Moreover, we found that all of the seven companies operated their pipe line and marine terminals almost entirely on a salaried basis. There were, of course, many jobbers, particularly in the fuel oil business along the Atlantic Coast, who were large enough to operate terminals, and the companies sometimes had the problem of deciding between a company and a jobber terminal operation. The issues in such cases, however, were of the same general character as those involved in connection with bulk plant facilities.

We found that many companies were making rapid progress in the use of direct shipments from terminals to service stations and other large customers and were thus developing their terminals as wholesale facilities. We shall treat this phenomenon as a by-passing of the wholesale level rather than as the establishment of a different kind of a wholesale outlet.

The various types of bulk plant outlets we found in common usage in the marketing programs of the seven companies were divided into five general categories as follows.

Company Operated Bulk Plants:

The facilities at the company operated bulk plants were owned or leased by the supplying company, and the plants were maintained and operated by regular employees of the company who were usually paid on a straight salary basis. The bulk plants ordinarily received their supplies by tank car, truck, or barge from refineries and marine and pipe line terminals. Products were usually distributed from the bulk plants by truck to service stations, farms, industrial plants, commercial accounts, city, state, and federal agencies, and, in the case of fuel oil, to homes. The area served from a bulk plant varied considerably, depending on such things as the population density and road conditions, but rarely exceeded 50 miles in radius and was not often in excess of 20 or 25 miles in radius.

Two principal methods of distribution were used by the company operated bulk plants in serving the various classes of consumer accounts. In the first method, products were delivered to customers by means of company trucks driven by company employees. In the second method, the deliveries were made by

---

[6] As noted earlier, because of limitations in the statistical records of certain of the companies it was necessary for us to group tank truck dealers with wholesale resellers in certain of our statistical analyses.

commission truck drivers [7] who were not regarded as company employees.

In addition to the various classes of consumer and industrial user accounts which were served by the two methods mentioned above, the company operated bulk plants also sold to various types of tank truck dealers. The tank truck dealers were in many respects counterparts of the commission truck drivers except that, instead of receiving a commission for their services, they bought products outright at the bulk plant and resold to the various types of final consumers by any means and at any price they chose. Finally, the larger company operated bulk plants were also sometimes used as distributing points for sales to the smaller branded and unbranded jobbers. In such cases, the shipments to the bulk plants of the jobbers were usually made by rail, large truck transports, or barge.

In the light of the foregoing discussion, it will immediately be recognized that a company's program of integration into wholesale marketing activities was affected in the first instance by the decision to use a company operated bulk plant rather than some other type of wholesale outlet and in the second instance by decisions made with respect to how the bulk plant was managed; that is, decisions with regard to the relative volumes sold to final consumers, service stations, tank truck dealers, and jobbers, and decisions with regard to the usage of company trucks versus commission truck drivers. Some of the more important variations in the practices of the seven companies with respect to the operation of their bulk plants will be noted in later discussion.

Commission Distributorships, Independent:

All the companies had some type of arrangement for operating bulk plants on a commission basis. The operators of the plants were usually called commission distributors, bailees, consignees, or commission agents. Most of the companies, however, were avoiding the use of the word "agent" because they were anxious that the operators of the plants should be regarded as independent businessmen and not

have the legal status of company employees. As employees the bulk plant operators would have become eligible for employee benefits, and as employers the companies would have had to assume the responsibility for the payment of Social Security taxes for the bulk plant labor force and for seeing that the operators complied with the wage and hour laws in the management of the plants. The Indiana Company was an exception to the general rule and operated its commission bulk plants with company employees. The Indiana Company's commission distributors will therefore be treated as a separate type of outlet, and it will be understood that all references to general practices in the following paragraphs are exclusive of the Indiana Company.

The buildings, tanks, and land at the commission bulk plants were in the great majority of cases owned or leased by the supplying company and rented to the commission distributor. Occasionally a commission distributor owned his plant himself or leased it from a third party, but in such cases he usually arranged to lease the facilities to his supplier and to rent them back from him at the time the commission distributorship was established. Practices with regard to trucks and other bulk plant equipment varied somewhat from company to company, but usually the commission distributor provided his own trucks, or at least the chassis, as well as other portable equipment and supplies.

The commission distributors obtained their stocks on a consignment basis and resold to customers at prices specified by the supplying company. In some sections of the country the commission distributor was paid a flat rate of so much per gallon of products delivered regardless of the distance of the customer from the bulk plant. In 1950 the usual rate on gasoline was between $1\frac{1}{2}$ and $1\frac{3}{4}$ cents per gallon. In other sections of the country, notably the territory in which the Indiana Company operated and the Rocky Mountain region, the distributor was paid one rate for deliveries of gasoline (and sometimes other products) to cutomers close to his plant and a slightly higher rate for deliveries outside some specified radius, such as 15 miles. Where this plan of payment was used there was usually, but not always, a differential in the price structure between dealer and consumer tank wagon prices;

---

[7] Other names commonly used included commission marketers, commission salesmen, commission tank wagon salesmen, commission route salesmen, and tank truck distributors.

in areas where the flat commission rate was used the dealer and consumer tank wagon prices were generally the same.

It was a fairly common practice for the supplying companies to require their distributors to relinquish, say, ½ cent per gallon of their commission on deliveries to service stations owned or leased by the supplying company on the grounds that (a) such sales could be made a good deal more easily than could sales to contractor stations, and (b) the supplying company was entitled to some compensation for its investment in the station properties.

The commission distributor delivered products to the same general types of consumers and industrial users as did the company operated bulk plants, and the distributor was usually free to make whatever arrangements he wished with regard to the use of his own trucks or the hiring of commission truck drivers. Like the company operated bulk plants, the commission distributors also delivered products "under the rack" to tank truck dealers and occasionally made shipments to the bulk plants of the smaller branded or unbranded jobbers.

The commission distributors frequently acquired service stations of their own which they operated with salaried employees or rented out to dealers in much the same manner as did the supplying companies. It was usually the practice of the supplying companies to furnish the service station customers of their commission distributors with pumps, tanks, compressors, and various other pieces of equipment. The supplying companies also usually assumed the responsibility for maintaining the equipment, removing it from the premises of lost accounts, and installing it on the premises of new accounts. In addition, the supplying companies usually maintained a staff of sales representatives to aid the commission distributors and their service station customers in developing better methods of merchandising and sales promotion.

As a corollary to the fact that stocks were handled at the commission bulk plants on a consignment basis, the supplying companies usually performed a number of the functions associated with the operation of the plants. Among other things, the suppliers financed the inventories, carried the cost of inventory in-surance, absorbed inventory profits and losses, absorbed stock losses up to certain allowable maximums, absorbed credit losses, financed accounts receivable, and performed billing functions for certain classes of trade. The suppliers also audited the accounts of the commission distributors and aided them in setting up suitable bookkeeping methods.

The agreements with commission distributors usually covered a period of one year and were automatically renewable unless one party or the other gave notice of intention to terminate some stated number of days, frequently between 5 and 60, prior to the anniversary date of the contract. Various other types of cancellation provisions were also used; the agreements of some companies, for example, were subject to termination at any time by either party without notice or with notice of as little as five days. In cases where a distributor owned his plant and leased it to and back from a supplier, the lease to the supplier sometimes covered a period of three to five years even though the distributorship agreement covered only one year. This practice was used because the supplying companies were generally reluctant to incur the costs involved in setting up a distributorship and in consigning stocks to a bulk plant unless they could be assured of a reasonably long-term arrangement.

Commission Distributors, Company Employees:

The Indiana Company was the only one of the seven companies that treated its commission distributors as company employees. The distributors were eligible for retirement annuities and all other employee benefits with the exception of paid vacations and sickness and disability payments. These latter benefits were not provided to the distributors because the company did not wish to assume the implied responsibility for maintaining the operation of the plants during the absence of the distributors. The executives of the company regarded the problem of hiring a man to operate the plant of a distributor during his absence as somewhat akin to that of locating a tenant to live temporarily in somebody else's house. The commission distributors were represented in negotiations with the company through an employee union, a fact which further distinguished them from the commission distributors of the other companies who were usually not unionized.

The buildings, tanks, and all equipment at the bulk plants, with the exception of truck chassis, were owned or leased by the Indiana Company. The commission distributors owned the truck chassis and received a rental fee from the company to cover their cost and maintenance. The commission distributors were not encouraged to build or acquire control of service stations in the area in which they operated and few, if any, of them did so. It was the general policy of the Indiana Company to avoid exposure to the possible loss in volume and representation which could arise if a large distributor, controlling several service stations, elected to transfer his business to some other supplier.

The commissions which the Indiana Company paid to its distributors were slightly lower than those paid by the other companies to their distributors. It was believed that the differential was justified in view of the employee benefits the Indiana Company distributors received and in view of the fact that the company did very little by-passing of its bulk plants with direct shipments from terminals and thus gave nearly all its station business to the distributors. The commission rates were graduated to provide higher rates for deliveries to farm and other customers at some distance from the plant, and throughout most of the territory in which the Indiana Company posted tank wagon prices, a differential was maintained between dealer and consumer tank wagon prices. The executives of the company were anxious that the distributors should give a good deal of attention to and be properly compensated for the development of the farm market, and an extensive accounting and record keeping system was maintained in the bulk plants as a basis for directing and controlling the sales efforts of the distributors.

It is apparent from the above discussion that there was a much closer tie between the Indiana Company and its distributors than there was between the other companies and their commission distributors. The commission bulk plants of the Indiana Company could, indeed, be regarded as a special type of company operated bulk plant. We have chosen, however, to treat them as a separate type of outlet in drawing comparisons among the seven companies because the plants were more nearly the counterparts of the commission distributorships of the other companies than they were counterparts of the salary operated bulk plants.

Branded Gasoline Jobbers:

We shall define a branded gasoline jobber as one who maintained and operated a bulk plant or terminal and who purchased gasoline for resale under the brand name of his supplier. It will be understood that the definition includes those who purchased only gasoline from the supplier and those who purchased both gasoline and fuel oil, regardless of whether the fuel oil was sold on a branded or unbranded basis. In the companies we studied the development of brand names in connection with the merchandising of fuel oil had not progressed sufficiently far to warrant distinctions between types of outlets on the basis of branding practices. We shall therefore treat bulk plant and terminal operators who purchased only fuel oil for branded or unbranded resale simply as "jobbers." Accounts purchasing gasoline for unbranded resale and fuel oil for branded resale (a rare circumstance) will be treated as "unbranded jobbers."

The seven companies all made use of branded jobbers for some aspect of their marketing programs. In nearly all cases the branded jobbers owned or leased the buildings, tanks, trucks, and equipment at their plants. In a few cases, however, the suppliers owned or leased the plants and rented them to the jobbers. Sinclair was somewhat of an exception to the general rule in that it leased substantial numbers of its bulk plants to jobbers; in 1950 the company had 465 branded and unbranded jobbers [8] of which 139 were operating plants leased from Sinclair. In addition to their bulk plant facilities, the branded jobbers frequently owned or leased service stations in the area of their plants which they operated with their own employees or rented to dealers. Pumps, tanks, compressors, and other marketing equipment used by the service station customers of the branded jobbers were usually furnished,

---

[8] Only 10 or 12 of the total were unbranded jobbers.

installed, removed, and maintained by the jobber rather than by the supplier as in the case of the customers of commission distributors.

The branded jobbers customarily bought products from their suppliers on one or the other of two bases. Under the first method of sale, the jobber bought at a stated discount off the posted tank wagon price of the supplier or, if the supplier was not one of the leading marketers in the area, at a stated discount off the prices of one of the leading marketers. The contracts usually, but not always, provided that when the tank wagon prices were temporarily depressed below the "normal levels," the supplier and the jobber would share the amount of the depression but that the jobber would at all times be guaranteed a certain minimum margin. A typical jobber contract in 1950 provided for the sale of gasoline to the jobber at $2\frac{1}{2}$ cents below the tank wagon prices, for the splitting of price cuts equally between the supplier and the jobber until the jobber's margin was reduced to $1\frac{1}{2}$ cents per gallon, and for the bearing of all further price cuts by the supplier alone. Similar provisions, although with different discounts and different minimums, were made for the sale of various other products to the jobber.

Under the second method of sale, the branded jobber bought at the supplier's delivered tank car price or sometimes at the supplier's tank car price, f.o.b. point of shipment, with freight allowed to the jobber's destination or with freight allowed up to a certain specified maximum. The jobber's margin under this method of sale was dependent upon the spread which from time to time existed between the tank car prices and the tank wagon prices at his particular location. Ordinarily in contracts of this type, the jobber was not guaranteed a minimum margin.

It was the practice of several of the companies to give their branded jobbers a choice between the two methods of sale, as they might from time to time elect. In the case of gasoline, the first method of sale was clearly predominant, while in the case of fuel oil the second method was probably the more commonly used. Other products, such as lubricating oils, greases, and antifreeze, were nearly always sold at the supplier's prevailing price for carload or less than carload lots, f.o.b. point of shipment,

with freight allowed to destination or up to a certain specified maximum. Many jobber arrangements provided for variations in the method of sale depending on the product; frequently, for example, the first method was used for gasoline and the second method for kerosene, fuel oil, and all other products.

Most of the branded jobber contracts contained some statement as to the maximum and minimum amounts of gasoline, fuel oil, and sometimes other products to be purchased each year. Moreover, maximum figures were frequently set (particularly in the case of fuel oil) on the fraction of the annual requirements that the supplier would be obligated to deliver in any one month. The maximum-minimum figures were usually regarded as merely rough estimates and were included in the contracts primarily as a means (a) of providing the supplier with some protection during times of shortages such as, for example, sometimes developed in the case of fuel oil during an unusually severe winter, and (b) of assuring that the jobber would buy in sufficient quantities to warrant the price schedule offered to him. The minimum figures were usually set far below the quantities the jobber was expected to purchase, and action was rarely, if ever, initiated against a jobber who for one reason or another failed to take his minimum quantities in any given year.

The branded jobbers resold to the same general types of consumers and industrial users as did the company operated bulk plants and the commission distributors. In addition, sales were made to tank truck dealers and occasionally to other, smaller jobbers. As in the case of the company operated and commission plants, the branded jobbers made deliveries to customers in their own trucks or made use of commission truck drivers as circumstances warranted.

Practices varied widely among the seven companies with regard to the granting of exclusive territories to branded jobbers. Only in the case of The Ohio Oil Company did we find that it was the supplier's practice to include in the jobber franchises an explicit statement of the territory in which the jobber was given the exclusive right to distribute the supplier's products. Some of the companies, however, made it a general practice to set up only one jobber in a given area and to avoid the duplication of company operated, commission, and jobber outlets in the same market territories.

On the other hand, some of the companies had in earlier years deliberately set up one or more jobbers in the same area as a means of getting more intense coverage of the market or as a means of guarding against loss of representation in case a jobber should transfer his business to another supplier. Moreover, it was not uncommon for a company to establish jobbers in an area while it was in the process of breaking into a market and later, as the volume of business expanded, to set up bulk plants of its own for salary or commission operation. In 1952 there was, however, some indication in the companies we studied of a general trend, very strong in some cases, toward the gradual elimination of dual distribution arrangements.

There was nothing in the contracts we studied which precluded the branded jobber from handling the products of other companies, and, as already noted, the minimum quantities stated in the contracts were usually set at very low levels and were not, we were told, designed to have the effect of excluding the products of other suppliers. As a practical matter, the branded jobbers rarely, if ever, found it desirable to handle the gasolines of more than one supplier. It was not uncommon, however, for a branded jobber to secure his fuel oil from a different source than his gasoline or from more than one source. In addition, the jobbers frequently handled the lubricating oils of more than one supplier.

The jobber sales contracts were customarily written for a period of one year but were automatically renewable unless one party or the other gave notice of his intention to terminate at some stated interval, usually 30, 60, or 90 days, prior to the anniversary date of the contract. In some cases the contracts included a provision that the supplier should have the option of matching any offer that the jobber might receive for his business and properties, or any part thereof, during the duration of the supply agreement. These provisions were, of course, included so that the supplier might have some protection against the loss of the volume which had been built up under his brand name if the jobber found it necessary or desirable to close out his business.

Unbranded Gasoline Jobbers:

We shall define an unbranded gasoline jobber as one who maintained and operated a bulk plant or terminal and who purchased gasoline for resale under a brand name other than that of his supplier. As noted earlier, we shall include in the category of unbranded jobbers all firms purchasing gasoline for resale under brand names other than those of their suppliers, regardless of the bases upon which they purchased and resold fuel oil and other products.

The unbranded jobbers were rarely used in the marketing programs of the seven companies we studied, and as a result the relationships between them and the companies were far more informal and far less standardized than in the case of branded jobbers. In some cases the unbranded jobbers shopped around among several sources of supply and purchased spot cargoes wherever they could negotiate the most favorable arrangement at the moment. In other cases, they entered into contracts with suppliers for the purchase of all or part of their requirements for some specified period of time. The sales agreements in these instances varied from case to case but sometimes carried many of the same provisions used in the agreements with branded jobbers.

The unbranded gasoline jobbers usually bought their gasoline, as well as other products, at the tank car prices of their suppliers rather than at a discount off the tank wagon prices in their localities. Suppliers rarely entered into arrangements to split the losses on subnormal gasoline tank wagon prices with these jobbers or offered them guarantees of minimum margins. Fuel oil and other products were sold to unbranded gasoline jobbers in much the same manner as they were to branded gasoline jobbers.

In respects other than those noted above, the unbranded gasoline jobbers conducted their businesses in much the same general manner as did the branded gasoline jobbers.

Fuel Oil Jobbers:

There were many operators of bulk plants and terminals who handled only fuel oil or who purchased their gasoline from one source and their fuel oil from another. From the standpoint of the company supplying the fuel oil, these accounts could not be classed as either branded or unbranded gasoline jobbers. Moreover, as noted earlier, we did not find it practical to draw a distinction between branded and unbranded fuel oil outlets because such a distinction had not yet assumed much significance in the operations of the companies we studied. We shall therefore make use of the term "fuel oil jobber" to designate operators of bulk plants and terminals to whom the supplier sold only fuel oil, regardless of whether the oil was resold on a branded or unbranded basis. It will be recognized that this definition could include accounts which from the standpoint of the company supplying gasoline might be classed as either branded or unbranded gasoline jobbers.

The fuel oil jobbers provided their own plant facilities and equipment and bought their fuel oil supplies on much the same bases as did the branded and unbranded gasoline jobbers. Sales were made largely to farm, home, industrial, and commercial accounts, and deliveries were made either in trucks driven by salaried employees of the jobber or commission truck drivers.

III. CONSIDERATIONS AFFECTING THE SELECTION OF WHOLESALE OUTLETS

We found that the marketing programs of the seven companies at the wholesale level of the industry tended to evolve from a continuing series of multiple-choice decisions: that is, decisions as to whether company operated bulk plants, commission distributors, branded jobbers, unbranded jobbers, or direct shipments from refineries or terminals would be used to serve particular market areas. Each of these decisions had the potentiality of altering a company's integration pattern in one or another of several different respects. A decision to use a commission distributor in lieu of a company operated bulk plant, for example, while it did not alter the level of the market in which a company sold, did alter the intensity of integration because the commission distributors were generally subject to a slightly lesser degree of control than were company employees. Similarly, the choice of a branded jobber over an unbranded jobber did not alter the level of

the market in which a company sold but did alter the intensity of integration because the branded jobbers customarily had far closer ties with their suppliers than did unbranded jobbers. A decision to use a commission distributor in preference to a branded jobber, on the other hand, altered both the level of the market in which a company sold and the intensity of its integration program with respect to the particular area of the market involved in the choice.

Although the various types of wholesale outlets were used in the marketing programs of the seven oil companies in many different ways and in many different combinations, we found that the basic considerations influencing the selection of outlets were of the same general character in all the companies. In the following paragraphs we shall outline some of the more important of these considerations and will attempt to indicate the manner in which the problem of outlet selection was usually approached by the executives of the companies. The discussion will relate primarily to gasoline because the economics of the gasoline situation usually determined the type of outlet used. A concluding section of the discussion will treat briefly certain special factors relating to the selection of wholesale outlets for fuel oil alone.

Comparative Costs:

The first and perhaps most important factor influencing the selection of outlets was the relative cost of doing business through one type of outlet as opposed to another. Consider first the choice between a commission distributor and a branded jobber. On sales through the commission distributor the supplier realized a higher price than he did on sales to the branded jobber. In the case of gasoline, for example, on sales through the commission distributor the supplier realized the tank wagon price less the distributor's commission of about 1½ to 1¾ cents per gallon. On sales to the branded jobber, on the other hand, the supplier usually realized the tank wagon price less the 2½ to 2¾ cents discount customarily allowed to the jobber. By selling through the commission distributor the supplier thus received about 1 cent more per gallon of gasoline sold than he did by selling to the branded jobber. Higher realizations were likewise secured in the case of other products sold through the commission distributor.

In the operation of the commission bulk plant, however, the supplier incurred a number of costs which he did not have in selling to the branded jobber. First, the commission bulk plant required a capital investment in the bulk plant properties, or the payment of rentals in the case of leased facilities, a capital investment in the bulk plant inventories, and a capital investment in the pumps, tanks, compressors, and other units of marketing equipment customarily furnished to the service station customers of the commission distributor. In addition, the supplier incurred extra operating costs in connection with the distributor business for such things as: the removal, installation and maintenance of marketing equipment at service stations; inventory insurance; stock losses; credit losses; billing, accounting, and auditing services; and the maintenance of sales personnel to aid the distributor in developing his sales promotion and merchandising methods.

The incremental capital costs, and to a considerable extent the incremental operating costs, connected with the commission distributor operation were, however, relatively fixed irrespective of volume changes. As the volume of business done by the bulk plant increased, the per gallon value of the extra costs incurred in connection with the establishment and operation of the plant declined and at some point became equal to the differential between the realization on sales through the commission distributor versus sales to the branded jobber. In other words, in each individual bulk plant situation there was always a break-even volume below which it was cheaper for the supplier to operate through a branded jobber and above which it was cheaper for him to operate through a commission distributor. In most cases it was not too difficult to estimate the break-even volume or, conversely, knowing the volume of operation, to determine whether it was more profitable for the supplier to operate with the commission or branded jobber arrangement. The preparation of estimates of this type was usually one of the first steps taken by a supplier in deciding between a commission distributor or branded jobber operation.

Similar cost considerations entered into the evaluation of company operated bulk plants versus commission bulk plants. The gross realization secured on sales through company operated and commission bulk plants was exactly the same. Likewise there were no significant differences in the capital costs associated with the ownership of the bulk plant properties, the inventories, and the marketing equipment for service stations. The operating costs in the two situations differed, however, in that in the case of the company operated plant the supplier paid the wages of the plant manager and his crew, whereas in the case of the commission plant the supplier paid the distributor a commission of so much per gallon of products sold to cover the labor costs involved in managing and running the plant. In the case of the company operated plant the total wages of the labor force included not only straight salaries but also overtime payments and the value of whatever employee benefits the bulk plant employees were eligible to receive.[9]

The total labor costs for the company operated plant were in large measure fixed on an annual basis, and the per gallon labor costs were thus subject to considerable reduction as the volume of business done by the station increased. The rates paid to the commission distributor, on the other hand, were usually fixed on a per unit basis and hence remained the same (on a per unit basis) regardless of the volume of business done by the plant. Once again therefore there was in every situation a break-even volume below which it was cheaper for a supplier to sell through a commission distributor and above which it was cheaper for him to use salaried employees.

The choice between branded and unbranded gasoline jobbers was usually determined on other than direct cost considerations, as will be noted below. At this point, however, it may be observed that on sales to unbranded jobbers the supplier usually realized a slightly lower average price than he did on sales to branded jobbers. The unbranded jobber usually felt that he was entitled to a somewhat lower price because he secured no benefit from the supplier's advertising program. Rarely, however,

---

9 As noted earlier, certain costs of this type were also incurred in connection with the Indiana Company's commission distributorships.

was a company in a position to make any savings in its over-all advertising costs by selling to unbranded jobbers unless it was in a position to consider conversion of its entire business to an unbranded operation. The unbranded jobbers were also in a slightly stronger bargaining position with respect to price than were the branded jobbers. Once a branded jobber had built up a business under the name of his supplier, he was not likely to switch his business to another company unless he could secure a substantial price concession or other benefits of importance by doing so. An unbranded jobber, on the other hand, was usually in a position where he could switch fairly easily, at least in times of normal or abundant supply, from one supplier to another depending on where he could make the most favorable buying arrangement at the moment.

Intangible Factors:

The selection of wholesale outlets was rarely made solely on the basis of comparative costs alone; in most cases a variety of intangible considerations were also involved. Over the long run these intangible considerations were usually reflected in one way or another in the prices realized or costs incurred by the supplier. We have set them in a separate category, however, because for the most part they represented things which could not be reduced easily to quantitative terms in individual bulk plant problems.

Security of Sales Position: One of the most important intangible factors was the relative security of sales position offered by the different types of outlets. The highest degree of security was afforded by the company operated bulk plants and by the employee operated commission bulk plants of the Indiana Company, because under both of these arrangements the entire bulk plant operation was fully controlled by the supplier. The commission bulk plant, independently operated, offered the next highest degree of security. Although the supplier usually owned or leased the facilities of these plants, they offered a slightly lesser degree of security than did the employee operated plants because the operators were independent agents and were not bound to the sup-

plier by such things as employee benefits and pension plans. The commission distributors were often regarded by their local communities as being in business for themselves and were frequently able to build close ties with many of their customers. As a result, they were sometimes in a position to take a good deal of business with them if they transferred to another supplier.

The branded jobber, in turn, afforded the supplier a significantly lesser degree of security of sales position than did the independently operated commission bulk plant. The branded jobber usually owned his own bulk plant, supplied the equipment for his own and dealer service stations, carried his own receivables, leased or owned service stations in his own name, and was in all other respects completely independent. His relations with his supplier were bound only by a sales contract which was subject to renegotiation at each anniversary date. As a result, the branded jobber usually thought and acted in a quite different manner from the way the commission distributor acted. He could switch brands at practically no cost to himself, since signs and paint were usually furnished by the supplier, and consequently was always in a somewhat stronger bargaining position than was the commission distributor. An unscrupulous branded jobber could even purchase bulk products from other sources and sell them under the brand name of his contracted supplier, when the price was right, with little or no fear of, or regard for, detection.

Of perhaps even greater importance was the fact that in a branded jobber's territory the supplier could not easily assure the continuity of his brand name through the purchase or lease of retail outlets. The acquisition of stations by a supplier was usually viewed with hostility and suspicion by the branded jobber because once the supplier had acquired control of a sufficient number of stations in a territory, there was always the chance that he would enter the market with bulk plants of his own and leave the jobber high and dry. Moreover, the margin granted to jobbers absorbed such a large share of the total margin between the tank car and service station price of gasoline that it was often difficult for the supplier to acquire and rent stations to dealers on a basis which would yield an adequate return on the station investment. The jobber was usually anxious to handle on his own account the high-volume stations which were capable of paying a good return, and the jobber often had the first chance to consider such sites because the supplier was not often in a position to support any very large sales staff in jobber territory.

The companies we studied had all experienced situations in which they had been taken completely out of a market through loss of a jobber to another company and, conversely, had experienced situations in which they had taken a competitor completely out of a market by the purchase of one of his jobbers. The process of regaining position in the market in such cases was often a long and expensive one and always entailed extra costs to re-establish brand name recognition in the territory. As noted earlier, to reduce the hazards involved in the loss of branded jobbers, some companies had established multiple jobberships in the same territory or had used branded jobbers in combination with company operated or commission bulk plants. The resulting competition between outlets selling under the same brand had in the experience of several of the companies, however, proved a source of constant irritation and dissatisfaction on the part of all concerned.

The difference in security of sales position offered by commission distributors as contrasted with branded jobbers is important, but it should not be overemphasized. Most of the companies reported that as a practical matter their turnover of branded jobbers was fairly low. In one company with over 500 branded jobber accounts where we were able to secure turnover figures, we found that only 4.7% of the accounts were lost in 1949 and 7.5% in 1950. A second company with about 700 jobbers lost 1.4% of its accounts in 1950 and 1.9% in 1951. Another company with over 700 branded jobbers estimated its average loss at about 12 accounts per year or about 1.7%. It was generally agreed among the executives with whom we talked, however, that the turnover among branded jobbers was substantially higher than among commission distributors. One of the companies which normally carried over 1,000 commission distributors, for example, reported a loss of only six distributors to other suppliers in the entire period 1946 to 1950, inclusive, or an average loss of about 0.1% per annum.

The unbranded gasoline jobber offered the supplier the lowest degree of security of sales position of any of the major types of wholesale outlets. As noted above, the unbranded jobber was in a position to, and frequently did, shift his sources of supply in accordance with the buying opportunities that were from time to time available to him. The connections with the unbranded jobbers were, in general, so lacking in stability that none of the seven companies regarded the unbranded jobber as a satisfactory means of developing the gasoline market. Some of the companies had, however, supplied a few unbranded jobbers for a period of many years merely as a means of disposing of gasoline they could not otherwise sell or merely because they were reluctant to break off a long-established relationship.

Planning of Operations: A second intangible consideration which influenced the seven companies in their selection of wholesale outlets had to do with the planning of refinery runs and the management of refined products stock positions. As noted in Chapter Eleven, a refiner can make some significant gains in operating costs by maintaining reasonably uniform refinery yields and by building stocks of refined products to meet seasonal variations in demand. Moreover, it is important that the stocks be maintained as close to the market as possible in order to avoid peaks and valleys in the requirements for transportation facilities. Both the company operated and commission distributor bulk plants offered a distinct advantage in this respect because as long as the supplier controlled both the bulk plant facilities and the inventories, he could plan refinery runs and shipments to secondary storage points close to the market in a manner to secure the lowest possible over-all cost for manufacturing and distribution.

The branded jobber, on the other hand, often tried to time his purchases to take advantage of fluctuations in products prices. As a result, he sometimes held off buying in anticipation of a price drop at just the times when the supplier's refinery stocks were pressed to capacity or, conversely, bought heavily in anticipation of a price rise at just the times when the supplier was least able to meet his requirements. As a supplier increased the volume he sold through branded jobbers therefore, he tended to reduce his ability to manage his refinery runs and stock positions effectively. The unbranded jobbers presented even greater problems in this respect than did the branded jobbers.

Pricing Practices: A third important consideration influencing the selection of wholesale outlets was the degree of control which the supplier could exercise in the case of each outlet over the tank wagon prices at which his products were sold to dealers and other customers. In the case of company and commission operated bulk plants, the supplier owned the bulk plant inventories and had complete control over selling prices at all times. The branded jobbers, on the other hand, were free to resell the products they purchased at any prices they chose. In an effort to secure new business or to hold existing accounts, the jobbers sometimes began to shade their prices to dealers or other customers and thereby set in motion price wars which eventually led to a temporary depression in the tank wagon price structure in the area.

A certain number of price wars were inevitable, but through careless or unsound price strategy the jobbers could easily precipitate more of them than was desirable or healthy. The price cuts were not a matter of indifference to the supplier because the typical jobber contract provided for guaranteed minimum margins and the splitting of price cuts with the branded jobber. Some companies took the position that as long as they had to share the responsibility for price developments at the tank wagon level, they might as well use the commission distributor plan and thus gain an opportunity to make sure that sound pricing practices were used.

On the other hand, one or two of the companies we studied took the position that jobbers offered the same advantages in the pricing field as did dealer operated service stations. In other words, it was believed that the jobber could do a more effective job in quickly adjusting prices to the competitive necessities of local situations than could a supplier operating through his own bulk plants.

Direction of Sales Effort: A fourth intangible consideration was the relative degree of influence which could be exercised by the supplier over the sales program of each type of outlet. In the case of company operated bulk plants, the supplier could exercise a strong degree of control over such things as the markets the bulk plant employees solicited, the products they pushed, and the standards of service required of dealer service stations in the territory. The commission bulk plants operated by company employees (Indiana Company) were susceptible to a slightly lesser degree of sales control, because the earnings of the distributors were tied to the sales volume of individual products, and it was difficult to induce them to do work which did not yield immediate sales results or to push the products at the lower end of the scale of commission rates. The commission bulk plants operated by nonemployees, in turn, offered the supplier a slightly lesser degree of control than did the commission plants operated by company employees.

The branded jobbers were free to develop their markets in any way they chose, and it was usually difficult for the supplier to influence the nature and direction of their selling effort in any major degree. The weaker jobbers sometimes followed the path of least resistance and did not put forth the effort necessary to realize the sales potential of their territories on particular products. One of the companies, for example, reported the following ratios of motor oil to gasoline sales for its branded jobbers as contrasted with its commission distributors and company operated bulk plants:

Year	Branded Jobbers	Company Operated and Commission Bulk Plants [10]
1939	1.40	2.27
1940	1.25	2.21
1941	1.51	2.25
1942	1.23	2.20
1943	1.42	2.53
1944	1.47	2.63
1945	1.44	2.60
1946	1.78	2.37
1947	1.89	2.50
1948	1.68	2.28
1949	1.57	2.20

[10] May include some sales direct from refineries and terminals to large consumers.

The company also reported that the high ratios for the company operated and commission bulk plants were obtained largely in the commission bulk plant territories. These ratios were realized despite the fact that the commission rate on motor oils for the distributor was only about 10% of the invoiced value, whereas the discount offered the branded jobbers was about 20% off the tank wagon price. The company's commission distributors had been protesting the low commission on motor oils, but they nonetheless continued to push the motor oils more aggressively than did the branded jobbers.

Relative Sales Effectiveness: A fifth very important factor influencing the selection of wholesale outlets was the relative sales effectiveness of each type of outlet in different market situations. Several of the companies had found that in the small towns and rural areas the branded jobbers were viewed in a quite different light by the populace than were the salaried employees of a large company. The branded jobbers had the status of independent businessmen and, as such, were often more readily accepted in the small communities and able to establish closer ties with their customers than were company employees. Similarly, the commission distributors, who at least had the status of quasi-independent businessmen, were often able to do a more effective job than were the salaried employees of the suppliers. The unbranded jobbers, the most independent of all the outlets, enjoyed somewhat the same standing in the small communities as did the branded jobbers, but were usually at a slight disadvantage relative to the branded jobbers because their brands were not so well recognized as those of the large suppliers. The selling advantages enjoyed by the jobbers and commission distributors by virtue of their independent or quasi-independent status tended to decrease as the size of the city increased and the selling job became less personalized in nature.

Questions of Public Policy: A final factor of no small importance was the question of public policy. All other things being equal, or nearly equal, several of the companies were, in 1952, tending to use commission distrib-

utors or branded jobbers wherever they could in lieu of company operated bulk plants in order to retain in existence as many independent or quasi-independent businessmen as possible.

Competitive Pressures:

It should not be inferred from the discussion in the two foregoing sections that the selection of wholesale outlets was always a deliberate, rational process or entirely a matter of free choice on the part of a supplier. In a great many cases, the hand of a supplier was forced in the type of arrangements he made with his outlets by the offers of competitive suppliers. Each supplier was interested in securing the best possible managers for his bulk plants, and the companies frequently bid against each other for the services of the better distributors or jobbers. For example, if an outstanding commission distributor wished to buy his bulk plant and convert it to a branded jobber operation, the supplier sometimes had to meet the request to keep the distributor from transferring to another company and perhaps taking a large number of his customers along with him. Conversely, a good jobber sometimes wished to take his money out of his bulk plant facilities or to gain the security offered by a commission distributorship and accordingly requested his supplier to set him up on a commission basis. In such cases, it was usually not hard for a jobber to get offers from another company if his supplier refused.

One of the companies reported that the pressure to convert commission distributors to jobbers was particularly strong in the period following World War II. The pressure arose from the fact that jobber margins tended to increase in the postwar period while commission rates, which were generally less flexible than jobber margins, remained fairly stable. As a result, the discrepancies between jobber margins and commission rates increased to the point where many distributors believed that they were no longer offset by the extra services offered by suppliers to distributors above and beyond those offered to jobbers.

The discrepancy between jobber margins and commission rates was particularly noticeable in the case of fuel oil, which was of little significance in the marketing operations of distributors and jobbers prior to the war but of great significance thereafter. In 1950 a typical jobber margin on fuel oil was 3.0 cents per gallon as contrasted with a commission rate of 1.8 cents per gallon. Moreover, in the case of fuel oil the supplier could not point to equipment furnished, installed, removed, and maintained in dealer service stations as justification for the difference as he could in the case of gasoline. Likewise it could not be claimed that the assistance of sales representatives was of any great significance in connection with the merchandising of fuel oil. In recognition of these facts, some suppliers had received many requests from distributors for conversion of their business, or at least the fuel oil portion thereof, to a jobber basis.

One company gave the following example of a situation in which its choice of outlets was determined largely by competitive necessity. When the company decided to develop extensive marketing operations in New York City in the late 1930's, it found that nearly all the better service station locations had already been tied up by jobbers and other major companies. In this situation, the company would have preferred to purchase existing jobbers, thus acquiring their controlled outlets, and to convert the jobbers to commission distributors. It found, however, that the commission distributorships were not attractive to the jobbers because they had already made their investments in bulk plant and marketing facilities and would merely have been trading a 2.5 cents per gallon jobber margin for a 1.5 cents per gallon gasoline commission. Moreover, the jobbers could see little point in selling their facilities and equipment to the supplier at necessarily depreciated values while the properties were still capable of producing high earnings. The supplier was forced therefore to secure his distribution in the New York area by means of branded jobber arrangements.

Fortuitous and Special Circumstances:

In addition to comparative costs, various intangible considerations, and competitive pressures, the selection of wholesale outlets was influenced to a very significant extent by special circumstances that happened to be present in particular situations. A company establishing a wholesale outlet in a new area might decide to use a branded jobber or a commission distributor simply because one happened to be available who was dissatisfied with his existing supplier and wished to make a change. Similarly, a company might decide against building a bulk plant of its own in a particular town because an attractive location with good access to transportation facilities could not be secured or because the supplier happened to be hard pressed for capital funds at the time the action was contemplated. A company sometimes took over a string of marketing facilities, including company operated, commission, and jobber bulk plants, from another supplier who was withdrawing from the territory. In such a case, the pattern of distribution set up by the buyer was inescapably influenced by existing arrangements and the general marketing policies of the seller.

Suppliers also frequently converted one type of outlet to another, not so much as a matter of marketing strategy, but rather as a means of taking care of special situations. Jobbers, for example, often wished to sell their properties in order to retire, to settle their estates, or to anticipate tax problems. In such cases the supplier sometimes had no alternative other than to buy, if he wished to retain the distribution that had been built up under his brand name, and might set up a company operated or commission bulk plant depending on whether a good commission distributor was available to do the job.

An example of the influence of fortuitous circumstances in the selection of wholesale outlets may be drawn from an experience of the Gulf Oil Corporation. In 1946 the company entered a new market in a large midwestern city by signing a supply contract with a branded jobber who, in addition to his bulk plant facilities, owned or controlled a string of 30 service stations in the area. The jobber had become dissatisfied with his existing supplier for several reasons, including the fact that the supplier had multiple wholesale outlets in the area in competition with one another. Gulf's decision to make use of a branded jobber in this case, and indeed its decision to enter this particular market at this particular time, was influenced to a considerable extent simply by the fact that a strong jobber with good facilities was available.

The contract signed with the jobber was a perpetual one, requiring a one-year notice by Gulf and a two-year notice by the jobber to effect cancellation. The contract also provided that Gulf should have a first refusal option in the event that the jobber received an offer for the purchase of his properties from some other company. Initially the contract provided for the sale of gasoline to the jobber at $2\frac{1}{2}$ cents off the prevailing tank wagon price, but in 1950 the margin was increased to $2\frac{3}{4}$ cents to enable the jobber to meet competition in the area more effectively.

In 1946 and prior years the jobber had had a gasoline sales volume of about 3,600,000 gallons a year. During his first three years with Gulf, however, the jobber increased his representation from 30 to 109 service station outlets and his volume as follows:

Year	Gasoline	Motor Oils
1947	6,912,000 gallons	127,000 gallons
1948	12,584,000	124,000
1949	13,831,000	152,000

The Gulf management attributed the growth of the business to the "almost unparalleled enterprise on the part of the principal officers of the jobber corporation and the immediate acceptance of the Gulf brand by the public in an area contiguous to our traditional marketing territory but previously untapped."

From a financial standpoint, the business was profitable to both Gulf and the jobber. During the first three full years of the contract, the Gulf marketing department earned an estimated total profit of $1,065,000 before taxes and of $639,000 after taxes on the volume of products sold. In computing this profit, it was assumed that gasoline was transferred from the Gulf refineries to the marketing department at 4% beneath the low of the prices quoted in *Platt's Oilgram Price Service*. Actually, the gasoline was supplied by exchange arrangements with a place differential in favor of Gulf of 0.40 cents per gallon at one point and of 0.275 cents per gallon at another point; these differentials were included in the estimated profit figures. Some indication of the profitability of the business to the jobber may be secured from the fact that his books for the year ending October 31, 1949, showed a profit after taxes of $75,000.

The jobber offered his properties for sale in 1950 because the two principal stockholders had extensive interests in other fields and were anxious to devote their full time to other affairs. Moreover, the jobber had become dissatisfied with his arrangements with Gulf and had become dubious about the long-run ability of the independent jobber to withstand the competitive and economic pressures at work in the industry. The Gulf Oil Corporation therefore, although it certainly had little cause for dissatisfaction with the existing arrangement, found it necessary to purchase the properties for $1,500,000 and operate them with salaried employees.

The decision of the Gulf management in this case was influenced by several considerations. In the first place, the jobber was Gulf's sole channel of distribution in the area for all products other than industrial lubricants, which Gulf sold direct to customers, and it was clear that if Gulf did not make the purchase some other company would, thus depriving Gulf of its representation in an important petroleum market. The business was important to Gulf because it appeared that it could very well form the nucleus for any future expansion the company might wish to undertake in the surrounding area.

Moreover, the properties included one of the best chains of stations in the territory. The 109 stations, of which 14 were owned by the jobber stockholders or their relatives, 78 were leased, and 17 were signed under supply contracts, were modern in design, attractive, and strategically located, and it was evident that the development of similar representation would cost Gulf considerably more than the purchase price. Finally, analysis of the situation indicated that Gulf could operate the business profitably on a salaried basis. It was anticipated that a gasoline sales volume of 13,500,000 gallons a year could be secured and that the marketing department's profit after taxes would be at least $62,345 a year, even on the basis of very conservative estimates with respect to the wholesale margin. The cash return on the $1,500,000 investment was estimated at 11.66% per annum and the payout period at 8.6 years.

On the basis of the foregoing facts, it would appear that Gulf's original decision to use a jobber outlet in the area was largely a matter of taking advantage of the opportunities of the moment and that its later decision to convert the outlet to a salaried operation was largely a matter of meeting the exigencies created by the jobber's decision to sell.

Considerations Influencing the Selection of Outlets for Kerosene and Distillate:

The outlets which a company used for the distribution of its kerosene and distillate were largely determined by the outlets which it selected for the distribution of gasoline. A company rarely established a company operated bulk plant or set up a commission distributorship without making provision for the sale of kerosene and distillate as well as gasoline, at least in those areas of the country where it had any appreciable volume of kerosene and distillate to sell. As suggested in earlier discussion, the selection of wholesale outlets usually rested on considerations relating to kerosene and distillate as well as gasoline, although the considerations relating to kerosene and distillate were usually of secondary significance. Many factors which were important in the selection of gasoline outlets, however, such as brand name representation or the supplying of equipment to dealers, sometimes had a quite different degree of significance or no significance at all with respect to the distribution of many of the kerosene and distillate products.

A company sometimes developed a quite different pattern of wholesale outlets for kerosene and distillate than for gasoline because it sold fuel oil to many types of accounts which did not handle its gasoline. The home fuel oil business was closely associated with the sale and maintenance of home fuel oil burners, and many firms which specialized in these activities did not engage in the distribution of gasoline. The suppliers sold to these fuel oil specialists because in some sections of the country the specialists had been able to capture a fairly large share of the market, and the suppliers had to sell to them to secure adequate distribution for their fuel oil output. Moreover, since brand names were of less significance in the marketing of fuel oil than in the marketing of gasoline, it was often possible for a supplier to use dual outlets for fuel oil even though he might be avoiding the use of dual outlets in the distribution of his gasoline.

IV. DIFFERENCES AND SIMILARITIES IN THE POSITIONS OF THE COMPANIES IN 1950

Although the underlying considerations which influenced the seven companies in their selection of wholesale outlets were much the same, differences in practices among the companies arose from differences in the way in which the considerations were evaluated and balanced one against another in individual cases. One company, for example, might calculate its costs quite differently from the way another did and thereby arrive at different conclusions as to the break-even volumes at which it was desirable for a supplier to switch from jobber to commission operation or from commission operation to salary operation. The executives of one company might also hold very different views from those held by the executives of another company with respect to the significance to be assigned to the various intangible and competitive considerations which entered into the decisions on wholesale outlets. Likewise, the impact of various fortuitous and special circumstances, of course, varied widely from one company to another. Finally, some variations in practice were an inherent product of differences in the economic characteristics of the territories in which the companies operated.

It is not surprising therefore that the arrangements of the seven companies with respect to the usage of the different types of outlets should reflect both strong similarities and strong differences. As a means of illustrating the similarities and differences which continually characterized the positions of the seven companies with respect to their wholesale distribution activities, in the following paragraphs we shall outline briefly some of the more important similarities and differences which we found in their arrangements for the distribution of gasoline in 1950.[11] The year 1950 was selected as a point of analysis because it is the last year for which we collected statistics on the proportion of each company's

---

[11] In the interests of simplicity, we shall not undertake a parallel analysis of distribution arrangements for kerosene and distillate. Information with regard to the kerosene and distillate programs of the companies may be found, however, in Chapter Twelve, Exhibits XII-19 to XII-26, and in the Appendix, Tables 9–15.

EXHIBIT XV-3. SEVEN OIL COMPANIES

Proportions of Gasoline Volume Sold through or to Various Types of Wholesale Outlets in Selected Years:
1935–1952

Companies		Through Refineries & Terminals	Through Company Operated Bulk Plants *	Through Commission Distributors	To Branded Jobbers	To Unbranded Jobbers
Gulf†	1935	15.7%	43.6%	40.7%	4.2%	1.5%
	1940	21.5	37.6	40.9	7.5	5.1
	1946	24.5	37.6	37.9	5.4	8.3
	1950	19.7	39.8	40.5	8.6	6.0
Sinclair ‡	1935	30.3	32.6	37.1	N.A.	N.A.
	1940	29.5	22.9	47.6	N.A.	N.A.
	1946	37.9	18.0	44.1	N.A.	N.A.
	1950	35.9	27.8	36.3	18.7	2.7
The Ohio Oil Company	1935	N.A.	N.A.	N.A.	N.A.	N.A.
	1940	9.3	57.5	33.2	13.0	17.2
	1946	26.9	35.6	37.5	15.6	15.3
	1950	38.8	15.2	46.0	23.1	8.9
Atlantic §	1949	77.2	21.3	1.5	23.0	2.1
	1950	78.6	20.5	0.9	23.9	2.7
	1951	83.7	15.7	0.6	23.9	2.4
	1952	85.4	14.1	0.5	23.2	2.6
Sohio ‖	1935	N.A.	N.A.	N.A.	14.3	—
	1940	N.A.	N.A.	N.A.	18.0	—
	1946	N.A.	N.A.	14.9	16.0	—
	1950	N.A.	N.A.	14.8	10.6	—
					To All Jobbers	
The Texas Company **	1948	31.5	34.1	34.3	16.1	
	1949	29.6	36.5	33.9	15.9	
	1950	26.5	40.9	32.6	17.3	
	1951	28.8	41.3	29.9	15.5	
					To All Wholesale Resellers	
Indiana Company ††	1935	16.3	35.5	48.2	N.A.	
	1940	19.8	26.3	53.9	14.7	
	1946	14.7	23.5	61.8	10.0	
	1950	17.6	22.3	60.1	9.9	

Note: The figures in the first two columns of this exhibit include the volumes sold to branded and unbranded jobbers which are shown in the last two columns.

* Includes sales through commission truck drivers.

† Some tank truck dealers are included with both branded and unbranded jobbers.

‡ Some tank truck dealers are included with unbranded jobbers.

§ Note that data do not cover same years as for other companies.

‖ Figures for commission distributors include small volume sold through commission truck drivers operating from company operated bulk plants.

** Note that data do not cover same years as for other companies. Volume sold to unbranded jobbers reported to be very small.

†† Volume sold to unbranded jobbers reported to be very small.

SOURCE: See Chapter Twelve, Exhibits XII–19 to XII–26, and Appendix, Tables 9–15.

gasoline volume that was sold to or through the various wholesale outlets.[12]

The proportions of each company's gasoline volume which were sold through or to the various types of wholesale outlets in 1935, 1940, 1946, and 1950 are shown in Exhibit XV-3. These data are a recapitulation of the figures

[12] The year 1951 will be used in the analysis for The Texas Company.

given in the balance of operations analyses for the individual companies in Chapter Twelve, Exhibits XII-19 to XII-26. In Exhibit XV-3, however, we have combined the figures for sales through commission truck drivers and sales through company operated bulk plants, because the commission truck drivers usually operated from and drew the large majority of their volume through company operated bulk plants.[13] The commission distributors and jobbers also used commission truck drivers, but the supplying companies had figures only for the total amounts shipped to such accounts, which included the volume subsequently distributed through commission truck drivers.

In appraising the figures in Exhibit XV-3, it should be noted that the first three columns add to 100% and represent a breakdown of each company's total gasoline sales by method of sale. The figures do not, however, represent the relative volumes which may have been transhipped by each type of outlet, because all the volume at one time or another passed through the refineries and nearly all of it passed through terminals en route to the various types of bulk plants. In addition, there were occasionally transhipments between company operated bulk plants or between company operated bulk plants and commission distributor bulk plants. The figures therefore measure only the relative usage made of the three types of outlets *as points of sale to customers*.

It should also be noted that the volumes shown for branded and unbranded jobbers are duplicated in the first three columns because the jobbers drew their volumes from one or another of the first three types of outlets and particularly from refineries and terminals. Exhibit XV-3 thus presents a mixed comparison of three methods of sale versus two types of customers. Such a comparison is entirely appropriate, however, because as indicated earlier, the marketing programs of the companies characteristically evolved from a series of multiple-choice problems involving at least the last four outlets covered by the table.

Additional data on the practices of the companies with respect to the usage of the various types of wholesale outlets is presented in Exhibits XV-4 and XV-5. Exhibit XV-4 contains an analysis of the number of the different types of outlets which each company employed in its marketing program. In this tabulation we found it necessary to group terminals and company operated bulk plants together in certain cases because the companies reported that nearly all their terminals operated as bulk plants and that they could not draw a clear line of demarcation between the two types of

outlets. Exhibit XV-5 contains such data as were available on the average monthly gasoline sales made to or by the various types of outlets.

Similarities in Positions:

As a first point of similarity in 1950, it may be noted that unbranded jobbers played a relatively insignificant role in the distribution programs of all seven companies. In each case the volume of gasoline sold to unbranded jobbers was less than 10% of the company's total gasoline sales. The number of unbranded jobbers was likewise a small fraction of the total outlets in each company's marketing program except in the case of The Ohio Oil Company where unbranded jobbers comprised 30.5% of the total outlets. It will be noted that the number of unbranded outlets is not shown separately in Exhibit XV-4 for Gulf, The Texas Company, Sinclair, or Sohio, but in these cases we were told that the number was extremely small.

A second point of similarity may be noted in the fact that branded jobbers were substantially more important in the marketing programs of all the companies than were unbranded jobbers. In no case, however, did sales to branded jobbers account for more than 25% of a company's total gasoline sales volume.

A third point of similarity appears in the fact that as a group the companies made far more use of company bulk plants, salary and commission operated, than they did of branded jobbers. The combined volume sold by company and commission operated bulk plants was two to ten times the volume sold to branded jobbers in all cases except that of Atlantic where the volume sold *to* branded jobbers was slightly greater than the volume sold through company and commission operated bulk plants.[14] It must, of course, be remembered that in the case of all the companies some part of the *sales through* company and commission bulk plants were *sales to* branded jobbers, although in most cases the branded jobbers drew their gasoline shipments from the refineries and terminals of their suppliers.

Finally, it may be observed that commission

---

[13] In some cases commission truck drivers also operated from refineries or terminals.

[14] As will be noted later, Atlantic had developed the by-passing technique to such a high degree that it did not have so much need for company and commission operated bulk plants as did the other companies.

distributors in 1950 handled a somewhat larger share of each company's gasoline volume than did company operated bulk plants in all cases where data were available except that of Atlantic and The Texas Company.

Differences in Positions:

The differences in the programs of the seven companies with respect to the usage of the various types of wholesale outlets were far more pronounced than were the similarities. First, Exhibit XV-3 indicates that there were wide variations among the companies with respect to the relative volumes sold through or to the different types of outlets. The Gulf Oil Corporation, for example, sold about ten times as much gasoline through company operated and commission bulk plants as it did to branded jobbers. At the other end of the scale, Atlantic in 1950 sold approximately the same amount through company and commission operated bulk plants as it did to branded jobbers. The positions of the other companies were scattered between these two extremes. It may likewise be noted that the Indiana Company sold about three times as much volume through commission operated as it did through company operated bulk plants whereas Atlantic sold about 20 times as much through company operated plants as it did through commission operated plants. Once again the positions of the other companies varied between the two extremes.

A second very significant point of difference among the companies lay in the extent to which each had developed the technique of by-passing bulk plants with direct shipments from refineries and terminals to service stations. We were not able to secure direct data on the volumes handled by the by-pass method for each company, but comparisons of some of the extreme cases may easily be drawn by inference from Exhibit XV-3.

The Atlantic Refining Company, for example, sold 78.6% of its gasoline volume in 1950 from refineries and terminals.[15] If it is assumed that the branded and unbranded jobbers were all supplied from refineries and terminals, the company shipped at least 52.0% (78.6% less 26.6%) of its volume direct from refineries and terminals to (a) service stations,

(b) consumers and industrial users, and (c) wholesale resellers other than jobbers. If we further assume that all the company's sales to groups (b) and (c) (see Appendix, Table 13) were made from refineries and terminals, which was probably not the case because many sales to consumers and industrial users were made from bulk plants, there still remains a minimum of 31.1% of the company's gasoline volume which must have gone direct from refineries and terminals to service stations. In view of the company's pipe line distribution facilities (See Chapters Seven and Nine), it is probable that the gasoline volume handled by the by-passing method was closer to the 52.0% figure than the 31.1% figure.

By way of contrast, the Indiana Company sold only 17.6% of its gasoline volume from refineries and terminals to all types of customers. If we recognize that some portion (actually probably a very high portion) of the 9.9% of the company's volume sold to jobbers[16] and that some portion of the 34.3% of the company's volume sold to industrial, household, and other consumers (see Appendix, Table 14) was shipped direct from refineries and terminals, it is readily apparent that the Indiana Company could not possibly have shipped more than about 5% or 6% of its gasoline volume directly from refineries and terminals to service stations. By similar analysis it may be determined that the Gulf Oil Corporation did not ship more than about 10% of its gasoline directly from refineries and terminals to service stations.

It seems reasonable to conclude therefore that Atlantic handled at least three to ten times as much of its gasoline volume by the by-passing method as did the Indiana Company and Gulf. Much of the difference in the situation of the companies may be explained by the fact that Atlantic had had an extensive pipe line system for over 20 years and had long been in the process of weeding out bulk plant locations and by the fact that the company had confined its marketing to a compact territory close to its pipe line and marine terminals.

The data in Exhibit XV-4 reveal that there were also some wide differences among the

---

[15] Including shipments to company operated service stations.

[16] In the case of the Indiana Company this figure includes all types of wholesale resellers (see Appendix, Table 14).

Exhibit XV-4. Seven Oil Companies

Analysis of Wholesale Outlets for Gasoline by Type: 1935–1952 *

Number of Outlets

	1935	1936	1937	1938	1939	1940	1941	1942	1943	1944	1945	1946	1947	1948	1949	1950	1951	1952
Gulf Oil Corporation: Total	1,131	1,178	1,213	1,232	1,252	1,345	1,367	1,293	1,348	1,363	1,382	1,348	1,344	1,368	1,389	1,451	1,488	1,485
Co. Operated Terminals and Bulk Plants	160	163	159	150	171	198	203	187	222	245	272	253	250	248	240	256	256	277
Commission Distributors	871	910	944	967	961	1,024	1,039	984	1,007	1,002	992	975	964	980	1,003	1,037	1,057	1,023
Branded Jobbers†	100	105	110	115	120	123	125	122	119	116	118	120	130	140	146	158	175	185
The Texas Company: Total	2,052	2,129	2,197	2,299	2,345	2,474	2,454	2,419	2,387	2,409	2,437	2,473	2,436	2,351	2,272	2,202	2,155	
Co. Operated Terminals and Bulk Plants	298	291	291	279	275	278	277	270	268	267	273	278	283	272	253	253	252	
Terminals‡	29	27	28	28	29	30	30	28	30	30	29	23	22	22	21	21	16	
Bulk Plants‡	269	264	263	251	246	248	247	242	238	237	244	255	261	250	232	232	236	
Commission Distributors	1,390	1,412	1,428	1,463	1,462	1,505	1,507	1,473	1,442	1,431	1,425	1,427	1,400	1,341	1,291	1,244	1,210	
Branded Jobbers†	364	426	478	557	608	691	670	676	677	711	739	768	753	738	728	705	693	
Sinclair Oil Corporation: Total	2,367	2,358	2,375	2,379	2,351	2,272	2,260	2,150	2,104	2,072	2,080	2,115	2,102	1,925	1,851	1,894	1,890	1,952
Co. Operated Terminals and Bulk Plants	255	227	180	154	135	119	116	139	140	130	128	155	183	211	229	235	236	248
Terminals	8	8	9	8	7	7	7	14	18	19	22	24	29	43	50	56	56	58
Bulk Plants	247	219	171	146	128	112	109	125	122	111	106	131	154	168	179	179	180	190
Commission Distributors	1,728	1,762	1,792	1,811	1,780	1,720	1,696	1,562	1,518	1,489	1,496	1,492	1,459	1,257	1,174	1,194	1,179	1,217
Branded and Unbranded Jobbers†	384	369	403	414	436	433	448	449	446	453	456	468	460	457	448	465	475	487
The Ohio Oil Company: Total										222	256	259	306	321	325	325	350	360
Co. Operated Bulk Plants										74	81	88	100	96	86	56	59	51
Commission Distributors										13	22	24	43	47	67	88	94	111
Branded and Unbranded Jobbers										135	153	147	163	178	172	181	197	198
Branded										51	62	52	68	93	82	82	78	76
Unbranded										84	91	95	95	85	90	99	119	122

EXHIBIT XV-4 (CONTINUED)

	1935	1936	1937	1938	1939	1940	1941	1942	1943	1944	1945	1946	1947	1948	1949	1950	1951	1952
The Atlantic Refining Company: Total															360	350	442	430
Co. Operated Terminals and Bulk Plants															170	151	154	148
Terminals							37	37	38	40	49	39	38	41	41	42	44	46
Bulk Plants							232	228	210	200	197	191	167	153	129	109	110	102
Commission Distributors															21	13	8	8
Branded and Unbranded Jobbers															169	186	280	274
Branded															154	170	263	257
Unbranded															15	16	17	17
Standard Oil Company (Indiana): Total							4,210	4,091	4,163	4,143	4,163	4,235	4,242	4,199	4,202	4,179	4,258	4,267
Co. Operated Terminals and Bulk Plants	164	165	165	163	165	167	168	164	166	167	169	172	176	177	165	184	227	242
Terminals	5	6	6	6	8	11	14	14	14	14	15	15	19	20	22	23	24	27
Bulk Plants	159	159	159	157	157	156	154	150	152	153	154	157	157	157	143	161	203	215
Commission Distributors	3,825	3,817	3,811	3,775	3,756	3,733	3,704	3,595	3,660	3,677	3,707	3,771	3,778	3,760	3,776	3,764	3,772	3,769
Branded and Unbranded Jobbers							338	332	337	299	287	292	288	262	261	231	259	256
Branded							332	326	331	293	279	285	280	254	254	224	253	252
Unbranded							6	6	6	6	8	7	8	8	7	7	6	4
Standard Oil Company (Ohio): Total							339	345	341	343	369	405	415	401	345	357	356	359
Co. Operated Terminals and Bulk Plants	160	167	170	170	170	166	163	160	158	157	163	172	173	176	173	177	176	177
Commission Distributors	24	51	71	75	77	78	80	84	83	81	90	105	109	110	108	109	109	110
Branded Jobbers†							96	101	100	105	116	128	133	115	64	71	71	72

Note: Blank spaces indicate data not available.

* Since the seven companies did not classify their wholesale outlets in precisely the same manner, it was necessary to make certain approximations in developing the figures for this exhibit. The data are intended to represent only those outlets handling gasoline (and other products) for the supplying company, but in one or two cases a very small number of outlets handling only kerosene and distillate may have been included in the figures for branded jobbers.

† Number of unbranded jobbers reported to be very small.

‡ Figures for terminals include only those operated by the refining department. Terminals operated by the sales department were included with bulk plants, but the number of such terminals was small relative to the total number of bulk plants.

SOURCE: Company records.

EXHIBIT XV-4 (CONTINUED)
Analysis of Wholesale Outlets for Gasoline by Type: 1935–1952*
Percentage of Total Outlets

	1935	1936	1937	1938	1939	1940	1941	1942	1943	1944	1945	1946	1947	1948	1949	1950	1951	1952
Gulf Oil Corporation: Total	100.0	100.0	100.0	100.0	100.0	100.0	100.0	100.0	100.0	100.0	100.0	100.0	100.0	100.0	100.0	100.0	100.0	100.0
Co. Operated Terminals and Bulk Plants	14.2	13.8	13.1	12.2	13.7	14.7	14.9	14.5	16.5	18.0	19.7	18.8	18.6	18.1	17.3	17.6	17.2	18.6
Commission Distributors	77.0	77.3	77.8	78.5	76.8	76.1	76.0	76.1	74.7	73.5	71.8	72.3	71.7	71.7	72.2	71.5	71.0	68.9
Branded Jobbers†	8.8	8.9	9.1	9.3	9.5	9.2	9.1	9.4	8.8	8.5	8.5	8.9	9.7	10.2	10.5	10.9	11.8	12.5
The Texas Company: Total	100.0	100.0	100.0	100.0	100.0	100.0	100.0	100.0	100.0	100.0	100.0	100.0	100.0	100.0	100.0	100.0	100.0	
Co. Operated Terminals and Bulk Plants	14.5	13.7	13.2	12.1	11.7	11.2	11.3	11.2	11.2	11.1	11.2	11.2	11.6	11.6	11.1	11.5	11.7	
Terminals‡	1.4	1.3	1.2	1.2	1.2	1.2	1.2	1.2	1.2	1.2	1.2	0.9	0.9	1.0	0.9	1.0	0.7	
Bulk Plants‡	13.1	12.4	12.0	10.9	10.5	10.0	10.1	10.0	10.0	9.9	10.0	10.3	10.7	10.6	10.2	10.5	11.0	
Commission Distributors	67.8	66.3	65.0	63.7	62.4	60.9	61.4	60.9	60.4	59.4	58.5	57.7	57.5	57.0	56.9	56.5	56.1	
Branded Jobbers†	17.7	20.0	21.8	24.2	25.9	27.9	27.3	27.9	28.4	29.5	30.3	31.1	30.9	31.4	32.0	32.0	32.2	
Sinclair Oil Corporation: Total	100.0	100.0	100.0	100.0	100.0	100.0	100.0	100.0	100.0	100.0	100.0	100.0	100.0	100.0	100.0	100.0	100.0	100.0
Co. Operated Terminals and Bulk Plants	10.8	9.6	7.6	6.5	5.7	5.2	5.1	6.5	6.7	6.3	6.2	7.3	8.7	11.0	12.4	12.4	12.5	12.7
Terminals	0.3	0.3	0.4	0.3	0.3	0.3	0.3	0.7	0.9	0.9	1.1	1.1	1.4	2.2	2.7	3.0	3.0	3.0
Bulk Plants	10.5	9.3	7.2	6.2	5.4	4.9	4.8	5.8	5.8	5.4	5.1	6.2	7.3	8.8	9.7	9.4	9.5	9.7
Commission Distributors	73.0	74.7	75.4	76.1	75.7	75.7	75.1	72.6	72.1	71.8	71.9	70.6	69.4	65.3	63.4	63.0	62.4	62.3
Branded and Unbranded Jobbers†	16.2	15.7	17.0	17.4	18.6	19.1	19.8	20.9	21.2	21.9	21.9	22.1	21.9	23.7	24.2	24.6	25.1	25.0
The Ohio Oil Company: Total										100.0	100.0	100.0	100.0	100.0	100.0	100.0	100.0	100.0
Co. Operated Bulk Plants										33.3	31.6	34.0	32.7	29.9	26.5	17.2	16.9	14.2
Commission Distributors										5.9	8.6	9.2	14.0	14.6	20.6	27.1	26.8	30.8
Branded and Unbranded Jobbers										60.8	59.8	56.8	53.3	55.5	52.9	55.7	56.3	55.0
Branded										23.0	24.2	20.1	22.2	29.0	25.2	25.2	22.3	21.1
Unbranded										37.8	35.6	36.7	31.1	26.5	27.7	30.5	34.0	33.9

EXHIBIT XV-4 (CONTINUED)

	1935	1936	1937	1938	1939	1940	1941	1942	1943	1944	1945	1946	1947	1948	1949	1950	1951	1952
The Atlantic Company: Total															100.0	100.0	100.0	100.0
Co. Operated Terminals and Bulk Plants															47.2	43.1	34.9	34.4
Terminals															11.4	12.0	10.0	10.7
Bulk Plants															35.8	31.1	24.9	23.7
Commission Distributors															5.8	3.7	1.8	1.9
Branded and Unbranded Jobbers															47.0	53.2	63.3	63.7
Branded															42.8	48.6	59.5	59.8
Unbranded															4.2	4.6	3.8	3.9
Standard Oil Company (Indiana): Total							100.0	100.0	100.0	100.0	100.0	100.0	100.0	100.0				
Co. Operated Terminals and Bulk Plants							4.0	4.0	4.0	4.0	4.1	4.1	4.1	4.2				
Terminals							0.3	0.3	0.3	0.3	0.4	0.4	0.4	0.5				
Bulk Plants							3.7	3.7	3.7	3.7	3.7	3.7	3.7	3.7				
Commission Distributors							88.0	87.9	87.9	88.8	89.0	89.0	89.1	89.6				
Branded and Unbranded Jobbers							8.0	8.1	8.1	7.2	6.9	6.9	6.8	6.2				
Branded							7.9	8.0	8.0	7.1	6.7	6.7	6.6	6.0				
Unbranded							0.1	0.1	0.1	0.1	0.2	0.2	0.2	0.2				
Standard Oil Company (Ohio): Total							100.0	100.0	100.0	100.0	100.0	100.0	100.0	100.0				
Co. Operated Terminals and Bulk Plants							48.1	46.4	46.3	45.8	44.2	42.5	41.7	43.9				
Commission Distributors							23.6	24.3	24.4	23.6	24.4	25.9	26.3	27.4				
Branded Jobbers†							28.3	29.3	29.3	30.6	31.4	31.6	32.0	28.7				

Note: Blank spaces indicate data not available.

* Since the seven companies did not classify their wholesale outlets in precisely the same manner, it was necessary to make certain approximations in developing the figures for this exhibit. The data are intended to represent only those outlets handling gasoline (and other products) for the supplying company, but in one or two cases a very small number of outlets handling only kerosene and distillate may have been included in the figures for branded jobbers.

† Number of unbranded jobbers reported to be very small.

‡ Figures for terminals include only those operated by the refining department. Terminals operated by the sales department were included with bulk plants, but the number of such terminals was small relative to the total number of bulk plants.

SOURCE: Company records.

EXHIBIT XV-5. SEVEN OIL COMPANIES
Comparison of Gasoline Sales Volumes of Wholesale Outlets: 1935–1952*

Average Monthly Gasoline Sales per Outlet (Gallons)

	1935	1936	1937	1938	1939	1940	1941	1942	1943	1944	1945	1946	1947	1948	1949	1950	1951	1952
Gulf Oil Corporation																		
Commission Distributors	43,320					55,629						77,539			92,386	96,271	101,424	112,872
Branded Jobbers	38,395					84,427						89,425			136,476	134,705	121,620	127,343
The Texas Company																		
Co. Operated Bulk Plants †														390,691	461,656	523,212	575,815	
Commission Distributors														73,267	76,963	77,730	81,172	
Branded Jobbers														62,246	63,963	72,655	73,692	
Sinclair Oil Corporation																		
Co. Operated Terminals and Bulk Plants																		
Terminals	143,185					266,735				361,200	396,568	290,409	289,734	281,061	278,901	336,151	386,953	392,157
Bulk Plants	308,875					433,500				1,374,394	1,188,250	704,666	615,276	458,255	463,750	500,374	627,640	610,633
Commission Distributors	137,820					256,312				187,772	232,253	214,515	228,431	235,708	227,266	284,771	312,073	325,463
Branded and Unbranded Jobbers	22,414					34,759				31,980	35,011	46,137	46,298	54,586	55,307	84,595	81,282	81,559
The Ohio Oil Company																		
Co. Operated Bulk Plants										39,927	58,242	61,145	53,209	46,413	55,632	61,980	70,391	75,914
Commission Distributors										21,675	23,325	42,667	21,404	33,066	26,944	40,236	30,820	30,128
Branded and Unbranded Jobbers										27,048	29,581	31,930	30,370	37,215	40,343	42,242	43,241	43,685
Branded										29,482	33,029	45,672	42,754	48,770	63,469	67,375	68,880	71,248
Unbranded										•25,570	27,231	24,408	21,506	24,572	19,273	21,425	26,436	26,514
The Atlantic Refining Company																		
Co. Operated Terminals and Bulk Plants															389,941	460,033	466,071	500,405
Terminals															1,200,580	1,252,830	1,336,290	1,347,650
Bulk Plants															132,294	154,550	117,981	118,313
Commission Distributors															59,142	61,077	65,125	51,125
Branded and Unbranded Jobbers															122,005	120,655	80,175	83,452
Branded															122,844	118,735	77,452	80,011
Unbranded															113,400	141,062	122,294	135,470
Standard Oil Company (Indiana)																		
Co. Operated Bulk Plants	215,373	233,181	221,228	189,511	201,684	200,914	206,864	172,225	145,341	146,794	182,683	211,113	218,894	232,761	253,446	244,783	210,812	203,700
Commission Distributors	12,131	13,633	15,029	15,320	16,258	17,203	18,153	16,856	15,040	15,546	16,705	23,114	24,062	26,032	27,393	28,296	29,885	31,485
Standard Oil Company (Ohio)																		
Branded Jobbers							83,454	66,395	52,080	60,501	64,358	68,796	83,738	91,914	137,267	100,958	86,415	86,333

Note: Blank spaces indicate data not available.

* See footnotes to Exhibit XV-4 for notations on numbers of different types of wholesale outlets used as divisors in developing data for this exhibit.

† Volume figures are for bulk plants alone, but a certain number of terminals operated by the sales department were included in the count of bulk plants. The number of such terminals was not enough to influence the average volume figures significantly.

SOURCE: Company records.

companies with respect to the relative numbers of the different types of wholesale outlets used in their marketing programs in 1950. In the case of the Indiana Company, company operated bulk plants and terminals constituted 4.4% of the total outlets, whereas in the case of Sohio they constituted 49.6%. Commission distributors ranged in number from 3.7% of total outlets in the case of Atlantic to 90.1% in the case of the Indiana Company. In making this comparison, it must, of course, be remembered that the Indiana Company's commission distributors were company employees, or nearly so, and lay somewhere in between the company operated and commission bulk plants of the other companies in terms of the intensity of integration afforded. The number of branded jobbers ranged from 5.3% of total outlets in the case of the Indiana Company to 48.6% in the case of Atlantic. The number of unbranded jobbers was not known in all cases but the range was at least from 0.2% of total outlets in the case of the Indiana Company to 30.5% in the case of The Ohio Oil Company.

From Exhibit XV-5 it may be seen that there were some wide differences among the companies in terms of the average size of the different types of outlets as measured by the gasoline volume sold to or through them. The company operated bulk plants of The Texas Company had an average monthly gasoline sales volume of 523,212 gallons whereas the average monthly gasoline volume of The Ohio Oil Company's operated bulk plants was only 61,980 gallons. The commission distributors of the Gulf Oil Corporation had an average monthly gasoline sales volume of 96,271 whereas in the case of the Indiana Company the average volume of commission distributors was 28,296 gallons per month. The branded jobbers of the Gulf Oil Corporation had an average sales volume (as measured by shipments from Gulf) about twice that of The Ohio Oil Company branded jobbers, and the unbranded jobbers of Atlantic had an average volume about seven times that of the unbranded jobbers of The Ohio Oil Corporation.

Exhibit XV-5 also reveals that there were some significant differences among the companies in terms of the relative size of the different types of outlets in each company's program. For example, the branded jobbers of Gulf, The Ohio Oil Company, and Atlantic had average gasoline sales about 50% greater than did the commission distributors of the three companies. The branded jobbers of The Texas Company, on the other hand, had an average volume slightly less than that of the company's commission distributors. Moreover, the company operated bulk plants of the Indiana Company had an average gasoline sales volume almost nine times that of the company's commission distributors, whereas in the case of The Ohio Oil Company the company operated bulk plants had an average monthly volume only about 50% larger than that of the company's commission distributors.

The maps in Chapter Twelve, Exhibits XII-4 and XII-8, reveal a striking contrast in the relative density of bulk plants maintained by The Texas Company and the Indiana Company. The maps indicate that throughout the Indiana Company's territory the ratio of the Indiana Company to The Texas Company bulk plants was about 40 to 1. This circumstance arose from some very fundamental differences in the marketing and product policies of the two companies. The Texas Company with its program of national distribution had long made it a policy to concentrate on the large volume locations and, in effect, to "skim the cream from the market." The Indiana Company, on the other hand, made a basic policy decision shortly after World War I to cultivate the farm market very intensively as a means of capitalizing on the new and expanding market which followed as an adjunct to the development of the tractor and the general mechanization of farming activities. This policy was maintained throughout the following 30 years, and in 1950 the Indiana Company had a substantially stronger position in the farm than any other market it served. As a means of serving the farm market, it was necessary for the company to maintain a far larger number of bulk plants per square mile than it was for The Texas Company with its policy of concentrating on large volume outlets and customers.

There was also a significant difference in the product policies of the two companies which had a bearing on the density of bulk plant locations. The Texas Company throughout its history had made every effort to maximize its gasoline yields and had, prior to 1950, made little attempt to develop a strong marketing program for kerosene and distillates. As one of the executives expressed it, the company's operations were based on a "gasoline economy." It will be recalled that during the early years of the company's history, the kerosene market was dominated by the Standard Oil group, and The Texas Company got its start by concentrating on the new market which was then developing for gasoline. The Indiana Company, on the other hand, was heavily entrenched in the kerosene business long before the automobile was invented, and fairly early in the 1930's the company decided to cultivate actively the market, which was then beginning to expand very rapidly, for petroleum heating fuels on farms and in city homes. The extensive sale of fuel oils required deliveries to far more locations and led to the maintenance of more bulk plants than did the sale of gasoline to service stations and large customers, the prime forte of The Texas Company.

V. CHANGES IN THE USAGE OF WHOLESALE OUTLETS FOR GASOLINE

We found that the various factors which influenced the selection of wholesale outlets were subject to change with the passage of time. Fluctuations in the jobber margin relative to the commissions normally granted distributors, for example, occasionally altered the boundary line between the market situations a company normally handled with branded jobbers and those it normally handled with commission distributors. Similarly, changes in population, changes in the relative importance of farm and industrial activities, the development of the market for domestic heating oils, and many other things from time to time caused the companies to alter their distribution arrangements.

In the following paragraphs we shall outline some of the more important changes which the seven companies made in the years covered by our data with respect to their usage of the different types of wholesale outlets for the distribution of gasoline. It will be noted that just as there were both differences and similarities in the positions of the companies in 1950, so too were there both marked differences and

marked similarities in the changes which the companies made in their programs.

The analysis of changes will be based on the summary figures in Exhibits XV-3 to XV-5. These data are fragmentary in some cases and do not permit rigorous and precise conclusions as to trends. They do suffice, however, to give a fairly good general indication of the direction in which the companies moved with regard to their usage of the different types of wholesale outlets in the years for which data were available. The principal conclusions which we believe may be drawn from the exhibits are as follows.

Unbranded Jobbers:

Unbranded jobbers played a small and generally declining part in the marketing programs of the companies throughout the period 1935–1950. The Ohio Oil Company, which made the most use of branded jobbers, decreased its sales to such accounts from 17.2% to 8.9% of the total gasoline volume in the period 1940–1950. It may likewise be inferred from the figures in Exhibit XV-3 that a decline in sales to unbranded jobbers took place in the case of the Indiana Company. The Gulf Oil Corporation increased its usage of unbranded jobbers, but the increase was small and probably due largely to random circumstances.[17]

Separate figures on the number of unbranded jobbers used by the companies were available in only three cases. The Ohio Oil Company increased the number of its unbranded jobber accounts by about 50% in the period 1944–1952, but unbranded jobbers as a proportion of the company's total wholesale outlets decreased from 37.8% to 33.9%. The Indiana Company held the number of its unbranded jobbers nearly constant in the period 1941–1952, as did Atlantic in the period 1949–1952.

Figures on the changes in the average monthly sales of gasoline per unbranded jobber account were available only in the case of Atlantic (1949–1952) and The Ohio Oil Company (1944–1952). The records in the case of both companies show no significant changes. It must, of course, be remembered that the un-

---

[17] Although the increase was small in percentage points, it had the effect of quadrupling the proportionate share of the company's volume sold to unbranded jobbers.

branded jobbers often drew their products from more than one source of supply and that the total volume of their sales might be quite different from their average monthly receipts from any single supplier.

Branded Jobbers:

Branded jobbers approximately maintained their relative positions in the distribution programs of the six companies for which records were available, if the programs of the six companies are viewed as a whole. The Ohio Oil Company increased the proportion of its gasoline sold to branded jobbers from 13.0% to 23.1% in the period 1940–1950. The records for Gulf show a slight increase and the records for Sohio and the Indiana Company a slight decrease in the usage of branded jobbers, but in these three cases the changes were minor and probably due largely to random circumstances. The records of Atlantic for the years 1949–1952 and of The Texas Company for the years 1948–1951 reflect no appreciable change in the proportion of gasoline volume sold to branded jobbers.

Four of the companies, Gulf (1935–1952), The Texas Company (1935–1951), Sinclair (1935–1952),[18] and Atlantic (1949–1952), increased the number of their branded jobbers both in absolute terms and also as a relative proportion of their total wholesale outlets. The Ohio Oil Company (1944–1952) increased the absolute number but made no significant change in the relative number of its branded jobbers. Two other companies, the Indiana Company (1941–1952), and Sohio (1941–1952), moved in the opposite direction and reduced both the absolute and relative number of their branded jobber outlets.

In the case of three companies average monthly gasoline sales per branded jobber showed an increase. Average monthly shipments per branded jobber more than tripled in the case of Gulf (1935–1952); more than doubled in the case of The Ohio Oil Company (1944–1951); and increased slightly in the case of The Texas Company (1948–1951). It is particularly interesting to note that in the case of

Gulf and The Ohio Oil Company average monthly shipments per branded jobber increased more than did average monthly shipments per commission distributor. On the other hand, Atlantic's average monthly shipments per branded jobber showed a decrease in the period 1949–1952. Sohio's average monthly shipments per branded jobber fluctuated during the period 1941–1952, but were about the same in 1952 as in 1941. The seventh company, Sinclair, was not able to show monthly sales to branded jobbers as a separate item.

Commission Distributors:

Commission distributors approximately maintained their positions in the programs of the six companies for which records were available, if the six companies are viewed as a whole. Gulf and Sinclair sold about the same proportions of their gasoline through commission distributors in 1950 as they did in 1935. The Ohio Oil Company (1940–1950) and the Indiana Company (1935–1950) made significant increases in their usage of commission distributors. The Texas Company (1948–1952) made a slight decrease in its usage of commission distributors, and Atlantic made no appreciable use of commission distributors at any time in the period 1949–1952.

Three of the companies, Gulf (1935–1952), Sohio (1935–1952), and The Ohio Oil Company (1944–1952), increased the number of their commission distributors, but only in the cases of Sohio and The Ohio Oil Company did the commission distributors become a larger proportion of the total wholesale outlets; in the case of Gulf the commission distributors became a slightly smaller proportion of the total wholesale outlets. Three other companies, Sinclair (1935–1952), Atlantic (1949–1952), and The Texas Company (1935–1951), decreased the absolute and proportionate number of their commission distributors. The Indiana Company (1935–1952) followed a third course of action and held the number of its commission distributors approximately constant.

In the case of five companies, average monthly gasoline shipments per commission distributor showed an increase. Average monthly shipments per commission distributor

---

[18] This conclusion may be drawn by inference in the case of Sinclair, even though separate figures are not shown for branded jobbers, because the number of unbranded jobbers was known to be a very small part of the total.

increased about 2.5 times in the case of Gulf (1935–1952) ; about 2.8 times in the case of Sinclair (1935–1952) ; about 1.4 times in the case of The Ohio Oil Company (1944–1952) ; about 2.5 times in the case of the Indiana Company (1935–1952) ; and about 1.1 times in the case of The Texas Company (1948–1951). Atlantic, on the other hand, had slightly smaller average monthly shipments per commission distributor in 1952 than in 1949. Records were not available for the seventh company, Sohio.

Company Operated Bulk Plants:

The usage of company operated bulk plants apparently declined in the gasoline marketing programs of the six companies for which data were available. The net decline in proportionate volume sold through company operated bulk plants was minor in the case of Gulf (1935–1950) and Sinclair (1935–1950) ; of considerable significance in the case of Atlantic (1949–1952) and the Indiana Company (1935–1950) ; and of very great importance in the case of The Ohio Oil Company (1940–1950). The Texas Company (1948–1951) increased its usage of company operated bulk plants. No data were available for the seventh company, Sohio.

It was not possible to secure figures on the number of company operated bulk plants as distinct from terminals in the case of several of the companies, but when it is remembered that the terminals in each case were a relatively small fraction of the total bulk plants and terminals, inferences may be drawn from the combined figures in Exhibit XV-4 with regard to changes in the number of company operated bulk plants.

Gulf probably increased both the absolute and relative number of its company operated bulk plants in the period 1935–1952, because the changes in Exhibit XV-4 are too great to be accounted for by terminals alone. The Indiana Company (1935–1952) likewise increased both the absolute and relative number of its company operated bulk plants. Sinclair at first decreased and then increased both the absolute and relative number of company operated bulk plants used in its program in the period 1935–1952. On the other hand, Atlantic decreased the absolute number of its company operated bulk plants in the period 1941–1952. The

Ohio Oil Company at first increased and then decreased the absolute number of its company operated bulk plants, but the number of company operated bulk plants as a percentage of total outlets declined throughout most of the period 1944–1952. Sohio and The Texas Company made no significant change in their usage of company operated bulk plants, so far as may be determined from our data.

Average monthly gasoline sales through company operated bulk plants increased about 2.4 times in the case of Sinclair (1935–1952), about 1.9 times in the case of The Ohio Oil Company (1944–1952), and about 1.5 times in the case of The Texas Company (1948–1951). The company operated bulk plants of the Indiana Company experienced a decline and later an increase in average monthly gasoline sales, but there was no significant net change for the period 1935–1952 as a whole. The company operated bulk plants of Atlantic, however, had slightly lower average monthly gasoline sales in 1952 than in 1949. Separate data on company operated bulk plants were not available for the other companies.

VI. FUTURE OBJECTIVES OF THE COMPANIES

It was the general policy of all seven of the companies to study each marketing situation on an individual basis and to select the type of wholesale outlet which the executives believed would be best suited to it in the light of all the considerations noted earlier in the chapter. In other words, the companies were not seeking to concentrate on any one or two types of wholesale outlets; their objective was rather to secure the *best combination* of the various types of wholesale outlets for the market situations with which they were confronted.

It should not be inferred that the policies and objectives of the seven companies with regard to the usage of the different types of outlets were identical. Just as there were both marked differences and marked similarities in the distribution arrangements of the companies in 1950 and in the changes made in their programs, so too were there both differences and similarities in the policies and objectives of the companies with regard to the usage of the different types of outlets. In general, however, it may be said that the policies the companies were following in 1952, and expected to follow in the immediate future, were somewhat as outlined below and that the differences which existed among the companies were largely a reflection of (a) differences in the character of the markets served, and (b) differences in the relative significance which the executives of each company assigned to the various factors affecting the selection of wholesale outlets.

Unbranded jobbers were regarded as the least desirable type of gasoline outlet and were used for the most part only as a last resort or as a temporary expedient while a company was in the process of developing other marketing arrangements. It was generally agreed by the marketing executives of the seven companies that the unbranded jobber had little to offer a company which was already committed to a branded program. Most of the companies therefore, while willing to continue unbranded jobber relationships of long standing were reluctant to take on new unbranded accounts or to build any major part of their marketing programs around them.

Branded jobbers were generally used along the fringes of a company's regular territory, in sparsely settled areas, and in other situations where it was believed (a) that the jobber could do a more effective selling job, or (b) that the volume of business done per outlet would not be sufficient to justify the supplier in making an investment in bulk plant or station facilities and in setting up the organization necessary to check inventories, audit books, supervise the installation, renewal, and maintenance of dealer equipment, provide sales assistance, and perform the various other functions and services usually associated with commission operated plants. In other words, the branded jobbers were used in relatively low-volume locations where it was believed that the extra costs associated with a commission distributorship would not be covered by the gains in realization secured on sales through commission distributors versus branded jobbers. It was believed that the branded jobbers could maintain profitable operations in these locations because they often engaged in various side line activities, such as a Coca-Cola or farm equipment distributor-

ship, which helped to cover their overhead and fixed costs.

The suppliers also tended to make use of branded jobbers in areas where their supply arrangements were insecure and where they were not ready to make capital commitments of their own. One of the companies, for example, initiated in 1950 a program of marketing expansion into two new areas outside its traditional territory through the use of branded jobbers. At that time the company was a buyer in the domestic market for both crude oil and refined products, and it appeared that, directly or indirectly, the additional supply of products for the expansion would have to come through purchase arrangements. There was a possibility, however, that the further development of Canadian or domestic reserves might in the future put the company in a position to expand its refining operations to the point where it could supply products for the new territories. The use of branded jobbers to gain access to the new markets provided a means by which the company could avoid a heavy financial commitment of its own until its crude oil and refined products situation had clarified. Moreover, it was currently possible to buy refined products in the wholesale market and to resell to jobbers on a reasonably profitable basis. It was anticipated that the jobber business might be purchased at a later date if the market developed satisfactorily and if the company found itself in the future in a position to supply refined products to the two areas.

Another general use made of branded jobbers was to accomplish marketing expansion at times when a supplier did not have capital funds available to build or acquire facilities of his own. In the words of an executive of one of the companies, branded jobbers were regarded as a "quick and inexpensive means of getting distribution." A further use made of branded jobbers was in situations where there was an extreme seasonality in the business, and where it was impossible to sustain the bulk plan operation on a year-around basis without engaging in supplementary activities.

All the companies, except the Indiana Company and Atlantic, generally tried to use commission distributorships (operated by non-company employees) for bulk plants of intermediate size; that is, for plants where the volume was large enough so that the extra costs associated with distributor as contrasted with jobber operation would be more than covered by the higher realizations secured on the distributor sales but where the volume was not sufficient to justify or require operation of the plant with salaried employees.

It was believed that the commission bulk plants could be operated successfully in a great many situations where company operated bulk plants could not. The commission distributor frequently did not incur costs for such things as employee benefits, workmen's compensation, pension plans, group insurance, and chain store taxes, or at least did not incur them to the same degree as did a supplier in the case of a company operated plant. The commission distributor could usually adjust his labor costs to local conditions more easily than could a large supplier and frequently could use his own family as a part of his labor force, thus avoiding the payment of overtime wage rates during periods of peak activity. Furthermore, the commission distributor, like the branded jobber, was often in a position to engage in various side line activities to aid in supporting the smaller volume plants. Finally, as noted earlier, there was considerable thinking to the effect that commission distributors could actually do a more effective selling job in the small towns and rural areas than could company employees.

The Indiana Company had somewhat the same general policies and objectives with respect to the usage of commission distributors as did the other companies. As noted earlier, however, the Indiana Company's commission distributors differed from those of the other companies in that they had the status of company employees. Atlantic differed from all the other companies in that it made little use of commission distributors and did not anticipate that it would develop any large volume of sales through such outlets in the near future.

Company operated bulk plants were ordinarily used by the companies at points where the volume of business was large. This practice had developed for three principal reasons. In the first place, as noted earlier, at the large volume plants the unit cost for wages and salaries frequently dropped below the level of the commissions paid to distributors. Second, in connection with the operation of the big bulk plants in metropolitan centers it was frequently necessary to have technical specialists available to handle the large industrial accounts, and it had been the experience of most of the companies that this type of selling could best be handled through salaried employees. Finally, salaried employees were used at the large plants because the companies did not wish, at such points, to risk the loss of accounts which sometimes resulted when distributors or jobbers transferred to other suppliers.

All the companies were developing arrangements for the by-passing of bulk plants with direct shipments to service stations from refineries and terminals as fast as their individual circumstances would permit. The by-passing technique was regarded as an inescapable consequence of the development of the products pipe line, the increasing size of service stations, the building of better roads, and the improvement of truck transport equipment. The companies were likewise increasing their direct shipments to large commercial accounts. The policies of the companies varied with regard to the prices charged these accounts, but it was generally believed that ultimately much of the commercial business would have to be done at jobber prices or better than jobber prices, depending on the size and nature of the account (see Chapter Nine).

It was recognized that the by-passing arrangements would inevitably lead to the elimination of many bulk plants of all types, company, commission, and jobber operated. It was believed, however, that in situations where the by-passing technique offered lower costs of distribution, the pressure of competition would make it impossible for the industry or any company in it to retain the bulk plant operation as part of the distribution process. At the same time, it was generally agreed that in the foreseeable future there would always be a substantial place for the bulk plant operation as a means of serving effectively the rural markets and the home market for heating fuels.

The policies and objectives of the companies with respect to the usage of the various types of wholesale outlets for the distribution of kerosene and distillate were much the same as in the case of gasoline, a necessary consequence of the fact that the two groups of products were usually handled through the same bulk plants. The companies were, however, much more inclined to sell kerosene and distillate on an unbranded basis than they were gasoline and often sold kerosene and distillate to outlets which did not handle their gasolines. Moreover, the by-passing technique was for obvious reasons much less applicable to kerosenes and distillate than it was to gasolines.

VII. SUMMARY

1. The structures of the seven companies were uniform with respect to the *depth* of integration into marketing activities; all the companies were and had been for some time selling to wholesale resellers, retail resellers, and consumers and industrial users. There were, however, wide differences among the companies with respect to *extent* of integration or the relative volumes of refinery output sold at the three levels of the market. All the companies made certain changes in their extent of integration between 1935 and 1950. Some of the companies made changes which reflected further integration while others made changes which reflected disintegration. The integration programs of the companies for gasoline were distinctly different from those for kerosene and distillate, but the general direction of the changes which each company made between 1935 and 1950 was approximately the same for the two groups of products.

2. The integration patterns of the seven companies at both the wholesale and retail level of the market were not so much a result of decisions made explicitly with respect thereto as they were a product of practices and policies with regard to the usage of different types of wholesale and retail outlets. These practices and policies, in turn, usually evolved from a continuing series of multiple-choice decisions with respect to the types of outlets to be used in particular situations. The executives of the companies usually studied each market location as a separate case and made their decisions in the light of a fairly large number of business and economic considerations. Important among the factors influencing the decisions on wholesale outlets were cost and volume considerations, various intangible considerations such as the relative security of market position afforded by the outlets under consideration, competitive pressures, and various fortuitous and special circumstances.

3. The positions of the companies in 1950, the changes they made between 1935 and 1950, and their future objectives with regard to the usage of different types of wholesale outlets reflected both strong similarities and strong differences. The similarities arose from the fact that the selection of market outlets was in the case of all the companies influenced by the same general set of business and economic considerations. The differences arose from the fact that the companies faced somewhat different market problems and the fact that the executives of each company evaluated and judged the considerations pertinent to the problem of outlet selection in different ways.

4. The policies and objectives of the seven companies with respect to the different types of wholesale outlets seemed to assure a continuing position in the industry for the commission distributor, the branded gasoline jobber, and the fuel oil jobber. The unbranded gasoline jobber, on the other hand, had little place in the marketing programs of the seven companies, and it appeared that he would have an even smaller position therein in the future. The branded gasoline jobber was used primarily at the small volume locations on the fringes of the supplier's market territory and in special situations where it was believed that he could do a more effective selling job than company or commission operated bulk plants. The inevitable development of the by-passing technique in those situations where it permitted lower distribution costs seemed to indicate that a declining portion of the industry's volume would be handled by all types of bulk plants and particularly those in or near large metropolitan centers.

CHAPTER SIXTEEN

Analysis of Integration Patterns: Retail Marketing Activities

Just as the integration patterns of the seven companies at the wholesale level of the industry tended to evolve from a continuing series of multiple-choice decisions with respect to the types of wholesale outlets to be used in particular situations, so too did the integration patterns of the companies at the retail level of the industry tend to evolve from multiple-choice decisions with respect to the types of retail outlets to be used at particular market locations. A decision to acquire or lease the properties of a contractor station and to convert it to dealer operation, for example, increased the intensity of the supplier's forward integration program because it gave him control over the physical facilities of the station. Likewise a decision to convert a dealer station to company operation altered the level of the market at which a company sold, and also increased the intensity of integration because the supplier thereby gained complete control over the operations as well as the physical facilities of the station.

In discussing the practices and policies of the seven companies with respect to the various types of retail outlets, we shall follow the same procedure of analysis as was used in connection with the discussion of wholesale outlets in Chapter Fifteen. Attention will first be directed to the various types of retail outlets which we found in the programs of the seven companies. We shall then discuss the general considerations which influenced the companies in their selection of outlets. Finally, we shall analyze some of the differences and similarities in the present positions, recent programs, and future objectives of the companies with respect to the usage of the different outlets.

I. The Types of Retail Outlets

We shall define a "retail outlet" as an intermediary engaged in the distribution of gasoline and/or kerosene and distillate which does not operate a bulk plant or terminal. This definition includes all the various types of gasoline service stations. In addition, it embraces the tank truck dealers and commission truck drivers who take deliveries from the bulk plants, terminals, or refineries of their suppliers and haul directly to service station, farm, commercial, and household accounts. The classification of tank truck dealers and commission truck drivers as retail outlets is a rather arbitrary one; as far as their activities in the distribution of gasoline to service stations are concerned, they might equally well be treated as wholesale intermediaries.

Company Operated Stations:

The physical facilities at the company operated stations were owned or leased by the supplier, and the stations were maintained and operated by company employees. In the great majority of cases, the station operators were paid on a straight salary basis, but in a few instances, notably in the case of Sohio, we found that the station operators received a part of their compensation on a commission basis. The company operated stations represented the highest possible extent and intensity of integration for a supplier, because through such stations the supplier carried his products all the way to the final consumer and maintained full control of selling prices, merchandising methods, and standards of service.

Dealer Operated Stations:

The facilities at the dealer operated stations were owned or leased by the supplier but were rented to dealers for operation. We found that these stations could be divided into three general categories depending on the nature of the equity held by the supplier in the property: (a) company owned stations, (b) three-party lease stations, and (c) two-party lease stations. The company owned stations were those in which the supplier owned both land and building or owned the building and leased the land. Situations in which the supplier owned the land and leased the building were extremely rare. Three-party lease stations were those in which the supplier leased the land and buildings from parties other than the station operator. Two-party lease stations were those in which the dealer owned or leased the station, leased it to the supplier, and then leased it back from the supplier for operation.

Of the various types of dealer operated stations, the company owned units represented the highest intensity of integration because in such cases the supplier had permanent control over at least the facilities and often both the land and facilities. In cases where the land was leased, the intensity of integration was, of course, less than in cases where both land and buildings were owned. The three-party and two-party lease stations offered a vast range of possibilities for variations in the intensity of integration depending on the duration of the leases, the provisions for lease cancellation, and the nature of whatever renewal options might be included in the contract.

The company owned and three-party lease stations were rented to dealers under a variety of different arrangements. Ordinarily, however, the contracts were written for a period of one year and were automatically renewable unless one party or the other gave notice of a desire to terminate at some stated interval prior to the anniversary date, usually 10 to 30 days. Many different types of rental payments were used; one common arrangement was for the dealer to pay the supplier a minimum monthly rental plus so much per gallon on all gasoline sold or on all gasoline sold over a certain minimum amount. Occasionally the per gallon rental was graduated to provide for one rate on all sales below a certain volume and another rate for all sales above that volume. In still other cases, the contract provided only for a fixed monthly rental payment by the dealer, regardless of the volume sold.

Two-party lease stations were usually leased to the supplier for a period of three to ten years. In some cases, however, the suppliers leased the stations for only a one-year period and included in the contracts a number of renewal options, sometimes as many as fourteen. The rentals paid by the supplier to the dealer were of many types, but often consisted of a guaranteed monthly minimum plus a fee of so much per gallon of gasoline sold through the station. The two-party lease stations were rented back by the supplier to the dealer on much the same basis as the company owned and three-party lease stations were rented to dealers. In some cases the rentals paid by the supplier to the dealer and by the dealer to the supplier were arranged to equalize or "wash out"; in other cases there was a differential between the two rentals in favor of the dealer. These differentials were used by some of the companies as a means of competing for the better dealer accounts. Moreover, it was contended that the two-party lease operator was entitled to some benefits in return for placing his station under lease to the supplier for an extended period of time.

The dealers, regardless of whether the station was a company owned, three-party lease, or two-party lease outlet, usually purchased their gasoline from suppliers under a sales contract or supply agreement. These arrangements usually extended for a period of one year and were automatically renewable unless one of the parties gave notice of his intention to terminate at some stated interval, often 30 days, prior to the anniversary date. All the contracts we studied stated that the sales price for gasoline would be the supplier's regular, delivered tank wagon price to dealers for the location in question. So far as any contractual relationships were concerned, the dealer was free to resell to his customers at any price he chose. All the contracts, except those of the Gulf Oil Corporation, set maximum and minimum quantities on the volume of gasoline to be purchased by the dealer. We were informed that the minimums were usually far below the average volume purchased by each dealer and that the maximum and minimum clauses rarely, if ever, had any practical significance other than to relieve the supplier of a possible implied obligation to deliver more than the maximum in times of severe shortage.

The suppliers usually furnished equipment, such as pumps, tanks, and air compressors, to the dealers under equipment rental agreements at a nominal fee of $1.00 per year. The amount of the equipment the supplier furnished was largely determined by the size and value of the station; in the case of the better stations it was not uncommon to furnish also lubricating lifts, air hose stands, and various other facilities at nominal rentals. Offers of special equipment were one means by which the suppliers competed for the better dealers. In nearly all cases the suppliers assumed the responsibility for the installation, maintenance, and removal of the equipment.

Contractor Stations:

The facilities at the contractor stations were owned or leased by the station operator, and the supplier had no equity whatsoever in the properties. Suppliers sold to these outlets under supply contracts which had essentially the same provisions as did the dealer sales agreements with respect to such things as duration, cancellation, prices, and maximum and minimum quantities. In several of the companies, precisely the same forms were used to negotiate supply agreements with both dealer and contractor stations. The suppliers also furnished equipment to contractor stations on about the same terms, and often under the same contracts, as they did to dealers. A supplier was, of course, less likely to furnish the more elaborate pieces of equipment to contractor stations than to dealer stations because his connections with contractor stations were usually more tenuous than with dealer stations.

Contractor stations were of two general types: undivided accounts and divided accounts. The former handled the gasolines of only one supplier whereas the latter, sometimes called split-pump stations, handled the gasolines of two or more suppliers. In the case of the undivided accounts there was usually a stronger tie between supplier and station operator than in the case of the divided accounts.

Commission Truck Drivers: [1]

Although the commission truck drivers hauled products to both final consumers and service stations and strictly speaking might be regarded as a method of sale rather than a type of outlet, we have classed them as a retail outlet because in many respects they were the counterpart at the retail level of the industry of the commission distributors at the wholesale level. The commission truck drivers were not regarded as company employees and usually owned their own trucks. In some cases, however, they merely owned the truck chassis and the tanks were furnished by the supplier; in a few cases the trucks were furnished entirely by the supplier. Most of the commission truck drivers had only one truck, but some operated a fleet of several trucks. In addition, some of the larger commission truck drivers occasionally owned or leased one or more service stations or had supply agreements with contractor service stations. [2]

The commission truck drivers received a fee of so much per gallon of products delivered. The commission rates varied depending on the prevailing pricing practices in the area in which the commission truck driver operated. In 1950 one of the companies was paying its commission truck drivers in a mid-western state 0.5 cent per gallon on deliveries for resale, 1.5 cents per gallon on deliveries to farmers, and 1.25 cents per gallon on deliveries to other consumers. The commission schedules also sometimes provided for variations in the rates depending on the distance of the customer from the bulk plant. The supplier in all cases controlled the prices at which sales were made to customers.

The territories in which the commission truck drivers were permitted to operate were usually prescribed in their contracts, although the suppliers often reserved the right to make

---

[1] Other names commonly used included commission marketers, commission salesmen, commission tank wagon salesmen, commission route salesmen, and tank truck distributors.

[2] The ownership or leasing of service stations represents vertical integration on the part of the commission truck driver. A commission truck driver owning or leasing service stations might be classified as a service station operator with backward integration into transportation activities, particularly if his service station activities are large relative to his trucking business.

deliveries in such territories by other means without obligation to the commission truck drivers. The agreements with the commission truck drivers customarily ran for a period of one year and were automatically renewable unless one of the parties gave notice of intention to terminate at some stated interval prior to the anniversary date.

Tank Truck Dealers:

As noted in Chapter Fifteen, the tank truck dealers performed essentially the same functions as did the commission truck drivers. They differed from commission truck drivers, however, in that they always furnished their own trucks and tanks and, instead of receiving a commission on deliveries, they bought products outright at the bulk plants of their suppliers and resold to customers by any means and at any price they chose. As in the case of the commission truck drivers, many of the tank truck dealers operated only one truck but some operated several. Some of the larger ones also owned or leased one or more service stations which they either operated with their own employees or rented out to dealers.[3]

II. CONSIDERATIONS AFFECTING THE SELECTION OF RETAIL OUTLETS

We found that the selection of retail outlets for particular market locations was influenced by the same general types of considerations as was the selection of wholesale outlets. In other words, the decisions of the suppliers were usually developed from balancing, one against another, whatever cost and volume considerations, intangible factors, competitive pressures, and special circumstances were pertinent to the particular situation at hand. In the following paragraphs we shall not attempt to discuss each of these influences in any great detail, but shall merely illustrate the manner in which they entered the problem of outlet selection. Most of

---

[3] The ownership or leasing of service stations represents vertical integration on the part of the tank truck dealer. A tank truck dealer owning or leasing service stations might be classified as a service station operator with backward integration into transportation activities, particularly if his service station activities are large relative to his trucking business.

the discussion will relate to the selection of service stations for the distribution of gasoline. A concluding section will then deal briefly with the factors influencing decisions relating to the usage of company trucks, commission truck drivers, and tank truck dealers, particularly in the distribution of domestic heating fuels.

Cost and Volume Considerations:

As in the case of wholesale outlets, the selection of retail outlets was influenced in the first instance by cost and volume considerations. A supplier, for example, usually realized the same price on deliveries to both contractor and dealer stations. In the case of the dealer stations, however, the supplier had not only the problem of covering his selling and delivery costs, but likewise the problem of securing a high enough station rental from the dealer to pay him a reasonable return on his investment in the properties or to cover his lease obligations to the property owner. The first problem in considering whether to use contractor stations or to establish dealer outlets in a particular locality was nearly always therefore simply the question of whether the volume prospects were sufficiently attractive so that the dealer would be able to pay the supplier an adequate station rental.

Cost and volume considerations were likewise important factors in the choice between dealer and company operated stations. In connection with both types of station, the supplier had approximately the same situation so far as ownership costs were concerned. By selling through company operated stations, however, the supplier realized a higher price for his products than he did in selling to dealer stations; he also incurred as additional expenses the costs of manning and operating the stations. A substantial part of these additional expenses were fixed irrespective of volume changes. The per gallon costs of station operation thus tended to decline as the volume increased and at some point became less than the incremental revenue the supplier secured from selling at retail prices rather than at tank wagon prices. In other words, in most situations there was a break-even volume above which the supplier made more money by selling through company operated stations at retail prices than by selling to dealers at tank wagon prices.

Intangible Factors:

Various intangible factors were often fully as important in the selection of retail outlets as were cost and volume considerations. In the first place, the various types of retail stations varied widely in the degree of security they afforded the supplier with regard to his sales representation in a particular locality. The degree of security was usually at a minimum in the case of divided contractor accounts and less in the case of both divided and undivided contractor accounts than in the case of all types of dealer and company operated stations. The latter types of stations varied in the degree of security they afforded depending on the nature of the equity the supplier held in the station properties.

All the companies reported that there was considerable turnover among their contractor stations. Each supplier was continually striving to replace his weaker stations with stronger ones and thus improve the average quality of his retail representation. As a result, the suppliers were continually taking contractor stations from and losing them to each other. Two companies were able to give us figures on the turnover among their retail outlets. In the first case, the data showed that the company lost about 10% of its contractor stations per year in the period 1946–1951, inclusive. In the second case, the data showed that the company lost about 5.1% of its contractor accounts in 1949 and 6.1% of its contractor accounts in 1950.

The seven companies reported that there was likewise some turnover in their dealer accounts but that it was substantially less than in the case of contractor stations. One company, for example, lost 0.8% of its dealers in 1949 and 2.2% in 1950. Another company lost 2.8% of its dealers in 1950 and 2.1% in 1951. The turnover of dealer accounts resulted from competition among suppliers for the better station managers and from the fact that the dealers occasionally left the business to take other employment or for a variety of other reasons. The loss of a dealer account was less serious than the loss of a contractor station of equal importance, because in the former case the company still retained the physical facilities and the market location. As a result, there was considerable reason for a supplier to purchase or lease the facilities at market locations which were particularly important to his sales program and to operate the stations with dealers or company employees.

A second important intangible factor influencing the selection of retail outlets was the degree of control which the supplier could exercise over the appearance of and service offered by the station. In the case of the contractor stations, the supplier could do little to influence station operating procedures, and one poorly run station operating under his brand name often had an adverse influence on his stations in the surrounding area. In the case of dealer stations, the supplier was in a better position to make sure his brand name was represented to the public in the manner he wanted because he controlled the physical facilities and could usually terminate the dealer agreement on any annual anniversary date if the operating conditions at the station were not to his liking. Company operated stations afforded the supplier complete control over standards of service and cleanliness.

The points mentioned above tended to favor the use of company operated over dealer operated stations and of dealer operated over contractor stations. There were, on the other hand, intangible factors which favored the use of both dealer and contractor stations over company operated stations. As pointed out in Chapter Nine, one of the major reasons many of the companies withdrew from the usage of company operated stations in the 1930's was because they found that independently operated stations, dealer or contractor, could do a more effective job in adjusting prices to meet local conditions than could company operated stations. Moreover, most of the companies had found that it required a good deal of supervisory effort to get company employees to do as aggressive a selling job as that done by good dealers or contractors because the incomes of the latter were directly dependent on their personal efforts. As noted earlier, only one of the seven companies, the Standard Oil Company (Ohio), had found it practical to use an incentive plan of wage payment in compensating its station employees.

Competitive Pressures:

In a great many cases the selection of retail outlets was determined more by the exigencies and requirements of particular situations than it was by long-run policies or marketing strategies. Suppliers were continually bidding against each other in their efforts to secure the better locations for their retail outlets. As a result, the decisions a supplier made with regard to the purchase or leasing of property and with regard to the terms on which his leases were negotiated were often simply a matter of competitive necessity. Moreover, questions of whether a contractor station could be converted to a dealer operation and of the terms on which the conversion could be made were often dictated by the offers to the contractor of competing suppliers.

The influence of competitive pressures on the selection of retail stations was particularly manifest in connection with two-party lease arrangements. The offer of a two-party lease arrangement with a differential in the lease rentals in favor of the lessee was often a very effective means by which one supplier took contractor stations from another. If a supplier found that one of his contractor stations had received such an offer from a competitor, he often found it necessary to make a comparable offer and to convert the station to a two-party lease dealer operation in order to retain the market location.

The owners of contractor stations also occasionally asked their suppliers to make fairly extensive equipment installations or facilities improvements for them. In such cases, two-party leases were frequently negotiated, with or without differentials in the rentals, in order that the supplier might be assured of the account for a sufficient period of time to make his investment worth while. Similarly, the owners of contractor stations sometimes asked their suppliers to enter into two-party lease arrangements in order that they might use the lease to the supplier as a basis for establishing credit and borrowing money from local banks to make improvements of their own in the station properties. If a supplier refused to accede to such requests, the contractor could, and often did, take his problem and his business to a competing company.

Fortuitous and Special Circumstances:

There were a vast number of special circumstances which influenced the selection of retail stations in one way or another. As in the case of wholesale outlets, the selection was often determined by the particular type of station that happened to be available at a particular location at a particular time.

The selection of retail outlets was also much influenced by the financial situation of the supplier and the access which he had to capital funds for marketing expansion. None of the companies had unlimited capital resources, and such funds as they did have were necessarily allocated among their producing, refining, transportation, and marketing divisions in accordance with the investment opportunities in and requirements of each division. There was always therefore some definite upper limit on the number of service station properties a supplier could acquire in any given period of time. If the supplier wished to increase further the density of his outlets or the geographic area in which he was represented, he could next make use of various types of leasing arrangements. There was, however, a very real upper limit on the extent of the lease commitments which it was prudent for a company to make in view of the hazards of population shifts and of alterations in roads and traffic patterns. When that limit was reached, contractor stations became extremely important as a means of accomplishing further marketing expansion.

Considerations Influencing the Usage of Commission Truck Drivers and Tank Truck Dealers:

The problem of outlet selection with respect to commission truck drivers and tank truck dealers was in reality a matter of deciding on the method of delivery to be used in moving products out of company or commission operated bulk plants; that is, a matter of deciding whether the hauling should be done by company trucks, commission truck drivers, or tank truck dealers. These decisions affected a supplier's integration pattern: the use of commission rather than company trucks affected the intensity of integration, and a decision to sell to tank truck dealers in lieu of making deliveries via company or commission trucks altered the level of the market at which a company sold.

So far as gasoline was concerned, decisions with respect to the usage of company trucks, commission truck drivers, and tank truck dealers rested largely on the relative trucking costs and the accessibility of the customers under consideration. Many of the costs involved in maintaining and operating company trucks were fixed irrespective of volume changes, and as a result unit delivery costs tended to decline as the volume handled increased. In markets where the volume was such that the unit delivery costs were less than the rate per gallon paid to commission truck drivers or the margin allowed to tank truck dealers, it was to a supplier's advantage to make deliveries in his own equipment.

The equipment and operations required to make deliveries efficiently to service stations and large customers in the heart of a bulk plant territory, however, were often very different from those required to make deliveries to small customers on the fringes of the territory or where road conditions made it impossible to use large trucks. As a result, if a supplier adjusted his operations and equipment to handle the large volume business in the center of his territory, his costs for deliveries to customers in the fringe markets were often so high that he could secure a better net realization by turning the business over to commission distributors or tank truck dealers whose operations and equipment were deliberately geared to the requirements of the small volume or remote markets. Some suppliers, of course, set up delivery facilities to handle both types of markets.

The extent to which a supplier made use of commission truck drivers or tank truck dealers in his gasoline business was influenced by many other considerations. One important factor was the availability of commission truck drivers or tank truck dealers in the bulk plant area. If a commission truck driver or a tank truck dealer had a string of service stations in a section of the market where a supplier had few outlets of his own, the supplier was likely to sell through or to him simply as a means of getting market representation.[4] Commission truck drivers and tank truck dealers, and par-

ticularly the former, were also often employed in markets where there were seasonal peaks in the gasoline demand which a supplier could not handle readily with his own equipment.

The choice between commission truck drivers and tank truck dealers rested on somewhat the same general types of consideration as did the choice between commission distributors and branded jobbers at the wholesale level of the industry. The margin allowed to tank truck dealers, for example, was usually slightly higher than the commission paid to commission truck drivers, but in connection with sales through the latter the supplier incurred certain costs, some fixed irrespective of volume changes, which he did not have in selling to tank truck dealers. As a result, the preferred arrangement from the supplier's standpoint depended somewhat on the volume involved. In areas where the supplier had supply contracts with service stations, it was, of course, desirable for him to make deliveries through commission truck drivers or his own trucks.

Decisions with respect to the usage of company trucks, commission truck drivers, and tank truck dealers in the distribution of domestic heating fuels,[5] the most important of the kerosene and distillate products, were influenced by a number of factors which were not present in the case of gasoline. As was noted earlier, the distribution of domestic heating fuels was closely associated with the sale of oil burners and the servicing of oil burners. In times of intense competition, for example, many fuel oil dealers sold burners at cost as a means of securing fuel oil contracts. Moreover, many customers in signing fuel oil contracts were more interested in the reliability of burner service the dealer would supply than in the oil that he carried. As a result, the extent to which a company used its own trucks for the direct delivery of fuel oil to customers was heavily influenced by the extent to which it was willing to become engaged in the auxiliary businesses of burner sales and burner serv-

---

4 See footnotes 2 and 3.

5 There were three main categories of heating fuels: (a) kerosene and light distillates (No. 1 fuel oils), (b) middle distillates (No. 2 and No. 3 fuel oils), and (c) residual fuel oils. The products in group (a) were used for space heaters, those in group (b) in domestic oil burners for central heating and in Diesel engines, and those in group (c) in specialized oil burners in industrial and commercial plants.

ice. The association of the oil delivery, burner sale, and burner service businesses was particularly important in the rural markets where the customer did not have many firms to which he could turn for burner service as he sometimes did in the metropolitan markets.[6]

Seasonal variations in market demand had a particularly important influence on the relative usage which a supplier made of company trucks, commission truck drivers, and tank truck dealers in the distribution of kerosene and distillate. In a market where there was a seasonal peak in the gasoline demand in the summer, a supplier sometimes found it desirable to engage in the direct distribution of heating fuels in the winter in order to keep his equipment and personnel employed on a year-round basis. There were, however, some definite limits on the extent to which equipment and personnel used in the gasoline business could be transferred to the fuel oil business. The large trucks used in delivering to service stations could not reach many household locations; the specialized hoses and metering equipment often used for fuel oil deliveries were not needed in the gasoline business; and the selling of fuel oil to home owners required differently trained personnel than did the bulk delivery of gasoline to service stations.[7]

In markets where there was a large seasonal peak in the winter demand for fuel oil, suppliers frequently employed commission distributors or sold to tank truck dealers in order to avoid carrying idle equipment or personnel through the summer months. Moreover, the fuel oil demand was heavily dependent on weather conditions and often varied sharply from one week to the next. In addition, road conditions sometimes greatly reduced the speed at which deliveries could be made and the number of stops per day that could be handled by a single truck. As a result there were weeks during the winter when the delivery capacity required by a supplier might be fully two or three times as much as in other weeks. The easiest way to handle these fluctuations in delivery requirements was by working the trucking equipment longer hours. In the case of com-

pany employees, however, the working of longer hours involved overtime wage payments or the hiring of additional personnel. An independent commission distributor or tank truck dealer could, on the other hand, work any number of hours per day his business might require without incurring additional out-of-pocket costs.

Other factors which influenced a supplier's choice among company trucks, commission truck drivers, and tank truck dealers in the distribution of both gasoline and domestic fuel oil were not greatly different from those which have been discussed in earlier sections as influencing the selection of wholesale outlets and service stations; cost and volume considerations, various intangible factors, competitive pressures, and matters of expediency and chance were all important.

III. DIFFERENCES AND SIMILARITIES IN THE POSITIONS OF THE COMPANIES IN 1950

The foregoing discussion of the types of factors which influenced suppliers in their selection of retail outlets has not been intended to be exhaustive but merely to indicate that the decisions a supplier made in each market locality were derived from the sifting and balancing of a fairly large number of business, competitive, and economic considerations. The sifting and balancing process was handled differently in each of the companies, depending on the relative emphases the executives attached to the various factors pertinent to the problem and on the characteristics of the markets in which the company operated. As a result, the positions of the seven companies at any given time with respect to the usage of the different types of retail outlets usually reflected both differences and similarities. To illustrate the point, we shall present a brief comparison of the positions of the companies in 1950.

Service Stations: [8]

Comparative data on the positions of the six companies with respect to the usage of the various types of service stations are shown in

---

[6] See Harvey P. Bishop, *Retail Marketing of Furnace Oil* (Boston, Division of Research, Harvard Graduate School of Business Administration, 1946).

[7] Ibid., p. 28.

[8] The discussion will relate to only six of the companies, since data from The Atlantic Refining Company on the number of different types of stations were not available for publication.

Exhibits XVI-1, XVI-2, and XVI-3. The first exhibit shows the number of stations of each type used by each company and a percentage breakdown of each company's total stations by type. The second exhibit shows the average monthly gasoline sales to or through each type of station. The third exhibit shows the gasoline sales to each type of station as a percentage of total gasoline sales to all types of service stations.

The data reveal at least three significant similarities in the usage which the companies were making of the different types of stations in 1950. First, it is apparent that all the companies except the Indiana Company used a far larger number of contractor than dealer stations and a far larger number of dealer than company operated stations. In the programs of the five companies (Indiana Company excepted) contractor stations accounted for 60% or more of the total stations; dealer operated stations accounted for between 13.0% and 38.6% of the total stations; and in no case did company operated stations account for more than 7.1% of the total stations.

A second point of similarity appears in the fact that in the case of each company average monthly gasoline sales through company operated stations were far greater than to dealer operated stations, and average monthly gasoline sales to dealer operated stations were far greater than to contractor stations. In each instance, average monthly gasoline sales through company operated stations were at least twice the average monthly sales to dealer operated stations, and average monthly sales to dealers were at least three times as large as average monthly sales to contractor stations (see Exhibit XVI-2).

A third point of similarity may be noted in the fact that five of the six companies (Sohio excepted) made less than 4.1% of their total service station sales of gasoline through company operated stations (see Exhibit XVI-3).

Notwithstanding these three general similarities in integration patterns, there were a number of marked differences in the programs of the individual companies. It will be noted, in the first place, that whereas company operated stations amounted to less than 1% of the total number of stations in the case of five of the companies, in the case of the Standard Oil Company (Ohio), company operated stations amounted to over 7% of the total. In other words, company operated stations were numerically about seven times as important in Sohio's program as in the program of any of the other companies. Similarly, it may be noted that dealer operated stations ranged from 13.0% of the total in the case of Sohio to 61.9% of the total in the case of the Indiana Company and that contractor stations ranged from 37.8% of the total in the case of the Indiana Company to 81.8% of the total in the case of Gulf.

There were likewise some wide differences among the individual companies with respect to average monthly sales to or through each type of station. Sohio's company operated stations handled about twice the volume of the Indiana Company's company operated stations; Sohio's dealer operated stations handled about 2.6 times the volume of Sinclair's dealer operated stations; and Sohio's contractor stations handled about 2.8 times as much volume as did The Ohio Oil Company's contractor stations. It may further be noted that whereas the company operated stations of The Texas Company and Sinclair handled about 4.5 times the average monthly volume of their dealer operated stations, the company operated stations of Sohio and the Indiana Company handled only about twice the volume of their dealer operated stations. Similarly, whereas the dealer operated stations of The Ohio Oil Company handled over five times the average monthly volume of its contractor stations, Gulf's dealer operated stations handled only slightly more than three times the volume of its contractor stations.

Finally, there were very significant differences in the proportions of each company's total sales to or through service stations which were handled by the different types of outlets. Whereas Sohio made over 30% of its total station sales through company operated stations, none of the other companies made over 4.1% of its station sales through such outlets. Furthermore, sales to dealer operated stations ranged from 28.0% of total station sales in the case of Sohio to 87.6% of total station sales in the case of the Indiana Company, and sales to contractor stations ranged from 11.4% of total station sales in the case of the Indiana Company to 56.7% of total station sales in the case of Gulf. It will also be noted that whereas The Texas Company, Sinclair, The Ohio Oil Company, and the Indiana Company made a substantially larger share of their total sales to dealer stations than to contractor stations, Gulf and Sohio reversed the relationship and made a substantially larger proportion of their total station sales to contractor stations than to dealer stations.

Commission Truck Drivers and Tank Truck Dealers:

We were not able to gather much statistical data with regard to the usage which the seven companies made of commission truck drivers and tank truck dealers in their marketing programs. We were informed, however, that these two types of outlets were relatively unimportant in the gasoline distribution programs of the seven companies. In addition, we were told by the companies selling through or to commission truck drivers and tank truck dealers that such outlets figured more significantly in the distribution of kerosene and distillate than in the case of gasoline. Finally, we were informed by the companies using commission truck drivers and tank truck dealers that in the case of both gasoline and kerosene and distillate, their sales to tank truck dealers were appreciably greater than their sales through commission truck drivers.

The above three facts were at least partially substantiated by statistical data we were able to secure from Atlantic, The Ohio Oil Company, and The Texas Company. As may be seen from the Appendix, Table 13, in 1950 Atlantic sold 0.5% of its gasoline and 0.8% of its kerosene and distillate through commission truck drivers; in the same year the company sold 2.9% of its gasoline and 13.6% of its kerosene and distillate to tank truck dealers. Similarly, The Ohio Oil Company in 1950 sold 2.5% of its gasoline and 4.7% of its kerosene and distillate through commission truck drivers whereas it sold 4.8% of its gasoline and 6.9% of its kerosene and distillate to tank truck dealers (see Appendix, Table 12). The Texas Company in 1951 sold 0.5% of its gasoline and 6.0% of its kerosene and distillate through tank truck dealers and made very little use of commission truck drivers for either product.

We found from interviews with the execu-

tives of the seven companies that there were some significant differences in the practices of the companies with respect to the usage of commission truck drivers and tank truck dealers. The Indiana Company, for example, made no significant usage of commission truck drivers or tank truck dealers in any part of its distribution program. As noted earlier, it had been the policy of the Indiana Company to cultivate its market very intensively, and the company had therefore developed its own trucking facilities to handle both large and small buyers throughout its territory. Likewise The Texas Company made no use of commission truck drivers in the distribution of its gasoline. As pointed out earlier in the chapter, it was the policy of The Texas Company to seek large volume outlets for its gasoline business, and as a result most of its gasoline deliveries were such that they could be handled more economically with company trucks than with commission truck drivers. The Texas Company also differed from the other companies in that nearly all its sales of kerosene and distillate from company bulk plants were made to tank truck dealers. This practice was, of course, related to the company's decision to minimize its middle distillate cut and to concentrate primarily on the marketing of gasoline. As of 1950 the company had made no major effort to develop the home fuel oil business on its own account.

IV. CHANGES IN THE USAGE OF RETAIL OUTLETS FOR GASOLINE

The various factors which affected the selection of retail outlets were subject to change with the passage of time in much the same manner and for much the same reasons as were the factors which influenced the selection of wholesale outlets. As in the case of the wholesale outlets, the changes which the individual companies made were sometimes parallel in timing and direction but in other instances were markedly dissimilar in either or both timing and direction. The following paragraphs will direct attention to some of the more important of these changes. Inasmuch as our historical data with regard to commission truck drivers and tank truck dealers were very fragmentary, the discussion will be confined

EXHIBIT XVI-1. SEVEN OIL COMPANIES

Analysis of Service Stations by Type: 1935–1952

Number of Stations

	1935	1936	1937	1938	1939	1940	1941	1942	1943	1944	1945	1946	1947	1948	1949	1950	1951	1952
Gulf Oil Corporation: Total			32,945	33,596	34,033	34,317	31,303	28,500	26,267	26,538	27,793	30,833	31,972	31,588	32,541	33,943	34,207	34,131
Company Operated Stations	531	130	116	121	163	241	387	431	509	375	335	367	338	313	270	229	200	191
Dealer Operated Stations			6,951	7,309	7,637	7,524	7,073	5,506	5,156	5,406	5,611	5,478	5,296	5,279	5,613	5,958	6,278	6,483
Two-Party Lease			1,876	1,658	1,513	1,421	1,220	859	586	508	513	464	312	224	226	228	195	184
Three-Party Lease	2,946	4,099	5,075	5,651	6,124	6,103	5,853	4,647	4,570	4,898	5,098	5,014	4,984	5,055	5,387	5,730	6,083	6,299
Contractor Stations	31,027	28,512	25,878	26,166	26,233	26,552	23,843	22,563	20,602	20,757	21,847	24,988	26,338	25,996	26,658	27,756	27,729	27,457
Undivided Accounts	27,364	25,531	23,910	24,675	25,082	25,680	23,367	22,133	20,226	20,392	21,519	24,778	26,230	25,893	26,571	27,699	27,678	27,376
Divided Accounts	3,663	2,981	1,968	1,491	1,151	872	476	430	376	365	328	210	108	103	87	57	51	81
The Texas Company: Total								41,026	36,530	38,312	40,345	43,937	43,731	41,873	41,820	40,281	40,228	
Company Operated Stations	61	56	57	48	33	6	9	3	3	1	1	2	5	3	3	3	3	
Dealer Operated Stations	11,347	7,098	6,994	7,722	7,828	8,147	8,243	7,242	6,760	6,732	7,070	8,220	9,355	9,874	10,371	10,922	11,568	
Contractor Stations								33,781	29,767	31,579	33,274	35,715	34,371	31,996	31,446	29,356	28,657	
Sinclair Oil Corporation: Total	24,042	25,277	27,423	29,951	29,300	28,182	27,167	21,371	19,567	17,656	18,476	20,811	21,227	18,511	18,793	20,833	21,819	23,144
Company Operated Stations	203	21	6	6	4	17	20	34	18	6	4	5	9	7	5	11	13	8
Dealer Operated Stations	8,840	7,413	8,068	9,283	10,012	9,952	9,626	7,126	6,459	6,192	6,406	6,904	7,482	6,674	7,079	7,940	8,572	9,324
Two-Party Lease	2,636	923	1,066	1,676	2,097	2,232	2,310	1,693	1,264	1,036	1,281	1,977	2,609	2,142	2,516	3,156	3,164	3,560
Three-Party Lease	6,204	6,490	7,002	7,607	7,915	7,720	7,316	5,433	5,195	5,156	5,125	4,927	4,873	4,532	4,563	4,784	5,408	5,764
Contractor Stations	14,999	17,843	19,349	20,662	19,284	18,213	17,521	14,211	13,090	11,458	12,066	13,902	13,736	11,830	11,709	12,882	13,234	13,812
Undivided Accounts	14,445	17,394	18,828	20,060	18,741	17,788	17,112	13,895	12,771	11,221	11,822	13,541	13,323	11,570	11,606	12,792	13,175	13,749
Divided Accounts	554	449	521	602	543	425	409	316	319	237	244	361	413	260	103	90	59	63
The Ohio Oil Company: Total			3,066	3,461	3,587	3,122	2,302	1,955	1,334	1,327	1,443	1,749	1,752	1,653	1,789	1,757	1,788	1,877
Company Operated Stations			16	15	28	41	62	89	60	11	10	9	5	10	10	7	5	7
Dealer Operated Stations			939	947	1,058	962	729	485	443	485	542	622	653	632	664	679	698	763
Contractor Stations			2,111	2,499	2,501	2,119	1,511	1,381	831	831	891	1,118	1,094	1,011	1,115	1,071	1,085	1,107
The Atlantic Refining Company: Total				11,835	11,324	10,693	10,395	8,687	7,887	7,590	7,671	7,883	7,698	7,158	7,637	7,157	6,933	6,601
Standard Oil Company (Indiana): Total					20,329	19,783	18,952	14,510	14,536	14,811	15,753	17,158	16,943	16,330	16,492	16,251	15,906	15,783
Company Operated Stations	1,950	178	0	0	0	0	0	0	0	0	0	0	43	50	49	50	49	45
Dealer Operated Stations					7,734	8,985	8,907	7,026	6,613	6,692	7,727	8,683	9,072	9,365	9,802	10,064	10,725	11,038
Contractor Stations					12,595	10,798	10,045	7,484	7,923	8,119	8,026	8,475	7,828	6,915	6,641	6,137	5,132	4,700*
Standard Oil Company (Ohio): Total	4,990	4,930	5,031	5,043	5,022	5,003	4,955	4,798	4,456	4,373	4,277	4,487	4,610	4,565	4,514	4,580	4,575	4,612
Company Operated Stations	398	284	245	257	260	261	288	337	372	324	290	293	322	315	312	325	333	341
Dealer Operated Stations	369	497	557	569	592	602	603	510	408	460	526	559	555	567	581	595	613	641
Contractor Stations	4,223	4,149	4,229	4,217	4,170	4,140	4,064	3,951	3,676	3,589	3,461	3,635	3,733	3,683	3,621	3,660	3,629	3,630

Note: Blank spaces indicate data not available. Dash (—) indicates less than 0.05%.

*Estimated.

SOURCE: Company records.

EXHIBIT XVI-1. (CONTINUED)

Analysis of Service Stations by Type: 1935–1952

Percentage of Total Stations

	1935	1936	1937	1938	1939	1940	1941	1942	1943	1944	1945	1946	1947	1948	1949	1950	1951	1952
Gulf Oil Corporation: Total			100.0	100.0	100.0	100.0	100.0	100.0	100.0	100.0	100.0	100.0	100.0	100.0	100.0	100.0	100.0	100.0
Company Operated Stations			0.4	0.4	0.5	0.7	1.2	1.5	2.0	1.4	1.2	1.2	1.1	1.0	0.8	0.7	0.6	0.6
Dealer Operated Stations			21.1	21.7	22.4	21.9	22.6	19.3	19.6	20.4	20.2	17.8	16.6	16.7	17.3	17.5	18.3	19.0
Two-Party Lease			5.7	4.9	4.4	4.1	3.9	3.0	2.2	1.9	1.9	1.5	1.0	0.7	0.7	0.6	0.5	0.5
Three-Party Lease			15.4	16.8	18.0	17.8	18.7	16.3	17.4	18.5	18.3	16.3	15.6	16.0	16.6	16.9	17.8	18.5
Contractor Stations			78.5	77.9	77.1	77.4	76.2	79.2	78.4	78.2	78.6	81.0	82.3	82.3	81.9	81.8	81.1	80.4
Undivided Accounts			72.6	73.5	73.7	74.9	74.7	77.7	77.0	76.8	77.4	80.3	82.0	82.0	81.6	81.6	80.9	80.2
Divided Accounts			5.9	4.4	3.4	2.5	1.5	1.5	1.4	1.4	1.2	0.7	0.3	0.3	0.3	0.2	0.2	0.2
The Texas Company: Total								100.0	100.0	100.0	100.0	100.0	100.0	100.0	100.0	100.0	100.0	100.0
Company Operated Stations								—	—	—	—	—	—	—	—	—	—	—
Dealer Operated Stations								17.7	18.5	17.6	17.5	18.7	21.4	23.6	24.8	27.1	28.8	
Contractor Stations								82.3	81.5	82.4	82.5	81.3	78.6	76.4	75.2	72.9	71.2	
Sinclair Oil Corporation: Total	100.0	100.0	100.0	100.0	100.0	100.0	100.0	100.0	100.0	100.0	100.0	100.0	100.0	100.0	100.0	100.0	100.0	100.0
Company Operated Stations	0.8	0.1	—	—	—	0.1	0.1	0.2	0.1	—	—	—	—	—	—	0.1	0.1	—
Dealer Operated Stations	36.8	29.3	29.4	31.0	34.2	35.3	35.4	33.3	33.0	35.1	34.7	33.2	35.3	36.1	37.7	38.1	39.3	40.3
Two-Party Lease	11.0	3.6	3.9	5.6	7.2	7.9	8.5	7.9	6.5	5.9	6.9	9.5	12.3	11.6	13.4	15.1	14.5	15.4
Three-Party Lease	25.8	25.7	25.5	25.4	27.0	27.4	26.9	25.4	26.5	29.2	27.8	24.7	23.0	24.5	24.3	23.0	24.8	24.9
Contractor Stations	62.4	70.6	70.6	69.0	65.8	64.6	64.5	66.5	66.9	64.9	65.3	66.8	64.7	63.9	62.3	61.8	60.6	59.7
Undivided Accounts	60.1	68.8	68.7	67.0	64.0	63.1	63.0	65.0	65.3	63.6	64.0	65.1	62.8	62.5	61.7	61.4	60.4	59.4
Divided Accounts	2.3	1.8	1.9	2.0	1.8	1.5	1.5	1.5	1.6	1.3	1.3	1.7	1.9	1.4	0.6	0.4	0.2	0.3
The Ohio Oil Company: Total			100.0	100.0	100.0	100.0	100.0	100.0	100.0	100.0	100.0	100.0	100.0	100.0	100.0	100.0	100.0	100.0
Company Operated Stations			0.5	0.4	0.8	1.3	2.7	4.6	4.5	0.8	0.7	0.5	0.3	0.6	0.6	0.4	0.3	0.4
Dealer Operated Stations			30.6	27.4	29.5	30.8	31.7	24.8	33.2	36.6	35.6	35.6	37.3	38.2	37.1	38.6	39.0	40.6
Contractor Stations			68.9	72.2	69.7	67.9	65.6	70.6	62.3	62.6	61.7	63.9	62.4	61.2	62.3	61.0	60.7	59.0
Standard Oil Company (Indiana): Total					100.0	100.0	100.0	100.0	100.0	100.0	100.0	100.0	100.0	100.0	100.0	100.0	100.0	100.0
Company Operated Stations					0	0	0	0	0	0	0	0	0.3	0.3	0.3	0.3	0.3	0.3
Dealer Operated Stations					38.0	45.4	47.0	48.4	45.5	45.2	49.1	50.6	53.5	57.4	59.4	61.9	67.4	69.9
Contractor Stations					62.0	54.6	53.0	51.6	54.5	54.8	50.9	49.4	46.2	42.3	40.3	37.8	32.3	29.8
Standard Oil Company (Ohio): Total	100.0	100.0	100.0	100.0	100.0	100.0	100.0	100.0	100.0	100.0	100.0	100.0	100.0	100.0	100.0	100.0	100.0	100.0
Company Operated Stations	8.0	5.8	4.9	5.1	5.2	5.2	5.8	7.0	8.3	7.4	6.8	6.5	7.0	6.9	6.9	7.1	7.3	7.4
Dealer Operated Stations	7.4	10.1	11.1	11.3	11.8	12.0	12.2	10.6	9.2	10.5	12.3	12.5	12.0	12.4	12.9	13.0	13.4	13.9
Contractor Stations	84.6	84.1	84.0	83.6	83.0	82.8	82.0	82.4	82.5	82.1	80.9	81.0	81.0	80.7	80.2	79.9	79.3	78.7

EXHIBIT XVI-2. SIX OIL COMPANIES

Comparison of Gasoline Sales Volume of Service Stations: 1935–1952

Average Monthly Gasoline Sales (Gallons)

	1935	1936	1937	1938	1939	1940	1941	1942	1943	1944	1945	1946	1947	1948	1949	1950	1951	1952
Gulf Oil Corporation: All Stations	14,032					2,659						3,891			4,514	4,709	5,092	5,467
Company Operated Stations						15,481						20,391			28,077	28,854	30,710	33,204
Dealer Operated Stations						4,901						9,101			10,093	10,500	11,384	12,185
Contractor Stations						1,907						2,507			3,100	3,268	3,476	3,688
The Texas Company: All Stations														4,087	4,339	4,686	5,089	
Company Operated Stations														46,920	43,656	45,138	41,167	
Dealer Operated Stations														9,095	9,515	10,088	10,920	
Contractor Stations														2,537	2,629	2,673	2,731	
Sinclair Oil Corporation: All Stations	2,029					2,250						3,309				4,225	4,445	4,603
Company Operated Stations	12,361					7,207						9,101				36,271	28,542	34,082
Dealer Operated Stations	3,524					4,246						6,602				7,644	8,005	8,294
Contractor Stations	1,008					1,155						1,672				2,092	2,116	2,094
The Ohio Oil Company: All Stations							2,307	2,195	2,484	2,377	2,580	3,056	3,583	4,309	4,347	4,968	5,060	4,556
Company Operated Stations							5,221	4,489	6,020	20,520	9,727	13,999	17,467	9,327	25,200	33,999	39,762	24,818
Dealer Operated Stations							4,516	5,154	4,467	4,264	4,936	6,644	7,447	8,485	8,635	9,811	10,312	10,992
Contractor Stations							1,122	1,008	1,171	1,035	1,067	970	1,213	1,648	1,609	1,709	1,520	1,484
Standard Oil Company (Indiana): All Stations			6,815	6,167	3,444	3,577	3,857	3,983	3,234	3,140	3,574	4,774	4,984	5,516	5,856	6,080	6,654	7,028
Company Operated Stations													26,534	28,280	24,073	19,390	21,427	23,878
Dealer Operated Stations					6,220	5,831	6,332	6,367	5,271	5,170	5,807	7,858	7,833	8,194	8,519	8,600	8,768	8,996
Contractor Stations					1,741	1,702	1,661	1,745	1,533	1,470	1,424	1,617	1,564	1,728	1,787	1,843	2,095	2,245
Standard Oil Company (Ohio): All Stations		3,406	3,695	3,648	4,051	4,398	5,268	4,920	3,931	3,768	4,683	6,917	7,033	8,090	8,597	9,329	9,704	10,366
Company Operated Stations		14,308	16,671	16,356	18,067	19,835	23,832	22,008	14,011	14,280	20,419	34,941	32,946	37,167	37,951	40,677	41,779	44,794
Dealer Operated Stations		7,127	8,496	8,187	8,945	9,977	11,846	11,927	10,835	9,960	11,052	15,478	15,867	17,982	18,753	20,076	21,086	22,627
Contractor Stations		2,214	2,311	2,261	2,483	2,614	2,976	2,559	2,144	2,027	2,396	3,341	3,484	4,080	4,439	4,798	4,837	5,008

Note: Blank spaces indicate data not available.

SOURCE: Company records.

EXHIBIT XVI-3. SIX OIL COMPANIES

Percentage of Total Station Sales of Gasoline Made by Each Type of Station: 1935–1952

	1935	1936	1937	1938	1939	1940	1941	1942	1943	1944	1945	1946	1947	1948	1949	1950	1951	1952
Gulf Oil Corporation: All Stations	100.0%					100.0%						100.0%			100.0%	100.0%	100.0%	100.0%
Company Operated Stations	11.1					4.1						6.2			5.1	4.1	3.7	3.4
Dealer Operated Stations	}88.9					40.4						41.6			38.6	39.2	41.0	42.3
Contractor Stations						55.5						52.2			56.3	56.7	55.3	54.3
The Texas Company: All Stations														100.0%	100.0	100.0	100.0	
Company Operated Stations														0.1	0.1	0.1	0.1	
Dealer Operated Stations														52.5	54.4	58.4	61.7	
Contractor Stations														47.4	45.5	41.5	38.2	
Sinclair Oil Corporation: All Stations	100.0					100.0						100.0				100.0	100.0	100.0
Company Operated Stations	5.1					0.2						0.1				0.5	0.4	0.3
Dealer Operated Stations	63.9					66.6						66.2				68.9	70.7	72.6
Contractor Stations	31.0					33.2						33.7				30.6	28.9	27.1
The Ohio Oil Company: All Stations							100.0%	100.0%	100.0%	100.0%	100.0%	100.0	100.0%	100.0	100.0	100.0	100.0	100.0
Company Operated Stations							6.1	9.3	10.9	7.1	2.6	2.4	1.4	1.3	3.2	2.7	2.2	1.7
Dealer Operated Stations							62.0	58.3	59.7	65.6	71.9	77.3	77.5	75.3	73.7	76.3	79.6	82.2
Contractor Stations							31.9	32.4	29.4	27.3	25.5	20.3	21.1	23.4	23.1	21.0	18.2	16.1
Standard Oil Company (Indiana): All Stations			100.0%	100.0%	100.0%	100.0	100.0	100.0	100.0	100.0	100.0	100.0	100.0	100.0	100.0	100.0	100.0	100.0
Company Operated Stations			0	0	0	0	0	0	0	0	0	0	1.4	1.6	1.2	1.0	1.0	1.0
Dealer Operated Stations			55.2	62.6	68.7	74.0	77.2	77.4	74.2	74.4	79.7	83.3	84.1	85.2	86.5	87.6	88.8	89.5
Contractor Stations			44.8	37.4	31.3	26.0	22.8	22.6	25.8	25.6	20.3	16.7	14.5	13.2	12.3	11.4	10.2	9.5
Standard Oil Company (Ohio): All Stations	100.0	100.0%	100.0	100.0	100.0	100.0	100.0	100.0	100.0	100.0	100.0	100.0	100.0	100.0	100.0	100.0	100.0	100.0
Company Operated Stations	29.5	24.2	22.0	22.9	23.1	23.5	26.3	31.4	29.8	28.1	29.6	33.0	32.7	31.7	30.5	30.9	31.3	31.6
Dealer Operated Stations	15.6	21.1	25.4	25.3	26.0	27.3	27.4	25.8	25.2	27.8	29.0	27.9	27.2	27.6	28.1	28.0	29.1	30.4
Contractor Stations	54.9	54.7	52.6	51.8	50.9	49.2	46.3	42.8	45.0	44.1	41.4	39.1	40.1	40.7	41.4	41.1	39.6	38.0

Note: Blank spaces indicate data not available.

SOURCE: Company records.

to changes with respect to the usage of the various types of service stations. The discussion will in each instance relate to those years for which data were available, but will for the most part cover changes in the period 1935 to 1952.

Total Number of Stations:

Five of the seven companies reduced the total number of their retail outlets in the period from about 1938 to 1952. The amount of the reduction varied considerably, however, from one company to another. The greatest reductions were made by The Ohio Oil Company and Atlantic which reduced the total number of their stations by about 40%; the least reduction was made by Sohio which reduced the number of its stations by only about 8%. Gulf decreased the total number of its stations between 1939 and 1943 but increased the number thereafter so that for the period 1938–1950 the net change was not appreciable. The Texas Company made no appreciable change in the total number of its stations between 1942 and 1951, the years for which data were available.

Number of Different Types of Stations:

The most significant change which occurred with respect to the number of the different types of stations in the programs of the companies was a marked decrease in the number of company operated stations.[9] Exhibit XVI-1 shows that some decrease occurred in the case of each company in the period from about 1935 to 1952, but the executives of the companies informed us that a far more significant decrease in the number of company operated stations took place between 1930 and 1935, a point which was substantiated in the case of the four companies for which data on the number of company operated stations back to 1929 were available. The reasons for the withdrawal from company operated stations have already been discussed in Chapter Ten.

The records of Sinclair and Gulf show that the number of company operated stations reached a low point in 1938 or 1939, rose sig-

---

[9] The discussion in the following paragraphs will relate to only six of the companies, since data from The Atlantic Refining Company on the number of different types of stations were not available for publication.

nificantly during the war years, and declined again thereafter. This sequence of events may be explained in part by the fact that the elimination of company operated stations may have been pressed too far during the middle 1930's and in part by the fact that it was necessary to convert a number of dealer stations to company operation during the war years because the Selective Service Act plus the attractive wage rates available in manufacturing plants made it difficult to secure good dealers.

The Standard Oil Company (Ohio) followed a strikingly different course from the other companies in that it reduced the number of its company operated stations only very slightly after 1935. The Gulf Oil Corporation also differed from the other companies in that, although it reduced the number of its company operated stations very sharply in the 1930's, it continued to use a larger proportion of company operated stations in its program than did the other companies. The Sohio situation can be explained largely by the company's long-standing policy of cultivating a small geographic market very intensively which naturally tended to give it more large-volume service station locations than was true in the case of the other companies. We found no particularly strong reason why the Gulf experience should have differed from that of the other companies and were informed that the company contemplated further reductions in the number of its company operated service stations in the future (see Chapter Seventeen).

The records in Exhibit XVI-1 reveal that the six companies followed two different programs with respect to the relative usage made of dealer and contractor stations. The programs of The Texas Company, the Indiana Company, The Ohio Oil Company, and Sohio reflect an increase in intensity of integration in that in each case an exchange of contractor for dealer stations took place in the years covered by our data. Gulf (1937–1952) and Sinclair (1935–1952), on the other hand, made no major changes in the relative numbers of their dealer and contractor stations.

The records for Gulf and Sinclair show that the two companies decreased significantly the relative number of divided contractor accounts used in their marketing programs. We were also told that a similar decline occurred in the relative number of divided contractor accounts used by the other companies.

The records for Gulf and Sinclair also reflect two distinctly different policies with respect to two-party leases. Gulf reduced substantially its usage of two-party leases between 1935 and 1952, whereas Sinclair increased its usage of such arrangements.

Average Monthly Gasoline Volume:

The average monthly gasoline volume handled by all types of stations in the programs of four of the companies increased substantially in the years for which data were available, a circumstance which followed as a corollary of the fact that the companies were expanding their volume of operations in accordance with the growth of the industry but at the same time were reducing the total number of their retail outlets. The records of The Texas Company and the Indiana Company show an increase in the average monthly gasoline volume of dealer and contractor stations but a slight decrease in the average monthly volume of company operated stations. In both of these cases, however, our data cover only a very short period of time; had records for the company operated stations been available over a longer period, it is probable that they would have shown an increase in average monthly gallonage similar to that found in the other companies.

In the case of all six companies, the average monthly gasoline volume handled by dealer stations increased more than the average monthly volume handled by contractor stations. In the case of three companies, Sinclair, The Ohio Oil Company, and Sohio, the average monthly volume handled by company stations increased more than the average monthly volume handled by dealer stations, but in the case of three other companies, Gulf, The Texas Company, and the Indiana Company, company operated stations did not increase their volume as much as did dealer operated stations.

Proportion of Total Station Sales by Type of Station:

The six companies either reduced or held approximately constant the percentage of their total station sales of gasoline made through company operated stations in the years covered by our data. The records for Gulf (1935–1952), Sinclair (1935–1952), and The Ohio Oil Company (1941–1952) show a significant reduction in the proportion of total station sales made through company operated stations (see Exhibit XVI-3). The Indiana Company decreased the proportion of its total station sales made through company operated stations from about 40% to zero sometime between 1931 and 1937, and thereafter sold none or only a very small fraction of its volume through such stations. The experience of Sohio was again different from that of the other companies in that the proportion of its total station sales of gasoline made through company operated stations remained fairly constant between 22.0% and 31.7% throughout the period 1935–1952.

Two of the companies, Sinclair and Gulf, held the proportions of their total station sales of gasoline made to dealer and contractor stations approximately constant, a circumstance which followed from the fact that the companies made no major changes in the relative numbers of the two types of stations in their programs and in view of the fact that the average monthly gallonage sold to dealer stations increased only slightly more than did the average monthly gallonage sold to contractor stations. In the case of Sohio, The Ohio Oil Company, the Indiana Company, and The Texas Company, an increase took place in the relative volume sold to dealer stations, chiefly at the expense of the relative volume sold to contractor stations. These changes paralleled the changes in the relative numbers of dealer and contractor stations in the programs of the four companies as noted above.

V. FUTURE OBJECTIVES OF THE COMPANIES

The executives of the seven companies were approaching the problem of outlet selection at the retail level in much the same manner as at the wholesale level. In other words, they usually studied each individual market location as a separate case and made their decisions in the light of their judgments of all the various factors mentioned earlier in the chapter. As in the case of the wholesale outlets, there were differences in the policies and objectives of the companies which stemmed largely from differences in the market situations they faced and from differences in the relative emphasis which the executives of each company placed on the different factors which related to the problem.

In the following paragraphs, we shall outline what we found to be the general objectives of the seven companies with respect to the various types of retail outlets, subject always to the proviso that there were very real differences among the companies with respect to the vigor with which the individual objectives were pursued, as is amply evident from the preceding analysis of the positions of the companies in 1950 and the changes in position in the years covered by our data. We shall also direct attention to certain points on which there was a marked divergence in the policies of the seven companies. As in the preceding section, the discussion will relate solely to the usage of service stations inasmuch as we did not have an opportunity to gather much information concerning the future plans of the companies with regard to commission truck drivers and tank truck dealers.

Company Operated Stations:

In general, the seven companies were planning to use company operated stations in only a small number of very high volume locations. It was believed by all the executives with whom we talked that only in such locations could company operated stations develop a net return to the supplier equal to or better than that which could be secured by selling to dealer operated stations. Regardless of how the net return compared with that which could be secured from dealer operation, most of the companies were also planning to use company operated stations in a few selected spots for training dealers, testing merchandising methods, and establishing standards of service and cleanliness. Finally, some of the companies were planning to make occasional usage of company operated stations for promotional purposes; it was believed that a smart, well-run station at a strategic location enhanced the prestige of the supplier and had sufficient advertising values to justify operating losses up to a certain point.

As noted in earlier discussion, Sohio had a very different situation with respect to company operated stations than did the other companies. As may be seen from the figures on average monthly volume handled, however, Sohio like the other companies was using, and planned to continue using, company operated stations primarily at very large volume locations. In other words, it appears that Sohio's policies and objectives were not fundamentally different from those of the other companies; because of its unique marketing situation Sohio merely had more opportunities for the use of company operated stations than did the other companies.

Dealer Operated Stations:

The seven companies planned to continue using dealer operations at company owned or leased locations, except in the very few cases which warranted company operations for one of the reasons noted above. It was generally believed that dealers would in the future, as in the past, be able to operate successfully many stations which could not be operated by company employees. The chief advantage of the dealer operation over company operation was believed to lie in the personal incentives which the dealership provided and the fact that the dealer was in a better position to adjust working hours to the requirements of the business than was a supplier using company employees to manage stations. In other words, the average dealer did not expect the business to pay him or members of his family the equivalent of overtime wages for work which he or members of his family did in excess of 40 hours per week. The analyses which several of the companies had made of company versus dealer operation revealed that the dealer, because of his willingness to work overtime and the incentives provided by independent operation, was usually able to handle a given volume of business with fewer men than could a company operated station.

The seven companies were, in general, making an effort to purchase or acquire leases on as many of the better service stations as they reasonably could. In other words, for the better than average locations, the suppliers usually preferred dealer to contractor operations. There was, however, a considerable tendency in 1952 for the companies to acquire control of the stations by lease arrangements rather than by outright ownership. It was generally believed by the executives with whom we talked that the return it would be possible to secure in the future on marketing investments would be relatively low and that an integrated company was therefore well advised to conserve "its own money" for investment in other phases of the business. As a result, a good deal of attention was being given to the development of the so-called lessor-built stations.

Under a typical lessor-built arrangement, the supplier induced the owner of an attractive piece of property to lease it to the supplier for, say, 10 years. The landowner was then encouraged to take his lease to a local bank and on the strength thereof to borrow the money necessary to build a station. The station was then leased to the supplier and rented back to the owner or some third party for a dealer operation. It will be recognized that the tendency of suppliers to hold their marketing properties by lease rather than ownership arrangements represented a decrease in intensity of integration.

With regard to the usage of two-party leases, we found some differences in the policies and objectives of the seven companies which went a good deal beyond matters of degree. It was the policy of Sinclair to use two-party leases, with or without differentials in the rentals, whenever it was necessary to do so in order to meet competition and to hold onto the better class of service stations. The Texas Company, The Ohio Oil Company, and the Indiana Company planned, in so far as we could determine, to continue using two-party leases whenever it was necessary to do so for four major purposes: First, the companies planned to use two-party leases with a differential in the rentals as a competitive weapon and as a means of holding onto the better service stations. Second, when loans were made to or major equipment installations made for a contractor, it was planned to make use of two-party leases, often on a "washout" basis with no differentials in the rentals, as a means of making sure that the contractor stayed with the supplier for a reasonable period of time after the installation was made. Third, it was planned to grant two-party leases in cer-

tain cases when the owners of contractor stations wished to have them as a basis for borrowing money to make improvements in their property. Fourth, it was planned to use two-party leases in connection with lessor-built stations when the landowner or some member of his family wished to operate the station.

By way of contrast, the Gulf Oil Corporation had decided to abandon the usage of two-party leases and was planning to continue the elimination of such stations from its program as rapidly as it could.[10] Atlantic made occasional usage of two-party leases in connection with the latter three purposes noted above, but in no case granted a differential in the rentals in favor of the station operator. Sohio had a few two-party lease accounts in 1952 and, like Atlantic, planned to make occasional use of them in the future for the latter three of the four purposes noted above. The executives of Sohio, however, were firmly opposed to the practice of granting differentials in the rentals to the station operators. They further believed that if competitors began to make extensive use of lease differentials in the state of Ohio it would be because there was too wide a spread between the tank wagon and tank car prices and that the way to meet the situation would be by prompt and vigorous reductions in the tank wagon prices.

Contractor Stations:

All seven of the companies anticipated that they would continue to make extensive usage of contractor stations in their marketing programs. They planned to use contractor stations, first, as a means of extending their market representation beyond the limits they could reach with purchase and lease arrangements, and, second, as a means of obtaining market representation at points where the volume was not large enough to provide adequate coverage of the ownership or leasehold costs associated with dealer operation. It was believed that contractors could afford to operate the latter locations because they frequently engaged in side-line businesses and, like the dealers, were able to work out many special ar-

---

10 Two-party leases with differentials in the rentals in favor of the station operator may have been thought to be vulnerable to charges of price discrimination.

rangements for adjusting working hours to the requirements of the business.

The suppliers definitely preferred undivided to divided contractor accounts and were seeking to eliminate the latter from their programs as rapidly as they could. Moreover, it was anticipated that the opportunity to use divided accounts would continue to decline in the future, as it had in the past, as a result of general recognition on the part of the contractor station operators that they could reduce their inventory costs and simplify their purchase, supply, and promotion problems by dealing with only one gasoline supplier.

VI. SUMMARY

1. The integration patterns of the seven companies at the retail level of the industry evolved in much the same general manner as at the wholesale level of the industry. The executives of the companies usually studied each market location as a separate case and made their decisions in the light of a fairly large number of business and economic considerations. In some cases, the decisions were controlled by long-run company policies and general management strategies. In many instances, however, the decisions were made almost entirely in the light of the exigencies and competitive pressures of the moment.

2. In the years covered by our data, the integration programs of the seven companies at the retail level of the industry reflected both strong similarities and strong differences, just as they did at the wholesale level of the industry. The experience of the seven companies also provided ample evidence that the companies had frequently employed both increases and decreases in depth, extent, and intensity of integration as a means of adjusting their operations to meet new competitive and economic conditions. The net changes made in the years covered by our data represented further integration for some companies and less integration for others.

3. The policies and objectives of the seven companies with respect to the different types of retail outlets seemed to assure a continuing position in the industry for the dealer operated and contractor station. There seemed to be some indication, however, that the dealer operated station, a quasi-independent business opportunity, might gain somewhat in the future at the expense of the contractor station, a strictly independent business opportunity. Contractor stations were used extensively to handle business at small volume locations and were therefore particularly vulnerable to periods of depression, rising costs, or increases in the intensity of competition.

CHAPTER SEVENTEEN

The Fluidity of Integration Patterns

ONE of the most striking things about the integration patterns of the seven companies revealed by our research was that the patterns were of a highly fluid character. Certain of the changes which the companies made in their patterns have been discussed in the preceding chapters, and attention has been directed to the fact that the companies characteristically had both marked differences and similarities in their programs and to the fact that the changes which they made often differed significantly in both timing and direction. It has likewise been noted than a good deal of trial and error was associated with the integration process and that the individual companies often made changes which represented disintegration as well as further integration. In other words, the companies were continually skirmishing along the boundaries of their operations, sometimes advancing and sometimes retreating in terms of the activities which they performed at each level of the industry.

In this chapter we shall attempt to summarize, on the basis of all the preceding discussion, some of the more important of the general circumstances which brought about changes in the integration patterns of the seven companies and which determined the nature and form of a company's structure at any given moment. Our preliminary study of this matter immediately revealed that we were here dealing with nearly the entire range of business, economic, social, human, and other considerations which influenced management decisions. We found, in fact, that there were few, if any, significant aspects of a company's operations or of business life in the oil industry which did not relate in one way or another to the formation of integration patterns.

It was therefore apparent that we could not possibly undertake in this volume a comprehensive summary and discussion of each of the many determinants of integration patterns which we found at work in the experience of the seven companies and to which reference has been made in the analysis of specific integration decisions in earlier chapters. We shall, however, attempt to carry the discussion far enough to indicate the general character of the process by which the patterns of the companies evolved and the nature and range of the factors which influenced the extent, timing, and direction of the changes made in the patterns.

I. THE PROCESS BY WHICH INTEGRATION PATTERNS EVOLVED

We found that the integration patterns of the companies usually evolved: (a) as the result of general company policies with respect to the balance which should be maintained among activities at the different levels of the business, and (b) as the summation of the management decisions, made one by one, on a vast number of individual business problems as they arose. In the case of all the companies it was very clear that both of these things were a part of the general process by which the company's integration pattern altered its form and shape.

Company Policies with Respect to Integration Patterns:

The companies all had certain policies, which were endorsed in varying degrees by individual members of their executive groups, regarding the balance which should be maintained among operations at successive levels in the company's structure. As noted in Chapter Thirteen, for example, the executives of the companies usually had some general idea as to the proportion of refinery runs which should be supplied from a company's own crude oil production. Similarly, the company executives usually had some general objectives with regard to the proportion of the refinery output which they would like to distribute through the so-called "controlled outlets"; that is, bulk plants or service stations where the facilities were owned or held under lease by the company. Moreover, the executives of companies which had arrived at what was thought to be a reasonably satisfactory balance of operations gave considerable attention to expansion on a balanced basis. When the executives of one of these companies contemplated an addition to refinery facilities, for example, they at the same time gave thought to the investments in crude oil producing, transportation, and marketing facilities which would likewise have to be made if the company were to retain its existing structure.

These general policies with respect to integration patterns represented management strategies concerning the structures which would yield maximum competitive strength and earning power, minimize the risks associated with capital investments in the different phases of the business, and afford maximum protection against the fluctuations in prices, demand and supply, and all the other vicissitudes of fortune which are inevitably associated with any business enterprise. In a general way, the policies reflected a long-term net evaluation of all the many factors discussed later in the chapter which had a bearing on integration decisions.

While all the companies we studied had at least some policies with regard to their integration patterns, the policies were for the most part fragmentary and loosely defined. Most of the executives with whom we talked had well-formed ideas with respect to two or three key ratios, such as the ratio of crude oil production to refinery runs or the amount of drilling the company should attempt to do with its own rigs, but beyond that they had no strong convictions with regard to the relationships which should be maintained among their particular company's activities in different phases of the business. In none of the companies did we find that the executives had arrived at a complete conception as to just what balance should be established among activities at all levels of the business from the exploration for oil to the selling of refined products to customers.

Moreover, in those cases where a general policy had been developed with respect to a desired balance among certain activities, the optimum ratio was usually expressed as lying somewhere within a fairly wide range rather than as a definite figure.

It should not be inferred from the foregoing discussion that the lack of more explicit and more clearly defined policies with respect to integration patterns represented a management deficiency on the part of the companies studied. To a considerable extent the situation described merely reflected the fact that the companies were still in the process of experimenting with different types of integration arrangements. It may also indicate that within certain fairly broad limits one integration pattern is just about as good, all things considered, as another.

The Summation of Individual Management Decisions:

We found considerable evidence to indicate that the integration patterns of the seven companies were formed and altered simply as the net result of the day-to-day decisions which the company executives made on individual business problems. The executives of the companies were faced with a continuing series of problems such as whether to lease a particular piece of oil property; whether to build, enlarge, or extend a crude oil trunk or products pipe line; whether to enlarge and modernize a refinery; whether to build, buy, or lease a terminal, bulk plant, or service station at a particular market location; and whether to take on a particular new jobber, dealer, or contractor station account. Each of these problems was faced as it arose and solved in the light of all the business, economic, competitive, and other considerations which were pertinent to the case. The summation of these decisions, of course, had a direct bearing on a company's integration pattern.

To a considerable extent therefore we found that a company's integration pattern at any given moment simply represented the net solution of the whole matrix of business problems which the management had faced prior to that date. It will be recalled, for example, that the Standard Oil Company (Indiana) built its products pipe line to Indianapolis not as the result of a policy decision to increase the proportion of the company's refinery output transported via company pipe lines but rather as a means of solving a very difficult competitive problem which the company faced at that time in the Indianapolis area.

Similarly, the Standard Oil Company (Ohio) was prompted to engage in crude oil production at the particular time it did by tax considerations of the moment as well as by long-run policy considerations. It may also be noted that Sinclair purchased the Wood River refinery in 1950 to solve a supply problem in the St. Louis area despite the fact that the acquisition worked against the long-run balance which the company was seeking to establish as a matter of policy between its crude oil production and refinery runs.

Relative Significance of Company Policies Versus Individual Decisions in the Shaping of Integration Patterns:

The relative significance of these two broad influences, company policies and the summation of individual decisions, in the shaping of integration patterns was somewhat difficult to assess. The two influences were, of course, not mutually exclusive, because the decisions on the day-to-day specific problems were inevitably made in the light of the long-run policies. The problem of evaluating the relative significance of the two influences was thus a matter of deciding to what extent the management decisions which altered integration patterns were a result of general policy considerations as contrasted with the cost, profit, competitive, and other considerations pertinent solely to the case at hand.

Our final conclusion was that the integration patterns of the seven companies we studied were formed and altered somewhat more as a consequence of the individual decisions made on the continuing series of day-to-day problems which the company executives faced than they were by company policies with respect to the balance of operations desired at different points in the company's structure. In other words, the executives made their decisions largely on the basis of what appeared to be the most efficient and profitable thing to do in individual cases and were influenced only secondarily by general company policies with respect to integra-

tion arrangements. The president of the Gulf Oil Corporation summarized the general situation we found in most of the companies very concisely with the comment: "We have no policies with respect to integration or balance of operations which we would lose money to keep."

Both the company policies with respect to integration arrangements and the management decisions on individual problems were influenced by a myriad of considerations, some of the more important of which will be summarized in the following sections of this chapter. In a sense, it might be said that the company policies represented a *general*, long-run evaluation of these considerations while the decisions on the individual integration problems represented a *specific*, short- and long-run evaluation of these factors.

II. Investment, Cost, and Profit Considerations

The most important factors which influenced the formation and alteration of integration patterns were investment, cost, and profit considerations. We include in this category all the many factors normally involved in the exploration of such questions as: what investments will yield the best return on the stockholder's dollar, and what is the most economical and effective way to do the job at hand? The influence of the investment, cost, and profit considerations on integration patterns was manifested through the part which they played in the analysis of capital investment proposals, in comparative studies of alternative operating procedures, and in functional profit and loss statements.

Analysis of Capital Investment Proposals:

As one part of their analyses of capital investment proposals, it was the general practice of the seven companies to calculate either or both of two figures: (a) the payout period for the investment; that is, the number of years required for the cost savings or incremental cash income secured from an investment to return the original outlay, or (b) the anticipated return per annum which would be earned on the investment over the life of the property. These figures served to summarize the various estimates with respect to operating costs, volumes, selling prices, buying prices, and taxes that might be pertinent to a particular investment project.

In making up their annual capital budgets, the companies used the payout and return on investment figures as an aid in contrasting one investment opportunity versus another and in selecting the particular projects which should be supported during the coming year. Moreover, as new projects arose during the course of the year, payout and return on investment figures were usually prepared as one means of deciding whether supplemental capital appropriations should be made for them. The relative attractiveness of a company's investment opportunities in the different phases of the business, as measured by payout and return on investment figures, thus had a great deal to do with the extent and timing of its expansion program at the separate levels of the industry and a corresponding bearing on the formation and alteration of its integration pattern.

The companies did not, of course, make their capital investment decisions on the basis of payout and return on investment figures alone. Frequently an investment with a long payout period or one promising little or no return was selected over others with better financial prospects because certain nonfinancial factors, such as those discussed in later sections of the chapter, were considered to be of overriding importance. Moreover, some of the companies tended to make their allocations of capital funds to the various functional departments, such as producing, refining, transportation, and marketing, partially in terms of what was necessary to maintain a competitive operation in each area and to permit expansion at the normal rate of growth for the industry. The payout and return on investment figures were then used primarily to evaluate the relative desirability of the various projects within each department. Under this procedure, investments in one department were subject to only an indirect comparison with investments in another. Finally, we observed that the return on investment figures for individual projects were sometimes (and perhaps not so often as they should have been) evaluated in the light of the business risks connected with the projects. An investment offering a return of 8% per annum,

for example, might be selected in preference to one offering a possible return of 15% per annum because the higher return offered by the latter was judged to be insufficient to compensate for the greater risks which it entailed.

Managerial practices with respect to the calculation and interpretation of the payout and return on investment figures varied considerably from company to company and sometimes from department to department within a single company. In a number of cases we found that the companies were using practices which were not entirely sound from a technical standpoint. Some of the companies, for example, relied very heavily on the payout figures to measure the relative desirability of different projects and gave little or no attention to return on investment estimates. Actually, of course, payout figures are useful primarily as measures of the risks associated with capital commitments and may be very misleading as measures of the relative financial returns which can be earned on investments, except in cases where it can be assumed that the useful life of all projects under consideration is about the same.[1]

In addition, we found that some of the companies computed their return on investment figures by dividing the estimated average annual cost saving or incremental income after depreciation and taxes by the original value of the investment rather than by the average depreciated value. This procedure produced noncomparable figures in cases where some of the investments under consideration were comprised in large part of land or other nondepreciable property while others were comprised almost entirely of depreciable property.

Regardless of the budgetary procedures or managerial practices used in connection with the payout and return on investment figures, however, it was clear beyond all reasonable doubt that all the companies were guided to a very significant degree in their capital allocations and thus in the formation and alteration

---

[1] The payout period is the number of years necessary to recover the capital outlay for a new project; it does not indicate what may be earned on the investment over the useful life of the property. If the economic life of an investment extended only one year beyond the payout period, for example, the return earned would be quite different from what it would be if the economic life extended for 10 years beyond the payout period.

of their integration patterns by evaluations of the relative financial attractiveness of the individual investment prospects which were from time to time open to them at the different levels of the industry.

Comparative Studies of Alternative Operating Procedures:

A second important way in which cost and profit considerations influenced the formation and alteration of integration patterns was through the part which they played in comparative studies of alternative operating procedures. Studies of alternative operating procedures were often part and parcel of the analyses of capital investment proposals discussed above. In addition, however, studies of alternative operating procedures often influenced integration arrangements in situations where no new capital commitments were involved. A typical example of how such studies were made and how they influenced integration patterns may be found in an examination which the Gulf Oil Corporation made of its company operated service stations in 1949 and 1950.

As was noted in Chapter Sixteen, throughout the period 1935–1952 Gulf maintained a substantially larger number of company operated service stations in its marketing program than did any of the companies studied except Sohio. In 1948 Gulf had 313 company operated stations, of which 298 were in operation during the year. In the early part of 1949 a careful study was made of each of these stations to determine whether Gulf could increase its profits by converting some of them to dealer operations. Profit and loss statements were prepared for each station similar to that shown in Exhibit XVII-1. These statements were designed to reflect retail operations alone; wholesale profits were excluded from the figures because it was assumed that the wholesale profits would be secured regardless of whether a station was company or dealer operated.

Each station was credited with the margin on gasoline and other products that an independent dealer would enjoy. Each station was charged with its actual operating expenses and a rental representing what the Gulf division sales office believed could be obtained for the station if it was leased to a dealer. No charge

was made for station and equipment maintenance or for ownership costs because it was assumed that those expenses would be the same under either company or dealer operation. Moreover, no attempt was made to distribute to the individual stations the division and general office overhead which was required for their supervision. To the actual salaries, wages, and commissions paid at the stations, 11% was added to cover social security payments, group insurance, state and federal employment insurance, workmen's compensation, and annuities and benefits. Later analysis indicated that this figure should have been 7.5%, but the calculations were not revised because it appeared that the difference in the results for an individual station would not have amounted to more than about 3.2% of its payroll.

The study revealed that only 31 of the 298 stations were earning a profit in the sense that they were producing more income than the estimated rental which could have been secured from a dealer. During 1949, 59 of the stations were converted to dealer operation, and at the end of the first six months of 1950 a second study was made. Some of the significant facts developed in the two studies are tabulated below:

	1948	1st 6 months 1950
Number of company operated stations	298	239
Number showing a retail profit:		
After dealer rental [2]	31	133
Before dealer rental	176	213
Net retail profit or (loss):		
After dealer rental [2]	($1,189,000)	($55,407)
Before dealer rental	228,041	568,525
Net retail profit or (loss) per gallon gasoline:		
After dealer rental [2]	($.012)	($.002)
Before dealer rental	$.006	$.015

Analysis of the detail figures indicated that the reduction of 1.0 cent per gasoline gallon in the loss after dealer rental in the first six months of 1950 as contrasted with 1948 was the net result of an increase of 0.5 cent per

[2] After deducting from the station profits the estimated rentals that could be secured by leasing the station to a dealer.

EXHIBIT XVII-1. GULF OIL CORPORATION

Example of Profit and Loss Analysis of Company Operated Service Station

PROFIT & LOSS STATEMENT—COMPANY OPERATED SERVICE STATION
RETAIL BASIS
GULF 2077

ESTIMATED ☐   ACTUAL ☒   DATE __7/20/50__

PERIOD COVERED __1st 6 mos. 1950__

LOCATION __Cleveland & Hudson__
TOWN __Columbus, Ohio__
DISTRICT __Columbus__
BULK PLANT __Columbus__

NEW OUTLET PROPOSED FOR SALARY OPERATION ☐
DEALER OPERATED OUTLET PROPOSED FOR SALARY OPERATION ☐
SALARIED OUTLET PROPOSED FOR L-3 OPERATION ☐

THIS FORM TO BE SUPPORTED BY FORM 1385 AND, IN THE CASE OF NEW OUTLETS, BY FORM 2045.

	ANNUAL GALLONS	RETAIL MARGIN FOR June	RETAIL GROSS OPERATING INCOME	¢ PER GAL. GASOLINE
GOOD GULF	77,814	4.0	$ 3,113	XXX
NO-NOX	35,724	4.5	1,608	XXX
TRAFFIC				XXX
TOTAL GASOLINE	113,538	XXX	4,721	4.2
ALL OTHER PRODUCTS AND SERVICES	XXX	XXX	5,752	5.0
PARKING	XXX	XXX		
TOTAL	XXX	XXX	$ 10,473	9.2

SERVICE STATION EXPENSES (PER FORM 1385)

SALARIES, WAGES AND COMM.	$ 9,243		
STATION MAINTENANCE			
ALL OTHER EXPENSES	1,864		
TOTAL SS OPERATING EXPENSES		11,107	9.8
RETAIL PROFIT BEFORE RENTAL		(634)	(.6)
LESS: ESTIMATED DEALER RENTAL VALUE OF STATION	240	1,440	1.3
NET RETAIL PROFIT OR LOSS		$ (2,074)	(1.8)

COMPLETE THIS SECTION ONLY WHEN THIS FORM IS NOT ACCOMPANIED BY FORM 2045

OCCUPANCY EXPENSE	6 Months		GROSS INVESTMENT	
INTEREST ON INVESTMENT—LAND (4%)	$ 488		LAND	$ 24,394
" " " —BLDGS. & EQUIP. (2%)	157		BUILDINGS	11,044
DEPRECIATION—BUILDINGS (5%)	276		EQUIP.—PETROLEUM	3,820
" —PETROLEUM EQUIPMENT (X%) 10	191		—SALESROOM	799
" —SALESROOM EQUIPMENT (20%)	80		TOTAL	$ 40,057
SUBTOTAL INTEREST & DEPRECIATION	$ 1,192			

AVERAGE PRICES FOR

				DEALER	SS
TAXES (REAL ESTATE)	75				
INSURANCE, FEES, ETC.	23				
RENT PAID			GOOD GULF	15.00	19.00
TOTAL OCCUPANCY EXPENSE	$ 1,290				

APPROVED:

WC Donalson
SERVICE STATION DEPT.

R M Muller
MANAGER
Retail

Sales Analysis
MHM

SOURCE: Gulf Oil Corporation.

gallon in the gasoline margin, a decrease of 0.7 cent per gasoline gallon in operating expenses, and a reduction of 0.2 cent per gasoline gallon in the margin on products other than gasoline. The average volume of products sold per month per station was approximately the same for the two periods. Analysis of the figures also revealed that the chief means by which dealer operations would have gained an advantage over company operations was through working longer hours and using a smaller number of people to do the same sales job. Of the 267 stations which showed a loss after dealer rental in 1948, 33% would have shown a profit with one less man, 33% a profit with 2 less men, 19% a profit with 3 less men, and 15% a profit with 4 or more less men.

On the basis of the two studies, the marketing department recommended that a very small number of company stations be selected for continued operation by salaried employees. It was believed that a small number of such stations might be desirable to aid in setting standards for cleanliness and service and for training purposes. It was anticipated that some of these stations might be operated at a loss, although it was believed that much could be done to improve their present showings. It was proposed that monthly profit and loss statements be prepared on these stations in order that the Gulf management might be continually apprised of the cost of the intangible benefits that were derived from them.

A second recommendation was that the sales divisions should be given three to six months to put the remainder of the company stations on a profitable basis and that at the end of that time any stations still showing a loss should be considered for conversion to dealer operation. Finally, it was recommended that the Gulf management formulate a general policy for the guidance of all sales divisions with regard to when and where company stations should be used. It was suggested that the management might decide to have one company station in each city where the company had a district sales office, in each state capital, and in other major cities where they could be operated at a profit. It was also suggested that the stations should be so located as to secure the greatest advertising value as well as the best possible operating profit.

As a direct result of the two studies of the relative profitability of company and dealer operations therefore the Gulf management embarked on a program which would, in time, alter the company's integration pattern by reducing the intensity of its forward integration into retail marketing activities.

Functional Profit and Loss Statements:

All the companies we studied made at least a partial attempt to determine profit and loss figures for their operations at the successive levels of the business such as producing, transportation, refining, or marketing. These functional profit and loss figures were an attempt to measure what the company *was actually earning* on its various operations, whereas the analyses of capital investment proposals and studies of alternative operating procedures, discussed above, were estimates of what the company might *expect to earn* by making particular investments or particular rearrangements in its methods of doing business.

On the whole, we found that the functional profit and loss figures played a relatively minor part in the formation and alteration of integration patterns in the companies we studied. To be sure, the functional profit and loss figures served to give the executives of the companies a general, long-run impression of the approximate profitability of their operations at the successive levels of the business. In making decisions on new investments and methods of operation, however, the executives were far more heavily influenced by the projected estimates of what *might be earned or saved* by the particular project at hand than they were by the past record of what *had been earned* in the different departments of the business.

Difficulties in Establishing Functional Profit and Loss Figures: The executives of the companies attributed their reluctance to make more extensive use of functional profit and loss figures in reaching decisions on integration arrangements partially to the inherent difficulties involved in making an accurate separation of profits by departments. We found considerable opinion to the effect that the separation could only be made on the basis of a series of highly academic, "pretend as if we were different than we are" assumptions. It was contended that the entire strategy and purpose of vertical integration was to relate investments in different phases of the business to each other in such a way that the resulting organization could (a) secure more profit per dollar invested over the long run, or (b) operate with less risk than could any of the individual units of the structure standing by itself alone.

The problem of profit separation in an integrated company thus required, in the final analysis, a determination of just how much of the incremental profit and just how much of the risk reduction achieved from the vertical combination was properly attributable to each of the component parts. Many of the executives with whom we talked were of the opinion that this problem was not unlike that of trying to decide just what percentage of a race horse's performance should be credited to the horse and what percentage to the jockey; in most circumstances the two in combination could turn in a better, and certainly more reliable, performance than could either one alone.

The determination of satisfactory prices for the transfer of crude oil and refined products among departments was generally regarded as the most critical difficulty in making a functional profit separation. In the case of crude oil, the practices of the companies varied, but in principle the procedure used by most of the companies was approximately as follows: Crude oil was "sold" by the producing department to a crude oil trading department at the posted prices in the field at the time the oil left the lease. The oil was then held by the crude oil trading department until it was charged to the refinery stills. At that time, it was billed to the refining department at the current posted field price at the point of origin plus transportation costs, plus taxes, plus a few cents a barrel handling charge to cover the expenses of the crude oil trading department. The crude oil trading department thus absorbed any gains or losses arising from price fluctuations between the date of production and the date of charging to the refinery stills. The crude oil pipe line department, if one was involved, developed its profit from the difference between the pipe line tariffs and the pipe line operating expenses.

For the most part, the executives of the companies were reasonably well-satisfied with the statement of producing and crude oil pipe line earnings which resulted from the above procedure. The posted field prices for crude oil were generally used in the settlement of royalty interests, for the calculation of federal and state taxes, and for many other purposes. Moreover, the statement of pipe line earnings which developed from simply treating the pipe line tariffs as the gross revenue of the pipe line department was generally in accord with that which the companies were required to file with the Interstate Commerce Commission for their common carrier lines. As a practical matter therefore it would have been extremely difficult to make any approach to the determination of producing department and crude oil pipe line earnings other than that outlined above.

It was well recognized, however, that the procedure did not always result in an equitable distribution of profit to the producing, crude oil transportation, and refining departments. Assume, for example, that an integrated oil company made a major crude oil discovery in a remote area, such as the Williston Basin, which had only rail transportation facilities to refining centers. The initial posted prices for crude oil in the field would of necessity be set low enough so that the crude oil could move out by rail and yet have a delivered price at refining centers which would be competitive with that of crude oil drawn from other sources. The integrated company might next build a crude oil trunk line connecting one of its refineries to the field and set pipe line tariffs which were well below the rail rates, particularly if it was subject to the pipe line consent decree and thus precluded from drawing dividends from the pipe line in excess of 7% of the ICC valuation of the pipe line properties. Under such circumstances, the buyers of crude oil would, of course, bid up the price in the new field until the field price plus the pipe line tariff once again equalized at refining centers against crude oil drawn from other sources.

In a situation of this kind, the earnings of the integrated oil company would be substantially increased, and the incremental profit arising from the advance in crude oil prices would be credited solely to the producing department, if the accounting was done as described above. From both a practical and a theoretical standpoint, however, it might well be argued that some of the incremental profit should be assigned to the transportation department and might indeed have been exacted by that department through higher tariffs had it not been for the limitations imposed by the pipe line consent decree. Moreover, the integrated company might have been in a position to build the pipe line only by virtue of the fact that it had a refinery at the other end of the line capable of absorbing a large share of the line throughput, a circumstance which would give the refining department a claim to the incremental income. Finally, the refinery might have been able to take additional crude oil only because the company had marketing properties in the area capable of disposing of the additional refined products output, a circumstance which might justify the marketing department in a claim for a share of the incremental income.

A fairly recent example of a situation in which the use of posted field prices for the segregation of producing department earnings may not prove entirely satisfactory may be found in the Platte Pipe Line, discussed in Chapter Seven, which runs from the producing fields in Wyoming to the St. Louis refining area. The companies who built the line will be enabled as a result of its construction to increase substantially their crude oil production in Wyoming and will thus increase their producing department earnings. Moreover, many small independent producers in Wyoming will be enabled to increase their output and earnings as a result of the construction of the line because the line will give them an outlet for their shut-in production. It might be argued therefore that the profits generated by the pipe line investment for the builders and other producers will be far greater than will ever be reflected in the profit and loss statements which the pipe line company will file as a common carrier with the Interstate Commerce Commission. Situations of this kind in which a profit opportunity springs from the interrelationship of two or more investments, rather than solely from one of them alone, are multitudinous in any large, integrated oil com-

pany, if its operations and capital investments are soundly conceived.

The complexities of the crude oil trading operations give birth to still further difficulties in connection with the separation of producing and refining department earnings on the basis of posted field prices. An integrated oil company may often dispose of its crude oil in one section of the country at the expense of its refining operations in another area, although on the combined transaction it may benefit. For example, a company might agree to sell a quantity of crude oil in Wyoming at the posted field price in Wyoming subject to a stipulation that it accept an equal quantity of Texas coastal crude oil from the buyer at the posted price in Texas. The company might then run the Texas coastal crude oil to its Gulf Coast refinery even though the use of such crude oil might involve higher transportation costs, lower yields, and the purchase of more blending stocks to meet the current market octane requirements than would have been the case had the refinery been allowed to purchase crude oil from the best market source. A company would not, of course, enter into such a transaction unless the gains arising from its ability to sell crude oil in Wyoming outweighed the losses taken on its refining activities. In deals of this kind, however, it is clear that transfers of crude oil at the posted prices in the field do not always result in an accurate division of profits between producing and refining departments.

All the executives with whom we discussed the matter agreed that it was far more difficult to establish satisfactory prices for the transfer of refined products between their refining and marketing departments than it was to establish prices for the transfer of crude oil between their producing and refining departments. It was freely granted that the tank car prices published in *Platt's Oilgram Price Service* and the *Chicago Journal of Commerce* were probably as good a representation as could be secured of the spot quotations on individual cargoes for immediate shipment. The executives were equally agreed, however, that the published quotations did not necessarily represent the prices at which their marketing departments would be able to buy refined products if operated on a nonintegrated basis nor the prices at which their refining departments would be able to sell if operated on a nonintegrated basis. It was pointed out that the marketing departments would be able to obtain certain price concessions by negotiating long-term contracts for large quantities and that the refining departments would not be able to secure the quoted tank car prices without incurring some selling expenses or at least paying brokerage fees of about $\frac{1}{8}$ of a cent per gallon.

As a result, the companies which attempted to separate refining and marketing earnings usually made their transfers at some discount, often $\frac{1}{8}$ to $\frac{3}{8}$ of a cent on gasoline, off the low of the published tank car quotations. The discount was sometimes a fixed amount, but in other cases it was subject to adjustment by some one individual or committee in accordance with the current state of the market. Companies following the latter practice took the position that the price should be closer to the low of the published quotations in times when products were short than in times when products were in ample supply.

In all cases the amount of the discount was an arbitrary judgment, and it was generally agreed that the transfer price thereby established could not at the best have an accuracy of more than plus or minus $\frac{1}{10}$ of a cent on gasoline for any stated period of time such as a quarter or a year. On transfers of 1.9 billion gallons of gasoline per year, which was about the average in 1950 for the seven companies studied, an error of plus or minus $\frac{1}{10}$ of a cent in the transfer price would have produced an error for each company of plus or minus $1,900,000 in the profit separation.

It is important to note that the fundamental problem involved in establishing satisfactory prices for the transfer of refined products from the refining to the marketing department of an integrated oil company cannot be solved merely through the accumulation of additional data on market quotations. Integration between the refining and marketing levels of the industry has progressed to the point where a large proportion of the refined products manufactured in the United States are not traded in the tank car markets. As noted in Chapter Two, for example, in 1950 at least 95.5% of the gasoline and naphtha was produced by companies engaged in both refining and wholesale marketing; these companies, in turn, characteristically sold about 81.8% of their output through their own bulk plants and terminals.

The best possible tank car quotations on gasoline could in 1950 therefore have reflected the movement of only about 20% of the total gasoline output. The basic difficulty in establishing satisfactory transfer prices for the separation of refining and marketing earnings arises from the fact that the spot quotations on about 20% of the volume sometimes are and sometimes are not good indicators of what the long-term contract prices "would have been if" the refining and marketing departments of the large integrated companies had been operating on a nonintegrated basis. In general, it can be said that a functional separation of earnings in any industry becomes increasingly difficult as the degree of vertical integration increases and the relative volume of products traded in the intermediate markets declines.

The separation of refining and marketing earnings presented the same general problem to the companies in situations involving interrelated investments as noted above in connection with the separation of producing and refining earnings. The companies sometimes built or acquired refining facilities to assure a source of supply for a highly profitable marketing operation even though it was anticipated that the refining activity might not be particularly profitable in its own right. Conversely, marketing facilities were sometimes established primarily to reduce the risk of loss in volume by a refinery in times of slack demand. In situations of this kind, where one investment was made to support or reduce the risk on another, it was extremely difficult to decide how much of the profit earned on the combined operation should be attributed to each.

As in the case of crude oil, there were also situations where it was difficult to assign the cost savings and profits arising from the use of a particular pipe line facility. The Texas Company, for example, owned a share in the Great Lakes Pipe Line Company and shipped products from its refinery at Tulsa to its market outlets in the North Central states far more cheaply than would have been possible by rail carriers. The Great Lakes Pipe Line operated as a common carrier, and its tariffs were set to hold earnings at about 7% of the ICC valuation of the properties. In this case, it was a moot question as to whether The Texas Company's savings in transportation costs arising from the use of the line should be attributed to the refining, transportation, or marketing departments.

A second general problem which the companies had encountered in connection with the development of departmental profit and loss figures was that of allocating various items of administrative overhead and general expense. All the companies had executive officers and certain departments such as the accounting, financial, and industrial relations departments whose services were used by all the major operating departments. The distribution of the cost of these services to the producing, transportation, refining, and marketing departments was necessarily arbitrary. The executives with whom we talked, however, were unanimous in the opinion that the problem of allocating expenses was of minor significance relative to the problem of determining satisfactory transfer prices discussed above.

A third type of problem which arose in connection with the development and use of departmental profit figures was that of determining the capital investment underlying the operations of each department. A determination of the capital investment was necessary as a means of evaluating the return earned on operations in one area as contrasted with another. In the case of physical plant and equipment, the separation could be made fairly easily, although there were certain facilities such as finished products storage tanks which had to be assigned arbitrarily to one department or another. The assignment of cash and other liquid assets to individual departments was more difficult. The money tied up in inventories to meet seasonal fluctuations in demand, for example, might properly be regarded as capital invested in the refining department or as capital invested in the marketing department. As in the case of the problem of expense allocation, however, the executives of the companies were agreed that the problem of dividing capital investments among departments was negligible compared with the problem of determining transfer prices.

A final general problem which existed in connection with the development and use of departmental profit figures (although rarely recognized explicitly by the executives with whom we talked) was that of properly evaluating the business risks associated with the operations of each department. The return on any business venture can only be appraised relative to the risks incurred. Government bonds, for example, are expected to earn a lower return than speculative industrial stocks. Similarly, in an integrated oil company a 5% return on certain marketing investments might be substantially better than an 8% return on certain producing activities because the long-term risks associated with the former might be substantially less than with the latter. In view of the fact, however, that investments are often made in one department of an integrated oil company as a means of reducing the risks to which another department is exposed, the problem of appraising returns relative to risks incurred in individual areas is exceedingly difficult.

Profit Accounting Practices of the Seven Companies: The practices of the seven companies with regard to profit statements for their crude oil producing and crude oil pipe line departments were fairly uniform. All the companies prepared profit statements for their producing departments, using the posted prices in the field for transfer purposes. The resulting figures were regarded as a reasonably satisfactory indication of the general level of profits earned in producing operations, subject to the reservations noted above. The seven companies likewise prepared profit statements for their crude oil pipe line departments or subsidiary pipe line companies, using the pipe line tariffs as the gross income of the pipe line activity. It was well recognized, however, that the resulting figures were not necessarily a fair indicator of the value of crude oil pipe line investments to an integrated oil company.

The practices of the companies with respect to the preparation of profit statements for their products pipe line departments were subject to considerable variation depending on the manner in which the lines were operated. The common carrier lines and some of the private lines were handled in the manner described above for crude oil pipe lines. In other cases, however, the products pipe lines were simply treated as service activities and no attempt was made to develop separate profit statements for them.

With respect to the separation of refining and marketing earnings, the practices of the seven companies varied widely. Three of the companies, Sinclair, Atlantic, and The Ohio Oil Company, made no separation of refining and marketing profits in their regular financial records. For accounting purposes, products were transferred from the refining to the marketing departments at refinery cost. The practice of Sinclair differed slightly from that of the other two companies in that it did make quarterly statistical studies of the profits earned by each bulk plant and sales division under assumptions as to the prices at which they "would have been able to buy if" they had been operating as large independent jobbers. The company did not, however, reverse the procedure and in like manner prepare quarterly estimates on the profitability of its refineries.

Three of the remaining companies, Gulf, the Indiana Company, and The Texas Company, made a separation of their refining and marketing earnings on the basis of transfer prices which were derived from published market quotations. Sohio likewise made a separation of refining and marketing earnings but its transfer prices were usually related to or derived from the company's own selling prices to its Fleet-Wing jobbers.[3] The executives of all four of these companies, viewed the results of the separation with a good deal of skepticism. For the most part they regarded the profit figures for the individual departments as a matter of general, academic interest rather than as an accurate measure of the profit performance of the departments. In most of their thinking and planning, they placed primary reliance upon the combined figures for refining and marketing profits.

The executives of the seven companies were not disposed to place heavy emphasis on departmental profit figures for three reasons in addition to those noted above. In the first place, it had been the experience of several of the companies that undue attention to departmen-

tal profit figures often led to serious dissension among their executive personnel over the establishment of transfer prices, particularly for the transfer of refined products between the refining and marketing departments. A few small losses in executive working relationships could, of course, easily offset any gains that might be made through the development and use of the departmental profit analyses.

Of even greater importance was the doubt which existed in the minds of many of the executives as to whether concentration on departmental profit figures was a sound management philosophy for an integrated oil company. In the final analysis, many decisions had to be made in terms of what produced the greatest net advantage for the company as a whole. If, however, departmental profit figures were available in the formal financial records and were given much attention by top management, there was a real danger that "departmental thinking" would emerge and control management action, particularly in cases where the facts were not clear-cut and the use of judgment was required. Finally, as noted earlier, many of the executives were of the opinion that integration decisions should be made more in the light of anticipated future earnings on individual projects rather than in the light of the past earning performance of the company in different phases of the business.

In the light of the foregoing discussion, it is not difficult to understand why functional profit and loss figures played only a minor role in the formation and alteration of integration patterns. In making decisions on specific integration problems, the executives of the companies generally preferred to rely upon payout and return on investment estimates and special profit studies along the lines of that made by the Gulf Oil Corporation of its company operated service stations. In such studies it was possible to take into account whatever special interrelationships of risks and profits might be pertinent to the problem at hand. The executives of the companies had likewise found that functional profit figures were not necessary as a means of evaluating performance in the various operating areas; many of the same objectives could be accomplished through the use of budgets, standards of cost performance, and various other devices.

---

[3] Sohio distributed its products to jobbers through a wholly-owned subsidiary, the Fleet-Wing Corporation. The Fleet-Wing Corporation had accounts in New York, Maryland, Pennsylvania, West Virginia, Michigan, and Indiana, as well as in Ohio.

III. COMPETITIVE PRESSURES

It was readily apparent that the integration patterns of the companies we studied were to a considerable extent formed and shaped by competitive pressures of many different types. The analysis and appraisal of these pressures, of course, often involved investment, cost, and profit considerations of the types discussed above. There were many moves which were made for investment, cost, or profit considerations, however, which did not necessarily involve competitive pressure, and there were likewise many moves made under competitive pressure where investment, cost, and profit considerations were of secondary importance. For these reasons we have chosen to treat the changes in integration patterns which took place primarily in response to competitive pressures as a separate topic.

We found that competitive pressures influenced integration patterns in at least three general ways. First, companies frequently altered their integration patterns as part of a defensive effort to offset actions taken by one or more of their competitors; second, companies altered their patterns as part of an offensive effort to improve their positions in the market; and, third, integration patterns were frequently altered somewhat by default simply because expansion at one level of the industry could be accomplished more easily than at another.

Offsetting the Moves of Competitors:

Numerous examples may be found throughout the earlier chapters of this book of situations in which a company altered its integration pattern as a result of actions taken defensively to offset the moves of one or more competitors. The best example of an industry-wide situation in which a great many companies made defensive changes in their integration arrangements may be found in the scramble for wholesale and retail outlets which took place between about 1920 and 1935 under the pressure of large crude oil supplies. From the discussion in Chapter Four, it will be recalled that companies with large crude oil supplies on their hands were prompted to integrate forward and acquire market outlets as a means of disposing of their output. In so doing they not only built

outlets of their own but also struggled to capture the jobbers and contractor stations of companies already established in the market. The established companies, in turn, then found it necessary to replace many of their jobber or contractor stations with company owned or leased facilities and thereby greatly increased the general intensity of their forward integration into marketing activities.

Many examples may likewise be found of specific major projects which were undertaken as defensive moves to offset the actions of competitors. As was noted in Chapter Three, the Standard Oil group built its first big crude oil trunk lines to the Atlantic seaboard in response to the competitive threat implicit in the line which had just been completed by the Tidewater Pipe Line Company. The Standard Oil Company (Indiana) built its products pipe line from Whiting to Indianapolis because of the inroads being made on its markets by competitors which had developed low-cost methods of transportation from the Mid-Continent area or which had taken advantage of the newly discovered crude oil in Illinois to set up refining facilities close to the market (see Chapter Seven). Similarly, The Atlantic Refining Company built its Keystone Pipe Line system in Pennsylvania in 1931 partially because two competitors, the Esso Standard Oil Company and the Sun Oil Company, had each established pipe line transportation facilities through the central part of the company's marketing territory.

A somewhat different manifestation of the working of competitive pressures on the formation of integration patterns may be found in the decisions which all the companies were continually making with regard to their wholesale and retail market outlets. As noted in Chapters Fifteen and Sixteen, the type of arrangement negotiated with a particular wholesale or retail outlet was not always a matter of free choice on the part of the supplier; on the contrary, the decision was often controlled by the offers which competitors were making for the same outlet or which the owner of the outlet was in a position to secure from competitive suppliers if he chose to do so. As a result, the integration patterns of the companies in the marketing field were continually evolving under the actions and influences of competitors.

Offensive Competitive Actions:

It follows as a corollary of the above that the integration patterns of the companies were also frequently altered, not as a means of defending an existing position, but rather as a means of improving a company's competitive strength and extending its existing position. An example of an industry-wide development which produced alterations in integration patterns was the by-passing of bulk plants with direct shipments from refineries and terminals to service stations, discussed in Chapter Nine. The companies first developing the by-passing technique in a particular market area were not prompted so much by any need to defend their existing positions as they were by a desire to cut their costs of distribution and thus improve their existing positions. At a later date, of course, other firms were forced to set up by-passing arrangements to hold their markets, and the integration process thus assumed regenerative characteristics.

A good example of a specific major project undertaken as an offensive competitive action may be found in the building of the Plantation Pipe Line by the Standard Oil Company (New Jersey), the Standard Oil Company (Kentucky), and the Shell Oil Company in the years 1940 to 1942. Before that time the markets in the Southeastern section of the United States had been served largely by rail transportation or by truck transports operating from tidewater or river terminals. The Plantation Pipe Line cut through the heart of the territory from Baton Rouge, Louisiana, to Greensboro, North Carolina, and thereby put the builders in a position to cut their costs and increase their share of the market. One of the defensive responses to the action by other companies may be found in the almost simultaneous building of the Southeastern Pipe Line by the Gulf Oil Corporation and the Pure Oil Company which extended from Port St. Joe, Florida, to Chattanooga, Tennessee. The Plantation line was initiated in 1940 and the Southeastern line in 1941; both began operations in 1942.

Ease of Expansion at Different Levels of the Industry:

Competitive pressures influenced the formation of integration patterns in a third and somewhat more subtle way in that they determined the relative resistance to expansion which an integrated company encountered at one level of the industry as contrasted with another. An integrated oil company is usually anxious to grow and to expand its operations wherever it can on a profitable basis. At any given time, however, an integrated company may have more competitive strength and find it easier and more profitable to expand at one level of the business than at another.

In recent years, for example, the large, integrated companies have generally had greater competitive strength at the refining level than they have had at the producing and marketing levels of the industry. At the refining level, the large, integrated companies have had all the advantages that come from size and at least partially assured crude supplies and market outlets for refined products. Characteristically, they have also had the financial resources necessary to keep pace with the continual advances in refining technology (see Chapter Nineteen). In the producing field and in many areas of the marketing field, however, the relative competitive strength of the integrated and nonintegrated companies has been much more evenly balanced. It is therefore not hard to understand why the structure of the typical integrated oil company has been large at the refining level and has tapered toward the producing and marketing ends.

IV. CHANGES IN ECONOMIC, LEGAL, AND POLITICAL CONDITIONS

Another general set of influences which had a great deal to do with the formation and alteration of integration patterns was the changes which from time to time took place in the economic, legal, and political conditions in the oil industry. The most dramatic example of an economic and legal development which produced changes in integration patterns may be found in the adoption of the conservation laws by the various producing states. The adoption of these laws changed the entire character of the oil producing business. Among other things, the laws brought under control the large crude oil supplies which had previously been generating a great deal of both forward and backward integration; tended to equalize the positions of integrated and nonintegrated oil producers with respect to the disposition of their output in times of large supplies; reduced the severity of the fluctuations in the price of crude oil; lengthened the payout periods on producing investments; accentuated somewhat the need for backward integration by a refiner; and reduced somewhat the need for forward integration by a crude oil producer (see Chapter Four).

The effect which the prorationing laws had on the integration patterns of individual companies has been amply illustrated in the discussion in earlier chapters. At this point it need merely be recalled that the conservation laws had the immediate effect of sharply reducing the crude oil ratios of Gulf, and Sinclair; led Atlantic and the Indiana Company to intensify their oil finding and producing efforts; and prompted Sinclair, for a number of years at least, to reduce its emphasis on crude oil producing as contrasted with refining and marketing activities.

The tax laws provide good examples of legal developments which had a strong influence on integration patterns. There is no question that such things as the provisions in the tax laws for the expensing of intangible development costs, the acceptance of "discovery value" in lieu of "cost value" as a basis for depletion, and the later adoption of the statutory depletion allowance, had a great deal to do with the extent of the capital commitments integrated oil companies were willing to make in their crude oil producing operations. Moreover, in times of high taxes and particularly when they are exposed to excess profits taxes, many integrated oil companies tend to accelerate their crude oil producing efforts because at such times they can expand their "crude oil producing plants" at a lower net out-of-pocket cost after taxes than would otherwise be the case. A specific example of a major change in an integration pattern the timing of which was prompted in considerable measure by the excess profits tax was that made by the Standard Oil Company (Ohio) when it entered the crude oil producing field in 1942 (see Chapter Eight).

The chain store taxes which were adopted by many states during the early 1930's provide a further example of the influence of tax laws on integration patterns. As noted in Chapter Ten, the withdrawal from company operated service stations by many integrated oil companies was well under way long before the chain store taxes came into being. There is no question, however, that the adoption of the chain store taxes tended to accelerate the withdrawal in many cases and served to prompt it in the case of at least a few companies. Mention might also be made of the provisions in the tax laws for accelerated amortization which in recent years have had a strong influence on integration decisions, particularly with respect to refinery expansion and the building of new pipe lines.

Another example of legal and judicial influences on the formation and alteration of integration patterns may be found in the various regulatory provisions which have from time to time been imposed by the Interstate Commerce Commission with respect to pipe line earnings and pipe line operations. Of particular importance was the pipe line consent decree in 1941, resulting from action brought by the Department of Justice. As noted in Chapters Seven and Fourteen the limitations on dividends to shipper owners, coupled with the rising capital costs which were associated with the technological advances in pipe line design, unquestionably reduced the relative attractiveness of pipe line investments and tended to prompt increased usage of joint ownership arrangements.

The wage and hour laws were another type of legislation which had some bearing on the formation of integration patterns, particularly in the marketing field. After the adoption of the laws, for example, many of the companies we studied found that they could no longer operate some of their bulk plants and service stations on a competitive basis with independent distributors or dealers. The independent operators often proved able to adjust their own working hours, to employ members of their families, and to make various arrangements for part-time help in such a way that they could secure lower labor costs per gallon than could a large company operating with salaried employees subject to the wage and hour laws. Similarly, the independent operators often proved able and willing to handle activities which were subject to abrupt and unpredictable fluctuations, such as the distribution of fuel oil to home owners, at a lower net cost than could large companies whose employees were covered by maximum hour legislation.

Finally, it was apparent that political and public sentiment had a strong bearing on the integration patterns of the companies we studied. In recognition of the public and political sentiment from time to time arising against big business, the protective attitude found in many circles with regard to little business, and the fact that the various types of jobbers were numerous and politically vocal, some of the companies took the position that they should continue to use independent marketing organizations in their distribution programs wherever they could even though in some cases slight extra costs might be involved in doing so.

The Standard Oil Company (Ohio), for example, maintained its Fleet-Wing organization and jobber distribution partially because some of the executives believed that it would be politically undesirable for the company to hold a large share of the market in the state of Ohio and at the same time to refuse to sell to independent marketers.[4] Similarly, some of the companies went out of their way to take care of little refiners in their pipe lines even though the lines were in some cases operated under conditions such that there was no legal necessity to do so. A further example of political influences on integration patterns may be found in the agitation with regard to crude oil imports which arose from time to time in the period following World War II among the independent oil producers. This agitation had a considerable bearing on the management decisions some of the large companies made with regard to imports of crude oil from their foreign producing operations, and the domestic crude oil buying programs of the companies were affected accordingly.

V. THE INFLUENCE OF PERSONALITIES

Innumerable examples could be cited of situations in which the direction of a company's

growth and development and the character of its integration arrangements were shaped by the personal philosophy of an individual executive. It will be recalled from Chapter Three that the philosophy of Mr. Andrew W. Mellon, as later reflected in the thinking of Mr. W. L. Mellon, had much to do with the general policy of vertical integration into all phases of the oil business which the Gulf Oil Corporation followed almost from the date of its inception. In the Sinclair Oil Corporation, the convictions of Mr. Harry F. Sinclair with regard to the effect of the prorationing laws on the crude oil producing business had a great deal to do with the shift in the balance between the company's crude oil producing and refining operations which took place during the 1930's (see Chapter Thirteen).

In The Atlantic Refining Company, the great personal interest which Mr. J. W. Van Dyke developed in tanker construction and operation in the later years of his life undoubtedly led the company to make heavier commitments in tanker transportation activities than might otherwise have been the case, although these investments did not ultimately result in a larger marine activity than the company could use effectively. In the case of The Texas Company, attention has already been directed in Chapter Thirteen to the personal interest of Mr. R. C. Holmes in refining activities and to the bearing which it had on some of the changes which took place in the company's integration pattern in the late 1920's and early 1930's. In the Standard Oil Company (Indiana) there is no question that Colonel R. W. Stewart's personal convictions and ambitions had a great deal to do with the company's efforts to seek a strong crude oil producing position during the early 1920's.

Although the Union Oil Company was not one of the seven companies which we studied in detail, its history provides a particularly good example of the influence of personalities on integration patterns.[5] The Union Oil Company was formed in 1890 through a merger of three firms, the Hardison and Stewart Oil Company, the Sespe Oil Company, and the Torrey Canyon Oil Company. The latter two firms were

---

[4] The Sohio executives had many reasons in addition to the one stated for the maintenance of the Fleet-Wing organization. Among other things, for example, the executives pointed out that Fleet-Wing provided the company with a brand name which could be used outside the state of Ohio and gave the management group valuable information concerning trends and conditions in the jobber market.

[5] Information drawn from F. J. Taylor and E. M. Welty, *Black Bonanza* (New York, Whittlesey House, McGraw-Hill Book Company, Inc., 1950).

largely producing organizations, but the Hardison and Stewart Oil Company was engaged in producing, transportation, refining, and marketing activities. The Hardison and Stewart Oil Company also owned the Mission Transfer Company which had storage tanks, pipe lines, and a small refinery and was engaged primarily in transporting and marketing the output of other oil producers.

Mr. Thomas R. Bard, who had previously been vice president of the Mission, Sespe, and Torrey companies and who had a financial interest in the latter two, was made president of the new organization. Mr. Lyman Stewart, who with his family owned 51% of the stock of the Hardison and Stewart Oil Company and an interest in the Sespe and Torrey companies, was elected vice president. The treasurer's office went to Mr. W. L. Hardison, who with certain associates held the remaining stock in the Hardison and Stewart Oil Company and an interest in the Sespe and Torrey companies. The merger arrangement provided that the merged companies would exchange their stock for Union Oil Company stock and would turn over their properties to the new company for development and operation. Fifty-three per cent of the Union stock was assigned to the Hardison and Stewart Oil Company and 47% to the Sespe and Torrey companies thus giving Mr. Lyman Stewart and Mr. W. L. Hardison technical control of the new organization. At the same time, however, an agreement was negotiated with Mr. Bard which gave him the right to name the majority of the directors to the Sespe and Torrey boards and which, in turn, gave him a slight majority representation on the Union Oil Company board.

Almost from the outset a strong divergence developed in the business philosophies of Mr. Bard and Mr. Stewart. Mr. Stewart was anxious to expand the Union Oil Company's operations as rapidly as circumstances would permit and strongly favored the aggressive development of refining, marketing, and transportation activities as well as crude oil production. Mr. Bard, on the other hand, favored a more conservative policy of growth and expansion and was strongly convinced that the company should stick fairly closely to crude oil producing and keep its commitments in refining, marketing, and transportation to a minimum.

For eight years a bitter battle was waged between the two groups of officers and stockholders, one headed by Mr. Stewart and the other by Mr. Bard, over the policies and management of the Union Oil Company. In 1898 Mr. Lyman Stewart and his associates were finally able to gain control of the company, although by an extremely thin margin, and in the following year won a decisive victory over the Bard interests. Thereafter, the Union Oil Company's policy of growth and development was shaped in accordance with Mr. Lyman Stewart's thinking, and the company developed as an integrated concern active at all levels of the industry. Had Mr. Bard and his associates won control in 1898, it seems quite clear that the company's integration pattern might have evolved in a very different way from that which it actually did under the Stewart administration.

We found that individual personalities had a strong bearing on the integration patterns of all the companies we studied through the part which they played in decisions on capital appropriations. It was the practice of all the companies to have periodic management meetings at which decisions were made as to the capital funds to be allotted for expenditure to each major department. Each department presented the cost and investment analysis of the projects it wished to undertake along with its appraisal of the intangible considerations which might be related to the projects. Ordinarily, however, the sum of the funds requested by the departments was substantially greater than the company could reasonably afford to spend in any given period of time. As a result, the available funds had to be apportioned among departments in accordance with the estimated returns on investments and the relative urgency of the various undertakings. Needless to say, the strength of the individuals leading the various departments and the persuasiveness with which they were able to argue their causes had a great deal to do with how the money was allocated and a corresponding bearing on the timing and character of the changes which occurred in a company's integration pattern.

A final and more subtle way in which personalities influenced the formation of integration patterns was through the part which they played in determining a company's collective managerial skill in the different phases of the oil business. Rarely did a company have equal managerial skill in conducting operations at all levels of the industry. Some companies, for example, had managerial groups which were particularly adept at oil finding and producing, while others had outstanding managerial competence in refining, marketing, or transportation activities. As a general rule, a company quite naturally tended to compete the most effectively, to find the most favorable investment opportunities, and to expand the most rapidly in the areas in which its executives were particularly competent. Indeed, a few companies took the position that, all other things being equal, they should deliberately direct their capital funds into the fields in which their management groups happened to be particularly competent, because in such areas they could secure a higher return with less risk per dollar invested than they could in other areas of the business.

The managerial competence of a company in a particular field tended to perpetuate itself from year to year. A skillful group of oil finding men, for example, tended to attract and train well the younger men in the industry who were interested in oil finding work. Similarly, an able group of refining or marketing executives tended to attract the outstanding younger men in the industry who were interested in those fields. We found many examples, however, of situations in which a company's prime field of managerial competence shifted, either slowly over a long period of time or abruptly as a result of some change in administration. In nearly all cases, the shifts in prime field of managerial competence were accompanied sooner or later by corresponding shifts in a company's integration pattern.

VI. OTHER INFLUENCES

The foregoing parts of this chapter have outlined some of the important considerations which influenced the formation and alteration of the integration patterns of the companies we studied. From this point onward, the list of influences could be extended almost indefinitely until it encompassed nearly all the competitive, economic, technological, legal, social, political, and human considerations which comprised the business environments in which the various companies operated. In this concluding section of the chapter, we shall merely mention a few of these other influences in an effort to suggest the character and range of them. It should not be inferred, however, that those which we cover were necessarily of any greater significance than a dozen others which we shall have to leave out.

Normal Growth and Expansion:

We found that many shifts and changes in integration patterns took place simply as a part or a consequence of a company's normal process of growth and expansion. A particularly good example may be found in connection with pipe line transportation activities. A company sometimes had a refining operation at one point and a marketing activity at another, but lacked sufficient volume to warrant the building of a products pipe line to connect the two together and therefore relied upon rail transportation service. If the company's business grew at the normal rate for the industry, it sometimes found at a later date that it had enough volume to assure a favorable return on a pipe line investment. Accordingly, steps were taken to build the pipe line, and the company thereby increased its integration into pipe line activities. In situations of this kind, normal growth put the company in a position to take advantage of a lower cost method of transportation, and the competitive desirability of making the change occasioned an alteration in integration pattern. Similarly, the normal development of a crude oil producing field often prompted the building of a crude oil trunk line when the volume reached the point where it would warrant the investment, and the normal growth of a refinery activity often necessitated the extension of crude oil trunk lines as a means of securing adequate crude oil supplies for the enlarged operation.

Integration patterns in the marketing field were particularly subject to change as a result of normal growth in sales volume. As noted in Chapters Fifteen and Sixteen, a company's relative cost of doing business through one type of wholesale or retail outlet as contrasted with another was often dependent in the first instance upon the volume of business done at the point in question. In their efforts to secure the lowest possible cost of distribution and to keep their marketing operations competitive with those of nonintegrated firms, the integrated companies were frequently compelled to alter their distribution arrangements as their volume of business increased. Similarly, as noted in Chapter Nine, the by-passing of bulk plants usually occurred at points where a service station or a commercial account had developed such a large volume of business that it was in a position to take direct shipments from a terminal or a refinery. Finally, it will be recalled from Chapter Nine that independent marketers sometimes undertook backward integration into refining simply as a consequence of the fact that their businesses had grown so large and their products requirements so great that they could no longer rely upon purchases in the tank car markets, in which a relatively small volume of products was traded, as a means of supply.

Changes in Products and Markets:

Fundamental changes in products and markets had an important influence on integration arrangements at many points in the industry's history. As long as the major product of the industry was kerosene, a product which was characteristically sold through grocery stores, hardware stores, and other multipurpose outlets, very few oil companies made any significant effort to engage in retailing activities. As soon as gasoline, a product which could be sold effectively through unipurpose outlets, became the primary product of the industry, however, a strong movement toward forward integration into retailing operations took place for the reasons outlined in Chapter Nine.

It will likewise be recalled from the discussion in Chapter Thirteen that The Texas Company's integration pattern underwent a major alteration in the period from about 1910 to 1926 partially as a result of the tremendous growth which took place in the gasoline markets at that time. Whereas before 1909 the company had usually been a seller of crude oil on balance, in the period 1910 to 1926 it was drawn by the expansion in its gasoline marketing operations into a position where it was frequently a buyer of both crude oil and refined products.

A recent example of a change in products

and markets which prompted changes in integration patterns may be found in the growth of the domestic fuel oil business during the last two decades. Before the middle 1930's the middle distillates were used primarily for industrial purposes, and most of the integrated oil companies disposed of the large bulk of their output of such products by direct shipments from refineries. With the great expansion in the use of fuel oils for home heating purposes, however, a number of the companies found it desirable to carry their distillates through their bulk plants, to engage in burner sales and burner maintenance activities, and in some instances to participate in truck deliveries to the homes of consumers.

Technological Developments:

Technological developments often prompted alterations in integration patterns in the sense that they sometimes created new situations in which an integration step would permit economies in operation. The most dramatic example may be found in the technological development of the products pipe line which has been discussed in earlier chapters. Before 1931 most oil companies participated to a relatively small extent in products transportation activities and relied heavily upon rail carriers. As soon as the products pipe line became technologically possible, however, a broad movement toward integration into products transportation activities was launched.

A second example of a major technological development which produced alterations in integration patterns may be found in the evolution of refining techniques. As will be noted in Chapter Nineteen, the advance of refining technology required a steady increase in the capital funds which had to be committed to refinery plant facilities in order to maintain a fully competitive operation. As the refinery investment increased in magnitude, it became increasingly important for a company to have its crude oil sources and its market outlets assured in order to protect and reduce the risk associated with its capital commitment.

Historical and Accidental Influences:

We found unmistakable evidence that historical and accidental influences had much to do with the evolution of the integration patterns of the companies we studied. Earlier chapters have directed attention to the fact that all the companies made many very important changes in their integration patterns at various points in their histories. The integration patterns in 1952, however, still bore in most cases at least some imprint of the historical antecedents of the companies. For example, three of the companies which originated chiefly as crude oil producers, The Ohio Oil Company, the Gulf Oil Corporation, and The Texas Company, still had very strong crude oil positions in 1952, even though they did not maintain them at the same level throughout their entire records. Conversely, the three companies which originated chiefly as refining and marketing organizations, The Atlantic Refining Company, the Standard Oil Company (Ohio), and the Standard Oil Company (Indiana), were still very strong refining and marketing organizations in 1952. The Sinclair Oil Corporation provides an exception in that it originated with a strong crude oil position but was relatively short of crude oil in 1952.

Some rearrangements in integration patterns we found to be entirely matters of historical accident. An excellent example may be found in the purchase of the Transcontinental Oil Company by The Ohio Oil Company in 1930. Transcontinental and The Ohio Oil Company both held extensive producing properties in the highly prolific Yates field in West Texas, and it was, in fact, on a tract purchased by the latter from the former that the Yates discovery well was drilled. In 1930 when the Transcontinental Oil Company became available for sale, its producing properties included 119 wells in the Yates field and 329 oil and gas wells in various fields in the states of Louisiana, Arkansas, Kansas, Oklahoma, Colorado, and Wyoming. In 1929 the company had a net crude oil production of about 31,500 barrels per day.

The management of The Ohio Oil Company was very anxious to secure the Transcontinental producing properties and entered into the purchase agreement for that reason. Forty million dollars par value of newly issued stock in The Ohio Oil Company was exchanged for the Transcontinental properties. As a part of the transaction, The Ohio Oil Company also acquired the Transcontinental's refining, mar-

keting, and transportation properties in the Southwest. Transcontinental had three refineries with an aggregate refining capacity of 12,500 barrels per day located at Fort Worth, Texas; Bristow, Oklahoma; and Boynton, Oklahoma. The company's marketing properties included 96 bulk plants and 376 service stations through which it sold about 40% of its gasoline, kerosene, and motor oil under the brand name "Marathon" in the states of Missouri, Kansas, Tennessee, Oklahoma, Texas, Arkansas, and Iowa. Transportation facilities were limited to crude oil gathering lines which connected the three refineries to near-by oil fields.

The Transcontinental refining and marketing properties proved to be of little value in The Ohio Oil Company's operations and were subsequently sold. The Boynton refinery was dismantled and sold for junk immediately after the purchase; the Bristow plant was sold in 1939 after a period of unprofitable operations; and the Fort Worth refinery was sold in 1941, partially as a result of the decline in the output of the Ranger field from which it drew its crude oil supply. The Transcontinental marketing operations were never profitable to The Ohio Oil Company, but the facilities in the vicinity of the refineries were maintained until the refineries were sold.

The Ohio Oil Company thus made two rearrangements in its integration pattern, one when the Transcontinental refining and marketing properties were acquired and a second when they were liquidated, which were merely an accidental consequence of the purchase of the Transcontinental producing properties.

Finally, but by no means of least importance, it was apparent that some rearrangements in integration patterns could best be classified simply as matters of fortuitous circumstance. As noted in Chapter Four, the fact that the discoveries of the big Oklahoma and West Texas oil fields in the middle 1920's and the East Texas field in 1930 all happened to come so close together in point of time generated powerful forces for both forward and backward integration throughout the entire industry and brought about very significant rearrangements in the integration patterns of some companies. Many examples may likewise be found of situations in which a particularly fortunate crude oil discovery by an individual company produced a major rearrangement in the company's integration pattern.

It will be recalled from the discussion in Chapter Thirteen, for example, that during the 1930's the Gulf Oil Corporation's crude oil ratio was declining and the company was anxious to develop additional production. In 1934, after seven years of negotiation, Gulf and the Anglo-Iranian Oil Company were able to arrange a concession for exploration in the tiny Shaikdom of Kuwait on the Persian Gulf. Exploration was begun in 1934 by the Kuwait Oil Company, Ltd. (jointly owned subsidiary of Gulf and the Anglo-Iranian Oil Company), and oil was discovered in 1939, but it was not until after World War II that drilling operations were commenced in earnest. In 1946 the Kuwait Oil Company brought in what ultimately proved to be fabulously productive oil fields. By the end of 1946 the company was producing 30,000 barrels per day from 9 wells, or an average of over 3,000 barrels per day per well.[6] The Kuwait properties subsequently proved of immense value to the Gulf Oil Corporation and did much toward re-establishing its position as a strong crude oil producing company.

VII. SUMMARY

1. The formation and alteration of integration patterns is essentially a process by which a corporation adapts itself to the total business environment in which it operates. The business environment in the oil industry is constantly changing, and as a result the integration patterns of the oil companies remain fluid in character and are constantly undergoing rearrangement as the managements seek the optimum responses to new conditions. The forces and circumstances which influence the formation of integration patterns are multitudinous and include investment, cost, and profit considerations, competitive pressures, changes in economic, legal, and political conditions, managerial personalities, historical and accidental developments, normal growth in the volume of business, changes in markets and products, and new technological developments.

[6] Craig Thompson, *Since Spindletop*, privately printed by the Gulf Oil Corporation, 1951.

2. A company's integration pattern is a reflection of its management's strategy concerning the balance of operations which will yield maximum competitive strength and earning power, minimize the risk associated with capital investments, and offer maximum protection against the fluctuations in price, demand and supply, and all the other vicissitudes of fortune which are inevitably associated with any business enterprise.

Integration patterns are also formed and shaped simply as the net result of the day-to-day decisions which a company's executives make on individual business problems. A company's integration pattern at any given moment may thus be regarded as the net solution of the whole matrix of business problems which the management has faced prior to that date.

The integration patterns of the seven companies we studied were formed and shaped somewhat more as a consequence of the individual decisions made on the continuing series of day-to-day problems which the executives faced than they were by general management strategies with respect to integration arrangements. These two broad influences on integration patterns, the summation of individual decisions and general management strategies, were not found to be mutually exclusive, however, because the day-to-day decisions were made in the light of long-run policies and the long-run policies were formulated in the light of what was learned from dealing with the day-to-day problems.

3. The executives of the seven companies were generally of the opinion that decisions on new capital investments and methods of operation should be made primarily in the light of what the new arrangements might be expected to earn or save for a company in the future rather than in the light of what a company had earned in different departments of the business in the past. As a result, records of profits and losses by functional departments played only a minor role in the formation and alteration of integration patterns. It had also been the experience of the companies that it was difficult to make a fully satisfactory separation of profits by functional departments, chiefly because of

the problems involved in determining transfer prices, and that undue attention to departmental results often led to serious dissension among their executive personnel. Moreover, since many integration decisions had to be made in the light of what yielded the greatest net advantage to the company as a whole, there was considerable question as to the wisdom of concentrating any very large amount of executive attention on records of earnings by functional departments.

4. The formation and alteration of integration patterns is a manifestation of the working of competition in the oil industry. Many rearrangements in integration patterns are initiated as defensive responses to competitive pressure or as a means of initiating new competitive pressure. Moreover, the alterations which take place in a company's integration pattern as it grows and expands reflect to a considerable degree the differences in the competitive resistance to expansion which it encounters at different levels of the industry. The degree of fluidity found in the integration patterns of the oil companies might therefore be taken as one very important measure of the general intensity of competition in the oil industry.

PART FOUR

The Participation of the Small Refiner
in the Oil Industry

THE PRECEDING chapters have discussed the forces and circumstances which have tended to foster the growth and development of large, integrated companies in the oil industry. Attention has also been directed to the integration patterns of the large companies and to the nature of the process by which the patterns are formed and altered in accordance with changing conditions. The purpose of Part Four of the book is to examine the changes which have taken place in the participation of small refiners in the affairs of the oil industry and to analyze the reasons for the changes. Part Four is therefore a study of the adaptation of small firms to the conditions of the oil industry, just as Part Three was a study of the adaptation of large firms to the conditions of the industry.

CHAPTER EIGHTEEN

The Characteristics of the Small Refiner and the Extent of His Participation in the Oil Industry

THE OBJECTIVES of this chapter are to describe some of the important characteristics of the small refining company and to present our findings with regard to the changes which took place in the participation of small refining firms in the affairs of the industry in the period 1920–1950. The first section of the chapter will consider briefly the nature of the small refining activity and wherein it differs from the small producing, the small marketing, and the large refining businesses. The second section of the chapter will examine changes over a 30-year period in the population, aggregate plant capacity, number of plants, plant size, cracking capacity, and location of small refiners. The remaining chapters in Part Four will then describe some of the forces and circumstances which brought about the changes in the participation of small refiners in the industry.

I. THE CHARACTERISTICS OF THE SMALL REFINER

We shall define a "small refining company" as any firm not included among the top 30 in the industry in terms of refining capacity. This definition is necessarily an arbitrary one, but our research indicated that it was at about this point that refining firms changed in character with regard to such important factors as the nature of integration arrangements, the size and type of plant equipment, the geographic scope of operations, brand name advertising programs, and the breadth of stock ownership. We used refining capacity as a measure of size in preference to other commonly used measures, such as dollar sales volume, book value of assets, or number of employees, because refining capacity figures have been widely used in

the oil industry and because they are available over a long period of years.

The maximum size of the small refiner as established by the above definition changed from year to year in accordance with changes in the composition of the large company group and the size of the smallest company included therein. As will be noted later, for example, the Solar Refining Company was the thirtieth largest company in the industry in 1920 and its refining capacity was 6,500 barrels per day whereas in 1950 the Consumer Cooperative Association was the thirtieth largest company and its refining capacity was 25,900 barrels per day.

The discussion in Part Four will be confined largely but not exclusively to the "small refining companies." At some points in later chapters we shall also draw upon the experiences of a few companies among the 30 largest in the industry. These companies are completely or substantially nonintegrated and are among the smaller of the 30 largest companies. The experiences of these larger, substantially nonintegrated firms are of interest because their business methods are often much like those of the small refiners and differ appreciably from those of the large, integrated companies.

A small refining venture usually represents a very appreciable business undertaking from a financial and operating standpoint. The annual sales volume of a company with a refining capacity of 5,000 barrels per day might, for example, exceed $6,000,000. The formation of such a company might entail an initial capital investment of from less than one to several million dollars depending upon the time the company was organized and the type of refinery equipment it employed. One small company we visited, with a refinery of 8,000 barrels per day capacity, had a net worth of approximately $4,000,000 and total assets valued in excess of $8,000,000. A different company, with a refining capacity at the upper limit of the small refiner category, had a net worth of roughly $10,000,000 and total assets of $20,000,000. As will be noted in Chapter Twenty-One, however, there have at times been some very small and poorly equipped firms that were financed for less than $100,000. Another indication of the size of small refining companies may be inferred from the fact that the number of employees may range from less than 50 up to as many as several hundred. Most of the small refining companies are incorporated, and in many instances the stock ownership is closely held despite the heavy financial commitments ordinarily undertaken by the firms.

The data reported in Chapter Two reveal that the vertical integration arrangements of the small companies frequently differed in two important respects from those of the large companies. Whereas all but a very few large companies participated in the activities at all principal levels of the industry, small companies frequently omitted one or more of the principal industry activities other than refining. Moreover, although their marketing operations were comparatively large, the small *integrated* refiners did not usually participate in producing and transportation activities to so great an extent as did the large companies.[1]

Notwithstanding the fact that the small refiners typically have had a far lesser degree of vertical integration than their large competitors, the small firms have frequently employed all the various types of vertical integration arrangements. A total of 77 companies with refining capacities below 25,000 barrels per day reported their integration arrangements to us in response to the industry survey described in Chapter Two. Of the 77 companies, 45 were

engaged in oil producing activities, 47 were participating in wholesaling activities, 35 were conducting retailing operations, and 50 were participating in pipe line transportation activities. Only 13 of the respondent companies with refining capacities under 25,000 barrels per day were not engaged in at least one major activity in addition to refining. Since 70 firms with refining capacities of less than 25,000 barrels per day did not respond to the survey, it is conceivably possible that somewhat more than half of the smaller firms were completely nonintegrated. It seems much more likely, however, that at least some of the nonrespondents were integrated and that the number of completely nonintegrated refiners in 1950 with refining capacities of less than 25,000 barrels per day was probably not greater than one-third of the total number of such firms.

The plant facilities of the small refiners have usually differed in two major respects from those of their large competitors. The plants of the small firms have generally been of a much smaller size and less well equipped than the plants of the large companies. In 1950, for example, the average size of the small companies' plants was only 4,600 barrels per day as compared with an average size of 38,000 barrels per day for the plants of large companies. Moreover, approximately one-half of the small refiners did not own any thermal or catalytic cracking facilities whereas all the large companies owned cracking processes.[2] The lack of cracking facilities usually prevented the small refiners from obtaining as large a yield of light end products and as high a quality of gasoline as the better equipped firms.

Since the small refiner has typically owned a single plant whereas the large companies have usually owned several plants, the differences in total refining capacity between small and large concerns have been far greater than figures on average plant size might suggest. On January 1, 1950, the total refining capacity of small firms ranged from less than 100 to 25,000 barrels per day. The average refining capacity of all small companies was approximately 5,000 barrels per day and the typical or median figure was roughly 3,000 barrels per day. The 30 large companies, on

---

[1] Some very small companies were integrated into nonrefining activities to a much greater extent than were other much larger refining companies. For example, one very small company had net crude oil production exceeding 80% of its refinery runs. One large firm with a refining capacity over 70 times as large as the smaller company, on the other hand, had net crude oil production of less than 30% of its refinery runs. Moreover, the smaller company sold a much higher proportion of its gasoline through its own wholesaling facilities than did the larger company.

[2] The source of these data will be discussed at a later point in the chapter.

EXHIBIT XVIII-1. RELATIVE PARTICIPATION OF 30 LARGEST AND ALL
SMALL COMPANIES: PRODUCING, REFINING, AND
MARKETING ACTIVITIES: 1950

	Quantities (1,000 bbls.)			Percentages of Industry Totals		
	United States Totals	30 Largest Companies	All Other Smaller Companies	United States Totals	30 Largest Companies	All Other Smaller Companies
Net Crude Oil Production	1,726,877	1,013,887	712,990	100.0%	58.7%	41.3%
Refinery Runs	2,094,967	1,893,102	201,765	100.0	90.4	9.6
Terminal and Bulk Plant Sales of Light Oil Products	1,661,000	985,113	675,887	100.0	59.3	40.7
Sales of Gasoline through Owned or Leased Service Stations	480,000	275,395	204,605	100.0	57.4	42.6

Note: Includes only companies engaged in refining activities and replying to the industry survey discussed in Chapter Two.
SOURCE: See Chapter Two.

the other hand, had refining capacities ranging from 25,000 to over 775,000 barrels per day. The average capacity of the large companies was 190,000 barrels per day and the median or typical figure was roughly 100,000 barrels per day.[3]

As noted in Chapter Two, the total number of active refining companies in 1950 did not exceed 179; it follows therefore (by virtue of our definitions) that the number of active small refiners did not exceed 149. There were, on the other hand, many thousands of small firms engaged in producing and marketing activities. At least 8,000 to 10,000 and possibly more than 12,000 firms and individuals were engaged in the production of oil.[4] More than 17,000 jobbers, commission agents, or other types of distributors operated the bulk stations and terminals at the wholesaling level of the industry, and these facilities were owned or leased by approximately 10,000 companies and individuals.[5] Most of the 188,000 service stations were independently operated, and the

retail outlets were owned by thousands of concerns or individuals.[6]

The small refiners have not only been fewer in number, but they have also conducted a smaller share of the industry's operations than small producers or marketers. The relative participation of large and small companies at several levels of the industry in 1950 is suggested by Exhibit XVIII-1. For purposes of illustration, we are here assuming that a small producer, wholesaler, or retailer is any company outside the 30 largest engaged in any of these activities. The data for the 30 largest companies were drawn from Chapter Two and pertain only to companies engaged in refining. Thus, the figure of 1,013,887,000 barrels shown for the 30 largest producing companies is a summation of the oil production of the 30 largest integrated refining companies ranked on the basis of net crude oil production. The figures reported in the exhibit for the 30 largest companies in various activities do not therefore include several, large nonintegrated producing and marketing concerns, nor do they include possibly one or two refiners with capacities ranging from 25,000 to 40,000 barrels per day that did not reply to the survey and which might have been among the 30 largest firms on the basis of refinery runs.

[3] See footnote 2.
[4] The number of producing firms was estimated primarily from data supplied by the U. S. Bureau of Old Age and Survivors' Insurance, Federal Security Agency of the Social Security Administration. A second source of information on the number of producers was the *International Petroleum Register*, Charles J. Penn, Editor, Los Angeles, California, published annually by Mona Palmer, Twenty-Eighth Edition, 1950.
[5] The number of jobbers, commission agents, and companies owning these facilities were estimated from data in the following publications: U. S. Census of Business, 1948, Volume IV, *Wholesale Trade-General Statistics: Commodity Line Sales Statistics*, "Petroleum Bulk Stations" (Government Printing Office, 1952); U. S. Bureau of Mines,

annual Information Circulars entitled *Petroleum Refineries, Including Cracking Plants, in the United States*; U. S. Department of Agriculture, Farm Credit Administration, *Petroleum Operations of Farmer Cooperatives* by J. Warren Mather, Circular C-139, May 1951; and the *International Petroleum Register*, Charles J. Penn, Editor, op. cit.

[6] Number of service stations obtained from U. S. Census of Business, 1948, Volume IV, op. cit.

The omission of these companies does not, however, affect the results appreciably.

As may be seen in the exhibit, small refiners conducted less than 10% of the industry's refining operations whereas small producers accounted for 41% of the country's oil production and small marketers conducted slightly more than 40% of the industry's wholesaling and retailing activities through their own facilities. Moreover, a significant proportion of the products volume sold through the owned or leased marketing facilities of the 30 largest companies was also handled by independent businessmen such as commission agents or dealers.

The functional relationship which has been established between the small refiners and the large, integrated companies has also been very different from that established between the small producers and small marketers and the large, integrated companies. The large, integrated companies constitute the most important market outlet for the small oil producers in the industry. The large companies also rely upon commission agents, distributors, consignees, and jobbers to distribute products in certain areas and to perform certain types of jobs at the wholesale level of the industry, and they depend very heavily upon independent service station operators and fuel oil dealers at the retail level of the industry (see Chapters Fifteen and Sixteen).

At the refining level of the industry, however, the activities of the small firms tend to duplicate rather than to complement those of the large companies. Since the large companies usually keep their refining capacities in approximate balance with their own sales requirements, the large companies do not provide a very substantial market for independently supplied products. Small refiners do, of course, often sell products to the large integrated companies. Some of the reasons why large companies purchase products from small refiners were discussed in Chapter Fourteen, and in Chapter Twenty-Three we shall see that some small firms specialize in the sense that they meet the unusual products needs of the large, integrated companies. On balance, however, the small refiners supply only a small part of the products requirements of the large companies whereas the small producers play an important role in supplying crude oil to the large, integrated companies and the small marketers sell a substantial portion of the products refined by the large, integrated companies.

Entry into the refining business has characteristically been blocked by more significant obstacles than entry at the other levels of the industry. As noted above, a small refining company may represent an investment ranging up to several million dollars. It would be, for example, very difficult to finance a business with a modern plant of 5,000 barrels per day capacity for much less than $3,000,000.[7]

Oil producing properties, on the other hand, can sometimes be purchased for as little as a few thousand dollars. Some new firms become established fairly inexpensively by acquiring acreage in new fields where the large companies overlook or are unable to lease all the properties. The costs to a wildcatter of securing oil production can range from practically nothing to a great deal of money depending upon his drilling success and the various producing arrangements by which he may secure acreage and drilling funds (see Chapter Thirteen). Based upon the industry-wide drilling experience for new-field wildcats in the period from 1944 to 1951, a wildcatter using only his own funds would on the average have to invest approximately $300,000 to find a new oil field.[8] The net capital outlay after taxes would, of course, be substantially less if the wildcatter had other income against which he could offset intangible drilling and development costs for tax purposes.

The amount of capital required to establish a small marketing operation is likewise not in the same order of magnitude as that needed for a small refining enterprise. One large com-

---

[7] A discussion of the historical cost of refineries is included in Chapter Nineteen. The effect of size and type of equipment on plant investment costs is considered in Chapter Twenty.

[8] Estimated from data developed from Frederic H. Lahee, "Exploratory Drilling in 1951," *Bulletin of the American Association of Petroleum Geologists*, Vol. 36, No. 6, June 1952, pp. 977–995, and *Petroleum Data Book*, Second Edition, 1948, p. D-4. Average depth of exploratory hole, 1944 to 1951, was around 4,000 feet and the average drilling cost for a 3,000–5,000 foot hole was approximately $30,000 in 1947. Since, in the period from 1944 to 1951, only one well out of 8.6 drilled in the new field category was successful, an average drilling expense of approximately $260,000 would have been required for each discovery well. Many new fields were of such a small size, however, that they would not support a payout.

pany reported that it could erect, equip, and stock a fully modern bulk plant in a rural community for approximately $32,000 in 1951. The company also reported that many of its branded jobbers purchased or erected less well-equipped bulk plant facilities, used secondhand trucks, and entered into business with total capital outlays ranging from $5,000 to $10,000. Commission agents and consignees leasing bulk plant facilities from the large companies ordinarily invest only in one or more trucks. Several large companies reported total investment costs for service stations in 1951 ranging from $30,000 to $80,000 in city environments. All but a few of these stations were leased to independent dealers whose only capital outlay was the funds for inventories which ranged up to about $7,500. The leasing of land and the use of concrete block construction and less elaborate equipment enables a small businessman to build and operate a service station with an investment considerably below $30,000 to $80,000. Capital requirements for small marketers are therefore not likely to exceed $50,000.

A scarcity in the type of executive talent necessary to manage a refining enterprise and particularly the technical competency necessary to deal with the intricate manufacturing process is another obstacle to entry into the refining business. The entire range of management problems encountered by a refiner is, in fact, likely to be more complex than that encountered by small businessmen at other levels of the industry. One small refiner summarized the conditions of entry into the refining business as follows: "The technical know-how necessary to operate a modern refinery and the money needed to build one are the two biggest safeguards of our competitive position. They really keep the population down."

II. The Changes in the Position and Participation of Small Refiners in the Industry, 1920–1950

In this section we shall present such statistical data as we were able to accumulate with regard to the changes in the position and participation of small refiners in the industry between 1920 and 1950. Specifically, we shall report on the changes in (a) the number of

small refiners, (b) the proportion of the industry refining capacity held by small firms, (c) the proportion of the industry plants held by small companies, (d) the average size of plants owned by small refiners, (e) the proportion of the industry cracking capacity owned by small companies, and (f) the shifts in the location of the industry operating capacity and plants.

Number of Small Refiners in the Industry:

In so far as we could determine, accurate historical records on the refining population have not been collected and published by either government or industry organizations. It is therefore very difficult at this juncture to reconstruct with any high degree of accuracy the number of refining companies at different points in the industry's history. Since 1918, however, the U. S. Bureau of Mines has with only a few interruptions been publishing annual information on the *refineries* in the industry.[9] From these Bureau of Mines refinery statistics it is possible to prepare approximations of the refining population in different years by grouping refineries together by companies.

One such study of the refining population prepared from U. S. Bureau of Mines records by the Coordination and Economics Department of the Standard Oil Company (New Jersey) shows the following number of refining companies at ten-year intervals from 1920:[10]

Year	Total Number of Active and Inactive Refining Companies	Number of Active and Inactive Small Refining Companies
1920	274	244
1930	260	230
1940	383	353
1950	223	193

The preparation of the population data from Bureau of Mines records, which list each individual refinery and the name of its owner, in-

---

9 U. S. Bureau of Mines, annual Information Circulars entitled *Petroleum Refineries in the United States* and *Petroleum Refineries, Including Cracking Plants, in the United States.*

10 This study was prepared by C. M. Furcht, Coordination and Economics Department, Standard Oil Company (New Jersey), and was reported in a company memorandum, "Growth and Structure of U. S. Refining Industry, 1920–1950." The Jersey Company study developed only figures for the total number of active and inactive firms. To obtain figures on the active and inactive small refining companies, we merely subtracted 30 from the Jersey Company totals.

volved several steps. Since quite a few companies owned more than one plant, it was first necessary to determine the number of companies as distinct from the number of plants. It was then necessary to ascertain which of the companies listed as owning refineries were subsidiaries of affiliates of still other refining companies. A company was not counted as a separate firm in the industry if it could be determined from published sources that 50% or more of its voting stock was owned by another refining company. The resulting figures should be accepted only as fairly close approximations to the actual number of firms because of the lack of adequate published information on company stockholding arrangements, particularly for the smaller firms, and because of certain inevitable inaccuracies in the primary source data on refineries.

It was reported in Chapter Two that our own survey of refining companies revealed that the number of active refining firms on December 31, 1950, did not exceed 179. The figures prepared by the Standard Oil Company (New Jersey) show 223 active and inactive firms on January 1, 1950. Since 37 of these firms were inactive (plants shut down), the Jersey Company figures show 186 active refining firms on January 1, 1950. The discrepancy of 7 firms (186–179) between the Jersey Company and the Chapter Two figures may be explained by changes in the refining population occurring during the year 1950.

On the basis of the Jersey Company study, several observations may be made concerning the changes in the small refining population. The first observation is that the number of small firms was less in 1950 than in any of the preceding years studied and approximately 20% less than in 1920. There was, however, no consistent long-term downward trend over the entire period, as evidenced by the fact that the number of small firms was less in 1930 than in 1920, substantially greater in 1940 than in 1930, and appreciably less in 1950 than in 1940.

Although yearly turnover figures summarizing individual company entries and exits are not available, the figures at ten-year intervals suggest the possibility that the refining population fluctuated widely within comparatively short time periods. As further evidence

of short-term movements in the population, statistics presented later in the chapter show that the total number of refineries in the United States as well as the number of refineries in certain areas sometimes fluctuated widely within very short time periods. As one important explanation of these short-term movements in the number of firms, Chapter Twenty-One will discuss the abrupt expansions and contractions in the refining population caused by the discovery and development of new oil fields.

Another observation that may be made from the population data is that a precipitous decline occurred in the number of small firms between 1940 and 1950. As of January 1, 1950, the number of small firms was only 55% as large as it was 10 years before. As Chapters Nineteen, Twenty, and Twenty-Two will show, the advances in refinery technology played a very important role in bringing about this recent decline in the number of small firms.

Proportion of the Industry's Refining Capacity Held by Small Refiners:

The changes which took place in the proportion of the industry refining capacity held by small firms can be measured with somewhat more precision than can changes in the number of small firms. As noted above, one of the difficulties encountered in determining the number of small firms from U. S. Bureau of Mines reports on refineries arises because the stockholding arrangements of small companies in other refining concerns are not always disclosed in published sources. With the aid of the American Petroleum Institute, however, we were able to reconstruct records of the stockholding arrangements of the larger companies in the industry over a period of years. We then accumulated the refining capacity of the 30 largest companies in the industry from U. S. Bureau of Mines records of refineries in much the same way that the Jersey Company estimated the number of firms from the same records. The refining capacity held by small refiners was derived by subtracting the refining capacity held by the 30 largest companies from the total industry capacity.

The data on the refining capacity held by small firms indicate that the small refiners were unable to maintain a rate of growth commensurate with that of the industry. As a result, their proportionate share of the total industry capacity declined. In the period 1920–1950 the industry more than quadrupled in size (see Exhibit XVIII-2). In only six years between 1918 and 1951 did refinery runs fail to surpass the level reached in the immediately preceding year. Five of the years in which setbacks were suffered were those of depressed economic conditions, 1930–1932, 1938 and 1949, and one was the full year of wartime adjustment, 1942. The total operating and shutdown refining capacity at the beginning of each year grew even more consistently than did refinery runs, registering a gain over the immediately preceding year in all but two cases, 1933 and 1943. Over the entire period, the largest single jump in physical capacity during any five-year period occurred after World War II when capacity was increased by 1,648,000 barrels per day between January 1, 1946, and January 1, 1951.

The decline in the share of the industry refining capacity held by small refiners between 1920 and 1950 may be seen in Exhibit XVIII-3. Over the 30-year period the small refiners lost approximately one-half of the proportionate position they held on January 1, 1920. In 1920 the small refiners owned 434,000 barrels per day of refining capacity, which amounted to 28.4% of the industry capacity. In 1950 the small refiners owned 995,000 barrels per day of refining capacity, which represented only 14.9% of the industry total. While the small refiners more than doubled their physical capacity over the 30-year period, they failed to keep pace with the large companies in a struggle for a proportionate share of the greatly increased capacity of the industry.

The most marked decline in the proportionate ownership of refining capacity by small firms occurred in the period from 1925 to 1930. In this one short span of years, the capacity of the small refiners fell from 29.4% to 19.5% of the industry total. The period immediately preceding 1930 was marked by a number of significant mergers and acquisitions by some of the larger companies. When two or more of the large companies joined their operations together, the larger of the small refiners were automatically brought into the top 30 companies and the aggregate capacity of the large

company group was increased. It was also during the years immediately preceding 1930 that great supplies of crude oil pressed forward into the markets, causing a number of new and expanding firms to gain strong footholds among the 30 largest companies in the industry.[11]

The next marked decline in proportionate ownership of refining capacity by small firms occurred between 1940 and 1950. In this 10-year period the share of the industry capacity owned by small firms declined from 20.4% to 14.9% of the total. The explanation of this decline may be found in the fact that the large companies expanded far more rapidly than the small firms to meet the unprecedented demand for refined products during and after World War II. As noted above, a drastic reduction in the number of small firms also took place during this period. The disappearance of small firms did not, however, contribute to the proportionate decline in capacity ownership by small firms to nearly the same extent as did the expansion of the large firms.

The foregoing discussion has dealt with the share of the *operating and shutdown* refining capacity owned by small firms. Exhibit XVIII-4 reveals the share of the industry *operating* capacity held by small refiners. The figures on ownership of operating capacity are important because they provide a better indication of the share of the industry products produced by small firms than do the figures on operating and shutdown capacity.[12] The share of the in-

---

[11] The substantial decline in the proportionate holdings of refining capacity by small firms which appears in our data between 1925 and 1930 may also be attributed partially to the manner in which refinery statistics were reported by the Bureau of Mines. A large number of small plants entered the industry in the early 1920's and many were shut down permanently before 1925. Since the Bureau of Mines continued to list plants until they had been shut down for at least five years, the plants did not become eligible for deletion until the 1925–1930 period. For all practical purposes, however, the capacity of these plants was withdrawn in the 1920–1925 period (see comments in U. S. Bureau of Mines, *Petroleum Refineries in the United States*, January 1, 1928, and January 1, 1931, Information Circulars 6065 and 6485).

[12] Beginning in 1938 the Bureau of Mines defined operating capacity as that portion of a plant's capacity actually being utilized; all unutilized capacity was considered shutdown capacity. Before 1938, however, the total capacity of any plant charging crude oil was listed as operating capacity even though some stills might have been closed down. (See U. S. Bureau of Mines, *Petroleum Refineries, Including Cracking Plants, in the United States*, January 1, 1938, Information Circular 7034).

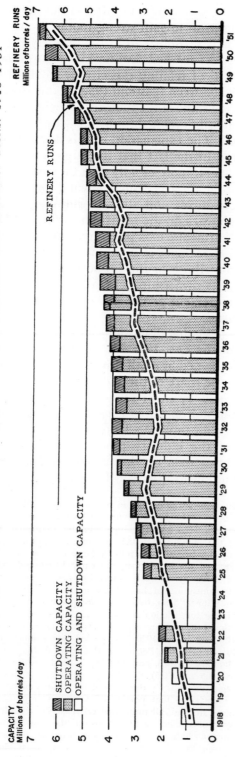

EXHIBIT XVIII-2. OPERATING AND SHUTDOWN REFINING CAPACITY AND REFINERY RUNS: 1918–1951

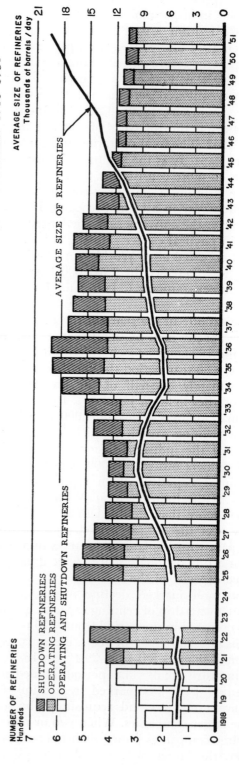

NUMBER OF OPERATING AND SHUTDOWN REFINERIES AND AVERAGE SIZE OF REFINERIES: 1918–1951

SOURCE: Number and capacity of refineries from Annual Circulars of U. S. Bureau of Mines, *Petroleum Refineries, Including Cracking Plants, in the United States, 1918–1951;* refinery runs from American Petroleum Institute, *Statistical Bulletins,* Vol. XXXII, No. 31 and Vol. XXXIII, No. 21.

EXHIBIT XVIII-3. CUMULATIVE TOTAL REFINING CAPACITY BY COMPANY SIZE GROUPS:
1920–1950

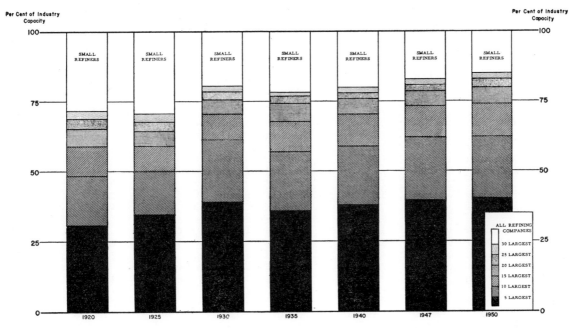

EXHIBIT XVIII-4. CUMULATIVE OPERATING CAPACITY BY COMPANY SIZE GROUPS: 1925–1950

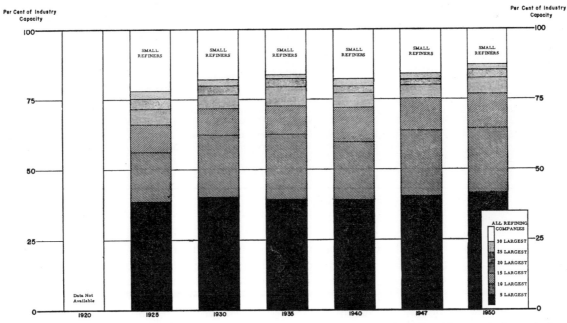

Note: Companies were grouped according to total operating and shutdown crude oil capacity (January 1 of years indicated, except May 1, 1925). From 1920 to 1935 operating capacity includes shutdown capacity of operating plants; thereafter figures include only operating capacity of operating plants.

SOURCE: Derived from U. S. Bureau of Mines records. See Appendix, Table 23, for data.

EXHIBIT XVIII-5. DIFFERENCES BETWEEN 1920 AND 1950 IN THE MEMBERS AND CAPACITY OF THE "LARGE" COMPANY GROUP

30 Largest Companies 1920	Percentage of Industry Capacity*	30 Largest Companies 1950	Percentage of Industry Capacity* 16 Successors to the 30 Largest Companies in 1920	Companies Not Among the 30 Largest in 1920
1. Standard Oil Company of New Jersey	9.5%	1. Standard Oil Company (New Jersey)	11.7%	
2. Standard Oil Company of California	7.6	2. Socony-Vacuum Oil Company, Inc.	7.9	
3. Standard Oil Company of Indiana	4.7	3. The Texas Company	7.4	
4. The Texas Company	4.6	4. Standard Oil Company (Indiana)	7.1	
5. Gulf Oil Corporation	4.6	5. Gulf Oil Corporation	6.8	
6. Union Oil Company of California	4.2	6. Standard Oil Company of California	5.7	
7. The Atlantic Refining Company	3.6	7. Shell Oil Company	5.5	
8. Sinclair Consolidated Oil Corporation	3.3	8. Sinclair Oil Corporation	4.5	
9. Royal Dutch Company	3.1	9. Cities Service Company	2.9	
10. Magnolia Petroleum Company	3.1	10. Tide Water Associated Oil Company	2.8	
11. Midwest Refining Company	3.0	11. Sun Oil Company	2.6	
12. Associated Oil Company	2.8	12. Phillips Petroleum Company		2.6%
13. Standard Oil Company of New York	1.7	13. The Atlantic Refining Company	2.4	
14. Cities Service Company	1.7	14. Union Oil Company of California	2.2	
15. Ohio Cities Gas Company	1.4	15. Pure Oil Company	1.7	
16. General Petroleum Corporation	1.3	16. Richfield Oil Corporation		1.5
17. Pierce Oil Corporation	1.3	17. The Standard Oil Company (Ohio)	1.4	
18. Tide Water Oil Company	1.3	18. Continental Oil Company		1.4
19. Cosden & Company	1.3	19. Ashland Oil & Refining Company		.9
20. Vacuum Oil Company	1.1	20. Petrol Refining Company		.7
21. Sun Company	.9	21. The Ohio Oil Company		.7
22. Standard Oil Company (Kansas)	.8	22. Mid-Continent Petroleum Corporation	.7	
23. Indian Refining Company	.7	23. Sunray Oil Corporation		.6
24. American Oilfields Company	.7	24. Eastern States Petroleum Company, Inc.		.5
25. Mid-Co. Gasoline Company	.6	25. Republic Oil Refining Company		.5
26. Pan-American Petroleum & Transport Company	.6	26. Skelly Oil Company		.5
27. White Eagle Oil & Refining Company	.6	27. Crown Central Petroleum Corporation		.5
28. Constantin Refining Company	.6	28. The Globe Oil & Refining Company		.5
29. The Standard Oil Company of Ohio	.6	29. Taylor Refining Company		.5
30. The Solar Refining Company	.4	30. Consumers Cooperative Association		.4
Total	71.6%		73.3%	11.8%

* Figures as of January 1, 1920, and January 1, 1950.

SOURCE: Derived from U. S. Bureau of Mines records.

dustry operating capacity held by small companies declined appreciably, but the changes were not so marked as they were in the case of operating and shutdown capacity. The proportion of the operating capacity declined in every year studied after 1925 except 1940 when the small refiners achieved a slight improvement in their proportionate holdings. In 1950 the small refiners held less than one-third as much of the industry operating capacity as did the five largest companies. Thus it may be concluded that there was a decline in the 1920–1950 period in the proportionate participation of small firms in refining activities.

A cross-comparison of Exhibits XVIII-3 and XVIII-4 reveals that the small refiners held a lesser share of the industry operating capacity than they did of total refining capacity in each year for which data were compiled. The fact that the small refiners held a lesser proportion of operating capacity than they did of total capacity is explained partially by the fact that their plants were operated at lower levels of throughput than those of the large companies and partially by the fact that the small firms often held a fairly large number of completely shutdown plants. The effect on refinery operating costs of running plants at levels below capacity will be discussed in Chapter Twenty.

The data on the operating and shutdown refinery capacity held by large firms show that the 30 largest companies in 1920 owned 71.6% of the industry capacity whereas the 30 largest companies in 1950 owned 85.1% of the industry capacity (see Exhibit XVIII-5). It should not be inferred, however, that the change in the relative holdings of refining capacity by large firms was all due to growth on the part of the 30 largest companies in 1920 and lack of growth on the part of small refiners.

Of the 30 largest companies in 1920, two later became defunct.[13] The 28 remaining companies by virtue of mergers and purchases of refineries comprised only 16 companies in 1950, and each of these 16 concerns was among the 30 largest firms in 1950. As shown in Exhibit XVIII-5, these 16 companies, in many cases under new corporate names, owned only 73.3% of the industry refining capacity in 1950. Therefore 14 new firms owning 11.8% of the industry refining capacity were also among the 30 largest companies in 1950. A large part of the decline from 28.4% to 14.9% of the industry refining capacity experienced by small refiners over the 30-year period may be explained by the fact that 14 small companies moved into the large company group and thereby added 11.8% to the capacity of the large company group.

Proportion of the Total Number of Refineries Owned by Small Firms:

The proportion of the industry's refineries held by small firms in 1950 was at its lowest

EXHIBIT XVIII-6. REFINERIES OWNED BY LARGE AND SMALL COMPANIES: 1920–1950

	Number			Percentage of Industry		
Year	Industry	Large Companies	Small Refiners	Industry	Large Companies	Small Companies
1920	373	99	274	100.0%	26.5%	73.5%
1925	550	120	430	100.0	21.8	78.2
1930	412	155	257	100.0	37.6	62.4
1935	631	178	453	100.0	28.2	71.8
1940	547	154	393	100.0	28.1	71.9
1947	399	148	251	100.0	37.1	62.9
1950	367*	149	218	100.0	40.6	59.4

* Figure as of January 1, 1950. The Chapter Two figure (331) was for operating companies as of December 31, 1950.
SOURCE: Derived from U.S. Bureau of Mines records.

point in 30 years.[14] As may be seen in Exhibit XVIII-6, the percentage of the plants owned by small refiners in the period 1920–1950 ranged from 78.2% of the industry plants in 1925 to 59.4% of the plants in 1950. Throughout the 30-year period, therefore, the proportion of the industry plants owned by small firms was far greater than the proportion of the industry refining capacity owned by small firms.

The fluctuations in the actual number of plants owned by small firms were far more appreciable than the fluctuations in the proportion of plants owned by small firms (see Exhibits XVIII-6 and XVIII-7). Wide fluctuations in the number of plants have, moreover, occurred over relatively short periods of time. For example, between 1920 and 1925 the number of plants increased by 57%; between 1925 and 1930 the number declined by 40%; between 1930 and 1935 the number again increased by 76%; and between 1940 and 1947 the number declined by 36%. As noted above, Chapter Twenty-One will discuss some of the important causes for short-run changes in the number of plants and firms.

Whereas the small refiners seldom owned more than a single plant, the large companies were typically multiplant operators. The approximate number of small refiners and the number of plants which they owned at 10-year intervals from 1920 to 1950 were as follows:

---

[13] The Mid-Continent Gasoline Company and the Constantin Refining Company passed into receivership proceedings before 1925.

[14] Data on refineries owned by small companies were compiled from annual Information Circulars of the U. S. Bureau of Mines entitled *Petroleum Refineries, Including Cracking Plants, in the United States* in the same manner that data on capacity were determined.

Year	Number of Small Refiners	Plants Owned by Small Refiners
1920	244	274
1930	230	257
1940	353	393
1950	193	218

Typically therefore the small refiner owned only a single plant. In contrast, the average number of plants owned by the 30 large companies varied from about 5 to 6 between 1930 and 1950. Moreover, the average number of plants owned by the 5 largest companies ranged from about 10 to 13 in this same period. There was a noticeable uptrend in plant holdings by large firms from 1920 to 1935 during a period of mergers and general expansion, and there was a downward trend in evidence between 1935 and 1950. As we shall observe in later chapters, the large companies were sometimes forced to close down their small plants for much the same reasons as small companies.

Average Size of Plants Owned by Small Refiners:

Throughout the period 1920–1950 the small refiner increased the average size of his plant. As may be seen in Exhibit XVIII-7, whereas the average size of the plants owned by the small refiners was about 1,600 barrels per day in 1920, the average size in 1950 was about 4,600 barrels per day.[15]

The small refiner did not, however, increase the average size of his plant as much as did his larger competitors. As a result, the discrepancy in plant size between large and small companies increased. As noted above, the average plant of the small refiner increased in size from 1,600 barrels per day in 1920 to 4,600 barrels per day in 1950, an increase of 190%. Meanwhile, the average size of the plants owned by the large companies increased from approximately 11,000 barrels per day in 1920 to 38,000 barrels per day in 1950, an increase of 245%. Between 1940 and 1950, however, the small refiners maintained a rate of plant growth exceeding that of the larger companies, registering an increase of 90% in the average size of plants between 1940 and 1950 as compared

with an increase of 60% for the plants of the large companies.[16]

The fact that there have been sound technological reasons for building oil refineries of a much larger size than oil producing "plants" or oil marketing "plants" is an important factor in explaining why the industry cannot sustain a large number of small refining firms whereas it can and does sustain thousands of small producers and marketers. By 1950 the average-size refinery in the industry had reached a capacity of nearly 20,000 barrels per day (see Exhibit XVIII-2). To maintain such a plant in operation, the oil output of approximately 2,000 producing wells was required. Moreover, the average-size plant in the industry yielded enough gasoline and naphthas to supply completely approximately 80 terminals and bulk plants and over 1,100 service stations.[17]

The technological and economic reasons for building large refineries also help to explain why a large share of the industry refining capacity is held by a fairly small number of companies. In 1950 for example, there were 47 refineries with capacities of 40,000 barrels per day or more. Even if each of these plants had been owned by a separate company, 64.2% of the industry capacity would have been held by only 47 companies. As another means of illustrating the significance of the high proportion of the industry capacity represented by large plants, Exhibit XVIII-8 compares the capacity of the 30 largest plants with the capacity of the 30 largest firms in 1950. The 30 largest plants, all with capacities in excess of 50,000 barrels per day, accounted for 52.6% of the industry capacity. The 30 largest firms, which owned 119 plants in addition to the 30 largest plants, held 85.1% of the industry capacity. It is also interesting to note that the entire 218 plants owned by the small refiners had a combined capacity equal to only about 90% of that

---

[15] Average plant size figures calculated from data reported in annual Information Circulars of the U. S. Bureau of Mines entitled *Petroleum Refineries, Including Cracking Plants, in the United States.*

[16] The increase in the average size of plants reflects not only the enlargement of refineries but also the disappearance of many small plants that depressed the average in preceding years.

[17] Number of producing wells, bulk stations and terminals, and service stations needed to supply or distribute the products of a 20,000 barrels per day plant estimated on the basis of the average crude oil output per well and the average sales of gasoline through marketing facilities in the United States in 1950 (see Chapter Two).

Exhibit XVIII-7. Number and Capacity of Refineries by Company Size Groups: 1920–1950

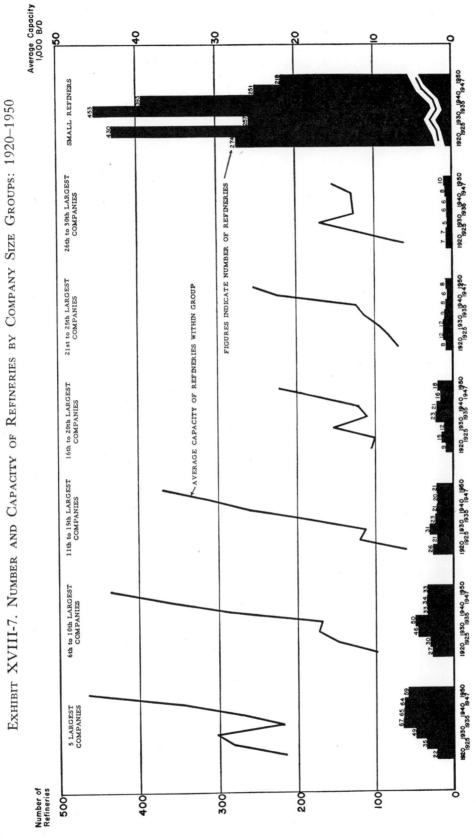

Source: Derived from U. S. Bureau of Mines records. See Appendix, Table 23, for data.

EXHIBIT XVIII-8. CUMULATIVE TOTAL REFINING CAPACITY
30 Largest Companies Versus 30 Largest Plants: 1950

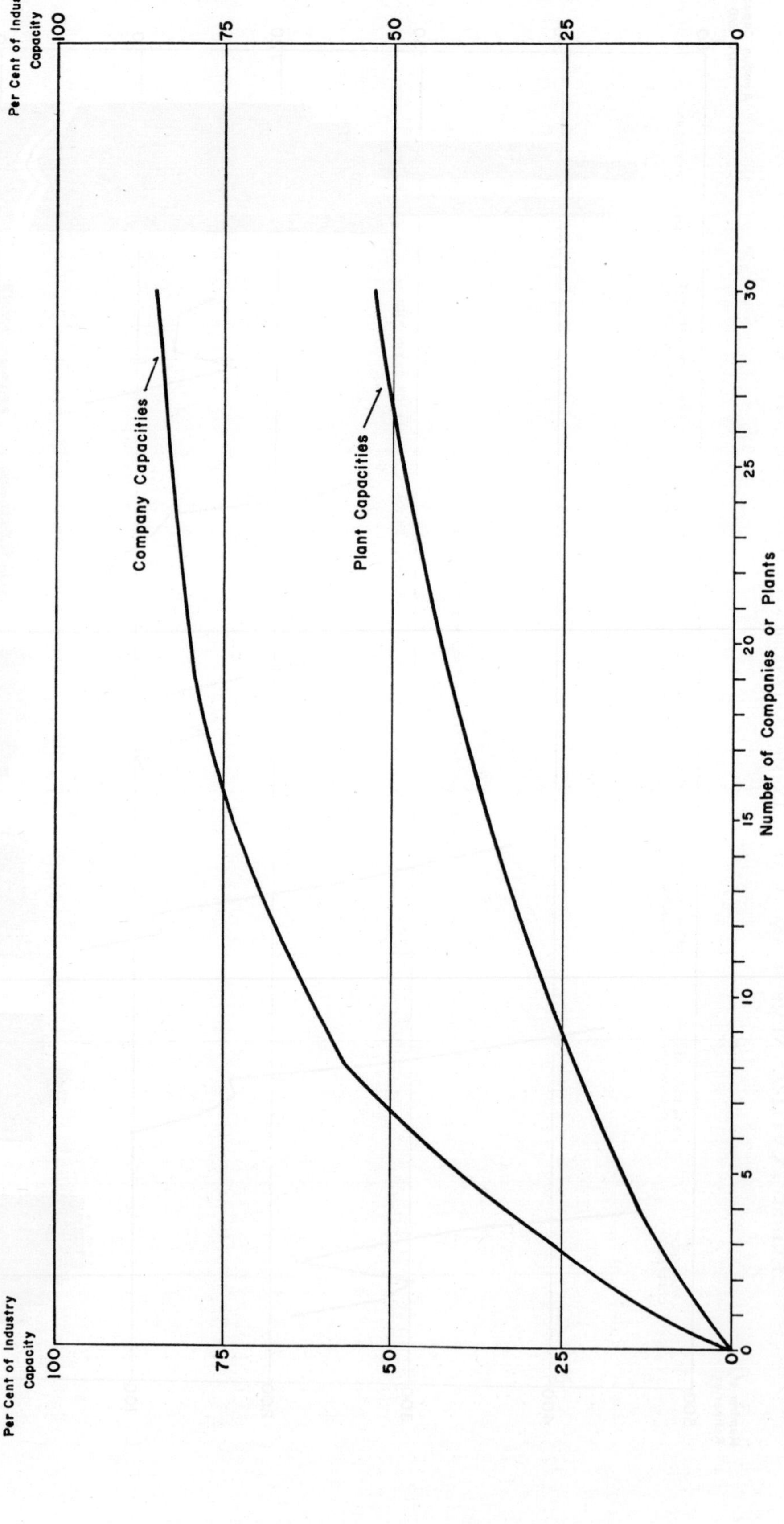

Per Cent of Industry Capacity

Company Capacities

Plant Capacities

Number of Companies or Plants

SOURCE: Derived from U. S. Bureau of Mines records.

Exhibit XVIII-9. Cracking Capacity of Small Refiners: 1935–1950

Year	Proportion of Industry's Crude Oil and Cracking Capacity Held by Small Refiners		Cracking Capacity per Barrel of Crude Oil Capacity		
	Percentage of Crude Oil Capacity	Percentage of Cracking Capacity	Small Companies	Large Companies	Small Companies as Percentage of Large
1935	21.6%	9.3%	.23 bbl.	.63 bbl.	36.5%
1940	20.4	12.2	.14	.25	56.0
1947	17.7	14.9	.23	.28	82.1
1950	14.9	13.0	.24	.28	85.7

Source: Derived from U.S. Bureau of Mines records.

of the five largest plants in the industry and equal to only about 75% of that of the two biggest companies in the industry.

Cracking Capacity of the Small Refiner:

The small refiners in the period 1935–1950 steadily improved their position relative to large companies with respect to the proportionate ownership of cracking facilities, but the disparity between large and small refiners was still appreciable in 1950. The small refiners were therefore at a disadvantage relative to the large firms in manufacturing high octane gasolines and increasing the percentage yields of the higher-price, light end products. As shown in Exhibit XVIII-9 the small refiners owned 37% as much cracking capacity per barrel of crude oil capacity as did the 30 largest companies in 1935, 56% as much cracking capacity per barrel of crude oil capacity as did the large companies in 1940, and 86% as much cracking capacity per barrel of crude oil capacity as did the large companies in 1950.[18]

The improvement in relative holdings of cracking facilities shown by the small refiners reflects not only the installation of new and expanded cracking plants but also the disappearance of many small firms that did not own cracking facilities. Information compiled from a Department of Commerce study indicates, for example, that approximately 140 firms without cracking plants went out of business be-tween January 1, 1940, and October 1, 1946, whereas only 30 companies with cracking facilities disappeared as a result of mergers, the sale or dismantling of refineries, or the dissolution of firms.[19]

Much of the new cracking capacity added after 1935 by small refiners consisted of thermal reforming processes designed to upgrade the quality of straight-run gasoline. The small firms, for reasons to be cited in Chapter Nineteen, lagged behind the large companies in the construction of catalytic processes which in many cases offer higher quality products, improved product yields, and greater process flexibility. Whereas 29 of the 30 largest companies owned catalytic processes in 1950, less than 20 of the 149 small refiners owned catalytic cracking and reforming units.[20]

As noted earlier in the chapter, approximately one-half of the small refiners did not have any cracking facilities whatsoever in 1950. Many of the plants without cracking facilities were very small and were, in quite a few cases, shut down. Since many of the noncracking plants were very small, the share of the industry's cracking facilities owned by all small firms was somewhat higher than might be anticipated from the fact that one-half of the small refiners had no cracking facilities. As shown in Exhibit XVIII-9, in 1950 the small firms owned 13.0% of the industry cracking capacity and 14.9% of the industry crude oil capacity.

[18] Derived from annual Information Circulars of the U. S. Bureau of Mines, *Petroleum Refineries, Including Cracking Plants, in the United States.* Beginning in 1938 the Bureau of Mines changed the basis of reporting cracking capacity from cracking stock charged to cracked gasoline produced (see U. S. Bureau of Mines, *Petroleum Refineries, Including Cracking Plants, in the United States,* January 1, 1938, Information Circular 7034).

[19] U. S. Department of Commerce, *U. S. Petroleum Refining: War and Postwar,* Industrial Series No. 73, prepared by Winona Patton, Industry Division, Office of Domestic Commerce (Washington, Government Printing Office, 1947).

[20] Prepared from information contained in "North American Operating Refineries," *The Oil and Gas Journal,* Vol. 48, No. 46, March 23, 1950, pp. 305–322.

Location of Small Refiners:

Throughout the period 1920–1950 the plants of the small firms were characteristically situated at various inland points near sources of crude oil supply, such as the Mid-Continent and the Rocky Mountain areas. While the large companies likewise owned smaller plants in the less densely populated areas of the country, a far greater portion of their capacity was represented by the large plants situated at points from which great metropolitan areas could be supplied economically, such as the Gulf and East Coasts and the metropolitan areas of the Middle West. As a means of illustrating the regional changes in refining activity, Exhibit XVIII-10 has been prepared. The exhibit shows, for seven selected years between 1920 and 1950, the percentage of the industry operating capacity, the number of operating refineries, and the average size of the operating plants in 13 areas of the country.[21]

As might be anticipated in view of the decline in the share of operating capacity held by small firms, the operating refining capacity in the areas where small firms have participated most actively has declined relative to that of other areas better situated with respect to metropolitan markets. This observation pertains only to the prominence of individual refining areas relative to the capacity of the industry. Actually, each of the 13 areas defined on the map showed an over-all increase in total physical capacity over the 30-year period.

The most serious decline in proportionate position was suffered by the Mid-Continent area which includes the Oklahoma-Kansas-Missouri, inland Texas, and Arkansas-Louisiana inland areas of the map. The proportion of the industry operating capacity in the Mid-Continent area declined from 33.0% in 1920 to 13.1% in 1950. Meanwhile, the Gulf Coast refining region emerged as the most important in the nation, with operating capacity increasing from 15.2% to 30.7% of the industry total. Four other areas—the East Coast area; the Metropolitan Lake Shore area; the metropolitan

area including Wood River, Illinois, Indianapolis, Indiana, and Cincinnati, Ohio; and the Michigan area—contained an appreciably greater proportion of the industry operating capacity in 1950 than they did in 1920. Of the areas showing an increase, only the Michigan area had a substantial amount of small refining activity. Each of the five areas showing a decline in proportionate holdings of operating capacity, on the other hand, had a considerable amount of small refining activity.

It may be observed from Exhibit XVIII-10 that the number of operating refineries in a particular region sometimes changed dramatically over very brief periods of time. For example, the number of operating refineries located at inland points in Texas increased from 64 to 91 between the years 1930 and 1935; by 1940 the number of operating refineries had declined to 72, and by 1947 the number of refineries had fallen to 49. Similarly, in the southern Great Lakes area, excluding the metropolitan areas of Wood River, Indianapolis, and Cincinnati, the number of operating refineries increased from 17 in 1935 to 31 in 1940 and then fell off rapidly to only 19 in 1947. In the Oklahoma-Kansas-Missouri area the number of operating refineries dropped from 124 in 1920 to 76 in 1925. Thereafter the decline was more gradual but continuous. Some of the reasons for the marked changes which took place over very short periods of time in the number of refineries in specific areas will be discussed in Chapter Twenty.

It is interesting to note that there have been significant regional differences in the average size of refineries since 1920. As shown in Exhibit XVIII-9, the regional size differentials have tended to become even more pronounced in recent years. Gulf Coast refineries attained an average operating capacity of 65,900 barrels per day in 1950. In contrast, refineries in the Oklahoma-Kansas-Missouri area had an average operating capacity of approximately 13,300 barrels per day, while the refineries at inland points in Texas had an average operating capacity of only 6,400 barrels per day. The marked disparities in size suggest the possibility that a premium was placed on the efficiency of large-scale manufacturing in metropolitan supply areas while other cost factors were of greater importance in the less densely

---

[21] The data for Exhibit XVIII-10 were derived from annual Information Circulars of the U. S. Bureau of Mines, *Petroleum Refineries, Including Cracking Plants, in the United States.* The 13 refining areas shown in Exhibit XVIII-10 do not, however, coincide with the U. S. Bureau of Mines refinery districts.

EXHIBIT XVIII-10. GEOGRAPHIC SHIFTS IN LOCATION OF U.S. REFINING
CAPACITY AND NUMBER AND SIZE OF PLANTS: 1920–1950

(Operating Capacity and Operating Plants Only)

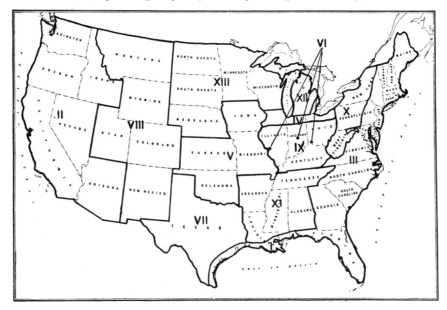

I. GULF COAST AREA

	1920	1925	1930	1935	1940	1947	1950
Number of Plants	20	23	18	25	35	36	29
Average Size of Plants (B/D)	11,555	19,829	36,927	30,200	33,403	43,441	65,922
Capacity as a % of U. S. Total	15.2%	18.2%	18.3%	20.9%	27.8%	29.3%	30.7%

II. WEST COAST AREA

	1920	1925	1930	1935	1940	1947	1950
Number of Plants	41	56	54	64	74	54	52
Average Size of Plants (B/D)	7,568	11,693	16,476	11,866	10,853	17,924	20,607
Capacity as a % of U. S. Total	20.2%	26.1%	24.5%	21.0%	19.2%	18.2%	17.2%

III. EAST COAST AREA

	1920	1925	1930	1935	1940	1947	1950
Number of Plants	22	17	24	25	23	23	22
Average Size of Plants (B/D)	9,410	23,218	25,208	24,540	26,839	35,193	42,059
Capacity as a % of U. S. Total	13.5%	15.8%	16.6%	17.0%	14.8%	15.2%	14.8%

IV. METROPOLITAN LAKE SHORE

	1920	1925	1930	1935	1940	1947	1950
Number of Plants	12	15	16	16	21	17	18
Average Size of Plants (B/D)	6,017	7,660	15,487	19,453	19,238	30,181	34,923
Capacity as a % of U. S. Total	4.7%	4.6%	6.8%	8.6%	9.6%	9.6%	10.2%

V. MID–CONTINENT AREA (Northern Region)

	1920	1925	1930	1935	1940	1947	1950
Number of Plants	124	76	60	54	44	43	37
Average Size of Plants (B/D)	2,781	4,715	7,283	7,880	8,286	9,816	13,287
Capacity as a % of U. S. Total	22.5%	14.4%	12.1%	11.8%	8.7%	7.9%	7.9%

VI. METROPOLITAN WOOD RIVER, INDIANAPOLIS AND CINCINNATI

	1920	1925	1930	1935	1940	1947	1950
Number of Plants	3	4	3	6	6	8	8
Average Size of Plants (B/D)	9,666	12,675	27,000	13,833	16,350	26,512	33,538
Capacity as a % of U. S. Total	1.9%	2.0%	2.2%	2.3%	2.3%	4.0%	4.3%

VII. MID–CONTINENT AREA (Texas Inland)

	1920	1925	1930	1935	1940	1947	1950
Number of Plants	52	52	64	91	72	49	38
Average Size of Plants (B/D)	2,842	2,877	3,962	3,229	3,546	5,502	6,366
Capacity as a % of U.S. Total	9.7%	6.0%	7.0%	8.1%	6.1%	5.0%	3.9%

VIII. ROCKY MOUNTAIN AREA

	1920	1925	1930	1935	1940	1947	1950
Number of Plants	14	19	32	68	75	51	44
Average Size of Plants (B/D)	4,778	7,072	4,475	1,236	1,401	3,129	5,470
Capacity as a % of U. S. Total	4.4%	5.4%	4.0%	2.3%	2.5%	3.0%	3.8%

IX. SOUTHERN GREAT LAKES AREA
(Excludes Metropolitan Centers in Area VI.)

	1920	1925	1930	1935	1940	1947	1950
Number of Plants	18	19	18	17	31	19	18
Average Size of Plants (B/D)	2,233	2,797	4,957	3,983	3,898	7,768	10,241
Capacity as a % of U. S. Total	2.6%	2.2%	2.4%	1.9%	2.9%	2.8%	2.9%

X. APPALACHIAN AREA

	1920	1925	1930	1935	1940	1947	1950
Number of Plants	58	54	48	38	31	24	20
Average Size of Plants (B/D)	1,165	1,509	2,129	3,353	3,595	4,974	5,862
Capacity as a % of U. S. Total	4.4%	3.2%	2.8%	3.5%	2.6%	2.2%	1.9%

XI. MID–CONTINENT AREA
(Arkansas-Louisiana Inland)

	1920	1925	1930	1935	1940	1947	1950
Number of Plants	7	27	17	13	16	16	14
Average Size of Plants (B/D)	1,657	2,017	6,698	5,642	5,700	5,112	5,639
Capacity as a % of U. S. Total	0.8%	2.0%	3.1%	2.0%	2.2%	1.5%	1.3%

XII. MICHIGAN (Excludes Detroit Area)

	1920	1925	1930	1935	1940	1947	1950
Number of Plants	—	—	4	10	21	14	13
Average Size of Plants (B/D)	—	—	1,875	2,005	2,311	3,807	4,367
Capacity as a % of U. S. Total	—	—	0.2%	0.6%	1.1%	1.0%	0.9%

XIII. NORTHERN PLAINS AREA

	1920	1925	1930	1935	1940	1947	1950
Number of Plants	2	1	—	8	10	7	7
Average Size of Plants (B/D)	1,000	1,000	—	67	804	2,373	2,110
Capacity as a % of U. S. Total	0.1%	0.1%	—	0.1%	0.2%	0.3%	0.2%

Note: Figures for 1920 are for operating and shutdown plants. Data for operating plants in 1920 are not available.

SOURCE: Derived from U. S. Bureau of Mines records

populated areas. The relative importance of processing and other types of costs to the competitive well-being of refineries will be considered at various points throughout the remainder of Part Four.

III. SUMMARY

1. For the purposes of discussion in Part Four of the book, we shall use the term "small refiner" to describe any company not among the largest 30 in terms of refining capacity. While the small refining company has typically represented a substantial business enterprise from a financial and operating standpoint, it has had a lesser degree of integration and has owned both smaller and less well-equipped plants than have the large companies. The small refining companies also have been far fewer in number, have conducted less of the industry's operations, have developed weaker functional relationships with the large companies, and have encountered more formidable obstacles in entering the industry than have small producers and small marketers.

2. The number of active and inactive small refining companies declined approximately 20% in the period 1920–1950. There was, however, no consistent long-term downward trend in the number of small firms as evidenced by the fact that the number of firms in 1920 and 1940 was greater than the number of firms in 1930 or 1950. A very marked decline of about 45% occurred in the small refiner population between 1940 and 1950.

3. There was a proportionate decline in the participation of small firms in the affairs of the industry in the period 1920–1950. The small refiners owned 28.4% of the industry refining capacity in 1920 and only 14.9% of the industry capacity in 1950. The most appreciable decline in the proportionate ownership of facilities by small firms occurred between 1925 and 1930, but there was also a significant reduction between 1940 and 1950. In every year for which data were compiled, the small refiners owned a smaller share of the industry operating capacity than they did of operating and shutdown refining capacity.

4. The small refiners owned a smaller proportion of the industry refineries in 1950 than at any other time over the preceding 30 years. The actual number of plants owned by small firms was, moreover, subject to very appreciable fluctuations over very short periods of time. Throughout the 1920–1950 period small companies characteristically owned a single plant whereas the large companies typically engaged in multiplant operations.

5. The small refiner increased the average size of his plant considerably over the period 1920–1950, but the disparity in the size of plants owned by large and small firms increased because the large companies maintained a rate of plant growth greater than that of the small firms. In 1950 the average capacity of the 149 plants owned by 30 large companies was approximately 38,000 barrels per day whereas the average capacity of the 218 refineries owned by the small refiners was only 4,600 barrels per day.

6. Between 1935 and 1950 the small refiners improved their position relative to the large companies with respect to the ownership of the industry cracking capacity. Whereas the small refiners owned only 37% as much cracking capacity per barrel of crude oil distillation capacity as the large companies in 1935, the small firms owned 87% as much cracking capacity per barrel of crude oil capacity as the large firms in 1950. Approximately one-half of the small refiners in 1950 did not, however, own any cracking processes.

7. As might be anticipated from the decline in the proportionate participation of small firms, the refining areas where small firms were most active lost ground proportionately to other refinery centers better situated to supply metropolitan consuming areas. For example, operating capacity in the Mid-Continent area declined from 35.1% of the industry total in 1920 to 13.3% in 1950; meanwhile, operating capacity along the Gulf Coast increased from 15.2% to 30.7% of the industry total. A study of plant location reveals, moreover, that the number of small refineries in certain areas close to sources of crude oil supply changed markedly over some very short periods of time.

CHAPTER NINETEEN

The Impact of Technological Change on the Opportunities for the Small Refiner

ONE of the most important factors contributing to the decline in the proportionate participation of the small refiner has been the continual advance in refinery technology which has taken place since 1900. The development of refinery processes has been highly dynamic, and the state of the refining art has been undergoing change at a seemingly ever-accelerating pace. It was a widely held view among "refiners" in 1952 that it was impossible to build a completely modern refinery. Although all the latest developments might be embodied in the design of a new plant, the refinery would inevitably be obsolete in some respects before it was erected and on stream. During the course of our field research, the former president of a small refining company which had gone out of business summarized the nature of the problem posed by technological advancement in these words: "During our entire history, we were under continued financial strain because of the need for more and more brick, mortar, and steel at the refinery. It was a hopeless treadmill."

The advances in refinery technology have resulted in improved yields of desired products, higher quality products, lower operating costs for particular operations, and greater process flexibility. To remain competitive therefore a refiner has been under strong compulsion to make basic changes continually in his refinery equipment. As later discussion will point out, the changes have called for very substantial capital outlays for plant equipment. The refiners who have lacked the money or the willingness to spend it have inevitably fallen by

NOTE: The factual data concerning the historical refineries discussed in this chapter were developed in conjunction with the Standard Oil Development Company. The authors alone, however, assume full responsibility for the analysis and interpretation of the data.

the wayside or at best continued in business under severe handicaps.

In this chapter we shall: (a) trace briefly the major developments in refinery technology over the period 1910–1950, (b) examine the economic significance of the changes and the corollary competitive pressures which were placed upon refiners to adopt them, and (c) appraise the magnitude of the dollar increases in capital investment which were required to maintain a competitive operation in the refining business.

I. THE EVOLUTION OF REFINERY EQUIPMENT

Over a long span of years, technological progress in the refining industry has been characterized by a series of ascending plateaus of accomplishment. A principal discovery has often been followed by a period during which more gradual improvements were made. Eventually, another major discovery then raised the stage of the refining art to an entirely new plane. In order to trace the evolution of refinery equipment, we determined the capital costs, equipment make-up, and operating characteristics of representative refineries at six selected time points in the period 1910–1950. Each of the time points selected for study lay within the span of years in which a new plateau of refinery technology was attained.

The representative refineries that we shall consider as a means of illustrating successive plateaus of technological progress were distinguished from one another by the commercialization of one or more principal pieces of processing equipment as indicated in Exhibit XIX-1. Beginning with shell stills in 1910, the rising plateaus were defined by Burton pressure stills in 1915; pipe stills, fractionating towers, and tube and tank thermal cracking in 1927; combination units, reforming, and visbreaking in 1935; and fluid catalytic cracking, nonselective polymerization, and vacuum distillation in 1946 and 1950.

There are two refineries shown for the year 1950; one plant is of conventional design and the second is a catalytic combination unit. The conventional refinery was more typical of the modern plants in existence in 1950 and was on a somewhat higher level of the same technological plateau as the 1946 plant. While there was little basic change in the equipment comprising the 1946 and 1950 conventional refineries, it was considered desirable to carry the analysis as far forward as our data would permit. The catalytic combination unit refinery, already feasible in 1950, portends the next higher plateau of refinery technology which might be reached if this type of plant is adopted generally by the industry.

The process equipment shown in Exhibit XIX-1 for each plant was representative of the most modern in existence at the time. In most cases, the years shown predate somewhat those in which the new processes gained widespread commercial acceptance.

It was assumed that each of the refineries was designed exclusively for manufacturing the prime petroleum fuels, i.e., gasoline, kerosene, distillate, and residual fuel oils. The prime fuels have usually been manufactured by virtually all refining companies, and most firms have restricted their operations solely to these prime fuels. The equipment in the different refineries was selected to give over-all product yields consistent with those of the period being considered. It should be noted that there was some latitude in the selection of the particular pieces of processing equipment which would give the desired product yields at the different time points. The particular pieces of equipment included in the seven refineries are therefore representative of the state of the art at the time period under consideration but do not include all the new and important process discoveries that might possibly have achieved substantially the same objectives.

The discussion which follows is confined to the sweeping changes brought about in the principal processing components of prime fuel refineries. At this point, we can merely mention that other pieces of processing equipment, such as pumps, condensers, and heat exchangers, have also undergone continued mechanical improvement since their first appearance; that special metal alloys have been developed and compounded to withstand extreme conditions of heat and temperature; and that many progressive steps have been taken in the development of refinery control mechanisms and instrumentation. In fact, a succession of little steps was necessary to make possible each of the major advances which marked the beginning of a new and higher plateau of technology. Moreover, it should be recognized that the changes brought about in the major pieces of processing equipment at prime fuel refineries, as discussed in subsequent paragraphs, were paralleled by no less impressive innovations in the manufacturing processes for lubricating oils and waxes and in the treating processes for various refined products.

1910 Refinery—Shell Stills:

Exhibit XIX-2 is a picture of one of the most modern refineries in existence in the year 1910. The principal processing equipment in the 1910 refinery was a battery of horizontal, cylindrical stills, called shell stills, into which crude oil was charged on a continuous basis.

In order to permit continuous operations, several shell stills were connected in series with each still located at a lower level than the preceding one. The crude oil flowed by gravity feed from one still to the next. Fires at progressively higher temperatures were built under succeeding stills. The lowest boiling point constituents of the crude oil were vaporized in the first still; the residue flowed to the next still where kerosene vapors were extracted at a somewhat higher temperature; higher boiling point fractions were removed in succeeding stills until only a heavy residue remained. The vapors passing from the various stills passed through condensers in which they were cooled and returned to a liquid state, and the various liquids then flowed directly to storage tanks.

Distillation in the battery of stills effected only a rudimentary separation of the products. The heavy residue remaining in the last still was heated until only a petroleum coke remained. To permit continuous operations, the

EXHIBIT XIX-1. REFINERY EQUIPMENT OF SEVEN REPRESENTATIVE REFINERIES: 1910–1950

Process	1910 Refinery	1915 Refinery	1927 Refinery	1935 Refinery	1946 Refinery	1950 Conventional Refinery	1950 Combination Unit Refinery
Distillation	Shell Stills	Shell Stills	Pipe Stills	Combination Unit Includes: Pipe Stills	Atmospheric and Vacuum Pipe Stills	Atmospheric and Vacuum Pipe Stills	Catalytic Combination Unit Includes: Atmospheric Pipe Still
Cracking	None	Burton Pressure Stills	Thermal Cracking (Tube and Tank)	Thermal Cracking Reforming Visbreaking	Fluid Catalytic Cracking	Fluid Catalytic Cracking Visbreaking	Thermal Reforming Fluid Catalytic Cracking Fractionation
Light Ends Recovery	None	None	Absorption Plant	Absorption Plant Stabilizer	Absorption Plant Splitter Debutanizer Nonselective Polymerization	Stabilizer Absorber Splitter Debutanizer Nonselective Polymerization Polymer Rerunning	Light Ends Recovery
Treating							
Natural Naphtha	Doctor Treat	Doctor Treat	Doctor Treat	Gray Vapor — Phase Treating	Copper Chloride and Air Sweetening	Continuous Caustic and Water Wash Copper Chloride	Caustic and Water Washed and Doctor Sweetened
Cracked Naphtha	None	Batch Acid, Caustic	Continuous Acid, Caustic	Gray Vapor — Phase Treating	Copper Chloride and Air Sweetening	Clay Treat Copper Chloride	Caustic and Water Washed and Doctor Sweetened
Kerosene	Batch Acid, Caustic	Batch Acid, Caustic	Batch Acid, Caustic	Continuous Caustic and Water Wash	Continuous Caustic and Water Wash	Continuous Caustic and Water Wash Sand Filter Clay Strain	None
Heating Oil	None	None	None	Continuous Acid, Caustic	Sand Filter	Continuous Caustic and Water Wash Sand Filter Clay Strain	Continuous Caustic and Water Wash

heavy residue was diverted alternately to two or more stills. While one batch was being reduced to coke and cleaned out, a second still was filled with another run of the heavy liquid residue.

No very sharp separations could be made between products of different boiling point ranges by means of the distillation process employed by the 1910 refinery. Gasoline fractions often included some kerosene fractions, while kerosene was diluted with both gasoline and distillate fuels. Some redistillation of the primary fractions was employed to obtain cleaner cuts. One redistillation process used was the forerunner of the modern fractioning tower. Vapors were passed through inclined tubes in which the highest boiling point products were condensed and returned to the still for redistillation, thereby effecting a cleaner separation of products.

While the 1910 refinery was very elementary compared with those of later years, it represented a distinct advance over the units utilized in the very early years of the industry. Initially, crude oil was batch-distilled in vertical cylindrical stills called "cheesebox stills." In these stills, only one batch of crude oil could be processed at one time. As the fire beneath the still increased the temperature of the oil, products of successively higher boiling point ranges were vaporized. These products were condensed and passed to storage tanks. At predetermined points, gauged by the gravity of the distillate, the flow of condensed products was diverted to different storage tanks. Since the products were somewhat co-mingled, the kerosene was frequently "weathered" (allowed to stand in the open) to permit the volatile gasoline fractions to evaporate. The very early stills had to be shut down frequently to permit the coke deposits to be removed.

In the period before 1900 cheesebox stills were gradually superseded by horizontal shell stills, which offered advantages in terms of fuel economy and reductions in other unit cost elements through the increased scale of operations. The early shell stills, like the cheesebox stills, however, permitted the processing of only one batch at a time. As the demand for petroleum products increased, the batch-operated stills proved inadequate to supply the growing market. The fact that domestic refinery runs increased from 142,000 to 331,000 barrels per day in the period from 1899 to 1909 indicates the magnitude of the problem posed by increasing demand.[1] A continuous method of operation which would greatly increase the total productive capacity of the industry was a necessity. The 1910 refinery described above embodied the first significant advancement in refinery technique, continuous processing.

1915 Refinery—Burton Pressure Stills:

The basic processing equipment of the 1915 refinery is pictured in Exhibit XIX-3. The 1915 refinery differed from the 1910 refinery principally through the addition of batch-operated, Burton pressure stills. The Burton pres-

sure stills were similar to the old batch-operated distillation stills, except that higher temperatures and pressures were employed to break down the molecules of straight-run gas oil into a cracked gasoline and a fuel oil heavier than the original charging stock. The new process was termed thermal cracking.

With advent of thermal cracking, petroleum refining underwent a very significant change. Thermal cracking was generally carried on as a supplementary processing operation to simple distillation, using one of the straight-run products as a charging stock. Simple distillation had merely separated some of the component products which were already present in crude oil whereas thermal cracking broke down the molecular structures of certain of the crude oil constituents and thereby converted heavy oil products into light ones.

The commercialization of thermal cracking was made necessary by the rapidly expanding market for automotive fuels. With the popularization of the automobile, refiners would have been confronted with the necessity of building up huge stocks of other unwanted by-products in order to satisfy the demand for gasoline unless a method had been found to increase the relative output of gasoline from each barrel of crude oil run. In the 15-year period 1899–1914 gasoline production was increased well over fourfold, and by 1918 the increase from 1899 was over twelvefold.[2] With the addition of Burton stills, the 1915 refinery yielded 35% more gasoline per barrel of crude oil run than did the 1910 refinery.

1927 Refinery—Pipe Stills, Fractionating Tower, Tube and Tank Thermal Cracking:

A picture of a modern, well-equipped refinery in the year 1927 is shown in Exhibit XIX-4. The 1927 refinery represented a radical improvement over the earlier methods of crude oil processing and incorporated three major advances: (a) pipe stills, (b) multiple level fractionating towers, and (c) tube and tank thermal cracking units.

The pipe still, which replaced the shell stills of the 1915 refinery, was first introduced to commercial practice in about 1912. In the pipe stills crude oil flowing continually through heated pipes was raised to a temperature which

---

[1] National Industrial Conference Board, Inc., *The Petroleum Almanac* (New York, 1946), p. 96.

[2] Ibid.

would completely vaporize all the desired products except some of the heaviest fuel oil. Pipe stills resulted in substantial unit savings in labor and fuel costs and paved the way for the very large capacity petroleum refineries which were later developed.

In the 1927 refinery the hot oil vapors from the pipe stills were passed into multiple level fractioning towers (commonly called bubble towers) where the condensation and separation of the petroleum vapors took place.[3] In the multiple level fractionating tower the rising vapors from the pipe still heater were washed and cooled by descending condensate as the ascending vapors bubbled through trays of liquid. The temperature in the column was regulated by the amount of reflux or distillate pumped back into the column for refractionation. The multiple level fractionating process made it possible to recover gasoline from the top of the column, and kerosene and light fuel oil distillates of closely defined boiling point ranges as side cuts at progressively lower levels of the column.[4] The fractionating tower eliminated a major portion of the costly rerunning of products which was formerly necessary and yielded products of closely defined specifications. The pipe still and fractionating tower have remained the predominant types of distillation equipment in refineries, al-

though numerous refinements have been made since 1927.

The tube and tank cracking process, the third major new feature of the 1927 refinery, was among the earliest of the continuously operating thermal cracking units.[5] Some of the improvements incorporated in its design were: (a) the heating of the charging stock in small tubes beneath the still to enhance heat transmission and to reduce the danger of explosion that existed when a large volume of oil was heated simultaneously; (b) the forced circulation of the oil in the heater tubes to impede the building up of coke, since coking had severely limited the length of runs and prevented deep cracking in older systems, and (c) the attainment of higher cracking pressures than was possible in the very early adaptations of the thermal cracking process.

Continuous cracking was necessary to supply the greatly increased demand for motor fuel. In addition to an over-all increase in demand for petroleum products in the years during and after World War I, the relative demand for gasoline continued to grow much more rapidly than that of other products. As a result of the growth in the automotive market, the consumption of gasoline was, by 1925, over 36 times as large as 1900 and over twice as large as 1920.[6] Moreover, the scarcity of crude oil that prevailed during World War I raised questions concerning the adequacy of our domestic crude oil reserves to meet the needs of the rapidly growing motoring public. Since cracking yielded a higher proportion of gasoline from each barrel of crude oil, it was viewed as an important oil conservation measure.

It was also in the 1920's that attention was first given to the ability of gasoline to resist knocking in engines. Tetraethyl lead was first introduced into motor fuels in 1923, and an octane scale was devised in 1927. The octane rating of gasoline is an objective measure of

[3] The fractionating tower, which made a sharper separation of products of different boiling point ranges possible, underwent many mutations from its embryonic stages as an inclined exposed vapor line. In all types of towers, vapors are passed into the towers directly from heating units. In the earlier towers, the condensation of higher boiling point vapors for subsequent redistillation was dependent upon cooling from contact with the tower shell. In a later development, the rising vapors were scrubbed and cooled by descending liquids, which were also being purified. At first, towers were packed with inert materials and, later, various enclosed metal plate arrangements were used to serve the same purpose. By counterflow of descending liquids and ascending vapors, the lowest boiling point constituents of the liquid were transformed into vapors and the highest boiling point constituents of the vapors were condensed into a liquid state. This continuous redistillation of products ensured that a minimum commingling of products of different boiling point ranges would take place. These processes aided materially in improving quality control.

[4] In an earlier system the oil vapors were fractionally condensed in a series of interconnected fractionating towers. From the first tower, that of the highest temperature, condensed residue was removed and all the lower boiling point vapors then passed on to the next tower. From the second tower unvaporized heavy distillates were obtained; from the third tower light fuel oil, and so on until only gasoline vapor remained.

[5] The cracking process was first made continuous with the development of the Dubbs process in 1921. As a part of this process the coke-forming materials which had caused frequent shutdowns were segregated from the clean products. The Dubbs and similar processes increased the yield of gasoline, permitted the cracking of heavier charging stocks, and increased the duration of the noninterrupted operating cycle.

[6] Consumption figures based upon gasoline production figures reported in National Industrial Conference Board, Inc., *The Petroleum Almanac* (New York, 1946), p. 96.

its ability to resist knocking in combustion engines. It was found that thermal cracking not only doubled the yield of gasoline from a barrel of crude oil but also yielded a product of a greatly superior antiknock quality. Although antiknock considerations were becoming of importance in 1927, they did not yet provide the great stimulus to the construction of cracking equipment that they were to foster in subsequent years.

1935 Refinery—Combination Unit, Reforming and Visbreaking:

The refinery shown in Exhibit XIX-5 was comprised of the most modern equipment available in the year 1935. The basic processing equipment was a combination unit which included crude oil distillation, thermal cracking, reforming, and visbreaking among its functions.

Beginning in the late 1920's and extending up to the present time, there has been a tendency to consolidate different refinery operations into so-called "combination units." Combination units have often offered several advantages over the conventional refineries in which each principal refining operation was conducted in a single unit. The advantages have included; (a) better heat exchange and the use of surplus heat from one step in the process at some other desired point; (b) reductions in refinery operating labor costs; and (c) reductions in construction and operating costs which were made possible through the use of a single piece of equipment common to several operations whenever possible; for example, one bubble tower might be used to fractionate both straight-run and cracked products and one furnace might be used to supply the heat required at several stages in the refining process.

The 1935 refinery had a combination unit for crude oil distillation, thermal cracking, thermal reforming, and visbreaking. Thermal reforming was used to crack straight-run gasoline and served to raise the octane number of the gasoline. Visbreaking was used for the mild cracking of heavy fuel oil and served to increase the free-flowing characteristics of the fuel oil and to increase the gasoline yield of the refinery as a whole.

Throughout the late 1920's and early 1930's the demand for higher antiknock (octane) gasolines gave an added impetus to the construction of cracking plants.[7] The development of higher compression ratio automotive engines, which enhanced operating efficiency, would not have been possible on the type of gasoline yielded by simple distillation. Meanwhile, the relative growth in the demand for gasoline and the higher price it commanded continued to exert a pressure for higher gasoline yields, as it had since the turn of the century. The large increases in the cracking capacity of the industry during the late 1920's and early 1930's were an outgrowth of these economic factors.

1946 Refinery—Fluid Catalytic Cracking, Non-selective Polymerization, and Vacuum Distillation:

The refinery pictured in Exhibit XIX-6 was made up of equipment representative of the most modern in existence during 1946. It was distinguished from the refineries of previous years principally by the addition of a fluid catalytic cracking unit, which replaced the older thermal cracking processes, and by a polymerization unit, which yielded a high octane gasoline from gaseous by-products.

The fluid catalytic cracking unit performed the cracking operation on vaporized gas oil in the presence of a catalyst which speeded the chemical reaction without undergoing any chemical change itself, except possibly contamination.[8] With the aid of a catalyst, the rate of cracking was increased, more moderate temperatures and pressures were employed than in thermal cracking, and greater yields of higher octane gasoline were obtained. The pressure toward achieving a higher quality gasoline product was a most important one in

---

[7] The efforts to secure higher octane numbers also resulted in the development and installation of vapor phase cracking processes during these same years. In vapor phase cracking, high temperatures or pressures were applied in chambers containing vaporized gas oil rather than chambers containing the liquid itself.

[8] The first commercially successful catalytic cracking process, the Houdry process, was put into operation in 1935. There were several commercial adaptations of the catalytic cracking process, employing various methods for commingling a catalyst with petroleum vapors and for reactivating the catalyst when it became coated with carbon. The variations included the Houdry, Thermofor, Cycloversion, Suspensoid, and Fluid processes, as well as various later adaptations of these processes.

EXHIBIT XIX-2. 1910 REFINERY—SHELL STILL

Courtesy: Standard Oil Company (New Jersey).

EXHIBIT XIX-3. 1915 REFINERY—BURTON PRESSURE STILLS

Courtesy: Standard Oil Company (Indiana).

EXHIBIT XIX-4. 1927 REFINERY—PIPE STILLS, FRACTIONATING TOWER,
TUBE AND TANK THERMAL CRACKING

Courtesy: Standard Oil Company (New Jersey).

EXHIBIT XIX-5. 1935 REFINERY—COMBINATION UNIT (DISTILLATION, THERMAL
CRACKING, REFORMING, AND VISBREAKING)

Courtesy: Standard Oil Company (Indiana).

EXHIBIT XIX-6. 1946 REFINERY—ATMOSPHERIC AND VACUUM DISTILLATION, FLUID
CATALYTIC CRACKING, AND NONSELECTIVE POLYMERIZATION

Courtesy: Standard Oil Company (New Jersey).

Exhibit XIX-7. 1950 Refinery—Fluid Catalytic Cracking Unit

Courtesy: Standard Oil Company (New Jersey).

fostering the development of catalytic processes.[9]

The catalytic polymerization unit in the 1946 refinery recombined the molecules of highly volatile gases into more stable liquid products; in a sense therefore polymerization was the reverse of cracking.[10] In the manufacture of motor fuels by cracking, large quantities of by-product gases were released. Initially, these refinery gases were either wasted or burned as refinery fuel. As refiners carried on deeper cracking to meet the demand for a high octane gasoline product, gas losses became prohibitive. Catalytic polymerization provided a means for converting the gases into a polymer gasoline. Polymer gasoline not only increased the total yield of gasoline from cracking operations but was itself a high octane product valuable for blending purposes.

The 1946 refinery also included equipment for the vacuum distillation of petroleum products in addition to the atmospheric distillation which had been performed in the earlier refineries. Vacuum distillation was developed as a means of reducing the temperature at which different products would vaporize. Vacuum distillation helped to avoid the undesired decomposition or cracking of heavier petroleum fractions. Vacuum distillation, along with catalytic cracking, made possible higher yields of distillate fuel oils when conditions warranted. The increased yield of middle distillates was essential to supply the greatly increased demand for domestic heating oils which developed subsequent to 1935.

---

[9] Another important method for increasing the octane value of gasoline was the catalytic reforming of gasoline fractions. This process was first commercially introduced in 1940. While reforming was not required from a quality standpoint in the 1946 refinery, which included catalytic cracking among its processing equipment, the catalytic reforming process was gaining widespread attention as one means of obtaining an increase in octane numbers in refineries which did not have catalytic cracking. Investments for catalytic reforming processes were on a generally lower scale than those for catalytic cracking. The Houdry, Cycloversion, Platforming, Fluid Hydroforming, Thermofor, and Atlantic processes are among the more important of the catalytic reforming processes developed in recent years. Other catalytic processes, such as hydrogenation, one of the first commercially adapted catalytic processes, dehydrogenation, cyclization, isomerization, alkylation, and aromatization have aided the refiner in his efforts to achieve higher octane products.

[10] The first catalytic polymerization unit was introduced commercially in 1935. Thermal polymerization plants predated the first catalytic installations.

1950—Conventional Refinery—Fluid Catalytic Cracking, Nonselective Polymerization, Vacuum Distillation, and Visbreaking:

A fluid catalytic cracking unit typical of the one included in the 1950 refinery is shown in Exhibit XIX-7. The basic processing equipment included in the 1950 conventional refinery was similar to that of the 1946 refinery. The 1950 refinery was on essentially the same plateau of technological progress as the 1946 refinery, although later improvements were incorporated into the design of some of its equipment and a few supplementary pieces of processing equipment were added. In the 1950 fluid unit, for example, the reactor and the regenerator were placed on the same horizontal level and the height and complexity of these units were reduced. The changes permitted the cracking operation to be carried on with greater efficiency.

The 1950 conventional refinery also included equipment for the visbreaking or cracking of heavy fuel oil. The visbreaking process has already been discussed in connection with the 1935 plant. Other differences between the 1950 and 1946 plants were the addition of a stabilizer and a polymer rerunning tower to the light ends processing equipment and several variations in the treating processes for particular refined products. The supplementary pieces of equipment, in addition to certain changes made in the design of principal pieces of processing equipment, constituted the primary differences between the 1946 and 1950 conventional refineries.

1950 Combination Unit Refinery—Catalytic Combination Unit Includes Pipe Still, Thermal Reforming, Fluid Catalytic Cracking, Fractionation, and Light Ends Recovery:

The second 1950 refinery represents the same general type of advance in technology as the earlier combination unit refinery of 1935. It was included in this analysis primarily to emphasize the fact that the search for new and improved methods is a continuing process. In many respects, the combination unit refinery represented an alternative choice to the 1950 conventional refinery. Although the catalytic combination unit was not then widely adopted because of the tendency to add individual pieces of equipment such as catalytic cracking units to existing refineries, there were certain locations and circumstances under which combination units were installed in existing plants.

Because processing equipment was consolidated wherever possible in the design of the combination unit and many "frills" were eliminated, the 1950 combination unit refinery had much lower investment and operating costs than did the 1950 conventional refinery. On the other hand, the combination unit refinery sacrificed sales realizations because its typical products yields were not so advantageous as those of the conventional plant and because its flexibility to vary the yield of particular products over a wide range was likewise decreased. The combination unit refinery had only an atmospheric pipe still in contrast to atmospheric and vacuum stills in the 1946 and 1950 conventional refineries. The combination unit did not include polymerization equipment among its facilities and the various treating processes were greatly simplified. For certain purposes, however, its generally lower scale of investment and operating costs made the combination unit refinery a distinctly better plant than the 1950 conventional plant.

It is evident from the foregoing discussion of typical refineries spaced over a 40-year period that even more remarkable strides were made in technology in the period 1930–1950 than in the preceding years of the twentieth century. Before 1930 most of the advances were essentially mechanical in nature. With the growing knowledge of petroleum chemistry, the refining process became ever more intricate, relying to a much greater extent upon the realignment of petroleum molecules as a means of obtaining the desired products. In retrospect, it appears that the search for improved technology at the refining level of the industry has not only been relentless; the pace has also been accelerating.

II. The Economic and Competitive Significance of the Refinery Process Improvements

As each of the new and improved processes described in the preceding paragraphs became commercially feasible, very strong competitive pressures were exerted for its acceptance and installation by the industry. The gains offered by the new developments were such that it was incumbent upon refiners either to provide the funds for process improvements or to suffer losses in competitive position. The commercialization of new processes followed a fairly uniform pattern. Initially, some one company or group of companies installed a newly developed process with the expectation of gaining a competitive advantage over other firms. As soon as a new process gained a foothold in the industry, strong pressures were exerted on the remaining refiners to offset the competitive advantages secured by the pioneering group.

The competitive advantages secured by the refiners employing new processes resulted from the greater plant efficiency made possible by the new developments. The new equipment usually influenced plant efficiency in one or another of three general ways: (a) by yielding a mix of products with a higher sales realization, (b) by improving the quality of products, and (c) by reducing the unit processing costs incurred to obtain a particular yield of products of stipulated quality specifications.

These several aspects of plant efficiency were to a large extent interdependent. For example, a further processing step and hence increased unit costs were usually necessary to increase the yield and to improve the quality of gasoline beyond that attainable with a straight-run distillation unit. As a compensating factor to the increased costs, sales realization values were likewise higher since gasoline commanded a higher price than the gas oil charging stock and because a price differential was usually secured for gasoline of premium quality. In appraising the relative efficiency of refineries built at different time points over a 40-year period therefore, it would be meaningless to base the comparison on any single factor such as operating costs. Costs, product yields, and product quality must all be considered.

The reasons why individual pieces of new equipment were installed by particular companies were subject to wide variations. During our field research, for example, each of the following reasons for the installation of catalytic cracking facilities was cited by one company or another. One company was interested solely in the improved quality of gasoline which a catalytic cracking unit made possible. The company had no intention of varying its yield of refined products after the addition of the new unit. Another company desired not only a higher quality gasoline product but also a higher yield of gasoline to supply its gasoline requirements. Still another company was much interested in the flexibility offered by a catalytic unit to shift yields on a seasonal basis.

In other cases, the motivation for the installation of a catalytic cracking unit was primarily to adjust for shifts which had taken place in the demand for products which could alternatively be used as charging stocks for the new units. Still other companies advanced the reasoning that the increased sales resulting from the quality advantage secured from a new unit would lead to a higher rate of throughput on all principal processing units at a refinery, thereby effecting cost savings on other cracking and noncracking operations. In each situation, a refiner might or might not have anticipated a price premium for his improved gasoline product. Thus, the various competitive advantages made possible by any one type of equipment were weighted very differently in individual company situations. In this chapter, we can merely summarize the advantages the various processes offered, and recognize that the advantages assumed varying degrees of importance for different refiners.

Improvements in Product Yields and Sales Realizations:

As the relative demand for different refined products changed, it was necessary for refiners to install new processing equipment capable of extracting products from the various crude oils in conformance with market requirements. Exhibit XIX-8 shows the proportion of different principal products extracted from a barrel of crude oil at various times since 1899 and the product yields of the seven representative refineries discussed earlier in the chapter. The chart shows the marked growth in the demand for automotive gasoline, beginning about the time of World War I, and the sharp decline in the demand for kerosene which took place with the electrification of homes and industrial plants. The chart also reflects the increase in distillate demand for home heating purposes beginning in the 1930's and the more recent reduction in the demand for residual fuel oils

which accompanied the increase in the use of natural gas for heating purposes and the development of Diesel equipment for railroads.

In most cases, the seven representative refineries had refinery yields of light end products somewhat in excess of average yields throughout the United States. Two refineries, the 1915 and 1927 plants, had gasoline yields approximately equal to the United States average yields; the five other refineries had gasoline yields which were higher than the United States averages. The 1946 plant and the 1950 conventional refinery also had yields of gas oil and distillates in excess of United States average yields. All plants equalled or bettered the national average yield of kerosene. Only with respect to heavy fuel oil were the yields of the seven refineries consistently below United States averages. The generally higher proportion of light end products extracted from each barrel of crude oil by the historical refineries is explained principally by the fact that the plants incorporated advanced processes somewhat sooner than did most refineries in the industry.

The shifts in product yields brought about through new refining equipment have meant large savings in natural resources as well as dollar savings to consumers. Consider, for example, the relative cost in natural resources and in dollars of providing gasoline for the motoring public on the basis of the refinery yields which prevailed in the early part of the present century. In the period 1914–1945 as a whole, the use of cracking facilities approximately doubled the yield of gasoline obtained from crude oil [11] and thus made it possible to meet the requirements of the gasoline market with about one-half as much crude oil as would otherwise have been the case.

Refiners were motivated to take advantage of the improved product yields offered by the successively more advanced refineries because they could then derive a higher revenue from the sale of products made from each barrel of crude oil processed. In order to compare the relative sales realizations of the seven representative refineries, the product yields of each re-

[11] U. S. Bureau of Mines figures on the production of gasoline broken down by production method, such as straight distillation and cracking, reported in National Industrial Conference Board, *The Petroleum Almanac* (New York, 1946), p. 71.

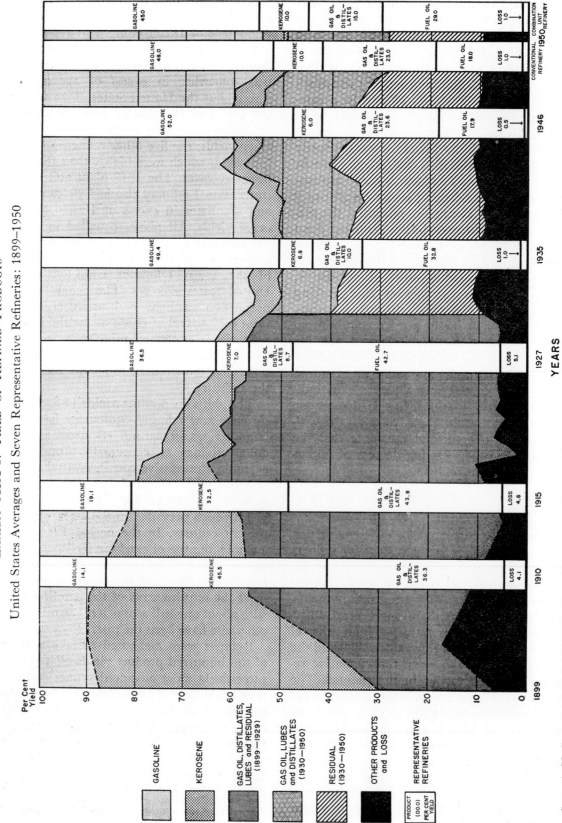

EXHIBIT XIX-8. YIELD OF REFINED PRODUCTS
United States Averages and Seven Representative Refineries: 1899–1950

SOURCE: U. S. average yields (1889–1944) from National Industrial Conference Board, *The Petroleum Almanac*, (National Industrial Conference Board, New York, 1946)
U. S. average yields (1945–1950) from American Petroleum Institute, *Statistical Bulletin*, Vol. XXXII, No. 31.

finery were priced on the basis of average prices existing in the New York cargo market for the year 1950. In making the comparison, it was necessary to assume that each of the earlier refineries could make products of a competitive quality in 1950, which actually was not the case (see later discussion in chapter). The sales realization values per barrel of crude oil processed were as follows: [12]

1910 Refinery	$3.92
1915 Refinery	3.94
1927 Refinery	3.52
1935 Refinery	3.96
1946 Refinery	4.25
1950 Refinery (Conventional)	4.20
1950 Refinery (Combination Unit)	3.99

Sales realizations ranged from a low of $3.52 for the 1927 refinery to $4.25 for the 1946 plant, a difference of 73 cents per barrel. The modern refineries which might have been erected after World War II had unit realizations ranging from 3 cents to 73 cents per barrel in excess of the earlier plants. In appraising these differences, it is helpful to note that a 1 cent differential per barrel amounts to an incremental income of over $90,000 yearly for a 25,000 barrels per day plant.

It should be remembered that a comparison based upon 1950 products and prices is purely hypothetical, since the generally inferior products of the older plants would have posed insurmountable marketing problems in 1950. The comparison of sales realization values, however, dramatizes the superiority of the modern refinery in serving the products markets which evolved in the United States and evidences the corollary pressure which was exerted upon refiners to make new process investments.

Improvements in Product Quality:

The effort to obtain higher quality products has been another very significant factor in moti-

vating investments for new and improved pieces of refinery equipment. Although decided quality improvements have been made in all the prime petroleum fuels, the achievements in gasoline have undoubtedly been those of paramount importance to the competitive position of refiners. Lacking space to examine the changes brought about in each one of the refined products, we have singled out gasoline for special consideration.

The race for a higher gasoline octane number, which is one measure of gasoline quality, has been such a prominent aspect of the competitive situation that it has often been referred to as "octane competition." The United States average octane rating of regular and premium gasoline, the average compression ratio of automobile engines, and the thermal efficiency of gasoline in years for which data were available throughout the period 1899–1950 are shown in Exhibit XIX-9. The thermal efficiency of gasoline is reported in the average ton-miles of movement secured from a gallon of gasoline at a speed of 50 miles per hour. Octane numbers, compression ratios, and the thermal efficiency of gasoline have all risen markedly over the time periods for which data were available. The trend toward higher compression engines which are more efficient in terms of fuel utilization has required a continual increase in the octane level of gasoline.

As octanes have moved to ever higher levels, refiners have been compelled to make additions or alterations in their equipment which would allow them to meet or surpass competitive octane standards. In Exhibit XIX-9, the octane rating of the gasolines obtainable from the seven representative refineries are reported. The octane numbers are reported for clear gasoline, in which no tetraethyl lead was added, for gasoline in which 1.5 cubic centimeters of tetraethyl lead were added per gallon of gasoline, and for gasoline in which 3 cubic centimeters of tetraethyl lead were added per gallon of gasoline.[13] Since the addition of tetraethyl lead to gasoline substantially increased octane numbers, the maximum octane quality obtainable from each refinery was in excess of the clear, nonleaded product. On a nonleaded basis, octane ratings were improved from a range of

---

[12] The sales realization values were predicated upon the running of an Illinois crude oil to the 1910 and 1915 refineries and a 50/50 mixture of East and West Texas crude oils to the five other plants. Since Illinois crude oil had a somewhat higher refinery value than a mixture of East and West Texas crude oils and would undoubtedly have cost more per barrel delivered to the East Coast, the sales realizations for the 1910 and 1915 refineries are somewhat overstated.

[13] A 3 cubic centimeter lead content was the maximum amount permissible per gallon of gasoline.

EXHIBIT XIX-9. QUALITY IMPROVEMENTS IN GASOLINE: 1899–1950

U. S. Average Octane Numbers and Octane Numbers Obtainable by Seven Representative Refineries

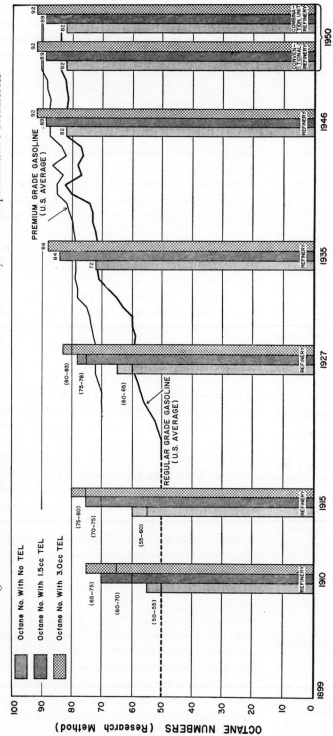

Average Engine Compression Ratios and Average Ton-Miles Per Gallon at 50 Miles Per Hour

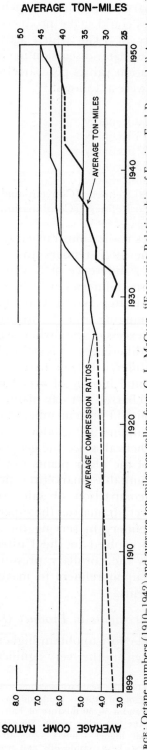

SOURCE: Octane numbers (1910–1942) and average ton-miles per gallon from C. L. McCuen, "Economic Relationship of Engine-Fuel Research," American Petroleum Institute, Mid-Year Meeting, Tulsa, Oklahoma, May 3, 1951. Octane numbers prior to 1910 assumed to have remained constant. Octane numbers (1943–1950) from Ethyl Corporation data. Average compression ratios from *Automotive Industries* and Ethyl Corporation Surveys.

about 50 to 55 in the 1910 refinery to 82 in the 1950 refineries. With maximum lead blending, the increase in octane quality was from a range of 67 to 75 in the 1910 plant to 92 in the 1950 refineries.[14]

The older refineries could not meet the United States average octane number standards that developed in the war and postwar period even with the addition of maximum quantities of tetraethyl lead. It might be noted, however, that the ability of the earlier refineries to meet octane standards varied in different geographic areas. In some regions, such as the East Coast and the Mid-West, octane numbers were frequently higher than the average for the entire United States. In other areas, such as the Rocky Mountain area, octane specifications were usually lower than the United States average.

Using United States averages as a measure, it is evident that only the postwar refineries were equipped to manufacture a gasoline of competitive quality in 1950. In certain areas, and with nearly maximum additions of tetraethyl lead, the 1935 refinery was also competitive from a quality standpoint. The cost of extra quantities of lead for blending purposes, however, created an extra cost for the 1935 refinery that the postwar plants did not have to bear.

Throughout the years, and particularly with the advent of catalytic cracking, the installation of new processes was necessary if a fully competitive gasoline product was to be obtained. The problem confronting the refiner has been that the premium gasoline of one day became the regular gasoline of the next; without the continual installation of new equipment and the expenditure of large sums of money therefore, the refiner was unable to make products that would meet competitive specifications.

After about 1935 the octane competition made possible by improved technology moved to the foreground as a contributor to the disappearance of small firms. Over a very brief span of years all the following changes took place in the refining industry:

1. The cracked gasoline capacity of catalytic cracking plants increased from 56,420 barrels per day on January 1, 1941, to 780,810 barrels per day on January 1, 1951. By January 1951 catalytic cracking capacity was slightly in excess of thermal cracking capacity.[15]
2. The United States average octane rating of regular grade gasoline increased from 74 in the period immediately before 1940 to 83.9 in 1950. The average octane rating of premium gasoline was raised from 82 to 90.4 during the same period.
3. The number of refining companies with either operating or shutdown facilities declined from 383 on January 1, 1940, to 223 on January 1, 1950. As reported in Chapter Two, the number of operating refining companies on December 31, 1950 did not exceed 179. The total number of refineries declined from 547 to 367 in the 10-year period.[16]
4. Between January 1, 1940, and October 1, 1946, approximately 140 firms without any cracking facilities, approximately 30 firms with thermal cracking facilities, and no firms with catalytic cracking units went out of business.[17]

These points provide a brief synopsis of the more recent stages of the "octane squeeze." As later discussion in the chapter will point out, very substantial sums of money were required to install the catalytic units which could yield competitive products. The great preponderance of the capital for new catalytic units was supplied by the larger companies. The large capital investments required for catalytic processes created a financial problem which made very definite inroads on the number of small firms engaged in refining.

The small firm was also particularly hard hit by the evolution of catalytic cracking because

---

[14] All octane numbers reported in this chapter were determined by the research testing method. Several methods are used to calculate the octane rating of fuels, of which the motor and research methods are two of the most important. The research method gives higher numbers for most fuels than the motor method. In general, the octane number of a gasoline is determined by ascertaining the volume per cent of isooctane in that mixture of isooctane and normal heptane which gives the same knock tendencies as the gasoline in question.

[15] U. S. Bureau of Mines, *Petroleum Refineries, Including Cracking Plants, in the United States,* January 1, 1951, I. C. 7163.
[16] See Chapter Eighteen.
[17] Ibid.

there were technical and economic difficulties encountered in adapting catalytic processes for use in very small refinery installations. The smallest technically feasible catalytic cracking unit was originally too large for installation in the plants of many very small refiners. It was, moreover, considerably more difficult for a small catalytic cracking unit to support a payout than it was for a large one.

It is extremely important to note that from a technological standpoint, catalytic processing equipment was readily accessible to the small firms. At no time during our field research did a small refiner express any dissatisfaction whatsoever with respect to either the granting of licenses on new processes or the royalty terms under which the licenses were available. It was rather the magnitude of the initial investment necessary for construction of the advanced processes that provided the obstacle to their employment by small firms.

The later introduction of catalytic reforming processes, such as platforming, to upgrade low-octane gasoline fractions offered a means by which the small companies could meet the octane challenge without the extremely large investments required for catalytic cracking units. Even with the various catalytic reforming processes, however, in which much of the product yield flexibility of catalytic cracking was lost, the cost of equipping a refinery to meet the requirements of the market was still very high.

One somewhat surprising factor is that the number of small refiners was not reduced to an even greater extent by the increase in octane numbers during and after World War II. One reason why many small refiners were able to operate satisfactorily is that they used methods other than catalytic cracking to improve the octane quality of their gasoline. Among the more common methods which were employed by small refiners to obtain gasolines of a salable quality without catalytic processes were: (a) the blending of maximum quantities of tetraethyl lead into gasoline stocks, (b) the employment of very deep thermal cracking, which yielded higher octane gasolines but led to excessive gas losses, (c) the use of polymerization plants to obtain a high octane blending stock from by-product refinery gases, (d) the purchase of high octane blending stocks such as

natural gasoline and catalytically cracked gasoline, and (e) the widespread installation of thermal reforming plants to up-grade the quality of low-grade gasoline. Some of the methods employed by small firms to obtain higher octane gasolines were often relatively expensive as compared with the incremental costs of catalytic cracking and seldom yielded gasolines comparable in quality with catalytic products.

A second important reason why the number of small refiners was not reduced to an even greater extent by the sharp increase in octane numbers after 1940 arose from the fact that a market existed for a third grade gasoline. In view of the specialized markets which existed for such a product (see Chapter Twenty-Three), it was not necessary for all refiners to meet the octane competition of the best-equipped companies. A third factor which helped some small refiners to operate quite successfully without catalytic processes was the use of selected crude oils that yielded a high quality straight-run gasoline.

A substantial rise in octane quality was not the only improvement brought about with respect to gasoline by advances in technology during the period 1910–1952. Other improvements included the minimization of gum-forming tendencies and changes in the vapor pressure of gasoline in order that vapor lock might be avoided and the starting characteristics of motor fuels improved. Gasolines were also tailored to perform more satisfactorily under particular regional or climatic conditions. As noted above, improvements in other products, which are too numerous to mention here, also contributed to the problem of a refiner in remaining competitive from a quality standpoint, although not to the same extent as did the changes in gasoline specifications.

Changes in Refinery Operating Costs:

The operating costs for the seven representative refineries discussed earlier in the chapter are shown in Exhibit XIX-10. The costs were calculated for refineries of 25,000 barrels per day capacity located on the East Coast. Thus, two variables which might have affected unit operating costs, size and location, have been eliminated from the study of historical costs.

The operating cost figures reflect the experience of one large refining company. They

EXHIBIT XIX-10. OPERATING COSTS OF SEVEN REPRESENTATIVE REFINERIES:
1910–1950

	1910 Refinery	1915 Refinery	1927 Refinery	1935 Refinery	1946 Refinery	1950 Conventional Refinery	1950 Combination Unit Refinery
Crude Capacity (Barrels per Day)	25,000	25,000	25,000	25,000	25,000	25,000	25,000
Operating Costs (Cents per Barrel): *							
Labor	2.9¢	4.2¢	3.0¢	4.4¢	10.2¢		54.0¢
Depreciation	2.9	3.5	4.0	5.4	11.2	76.6¢†	54.0¢
Other, Excluding Fuel Cost (See below)	3.8	7.8	6.1	11.2	35.6		
Fuel Cost	2.2	4.0	4.3	8.2	13.4	11.8	8.0
6% Return on Investment	2.9	3.5	4.0	5.3	11.2	16.1	10.5
Total Operating Costs plus 6% Return on Investment	14.7¢	23.0¢	21.4¢	34.5¢	81.6¢	104.5¢	72.5¢
Total Operating Costs plus 6% Return on Investment Adjusted to 1950 Cost Basis	N.A.	115.2¢	49.9¢	79.9¢	107.0¢	104.5¢	72.5¢
Fuel Costs Included above	Coal @ $1.80/Ton	Coal @ $2.00/Ton	Fuel Oil @ $.80/Bbl.	Fuel Oil @ $1.00/Bbl.	Fuel Oil @ $1.75/Bbl.	Fuel Oil @ $2.15/Bbl.	Fuel Oil @ $2.15/Bbl.
Data Used to Adjust to 1950 Cost Basis:							
Refinery Construction Cost Index (1939 = 100)	61	59	104	91	160	212	212
Coal (per ton)							$9.75
Basic Wage Rate		$.287	$.764	$.826	$1.505	$2.004	$2.004

* Operating costs include normal refinery burdens and 6% depreciation.
† See Chapter Twenty for a detailed cost breakdown on a 1950 refinery.

do not for any of the years considered necessarily reflect average or typical industry figures for 25,000 barrels per day refineries made up of the different pieces of processing equipment shown in Exhibit XIX-1. The 1910 and 1915 operating costs were calculated from cost statements for an East Coast refinery. The 1927 costs represent those of an actual Gulf Coast refinery adjusted to the East Coast location. The 1935, 1946, and 1950 operating costs were calculated to reflect processing costs reported by operating refineries for those years. In order to take cognizance of the varying plant investments in appraising operating costs, a 6% return on the different investments was added to the operating costs of each of the seven refineries.

The first observation that may be made from the data is that, on the basis of unadjusted dollars, unit operating costs plus a 6% return on investments were higher for successive refineries, with the notable exceptions of the 1927 refinery and 1950 combination unit refinery. It will be recalled that the 1927 refinery was the first of the historical plants to utilize pipe stills and continuous cracking. The 1950 combination unit refinery had substantially lower investment and operating costs because several operations were conducted in an integrated processing unit. The 1950 combination unit refinery was not, however, so well equipped as the 1950 conventional refinery with respect to refinery yields or the ability to shift yields over a wide range. On the basis of unadjusted dollars, unit operating costs plus a 6% return on investment increased from approximately 15 cents in 1910 to 73 cents for the 1950 combination unit refinery and to $1.05 for the 1950 conventional refinery.

A better comparison of unit operating costs for the representative refineries is afforded by cost figures which have been adjusted to a 1950 basis in accordance with changes in the price levels for different types of operating costs. We therefore adjusted costs for the earlier refineries to a 1950 basis in order to show how much it would have cost to operate these refineries in 1950, if the mode of operation had been the same as in the earlier year.[18] The operating costs of the representative refineries expressed in terms of 1950 price levels are shown at the bottom of Exhibit XIX-10. Unfortunately, the index data necessary to adjust the 1910 costs to a 1950 basis were not available.

The adjusted cost data reveal that since 1927 refiners have paid for improved yields and better products with higher operating costs. Operating costs increased from 50 cents per barrel of crude oil processed in the 1927 refinery to 80 cents per barrel in the 1935 refinery and to $1.05 in the 1950 conventional refinery. Only the 1950 combination unit refinery, adaptations of which were used very sparingly in the industry, had costs comparable with those of the pre-catalytic era.

In comparing the operating costs of the refineries, it is particularly interesting to note the great technical advance represented by the commercialization of pipe stills and continuous cracking units in the 1927 refinery. Operating costs, on a 1950 cost basis, declined from $1.15 in the 1915 refinery to only 50 cents in the 1927 plant.

The increases in over-all unit operating costs shown for the more modern refineries resulted from the fact that a greater number of processing operations were performed in the modern plants than in the earlier plants. It should not be inferred from an examination of either adjusted or unadjusted operating costs for the representative refineries, however, that little progress has been made in terms of cost reduc-

---

[18] Because of the lack of detailed historical records for individual cost components, it was necessary to make a rather rudimentary adjustment. Unit operating costs, excluding fuel, were broken down into three components; labor, depreciation, and other expenses. Unit labor costs were adjusted in accordance with the changes in a record of basic wage rates maintained by the Esso Standard Oil Company for an East Coast refinery. Depreciation was adjusted in accordance with a refinery construction cost index described at a later point in the chapter. Other expenses were inflated or deflated half on the basis of the wage index and half on the basis of the refinery construction cost index. Refinery fuel costs were adjusted to a 1950 basis in accordance with the changes in the price of either bituminous coal or fuel oil. The return on investment was adjusted by the refinery construction cost index. By adjusting these component costs, it was possible to obtain a rough approximation of the 1950 operating cost for each refinery.

tions on individual refinery operations. The costs of crude oil distillation were, for example, reduced by the conversion from batch operated to continuously operating shell stills and then by the advent of pipe stills; the continuous process for thermal cracking resulted in lower operating costs than did the earlier pressure stills; and better fractionating methods reduced the costs of rerunning products.

It should also be recognized in appraising operating costs over a long period of time that refineries have not remained constant in size. There has been an almost uninterrupted increase in the average size of plants. In Chapter Twenty, it will be shown that for refineries of any one type, the larger plants have lower unit operating costs. Thus, the over-all increases in plant size have also exerted a downward pressure on long-term operating costs for the industry which have not been reflected in the figures for the seven representative refineries.

Net Result of Changes in Quality, Yields, and Costs:

It may be concluded from the foregoing analyses that the modern plants were more efficient than older plants of the same size in two respects: the products yielded were of a superior quality and the refineries afforded a greater dollar value sales volume as a result of their ability to obtain a greater yield of high value products from crude oil. Both of these objectives were achieved, however, at generally higher unit processing costs to the refiner. These economic findings are summarized in Exhibit XIX-11 which brings together the quality, sales realization, and operating data already presented.

In the first place, as may be seen from the exhibit, only the modern plants were well-equipped to keep pace with the increases in octane numbers which, by 1950, had reached 83.9 for regular grade gasoline and 90.4 for premium grade gasoline. Secondly, the modern plants would in 1950 have been more profitable than the earlier plants. In the exhibit we have deducted the operating costs of the representative refineries, adjusted to a 1950 basis and including a 6% return on investment, from 1950 sales realizations. The difference represents the dollar increment which each refinery would have had to cover all other costs,

Exhibit XIX-11. Summary of Economics for Seven Representative Refineries: 1910–1950

	1910 Refinery	1915 Refinery	1927 Refinery	1935 Refinery	1946 Refinery	1950 Conventional Refinery	1950 Combination Unit Refinery
Crude Capacity (Barrels per Day)	25,000	25,000	25,000	25,000	25,000	25,000	25,000
Octane Quality (Research Method)*							
No TEL	50–55	55–60	60–65	72	82	82	82
1.5 c.c. TEL	60–70	70–75	75–78	84	89	89	89
3.0 c.c. TEL	65–75	75–80	80–83	88	92	92	92
1950 Sales Realization Values (Per Barrel of Crude Oil Processed)†	$3.92	$3.94	$3.52	$3.96	$4.25	$4.20	$3.99
Total Operating Costs plus 6% Return on Investment Adjusted to 1950 Cost Basis‡ (Per Barrel of Crude Oil Processed)	N.A.	1.15	.50	.80	1.07	1.04	.72
Increment to Cover All Other Costs and Provide Additional Profits over a 6% Return (Per Barrel of Crude Oil Processed)	N.A.	$2.79	$3.02	$3.16	$3.18	$3.16	$3.27

* See Exhibit XIX–9.
† Based on the assumption that the earlier plants could make salable products in 1950.
‡ See Exhibit XIX–10.

such as crude oil, and to provide additional profits over a 6% return on investment.

The per barrel increment increased from $2.79 in the 1915 refinery to $3.27 in the 1950 plant. It is apparent that the modern plants were more profitable despite the fact that a strong bias in favor of the older plants was introduced into the analysis by the admittedly invalid assumption that the older plants could make products of a salable quality in 1950. It may be concluded therefore that as the relative demand for different products has shifted and ever-improved product quality has been sought, a compelling pressure has been exerted upon refiners to install new equipment. In fact, the life of a refining company has been dependent, in large part, upon the willingness and capability of its owners to utilize elements of the continually improved refinery technology.

III. The Increasing Capital Requirements of the Refining Business

Thus far the discussion has centered upon the major process developments which have taken place in prime fuel refineries and on the forces and circumstances which led to their commercialization. The purpose of the following paragraphs is to discuss the nature of the financial problem imposed upon refiners by the changes in technology. The changing capital requirements are measured in terms of investment costs for the seven representative refineries considered in earlier sections of the chapter.

The investments required to erect "grass roots refineries" [19] with crude capacities of 25,000 barrels per day in selected years since 1910 are shown in Exhibit XIX-12. The investment figures for process equipment, utilities and general refinery offsites, and tankage are set forth separately for each refinery. Plant investments were for an East Coast location. The 1910 and 1915 refinery investments were based on original East Coast refinery cost records with certain adjustments; the 1927 and 1935 refinery investments were calculated from published costs for individual process units; the 1946 and 1950 refinery investments were built up from estimates of equipment costs. As noted previously, each of these refineries was representative of a sweeping change in refinery technology, and the equipment included in each refinery, as set forth in Exhibit XIX-1, was typical of the most modern equipment available in each year considered.

The first observation that may be made with respect to the plant investment figures is that the cost of building the representative plants increased from $4,400,000 for the 1910 refinery

[19] The term "grass roots refineries" is used in the industry to describe a situation in which a company buys a tract of land and builds a completely new refinery thereon.

EXHIBIT XIX-12. INVESTMENT COSTS FOR SEVEN REPRESENTATIVE REFINERIES:
1910–1950

	1910 Refinery	1915 Refinery	1927 Refinery	1935 Refinery	1946 Refinery	1950 Conventional Refinery	1950 Combination Unit Refinery
Capacity (Barrels per Day)	25,000	25,000	25,000	25,000	25,000	25,000	25,000
ORIGINAL COSTS:							
Process Equipment							
Distillation	$ 1,980,000	$ 1,980,000	$ 840,000	$ 3,800,000	$ 2,100,000	$ 2,400,000	$ 5,700,000
Cracking	—	640,000	1,200,000	(Thermal	3,400,000	3,800,000	(Catalytic
Light Ends	—	—	400,000	Combina-	2,300,000	4,500,000	Combina-
Finishing	240,000	200,000	140,000	tion Unit)	300,000	1,000,000	tion Unit)
Total Process Equipment	$ 2,220,000	$ 2,820,000	$ 2,580,000	$ 3,800,000	$ 8,100,000	$11,700,000	$ 5,700,000
Utilities and General Refinery Offsites	1,410,000	1,780,000	2,300,000	3,400,000	7,550,000	11,300,000	9,150,000
Tankage	770,000	770,000	1,120,000	900,000	1,450,000	1,500,000	1,150,000
Total Investment Cost	$ 4,400,000	$ 5,370,000	$ 6,000,000	$ 8,100,000	$17,100,000	$24,500,000	$16,000,000
Dollars per Barrel of Daily Capacity	$176	$214	$240	$324	$684	$980	$640
COSTS ADJUSTED TO 1950 BASIS:							
Total Investment Cost	$15,300,000	$19,300,000	$12,200,000	$18,900,000	$22,600,000	$24,500,000	$16,000,000
Dollars per Barrel of Daily Capacity	$612	$770	$489	$756	$905	$980	$640
Refinery Construction Cost Index (1939 = 100)	61	59	104	91	160	212	212

to $24,500,000 for the 1950 conventional refinery. Moreover, the investment costs for refineries erected in the intervening years rose in successive stages, with a very marked increase in evidence for the 1946 plant, the first plant with catalytic cracking facilities. The cost of the 1950 combination unit refinery was, however, one-third less than that of the 1950 conventional refinery. The 1950 combination unit refinery was the first interruption in the increasing capital cost trend in evidence among the seven representative refineries.

Since the differences in the original plant investment figures reflected not only the impact of technology but also changes in the value of the dollar, it was necessary to adjust all investment costs to a common dollar yardstick in order to isolate the increased capital costs traceable to advances in technology. The adjustment of earlier refinery construction costs to a 1950 cost basis was accomplished through the application of a refinery construction cost index maintained by the Standard Oil Development Company.[20] The adjusted investment

[20] The index was a composite of a refinery material cost index and a refinery construction labor cost index. The material cost index was the weighted average of individual indexes of materials entering into refinery con-

costs for each of the representative refineries are also shown at the bottom of Exhibit XIX-12.

The adjusted investment costs provide a somewhat different picture of the impact of

struction. The individual material indexes were weighted according to their pro rata share of refinery material cost as determined from actual costs.

The labor cost index was computed from union scale wage rates and productivity for the building trades. Labor productivity was estimated using data obtained from a survey of refinery construction contractors and field engineers of the Standard Oil Development Company. The labor cost index reflected not only changes in the individual worker's efficiency, but also changes in delivery time for material, efficiency of field management planning, and union regulations.

The material cost index and the labor cost index were combined in a 79%–21% ratio to obtain the refinery construction cost index. The material-to-labor ratio used was the average for construction of a typical refinery on a 1939 cost basis.

The refinery construction cost index was designed to measure the changes in the direct material and labor costs for construction of complete grass root refineries and did not consider changes in indirect costs such as the contractors' overheads and fees for engineering and other services. The index was, however, directionally correct for application to total refinery investments. It is recognized that this index, or any other, could not be completely correct, since the nature of refining equipment was in 1950 different from what it had been 40 years before. However, the materials and basic components making up the equipment were sufficiently similar so that the use of a continuous index was well within the accuracy required for the present study.

technological advance on investment requirements than do the unadjusted costs discussed above. The adjusted cost per barrel of capacity increased sharply between 1910 and 1915 but declined significantly when the pipe stills and continuous cracking represented in the 1927 refinery became commercially available. After 1927 investment costs increased steadily until in 1950 (for the conventional refinery) they were 100% above the 1927 level. The 1950 combination unit (which had not yet been generally adopted by the industry) would have permitted a significant investment cost saving over the 1950 conventional unit, but even the combination unit would have represented a 31% increase in investment costs over the 1927 plant.

Since the main focus of this chapter is on the changing scale of business opportunity brought about by changes in refinery technology, we have not considered the other financial responsibilities assumed in the operation of a refining business. The total investment necessary to engage in the refining business was, of course, considerably larger than plant investment costs because of the net working capital which was necessary to transact business. The inventories of crude oil and refined products held in storage at a refinery were, for example, a major investment cost component. In 1950, 10 days' supply of crude oil and 30 days' supply of refined products at a 25,000 barrels per day refinery would have represented an investment of over $3,000,000 in inventories. The plant investment figures alone, however, illustrate two very important factors about the nature of the refining venture: it was basically a high capital cost business, and with the exception of the 1950 combination unit refinery, it became progressively more so after 1927 in terms of adjusted costs because of the continual changes in technology.[21] The advances in technology since 1927 have therefore had the effect of erecting ever-larger barriers to entry into the refinery business.

Thus far the discussion has not set forth explicitly the amount of reinvestment necessary on the part of any going concern with a 25,000 barrels per day refinery to remain competitive from a technological standpoint. In reality, most active refineries are a conglomeration of old and new equipment. Processing changes are brought about continually by the addition of new equipment and by the adaptations and adjustments of the more obsolete pieces of equipment. At times, radical transformations are made in the design or functions served by the older pieces of equipment in order to avert the necessity of making entirely new installations.

Some measure of the magnitude of the continual reinvestment which was necessary to keep a 25,000 barrels per day refinery abreast of the latest technology over a long period of years may be obtained from Exhibit XIX-12.[22] Around 1915 an investment of $640,000 would have been required to install thermal cracking facilities; around 1927 a pipe still heater, greatly improved thermal cracking units, and adjustments in utilities would have required roughly $3,000,000; and during or after World War II a fluid catalytic cracking unit, light ends processing equipment, and utilities additions would have required roughly $9,000,000. In addition, the installation of a whole host of individual pieces of processing equipment, such as pumps and condensers, would have been required in the interim years. It is evident from the figures set forth in Exhibit XIX-12 that the maintenance of a fully competitive refinery involved substantial financial commitments in the period 1910–1950 and particularly during the years in which a new plateau of technology was reached.

The over-all magnitude of the refining investment and the impact of technological advancement in increasing the capital requirements are helpful in explaining some of the

---

[21] See Chapters Twenty-One and Twenty-Three for examples of refineries which were constructed with investment costs held to a minimum.

[22] One theoretical method for determining reinvestment costs would be to accumulate the costs of plant additions representing refinements in technique or basic processes for any one refinery of a constant *size* over a long period of years. As a practical matter, however, there are some serious limitations in this approach. One difficulty is that there are few, if any, refineries in existence which would lend themselves to this type of study. Moreover, the difficulty of determining what proportion of each capital expenditure is made to gain the advantage inherent in improved technology is practically insuperable. For example, a new condenser or heating unit might be required for maintenance purposes but still entail elements of improved technology. In Chapter Twenty-Two, the nature of the financial problem imposed by technology on several specific companies will be considered.

changing industry characteristics observed in Chapter Eighteen. Refining was essentially a million or multimillion dollar business. Even a modern skimming plant with a capacity of 1,000 barrels per day would have probably entailed an investment of around $300,000 in 1950. Such a plant would not, of course, have been in a position to produce gasoline of an acceptable octane quality. The plant investment required for a more competitive but still a very small plant would have almost assuredly exceeded $1,000,000 in 1950. To assure a portion of the crude oil supply or market outlets for such a refinery would have magnified the investment problem. It is small wonder therefore that few new firms were being organized to enter the refining business in the postwar period and that the ever-increasing demand for petroleum products was being met primarily by established companies with capital resources at their command.

Many of the *small companies* in the refining industry were organized in periods when financial requirements were less demanding than they were in 1950. An even greater number of *refineries* were constructed in time periods less costly than 1950. Many of these small companies have been closely held and of rather limited financial means. They have therefore been particularly vulnerable to the ever larger hurdles posed by technological progress. The problems posed for a family or a small group of business associates in raising $1,000,000 to meet the competitive pressures brought about by some change in technology have generally been greater than those faced by a large, established multimillion dollar firm in reinvesting $10,000,000 to meet the same challenge. Although both large and small companies have been confronted with the necessity of reinvesting very large sums of money in their plant establishments, there is little question but what the financial burden has been of more serious consequences to the small firm.

IV. SUMMARY

1. One predominant trait of the refining industry has been a highly dynamic tech-

nology. The advances in refinery technology have resulted in improved product yields, higher quality products, and lower operating costs for *particular operations* for the refiners which availed themselves of the new processes. Refiners seeking improved yields and higher quality products incurred somewhat higher unit operating costs as the refining process became more intricate, but they were compensated by a higher sales realization value per barrel of crude oil run. It was, moreover, necessary to add new processes in order to keep products at competitive standards. The superiority of the more modern plants exerted very strong competitive pressures for firms to spend the large sums of money required for new process installations.

2. Octane competition is a manifestation of improved technology which has created particularly difficult problems for the small refiner. The processes required to attain high-octane products have involved such huge amounts of money that the small firm has been hard pressed to remain in business with a gasoline product of competitive specifications. The small plant was especially vulnerable to competition from catalytically cracked products because of the technical and economic difficulties first encountered in adapting catalytic processes to small installations.

3. An examination of the changing capital requirements associated with the advances in refinery technology reveals: (a) refining has always been an inherently high capital cost business, and (b) it has become progressively more so as advances in refining have taken place. The advent of catalytic cracking processes was a particularly important factor in increasing the magnitude of the investment necessary to sustain a competitive enterprise. The small, closely held firms have been particularly vulnerable to and have suffered serious consequences from the impact of technological advancement because of the limited amounts of capital which have usually been available to them.

CHAPTER TWENTY

The Effect of Differences in Plant Facilities and Operating Practices on the Competitive Position of the Small Refiner

WE FOUND that the manufacturing operations conducted by small refining companies have frequently differed in three important respects from those of the large, integrated companies. The plants owned by the small refiners have usually been of much smaller size and have generally embodied different types of processing equipment than the plants of the large companies. In addition, small refiners have often developed operating practices quite different from those followed by large companies. In this chapter we shall consider the effect of these differences on the competitive position of the small firms.

The chapter will be subdivided into sections analyzing (a) the effect of size on the efficiency of refineries made up of the same types of processing equipment, (b) the effect of different types of processing equipment on the relative efficiency of refineries of the same size, (c) the effect of differences in both size and type of equipment on the efficiency of refineries, and (d) the effect of differences in certain operating practices on the efficiency of refineries of the same size. Throughout the first three sections it will be assumed that the various types of refineries studied might have been built and operated by a single company and that a uniform set of operating practices were employed with regard to such matters as the types and grades of crude oil charged, personnel staffing, basic wage rates, and employee benefits. The fourth section will then deal with the effects of differences in operating conditions.

NOTE: The factual data concerning the refineries discussed in the first three sections of this chapter were developed in conjunction with the Standard Oil Development Company. The authors alone, however, assume full responsibility for the analysis and interpretation of the data.

A study of *plant* efficiency is quite different from a study of the over-all effectiveness with which *companies* of different sizes and types carry out their refining operations. The quantitative analyses in this chapter are, to a large extent, concerned with the efficiency of plants and not the refining efficiency of companies. It is nonetheless possible to draw some inferences with respect to the relative strengths or weaknesses of large and small companies in their refining activities by relating the specific studies of plant efficiency presented in this chapter to the general characteristics of the plants owned by large and small companies.

As a practical matter, it would be very difficult to compare with any high degree of precision the efficiency with which different sizes and types of *companies* perform their manufacturing operations. One difficulty arises from the fact that many companies own several plants which may vary with respect to size, type of equipment, location, crude oil supplies, and markets served. The disparities in plant efficiency among the refineries of one company are therefore sometimes greater than the differences in over-all refining efficiency existing among companies.

The variety of vertical integration arrangements employed by different companies is a second factor which makes it difficult to compare the refining efficiency of companies. In an integrated company, it is often difficult to determine what aspect of the company's operations should be credited with the profit increases arising from a particular change in procedures. As one illustration, if unit processing costs are decreased at a refinery because of a greater crude oil throughput, should the credit be given to the crude oil supply department for providing additional crude oil, to the marketing department for increasing sales, or to the refining department for processing the additional crude oil? The accounting problems involved in determining departmental earnings in an integrated concern also make it difficult to compare the efficiency of any single operation such as refining.[1]

In a broad sense, plant efficiency might be viewed as including the significance of plant location. In the interests of simplicity, however, we shall defer to Chapters Twenty-One and Twenty-Three the discussion regarding the importance of plant location to the competitive position of small firms. In order to eliminate the effects of plant location on delivered crude oil prices, products prices, and operating costs, all individual analyses presented in this chapter are based upon refineries situated in the same locations.

I. THE EFFECT OF SIZE ON REFINERY EFFICIENCY

In the following paragraphs we shall examine the effect of size on refinery efficiency, *assuming that all other factors which affect efficiency are held constant.* In actual practice, "all other things" never are constant, and many things other than size may influence the competitive strength of a particular refinery or refining company. The consideration of one variable at a time, however, permits a much clearer analysis of the problem of refinery efficiency than would be possible if an attempt were made to consider all variables simultaneously.

In order to gauge the effect of size on refinery efficiency, the investment and operating costs for modern prime fuel refineries of five different crude oil capacities were determined. The analysis was based upon a study by a large company for refineries which might have been erected along the Gulf Coast in 1950. The refineries ranged in size from 10,000 to 200,000 barrels per day, consisted of equipment representative of the most modern available in the year 1950, and were of "conventional" design; that is, separate pieces of equipment such as pipe stills and catalytic cracking units performed the major processing steps rather than combination units in which several principal processing opera-

---

[1] See Chapter Seventeen.

EXHIBIT XX-1. PROCESSING EQUIPMENT FOR PRIME FUEL PRODUCTS REFINERIES, CONVENTIONAL DESIGN (10,000–200,000 BARRELS PER DAY): 1950

1. Two-Stage Atmospheric Vacuum Pipe Still
    Treating: Kerosene and Heating Oil — Caustic Wash, Sand Bed, and Clay Strain
2. Naphtha Stabilizer
    Treating: Naphtha — Caustic and Water Wash
3. Naphtha Reformer *
4. Visbreaker
    Treating: Heating Oil — Acid Treating Plant and Acid Concentration Plant
5. Naphtha Debutanizer
6. Fluid Catalytic Cracking Unit
    Light Ends Recovery: Gas Compression
                                    Absorber
                                    Splitter
                                    Debutanizer
                                    Rerun Tower
    Treating: Naphtha — Clay Treat
                 Kerosene and Heating Oil — Caustic Wash, Sand Bed, and Clay Strain
7. Nonselective Polymerization Plant (Including Stabilizer, Debutanizer, and Feed Pretreatment)
8. Copper Chloride Sweetening Facilities

Note: The refineries had the following capacities: 10,000, 30,000, 60,000, 100,000, and 200,000 barrels per calendar day.
    * Naphtha reformer not included in 10,000 and 30,000 barrels per day refineries.

tions were performed within certain pieces of equipment. A detailed summation of the processing equipment comprising the conventional refineries is given in Exhibit XX-1.

In order to restrict the analysis solely to the effect of size on refinery efficiency, the investment and operating costs were prepared on the assumption that the process equipment of the 200,000 barrels per day refinery could be scaled down to successively smaller capacities.[2] The 10,000 barrels per day refinery was thus a small-scale model of the larger plants, possessing the same flexibility of operation and product yield distribution as the larger plants. Under comparable operating conditions therefore, the sales revenue per barrel of products sold would have been identical for all refineries. Using a

---

[2] Exhibit XX-1 reveals that the omission of the naphtha reformer in the 10,000 and 30,000 barrels per day refineries was the only way in which the various refineries differed, except for size.

representative crude oil supply for prime fuel refineries—a 50/50 mixture of East and West Texas crude oils—the refinery yields were as follows:

Gasoline	48%
Kerosene	10
Heating Oil	23
Fuel Oil (or its equivalent)	19
	100%

In order to ascertain the investment and operating costs for the different sized refineries, it was necessary to make certain assumptions about their respective operations. It was assumed that the products of the 10,000 and 30,000 barrels per day plants would be moved from the refineries by tank car and tank truck for distribution in local markets. It was assumed that products of the larger refineries would exceed local requirements. It was therefore necessary to add waterfront docks to the facilities of the larger plants to permit the shipment of some proportion of the products output by tankers to a broad geographical market. The proportion of the products output to be moved by tankers was as follows: [3] 60,000 barrels per day plant, 50%; 100,000 barrels per day plant, 70%; and 200,000 barrels per day plant, 85%. It was assumed that the remaining output from each of the larger refineries would be moved by tank car and tank truck for sale in local markets.

It was further assumed that: (a) crude oil receipts at each refinery would be entirely by pipe line, (b) power would be purchased, (c) steam would be generated at 150 pounds per square inch gauge, and (d) approximately 50 barrels of refined products and crude oil storage capacity would be installed for each barrel of crude oil refining capacity for refineries of all sizes.

[3] The 60,000 barrels per day refinery was a marginal case regarding products shipments. That is, it could have been assumed that a plant of this size either might or might not have had dock facilities for shipping products. In the original analysis, data were prepared for 60,000 barrels per day refineries with and without docks. For purposes of simplicity, only the 60,000 barrels per day refinery with docks was included in the chapter. It is of interest to note that the total investment for a 60,000 barrels per day plant without docks was $40,000,000 compared with $41,000,000 for the refinery with docks. Operating costs for the plant without docks ranged from 4 cents less per barrel of crude oil processed with the refineries operating at 50% of capacity to 2 cents less per barrel with the refineries operating at 100% of capacity.

With the exception of the 10,000 barrels per day plant, each of the refineries was a realistic prototype of a refinery which might have been constructed in 1950.[4] As noted above, the 10,000 barrels per day refinery was a scaled down replica of the 200,000 barrels per day plant. In varying only the size of equipment, we held constant a great many factors that would not in practice have been held constant in the construction and operation of a modern 10,000 barrels per day plant. The 10,000 barrels per day plant, for example, contained equipment not usually found in a small refinery such as a visbreaker, a polymer plant, a vacuum distillation unit, and complete treating facilities. It suffered such marked disadvantages in investment and operating costs because of the inclusion of all these components of the larger plants that under ordinary circumstances it probably would not have been erected by a small refiner.

A small refiner would also usually operate a modern 10,000 barrels per day plant under an entirely different set of operating conditions from that assumed for the refineries in the analysis. Manpower requirements, wage rates, employee services, types of crude oil run, product yields, and tankage requirements are but a few of the factors that would undoubtedly be varied.

The 10,000 barrels per day plant used in this analysis is therefore a purely hypothetical plant, and *it is used only to illustrate the behavior of certain refining costs as the size of plant is varied over the entire scale from 10,000 to 200,000 barrels per day.* At a later point in the discussion, the cost characteristics of 10,000 and 25,000 barrels per day refineries which more nearly represent the type of plants which might have been constructed by small refiners in 1950 will be considered.

The Difference in Capital Costs for Conventional Refineries of Different Size:

The total capital investment costs for the five refineries ranging in size from 10,000 to 200,000 barrels per day are shown in Exhibit

[4] Depending upon the objectives being sought by a management, combination units rather than conventional refineries might, of course, have been erected. Conventional refineries often give better product yields and make easier the later installation of supplementary facilities such as an asphalt or a lubricating oil plant.

EXHIBIT XX-2. INVESTMENT COSTS AT A GULF COAST LOCATION FOR PRIME
FUEL PRODUCTS REFINERIES: 1950

Capacity, Barrels per Day	10,000	30,000	60,000	100,000	200,000
Investments ($1,000):					
Process Units	$ 6,100	$12,000	$19,100	$27,500	$ 50,300
Utilities and General Refinery Offsites	6,300	11,400	16,900	24,600	42,900
Tankage	600	1,600	3,000	4,900	9,800
Docks	—	—	2,000	4,000	6,000
Total	$13,000	$25,000	$41,000	$61,000	$109,000
Assumptions					
Crude Oil Delivered by Pipe Line (Barrels per Day)	10,000	30,000	60,000	100,000	200,000
Products Shipped Out by:					
Tank Car and Tank Truck (Barrels per Day)	10,000	30,000	30,000	30,000	30,000
Tanker (Barrels per Day)	—	—	30,000	70,000	170,000

XX-2. From the data it may be seen that total capital costs rise very sharply as the size of plant increases. Total investment costs in 1950 were $13,000,000 for the 10,000 barrels per day refinery, $25,000,000 for the 30,000 barrels per day refinery, and $109,000,000 for the 200,000 barrels per day plant. Thus, a company that wished to make a large-scale plant installation needed either a great accumulation of capital on hand or ready access to large amounts of money through borrowing or capital flotations. In view of the above discussion, however, it should be noted that the $13,000,000 investment cost shown for the 10,000 barrels per day plant was not a realistic cost for an actual plant but rather an indication of what the investment cost would have been if the equipment in the larger plants had been scaled down in size to 10,000 barrels per day.

Although the large plants required much larger capital outlays than the small ones, they cost less *per barrel of capacity* than did the small ones (see Exhibit XX-3). Costs ranged downward from $1,300 per barrel of capacity for the 10,000 barrels per day refinery to $545 per barrel of capacity for the 200,000 barrels per day plant. From the sharp downward sweep of the curve, it is evident that the most significant economies in the construction costs of refineries were realized between 10,000 and 60,000 barrels per day of capacity; above 60,000 barrels per day the investment cost curve declined much more slowly as the plant size increased. It may be observed, however, that investment costs per barrel of capacity continued to decline over the entire range up to

the 200,000 barrels plant. Thus, the most economically sized conventional refinery to erect in 1950, in terms of *investment cost per barrel of capacity*, lay somewhere beyond the 200,000 barrels per day refinery considered in this analysis.

Entirely apart from any consideration of relative operating costs, marked financial savings accrued from the erection of the larger sized refineries. When the decision is made to expend the amount of capital needed for a refinery of a certain size, a company either (a) uses accumulated funds and foregoes the opportunity to earn a rate of return on this money elsewhere in its operations,[5] or (b) raises money by borrowing or issuing stock, thereby incurring a tangible capital charge. In this discussion we shall use the term financial charge to describe either an assumed or an actual capital cost figured on the amount of the plant investment.

Since the large refineries cost considerably more than the smaller ones, the financial charges were much greater for the large plants than for the small ones. Since the investment cost per barrel of capacity declined in the case of the larger plants, however, the financial charges per barrel of crude oil processed were also less for the larger plants. For purposes of illustration, we assigned three different financial rates, 4%, 6% and 8%, to the amounts of capital required to erect the different sized refineries. The financial charges were then divided by the number of barrels of crude oil

---

[5] In a great many cases, the plant investment funds at the disposal of a management have been provided by retained earnings or through depreciation.

EXHIBIT XX-3. INVESTMENT COSTS, FINANCIAL CHARGES, AND DEPRECIATION
EXPENSES FOR CONVENTIONAL REFINERIES OF DIFFERENT SIZES: 1950

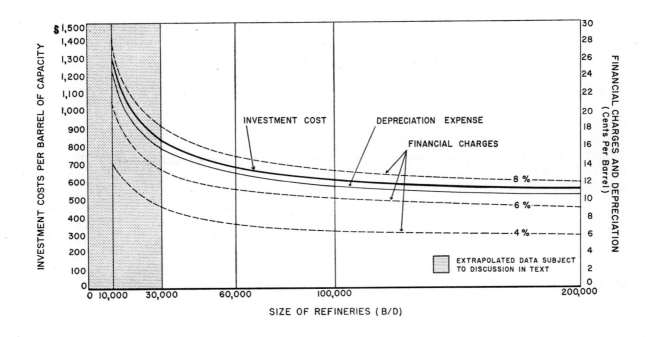

EXHIBIT XX-4. FIXED AND VARIABLE UNIT OPERATING COSTS, FINANCIAL CHARGES,
AND RETURN ON INVESTMENTS FOR CONVENTIONAL REFINERIES OF DIFFERENT SIZES: 1950

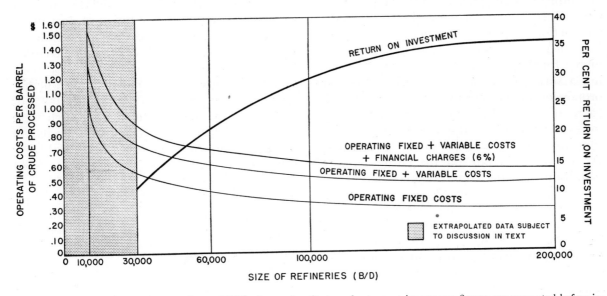

Note: Calculations assume operation at 100% of capacity. Costs and return on investment figures are computed before income taxes and financial charges.

processed in the different sized refineries and plotted on Exhibit XX-3.

The curves showing financial charges constitute a good measure of one advantage of size in petroleum refining. At a 6% rate, for example, financial charges declined from 21 cents per barrel of crude oil processed for the 10,000 barrels per day plant to 14 cents per barrel for the 30,000 barrels per day plant. Thereafter the savings were less pronounced, declining 3 cents per barrel between the 30,000 and 60,000 barrels per day plants, approximately 1 cent per barrel between the 60,000 and 100,000 barrels per day plants, and approximately 1 cent per barrel between the 100,000 and 200,000 barrels per day refineries.[6] In appraising the significance of the differences, it is important to note that a 1 cent saving per barrel amounted to $110,000 yearly for the 30,000 barrels per day plant and $730,000 yearly for the 200,000 barrels per day plant. The 7-cent differential per barrel of crude oil processed between the 10,000 and 30,000 barrels per day plants represented a financial saving of approximately $775,000 per year for the builder of the larger plant. At financial rates higher than 6% the savings were even more appreciable; at lower rates the savings were less significant (see Exhibit XX-3).

The decrease in investment cost per barrel of refining capacity realized in the larger plants also yielded a saving in operating costs through a reduction in unit depreciation charges. Since investment costs per barrel of capacity were higher for the smaller plants, a company owning a small plant had to set aside a higher proportion of the revenue received from each barrel of crude oil processed and sold in order to recover its initial capital outlay than did a company owning a larger plant. Assuming a 7% depreciation rate on the entire refinery establishment, the unit depreciation costs ranged downward from 25 cents per barrel crude oil processed for the 10,000 barrels per day plant to 16 cents per barrel for the 30,000 barrels per day plant and to 10 cents per barrel for the 200,000 barrels per day plant.[7] The unit depreciation charges reflect very clearly

the marked savings which resulted from the reductions made in investment costs per unit of capacity through the construction of larger scale plants.

In summation, an examination of the investment costs for different sized conventional refineries comprised of the same types of equipment reveals that the larger plants cost substantially more than smaller plants in total amount but that the investment costs declined per barrel of capacity as the size increased. Because of the declining capital cost per barrel of capacity, the financial charges per barrel of crude oil processed were lower for the large than for the small refineries. Moreover, the owner of a small plant had to set aside a higher proportion of the revenue received from each barrel of crude oil processed and sold in order to recover his initial capital outlay than did the owner of a large plant. Having established these characteristics of the refinery investment, we shall now turn to a consideration of the relative operating costs in the different sized refineries.

Operating Costs and Return on Investment:

An analysis of the costs incurred by the different sized refineries reveals that a high proportion of the total processing costs encountered over a normal operating range within any one refinery was accounted for by cost elements which were, for the most part, fixed in amount regardless of the level of crude oil throughput. For example, depreciation charges, burden, and overhead expenses were not likely to fluctuate greatly in total amount whether a refinery was operating at 50% or 100% of rated capacity. The cost elements which were fixed in total amount led to varying charges per barrel of crude oil processed; the higher the level of throughput, the lower the fixed costs per barrel of crude oil run. In contrast, other costs such as refinery fuel and chemicals were variable in total amount. The variable costs were approximately the same for each barrel of crude processed irrespective of the level of throughput.

For the conventional refineries ranging in size from 10,000 to 200,000 barrels per day and operating at 100% capacity the variable and fixed costs were divided approximately as follows:

---

[6] The financial charges were computed assuming that the refineries were operating at 100% capacity.

[7] Unit depreciation charges were computed assuming that the plants were operating at 100% of capacity.

Variable Costs

Chemicals (including catalyst and TEL[8])	19%	
Utilities and Fuel	8	27%

Fixed Costs[9]

Operating Labor and Supervision	10	
Repairs (labor and materials)	14	
Burdens (including payroll burden, refinery burden, and laboratory expense)	27	
Depreciation	22	73
Total Costs		100%

The breakdown is, of course, not precise for each of the different sized refineries. In general, fixed costs were somewhat lower in the large plants and somewhat higher in the small plants than the above figures indicate.

The unit processing costs for the different sized refineries, assuming that each refinery was operating at 100% of capacity, are shown in Exhibit XX-4. The operating costs are representative of those that would have been incurred by a large refining company if it had erected and operated the plants in the year 1950. The operating costs do not reflect the *average cost* experience of the entire industry for refineries ranging in size from 10,000 barrels per day to 200,000 barrels per day. It will

---

[8] Tetraethyl lead.

[9] All labor charges, whether direct or indirect, have been classified as fixed expenses. Supervisory expenses were clearly fixed in total amount for most companies. The assumption that a full operating labor force would be retained at less than full capacity operations was also consistent with the personnel policies of many oil companies.

In actuality, the manpower required to perform much of the work at any refinery does not vary greatly regardless of the amount of crude oil run, unless the refinery is operated intermittently or with particular pieces of processing equipment shut down completely. To assume intermittent operations would have completely altered the unit processing costs incurred over a time period, since the fixed costs which continued during the shutdown period would have had to be absorbed during the operating period. To assume that any of the pieces of processing equipment were shut down while others operated would have invalidated the assumption upon which the analysis was based: namely, that product yields would be held constant in the different sized refineries and at various levels of throughput in any one refinery.

In any event, since operating and supervisory labor amounted to only 10% of total costs, it is not believed that an assumption of no variability in labor costs would materially alter the economic conclusions that might be reached with a different set of assumptions. Total labor expenses, including operating labor, supervision, maintenance, overhead, and payroll burdens, amounted to approximately 30% of the total costs.

---

be recalled, for example, that the 10,000 barrels per day conventional refinery had such marked operating disadvantages that no refiner would actually have built such a plant. There were, moreover, no plants in existence in 1950 that fulfilled *precisely* the specifications of the larger refineries used in this analysis, although these plants were economically feasible. The cost figures serve, however, to show the effect of size of equipment on the behavior of costs.

The most important gains in unit operating costs made by the larger size refineries came about from the unit savings made on various fixed costs. The bottom line on Exhibit XX-4 shows the fixed costs per barrel of crude oil run for the different sized refineries when operating at 100% of capacity. Much like the investment cost curve per barrel of capacity, unit fixed costs declined very rapidly for refineries between 10,000 and 30,000 barrels per day but tended to decrease much less rapidly as larger and larger refineries were considered. Unit fixed costs varied from $1.09 per barrel for a 10,000 barrels per day refinery to as little as 29 cents per barrel for a 200,000 barrels per day plant. The decline in unit depreciation expense, which was one fixed cost component, has already been discussed. The savings in depreciation were proportionate to the savings in investment cost per barrel of capacity.[10] The unit cost curve for all fixed expenses indicates that other fixed cost components such as burden, labor, and supervision behaved in much the same manner as depreciation.

The unit savings in variable costs achieved by the larger size refineries did not contribute significantly to the economic superiority of the larger plants. Unit variable expenses for the different sized refineries operating at 100% of capacity were added to the unit fixed costs in Exhibit XX-4. It is evident from the vertical distance between the two lines, one line measur-

---

[10] In this analysis, the savings in unit depreciation expenses were *directly proportional* to total investments since a 7% rate on the total investment was used to cover depreciation and local taxes. In actuality, the savings would have been only *roughly proportional*. Although the rates of depreciation on any given piece of equipment would have been the same in all refineries, the different pieces of equipment would have represented varying proportions of the total cost in each refinery. It would therefore have been mere coincidence in actual practice if the total depreciation charges were the same percentage of each plant investment.

ing unit fixed costs and the other unit fixed costs plus unit variable costs, that variable costs were only slightly smaller for the larger than for the smaller plants. In fact, over the entire range from 10,000 to 200,000 barrels per day, unit variable costs declined only 3 cents per barrel of crude oil processed (from 21 cents to 18 cents). Thus, the unit savings made by the larger plants on fuel, chemicals, utilities, and tetraethyl lead were very small indeed in contrast to the unit savings realized on various fixed cost components.

Since it was assumed that the yield of products, and consequently the revenue per barrel of crude oil processed and sold, was identical for all the plants in this analysis, the differences in total operating costs were, in effect, the differences in unit profits before provision for state and federal income taxes. The magnitude of the differences, especially at the lower end of the size scale, indicates that the small plants were at a substantial profit disadvantage, *assuming that all factors other than size of facilities were constant.*

Between the 10,000 and 30,000 barrels per day plants, the difference in unit profit before taxes amounted to 56 cents per barrel of crude oil processed; between 30,000 and 100,000 barrels per day, the difference was 25 cents per barrel; and between 100,000 and 200,000 barrels per day, the profit differential was 5 cents per barrel of crude oil processed. While the incremental profit advantage fell off sharply for larger plants, the gains were significant over the entire range of size up to 200,000 barrels per day. For example, 5 cents per barrel amounted to $3,650,000 yearly on all the products yielded by a 200,000 barrels per day refinery.

The differences in unit profitability have not thus far been related to the amounts of capital required for the different plants. One method of taking capital investments into account is to assign a financial charge, say 6% to the relative amounts of capital necessary to build the different refineries. This financial charge can then be translated into a unit cost per barrel of crude oil processed and added to unit fixed and variable expenses for the refineries of different sizes.

The summation of unit fixed and variable expenses plus a 6% charge on the amounts of capital employed for the different sized plants is plotted in Exhibit XX-4. It is apparent from the data that total operating costs plus a financial charge declined from $1.15 per barrel for the 10,000 barrels per day plant to 88 cents per barrel for the 30,000 barrels per day plant and to 56 cents per barrel for the 200,000 barrels per day plant. As noted earlier, the 10,000 barrels per day plant is a hypothetical case, but the general slope of the curve in Exhibit XX-4 nevertheless provides an indication of the substantial economies resulting from large-scale refining.

A second method for taking into account differences in capital requirements in comparing unit processing costs is to compute the yearly profit for refineries of different sizes and to express these profits as a percentage of the respective investments. The rates of return on investments, before income taxes, for the refineries of different size are plotted on Exhibit XX-4 as the line sloping upward to the right. In computing the profitability of the refineries, average Gulf Coast cargo prices for the last 6 months of 1950 and the refinery yields given earlier in the chapter were used to calculate sales revenues.[11] From the sales revenues, processing costs and the delivered cost at the Gulf Coast of a 50/50 mixture of East Texas-West Texas crude oil were deducted. The difference represented the profit before taxes available to the various refineries. The profits were then expressed as a percentage of the original investment in each case.

It may be seen from Exhibit XX-4 that the rate of return on investment for refineries of different sizes rose sharply at first and then more slowly. Athough the curve was not extended to the 10,000 barrels per day plant because the return was negative, our data revealed that the largest gain in the rate of return was made between the plant sizes of 10,000 and 30,000 barrels per day, the increase being from minus 8% to 12% at 100% of capacity. Above 60,000 barrels per day the

---

[11] Refined products prices for the last 6 months of 1950 were used throughout the chapter because in the earlier months of the year the price structure was abnormally depressed as the refining industry emerged from the extremely low margin period of 1949. Since we were interested in the comparative profitability of the refineries for any given set of economic conditions, prices as of any date might have been selected for the analyses.

incremental gains were not so appreciable, but the rate of return continued to increase over the entire range up to 200,000 barrels per day, reaching a level of 36% for the largest sized refinery considered. These figures were computed before any consideration for federal or state income taxes, the effect of which would have been to narrow the differences in rate of return for the different sized plants.

Effect of Less than Capacity Operations on Refineries of Different Sizes:

The effect of size on refinery efficiency has thus far been measured only for the very particular case in which all refineries were operating at 100% of capacity. In this section, we shall analyze the effect of varying levels of crude oil throughput on the relative efficiency of the refineries of different sizes. Cost behavior over an operating range extending from 50% to 100% of capacity will be considered. All the cost data pertinent to the following analysis were prepared, assuming that no process units would be shut down and that the labor force would be held intact when refinery runs were reduced below full capacity.

Because of the high proportion of fixed costs incurred by the refineries, unit processing cost rose sharply at less than full capacity utilization. There were therefore some very significant cost advantages to be realized in operating a refinery of any rated capacity at a point as near to 100% of capacity as possible. In Exhibit XX-5 unit cost curves for the different sized refineries have been plotted to demonstrate the effect of less than full utilization of facilities on the behavior of unit costs. For each refinery, very great losses in efficiency were suffered at successively lower levels of utilization. Over an operating range from 100% to 50% of capacity, the unit costs of the 10,000 barrels per day refinery increased from $1.30 to $2.39 per barrel; those of the 100,000 barrels per day plant increased from 52 cents to 85 cents per barrel.

The marked cost differences for a refinery of any one size re-emphasize the importance to a refiner of having the greatest assurance possible that refinery runs will not be shut back below capacity because of a lack of continuity in either crude oil supplies or products markets. The unit cost figures also suggest that in many cases

it would be more economical for a refining company to build a small plant which it could be sure of operating at 100% of capacity than to build a large plant which it might have to operate at less than capacity. For example, at 60% of capacity, a 100,000 barrels per day plant had a unit operating cost of 74 cents per barrel, while a 60,000 barrels per day plant running the same volume of crude oil had a unit processing cost of only 60 cents per barrel. It was therefore desirable for a refiner to plan very carefully the size of plant he could justify building on the basis of an assured crude oil supply and permanence of market outlets.

The unit cost curves for refineries of different sizes as shown in Exhibit XX-5 reveal that the small plants would have been more vulnerable from a processing cost and profit standpoint to general declines in industry demand than would companies owning large plants. The large refineries not only had a decided unit processing cost advantage over the smaller plants of the same design at any comparable point below 100% of capacity, but the differential in unit costs grew larger at each successively lower level of throughput. The increasing unit cost disparity at less than capacity operations is a reflection of the fact that fixed costs constituted a greater percentage of total costs for small than for large capacity plants. Since the product yields were assumed to be the same in all cases, differences in unit operating cost were actually differences in unit profitability, and the small refineries would thus have suffered greater losses in profit when a decline in industry demand was experienced equally by all plants.

A further disadvantage of the smaller plants was the higher level of throughput which had to be attained in order to cover costs with revenues. The straight horizontal line in Exhibit XX-5 shows the margin per barrel of crude oil run which was available to the different refineries to cover operating costs and to provide a profit. The margin was ascertained by deducting the delivered cost of crude oil from the sales realization per barrel of crude oil run as determined on the basis of refinery yields and the average Gulf Coast products prices for the last 6 months in 1950. The unit margin remained constant regardless of the level of throughput in any refinery since it was assumed

EXHIBIT XX-5. UNIT COSTS AT VARYING LEVELS OF THROUGHPUT AND COMPARATIVE BREAK-EVEN POINTS FOR CONVENTIONAL REFINERIES OF DIFFERENT SIZES: 1950

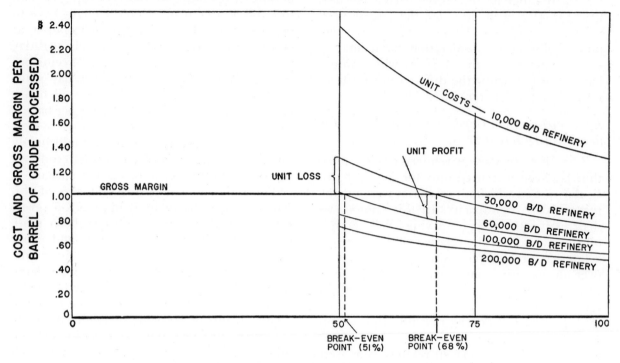

LEVEL OF THROUGHPUT (Percentage of Capacity)

EXHIBIT XX-6. RATES OF RETURN ON INVESTMENT AT VARYING LEVELS OF THROUGHPUT FOR CONVENTIONAL REFINERIES OF DIFFERENT SIZES: 1950

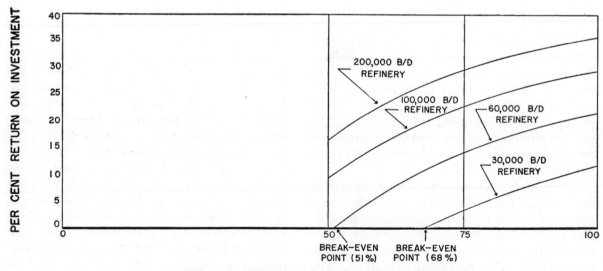

LEVEL OF THROUGHPUT (Percentage of Capacity)

that yields would not be varied at less than capacity operations. The point at which the margin line intersects the unit cost curve for any sized plant determines the level of throughput at which the unit margin was just adequate to cover unit costs in that plant. The intersection defines the so-called "break-even point." The vertical distance above the margin line to the unit cost curves on the graph measures the per unit losses at any level of throughput; the vertical distance below the margin line to the unit cost curves measures per unit profitability.

It is readily apparent from Exhibit XX-5 that the larger plants broke even at lower levels of throughput than did the smaller plants. Because of its marked inefficiencies, the 10,000 barrels per day refinery failed to cover its costs with the margin available at any point up to capacity.[12] The 30,000 barrels per day plant broke even with refinery runs at 68% of capacity, and the 60,000 barrels per day plant broke even at a 51% operating rate. The 100,000 and 200,000 barrels per day plants were profitable even at a 50% operating rate. These curves show very dramatically that the larger plants were better equipped cost and profit-wise to absorb a shut back in refinery runs than were the small plants.

The large plants also earned higher rates of return at all levels of throughput than did the smaller ones. In Exhibit XX-6 the percentage returns on investment are graphed for the refineries of different sizes and for varying levels of throughput at any one refinery.[13] These returns were before taxes, and they were determined for varying levels of throughput by the same general method described above to determine the rate of return at 100% of capacity. The curves originate at the break-even points for the various refineries and rise continually to 100% of capacity, at which point the greatest rate of return was received from each plant. The fact that the curves for successively larger refineries lie on top of one another clearly establishes the economic superiority of the larger

plants at each and every comparable level of throughput from 50% to 100% of capacity.

While the analysis in this section has pertained to the effect of size on efficiency for one very particular type of refinery, any of a number of other designs which might have been studied would have yielded the same basic conclusion that, for any single set of operating conditions, the larger plant of any one type had some very definite advantages over smaller refineries of the same basic design. Only the relative magnitude of the figures pertaining to any one type plant would have been changed.

Small companies have frequently been able to escape the processing cost disadvantages of smallness, however, because their plants have embodied different types of equipment than those of the large companies, and because they have often followed operating practices different from those of the large companies. A 2,000 barrels per day skimming plant would almost assuredly have lower unit processing costs than a 30,000 barrels per day refinery with catalytic cracking facilities, although the small plant could not, of course, produce gasoline of the same competitive quality as the large. Processing costs alone have not therefore always been of paramount importance in establishing the competitive position of the small firm.

II. THE EFFECT OF DIFFERENT TYPES OF PROCESSING EQUIPMENT ON THE EFFICIENCY OF REFINERIES OF THE SAME SIZE

The types of processing equipment employed in refineries affect efficiency by determining: (a) the extent to which a particular type of crude oil can be broken up into varying ratios of relatively high or low value products, (b) the operating costs per barrel of throughput, and (c) the quality of products. Each of these factors was discussed in Chapter Nineteen in terms of historical refineries of 25,000 barrels per day capacity. In the following paragraphs we shall first discuss, in somewhat more detail than was possible in Chapter Nineteen, the effect which different pieces of refinery equipment play in determining product yields and sales realization values. We shall then examine the economics of two modern refineries of the same size in which variances in the types of

---

[12] It should be remembered that the 10,000 barrels per day refinery used in this analysis was a hypothetical plant. It should not be inferred from the results obtained with this plant that a typical 10,000 barrels per day plant in the industry could not operate at a profit.

[13] The return on investment curve for the 10,000 barrels per day refinery was not plotted because the plant showed a negative return on investment at every point from 50% to 100% of capacity.

processing equipment caused differences in both operating costs and product yields. The improvement in the octane quality of gasoline achieved in successively more advanced plants was discussed in Chapter Nineteen, and we shall not consider this subject further in this chapter.

Differences in Products Yields and Unit Realizations:

It was observed in Chapter Nineteen that one of the major gains which has come about as a result of changes in refinery technology has been a comparative improvement in unit sales realizations, principally through the recovery of a higher proportion of light end products from each barrel of crude oil run. The product yield superiority of refineries composed of successively more modern pieces of processing equipment was discussed in terms of the typical yield of products which each of seven historical refineries was designed to produce. The realization values per barrel of crude oil run in the representative historical refineries ranged from $3.52 to $4.25 computed on the basis of New York harbor cargo prices in 1950 and the *typical product yields* of the several plants. This discussion established very clearly that the type of processing equipment used could result in very great differences in the typical revenues realized by several refineries of the same size. At this point we shall consider a further aspect of the shifts in product yields and sales realization values made possible by different types of equipment; namely, the *flexibility* of various types of processing equipment or the potentiality *to maximize or minimize the output of selected products.*

Almost every type of refinery has a certain amount of flexibility to alter the proportionate yield of different refined products from its "typical" yield structure. In fact, product yield flexibility has been sought in the design of a refinery in much the same manner as a generally favorable average yield of high value products. The economic advisability of varying products yields at a refinery has often shifted from day to day or seasonally along with changes in market prices, product specifications, the supply of the different types of crude oil available, and the cost structure at the refinery. One common adjustment has been to increase the yield of gasoline in the summer and heating oil in the winter in order to satisfy peak seasonal demands.

Since refining costs have varied with changes in product yields, and refined products prices themselves have been influenced in accordance with the relative amounts of different products thrown upon the market, the problem of deciding upon an optimum break-up of products with any particular pieces of processing equipment has been extremely complex. A further complication has been introduced by an economic consideration of the amounts of different products which should be stored to meet peak periods of product demand (see Chapter Eleven). The yield problem has been still further complicated by the alternative of installing supplementary pieces of equipment which could greatly enlarge the product flexibility of a refinery, although at a completely revised scale of unit operating costs.

At this point we shall examine the product yield flexibility of six typical refineries of the same size. Each of the six refineries is progressively more advanced in terms of its ability to reduce the relative output of residual fuel oil and generally to improve unit sales realizations. The equipment of the first refinery and the principal changes made in successively more advanced plants are as follows:

First refinery—atmospheric distillation and reforming units

Second refinery—add reduced crude or thermal cracking facilities

Third refinery—add catalytic cracking unit; eliminate reforming facilities

Fourth refinery—replace the atmospheric distillation unit with a two-stage, atmospheric and vacuum distillation unit; eliminate the reduced crude or thermal cracking facilities

Fifth refinery—add visbreaking facilities

Sixth Refinery—add a coking unit; eliminate the visbreaking facilities.

The product yields of the six refineries when operating for maximum gasoline, maximum distillate, and maximum heavy fuel oil production are shown in Exhibit XX-7. The yields were based upon a 50/50 mixture of representative East Texas-West Texas crude oils. Exhibit XX-7 also includes rough estimates of the refinery fuel requirements and the gas produc-

Exhibit XX-7. Product Flexibility of Typical Refineries

	Atmospheric Distillation, Reforming	Atmospheric Distillation, Reforming, Reduced Crude Cracking (Thermal)	Atmospheric Distillation, Catalytic Cracking, Reduced Crude Cracking (Thermal)	Atmospheric and Vacuum Distillation, Catalytic Cracking	Atmospheric and Vacuum Distillation, Catalytic Cracking, Visbreaking	Atmospheric and Vacuum Distillation, Catalytic Cracking, Coking
Maximum Gasoline (% Yields):						
Gasoline	31.0%	43.0%	51.8%	49.2%	50.2%	54.8%
Kerosene	5.0	5.0	5.0	5.0	5.0	5.0
Distillates	19.6	24.2	12.5	22.8	23.8	32.3
Residual Fuel Oil (before Refinery Fuel)	42.0	24.2	23.9	17.0	15.1	0.0*
Total	97.6	96.4	93.2	94.0	94.1	92.1
Refinery Fuel Required	3.0	7.5	7.0	4.0	4.0	5.0
Gas Produced (F.O.E.)†	2.0	3.5	‡	‡	‡	‡
Residual Fuel Oil Required	1.0	4.0	0.0	0.0	0.0	0.0
Residual Fuel Oil (after Refinery Fuel)	41.0	20.2	23.9	17.0	15.1	0.0
Maximum Distillate (% Yields):						
Gasoline	22.3	30.5	36.4	39.3	40.3	43.6
Kerosene	5.0	5.0	5.0	5.0	5.0	5.0
Distillates	32.6	41.0	39.5	34.4	39.3	44.4
Residual Fuel Oil (before Refinery Fuel)	37.4	20.0	15.7	16.2	10.4	0.0*
Total	97.3	96.5	96.6	94.9	95.0	93.0
Refinery Fuel Required	3.0	7.5	6.5	4.0	4.0	5.0
Gas Produced (F.O.E.)	2.0	3.5	4.0	†	†	†
Residual Fuel Oil Required	1.0	4.0	2.5	0.0	0.0	0.0
Residual Fuel Oil (after Refinery Fuel)	36.4	16.0	13.2	16.2	10.4	0.0
Maximum Fuel Oil (% Yields):						
Gasoline	22.3	30.5	36.4	39.3	40.3	43.6
Kerosene	5.0	5.0	5.0	5.0	5.0	5.0
Residual Fuel Oil (before Refinery Fuel)	70.0	61.0	55.2	50.6	49.7	44.4
Total (before Refinery Fuel)	97.3	96.5	96.6	94.9	95.0	93.0

Note: All yields based upon a 50/50 mixture of East and West Texas crude oils.

* The coking operation will produce roughly 3 pounds of coke per barrel of crude oil run.

† Fuel Oil Equivalent.

‡ Gas in excess of that required for refinery fuel will be produced. Gas produced in excess of refinery fuel requirements will be flared.

tion in each of the six plants when operated for maximum gasoline or maximum distillate production. It was assumed that any gaseous products would be fully consumed as refinery fuel before any liquid fuel oil would be deducted from refinery yields for use as a refinery fuel. In those cases where gas production exceeded refinery fuel requirements, it was assumed that the excess gas would be flared. In effect therefore product yield comparability among the different refineries was established after an adjustment had been made for the portion of the fuel oil yield which was required for refinery fuel in some of the plants. In order to simplify the comparison, the refineries did not include processes, such as polymerization, which convert refinery gases into gasoline.

The more advanced refineries in this study provided a much greater opportunity to vary the yields of particular refined products over a wide range, depending upon the economic advisability of maximizing or minimizing the yields of specific products. Since each of the six plants had an atmospheric crude oil distillation unit, any of the six plants could conceivably have cut back the yield of gasoline to as little as 22.3%, the lower limit in the least complicated plant, by shutting down certain units of equipment. Since gasoline was a comparatively high-price product, however, the upper range of yield potentiality on gasoline was likely to be more significant than the lower scale. The upper limit on gasoline production jumped from 31.0% in an atmospheric distillation process to 43.0% with thermal cracking. Catalytic cracking raised the upper yield limits on gasoline to between 49.2% to 54.8%. When a comparison is made of the relative flexibility of the plants with all process units in each refinery in operation, the plant with both thermal and catalytic cracking had the greatest range of flexibility on gasoline yields. It suffered by comparison, however, with several other plants when it was running for maximum gasoline production because its yields of distillates were reduced far below those of the more advanced plants.

One of the most significant advantages of the more advanced plants was their ability to cut back the output of the relatively low-price residual fuel oil. Again, presumably each of the six plants could, by equipment shutdowns when necessary, have yielded as much as 70% heavy fuel oil, which was the maximum yield from the atmospheric distillation unit. Because of the relatively low price of residual fuel oil in recent years, however, economic considerations have been much more likely to exert pressures for reducing its output. Before a reduction was made for refinery fuel, each of the more advanced plants offered a greater potentiality for curtailing the yield of residual fuel oil. The increased flexibility was gained regardless of whether the plants were running for maximum gasoline or maximum distillates production. Ultimately, with the addition of the coking unit, the yield of residual fuel oil was completely eliminated. While the distillation unit could not reduce the yield of heavy fuel oil below 37.4%, each of the plants with catalytic processes could cut the output of this product below 17.0%.

The plant, including both thermal and catalytic cracking units, possessed the greatest flexibility to alter the yield of distillates over a wide range. This plant could vary the yield of distillates from 12.5% to 39.5%, a range of 27%, which was greater than that attainable in any of the other plants, even with equipment shutdowns in the other plants. When the plant with thermal and catalytic cracking units was running for maximum distillate production, however, its yield of gasoline was not nearly so high as that of the more advanced plants.

The fact that the better equipped refineries were in a more favorable position to capitalize on the generally higher price scale which has evolved for the lighter petroleum products is evident from a comparison of the sales realizations per barrel of crude oil run which were afforded the six refineries on the basis of the refined products prices prevailing in selected months. The sales realizations per barrel of crude oil processed at maximum gasoline and maximum distillate production for each of the six refineries have been calculated on the basis of average Gulf Coast products prices for the five selected months in 1949, 1950, and 1951. The realization values are recorded in Exhibit XX-8.

The data show clearly that there was a greater potential to realize large unit revenues with the processes of the more advanced plants. In each of the five months, each successively more advanced plant offered a greater potential for revenue maximization than any preceding plant on the basis of either maximum gasoline or maximum distillate production.

In July 1950, for example, realizations of the different plants, on the basis of maximum gasoline production, ranged from $3.08 to $3.94 per barrel, a difference of 86 cents. In July 1949, when the refining industry was confronted with a recession of refined products prices of temporary duration, the advantage of the better equipped plants was even more striking. In this month realizations figured on the basis of maximum gasoline production ranged from $2.66 to $3.56 per barrel, a difference of 90 cents. The marked difference of 90 cents was explained largely by the ability of the refinery with the coking plant to eliminate completely the yield of heavy fuel oil, the price of which was depressed to a greater extent than that of other products.

The fact that each refinery had some product flexibility means that each plant had some defense against a sharp decline in the price of only one or two products. Likewise, each plant afforded some degree of opportunity to maximize the production of products which were abnormally high priced. The greater product flexibility of the better equipped plants, however, meant far stronger defenses and far greater revenue potentiality for these refineries.

It should not be inferred from the above discussion that the differences in unit sales reali-

Exhibit XX-8. Comparative Sales Realizations per Barrel of Crude Oil Run in Selected Months *

	Atmospheric Distillation, Reforming	Atmospheric Distillation, Reforming, Reduced Crude Cracking	Atmospheric Distillation, Catalytic Cracking, Reduced Crude Cracking	Atmospheric and Vacuum Distillation, Catalytic Cracking	Atmospheric and Vacuum Distillation, Catalytic Cracking, Visbreaking	Atmospheric and Vacuum Distillation, Catalytic Cracking, Coking †
Sales Realizations per Barrel, Maximum Gasoline Production:						
January 1949	$3.20	$3.46	$3.54	$3.63	$3.67	$3.86
July 1949	2.66	3.06	3.16	3.25	3.30	3.56
January 1950	2.85	3.17	3.25	3.35	3.39	3.60
July 1950	3.08	3.46	3.59	3.67	3.71	3.94
January 1951	3.09	3.45	3.55	3.64	3.69	3.93
Sales Realizations per Barrel, Maximum Distillates Production:						
January 1949	$3.15	$3.38	$3.54	$3.56	$3.65	$3.76
July 1949	2.59	2.94	3.12	3.14	3.25	3.42
January 1950	2.80	3.08	3.24	3.26	3.36	3.49
July 1950	2.97	3.28	3.48	3.52	3.62	3.76
January 1951	3.02	3.33	3.51	3.54	3.65	3.79

* Sales realizations computed from refinery yields given in Exhibit XX-7 and products prices reported for selected months in *Platt's Oil Price Handbooks.* (Average of highs and lows, Gulf Coast cargo prices.)

† Sales realizations based upon liquid products only.

zations reflected the actual disparity in profit before taxes available from refinery operations. As a general rule, the greater the yield of light end products taken from a barrel of crude oil, the higher the operating costs. The sales realization figures are presented principally to show that, for refineries of any one size, the entire range of opportunity for revenue maximization was greater as certain supplementary pieces of processing equipment were added.

Ordinarily the plants of small companies have not been so well equipped as those of their large competitors either to vary product yields or to capitalize upon the general price scale which has evolved for different refined products. Data were presented in Chapter Eighteen showing that small refining companies, as a group, have had a smaller share of cracking capacity in relation to their distillation capacity than large companies. Many of the plants held by small companies have been solely atmospheric distillation plants, thereby affording little product flexibility and little opportunity to increase the yield of the higher priced products.

It was also shown in Chapter Eighteen that the small companies have been particularly weak with respect to the ownership of catalytic cracking processes. In addition to the statistical comparisons which were made of the general plant aspects of large and small companies, the authors were given the opportunity to visit a number of refineries owned by large and small companies during the course of the field research on this project. The plant visitations confirmed the viewpoint that the small refiners were usually at a material disadvantage to the large companies in terms of the capabilities of the processing equipment employed to adjust yields and to maximize sales realizations. Elaborate and costly processes have been used very sparingly by small refiners. With a few notable exceptions therefore, the small refining company has been at a competitive disadvantage because of his inability to take as much out of any particular barrel of crude oil as his large competitors.

The Effect of Type of Processing Equipment on the Efficiency of Two Modern 25,000 Barrels per Day Refineries:

The foregoing discussion has provided a general indication of the advantages associated with different types of equipment. As a specific illustration, we shall at this point consider the economics of two 25,000 barrels per day re-

EXHIBIT XX-9. REFINERY EQUIPMENT FOR CONVENTIONAL AND COMBINATION UNIT REFINERIES OF 25,000 BARRELS PER DAY CAPACITY

Process	Conventional Refinery	Combination Unit Refinery
Distillation	Atmospheric and Vacuum Pipe Stills	Catalytic Combination Unit Includes: Atmospheric Pipe Still
Cracking	Fluid Catalytic Cracking Visbreaking	Thermal Cracking Fluid Catalytic Cracking
Light Ends	Stabilizer Absorber Splitter Debutanizer Nonselective Polymerization Polymer Rerunning	Fractionation and Light Ends Recovery
Treating		
Natural Naphtha	Continuous Caustic and Water Wash Copper Chloride	Caustic and Water Wash Doctor Sweeten
Cracked Naphtha	Clay Treat Copper Chloride	
Kerosene	Continuous Caustic and Water Wash Sand Filter Clay Strain	
Heating Oil	Continuous Caustic and Water Wash Sand Filter Clay Strain	Continuous Caustic and Water Wash

fineries of different design. One plant is of conventional design; the other is a combination unit refinery. The size of the plants was held constant in order that the effect of different types of equipment could be measured independently of the effect of size. The comparison is for plants in which there was no appreciable difference in the quality of products yielded. For example, the equipment of both refineries yielded gasolines of identical octane quality.

The 25,000 barrels per day conventional refinery was a scaled down replica of the 30,000 barrels per day refinery considered in the first section of this chapter. The equipment in the combination unit refinery was representative of the type which might have been used by a progressive small refiner in 1950 if he was building a new plant. The combination unit refinery contained a fluid combination unit in which atmospheric distillation, thermal reforming, and fluid catalytic cracking were performed. The combination unit refinery, however, omitted the visbreaking, polymerization, and vacuum distillation processes of the con-

ventional refinery. As a result of these changes, the combination unit had less product flexibility and lower yields of gasoline and heating oil than the conventional 25,000 barrels per day refinery. The average yield structure for which the refineries were designed to operate was as follows:

	Yield of Refined Products	
	Conventional Refinery	Combination Unit Refinery
Gasoline	48%	45%
Kerosene	10	10
Heating Oil	23	15
Fuel Oil Equivalent	19	30
	100%	100%

A detailed summary of the processing equipment included in the two plants is given in Exhibit XX-9.

The combination unit had investment costs substantially below those of the conventional refinery. As shown in Exhibit XX-10, the cost of process units was reduced from $11,700,000 to $5,700,000 and that of utilities from $11,300,-

EXHIBIT XX-10. INVESTMENT COSTS AT EAST COAST LOCATION FOR CONVENTIONAL AND COMBINATION UNIT REFINERIES OF 25,000 BARRELS PER DAY CAPACITY: 1950

	Conventional Refinery	Combination Unit Refinery
Process Equipment		
Distillation	$ 2,400,000	
Cracking	3,800,000	Combina-
Light Ends	4,500,000	tion Unit
Finishing	1,000,000	
Total Process Equipment	$11,700,000	5,700,000
Utilities and General		
Refinery Offsites	11,300,000	9,150,000
Tankage	1,500,000	1,150,000
Total Investment Cost	$24,500,000	$16,000,000
Investment Cost per Barrel of Capacity	$980	$640

000 to $9,150,000.[14] The $350,000 saving in tankage was made because the combination unit required less intermediate or processing tankage than the conventional refinery. The total investment cost was reduced from $24,-500,000 to $16,000,000 or from $980 to $640 per barrel of capacity. With a financial charge of 6% on the original investment, the combination unit represented a financial saving of $510,000 yearly.

The combination unit refinery not only entailed a considerably smaller capital outlay than the conventional refinery; it also had a much lower scale of operating costs. Unit processing costs for the two refineries at levels of throughput from 50% to 100% of capacity are plotted in Exhibit XX-11. The vertical distance between the sloping lines reveals that at 100% of capacity the combination unit had a unit processing cost advantage of 26 cents per barrel; at a 50% level of throughput the advantage was even more pronounced, amounting to 48 cents per barrel. The fact that the disparity in operating costs increased continually at points further below capacity was a reflection of the fact that fixed cost elements con-

stituted a higher proportion of total costs in the conventional refinery.[15] The combination unit refinery was therefore considerably less vulnerable cost- and profit-wise to conditions which might cause runs to be shut back below capacity.

Because of the greater yield of high value products obtainable from the conventional refinery, its unit sales realization was higher than that of the combination unit refinery. As shown by the horizontal lines in Exhibit XX-11, the combination unit suffered losses in realization value (and also losses in unit margins) amounting to 22 cents per barrel as contrasted with the conventional refinery. The margins were determined by subtracting the delivered cost of a 50/50 mixture of East and West crude oil at an East Coast location from the revenue per barrel of products based upon average New York cargo pieces for the last six months of 1950.[16] The points at which the unit margin lines intersect the unit cost curves for the respective refineries determine the level of crude oil throughput which these two refineries had to maintain in order to break even. With a break-even point of 55% compared with 70% for the conventional refinery, the combination unit was in a stronger profit position on the basis of 1950 costs and prices.

When the profits before taxes at various levels of throughput are expressed in terms of a rate of return on the original investments, the advantages of the combination unit are readily apparent. As shown in Exhibit XX-12, the rate of return at 100% of capacity during the last six months of 1950 would have been 18% for the combination unit and 10% for the conventional refinery.[17]

The foregoing analysis of two modern refineries of the same crude oil capacity has shown that initial capital investments, operating costs, and sales realizations can vary greatly for two refineries of the same size com-

---

[14] Utilities were included under the assumption that power would be purchased and steam generated at 150 pounds per square inch gauge.

[15] The division of fixed and variable costs for the two refineries was made under the same assumptions used in the earlier analysis of conventional refineries of different sizes.

[16] Spot charter tanker rates for movements from the Gulf to East Coasts for the last six months of 1950 were added to the delivered cost of crude oil to the Gulf Coast to arrive at the delivered cost of crude oil at an East Coast location.

[17] Rates of return were determined before provision for federal and state income taxes.

EXHIBIT XX-11. UNIT COSTS AT VARYING LEVELS OF THROUGHPUT AND COMPARATIVE
BREAK-EVEN POINTS FOR CONVENTIONAL AND COMBINATION UNIT REFINERIES
OF 25,000 BARRELS PER DAY CAPACITY: 1950

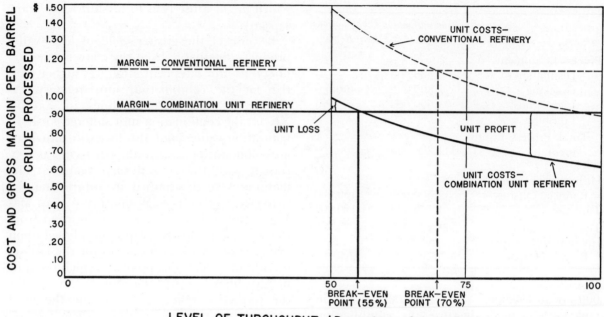

EXHIBIT XX-12. RATES OF RETURN AT VARYING LEVELS OF THROUGHPUT
FOR CONVENTIONAL AND COMBINATION UNIT REFINERIES
OF 25,000 BARRELS PER DAY CAPACITY: 1950

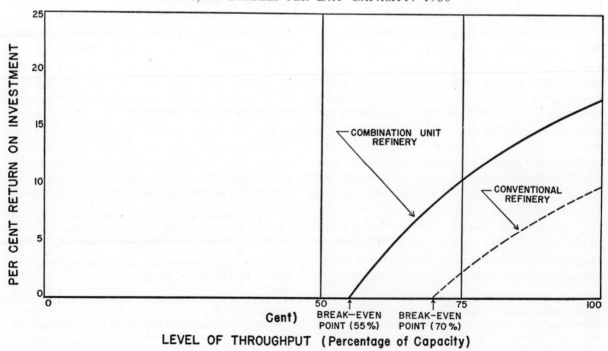

prised of different pieces of processing equipment. In this particular case, a combination unit more than recouped losses in sales realization relative to a conventional refinery by the gains which it made in terms of operating and investment costs. Since the combination unit refinery contained equipment representative of that which might have been employed by a progressive small refiner, the comparison gives some insight into the means by which the small refiner has often been able to offset at least a portion of the disadvantages of smallness in refinery processing through use of different types of equipment.

III. Comparative Analysis of a Typical Small vs. a Typical Large Refinery, Both of Modern Design

In the two preceding sections of this chapter we examined first the effect of size and second the effect of different types of processing equipment on refinery efficiency. In this section we shall broaden the analysis to include the effects of both size and type of equipment. For purposes of illustration, two refineries which were typical of those among the most modern developed in 1950 will be used. One typifies the type of plant which might have been built by a small refiner and the other is the type of plant which might have been erected by a large refining company.

The first plant is a 10,000 barrels per day fluid combination unit refinery which is a smaller replica of the 25,000 barrels per day combination unit refinery discussed in the preceding section. As representative of the type of plant which might have been employed by a larger company, the 30,000 barrels per day conventional refinery described in the first section of this chapter will be used. The investment and operating costs are for a Gulf Coast location as of 1950.

It should be noted at the outset that this analysis portrays a very particular case situation. Both of these plants were extremely modern, and in actuality there were no plants owned by either large or small companies which precisely duplicated these facilities. As was pointed out in Chapter Eighteen, only a few of the small refiners owned catalytic cracking units in 1950.

While most of the larger plants in the industry were of conventional design, a 30,000 barrels per day combination unit might have been used instead of a conventional refinery as the modern, large-size plant. In the preceding section it was observed that a 25,000 barrels per day combination unit refinery offered some very distinct advantages over a conventional refinery of the same size in terms of capital investments and operating costs; a 30,000 barrels per day combination unit would have showed the same advantages over a conventional refinery of the same size. Moreover, a plant larger than the 30,000 barrels per day conventional refinery might have been used to contrast with the 10,000 barrels per day combination unit refinery. Cross-reference to the first section of the chapter will reveal the extent to which an even larger conventional refinery would have realized added advantages over the 30,000 barrels conventional refinery used. It is believed, however, that the two plants selected give a realistic, but particularized, comparison of modern plants which might have been built in 1950 by large and small companies. The analysis assumes that the wage scale for refinery labor, the delivered cost of crude oil, the selling prices of refined products, and all other operating practices were the same for the large and the small companies, which would not necessarily be the case.

Comparative Investment Costs and Financial Charges:

As shown in Exhibit XX-13 a 30,000 barrels per day conventional refinery entailed an initial capital outlay somewhat over three times as large as a 10,000 barrels per day combination unit plant. The investment cost per barrel of capacity was therefore somewhat greater for the larger conventional refinery: $833 per barrel as compared with $780 per barrel for the combination unit plant. Using an interest rate of 6%, yearly financial charges were $468,000 for the small plant and $1,500,000 for the larger plant. The financial charges at a 6% rate amounted to approximately 13 cents per barrel of crude oil processed for the 10,000 barrels per day plant and 14 cents per barrel of crude oil processed for the 30,000 barrels per day refinery. It is evident therefore that the smaller plant had a financial advantage of

EXHIBIT XX-13. INVESTMENT COSTS AT GULF COAST LOCATION FOR 10,000 BARRELS PER DAY COMBINATION UNIT REFINERY AND 30,000 BARRELS PER DAY CONVENTIONAL REFINERY: 1950

	Combination Unit Refinery	Conventional Refinery
Capacity (Barrels per Day)	10,000	30,000
Investments		
Process Units	$2,800,000	$12,000,000
Utilities and General Refinery Offsites	4,550,000	11,400,000
Tankage	450,000	1,600,000
Total	$7,800,000	$25,000,000
Investment Cost per Barrel of Capacity	$780	$ 833

roughly 1 cent per barrel at 100% of capacity; at 50% of capacity the financial advantage of the smaller plant was 2 cents per barrel.

Comparative Profitability of the Two Plants:

The larger plant had a greater profit potential per barrel of crude oil processed than the smaller plant. As shown in Exhibit XX-14, the operating costs of the larger plant were approximately the same as those of the smaller plant with refinery runs at 100% of capacity and approximately 1 cent less with refinery runs at 50% of capacity. The difference in operating costs alone does not, however, provide an equitable basis for comparing the profitability of the refineries, since the 10,000 barrels per day combination unit had less desirable product yields. On the basis of average products prices for the last six months of 1950, the loss in sales realization values arising from differing yields amounted to approximately 19 cents per barrel of crude oil run. When this relative loss is superimposed upon the unit processing costs of the smaller plant, as is shown in Exhibit XX-14, it is evident that the unit profit advantage before taxes and financial charges of the larger plant amounted to approximately 18 cents per barrel at levels of throughput ranging from 50% to 100% of capacity. Thus, the larger plant held a substantial advantage, principally because of its

better product yields and also because of its slightly lower unit process cost, which was more than adequate to offset the somewhat higher unit financial charges.

The improved yields of higher price products permitted the 30,000 barrels per day refinery to break even at an appreciably lower level of throughput than the smaller plant. Based on 1950 costs and prices, as shown in Exhibit XX-15, the 30,000 barrels per day refinery earned a profit when throughput was maintained at levels above 68% of capacity. In contrast, the 10,000 barrels per day refinery needed to run at 88% of capacity before its unit processing costs were covered by unit realizations less crude oil and transportation costs. Therefore the larger plant was less vulnerable to the forces and circumstances which might cause refinery runs to be curtailed.

A company owning the larger plant was assured, all other things being equal, of a higher rate of profitability on its original capital investment than a company owning the smaller one at each and every comparable level of throughput from 50% to 100% of capacity. The rates of return on investments before taxes, based on 1950 costs and prices, are plotted in Exhibit XX-16. This chart shows that at 100% of capacity a company using a modern 30,000 barrels per day conventional refinery would have earned a return on its investment approximately 8 percentage points higher than a refiner using an efficient, smaller, and different type of plant. This analysis reveals that a company which could afford to make the greater initial capital outlay and which had the input and output assurances that a larger plant would require had certain advantages over the small refiner from the time the plants were built.

The relative cost and profitability figures presented in this section illustrate *one concrete example* of the basic disadvantage which a progressive small refiner might have suffered in competition with a larger company also owning modern facilities if only size and type of equipment were different in the two situations. As will be noted later, there are many ways by which small refiners are often able to offset the disadvantages associated with the size and type of equipment they customarily employ.

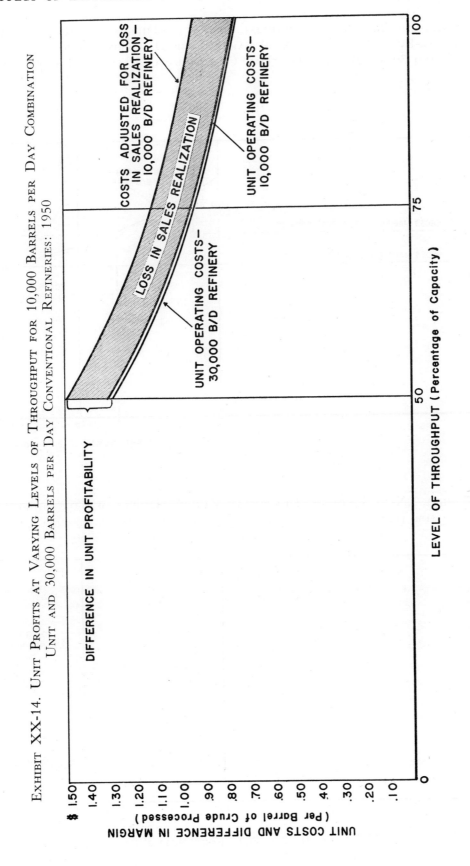

Exhibit XX-14. Unit Profits at Varying Levels of Throughput for 10,000 Barrels per Day Combination Unit and 30,000 Barrels per Day Conventional Refineries: 1950

EXHIBIT XX-15. UNIT COSTS AT VARYING LEVELS OF THROUGHPUT AND COMPARATIVE
BREAK-EVEN POINTS FOR 10,000 BARRELS PER DAY COMBINATION UNIT
AND 30,000 BARRELS PER DAY CONVENTIONAL REFINERIES: 1950

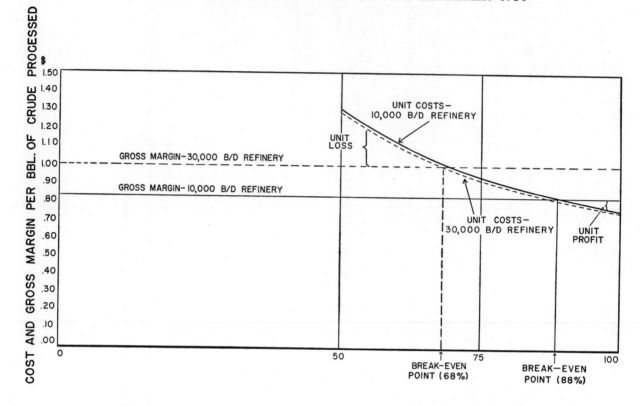

EXHIBIT XX-16. RATES OF RETURN AT VARYING LEVELS OF THROUGHPUT
FOR 10,000 BARRELS PER DAY COMBINATION UNIT AND 30,000
BARRELS PER DAY CONVENTIONAL REFINERIES: 1950

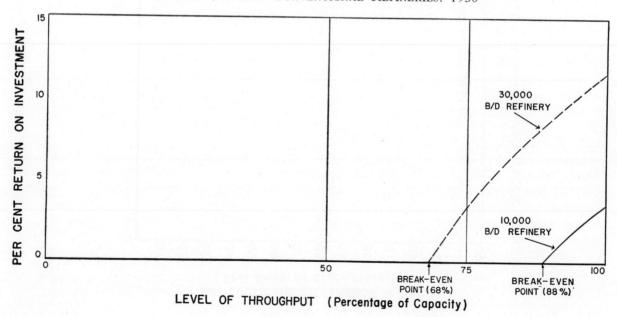

IV. The Effect of Differences in Operating Practices

The analyses presented thus far in the chapter have indicated that the small plant is under a considerable handicap relative to the larger one when both are operated in accordance with the same practices. The small refiners have, however, often been able to offset their disadvantage of size by adopting operating practices at their plants which are different from those of large companies. Many small refiners have run premium-grade crude oils to secure a range of products differing from those obtained by large companies. Small refiners have frequently employed fewer personnel per barrel of crude oil throughput, paid lower hourly wage rates, and offered fewer fringe benefits to employees than have large companies. Moreover, the fact that the employees of some small refiners have been organized by industrial or company unions rather than craft unions has allowed them greater freedom in making work assignments to a given employee than has been possible in certain large companies.

Small companies have frequently held down the sizes of supporting activities such as the accounting, purchasing, warehousing, research, medical, and maintenance departments. In many cases, moreover, such supporting services have been purchased by small refiners rather than staffed and maintained by the companies themselves. Many small refiners have operated with fewer or smaller offsite facilities such as docks, tankage, repair shops, and office buildings than have large companies. It has often proved more beneficial for the small refiner to provide only an irreducible minimum of such offsite facilities and to rent the remainder from outsiders rather than to own and operate all the various adjuncts to a refinery operation. Finally, substantial savings have often been made by small refiners through the selection of less costly real estate sites and through shortcuts in the construction, design, and upkeep of facilities.

As a means of illustrating some of the arrangements by which the small refiner has improved or can improve his competitive position relative to large firms, we shall draw upon a study which the Zephyr Oil Company [18] prepared in the early part of 1953. The study set up a series of five case comparisons summarized in Exhibit XX-17, in which (a) refinery size, (b) type of crude oil and products, (c) manpower, (d) offsite facilities, and (e) product yields were varied. The refineries used in the case comparisons were modern plants that might have been erected at a selected location.

In computing the investment costs, operating expenses, and profitability of the plants, 1953 costs and prices were utilized. Operating costs were based upon total refinery personnel, including all process, oil movement, utility, mechanical, supervisory, and overhead labor. Payroll burden was calculated as a percentage of the total payroll and included allowances for fringe benefits. Contract labor and maintenance overtime costs were computed in accordance with the number and kinds of personnel allocated to the various situations. Other major items reflected in the operating costs included appropriate amounts for repair materials, chemicals, catalysts, lead costs, research costs, and purchased utilities; and a charge based upon the investments to cover depreciation and local taxes. In addition, administrative and general expenses, supplies, and other expenses were included. The total operating costs were developed on an ex-fuel basis. Accordingly, the product realization values were calculated after deducting the refinery fuel required for each case. Crude oil and products prices were based upon 1953 prices at the Gulf Coast, plus an estimated long-range freight cost to the selected refinery site.

As a starting point for the analysis (see Exhibit XX-17, "Zephyr Case"), the study compared the advantages of 100,000 and 25,000 barrels per day plants which might have been built and operated under similar operating practices. The 100,000 barrels per day plant was a refinery including two-stage (atmospheric and vacuum) distillation, catalytic reforming, catalytic cracking, residuum reduction, nonselective polymerization, and sour product finishing facilities. The 25,000 barrels per day plant was a simpler refinery with atmospheric crude distillation, thermal reform-

---

[18] Fictitious name of a large refiner which made available to the authors the data upon which much of the discussion in this section is based.

ing, and catalytic cracking facilities, as well as equipment for residuum reduction, nonselective polymerization, and product finishing. Both refineries were designed to process sour crude oil and to yield products as shown below: [19]

Zephyr Case	Per Cent Yields (*Liquid Volume*)	
	100,000 B/D Refinery	25,000 B/D Refinery
Gasoline	42.1%	41.2%
Middle Distillates	49.0	48.9
Bunker Fuel	0.0	0.0
Excess Gas (above fuel requirements)	2.9	4.2
Thermal Coke (tons per day)	200 tons	60 tons

In both refineries it was planned that the output of bunker fuel oil (residual fuel oil) would be completely eliminated, although a small amount of excess gas and thermal coke would be made.

Since the Zephyr Case comparison was predicated upon uniform operating practices, the situation is analogous to those presented in the earlier part of this chapter dealing with the effects of size and type of equipment. As might be anticipated, the 100,000 barrels per day refinery would have shown some very appreciable advantages over the 25,000 barrels per day refinery. It is evident from Exhibit XX-17 that the larger plant could have yielded an attractive profit of 37.5 cents per barrel of crude oil processed and a return of 15.4% on an investment of $90,000,000.[20] In contrast, the smaller plant would have earned only 3.6 cents per barrel of crude oil processed and a return of 1.1% on the investment of $37,000,000. It should also be noted that the investment costs per barrel of capacity would have been 65% higher for the smaller plant than for the large. Having established these economic yardsticks for Zephyr Oil Company conditions of operation, further comparisons were made showing how the profitability and return on invest-

[19] The sour crude oil in both cases was essentially West Texas crude oil.

[20] Profits throughout this section were computed before federal income taxes but after a reasonable allowance for depreciation. Both profits and the percentage return on investments were computed with the plants operating at 100% of capacity.

ment of a 25,000 barrels per day plant could have been improved under a range of modified operating conditions.

Effect of Types of Crude Oil and Product Yields:

One of the ways by which a small refiner could have improved the profit performance of the 25,000 barrels per day plant was to run better types and grades of crude oil to somewhat different product yields than those on which the Zephyr Case was based. The large refiner would ordinarily operate with readily available crude oils and meet whatever market requirements for refined products developed. Thus, the large refiner would not be free to engage in selected crude oil operations. Small refiners were often confronted with different supply and market requirements and were therefore able to base their operations upon light sweet rather than sour crude oils. Light sweet crude oils are of a higher refinery value than sour crude oils because their constituents include greater proportions of light products, such as gasoline, and lesser proportions of corrosive sulphur compounds.

To evaluate the effect on refining economics of changing the types and grades of crude oil run to a refinery and the products derived therefrom, a 25,000 barrels per day refinery running sour crude oil was compared with a plant of the same size designed for processing of light sweet crude. All other operating practices were held constant in this comparison. The light sweet crude oil selected was representative of what might have been processed by a small refiner in South Texas. An "optimum" product yield was selected for the sweet crude oil refinery. The optimum product yield was that which afforded the greatest profit per barrel of crude oil processed. In contrast, the product yields of the sour crude oil refinery were based upon estimated market requirements. Comparative product yields, excluding refinery fuel, are shown on the top of page 582.

As shown in Exhibit XX-17 under the heading Case A, the sweet crude oil refinery would have offered some advantages over a sour crude oil refinery of the same size. A shift from a sour crude oil with no bunker fuel production to a light sweet crude oil with normal heavy fuel

EXHIBIT XX-17. EFFECT OF OPERATING PRACTICES ON REFINERY ECONOMICS

Comparison		Assumed Bases					Anticipated Results			
	Crude Oil Capacity B/D	Crude Oil Type	Product Yield Basis	Manpower Basis	Offsites Basis	Investment Cost per Barrel	Profit per Barrel*	Percentage Return on Investment*	Men per 1,000 Barrels of Crude Oil Capacity
Zephyr Case — Effect of Refinery Size	100,000	Sour	Market Requirements	Zephyr	Zephyr	$ 900	$0.375	15.4%	12.05
	25,000	Sour	Market Requirements	Zephyr	Zephyr	1,480	0.036	1.1	20.15
Case A — Effect of Type of Crude Oil and Products	25,000	Sour	Market Requirements	Zephyr	Zephyr	1,480	0.036	1.1	20.15
	25,000	Light Sweet	Optimum	Zephyr	Zephyr	1,000	0.109	4.0	14.95
Case B — Effect of Reduced Manpower	25,000	Light Sweet	Optimum	Zephyr	Zephyr	1,000	0.109	4.0	14.95
	25,000	Light Sweet	Optimum	Small Refiner	Zephyr	960	0.219	8.4	8.50
	25,000	Sour	Market Requirements	Zephyr	Zephyr	1,480	0.036	1.1	20.15
	25,000	Sour	Market Requirements	Small Refiner	Zephyr	1,440	0.165	4.4	12.20
Case C — Effect of Reduced Offsites	25,000	Light Sweet	Optimum	Small Refiner	Zephyr	960	0.219	8.4	8.50
	25,000	Light Sweet	Optimum	Small Refiner	Small Refiner	680†	0.267	14.5	7.48
Case D — Effect of Product Yields	25,000	Light Sweet	Optimum	Small Refiner	Small Refiner	680†	0.267	14.5	7.48
	25,000	Light Sweet	Maximum Middle Distillates	Small Refiner	Small Refiner	520†	0.214	15.2	6.84

* Profits and percentage returns on investments were computed after depreciation but before income taxes. Rental charges are included in operating costs. Indicated investment costs would be increased by about $200 per barrel of capacity if crude oil and refined products tankage and docks were owned rather than rented.

† Crude oil and refined products tankage and docks costing $5,000,000 are rented from others.

Case A	Per Cent Yields (Liquid Volume)	
	Sour Crude Oil Refinery	Light Sweet Crude Oil Refinery
Gasoline	41.2%	43.4%
Middle Distillates	48.9	43.4
Bunker Fuel	0.0	9.8
Excess Gas, Fuel Oil Equivalent (FOE)	4.2*	0.5
	94.3%	97.1%

* In addition, some thermal coke was produced.

production would have reduced the refinery investment by one-third, increased profits by 7.3 cents per barrel, and improved the rate of return on the plant investment by 2.9 percentage points.

The use of sweet crude oils would have permitted an appreciable saving in investment cost to be made on practically all individual pieces of processing equipment as well as on utilities. In the sweet crude oil refinery, moreover, thermal reforming would have been unnecessary, residuum reduction would not have been justified because of the relatively small percentage of bottoms in the crude oil, and treating facilities could have been curtailed.

Although not shown in Exhibit XX-17, the components contributing to the increase in profitability of 7.3 cents per barrel crude oil processed were an improvement in sales realization amounting to 4 cents per barrel and a reduction in operating costs of 25.3 cents per barrel arising principally from savings on labor and depreciation expenses. Offsetting the gross gain of 29.3 cents per barrel was an increased crude oil cost of 22 cents per barrel, leaving a net rise in profits of 7.3 cents per barrel. It might be noted therefore that the advantage of the sweet crude oil operation would have disappeared if the differential between the average sour crude oil price and the average sweet crude oil price had been roughly 7 cents greater than that existing early in 1953.

Effect of Reduced Manpower:

A second way in which small refiners could have improved their competitive positions was to employ fewer personnel per 1,000 barrels of crude oil capacity [21] than did large companies.

---

[21] For refineries of the same general size.

Consultations with other large and small refining companies revealed that the personnel requirements of small refiners per barrel of capacity were often less than those of the larger companies. Although we did not accumulate statistical evidence on this point during the course of our research, several small refiners did cite differences in staffing requirements as a principal source of competitive strength. Differences in manpower were explained partially by the greater flexibility which unions sometimes allowed small companies in planning the work assignments of employees and partially by the difficulty certain large companies experienced in "eliminating a job once it was created or releasing an employee once he was hired."

Case B in Exhibit XX-17 measures the effect on profitability of shifting from the "Zephyr" manning basis to a "small refiner" manning basis. Case B establishes, for both sour and sweet crude oil refineries of 25,000 barrels per day capacities, the important gains realizable with less operating personnel. The sweet crude oil refinery might have been operated by a small refiner with a 43% smaller workforce than was planned by the Zephyr Oil Company, thereby reducing the operating costs and increasing the profit of the small refiner by 11 cents per barrel. The saving would have improved the rate of return on investment earned by the small refiner by 4.4 percentage points. With respect to the sour crude oil refineries, the cost saving arising from reduced manpower needs (12.9 cents per barrel) would have been greater than in the sweet crude oil refineries, but the improvement in rate of return (3.3 percentage points) would not have been so large because of the greater total investment in the sour crude oil refineries.

It should be noted that wage and salary rates and employee benefits were identical for all case comparisons. Still further savings would, of course, have accrued to small refiners able to negotiate lower wage rates. The slight reductions in investment costs of $40 per barrel of capacity for both the sweet and sour crude oil refineries when running with reduced manpower were attributable to the fact that certain offsite facilities, such as cafeterias and office buildings, would have been somewhat smaller in size with fewer personnel.

Effect of Reduced Offsites:

A third way in which small refiners could have increased the attractiveness of the refining operation was by renting certain offsite facilities, by holding down their investments in offsites which they owned, and by purchasing selected services. Offsite facilities frequently rented by small refiners include docks, tankage, loading and warehousing facilities, land, and some buildings. The erection of small frame buildings for offices also often holds down investments in offsites. The use of steam boilers in process units, without spares, and the curtailment of tankage likewise decreases investment outlays in some instances. Services sometimes purchased at an over-all cost saving by small refiners include maintenance work as well as accounting and medical assistance.

The effect of reduced offsites was studied only for sweet crude oil refineries staffed on a small refiner manpower basis. As revealed in Case C, Exhibit XX-17, the switch to a smaller refiner basis for offsite practices would have meant a substantial saving of 30% in refinery investment costs, a profit increase of 4.8 cents per barrel, and a return on the refinery investment of 6.1 percentage points higher than could be secured with the offsite practices of the large company. The conversion to a small refiner basis for offsites would have reduced both depreciation and labor costs. On the other hand, rental and service charges would have been paid to outside organizations for services and leased facilities.[22] It was believed that a net gain would have accrued to the small refiner because outside specialists could have provided particular services and offsite facilities at lower costs than Zephyr in a 25,000 barrels per day plant.

By applying the several changes in operating practices discussed thus far, a small refiner could have built and operated a modern refinery of 25,000 barrels per day capacity and earned a rate of return on his investment almost as high as that secured by the Zephyr Oil Company with a 100,000 barrels per day plant. As noted above, a 100,000 barrels per day re-

finery running sour crude oil with Zephyr's operating practices could have been built for an investment of $900 per barrel and earned a 15.4% return on the owner's investment. By running light sweet crude oil, reducing manpower requirements, and holding offsites investments to a minimum, a small refiner could have erected a 25,000 barrels per day refinery at an investment cost of $680 per barrel of capacity and could have operated the plant to earn a 14.5% return on his investment. It is readily apparent therefore that despite an inherent disadvantage arising from small size, the small refiner could have done much to offset his handicap through his selection of operating practices.

Effect of Product Yields:

Still a fourth method by which a small refiner could have increased his profitability was through the careful selection of product yields. As a means of demonstrating the opportunity that existed for product specialists, Case D compares two refineries, each of 25,000 barrels per day capacity, that were specifically designed to fulfill different product yield objectives. Using identical types and grades of light sweet crude oil, one plant was designed for the production of an optimum product yield and the other for the production of maximum middle distillates. As noted above, the optimum product yield was defined as the one which maximized the profit per barrel of crude oil processed. Comparative product yields were as follows:

Case D	Per Cent Yields (Liquid Volume)	
	Optimum Yield	Maximum Middle Distillates
Gasoline	43.4%	27.8%
Middle Distillates	43.4	59.9
Bunker Fuel	9.8	9.0
Excess Gas (FOE), above refinery fuel requirements	0.5	0.8
	97.1%	97.5%

Both refineries were studied on the basis of "small refiner" manning and offsites practices (see Cases B and C).

The most significant finding of Case D, as

---

22 Because of the absence of specific information, expenses amounting to 10% per year on the estimated investment costs of rented facilities were assumed in figuring operating costs.

shown in Exhibit XX-17, was that the refinery maximizing middle distillates would have cost only three-fourths as much to build as the refinery running for optimum yields. The difference in investment costs would have been so marked that the refinery maximizing distillates production would have been able to earn an over-all return of 15.2% on the investment as compared with 14.5% for the other plant despite the fact that its profit would have been 5.3 cents less per barrel of crude oil processed. The savings in investment costs would have been accounted for principally by the much smaller catalytic cracking unit, the lesser amount of light ends processing equipment, the omission of the polymerization plant, and the attendant reductions in utilities and offsites needed to meet the changed yield objectives. The lower profit per barrel of crude oil processed earned by the refinery maximizing distillates production would have resulted from the fact that a gain in operating costs of 13.7 cents per barrel would have been more than compensated by a loss in sales realization value amounting to 19 cents per barrel.

For our purposes, the most important conclusion that might be reached on the basis of the study conducted by the Zephyr Oil Company is that small refiners could in 1953 have erected fully modern 25,000 barrels per day plants and earned rates of return on their investments which were comparable with those which the Zephyr Oil Company might have secured on the substantially greater investment needed for a 100,000 barrels per day plant. The opportunity to overcome the basic disadvantages of size existed because of differences in operating practices with regard to such matters as the types of crude oil run, manpower requirements, refinery offsites, and product yields.

Throughout the course of our field research, small refiners emphasized the importance to their success of the differences between their operations and those of the large companies.[23] Among the differences in operating conditions mentioned frequently were the factors studied by the Zephyr Oil Company. Many of these practices were, of course, applied with similar results in plants much smaller than 25,000 bar-

rels per day. The Zephyr study did not, moreover, take into consideration all the differences in operating practices which sometimes existed between large and small companies or between different large and different small companies.[24] It was assumed in all cases, for example, that there would be no reduction in wage rates, including all fringe benefits, under the small refiner mode of operation and that all process and offsite units would follow the same process, mechanical, and safety standards.

At this point we should like to modify the economic analyses presented in this chapter in accordance with the types of refineries that actually existed in the industry in the 1950's. The refineries cited throughout this chapter were all extremely modern plants whose investment costs were based upon 1950 or 1953 construction costs. All returns on investments were therefore rather low as compared with existing refineries because the calculations were based upon relatively high 1950 and 1953 investment costs. Moreover, the engineering standards for all plants in the analyses were set at very high levels. By making some compromises with these standards, companies employing the same basic processes could, and often did, operate at lower processing costs than those cited in this chapter.

One other important general qualification that should be made to the analyses presented in this chapter is that few small refiners possessed the types of modern processing equipment discussed. The analyses are more appropriate therefore as a means of gauging the competitive effectiveness of the small refiner if he were to take full advantage of the stage of the refining art as it existed in the early 1950's. Since only a handful of small refiners had catalytic and other advanced processes entailing higher unit processing costs, the small firms were likely to have processing costs on a generally lower scale than those reported in the foregoing cost analyses. At the same time, however, the small refiners were undoubtedly sacrificing dollar sales realizations and quality of products because of the comparatively inferior processes through which they achieved the lower operating costs.

---

[23] This concept will be treated more fully in Chapter Twenty-Three.

[24] It is, of course, true that significant differences in operating practices often existed within a group of large companies and within a group of small companies.

V. Summary

1. Large refineries have distinct economic advantages over small refineries of the same type and design. A study of conventional refineries ranging in size from 10,000 to 200,000 barrels per day revealed that the large plants had lower investment costs per barrel of capacity and lower unit operating costs than the small plants. The lower unit operating costs resulted primarily from the savings in depreciation charges associated with the smaller investment costs per barrel and from savings in labor and other fixed costs. Differences in variable costs likewise favored the large plants, but the savings were not so appreciable as they were on fixed costs. The large plants offered a higher rate of return on capital invested than the small plants at any comparable level of throughput from 50% to 100% of capacity. The large plants also broke even at lower levels of throughput than the small plants and were therefore less vulnerable profit-wise to the various circumstances which might cause reductions in refinery runs.

2. Well-equipped refineries have some significant advantages because they obtain higher quality products and more favorable product yields than refineries that are less well-equipped. Of particular importance from a quality standpoint is the ability of certain modern refinery processes to secure gasoline of a high octane quality. The better-equipped plants are usually able to secure higher refinery sales realizations because the *typical* yields include a large proportion of the higher value products such as gasoline and because the *flexibility* of the equipment permits yields of individual products to be adjusted over a wide range when market conditions warrant.

3. The economic characteristics of different sizes and types of equipment discussed in this chapter have presented a continuing dilemma to the small refiner. If he builds plants comparable in design with those of his large competitors, he may suffer significant disadvantages in terms of processing costs per barrel. If, on the other hand, he builds plants less well-equipped than those of his large competitors, he may be able to secure processing costs equal to or better than those of the large firms but only at the expense of significant losses in product quality and product yields. As a general rule, small refiners have characteristically followed the second course. As a result, their processing costs have been reasonably well in line with those of large firms, but they have operated at a disadvantage because of their inability to produce high-quality products and to obtain a favorable yield of higher price products.

4. Small refiners have often offset the inherent disadvantages arising from the size or type of equipment they employed by following operating practices differing from those of the large firms. Small firms have often improved their competitive positions by running different types and grades of crude oil than the large companies, selecting product yields very carefully, operating with lower manpower requirements than large companies, offering a reduced scale of wage rates and fewer fringe benefits to employees, renting some offsite facilities and holding others to a minimum, purchasing rather than providing certain services, and employing different process and engineering standards at their plants than large companies. One study revealed that by following certain of the practices outlined above, a small refiner could have built a modern 25,000 barrels per day refinery in 1953 and earned a percentage return on his investment approximately the same as a large company with different operating practices could have realized on a new 100,000 barrels per day plant.

CHAPTER TWENTY–ONE

Changes in the Refining Population Arising from the Discovery and Development of New Oil Fields

THROUGHOUT the history of the oil industry marked changes in the refining population have often occurred as a result of the discovery and development of new oil fields. The initial development of a new field is often characterized by a period of "flush" production during which the field has a very high producing potential. In some cases, particularly in the days before the adoption of the state conservation laws, oil was drawn from new fields in large volume and offered for sale in the fields at very low prices. The cheap crude oil, in turn, created an attractive refining opportunity and frequently resulted in the erection of many small plants in the immediate vicinity of the fields.[1] Although these plants were often of a rudimentary character, they could be operated profitably as long as the inexpensive crude oil was available. When the production of the new fields began to decline or arrangements were made to assimilate the new supplies in the national market, the cheap crude oil quickly disappeared, and most of the small refineries then vanished from the scene as rapidly as they had come.

A very early example of the refining activity prompted by the discovery and development of a new oil field may be found in the history of the Pennsylvania oil regions. Following the discovery of the first commercial oil well in 1859, vast quantities of crude oil were produced. Since there was no ready market, the price of crude oil at the well-head fell from $10 a barrel in January 1861 to as low as 10 cents a barrel at the end of the year.[2] Even at this price it was difficult to dispose of all the crude oil production since transportation facilities from the

field were wholly inadequate to carry what was then considered a "flood of oil." This large supply of low-price crude oil induced a number of people, many of limited financial means and lacking in former business experience, to enter the refining business. Fifteen plants were established in the oil regions by the end of 1860, and within three years 61 plants ranging in capacity from 15 to 300 barrels per day were interspersed throughout the new oil fields.[3] Initially, these field refineries enjoyed some marked transportation and crude oil price advantages over the refineries that were built in metropolitan centers.

Less than 15 years after the peak had been reached in this early refining boom, only a few plants remained in the oil fields. The great overbuilding of refinery capacity led to extensive price cutting on refined products. Particularly in the periods 1866 to 1867 and 1870 and 1875 there were sharp depressions in the refining business in which many plants were shut down. Many small refineries were also stranded without a crude oil supply as a result of the rapid shifts which took place in the centers of crude oil production. Finally, the extensive acquisition of plants by the Standard Oil group, begun in 1871, accounted for the disappearance of nearly all the plants which had managed to withstand the intense competition and the adverse effects of changing sources of crude oil supply. Many of these plants were shut down and dismantled subsequent to their purchase by the Standard Oil group. Thus in a relatively brief span of years the discovery and development of the early Pennsylvania oil fields caused a large turnover in the industry's refining population.

The basic story of the inrush and subsequent

---

[1] In the following discussion we shall refer to such plants as "field refineries."

[2] Paul H. Giddens, *The Birth of the Oil Industry* (New York, The Macmillan Company, 1938), p. 83.

[3] Ibid., p. 93.

disappearance of refineries in or near producing fields was relived time and time again throughout the ensuing years. Among the principal discoveries that set in motion fairly extensive local refining activity were the Ranger and East Texas fields in Texas; the Oklahoma City and Seminole fields in Oklahoma; the Kettleman Hills field in California; the Centralia, Salem-Lake Centralia, and Louden fields in Southern Illinois; the El Dorado field in Arkansas; and other scattered fields in Kansas, Michigan, and throughout the Rocky Mountain area. Of the many plants located in these areas only a comparatively few survived for more than a short period. That the building of plants in new oil fields has persisted down to the present time is evident from the reports of impending refining activity in the newly discovered Williston basin. In fact, the Standard Oil Company (Indiana) has already announced plans to construct a refinery at Mandan, North Dakota, to serve as an outlet for Williston basin crude oil.

As a means of clarifying the way in which the discovery and development of new oil fields caused sharp expansions and contractions in the refining population, we shall discuss the entrance and exit of refiners from two different oil producing areas. The first section of the chapter will describe the refining activity which followed the discovery of the East Texas field in 1930, and the second section will consider the refining activity which followed the discovery of several new oil pools in the Illinois basin in the late 1930's. In the concluding section of the chapter, we shall compare and contrast the East Texas and Illinois situations, discuss briefly the experiences of large companies with oil field refineries, and consider the effect of the prorationing laws and the advances in refinery technology on the refining opportunities arising from the discovery of new oil fields.

I. THE EXPERIENCE OF SMALL REFINERS IN THE EAST TEXAS FIELD

The rapid development of the East Texas oil field after its discovery on October 3, 1930, was marked by the greatest influx of refineries ever concentrated in a single area. Exhibit XXI-1 shows the location of the field refineries and their position with respect to other refineries scattered over a much larger area as of January 1, 1935. The first small refineries were constructed in the East Texas field early in 1931. There is no readily available record of the total number of plants built in the East Texas field during the next four or five years. Because of the transient character of many of these refining ventures, frequent changes in corporate title, transfers in ownership, and the unwillingness of some firms to respond to refining surveys, there were understandably some omissions of plants in the data compiled by interested organizations.[4] The total number of plants attracted to the area was probably in the neighborhood of 100. A compilation of plants prepared from a U.S. Bureau of Mines publication showed 76 refineries situated either within the confines of the East Texas field or very close by as of January 1, 1936.[5] The number of plants entering the area certainly exceeded 76, however, since some plants had been abandoned or dismantled before January 1, 1936.

In the four-year period after 1936, the number of operating and shutdown refineries listed by the Bureau of Mines for the East Texas producing area fell off sharply until only 14 plants remained on January 1, 1940. The number of operating and shutdown refineries and the operating and shutdown refining capacity in the East Texas field at yearly intervals from 1932 to 1940 are shown graphically in Exhibit XXI-2.[6] The oil production, price, and legal data shown in Exhibit XXI-2 will be considered at later points in the discussion.

Because of the large number of refineries which entered and subsequently left the East Texas area, this one situation accounted for

---

[4] Among the organizations publishing data on East Texas refineries were the U. S. Bureau of Mines, the Railroad Commission of Texas, *The Oil and Gas Journal*, and *The Oil Weekly*. We could not assemble fully accurate entry data from these sources, partially because of minor inconsistencies in the reported data but mainly because changes in corporate title and ownership made it impossible for us to follow the history of individual plants.

[5] Refinery data reported in this paragraph were compiled from annual publications of the U. S. Bureau of Mines entitled *Petroleum Refineries in the United States* and *Petroleum Refineries, Including Cracking Plants, in the United States*, January 1, 1931, to January 1, 1940, Information Circulars 6485, 6641, 6728, 6807, 6850, 6906, 6977, 7034, 7091, and 7124.

[6] The difficulties encountered by organizations seeking East Texas refinery statistics, as noted in the text, understandably led to some omissions of plants from Bureau of Mines records and to the retention of too many shutdown plants in some years.

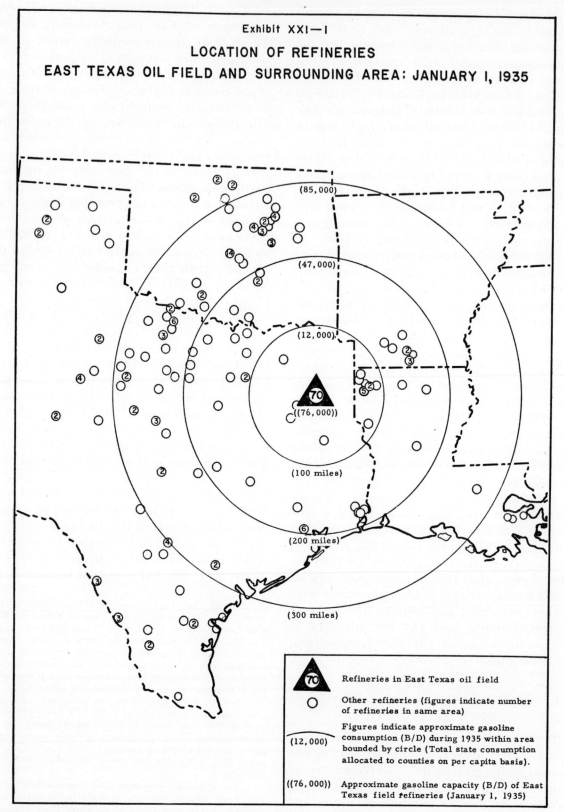

Exhibit XXI—I

LOCATION OF REFINERIES
EAST TEXAS OIL FIELD AND SURROUNDING AREA: JANUARY I, 1935

▲ 70 Refineries in East Texas oil field

○ Other refineries (figures indicate number of refineries in same area)

(12,000) Figures indicate approximate gasoline consumption (B/D) during 1935 within area bounded by circle (Total state consumption allocated to counties on per capita basis).

((76,000)) Approximate gasoline capacity (B/D) of East Texas field refineries (January 1, 1935)

SOURCE: Prepared from U. S. Bureau of Mines, *Petroleum Refineries, Including Cracking Plants, in the United States*, January 1, 1935, I. C. 6850.

a large share of the total entries and exits from the entire refining industry during the 1930's. Between January 1, 1930, and January 1, 1936, there was a net increase of 220 in the number of refineries throughout the entire United States. According to Bureau of Mines reports, at least 76 or one-third of these plants were built in the East Texas field. Between January 1, 1936, and January 1, 1940, the number of refineries in the United States declined from 632 to 547, a net decline of 85. In the immediate area of the East Texas field alone, the number of refineries reported by the Bureau of Mines statements fell by 62 during this period. The purpose of the following discussion is to explore the circumstances which brought about these marked changes in East Texas refining activities.

Circumstances Attracting Small Refiners to the East Texas Field:

An attractive opportunity was provided for refining activity in the East Texas area because there were huge supplies of crude oil available for local consumption, the crude oil could in one way or another be purchased at extremely low prices, and the crude oil was of such a quality that inexpensive, rudimentary plants could be used for processing. Small refiners were quick to recognize these advantages and set in motion the greatest oil field refining activity in the history of the industry.

One factor causing large quantities of crude oil to be made available for consumption in the East Texas area was the extraordinary nature of the new field and the speed with which it was developed. The East Texas field has proven to be the most prolific producing area ever discovered in the United States. Following its discovery, there were several factors which contributed to the extremely rapid development of the field. Since the producing sands were only 3,600 feet beneath the land surface, wells could be put down both quickly and inexpensively. The drilling time for a well usually was less than 20 days and the drilling costs seldom exceeded $10,000. Wells with a potential production of as high as 10,000 barrels of oil per day each were readied for production with total capital outlays of less than $20,000. After a well was completed, moreover, most operators produced oil as rapidly as possible in

order to prevent offsetting leaseholders from draining their properties. As shown in Exhibit XXI-2, the East Texas field was expanded so rapidly that production exceeded 500,000 barrels per day during one month of 1931 and provided over 15% of the total United States production in 1932 and over 20% in 1933.

The first refineries were erected in East Texas early in 1931 when producers, as a means of finding a market for the tremendous supply of new crude oil, elected either to engage in the refining business themselves or to make their oil available to others having the funds necessary to erect local plants. The great producing potential of the East Texas field could not be absorbed readily by existing refineries located outside the area because there were already large supplies of crude oil available from other sources and the country was entering a general business depression. Refiners outside the East Texas area were therefore unable to utilize all the new crude oil despite the hurried construction of economical transportation facilities which provided access to a broad territorial market for the oil. In fact, pipe line capacity from the East Texas field was overbuilt during the first 15 months of crude oil production in the area. Although crude oil production only occasionally exceeded 350,000 to 400,000 barrels per day in the years following 1931, 17 trunk lines and 35 gathering systems with an aggregate capacity for moving 1,000,000 barrels per day from the field were constructed in the East Texas district during 1931.[7]

With such an abundance of crude oil being thrust upon a market which was already amply supplied, it was inevitable that large quantities of East Texas crude oil should be made available to buyers at bargain prices. Even before the discovery of the East Texas field, the posted price of 36° gravity North Texas crude oil had declined from $2.29 per barrel in 1926 to 95 cents per barrel in 1930.[8] As shown in Exhibit XXI-2, the going price of East Texas crude oil fell to a low of 15 cents per barrel in 1931. Since refined products prices did not show a commensurate decline, refiners

---

[7] Joseph E. Pogue, *Economics of Pipe Line Transportation in the Petroleum Industry* (New York, American Petroleum Institute, 1932), p. 18.

[8] Crude oil prices reported in *Platt's Oil Price Handbook,* 1926 and 1930.

EXHIBIT XXI-2. A CHRONOLOGY OF THE EAST TEXAS OIL FIELD: 1931–1940

— New Conservation Acts

New Laws to Control Refining and Transportation

— Court Decisions Affecting Production

—·— Court Decisions Affecting Ref. and Trans.

Crude Oil Production — Actual, Allowable, and Hot Oil

SYMBOLS FOR COURT DECISIONS:

O Favorable to Conservation Efforts
● Unfavorable to Conservation Efforts
⊙ Laws Generally Upheld, but Procedures Violated in Enforcement

PRINCIPAL COURT DECISIONS AFFECTING CONTROL OF PRODUCTION:

1. Macmillan Case
2. Constantin Case
3. Danciger Case
4. Champlin Case
5. People's Case (July 19, 1932)
6. People's Case (October 24, 1932)
7. People's Case (March 17, 1933)
8. Rowan and Nichols Case
9. Hunt and Companion Cases
10. Second Danciger Case
11. Amazon Case
12. Amazon Case (C.A.)
13. Amazon Case (S.Ct.)

PRINCIPAL COURT DECISIONS AFFECTING CONTROL OF REFINING AND TRANSPORTATION:

a. Atlas Pipe Line Case
b. Panama Case
c. Panama Case (C.A.)
d. Culver Case
e. Blue Diamond Case
f. Panama Case (S.Ct.)
—Invalidated Sec. 9(c) N.I.R.A.
g. Phoenix and Primrose Case
h. Melton and Hercules Cases
i. Johnson Refineries Cases
j. Oil Refineries Case
k. Second Panama Case

Hot Oil — Actual Production (U.S. Bureau of Mines) Less Allowable Production (Railroad Commission of Texas)

Hot Oil — As Estimated by Oil Scouts of Major Companies

Average Barrels per Day (1,000s)

1000   800   600   400   200   0

Dollars per Bbl.

1.50   1.00   .50   0

Texas Conservation Act
Anti-Market Demand

Texas Market Demand Act

Texas Confiscation Act

Presidential Order Prohibiting Interstate Movement of Hot Oil, Authority Sec. 9(c) N.I.R.A.

Petroleum Code (N.I.R.A.)
Texas Refinery Control and Felony Bill, H.B.99
S.B.21 (Amends H.B.99)
Connally Hot Oil Act
Texas Truck Tender Shipping Bill

May 1, 1931-Effective Date, First East Texas Proration Order

Aug. 16 to Sep. 4, 1931 Martial Law Declared Field Shut Down

Dec. 18 to 31, 1932 Field Shut Down by Railroad Commission

Apr. 6 to 23, 1933 Field Shut Down to Take Potentials

Early July, 1934 East Texas Buying Program Initiated

May 27, 1935 N.I.R.A. Declared Unconstitutional

May 5, 1936 Madison Trial Begins

ACTUAL PRODUCTION

ALLOWABLE PRODUCTION

Not Available After September, 1938

Crude Oil Price

Average Barrels per Day (1,000s)

Dollars per Bbl.

1931 1932 1933 1934 1935 1936 1937 1938 1939 1940

EXHIBIT XXI-2 (CONTINUED)

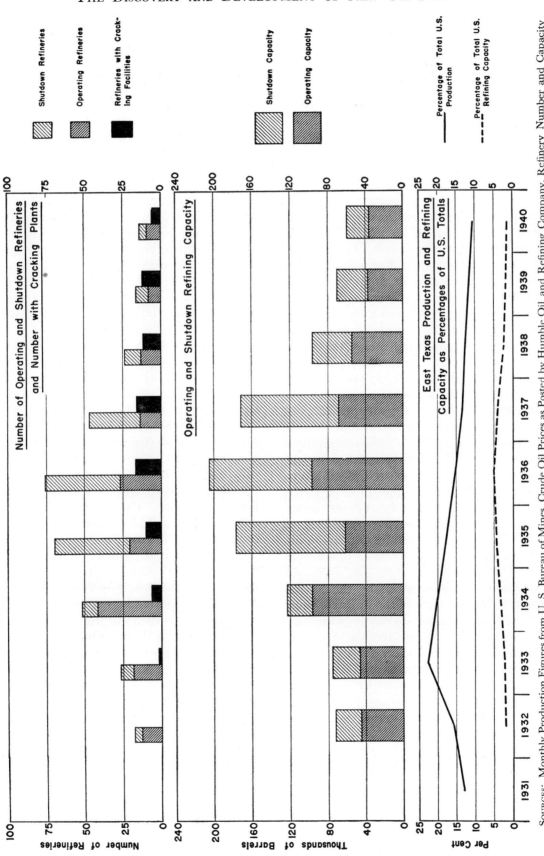

SOURCES: Monthly Production Figures from U. S. Bureau of Mines, Crude Oil Prices as Posted by Humble Oil and Refining Company, Refinery Number and Capacity Data from Annual Information Circulars Prepared by U. S. Bureau of Mines, *Petroleum Refineries, Including Cracking Plants, in the United States.*

rushed into the area with makeshift plants in order to convert the cheap crude oil into refined products. At one point in 1933, when efforts to curtail production temporarily collapsed, production in the field rose to nearly 1,000,000 barrels per day, and the price of crude fell as low as 10 cents per barrel.

Throughout the period from 1931 to 1936 there was also a very substantial volume of crude oil available for purchase at prices considerably below those posted in the field, and these bargain prices likewise attracted refiners to East Texas. It was during the development of the East Texas field that the prorationing laws were in their formative stages. The state of Texas, acting through the Railroad Commission of Texas, instituted its program to limit oil production in the East Texas field on May 1, 1931.[9] Following the issuance of the first order to limit production, many producers and refiners began a protracted and often bitter battle against the efforts of the state and others to regulate oil production. Whatever the merits of the opposing points of view may have been, it is undeniably true that great quantities of crude oil were produced and refined in defiance of the regulatory measures. Crude oil produced in excess of the allowables prescribed by the state conservation agency as well as oil stolen from the wells, tanks, or pipe lines of others was termed "hot" oil. The hot oil was generally available at prices ranging from 25% to 60% below the prices posted for legitimate oil.

The amount of hot oil produced in different time periods was influenced to some extent by the vacillating position taken by the federal courts regarding the right of the Railroad Commission of Texas to limit crude oil production and to some extent by the feeling of certain producers that they had the right to produce oil on their properties regardless of laws to the contrary. A court decision which was interpreted as being favorable to the prorationing effort often stemmed the flow of hot oil, at least temporarily; a decision considered unfavorable to the prorationing effort was frequently followed by the wide-open production of many wells.

The freedom with which refiners processed hot oil was also influenced by the legal atmosphere prevailing at the moment. At various times from 1932 to 1935, for example, refiners secured restraining orders in federal courts which prohibited members of the Railroad Commission's field staff from inspecting the operating records of refineries. The issuance of such a restraining order gave many refiners new confidence in their determination to process hot oil. Exhibit XXI-2 includes a chronological listing of state and federal legislation, major court decisions, and other pertinent developments which bore on the efforts of legislative, judicial, and administrative bodies either to foster or to retard the conservation efforts.

Exhibit XXI-2 also reveals that the greatest inrush of small refiners to the East Texas field coincided with the peak of hot oil activity in 1933 and 1934. Two estimates of the volume of hot oil available in the East Texas field are shown in the exhibit. One estimate of the hot oil production was derived by subtracting production allowables as prescribed by the Railroad Commission of Texas from actual production figures as reported by the U. S. Bureau of Mines. The difference between allowable and actual production provides only a minimum estimate of the hot oil available because much of the illegal production was not reported to the Bureau of Mines. The second estimate of hot oil production presented in the exhibit was prepared by oil scouts of major oil companies.[10] This second estimate of hot oil production was somewhat higher than the first because the oil scouts of The East Texas Engineering Association reported higher production figures in some periods than did the Bureau of Mines. While neither of these estimates should be accepted as a fully accurate accounting of the hot oil activity of the period, they do illustrate that a large quantity of inexpensive crude oil was finding its way into the markets. Through 1934, in fact, the amount of hot oil produced was generally sufficient to supply a large part or all of the operating refinery capacity of the East Texas plants (see Exhibit XXI-2).

It is not unreasonable to assume that some refiners built plants in East Texas for the express purpose of processing hot oil and that

---

[9] The Railroad Commission of Texas issued its first order to curtail production on April 4, 1931. This order was twice revised so that the program to limit production was postponed until May 1, 1931.

[10] Statement of Joseph E. Pogue, *T.N.E.C. Hearings*, Part 14, p. 7447 (Washington, Government Printing Office, 1941).

these firms had little or no intention of staying in the refining business after the time when the hot oil traffic was curbed. In any event the processing of hot oil was certainly a fairly prevalent practice. Some producers and refiners overtly defied the Railroad Commission as they proceeded with the production and processing of hot oil. Others built concealed pipe lines directly from producing wells to plants and by-passed the gauges which recorded the official production flow of oil wells. The building of some plants was probably motivated by the fact that it was sometimes easier for a producer to avoid legal and administrative restraints on his production if he could process his oil and sell it as refined products.

Even in 1935, when state and federal enforcement agencies were much more effective in prohibiting the production and processing of hot oil, one further opportunity for acquiring an inexpensive supply of crude oil was afforded some refiners. Under the terms of the Texas Confiscation Act, enacted May 11, 1935, hot oil was confiscated by the state and sold to the highest bidder at judicial sale. Under the terms of this act, the refined products made from confiscated hot oil which had been sold on the "court-house steps" were adjudged legal products which could be moved in intrastate commerce. Since the hot oil had frequently been stored in open earthen pits adjacent to the refineries of the owners prior to state confiscation and had lost some of the lighter fractions through evaporation, the oil did not bring high prices. Beginning in May 1935 millions of barrels of hot oil were confiscated by the state. The bulk of this contraband oil was repossessed by the original owners of the stored oil at an average price of about 20 cents per barrel.[11] Since legally produced crude oil sold at a posted price of $1 per barrel during this period, the price of 20 cents per barrel represented a substantial bargain. Throughout most of the period from 1931 to 1935 therefore, small refiners could in one way or another purchase ample supplies of crude oil at bargain prices.

The movement of refiners into the East Texas area was stimulated in no small part by the fact that the crude oil was of a relatively high refinery value. The crude oil was therefore particularly well-suited to the requirements of the small refiner who was either unable or unwilling to construct elaborate refinery processing facilities. The gasoline yield from a rudimentary skimming or topping operation amounted to 36% to 40% of the high-gravity crude oil.[12] Without the benefit of any treating after skimming, a third-grade gasoline of passable specifications could be obtained even from very elementary and inexpensive plant equipment. From a refining standpoint, the sole disadvantage of the crude oil was a fairly high wax content which made the fuel oil yielded from a skimming operation a generally undesirable, high cold-test product which congealed at 80° F. to 100° F. To process the East Texas crude oil, plants of 1,000 barrels per day capacity could nevertheless be put into operation for investments ranging from below $10,000 up to $25,000.

While there are no figures available which would indicate the precise nature of the profit opportunity afforded refiners by the cheap East Texas crude oil, enough information is available to indicate that there were periods from 1931 to 1936 when profits were exceedingly attractive in relation to the plant investments which had been made. The first group of refiners to move into the East Texas area was undoubtedly rewarded for its foresight. In July and August 1931 the going price of crude oil was approximately 15 cents per barrel. As noted above, most East Texas refiners performed a simple topping operation on this crude oil, obtaining 15 to 17 gallons of gasoline and 25 to 27 gallons of fuel oil from each barrel of crude oil. During this period of ample crude oil supplies, a very rough approximation of the monthly profit picture of a 1,000 barrels per day topping plant in the East Texas field was as shown at the top of page 594. A profit rate of $5,700 *per month* on a total business investment ranging from $10,000 to $25,000 is very attractive by any standards.

A trade magazine reported that many of the refineries on a full-time operation during this period were realizing net earnings which would

11 See "Texas Wins Big Hot Oil Confiscation Case," *The Oil Weekly*, Vol. 78, No. 2, June 24, 1935, p. 12, and "Hot Oil Runs Up," *The Oil Weekly*, Vol. 78, No. 10, August 19, 1935, p. 36.

12 H. H. King, "Rapid Refinery Development Takes Place in East Texas," *The Oil Weekly*, Vol. 62, No. 12, September 4, 1931, pp. 24–26.

APPROXIMATE MONTHLY PROFIT OF AN
EAST TEXAS REFINERY:

Sales Realization per Barrel of
Crude Oil Processed: [13]
16 gallons of gasoline at 4 cents
per gallon   64¢
26 gallons of fuel oil (sales re-
alization often negligible)   0   64¢
                                      ——
Expenses per Barrel of Crude Oil
Processed:
Crude oil   15¢
Gathering charges, refinery, and
marketing expenses [14]   30   45
                                      ——
Net Profit per Barrel of Crude
Oil Processed   19¢
Net Profit *per Month* (30,000 bar-
rels) $5,700

pay out the cost of the plants within 30 days.[15] The owner of a 10,000 barrels per day topping plant reported that a net profit of $50,000 for the month of August would have been earned had the crude oil supplies been available throughout the entire month.[16] As Exhibit XXI-2 reveals, crude oil supplies were temporarily cut off by the military shutdown of the field on August 17, 1931.

Most of the refiners who operated on hot oil or confiscated crude oil also fared extremely well financially. The refiners processing hot oil enjoyed such a marked advantage over other companies because of their cheap crude oil supply that they were able at times to sell refined products for less than the posted price of crude oil. In March 1934, for example, the products manufactured by an East Texas topping plant from one barrel of crude oil sold for around 75 cents, despite the fact that the posted price of crude oil was then $1 per barrel. At this time a very large supply of hot oil was available at prices ranging from 25 to 40 cents per barrel.[17] With a gross margin of 35 cents to 50 cents per barrel, the refiners processing hot crude oil

were able to pay off the investment costs of their plants in several months. The refiners that neglected to pay the state gasoline excise tax fared even better, unless they were among the few apprehended.[18] Similarly, the bargain price of approximately 20 cents per barrel for confiscated crude oil, compared with crude oil which cost $1 per barrel at posted prices, enabled the 20 to 25 small refiners still operating in 1935 to enjoy very lucrative operations until their low-price products touched off gasoline price wars in some southwestern cities.[19]

It should not be inferred from the above discussion that the East Texas refineries operated at or near capacity and profitably during the entire period from 1931 to 1935. Figures on refinery runs compiled by the Railroad Commission of Texas and the estimates of refinery runs reported by trade journals indicate that refinery throughputs fluctuated widely from month to month and that plant shutdowns were rather frequent. To a large extent the refiners operated their plants when cheap crude oil was available and shut back refinery runs when crude oil bargains could not be secured. In view of the low cost of plants and the abnormal crude oil price situation, however, payouts on plant investments could be and often were obtained in very short periods of time.

Circumstances Causing the Exit of Small Refiners from the East Texas Field:

After 1935 the number of plants listed by the Bureau of Mines in the East Texas area declined very rapidly. Between January 1, 1936, and January 1, 1940, the number of operating and shutdown refineries dropped off from a peak of 76 to only 14. The large number of shutdown plants reported in 1935 and 1936 indicates, moreover, that the refining activity had really passed into eclipse even more rapidly than the listing of both operating and shutdown plants would suggest. On January 1, 1936, for example, only 27 plants were in operation; three years later only 8 plants were processing crude oil. Actually, as noted above, there was considerable turnover in the ownership of

[13] For selling prices of refined products in East Texas, see H. H. King, "East Texas Highlights," *The Oil Weekly*, Vol. 12, No. 10, August 21, 1931, p. 62.

[14] Refining expenses on a skimming operation, excluding depreciation charges, approximated 10 cents per barrel of crude oil run. An expense estimate of 30 cents per barrel for gathering, refining, and marketing is therefore probably liberal.

[15] H. H. King, "Rapid Refinery Development Takes Place in East Texas," *The Oil Weekly*, Vol. 62, No. 12, September 4, 1931, pp. 24–26.

[16] Ibid., pp. 24–26.

[17] Jack Logan, " 'Hot' Oil Still Disturbing," *The Oil Weekly*, Vol. 72, No. 12, March 5, 1934, p. 7.

[18] See *Wright* vs. *State*, 71 S. W. (2d) 352; *Johnson & Burnham, mc. et al.* vs. *State et al.*, 95 S. W. (2d) 194.

[19] "Hot Oil Increases," *The Oil Weekly*, Vol. 78, No. 13, September 9, 1935, p. 54.

facilities and intermittent operation of plants throughout the period from 1931 to 1935. It was during 1935, however, that a net decline in both the total number of plants and in the number of operating plants became evident. Many of the discarded plants were left to rust away and the remains of some can still be seen in the East Texas area. Some plants were dismantled and sold at scrap prices. Still other plants were dismantled with the salvageable processing equipment being moved to new locations. Four of the major causes of the decline in refining activity were the disappearance of cheap crude oil, the inadequacy of plant facilities, the excess refining capacity in the East Texas area, and the failure of many of the small refiners to establish adequate marketing arrangements.

Disappearance of Cheap Crude Oil: The most important cause for the decline in refining activity was the increased effectiveness of the prorationing and other regulatory laws in removing the large supplies of low-cost crude oil which had originally attracted the refiners into the area. The enactment of the Refinery Control and Felony Bill on March 9, 1934, and the Truck Tender Shipping Bill on March 13, 1935, by the Texas Legislature, and the passage of the Connally Hot Oil Act by the United States Congress on February 22, 1935, did much to pave the way for effective regulation. Control over hot oil activities was accomplished by state and federal agencies with the aid of an intricate accounting or "tender" system which traced the movement of legally produced crude oil through the various stages of storage, transportation, and refining. Authorized tenders attesting to the legality of the crude oil and the products made therefrom were required of producers, refiners, and transporters before any crude oil or products could be moved in commerce. This system defined legal crude oil as that produced in conformance with the allowables set by the Railroad Commission of Texas.

The attainment of effective prorationing in the East Texas field not only cut back the amounts of crude oil available but also had the more important effect of compelling fairly strict adherence to the posted price structure for crude oil. In 1934 many East Texas refiners were unable to cover their crude oil require-

ments with purchases of legal production. At this time the pipe line connections owned by the small plants were connected to wells capable of producing only about 18,000 barrels of legal oil per day, although their actual refinery runs far exceeded this figure.[20] To meet the crude oil needs of responsible field refiners, the major companies offered to make available at posted prices 5% of the crude oil which they gathered by pipe line in the East Texas field. Only a relatively few refiners were able to accept this offer of the major companies and operate profitably, however, because of certain other inherent disadvantages which are discussed below.

Inadequacy of Plant Facilities: Once the supply of low-cost crude oil had been removed, the small refiners were unable to compete effectively in the industry because of their generally inefficient plant facilities. With few exceptions, the scores of refineries in the East Texas field were hastily constructed, inexpensive plants designed to skim the gasoline off the high-gravity East Texas crude oil. Plants were erected and put into operation in a period ranging from several weeks to several months after construction materials were on hand. Widespread utilization of secondhand equipment and accessories not originally intended for refinery use kept total investment costs for topping and skimming plants well under the $25,000 mark in many cases. Attesting to the makeshift nature of the plants, typical East Texas refineries were described as "cheeseboxes," "boiler refineries," "pot stills," "coffeepots," "teakettles," and even "smudge pots."

The absence of thermal cracking facilities exacted a considerable hardship on the skimming and topping plant operators. On January 1, 1936, only 17 out of 76 refineries had any thermal cracking facilities, and only a few of the 17 thermal units were of a modern type. The inefficient plant facilities resulted in the production of gasoline of low quality, did not permit the product yields necessary for profitable operations, and magnified the difficulties encountered in the disposal of fuel oils.

---

[20] Harry Harter, *East Texas Oil Parade* (San Antonio, Texas, Naylor Company, 1934), p. 129. Pipe line and refinery runs were reported in hearings before the Texas Legislature.

The gradual upgrading in octane numbers brought about by the widespread adoption of thermal cracking facilities by refiners in other regions caused the quality differential between the third-grade gasoline offered by most East Texas refiners and the regular grade of gasoline available on the market to widen. While third-grade gasoline did not perform so well in the higher compression engines which were introduced during the period, the marked price advantage afforded by third-grade gasoline was sufficient to attract patronage during the severe business depression of the early 1930's. Many large companies were in fact compelled to market a competitive third-grade gasoline in order to protect their market positions.

Beginning in the latter part of 1934, however, the price of the third-grade gasoline sold by East Texas refiners was elevated under the influence of effective prorationing and certain market stabilization programs,[21] and the price disparity between third-grade and regular grade gasoline was reduced. When the third-grade gasoline manufactured by East Texas refineries was no longer placed on the market at substantially lower prices than the regular grade gasoline of other companies, the East Texas refiners suffered serious losses in gallonage to companies employing thermal cracking processes. The substantial gains made in industry octane numbers in the period from 1934 to 1936 occurred just at the time that the East Texas refiners were suffering from the loss of cheap crude oil.

The lack of thermal cracking facilities afforded the topping and skimming plant operators little, if any, flexibility to increase the relative output of higher-price products at the expense of other low realization products. The most serious disadvantage was the inability to increase the yield of the relatively high-price gasoline product above 36% to 40% of refinery runs. The installation of cracking facilities would have made it possible to crack the generally undesirable fuel oil yield, thereby obtaining a maximum yield of 60% or more of gasoline. In 1935, when refined products prices had rebounded from the very low levels that characterized the industry in the immediately preceding years, the total sales realization value obtained by a typical skimming plant in East

Texas averaged $1.17 per barrel for the year.[22] On the basis of posted prices for crude oil, a margin of 17 cents per barrel remained to cover gathering charges and all refining, selling, and administrative expenses. On this margin, profitable operations were at best extremely unlikely. During the same period an East Texas plant with thermal cracking facilities was able, by increasing the gasoline yield up to 60% of refinery runs, to obtain a gross margin ranging as high as 32 cents above the posted price of crude oil. The incremental margin made available by the use of thermal cracking facilities, ranging up to 15 cents per barrel for this year and more in later periods, made it possible for plants with such facilities to operate profitably on crude oil purchased at posted prices whereas refiners without such facilities could not.

The failure to install thermal cracking facilities also magnified the fuel oil sales problem confronting East Texas refiners. Although the first few refiners moving into the area were able to negotiate long-term contracts to supply local railroads with fuel oil, the disposal of fuel oil constituted a major problem for most of the refiners. The local industrial market for fuel oil was not extensive, and the abundance of inexpensive natural gas cut deeply into the small market which was available. In distant industrial areas such as Chicago and the East Coast where the East Texas plants were at a freight disadvantage, fuel oils without the undesirable high cold-test characteristics of East Texas fuel oil were freely offered. Some fuel oil was consumed by oil producers as fuel to drive drilling rigs in East Texas, especially during the early development of the East Texas field when the supply of natural gas was cut off during compulsory field shutdowns. This market was, however, short-lived and not extensive.

The fuel oil problem was of such a serious nature that during the boom refining periods the practice of diverting huge stocks of fuel oil to earthen storage pits was widely fol-

---

[21] See later discussion in this chapter.

[22] Based on average yearly prices for refined products as reported for East Texas in *Oil Price Handbook for 1935* compiled by *National Petroleum News* and the following yield of products for skimming operations obtained from W. T. Ziegenhain, "Refining Value of East Texas Crude," *Oil and Gas Journal*, Vol. 29, No. 49, April 23, 1931, p. 24: gasoline, 37%; kerosene, 6%; distillates, 24%; and residual fuel oil, 30%.

lowed. These accumulated stocks evaporated or burned, were absorbed in fuel oil markets at low prices, rerun by the few plants having cracking facilities, or sold, largely through brokers, to refiners in other areas for rerunning. The fuel oil was ideally suited as a charging stock for thermal cracking units. Since few East Texas refiners owned cracking units, however, the output of fuel oil was much greater than it might otherwise have been. The lack of cracking facilities was not, however, the only factor contributing to the seriousness of the fuel oil problem. In 1935, for example, 23 plants were not even located on railroads where a reasonable possibility of moving the fuel oil to market existed.[23] These plants catered almost exclusively to the tank truck gasoline market.

The effects of the increase in gasoline octane ratings and the need for greater product flexibility on East Texas refiners are manifested by the fact that ultimately only the plants with cracking facilities were able to remain in operation. On January 1, 1936, 13 out of the 27 operating plants had cracking facilities; on January 1, 1937, 11 out of 14 operating plants had cracking units; on January 1, 1938, 11 out of 13 operating plants had cracking facilities; and by January 1, 1939, only 8 plants, all with cracking facilities, remained in operation. Thus, when the small refiners were confronted with the necessity of paying the posted prices for crude oil, the lack of cracking facilities was an important factor in prohibiting the skimming plant operators from continuing in business.

Excess Refining Capacity in the East Texas Area: Another reason why the East Texas refiners could not compete without the supplemental margin provided by low-cost crude oil was the great overbuilding of refining capacity in this one small area relative to the market for refined products which could be reached economically.

Price concessions on crude oil made it possible for the small refiners to compete at different times from 1931 to 1935 in almost every geographical region of the United States. Gasoline was the "money product" of the refineries, and railroad tank car shipments were possible to many distant points. These expensive shipments were possible only because a cheap supply of crude oil placed the refiners in a position to sell gasoline at refinery prices which could, in effect, absorb expensive hauling charges. When the refiners were compelled to base their operations and selling prices on crude oil purchased at higher prices, the area through which they could distribute competitively was greatly reduced in size.

The East Texas refineries were, of course, advantageously located to supply the market in the immediate vicinity of the plants, but this area had a very limited market potential in comparison with the total capacity of the local plants. The estimated daily consumption of gasoline in 1935 in successive 100-mile areas radiating from the midpoint of the East Texas refinery center is shown on the map, Exhibit XXI-1. On January 1, 1935, the refineries in East Texas had a gasoline capacity adequate to supply approximately 90% of the actual gasoline consumption in the entire 300-mile radius area outlined on the map. With other refinery centers located in Oklahoma, Arkansas, Louisiana, and other areas of Texas, the East Texas refiners were hardly in a position to reach this entire area at a transportation advantage over their competitors. Furthermore, it was obviously impossible for these refiners to secure anywhere near 90% of this gasoline market in competition with established refiners and marketers. It is evident from this analysis that refinery capacity was built up far beyond the point which would permit very many of the small refiners to sell their entire output in the small area surrounding their plants where they enjoyed a transportation advantage. The situation with respect to fuel oil has already been discussed. Such markets as did exist were not in East Texas.

The East Texas refiners were poorly located cost-wise to distribute their gasoline and other products over a wide geographic area. Yet, as noted above, they had to move far afield in search of outlets if they were to operate at any level approaching capacity. In moving products in a northerly direction, East Texas refiners were at a substantial transportation dis-

---

[23] Compiled from information reported in the U. S. Bureau of Mines, *Petroleum Refineries, including Cracking Plants, in the United States, January 1, 1935*, Information Circular 6850.

advantage in competing with other Mid-Continent refiners. In moving products to the South and East, the small refiners were confronted with competition from the large, efficient refineries on the Gulf and East Coasts. It was, moreover, considerably more costly for the small refiners to move refined products to the Gulf Coast by trucks or tank cars than it was for other companies to transport crude oil to the Gulf Coast by pipe line. In view of this economic disadvantage, it is not surprising that the number and capacity of East Texas refineries fell off rapidly after the supply of cheap crude oil was removed from the market.

Failure to Build Up Assured Outlets for Refined Products: The failure of the East Texas refiners to develop assured outlets, marketing organizations, and brand name programs was a third reason why the small firms could not survive without cheap crude oil. In marketing gasoline during the period from 1931 to 1935, virtually all the East Texas refiners sold exclusively in the tank car markets to jobbers and brokers. As long as the East Texas refiners could provide an inexpensive source of gasoline supply for bulk buyers, the failure to cultivate assured market outlets was of little consequence. In 1933 and 1934, for example, the ability of the East Texas refiners to put out a third-grade gasoline selling at the refinery gate for prices as low as 3 cents per gallon or less dominated the gasoline wholesale price market east of the Rockies, particularly in the area extending from the Southwest northward through the Midwest. When the refiners were no longer in a position to offer low-price gasoline, however, wholesalers did not hesitate to turn to other sources of supply as a means of getting higher quality products.

Beginning in November 1934 the major oil companies had become an important market for the gasoline output of East Texas refiners that agreed to participate in the market stabilization program sponsored under the Oil Code.[24]

This program brought higher prices and increased stability to the industry, a goal which many industry people and government officials were seeking at that particular time. The decision of the Supreme Court of the United States on May 27, 1935, in the Schechter Case, had the effect of invalidating the NIRA and the Code of Fair Competition for the Petroleum Industry.[25] Certain large companies, however, continued the intermittent purchase of "distress" quantities of gasoline from East Texas refiners until about August 1936. The buying program was halted at that time because the government questioned its legality, and the program was subsequently found to be in violation of the Sherman Anti-Trust Act during the so-called Madison trial.[26] During the trial it was alleged that more than 50% of the small refiners' gasoline output was moving into the hands of certain large companies for resale. The prohibition of sales to large companies was a serious setback to the refineries still remaining in the East Texas field. Since the small firms had not cultivated market outlets for gasoline, only a few companies were able to survive this important loss of gallonage.

It is apparent from the foregoing analysis of the factors causing the disappearance of small refiners from the East Texas field that a flood of cheap crude oil lent temporary support to firms that were in other respects under severe handicaps. When the support was removed, the ill-equipped plants were unable to compete with other refineries in terms of satisfactory product yields or quality. Even if the plants had been fully modern, however, the total re-

---

[24] The Code of Fair Competition for the Petroleum Industry was formulated under the National Industrial Recovery Act. The Oil Code became effective on October 1, 1933, and it remained in operation until the U. S. Supreme Court ruled the National Industrial Recovery Act unconstitutional on May 27, 1935. Under the Oil Code, various attempts were made to stabilize the industry through devices such as the regulation of oil production, the allocation of

refinery runs, and the governing of prices. In June 1934 the Planning and Coordination Committee recommended a buying program whereby the major companies would purchase 3% of their sales requirements from small refiners holding distress quantities of gasoline. Actual purchases in the East Texas area began in November 1934. The continuous flood of hot oil made administration of the Petroleum Code and the various plans sponsored under the Code extremely difficult.

[25] In *ALA Schechter Poultry Company* vs. *U. S.*, 295 U. S. 495, 55 S. Ct. 837, 79L Ed 1570, the Supreme Court invalidated the Code of Fair Competition for the Poultry Industry. The decision rendered in this case was interpreted as being applicable to Codes regulating the activities of other industries.

[26] See *U. S.* vs. *Standard Oil Company (Indiana) et al.*, 23 F. Supp. 937; 7 Cir., 105 F. 2d 809, and; *U. S.* vs. *Socony Vacuum Oil Co., Inc., et al.*, 310 U. S. 150, 60 S. Ct. 811, 84L. Ed.

finery capacity in the area was far in excess of that which could be reasonably supported. Refinery capacity greatly exceeded local requirements, and a broad geographic area could be reached only at a transportation disadvantage. The failure of the field refiners to cultivate assured market outlets added to their problems. Under the combined impact of all these disadvantages, the number of firms that survived the loss of the inexpensive crude oil supply was naturally small.

II. THE EXPERIENCE OF SMALL REFINERS IN THE ILLINOIS BASIN OIL FIELDS

A second and more recent example of the entry and exit of small refiners from the industry in response to the discovery and development of an important oil field may be found in the Illinois basin situation. The Illinois refining boom was exceptionally short-lived, beginning in 1938 and suffering a serious decline only two years later. Exhibit XXI-3 shows the location of the new refineries in the Illinois basin area and the location of other refineries which were already established before the new crude oil discoveries.

The Illinois refining activity involved the construction of 18 small plants in the state of Illinois and 5 in adjacent states. Of the 18 Illinois plants, 14 were located in or within several miles of new producing fields. On January 1, 1940, the boom was at a crest with 17 of the new Illinois refineries in operation. One year later, only 6 of the 18 newly constructed Illinois plants were operating. On January 1, 1951, 4 of these Illinois refineries were operating, although at least 2 of these plants had been shut down for extended periods in the intervening years. Of the 5 small refineries attracted to the contiguous states of Indiana, Kentucky, and Missouri by the flush production of the Illinois fields, only the 3 in Indiana survived until January 1, 1941, and these plants were still in operation 10 years later. In total, therefore, the new Illinois fields attracted 23 small refineries, of which only 9 were in operation less than two and one-half years after the completion of the first plant. In the following discussion we shall trace the factors leading to this refinery development and to its very sudden decline.

Circumstances Contributing to the Entry of New Refineries in the Illinois Basin:

As was the case in the East Texas field, the small refineries were attracted to the Illinois basin area in 1938 and 1939 by an abundance of cheap crude oil. The resurgence of Illinois as an important producing state was marked by the discovery and extraordinarily rapid development of the Centralia, Salem-Lake Centralia, and Louden fields in the western section of the Illinois basin. The monthly production of the fields, total statewide production, and the posted prices of crude oil in the new fields for the period 1938 to 1942 are shown in Exhibit XXI-4. As the exhibit reveals, another group of newly discovered fields which were to the east of the Centralia and Louden fields also contributed to the upsurge in production and the attendant refinery activity.

There was active participation by many small crude oil operators in the new Illinois fields because capital costs were low. Wells in the shallower producing stratas could, for example, usually be completed in five or six days for as little as $15,000 to $18,000.[27] Unlike the East Texas situation, the crude oil production in the Illinois fields was not governed by prorationing laws. Production in the new fields was curbed somewhat only by voluntary conservation agreements among offsetting operators and by the limitations which certain crude oil purchasers placed upon the amount of oil they would gather by pipe line. Many producers, however, elected to produce their wells to capacity whenever a market existed for their crude oil, and this practice compelled offsetting leaseholders either to follow a similar course of action or to suffer underground losses of oil through drainage.

Despite the fact that outgoing pipe line capacity from the new fields was wholly inadequate to handle the unregulated, flush production in 1938 and 1939, oil was run from wells in large quantities as producers tried to get as large a share of the underground reserves as possible. Under these conditions producers were willing to accept very low prices for their oil. The depressed prices permitted compara-

---

[27] E. L. Barringer, "Transports Widen Markets for New Illinois Plants," *National Petroleum News,* Vol. 31, No. 1, January 4, 1939, p. 21.

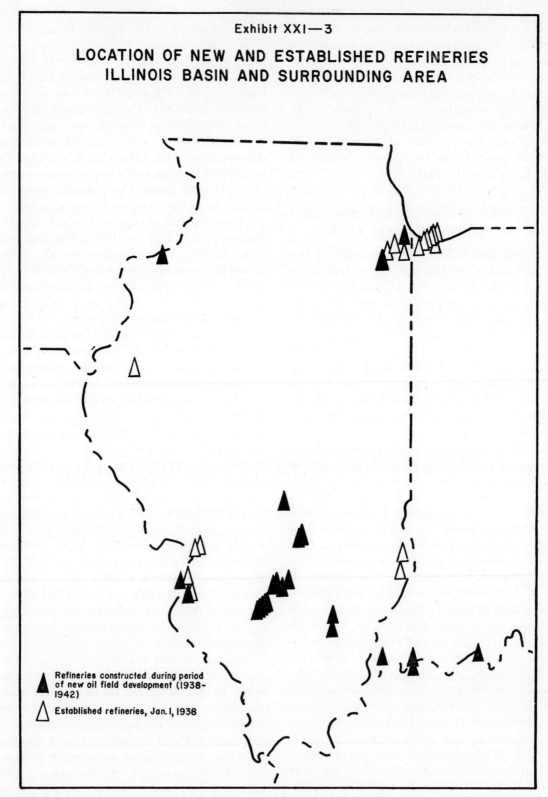

Exhibit XXI—3

LOCATION OF NEW AND ESTABLISHED REFINERIES
ILLINOIS BASIN AND SURROUNDING AREA

▲ Refineries constructed during period of new oil field development (1938-1942)

△ Established refineries, Jan. I, 1938

SOURCE: Prepared from data included in U. S. Bureau of Mines, *Petroleum Refineries, Including Cracking Plants, in the United States*, 1938–1941, I. C. 7034, 7091, 7124, and 7161, and from Illinois Basin Map, *Supplement* to *The Oil and Gas Journal*, October 26, 1939.

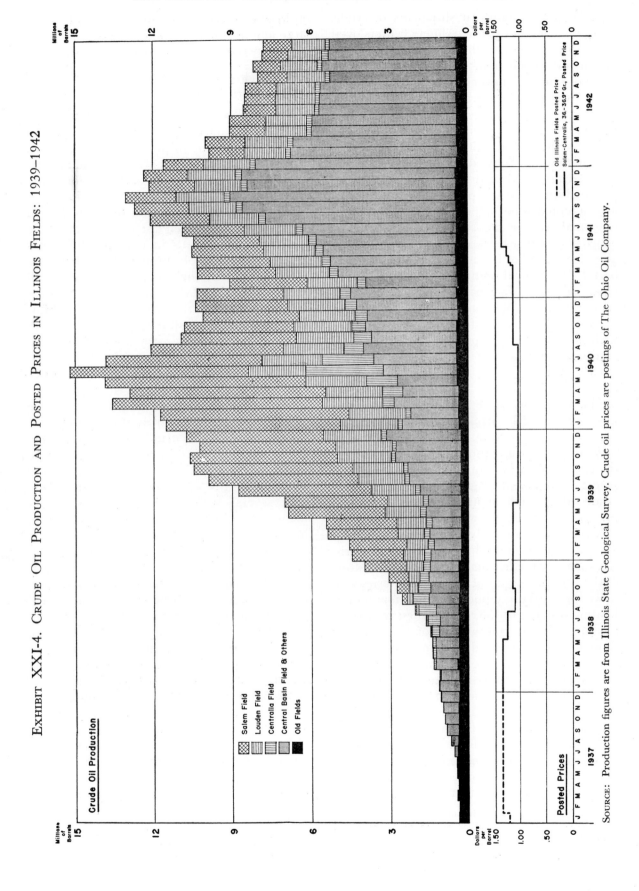

EXHIBIT XXI-4. CRUDE OIL PRODUCTION AND POSTED PRICES IN ILLINOIS FIELDS: 1939–1942

Crude Oil Production

Salem Field
Louden Field
Centralia Field
Central Basin Field & Others
Old Fields

Posted Prices

Old Illinois Fields Posted Price
Salem-Centralia, 36.–36.9° Gr., Posted Price

SOURCE: Production figures are from Illinois State Geological Survey. Crude oil prices are postings of The Ohio Oil Company.

tively expensive tank car shipments of crude oil to be made to existing refinery centers over a wide area and drew other refiners to the scene of the oil production. Although the posted price of crude oil never fell below $1.05, even during the flush production stages in the new fields, at least one large company purchasing on gathering systems employed a price scale whereby the posted price was paid for a certain amount of allocated production and a discounted price was paid for oil taken over the prorated quota. In sharp contrast to the generally accepted scale of posted prices, however, one small refiner reported that his company actually purchased oil during the period of abundant supplies for as little as 45 cents per barrel. Other small refiners contracted for purchases at 60 cents per barrel, and a price of 80 cents was quite common.

The small refiners entered the Illinois basin with small, poorly equipped plants. In fact, the equipment for some of the plants was moved from East Texas where the refinery boom had ended. The average crude oil charging capacity of the 18 newly erected refineries in Illinois was less than 2,000 barrels per day, and thermal cracking facilities were installed at only two of these plants. Only four refineries, including the two with cracking units, had lead-blending plants to upgrade their gasoline output.[28] With crude oil available at more than 20 cents below posted prices, the skimming plants were able to operate profitably for a period by selling a low octane gasoline which was made competitive on a price rather than a quality basis. Most of the gasoline output of the new refineries was moved in trucks to jobbers within a maximum hauling distance of 150 to 200 miles; railroads, meeting the rate competition of truckers for short hauls, also secured an important part of the gasoline traffic. Fuel oils were moved by tank cars to industrial markets over a wider area. Although the new refineries were near some of the largest gasoline consuming areas in the Middle West, including St. Louis and Chicago, these markets could be entered only at a competitive cost disadvantage relative to the large, efficient plants located in or near these cities. Sales efforts were therefore concentrated

on local markets where the influence of such a large amount of low-grade gasoline was a disruptive market force for over two years.

Circumstances Contributing to the Exit of the Illinois Basin Refineries:

The flush producing wells in the new fields, as has been characteristic of Illinois production, showed a rapid rate of production decline. Oil production in the new fields was found at varying depths in several sand and limestone substructures. The drop in well production averaged around 10% per month on open flow in the sand zones and even faster in the limestone formations. The wells in one limestone substructure, for example, produced at a daily rate of less than half their initial rate within 20 days.[29] Therefore, the large production increases shown for the new fields in Exhibit XXI-4 were made possible only by the discovery of continually deeper formations and by the rapid drilling of a large number of new wells to offset the production declines of older wells. The new fields were fairly well defined and drilled up by the summer of 1940, and crude oil production fell off sharply after that time.

Meanwhile, the demand for Illinois crude oil had been increased by the provision of pipe line facilities which could transport the crude oil economically to more distant refineries. Since several trunk lines moving Mid-Continent and older Illinois crude oils passed through or near the new fields, a relatively small amount of new trunk line construction was required to provide a broad refining market for the crude oil. As the network of gathering systems and connecting lines was completed, more and more producers were given the opportunity to sell their output at posted prices.

The gradual disappearance of bargain price crude oil made it increasingly difficult for the skimming plant operators in the Illinois basin to offset their comparative plant inefficiency by savings on crude oil purchases. As noted above, only two plants had thermal cracking facilities. The lack of cracking facilities placed the 16 new skimming plants in Illinois at an inherent disadvantage of 18 to 20 cents per barrel of crude oil processed in comparison with established refineries in the Illinois-Indiana

---

[28] "Illinois New Flush Crude Not a Menace to Markets," *National Petroleum News*, Vol. 32, No. 13, March 27, 1940, p. 34.

[29] Ibid., p. 29.

regions.[30] This disadvantage arose largely from the fact that the skimming plants could secure a gasoline yield of only about 30% whereas refineries with cracking units could secure a gasoline yield of 60% to 70%.[31]

During 1940 the skimming plant operators encountered serious problems when they were no longer able to buy crude oil for 20 cents below posted prices. To compensate for the loss in margin brought about by increasing crude oil prices, the refiners necessarily advanced the selling prices of their refined products. Jobber and consumer resistance followed in the wake of the gasoline price increases, however, since the gasoline output of all but a few of the plants was of a substandard quality. With lead-blending facilities at only four Illinois plants, most of the refiners were turning out a third-grade gasoline. The reduced operating margin and the reluctance of marketers to purchase the gasoline output on other than a discount basis were the important factors contributing to the drastic decline in refining activity which occurred less than two and one-half years after the boom was initiated.

Several of the small field refiners actually suffered bankruptcies or passed through reorganizations prior to the time when the peak of production was reached in mid-1940. The reasons most frequently cited for these failures were undercapitalization and technical incompetency. Typically, a businessman and his friends and associates would erect a small skimming plant costing about $60,000. The magnitude of the other capital requirements, including working capital to finance inventories and accounts receivable, which might approach the cost of the plant in total amount, was sometimes not given adequate recognition in the initial planning. The result was a "shoe-string" operation involving a delay in meeting financial commitments and culminating in bankruptcy. The lack of capital and technical proficiency also contributed to the quality problems experienced on refined products.

The difficulties of the small refiners were occasioned not only by the disappearance of low-cost crude oil but also at a later stage by difficulties in getting any crude oil at all. The difficulty in securing crude oil supplies was caused by the rapid exhaustion of the Illinois fields and the unwillingness of some small producers to sell crude oil to small refiners when they had the alternative of supplying large companies. The news of refinery bankruptcies, which sometimes involved losses to the crude oil producers supplying the plants, was quickly circulated and with adverse effects on the business relationships between producers and the remaining small field refiners. One small refiner who had operated in the Illinois field believed the small producers preferred to sell to the larger companies because the large companies had absorbed expensive trucking charges on the movement of crude oil from wells before pipe line connections were built. Small refiners were generally unwilling to absorb crude oil hauling charges. Another small Illinois refiner believed that some of the field refiners were considered less desirable crude oil customers than large companies because the small refiners sometimes visited producers and pipe line companies and argued for further discounts off posted crude oil prices, basing their complaints upon such factors as an excessive b. s. and w. content in the crude oil.[32] The small refiner believed that the large companies, on the other hand, rarely if ever voiced such complaints.

Finally, very few of the small refiners constructed their own pipe line gathering systems as a means of gaining access to a continuing supply of crude oil at the well-head. The failure of the small refiners to develop gathering systems was explained by the magnitude of the capital investment required and by the fact that some small producers were not interested in selling to the small Illinois refiners.

The refiners who passed out of business with an adjustment in economic conditions in the Illinois region were, in general, opportunists who depended upon cheap crude oil as their principal source of competitive strength. Some companies realized good profits as a result of the abnormal crude oil price situation. In not all cases, however, were payouts on the original plant investments secured.

---

[30] Ibid., p. 28. See also discussion in Chapter Twenty treating the effect of types of refinery equipment on refinery sales realizations.

[31] "Illinois New Flush Crude Not a Menace to Markets," op. cit., p. 34.

[32] The proportion of basic sediment and water permitted per barrel of crude oil was regulated by contracts. Excessive amounts indicated an inferior crude oil.

III. THE CHARACTER OF THE BUSINESS
OPPORTUNITY PRESENTED TO REFINERS
BY THE DISCOVERY AND DEVELOPMENT
OF NEW OIL FIELDS

In this section we shall first draw upon the East Texas and Illinois situations as a means of clarifying the character of the business opportunity afforded small refiners by the discovery of new oil fields. We shall then examine briefly what the experience of large companies has been with regard to the building of plants in new producing areas. Finally, we shall consider how the widespread adoption of the prorationing laws and the advances in refinery technology have limited the opportunities for oil field refining ventures.

The Transitory Business Opportunity Afforded Refiners by New Oil Fields:

The East Texas and Illinois situations shed a great deal of light on the character of the business opportunity presented to refiners by the discovery and development of new oil fields. The circumstances causing the appearance and disappearance of refineries in the two areas were in some respects similar and in some respects dissimilar. The most important point to be observed about both situations, however, is that the oil field discoveries provided a business opportunity of a transitory character.

The fact that the business opportunity afforded refiners was a transitory one may be deduced from the most significant similarity between the East Texas and Illinois situations. The economic lives of most of the refiners in the two areas were limited to the periods in which they could purchase abundant supplies of cheap crude oil. A substantial competitive advantage in the form of cheap crude oil was in fact absolutely essential if the refiners were to overcome their many serious handicaps. Since it was unavoidable that the cheap crude oil supply should at some time disappear, it was likewise inescapable and entirely proper that most of the refiners should go out of business. It should not by any means be inferred that the business opportunity provided in the new fields was not a good one. As some people commented during the decline of the East Texas refining activity, "the small refiners got theirs while the getting was good."[33] It was likewise true that some of the Illinois refiners fared quite well financially.

Other similarities between the East Texas and Illinois situations also point to the transient character of the business opportunity. All but a few refineries in both situations were inexpensive skimming plants and not properly equipped to meet the standards of efficiency set by their competitors in terms of product quality or product yields. The fact that plant investments could be held at low levels was, however, essential to the financial attractiveness of the oil field refining ventures. Another similarity between the two situations arose from the fact that many of the plant operators in East Texas and Illinois were of limited financial means, inexperienced, and technically untrained. They were therefore at a natural disadvantage in a complex, high capital-cost business. One further similarity was the reliance which East Texas and Illinois refiners placed upon price-cutting as a means of disposing of their products; little attention was directed toward the development of brand names or strong bonds with market outlets. Many of the circumstances common to these two situations have been evident in other oil field refinery developments throughout the history of the industry.

The East Texas and Illinois refinery experiences were also marked by some important dissimilarities. One noteworthy difference may be found in the circumstances causing the disappearance of the large quantities of cheap crude oil. The abundant flow of crude oil from the East Texas field was halted by the enactment and enforcement of prorationing measures. The attainment of effective prorationing undoubtedly hastened the decline of the local refining activity, but it also resulted in a tremendous physical and economic gain in the utilization of an important store of natural resources. In Illinois, on the other hand, no prorationing act was in effect, and the flush production was stemmed largely by the natural exhaustion of reservoir pressures and the rapid exploitation of the relatively limited amounts of oil in the different producing strata.

[33] L. E. Bredberg, "Hope for More Effective Regulation Spreading in East Texas Following New Developments," *Oil and Gas Journal,* Vol. 32, No. 44, March 22, 1934, p. 8.

Another significant dissimilarity between the East Texas and Illinois situations may be found in the location of the refineries with respect to principal marketing areas. The marketing and transportation difficulties encountered by the East Texas refiners because of the large refining capacity they built at an inland location have already been noted. The Illinois refiners were in a much better geographical position with respect to large consuming areas, but their marketing problems were no less acute, except possibly with regard to heavy fuel oil. Refining capacity in the Illinois-Indiana region was already more than adequate to supply the metropolitan areas which were near the new field refineries. The small refiners were therefore confronted with the task of breaking into these metropolitan markets in direct competition with established companies owning larger, more efficient refineries even better situated in many cases to supply the metropolitan areas at low transportation costs. With few exceptions, the new Illinois plants were not adequately equipped to turn out products which could enter these or any other markets on a competitive basis.

The Experience of Large Companies with Oil Field Refineries:

It is important to note that many large companies have had much the same type of experience with oil field refineries as have the small firms. Large companies have built many small plants in producing regions to take advantage of cheap crude oil and as a means of supplying particular inland areas at lower transportation costs than competitors. In general, however, the larger companies have not exploited this particular type of business opportunity to the same degree as have the small companies. For example, only one major company constructed a refinery in the East Texas oil field.

The large companies constructing oil field refineries have not been immune to adverse shifts in economic circumstances, such as those which impinged upon the small refiners in East Texas and the Illinois basin, and they have frequently abandoned plants which at one time provided outlets for new oil fields. One need merely look to the history of some of the larger companies to see that many of the plants dismantled or sold over the past thirty years were originally built to provide an outlet for newly discovered oil fields. Exhibit XXI-5 shows, for example, the plants abandoned by the Standard Oil Company (New Jersey), the Sinclair Oil Corporation, and the Cities Service Corporation in the period from January 1, 1920 to January 1, 1950. The experiences of these three large companies alone show a number of plant abandonments in the producing areas of Texas, Oklahoma, Wyoming, Kansas, Louisiana, Montana, and Pennsylvania.

Large companies have been compelled to abandon oil field refineries for many of the same reasons as have the small companies. The factors have included the exhaustion of local crude oil supplies, the overcapacity of refining facilities in a particular region, problems in the disposal of by-products, the comparative inefficiency of small plants, and the difficulties encountered in meeting competitive quality standards on gasoline. In addition, the decision by the management of a large company to abandon a small refinery has sometimes been made as a matter of alternative choice. For example, rather than continuing a small, relatively inefficient plant in operation, the management of a large company may decide to service its outlets in a localized region either from a large, modern refinery at some distance from the market or by means of product exchanges arranged with other companies. These considerations have been particularly important in recent years as a result of management decisions that particular small refineries would not yield an adequate rate of return on the investment required for catalytic cracking facilities (see Chapter Nineteen).

Despite the numerous plants they have abandoned in producing areas, the large companies have often been able to withstand the loss of cheap crude oil for longer periods than have many of the small refiners. There are, of course, many explanations for the greater competitive strength exhibited by the oil field refineries of certain large companies. The advantages of the large companies have included greater financial stability, the availability of company owned crude oil production, and the existence of strong marketing organizations. Nonetheless, both large and small companies for many of the same basic reasons have been forced to

EXHIBIT XXI-5. PLANT ABANDONMENTS BY SELECTED OIL COMPANIES: 1920–1950 *

Standard Oil Company (New Jersey)			Cities Service Corporation		Sinclair Oil Corporation	
Subsidiaries and Affiliates	Location of Plants	Capacity B/D	Location of Plants	Capacity B/D	Location of Plants	Capacity B/D
Humble Oil and Refining Company	Hearne, Texas	8,000	Independence, Kansas	2,500	Chanute, Kansas	2,000
	Burkburnett, Texas	4,000	Oklahoma City, Oklahoma	2,500	Vinita, Oklahoma	10,000
	Breckenridge, Texas	1,500	Warren, Pennsylvania	680	Cushing, Oklahoma	6,500
	Chilton, Texas	4,500	Cushing, Oklahoma	5,000	Rodeo, California	200
	McCamey, Texas	15,000	Gainesville, Texas	3,600	Muskogee, Oklahoma	1,200
	Neches, Texas	5,000	Okmulgee, Oklahoma	4,000	Mekaux, Louisiana	20,000
	Ingleside, Texas	31,500	Bossier City, Louisiana	23,000	West Tulsa, Oklahoma	4,500
Esso Standard Oil Company	Parkersburg, West Virginia	6,000	East Braintree, Massachusetts	20,000	Phoenix, Arizona	1,000
					Vinvale, California	10,000
Carter Oil Company	Lovell, Wyoming	2,500	Petty Island, New Jersey	20,000	El Paso, Texas	5,000
	Newcastle, Wyoming	1,900			Gladewater, Texas	4,000
	Billings, Montana	11,000			Fort Worth, Texas	6,500
					Sand Springs, Oklahoma	7,200
					Coffeyville, Kansas	11,000
					Kansas City, Kansas	12,000

* Includes plants dismantled or sold.

SOURCE: C. M. Furcht, "Growth and Structure of U.S. Refining Industry, 1920–1950," Company memorandum, Standard Oil Company (New Jersey). Plant capacities were in some cases secured directly from the companies.

abandon a great many of the plants which were built in new producing fields.

Effect of the Prorationing Laws and Advances in Refinery Technology:

The adoption of the prorationing laws and the substantial gains in refinery technology have since about 1935 or 1940 greatly reduced the opportunities for refiners associated with the discovery and development of new oil fields. The prorationing laws, by providing for the orderly development of new oil fields, have had the effect of greatly reducing or eliminating the substantial quantities of cheap crude oil which were available at newly discovered fields in the past.[34] Therefore one of the most important incentives for refiners to build plants at the point of crude oil production no longer exists. To the extent that the prorationing laws have restricted the opportunity for oil field refining activities, they have also been responsible for some of the contraction in the refining population since about 1940. The discovery and development of new oil fields, of course, still provides the opportunity for some local refining activity. It is possible, for example, for a comparatively few refiners to build plants in a new field for the purpose of supplying local markets for refined products at a combined

crude oil and refined products transportation advantage over more distant refineries (see Chapter Twenty-Three).

The opportunity for extensive refinery construction in new oil fields has also been reduced by the sweeping changes in refinery technology. Particularly since the advent of catalytic cracking processes, refiners without modern facilities have experienced difficulties in meeting octane standards on gasoline even with crude oils of a high refinery value. The new processes have, moreover, been essential for the improvement of product yields (see Chapters Nineteen and Twenty). The investment problem confronting field refiners in recent years has therefore been of an entirely different order of magnitude than in the past.

IV. SUMMARY

1. Throughout the history of the oil industry, sharp expansions and contractions in the refining population have often resulted from the discovery and development of new oil fields. Particularly before the adoption of the prorationing laws, the early development of a new oil field was often attended by abundant supplies of very inexpensive crude oil. Small refineries were frequently constructed in the vicinity of new fields because of the unusual profit opportunity presented by the cheap crude oil. The abnormal crude oil

---

[34] See Chapter Four for a discussion of the evolution of the prorationing laws.

supply situation more than compensated for the fact that the field refineries were usually poorly equipped and inefficient. When crude oil production in the new fields began to decline or was assimilated in the national market, the cheap crude oil quickly disappeared and many of the small plants were dismantled or abandoned.

2. The extensive refining activity in East Texas during the 1930's provides an excellent example of the opportunity presented to refiners by the discovery and development of a new oil field. Small refiners rushed into the East Texas area with inexpensive plants to convert an oversupply of cheap crude oil into products on a temporary but lucrative basis. When the abundant supplies of cheap crude oil disappeared, primarily because of the development of the prorationing laws, the rudimentary skimming and topping plants were unable to compete satisfactorily in terms of product quality or product yields. Even if the plants had been fully modern, however, the great overbuilding of refining capacity in the East Texas area would have made it exceedingly difficult for more than a very few plants to have survived. The failure of the refiners to cultivate assured market outlets and a particularly difficult situation with respect to the disposal of heavy fuel oil contributed to the problems of the small firms. Under the combined weight of these circumstances, there was a mass withdrawal of small refiners from the East Texas area.

3. A second and more recent example of oil field refining activity was found in the Illinois basin situation. Again, an inexpensive crude oil supply was the stimulus to refinery investments. Most of the new firms operated profitably for a period. Although Illinois production was unregulated, the rapid exhaustion of underground reserves and an extensive outgoing pipe line system soon combined to force actual crude oil prices up to posted levels. The plants of the Illinois refiners were not properly equipped to operate profitably on crude oil purchased at posted prices, and they encountered sales resistance when they attempted to recover the increased costs of crude oil with higher prices for refined products because their gasolines were usually of poor quality. The fact that the small plants were surrounded by large, efficient plants placed them in a poor competitive position. Several of the firms suffered bankruptcies because of undercapitalization and inexperienced managements. Finally, some of the refiners were left without a source of crude oil supply because local supplies of crude oil played out very quickly and because certain small producers preferred to sell to large, well-established companies which proved to be better credit risks than some of the small firms. This body of circumstances resulted in an abbreviated refining boom in the Illinois basin area.

4. The business opportunity afforded refiners by the discovery and development of new oil fields has necessarily been of a transitory character. The abundance of cheap crude oil, upon which the small refiners usually relied to offset their basic plant deficiencies and to enable them to reach broad geographic markets for their products, inevitably disappeared as the development of the fields proceeded. It was therefore entirely proper that the small refiners should have had only temporary economic lives. It is important to note that the economic lives of the refineries which the large companies built in producing fields have been limited in much the same way and by many of the same circumstances as have the lives of the refineries of the small companies.

5. Since large supplies of cheap crude oil are less likely to come onto the market in new oil fields being developed under prorationing measures, the prorationing acts have reduced and are likely to continue to restrict the opportunity to refiners arising from the discovery and development of new oil fields. The advances in refinery technology, particularly catalytic cracking processes, have also tended to restrain the building of the low-cost plants which typified oil field refining developments in the past. By reducing the opportunity for firms to engage in temporary oil field refining ventures such as those described in this chapter, these changes have effected a permanent contraction in the refining population.

CHAPTER TWENTY-TWO

Circumstances Causing the Disappearance of Three Small Refining Companies

THE preceding chapters in Part Four have dealt with certain broad economic conditions which contributed to the decline in the proportionate participation of small refiners in the affairs of the oil industry. These conditions included the growing capital requirements arising from advances in technology, the competitive disadvantages sometimes arising from the size and type of refinery equipment owned by small companies, and the circumstances surrounding the discovery and development of new oil fields. Attention was also directed in Chapters Five and Six to the highly unstable character of the refining gross margin and to the problems which it presented to nonintegrated refining companies. In this chapter, we shall analyze three specific company situations as a means of illustrating the manner in which these and other forces have brought about a reduction in the proportionate participation of small firms in refining activities.

The chapter will begin with a brief account of the circumstances which culminated in the postwar disappearances of the Aetna Oil Company, the Wood River Oil and Refining Company, and the Allied Oil Company. After each of these three situations has been discussed separately, the factors in evidence in the three cases will be compared and contrasted as a means of defining some of the important broad influences to which small refining companies have sometimes succumbed.

I. AETNA OIL COMPANY

During November 1949 Mr. W. T. Davis, president of the Aetna Oil Company, made a decision which paved the way for the Aetna Oil Company to be merged into the Ashland Oil & Refining Company. The Aetna Oil Com-

pany was an integrated concern engaged in refining, marketing, river tanker transportation, crude oil gathering, and to a much lesser extent crude oil producing operations. On January 16, 1950, the effective date of the merger, this small business activity ceased to exist as a separate entity.

The Aetna Oil Company was organized in 1917 by James "King" Duffy, a New England promoter, and was financed by Commodore E. C. Benedict, a New York millionaire.[1] The company's first refining facilities at Louisville, Kentucky, consisted of batch-operated shell and steam stills with a crude oil charging capacity of 1,000 barrels per day. The refinery was modernized and enlarged on several occasions and in 1949 the main processing equipment consisted of a combination skimming and thermal cracking unit with a crude oil capacity of 8,000 barrels per day.

The company integrated forward into marketing operations early in its history, making its first property acquisitions in the early 1920's. In 1949 the company distributed about 75% of its gasoline output through its own bulk plants and service stations or by sale to jobbers that resold under the Aetna brand name. The company's principal retail marketing territory was comprised of central and western Kentucky,

---

[1] In July 1921 the original venture ended in bankruptcy proceedings, and the administrators of the Benedict estate purchased the company for the bond or preferred stock interest of $250,000 plus $29,000 in cash. The company was recapitalized for $300,000 and renamed the Louisa Company of Kentucky. It subsequently became one of many widely scattered and diversified Benedict interests owned by the Louisa Company, a Delaware holding company. In 1927 the marketing division was known as the Aetna Oil Service and the manufacturing division as the Louisa Company of Kentucky. At this time both were combined into Aetna Oil Service, Inc. Later the name was changed to the Aetna Oil Company. For purposes of simplification the name Aetna Oil Company will be used throughout this discussion.

Louisville, and southern Indiana. The company constructed crude oil gathering lines in the Illinois basin and thereafter engaged in crude oil gathering activities. In 1949 the company also owned barges which were used to transport the company's crude oil and refined products to and from the Louisville refinery, which was located on the Ohio River.

In January 1932 when the Aetna Oil Company was in a critical financial position, a change in management was made which caused Mr. W. Abbott to be elected vice president and treasurer and Mr. W. T. Davis to be elected secretary of the company. Mr. Abbott had joined the company in 1923 as an oil burner salesman and had later served as head of the oil burner division, as an executive in the crude oil supply department, and as an assistant general manager. Mr. Davis, a graduate of the Massachusetts Institute of Technology, had been employed temporarily at the Aetna refinery for a period of 15 months beginning in January 1924. He had joined Aetna on a permanent basis in 1928 serving first as service station supervisor, later as head of all company engineering, and in 1931 as refinery superintendent.

In 1935 Mr. Abbott was elected president and treasurer and Mr. Davis vice president and secretary of the company. In practice, the two men functioned as co-administrators of the company during the years from 1932 through 1941. From 1932 through 1938, Mr. Davis administered refining, transportation, and accounting activities and Mr. Abbott supervised all sales and crude oil supply operations; from 1939 through 1941 Mr. Davis handled sales activities in addition to his other functions while Mr. Abbott devoted his time exclusively to crude oil supply operations. Upon the death of Mr. Abbott in 1941 Mr. Davis was elected president of the Aetna Oil Company.

Messrs. Abbott and Davis acquired ownership control of the Aetna Oil Company in 1936. From 1921, when Aetna had passed through bankruptcy proceedings, until 1936 the company had been owned by the Benedict estate. The executors of the Benedict estate realized that it was only through the untiring management efforts of Messrs. Abbott and Davis that the company had been revitalized after the company's second financial crisis in 1932. In the early part of 1936 therefore the adminis-

trators of the Benedict estate offered Messrs. Abbott and Davis an option to purchase control of the company which they had managed with such success. In 1934 the executors had already given both Mr. Abbott and Mr. Davis 250 shares of common stock for their services to the company. At that time, the company had outstanding 1,500 shares of no par common stock. The 1936 purchase option stipulated that Messrs. Abbott and Davis purchase the remaining 1,000 shares of common stock for $50,000 and 1,000 of the 5,000 outstanding shares of 6% cumulative preferred stock at a price of $100 per share.

In view of the company's operating and financial history, it was very difficult indeed for both Mr. Abbott and Mr. Davis to raise the funds necessary to exercise the stock purchase option. Mr. Davis managed to raise his portion of the necessary capital by borrowing from his father, by securing a loan on his life insurance policy, and by obtaining a personal loan from the banks. Mr. Abbott also borrowed heavily to raise his share of the necessary capital. In 1936 each purchased 355 additional shares of common stock for $17,750 and preferred stock valued at about $28,000. They were successful in selling to their friends and associates the remainder of the stock necessary to exercise the purchase option. Within a year 72.5 of the shares sold to outsiders were purchased and retired by the company. Consequently, Mr. Abbott and Mr. Davis each owned 42½% of the 1,427.5 shares of common stock outstanding. Following the death of Mr. Abbott in 1941 the large block of Aetna stock in his estate was administered by a Louisville bank which served in the capacity of trustee.

After the United States entered World War II Mr. Davis felt that government controls over petroleum supplies and markets were doing a fairly effective job in defining Aetna's activities and decided that his greatest contribution to the war effort might be made as a member of the armed services. Consequently, Mr. Davis enlisted in the Army and was called to active duty for a period of three years beginning December 1942. During most of this period he served in the China-Burma-India theater of operations. To manage the company in his absence, Mr. Davis set up a management committee composed of three vice presidents. Late in

EXHIBIT XXII-1. AETNA OIL COMPANY

Selected Financial and Operating Data: 1932–1949

Balance Sheet and Income Statement Items

($1,000)

Year Ending December 31 Except as Noted	Sales	Net Income	Net Working Capital	Plant, Property, & Equipment		Funded Debt	Capital Stock & Surplus	Total Assets
				Gross	Net			
1932	$ 1,333	$(230)	$ 88	$1,251	$ 634	$1,876	$1,361	$1,097
1933*	1,172	(208)	4	1,250	538	—	706	956
1934	1,365	(32)	45	1,258	502	—	686	970
1935	2,022	43	141	1,242	466	—	729	993
1936	2,587	219	221	1,326	507	—	863	1,173
1937	3,134	198	219	1,418	610	7	999	1,476
1938	3,274	8	83	1,540	694	2	988	1,499
1939	3,975	508	368	1,688	769	—	1,367	1,873
1940	4,508	295	346	2,001	1,007	121	1,442	2,288
1941	6,863	415	792	2,201	1,122	360	1,793	3,110
1942	7,268	299	774	2,687	1,464	457	2,053	3,493
1943	7,386	219	978	2,728	1,370	394	2,236	3,675
1944	8,587	246	982	2,782	1,280	332	2,343	3,804
1945	7,468	199	1,068	2,954	1,336	267	2,554	3,888
1946	10,733	267	1,302	3,140	1,427	194	2,667	4,519
1947	13,584	725	1,339	3,737	1,964	143	3,383	5,990
1948	14,017	662	2,070	5,071	3,019	1,015	4,252	9,752
1949†	9,833	95	2,082	5,339	2,972	866	4,244	8,425

Crude Production, Refinery Runs, Refinery Yields, and Sales of Refined Products

(1,000 bbls.)

Year	Net Crude Oil Production	Refinery Runs	Yield of Products				Sales of Refined Products				
			Gasoline	Kerosene	Distillates	Residual Fuel Oil	Total	Gasoline	Kerosene	Distillates	Residual Fuel Oil
1939	50	1,360	690	86	178	463	1,530	845	87	159	439
1940	26	1,927	839	129	272	611	1,932	984	130	283	535
1941	43	2,575	1,067	221	410	805	2,623	1,297	211	355	760
1942	68	2,428	917	293	409	746	2,643	1,164	304	472	703
1943	33	2,264	765	287	343	805	2,637	1,060	325	338	914
1944	62	2,504	963	263	375	803	3,019	1,389	306	379	945
1945	182	2,246	877	209	340	736	2,506	1,162	238	326	780
1946	113	2,598	929	251	381	888	3,415	1,675	353	329	1,058
1947	78	2,364	922	238	334	801	3,237	1,517	301	432	987
1948	222	1,559	632	148	249	475	2,503	1,145	143	358	857
1949†	171	1,529	423	111	247	446	1,830	941	108	263	518

* For 14 months ending February 28, 1934. The marked difference between the net worth as of December 31, 1932, and February 28, 1934, is due to a financial reorganization effective as of May 31, 1933.

† For 9 months ending September 30, 1949.

SOURCE: Aetna Oil Company.

1945 Mr. Davis resumed active management of the Aetna Oil Company.

Under the joint administration of Messrs. Abbott and Davis, the Aetna Oil Company developed into a profitable refining business. Although the company was unprofitable from 1932 to 1934, in 1935 it realized what was for the Aetna Oil Company a very substantial profit of $43,000. After 1935 the company was profitable each year, with a high point in earnings of $725,000 being reached in the year 1947. Selected financial and operating data illustrating the company's growth are shown in Exhibit XXII-1.

Circumstances Motivating the Merger Decision:

A group of factors, some affecting the operations of the Aetna Oil Company and others of personal concern to Mr. Davis, culminated in the decision whereby the Aetna Oil Company was merged into the Ashland Oil & Refining Company in 1950. Some of these circumstances originated many years prior to 1950, others were problems of immediate concern, and still others were uncertainties about the future.

Impact of Technological Advancement: One important factor leading to the withdrawal of Aetna was the unwillingness of Mr. Davis to recommend the capital expenditures for certain refinery equipment which the company needed to keep pace with the postwar octane competition on gasoline. Throughout its history the Aetna Oil Company had made numerous plant additions, improvements, and replacements as a result of basic developments which were made in refinery processing techniques. In the postwar period, however, the management was confronted with the necessity of making an investment which dwarfed any previous outlay for plant facilities.

Mr. Davis noted that throughout the years refining had been the most successful and profitable of the company's operations. Transportation activities had also been quite profitable. Neither crude oil producing nor marketing activities had yielded returns comparable with those realized on refining and transportation operations. The principal processing equipment used by the company consisted of a combination skimming and thermal cracking unit with a crude oil charging capacity of 8,000 barrels per day. The vice president in charge of refinery operations was highly regarded in the industry as an outstanding technical man, and Aetna's refinery equipment was kept in excellent operating condition. The company's refinery was not, however, equipped to produce the high octane gasolines made available by catalytic cracking processes.

As World War II progressed it became evident that the struggle for higher octane numbers on gasoline would be an integral part of the postwar competitive picture. At first the company officers felt there was a strong possibility that a surplus of high octane blending stocks might develop because of the large amount of cracking equipment built by other companies during the war years.[2] Later, when it became evident that such a surplus would

not materialize, the management considered the purchase of a catalytic cracking unit.

Immediately after the war Aetna had construction cost estimates for catalytic cracking units prepared by several refinery engineering firms, including the M. W. Kellogg Company and Universal Oil Products. The management was interested in catalytic cracking units in sizes ranging from 3,000 to 6,000 barrels per day of charging stock capacity. In addition, it was anticipated that if the cracking unit were installed, the company's crude oil distillation equipment would be enlarged to handle between 10,000 and 20,000 barrels of crude oil per day. The estimates for catalytic cracking units ranged between $4,000,000 and $8,000,000, and there was no guarantee that actual construction costs would not exceed the estimates by a considerable amount. In view of the postwar construction boom, the management was much disturbed about its inability to get a firm construction bid as a basis for planning.

While it would have been possible for the company to have borrowed approximately 75% of the plant cost, Mr. Davis and several of the minority stockholders were unwilling "to assume the risks involved in such a large expenditure." The situation presented a dilemma since the management also felt the installation of a catalytic cracking unit was a necessity if the company were to assure its competitive position over the long run. To meet octane requirements in the postwar period the company had relied temporarily upon blending stocks supplied by two major oil companies. This buying arrangement was considered merely a stop-gap measure since the possible curtailment of outside supplies of high octane stocks would have placed Aetna at a severe quality disadvantage in marketing its gasoline.

Consideration of a Pension Plan: A second reason for the merger arose from the reluctance of the management to commit the company funds necessary to initiate and carry forward a pension plan for employees. After the war pension plans were widely adopted in the oil and other industries, and there were therefore very strong pressures on the Aetna management to install a pension plan for its employees. Mr. Davis was sympathetic to the need for an adequate pension plan and felt that a pension

---

[2] During the period in which Mr. Davis was a member of the armed services he was kept well informed of company affairs through long letters and memoranda prepared by officers of the Aetna organization. He was therefore cognizant of the octane problem which was developing for the Aetna Oil Company.

program was both inevitable and advisable. He was, however, somewhat dismayed by the large cash outlay which would have been necessary to fund past service benefits. Depending upon the terms selected, an initial investment of $400,000 to $600,000 would have been required. In view of the company's size, Mr. Davis and the other owners felt an expenditure of such magnitude could not be afforded.

Personal Desires of Mr. Davis: A third reason for the merger decision lay in Mr. Davis' strong personal desire to ease the strain of his business life. Aetna was on the brink of bankruptcy when Messrs. Abbott and Davis assumed management control of the company in 1932. At that time current liabilities totaled $395,000, of which two-thirds were overdue. The task of rebuilding the company's financial and competitive strength was a demanding one for the two executive officers. During the first six or seven years that they managed the company, they often worked as many as 20 hours per day. Mr. Davis lost weight and suffered from frequent headaches, indigestion, and insomnia. In 1937 Mr. Davis took a much needed rest, but upon his return to Louisville the Ohio Valley was subjected to the worst flood in its history. The refinery was shut down for a month, and the losses were heavy. After surmounting this misfortune Mr. Davis suffered a relapse. In May 1937 he went to Sea Island, Georgia, for a month's rest; when he returned to work, he suffered a second relapse and was eventually sent to the Johns Hopkins Hospital, with the thought that he might be forced to give up his business career forever. He was completely exhausted and remained at the hospital from August to November 1937. During his recuperative period he reflected at length upon a management reorganization of the company which would subdivide the company into four departments, with a capable man in charge of each. By the end of 1939 this management objective had been attained.

While he was in the Army and detached from day-to-day operating pressures, Mr. Davis had ample opportunity to reflect upon his past life and upon what he would prefer his life to be in the future. As a boy Mr. Davis had spent long and very enjoyable periods on his grandfather's farm, and he looked favorably upon the possibility of engaging in some farming activity in the future. It was during the war period that the possibility of selling his interest in the Aetna Oil Company first occurred to Mr. Davis. The physical and nervous strain of building a successful refining business had seriously affected his health in the past. It was considered necessary that he avoid business pressures in the future which might cause a recurrence of these ailments.

Mr. Davis further recognized that through overattention to his work, he had failed to achieve a successful domestic life. He was most anxious that his future work should not jeopardize the happiness of his second marriage. The desires and ambitions of Mr. Davis to ease the strain of his business life therefore had their origin many years prior to 1949 and particularly during the periods in which Mr. Davis' health and domestic life were impaired by constant overwork.

Tax and Estate Considerations: Mr. Davis wished to diversify his personal holdings and was concerned about the impact which inheritance taxes would make upon his estate in the event of his death. Moreover, the officers of a Louisville bank, which held $45\frac{1}{2}\%$ of Aetna's stock in trust for the Abbott estate and two minority stockholders, were anxious to sell this large interest in the company for cash in order to diversify the investment portfolios of their clients.

The bulk of Mr. Davis' estate was represented by the equity which he had built up in the Aetna Oil Company. In merger proceedings with the Ashland Oil & Refining Company, a cash value of approximately $2,000,000 was attached to Mr. Davis' common stockholdings.[3] If this figure is taken as indicative of a fair market value which might have been assigned to the stock by the Bureau of Internal Revenue for inheritance tax purposes in the event of Mr. Davis' death, the tax liability would have been substantial under the tax provisions existing in 1949. To meet the large tax liability, it would have been necessary for the estate to liquidate some of Mr. Davis' holdings in the Aetna Oil

---

[3] In view of the tax advantages of a statutory merger, however, Mr. Davis ultimately accepted Ashland securities having an estimated market value of less than the agreed-upon cash price.

Company. Inasmuch as the stock was closely held, Mr. Davis feared that a sale might have to be made under distress conditions and that the price realized for the stock would be considerably less than its true worth. It was also possible, because of the close identity of Mr. Davis with the Aetna firm, that his death might have had a very serious depressing effect on the market price of the Aetna stock.

Mr. Davis had been aware of the inheritance tax problem for some time and had been taking steps to prepare his estate for this burden. For many years he had attempted to keep pace with the growth in his estate by taking out life insurance policies adequate to meet the inheritance tax liability that would fall due upon his death. As the total face value of the insurance increased and as Mr. Davis became older, insurance premiums reached staggering figures. He later reduced his insurance coverage to $60,000, realizing that an expensive insurance program would not be a practical means of meeting the growing tax liability. Moreover, he felt that there were sufficient funds in his estate to provide adequately for his family.

Ultimately Mr. Davis turned his attention to other means of diversifying his personal holdings and preparing his estate to meet inheritance taxes. Mr. Davis was very much impressed with the possibility of arranging a tax-free statutory merger of Aetna with a widely held, listed corporation as one method of achieving an orderly liquidation of his large stock interest in Aetna. Such a move would postpone any capital gains tax liability until the newly acquired stock was sold. Mr. Davis recognized that a widely held stock could be disposed of much more readily than could Aetna stock in order to raise the funds which would be necessary to meet the inheritance taxes. An outright cash sale of Aetna stock was also considered by Mr. Davis. The proceeds from a cash sale of Aetna stock would, however, have been immediately taxable at capital gains rates.

Crude Oil Supply Problems: A fifth reason for the merger decision was the management's concern over the large sums of money which would have been required to build up crude oil reserves to a point where uncertainties about the continuity of crude oil supplies in the future would be removed. Before 1939 the company had relied heavily upon major companies as a source of crude oil supply. Subsequent to 1939 Aetna's crude oil supply was obtained largely from the Illinois basin, where the company owned approximately 90 miles of gathering lines. Ownership of this gathering system made it possible for the company to make approximately 95% of its crude oil purchases at the well-head. The arrangements with independent producers for purchases of oil at the well-head provided in some cases that Aetna would supply loans and equipment for developing the producing properties. The oil gathered in Aetna's line was delivered largely to the Sohio Petroleum Company which returned oil to Aetna on the Ohio River at points from which it could be moved into Louisville economically by barge.

In the postwar period Aetna purchased some small producing properties and engaged in a modest way in the development of oil leases. The company also obtained fractional interests in some properties as a result of the financial assistance which it extended to small producers located on the company's gathering line. Net crude oil production, however, never amounted to more than 15% of refinery runs.

Crude oil was in very short supply after World War II, and the Aetna management was concerned that the maintenance of adequate crude oil supplies might pose serious problems in the future. Since the company was dependent upon outside purchases for approximately 90% of its refinery requirements, the hazard of future shortages developing was considered a very real one. To develop an appreciable amount of company owned production would have involved expenditures which, it was believed, would far outstrip the financial resources of the company. While the crude oil supply problem was not an immediately pressing one, it nevertheless influenced management thinking about a possible merger.

Minor Considerations: A refinery fire in 1948 and a poor profit showing in 1949 were of some, but distinctly minor, significance in influencing the merger decision. The 1948 refinery fire halted production for approximately three months and affected operations adversely. During this period it was necessary for Aetna to purchase large amounts of products from outside sources at a time when they were scarce and high in price. The property loss was largely covered by insurance, and the adverse effects on operations were likewise in part offset by use and occupancy insurance. Nevertheless, Mr. Davis stated that the fire involved a cost to the company of several hundred thousand dollars.

Aetna suffered a sharp curtailment in profits during 1949 as a result of the marked contraction which took place in the refiner's margin during the year. As noted in Chapter Six the decline in the refiner's margin during 1949 was caused largely by an abnormally depressed price for residual fuel oil. Prices in the Aetna market area for residual fuel oil, which represented approximately 25% of Aetna's refinery output, fell from a high point of $2.50 a barrel in 1948 to a low point of 60 cents a barrel in 1949. It is important to note that the lack of vacuum distillation, catalytic cracking, coking, or asphalt facilities at the Aetna plant impaired the company's ability to counteract this market situation. Without any of these processes the company was severely limited in the steps it could take to reduce the output of the low-priced residual fuel oil. The Aetna officers were, however, of the opinion that the depressed market conditions would be of temporary duration, and residual prices had in fact rebounded somewhat by November 1949, the date of the merger decision. Largely as a result of the fire and the 1949 market situation, the net income realized by Aetna fell from $725,000 in 1947 to $662,000 in 1948 and $95,-000 for the nine months ending September 30, 1949. These circumstances, while transitory, had some effect in motivating the management toward the merger action.

The Merger Terms:

The merger agreement consummated between the Aetna Oil Company and the Ashland Oil & Refining Company enabled the Aetna shareholders to close out their interests in the company with creditable gains on their original investments. As noted earlier, in 1936 Messrs. Abbott and Davis and their associates purchased 1,000 shares of Aetna common stock for $50,000 and 1,000 shares of Aetna preferred stock for $100,000. Previously, Mr. Abbott and Mr. Davis had each been given 250 shares of Aetna common stock. In subsequent years several changes were made in Aetna's capital stock structure. The company's common stock was split 50 for 1 in 1946, and on September 30, 1949, there were 71,375 common shares outstanding. The original 6% cumulative preferred stock issued in 1934 had been retired by 1945, and, in 1946, 4,996¼ shares of 4% cumulative, $100 par value, preferred stock were declared by the company as a dividend to common shareholders. Therefore, both the Aetna common and preferred stock issues outstanding in 1949 were a direct outgrowth of a $50,000 common stock investment made in 1936.

The Aetna preferred and common stock was acquired by the Ashland Oil & Refining Company in return for $1,884,000 in cash and $2,-662,000 par value Ashland preferred stock. The cash was paid to the trustees for the Abbott estate and the two minority stockholders. Mr. Davis and the other minority stockholders exchanged their holdings of Aetna preferred and common stock for a mixture of Ashland $5.00 cumulative preferred stock and Ashland $1.20 cumulative convertible preferred stock. Thus, a total common stock investment of $50,000 made in Aetna common stock in 1936 brought a price of approximately $4,546,000 in 1949. Mr. Davis personally received preferred stock of Ashland with a stated value of $1,859,467.50 and a market value of somewhat less than this amount. Cash dividends which had been received on the Aetna stock over the 13-year period prior to the merger supplemented the owners' return on their original investment. The cash dividend record of Aetna over this entire time period is not readily available. From January 1, 1946, to September 30, 1949, however, it is known that cash dividends amounted to $114,438.

II. The Wood River Oil and Refining Company

The Wood River Oil and Refining Company provides a second illustration of the circumstances causing the postwar disappearance of a small refining company. In June 1950 the management of the Wood River Oil and Refining Company sold the company's refinery at Hartford, Illinois, a small products pipe line in Illinois, and two refined products terminals to

EXHIBIT XXII-2. WOOD RIVER OIL AND REFINING COMPANY

Selected Financial and Operating Data: 1945–May 31, 1950

(000's)

| Year | Gross Operating Income | Net Income | Total Assets | Net Working Capital | Plant, Property, and Equipment | | Long-Term Debt | Surplus Reserves | Capital Stock and Surplus | Refinery Runs (bbls.) | Sales of Refined Product (bbls.) |
					Gross	Net					
1945	$ 8,767	$ 82	$ 4,631	$1,039	$ 2,995	$ 1,855	$1,989	$ 500	$ 655	3,618	3,635
1946	11,691	607	7,614	546	4,595	3,207	3,208	500	1,434	5,054	4,960
1947	23,001	2,577	13,333	1,269	7,431	5,642	4,133	—	4,075	7,066	6,732
1948	38,775	2,781	18,675	1,463	11,154	8,430	3,695	1,250	7,036	7,867	8,641
1949	22,388	(319)	19,895	2,006	14,576	10,811	5,871	1,250	6,862	6,070	5,815
May 31, 1950	10,110	252	20,170	2,572	14,674	10,446	5,329	1,250	7,107	2,645	2,524

SOURCE: Wood River Oil and Refining Company.

the Sinclair Oil Corporation for $15,500,000. The company's participation at the refining level of the industry was thus brought to an end. The company continued, however, to operate its remaining producing, marketing, and transportation properties.

The Wood River Oil and Refining Company, Inc., was organized in January 1940 with an authorized capital of $15,000, consisting of 15,000 shares of common stock, $1.00 par value. The principal owners and their shareholdings were Mr. O. H. Ingram, 5,000 shares; Mr. I. O'Shaughnessy, 5,000 shares; and Mr. Fred Koch, 3,750 to 5,000 shares. Mr. Ingram, who initiated the project, had a large personal fortune and was president of the Ingram Products Company which was engaged in certain operations in the textile industry. Mr. O'Shaughnessy was president of the Globe Oil and Refining Company which owned a shutdown refinery in Blackwell, Oklahoma. Mr. O'Shaughnessy was convinced that the St. Louis area, readily accessible to river and pipe line transportation, was an excellent site for a refinery and therefore joined as a partner in the venture. Mr. Fred Koch was president of the Winkler-Koch Engineering Company and the Koch Engineering Company, Inc., firms of refinery consulting engineers which had designed and constructed refinery improvements as well as complete refineries in the United States, Europe, and Asia. Mr. Koch had always wanted to enter the refining industry but had never had access to the capital required to do so. He thus welcomed an opportunity to join the firm.

As a result of a disagreement over management policies in 1944 Mr. Ingram and Mr.

Koch bought out Mr. O'Shaughnessy's interest in the company. In 1950 Mr. Ingram and Mr. Koch each owned about 40% of the common stock; Mr. Koch had been elected president of the company and was primarily responsible for the management of its affairs.

The Wood River refinery was completed in 1941 at a cost of about $2,000,000. It was financed by a bank loan of about $1,000,000 and personal notes of the owners aggregating about $1,000,000. The original refinery consisted of combination topping and thermal cracking units with a crude capacity of 15,000 barrels per day; by 1950 the crude capacity had been doubled and new processing equipment including a fluid catalytic cracking unit had been added. Throughout most of the postwar period the company was extremely profitable. Total assets increased to $20,170,000 and the stockholders' equity to $8,357,000. In 1950 there was over $6,000,000 in notes and loans outstanding, but during the entire period from 1941 to 1950 no new equity capital was added to the business. Selected financial and operating data for the Wood River Oil and Refining Company are shown in Exhibit XXII-2.

Circumstances Prompting the Sale:

The principal reasons why the owners were willing to accept the offer of the Sinclair Oil Corporation of $15,500,000 for the refinery, the two terminals at Peru and Rockford, Illinois, and the products pipe line connecting the terminals were as follows:

Marketing Problems: A very important factor leading to the sale of the refinery was the owners' concern that the refinery output could not be marketed successfully in the future. When the company was formed in 1940, it took over the marketing accounts of the Globe Oil and Refining Company. During the war the company's refinery throughput was restricted by government regulations and products output was allocated to customers at a stipulated scale of prices which provided a reasonable profit margin. In the immediate postwar period there was a general shortage of petroleum products, and the company had no difficulty in selling its output on favorable terms.

Lulled into a sense of security by the sellers' market which prevailed throughout most of its history, the company made no strong effort to develop an aggressive marketing program with independent jobbers. There was, however, some feeling in the management group that such an effort should be made. In the immediate postwar period the company had among its sales accounts two very large customers, the Illinois Farm Bureau, a cooperative, and the Mid-Continent Petroleum Corporation. The company sold to these two customers at a price somewhat under the low of the *Chicago Journal of Commerce* quoted prices until a shortage of products developed early in 1948, at which time the low of the market price was charged. The Wood River management understood that Mid-Continent purchased from Wood River for two reasons. First, it was believed that the Mid-Continent management desired to concentrate on the refining and sale of lube oils but recognized that it was necessary to build up gasoline sales in order to increase lube oil sales. The Mid-Continent Petroleum Corporation had insufficient refining capacity and could not accomplish its objectives in the lube oil market without an outside source of supply for gasoline. Second, it was believed that the management of Mid-Continent wished to keep its own refinery output slightly smaller than its sales volume in order to assure capacity operations in times of slack demand.

In the latter part of 1948 market conditions in the petroleum industry changed drastically, and an oversupply of crude oil, gasoline and fuel oils developed. During this period the Mid-Continent Petroleum Corporation installed additional refining equipment of its own and was thus able to stop purchasing from the Wood River Oil and Refining Company. The Illinois Farm Bureau also acquired a small refinery to supply its own needs, possibly, Mr. Koch believed, because Wood River had charged it the low of the market prices during the period of products shortage earlier in the year. Meanwhile, the Wood River Oil and Refining Company lost a number of its small jobber accounts. These firms did not hesitate to switch to other sources of supply when differentials in price of as little as one-eighth of a cent per gallon were offered. Finally, the distributors of major companies who had been encouraged by their suppliers to buy part of their requirements from Wood River in the period of shortage were urged to place all their business with their regular sources of supply. The depressed market conditions continued into 1949, and in that year the Wood River Oil and Refining Company had a net loss of $319,000.

Faced with these difficulties, the Wood River Oil and Refining Company took certain steps to strengthen the management of its marketing organization. The weaknesses in this department had been recognized for some time, but changes had not been made because the need for them was not urgent. A belated effort was then made to develop an effective jobber program. The company designed a trade mark and began selling under the Wood River brand name. In addition, numerous cards, pamphlets, and other units of a "sales package" were developed to describe the Wood River sales program to independent jobbers. In a further attempt to introduce stability into its market activities, the company organized a wholly owned subsidiary to build two company owned and operated service stations in the Chicago area in 1949.

In looking to the future the owners believed that the company would have to market 50% of its gasoline output through company owned and operated service stations to assure stability in the refinery operations. It was estimated that these service stations would need a volume of 100,000 gallons a month to operate on a profitable scale and would cost $65,000 each, $50,000 for buildings and equipment and $15,000 for land. To market one-half the gasoline output of 450,000 barrels per month through such stations would thus have required a total capital expenditure of $6,500,000. The management also believed that the company needed at least two additional products terminals which would cost from $300,000 to $700,000 each.

Crude Oil Supply Problems: The owners of the company were also concerned about their ability to secure adequate crude oil supplies for the refinery in the future. Originally, the Globe Oil and Refining Company purchased crude oil for the Wood River Oil and Refining Company and for its own use. Mr. Koch asserted that operations were impeded during this period because the crude oil made available to Wood River was often high-priced and of an undesirable refinery value. During the war period government allocations assured the company of a continuous supply of 14,700 barrels of crude oil per day. This supply was adequate to meet the refinery's requirements prior to its enlargement to a capacity of 30,000 barrels per day in 1948. After the war neither of these sources was available and the problem of securing an adequate supply of crude oil was one of the most difficult ones which the company faced.

The location of the refinery at Hartford made available the facilities of six common carrier pipe lines, the Stanolind, Magnolia, Ajax, Sinclair, and Shell lines, and also gave the company access to crude oil via excellent river and rail transportation routes. The company could obtain crude oil from almost any point in Illinois, Louisiana, Texas, Oklahoma, Kansas, New Mexico, and Wyoming by pipe line. Furthermore, crude oil could be brought up the Mississippi River at a reasonable cost from Mississippi, Louisiana, and Arkansas fields or from abroad. Despite these advantageous transportation arrangements the management was much concerned about its postwar reliance on crude oil contracts with large suppliers as a means of assuring a permanent crude oil supply. The possible inability to negotiate a renewal on an important crude oil contract would have been ruinous to the company's operation.

As one means of alleviating the supply problem the company had integrated backward into crude oil pipe line gathering systems. In 1946 the company acquired the Rock Island Oil Company, Inc., which had a pipe line gathering system in the oil fields near Duncan, Oklahoma. Some of the producers on this line later switched their connections to a competing line which was built by a larger company. Subsequent discoveries in the area more than offset the loss, however, and this system gave the company access to about 17,000 barrels of crude oil per day which were available to the Hartford refinery in 1948. Similarly, in the latter part of 1948 Wood River purchased a one-half interest in a West Texas gathering system which was previously owned by an individual. This venture was, however, unsuccessful in augmenting the company's crude oil supply. At about the time of the purchase the producers on the line signed contracts to sell their output to a major oil company. The previous owner of the gathering system had been buying from independent producers at discounts below the posted prices. The independent producers chose to sell to a larger concern which could give them greater assurance of a continuing market in the industry plus a price increase up to posted levels. Subsequently, Wood River disposed of its interest in this line.

As a second means of solving the crude oil supply problem the company made substantial expenditures, financed out of earnings, in an effort to develop some crude oil production of its own. These efforts were only partially successful. The company's net crude oil production was less than 1,000 barrels per day in 1950. At the close of 1949 the company's net investment in producing properties was $2,830,000. During the period 1945 to 1949 the net loss on producing operations amounted to $718,847. The company also had control of several thousand additional barrels of crude oil per day from the producing properties owned by certain stockholders and associates of the company. The owners of the company anticipated that securing an adequate supply of crude oil would continue to present financial and operating difficulties.

Debt Structure: A point of much concern to the owners was the existing debt structure of the company and the difficulties involved in securing further financing. As noted above, the company had loans and bank notes outstanding in 1950 amounting to more than $6,000,000. Most of this indebtedness was incurred in the period from 1947 to 1950 to permit the construction of the products pipe line, the pipe line terminals, a perco-reforming unit, and a fluid catalytic cracking unit. This debt structure was considered by the management to be an "imposing burden which hung over the company." Relations with the refinery union were unpredictable, and the management continually feared a work stoppage which, in view of the interest commitments and principal repayments on the debt, would have been ruinous to the company. Furthermore, the company was more vulnerable to a possible sustained period of operating losses than other companies employing a larger share of equity capital.

Despite the heavy expenditures which had been made for equipment in the postwar period, large additional capital outlays appeared necessary to permit the development of the company's marketing program and to assure adequate supplies of crude oil. As noted above, the estimates of required funds amounted to millions of dollars. The management also believed that additional working capital was needed to enlarge the company's crude oil and refined products inventories. Larger crude oil inventories would have permitted greater flexibility in scheduling refinery runs on the various types of crude oil received, and larger products inventories would have permitted the company to build stocks of gasoline and fuel oil in the respective off seasons and thus have permitted the company to take advantage of seasonal variations in price.

The owners of the company and their associates already held company notes in the amount of $1,261,000, and they were reluctant to invest additional sums in the firm. Early in 1950, the common stock market was somewhat depressed, and it was considered extremely doubtful that a stock issue by a little-known firm such as the Wood River Oil and Refining Company could be floated successfully, particularly in view of the fact that the company lacked a prewar earnings record.

Desire to Sell Products Pipe Line and Terminals: The management was anxious to dispose of the company's products pipe line and the terminaling facilities on the line because the system had failed to fulfill the company's expectations with respect to its original purpose. The company had constructed a short, 8-inch products pipe line of 30,000 barrels a day capacity from Peru, Illinois, to Rockford, Illinois, in 1946 and 1947. Total expenditures for the pipe line from 1946 through June 1950 were $1,878,000. Refined products terminals were erected at the two end points of the line, and products were moved from the refinery at Hartford to Peru by barge transportation. The management had hoped that this products pipe line would permit the company to move products to the Rockford terminal at competitive transportation costs and to develop a substantial market in that area. At a later date the management planned to extend the pipe line to Madison, Wisconsin, and the right of way was secured for this purpose. Sales in the Rockford area, however, proved disappointing to the management; although burning oil sales for home heating purposes were excellent, gasoline sales were very poor. The management attributed the failure of the project to the difficulty involved in securing satisfactory market outlets for gasoline. Since the entire program proved unsuccessful, the management was most anxious to dispose of its products pipe line and the attendant terminaling facilities.

Other Interests of the Owners: The two principal owners of the Wood River Oil and Refining Company "had gotten pretty sick of the refining business during the unprofitable period in 1949" and they had other business affairs to claim their attention. Mr. Ingram had never participated actively in the management of the company. Shortly after its formation he developed a river barge transportation business, and the refinery thereafter was of interest to him primarily as a source of supply of transportable products. The barge business came to have a great personal interest to Mr. Ingram, and he was entirely willing to turn his attention to it after the unprofitable period in 1949. Mr. Koch had a somewhat greater interest in continuing the refining business, but he also had his two consulting firms to manage, a new refining venture to plan, as well as the continuation of the marketing operation of the Wood River Oil and Refining Company.

Inheritance Taxes and Investment Considerations: Both Mr. Koch and Mr. Ingram recognized that a difficult inheritance tax problem would arise if one of them should die since neither of their estates could have been settled without a forced sale of stock to get the funds necessary to pay the inheritance taxes. The financial advisor to Mr. Ingram, who also served as a member of the Wood River Oil and Refining Company board of directors, owned 15,000 shares of common stock in the company as a result of a nominal investment which he had made in 1940. The financial advisor was nearing 60 years of age and he was most anxious to convert his holdings into liquid assets in order to put his estate in order. In 1950 these shares were valued at more than $400,000.

Adequacy of the Sales Price:

The price offered by the Sinclair Oil Corporation provided the Wood River owners an opportunity to get out of the refining business with a substantial profit for their efforts. The price of $15,500,000 covered the refinery, the terminals at Peru and Rockford, and the products pipe line connecting the two terminals. In 1950 the company's gross investment in these properties was less than $12,000,000. Moreover, at the time of the sale, the company had other assets valued at about $11,000,000, which was roughly the amount of the company's current liabilities and outstanding debts. The purchase price of $15,500,000 would therefore have enabled the company to close its books with a net profit for the 10-year period of about $15,000,000 over and above the $15,000 of capital initially paid in by the owners. On the sales transaction the company realized $6,000,000 in excess of the book value of the refinery, terminals, and refined products pipe line before providing for federal and state taxes. No record is available of the dividends paid out during the 10-year period, but they were presumably small.

The Wood River Oil and Refining Company continued its small business participation after the sale of its refinery, products pipe line, and terminals to the Sinclair Oil Corporation. Mr. Ingram, however, withdrew from the company in order to devote his time to his barging and other business interests. In 1950 Wood River continued to press its search for crude oil and engaged in the active planing of a future refinery activity. Moreover, the company purchased a 60,000-acre ranch in Montana, and became thereby engaged in both the oil and ranching businesses. In 1952 the company announced plans to construct a 15,000 barrels per day refinery in the Chicago area.

III. ALLIED OIL COMPANY [4]

The experience of the Allied Oil Company provides a third example of the circumstances which culminated in the postwar disappearance of a small refining company. Early in 1948 Messrs. W. W. Vandeveer and F. R. Newman decided to merge their company into the Ashland Oil & Refining Company. When the merger was consummated on August 3, 1948, the refining population was reduced by one.

The decision of the Allied owners to merge their firm with the Ashland Oil & Refining Company stemmed largely from the personal financial pressures to which the principal owners were subjected as the Allied Oil Company grew and expanded its operations. In the following paragraphs we shall trace the growth of the corporation and the problems which arose therefrom.

The Growth of the Allied Oil Company:

The Allied Oil Company was founded in 1925 as a small fuel oil marketing organization. As opportunities arose in later years, the company integrated backward in successive stages into products transportation, refining, crude oil transportation, and crude oil producing activities. By 1948 the company's annual sales volume had grown to approximately $50,000,000 and its net worth to about $10,000,000.

Fuel Oil Marketing: In 1925 several factors combined to create a favorable opportunity for marketing industrial fuel oil in northeastern Ohio. The various refiners supplying industrial fuel oil to this area were engaged in the change-over from distillation to cracking processes. Much of the burning equipment in use by industrial fuel oil consumers had been

---

[4] Certain of the facts in the following discussion were drawn from an unpublished case study on the Allied Oil Company prepared by J. Keith Butters, and a publication by J. Keith Butters, John Lintner, William L. Cary, assisted by Powell Niland entitled *Effects of Taxation: Corporate Mergers* (Boston, Division of Research, Graduate School of Business Administration, Harvard University, 1951).

designed for straight-run fuels, and these consumers were experiencing considerable difficulty in using the cracked residues produced by the new refinery facilities. The organizers of the Allied Oil Company intended that the company should function as a specialist in providing fuel oils which would operate satisfactorily in the various types of industrial oil burners.

Allied was subsequently able to operate as an effective middleman between the large number of refiners located on the periphery of the Ohio market and the fuel oil customers in the area. From the viewpoint of the refiner, residual fuel oil in the 1920's was strictly a by-product of gasoline manufacture; it had to be disposed of rapidly since most refiners had limited storage space. Refiners typically sold their fuel oil in whatever market appeared most attractive at the time without trying to develop a continuing relationship with specific purchasers. Allied, on the other hand, maintained sufficient sources of supply for the various kinds of fuel oil needed by its customers in order that it might fulfill all orders without delay. Just as Allied was able to provide a steady source of supply to its customers, so also was it a convenient sales outlet for the excess supplies of fuel oil accumulated by refiners in its area.

The company's fuel oil marketing business grew steadily, and by 1948 Allied was the largest independent fuel oil marketer in the lower Great Lakes area, eastern Ohio, western Pennsylvania, and parts of West Virginia. The marketing area constituted one of the most concentrated outlets for industrial fuel oil in the United States. In 1948 the company had 300 industrial accounts, including several of the larger steel companies. Allied purchased from many large and small refining companies to meet its fuel oil sales requirements.

Transportation and Terminaling Facilities: During the boom period in 1928 and 1929 the management had to ship hundreds of tank cars of fuel oil by rail from refining points in the Mid-Continent and from eastern seaboard areas to supply the peak demands of the steel industry. It was during this period that the management became acutely conscious of the contribution which low-cost transportation facilities could make to the company's profits.

In the fall of 1929, after a survey of the potentialities of water transportation had been completed, the company erected a large products terminal at Cleveland, Ohio, and purchased its first lake tanker. Both terminal and tanker were designed to handle dirty products. Soon after the vessel was acquired, Allied experienced a demand from other oil companies to serve as a contract carrier in the movement of gasoline and other petroleum products on the Great Lakes, and subsequently the company purchased additional vessels for the transportation of both clean and dirty products. In 1948 the company owned six lake-going vessels, the largest independent fleet of tankers on the Great Lakes, and chartered additional lake vessels. Allied also owned a 50% interest in Allied-Ashland Tankers, Inc. In February 1948 Allied-Ashland Tankers purchased two "T-2" ocean-going tankers which were chartered to the Standard Oil Company (New Jersey) for a period of five years.

As the size and area of its fuel oil marketing operation increased over the years, Allied added to its fuel oil terminaling facilities. In 1948 it owned and operated terminals in Cleveland, Ohio, Follansbee, West Virginia, and Erie, Pennsylvania. The company also leased a terminal at Kobuta, Pennsylvania, on the Ohio River near Pittsburgh.

Refining Operations: The third major phase of the company's expansion was begun in the latter part of 1936 when the company undertook the wholesale marketing of the entire output of a leased refinery at Canton, Ohio. In 1936 a promoter secured a lease on a small refinery from the first mortgage bondholders of a defunct organization, and he requested Allied to undertake the sale of the entire refinery fuel oil output. Meanwhile, the Allied management had been considering the possibility of entering the gasoline jobbing business. The management felt there was a profitable opportunity for well-managed independent gasoline distributors in the area. Moreover, certain other independent distributors were experiencing difficulties in finding adequate and stable sources of supply at what they deemed reasonable prices. Several of these distributors had encouraged the company to undertake gasoline terminaling operations at Cleveland. The proposal to re-open the refinery offered the Allied management an opportunity to experiment in the gasoline supply business without making a heavy fixed commitment. Accordingly, the management arranged to market not only the entire fuel oil output but also the entire gasoline output of the Canton refinery. Allied encountered no difficulty in marketing the gasoline output, and when the promoter worked into financial difficulties late in 1937, Allied assumed his lease obligation and subsequently operated the refinery for its own account.

Refinery operations were benefited materially by the discovery of crude oil in southern Illinois in 1938,[5] and in the spring of 1940 Allied purchased the physical assets of the refining company from the first mortgage bondholders. The crude oil charging capacity of the refinery was increased from 2,000 to 7,000 barrels per day and thermal cracking capacity to 3,500 barrels per day; in addition condensing equipment and a polymerization plant were added. The refinery expansion was financed chiefly from profits derived from low-price crude oil which became available during the early development of the new Illinois basin fields. The management doubted that an expansion program would have been attempted except for this unusual situation. During this period, however, refinery operations resulted in a satisfactory profit each year even when figured on the basis of normal crude oil prices, and no difficulty was encountered in selling the entire gasoline and fuel oil output. In fact, the company had to buy some gasoline in the open market to supply the demand. By 1943 the skimming capacity of the refinery had been expanded to 12,000 barrels per day, and the cracking capacity remained at 3,500 barrels per day.

In 1948 the refinery was processing approximately 10,000 barrels of crude oil per day and the cracking plant was not in operation. The management considered it economically advisable under the market conditions existing in 1948 to manufacture only straight-run gasoline. Therefore substantial quantities of natural gasoline and high octane blending stocks were purchased from other companies to complete the manufacture of competitive grades of gaso-

line. During 1947 fuel oil produced at the refinery supplied about 25% of the requirements of the company's marketing program. Allied owned and operated a pipe line direct from the refinery to two large steel mills located in the Canton area through which it delivered fuel oil direct from the refinery to the consumers. A substantial portion of the refinery gasoline output was sold in tank car lots to independent jobbers who resold under their own brand names. Lesser quantities of gasoline were sold direct to large commercial accounts such as public transportation companies, truck lines, and other oil companies. Allied did not own or operate any service stations.

Crude Oil Purchasing, Crude Gathering Lines, and Production: The discovery of new fields of crude oil in southern Illinois beginning in 1937 caused a sharp upturn in Allied's growth. A small gathering line which connected a number of independent leases in the Salem-Lake Centralia field was acquired. In addition, a crude oil terminal was erected at Toledo, Ohio. With the completion of these facilities, Allied was able to purchase crude oil at the well-head adequate to supply its requirements at the Canton refinery plus additional quantities which were resold to Canadian refiners through the Toledo terminal. The facilities of two common carrier pipe line systems were used to reach the Canton refinery and the Toledo terminal. The purchase and expansion of the refinery has already been noted as one outgrowth of the new Illinois fields. Thus a large measure of the company's expenditures on facilities expansion between 1939 and 1948 was induced by the flush Illinois production.

In 1943 Allied acquired a small gathering system in the East Texas field and extended its purchasing operations to the Mid-Continent and Texas areas. By 1948 the company was gathering oil in Illinois, Indiana, Oklahoma, Texas, and Louisiana. Allied did not engage in trunk pipe line transportation but owned and operated 170 miles of gathering lines.

The Allied management did not regard the production of crude oil as one of the company's principal activities. In connection with its activities relating to the purchase of crude petroleum from independent producers, how-

---

[5] The refining activity touched off by the discovery of the new Illinois fields is discussed in Chapter Twenty-One.

EXHIBIT XXII-3. ALLIED OIL COMPANY

Selected Financial and Operating Data: 1933-1948

Selected Balance Sheet and Income Statement Items

($1,000)

Year	Net Sales	Net Income After Taxes	Total Assets	Net Working Capital	Capital Stock and Surplus	Total Debt	Ratio of Current Assets to Current Liabilities	Ratio of Net Worth to Debt
1933	$ 1,845	$ 79	$ 764	$ 164	$ 490	$ 274	1.7	1.79
1934	2,042	115	1,107	98	541	566	1.2	0.96
1935	2,468	113	863	203	649	214	2.0	3.04
1936	3,054	149	1,258	276	717	541	1.5	1.33
1937	4,773	107	1,616	175	794	822	1.3	0.97
1938	4,041	187	1,596	320	961	656	1.6	1.51
1939	8,357	667	2,666	425	1,544	1,122	1.4	1.38
1940	13,875	596	4,188	598	2,010	2,177	1.3	0.92
1941	22,400	880	5,817	1,008	2,343	3,474	1.3	0.67
1942	25,235	881	7,471	2,153	3,093	4,378	1.7	0.71
1943	28,535	899	9,001	1,884	3,732	5,269	1.5	0.71
1944	33,302	1,210	9,281	2,719	4,546	4,735	1.8	0.96
1945	30,135	1,163	N.A.	N.A.	N.A.	N.A.	N.A.	N.A.
1946	27,649	945	N.A.	N.A.	N.A.	N.A.	N.A.	N.A.
1947	40,177	1,768	19,991	5,435	8,884	11,107	1.8	0.80
1948*	14,227	1,089	21,100	6,293	9,974	11,127	1.9	0.90

* Balance sheet items, March 31. Income statement items, 3 months.

SOURCE: J. Keith Butters, John Lintner, and William L. Cary, assisted by Powell Niland, *Effects of Taxation: Corporate Mergers* (Boston, Division of Research, Graduate School of Business Administration, Harvard University, 1951), pp. 39–40.

Crude Oil Production, Purchases, and Sales and Refinery Runs

(1,000 bbls.)

Year	Net Crude Oil Production	Gross Crude Oil Production	Crude Purchases at Well-head	Other Crude Purchases	Crude Oil Sales	Refinery Runs
1943	177	438	4,833	2,761	4,934	2,677
1944	233	518	6,629	2,861	6,835	2,811
1945	312	630	7,068	3,035	6,542	2,871
1946	430	872	6,170	701	5,028	2,788
1947	567	1,131	4,557	799	2,609	3,224
1948*	128	334	1,240	182	344	965

* 3 months.

SOURCE: Prospectus of Ashland Oil & Refining Company, July 30, 1948, p. 7.

ever, it participated in a substantial number of exploratory ventures through which it acquired fractional interests in various crude oil producing properties. Moreover, in 1947 Allied purchased interests in two small producing properties, one in Oklahoma and the other in Illinois.

The magnitude of the expansion described above is evident from the growth in the company's sales and assets as shown in Exhibit XXII-3. Sales increased from $4,041,000 in 1938 to an annual rate of approximately $50,000,000 in 1948. Total assets increased from $1,596,000 to $21,100,000 in the same period. The expansion posed serious financial problems for the company and its principal owners which ultimately culminated in the merger decision.

Effects of Expansion on the Financial Position of the Allied Oil Company:

Allied was continually in a tight financial position throughout its history largely because the rapid expansion of the firm was not accompanied by the bringing of new outside equity capital into the business.

The initial capitalization of the Allied Oil Company amounted to $30,000. Of this amount $10,000 was supplied by Messrs. Vandeveer and Newman and $20,000 by an associate who, within a few years, sold his interest to the two active partners. No additional equity capital was provided from the outside at any time; the company's growth was financed entirely by the reinvestment of earnings and by borrowing, which was a relatively unimportant factor prior to 1940. The company issued stock in lieu of cash dividends to conserve working capital. Except in 1936 and 1937, when the undistributed profits tax was in effect, dividend distributions were small.

Subsequent to 1940 the company incurred a heavy fixed indebtedness to permit its expansion. Prior to this date long-term debt exceeded $100,000 only in 1937. In 1940 the company's fixed indebtedness rose to $300,000, and by the end of 1942 the amount outstanding was $1,415,000. The increase resulted largely from the sale of $1,250,000 of 4% sinking fund debentures to an insurance company early in 1942. The loan was refinanced in 1947 by the sale to the same company of $4,000,000 of $3\frac{1}{2}$% sinking fund debentures. As evidence of the company's strained financial position, Exhibit XXII-3 shows that the ratio of current assets to current liabilities was consistently less than two to one after 1933 and that total current and long-term indebtedness exceeded the owners' book equity in the company during most of this period.

Despite the heavy capital expenditures which were made between 1939 and 1948, the management believed that substantially more money would be required in the near future if the firm were to remain fully competitive. The upward surge in octane numbers after the war placed the company in the potentially vulnerable position of relying upon the purchase of high octane blending stocks to meet competitive gasoline standards. The management estimated that installation of a catalytic process at the Canton refinery would cost between $2,500,000 and $5,000,000. Other large capital needs were forecast for the company's tanker fleet and crude oil production division. These company requirements were, however, not considered insurmountable and they were definitely secondary to the financial problems impinging upon the owners as causal factors for the merger.

Effects of Expansion on the Personal Financial Position of the Two Principal Owners:

It is ironic that the success enjoyed by the Allied Oil Company in expanding its facilities and profits placed both of its principal owners in a vulnerable financial status. Throughout the company's history, the two principal owners retained equal ownership interest in the concern and all important decisions were reached jointly. In 1948 Messrs. Vandeveer and Newman each owned approximately 47% of the company's common stock. Although the original investment in the company in 1925 was only $30,000, on March 31, 1948, the company's stock had a book value of approximately $10,000,000, and this figure was considered a very conservative estimate of the stock's true worth. The Allied stock was all closely held and did not have an established position in the securities markets.

The death of either of the principal owners would have posed serious financial problems for the heir of the deceased and possibly for the surviving owner. With an assumed valuation of $5,000,000 placed on the holdings of either owner, the federal estate taxes would have amounted to about $2,400,000 for Mr. Newman, who was unmarried, and a minimum of $1,000,000 for Mr. Vandeveer. Neither owner had been able to accumulate liquid assets sufficient to meet the inheritance taxes which would have been payable on his holdings of Allied stock. Since most of the liquid funds held by the owners would also have been subject to an inheritance tax rate of over 50% before they could be applied to the tax levied on the Allied stock, the owners did not have any reasonable expectation of accumulating adequate outside funds. As a matter of fact, the Allied stock itself constituted the principal personal wealth of each owner. Therefore, a forced sale of stock, possibly at a price far below that which the owners considered a fair price for their holdings, would have been necessary to raise the funds necessary to meet inheritance taxes.

It was also possible that the death of either owner would have raised a difficult financial problem for the survivor should he have desired to purchase most or all of the decedent's stock in order to protect his own investment in the company. The purchase of a large block of the deceased's stock by the surviving owner would have given the greatest assurance to the survivor that he would not have had to contend with a strong minority stockholder who might be objectionable in some way. Neither owner had personal resources adequate to make such a purchase. Either surviving owner would, however, have been able to purchase enough stock to retain a majority interest in the company. As Allied continued to expand and its stock to increase in value, the inheritance tax problem confronting the owners was expected to become even more severe.

The Merger with the Ashland Oil & Refining Company:

A tax-free merger with the Ashland Oil & Refining Company was arranged in 1948 largely as a means of putting the estates of the two principal Allied owners in order. Several alternatives to a merger had been previously considered and discarded as being either not feasible or unattractive to the principal owners. These alternatives included a public sale of stock, the sale of stock to employees, substantial stock gifts to reduce the size of estate taxes, and sale or gifts of stock to either a new or established charitable foundation. A public issue of Allied stock, including a portion of the holdings of the principal owners, was considered the best alternative to a merger. A public sale of stock was not undertaken primarily because the owners were at first reluctant to accept the thought of bringing outsiders into the company and later by the fact that better terms could be secured by the owners for their stock via the merger route. In contrast to the Allied situation, the stock of the Ashland Oil & Refining Company had a ready market since its securities were listed and actively traded. At the time of the merger Ashland was a somewhat larger concern than Allied and was also integrated to some extent into all principal phases of the oil industry.

The merger agreement, which was tentatively agreed upon by the two boards of directors on July 6, 1948, and later consummated with the approval of both groups of stockholders, provided that the entire capital stock of Allied be exchanged for 200,000 shares of a new issue of $1.20 Ashland cumulative convertible preferred stock and 357,500 shares of Ashland common stock. Messrs. Vandeveer and Newman each received 93,720 shares of Ashland preferred stock and 167,522 shares of Ashland common stock. The stock received by each owner had a market value of approximately $5,750,000 on July 6, 1948. Subsequently, as a part of the merger agreement, Messrs. Vandeveer and Newman

each sold 50,000 shares of their preferred stock in a public offering for gross proceeds of $1,-200,000. They each netted about $850,000 in cash from the sale of stock after deductions had been made for underwriting costs and the applicable capital gains tax. Thus, each Allied owner received $850,000 in cash and $4,550,000 in marketable Ashland shares for his prior stock interest in Allied. In the year following the merger, dividends of over $250,000 were paid on the Ashland stock received by each owner, excluding the $1.00 dividends on the 50,000 preferred shares which were sold under agreement. The cash income represented a substantial increase over the $75,000 to $100,000 yearly income the owners had received as salaries and dividends from Allied prior to the merger.

IV. Comparison of the Aetna, Wood River, and Allied Situations

The merging of the Aetna Oil Company and the Allied Oil Company into the Ashland Oil & Refining Company and the sale of the refinery owned by the Wood River Oil and Refining Company to the Sinclair Oil Corporation reduced the refining population by three and led directly to a greater concentration of refining capacity in the industry. Grouped together, the three exits accounted for a reduction of about 1.5% in the refining population and transferred less than 1% of the industry's refining capacity into the hands of remaining companies. It is through the duplication of withdrawals such as these, however, that changes in business population and concentration are brought about.

The withdrawals cited in this chapter illustrate two general ways by which companies have discontinued their participation in the refining segment of the industry. One medium is through the complete disappearance of a corporation or partnership engaged in the refining activity. The disappearance may be accomplished by voluntary or involuntary dissolution, by the merger of a refining company into another surviving corporation, or by sale of assets or stock to an entirely new organization. The Aetna and Allied cases illustrate the disappearance of corporate entities. A second general way in which companies disappear from the refining industry is through the elimination of refining activities by corporations or partnerships which nevertheless continue their business participation in other lines. The Wood River situation is an example of this second type of disappearance. In the case of either type of disappearance the refining facilities may or may not be continued in operation. The fact that the plants formerly owned by the Aetna, Wood River, and Allied companies were continued in operation illustrates an adage in the industry attesting to the relative longevity of plants in comparison with companies: "Refiners may come and go, but old refineries never die."

The three cases cited in this chapter shed considerable light on the complex group of circumstances which sometimes are responsible for the disappearance of small refining companies. For purposes of analysis, the diverse factors at work in these three situations may be divided into two broad categories: (a) the wide range of financial and nonfinancial problems confronting the owner-manager of a small industrial firm, and (b) the particular economic and financial pressures that make it difficult to sustain a small refining business on a fully competitive and profitable basis. At times the cumulative weight of these problems becomes so distressing that it results in a withdrawal decision which may be made either willingly or regretfully and under either profitable or unprofitable circumstances.

The Importance of Personal Factors:

Personal considerations which bore little direct relation to the competitive positions of the firms played an important part in causing all three companies to withdraw from the refining industry. As is characteristic of small businesses, the stock of each of these corporations was closely held. Moreover, in each case one of the principal stockholders was also the chief operating executive of the company, and the well-being of each of the companies was identified very closely with one or more owner-managers. The personal considerations which were important in the three situations were of both a financial and a nonfinancial character.

Personal Considerations, Financial: The desire of principal stockholders to exchange their valuable holdings in closely held organizations for either more marketable securities or for cash was very much in evidence in each of the three situations. The difficult financial problem posed for the two principal owners of Allied by the rapidly rising value of their stock holdings in that organization has already been treated in detail. Neither owner held liquid or readily convertible assets adequate to meet the inheritance taxes which would have been levied against his Allied holdings in the event of his death. Personal tax considerations were therefore prominent factors in motivating the decision to raise cash and secure a listed stock through the merger terms arranged with the Ashland Oil & Refining Company. Whether, with both its active owner-managers approaching retirement age, Allied would have discontinued its business participation at some future date even with a much more lenient inheritance tax structure is now impossible to foretell. In any event, the discontinuance was certainly greatly accelerated by tax problems.

In the Aetna case the desire which Mr. Davis had to diversify his personal holdings was definitely secondary to other considerations in prompting his merger decision. Again, however, his estate would have been in no position to meet inheritance taxes without liquidating a large share of his Aetna holdings. The possibility that a forced sale of stock might be made at distress prices disturbed Mr. Davis, just as it did Messrs. Vandeveer and Newman.

The desire which the officers of the Louisville bank had to liquidate the Aetna stock held in trust for their clients was also a very important factor in setting the stage for the Aetna-Ashland merger. With the probable objective of building balanced investment portfolios for its clients, the Louisville bank was anxious to sell its Aetna holdings for cash. The impending sale of such a large block of shares would have brought a strong minority interest into the organization which might or might not have cooperated fully with the present management. The desire of the bank to liquidate its trust holdings of Aetna stock was therefore one more important factor of concern to Mr. Davis at the time he was considering the disposition of his Aetna holdings. Should the trust holdings have been sold to another oil company without a subsequent merger involving the exchange of the remaining Aetna stock, the

Aetna Oil Company might have continued in existence as a separate concern, although for all practical purposes it would have been closely affiliated with a larger organization.

The desire to diversify personal holdings was also an important consideration underlying the sale of the Wood River refinery to the Sinclair Oil Corporation. The financial advisor to Mr. Ingram held 15,000 shares or 3% of the Wood River stock. In addition to being the personal financial advisor to a stockholder owning over 40% of the company's stock, the minority stockholder was also a member of the Wood River board of directors. His influence on the company's activities was therefore greater than a 3% stock interest might indicate. The financial advisor was 60 years of age in 1950, and his Wood River stock holdings, which were ultimately purchased by the company for approximately $405,000, constituted an important part of his personal estate. In order to put his estate in order, he was most anxious to convert his Wood River holdings into liquid assets. The sale of the refinery, the company's most valuable asset, placed the company in a liquid position, thereby enabling it to retire the shares of the owners wishing to withdraw from the business. The financial advisor, foreseeing this possibility, strongly recommended the sale of the refinery. Moreover, neither Mr. Koch nor Mr. Ingram had sufficient outside funds to meet the inheritance taxes that would have fallen due on their Wood River holdings in the event of their demise, and they were anxious to guard against the possibility of a forced sale of stock at some future date. Therefore the inheritance tax problem was common to all three situations.

The influence of personal financial considerations similar to those witnessed in these three cases is felt frequently throughout industry and sometimes with the same end results on the business population. In putting estates in order, a certain amount of liquidity is necessary to meet tax levies and a diversification of holdings is often deemed preferable to having all one's "eggs in one basket." Mergers or the sale of company assets are means by which the owners of closely held organizations can secure either readily marketable securities or cash. Other means of meeting personal financial objectives, which might permit a small firm to continue in business, are sometimes impractical or less desirable alternatives.

Personal Considerations, Nonfinancial: Quite apart from personal financial problems, the ambitions, business interests, and desires of principal stockholders were important factors in causing the Aetna and Wood River disappearances. The significance of personal considerations of a nonfinancial character was most clearly marked in the Aetna situation. Mr. Davis was most anxious to ease the strain of his business life. His health had suffered serious setbacks under the burden of building a successful enterprise, and it was considered a physical necessity that he be relieved of such tensions in the future. Moreover, Mr. Davis was anxious to avoid a strenuous business life which would interfere with his plans to achieve a happy domestic life, a goal which he had not realized in the past. Moreover, as a result of boyhood experience, Mr. Davis was anxious to engage in some type of agricultural endeavor.

A shift in the business interests of an important stockholder was a significant causal factor for the sale of the Wood River refinery. As noted earlier, Mr. Ingram, one of the two principal Wood River stockholders, had developed a river barging business subsequent to the organization of the Wood River Oil and Refining Company. Mr. Ingram was completely fascinated by the barging business, and he wished to concentrate his management attention and resources on the petroleum transportation activity as well as on his diversified interests in other industries.

It is important to note that the small, closely held company is more vulnerable to personal problems such as those outlined above than is the large corporation. Since the owners and managers of small companies are frequently the same individuals, a problem encountered as a stockholder is readily transmitted into management action and vice versa. Moreover, nonbusiness problems affect both management and stockholder decisions simultaneously, and it is a relatively simple matter for any of a wide range of personal problems to cause the discontinuance of the firm. The diversity and demanding nature of the personal problems confronting the owner-managers of the Aetna, Wood River, and Allied companies are not by any means all-inclusive, but they do portray the significance of personal considerations. In the larger corporations, the individual stockholder or management official is frequently confronted with similar or identical problems. In a large corporation, however, the individual stockholder can usually liquidate his stock interest without affecting the longevity of the firm; the individual management official is seldom as essential to continued company operations as he often is in a small firm.

It should not be inferred from the experience of the Aetna, Wood River, and Allied companies or from the foregoing discussion that all small refining firms are closely held and owner-managed. The predominant type of corporate structure for small refiners is, however, that in which a company is owned by a relatively few people and in which one of the principal owners also serves as chief operating executive. A great many small refining companies are thus more directly vulnerable to personal problems of a financial or nonfinancial nature than are large corporations.

Problems Confronting the Companies:

In addition to the personal problems involved in the Aetna, Wood River, and Allied situations, there were difficulties encountered by the corporations themselves which were instrumental in causing the disappearances. These company difficulties arose from certain evolutionary developments in the refining industry which caused financial problems to develop in the small companies and from the lack of substantial vertical integration which, among other things, contributed to the poor profit showings of Aetna and Wood River in 1949.

Evolutionary Developments Causing Financial Problems: The intense octane competition in the postwar period placed each of the companies in a position where the managements believed it would be necessary to make extremely large expenditures at their refineries. The development of catalytic cracking processes which offered increased yields of high octane gasoline and greater product flexibility has already been discussed in Chapters Nineteen and Twenty. The company situations reported in this chapter illustrate the effect which this technological advance had on three small

companies. While the response to the evolution of catalytic cracking processes was not the same by the three companies, the net result in each case was a financial burden which the owners were unwilling to assume. The Wood River management actually spent approximately $4,000,000 in the postwar period to install various catalytic processes. The magnitude of these expenditures severely limited the extent to which the company could move in meeting other facilities requirements which the management likewise considered necessary. Moreover, these refinery equipment costs contributed in large part to the top-heavy, long-term debt structure of over $6,000,000 which the management was reluctant to carry into the future. The advance in refining technology was therefore an important cause for the sale of the Wood River refinery.

Unlike Wood River, both Aetna and Allied relied upon short-term purchases of high octane blending stocks to achieve competitive gasoline standards. Neither management was content, however, to plan its future operations without providing for the manufacture of its own supply through the installation of catalytic cracking facilities. Both managements feared that shortages of high octane blending stocks might develop in which their companies would be unable to procure outside supplies. The advent of catalytic cracking was one of the principal factors contributing to the disappearance of the Aetna Oil Company. The management refused to incur a financial burden estimated to range between $4,000,000 and $8,000,000 for new plant facilities, although it felt such an expenditure was absolutely mandatory if the company were to continue in business on a competitive basis. While the advent of catalytic cracking was probably of lesser importance in causing the Allied withdrawal than in the other two situations, the capital requirements which had been forecast for the Allied refinery constituted the most important nonpersonal reason for the merger.

The widespread adoption of employee pension plans was another evolutionary development in general business practice which contributed to the merger of the Aetna Oil Company. Although the management sympathized with the need for an equitable pension plan, the cash required to fund past service benefits would have amounted to between $400,000 and $600,000. Thus, Aetna was faced with the need for a total capital outlay ranging between $4,-400,000 and $8,600,000 for refinery improvements and an employee pension plan. The total requirement was considered an inadvisable burden for a company which, on December 31, 1948, already had a funded debt in excess of $1,000,000 and a total capital and surplus of only $4,244,000. A major shift would have been necessary in Aetna's capital base if the company had attempted to modernize its refinery and develop a pension plan.

The three companies found they were in a difficult financial position when the evolutionary developments, catalytic cracking and partially funded pension plans, called for such large capital outlays. It must, of course, be recognized that large companies faced these same pressures. The large companies were, however, better able to meet the financial problems. The yearly capital budget of a large company regularly amounts to millions of dollars. Thus, any one extraordinary outlay such as the cost of a catalytic cracking unit can be incurred at the expense of other items on the capital budget or with relatively minor adjustments, proportionately, in the firm's total borrowed and invested capital. On the other hand, the expenditures which the three small refining companies were called upon to make were entirely out of line with their capital structures, and none of them was in a good position to raise new equity capital.

Lack of Integration: The failure or inability to undertake adequate vertical integration was a further contributing factor to the disappearance of the three firms. The Wood River situation provides an excellent example of the serious difficulties which can and do arise if a company fails to develop a sound, aggressive sales program for gasoline. In the tight postwar gasoline market, Wood River acted largely as a supplemental supplier to other companies, selling a large portion of its total gasoline output to two large companies and through the distributors and outlets of other companies. Little concentrated effort was made by the Wood River management to cultivate its own outlets or to establish a definite sales tie-in with independent jobbers. Thus, Wood River was unprepared to meet the new set of competitive conditions which developed in the gasoline market in the latter part of 1948 and 1949. The two largest customers stopped purchasing from Wood River, and the distributors of other companies were called upon to curtail their outside purchases of gasoline. Wood River suffered appreciable losses in gallonage and profits when these changes came about.

The failure to develop a sound marketing program for gasoline was also an important factor in the failure of the Wood River products pipe line project. Controlled gasoline gallonage was not built up to a level which would permit pipe line throughput to be sustained at satisfactory levels. Consequently, the pipe line venture did not prove to be a successful one.

The Aetna Oil Company also suffered at times from a lack of integration. In 1948, for example, Aetna's earnings were depressed by a refinery fire which removed the source of assured supply for its marketing operation. In that year the demand for refined products was strong and the opportunities for profits great. While the refinery was being renovated following the fire, however, Aetna's marketing department was deprived of the advantages of backward integration into refining, and the company was compelled to make outside purchases of gasoline to meet its sales commitments to gasoline dealers, contractor stations, and distributors. The gasoline which Aetna was called upon to supply had to be obtained at high prices in the spot markets. The adverse effect upon profits was very depressing to the management, and it played a minor role in causing the merger decision.

Because of their lack of substantial integration, both Wood River and Aetna suffered particularly serious profit reverses during the period of depressed refining margins that prevailed throughout most of 1949 (see Chapter Six). The greatly reduced refining margin resulted from the abnormally low price of residual fuel oil and from lesser reductions in the prices of other products. Few refining companies were able to escape these market conditions completely unscathed. The profits of Wood River and Aetna were, however, much more seriously affected than were the profits of other more heavily integrated concerns. Seventeen major, integrated companies suffered a profit reduction of 28% in 1949 as compared with 1948.[6] In contrast, the net income of the Wood River Oil and Refining Company fell from $2,781,000 in 1948 to a net loss of $319,-000 in 1949. Since Wood River produced only a very small portion of its own crude oil requirements and sold almost exclusively at the tank car level, it was extremely vulnerable to the adverse fluctuations in the refiner's margin. Throughout this unprofitable period, a catalytic cracking unit was under construction at the Wood River plant. The slow rate of progress on this construction work was disconcerting to the management since the new equipment would have afforded much greater flexibility to cut back the yield of low-price heavy fuel oil. Unfortunately, the plant was not completed until 1950. The 1949 margin situation was partially responsible for the sale of the Wood River refinery; its effect was, however, principally psychological.

The profit of the Aetna Oil Company dropped from $662,000 in 1948 to $172,000 for the first 11 months of 1949. Aetna produced a somewhat higher percentage of its own crude oil requirements than Wood River, and it reached the tank wagon level of the industry in selling a portion of its gasoline and heating oil output. It was therefore less dependent upon the refiner's margin as a source of profits than was Wood River. Because of their lack of integration, neither company fared as well as did other more heavily integrated concerns.

Another example of the difficulties encountered as a result of a lack of integration may be found in the crude oil supply problems encountered by the Wood River Oil and Refining Company. The firm experienced crude oil purchasing problems at several points in its short life, and the management feared that these problems might recur in the future during periods of shortage. Wood River experienced crude oil buying problems with some of the crude oil producers located on its gathering system because the producers preferred to sell to larger companies who they believed were able to offer greater assurance of a continuing market. The company was also short of

crude oil because refinery capacity was expanded far beyond the volume of crude oil available on the company's crude oil gathering system in the postwar period. It should be noted, however, that in 1950 the company's pipe line system was hooked into producing wells capable of supplying approximately two-thirds of the company's refinery capacity. The company was, in fact, in a far better crude position than the typical refining company and fully as well or better off than some of the major companies.[7] Because Wood River's refinery runs were shut back in 1950, the crude oil gathered actually exceeded refinery runs. In considering the crude oil supply problem which the refinery expansion created, it should be recognized that the economics of the refinery operation and the desire to balance out equipment facilities provided strong motivations to accomplish the refinery enlargement.

The managements of Aetna, Wood River, and Allied were aware of the disadvantages arising from their lack of integration, but their desires to undertake further integration steps were thwarted by the amounts of money involved. Each of the managements felt that a more strenuous effort should be made to secure company-owned crude oil production. Therefore, the very large expenditures needed to engage more heavily in producing activities were of considerable concern in each case. The Wood River management was likewise disturbed by the large expenditures which it forecast as necessary to carry forward a program of growth in marketing. As noted above, both Aetna and Allied felt the need for major refinery installations. Allied also felt the need for expenditures in the other phases of its integrated operation, such as water transportation.

It should be noted that the problem of raising capital adequate to meet competitive pressures and to finance a program of corporate growth is common to small business in general. In petroleum refining, this general problem is, however, greatly accentuated by the nature of the refinery investment and the costs of building an integrated company. In the Aetna, Wood River, and Allied situations, the cost of keeping the refinery establishments competitive, the

---

[6] The 28% reduction in net income was calculated from financial data published by 17 of the leading integrated companies.

[7] The typical refinery had crude oil runs from wells equal to 52.1% of its refinery runs in 1950 (see Chapter Two).

lack of vertical integration, and the managements' feeling that the companies were helpless to move toward further integration because of financial limitations were all factors in the withdrawal decisions.

Profitable Financial Experience:

It is important to note that Aetna, Wood River, and Allied were all successful and profitable companies, and that each of these refining activities was ultimately terminated on very reasonable terms. In none of the situations could the withdrawal terms be interpreted as exacting any particular financial hardship on the owners.

During the period from 1935 to 1949 the Aetna Oil Company was a successful firm with an enviable earnings record. The financial burden necessary to install catalytic cracking facilities and to initiate a pension plan, the personal desires of Mr. Davis to ease the strain of his business life, and the desire of the Louisville bank to sell its trust holdings in Allied stock for cash were the most important factors ending the life of the enterprise. The $4,546,000 received in cash and Ashland stock in return for Aetna stock represented a very attractive return for the common stock investment of $50,000 made by the owners in 1936.

As a business venture the Wood River refinery was extremely successful and highly profitable under the particular set of economic circumstances which prevailed during World War II and particularly in the immediate postwar period. During these years the overriding industry need was for refining capacity which could satisfy the requirements of a wartime economy and the greatly increased consumer demand which was experienced after the war. With the advent of the new competitive forces in the postwar period, and the cumulative effect of ever-increasing capital requirements, the refining activity was liquidated on an entirely satisfactory basis which would have permitted the company to have closed its books with a net profit of approximately $15,000,000 over the original investment in the company.

The Allied Oil Company likewise provided a comfortable standard of living for its two principal owners, was consistently profitable, and permitted its owners to accumulate substantial estates. It was, in fact, the success of the organization which led to the personal estate problems confronting the owners. The Allied Oil Company was organized with a capitalization of $30,000 in 1925. In 1948 each principal Allied owner received $850,000 in free cash and $4,550,000 in marketable Ashland securities for his Allied stock holdings.

V. SUMMARY

1. The disappearence of the Aetna, Wood River, and Allied refining companies from the industry resulted from the interaction of a highly complex and diversified set of factors. These factors were of two broad types; one group pertained to the personal situations of the owner-managers and the other to the competitive positions of the companies. The personal considerations, which are by no means peculiar to refiners, included a wide range of problems of both a financial and nonfinancial character. In the three situations, personal considerations and company pressures were so intermingled and reinforcing that it is difficult to ascertain wherein the main stimulus to withdrawal originated.

2. In the Aetna case, company and personal problems were probably of about equal importance in prompting the merger with the Ashland Oil & Refining Company. The most serious company problem was the anticipation of expenditures far greater than any previous capital outlays. The financial problem resulted from the need or desire to meet two recent developments in the industry, the commercialization of catalytic cracking facilities and the institution of employee pension plans. As an example of the interdependency of management and stockholders' decisions, the risks which the company would have assumed in making these large expenditures could not easily be separated from the owners' concern over the value of their stockholdings. The major personal and stockholder problems were the desire of Mr. Davis to ease the strain of his business life and the desire of a Louisville bank to sell a large block of Aetna stock for cash. Personal estate problems, the psychological

impact of a refinery fire in 1948 and the poor profit showing in 1949, and the concern over the large capital requirements necessary to build up crude oil reserves were further contributors to the withdrawal.

3. In the Wood River situation, the decision to sell the refinery to the Sinclair Oil Corporation probably originated somewhat more in company problems than in personal considerations. The burdensome debt structure assumed at the time catalytic cracking and pipe line facilities were constructed, the serious loss of gasoline market outlets in the latter part of 1948, the unprofitable operations in 1949, and the thought that still more money was needed for the expansion of marketing and crude oil producing activities were probably the dominant factors motivating the sale. Inheritance tax considerations and a shift in business interests were, however, also important factors leading to the sales decision.

4. The merger of Allied into the Ashland Oil & Refining Company was a situation in which the personal problems of the principal owners overshadowed those confronting the corporation itself. In this case, the preparation of estates to meet inheritance taxes was a very important factor. The capital requirements forecasted for the company's refinery, transportation, and producing activities played a secondary role in the merger decision.

5. The economic circumstances to which the three small companies were exposed were no different from those confronting the large, integrated companies. The three small firms were, however, more vulnerable to these pressures because they were closely held and owner-managed, comparatively small, and lacking in substantial vertical integration. The fact that the three firms were closely held and owner-managed subjected the companies to the adverse effects of personal problems that the large, widely held companies administered by professional managements were able to avoid. The fact that the three companies were small made them less well-equipped than large companies to carry forward a program of growth in the various aspects of their operations. The lack of integration contributed to the precipitous decline in earnings shown by Wood River and Aetna in 1949 and led to serious postwar marketing problems for Wood River. Moreover, the desire of each of the three managements to further the extent of its company's vertical integration posed financial problems which the small firms were hard pressed to solve.

6. The three withdrawals may be attributed, at least in part, to the fact that the owners were able to close out their interests on a favorable financial basis. Each disappearance was arranged on terms which yielded cash or stock worth many times the original investments in the companies.

CHAPTER TWENTY-THREE

Interstices for the Small Refiner

THE preceding chapters in Part Four have discussed some of the general and specific forces which have contributed to abrupt changes in the refining population and which have brought about a general decline in the proportionate participation of small firms in refining activities. Notwithstanding these circumstances, however, there have been approximately 150 or more small refining companies present in the industry for a long period of time. During the course of our field research, it became evident that the capacity of these small firms to operate successfully rested, in no small part, upon their ingenuity in picking spots or niches at the refining level of the industry which were uniquely suited to the size and character of their operations. In this chapter, we shall refer to these spots or niches as "interstices" because they often represent nooks and crannies in the affairs of the oil industry which are not filled by the large, integrated companies. The tendency for small refiners to seek out one or more specialized orbits and the significance of such orbits to their well-being was aptly phrased by an executive of one small refining company as follows, "The small refiner has to have a gimmick if he is going to succeed."

Generally speaking, the interstices open to the small and substantially nonintegrated refiner represent activities in which the small firm either enjoys an advantage or is at no appreciable over-all disadvantage in competing with the large, integrated companies. The interstices arise in a multitude of ways, and it would be impossible to describe and illustrate all of the different types in any one volume. In this chapter therefore we shall merely select a few of the more important interstices for discussion as a means of illustrating the way in which many small refiners have been able to maintain successful operations despite the existence of economic conditions which have been generally favorable to the growth and development of large, integrated concerns.

I. GEOGRAPHIC SPECIALIZATION

Geographic specialization has been one of the most important and profitable of all the niches exploited by small refiners. The geographic specialist builds his plant away from established refining centers and thereby gains some definite transportation advantages over his large and small competitors in supplying refined products to the area immediately surrounding his plant. A study of the location and capacity of all domestic refineries reveals that many small plants are somewhat separated from other refineries and particularly from the large plants erected to supply metropolitan areas. These many isolated small plants are, in effect, filling geographic interstices in the industry. Most of the small, widely-dispersed plants are owned by small companies. Others are owned by large, integrated companies seeking the same general competitive advantages as the smaller firms.

The low transportation cost which the geographic specialist enjoys by virtue of his plant location frequently permits him to develop lower laid-down costs to nearby customers than can be secured by his competitors. It is important to recognize, however, that low transportation costs alone are not always sufficient to give a refiner a competitive advantage in the area surrounding his plant. A distant competitor may compensate for his transportation disadvantage with highly efficient refining or marketing facilities, or he may rely upon product exchanges or local purchases to enter an area on a competitive basis. To obtain an over-all advantage the geographic specialist must have a combination of refining, transportation, and marketing costs lower than those of competitors.

In many of the large marketing areas, competing companies have worked out a variety of ways of obtaining and delivering products to customers at costs which permit them to compete on equal terms with one another. There are nevertheless many small areas throughout the country where the market is not of sufficient size to warrant the attention or capital expenditures which would be needed for large companies to enter the areas at very low cost. In such areas, the small refiner may develop a combination of refining, transportation, and marketing costs that gives him an advantage over other firms. In general, there is an area circumscribed around the plant of the geographic specialist which he can serve at lower laid-down costs than remote refiners. The delineation of this area shifts continuously in accordance with every change brought about in the relative cost positions of the competing refiners. For example, the construction of products pipe lines into the marketing territory may reduce the area of geographical preference enjoyed by a local refiner. An improvement in refinery efficiency on the part of a local refiner may enlarge the area of his competitive advantage.

Because of the important part which location plays in determining a plant's relative cost position, the discussion at this point suggests a broader concept of refinery efficiency than was discussed in Chapters Nineteen and Twenty. Any plant can have a built-in advantage by virtue of its location which may offset, to some extent, the disadvantages suffered through relatively high processing costs or the losses in sales realization which come about from unfavorable product yields. Some small refiners have, in fact, been depending to a substantial degree upon the location of their plants to offset the advantages gained by other companies through the size and type of equipment used at their refineries.

In the following paragraphs, we shall draw upon the experience of two small companies as a means of illustrating the way in which small refiners sometimes may make use of an isolated geographic location in order to develop profitable operations in competition with larger concerns.

The Shallow Water Refining Company:

The Shallow Water Refining Company provides an excellent example of a geographic specialist. In January 1952 the company owned and operated the only refinery in western Kansas, a very small plant with a crude oil charging capacity of approximately 3,000 barrels per day. The firm was closely held and financial statements were not available for general distribution. The authors were told, however, that with the exception of the first few years following the company's incorporation in 1937, the firm enjoyed profitable operations throughout its history. The company's products included gasoline, kerosene, asphalt, roads oil, residual fuel oil, and a wide range of Diesel fuels. In 1950 the company owned net crude oil production amounting to approximately 30% of its average refinery runs of 2,100 barrels per day; the company did not own or lease any marketing facilities. Selected operating data covering the period from 1941 to 1950 are shown in Exhibit XXIII-1.

The nature of Shallow Water's geographic isolation from the refining and pipe line facilities of other companies is evident from Exhibit XXIII-2. The refinery at Shallow Water, Kansas, was operated on the crude oil available from nearby pools, and the distribution of refined products was confined to a relatively small marketing territory encircling the refinery. Geographically, the company's operations were thus self-contained within a relatively small marketing area. The refinery location and the limited geographical scope of Shallow Water's operations were the keys to a very successful small business opportunity.

Organization as a Specialist: The Shallow Water Refining Company was organized in 1937. In the preceding year The Atlantic Refining Company had brought in an exploratory well in western Kansas in what was later named the Shallow Water pool. The new pool was rather far removed from developed oil fields, pipe line transportation facilities, and refinery centers. Transportation rates via rail were prohibitive to any existing refinery area or to any main pipe line terminal. Furthermore, poten-

EXHIBIT XXIII-1. SHALLOW WATER REFINING COMPANY

Selected Operating Data: 1941–1950 (1,000 Bbls.)

Year	Net Crude Oil Production	Refinery Runs	Yield of Refined Products				
			Gasoline	Tractor Fuel, Distillates, and Kerosene	Diesel Oil	Fuel Oil and Surplus Cracking Stock	Asphalt
1941	—	575	141	36	102	123	152
1942	—	671	150	44	131	193	124
1943	—	603	144	31	111	139	147
1944	—	376	127	29	72	42	78
1945	—	638	187	71	115	114	116
1946	82*	638	159	46	134	99	160
1947	253	559	162	69	122	59	112
1948	346	651	201	76	143	65	131
1949	277	739	201	51	182	73	202
1950	234	770	247	39	181	51	206

* 1946 figure is for 5 months only.

SOURCE: Shallow Water Refining Company.

tial production in the new field was not sufficient to warrant the construction of a crude oil trunk line to an outlet point. Consequently, The Atlantic Refining Company had no immediate use for its new crude oil reserves.

One of the founders of the Shallow Water Refining Company was impressed with the possibilities of refining the crude oil in the area and serving marketing points near the proposed refinery site at a transportation advantage over existing companies. The nearest competitive refineries were then located in Wichita, Kansas. From its inception therefore the Shallow Water Refining Company was destined to fill two distinct economic gaps in the oil industry: (a) it was to provide the only feasible outlet for a relatively small amount of crude oil, and (b) it was to serve as an economical product supply point for the rural area of western Kansas.

Very little equity capital was supplied by the organizers of the company. The original and still existing capital stock capitalization of $50,000 was borrowed, largely from banks, by the organizers of the firm. The corporation itself incurred bank indebtedness for the remainder of its capital requirements. The inaugural policy of not securing equity financing for the company was adhered to throughout the corporate history. All expansion was financed through retained earnings or by outside borrowing. Originally there were several stockholders, but in April 1951 the corporation was owned solely by members and relatives of a single family.

The Shallow Water refinery was constructed in 1937, and for several years immediately thereafter the company's refining operations were very unprofitable. The entire decade of the 1930's was a difficult period for many refining companies, particularly the year 1938 which witnessed a sharp business recession. The Shallow Water Refining Company also suffered because the crude oil available in the area was not developed rapidly enough to permit full utilization of the refinery. After the first few years, however, operations were profitable, even during the generally depressed refining period in 1949.

The Company's Transportation Advantage: An executive of the Shallow Water Refining Company emphasized the company's prime competitive advantage in these words, "We literally exist on a freight differential over competing refineries." The Shallow Water management estimated that the company's delivered cost of crude oil was approximately the same as that of other refiners in the Kansas area. A single scale of prices for crude oil at the wellhead was generally adhered to throughout the state. A crude oil of the same general grade and quality was therefore available to various refiners in different fields at the same posted prices. In moving crude oil to its refinery, Shallow Water made use of company owned trucks,

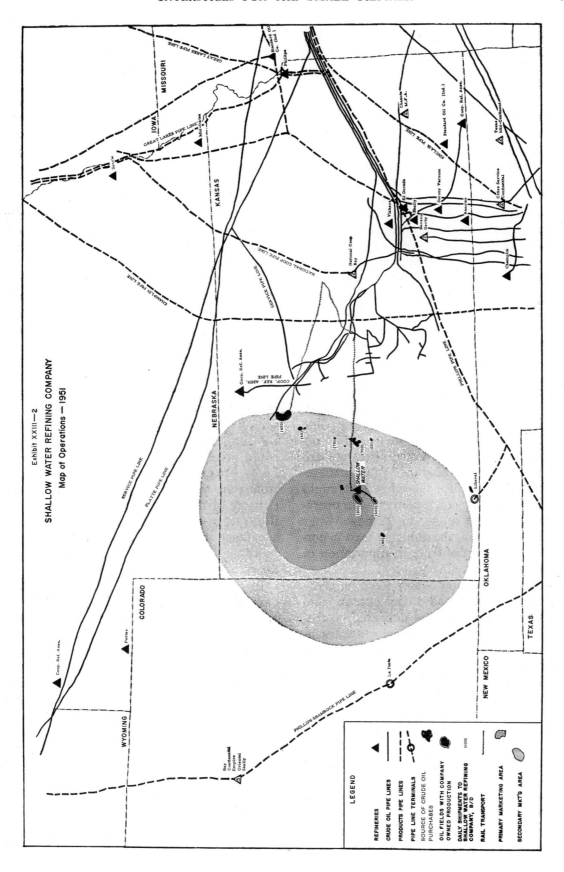

Exhibit XXIII—2

SHALLOW WATER REFINING COMPANY

Map of Operations — 1951

LEGEND

REFINERIES

CRUDE OIL PIPE LINES

PRODUCTS PIPE LINES

PIPE LINE TERMINALS

SOURCE OF CRUDE OIL
PURCHASES

OIL FIELDS WITH COMPANY
OWNED PRODUCTION

DAILY SHIPMENTS TO
SHALLOW WATER REFINING
COMPANY, B/D

RAIL TRANSPORT

PRIMARY MARKETING AREA

SECONDARY MKT'g AREA

the pipe line facilities of an affiliated company,[1] and railroad tank car transportation as shown in Exhibit XXIII-2. In April 1951 two very short trunk lines from the Shallow Water and Nunn pools delivered 700 barrels of crude oil per day to the refinery. The 700 barrels of crude oil comprised the company's gross crude oil production plus the output of four other wells not belonging to the company. Four hundred and fifty barrels of crude oil per day were supplied to the refinery by tank car from the Morrel pool. The Morrel pool was the most distant source of crude oil utilized and was located roughly 120 miles northeast of the refinery. The remainder of the crude supply, 1,200 barrels per day, was brought in by company trucks from pools in an area circling the refinery.

The company charged producers from which it gathered oil a portion of the cost of the truck transportation to the refinery. Shallow Water began making these charges to producers in the period after World War II. At this time producers in certain other fields, were shipping some of their oil production to rail points by truck at costs ranging up to 1 cent per barrel-mile. These producers did not have pipe line connections, and occasionally there was no demand for their oil at the posted prices prevailing in the fields. The Shallow Water management felt that if producers in other fields could absorb high trucking costs and remain in operation, the producers selling to Shallow Water were also capable of absorbing at least a portion of the high cost of truck transportation to the Shallow Water refinery.

Although the Shallow Water Refining Company had no particular advantage over its competitors with respect to the delivered cost of its crude oil, the company did enjoy a substantial advantage over competitors on the transportation of refined products. As may be seen in Exhibit XXIII-2, the Shallow Water plant was situated right in the midst of the company's comparatively small marketing area. The nearest competitive refinery center at Wichita, Kansas, was approximately 200 miles distant. Since no products pipe lines entered Shallow Water's marketing territory, competitors relied very heavily upon comparatively expensive railroad tank car movements as a means of reaching

the area. Unlike its competitors, Shallow Water was able to use tank trucks to deliver refined products directly from the refinery to outlets and consumers. Approximately 80% of the company's gasoline, Diesel fuel, kerosene, and distillate output was shipped by outside truck haulers and the remainder by company owned trucks. The company owned trucks also delivered substantially all of the company's asphalt production and were used to supply the refinery with about 1,700 barrels of crude oil per day. Because of its location and ability to use truck transports, Shallow Water could deliver refined products to most points in its marketing territory for 1.5 to 2 cents less per gallon than could competitors.

In quoting f.o.b. refinery prices for its products, however, the Shallow Water management found that it was not in a position to realize the full transportation advantage of 1.5 to 2 cents per gallon on each of its refined products. The extent to which the company could capitalize on its transportation advantage on gasoline, for example, depended upon a whole range of other competitive factors, such as the strength of brand name preferences and products quality. Similarly, the extent to which the company could price any product above the prevailing f.o.b. prices of competitive refiners shifted from time to time in accordance with general changes in market conditions. As a means of illustrating the nature of the transportation advantage and the various factors bearing upon it, we shall describe the pricing practices which the company used in April 1951.

In quoting gasoline prices, Shallow Water took advantage of roughly 60% to 70% of the 1.5 to 2 cent freight differential which it enjoyed over Wichita refiners. The refinery prices of gasoline in Wichita were usually based on the low of the Oklahoma Group 3 quotations published in the Chicago Journal of Commerce. Thus Shallow Water quoted prices f.o.b. its refinery about 1.25 cents above the prevailing low of the Oklahoma Group 3 prices. The management believed that it would not be possible for Shallow Water to retain a higher percentage of the freight advantage it enjoyed because of brand preferences which had been established for the gasolines distributed by many of the large companies.

All sales of gasoline by Shallow Water were

---

[1] The pipe line company was owned by the stockholders of the Shallow Water Refining Company.

therefore made at a price 1.25 cents above the Oklahoma Group 3 price except sales to extremely large-volume accounts such as those handling two million gallons per year and sales to customers on the eastern limits of Shallow Water's marketing territory where the competition from Wichita refiners was most severe. Sales were made to these groups of customers at a price of 0.25 cent below Shallow Water's posted prices. Shallow Water had a great many of these eastern area accounts early in 1951, but the company was replacing them as quickly as possible with other more profitable outlets located closer to the refinery.

Shallow Water sold a wide range of Diesel fuels, primarily to municipal power plants, at a price 1.5 cents above the Group 3 prices quoted in the Chicago *Journal of Commerce*. Since the company was under no brand name disadvantage in the sale of these products, it was able to realize a somewhat higher percentage of its average freight advantage on Diesel fuel sales than it could on gasoline sales.

On asphalt sales Shallow Water was able to realize the full transportation advantage which it enjoyed over its competitors, plus 0.5 cent per gallon. In submitting asphalt bids, it was the general practice of the Shallow Water management to estimate the bid prices of competitors as closely as possible on a f.o.b. refinery basis. Alternative transportation rates for the different refiners were then computed to the transportation center nearest to the intended point of use. These transportation costs were added to the estimated f.o.b. refinery prices of the competing asphalt marketers. To the lowest estimated delivered price of any competitor, Shallow Water added 0.5 cent per gallon. The justification for the incremental 0.5 cent per gallon margin will be discussed at a later point in the chapter.

On sales of heavy residual fuel oil, which represented only 7% of the company's product yield in 1950, the company had no apparent transportation advantage. Sales were made almost exclusively to railroads and the negotiations were often carried on in the following manner: the purchasing agents called the company and requested delivery of a stated number of barrels of fuel oil to a particular place at a quoted purchasing price. Since there were no other important markets for residual fuel

in the immediate vicinity, Shallow Water had little alternative other than to accept the terms prescribed by the railroads.

The significance to the company of its products transportation advantage can be more fully appreciated when the amount of the advantage is compared with selected operating costs of the company for the year 1950. The 1.5 to 2 cents per gallon freight advantage amounted to 58 to 77 cents per barrel of refinery runs. Since the company was unable to take full advantage of the average differential on all products, it actually realized an advantage of approximately 50 cents per barrel of refinery runs on the basis of the pricing practices prevailing in April, 1951. In comparison, the company's total refinery expenses, excluding crude oil, averaged 54.7 cents per barrel of refinery runs for the year 1950. Total administrative and selling expenses for the same period amounted to 26 cents per barrel. It is readily apparent from these figures that the profits directly attributable to the company's preferred geographic location were exceedingly attractive. In fact, the incremental margin secured from the locational advantage was more than adequate to offset any possible refinery processing cost disadvantage which this small plant may have had in relation to the large volume plants of its competitors. The transportation advantage, alone, assured the Shallow Water management that the company's total laid-down costs to selected marketing points in its territory could not be bettered by its most efficient competitors.[2]

Shallow Water's transportation advantage made the company less vulnerable profit-wise to the fluctuations in refinery margins which characterized the industry than might otherwise have been the case. The depressed margin period in 1949 was, for example, a generally unprofitable period for refining companies, especially those selling largely or exclusively in tank car markets. Although Shallow Water sold exclusively in the tank car markets, the transportation advantage permitted the company to maintain profitable operations on its refinery activity during this period. The company did not escape the sharp contraction in refiner's margin during 1949; it merely had

---

[2] These cost comparisons were based on the assumption that the costs of crude oil for Shallow Water and its competitors were equal to the posted prices in the fields.

"more margin to work on" than many companies selling on an f.o.b. refinery basis and Shallow Water was thus less vulnerable than many other refiners to a reduction in prices.

Geographic Location as a Means of Assuring a Crude Oil Supply: Shallow Water's geographic isolation also played an important role in assuring the company an adequate supply of crude oil. After 1937 the company's refinery provided the sole market outlet for the production of several small oil pools in western Kansas. Shortly after the discovery of the Shallow Water pool, which had attracted the Shallow Water Refining Company into the region, The Atlantic Refining Company brought in the Nunn pool, located 12 miles from the refinery. In later years, pools were discovered to the northeast of the refinery at distances ranging from 50 to 150 miles.

At one time the Shallow Water management considered its complete dependency upon the production of several small, widely scattered oil pools as more of a liability than an asset. In fact, assuring an adequate crude oil supply posed serious problems for the management throughout the entire period from 1937 to the end of World War II. During this period, the development of crude oil producing properties in the territory surrounding the refinery was not rapid enough to fulfill the company's requirements for crude oil. Oil wells in the territory were not prolific producers, and all the wells were "on the pump." Even in the period immediately following a discovery, wells in this area were not free-flowing. Moreover, a certain amount of drilling was necessary at all times to offset the natural rate of decline of producing wells. Until after World War II Shallow Water was entirely dependent upon other companies to maintain the production of the area. Since other companies might, at any time, have preferred to spend their money in more fruitful areas, there was always a hazard that the company might lose its crude oil supplies.

In the postwar years, exploratory and development work in the area made larger supplies of crude oil available to the company, and by 1951 the management considered the company's reliance upon small widely dispersed oil pools as a major source of strength. The re-

finery was so located geographically that it was the only economical outlet for the crude oil produced in the immediate area. An investment in crude oil pipe line facilities, which might move the oil to more distant markets on an economical basis, was not justified by the relatively small amounts of crude oil available from the scattered pools. In fact, the economics of the situation were such that Shallow Water could not conceivably replace costly truck transportation from the various pools with pipe lines on a profitable basis. In essence, therefore, the Shallow Water Refining Company solved the general problem of assuring an adequate crude oil supply, which is often of crucial significance to the small refiners, because its refinery was both strategically located and small. Its strategic location assured the company that whatever crude oil was available in the area would be diverted to the refinery. The small size of the refinery obviated the necessity of going far afield in search of supplementary supplies.

It was not until 1946 that the Shallow Water Refining Company participated in the crude oil producing activities of the region. At that time the company purchased producing properties yielding approximately 500 barrels of crude oil per day from The Atlantic Refining Company for $500,000. In subsequent years Shallow Water drilled a number of development wells, which added 150 barrels of crude oil per day to its crude oil supply. Participation in the drilling of development wells gave the company somewhat greater assurance that the oil production of the area would be maintained, since the company was no longer entirely dependent upon outside companies to offset the natural rate of decline in the producing field. In the year 1950 the company's net crude oil production amounted to 30% of refinery runs. The remainder of Shallow Water's crude oil requirements was purchased on division orders from other producers in the area.[3]

In the light of the foregoing discussion, it is apparent that the Shallow Water management

---

[3] A division order is in the nature of a supplemental contract to the oil lease. It sets forth the exact ownership of the working and royalty interests in a well. Thus, purchases "on division orders" are made from the original owners at the point of production. This type of supply contract is automatically renewable, although it can be cancelled by either party if the stipulated advance notice is given.

found a very effective interstice in the refining industry through its geographic specialization. The opportunity was uniquely suited to a small refining activity because of the limited amount of crude oil available in the area and because of the absence of large metropolitan markets for refined products.

Ashland Oil & Refining Company:

The Ashland Oil & Refining Company provides a second example of a company which was established and developed as a geographic specialist. Although the Ashland Oil & Refining Company experienced a phenomenal rate of corporate growth in the period during and after World War II which increased its refinery capacity to over 100,000 barrels per day, it was for many years a small refining company. Total refining capacity did not, for example, exceed 10,000 barrels per day until after 1940. From the very beginning of its corporate history, a transportation advantage over other refiners played an important part in the company's competitive success.

The Ashland Refining Company, predecessor company to the Ashland Oil & Refining Company, was organized as a geographic specialist. In 1924 Mr. Paul Blazer was commissioned to form a refining subsidiary for the Swiss Oil Corporation, an oil producing concern. Mr. Blazer immediately set out to find a refinery location which would give the new firm a transportation advantage over existing refining companies. Although the home offices of the Swiss Oil Company were in Lexington, Kentucky, this location was eliminated as a potential refinery site because several other refineries were already operating in the locality.

After investigating several possibilities, Mr. Blazer decided to buy a small plant owned by the Great Eastern Refining Company. The Great Eastern plant had a capacity of 500 barrels per day and was located near the town of Catlettsburg, Kentucky, on the bank of the Big Sandy River, four miles from the point where it joined the Ohio River. Mr. Blazer became interested in the Great Eastern refinery for several reasons. The plant was somewhat removed from any large refining center and an opportunity therefore existed for the delivery of refined products to the area immediately surrounding the plant at a transportation ad-

vantage over competitors. An economical supply of crude oil was available because the refinery was connected by pipe line to the oil fields of eastern Kentucky. Refined products could, moreover, be moved from the refinery inexpensively on the Ohio River, and a towboat and barge were available for making shipments. Finally, the Great Eastern refinery also had the additional advantage of being situated at the intersection of two railroads. In 1924 the Great Eastern Refining Company was experiencing financial difficulties, and its owners therefore decided to sell their refinery when an offer was made by Mr. Blazer.

By 1930 the Ashland Oil & Refining Company had acquired another plant and was running approximately 4,500 barrels of crude oil per day to two small refineries located four miles apart near Catlettsburg, Kentucky, and Kenova, West Virginia.[4] The gasoline output of the refineries was marketed under several different brand names principally within a radius of 150 miles surrounding the plants. A large portion of the products output was delivered by a fleet of trucks operating within a 50-mile radius of the refinery, an area where the company enjoyed a substantial transportation advantage over competitors. Products of the refineries were sold through owned or leased bulk plants and service stations and supplied to several hundred independent service stations under contract. In addition, several million gallons of refined products were sold annually to large oil companies that found it was more economical to purchase refined products from Ashland for local distribution in the area than it was to move refined products from distant refineries.

In the years following 1930 the Ashland Oil & Refining Company made increasing use of barge facilities for the movement of both crude oil and refined products. In 1940 the company shipped refined products from its Catlettsburg refinery to terminals on the Ohio River spaced between Louisville, Kentucky, and Pittsburgh, Pennsylvania. Refined products were moved to local markets from the river terminals and

---

4 The Ashland Oil & Refining Company was not actually incorporated until October 1, 1936, when the Swiss Oil Corporation and the Ashland Refining Company were consolidated. In the interests of simplicity, however, we shall refer to the company as the Ashland Oil & Refining Company throughout the remainder of the discussion.

from the refinery either by trucks or tank cars. In 1940 Mr. Paul Blazer, president of the Ashland Oil & Refining Company, reported to stockholders, "Much of the profit of your company is derived from its transportation facilities and the fact that our marketing operations are confined to an area within an economical shipping radius." [5]

Following the acquisition of its first refinery in 1924, the Ashland Oil & Refining Company was profitable in every year except 1931. In the depression year of 1931 the company suffered a loss of $44,000 on a consolidated basis, but the refining subsidiary actually earned a net profit of $126,000. In fact, information available in the company's annual reports from 1926 to 1932 reveals that losses on oil producing operations diluted refining earnings in four out of seven years. The financial success of the Ashland Oil & Refining Company and its remarkable growth in recent years are evident from the financial data shown in Exhibit XXIII-3. Net sales, for example, increased from $2,526,000 in 1925 to $8,046,000 in 1940 and $145,432,000 in 1950. Net income and total asset figures have likewise shown very large increases in recent years.

EXHIBIT XXIII-3. ASHLAND OIL & REFINING COMPANY

Selected Financial Information: 1925–1950
($1,000)

Year	Net Sales	Net Income	Total Assets
1925	$ 2,526	$ 824	$ 10,547
1930	4,735	71	8,874
1935	4,031	508	6,433
1940	8,046	697	8,332
1945	34,812	980	21,815
1950	145,452	10,004	103,684

In 1951 the management of the Ashland Oil & Refining Company still considered the geographic location of the river refinery near Catlettsburg, Kentucky, to be one of the company's major competitive advantages. Throughout its history the management was guided by the general policy of not marketing in an area unless Ashland could serve the area as efficiently as any other competitor from the combined standpoint of transportation and refining costs. Ashland was able to distribute the products of the Catlettsburg refinery economically because the

5 Ashland Oil & Refining Company, *Annual Report*, 1940.

marketing area it serviced was concentrated and serviceable by low-cost river barge movements. With the building of products pipe lines into Ashland's marketing territory after 1940, Ashland lost its transportation advantage over the companies having access to such facilities. It did, however, retain a transportation advantage over refiners not having access to pipe lines. It was believed that the transportation advantage ranged up to as much as 0.5 cent per gallon. Companies utilizing products pipe lines in the area held a large share of the market, but they were a definite minority in relation to the total number of companies marketing in the area.

A large share of the success of Ashland's principal river refinery at Catlettsburg, Kentucky, may be attributed to the fact that it was located right in the midst of the most distant marketing area served by many of the large refineries in the eastern part of the United States. Refined products reached the Catlettsburg area by two general movements: (a) products were often moved from Gulf Coast and Mid-Continent refineries in a northerly direction by pipe line or by barge along the Mississippi and Ohio Rivers, and (b) products were transported from East Coast points as far inland as the Ohio-Kentucky area. Thus Ashland's principal refinery was located in a peripheral marketing area for many companies, and Ashland realized a clear-cut advantage over some of these companies on products transportation costs. The transportation advantage was, of course, most pronounced in the area immediately encircling the Catlettsburg refinery because there were certain other refineries spaced along the Ohio River that enjoyed the same general transportation advantage as did Ashland.

The refinery location at Catlettsburg was particularly advantageous in times of shortages such as prevailed during several of the years following World War II because at such times distant refiners tended to concentrate their selling effort in the more profitable areas surrounding their own plants. When refined products were in ample supply, on the other hand, distant companies sometimes elected to dispose of part of their gallonage in remote areas at reduced prices and thus generated tough competition for Ashland. The state of Ohio, particularly, had been a "dumping ground" for distant refiners on several occasions. On balance, however, the river location at Catlettsburg proved to be a very important aspect of the company's financial success.

After World War II the Ashland Oil & Refining Company inaugurated a major expansion program in which seven small refineries were acquired. The small refineries were located at various points from Buffalo, New York, to St. Elmo, Illinois, and each was in a position to serve its immediate locality at low transportation costs. Whereas some companies relied upon one or more very large plants and products pipe lines to extend their marketing areas or to reduce costs, Ashland depended upon the advantages of small local refinery supply points to enlarge its marketing territory.

It is apparent from the foregoing discussion that the Shallow Water Refining Company and Ashland Oil & Refining Company developed along radically different routes in the decade prior to 1951. Shallow Water expanded slowly and confined its supply and marketing operations to one highly concentrated area. Ashland, on the other hand, acquired a number of small refineries, expanded outside its original market territory, and ultimately was compelled to draw its crude oil supplies from a number of different sources. Furthermore, Ashland integrated heavily into barge and tanker transportation. Both companies, however, illustrate the successful exploitation of the geographic interstices in the refining industry. The organizers of both companies visualized territorial gaps in the refining industry where small companies could gain a foothold through a transportation advantage over established companies. In both cases their appraisals were justified by the future success of their organizations.

Obviously, large refining companies competing in the Shallow Water and Ashland market territories were free to build small competitive refineries in the areas if they were disposed to do so. A large company may often, however, have other more profitable investment opportunities, such as in the expansion of crude oil producing operations, the renovation or enlargement of existing refineries, or the construction of pipe lines. In the small, localized areas where the large companies choose not to improve their competitive cost positions, the opportunity exists for small firms to engage in geographic specialization.

II. SPECIALIZATION IN RAW MATERIALS

The processing of particular types and grades of crude oil provides a second example of the interstices which small refiners have found in the affairs of the oil industry. The crude oil available from different fields has widely varying physical characteristics. Large refining companies must usually draw their crude oil supplies from widely scattered areas to obtain a sufficient supply to meet their requirements, and their raw material supply is therefore often composed of many different types and grades of crude oil. The small refiner can sometimes, because of his size, rely solely upon a narrow range of particular types and grades of crude oil of which the available supplies are very limited. As the following discussion will point out, operations based upon specialization in raw materials sometimes offer very attractive opportunities for small refining companies.

Maritime Oil Company:

The Maritime Oil Company provides an example of a very profitable small refining and marketing concern whose success was dependent to a very large degree upon the purchasing of a very special grade of crude oil which was available in only limited quantities. The company was organized as a marketing firm in 1924 to engage in the specialty business of "ship bunkering" along the Gulf Coast.[6] The company established ship bunkering stations in various cities, and the marketing activity subsequently proved quite profitable to the firm. It was not until 1938 that the Maritime Oil Company integrated backward into the refining business through the acquisition of a 5,000 barrels per day refinery located in Houston, Texas. From 1938 to the end of 1949 refining activities were likewise very profitable, although earnings on the refinery operation were not so high after about 1945 as they had been prior to that time. The Maritime Oil Company did not own any crude oil producing properties and its marketing facilities handled only fuel oil for ships except for one "floating service

---

6 "Ship bunkering" is a term used in the industry to describe the sale of fuel oil to ships.

station" that supplied gasoline to smaller pleasure and commercial crafts. The company also owned 4 towboats and 12 barges which it used to transport crude oil from different Gulf Coast ports to the Houston refinery and fuel oil from the refinery to market outlets.

The management attributed the firm's extremely profitable refining experience prior to about 1945 largely to the existence of very special types of crude oil which the company was able to acquire for processing. The refinery facilities owned by the Maritime Oil Company consisted solely of an atmospheric distillation unit and auxiliary equipment. There were no thermal or catalytic cracking processes at the plant. The special types of crude oil purchased by the company and charged to the relatively simple processing equipment yielded only two refined products. The most important product was a comparatively high octane gasoline. The straight-run gasoline obtained by the company had an octane quality of about 65 (A.S.T.M.—Motor Method) as compared with an octane rating of about 50 for the straight-run gasoline usually obtained from an ordinary crude oil. The straight-run gasoline of the Maritime Oil Company could, moreover, be raised to an octane rating somewhat higher than 65 by the addition of tetraethyl lead or blending stocks. The only other product yielded by the refinery from the particular types of crude oil used by the company was a special residual product used in certain kinds of Diesel engines. Since many smaller ships had Diesel engines, this Diesel product was a natural adjunct to the company's ship bunkering business.

The supply of crude oil permitting an operation such as the Maritime Oil Company developed was strictly limited. The company searched out crude oil supply points diligently, however, and purchased all its requirements. As an aid in locating specialized types of crude oil, the company performed laboratory tests on samples of oil obtained from wells scattered throughout the Gulf Coast area as well as from interior fields. The distillation tests frequently showed not only wide variations in the quality of crude oil obtained from different regions but also wide variations in the quality of crude oil obtained from different oil pools in the same region. Because of the limited amounts of very high gravity crude oil which yielded the

type and quality of products desired by the company, it would have been very difficult for a large company to have supported an operation solely upon the existence of such crude oil.

The procurement of very special grades of crude oil permitted the Maritime Oil Company to escape, at least temporarily, the impact of the technological advances represented by both thermal and catalytic cracking since it enabled the company to obtain a competitive grade of gasoline without a substantial investment in new facilities. Before World War II the "aviation gasoline cut" was exported, largely to England. The Diesel fuel oil was sold along the Gulf Coast largely through the bunkering stations owned by the Maritime Oil Company. During World War II the company's refined products were sold to the government or to others under allocations prescribed by the Petroleum Administration for War.

In the postwar period the economic and competitive conditions were no longer considered favorable to the type of specialty operation which the Maritime Oil Company had been conducting. The company sold its ship bunkering business in 1945 and about the same time encountered difficulties in purchasing the particular types of crude oil upon which its specialized refining operations were based. A very definite scarcity of all types of crude oil developed and, although it was possible for the company to purchase adequate amounts of crude oil, it could not always obtain the exact types desired. The company was compelled therefore to draw upon ordinary types of crude oil and to convert its refinery to the manufacture of four products: gasoline, mineral spirits, No. 2 heating oil, and No. 5 fuel oil. These products were sold almost exclusively to large oil companies, which also supplied Maritime with its crude oil requirements.

As highly selective crude oil became more scarce and octane requirements on gasoline moved upward, the Maritime Oil Company found that its refinery could not make a marketable gasoline product from the general run of crude oils which were available. In order to stay in business with a competitive gasoline product, the management considered an investment of approximately $1,000,000 for thermal cracking and attendant facilities to be absolutely necessary. Since the Maritime Oil Company was a partnership owned by two brothers, an investment of $1,000,000 was considered a very substantial sum. The brothers were financially secure as a result of prior operations, and it was, they believed, "hardly worth while to put $1 million into brick and mortar, especially with the income tax situation the way it was." One partner pointed out that if the company had owned or had access to its own crude oil supply, the owners might have reacted differently to the need for an investment in cracking facilities. The risk associated with the investment was, however, considered too great for a company existing as a nonintegrated refiner.

In the latter part of 1949 Maritime's refining operations became unprofitable because of the depressed market prices for refined products. Almost as soon as it was evident, around January 1, 1950, that refining operations could not be carried on at a profit, the management decided to shut down the company's plant. In August 1950 the partners leased the plant to another concern with a purchase option included in the lease terms. The lessee moved even further into a specialty line, its business being the preparation and manufacturing of petro-chemicals for further processing in the chemical industry. A very sizable capital outlay was made by the lessee to adapt the existing refinery equipment for new uses and to add new equipment. In the summer of 1951 the lessees exercised their purchase option on the plant in order to protect their substantial investment in processing facilities.

After the sale of the refinery the Maritime Oil Company continued to exist as a small business, but its operations were confined to even more specialized orbits than in prior years. The activities were of two types: a grease plant operation and a drumming and packaging business. The manufacture of greases was a simple process in which lubricating oils were worked into fatty oils. In the drumming and packaging business, lubricating oils were purchased and placed in containers ranging in size from one-quart cans to 55-barrel drums. Lubricating oils were packaged under the company's own brand name and for other companies. A plant for loading ships on the Houston ship channel was maintained by the company in connection with the drumming and packaging business. Greases

and lubricating oils were exported under the company's brand name to foreign markets, largely South America. In February 1952 the Maritime Oil Company was the only small company engaged in a drumming and packaging business west of Louisiana.

Other Crude Oil Specialists:

There are many other situations in which small refiners have developed operations based upon specialized raw materials. One of the best-known examples of capitalization on a particular grade of crude oil may be found in the experience of a group of small refiners located in the oil regions of Pennsylvania. These refiners have for years been making high quality, branded lubricating oils from a crude oil unusually well adapted to the manufacture of motor oils. Many of the branded lubricating oils sold by these small refiners have been advertised extensively over a wide geographical area. The consumer acceptance gained by "Pennsylvania Grade" lubricating oil has, in fact, often permitted these small refiners to sell their principal product at premium prices.

Small refiners in other areas have also sometimes geared their operations to the availability of particular types and grades of crude oil. The importance of a high gravity crude oil to the refiners in the East Texas field, for example, was discussed in Chapter Twenty-One. In addition, it may be observed that the extent to which a company can engage in the manufacture of certain petroleum product specialties, such as those discussed in the following section of this chapter, is sometimes a direct function of the types of crude oil it has available.

III. SPECIALIZATION IN PRODUCTS AND MARKETS

Specialization in particular products and markets has constituted a third general means by which small refiners have often found opportunities for successful and profitable operations. In the consumer gasoline markets, the large, integrated companies have developed very strong positions because they sell high-quality products, have the advantage of brand names for which strong consumer preferences have been established, and as a general rule have better located and more attractive service stations than do the small refiners. Recognizing the well-entrenched positions of the large concerns in the consumer gasoline market, some small refiners have elected to concentrate their activities on the commercial gasoline markets where brand identification is of little or no importance. Similarly, some small refiners have chosen to concentrate on the distillate and residual fuel oil markets where brand names are of minor significance and they can operate on equal terms with the large concerns.

In addition to seeking out markets for one or another of the major petroleum products which provide favorable competitive opportunities, some small refiners have employed further processing equipment to manufacture certain specialty petroleum products. Crude oil can be processed by suitable techniques into literally thousands of different end products. The characteristics of some of these products and the markets in which they are sold are such that a small refiner can manufacture and sell the products at no disadvantage to the largest concerns in the industry. Moreover, in some cases the markets for the specialty products are so small that the large companies cannot afford to devote a large share of executive time and attention to them

Bareco Oil Company:

The experience of the Bareco Oil Company provides an excellent example of the development of a specialty type product. Beginning in 1939 a large share of management attention and company resources were diverted to the task of establishing the Bareco Oil Company as a leader in the microcrystalline wax industry. At about the same time the company began to liquidate all its conventional refining and marketing properties. The experience of the company therefore illustrates the development of a specialty wax product and a concurrent step-by-step withdrawal from the manufacture and sale of other refined products.

The Bareco Oil Company was incorporated for the purpose of acquiring the refining and marketing facilities of the Barnsdall Oil Company.[7] Because of persistent losses on its refin-

---

[7] The Bareco Oil Company was actually organized under the corporate name of the Barnsdall Refining Corporation. The name was changed to the Bareco Oil Company on January 5, 1940. In the interests of simplicity, the firm will be re-

EXHIBIT XXIII-4. BARNSDALL OIL COMPANY

Selected Financial Information: 1933–1937

($1,000)

	Gross Sales	Net Income
Prior to Disposition of Refining and Marketing Properties:		
1933	$14,100	$(1,943)
1934	18,036	(1,029)
1935 (January 1 to May 31)	8,215	(548)
After Disposition of Refining and Marketing Properties:		
1935 (May 31 to December 31)	4,484	1,289
1936	11,101	2,263
1937	13,832	1,903

( ) Denotes loss.

SOURCE: Barnsdall Oil Company, *Annual Reports.*

ing and marketing operations, the management of the Barnsdall Oil Company decided in May 1935 to divorce completely these activities from the company's crude oil producing business. The sales and net income figures of the Barnsdall Oil Company for the years 1933 to 1937 are shown in Exhibit XXIII-4. The 1935 financial figures are segregated to show the results of operations before and after the disposition of refining and marketing properties. The net income figures reveal that the refining and marketing operations of the Barnsdall Oil Company were greatly diluting the earning capacity of the company's crude oil producing activities. Substantial losses were incurred by the Barnsdall Oil Company in 1932, 1934, and the first five months of 1935; immediately after the refining and marketing properties were shifted to the Bareco Oil Company, however, the Barnsdall Oil Company earned attractive profits. The common stock of the Bareco Oil Company was distributed to the stockholders of the Barnsdall Oil Company on a pro rata basis.

In 1935 the refining properties of the newly formed Bareco Oil Company consisted of three plants with an aggregate crude oil charging capacity of 18,000 barrels per day. The plants were located in Barnsdall and Okmulgee, Oklahoma, and Wichita, Kansas. The marketing facilities included approximately 200 owned or leased bulk stations and 500 owned or leased service stations. In addition, refined products were marketed through nearly 3,000 jobbers

---

ferred to as the Bareco Oil Company throughout the discussion.

and contractor stations that sold under the company's brand name "Be Square." Selected financial and operating data for the Bareco Oil Company for the period 1935 to 1950 are shown in Exhibit XXIII-5. In the following paragraphs we shall discuss first the development and nature of the specialty wax business and secondly the retrenchment program which the company followed with respect to its conventional refinery and marketing activities.

The Microcrystalline Wax Business: During the first five years of its history the Bareco Oil Company suffered heavy operating losses (see Exhibit XXIII-5). In 1939 Mr. O. L. Cordell was named president of the Bareco Oil Company and thereafter considerable emphasis was placed upon the development of a microcrystalline wax business.[8] Before 1939 the company secured only a small quantity of microcrystalline wax as a by-product of its process for manufacturing lubricating oil. The company subsequently developed a wide range of both soft and hard microcrystalline waxes.

Bareco's soft microcrystalline wax business was a direct outgrowth of the company's lubricating oil manufacturing operation at the Barnsdall refinery. Early in 1939 the Barnsdall refinery had a 5,000 barrels per day capacity and was a so-called "complete" plant in that it yielded a diversified line of petroleum products including such specialties as lubricating oil, paraffin wax, and a small quantity of microcrystalline wax.[9] The soft microcrystalline

waxes were extracted from petrolatum, an intermediate product secured in the manufacture of lubricating oils from residual fractions.[10] The management of the Bareco Oil Company decided to increase its output of soft microcrystalline waxes when it found that microcrystalline waxes had special qualities which suited them for applications in the paper, electrical, communication, textile, leather, chemical, and packaging industries.[11]

One important factor contributing to the development of Bareco's microcrystalline wax business was the fact that the company was able to enter heavily into the business with only a very modest capital expenditure. As noted above, the soft microcrystalline waxes were a by-product of the company's lubricating oil process. The lubricants which were produced at the Barnsdall refinery by a centrifuge operation were of the "conventional" type. After about 1935 the solvent extraction method for manufacturing lubricating oils came into vogue in the industry. Lubricants produced by the solvent method have a high viscosity index and certain other characteristics which cannot be attained from the "conventional" method of manufacture. The Barnsdall lubricating oil equipment was therefore becoming obsolete. Fortunately, however, the lubricating oil equipment was suitable for producing microcrystalline waxes by the centrifuge operation and the conversion to large-scale wax production could be made with small capital expenditures.

Bareco began the manufacture of hard microcrystalline waxes as the result of a new process brought to the attention of Bareco's research department in 1939. The new process permitted the reclamation of hard microcrys-

---

8 Mr. O. L. Cordell was employed as president of the Bareco Oil Company on January 1, 1939. Approximately one year later, after five years of heavy losses, the Bareco Oil Company went through a recapitalization plan whereby the Barnsdall Oil Company, the major Bareco creditor, again gained control of the common stock of the company. In 1940 and 1941 Mr. Cordell and his associates purchased a controlling interest in the firm from the Barnsdall Oil Company. In subsequent years the Barnsdall Oil Company entirely disposed of its minority interest in the Bareco Oil Company.

9 The solid waxes obtained from various petroleum fractions are of two major types: (a) paraffin waxes, produced from distillate fractions, and (b) microcrystalline waxes, produced from residual fractions and tank bottoms (see later discussion in text). The physical characteristics of the two types of waxes differ appreciably. The melting points of commercial paraffin waxes are, in general, much lower than those of microcrystalline waxes. Another important difference is that paraffin waxes are brittle products while microcrystalline waxes have plastic qualities. Although the total industrial production of paraffin waxes greatly exceeds that of microcrystalline waxes and many

companies offer paraffin waxes in their product lines, there are certain purposes for which microcrystalline waxes are superior to paraffin waxes.

10 One of the principal steps involved in the production of lubricating oils from residual fractions involves the extraction of petrolatum by either solvent or centrifuge processes. It is necessary to remove the petrolatum in order to secure lubricating oils which have free-flowing characteristics at low temperatures. When the by-product petrolatum is de-oiled by either a centrifuge or solvent extraction operation, a microcrystalline wax is obtained.

11 Most of the soft microcrystalline waxes were utilized in the paper industry for laminating various types and grades of paper. Other typical applications of microcrystalline waxes included: bakery, dairy, frozen and dehydrated food packaging; leather treatment; textile sizes; cable and wire insulation; cosmetics, salves, and ointments; rust preventatives; candles; and polishes.

EXHIBIT XXIII-5. BARECO OIL COMPANY

Selected Financial and Operating Data: 1935–1950

Balance Sheet and Income Statement Items

($1,000)

| Year | Gross Operating Income | Net Profit | Common Stock Dividends | Net Working Capital | Plant, Property, and Equipment | | Funded Debt | Capital Stock and Surplus | Total Assets |
					Gross	Net			
1935	$ 8,276	$ (484)	$nil	$ 1,730	$13,782	$5,736	$5,074	$2,809	$10,546
1936	13,413	(718)	nil	1,293	13,869	5,524	5,054	2,122	10,018
1937	14,819	(860)	nil	492	14,124	5,551	5,049	1,263	10,089
1938	13,891	(1,433)	nil	(1,499)	13,656	6,157	5,072	1,263	9,984
1939	13,929	(157)	nil	(1,319)	11,738	5,878	5,024	(170)	10,089
1940	10,585	(703)	nil	1,981	11,133	5,279	3,583	(327)	9,353
1941	12,699	222	nil	2,609	10,246	4,634	3,161	3,969	8,226
1942	14,166	587	nil	2,591	8,163	3,124	1,095	4,191	8,658
1943	10,393	456	nil	2,607	7,181	2,458	—	4,773	6,686
1944	11,302	602	205	3,527	5,963	1,639	—	5,229	6,470
1945	10,530	466	205	4,318	5,321	1,195	—	5,612	6,988
1946	10,863	555	368*	1,325	5,259	1,179	—	5,873	7,034
1947	14,392	1,179	367	1,861	4,801	1,433	—	2,755	4,143
1948	16,941	1,175	489	2,248	5,245	1,834	—	3,563	5,720
1949	13,401	140	204	2,500	5,264	1,787	—	4,340	6,394
1950	15,594	639	245	2,928	5,232	1,720	—	4,276	5,125
								4,670	6,166

( ) Negative figures.

* Plus capital distribution amounting to $3,284,520, which is approximately equivalent to the amount received by the company from the sales of the Corpus Christi refinery and petroleum marketing facilities.

Refinery Runs and Sales of Refined Products

(1,000 bbls.)

| Year | Refinery Runs | | | | | Sales of Refined Products | | | | | |
	Barnsdall Refinery	Okmulgee Refinery	Wichita Refinery	Corpus Christi Refinery	Total	Micro-crystalline Waxes	Gasoline & Naphthas	Distillate Fuels	Residuum	Lubricating Oils & Greases	Total
1935	1,277	1,327	1,056	—	3,660	1	2,490	550	367	215	3,622
1936	1,231	569	1,333	—	3,133	2	2,118	677	552	221	3,570
1937	1,219	717	1,735	40	3,711	3	2,565	802	609	225	4,204
1938	1,101	—	1,595	1,708	4,404	2	3,227	521	853	225	4,828
1939	1,245	—	1,686	1,895	4,826	6	3,383	552	1,285	294	5,520
1940	1,244	—	1,680	271	3,195	10	2,560	478	586	233	3,867
1941	1,327	—	1,705	1,518	4,550	15	3,399	470	810	229	4,923
1942	1,381	—	1,635	1,764	4,780	17	3,360	1,179	1,286	209	6,051
1943	1,143	—	1,312	—	2,455	61	1,925	462	500	368	3,316
1944	1,170	—	1,673	—	2,843	81	2,058	497	628	278	3,542
1945	1,112	—	1,714	—	2,826	57	2,071	512	570	253	3,463
1946	713	—	1,868	—	2,581	62	1,884	416	700	93	3,155
1947	—	—	2,495	—	2,495	71	1,667	494	697	13	2,942
1948	—	—	2,632	—	2,632	66	1,544	514	728	11	2,863
1949	—	—	1,975	—	1,975	58	1,362	358	546	7	2,341
1950	—	—	2,087	—	2,087	107	1,486	314	503	7	2,417

talline waxes from tank bottoms, the residue or sludge in crude oil storage tanks, with the aid of a solvent. Bareco's research department did some exploratory work on the new solvent process and the company was granted a patent on the process in July 1939.[12] Hard microcrystal-

line waxes had higher melting points than the soft microcrystalline waxes and were considered of a superior quality for certain purposes. The hard microcrystalline waxes were used largely

[12] In general, the process for the manufacture of micro-crystalline waxes from tank bottoms involved the distilla-

tion of tank bottoms to remove the lighter fractions; dissolving the residue material in a selective solvent, such as ethylene dichloride; and filtering to extract the microcrystalline wax.

EXHIBIT XXIII-5. (CONTINUED)

Income from Individual Facilities*
($1,000)

Year	Barnsdall Wax Plant	Barnsdall Refinery	Wichita Refinery	Okmulgee Refinery	Corpus Christi Refinery	Barnsdall Pipe Line	Refined Oils Purchased for Resale
1935	$ —	$ 20	$ 98	$103	$ —	$94	$19
1936	45	164	302	33	—	—	14
1937	64	132	409	(40)	(4)	—	16
1938	38	(73)	66	(9)	12	5	38
1939	124	346	298	(8)	433	21	2
1940	245	445	199	(2)	(103)	33	25
1941	330	494	414	—	280	1	42
1942	474	650	382	—	108	8	40
1943	814	612	302	—	—	(7)	31
1944	1,109	459	454	—	—	(1)	19
1945	898	347	451	—	—	—	14
1946	1,090	281	399	—	—	16	11
1947	1,084	—	1,382	—	—	36	10
1948	792	—	1,739	—	—	15	5
1949	396	—	124	—	—	40	3
1950	1,200	—	506	—	—	42	—

( ) Denotes loss.
* Before selling, general, and administrative expenses.

SOURCE: Bareco Oil Company.

to replace high-priced vegetable and mineral waxes as a raw material in the manufacture of items such as furniture polish.

Following the management decision to concentrate on the development of a microcrystalline wax business, production and sales increased very rapidly. As shown in Exhibit XXIII-5, the company's sales of microcrystalline waxes increased more than sevenfold in the three-year period beginning in 1938 and ending prior to World War II. During World War II Bareco became established as a leader in the microcrystalline wax business. During the war years many military applications were found for microcrystalline waxes as a waterproof coating for paper and other materials. As a result, Bareco's yearly wax sales jumped from 15,000 barrels in 1941 to 81,000 barrels in 1944, and the profit derived from the Barnsdall wax plant was larger than that from any other single facility owned by the company in the war years 1943 to 1945 (see Exhibit XXIII-5).

In 1946 the processing of crude oil was suspended at the Barnsdall refinery, and thereafter the plant was utilized solely for the production of microcrystalline waxes. A new plant was also erected at Barnsdall in 1946 for the manufacture of soft microcrystalline waxes by the solvent process which served to supplement the centrifuge process which the company had previously used. In the five-year period following the war, the company expanded the capacity of its microcrystalline wax manufacturing facilities by 50%. Through its concentration on a specialty-type product, Bareco became the proverbial "big fish in a little pond." The Bureau of Mines reported a total United States production of 405,000 barrels of microcrystalline waxes in 1950.[13] Bareco's sales of microcrystalline waxes amounted to 107,000 barrels for the same period.

The competitive situation in the microcrystalline wax industry differed greatly between the soft and hard waxes. In the soft microcrystalline field, at least five large companies were in competition with Bareco in 1951. In the hard microcrystalline wax category, the company had only two main competitors. In addition to these two groups of companies which competed directly with Bareco, there were other companies producing grades of microcrystalline waxes which were not directly competitive with Bareco's products. In general, Bareco's selling effort was concentrated on customers within the area in which it was at no substantial

[13] U. S. Bureau of Mines, "Petroleum and Petroleum Products," reprint from Minerals Yearbook, 1950 (Washington, Government Printing Office, 1951), p. 115.

freight disadvantage with respect to other refiners. Bareco, for example, could not ordinarily compete in the New England market because it had higher transportation costs than eastern refiners.

There were no particular features of the microcrystalline wax business which made it uniquely suited to the operations of a small firm. At the same time, however, the microcrystalline wax business was usually such a small part of the total operations of a large corporation that it did not warrant a large share of executive time and attention. The Bareco Oil Company could, for example, devote a large share of executive time to contacts with prospective customers. The selling job on microcrystalline waxes entailed very close cooperation between suppliers and prospective customers. In contrast to the paraffin waxes, the characteristics of microcrystalline waxes varied over a wide range and it was frequently necessary for a customer to test many grades of wax to find the one best suited to his specific needs. A customer seldom shifted his supplier after the initial sale was made because of the difficulties involved in establishing the exact grades and specifications necessary for his requirements. One large Bareco customer spent $25,000 for tests on Bareco waxes before placing an order.

The management of the Bareco Oil Company believed, moreover, that the company had a decided quality advantage over larger competitors because Bareco had been unusually successful in turning out a uniform product. The management believed that the large firms had difficulty in securing as uniform a product because they obtained petrolatum as a by-product of their own refinery operations. Any one refinery in a large company ordinarily ran several different types of crude oil yielding different types of petrolatum. The management believed that this nonuniformity in raw materials supply resulted in continual changes in the characteristics of the microcrystalline waxes produced by large companies. Bareco, on the other hand, purchased petrolatum from many refineries in the Mid-Continent area and was thus able to secure the particular raw material supplies it needed to secure stable wax specifications. Since Bareco's suppliers obtained petrolatum as a by-product of their lubricating oil processes and were anxious to dispose of it, Bareco experienced no difficulty whatsoever in purchasing adequate supplies.

Bareco's microcrystalline wax operation proved quite profitable to the company. In five of the seven years from 1944 to 1950 the income from the wax business exceeded that of all refined oil operations combined (see Exhibit XXIII-5). The microcrystalline wax business also helped to offset some of the profit fluctuations to which Bareco was exposed on its refining operations. In 1946, for example, profits on refining contracted but profits on the wax business increased. In 1949, a generally unfavorable year for refiners, the profits of both the wax and refined oil businesses declined, but the contribution of the wax department to company income before selling, general, and administrative expenses was over three times as large as the contribution of the refined oil business. Thus, for Bareco, product diversification was not only profitable in its own right but it also helped to stabilize the earning power of an otherwise nonintegrated oil refining company.

Liquidation of Refining and Marketing Properties: The history of the Bareco Oil Company after 1939 was marked not only by the development of the microcrystalline wax business but also by the company's step-by-step disposal of all refining and marketing properties. For the years 1935 to 1939 the Bareco Oil Company prepared departmental earnings statements on its refining and marketing activities. Since no actual sale outside the company was made on the refined products transferred from the refining department to the marketing department for sale, it was necessary for the company to use an admittedly arbitrary scale of transfer prices. In pricing product transfers from the refining to the marketing department, the company used the low of the market prices quoted in the *Chicago Journal of Commerce, National Petroleum News,* and *Platt's Oilgram.* Three sources were used to provide a more complete coverage of different products prices than could have been secured from one alone. There was a good deal of dispute and uncertainty in the industry as to what the low of the market quotations in these publications represented. Many people contended that the prices reflected the spot purchases of small quantities of refined products and that they were not indicative of the prices at which large buying organizations could contract for their requirements. Others felt that the average of the low prices or perhaps the average of the low and high quoted prices represented meaningful prices at which the intracompany transfer of products could be assumed to take place for the preparation and interpretation of departmental earnings statements. In any event, the net income by departments derived on the basis of the low of the quoted prices were as follows:

Net Income by Departments
($1,000)

Year	Marketing Department	Refining Department	Total Company
1935	$(224)	$(260)	$ (484)
1936	(399)	(319)	(718)
1937	(391)	(469)	(860)
1938	(468)	(955)	(1,433)
1939	(475)	318	(157)

( ) Denotes loss.

In the light of the results of the refining and marketing operations, Mr. Cordell reasoned that the company must discontinue direct marketing activities or be financially ruined in the very near future. The company sold its marketing facilities for the most part to independent operators. In isolated cases, major companies purchased the service station sites. On the sale of its marketing facilities, the company took heavy capital losses which were applied against the high operating profits earned during the war years. Sale of the facilities thus provided a dual source of funds: cash was realized from the sales and income taxes were reduced during a period of high tax rates. The marketing divorcement program was fully completed in 1946.

Whereas all marketing properties were abandoned as a result of a single policy decision made in 1939, individual refineries were, to a large extent, discarded only when profitable operations could no longer be secured. The Okmulgee, Oklahoma, plant was dismantled in 1937 principally because refinery capacity was in excess of the company's demand in the local area. The company salvaged all usable equipment at the dismantled plant for movement to the Barnsdall and Wichita refineries and a new plant which was under construction at Corpus Christi, Texas.

The Corpus Christi plant was built principally to take advantage of the deep water location on the Gulf Coast. It was expected that the location would offer economical transportation by tankers to a broad geographic market. Although the Corpus Christi plant was profitable in several years (see Exhibit XXIII-5), the plant lost money in 1940 and was shut down for 14 consecutive months prior to May 1, 1941, because of the depressed prices which existed for refined products in the Gulf Coast area. In September 1942 the Corpus Christi plant was sold to an agent representing the U. S. Army. The government dismantled the plant for intended relocation in Alaska.

The processing of crude oil was suspended at the Barnsdall refinery in 1946 and thereafter the plant was engaged solely in the manufacture of microcrystalline waxes. While refinery runs at Barnsdall were not completely terminated until 1946, the company had for several preceding years been in the process of transferring all of its refined oil manufacturing operations to the Wichita refinery. The management figured that only a small capital expenditure would be necessary for the company to route its entire crude oil supply and to transport some of the Barnsdall processing equipment to Wichita. It was expected that refining operations would prove more economical after the transfer because of the increased level of throughput which could be maintained at the Wichita plant.

Operation of the Wichita plant, the company's sole remaining refinery, was permanently discontinued in September 1952. The reasons for the action were set forth in the company's *Annual Report* for 1952 as follows:

Operation of the Wichita, Kansas, refinery was permanently discontinued in September, 1952. It was pointed out in our 1951 report that marketing conditions were adversely affecting the profits of this plant. Such conditions became more unfavorable in 1952, resulting in a loss for the first eight months of the year.

The abandonment of this operation was in harmony with the established policy of the Company of gradual liquidation of unprofitable refining and marketing properties which was begun in 1940, but interrupted insofar as the Wichita plant was concerned, by profitable operations during the war and post war periods. To continue the operation of this plant we were confronted with the necessity of making large expenditures for modernization in order to produce competitive products, principally higher octane gasoline, and to reduce the yield of residual fuel oil, the sale of which was becoming increasingly unprofitable, due to the almost complete dieselization of railroad motive power which formerly provided the major market for this product.

We were unsuccessful in our efforts to dispose of this property as a complete unit and the sale of the equipment by individual units or otherwise is now in process.

In retrospect, it appears that from the time the Bareco Oil Company was divorced from an integrated structure by the Barnsdall Oil Company, the Bareco Oil Company consistently followed a program of retrenchment in its unprofitable refined oil business. The withdrawal from the typical industry activities was, however, accompanied by the development of the specialty microcrystalline wax business. In the microcrystalline wax business the company was able to operate so successfully that it became one of the leading manufacturers in the field.

Shallow Water Refining Company:

A second example of product specialization may be found in the experience of the Shallow Water Refining Company. The geographic interstice which the Shallow Water Refining Company filled in western Kansas has already been discussed at an earlier point in the chapter. The company was also able to develop a very attractive asphalt and road oil business because the grades of crude oil readily available to the company were unusually well-suited for asphalt production and because the company was able to offer some services to its asphalt customers that competitors could not easily duplicate.

The crude oil available from the small oil pools surrounding the Shallow Water refinery (see map, Exhibit XXIII-2) had a very high asphaltic content which made it possible for the company to obtain relatively high yields of asphalt of fairly uniform specifications. In 1950 the company's refinery yield of asphalt was 27% of refinery runs whereas the industry-wide yield of asphalt was approximately 3% of refinery runs.[14] Since the characteristics and asphaltic content of crude oils were subject to wide regional variations and most large companies drew their supplies from many areas, the Shallow Water management felt that the large companies encountered greater difficulties in obtaining consistently as high a yield of asphalt or as uniform a product as could Shallow Water.

The most important end use of asphalt was road building, and the customers included municipalities and contractors. Service and cost considerations were of paramount importance to asphalt buyers in determining the suppliers with which they would place their business. Once a particular grade of asphalt was agreed upon, there was little or no question about its quality since a state inspector was permanently assigned to each refinery in Kansas to test for quality specifications. The Shallow Water Refining Company was in a position to supply its customers with a high quality of service and reasonably priced products. The nearness of the Shallow Water refinery to the points of use for its asphalt production enabled the company to work closely with customers and to tailor asphalt production to their particular requirements. Since there were many grades of asphalt which could, with the proper interchange of information between suppliers and customers, be adapted for specific needs, the customer service offered by Shallow Water was well-received by buyers. Originally the company had tried to sell its asphalt output through a broker, but this arrangement proved unsatisfactory because of the need for close cooperation between refinery personnel and customers to meet specific quality and scheduling requirements. Consequently, the company undertook to sell its asphalt directly and found that direct marketing proved to be much more effective than a brokerage arrangement.

Although the Shallow Water Refining Company deliberately overbid the lowest estimated delivery price of any of its competitors by 0.5 cent per gallon, the company still provided asphalt to customers at a very reasonable cost to them. Shallow Water was able to secure a

---

[14] Industry figure computed from U. S. Bureau of Mines, "Petroleum and Petroleum Products," reprint from *Minerals Yearbook, 1950* (Washington, Government Printing Office, 1951), p. 61.

premium of 0.5 cent per gallon on the sale of asphalt because the company offered two distinctive advantages to customers which were worth somewhat more than the price differential. In the first place, Shallow Water delivered heated liquefied asphalt directly from the refinery to customers by tank truck. Other companies marketing in the territory used tank cars equipped with coils through which steam was passed at destinations to permit the asphalt to be removed from the tank cars. Because of the reheating costs, the hot asphalt delivered by Shallow Water was worth from 0.8 cent to 1.5 cents per gallon more to contractors than asphalt which had solidified en route.

The second reason why Shallow Water was able to charge 0.5 cent per gallon more than competitors for asphalt lay in its ability to tie in shipments very closely with the road-building schedules of customers. Through the use of its own trucks and because of its nearness to the market, Shallow Water was able to schedule convenient quantities of asphalt for delivery to customers at the most advantageous time.

Leonard Refineries, Inc.:

Leonard Refineries, Inc., located in Alma, Michigan, provides another example of a small refining company for which asphalt was an important specialty product. The asphalt business in this case represented a partial solution to the company's disadvantageous position with respect to the sale of residual fuel oils.

The normal marketing area for the refinery's residual fuel oil output was Detroit, Michigan, which was located approximately 125 miles to the southeast of Alma. Several refineries were situated in the Detroit area, and the price structure for refined products in the entire Michigan peninsula was based upon the transportation costs involved in a general northerly flow of crude oil and refined products from Detroit and other southerly refining points. Since Detroit was the only large market for residual fuel oil in the entire area, it was necessary for Leonard Refineries to employ unattractive back hauling into an established refinery center in order to dispose of its residual output. The conversion of residual fuel oil into asphalt, however, helped the company to alleviate the problem by reducing the total yield of residual fuel oil that had to be moved into the Detroit area.

Furthermore, there was a strong local market for asphalt which permitted the company to realize a transportation advantage in the sale of the product.

Like Shallow Water, Leonard Refineries followed the practice of delivering heated asphalt in its own trucks directly to the construction locations of its customers. This practice was made possible by the proximity of the Leonard refinery to a substantial market for asphalt. By providing heated asphalt the Leonard company was likewise able to secure a somewhat higher price for its asphalt than could its competitors.

Leonard Refineries also cultivated an attractive specialty business through the utilization of by-product refinery gases. These gases were bottled and distributed as fuel for cooking, refrigeration, and heating purposes in the rural areas of Michigan.

Specialization by Types of Gasoline Accounts:

As noted above, the aggressive brand name programs on gasoline followed by the major companies have resulted in a strong consumer demand for branded gasoline. The branding programs have therefore been one of the principal elements of competitive strength for large companies. Small refiners, on the other hand, have generally lacked the financial resources necessary to carry out extensive brand name programs. Even with adequate financial resources, however, the small firm cannot usually avail itself of the same nationwide or regional advertising media used by the larger companies because the small firm generally sells in a fairly restricted market territory. Moreover, since small refiners characteristically sell only a small proportion of their gasoline output under their own brand names, it is difficult for a small firm to justify the expenditures for a concerted advertising effort of any magnitude, even to the extent that localized advertising media will permit. Thus, some measure of the small refiner's disadvantage in competing for the passenger car market stems from the fact that his controlled or branded gallonage is inadequate to warrant the financial outlay for an effective brand name program.

To avoid direct competition with the major oil companies in the brand-conscious service station markets, some small refiners have concentrated on other market segments where brand names are of little or no consequence in attracting patronage. Large commercial accounts for gasoline are an excellent example of the non-branded market. Gasoline purchases are a major business expense for commercial haulers such as those operating a fleet of taxicabs, trucks, or busses. Commercial accounts are therefore generally more interested in the price differential that may be obtained on an acceptable quality of gasoline than they are on brand identification. Commercial accounts frequently operate by accepting large bulk shipments of gasoline into their own storage facilities. The small refiners are sometimes able to enter commercial markets competitively by making bulk shipments to these large customers direct from their refineries at tank car prices. Of course, large companies also seek commercial business aggressively, but they are at a price disadvantage in those localities where their product passes through one more level of distribution than that of the small, local refiner. In territories where they rely upon distributors, for example, the large firms are often at a 1.5 to 2.5 cents per gallon price disadvantage in seeking commercial accounts.

The farm market has constituted a second important field in which small firms have often developed aggressive selling programs for gasoline. Farm accounts frequently accept bulk shipments of gasoline in amounts ranging upwards from 500 gallons. The small, local refining concern can, at times, appeal to the farm trade very effectively on a price or service basis. Moreover, small refiners are able to sell in these substantial markets without investing large sums of money in advertising and promotional programs or in retail marketing facilities.

Within the passenger car market itself many small refiners have developed a successful business by offering price concessions to offset the brand names of their larger competitors. An officer of one small refining company described two distinct classes of gasoline customers patronizing retail stations: "In the first group are those customers heavily impressed with branded products and influenced by good looking stations with polished rest rooms. A second group tends to suppress these interests in favor of price advantage of 1 to 2 cents per gallon." Historically, his company had appealed to the second group, although it had very fine service station

outlets in some localities. The management of this small company "operated under the assumption that there would always be a certain number of people preferring cut-rate products."

It should not be inferred from the foregoing discussion that small refiners completely avoid sales of gasoline under company brand names. While the small firm is generally at a significant disadvantage relative to the large in attracting consumers by brand name appeal, a great many small refiners enter into direct competition with the major companies on a brand name basis on at least a part of their gasoline output. Moreover, some small refiners make the sale of a branded gasoline product an important part of their business.

The Aetna Oil Company provides an example of a small refining company that specialized in the retail marketing of petroleum products under its own brand name.[15] The company's principal retail marketing territory included the areas of central and western Kentucky, Louisville, and southern Indiana. In 1949 gasoline distribution was effected largely through 39 bulk stations which served 220 company owned or leased service stations, 580 contract dealers, and approximately 2,000 consumer accounts. The company had maintained an interest in developing marketing properties since 1921.

Where it did not have bulk plant representation in its territory, the Aetna Oil Company had jobbers who purchased their requirements from Aetna and resold under the Aetna brand name. The company had 15 jobbers who served 75 owned or leased service stations, 200 contract dealers, and 500 consumer accounts. Aetna's direct and jobber distribution under its own brand name normally accounted for around 75% of its gasoline output. The remainder of the gasoline output was sold to others, largely on a wholesale basis, for resale under private brand names. Aetna also purchased at wholesale and resold through its branded outlets a complete line of tires, batteries, accessories, and antifreezes. The company did not manufacture but purchased and resold substantial quantities of lubricating oils.

---

[15] As noted in Chapter Twenty-Two, the Aetna Oil Company was merged into the Ashland Oil & Refining Company on January 16, 1950.

Another example of branded selling by small companies is provided by the experience of a group of small, Mid-Continent refiners. In the spring of 1935 seven small refiners in the Mid-Continent area began selling gasoline under a single brand name, Sovereign Service. The refiners' gasoline was actually sold largely to jobbers that were participating in the brand name program. The primary objectives of the marketing organization were to adopt a common color scheme for Sovereign Service stations, to engage in promotional work, and to improve service station rest room facilities.

In January 1951 four small Kansas refiners, including three of the original group, owned Sovereign Services, Inc. This organization was a nonprofit, cooperative corporation engaged in promoting the Sovereign Service brand name. The four owners shared the cost of the promotional work done by the organization. Each refiner, however, secured his own jobber accounts. At this time there were more than 500 service stations selling under the Sovereign Service brand name and almost 200 Sovereign jobbers. The Sovereign name was considered by the refiners to be an attractive inducement in soliciting jobber trade. Moreover, promotion of the Sovereign name was expected to attract consumer patronage, thereby enabling the refining firms and their jobbers to compete more effectively against companies selling gasoline under other well-known brand names.

IV. SPECIALIZATION IN MANAGEMENT SKILLS

Each of the interstices discussed thus far represents a business opportunity which was found to some extent through skillful management planning. We further observed that the success of some small companies was due in large part to particular skills of its principal executives. In the case of one small company we visited, for example, the ability of the principal executives to maintain very cordial relationships with the firm's large fuel oil buyers was considered as one of the company's main competitive strengths. Several cases came to our attention in which the management personnel were particularly adept in maintaining close relationships with large and small crude oil suppliers. Certain small companies are also very well-known for the competence of their manage-

ment personnel as refinery process engineers. During the course of our field research, the president of one small refining company commented that "the refining segment of the oil industry has been blessed with too many promoters and too few technically trained people." Expanding his remarks, he referred to the niche which exists for small refiners to specialize in refinery know-how.

As a means of illustrating the way in which particular management skills are used to advantage in certain small companies, we shall in the following paragraphs discuss how the operations of two companies have been aided by the technical proficiency of their managements.

Leonard Refineries, Inc:

Leonard Refineries specialized in the adaptation of new refinery processes for use in small plants. As noted above, the company's refinery was situated in Alma, Michigan, and the company drew its crude oil supply from Michigan and other fields. In view of the comparatively undesirable quality of the straight-run gasoline manufactured from Michigan crude oil, the management skill which permitted the company to be a leader in the tailoring of new and advanced refinery processes to the needs of the small firm was a vital factor in establishing the company's competitive strength.

The first small-scale catalytic polymerization and catalytic cracking units to be installed in the industry were erected at Leonard's Alma plant. The small "poly" plant entailed a capital outlay by the company of only $9,000.[16] Operation of the unit increased the company's total sales realization because it made available about 1,500 additional gallons of gasoline per day from the same quantity of crude oil, a 3.5% increase in gasoline yield.[17] The polymerized gasoline also led directly to lower operating costs by eliminating the need for costly benzol blending which had been used to obtain a competitive housebrand gasoline from the Michigan crude oil. In 1947 a thermofor catalytic cracking unit was constructed at the Leonard refinery. A refinery engineering firm had sub-

---

[16] "Leonard's 'Poly' Unit Eliminates Benzol Blending for Anti-Knock," *National Petroleum News*, Vol. 30, no. 32, August 10, 1938, p. R-378.

[17] *Ibid.*

EXHIBIT XXIII-6. ASHLAND OIL & REFINING COMPANY
Comparative Operating Refining Capacity

Location of Refinery	Previous Owner	Year Acquired by Ashland	Operating Capacity (B/D) At Time of Acquisition	1951
Niles, Ohio	Western Reserve Oil Company	1947	2,000	2,000
Canton, Ohio	Allied Oil Company	1948	10,000	17,000
Louisville, Kentucky	Aetna Oil Company	1950	8,000	10,000
Freedom, Pennsylvania	Freedom-Valvoline Oil Company	1950	4,000	5,000
Tonawanda, New York	Frontier Oil Refining Corporation	1950	9,000	15,000
Findlay, Ohio	National Refining Company	1950	9,000	14,000
St. Elmo, Illinois	Northwestern Refining Company	1950	4,500	4,500
			46,500	67,500

SOURCE: Ashland Oil & Refining Company.

mitted an original bid price in the amount of $2,500,000. By working closely with the engineering firm and making certain drastic alterations in the original plans, Leonard was able to have the unit completed at a total investment cost of slightly under $600,000.

Ashland Oil & Refining Company:

The Ashland Oil & Refining Company specialized in improving the efficiency of relatively old refineries and processing equipment. The nature of Ashland's geographic specialization and the resultant transportation advantage of the company were discussed in an earlier section of the chapter. The Ashland management, however, considered the company's over-all refining efficiency to be even more important than its geographic specialization as a point of competitive strength. The management of the company was very much interested in the redesign and renovations of refinery equipment and the company maintained an excellent staff of refinery engineers. The engineering staff played an important role in the success of the company's postwar expansion program during which seven small refineries were purchased or merged into the Ashland organization.

Improvements in the newly acquired refineries were along three general lines: In the first place, crude oil throughputs were frequently increased by the removal of "bottleneck" operations. In many cases, the limiting factor on crude oil throughput was relatively inexpensive equipment such as heat exchangers or pumps. Once the limiting factor on throughput was determined, it could usually be adjusted fairly easily. With the removal of each bottleneck operation, some other operation became the governing factor on maximum throughput. In planning the removal of bottlenecks therefore, the company usually set a definite upper limit on the amount of money to be spent. Since the increases in throughput were usually accomplished through certain modifications which did not involve replacing the basic processing units, relatively small capital expenditures were involved.

A measure of the company's success in increasing levels of throughput at the seven refineries acquired by the company after World War II is given in Exhibit XXIII-6. The total operating capacity of the seven plants was increased from approximately 46,500 barrels per day at the time of acquisition to 67,500 barrels per day in 1951, an increase of 45%. In view of the relatively high proportion of fixed costs incurred in a refining operation [18] the alterations in plant design and throughputs substantially improved the profitability of the plants.

The second major type of improvement which the Ashland engineering staff was frequently able to make at the refineries the company acquired was the reduction of refinery fuel consumption. Greater fuel economy was usually accomplished by adding supplementary heat exchangers. In other cases, however, more drastic alterations were necessary. The changes made at the National plant at Findlay, Ohio, provide a rather extreme example of how the company increased heat efficiency at the newly acquired refineries. The crude oil distillation and fractionating processes at the National plant were completely detached from the ther-

[18] See Chapter Twenty.

mal cracking unit, and distilled products had been permitted to cool before being charged to the thermal cracking unit. This arrangement made it necessary to reheat the products at the time they were charged to the cracking unit. By installing a heat exchanger and connecting the crude oil distillation and thermal cracking units with an insulated line, Ashland was able to cut fuel costs approximately in half.

A third type of cost reduction at the newly acquired refineries resulted from the elimination of excessive labor costs. Ashland followed the general rule of thumb that eight men should be required per thousand barrels of crude oil throughput. Of each group of eight men, five were generally operating men and three were maintenance men. Most of the increased throughput at refineries shown in Exhibit XXIII-6 was accomplished with little or no increase in total labor costs.

Ashland's refining operations were not only benefited by the type of cost savings outlined above, but also by the fact that plant investments were held at an absolute minimum. The company, for example, had a comparatively small amount of capital invested at Catlettsburg, Kentucky, where the company really had two interconnected refineries with an aggregate capacity of 45,000 barrels per day in 1950. Much of the basic equipment in the older refinery near Catlettsburg was material salvaged from dismantled refineries and was acquired at a low cost. The company's newer refinery near Catlettsburg included a distillation unit with a crude oil charging capacity of 26,000 barrels per day and a thermofor catalytic cracking unit with a charging stock capacity of 20,000 barrels per day. The refinery entailed a total investment cost of only $3,650,000 for the Ashland Oil & Refining Company. Of this amount, $2,150,000 was paid to the government for the thermofor catalytic cracking unit which had originally cost the Defense Plants Corporation approximately $16,000,000 to erect.

In addition to developing special managerial proficiencies, some small firms follow operating practices at their plants which are appreciably different from those followed by large companies. The effect of differences in operating practices was discussed at length in Chapter Twenty. At this point we shall merely note that the ability of small firms to operate with less "gold plated" refinery equipment and fewer offsite facilities, to operate with fewer personnel per barrel of crude oil capacity, to pay lower hourly wage scales, and to offer fewer fringe benefits than large companies are all further examples of ways by which small refiners are able to compete effectively with larger concerns.

V. Meeting Special Demand Situations

Many small refiners fill an important gap in the affairs of the industry by meeting special demand situations for refined products. When the demand for all refined products is generally strong, some small refiners bring their spare refining capacity into operation to help provide an adequate supply. Similarly, when the demand for a single product is unusually heavy, some small refiners shift their refinery yields to provide greater quantities of the needed product. Some small companies also help to fulfill the special demand situations of the large, integrated companies by supplying them with products when the refining capacity of the large companies is inadequate to meet the situation.

The specialists in meeting unusual product demands are, of course, induced to provide or cut back the marginal supplies of refined products for the industry by the continual shifts in products prices. When prices of products are generally strong or the price of one product is unusually high, an attractive profit opportunity is provided for the small refiners. When the demand is met and prices are corrected, the profit opportunity either disappears or at least its attractiveness is reduced, and the small refiners either shut back refinery runs or readjust their product yields.

As a means of illustrating the response of refiners to special demand situations, we shall discuss three types of operations: (a) the "in and outer" who provides spare capacity for the longer-run shifts in demand situations, (b) the small companies that shift refinery yields frequently to capitalize on short-term fluctuations in the demand picture, and (c) the small and substantially nonintegrated companies that meet certain special product needs of the large, integrated companies.

The "In and Outer":

The in and outer is an opportunist who specializes in the time periods in which he operates. The refining facilities of an in and outer are operated on an intermittent basis in accordance with the movement in the gross margin available to refining companies. When the gross margin is sufficient to permit profitable operations or to at least cover out-of-pocket costs, the in and outer continues in operation. When the margin falls below such a point, the plant is shut down until the price structure again improves. The in and outer performs a useful economic function by providing marginal or spare capacity for the industry on a stand-by basis.

The in and outer type of operation is most characteristic of companies owning plants which offer little flexibility to adjust refinery yields, since such firms are often the hardest hit by adverse fluctuations in the refining margin. The in and outer is therefore quite different from the specialist in adjusting refinery yields, and the in and outer is generally dependent upon longer-run changes in the demand-supply situation than are the product yield specialists.

The management alternative of operating on an in and outer basis is not readily available to large companies. Most large companies cannot easily afford to provide for unexpectedly heavy demands as a regular part of their operating policies because of the labor problems involved in cutbacks when the peak demands are satiated. Many large companies therefore prefer to stabilize their operations over long periods and to purchase from outsiders to meet peak demands. Moreover, many large companies and small companies feel a sense of responsibility to their established customers and labor forces which precludes the temporary shutdown of a company's entire refinery capacity during unprofitable periods.

During our field research we visited a small refining company that exemplified the policy of in and outer operations. The management had no intention of operating its plant continuously; rather, the maintenance of refinery runs only during the periods when the refining margin was "lush" was the accepted way of doing business. The investment in refinery facilities had been kept at comparatively low levels, the company had no assured source of crude oil supply, and refined products were sold exclusively at the refinery gate. In general, the experience of the company during alternate periods of plant operations and plant shutdowns was a barometer reflecting general business conditions in the refining segment of the oil industry.

The president of the company was sometimes criticized for a lack of customer responsibility. The president justified his unwillingness to supply customers during unprofitable periods with the following line of reasoning: "We make money. If we supplied products at a loss, we would eventually go out of business permanently and would never be in a position to supply anybody with products." The company had always been able to regain customers or secure new ones after a plant shutdown by appealing almost exclusively on a price basis. The in and outer type of operation proved to be a very profitable one for the company. Over the years the initial investment made by the owners in the refinery "was paid out many times over." In addition, members of the owning family drew salaries that permitted a comfortable standard of living to be maintained.

A second type of in and outer operation involves the intermittent operation of a stand-by refinery by companies owning more than one plant. In 1950 the Ashland Oil & Refining Company purchased a refinery at St. Elmo, Illinois, with a crude oil capacity of 4,500 barrels per day and a thermal cracking capacity of 2,300 barrels per day. In addition to the refinery, Ashland was interested in terminaling facilities which were a part of the purchase package. It was anticipated that the St. Elmo refinery, which represented a small investment, would be operated as a "fair weather" refinery. Under ordinary or depressed fuel oil conditions, it was doubtful that the plant could be operated on a profitable basis; when the prices for heavy fuel oil were high, however, profitable operations could be expected. Therefore the Ashland management planned to operate the refinery when the fuel oil market was strong and to shut down the plant when the market fell off.

In addition to the companies that operate their plants intermittently, there are many others that bring some idle capacity into use when refined products markets are particularly strong. Companies frequently own marginal refinery equipment which is a carry-over from earlier periods in their history. Particularly when fuel oil markets are strong, this added capacity can often be utilized effectively.

Specialists in Adjusting Refinery Yields:

A second type of adjustment to special demand situations is provided by the companies which shift their refinery yields frequently in accordance with very short-term fluctuations in the prices of various products. The specialists in adjusting refining yields differ from the "in and outer" and other companies maintaining spare capacity in that the *mix* of refined products they choose to place upon the market at any one time is considered of far greater importance than the total *quantity* of products made available in different time periods.

Some large companies estimate the future demands for their various refined products months in advance. They then hold their refinery yields at fairly stable levels and build up refined products inventories sufficient to meet their future requirements regardless of subsequent price movements. To a large extent, these companies place major emphasis upon economical refinery operations and the anticipated total demand for refined products in planning their refinery yields. Short-term price movements are often of minor importance since undue preoccupation with the daily or weekly movements in prices might leave the companies in short supply on one or more products at some future date.

Some small refiners, on the other hand, produce the particular mix of refined products which maximizes their sales realizations at the moment. Other small refiners govern their refinery yields partially by the existing price situation for refined products and partially by the anticipation of seasonal price increases on certain products which they produce for storage. Although it proves more costly from a manufacturing standpoint to adjust refinery yields frequently than it does to maintain fairly uniform yields, the product yield specialist is sometimes compensated with greater sales realizations than the companies that hold their refinery yields uniform.

The Eastern States Petroleum Corporation provides an excellent example of the specialist in meeting short-run demands for refined products. In 1951 the Eastern States Petroleum Company was a virtually nonintegrated refining company with plant facilities located in Houston, Texas. The company owned net crude oil production which was negligible in amount in comparison with its total refinery requirements and operated a truck rack at the refinery from which jobbers servicing the local Houston market were supplied. The company's refining capacity was nearly 50,000 barrels per day and the plant was extremely modern. Processing equipment included crude oil distillation, thermal cracking, fluid catalytic cracking, catalytic platforming, alkylation, and polymerization units. The equipment produced gasoline of a very high octane quality.

Products flexibility was an important aspect of Eastern States' operating success. Since it was economical for some large companies to even out their refinery yields over a long-term basis, a market was created for Eastern States to fill in the peak demands for various products by varying its refinery yields. The company's refinery was easily adapted to shifts in products yields because of the advanced refinery processes employed by the company.

Eastern States also tried, to the extent possible, to vary its sources of crude oil supply according to the seasonal demand for products. Since the posted prices of crude oils were not subject to seasonal variations, it was desirable to obtain a crude oil giving a high gasoline yield in the summer months and a crude oil having a high fuel oil yield in the winter months. The management doubted that major companies, in view of their long-term crude oil purchasing policies and obligations, were able to make use of selective purchasing in quite the same manner as Eastern States.

The Ashland Oil & Refining Company also adjusted its refinery yields rapidly to take advantage of short-term shifts in the prices of refined products. Refinery yields were planned in such a manner that the sales department could maximize sales realizations at all times. It required considerable refinery know-how to shift yields frequently, and Ashland's refinery superintendents were specially trained to alter refinery yields rapidly. Beyond shifting yields to capitalize on short-term market conditions,

Ashland also relied very heavily on its large products storage capacity to store those products on which a seasonal or longer-term price increase was expected.

A situation in 1949 serves as an excellent example of how the company adjusted refinery yields in accordance with market conditions. The price of heavy residual fuel oil, which Ashland sold largely to the steel industry, declined to less than half the market price of a year earlier. Ashland's principal refinery near Catlettsburg was so flexible that the yield of fuel oil was reduced to approximately 2% during the period of greatest oversupply. Partially as a result of this factor, Ashland's earnings from refinery operations suffered much less than those of the oil industry in general.[19]

Supplementing the Operations of the Large Companies:

An opportunity also exists for some small companies to meet the special needs of large, integrated companies. As noted in Chapter Fourteen, there were many reasons why large companies found it necessary and desirable to purchase a portion of their products requirements from other refiners. Among other things purchases were made because it was usually not possible to maintain a perfect balance between refining and marketing operations as facilities were expanded, to handle spot shortages, to meet seasonal variations in demand, to compensate for differences between product yields and market requirements, to take advantage of favorable buying opportunities, and to supply areas remote from their own refineries. While many of the reasons for which large companies have purchased products are of a temporary character, the large companies have provided an important market for certain small or substantially nonintegrated refining companies.

A group of substantially nonintegrated refiners with relatively large plants located along the Gulf Coast have specialized in supplying refined products to major companies. Refineries in this area have access to a broad geographic area for their products via economical transportation media. They can reach other Gulf Coast and Eastern seaboard destinations by tankers and inland points along the Mississippi

River and connecting waterways by barge. Furthermore, location of plant facilities along the Gulf Coast affords a wide range of alternative sources of crude oil supply to refiners dependent upon purchases for all or most of their requirements. The president of one nonintegrated company remarked, "It's not by accident that we're here. It's because of the different options it gives us in purchasing a crude supply. Domestically, there are coastal crudes and inland crudes moving to the Gulf Coast refining area. Furthermore, Venezuelan and Mexican crude can be depended upon as a buffer when the necessity arises." Other advantages offered by the Gulf Coast location are the comparatively cheap refinery fuel costs made possible by large supplies of natural gas, and the generally attractive heavy fuel oil markets offered by the shipping trade.

In the postwar period, some refiners in the Gulf Coast area found that the large, integrated companies provided at least a temporary means of averting the full impact of the rapid technological advancement taking place in the industry. Refineries without catalytic cracking facilities had large supplies of topped crude oil for which there was, at times, no ready fuel oil market at attractive prices. This heavy product was, however, convertible by catalytic cracking into gasoline and smaller amounts of fuel oil. Therefore, the practice developed whereby companies with catalytic cracking facilities in the area, primarily the large, integrated companies, purchased the topped crude as charging stocks for their catalytic cracking units. In so doing, the better equipped plants provided a market for a portion of a troublesome by-product manufactured by some of the noncatalytic cracking plants in the area.

Many inland refiners also sold large quantities of gasoline and some other products to major companies. These refiners were often able to capitalize on their geographically preferred position in reaching particular localized marketing areas. Major companies engaged in extensive distribution sometimes found it expedient to purchase from such companies over relatively extended time periods. For example, early in 1952 the Shallow Water Refinery Company was successful in negotiating long-range deals to supply two of the largest companies marketing in western Kansas. In addition, tem-

---

[19] See Ashland Oil & Refining Company, *Annual Report,* for year ending September 30, 1949.

porarily heavy market demands sometimes led large companies to rely on inland refineries as a supplemental source of products supply. The experience of the Wood River Oil and Refining Company in fulfilling such a demand has already been discussed in Chapter Twenty-Two.

VI. SUMMARY

1. Despite the existence of economic circumstances which are generally favorable to the growth and development of large integrated structures, there are many refining companies falling outside the large, integrated group which have fared very well in the industry. Our research indicated that an important aspect of the management job in such companies is the judicious selection of interstices or the particular fields of endeavor where the small refiner is either at an advantage or at no overriding disadvantage in competing with the large, integrated units. While the interstices summarized in the following paragraphs are by no means a comprehensive listing, they do illustrate some of the more important niches found by the small firms.

2. Geographic specialization is one of the most important niches exploited by small refining companies. The small refiners filling the territorial gaps in the industry are often in a position to supply the areas surrounding their plants at a marked transportation cost advantage over their competitors. Specialization by areas therefore sometimes grants the small firm a competitive edge which the large, integrated companies sometimes cannot overcome when they are compelled to move products from more distant sources of supply.

3. Specialization on raw materials is a second effective interstice sought out by some small refiners. A small refiner can sometimes, because of his very limited requirements, confine his supply of raw materials exclusively to desirable types and grades of crude oil which are comparatively scarce. Raw materials specialization permits some small companies using the less modern types of refinery equipment to obtain a higher quality gasoline product than would be available

from the general run of crude oils. Certain crude oils also lead easily to the development of specialty product lines such as asphalts, road oils, lubricating oils, and waxes. While highly selective crude oils are available to larger companies, the requirements of large companies are generally of such magnitude that they cannot base their operations entirely upon a narrow range of crude oils.

4. A very important interstice for small refiners is that achieved by concentrating on specialized products and markets. Some small refiners engage heavily in the production of one or more specialty products such as waxes, asphalts, road oils, and high-grade lubricating oils. The small companies are able to compete effectively with the large firms on these products because they devote a large share of management attention to what is often a small part of a large company's operation, or because they offer special services to customers which the large companies are unwilling or unable to provide. On gasoline, where the small refiners are at a disadvantage in the passenger car market because of the aggressive brand name programs of the large companies, the small firms sometimes select the market segments where brand names are of lesser importance. Typical market segments sought out by small refiners, largely on a price basis, are commercial and farm accounts.

5. The success of some small refining companies is due in large part to particular management skills which the firms are able to utilize effectively. One important specialized talent used to advantage by the principal executives of some small companies is technical proficiency. Technical know-how finds expression in the adaption of new refinery processes to the needs of the small firm, in maintaining high levels of efficiency at the refinery, and in the ability to adjust product yields rapidly in order to maximize sales realizations. No less important management skills are those which give some small companies an advantage in dealing with suppliers or customers.

6. The fulfillment of special market demand situations has also provided an attractive

opportunity for small companies. Some small refiners operate on an in and outer basis and thereby provide spare capacity to meet longer-run shifts in demand. Other small refiners shift their refinery yields frequently to take advantage of the short-term fluctua-

tions in the demand for various products. A third group of refiners, of which substantially nonintegrated firms on the Gulf Coast provide an excellent example, meet certain special product needs of the large, integrated companies.

PART FIVE

Summary and Conclusions

CHAPTER TWENTY-FOUR

The Growth and Development of Integrated Oil Companies

AT THE outset of this book we set three primary objectives for the study. The first objective was to find out what has prompted the extensive growth and development of large, integrated units in the oil industry. The second objective was to examine the processes by which the integrated structures have evolved and by which selected oil companies have acquired their distinguishing characteristics. The third objective was to determine what changes have taken place in the participation of small business at the refining level of the industry and why those changes have occurred. In this final chapter, we shall present a brief, summary statement of our general conclusions on each of these three matters.

I. THE ECONOMIC CLIMATE IN THE OIL INDUSTRY

Large, integrated units have gradually emerged as the predominant form of business organization in the oil industry because the economic climate in the industry has been generally favorable to the integration process for a long period of time. The experience of other industries provides ample evidence that vertical integration does not flourish and endure unless the underlying technological, economic, and business characteristics of an industry are favorable to it. In the oil industry the economic climate has been continually changing as the market has expanded and new circumstances have arisen, but on the whole the industry has remained, throughout most of its history, remarkably receptive to the integration process. The fact that the economic climate in the oil industry has been so favorable to vertical integration may be traced: (a) to certain general conditions which have been continually present in the industry, (b) to certain transitory conditions which have from time to time reinforced the general conditions, and (c) to a lack of serious obstacles to vertical integration.

The General Conditions Favorable to Vertical Integration:

The general conditions which have favored the growth and development of integrated oil companies have had their origin in three fundamental circumstances: the behavior of the profit opportunities at the different levels of the industry, the economic characteristics of the physical facilities which are used in the oil process, and the nature of the managerial job involved in planning and conducting oil industry activities.

Behavior of Profit Opportunities: The data examined in Chapters Five and Six provide strong evidence that the profit opportunities at the different levels of the oil industry have been continually fluctuating and that the movements at one level have frequently differed in both timing and direction from the movements at other levels. As a result, many of the important types of vertical integration have provided a means by which a company could do a great deal toward stabilizing its earnings experience. It is particularly important to note that the profit opportunities at the refining level of the industry, the central point in the oil process, have been extremely unstable, and that both forward and backward integration from the refining position have provided a very significant means by which greater stability could be secured.

Our research revealed that the causes of the

dissimilarities in the profit movements at the different levels of the oil industry have been to a considerable extent an inevitable corollary of our system of private enterprise and open competition. Among other things, the dissimilarities in profit movements have arisen because new capital does not flow uniformly and evenly into all phases of the business at all times, the prices of crude oil and refined products respond somewhat differently to changes in market conditions, demand-supply relationships at the successive levels of the industry are frequently somewhat different for short periods of time, there are differences in the mix of products handled at each level of the industry, and there are differences in the risks applicable to operations in the separate phases of the business.

The causes of the variations in profit opportunities have been of such a character that there has been little any individual firm could have done to gain protection from them except through vertical integration or through diversification into nonpetroleum activities. Moreover, the causes of the profit variations have been so numerous and so complex in their actions and interactions that it is difficult to imagine any means by which the profit variations might be removed from the industry. Even with extensive state or federal controls over such things as prices, capital expenditures, the selection of projects for investment, and entries to and exits from the industry (which would be highly undesirable from many standpoints), it is doubtful that the profit opportunities at the different levels of the industry could be held constant or compelled to move in unison.

As was pointed out in Chapter Five, the dissimilarities in profit opportunities at the different levels of the industry have not often been recognized explicitly by oil company managements as a reason for undertaking vertical integration programs. The various cases discussed throughout this book indicate that vertical integration moves have usually been viewed as a means of solving the problems or capitalizing on the opportunities of particular business situations. Once a company embarks on a program of vertical integration, however, it frequently gains in profit stability and is thereby enabled to plan and conduct its capital invest-

ment programs, its research programs, and many other aspects of its business on a more orderly and effective basis than might otherwise be the case. The dissimilarities in profit movements in the separate phases of the oil business have therefore constituted one of the important general conditions which have fostered the growth and survival of integrated companies.

In view of the character of the forces which underlie the dissimilarities in profit fluctuations in the separate phases of the business, there is every reason to suppose that such dissimilarities will characterize profit experience at the different levels of the industry for many years to come. It may be anticipated therefore that vertical integration will continue to constitute, as it has in the past, a significant means by which oil companies may realize the important economic values associated with increased stability of earnings.

Economic Characteristics of Physical Facilities: A second series of general conditions which has tended to create in the oil industry a climate favorable to vertical integration may be found in the economic characteristics of the physical facilities used in the oil process. Many of these facilities involve very large capital outlays, are highly specialized in terms of their economic utility, are extremely vulnerable to reductions in volume of throughput or output, and are heavily dependent for their competitive effectiveness upon supporting investments in other phases of the business. Investments in oil industry facilities have thus often been associated with a high degree of risk, and vertical integration has constituted one important means by which the risk might be reduced.

Consider, for example, the investment in a modern oil refinery. The capital outlay required in 1950 for a refinery of 20,000 barrels per day capacity, the average size of plant in the industry, was approximately $20,000,000. As was demonstrated in Chapter Twenty, substantial operating advantages were associated with larger plants ranging in size up to about 200,000 barrels per day capacity and requiring investments in excess of $100,000,000. An oil refinery has, however, a very limited economic utility. It can be used only for the processing of crude oil, and most of its output consists of a few standardized products. Moreover, the importance of inward and outward transportation costs is such that a refinery can draw crude oil and serve markets in only a relatively small geographic area.[1] The security of the large investment required for a refinery is therefore heavily dependent upon the continued competitive effectiveness of the plant *in* the petroleum industry and *in* a particular geographic area.

The continued competitive effectiveness of a refinery, in turn, rests heavily upon three things: maintenance of a high level of throughput, access to adequate supplies of crude oil at competitive prices, and satisfactory transportation arrangements for inward and outward shipments.[2] The maintenance of a high level of throughput is of crucial importance because processing costs per barrel may rise as much as 60% to 85% as the throughput falls from 100% to 50% of designed capacity/ (see Exhibit XX-5). Access to adequate supplies of crude oil at competitive prices is important because the cost of crude oil represents approximately 70% to 85% of the value of petroleum products, f.o.b. refinery (see Chapter Eight, page 232 and Exhibit VIII-2). Satisfactory crude oil and refined products transportation arrangements are important because transportation costs frequently represent as much as 25% of the delivered tank wagon prices for gasoline, the major petroleum product, and likewise a high proportion of the delivered tank car prices at which a refiner would normally sell to jobbers (see Exhibit VII-1). It is readily apparent therefore that the competitive effectiveness of a refinery is dependent not so much upon the managerial job done *inside* the refinery gate as it is upon the managerial job done *outside* the refinery gate to assure a high level of throughput, adequate crude oil supplies, and low-cost transportation service.

Vertical integration represents a means of reducing the risks associated with refinery investments because it serves to protect a refinery on the above matters: that is, on the

points where it has great competitive vulnerability. Integration forward into marketing activities constitutes one of the best means by which a refiner may guard against a forced reduction of throughput in times when the refined products markets are oversupplied, and backward integration into crude oil production constitutes one of the best means by which a refiner may be assured of adequate crude oil supplies at reasonable prices in times of crude oil shortages. Similarly, integration into transportation operations constitutes one of the best means by which a refiner may be assured of having the transportation facilities necessary to his situation. For example, once a refinery location has developed economic characteristics which permit or require the use of pipe lines to move crude oil inward, or refined products outward, a refiner often cannot afford to wait for the pipe line investments to be made by outside interests but must build the lines himself to keep his operations on a competitive basis.

The physical facilities used at other points in the oil process have in at least some degree the same general characteristics as do refinery facilities. Crude oil and refined products pipe lines require very large capital outlays, have a distinctly limited economic utility in terms of products carried, number of potential customers, and geographic area served, and are extremely vulnerable to reductions in throughput below designed operating capacity. Investments in pipe lines are therefore subject to significant risks which may be modified by ownership or control of the facilities lying at the two ends of the lines.

Individual marketing facilities usually require much smaller investments than do refineries and pipe lines, and the need to protect them with supporting investments in other phases of the business has generally been less than in the case of refineries and pipe lines. At the same time, however, marketing facilities are like refineries and pipe lines in the sense that they have a very limited economic utility and cost characteristics which make them vulnerable to reductions in the volume of business handled. Investors contemplating commitments in the larger marketing facilities therefore, such as pipe line and marine terminals, are often under considerable compulsion to assure their

---

[1] Refineries at tidewater locations would, of course, have greater options with respect to sources of crude oil and market outlets than would inland refineries.

[2] It is also highly important that the plant itself be kept abreast of technological advances in refining techniques. This point will be discussed later in the chapter.

sources of supply and their transportation service through various types of integration arrangements. Moreover, a marketing venture which involves the development of a brand name and the construction of bulk plants and service stations over a wide geographic area requires substantial capital outlays and is an extremely risky matter unless steps have been taken to assure adequate supplies of refined products at prices which will permit effective competition.

The investments required for the discovery and development of producing properties may be very small or very large, depending on the situation. The producing facilities are, in nearly all cases, highly specialized in the sense that they can supply only one product to one market. Moreover, since the costs of lifting oil are usually very small compared with those involved in finding and developing the properties, investments in crude oil production, like investments in refineries and pipe lines, are very vulnerable to any forced curtailment in output. As was noted in Chapter Four, before the development of the prorationing laws, producers were often under compulsion to undertake forward integration programs to protect their producing operations in times of crude oil surplus. In the United States since 1935 the prorationing laws have served to place the integrated and nonintegrated producer on approximately equal terms with respect to their ability to sell their output. Investors making large commitments in the development of new producing areas, however, are frequently under pressure to build pipe lines, refineries, or market outlets as a means of assuring recovery of their capital outlay in the producing business.

There is every reason to suppose that in the future the plant facilities used in the oil process will retain much the same economic characteristics they have had in the past. Indeed, the available evidence seems to indicate that plant facilities at all levels of the industry are becoming increasingly costly, increasingly specialized, and increasingly vulnerable to interruptions or curtailments in the volume at which they are designed to operate. It seems reasonable to conclude therefore that the economic characteristics of petroleum plant facilities will continue to constitute general conditions favorable to the integration process.

Nature of the Managerial Job: A third set of general conditions favorable to the growth and development of integrated companies has arisen from the character of the managerial job involved in planning and conducting oil industry activities. The nature of the managerial job has been such that important benefits have been available to the companies which were successful in developing integrated structures, together with sound techniques for administering their affairs on an integrated basis.

As was suggested by the discussion in the above paragraphs, the economic utility and competitive effectiveness of plant investments in the oil industry is often heavily dependent upon corollary investments in other phases of the business. When plant investments are being made by a series of nonintegrated companies operating at different levels of the industry, it is often very difficult to insure that the investments will be properly correlated time-wise, place-wise, and size-wise with respect to each other. Any single investment may therefore be placed in jeopardy or have its competitive effectiveness impaired through the failure of firms operating at other levels to make the necessary supporting investments at the proper times and in the proper places.

In an integrated company, management has the opportunity (which it may or may not exercise effectively) to plan capital investments on a coordinated basis and in such a manner that the commitments made at one level of the business will support and complement those made at other levels. In other words, an integrated company can, if its management is successful in operating on an integrated basis, do a more effective job of regulating and controlling the flow of capital funds into the business than can nonintegrated companies.

A second very important aspect of the managerial job in the oil industry is that of handling the logistical problems associated with the producing, refining, and distribution processes. These logistical problems are complicated by the seasonal characteristics of the demand for many petroleum products, the difficulties involved in predicting weather conditions and their effect on the consumption of heating oils, and the fact that there are very definite upper limits on the amount of crude oil and refined products which the storage facilities of the industry will accommodate at any given time. The management of an integrated company is in a position to have an intimate knowledge of activities at all levels of the business and can thus often do a more effective job of handling the problems of logistical planning and of adjusting operating programs to shifts and changes in market conditions than can the management of a nonintegrated company.

As noted in Chapter Eleven, for example, an integrated company can often make very effective use of inventory programs to offset the seasonal variations in the demand for petroleum products. The strategic use of inventories frequently makes it possible to secure more uniform crude oil runs, refinery yields, and transportation requirements and thereby permits important savings in operating and investment costs. Nonintegrated firms have difficulty in making equally effective use of seasonal inventories because they incur more risks in the building of seasonal stocks, often have their logistical plans disrupted by the efforts of their customers to anticipate changes in market prices, and are not in an equally good position to level out transportation requirements by accumulating inventories at storage points throughout their market territories.

A third important aspect of the managerial job in the oil industry is that of continually searching out capital investment opportunities which will yield a high rate of return relative to the business risks attendant thereon. In Chapter Eleven, attention was directed to the fact that an integrated company, by virtue of having activities in several different phases of the business, may frequently have a wider selection of favorable investment opportunities open to it than would be available to a nonintegrated company. In other words, an integrated company is often in a position to enhance the gains or reduce the risks associated with particular projects and can thus make certain types of investments which would appear unattractive to firms operating at only one level of the industry. By making a number of such investments over a long period of time, some of the integrated companies have been able to reduce their over-all operating costs, increase their competitive strength, and raise the level of the return earned on the capital funds at their disposal.

The foregoing and other characteristics of the managerial job which permit a company to realize gains through managing on an integrated basis show every evidence of continuing into the future. It is, in fact, reasonable to suppose that as the activities of the oil industry increase in size and complexity both at home and abroad, the managerial and operational gains made available by vertical integration to the management that has the wisdom, skill, and resources to take advantage of them will become increasingly important as general conditions favorable to vertical integration.

The Transitory Conditions Favorable to Vertical Integration:

The general conditions favorable to vertical integration in the oil industry have been reinforced by a continuing series of transitory conditions which have provided strong stimuli to the integration process during limited periods of time. These transitory conditions have arisen from the economic, legal, and political circumstances prevailing at given stages in the industry's history and have later disappeared from the scene or become of little consequence as new circumstances have developed. The continual emergence of new and different transitory conditions to replace those of earlier periods has been fully as significant in creating an economic climate favorable to vertical integration as the general conditions discussed in the preceding section.

Some of the more important of the transitory conditions which have fostered the growth and development of integrated oil companies are immediately apparent from a backward glance over the history of the industry. In the period before 1911 the existence of the Standard Oil Trust and its successor organizations constituted a stimulus to vertical integration on the part of smaller competitors. It will be recalled from the discussion in Chapter Three that the Gulf Oil Corporation as well as certain other strong independents undertook their early vertical integration programs as a means of escaping the dominance of the Standard Oil group and as a means of competing effectively with it. The significance of the Standard Oil group as a motivation for integration on the part of other firms was, of course, removed from the industry by the dissolution decree of 1911.

In the period from about 1911 to 1920 there were two important transitory conditions favorable to vertical integration. The first was the rapid development of the automobile and the correspondingly rapid growth in the demand for gasoline. As noted in Chapter Nine, the sudden emergence of the new market created a pressing need for the establishment of an entire new system of distribution facilities. Many refiners therefore integrated forward into marketing operations as a means of providing the market outlets necessary to the distribution of their gasoline and as a means of capitalizing on the profit opportunities which the new market presented.

The second transitory condition motivating vertical integration in the period 1911–1920 was World War I and the shortages of all petroleum products which were occasioned as a result thereof. During the war period, for example, both the Standard Oil Company (Indiana) and The Atlantic Refining Company were prompted to initiate crude oil producing activities as a means of assuring adequate crude oil supplies for their refining and marketing activities. It is significant that the rapid development of the automobile gasoline market created a temporary condition favorable to forward integration whereas the shortages of World War I created a temporary condition favorable to backward integration.

The period 1920–1935 witnessed the emergence of one of the most powerful transitory conditions favorable to vertical integration which the industry has ever experienced. The great crude oil supplies which were brought into existence during this period, largely as a result of fortuitous discoveries, fostered much new competition at the producing level of the industry and caused many crude oil producers to integrate forward into refining, marketing, and transportation activities as a means of securing and assuring an outlet for their production. The forward integration moves of the crude oil producers in turn, impelled established refiners and marketers to undertake various types of integration as a means of guarding their outlets from capture by newcomers to the market. Finally, the generally intense competitive conditions of the time prompted many companies to experiment with various types of integration in an effort to reduce their costs and improve their operating efficiency.

The large crude oil supplies were brought under control by the development of the conservation laws during the middle 1930's, and since that time there has been much less reason for a crude oil producer to integrate forward than there was in earlier years. The conservation laws in their turn, however, created a new condition favorable to vertical integration which still exists. As was noted from the experience of The Atlantic Refining Company and the Standard Oil Company (Ohio) in Chapter Eight, the conservation laws served to remove many of the opportunities which the refiner previously had had to buy crude oil at distress prices but did not protect him from the necessity of paying high prices in times of shortages. The conservation laws have thus been interpreted by the managements of some refining companies as a new, general condition favorable to backward integration.

World War II brought into being at least two important temporary conditions favorable to backward integration into crude oil production. The first was the enactment of the excess profits tax which, along with many other circumstances, was important in prompting the Standard Oil Company (Ohio) to embark on a major crude oil producing program in 1942 and which undoubtedly led many other companies to make larger commitments in crude oil production than might otherwise have been the case. As pointed out in Chapter Eight, the tax provisions for expensing intangible drilling costs are such that a company can expand its producing operations on a very favorable basis at times when it is exposed to high tax rates. In addition, the general inflationary forces at work during the war period suggested to some managements, notably that of The Atlantic Refining Company, the desirability of investing capital funds in crude oil producing properties as a hedge against a long-run depreciation in the value of the dollar.

The postwar period 1945–1950 likewise witnessed the development of at least two transitory conditions favorable to vertical integration. The very great expansion which took place in the demand for many petroleum products in the immediate postwar period created severe shortages for both crude oil and refined products which persisted until about 1949. These shortages prompted both refiners and marketers to integrate backward as a means of securing and protecting their sources of supply. Examples may be found in the backward integration programs of the farm cooperatives which were discussed in Chapter Nine. A second development in the postwar period which fostered forward integration programs by refining companies was the rapid growth in the use of the middle distillates for heating purposes. The development of the new heating oil markets created a profit opportunity which led many companies to establish terminal and bulk plant facilities for the distribution of distillates, to engage in burner sale and maintenance activities, and to participate in truck deliveries to the homes of consumers.

It is difficult to foretell the extent to which new transitory conditions such as those discussed above may continue to appear in the future. It seems reasonable to suppose, however, that as long as the industry remains free of government controls and retains its competitive characteristics, there will be a continuing series of transitory conditions appearing on the scene from time to time to reinforce the general conditions favorable to the growth and development of integrated companies.

The Absence of Serious Obstacles to Vertical Integration:

The presence of both general and transitory conditions favorable to vertical integration is not fully sufficient to explain the strong receptivity of the oil industry to the integration process. Many examples may be found of other industries in which the business and economic reasons for vertical integration have been almost as persistent and powerful as in the oil industry but in which relatively little vertical integration has ever taken place. Examination of these other industries reveals that they have usually been characterized by major obstacles to vertical integration which have not been present in equal degree in the oil industry. It appears therefore that the integration process has flourished and endured in the oil industry, not only because there have been continuing strong motivations for vertical integration, but

likewise because there have been relatively few serious obstacles to vertical integration.

The point may be illustrated by brief consideration of the forces for and against vertical integration in the cotton textile industry as contrasted with those found in the oil industry. Vertical integration has occasionally taken place in the cotton textile industry, but it has never developed as a dominant form of business organization to anywhere near the extent that it has in the oil industry. As was pointed out in Chapter One, the distinction between integrated and nonintegrated companies is a matter of degree, and there are an infinite number of fine gradations on the scale between the two extremes. So too it is in the case of industries, and if the oil industry lies toward one end of the scale, it is certainly true that the cotton textile industry lies well toward the other end.

The failure of the integration process to develop more strongly in the cotton textile industry cannot be attributed in any major degree to a lack of motivations for vertical integration. The cotton textile companies have faced many chronic problems, not unlike those from time to time confronting the oil companies, which have strongly suggested the desirability of further vertical integration. Among other things, vertical integration has offered cotton textile companies opportunities: (a) to stabilize gross margins and net profits in much the same manner as in the oil industry, (b) to achieve a better correlation of production to demand throughout the process and thereby to reduce the inventory maladjustments which have been a continuing problem of the industry, (c) to achieve important and necessary gains in the coordination of manufacturing, merchandising, and selling activities in order to meet the product requirements of customers more efficiently, (d) to reduce the excessive buying, selling, and handling costs arising from the transfer of products through the many levels of the industry, (e) to protect a mill's market connections in times of abundant supply, which have been fully as frequent in the textile as in the oil industry, and (f) to guard against sudden, adverse fluctuations in the prices at which a mill obtains its raw cotton supplies.

The gains to be realized from vertical integration in the cotton textile industry have long been recognized by economists and industry leaders,[3] and over the years textile companies have engaged in considerable experimentation with various types of integration arrangements.[4] Except in the case of certain products and except during certain time periods, however, these integration ventures have not been particularly successful. For the most part, and certainly in the field of highly styled merchandise, the integrated structures have failed to stand the test of competition and have been replaced with other arrangements.

The fact that the cotton textile industry has not been more receptive to the integration process may be traced to a number of circumstances. In the first place, integration by all types of textile companies into transportation activities has been restrained by the fact that the industry uses multipurpose transportation facilities which are dependent for economical operation upon the handling of a wide variety of shipments for many different customers. In the case of most railroads, textile products account for only a very tiny fraction of the total traffic, and a textile company integrating into railroad operations would obviously represent an extreme case of "the tail wagging the dog."

Forward integration into retail operations from any earlier position in the cotton textile process has been restrained by the fact that the great majority of the textile products are sold in multiproduct outlets, such as department stores and dry goods stores, where many other items are handled. Even the specialty clothing stores usually carry a wide line of accessories and, in addition, must offer their customers a far wider variety of fabrics and styles than any one textile mill or cutting and sewing plant

could hope to produce on an economical basis. As a result, forward integration into retail activities from any earlier position in the industry has usually meant extensive purchasing operations and entrance into many new lines of business which would tend to dwarf the original textile operation. The same general considerations apply with respect to forward integration by textile companies into wholesaling activities.

Forward integration by cotton growers into textile mill operations and backward integration by textile mills into cotton growing has been retarded by certain characteristics of cotton and the cotton growing process. Cotton is grown and prepared for market in a very large number of different staple lengths, grades, and varieties. The output from any one growing area normally falls into several different categories and may vary considerably from one year to the next depending on crop conditions. A spinning and weaving mill, however, ordinarily runs only one or two different types of cotton and may, in fact, purchase and blend cotton from several different sources in order to assure uniformity in its supplies. As a result, the normal cotton plantation can serve more effectively as a partial source of supply for the industry as a whole than it could as an exclusive source of supply for a single mill or for the small group of mills which might reasonably be brought under one management. Conversely, a textile mill can scarcely afford to place reliance on the output of any single farm area and can usually best assure its raw cotton supply by remaining free to buy from whatever source may offer the best supply of the particular grade the mill needs in a particular crop year.

A general obstacle to integration of the various manufacturing and distribution activities between the spinning and weaving and cutting and sewing operations arises from the fact that as cotton fabrics leave the mills they tend to fan out into a large number of different markets, many of which are susceptible to the influence of constantly changing fashions and require that a wide variety of items be offered for the customer's selection. Forward integration by a textile mill has thus often meant the assumption of style risks and the performance of many intricate merchandising functions which

---

[3] For a few examples see C. T. Murchison, "Requisites of Stabilization in the Cotton Textile Industry," *The American Economic Review*, Vol. XXIII, No. 1, Supplement, March 1933, p. 78; M. T. Copeland and E. P. Learned, *Merchandising of Cotton Textiles, Methods and Organization*, Business Research Studies No. 1, Division of Research, Harvard Business School, 1933; Royal Little, "Vertical Integration," abstract of a paper read before the National Textile Seminar, appearing in *Textile Industries*, June 1947, p. 80; and U. S. 80th Congress, 1st Session, *Hearings Before Subcommittee No. 2 of the House Committee on the Judiciary on H. R. 515, A Bill to Amend Sections 7 and 11 of the Clayton Act*, March and April 1947, Testimony of C. T. Murchison, President of the Cotton Textile Institute, p. 224.

[4] See H. S. Davis, G. W. Taylor, C. C. Balderston, and A. Bezanson, *Vertical Integration in the Textile Industries*, Industrial Research Department, Wharton School of Finance and Commerce and The Textile Foundation, Inc., Washington, D. C., 1938.

can often be handled better by specialists who are in a position to devote their full attention to the demand characteristics of individual markets. Conversely, since textile mills and finishing plants must for technological reasons restrict their operations to a relatively small number of different fabrics, backward integration by a cutting and sewing plant has often meant a loss in the plant's freedom to obtain the variety of different fabrics which may be required by its merchandising program. Moreover, all integrated companies operating in the field of highly styled garments may suffer competitive disadvantages because they span a long manufacturing cycle and are forced to make their decisions on style further in advance of the selling seasons than are nonintegrated concerns.

A final important obstacle to vertical integration by textile companies of all types has been the lack of financial resources to support integration programs. For at least the last quarter of a century, with the exception of World War II, the textile business has been expanding at a fairly slow rate, ample mill capacity has been present, and profits have been low relative to those available in other industries. The textile industry has, in fact, long been regarded as one of the "sick" industries in our industrial economy. The textile companies have thus not had ready access to the capital necessary for integration moves, even if they had desired to make them.

It is immediately apparent that most of the obstacles to integration in the cotton textile industry, cited above, have not been present in any significant degree in the oil industry. The crude oil and products pipe lines are unipurpose facilities, and the investment opportunity which they provide has not been particularly attractive to entrepreneurs not already engaged in the oil business. The distribution of gasoline, the principal product of the industry, has not involved the use of multipurpose retail and wholesale outlets to anywhere near the same degree as has the distribution of textile products. The modern service station has developed as a specialized outlet to serve the automobile trade. The customer does not demand a wide variety of gasoline from which to choose, and a service station can very easily draw its entire supply from a single, small refinery.

Similarly, the fact that the petroleum bulk plants characteristically handle only a narrow range of closely related products has made it easier for a refiner than for a textile firm to engage in wholesaling activities.

Crude oil, like cotton, is subject to many variations in type and grade, but it is nonetheless possible to run a refinery on the output of a single field, or even a single well, as long as the oil continues to flow. Backward integration therefore has constituted a more practical solution to the raw material supply problems of a refiner than it has to the raw material supply problems of a textile mill. Multiplicity of markets and the requirements of variety and style, which are among the most important obstacles to integration in the cotton textile industry, are not present in any important degree in the oil industry. A modern refinery may make as many as 2,000 different end products, but the great bulk of the refinery output stays in a few well-defined markets. Moreover, these markets do not require a wide variety of products, with the possible exception of the lube oil and tire, battery, and accessory markets, and fashions and styles are of negligible significance.

Finally, the oil companies have been living, for the most part, in a rapidly expanding economy and profits have generally been good, or at least certainly better than they have been in the cotton textile industry. The oil companies have thus been able to generate a large part of the capital required for integration and have had fairly easy access to outside capital when it was necessary.

Examination of other nonintegrated industries reveals a situation similar to that existing in the cotton textile industry. In other words, these industries have had many of the same motivations for integration as in the oil industry but have been characterized by major obstacles to integration which have not been present in the oil industry, or at least not in equal degree. It seems reasonable to conclude therefore that the receptivity of the oil industry to the integration process may be attributed fully as much to the lack of serious obstacles to integration as to the presence of strong motivations for integration.

It should not be inferred from the above discussion, however, that obstacles to integration have been *completely* absent from the oil industry. Such obstacles have from time to time appeared and have served to impede or reverse the integration process in precisely the same manner as in other industries. It will be recalled that refiners made little attempt to integrate forward into retail activities as long as the principal product of the industry was kerosene, an item which could best be distributed through multipurpose outlets. Similarly, the oil companies did not integrate into railroad transportation activities, beyond the ownership or leasing of tank cars, in the years before 1931 when refined products were moving from refineries to markets largely by rail. It was only after the products pipe line, a new, unipurpose facility offering important cost advantages, became available that a major movement toward integration into refined products transportation activities took place. It will also be recalled from Chapter Ten that the leasing out of company service stations took place fairly promptly in most companies after obstacles to forward integration appeared in the form of chain store taxes, wage and hour legislation, and the administrative difficulties involved in adapting pricing practices and working hours to the competitive necessities of local situations.

In the final analysis it appears that the nature and extent of vertical integration in an industry are inevitably controlled by the long-run balance of business and economic forces for and against the integration process. When the gains to be made from vertical integration outweigh the obstacles to it, many integration steps may be taken. On the other hand, when the balance of business and economic forces is unfavorable to vertical integration, such steps are rarely taken, and companies may, in fact, abandon integration arrangements that were made to meet the conditions of an earlier period. In the cotton textile and other nonintegrated industries, the balance has characteristically been about even or slightly negative, and relatively little vertical integration has ever taken place. In the oil industry, the balance has shifted and changed from time to time but has generally been favorable to the integration process. As a result, the oil companies have frequently found vertical integration to be a good solution to the management problems they have faced, and vertically integrated structures have gradually emerged as the predominant form of business organization in the industry.

II. THE FORMATION AND ALTERATION OF INTEGRATION PATTERNS

The second major purpose of our study was to examine the process by which integration patterns are formed and altered. Our general conclusion is that the process may be defined as a continuing series of changes or steps by which oil corporations have adapted themselves to the particular economic environment prevailing in the oil industry.

The process is closely akin to that which may be found at work throughout the entire world of living organisms. It has long been established in scientific fact and theory that living organisms are continually making a progressive adaptation to the physical environments in which they exist. As new conditions emerge, organisms which fail to make the necessary adaptations inevitably suffer a competitive disadvantage in nature's struggle for survival and, in some cases, gradually become extinct. So, too, it is in the economic world, and business corporations must continually alter their structures and seek new adaptations to the realities of their surroundings, if they are to remain strong and vigorous and able to withstand the relentless pressure of business competition.

Our examination of the structures of seven major oil companies and the manner in which they have evolved led us to a number of conclusions with regard to the underlying characteristics of the process by which integration patterns are formed and altered in the oil industry. These conclusions we shall summarize in the paragraphs which follow:

Our first conclusion is that the forces and circumstances which influence the formation of integration patterns are multitudinous. They include, among other things, investment, cost, and profit considerations; competitive pressures; changes in economic, legal, and political conditions; managerial personalities; historical and accidental developments; changes in markets and products; and new technological developments. Some of these forces and circumstances are conditions of the general environment in the oil industry and apply in at least some degree to nearly all oil companies, while others are more specialized and may relate to only a single company and its particular operating situation. At any given moment therefore, the particular combination of general and specific forces to which any one company is responsive may be somewhat different from the combinations to which other companies are responsive.

Our second conclusion is that the formation and alteration of integration patterns is a continuing process; it has been going on throughout the entire course of the industry's history and will probably continue for an indefinite period into the future. All the available evidence indicates that the oil companies have not been and are not moving toward any particular "integrated state" which, once having achieved, they will retain as a permanent form of organization. The patterns of the seven companies we studied have undergone many important changes and have rarely remained constant for any sustained period of time. As noted in the first section of the chapter, new motivations for and obstacles to integration are continually appearing and disappearing from the scene, and the parameters of the integration problem are thus constantly changing. It appears probable therefore that the integration patterns of the oil companies will remain, as in the past, fluid in character and subject to continual rearrangement as the company managements seek the optimum responses to new conditions.

Our third conclusion, which follows almost as a corollary of the second, is that the formation of integration patterns is a two-directional process involving both integration and disintegration. It will be recalled from the discussion and data in Chapter Twelve that the changes which the seven companies studied have been making in their producing, refining, transportation, and marketing arrangements have involved both increases and decreases in the depth, extent, and intensity of integration. Moreover, as was noted in Chapter Ten, there have occasionally been industry-wide developments, such as the leasing-out of service stations in the middle 1930's, which have brought about a general reduction in the amount of vertical integration present in the industry.

Since the economic climate in the oil industry has been generally favorable to the integration process, integration actions have been more common in the practice of individual companies than have disintegration actions. As a result, many oil companies have tended to develop basic structures which represent a fairly advanced form of vertical integration. These companies are, however, continually modifying the boundaries of their operations and are sometimes advancing and sometimes retreating in terms of the depth, extent, and intensity of integration involved in their activities.

Our fourth conclusion is that managerial action with respect to the formation of integration patterns is ordinarily taken in two related but very different kinds of ways. In the first place, the management of an integrated oil company usually has certain general policies with regard to the balance which should be maintained among its operations in various phases of the business and with regard to the kind of structure which will maximize competitive strength and earning power and minimize the business risks to which a company is exposed. Although these general policies are often fragmentary and loosely defined, they inevitably have a continuing general influence on the manner in which a company's integration pattern evolves.

The second way in which managerial action is taken with respect to the formation of integration patterns is through the day-to-day decisions which the executives make on individual business problems involving integration arrangements. To a considerable extent, a company's integration pattern at any given moment simply represents the net solution of the whole matrix of business problems which the management has faced prior to that time. Day-to-day decisions are, of course, frequently made in the light of long-run policies and long-run policies are inevitably formulated in the light of what is learned from handling day-to-day problems. On the whole, however, we gathered the impression that the integration patterns of the companies we studied were shaped somewhat more by the individual decisions made on the continuing series of day-to-day problems than they were by general management strategies.

Our fifth conclusion is that the formation of integration patterns in the oil industry has been characterized by a high degree of individualism. Just as any given physical environment fosters the growth and development of many different species of plant and animal life, so, too, has the oil industry fostered the growth and development of many different types of integrated structures. The records of the companies we studied indicate conclusively that there have always been many different integration arrangements in the oil industry which would permit profitable operation and effective competition.

Since the oil companies have all been operating in essentially the same economic environment, their patterns of growth and development have inevitably had many common characteristics. At the same time, however, it is abundantly clear that individual companies have frequently followed integration programs which were markedly dissimilar in either or both timing and direction. Moreover, when two or more companies have taken the same action at about the same time, it has often been for very different reasons. It appears therefore that the formation of integration patterns is fundamentally a process of progressive adaptation by which *individual companies* work out the particular structures best suited to their *own particular* external and internal situations.

Our final and perhaps most important conclusion is that the formation and alteration of integration patterns is a manifestation of the working of competition in the oil industry. As was noted in Chapter Seventeen, many integration actions are initiated as a means of reducing costs and increasing a company's competitive effectiveness. Conversely, many integration actions are initiated as a means of protecting a company's business against the onslaughts of competitors. Moreover, it is apparent that if profits were easily won and competition generally soft in the oil industry, there would be no particular reason for a company to alter continually its integration arrangements. As in the world of living organisms, changes in structure are most likely to occur when and where the struggle for survival is most intense. In our judgment therefore the degree of fluidity found in the integration patterns of the major oil companies is one excellent measure of the general intensity of competition in the industry.

III. The Participation of the Small Refiner in the Oil Industry

The third purpose of our research was to find out what changes have taken place in the activities of the small and substantially nonintegrated refiners as the integration process has gone forward in the oil industry and to determine why those changes have occurred. Our general conclusion is that over the past 30 years there has been a gradual contraction in the proportionate participation of the small and substantially nonintegrated refiners in the affairs of the oil industry. The change has been an appropriate and natural part of the evolution of the industry and could have been avoided only by placing strong, artificial restraints on the economic, technological, and competitive forces at work in the industry. The entire industry and the structures of individual companies in it have, however, been evolving in such a way that there are many promising fields of endeavor still open to the small refiner which will, in all probability, continue in existence for many years to come.

The Nature of the Changes:

The changes which have taken place in the activities of the small refiners were summarized in Chapter Eighteen. The most important fact established by our research was that in the period 1920–1950 the proportionate share of the industry's refining capacity held by small firms declined from about 28% to 15% of the total. The available evidence indicates that the small refiners suffered about two-thirds of their proportionate loss in position between 1925 and 1930 and about one-third between 1940 and 1950. Since the plants of the small refiners have characteristically operated at lower levels of capacity than have those of the larger companies, the share of the industry's activities conducted by the small refiners was probably less throughout the 30-year period than might be suggested by their plant capacities.

A second fact established by our data was that the small refiners have not kept pace with the large refiners in increasing the average size of their plants or in the installation of technologically improved facilities. In the period 1920–1950 the average size of the plants of the small refiners increased about 190% whereas the average size of the plants of the large companies increased about 245%. During the period of 1935–1950, the small refiners increased their share of the industry's cracking facilities, but they nonetheless owned a consistently smaller proportion of cracking facilities than they did of total refining capacity. Moreover, such cracking facilities as the small refiners did have were frequently of the thermal cracking type rather than of the newer, catalytic cracking type. As will be noted below, the failure of the small firms to increase the average size of their plants and to install new processing techniques in pace with the large firms was important because it undoubtedly impaired their competitive efficiency.

We also observed that the structure of the oil industry has been evolving in such a way that the small refiner has not developed close functional relationships with large firms to anywhere near the same degree as have small firms in other branches of the business. Small producers supply a very large share of the crude oil requirements of large companies and, in addition, continually participate with the large companies in various types of joint exploratory activities as described in Chapter Thirteen. Similarly, small marketers are responsible for both the wholesale and retail distribution of a substantial share of the refined products output of the large companies and have a definite place in the marketing strategy of the large companies. The small refiners, on the other hand, supply only a very small part of the products requirements of the large companies and have no really significant place in their operating programs.

Why the Changes Have Occurred:

Just as the growth and development of integrated oil companies has been a process of progressive adaptation on the part of the companies to the conditions of their economic environment, so too the decline in the participation of the small refiner in the affairs of the industry has been a product of changing economic and competitive conditions. In our judgment, it would be folly to think in terms of holding constant the position of small business in any one industry or, more particularly, in any one compartment of an industry. The

participation of small business should be expected to undergo change as an industry grows, new conditions develop, and the techniques of management advance. In our opinion therefore it is a matter of no great consequence that the small and substantially nonintegrated refiners should occupy a less prominent position in the affairs of the industry than they did 30 years ago; the important question is why did the changes occur?

Our first conclusion is that the decline in the proportionate participation of the small refiner may be attributed in large measure to the continued, rapid technological progress which has so long characterized the refining industry. The advances in refining technology have continually made available equipment which would permit improved product yields, higher quality products, and lower operating costs for particular operations. The superiority of the modern plants, together with certain economies of large size, has created a continuing and growing need for the refiner to reinvest large sums of money in plant facilities in order to maintain his operations on a competitive basis. The small refiner, like the small firm in many other industries, has often not had as ready access to large sums of new capital as have had the larger firms. Moreover, many small refiners as a matter of personal option have elected to withdraw the earnings of their businesses for personal use in lieu of plowing the funds back into new equipment. It has therefore been inevitable that a decline in the proportionate position of the small refiner should have gone hand in hand with the advance of refining technology.

A second major circumstance which contributed to the decline in the proportionate participation of the small refiner between 1920 and 1950 was the change which took place in the character of crude oil producing activities after the adoption of the conservation laws in the middle 1930's. In the period from about 1920 to 1935, it was a fairly frequent occurrence for major crude oil discoveries, coupled with the rapid development which took place under the rule of capture, to generate large quantities of cheap crude oil in local areas for limited periods of time. These abundant supplies of cheap crude oil created a fertile field of opportunity for the growth of small refining companies. The small refiners often went out of existence as a field passed beyond its period of flush production, but new discoveries elsewhere continually brought new crops of small refiners into existence.

The development of the conservation laws in the middle 1930's provided a means by which new oil fields could be developed in a more orderly manner, and since the adoption of the laws, the discovery and development of new fields have not often generated large, temporary supplies of cheap crude oil in local areas. The development of laws and engineering practices to conserve our natural resources has thus had the inevitable consequence, and properly so, of restricting one particular type of business opportunity for small refining ventures.

A third circumstance which contributed to the decline in the proportionate participation of the small refiner in the period 1920–1950 was the general success which has attended the vertical form of organization. As noted above, the oil industry has long been characterized by an economic climate favorable to vertical integration, and many companies have thus found vertical integration to be an effective means of dealing with the particular set of business risks and economic hazards associated with oil industry operations. Vertical integration has, for example, provided refining companies with a means of offsetting the violent fluctuations in profits associated with the refining business and with a means of realizing important managerial and operational gains.

Small firms have lagged behind the large companies in undertaking vertical integration for the same reasons that they have lagged behind in adopting new technological developments; that is, because they did not have ready access to the large amounts of capital which vertical integration required or because they elected to withdraw a relatively large share of their earnings from the business for personal use.[5] It is readily understandable therefore

that over the long run the large companies, which were financially able and willing to undertake integration when and where it could be used to advantage, should have gradually increased their proportionate share of the refining business at the expense of the small and substantially nonintegrated firms.

Finally, the decline in the proportionate position of the small refiners must be ascribed in large measure to the continuing pressure of competition in the oil industry. Had competition in the oil industry been generally weak and ineffective, the small refiners would have suffered no particular hardship from their tardiness in adopting new technological developments, the loss of the abundant supplies of cheap crude oil associated with the discovery of new oil fields, or their failure to make use of vertical integration to the same degree as did their larger competitors. Economic and technological circumstances, such as those discussed in the preceding paragraphs, compel adjustments in industry and corporate structures only when the pressure of competition is sufficiently strong to overcome the natural inertia which is associated in some degree with any human endeavor. Just as we hold the fluidity of integration patterns to be a measure of the intensity of competition in the oil industry, so, too, do we therefore hold the changes in the participation of the small refiners to be a manifestation of the working of effective competition.

The Continuing Opportunities for the Small Refiner:

Notwithstanding the decline which has taken place in the proportionate participation of the small refiners, there still remain many places in the industry where such firms can compete effectively and earn high rates of return on their capital investments. Moreover, the available evidence indicates that there is ample opportunity at the refining level of the industry for new firms to enter the business and to grow and prosper with either integrated or nonintegrated structures, *provided* that they select business situations which are well suited to the managerial and financial resources at their command.

In the first place, there are many situations in which the small refiner can operate success-

---

[5] It will be recalled from the data in Chapter Two that whereas the small refining companies had both integrated and nonintegrated structures in 1950, the large firms were exclusively of the integrated type. Moreover, the small integrated refining firms frequently did not conduct operations at each principal operating level of the industry nor did they typically engage in nonrefining activities to the same extent as did the larger companies, except possibly in the case of marketing.

fully in direct competition with much larger firms. Although the small refiner has certain inherent disadvantages associated with the size and type of his equipment, he can often obtain a combination of processing costs, product yields, and product quality which will permit him to earn a return on investment comparable with that of larger firms by virtue of his ability to hold his investment costs and certain of his operating costs, particularly indirect labor costs and fringe benefits, at lower levels than can the larger firms (see Chapter Twenty). Moreover, there are certain areas of the market in which petroleum products are sold largely on the basis of specifications and price; in these markets the small refiner is under no handicap from his inability to finance the building of a brand name or the construction of large chains of modern, attractive service stations. It may also be observed that the small refiner does not carry, to the same degree as do the larger firms, the responsibility for seeing that the public and the government services are adequately supplied with all types of petroleum products under all types of circumstances. As a result, the small refiner often has more freedom than do the large firms to take advantage of transient market conditions through suitable adjustments in product yields and prices.

Our research revealed that small refiners have been particularly successful when they have elected to operate in specialized segments of the market which are of relatively little interest to the large firms or in which the large firms are ill-equipped to compete. Some small refiners have done extremely well, for example, by confining their operations to isolated geographic areas which the large firms could not reach without incurring high transportation costs, by searching out special grades of crude oil which were not available in sufficient quantity to support a large-scale operation, or by searching out markets which were too small or too specialized in their requirements for quality or service to interest the large companies. Some small refiners have also profited by serving as marginal suppliers to the industry, operating in times of strong demand and favorable prices and closing down in times of depressed refining margins. Finally, some small firms have developed strong positions by utilizing effectively certain specialized managerial skills, such as exceptional proficiency in the arrangement and operation of refinery equipment.

In looking to the future, we would anticipate that the oil industry will continue to be characterized by an economic climate favorable to vertical integration and that the integrated companies will continue to occupy a very prominent position in the affairs of the industry. We would anticipate that the integrated companies will continue to make frequent changes in their structures which may involve either increases or decreases in depth, extent, and intensity of integration as new circumstances may warrant.

We would also anticipate that some of the existing opportunities for small firms in the refining industry may pass and that new opportunities may arise to take their place. On balance, the participation of small refiners in the industry may expand or contract, and whether it does or not will be of no great significance, so long as the changes do not result from unfair and illegal practices.

We would hope that the pressure of competition will continue sufficiently strong and the industry sufficiently free from controls so that all types of oil companies will be compelled to make whatever changes in structure and size may be required by the emergence of new technological and economic conditions.

LIST OF APPENDIX TABLES

TABLE 1. RETURN ON BORROWED AND INVESTED CAPITAL

	Producing				Marketing				Refining-Marketing (0–10%) [a]			
Year	Number in Group	Median	Inter-quartile Average	Arith-metic Average	Number in Group	Median	Inter-quartile Average	Arith-metic Average	Number in Group	Median	Inter-quartile Average	Arith-metic Average
1920	9	12.9%	14.2%	15.2%	2	*	*	*	6	14.1%	15.5%	16.0%
1921	16	3.8	4.5	3.8	3	*	*	*	9	2.4	2.1	1.8
1922	18	5.9	5.7	7.9	3	*	*	*	10	12.3	9.1	7.4
1923	19	3.3	3.0	5.1	2	*	*	*	12	3.7	3.5	2.2
1924	24	5.1	5.1	7.8	2	*	*	*	12	5.7	5.3	5.7
1925	24	7.1	7.9	13.3	4	19.7%	*	17.8%	13	5.8	4.8	5.3
1926	23	11.5	11.9	16.2	4	12.3	*	13.5	14	6.8	5.6	5.8
1927	26	4.1	4.7	7.5	4	10.4	*	9.6	13	3.7	3.3	1.2
1928	24	3.8	3.2	5.0	3	*	*	*	13	8.6	8.2	9.4
1929	27	9.4	8.6	13.2	4	13.9	*	13.7	12	4.8	5.7	6.8
1930	28	5.1	5.8	9.3	5	8.3	8.5%	6.6	10	2.0	0.4	(1.8)
1931	27	(0.1)	(0.7)	0.1	4	8.2	*	9.2	7	(2.9)	(2.8)	(0.9)
1932	30	1.9	2.7	6.5	5	7.2	8.8	7.7	6	(3.3)	(2.3)	(4.1)
1933	28	1.9	1.8	4.3	6	8.5	7.5	6.4	5	1.7	2.2	(1.7)
1934	26	6.3	7.0	9.7	6	8.7	8.6	6.4	5	(0.6)	(0.9)	(0.7)
1935	24	5.6	6.3	9.3	6	7.7	7.1	6.9	7	5.7	5.4	3.5
1936	30	9.1	9.1	13.0	6	11.5	9.6	9.7	7	6.4	6.8	7.7
1937	30	9.6	11.2	14.9	6	10.1	10.0	9.5	7	7.0	7.9	6.1
1938	31	9.2	9.6	11.9	6	8.5	7.7	7.5	8	0.4	(0.4)	(3.4)
1939	32	6.9	6.8	8.6	5	11.2	10.3	8.7	9	9.4	5.9	7.9
1940	32	6.1	6.0	7.0	4	10.3	*	9.9	11	5.9	5.4	5.9
1941	32	9.7	9.1	10.3	4	12.3	*	12.7	11	7.9	6.3	11.2
1942	32	9.4	9.1	10.2	4	8.4	*	9.0	11	7.6	8.3	8.3
1943	31	9.8	10.5	11.6	4	5.4	*	6.3	11	7.2	7.7	7.8
1944	31	10.7	11.5	11.8	4	7.7	*	7.3	8	10.6	10.7	11.0
1945	31	9.6	10.0	10.4	4	6.6	*	6.8	7	7.8	7.8	8.1
1946	31	9.5	10.0	11.3	4	10.7	*	11.9	7	10.0	10.9	10.4
1947	31	16.8	17.4	20.9	4	12.5	*	13.5	8	11.1	13.6	17.4
1948	28	24.6	24.9	24.9	3	*	*	*	9	23.4	22.9	21.9
1949	28	18.0	15.9	17.0	3	*	*	*	9	3.3	6.0	7.3
1950	27	11.8	13.4	13.9	3	*	*	*	7	10.1	9.0	9.1
1951	26	14.9	13.8	13.4	3	*	*	*	6	12.1	12.0	13.1
1952	23	11.2	12.5	11.9	2	*	*	*	5	11.2	11.8	12.4
1920–1934	349	4.7	4.9	8.1	57	10.4	10.8	11.1	147	4.4	4.3	4.0
1935–1952	530	10.1	10.7	12.8	75	9.9	9.6	9.7	148	7.9	8.7	9.2
1920–1952	879	8.5	8.7	10.9	132	10.3	10.1	10.3	295	6.8	6.6	6.6

Note: Net income was taken after taxes but before interest charges and income applicable to minority interests. Borrowed and invested capital included common stock, surplus, preferred stock, long-term debt, and the equity of minority stockholders in consolidated subsidiaries.

( ) Indicates negative figure.

SOURCE: See discussion in Chapter Five.

EARNED BY VARIOUS TYPES OF OIL COMPANIES: 1920–1952

Year	Producing-Refining-Marketing (10%–50%) [a] Number in Group	Median	Inter-quartile Average	Arith-metic Average	Producing-Refining-Marketing (50%–100%) [a] Number in Group	Median	Inter-quartile Average	Arith-metic Average	Producing-Refining-Marketing (100%–500%) [a] Number in Group	Median	Inter-quartile Average	Arith-metic Average
1920	2	*	*	*	3	*	*	*	1	*	*	*
1921	2	*	*	*	3	*	*	*	1	*	*	*
1922	2	*	*	*	6	8.3%	7.8%	6.4%	2	*	*	*
1923	1	*	*	*	7	7.4	7.2	6.0	2	*	*	*
1924	2	*	*	*	7	8.2	7.9	7.1	3	*	*	*
1925	2	*	*	*	9	9.2	9.7	11.4	4	11.3%	*	11.1%
1926	1	*	*	*	11	7.4	8.6	9.4	6	9.7	9.8%	9.9
1927	3	*	*	*	12	5.4	5.4	4.4	7	3.8	3.3	2.8
1928	3	*	*	*	12	7.6	7.6	7.3	8	5.5	5.2	4.5
1929	4	6.8%	*	7.6%	13	8.1	8.1	8.2	9	10.2	8.5	8.3
1930	4	3.6	*	4.0	12	3.2	3.1	2.8	9	3.2	3.3	1.6
1931	7	(0.7)	(1.3)%	(2.9)	11	(1.9)	(2.1)	(4.2)	10	(5.5)	(5.5)	(6.9)
1932	6	2.1	0.4	(0.5)	11	1.5	1.6	(0.3)	9	0.7	0.3	(0.5)
1933	9	(1.7)	(0.8)	(2.5)	9	1.9	2.4	2.5	9	(0.3)	(0.8)	(1.7)
1934	13	2.6	1.3	(1.5)	6	2.9	2.5	2.6	10	3.3	3.7	2.7
1935	14	4.7	4.9	5.2	7	4.2	4.1	4.2	9	7.8	7.0	5.8
1936	12	7.8	8.0	8.6	7	6.6	6.6	6.5	7	10.7	10.6	8.2
1937	13	8.3	8.1	8.3	7	8.7	8.8	8.8	7	12.6	12.8	11.4
1938	12	2.8	2.7	2.0	8	5.1	5.1	8.3	7	4.8	5.0	5.5
1939	11	3.5	4.0	4.3	9	5.6	5.7	9.6	6	5.7	5.7	5.6
1940	10	4.3	4.5	4.7	9	5.5	5.4	7.4	6	6.2	6.1	6.0
1941	11	7.7	8.3	8.8	8	8.9	8.9	9.0	6	9.4	9.2	9.2
1942	10	6.6	7.2	7.3	10	6.7	6.6	7.5	6	10.7	10.8	10.5
1943	10	8.7	8.7	8.9	10	8.1	8.3	9.0	6	9.8	9.8	9.8
1944	12	8.5	8.6	12.2	9	9.2	8.9	10.4	6	9.8	9.7	9.7
1945	12	9.8	9.9	10.0	9	9.4	8.5	9.4	7	11.3	11.3	11.3
1946	11	9.1	10.1	9.2	9	9.2	8.9	9.0	8	12.3	12.2	12.4
1947	11	14.0	15.2	15.7	11	13.1	12.4	12.8	7	19.9	19.6	19.6
1948	12	16.0	17.8	18.7	12	17.3	17.2	17.1	6	26.7	25.9	24.3
1949	13	10.8	11.0	12.0	11	10.9	10.7	10.8	6	16.3	16.5	16.2
1950	13	12.7	12.6	12.9	11	11.4	11.9	12.6	6	16.4	16.5	15.5
1951	10	12.0	12.0	12.3	12	12.4	12.6	12.7	7	15.3	15.2	14.6
1952	10	9.6	9.5	9.7	12	10.2	10.1	10.2	6	12.6	12.8	12.8
1920–1934	61	2.4	1.9	1.0	132	5.8	5.6	5.1	90	3.2	3.0	2.7
1935–1952	207	9.0	9.1	9.5	171	9.1	9.1	10.1	119	10.9	10.9	11.5
1920–1952	268	7.8	7.7	7.6	303	7.6	7.7	7.7	209	8.0	7.8	7.7

* Medians and arithmetic averages were not computed for groups of less than four. Interquartile averages were not computed for groups of less than five.

[a] Numbers in parentheses indicate domestic crude oil production as a percentage of domestic refinery runs. See Chapter Five for further discussion of method of grouping companies.

TABLE 2. GULF OIL CORPORATION

Producing, Refining, and Marketing Operations: 1901–1952

(All figures in 1,000 barrels except as noted)

Year	Net Foreign Production [a] (1)	Imports Own Foreign Production [b] (2)	Net Domestic Production (3)	Crude Oil Supply in U.S. (4)=(2)+(3)	Domestic Refinery Runs [c] (5)	Refined Product Sales [d] (6)	Refined Product Purchases [e] (7)	Sales Supplied from Own Refineries (8)=(6)−(7)	Ratio Crude Oil Supply in U.S. to Refinery Runs (9)=(4)÷(5)	% Product Sales Supplied from Own Refineries (10)=(8)÷(6)
1901			1,204	1,204						
1902			1,938	1,938	1,377				140.7%	
1903			2,158	2,158	2,308				93.5	
1904			2,923	2,923	2,909	2,232			100.5	
1905			3,361	3,361	3,923	3,310			85.7	
1906			1,617	1,617	3,930	3,589			41.1	
1907			3,345	3,345	3,751	3,448			89.2	
1908			4,714	4,714	4,752	3,138			99.2	
1909			6,645	6,645	7,132	5,199			93.3	
1910			6,709	6,709	9,124	5,139			73.5	
1911			7,685	7,685	9,998	6,797			76.9	
1912			7,425	7,425	9,698	7,407			76.6	
1913			9,032	9,032	12,008	9,788			75.2	
1914	768	655	11,114	11,769	13,147	11,576			89.5	
1915	871	976	12,215	13,191	15,797	15,750			83.5	
1916	829	1,211	13,666	14,877	16,967	16,161			87.7	
1917	1,199	1,194	16,335	17,529	18,175	17,661			96.4	
1918	1,282	1,758	17,770	19,528	17,146	16,425			113.9	
1919	4,281	4,505	16,602	21,107	20,278	18,425			104.1	
1920	11,021	9,595	19,507	29,102	24,952	23,471			116.6	
1921	17,201	13,237	17,740	30,977	30,157	24,809			102.7	
1922	24,771	18,687	24,017	42,704	36,688	36,147			116.4	
1923	7,192	7,192	32,807	39,999	33,487	29,604			119.4	
1924	10,118	9,306	28,194	37,500	33,789	30,724			111.0	
1925	6,587	3,416	31,301	34,717	36,130	32,449			96.1	
1926	10,616	6,815	33,582	40,397	44,933	37,745			89.9	
1927	12,520	9,515	42,252	51,767	52,553	43,811	126	43,685	98.5	99.7%
1926	17,927	15,578	45,139	60,717	59,130	51,562	3,705	47,857	102.7	92.8
1929	28,186	22,774	50,059	72,833	67,981	57,545	1,092	56,453	107.1	98.1
1930	21,419	20,866	42,747	63,613	67,696	56,000	655	55,345	94.0	98.8
1931	16,934	14,726	37,995	52,721	65,615	51,387	612	50,775	80.3	98.8
1932	14,338	12,546	35,123	47,669	53,441	44,921	712	44,209	89.2	98.4
1933	13,276	11,654	37,494	49,148	55,714	48,535	1,940	46,595	88.2	96.0
1934	13,944	10,547	35,640	46,187	56,374	48,035	3,067	44,968	81.9	93.6
1935	15,892	11,138	37,381	48,519	61,712	54,456	2,175	52,281	78.6	96.0
1936	14,073	12,400	41,760	54,160	71,686	63,884	4,643	59,241	75.6	92.7
1937	20,184	10,379	46,317	56,696	77,894	68,788	3,969	64,819	72.8	94.2
1938	11,515	10,687	40,804	51,491	76,117	70,455	2,256	68,199	76.7	96.8
1939	11,422	12,066	41,235	53,301	81,595	78,939	5,708	73,231	65.3	92.8
1940	16,552	15,531	46,041	61,572	90,586	81,702	2,616	79,086	68.0	96.8
1941	19,633	20,465	47,196	67,661	99,683	93,639	6,398	87,241	67.9	93.2
1942	9,973	3,936	46,655	50,591	82,300	87,715	7,712	80,003	61.5	91.2
1943	8,786	1,706	55,643	57,349	87,787	94,570	24,530	70,040	65.3	74.1
1944	16,189	8,808	68,930	77,738	103,903	115,722	21,860	93,862	74.8	81.1
1945	22,140	15,306	74,014	89,320	106,615	118,549	19,587	98,962	83.8	83.5
1946	28,945	23,840	75,124	98,964	125,016	125,587	15,082	110,505	79.2	88.0
1947	36,131	25,124	78,883	104,007	134,897	143,096	22,459	120,637	77.1	84.3
1948	53,259	27,173	86,154	113,327	140,558	146,964	27,529	119,435	80.6	81.3
1949	76,230	33,800	71,861	105,661	138,788	144,529	19,279	125,250	76.1	86.7
1950	103,056	38,846	74,635	113,481	163,657	168,361	19,383	148,978	69.3	88.5
1951	146,075	31,914	85,094	117,008	169,090	181,741	27,309	154,432	69.2	85.0
1952	170,478	36,652	81,828	118,480	166,141	186,445	33,769	152,676	71.3	81.9

Note: Blank spaces indicate data not available.

[a] Includes Gulf's share of Kuwait production but not Venezuela production which was sold under long-term contract beginning in 1938.

[b] These data, while representing essentially imports of the company from its own foreign production, include in the earlier years some amounts of crude oil purchased from others. In some cases therefore the amounts shown for imports of the company's own foreign production may exceed the amount of such production. In 1923 the company reported "imports of own foreign production" of 11,691,000 barrels versus a foreign production of only 7,192,000 barrels. In this year therefore the latter figure was used for imports. Column 2 may also exceed column 1 in some cases by virtue of withdrawals from inventories.

[c] Company reports it ran no crude oil under processing agreements for others.

[d] Figures may contain inaccuracies in early years of company's history.

[e] Includes products acquired under processing agreements.

Source: Gulf Oil Corporation.

TABLE 3. THE TEXAS COMPANY

Producing, Refining, and Marketing Operations: 1902–1952

(All figures in 1,000 barrels except as noted)

Year	Net Foreign Production [a] (1)	Imports Own Foreign Production (2)	Net Domestic Production [b] (3)	Crude Oil Supply in U.S. (4)=(2)+(3)	Domestic Refinery Runs [c] (5)	Refined Product Sales [d] (6)	Refined Product Purchases [e] (7)	Sales Supplied from Own Refineries (8)=(6)−(7)	Ratio Crude Oil Supply in U.S. to Refinery Runs (9)=(4)÷(5)	% Product Sales Supplied from Own Refineries (10)=(8)÷(6)
1902			216	216						
1903			2,672	2,672	43				6214.0%	
1904			3,855	3,855	318				1212.3	
1905			5,402	5,402	548				985.8	
1906			3,910	3,910	925				422.7	
1907			5,154	5,154	1,410				365.5	
1908			5,518	5,518	4,086				135.1	
1909			4,225	4,225	6,169				68.5	
1910			5,560	5,560	8,565				64.9	
1911			5,933	5,933	8,779				67.6	
1912			6,456	6,456	9,880				65.3	
1913	430		8,844	8,844	12,018				73.6	
1914	1,315		13,535	13,535	12,950				104.5	
1915	1,366		16,877	16,877	17,875				94.4	
1916	1,325		14,123	14,123	19,681				71.8	
1917	1,366		12,775	12,775	23,709				53.9	
1918	1,145		12,091	12,091	23,318				51.9	
1919	4,615		14,318	14,318	28,610				50.1	
1920	9,817		18,586	18,586	31,418				59.2	
1921	5,389		17,347	17,347	26,967				64.3	
1922	3,174		17,817	17,817	27,707				64.3	
1923	2,017		17,195	17,195	29,557				58.2	
1924	1,203		15,780	15,780	35,920				43.9	
1925	543		18,210	18,210	34,414				52.9	
1926	461		18,091	18,091	36,559		1,664		49.5	
1927	352		22,569	22,569	38,847		1,463		58.1	
1928	245		38,595	38,595	55,898		1,675		69.1	
1929	217		43,604	43,604	58,294	48,872	1,813	47,059	74.8	96.3%
1930	206		36,853	36,853	58,460	54,690	683	54,007	63.0	98.8
1931	180		29,296	29,296	59,476	47,007	3,143	43,864	49.3	93.3
1932	172		28,282	28,282	60,211	45,945	1,832	44,113	47.0	96.0
1933	165		30,854	30,854	65,449	51,200	1,882	49,318	47.1	96.3
1934	170		31,086	31,086	71,150	52,702	2,522	50,180	43.7	95.2
1935	80		37,646	37,646	76,276	60,938	1,735	59,203	49.4	97.1
1936			43,800	43,800	88,140	78,346	2,067	76,279	49.7	97.4
1937			49,525	49,525	96,424	86,619	3,148	83,471	51.4	96.4
1938			48,160	48,160	94,865	76,739	2,044	74,695	50.8	97.3
1939			63,428	63,428	100,467	79,605	2,188	77,417	63.1	97.3
1940			84,597	84,597	101,622	82,421	2,640	79,781	83.3	96.8
1941			73,734	73,734	115,241	93,948	1,895	92,053	64.0	98.0
1942	5,955		67,156	67,156	101,082	94,116	2,663	91,453	66.4	97.2
1943	6,616		74,549	74,549	111,221	100,085	2,017	98,068	67.0	98.0
1944	9,579		87,047	87,047	130,563	110,087	2,762	107,325	66.7	97.5
1945	17,409		89,225	89,225	127,948	115,267	5,458	109,809	69.7	95.3
1946	37,952		87,097	87,097	132,546	114,114	2,859	111,255	65.7	97.5
1947	37,872		92,740	92,740	139,079	126,070	4,485	121,585	66.7	96.4
1948	56,982	529	99,529	100,058	145,979	139,453	2,670	136,783	68.5	98.1
1949	72,064	5,386	91,818	97,204	151,038	142,047	912	141,135	64.4	99.4
1950	81,478	6,263	97,532	103,795	140,326 [f]	148,699	12,075 [f]	136,624 [f]	74.0 [f]	91.9 [f]
1951	105,954	3,332	111,429	114,761	175,969	163,492	1,716	161,776	65.2	99.0
1952	118,457		114,452		175,917					

Note: Blank spaces indicate data not available.

[a] Includes net interest in net foreign production of affiliated companies beginning in 1942.

[b] Includes net interest in net domestic production of affiliated companies beginning in 1942.

[c] Excludes crude run for others under processing agreements.

[d] Excludes refined products supplied to others under processing agreements. Includes shipments for export beginning in 1948. The amount of the export shipments was between 7 and 8 million barrels in 1948, 1949, and 1951; in 1950 it was slightly over 5 million barrels. Shipments for export were excluded prior to 1948.

[e] Includes products acquired under processing agreements. Includes purchases by refining department only. Data on other purchases not available but reported to be a small part of total supply.

[f] Operations influenced by a refinery strike.

Source: The Texas Company.

TABLE 4. SINCLAIR OIL CORPORATION

Producing, Refining, and Marketing Operations: 1919–1952

(All figures in 1,000 barrels except as noted)

Year	Net Foreign Production	Imports Own Foreign Production	Net Domestic Production	Crude Oil Supply in U.S.	Domestic Refinery Runs a	Refined Product Sales b	Refined Product Purchases c	Sales Supplied from Own Refineries d	Ratio Crude Oil Supply in U.S. to Refinery Runs	% Product Sales Supplied from Own Refineries
	(1)	(2)	(3)	(4)=(2)+(3)	(5)	(6)	(7)	(8)=(6)−(7)	(9)=(4)÷(5)	(10)=(8)÷(6)
1919	4,566	1,474	5,599	7,073	10,464				67.6%	
1920	9,445	3,058	6,607	9,665	11,738				82.3	
1921	7,496	2,044	5,743	7,787	8,558				91.0	
1922	2,519	906	7,396	8,302	9,152				90.7	
1923	6,445	2,288	6,993	9,281	11,851				78.3	
1924	9,842	5,042	6,175	11,217	18,519				60.6	
1925	4,475	1,643	9,059	10,702	25,855	27,448		27,448	41.4	
1926	2,686	2,200	11,241	13,441	28,054	28,199		28,199	47.9	
1927	2,765	1,592	14,704	16,296	30,307	29,811		29,811	53.8	
1928	2,394	748	13,629	14,377	33,433	33,078		33,078	43.0	
1929	2,442	889	16,182	17,071	35,729	34,181		34,181	47.8	
1930	1,953	0	14,835	14,835	36,358	33,417		33,417	40.8	
1931	1,588	0	14,754	14,754	35,628	31,463		31,463	41.4	
1932	1,254	0	22,531	22,531	36,078	30,424		30,424	62.5	
1933	1,108	0	25,292	25,292	43,376	36,790		36,790	58.3	
1934	1,111	0	24,833	24,833	44,975	41,704		41,704	55.2	
1935	1,983	0	24,753	24,753	51,906	52,157	7,015	45,142	47.7	86.6%
1936	2,059	0	25,333	25,333	57,720	55,716	6,478	49,238	43.9	85.3
1937	1,854	0	28,893	28,893	65,040	62,467	6,140	56,327	44.4	90.2
1938	345	0	24,121	24,121	64,616	62,981	4,613	58,368	37.3	92.7
1939	0	0	23,017	23,017	69,628	67,590	7,669	59,921	33.1	88.7
1940	0	0	24,107	24,107	68,001	68,608	8,385	60,223	35.4	87.8
1941	32	0	27,241	27,241	74,937	76,378	9,364	67,014	36.4	87.7
1942	365	0	26,049	26,049	71,163	75,554	8,157	67,397	36.6	89.2
1943	3,554	3,365	26,255	29,620	77,901	86,191	16,848	69,343	38.0	80.5
1944	10,605	10,605	27,354	37,959	95,344	114,532	28,544	85,988	39.8	75.1
1945	10,452	10,452	27,571	38,023	96,306	111,494	24,485	87,009	39.5	78.0
1946	9,786	9,786	26,825	36,611	92,296	93,000	9,986	83,014	39.7	89.3
1947	7,547	7,547	28,885	36,432	89,990	92,830	10,621	82,209	40.5	88.6
1948	5,473	5,473	33,671	39,144	96,782	93,887	12,398	81,489	40.4	86.8
1949	4,345	4,345	30,327	34,672	95,232	94,078	6,920	87,158	36.4	92.6
1950	3,571	2,114	31,692	33,806	115,672	108,463	6,774	101,689	29.2	93.8
1951	3,543	0	37,518	37,518	129,759	123,300	5,687	117,613	28.9	95.4
1952	3,680	0	40,230	40,230	132,281	129,897	5,917	123,980	30.4	95.5

Note: Blank spaces indicate data not available.

a Includes crude run by others for Sinclair under processing agreements. In 1951 excludes 1,341,000 run by Sinclair for others.

b Includes all domestic sales and shipments for export. Figures prior to 1931 are estimates.

c Does not include products acquired under processing agreements before 1950. Such products were included with yield of products from company refineries, but do not amount to more than 1% or 2% in any case.

d Includes products acquired from others under processing agreements before 1950. See footnote c.

SOURCE: Sinclair Oil Corporation.

TABLE 5. THE OHIO OIL COMPANY

Producing, Refining, and Marketing Operations: 1911–1952

(All figures in 1,000 barrels except as noted)

Year	Net Domestic Production [a]	Refinery Runs [b]	Refined Product Sales [c]	Refined Product Purchases [d]	Sales Supplied from Own Refineries	Ratio Crude Oil Supply in U.S. to Refinery Runs	% Product Sales Supplied from Own Refineries
	(1)	(2)	(3)	(4)	(5)=(3)−(4)	(6)=(1)÷(2)	(7)=(5)÷(3)
1911	14,988	0	0				
1912	14,094	0	0				
1913	13,100	0	0				
1914	12,524	0	0				
1915	11,257	0	0				
1916	11,441	0	0				
1917	11,874	0	0				
1918	10,854	0	0				
1919	10,670	0	0				
1920	9,639	0	0				
1921	10,878	0	0				
1922	13,280	0	0				
1923	12,487	0	0				
1924	12,679	211	203			6009.0%	
1925	12,998	434	477			2994.9	
1926	11,238	442	519			2542.5	
1927	11,339	1,439	1,419			788.0	
1928	13,252	1,931	2,027			686.3	
1929	18,257	2,375	2,030			768.7	
1930	20,918	3,577	3,704			584.8	
1931	22,091	6,512	5,967			339.2	
1932	20,270	5,058	5,094			400.8	
1933	19,860	4,828	4,846			411.4	
1934	17,904	4,813	4,908	383	4,525	372.0	92.2%
1935	18,301	5,440	5,378	428	4,950	336.4	92.0
1936	18,409	5,995	5,729	254	5,475	307.1	95.6
1937	22,450	6,142	5,810	422	5,388	365.5	92.7
1938	19,256	6,148	6,080	587	5,493	313.2	90.3
1939	20,553	6,301	6,679	1,199	5,480	326.2	82.0
1940	22,625	6,982	7,024	827	6,197	324.0	88.2
1941	24,059	6,358	6,458	890	5,568	378.4	86.2
1942	27,743	5,853	6,805	345	6,460	474.0	94.9
1943	29,745	6,395	6,920	594	6,326	465.1	91.4
1944	31,942	6,758	7,356	894	6,462	472.7	87.8
1945	32,825	7,002	7,771	905	6,866	468.8	88.4
1946	31,404	7,536	8,683	1,133	7,550	416.7	87.0
1947	33,050	8,667	9,936	1,576	8,360	381.3	84.1
1948	35,227	9,331	10,852	1,269	9,583	377.5	88.3
1949	28,112	10,675	10,982	446	10,536	263.3	95.9
1950	30,164	13,034	12,771	312	12,459	231.4	97.6
1951	33,711	13,297	13,243	314	12,929	253.5	97.6
1952	33,723	13,774	13,885	294	13,591	244.8	97.9

Note: Blank spaces indicate data not available.

[a] Foreign production amounted to 78,553 barrels in 1950, 94,028 barrels in 1951, and 134,777 barrels in 1952. None of this production was imported.

[b] Includes crude oil processed for The Ohio Oil Company by other refineries, but not crude oil processed by The Ohio Oil Company for others.

[c] Includes all domestic sales and shipments for export.

[d] Includes products acquired under processing agreements.

SOURCE: The Ohio Oil Company.

TABLE 6. THE ATLANTIC REFINING COMPANY
Producing, Refining, and Marketing Operations: 1912–1952
(All figures in 1,000 barrels except as noted)

Year	Net Foreign Production	Imports Own Foreign Production [a]	Net Domestic Production	Crude Oil Supply in U.S.	Domestic Refinery Runs [b]	Refined Product Sales [c]	Refined Product Purchases	Sales Supplied from Own Refineries	Ratio Crude Oil Supply in U.S. to Refinery Runs	% Product Sales Supplied from Own Refineries
	(1)	(2)	(3)	(4)=(2)+(3)	(5)	(6)	(7)	(8)=(6)−(7)	(9)=(4)÷(5)	(10)=(8)÷(6)
1912	0		0	0	15,489	13,622				
1913	0		0	0	13,924	12,498				
1914	0		0	0	8,949	9,458				
1915	0		0	0	10,970	10,010				
1916	175		0	0	11,654	12,551				
1917	719		0	0	14,278	15,216				
1918	550		1	1	16,073	18,899			0.1%	
1919	977		84	84	17,241	16,713			0.5	
1920	1,256		300	300	18,088	17,555			1.7	
1921	1,093		972	972	18,128	16,956			5.4	
1922	1,200		1,944	1,944	20,258	19,942			9.6	
1923	865		2,517	2,517	22,290	21,991			11.3	
1924	779		3,290	3,290	22,492	23,841			14.6	
1925	595		2,047	2,047	23,234	24,857			8.8	
1926	371		2,200	2,200	22,277	27,135			9.9	
1927	255	(None	5,947	5,947	23,498	26,669			25.3	
1928	194	before	8,851	8,851	25,586	28,963			34.6	
1929	111	1948)	5,021	5,021	26,221	26,858	5,811	21,047	19.1	78.4%
1930	19		3,305	3,305	25,959	23,475	3,847	19,628	12.7	83.6
1931	0		2,610	2,610	27,730	23,636	1,960	21,676	9.4	91.7
1932	0		4,295	4,295	25,532	21,628	754	20,874	16.8	96.5
1933	0		7,552	7,552	26,780	22,668	1,059	21,609	28.2	95.3
1934	0		9,499	9,499	29,161	23,739	1,109	22,630	32.6	95.3
1935	0		9,228	9,228	30,203	26,469	686	25,783	30.6	97.4
1936	0		9,836	9,836	33,258	29,040	784	28,256	29.6	97.3
1937	0		12,406	12,406	35,276	31,086	1,103	29,983	35.2	96.5
1938	0		12,203	12,203	34,521	31,122	751	30,371	35.3	97.6
1939	0		13,052	13,052	37,269	32,805	1,962	30,843	35.0	94.0
1940	0		13,496	13,496	37,834	33,702	1,038	32,664	35.7	96.9
1941	0		15,091	15,091	41,342	36,213	1,172	35,041	36.5	96.8
1942	0		14,515	14,515	25,486	32,697	10,319	22,378	57.0	68.4
1943	0		17,678	17,678	34,281	34,949	7,426	27,523	51.6	78.7
1944	0		24,631	24,631	40,646	40,335	6,815	33,520	60.6	83.1
1945	11		24,750	24,750	43,054	40,692	4,777	35,915	57.5	88.3
1946	10		23,567	23,567	44,656	40,129	2,142	37,987	52.8	94.7
1947	13		24,320	24,320	50,322	48,407	2,152	46,255	48.3	95.6
1948	316	344	27,347	27,691	53,271	47,832	2,989	44,843	52.0	93.7
1949	1,916	2,051	23,901	25,952	52,718	49,574	1,934	47,640	49.2	96.1
1950	4,383	4,228	25,903	30,131	57,948	55,180	2,441	52,739	52.0	95.6
1951	3,670	3,768	31,780	35,548	63,342	59,929	1,888	58,041	56.1	96.8
1952	3,488	3,433	33,827	37,260	64,796	62,273	2,703	59,570	57.5	95.7

Note: Blank spaces indicate data not available.

[a] Imports of own production may be greater than net foreign production due to closing the books of Venezuelan Atlantic Refining Company as of November 30 each year, but importing some December production.

[b] Company reports no crude handled for or by others under processing agreements.

[c] Includes all domestic sales and shipments for export. Unusual sales at government direction in years 1942–1945, inclusive, have been excluded. Figures prior to 1928 may include some products purchased abroad and resold abroad, particularly in the period 1920–1928.

SOURCE: The Atlantic Refining Company.

TABLE 7. STANDARD OIL COMPANY (INDIANA)

Producing, Refining, and Marketing Operations: 1930–1952

(All figures in 1,000 barrels except as noted)

Year	Net Foreign Production	Imports Own Foreign Production	Net Domestic Production [a]	Crude Oil Supply in U.S.	Domestic Refinery Runs	Refined Product Sales	Refined Product Purchases [b]	Sales Supplied from Own Refineries [c]	Ratio Crude Oil Supply in U.S. to Refinery Runs	% Product Sales Supplied from Own Refineries [c]
	(1)	(2)	(3)	(4)=(2)+(3)	(5)	(6)	(7)	(8)=(6)−(7)	(9)=(4)÷(5)	(10)=(8)÷(6)
1930	42,387	7,309	12,691	20,000	58,917	93,579	3,375	90,204	34.0%	96.4%
1931	37,986	3,319	11,880	15,199	54,858	85,545	3,308	82,237	27.7	96.1
1932	14,749	2,349	10,676	13,025	47,336	75,439	4,427	71,012	27.5	94.1
1933			11,229	11,229	49,833	72,850	28,449	44,401	22.5	61.0
1934			14,206	14,206	56,649	79,554	28,736	50,818	25.1	63.9
1935			19,317	19,317	66,057	83,573	25,894	57,679	29.2	69.0
1936	(None	(None	26,739	26,739	74,683	94,827	30,497	64,330	35.8	67.8
1937	after	after	33,534	33,534	86,989	95,288	19,054	76,234	38.6	80.0
1938	1932)	1932)	31,820	31,820	86,992	90,658	13,725	76,933	36.6	84.9
1939			32,021	32,021	95,814	103,232	14,363	88,869	33.4	86.1
1940			33,266	33,266	104,481	106,069	16,101	89,968	31.8	84.8
1941			39,566	39,566	111,147	117,737	19,351	98,386	35.6	83.6
1942			41,858	41,858	104,204	116,036	15,341	100,695	40.2	86.8
1943			52,421	52,421	107,591	121,626	21,794	99,832	48.7	82.1
1944			64,319	64,319	113,800	139,557	32,606	106,951	56.5	76.6
1945			66,304	66,304	113,596	139,281	33,701	105,580	58.4	75.8
1946			66,202	66,202	124,429	132,639	18,087	114,552	53.2	86.4
1947			72,225	72,225	134,664	147,888	20,058	127,830	53.6	86.4
1948			83,069	83,069	156,207	159,061	18,844	140,217	53.2	88.2
1949			69,227	69,227	150,049	163,688	14,469	149,219	46.1	91.2
1950			74,796	74,796	168,656	188,045	26,416	161,629	44.4	86.0
1951			90,448	90,448	187,646	207,774	26,973	180,801	48.2	87.0
1952			91,871	91,871	185,326	211,673	29,310	182,364	49.6	86.2

[a] Includes company's net interest in net domestic production of affiliated companies for years 1937–1952, inclusive.
[b] Does not include purchases of parent company prior to 1945. In the period 1930–1932, inclusive, the parent company apparently had large product purchases or transfers from its foreign refineries. For the period 1945–1950, inclusive, purchases of the parent company were about 15% of total purchases. Includes products acquired under processing agreements.
[c] Figures are overstated prior to 1945 and particularly in years 1930–1932, inclusive, because data on product purchases of parent company were not available. See preceeding footnote.

SOURCE: Standard Oil Company (Indiana).

TABLE 8. STANDARD OIL COMPANY (OHIO)

Producing, Refining, and Marketing Operations: 1929–1952

(All figures in 1,000 barrels except as noted)

Year	Net Domestic Production	Refinery Runs	Refined Product Sales	Refined Product Purchases [b]	Sales Supplied from Own Refineries	Ratio Crude Oil Supply in U.S. to Refinery Runs	% Product Sales Supplied from Own Refineries
	(1)	(2)	(3)	(4)	(5)=(3)−(4)	(6)=(1)÷(2)	(7)=(5)÷(3)
1929	0		10,059				
1930	0	9,823	9,985				
1931	0	9,703	10,212				
1932	0	13,141	10,084				
1933	0	12,348	9,426				
1934	0	11,942	9,366				
1935	0	11,878	11,556				
1936	0	12,762	12,656				
1937	107	13,642	13,169			0.8%	
1938	172	15,191	14,351			1.1	
1939	265	16,792	16,517			1.6	
1940	198	19,813	18,583			1.0	
1941	164	24,948	22,704			0.7	
1942	682	24,785	24,667			2.8	
1943	2,062	25,802	26,878			8.0	
1944	3,772	27,256	27,289	3,651	23,638	13.8	86.6%
1945	7,545	27,079	26,532	4,005	22,527	27.9	84.9
1946	8,965	30,510	30,332	2,331	28,001	29.4	92.3
1947	9,626	34,046	33,456	3,625	29,831	28.3	89.2
1948	11,418	29,456 [a]	34,105	8,422 [a]	25,683 [a]	38.8 [a]	75.3 [a]
1949	11,137	31,918	33,018	2,540	30,478	34.9	92.3
1950	11,035	39,262	37,624	2,237	35,387	28.1	94.1
1951	11,694	43,402	40,308	2,509	37,799	26.9	93.8
1952	12,413	43,360	41,222	1,859	39,363	28.6	95.5

Note: Blank spaces indicate data not available.
[a] Operations influenced by a refinery strike.
[b] Includes products acquired under processing agreements.

SOURCE: Standard Oil Company (Ohio)

TABLE 9. GULF OIL CORPORATION
Balance of Operations in Selected Years

	Thousands of Barrels						Percentage Breakdowns					
	1929	1935	1940	1946	1949	1950	1929	1935	1940	1946	1949	1950
CRUDE OIL OPERATIONS												
Total new supply of crude oil in U.S.	66,451	56,178	94,884	128,211	145,790	161,592	100.00%	100.00%	100.00%	100.00%	100.00%	100.00%
Net domestic production	50,059	37,381	46,041	75,124	71,861	74,635	75.33	66.54	48.52	58.59	49.29	46.19
Imports own foreign production	22,774	11,138	15,531	23,840	33,800	38,846	34.27	19.82	16.37	18.60	23.18	24.04
Net purchases a	(6,382)	7,659	33,312	29,247	40,129	48,111	(9.60)	13.64	35.11	22.81	27.53	29.77
Total net foreign production b	28,186	15,892	16,552	28,945	76,230	103,056						
REFINED PRODUCTS OPERATIONS												
Total new supply refined products in U.S.	57,521	57,626	85,545	132,528	148,075	171,554	100.00	100.00	100.00	100.00	100.00	100.00
Yield of refined products from refineries c	56,429	55,451	82,929	117,446	128,797	151,832	98.10	96.23	96.94	88.62	86.98	88.50
Imports from company's foreign refineries	0	0	0	0	0	340	0	0	0	0	0	0.20
Purchases of refined products d	1,092	2,175	2,616	15,082	19,278	19,382	1.90	3.77	3.06	11.38	13.02	11.30
Gasolines	554	1,568	758	8,851	11,037	7,002	0.96	2.72	0.89	6.68	7.45	4.09
Kerosene and distillate (1940–1950)	70	100	824	3,892	3,354	5,405	0.12	0.17	0.96	2.94	2.27	3.15
Residual (Incl. distillate 1929–1935)	459	409	830	2,057	4,597	6,406	0.80	0.71	0.97	1.55	3.10	3.73
Other products	9	98	204	282	290	569	0.02	0.17	0.24	0.21	0.20	0.33
Domestic refinery runs e	67,981	61,712	90,586	125,016	138,788	163,657						
TRANSPORTATION OPERATIONS												
Total crude oil receipts at refineries f	69,590	62,800	91,330	125,860	139,680	162,840	100.00	100.00	100.00	100.00	100.00	100.00
Via company facilities	61,130	56,450	78,830	110,270	133,050	133,900	87.84	89.89	86.31	87.61	95.25	82.23
Company owned pipe lines g	46,030	46,850	69,150	94,580	90,040	100,080	66.14	74.60	75.71	75.14	64.46	61.46
Company marine equipment h	15,100	9,600	9,680	15,690	43,010	33,820	21.70	15.29	10.60	12.47	30.79	20.77
Via outside facilities	8,460	6,350	12,500	15,590	6,630	28,940	12.16	10.11	13.69	12.39	4.75	17.77
Marine equipment	7,820	1,690	6,290	10,670	5,200	18,530	11.24	2.69	6.89	8.48	3.73	11.38
Tank cars, trucks, and others i	640	4,660	6,210	4,920	1,430	10,410	0.92	7.42	6.80	3.91	1.02	6.39
Total products shipments from refineries f	48,780	54,890	83,500	117,610	133,980	155,050	100.00	100.00	100.00	100.00	100.00	100.00
Via company facilities	39,820	37,200	55,580	72,550	89,840	97,060	81.63	67.77	66.56	61.69	67.05	62.60
Company owned pipe lines g	0	1,340	4,000	12,740	14,950	16,400	0	2.44	4.79	10.83	11.16	10.58
Company marine equipment h	35,220	33,750	48,480	46,100	56,330	57,930	72.20	61.49	58.06	39.20	42.04	37.36
Pipe line and marine j	0	0	0	3,700	4,200	6,550	0	0	0	3.15	3.13	4.22
Truck k	4,600	2,110	3,100	10,010	14,360	16,180	9.43	3.84	3.71	8.51	10.72	10.44
Via outside facilities	8,960	17,690	27,920	45,060	44,140	57,990	18.37	32.23	33.44	38.31	32.95	37.40
Pipe line	0	970	2,220	3,480	6,820	8,860	0	1.77	2.66	2.96	5.09	5.71
Marine equipment	750	6,630	12,740	28,530	27,720	39,960	1.54	12.08	15.26	24.25	20.69	25.78
Rail	8,210	10,090	12,960	13,050	9,600	9,170	16.83	18.38	15.52	11.10	7.17	5.91

Note: Blank spaces indicate data not available.

a Includes purchases abroad for import and shipments abroad from U.S. stocks.

b Includes Gulf's share of Kuwait production, but excludes production of Mene Grande Oil Company sold under long-term contract.

c Excludes fuel oil used for refinery heat and yield from crude oil run under processing agreements for others.

d Excludes semifinished stocks but includes products acquired under processing agreements.

e Excludes crude oil run for others under processing agreements.

f Excludes shipments between Gulf refineries.

g Includes all pipe lines in which company had stock interest. Shipments from refineries via pipe lines include a substantial volume moving through short lines from refineries to near-by sales terminals.

h Includes tankers under long-term charter (usually five years or over).

i May include a very small volume moving via company trucks.

j By tanker to Port St. Joe and thence through Southeastern pipe line. In some instances the marine portion of the haul may have been via outside tankers.

k It was not possible to separate the volume moved via company and outside trucks. Total arbitrarily classed as a movement via company facilities.

TABLE 9. GULF OIL CORPORATION (CONTINUED)

Balance of Operations in Selected Years

	Thousands of Barrels						Percentage Breakdowns					
	1929	1935	1940	1946	1949	1950	1929	1935	1940	1946	1949	1950
MARKETING OPERATIONS												
Total sales refined products [1]	57,546	54,456	81,702	125,587	144,529	168,361	100.00	100.00	100.00	100.00	100.00	100.00
Gasolines	22,832	26,491	39,761	57,001	65,468	70,541	39.68	48.65	48.67	45.39	45.30	41.90
Kerosene and distillate	7,430	8,707	13,820	26,039	32,743	43,586	12.91	15.99	16.92	20.73	22.65	25.89
Residual	25,036	16,960	24,310	37,058	41,157	47,460	43.50	31.14	29.75	29.51	28.48	28.19
Other	2,248	2,298	3,811	5,489	5,161	6,774	3.91	4.22	4.66	4.37	3.57	4.02
Gasoline sales by method of sale: Total [m]		26,491	39,761	57,001	65,468	70,541		100.00	100.00	100.00	100.00	100.00
From refineries and terminals		4,152	8,553	13,945	12,923	13,922		15.67	21.51	24.46	19.74	19.74
From company operated bulk plants		11,511	14,737	21,093	25,402	27,372		43.46	37.06	37.00	38.80	38.80
Through commission truck drivers		48	196	363	668	723		0.18	0.49	0.64	1.02	1.02
Through commission distributors		10,780	16,275	21,600	26,475	28,524		40.69	40.94	37.90	40.44	40.44
Gasoline sales by type customer: Total		26,491	39,761	57,001	65,468	70,541		100.00	100.00	100.00	100.00	100.00
To wholesale resellers		2,646	6,449	13,180	11,710	11,904		9.99	16.22	23.12	17.89	16.87
Brokers, refiners, cargo buyers, export [n]		1,140	1,442	5,337	3,811	1,618		4.31	3.63	9.36	5.82	2.29
Unbranded jobbers and tank truck dealers		409	2,040	4,777	2,206	4,205		1.54	5.13	8.38	3.37	5.96
Branded jobbers and tank truck dealers		1,097	2,967	3,066	5,693	6,081		4.14	7.46	5.38	8.70	8.62
To retail resellers		17,061	25,008	32,143	39,807	43,783		64.40	62.90	56.39	60.80	62.07
Contractor stations		{17,061	14,472	17,901	23,621	25,909		64.40	36.40	31.40	36.08	36.73
Dealer operated stations			10,536	14,242	16,186	17,874			26.50	24.99	24.72	25.34
To consumers and industrial users [o]		6,784	8,304	11,678	13,951	14,854		25.61	20.88	20.49	21.31	21.06
Company operated stations		2,129	1,066	2,138	2,166	1,888		8.04	2.68	3.75	3.31	2.68
Industrial, household, and other		4,655	7,238	9,540	11,785	12,966		17.57	18.20	16.74	18.00	18.38
Kerosene and distillate sales by method of sale: Total [o]		8,707	13,820	26,039	32,743	43,586		100.00	100.00	100.00	100.00	100.00
From refineries and terminals		4,217	7,547	13,778	17,419	21,949		48.44	54.61	52.92	53.20	50.36
From company operated bulk plants		2,810	3,597	7,497	10,676	15,075		32.27	26.03	28.79	32.61	34.59
Through commission truck drivers		243	129	264	256	362		2.79	0.93	1.01	0.78	0.83
Through commission distributors		1,437	2,547	4,500	4,392	6,200		16.50	18.43	17.28	13.41	14.22
Kerosene and distillate sales by type customer: Total		8,707	13,820	26,039	32,743	43,586		100.00	100.00	100.00	100.00	100.00
To wholesale resellers		4,071	8,934	15,701	18,992	25,768		46.75	64.64	60.30	58.01	59.12
Brokers, refiners, cargo buyers, export [n]		190	252	3,333	1,996	2,137		2.18	1.82	12.80	6.10	4.90
Jobbers and tank truck dealers		3,881	8,682	12,368	16,996	23,631		44.57	62.82	47.50	51.91	54.22
To retail resellers		948	1,046	1,767	1,723	1,990		10.89	7.57	6.79	5.26	4.57
Contractor stations } Dealer operated stations		948	1,046	1,767	1,723	1,990		10.89	7.57	6.79	5.26	4.57
To consumers and industrial users		3,688	3,840	8,571	12,028	15,828		42.36	27.79	32.91	36.73	36.31
Company operated stations		16	5	9	7	7		0.18	0.04	0.03	0.02	0.02
Industrial, household, and other		3.672	3.835	8,562	12,021	15,821		42.18	27.75	32.88	36.71	36.29

[1] Includes all domestic sales and shipments for export.
[m] Breakdown for 1949 derived from 1950 experience.
[n] Includes cargo sales to U.S. Government. Sales to post offices, forestry offices, and other local government agencies treated as sales to consumers and industrial users.

[o] Breakdown for 1949 derived in part from 1950 experience.

SOURCE: Gulf Oil Corporation.

TABLE 10. THE TEXAS COMPANY
Balance of Operations in Selected Years

	Thousands of Barrels						Percentage Breakdowns					
	1929	1935	1940	1946	1949	1951	1929	1935	1940	1946	1949	1951
CRUDE OIL OPERATIONS												
Total new supply of crude oil in U.S.	NA	78,541	107,749	133,485	155,464	175,479	100.00%	100.00%	100.00%	100.00%	100.00%	100.00%
Net domestic production[a]	43,604	37,646	84,597	84,072	88,829	107,593	NA	47.93	78.51	62.98	57.14	61.31
Imports own foreign production	265	65	0	0	5,387	3,332		0.08	0.00	0.00	3.46	1.90
Net purchases[b]	NA	40,830	23,152	49,413	61,248	64,554		51.99	21.49	37.02	39.40	36.79
Total net foreign production[a]	217	80	0	1,056	7,452	8,537						
REFINED PRODUCTS OPERATIONS												
Total new supply of refined products in U.S.	59,351	76,810	103,432	134,145	152,499	177,589	100.00	100.00	100.00	100.00	100.00	100.00
Yield of refined products from refineries[c]	57,538	75,075	100,792	131,286	149,935	173,930	96.95	97.74	97.45	97.87	98.32	97.94
Imports from company's foreign refineries	0	0	0	0	1,652	1,943	0.00	0.00	0.00	0.00	1.08	1.09
Purchases of refined products[d]	1,813	1,735	2,640	2,859	912	1,716	3.05	2.26	2.55	2.13	0.60	0.97
Gasolines	718	1,725	938	2,301	444	1,321	1.21	2.25	0.91	1.72	0.29	0.74
Kerosene and distillates	4	1	4	0	1	20	0.00	0.00	0.00	0.00	0.00	0.01
Residual	1,033	0	1,688	503	453	208	1.74	0.00	1.63	0.37	0.30	0.12
Other products	58	9	10	55	14	167	0.10	0.01	0.01	0.04	0.01	0.10
Domestic Refinery Runs[e]	58,294	76,276	101,622	132,546	151,038	175,969						
TRANSPORTATION OPERATIONS												
Total crude oil receipts at refineries	60,462	75,594	101,968	126,443	144,355	168,910	100.00	100.00	100.00	100.00	100.00	100.00
Via company facilities	56,211	73,398	99,326	119,342	128,424	149,106	92.97	97.09	97.41	94.38	88.96	88.28
Company owned pipe lines[f]	53,776	58,995	86,561	104,790	91,200	110,775	88.94	78.04	84.89	82.87	63.18	65.58
Company marine equipment[g]	2,435	14,403	12,765	14,552	37,224	38,331	4.03	19.05	12.52	11.51	25.78	22.70
Via outside facilities	4,251	2,196	2,642	7,101	15,931	19,804	7.03	2.91	2.59	5.62	11.04	11.72
Total products shipments from refineries	59,563	71,592	96,859	126,537	142,502	162,931	100.00	100.00	100.00	100.00	100.00	100.00
Via company facilities	35,849	47,210	57,930	78,165	94,310	121,063	60.19	65.94	59.81	61.77	66.18	74.30
Company owned pipe lines[f]	3,915	4,764	5,857	15,630	21,028	34,072	6.57	6.65	6.05	12.35	14.76	20.91
Company marine equipment[g]	31,934	42,446	52,073	62,535	73,282	86,991	53.62	59.29	53.76	49.42	51.42	53.39
Via outside facilities	23,714	24,382	38,929	48,372	48,192	41,868	39.81	34.06	40.19	38.23	33.82	25.70
Pipe line	0	31	38	40	1,677	2,312	0.00	0.04	0.04	0.03	1.18	1.42
Marine	17	141	2,638	2,897	5,467	4,390	0.03	0.20	2.73	2.29	3.84	2.69
Rail	21,551	22,077	32,084	24,285	19,056	16,333	36.18	30.84	33.12	19.19	13.37	10.03
Truck	2,146	2,133	4,169	21,150	21,992	18,833	3.60	2.98	4.30	16.72	15.43	11.56

Note: Blank spaces indicate data not available.

[a] Crude oil and condensate.

[b] Includes purchases abroad for import and shipments abroad from U.S. stocks.

[c] Includes fuel oil used for refinery heat but excludes yield from crude oil run under processing agreements for others.

[d] Includes purchases by refining department only. Data on other purchases not available but reported to be a small part of total supply. Excludes semifinished stocks, but includes products acquired under processing agreements.

[e] Excludes crude oil run for others under processing agreements.

[f] Includes all pipe lines in which company had a stock interest.

[g] Includes tankers under long-term charter (over 10 years).

TABLE 10. THE TEXAS COMPANY (CONTINUED)

Balance of Operations in Selected Years

	Thousands of Barrels						Percentage Breakdowns					
	1929	1935	1940	1946	1949	1951	1929	1935	1940	1946	1949	1951
MARKETING OPERATIONS												
Total sales refined products h					142,047	163,492					100.00	100.00
Gasolines					83,774	93,979					58.98	57.48
Kerosene and distillate					16,785	23,790					11.82	14.55
Residual					27,392	29,784					19.28	18.22
Other					14,096	15,939					9.92	9.75
Gasoline sales by method of sale: Total					83,774	93,979					100.00	100.00
From refineries and terminals and for export					24,784	27,091					29.58	28.83
From company operated bulk plants					30,601	38,826					36.53	41.31
Through commission distributors					28,389	28,062					33.89	29.86
Gasoline sales by type customer: Total					83,774	93,979					100.00	100.00
To wholesale resellers					20,192	21,338					24.10	22.71
Brokers, refiners, cargo buyers, export i					6,405	6,265					7.64	6.67
Branded and unbranded jobbers					13,304	14,590					15.88	15.53
Tank truck dealers (peddlers)					483	483					0.58	0.51
To retail resellers					51,811	58,455					61.85	62.20
Contractor stations					23,618	22,363					28.19	23.80
Dealer operated stations					28,193	36,092					33.66	38.40
To consumers and industrial users					11,771	14,186					14.05	15.09
Company operated stations					37	35					0.04	0.04
Industrial customers					8,702	11,043					10.39	11.75
Farm, household, and other					3,032	3,108					3.62	3.30
Kerosene and distillate sales by method of sale: Total					16,785	23,790					100.00	100.00
From refineries and terminals and for export					12,258	18,931					73.03	79.58
From company operated bulk plants					1,489	1,904					8.87	8.00
Through commission distributors					3,038	2,955					18.10	12.42
Kerosene and distillate sales by type customer: Total					16,785	23,790					100.00	100.00
To wholesale resellers					10,843	14,953					64.60	62.85
Brokers, refiners, cargo buyers, export i					2,963	3,281					17.65	13.79
Branded and unbranded jobbers					6,525	10,240					38.87	43.04
Tank truck dealers (peddlers)					1,355	1,432					8.08	6.02
To retail resellers					989	937					5.89	3.94
Contractor stations					704	579					4.19	2.44
Dealer operated stations					285	358					1.70	1.50
To consumers and industrial users					4,953	7,900					29.51	33.21
Company operated stations					0	0					0.00	0.00
Industrial customers					3,968	7,016					23.64	29.49
Farm, household, and other					985	884					5.87	3.72

h Includes all domestic sales and shipments for export but excludes refined products supplied to others under processing agreements.

i Probably includes cargo sales to U.S. Government. Sales to post offices, forestry offices, and other local government agencies probably treated as sales to consumers and industrial users.

SOURCE: The Texas Company.

TABLE 11. SINCLAIR OIL CORPORATION
Balance of Operations in Selected Years

	Thousands of Barrels						Percentage Breakdowns					
	1929	1935	1940	1946	1949	1950	1929	1935	1940	1946	1949	1950
CRUDE OIL OPERATIONS												
Total new supply of crude oil in U.S.	36,484	42,853	71,125	92,086	96,253	110,771	100.00%	100.00%	100.00%	100.00%	100.00%	100.00%
Net domestic production	16,173	26,041	26,593	28,636	32,126	33,866	44.33	60.77	37.39	31.10	33.39	30.57
Crude oil	16,173	24,753	24,107	26,825	30,327	31,692	44.33	57.76	33.89	29.13	31.51	28.61
Natural gasoline a		1,288	2,486	1,811	1,809	2,174		3.01	3.50	1.97	1.88	1.96
Imports own foreign production	889			9,786	4,345	2,114	2.44			10.63	4.51	1.91
Net purchases b	19,422	16,812	44,532	53,664	59,772	74,791	53.23	39.23	62.61	58.27	62.10	67.52
Total net foreign production	2,442	1,983		9,786	4,345	3,571						
REFINED PRODUCTS OPERATIONS												
Total new supply refined products in U.S.	36,291	54,138	70,103	96,050	95,912	110,609	100.00	100.00	100.00	100.00	100.00	100.00
Yield of refined products from refineries c	34,488	46,996	61,717	86,064	88,991	103,610	95.03	86.81	88.04	89.60	92.78	93.68
Imports from company's foreign refineries		127				225		.23				.20
Purchases of refined products d	1,803	7,015	8,386	9,986	6,921	6,774	4.97	12.96	11.96	10.40	7.22	6.12
Gasolines	949	5,503	3,219	3,428		768	2.62	10.17	4.59	3.57		0.69
Kerosene and distillate	501	1,019	3,953	4,400		2,382	1.38	1.88	5.63	4.58		2.15
Residual		11	775	1,968		3,311		0.02	1.11	2.05		3.00
Other products	353	482	439	190		313	0.97	0.89	0.63	0.20		0.28
Domestic refinery runs e	35,729	51,906	68,011	92,296	95,109	110,797						
TRANSPORTATION OPERATIONS												
Total crude oil receipts at refineries	36,379	55,923	67,829	92,688	95,121	111,312	100.00	100.00	100.00	100.00	100.00	100.00
Via company facilities	6,486	50,005	58,169	92,070	92,799	104,291	17.83	89.42	85.76	99.33	97.56	93.69
Company owned pipe lines f		43,045	51,234	69,963	66,451	77,910		76.97	75.54	75.48	69.86	69.99
Company tankers g	6,486	6,960	6,935	22,107	26,348	26,381	17.83	12.45	10.22	23.85	27.70	23.70
Via outside facilities	29,893	5,918	9,660	618	2,322	7,021	82.17	10.58	14.24	0.67	2.44	6.31
Total products shipments from refineries	34,722	48,471	61,664	85,910	89,397	104,731	100.00	100.00	100.00	100.00	100.00	100.00
Via company facilities	12,655	11,756	13,689	28,606	51,816	58,915	36.45	24.25	22.20	33.30	57.96	56.25
Company owned pipe lines f		478	803	12,140	27,836	35,067		0.99	1.30	14.13	31.14	33.48
Company tankers g	12,655	11,278	12,886	16,466	23,980	23,848	36.45	23.26	20.90	19.17	26.82	22.77
Via outside facilities h	22,067	36,715	47,975	57,304	37,581	45,816	63.55	75.75	77.80	66.70	42.04	43.75
MARKETING OPERATIONS												
Total sales refined products i	34,181	52,157	68,608	93,000	94,078	108,463	100.00	100.00	100.00	100.00	100.00	100.00
Gasolines	21,024	29,838	35,854	44,589	47,361	52,410	61.51	57.21	52.26	47.94	50.35	48.32
Kerosene and distillate	3,901	12,163	16,374	23,725	25,189	31,879	11.41	23.32	23.86	25.51	26.77	29.39
Residual	5,791	7,254	13,418	20,410	18,478	19,602	16.94	13.91	19.56	21.95	19.64	18.07
Other	3,465	2,902	2,962	4,276	3,050	4,572	10.14	5.56	4.32	4.60	3.24	4.22
Gasoline sales by method of sale: Total	21,024	29,838	35,854	44,589	47,361	52,410	100.00	100.00	100.00	100.00	100.00	100.00
From refineries	6,590	8,250	9,037	11,369	9,152	8,927	31.34	27.65	25.21	25.50	19.32	17.03
From terminals	2,255	706	867	4,832	6,624	8,006	10.73	2.37	2.42	10.84	13.99	15.28
From company operated bulk plants j	12,179	9,726	8,202	8,029	11,623	14,564	57.93	32.60	22.87	18.01	24.54	27.79
Through commission distributors		11,066	17,082	19,666	18,551	19,053		37.08	47.64	44.10	39.17	36.35
Through exchanges k		90	660	693	1,411	1,860		0.30	1.86	1.55	2.98	3.55
Gasoline sales by type customer: Total l		29,838	35,854	44,589	47,361	52,410		100.00	100.00	100.00	100.00	100.0
To wholesale resellers		8,614	10,064	16,084		17,893		28.87	28.07	36.07		34.14
Brokers, refiners, cargo buyers, export						6,654						12.70
Unbranded jobbers and tank truck dealers						1,428						2.72
Branded jobbers						9,811						18.72
To retail resellers		13,223	18,077	19,662		25,034		44.32	50.42	44.10		47.77
Contractor stations		4,321	6,007	6,639		7,697		14.48	16.75	14.89		14.69
Dealer operated stations		8,902	12,070	13,023		17,337		29.84	33.67	29.21		33.08
To consumers and industrial users		8,001	7,713	8,843		9,483		26.81	21.51	19.83		18.09
Company operated stations		717	35	13		114		2.40	0.10	0.03		0.22
Industrial, household, and other		7,284	7,678	8,830		9,369		24.41	21.41	19.80		17.87
Kerosene and distillate sales by method of sale: Total	3,901	12,163	16,374	23,725	25,189	31,879	100.00	100.00	100.00	100.00	100.00	100.00
From refineries	1,736	4,313	4,842	11,488	6,961	8,562	44.50	35.46	29.57	48.42	27.63	26.86
From terminals	631	2,682	1,863	2,504	6,112	8,688	16.18	22.05	11.38	10.55	24.26	27.25
From company operated bulk plants		3,139	4,976	4,476	5,123	6,781		25.81	30.39	18.87	20.34	21.27
Through commission distributors	1,534	2,022	4,471	5,101	6,820	7,222	39.32	16.62	27.30	21.50	27.08	22.66
Through exchanges k		7	222	156	173	626		0.06	1.36	0.66	0.69	1.96

Kerosene and distillate sales by type customer: (not available)

Note: Blank spaces indicate data not available.

a Natural gasoline transported to refineries via pipe lines commingled with crude oil.

b Includes purchases abroad for imports and shipments abroad from U.S. stocks.

c Excludes fuel oil used for refinery heat and yield of crude oil run under processing agreements for others.

d Excludes semifinished stocks but includes products acquired under processing agreements.

e Excludes crude oil run for others under processing agreements. In 1950 includes 475,000 barrels run for Sinclair by another refinery.

f Includes all pipe lines in which company had a stock interest.

g Includes tankers under long-term charter.

h Includes shipments via company trucks, but such shipments were negligible relative to the total.

i Includes all domestic sales and shipments for export.

j Includes sales through commission truck drivers working out of company bulk plants.

k Products received in exchanges and resold through facilities of the partner in the exchange. Products received in exchange and resold through Sinclair facilities were included as sales by such facilities.

l Company divides its sales into two major categories: *wholesale sales* and *bulk plant sales*. The breakdowns here shown assume that the same proportion of the *wholesale sales* (4.79%) went to industrial, household, and other consumers in 1935, 1940, 1946, and 1950 as in 1951. In addition, the breakdown of sales "to wholesale resellers" for 1950 is based on 1951 ratios. Sales to U.S. military services were treated as a cargo sale.

SOURCE: Sinclair Oil Corporation

TABLE 12. THE OHIO OIL COMPANY
Balance of Operations in Selected Years

	Thousands of Barrels					Percentage Breakdowns				
	1935	1940	1946	1949	1950	1935	1940	1946	1949	1950
CRUDE OIL OPERATIONS										
Total new supply of crude oil in U.S.	4,229	5,810	8,247	12,153	11,591	100.00%	100.00%	100.00%	100.00%	100.00%
Net domestic production	18,301	22,625	31,404	28,112	30,164	432.75	389.41	380.79	231.32	260.24
Net purchases (sales) a	(14,072)	(16,815)	(23,157)	(15,959)	(18,573)	(332.75)	(289.41)	(280.79)	(131.32)	(160.24)
Total net foreign production	0	0	0	0	79					
REFINED PRODUCTS OPERATIONS										
Total new supply refined products in U.S.	5,771	6,713	8,520	10,825	13,258	100.00	100.00	100.00	100.00	100.00
Yield of refined products from refineries b	5,343	5,886	7,387	10,379	12,946	92.58	87.68	86.70	95.88	96.65
Purchases of refined products c	428	827	1,133	446	312	7.42	12.32	13.30	4.12	2.35
Domestic refinery runs d	5,440	6,982	7,536	10,675	13,034					
TRANSPORTATION OPERATIONS										
Total crude oil receipts at refineries	5,430	6,101	7,571	10,639	13,247	100.00	100.00	100.00	100.00	100.00
Via company facilities (pipelines) e	4,456	5,853	7,088	10,435	12,952	82.06	95.94	93.62	98.08	97.77
Via outside facilities	974	248	483	204	295	17.94	4.06	6.38	1.92	2.23
Total products shipments from refineries	5,349	5,820	7,436	10,447	12,892	100.00	100.00	100.00	100.00	100.00
Via company facilities (trucks)	0	0	250	320	492	0	0	3.36	3.06	3.82
Via outside facilities	5,349	5,820	7,186	10,127	12,400	100.00	100.00	96.64	96.94	96.18
MARKETING OPERATIONS										
Total sales refined products f	5,377	7,025	8,682	10,982	12,770	100.00	100.00	100.00	100.00	100.00
Gasolines	3,475	4,345	4,337	5,813	6,839	64.63	61.85	49.96	52.93	53.56
Kerosene and distillate	828	790	1,268	2,147	2,596	15.40	11.25	14.60	19.55	20.33
Residual	313	690	1,645	1,410	1,488	5.82	9.82	18.95	12.84	11.65
Other	716	1,200	1,432	1,612	1,847	14.15	17.08	16.49	14.68	14.46
Gasoline sales by method of sales: Total g		3,282	4,337	5,813	6,839		100.00	100.00	100.00	100.00
From refineries		307	997	1,402	1,642		9.36	22.99	24.12	24.00
From terminals		0	169	546	1,010		3.90	9.39	14.77
From company operated bulk plants		1,793	1,110	1,189	873		54.63	25.59	20.45	12.77
Through commission truck drivers		94	433	181	168		2.86	9.98	3.11	2.46
Through commission distributors		1,088	1,628	2,495	3,146		33.15	37.54	42.93	46.00
Gasoline sales by type customer: Total g		3,282	4,337	5,813	6,839		100.00	100.00	100.00	100.00
To wholesale resellers		1,489	2,139	2,425	3,046		45.37	49.32	41.71	44.54
Brokers, refiners, cargo buyers i		307	141	134	536		9.35	3.25	2.31	7.84
Unbranded jobbers		565	662	496	606		17.22	15.27	8.53	8.86
Branded jobbers		428	678	1,486	1,577		13.04	15.63	25.55	23.06
Tank truck dealers (peddlers)		189	658	309	327		5.76	15.17	5.32	4.78
To retail resellers		1,300	1,491	2,150	2,426		39.61	34.38	36.99	35.47
Contractor stations		442	310	512	523		13.47	7.15	8.81	7.65
Dealer operated stations		858	1,181	1,638	1,903		26.14	27.23	28.18	27.82
To consumers and industrial users		493	707	1,238	1,367		15.02	16.30	21.30	19.99
Company operated stations		84	36	72	68		2.56	0.83	1.24	0.99
Industrial, household, and other		409	671	1,166	1,299		12.46	15.47	20.06	19.00
Kerosene and distillate sales by method of sale: Total h		482	1,268	2,147	2,595		100.00	100.00	100.00	100.00
From refineries		210	88	249	206		43.57	6.94	11.60	7.94
From terminals		0	6	58	58			0.47	2.70	2.24
From company operated bulk plants		137	185	385	330		28.42	14.59	17.93	12.72
Through commission truck drivers		16	93	77	123		3.32	7.34	3.59	4.74
Through commission distributors		119	896	1,378	1,878		24.69	70.66	64.18	72.36
Kerosene and distillate sales by type customer: Total h		482	1,268	2,147	2,595		100.00	100.00	100.00	100.00
To wholesale resellers		345	997	1,535	1,800		71.58	78.63	71.49	69.37
Brokers, refiners, cargo buyers i		210	23	233	182		43.58	1.81	10.85	7.01
Unbranded jobbers		82	756	541	525		17.01	59.62	25.20	20.23
Branded jobbers		22	107	654	913		4.56	8.44	30.46	35.19
Tank truck dealers (peddlers)		31	111	107	180		6.43	8.76	4.98	6.94
To retail resellers		50	58	88	101		10.37	4.57	4.10	3.89
Contractor stations		33	34	52	56		6.84	2.68	2.42	2.16
Dealer operated stations		17	24	36	45		3.53	1.89	1.68	1.73
To consumers and industrial users		87	213	524	694		18.05	16.80	24.41	26.74
Company operated stations		1	1	1	1		0.21	0.08	0.05	0.04
Industrial, household, and other		86	212	523	693		17.84	16.72	24.36	26.70

Note: Blank spaces indicate data not available.

a Includes purchases abroad for import and shipments abroad from U.S. stocks.

b Excludes fuel oil used for refinery heat and yield from crude oil run under processing agreements for others.

c Excludes semifinished stocks but includes products acquired under processing agreements.

d Excludes crude oil run for others under processing agreements but includes crude oil run by others under processing agreements.

e Includes all pipe lines in which company had a stock interest.

f Includes all domestic sales and shipments for export.

g Figures for 1940 exclude 1,063,000 barrels of gasoline sold in Southwest area from which company withdrew prior to 1943. No breakdown by type of customer available on this volume. Breakdown of sales by method in 1940 is based in part on 1941 experience.

h Figures for 1940 exclude 308,000 barrels of kerosene and distillate sold in Southwest area from which company withdrew prior to 1943. No breakdown by type of customer is available on this volume. Breakdown of sales by method in 1940 is based in part on 1941 experience.

i Probably includes cargo sales to U.S. Government. Amount of such sales reported to be a very small part of total sales.

SOURCE: The Ohio Oil Company.

TABLE 13. THE ATLANTIC REFINING COMPANY
Balance of Operations in Selected Years

	Thousands of Barrels						Percentage Breakdowns					
	1929	1935	1940	1946	1949	1950	1929	1935	1940	1946	1949	1950
CRUDE OIL OPERATIONS												
Total new supply of crude oil in U.S.	24,856	29,898	39,000	44,124	52,998	58,260	100.00%	100.00%	100.00%	100.00%	100.00%	100.00%
Net domestic production	5,021	9,228	13,496	23,567	23,901	25,903	20.20	30.86	34.61	53.41	45.10	44.46
Imports own foreign production	107				2,051	4,228	0.43				3.87	7.26
Net purchases [a]	19,728	20,670	25,504	20,557	27,046	28,129	79.37	69.14	65.39	46.59	51.03	48.28
Total net foreign production	111			10	1,916	4,383						
REFINED PRODUCTS OPERATIONS												
Total new supply refined products in U.S.	27,259	26,459	34,730	41,983	49,545	55,593	100.00	100.00	100.00	100.00	100.00	100.00
Yield of refined products from refineries [b]	21,448	25,773	33,692	39,841	47,611	53,152	78.68	97.41	97.01	94.90	96.10	95.61
Purchases of refined products [c]	5,811	686	1,038	2,142	1,934	2,441	21.32	2.59	2.99	5.10	3.90	4.39
Gasolines			190	1,097	536	602			0.55	2.61	1.08	1.08
Kerosene and distillate			51	447	173	138			0.15	1.06	0.35	0.25
Residual			495	201	868	1,425			1.42	0.48	1.75	2.56
Other			302	397	357	276			0.87	0.95	0.72	0.50
Domestic refinery runs [d]	26,221	30,203	37,834	44,656	52,718	57,948						
TRANSPORTATION OPERATIONS												
Total crude oil receipts at refineries	26,028	29,715	38,060	44,096	52,605	57,657	100.00	100.00	100.00	100.00	100.00	100.00
Via company facilities	14,755	24,183	37,466	38,494	44,212	47,577	56.69	81.38	98.44	87.30	84.05	82.52
Company owned pipe lines [e]			7,626	5,361	11,258	8,295			20.04	12.16	21.40	14.39
Company tankers	14,755	24,183	29,840	33,133	32,954	35,080	56.69	81.38	78.40	75.14	62.65	60.84
Term charter tankers						4,202						7.29
Via outside facilities	11,273	5,532	594	5,602	8,393	10,080	43.31	18.62	1.56	12.70	15.95	17.48
Total products shipments from refineries	24,299	26,870	33,982	40,714	48,487	55,117	100.00	100.00	100.00	100.00	100.00	100.00
Via company facilities		13,247	23,445	27,982	36,850	38,815		49.30	68.99	68.73	76.00	70.42
Company owned pipe lines [e]		4,311	9,878	11,550	15,692	17,462		16.04	29.07	28.37	32.36	31.68
Company and term charter tankers [f]		4,274	9,134	9,130	13,450	12,803		15.91	26.88	22.43	27.74	23.23
Company trucks		4,662	4,433	7,302	7,708	8,550		17.35	13.04	17.93	15.90	15.51
Via outside facilities		13,623	10,537	12,732	11,637	16,302		50.70	31.01	31.27	24.00	29.58
MARKETING OPERATIONS												
Total sales refined products [g]	25,985	26,460	33,695	40,129	49,574	55,180	100.00	100.00	100.00	100.00	100.00	100.00
Gasolines	14,456	14,838	17,525	19,471	23,523	24,084	55.63	56.08	52.00	48.52	47.45	43.65
Kerosene and distillate	3,503	3,224	6,950	10,850	13,222	16,702	13.48	12.18	20.63	27.04	26.67	30.27
Residual	4,458	5,763	7,095	5,971	7,974	8,824	17.16	21.78	21.06	14.88	16.09	15.99
Other	3,568	2,635	2,125	3,837	4,855	5,570	13.73	9.96	6.31	9.56	9.79	10.09
Gasoline sales by method of sale: Total		14,838	17,525	19,471	23,523	24,084		100.00	100.00	100.00	100.00	100.00
From refineries					4,087	3,880					17.37	16.11
From terminals					14,064	15,034					59.79	62.43
From company operated bulk plants					4,876	4,813					20.73	19.98
Through commission truck drivers					141	130					0.60	0.54
Through commission distributors					355	227					1.51	0.94
Gasoline sales by type customer: Total		14,838	17,525	19,471	23,523	24,084		100.00	100.00	100.00	100.00	100.00
To wholesale resellers [h]		7,402	7,314	8,985	8,062	8,084		49.88	41.73	46.15	34.27	33.57
Brokers, refiners, cargo buyers, export [i]					1,473	977					6.26	4.06
Unbranded jobbers		(see footnote h)			486	645		(see footnote h)			2.07	2.68
Branded jobbers					5,405	5,767					22.97	23.94
Tank truck dealers (peddlers)					698	695					2.97	2.89
To retail resellers		6,263	9,483	10,091	11,962	12,469		42.21	54.12	51.82	50.85	51.77
Contractor stations					5,568	5,612					23.67	23.30
Dealer operated stations					6,394	6,857					27.18	28.47
To consumers and industrial users					3,499	3,531					14.88	14.66
Company operated stations		1,173	728	395	245	200		7.91	4.15	2.03	1.04	0.83
Industrial customers [h]		(see footnote h)			2,008	2,261		(see footnote h)			8.54	9.39
Farm, household, and other [h]					1,246	1,070					5.30	4.44
Kerosene and distillate sales by method of sale: Total		3,224	6,950	10,850	13,222	16,702		100.00	100.00	100.00	100.00	100.00
From refineries					3,217	3,678					24.33	22.02
From terminals					7,327	9,206					55.41	55.13
From company operated bulk plants					2,466	3,620					18.65	21.67
Through commission truck drivers					129	129					0.98	0.77
Through commission distributors					83	69					0.63	0.41
Kerosene and distillate sales by type customer: Total		3,224	6,950	10,850	13,222	16,702		100.00	100.00	100.00	100.00	100.00
To wholesale resellers [h]		2,256	4,658	9,634	9,993	12,461		69.98	67.02	88.79	75.58	74.61
Brokers, refiners, cargo buyers, export [i]					391	713					2.96	4.27
Jobbers		(see footnote h)			7,232	9,479		(see footnote h)			54.70	56.75
Tank truck dealers (peddlers)					2,370	2,269					17.92	13.59
To retail resellers		963	2,289	1,214	109	95		29.87	32.94	11.19	0.82	0.57
Contractor stations					80	65					0.60	0.39
Dealer operated stations					29	30					0.22	0.18
To consumers and industrial users					3,120	4,146					23.60	24.82
Company operated stations		5	3	2	1			0.15	0.04	0.02	0.01	
Industrial customers [h]		(see footnote h)			1,740	2,574		(see footnote h)			13.16	15.41
Farm, household, and other [h]					1,379	1,572					10.43	9.41

Note: Blank spaces indicate data not available.

[a] Includes purchases abroad for import and shipments abroad from U.S. stocks.

[b] Excludes fuel oil used for refinery heat.

[c] Excludes semifinished stocks.

[d] Company reports no crude oil runs for or by others under processing agreements in these years.

[e] Includes all pipe lines in which company had a stock interest.

[f] Includes tankers under long-term charter (usually 10 years or over).

[g] Includes all domestic sales and shipments for export.

[h] For the years 1935, 1940, 1946 the category wholesale resellers includes sales to industrial, farm, household, and other consumers.

[i] Probably includes cargo sales to U.S. Government. Sales to post offices, forestry offices, and other local government agencies probably treated as sales to consumers and industrial users.

SOURCE: The Atlantic Refining Company.

TABLE 14. STANDARD OIL COMPANY (INDIANA)

Balance of Operations for Selected Years

	Thousands of Barrels				Percentage Breakdowns			
	1935	1940	1946	1950	1935	1940	1946	1950
CRUDE OIL OPERATIONS								
Total new supply of crude oil in U.S.	67,205	111,472	131,402	171,496	100.00%	100.00%	100.00%	100.00%
Net domestic production [a]	19,317	33,266	66,202	74,796	28.74	29.84	50.38	43.61
Net purchases [b]	47,888	78,206	65,200	96,700	71.26	70.16	49.62	56.39
REFINED PRODUCTS OPERATIONS								
Total new supply refined products in U.S.	86,025	112,740	133,485	189,533	100.00	100.00	100.00	100.00
Yield of refined products from refineries [c]	60,131	96,639	115,398	163,117	69.90	85.72	86.45	86.06
Purchases of refined products [d]	25,894	16,101	18,087	26,416	30.10	14.28	13.55	13.94
Gasolines			6,904	6,491			5.17	3.43
Kerosene and distillates			1,426	2,980			1.07	1.57
Residual			8,613	15,934			6.45	8.41
Other products			1,144	1,011			0.86	0.53
Domestic refinery runs	66,057	104,481	124,429	168,656				
TRANSPORTATION OPERATIONS								
Total crude oil receipts at refineries	64,057	105,641	125,561	169,288	100.00	100.00	100.00	100.00
Via company facilities	55,501	84,299	115,050	161,239	86.64	79.80	91.63	95.25
Company owned pipe lines [e]	54,578	76,961	110,420	150,424	85.20	72.85	87.94	88.86
Company marine equipment	126	6,732	3,742	9,793	0.20	6.37	2.98	5.79
Term charter vessels	797	606	888	1,022	1.24	0.58	0.71	0.60
Via outside facilities	8,556	21,342	10,511	8,049	13.36	20.20	8.37	4.75
Total products shipments from refineries	60,522	95,721	121,291	169,825	100.00	100.00	100.00	100.00
Via company facilities	11,796	47,089	58,895	102,232	19.49	49.19	48.56	60.20
Company owned pipe lines [e]	166	4,784	11,306	34,719	0.28	5.00	9.32	20.44
Company marine equipment	9,401	22,976	28,616	35,956	15.53	24.00	23.59	21.17
Term charter vessels	2,229	19,329	15,390	26,911	3.68	20.19	12.69	15.85
Trucks [f]	N.A.	N.A.	3,583	4,646	0.00	0.00	2.96	2.74
Via outside facilities	48,726	48,632	62,396	67,593	80.51	50.81	51.44	39.80
Pipe line	0	0	1,568	4,381	0.00	0.00	1.29	2.58
Marine	9,602	5,641	12,601	6,317	15.87	5.90	10.39	3.72
Rail and truck [f]	39,124	42,991	48,227	56,895	64.64	44.91	39.76	33.50
MARKETING OPERATIONS								
Total sales refined products [g]	43,987	54,956	71,470	94,444	100.00	100.00	100.00	100.00
Gasolines	27,535	34,045	40,291	50,621	62.60	61.95	56.38	53.60
Kerosene and distillate	7,094	10,304	15,317	26,873	16.13	18.75	21.43	28.45
Residual	4,678	5,703	8,743	8,534	10.63	10.38	12.23	9.04
Other	4,680	4,904	7,119	8,416	10.64	8.92	9.96	8.91
Gasoline sales by method of sale: Total	27,535	34,045	40,291	50,621	100.00	100.00	100.00	100.00
From refineries and terminals	4,493	6,742	5,917	8,931	16.32	19.80	14.69	17.64
From company operated bulk plants	9,784	8,955	9,470	11,260	35.53	26.31	23.50	22.25
Through commission distributors	13,258	18,348	24,904	30,430	48.15	53.89	61.81	60.11
Gasoline sales by type customer: Total	27,535	34,045	40,291	50,621	100.00	100.00	100.00	100.00
To wholesale resellers [h]	15,533	4,994	4,028	5,012	56.41	14.67	10.00	9.90
To retail resellers	6,697	20,221	23,318	27,959	24.32	59.39	57.87	55.23
Contractor stations	4,715	5,252	3,915	3,231	17.12	15.42	9.71	6.38
Dealer operated stations	1,982	14,969	19,403	24,728	7.20	43.97	48.16	48.85
To consumers and industrial users		8,830	12,945	17,650		25.94	32.13	34.87
Company operated stations	5,305	0	91	277	19.27	0.00	0.23	0.55
Industrial, household, and other [h]		8,830	12,854	17,373		25.94	31.90	34.32
Kerosene and distillate sales by method of sale: Total	7,094	10,304	15,317	26,873	100.00	100.00	100.00	100.00
From refineries and terminals	1,405	3,303	4,110	6,878	19.80	32.06	26.83	25.59
From company operated bulk plants	1,325	1,255	1,035	1,626	18.68	12.18	6.76	6.05
Through commission distributors	4,364	5,746	10,172	18,369	61.52	55.76	66.41	68.36
Kerosene and distillate sales by type customer: Total	7,094	10,304	15,317	26,873	100.00	100.00	100.00	100.00
To wholesale resellers	207	486	604	1,011	2.92	4.72	3.94	3.76
To consumers and industrial users	6,887	9,818	14,713	25,862	97.08	95.28	96.06	96.24

Note: Blank spaces indicate data not available. Data are for the parent company and consolidated subsidiaries except in the case of marketing operations, in which case the data are for the parent company only.

The parent company and its three subsidiaries, the Pan American Petroleum Transport Company, the Pan-Am Southern Corporation, and the Utah Oil Refining Company, had quite different marketing situations and different practices with respect to vertical integration in the marketing field. It was decided therefore that the analysis of marketing activities should be confined to the parent company.

[a] Includes net interest in net domestic production of affiliated companies in all years except 1935. The amount of such production in most years was less than 2,000,000 barrels.

[b] Includes purchases abroad for import and shipments abroad from U.S. stocks.

[c] Exclusive of fuel oil used for refinery heat. No crude oil was run under processing agreements for others.

[d] Exclusive of semifinished stocks. Does not include purchases of parent company in 1935 and 1940. For the period 1945 to 1950, purchases of the parent company were about 15% of total purchases. Includes products acquired under processing agreements.

[e] Includes all pipe lines in which company had a stock interest.

[f] Shipments via company trucks included with outside trucks in 1935 and 1940.

[g] Includes all domestic sales and shipments for export. Data are for parent company only.

[h] Sales to wholesale resellers and to industrial, household, and other customers grouped together in 1935.

SOURCE: Standard Oil Company (Indiana).

TABLE 15. STANDARD OIL COMPANY (OHIO)
Balance of Operations in Selected Years

	Thousands of Barrels				Percentage of Breakdowns				
	1935	1940	1946	1950	1929	1935	1940	1946	1950
CRUDE OIL OPERATIONS									
Total new supply of crude oil in U.S.	11,878	19,813	30,510	39,262	100.00%	100.00%	100.00%	100.00%	100.00%
Net domestic production		198	8,965	11,035			1.00	29.38	28.11
Net purchases	11,878	19,615	21,545	28,227	100.00	100.00	99.00	70.62	71.89
Total net foreign production									
REFINED PRODUCTS OPERATIONS									
Total new supply refined products in U.S.	10,954	20,161	29,984	38,305	100.00	100.00	100.00	100.00	100.00
Yield of refined products from refineries[a]	10,576	17,856	27,653	36,068	100.00	96.55	88.57	92.23	94.16
Purchases of refined products[b]	378	2,305	2,331	2,237		3.45	11.43	7.77	5.84
Gasolines	130	1,584	1,263	875		1.19	7.85	4.21	2.28
Kerosene and distillate	19	167	128	142		0.17	0.83	0.43	0.37
Residual	168	462	837	1,017		1.53	2.29	2.79	2.66
Other products	61	92	103	203		0.56	0.46	0.34	0.53
Domestic refinery runs[c]	11,878	19,813	30,510	39,262					
TRANSPORTATION OPERATIONS									
Total crude oil receipts at refineries	12,809	21,828	30,458	39,901	100.00	100.00	100.00	100.00	100.00
Via company facilities	2	18,727	28,069	39,363		0.02	85.79	92.16	98.65
Company owned pipe lines[d]		18,667	21,367	34,376			85.52	70.16	86.15
Company marine equipment			6,628	1,962				21.76	12.44
Company trucks	2	60	74	25		0.02	0.27	0.24	0.06
Via outside facilities	12,807	3,101	2,389	538	100.00	99.98	14.21	7.84	1.35
Total products shipments from refineries	10,566	18,955	29,536	36,547		100.00	100.00	100.00	100.00
Via company facilities	2,480	12,127	21,524	27,911		23.47	63.98	72.87	76.37
Company owned pipe lines[d]		7,759	14,446	16,731			40.94	48.91	45.78
Company marine equipment			617	2,212				2.09	6.05
Company trucks	2,480	4,368	6,461	8,968		23.47	23.04	21.87	24.54
Via outside facilities	8,086	6,828	8,012	8,636		76.53	36.02	27.13	23.63
MARKETING OPERATIONS									
Total sales refined products	11,556	18,583	30,332	37,624	100.00	100.00	100.00	100.00	100.00
Gasolines	6,666	10,852	15,755	19,352	59.88	57.68	58.40	51.95	51.44
Kerosene and distillate	893	1,724	4,760	7,977	9.65	7.73	9.28	15.69	21.20
Residual	3,301	5,072	8,208	8,413	20.21	28.57	27.29	27.06	22.36
Other	696	935	1,609	1,882	10.26	6.02	5.03	5.30	5.00
Gasoline sales by method of sale: Total	6,666	10,852	15,755	19,352		100.00	100.00	100.00	100.00
Through commission distributors[e]			2,348	2,865				14.90	14.80
All other			13,407	16,487				85.10	85.20
Gasoline sales by type customer: Total	6,666	10,852	15,755	19,352		100.00	100.00	100.00	100.00
To wholesale resellers	1,283	3,190	4,040	3,127		19.25	29.40	25.64	16.16
Brokers, refiners, cargo buyers	332	1,239	1,524	1,079		4.98	11.42	9.67	5.58
Unbranded jobbers	0	0	0	0		0	0	0	0
Branded jobbers	951	1,951	2,516	2,048		14.27	17.98	15.97	10.58
To retail resellers	3,341	4,808	5,942	8,430		50.12	44.32	37.71	43.56
Contractor stations	2,601	3,092	3,470	5,017		39.02	28.50	22.02	25.92
Dealer operated stations	740	1,716	2,472	3,413		11.10	15.82	15.69	17.64
To consumers and industrial users	2,042	2,852	5,773	7,795		30.63	26.28	36.65	40.28
Company operated stations[f]	1,397	1,478	2,925	3,777		20.96	13.62	18.57	19.52
Industrial, household, and other[g]	645	1,374	2,848	4,018		9.67	12.66	18.08	20.76
Kerosene and distillate sales by method of sale: Total (breakdown not available)	893	1,724	4,760	7,977					
Kerosene and distillate sales by type customer: Total	893	1,724	4,760	7,977		100.00	100.00	100.00	100.00
To wholesale resellers	571	1,147	3,221	3,215		63.94	66.53	67.67	40.30
Brokers, refiners, cargo buyers	524	1,014	2,409	2,011		58.68	58.82	50.61	25.21
Jobbers	47	133	812	1,204		5.26	7.71	17.06	15.09
To retail resellers	46	48	74	126		5.15	2.79	1.55	1.58
Contractor stations[h]	36	31	43	75		4.03	1.80	0.90	0.94
Dealer operated stations	10	17	31	51		1.12	0.99	0.65	0.64
To consumers and industrial users	276	529	1,465	4,636		30.91	30.68	30.78	58.12
Company operated stations[f]	10	7	15	27		1.12	0.41	0.32	0.34
Industrial, household, and other[g]	266	522	1,450	4,609		29.79	30.27	30.46	57.78

Note: Blank spaces indicate data not available.

[a] Excludes fuel oil used for refinery heat and yield from crude oil run under processing agreements for others.

[b] Excludes semifinished stocks but includes products acquired under processing agreements.

[c] Excludes crude oil run for others under processing agreements.

[d] Includes all pipe lines in which company had a stock interest.

[e] Includes sales by commission truck drivers operating out of company operated bulk plants.

[f] In 1935 the figures include a relatively small volume sold through company stations operated on a straight commission basis.

[g] Includes a relatively small volume sold to tank truck dealers (peddlers). Also includes sales to U.S. Government, because company treats such business as sales by the retail department rather than as sales by the wholesale department.

[h] Kerosene and distillate sales to contractor stations in all years were derived from kerosene and distillate to gasoline ratio for dealer stations. In view of the fact that many contractor stations were in rural areas where the ratio was high, the figures are probably a minimum estimate

SOURCE: Standard Oil Company (Ohio).

TABLE 16. GULF OIL CORPORATION

Capital Expenditures by Departments: 1910–1952

Year	Capital Expenditures ($1,000)								Capital Expenditures — Percentage of Total						
	Production[a]	Manufacturing	Marketing	Domestic Pipe Lines	Marine	Other	Related Business Investments[b]	Total	Production	Manufacturing	Marketing	Domestic Pipe Lines	Marine	Other	Related Business Investments
1910	$ 2,912	$ 380	$ 64	$ 1,216		$ 159		$ 4,731	61.55%	8.03%	1.35%	25.71%		3.36%	
1911	2,380	809	83	993	$ 48	106		4,419	53.86	18.31	1.88	22.47	1.08%	2.40	
1912	2,980	760	261	819	662	194		5,676	52.50	13.39	4.60	14.43	11.66	3.42	
1913	4,774	434	458	651	252	238		6,807	70.13	6.38	6.73	9.56	3.70	3.50	
1914	4,427	792	1,021	1,837	616	6		8,699	50.89	9.10	11.74	21.12	7.08	0.07	
1915	4,427	1,529	1,515	2,126	593	114		10,304	42.96	14.84	14.70	20.63	5.76	1.11	
1916	10,395	1,020	952	1,100	1,495	3		14,965	69.46	6.82	6.36	7.35	9.99	0.02	
1917	14,584	4,768	1,888	4,379	3,409	704		29,732	49.05	16.04	6.35	14.73	11.46	2.37	
1918	13,044	1,416	790	2,634	747	149		18,780	69.46	7.54	4.21	14.02	3.98	0.79	
1919	20,176	1,856	5,038	9,272	3,741	1,446		41,529	48.58	4.47	12.13	22.33	9.01	3.48	
1920								46,334							
1921								36,765							
1922	21,929	5,010	5,729	5,395	350	272		38,685	56.69	12.95	14.81	13.95	0.90	0.70	
1923	24,136	11,288	9,525	6,282	983	891		53,105	45.45	21.26	17.93	11.83	1.85	1.68	
1924	14,011	4,917	15,854	5,382	587	1		40,752	34.38	12.07	38.90	13.21	1.44	0.00	
1925	21,094	6,938	8,126	5,676	818	0		42,652	49.46	16.26	19.05	13.31	1.92	0.00	
1926	35,155	5,031	15,768	7,517	3,177	0		66,648	52.75	7.55	23.66	11.28	4.76	0.00	
1927	26,049	10,097	15,067	13,357	2,462	0	$ 324	67,356	38.67	14.99	22.37	19.83	3.66	0.00	0.48%
1928	27,572	5,536	8,749	4,260	2,112	0	1,451	49,680	55.50	11.14	17.61	8.58	4.25	0.00	2.92
1929	22,016	29,638	15,468	9,930	2,439	0	151	79,642	27.64	37.22	19.42	12.47	3.06	0.00	0.19
1930	16,142	27,759	22,403	13,478	247	662	1,942	82,633	19.54	33.59	27.11	16.31	0.30	0.80	2.35
1931	7,947	12,771	8,623	4,070	622	13	3,647	37,693	21.08	33.88	22.88	10.80	1.65	0.03	9.68
1932	9,973	1,713	2,760	652	4	210	3,919	19,231	51.86	8.91	14.35	3.39	0.02	1.09	20.38
1933	11,245	2,436	4,220	556	4	205	2,639	21,305	52.78	11.43	19.81	2.61	0.02	0.96	12.39
1934	15,017	3,549	4,525	368	419	699	2,226	26,803	56.03	13.24	16.88	1.37	1.56	2.61	8.31
1935	26,116	3,596	4,758	663	589	1,098	1,363	38,183	68.40	9.42	12.46	1.74	1.54	2.87	3.57
1936	33,832	5,287	10,545	4,587	4,420	439	2,097	61,207	55.27	8.64	17.23	7.49	7.22	0.72	3.43
1937	44,937	7,731	13,450	3,211	4,067	817	2,656	76,869	58.46	10.06	17.50	4.18	5.29	1.06	3.45
1938	33,637	7,949	6,997	905	477	168	1,778	51,911	64.80	15.31	13.48	1.74	0.92	0.32	3.43
1939	29,833	3,389	8,501	1,186	34	210	2,888	46,041	64.80	7.36	18.46	2.58	0.07	0.46	6.27
1940	37,619	6,017	9,111	2,672	973	387	1,895	58,674	64.12	10.25	15.53	4.55	1.66	0.66	3.23
1941	29,926	4,903	11,829	4,152	2,103	237	965	54,115	55.30	9.06	21.86	7.67	3.89	0.44	1.78
1942	20,671	12,644	4,754	2,207	9,385	322	3,222	53,205	38.85	23.76	8.93	4.15	17.64	0.61	6.06
1943	29,229	10,746	1,445	1,181	12,122	207	2,831	57,761	50.60	18.61	2.50	2.04	20.99	0.36	4.90
1944	65,826	6,951	6,279	2,890	23	449	4,609	87,027	75.64	7.99	7.21	3.32	0.03	0.51	5.30
1945	70,448	21,038	8,404	8,010	10	1,154	4,812	113,876	61.86	18.48	7.38	7.03	0.01	1.01	4.23
1946	61,684	11,252	16,666	4,507	8,343	1,954	6,554	110,960	55.59	10.14	15.02	4.06	7.52	1.76	5.91
1947	105,677	19,963	29,368	6,113	17,094	2,034	13,334	193,583	54.59	10.31	15.17	3.16	8.83	1.05	6.89
1948	150,419	40,021	15,384	4,666	22,081	2,841	22,574	257,986	58.31	15.51	5.96	1.81	8.56	1.10	8.75
1949	118,803	23,681	16,647	1,456	710	1,406	23,610	186,313	63.77	12.71	8.94	0.78	0.38	0.75	12.67
1950	90,465	6,547	24,611	3,215	47	942	11,056	136,883	66.09	4.78	17.98	2.35	0.03	0.69	8.08
1951	117,552	24,679	25,521	10,426	1,779	1,901	11,361	193,219	60.84	12.77	13.21	5.40	0.92	0.98	5.88
1952	139,680	28,327	20,925	8,265	4,565	2,056	20,069	223,887	62.39	12.65	9.35	3.69	2.04	0.92	8.96

[a] Domestic and foreign: includes intangible development and dry hole costs. Includes investments in Kuwait beginning in 1945.

[b] Includes small investments in and advances to Kuwait Oil Company, Ltd., before 1945. For period 1945–1952 investments in Kuwait Oil Company, Ltd., were included with production expenditures.

SOURCE: Gulf Oil Corporation.

TABLE 17. THE TEXAS COMPANY

Capital Expenditures by Departments: 1927–1951

Year	Capital Expenditures ($1,000)							Capital Expenditures — Percentage of Total					
	Production[a]	Manufacturing	Marketing	Pipe Lines	Marine	Other	Total	Production	Manufacturing	Marketing	Pipe Lines	Marine	Other
1927	$ 25,479	$ 9,000	$ 8,624	$ 2,263	$ 57	$1,255	$ 46,678	54.58%	19.28%	18.48%	4.85%	0.12%	2.69%
1928	35,298	11,660	10,596	13,890	786	703	72,933	48.40	15.99	14.53	19.04	1.08	0.96
1929	33,440	27,846	19,055	12,661	176	1,660	94,838	35.26	29.36	20.09	13.35	0.19	1.75
1930	21,356	14,259	21,117	1,390	118	1,435	59,675	35.79	23.89	35.39	2.33	0.20	2.40
1931	5,484	2,538	10,011	4,155	88	1,409	23,685	23.15	10.72	42.27	17.54	0.37	5.95
1932	6,582	1,912	9,999	802	496	134	19,925	33.03	9.60	50.18	4.03	2.49	0.67
1933	9,245	2,532	5,396	1,020	244	159	18,596	49.71	13.62	29.02	5.49	1.31	0.85
1934	20,800	2,261	5,903	1,283	2,199	1,752	34,198	60.82	6.61	17.26	3.75	6.43	5.13
1935	20,619	3,765	5,318	1,203	1,122	136	32,163	64.11	11.71	16.53	3.74	3.49	0.42
1936	26,178	5,254	8,429	2,492	6,442	322	49,117	53.30	10.70	17.16	5.07	13.12	0.65
1937	32,347	8,726	8,711	5,574	4,558	181	60,097	53.82	14.52	14.50	9.28	7.58	0.30
1938	29,108	7,830	5,983	2,891	3,097	626	49,535	58.76	15.81	12.08	5.84	6.25	1.26
1939	37,544	8,215	5,538	3,454	6,473	230	61,454	61.09	13.37	9.01	5.62	10.53	0.38
1940	45,500	7,304	7,700	3,095	10,013	112	73,724	61.72	9.91	10.44	4.20	13.58	0.15
1941	35,954	6,939	6,161	3,200	8,575	97	60,926	59.01	11.39	10.11	5.25	14.08	0.16
1942	31,437	15,753	3,705	8,865	1,354	70	61,184	51.38	25.75	6.06	14.49	2.21	0.11
1943	47,916	33,588	629	5,271	20,471	19	107,894	44.41	31.13	0.58	4.89	18.97	0.02
1944	63,730	24,857	1,693	3,800	6,093	200	100,373	63.49	24.76	1.69	3.79	6.07	0.20
1945	55,651	15,708	3,939	1,342	35	341	77,016	72.26	20.40	5.11	1.74	0.05	0.44
1946	50,356	11,062	14,033	4,515	2,260	184	82,410	61.11	13.42	17.03	5.48	2.74	0.22
1947	81,437	16,247	29,229	9,107	13,976	324	150,320	54.18	10.81	19.44	6.06	9.30	0.21
1948	112,688	57,854	23,098	27,342	10,526	305	231,813	48.61	24.96	9.96	11.80	4.54	0.13
1949	92,020	59,866	20,491	25,946	21,215	870	220,408	41.75	27.16	9.30	11.77	9.63	0.39
1950	94,353	26,908	22,613	5,821	3,311	253	153,259	61.56	17.56	14.75	3.80	2.16	0.17
1951	130,980	18,735	29,763	12,156	4,853	1,317	197,804	66.22	9.47	15.05	6.14	2.45	0.67

[a] Domestic and foreign; includes dry hole costs.

SOURCE: The Texas Company.

TABLE 18. SINCLAIR OIL CORPORATION

Capital Expenditures by Departments: 1927–1952

Year	Capital Expenditures ($1,000)							Capital Expenditures — Percentage of Total					
	Production[a]	Manufacturing	Marketing	Pipe Lines	Marine	Other	Total	Production	Manufacturing	Marketing	Pipe Lines	Marine	Other
1927	$13,539	$ 5,504	$ 2,855	$ 66	$ 31	—	$ 21,995	61.56%	25.02%	12.98%	0.30%	0.14%	—
1928	12,456	6,030	2,606	29	17	$ 30	21,168	58.84	28.49	12.31	0.14	0.08	0.14%
1929	16,245	12,423	12,878	3	419	79	42,047	38.63	29.54	30.63	0.01	1.00	0.19
1930	15,394	9,329	6,850	2,374	1,553	108	35,608	43.23	26.20	19.24	6.67	4.37	0.30
1931	6,558	8,673	1,617	3,471	1,000	209	21,528	30.46	40.29	7.51	16.12	4.65	0.97
1932	7,261	1,485	1,956	618	0	36	11,356	63.94	13.08	17.22	5.44	0	0.32
1933	5,843	5,090	3,771	1,008	0	36	15,748	37.10	32.32	23.95	6.40	0	0.23
1934	9,909	3,259	4,206	311	11	43	17,739	55.86	18.37	23.71	1.76	0.06	0.24
1935	11,531	1,921	3,512	553	5	224	17,746	64.98	10.82	19.79	3.12	0.03	1.26
1936	18,935	3,702	3,915	823	78	279	27,732	68.28	13.35	14.12	2.97	0.28	1.00
1937	17,551	7,537	6,222	1,474	89	540	33,413	52.53	22.56	18.62	4.41	0.27	1.61
1938	10,930	2,802	5,072	579	6	60	19,449	56.20	14.40	26.08	2.98	0.03	0.31
1939	12,754	2,397	4,202	1,342	491	41	21,227	60.08	11.29	19.80	6.32	2.32	0.19
1940	15,399	5,158	5,570	1,621	3,643	21	31,412	49.02	16.42	17.73	5.16	11.60	0.07
1941	25,661	3,027	4,473	4,125	17,619	32	54,937	46.71	5.51	8.14	7.51	32.07	0.06
1942	13,979	11,339	1,983	12,980	5,485	547	46,313	30.19	24.48	4.28	28.03	11.84	1.18
1943	20,073	27,461	1,609	8,322	16	313	57,794	34.73	47.52	2.78	14.40	0.03	0.54
1944	29,617	8,839	1,753	6,552	50	42	46,853	63.21	18.87	3.74	13.98	0.11	0.09
1945	34,556	3,579	4,654	5,383	45	218	48,435	71.35	7.39	9.61	11.11	0.09	0.45
1946	23,213	13,910	15,517	7,013	3,604	65	63,322	36.66	21.97	24.50	11.08	5.69	0.10
1947	28,238	37,175	15,125	13,261	222	41	94,062	30.02	39.52	16.08	14.10	0.24	0.04
1948	38,712	33,397	11,261	19,404	119	38	102,931	37.61	32.45	10.94	18.85	0.11	0.04
1949	36,322	15,591	18,801	4,869	125	91	75,799	47.92	20.57	24.80	6.42	0.17	0.12
1950	47,377	22,627	16,049	5,455	65	3,439	95,012	49.86	23.82	16.89	5.74	0.07	3.62
1951	75,624	6,834	20,116	13,289	1,522	950	118,335	63.90	5.78	17.00	11.23	1.29	0.80
1952	76,953	26,119	18,527	51,600	7,407	528	181,134	42.48	14.42	10.23	28.49	4.09	0.29

[a] Includes intangible development costs.

SOURCE: Petroleum Department, Chase National Bank, for intangible development costs, 1935–1950. Sinclair Oil Corporation for all other figures.

TABLE 19. THE OHIO OIL COMPANY

Capital Expenditures by Departments: 1925–1952

Year	Capital Expenditures ($1,000)					Capital Expenditures — Percentage of Total			
	Production [a]	Manufacturing	Marketing	Pipe Lines [b]	Total	Production	Manufacturing	Marketing	Pipe Lines
1925	$11,738	$ 16	$ 29	0	$11,783	99.62%	0.13%	0.25%	0
1926	10,867	2,331	53	0	13,251	82.01	17.59	0.40	0
1927	9,233	1,973	71	0	11,277	81.87	17.50	0.63	0
1928	6,730	167	450	0	7,347	91.60	2.27	6.13	0
1929	14,506	321	1,303	0	16,130	89.93	1.99	8.08	0
1930 [c]	11,410	2,529	*	$ 4,276	18,215	62.64	13.88	*	23.48%
1931	9,101	586	*	516	10,203	89.20	5.74	*	5.06
1932	8,759	1,672	*	2,072	12,503	70.06	13.37	*	16.57
1933	5,422	1,026	1,334	4,697	12,479	43.45	8.22	10.69	37.64
1934	3,335	1,000	*	662	4,997	66.74	20.01	*	13.25
1935	7,311	822	*	212	8,345	87.61	9.85	*	2.54
1936	11,347	1,192	*	519	13,058	86.90	9.13	*	3.97
1937	14,730	1,422	*	1,091	17,243	85.42	8.25	*	6.33
1938	11,538	139	625	631	12,933	89.21	1.08	4.83	4.88
1939	6,615	208	587	3,388	10,798	61.26	1.93	5.44	31.37
1940	6,871	413	741	1,881	9,906	69.36	4.17	7.48	18.99
1941	11,753	467	467	2,028	14,715	79.87	3.17	3.17	13.79
1942	8,442	293	203	1,703	10,641	79.34	2.75	1.91	16.00
1943	9,151	66	165	1,219	10,601	86.32	0.62	1.56	11.50
1944	15,835	1,401	417	1,233	18,886	83.84	7.42	2.21	6.53
1945	13,816	914	1,796	995	17,521	78.85	5.22	10.25	5.68
1946	11,604	724	2,326	1,426	16,080	72.16	4.50	14.47	8.87
1947	18,169	6,260	2,570	1,586	28,585	63.56	21.90	8.99	5.55
1948	19,988	9,813	1,851	2,743	34,395	58.11	28.53	5.38	7.98
1949	20,260	4,050	3,774	1,819	29,903	67.75	13.55	12.62	6.08
1950	20,044	996	3,340	9,068	33,448	59.92	2.98	9.99	27.11
1951	23,196	1,016	3,903	13,103	41,218	56.28	2.46	9.47	31.79
1952	27,481	2,631	6,184	12,421	48,717	56.41	5.40	12.69	25.50

* Expenditures for marketing properties are included in refining figures.
[a] Includes dry hole costs, and nominal amounts for administrative facilities and investments of gas utility subsidiaries.
[b] Pipe line properties did not come under the control of The Ohio Oil Company until after 1930.
[c] Figures for 1930 do not include the purchase of the assets of the Transcontinental Oil Company with common stock of The Ohio Oil Company having a stated value of $40 million and do include purchase of the stock of the Illinois Pipe Line Company with preferred stock of The Ohio Oil Company valued at $58 million.

SOURCE: The Ohio Oil Company.

TABLE 20. THE ATLANTIC REFINING COMPANY

Capital Expenditures by Departments: 1925–1952

Year	Capital Expenditures ($1,000)							Capital Expenditures — Percentage of Total					
	Production [a]	Manufacturing	Marketing	Pipe Lines	Marine	Other	Total	Production	Manufacturing	Marketing	Pipe Lines	Marine	Other
1925	$ 3,096	$ 5,047	$ 2,996	0	$ 729	$ 14	$11,882	26.06%	42.48%	25.21%	0	6.13%	0.12%
1926	5,602	4,366	3,205	0	475	3	13,651	41.04	31.98	23.48	0	3.48	0.02
1927	5,209	5,000	2,956	0	1,769	2	14,936	34.88	33.48	19.79	0	11.84	0.01
1928	4,421	2,394	3,270	$ 8,962	677	6	19,730	22.41	12.13	16.57	45.43%	3.43	0.03
1929	4,135	3,777	9,339	855	508	12	18,626	22.20	20.28	50.14	4.59	2.73	0.06
1930	2,993	3,091	8,312	1,039	1,995	7	17,437	17.16	17.73	47.67	5.96	11.44	0.04
1931	3,958	4,334	4,712	8,503	840	5	22,352	17.71	19.39	21.08	38.04	3.76	0.02
1932	7,072	1,211	2,883	381	128	8	11,683	60.53	10.37	24.68	3.26	1.09	0.07
1933	4,321	1,202	2,260	591	207	23	8,604	50.22	13.97	26.27	6.87	2.40	0.27
1934	7,329	4,210	3,955	388	395	21	16,298	44.97	25.83	24.27	2.38	2.42	0.13
1935	5,541	1,088	3,697	2,566	772	24	13,688	40.48	7.95	27.01	18.75	5.64	0.17
1936	9,755	3,700	3,443	2,039	105	36	19,078	51.13	19.39	18.05	10.69	0.55	0.19
1937	14,282	7,825	5,570	4,535	2,255	37	34,504	41.39	22.68	16.14	13.14	6.54	0.11
1938	11,517	1,552	5,634	408	2,927	31	22,069	52.19	7.03	25.53	1.85	13.26	0.14
1939	6,296	3,114	4,434	332	2,309	21	16,506	38.14	18.87	26.86	2.01	13.99	0.13
1940	6,794	2,680	4,978	411	3,118	66	18,047	37.65	14.85	27.58	2.28	17.28	0.36
1941	11,559	3,015	6,347	834	5,891	48	27,694	41.74	10.89	22.92	3.01	21.27	0.17
1942	6,739	4,574	1,906	1,069	4,191	36	18,515	36.40	24.71	10.29	5.77	22.64	0.19
1943	23,227	10,406	413	515	3,612	24	38,197	60.81	27.24	1.08	1.35	9.46	0.06
1944	21,257	9,477	1,268	334	10	15	32,361	65.69	29.28	3.92	1.03	0.03	0.05
1945	27,830	3,250	3,440	130	6,018	38	40,706	68.37	7.98	8.45	0.32	14.79	0.09
1946	23,506	5,703	7,496	1,096	3,908	115	41,824	56.20	13.64	17.92	2.62	9.34	0.28
1947	19,841	11,861	12,509	2,132	351	174	46,868	42.33	25.31	26.69	4.55	0.75	0.37
1948	35,427	10,325	8,126	3,559	385	198	58,020	61.06	17.80	14.01	6.13	0.66	0.34
1949	30,478	5,734	7,663	9,675	121	143	53,814	56.63	10.66	14.24	17.98	0.22	0.27
1950	31,159	4,411	6,792	1,254	37	442	44,095	70.67	10.00	15.41	2.84	0.08	1.00
1951	44,680	9,527	12,184	10,074	1,895	621	78,981	56.57	12.06	15.43	12.75	2.40	0.79
1952	45,372	16,262	14,121	4,523	569	712	81,559	55.63	19.94	17.31	5.55	0.70	0.87

* Includes dry hole costs.

SOURCE: The Atlantic Refining Company.

TABLE 21. STANDARD OIL COMPANY (INDIANA)
Capital Expenditures by Departments: 1936–1952

Year	Capital Expenditures ($1,000)						Capital Expenditures — Percentage of Total				
	Production [a]	Manufacturing	Marketing	Transportation [b]	Other	Total	Production	Manufacturing	Marketing	Transportation	Other
1936	$ 20,963	$10,536	$ 6,546	$11,871		$ 49,916	42.00%	21.11%	13.11%	23.78%	
1937	36,132	11,800	8,326	7,092	$ 301	63,651	56.77	18.54	13.08	11.14	0.47
1938	19,910	7,115	5,781	4,557	131	37,494	53.10	18.98	15.42	12.15	0.35
1939	18,167	5,236	7,450	6,945	91	37,889	47.95	13.82	19.66	18.33	0.24
1940	22,306	7,991	9,168	10,118	73	49,656	44.92	16.09	18.46	20.38	0.15
1941	44,297	6,049	10,814	11,918	222	73,300	60.43	8.25	14.76	16.26	0.30
1942	17,117	23,003	5,064	4,461	1,693	51,338	33.34	44.81	9.86	8.69	3.30
1943	47,202	42,065	2,453	9,070	165	100,955	46.76	41.67	2.43	8.98	0.16
1944	59,981	17,505	2,890	14,402	328	95,106	63.07	18.41	3.04	15.14	0.34
1945	51,420	17,161	5,461	7,969	95	82,106	62.63	20.90	6.65	9.71	0.11
1946	66,031	50,093	19,108	26,140	418	161,790	40.81	30.96	11.81	16.16	0.26
1947	85,313	70,178	18,883	51,862	850	227,086	37.57	30.90	8.32	22.84	0.37
1948	111,242	83,402	10,210	54,866	4,953	264,673	42.03	31.51	3.86	20.73	1.87
1949	64,231	50,064	12,127	13,788	2,570	142,780	44.99	35.06	8.49	9.66	1.80
1950	79,029	15,509	23,353	17,829	1,093	136,813	57.76	11.34	17.07	13.03	0.80
1951	119,345	20,828	20,579	30,669	6,430	197,851	60.32	10.53	10.40	15.50	3.25
1952	112,859	48,101	18,709	31,721	9,483	220,874	51.10	21.78	8.47	14.36	4.29

[a] Dry hole costs included, 1940 through 1952. Information on dry hole cost not available prior to 1940.
[b] Includes motor equipment and ocean, lake, and river terminals beginning in 1947. Prior to 1947 such expenditures were considered a part of the facility by which used.

SOURCE: Standard Oil Company (Indiana).

TABLE 22. STANDARD OIL COMPANY (OHIO)
Capital Expenditures by Departments: 1929–1952

Year	Capital Expenditures ($1,000)						Capital Expenditures — Percentage of Total				
	Production [a]	Manufacturing	Marketing	Transportation	Other	Total	Production	Manufacturing	Marketing	Transportation	Other
1929	0	$ 1,852	$3,357			$ 5,209	0	35.55%	64.45%		
1930	0	2,974	2,154			5,128	0	58.00	42.00		
1931	0	2,442	1,668			4,110	0	59.42	40.58		
1932	0	318	529			847	0	37.54	62.46		
1933	0	321	422			743	0	43.20	56.80		
1934	0	832	1,066			1,898	0	43.84	56.16		
1935	0	685	511			1,196	0	57.27	42.73		
1936	0	1,115	1,661			2,776	0	40.17	59.83		
1937	$ 423	2,389	2,210	$1,908		6,930	6.10%	34.48	31.89	27.53%	
1938	239	774	2,522	2,391	$ 35	5,961	4.01	12.98	42.31	40.11	0.59%
1939	140	1,409	919	3,101	88	5,657	2.47	24.91	16.24	54.82	1.56
1940	66	1,589	1,575	4,753	73	8,056	0.82	19.72	19.55	59.00	0.91
1941	213	2,770	3,142	2,497	176	8,798	2.42	31.49	35.71	28.38	2.00
1942	4,687	2,857	916	2,129	93	10,682	43.88	26.74	8.58	19.93	0.87
1943	8,501	6,461	379	1,399	51	16,791	50.63	38.48	2.26	8.33	0.30
1944	16,523	2,400	1,345	1,940	106	22,314	74.05	10.75	6.03	8.69	0.48
1945	16,323	2,354	2,108	2,332	152	23,269	70.15	10.12	9.06	10.02	0.65
1946	14,049	1,517	5,047	2,725	267	23,605	59.52	6.43	21.38	11.54	1.13
1947	20,176	1,821	7,155	1,879	195	31,226	64.61	5.83	22.91	6.02	0.63
1948	17,367	5,455	4,133	3,168	228	30,351	57.22	17.97	13.62	10.44	0.75
1949	15,305	17,873	3,187	1,934	432	38,731	39.52	46.15	8.23	4.99	1.11
1950	12,204	16,102	4,234	625	139	33,304	36.64	48.35	12.71	1.88	0.42
1951	25,234	9,293	6,155	1,136	271	42,089	59.95	22.08	14.62	2.70	0.65
1952	16,296	5,603	6,023	1,557	223	29,702	54.86	18.86	20.28	5.24	0.76

Note: Blank spaces indicate data not available.
[a] Domestic and foreign; includes dry hole costs.

SOURCE: Standard Oil Company (Ohio).

TABLE 23. NUMBER, CAPACITY, AND AVERAGE SIZE OF THE REFINERIES OWNED BY SELECTED GROUPS OF REFINING COMPANIES: 1920–1950

	Amounts							Percentage of Industry						
	1920	1925	1930	1935	1940	1947	1950	1920	1925	1930	1935	1940	1947	1950
Total Refining Capacity (B/D):														
1st to 5th largest companies	473,300	985,500	1,482,000	1,462,600	1,764,300	2,206,020	2,734,600	30.9%	34.5%	39.4%	36.0%	38.1%	39.6%	40.8%
6th to 10th largest companies	264,600	441,800	819,000	847,000	947,100	1,245,700	1,434,700	17.3	15.5	21.7	20.9	20.5	22.4	21.4
11th to 15th largest companies	161,780	256,000	349,500	437,700	542,300	618,500	775,600	10.6	9.0	9.3	10.8	11.7	11.1	11.6
16th to 20th largest companies	95,500	150,400	187,000	256,500	256,600	275,850	399,600	6.2	5.3	5.0	6.3	5.5	5.0	6.0
21st to 25th largest companies	56,500	98,500	113,500	102,500	99,500	132,500	202,500	3.7	3.4	3.0	2.5	2.1	2.4	3.0
26th to 30th largest companies	44,400	81,700	85,500	76,000	77,000	103,000	154,325	2.9	2.9	2.1	1.9	1.7	1.8	2.3
Small Refiners	434,485	839,942	729,085	876,200	941,846	987,912	994,975	28.4	29.4	19.5	21.6	20.4	17.7	14.9
Total Industry	1,530,565	2,853,842	3,765,585	4,058,500	4,628,646	5,569,482	6,696,300	100.0	100.0	100.0	100.0	100.0	100.0	100.0
Operating Capacity (B/D):														
1st to 5th largest companies		970,500	1,468,000	1,444,300	1,666,300	2,172,535	2,614,569		38.6	40.4	40.0	39.7	40.7	42.0
6th to 10th largest companies		441,400	795,500	813,000	841,600	1,220,700	1,416,488		17.6	21.9	22.5	20.1	22.9	22.8
11th to 15th largest companies		248,500	348,500	366,700	513,300	618,500	751,600		9.9	9.6	10.1	12.2	11.6	12.0
16th to 20th largest companies		144,500	184,500	248,500	218,600	265,500	321,675		5.8	5.1	6.9	5.2	5.0	5.2
21st to 25th largest companies		85,500	109,500	102,500	98,000	117,500	166,500		3.4	3.0	2.8	2.3	2.2	2.7
26th to 30th largest companies		73,500	85,500	51,000	75,000	79,400	131,325		2.9	2.3	1.4	2.8	1.5	2.1
Small Refiners		547,917	643,325	588,749	783,894	862,264	820,841		21.8	17.7	16.3	17.7	16.1	13.2
Total Industry		2,511,817	3,634,825	3,614,749	4,196,694	5,336,399	6,222,998		100.0	100.0	100.0	100.0	100.0	100.0
Cracking Capacity (B/D):														
1st to 5th largest companies			679,265	1,015,619	415,440	610,049	756,007			43.6	46.0	39.7	40.3	41.5
6th to 10th largest companies			431,000	563,200	232,409	358,750	370,700			27.6	25.5	22.2	23.7	20.4
11th to 15th largest companies			56,400	202,700	146,599	160,690	237,400			3.6	9.2	14.0	10.6	13.0
16th to 20th largest companies			80,000	150,650	81,974	100,689	115,980			5.1	6.8	7.8	6.6	6.4
21st to 25th largest companies			48,300	53,000	23,371	38,500	65,675			3.1	2.4	2.2	2.6	3.6
26th to 30th largest companies			35,075	19,000	19,150	20,150	37,370			2.3	0.8	1.9	1.3	2.1
Small Refiners			229,000	205,100	127,271	225,814	237,551			14.7	9.3	12.2	14.9	13.0
Total Industry			1,559,040	2,209,269	1,046,214	1,514,622	1,820,683			100.0	100.0	100.0	100.0	100.0
Number of Plants:														
1st to 5th largest companies	22	35	49	67	65	64	59	5.9	6.4	11.9	10.6	11.9	16.1	16.1
6th to 10th largest companies	27	30	46	50	33	34	33	7.2	5.4	11.2	7.9	6.0	8.5	9.0
11th to 15th largest companies	26	21	31	23	21	20	21	7.0	3.8	7.5	3.7	3.8	5.0	5.7
16th to 20th largest companies	9	15	12	23	21	16	18	2.4	2.7	2.9	3.6	3.8	4.0	4.9
21st to 25th largest companies	8	12	12	9	6	6	8	2.1	2.2	2.9	1.4	1.5	1.5	2.2
26th to 30th largest companies	7	7	5	6	6	8	10	1.9	1.3	1.2	1.0	1.1	2.0	2.7
Small Refiners	274	430	257	453	393	251	218	73.5	78.2	62.4	71.8	71.9	62.9	59.4
Total Industry	373	550	412	631	547	399	367	100.0	100.0	100.0	100.0	100.0	100.0	100.0
Average Size of Plants (B/D):														
1st to 5th largest companies	21,514	28,157	30,245	21,830	27,143	34,469	46,349							
6th to 10th largest companies	9,800	14,710	17,804	16,940	28,700	36,638	43,476							
11th to 15th largest companies	6,222	12,190	11,274	19,030	25,824	30,925	36,933							
16th to 20th largest companies	10,611	10,027	15,583	11,152	12,219	17,241	22,200							
21st to 25th largest companies	7,063	8,208	9,458	11,389	12,438	22,083	25,312							
26th to 30th largest companies	6,343	11,672	17,100	12,667	12,833	12,875	15,432							
Small Refiners	1,585	1,953	2,837	1,934	2,397	3,936	4,564							
Large Companies	11,072	14,532	19,590	17,878	23,940	30,957	38,263							
Average Size — All Plants	4,103	5,189	9,140	6,432	8,462	13,959	18,246							

SOURCE: Derived from U.S. Bureau of Mines Records. See discussion in Chapter Eighteen.

INDEX

(Page numbers in **bold face** type refer to exhibits or tables)

service stations (*cont.*)
  contractor stations (*cont.*)
    proportion of total station sales of gasoline made to, six oil companies, 484, 491, **489**
  dealer operated stations
    average monthly gasoline sales per station, six oil companies, 484, 491, **488**
    considerations influencing use of, 479–480
    cost advantages of, 293
    future objectives with respect to use, seven oil companies, 492–493
    method of operation, 477–478
    number in programs of six oil companies, 484, 490, **486–487**
    number owned or leased by various types of integrated companies (1950), **32–33**
    proportion of total station sales of gasoline made to, six oil companies, 484, 491, **489**
    sales of gasoline through, as per cent refinery yields for various sizes of refining companies (1950), **43**
    sales of gasoline through, as per cent refinery yields for various types of integrated companies (1950), **42**
    volume of gasoline sold through, by various types of integrated companies (1950), **34–35**
  development of (1914–1926), 101–102, 268–270
  differences and similarities in positions of six companies with respect to use of different types, 483–485
  divided accounts, 478, 480, 490, 494
  equipment furnished by suppliers, 478
  growth in sales under leasing programs, 293–294
  increased storage capacity (1929–1952), **275–276**
  independent dealers, advantages of, 293–294
  intense competition for dealers (1920's and 1930's), 270–271
  investment required (1951), 523
  large volume stations, effect on by-passing of bulk plants, 273
  leasing of, 289–290, 293
  lessor-built arrangements, 492–493
  number owned or leased by various types of integrated companies (1950), **32–33**
  overbuilding of, in late 1920's and early 1930's, 150–151, 242, 290
  sales of gasoline through company owned or leased stations as per cent refinery yields for various sizes of refining companies (1950), **43**
  sales of gasoline through company owned or leased stations as per cent refinery yields for various types of integrated companies (1950), **42**
  selection of. *See* retail outlets
  self-service stations, contributor to by-passing of bulk plants, 273
  three-party lease arrangements, 477
  turnover of accounts, 480
  two-party lease arrangements, 477, 481, 491, 493
  types of arrangements with suppliers as illustration of intensity of integration, 14
  undivided accounts, 478, 480, 490, 494
  volume of gasoline sold through, by various types of integrated companies (1950), **34–35**
  See also retail outlets
Sespe Oil Company, 510–511
Shallow Water Refining Company, 633–639
  asphalt business, 650–651
  crude oil producing activities, 638
  geographic specialization, 636–639
  map of operations (1951), **635**
  operating data (1941–1950), **634**
  organization and development (after 1937), 633–634
  product specialization, 650–751
Sharon Drilling Company, acquired by Standard Oil Company (Ohio) (1946), 249
Shell Oil Company
  reasons for participation in construction of Plantation Pipe Line, 508
  selected financial and operating data compared with other large oil companies (1952), **332**

Shell Oil Company (*cont.*)
  share of gasoline market held in Indiana (1926–1952), **108–109**
  share of gasoline market held in Ohio (1926–1952), **106–107**
  share of gasoline market held in Pennsylvania (1926–1952), **110–111**
  share of U.S. gasoline market, 1926, 1933, 1934, and 1935, **104**
Sherman Antitrust Act of 1890, 57
Show Me Distributing Company, acquired by The Ohio Oil Company, 101
Simrall Corporation, purchase of interest in, by Standard Oil Company (Ohio), 246
Sinclair Crude Oil Purchasing Company, 258, 261
  half-interest in, sold to Indiana Company by Sinclair (1930), 389
Sinclair, Harry F.
  influence on integration pattern of Sinclair Oil Corporation, 383, 510
  participation in Continental Trading Company, Ltd., purchase and sale of crude oil contracts (1921), 260
Sinclair Oil Corporation
  assets, total, compared with other large oil companies (1952), **332**
  balance of operations in selected years (1929–1950), 353–365, **356, 692**
  bulk plants. *See* wholesale outlets
  capital expenditures by departments compared with those of six other companies (1927–1952), **368–369, 698**
  commission distributors. *See* wholesale outlets
  competitive position in postwar market, 307
  construction of terminals on Plantation Pipe Line (1951), 307
  construction of terminals on Southeastern Pipe Line (1951), 307
  Crown Petroleum Company, acquisition of, 13, 308
  crude oil gathering activities
    crude oil gathered as per cent domestic production (1935–1952), **418–419**
    crude oil gathered plus imports as per cent domestic refinery runs (1935–1952), **418–419**
    practices and policies compared with six other companies, 415–420
  crude oil operations in Venezuela, 305
  crude oil production
    domestic production compared with other large oil companies (1952), **332**
    foreign production, compared with other large oil companies (1952), **332**
    producing, refining, and marketing operations (1919–1952), 343, **346, 684**
    program initiated in 1949 as example of horizontal and vertical integration, 8
    Wyoming crude oil production, problem of finding an outlet for, after World War II, 307–308
  crude oil purchasing problems after World War II, 307
  crude oil ratio, 497, 514
    affected by decline in expenditures for crude oil production (1931–1939), 382
    affected by management appraisal of significance of prorationing laws in 1930's, 381–382
    affected by purchase of The Prairie Oil and Gas Company, 381
    comparison of changes with those of other companies, 388–390
    comparison with five other companies (1919–1952), **351**
    decision to buy crude oil rather than to maintain production in 1930's, 382
    decision to increase production (1949), 381, 382–383
    decline in ratio (1922–1939), 381
    domestic production plus imports as per cent domestic refinery runs (1924–1952), **418–419**

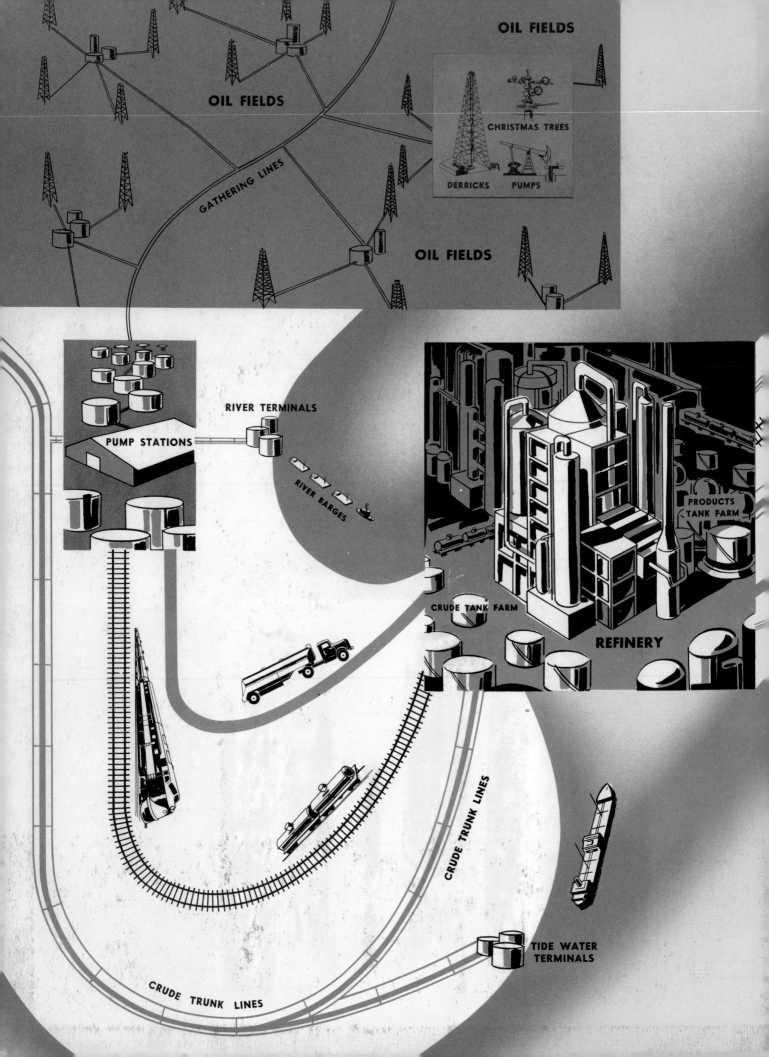

OIL FIELDS

OIL FIELDS

OIL FIELDS

GATHERING LINES

CHRISTMAS TREES

DERRICKS   PUMPS

RIVER TERMINALS

PUMP STATIONS

RIVER BARGES

CRUDE TANK FARM

PRODUCTS TANK FARM

REFINERY

CRUDE TRUNK LINES

CRUDE TRUNK LINES

TIDE WATER TERMINALS